W9-BHT-392

Toolbars

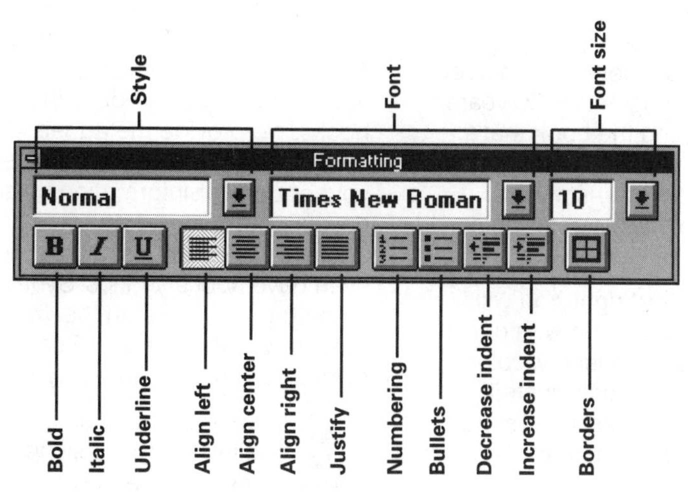
Style
Font
Font size
Formatting
Normal
Times New Roman
10
Bold
Italic
Underline
Align left
Align center
Align right
Justify
Numbering
Bullets
Decrease indent
Increase indent
Borders

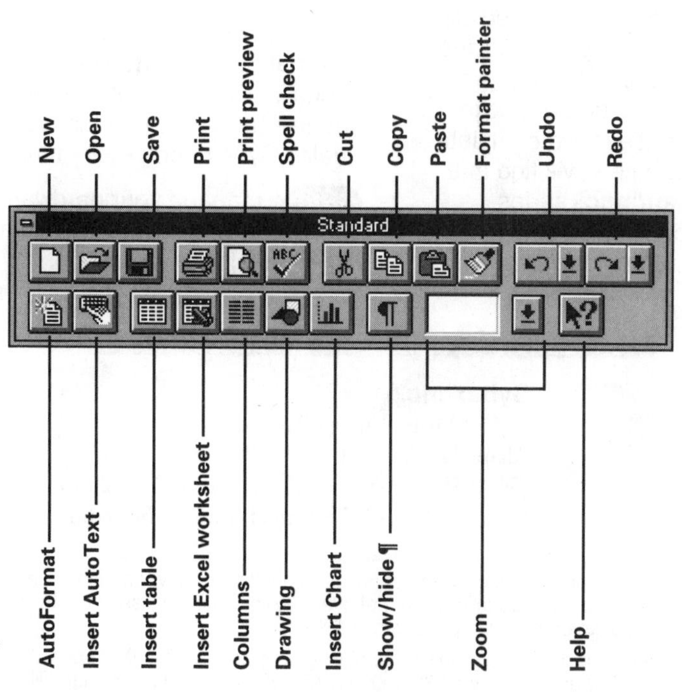
New
Open
Save
Print
Print preview
Spell check
Cut
Copy
Paste
Format painter
Undo
Redo
Standard
AutoFormat
Insert AutoText
Insert table
Insert Excel worksheet
Columns
Drawing
Insert Chart
Show/hide ¶
Zoom
Help

Mastering Word 6 for Windows™

Special Edition

Second Edition

Ron Mansfield

San Francisco ▲ Paris ▼ Düsseldorf ▲ Soest

Acquisitions Editors: Dianne King, Kristine Plachy
Developmental Editors: Sarah Wadsworth, Brenda Kienan
Editors: David Krassner, Laura Arendal
Technical Editors: Tanya Strub, Richard Nollet
Book Designer: Helen Bruno
Chapter Art: Helen Bruno
Screen Graphics: Cuong Le
Desktop Production: Ann Dunn, Molly Sharp
Production Assistant: Emily Smith
Indexer: Matthew Spence
Cover Designer: Design Site
Cover Photographer: Mark Johann
Cover photo art direction: Ingalls + Associates

Second edition updated by Christian Crumlish.

Screen reproductions produced with Collage Plus.

Library of Congress Card Number: 94-69306
ISBN: 0-7821-1639-6

Manufactured in the United States of America
10 9 8

To
Teachers

►► Acknowledgments

You are holding a miracle of cooperation and the product of one of the hardest-working book crews on earth. Hats off to the *entire* Sybex crew. You put this on the shelves in record time!

David Krassner deserves a special attaperson for efforts above and beyond any editor's job description. Guy Hart-Davis made Part Five a reality and a delight to read. Thanks, Guy, for those long nights and weekends. Tanya "the Whirlwind" Strub did an outstanding job of technical editing with incredible speed and accuracy. And Sarah Wadsworth and Dusty Bernard provided additional editing down the stretch when we needed it most.

I'd also like to thank Christian Crumlish for preparing this edition.

Contents at a Glance

Table of Contents

►► Introduction

Word 6 for Windows is a major upgrade to an already full-featured program. Word can integrate information from non-Word programs (spreadsheets, databases, graphics sources, etc.) and assure that Word documents are automatically updated when those outside information sources change.

Regardless of whether you are a seasoned Word user or a first-timer, this book is for you. For those who are already familiar with Word's functionality, you'll find plenty of tips to help you streamline your work. We've highlighted features new to Word 6 so you can quickly find the information you need to see what has changed and how. New Word users will appreciate the many tutorials, each carefully designed to illustrate a particular feature or skill in Word. In addition, there are tips to turn you into a competent Word wonk quickly and warnings to keep you from making "rookie" mistakes.

Any product with so many features can be a little intimidating at first. But mastering Word is a bit like playing chess or the piano—you can spend the rest of your life learning new tricks and techniques every day.

►► What You Need for the Practice Exercises

If you haven't already installed Word 6, either follow Microsoft's instructions or read Appendix A of this book.

This book assumes that you have used Windows at least briefly and that you know how to click, drag, select text, and make menu choices. The first part of the book *reviews* these concepts, but you might want to keep your Windows manuals within reach if you are just getting started.

If you want to practice saving work to floppies, find a spare diskette before you settle down to work.

Let's do it!

►► Where to Go from Here

The book's organization is fairly straightforward, except for a detour to Appendix A if you need to install Microsoft Word. Here's an overview of each section.

► Part One: Up and Running

Part One helps you dive right in. Sit at a computer when you read it. You'll soon be creating, saving, and printing impressive documents, beginner or not. Word offers a number of different ways to view and move through your documents. Part One will introduce you to these time-saving techniques. Chapter 1 gives a comprehensive overview of all the new features in Word 6; you may wish to use Chapter 1 as a jumping-off point to other sections of the book for topics that interest you.

Part One also covers Word's graphics features—both new and old. You'll learn to create, import, position, and size graphic elements. The process of flowing text around graphics is illustrated. We'll also try to make some sense out of the growing collection of graphics and font standards (TIFF, PICT, EPS, TrueType, etc.) and show how they relate to Word 6 for Windows.

You'll explore printing issues and see how your choice of printers and printing options affects the final look of your documents.

Word's unique Find File command and Summary Info features are demonstrated in Part One. You'll see how they work together to help you organize your hard disk and find misplaced files.

► Part Two: Formatting Fundamentals

Part Two shows you how to look great in print. It is organized to help you quickly find illustrated answers to specific questions. You'll learn the fundamentals of formatting characters, lines, paragraphs, and sections. Tabs, tables, styles, style sheets, headers, footers, hyphenation, and page numbering are also covered here. Those of you who need to create footnotes will find out how in Part Two.

There are numerous step-by-step "recipes" for getting the results you desire. You'll also see plenty of illustrations of the techniques at work.

▶ Part Three: Time Savers

As you might expect, Part Three is filled with tips and techniques. Here you will learn how Word 6 makes envelope and label printing a snap, and you'll learn to find and replace text or styles. Word 6 offers an incredible variety of templates and Wizards. You'll see how to use them to create:

- Awards
- Brochures
- Business cards
- Calendars
- Directories and lists
- Forms
- Invitations
- Letterheads and envelopes
- Manuals
- Memos
- Multicolumn newsletters
- Newspaper and magazine ads
- Overhead slides
- Postcards
- Posters
- Reports and proposals
- Signs
- Three-fold mailers
- And much more

We'll also demystify Word's new AutoText features and show how to create templates for repetitive tasks. Then you'll learn how to improve your documents' contents with Word's built-in thesaurus and Spelling and Grammar checkers. If you write or work on long, complex documents, be sure to read about Word's outlining features in Part Three, as well.

▸ Part Four: Desktop Publishing

Because some desktop publishing projects can be quite complex, you'll see how to work with Word's new Master Documents. Word's table-of-contents and indexing features are explored here as well. If you and others collaborate on big jobs, Part Four will show you how to give documents a uniform look and feel, even when they have multiple authors.

There's a chapter on how to print documents on specialty paper stock, and then there's the Document Shop, which provides step-by-step instructions on how to prepare all kinds of useful documents.

▸ Part Five: Power Tools

Finally, Part Five deals with topics of interest to advanced users of Word. Few other programs offer as much opportunity for customization. Word lets you rearrange menus and Toolbars, change default settings, modify dictionaries and grammar rules, and much, much more.

Part Five also contains chapters describing Word's text- and voice-annotation features, and the print-merge feature for personalized mailings and similar documents. In Chapter 28 you'll actually set up a simple, personalized mailing project and create some mailing labels, envelopes, and postcards.

Chapter 29 presents Microsoft Graph, which can be used to create charts in a variety of formats from data in your Word documents.

If your computer is on a network with others, read about Word's e-mail and other network tools in Chapter 31.

And don't miss Chapter 30. It details ways to use Object Linking and Embedding to automatically update documents when things change elsewhere.

Chapter 32, 33, and 34 are packed with information about field codes, forms, and macros (including some helpful WordBasic advice).

▶ Appendices

To top it all off, the appendices function as a handy reference section. In addition to installation instructions, a complete list of word commands, and character sets, there's also a primer for former WordPerfect users, complete field code and switch information, and detailed coverage of WordBasic commands by category.

▶▶ Book Conventions

We've used some standard conventions and typographer's tricks to make the book easier to read. While most of them will be obvious, scan the next few paragraphs just in case.

▶ About the Examples and Exercises

The book contains a number of exercises and lists of steps that you may want to try as you read along. Whenever you need to hold down one key, then press another, you'll see the keys separated by pluses. For instance, *Ctrl+S* means hold down the Ctrl key while pressing the S key. Boldface text usually indicates things you are expected to type. Also, some keys (such as the arrow keys and the Enter key) are indicated by icons. The icon for the Enter key is ↵. So, if you are being asked to type Mark Twain's name and then press the Enter key in an exercise, you'll read something like "Type **Mark Twain** then press ↵."

▶ Menu Commands

As a shortcut and an eye-catcher, we've used a special convention to indicate menu commands. When we want you to choose a menu command, it will follow this pattern: *menu name* ➤ *command*. Also, to help you out, we have underlined the *hot key* for the menu and the command. Pressing the hot key letter is the same as choosing the command. For example, if we want to choose the Save command from the File menu, we will say "Choose File ➤ Save." In this case, if you were to hit the Alt key to highlight the menu bar, and then press the *F* and *S* keys, it would be the same as choosing the command from the menu with the mouse.

► Tips, Warnings, Notes, and New

Throughout the book you'll find notes, tips, warnings, and discussions of new features. They are marked so they're easy to spot.

Because so many things have changed in Word 6, we've added this "New" icon in the margin to help experienced Word users spot differences. If you are a longtime Word user, it will be a good idea to skim each chapter looking for these easy-to-spot items.

► Fast Tracks

Fast Tracks summarize the important steps, keystrokes, and menu commands for major Word features. You'll find them at the beginning of each chapter. Think of them as bite-sized how-to instructions that can often save you a trip through the entire chapter.

PART ONE

Up and Running

▶ ▶ **CHAPTER 1**

What's New in Word 6

Word 6 is a *major* upgrade of the Word for Windows software. Most of the changes make life easier for both new and experienced users. A few things will take some getting used to. Let's have a look at what's new.

By the way...see that icon in the margin? You'll see it throughout the book. That's your signal that what's being discussed in the paragraph is *new* in Word 6.

More and Better Toolbars

Word now provides eight Toolbars containing buttons that you click to execute commands or bring up dialog boxes. Three of these can be seen in Figure 1.1.

Toolbars can be placed anywhere you like, and their shape can be changed. Incidentally, Word no longer has a ribbon. It is now called the Formatting Toolbar. Virtually every chapter of this book contains information about Word's new Toolbars.

Easier-to-Use Horizontal Ruler

If you've ever struggled with the tiny first line indent triangles in older Word for Windows versions, you'll appreciate the new, large, "euro-styled" margin handles of Word 6. See Chapters 2 and 3.

FIGURE 1.1

New Toolbars, rulers, and an improved status area are just a few of the improvements in Word 6.

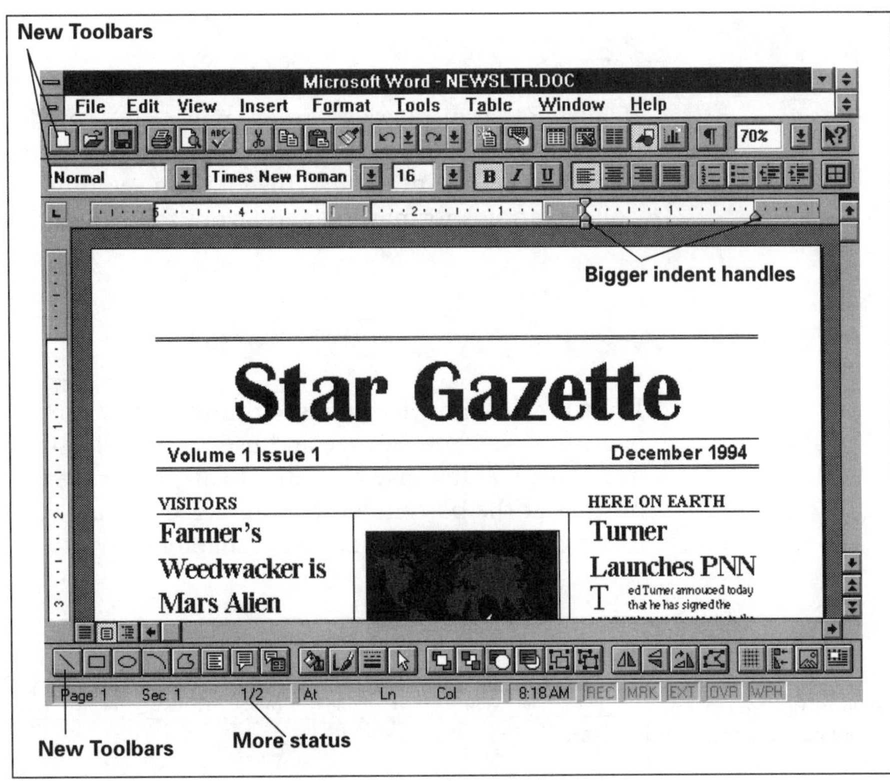

▸▸ Vertical Ruler

The vertical ruler lets you see and adjust header and footer positions. It also lets you change table row heights. Vertical rulers are automatically displayed in Page Layout and Print Previews. See Chapter 3 and others.

▸▸ Improved Status Bar

The status bar at the bottom of the screen provides much more information than before. Keep one eye down there when you work. Word will often tell you what it expects next. See Chapter 2.

▸▸ Full Screen View

Realizing that display screens are never big enough, Word's creators have added a Full Screen option that removes virtually all the clutter—Toolbars, status info, etc. This lets you see more of the page when doing complex formatting and layout tasks. See Chapter 3.

▸▸ Improved Print Preview

Print Preview now lets you see thumbnail sketches of up to eighteen pages at once. You can see and use rulers in Print Preview, as illustrated in Figure 1.2. It's easy to switch to any other view you desire with view buttons at the bottom left of your screen. And, best of all, you can edit text right in Print Preview! See Chapter 4.

FIGURE 1.2 ▸

Print Preview lets you see up to eighteen thumbnails. You can even edit in Print Preview.

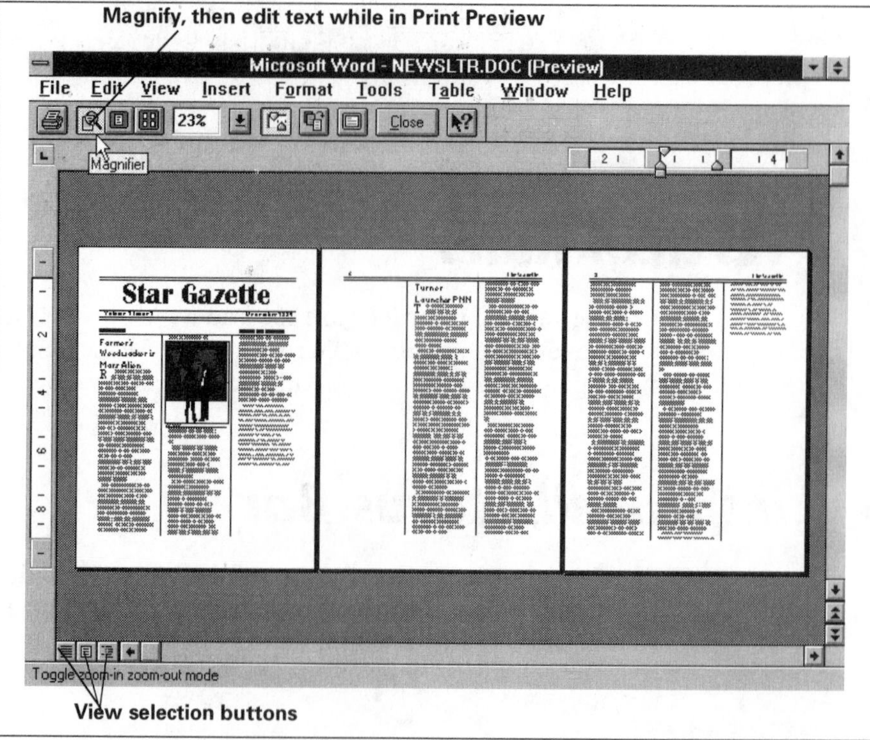

▶▶ New "Tab-Organized" Choices

Word now "rounds up" collections of choices and displays them in cleverly designed dialog boxes like the one in Figure 1.3. Clicking on tabs lets you see additional choices.

FIGURE 1.3 ▶

Clicking on "tabs" lets you see more choices.

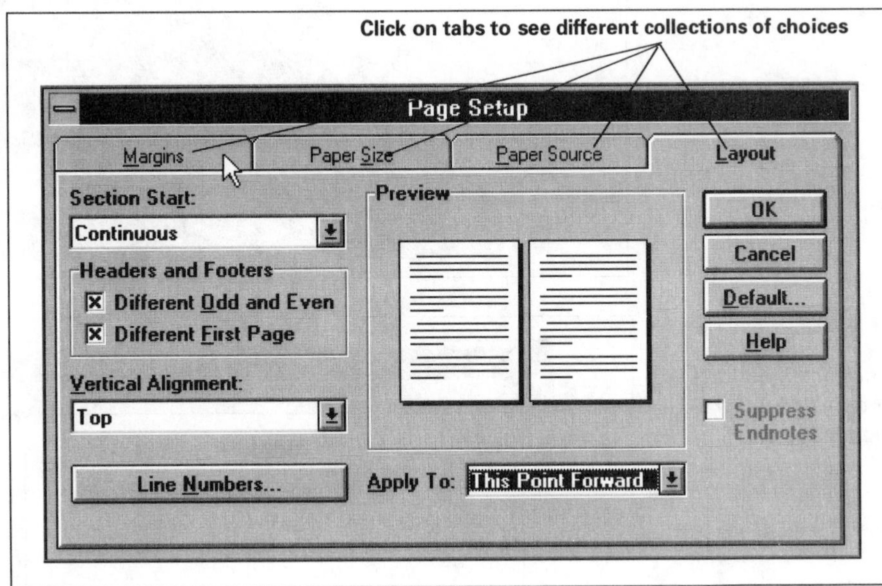

▶▶ Demos

Word can demonstrate itself for you. There are demos for new Word users, experienced folk, and WordPerfect converts, as illustrated in Figure 1.4. See Chapter 2.

▶▶ Tip of the Day

Here's a painless way to master Word. Each time you start the program, it will display a helpful tip like the one in Figure 1.5.

Tips can be turned off if you tire of them. See Chapter 2.

FIGURE 1.4

Word will even demonstrate itself for you.

FIGURE 1.5

Each time you start Word, it gives you a handy tip.

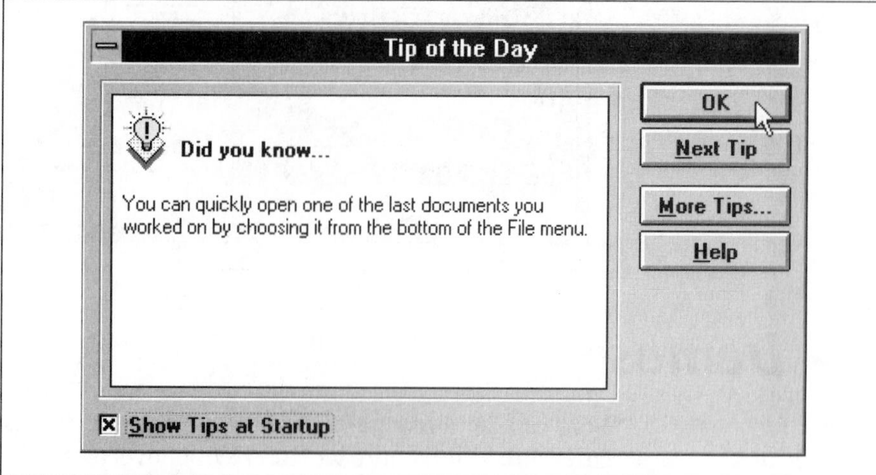

▸▸ Multilevel Undos and Redos

How many times have you wished you could rewrite history? Well, Word 6 lets you. It records all of your actions, then lets you list them in a drop-down menu like the one shown in Figure 1.6.

You can selectively undo one or many earlier actions. A related Redo feature lets you "undo undos." See Chapter 2.

FIGURE 1.6

You can undo (and redo) many generations of changes.

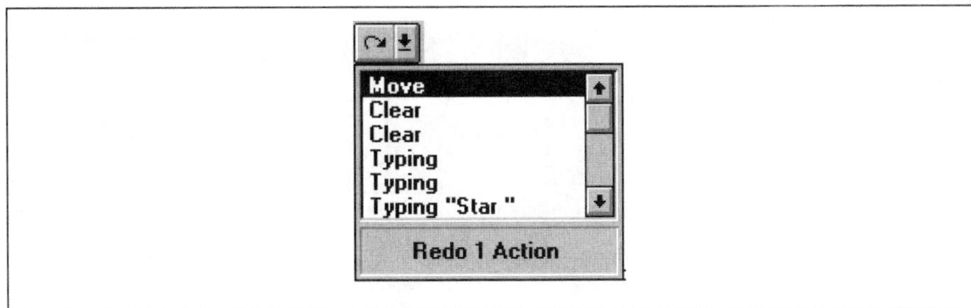

▶▶ Smart Cut and Paste

Cut, paste, and drag-and-drop now adjust white space automatically. For instance, if you select a word and a space and move the selected text to the end of a sentence, Word will eliminate the unwanted space between the word and the period.

▶▶ Much-Improved Find and Replace

Word 6 offers a much more robust Find and Replace command (see Figure 1.7). You can now search for text containing specific formatting characteristics (fonts, paragraph settings, styles, etc.). You can easily look for special characters and other items (paragraph marks, tabs, graphics, white space, etc.). And you can specify complex replacements as well.

There is also a "Sounds Like" search option that looks for words that sound alike but are spelled differently. See Chapter 20.

▶▶ Unequal Column Widths

Not only does Word 6 let you create side-by-side columns of different widths, it makes them easy to set up and adjust. As you can see in Figure 1.8, the new Columns dialog box lets you pick from predefined column choices or specify your own. Very slick. See Chapter 22.

FIGURE 1.7 

You won't recognize Find and Replace. It is far more robust.

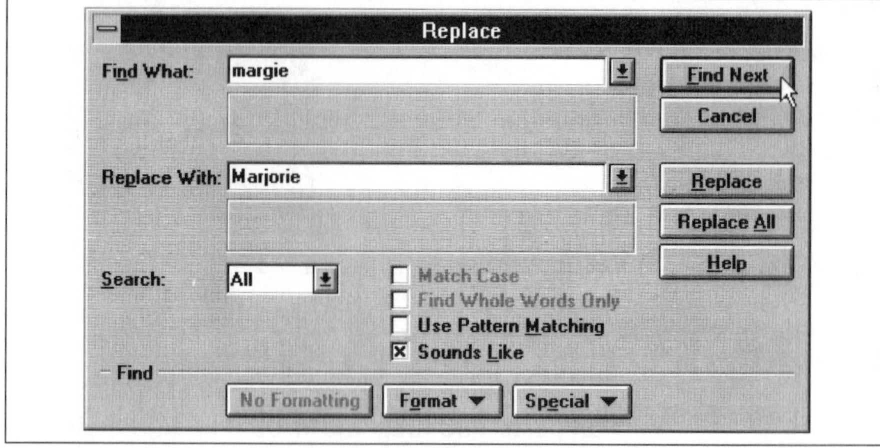

FIGURE 1.8 

Side-by-side columns can now have different widths.

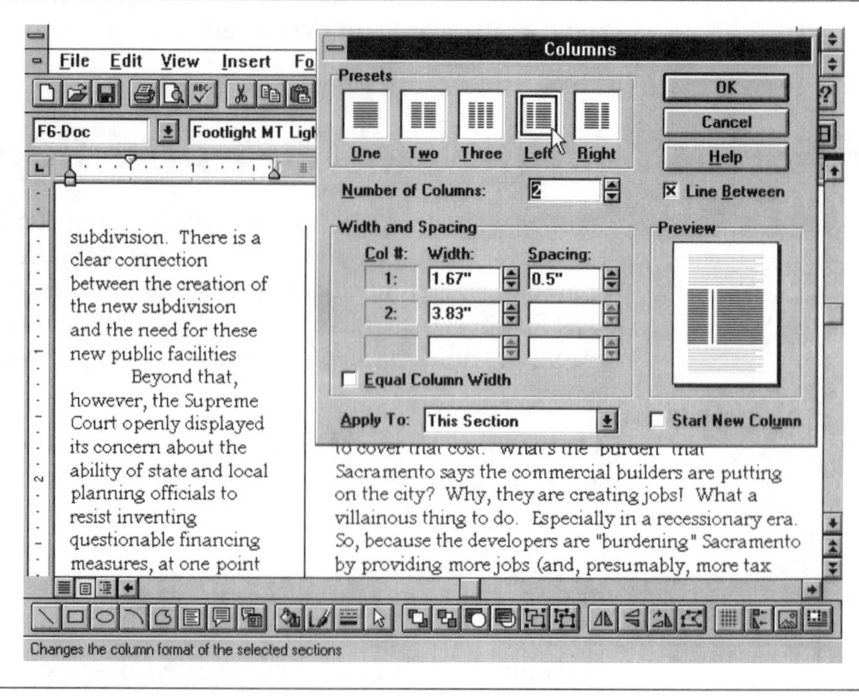

►► The "Other" Button Mouse Menus

Microsoft has finally ordained the use of that extra mouse button you've been wondering about since you bought your computer. It can be used to bring small menus into view while working in text. The menus list commonly used commands that you might like to use at that particular point in a document. In Figure 1.9, for instance, the menu includes font, paragraph, and bullet choices.

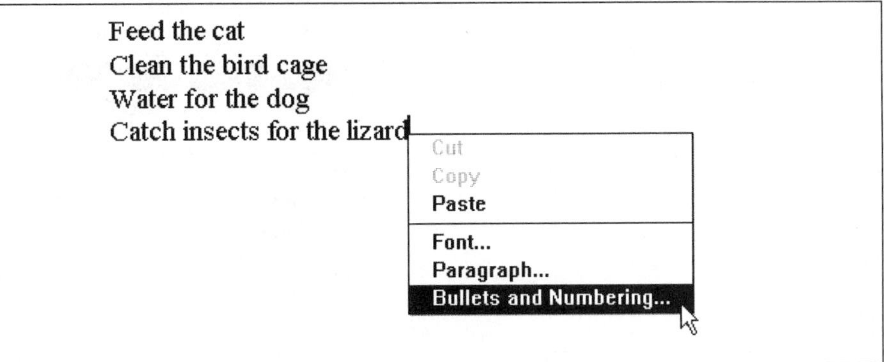

FIGURE 1.9 ►

Use your "other" mouse button to see mini menus right in the document.

Normally the right mouse button reveals these lists. If you are left-handed, however, you can use the Windows Control panel to make the right button your "primary" button and the left button will produce menus instead. See Chapter 2.

►► A Table Menu

Tables have always been Word's strong suit, but table features and commands were widely scattered. Word 6 collects most of them on a single new Table menu, shown in Figure 1.10. See Chapter 11.

►► Automatic Table Formatting

Borrowing from Microsoft Excel's spreadsheet formatting prowess, Word 6 makes it easy to apply elegant predefined formats to tables. As you can see in Figure 1.11, the Table AutoFormat dialog box even lets you see what formats look like before you apply them. See Chapter 11.

FIGURE 1.10

Word's new Table menu gathers all the table commands under one roof.

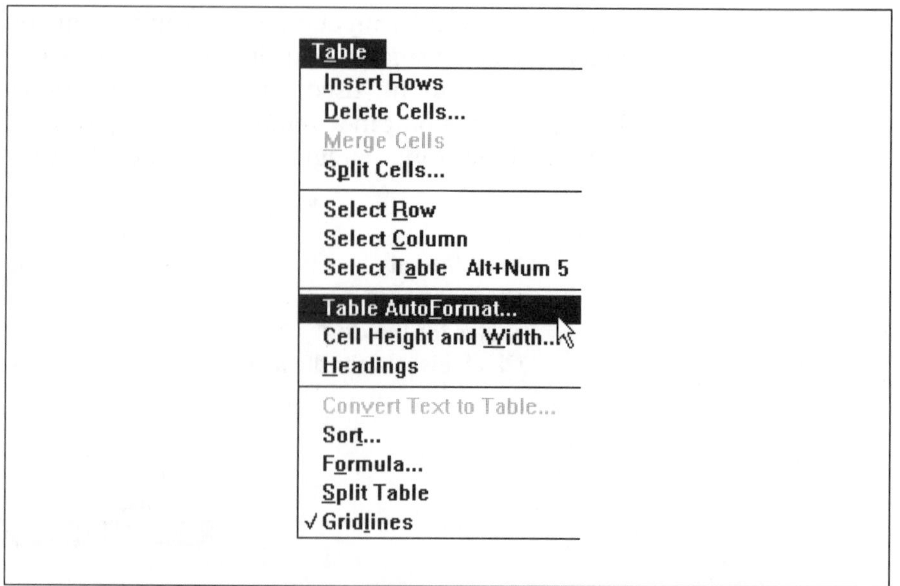

FIGURE 1.11

Now it's easy to apply predefined formats to Word tables.

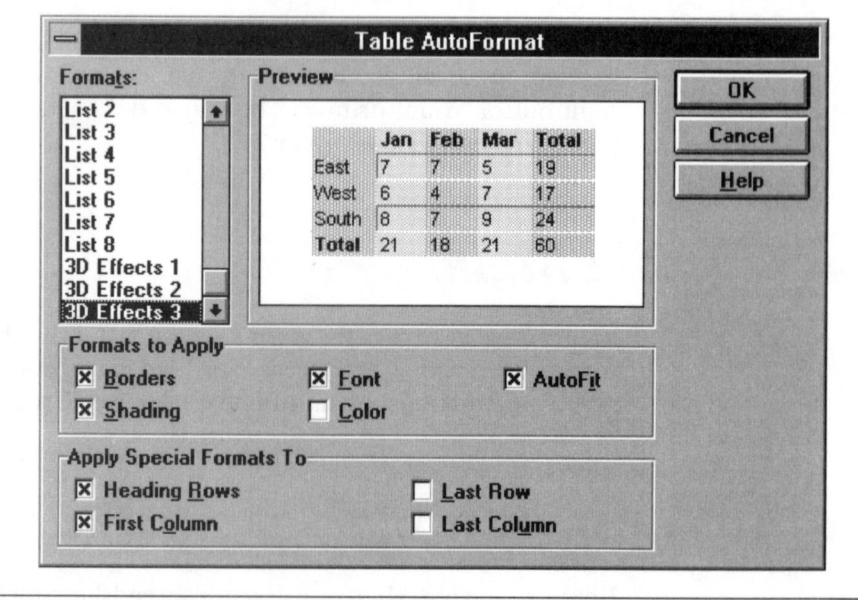

►► Wizards

Imagine having an assistant who can ask you a few questions and then create a complex, personalized document while you watch. That's exactly what Word's wizards do for you. There are wizards for creating awards, agendas, calendars, fax cover sheets, letters, memos, newsletters, resumes, and more. Figure 1.12 shows the Agenda wizard at work. See Chapters 16 and 27.

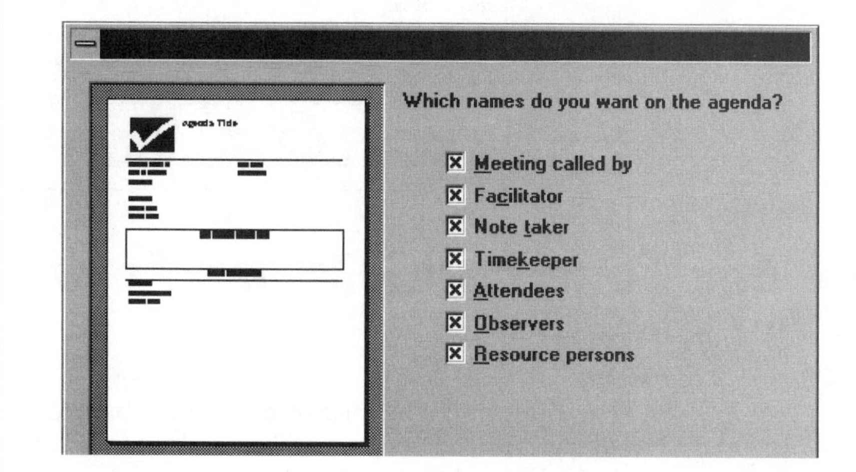

FIGURE 1.12 ►

Wizards ask questions and then set up complex documents with little or no further intervention.

►► Prewritten Business Letters

Word's Letter wizard lets you choose from dozens of "canned" business documents and formats, for everything from past-due notices to product upgrade sales letters. (I wonder where they got *that* idea?) All you need to do is pick a letter, fill in a few blanks, and print. Figure 1.13 shows just a few of the choices. See Chapters 16 and 27.

FIGURE 1.13

Some wizards even include boilerplate text. Fill in a few blanks, and you can print finished letters and other documents.

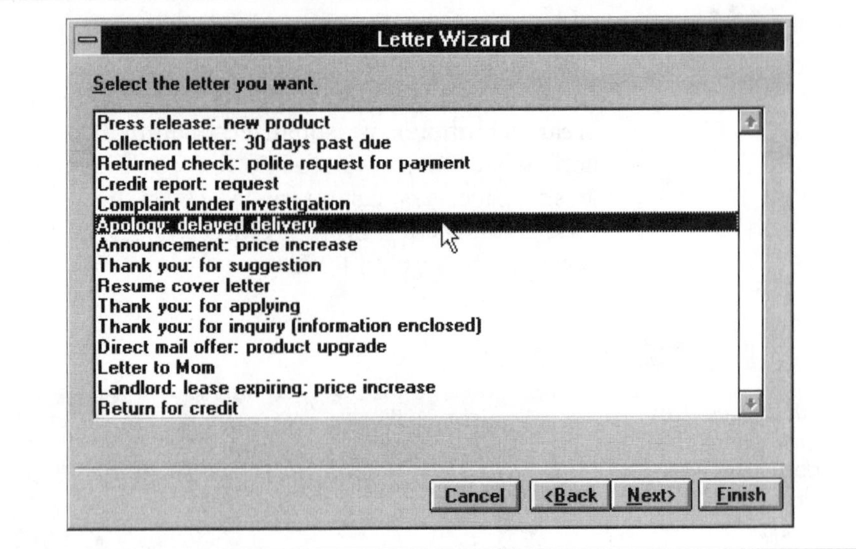

►► Bar Code and FIM Marks on Envelopes

Envelope and label printing, once the bane of word processor users everywhere, is a snap with Word 6. You can now even include delivery-point bar codes and FIM-A courtesy reply coding to speed up mail delivery and postage-free, reply-mail processing, as shown in Figure 1.14. See Chapter 15.

►► Drag-and-Drop across Windows

Sometimes it's the little things that make life easier. If you are a drag-and-drop addict, like I am, you'll be pleased to know that you can now drag from one document window to another.

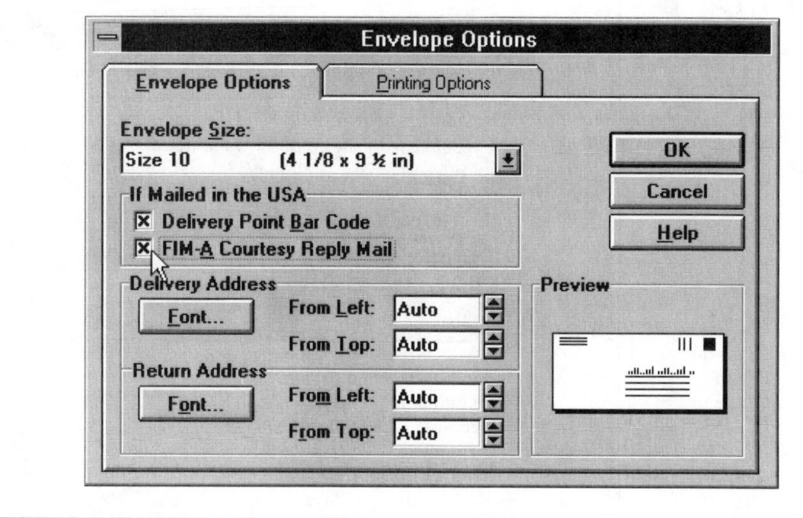

FIGURE 1.14 *There are many new envelope and label options, including bar codes.*

►► AutoCorrect

I don't know about you, but I often type "teh" instead of "the" and waste time correcting things like that at the end of a project. And I often wish I could type acronyms like *DRD* and have my computer type out *Department of Redundancy Department*. Word 6 can do that and more thanks to the AutoCorrect feature. Use Word's predefined collection of things to watch for, and add your own, as shown in Figure 1.15. See Chapter 17.

►► AutoText

AutoText is actually a beefed-up replacement for Word's old Glossary feature. But they still haven't gotten the name right. AutoText lets you create boilerplate text, graphics, and other document elements, then paste them at will. Store just about anything you want this way (logos, tables, etc.), then paste them with a few mouse clicks or keystrokes. Now if we could just find a better name for this handy feature. See Chapter 17.

FIGURE 1.15 ►

Word can watch over your shoulder and automatically correct mistakes that you make often.

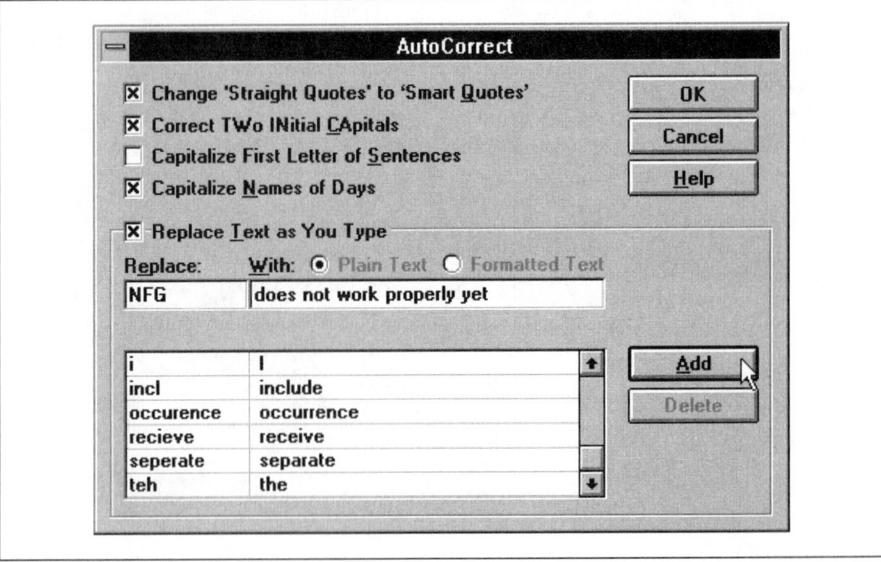

►► AutoFormat

AutoFormat looks for ways it can improve the overall appearance of a document, and when asked, will suggest changes. For example, it will look for and offer to remove unnecessary spaces as shown in Figure 1.16. See Chapter 14.

FIGURE 1.16 ►

AutoFormat suggests improvements to the appearance of your documents.

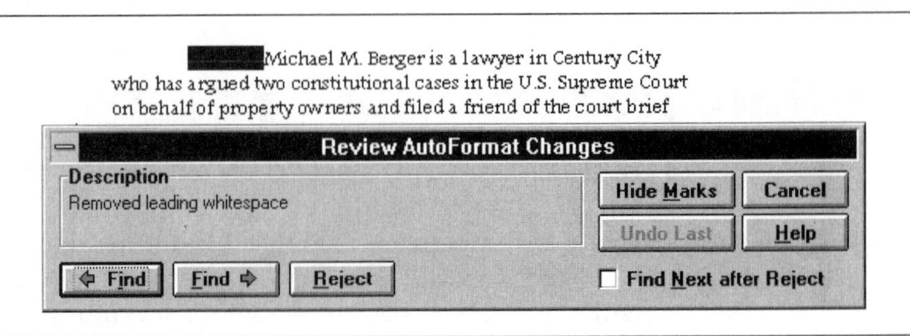

AutoFormat will work while you type or after you've finished. You can review each change or give AutoFormat carte blanche.

►► AutoCaption

Technical writers rejoice. AutoCaption will make your life easier. From now on, when you create documents containing illustrations, equations, tables, and other elements that need sequential numbering and in-text callouts, Word can help. It will even renumber all references as needed when you add or delete things as shown in Figure 1.17. See Chapter 25.

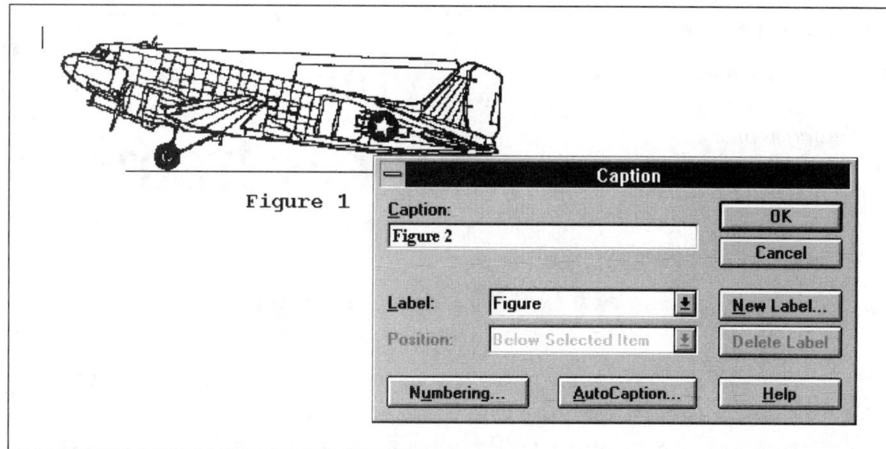

FIGURE 1.17 ►

AutoCaption helps you keep figure numbers straight in text and captions.

►► Automatic Cross-Referencing

Cross references tell the people who read your documents where to look for additional information on a subject. Word 6 automates the cross-referencing procedure, so that when the document changes, you won't need to manually change all of the cross references. As you can gather from Figure 1.18, you can cross-reference headings, figures, tables, and much more. See Chapter 25.

►► Copy Formatting More Easily

A cute little "Format Painter" button and mouse pointer let you select formatting from one part of your document and apply it elsewhere as shown in Figure 1.19. See Chapter 14.

FIGURE 1.18

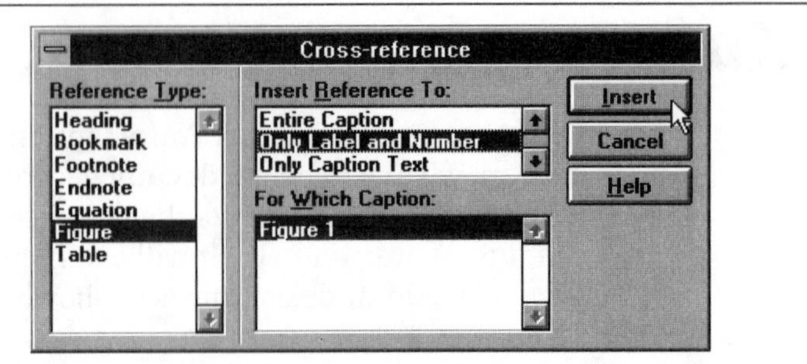

Word 6 lets you create automatic cross-references that are updated automatically when you alter your documents.

Cross-reference
Reference Type:
Heading
Bookmark
Footnote
Endnote
Equation
Figure
Table
Insert Reference To:
Entire Caption
Only Label and Number
Only Caption Text
For Which Caption:
Figure 1
Insert
Cancel
Help

FIGURE 1.19

The Format Painter button lets you apply formatting from one part of your document to another.

Make Big
Money from
Did you know
that there are
always openings
in the canning
industry? We
need

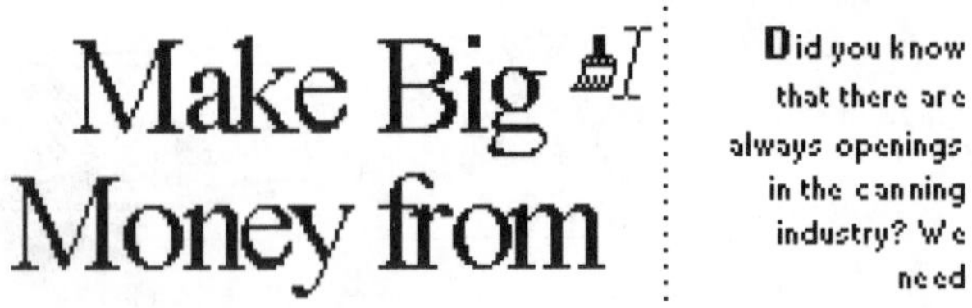

▸▸ Automatic Drop Caps

Once the exclusive tools of skilled printers who hand-set type, drop caps add allure and an air of elegance. They are a snap with Word 6. Figure 1.20 shows a few of the many drop-cap effects you can create. See Chapter 9.

FIGURE 1.20

Drop caps add style and visual interest. Word 6 makes them easy to create.

Word's new Drop Cap feature automatically creates frames, increases the size of the initial. It will place drop caps in the text or in the margin as shown here.
Drop caps can be created in a number of ways. This one was made by selecting just the letter D in 12 point New Century Schoolbook text and increasing it to 25 points.
Large initial
Graphics can be used as drop caps too. This butterfly was pasted from the scrapbook, reduced in size, framed, then dragged into place from Print Preview. The From Text option was set to 0 in the Frame dialog box to tighten things.
Entire words can be dropped. This example was created with the Frame command on Word's Insert menu. First the word Entire was selected.

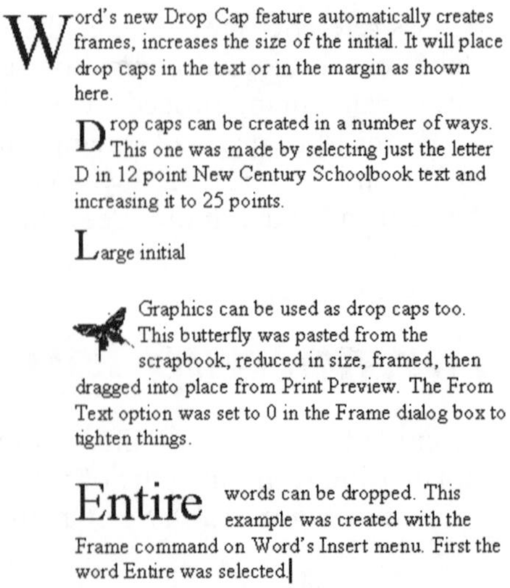

▶▶ Easier Mail Merges

"Quick! We need to get this personalized letter to all of our customers who purchased car seat model N-124. It needs to be in the mail tonight."

Now, with the help of the Mail Merge Helper, rush jobs like this can be accomplished almost as a matter of routine. The helper asks necessary questions and leads you through the process of setting up main documents, data, and the other necessary elements for a successful merge project. As you can see in Figure 1.21, the process is quite straightforward. See Chapter 28.

FIGURE 1.21 ▶

Word will lead you through all of the necessary merge steps.

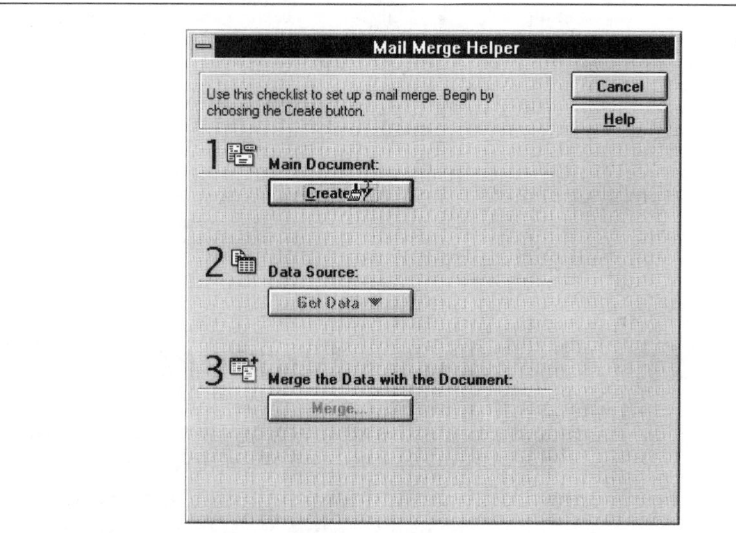

▶▶ More Online Help

Perhaps because there are so many new features, Word comes with even more online help than before. And it is organized for easy access by pros and beginners. Figure 1.22 shows the veritable tip of the help iceberg. See Chapter 2.

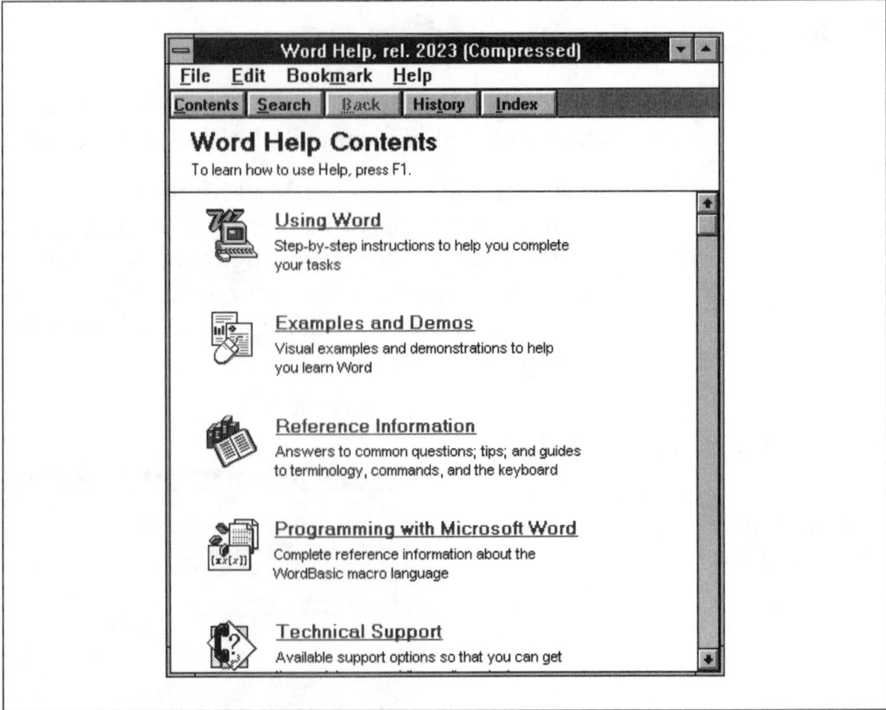

FIGURE 1.22

Word 6 provides plenty of online help.

►► Better Drawing Features

One of the reasons so many people like Windows is its graphics prowess. Word 6 takes advantage of those strengths by adding new and improved drawing features, such as the ones shown in Figure 1.23. You may not even need a separate drawing program for everyday illustration tasks. See Chapter 5.

►► More "Canned" Styles

Word has always offered pre-configured styles—collections of formatting decisions for things like headings, glossary entries, etc. Word 6 has more and better predefined styles. See Chapter 14.

FIGURE 1.23

Check out Word's improved drawing features.

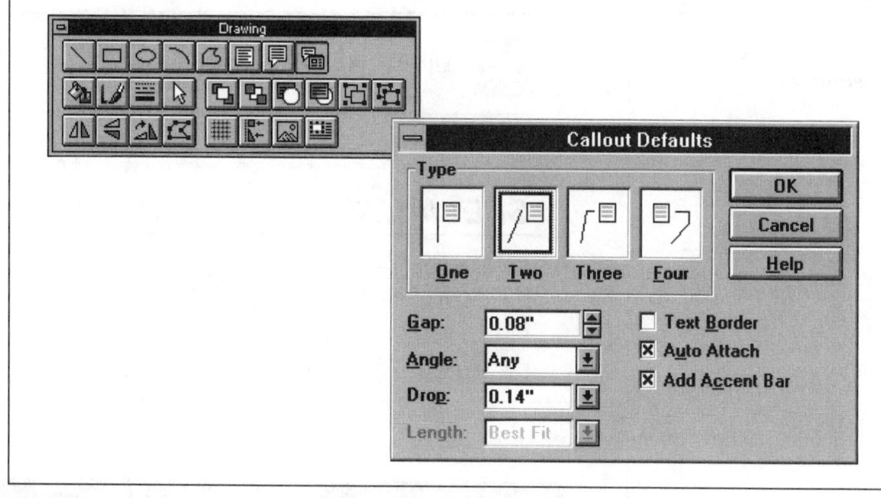

►► Style Gallery

Word's Style Gallery lets you preview your text using a variety of styles so that you can pick just the right one. It's quick and easy and removes much of the guesswork. See Chapter 14.

►► Better Page and Section Break Markers

Speaking of guesswork, have you ever tried to remember what a section break looked like (as opposed to a forced page break, or perhaps a column break)? Well, Word 6 makes it easy to tell them apart—they display their names, as shown here in Figure 1.24. See Chapter 8.

►► More Workgroup Features

If you work with others, and find yourself passing around files, you'll like Word's improved annotation feature (shown in Figure 1.25) and other workgroup features like Master Documents.

FIGURE 1.24

Breaks now speak for themselves.

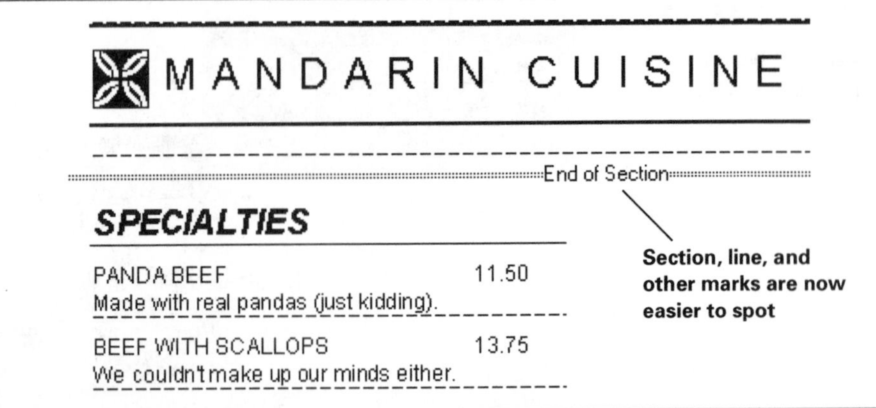

FIGURE 1.25

Word 6 is great when you need to collaborate.

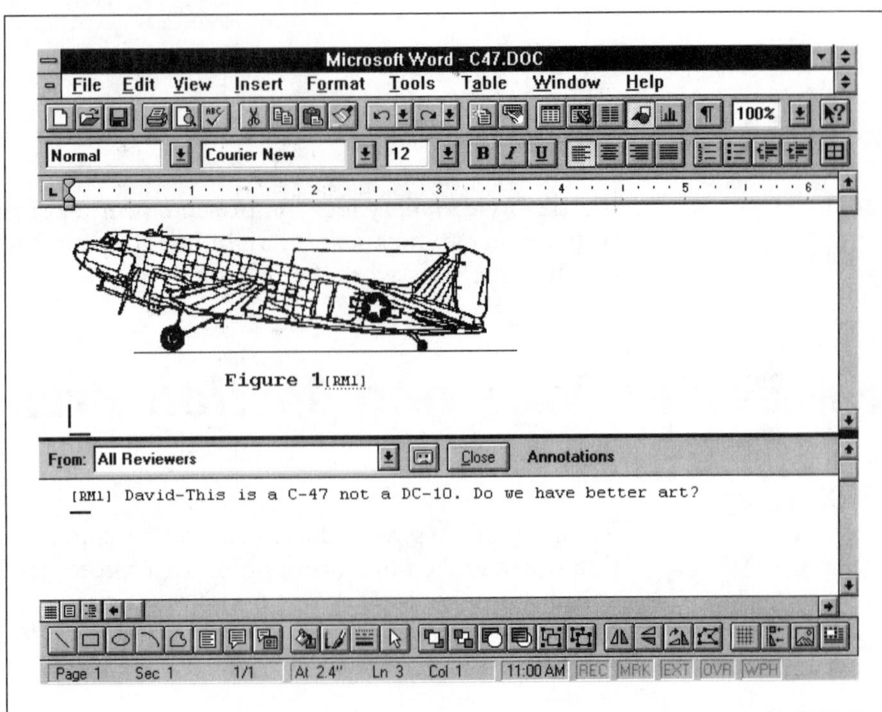

These features make it easy for different people to work on different parts of the job, then combine their efforts flawlessly. See Chapter 24.

▶▶ New Mail-Related Features

There are several new mail-related features for those of us with e-mail systems. For example, Word now makes it easy to create mail routing slips. See Chapter 31.

▶▶ List Multiple File Extensions

Here's another one of those nice little extras. When using an Open command, have you ever wanted to see a list of all the files ending in .DOC *and* .TXT? Or have you ever wanted to see just your graphics files in an open dialog box? Word now lets you specify more than one file extension at once in many dialog boxes, as illustrated in Figure 1.26.

FIGURE 1.26

You can now filter for mutiple file extensions in the dialog boxes.

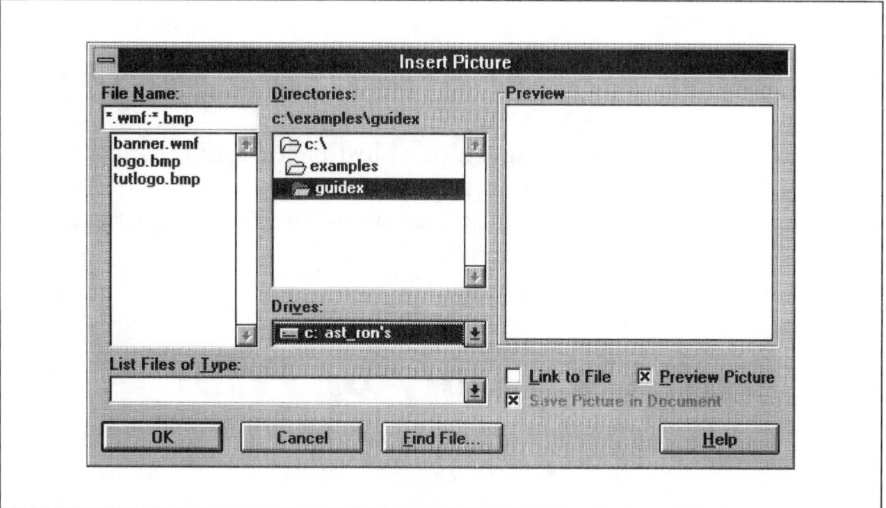

▶▶ Improved Page Numbering

You'd be hard-pressed to think of a page-numbering scheme you couldn't accomplish with Word 6. And, as you can see in Figure 1.27, you needn't be a rocket scientist to number pages like one. See Chapter 12.

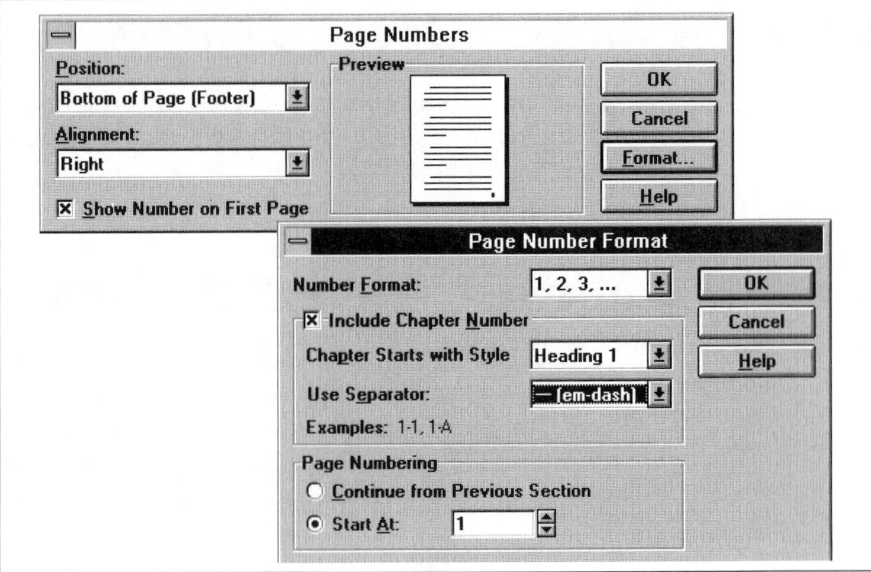

FIGURE 1.27 ►

Word offers plenty of easy-to-understand page-numbering options.

►► Print Nonconsecutive Pages

Now you can print just pages 3 and 9 and 11 without issuing multiple print commands or throwing out unwanted pages. Word lets you specify noncontiguous pages and page ranges in a single print command. See Chapter 4.

►► Print Odd-Only or Print Even-Only Pages

If you print two-sided projects on a typical printer, you'll love this new feature. Word 6 lets you print just odd numbered pages, then load them back in the tray upside down and print the even pages on the backsides. Cool. See Chapter 4.

▶▶ Improved Find File

It's on the server somewhere.... Word's new Find File lets you quickly locate files containing the information you need, even if Word didn't create the files. It's even possible to "peek inside" files without loading them, as shown in Figure 1.28. See Chapter 7.

FIGURE 1.28

Find File is fast and powerful.

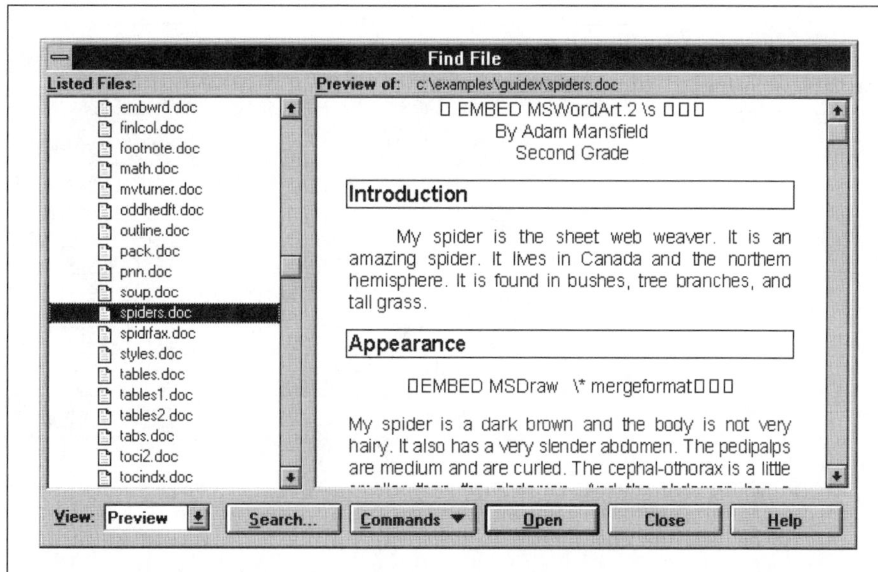

▶▶ In-Place Editing of Embedded Objects (OLE-2)

If you embed OLE objects (drawings, charts, and other items created by different programs), Word 6 lets you edit them from within Word by double-clicking. See Chapter 30.

▸▸ Improved Symbol and Special Character Insertion

To enter special characters like © and ® or special symbols like ¶, use Word's improved Insert ➤ Symbol… command. As shown in Figure 1.29, it has two tabs, an easier way to select fonts, and more. See Chapter 9.

FIGURE 1.29 ▸

The Insert ➤ Symbol… command has been improved.

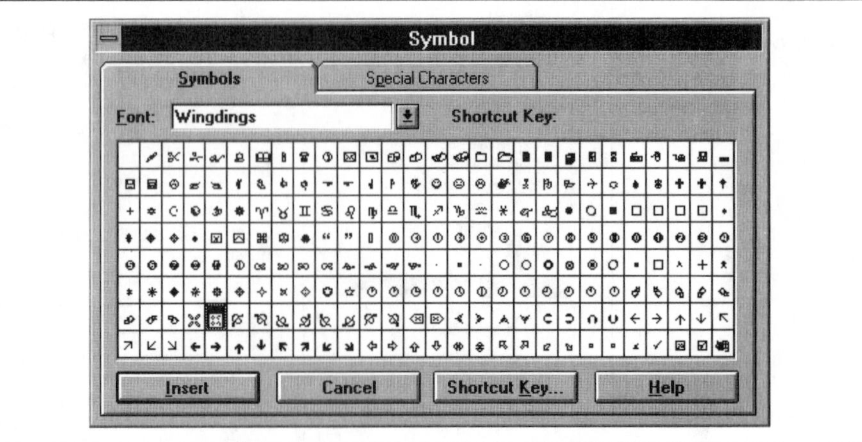

▸▸ More Border, Line, and Shading Choices

Word 6 offers more border, shading, and line options than its predecessors. Moreover, the choices have been consolidated, as you can see in Figure 1.30. See Chapter 10.

▸▸ Automatically Change Capitalization

Word makes it a snap to change the case of selected text. Choices now include Sentence case, all lowercase, all uppercase, Title case, and

FIGURE 1.30

Border, shading, and line choices have been increased and consolidated.

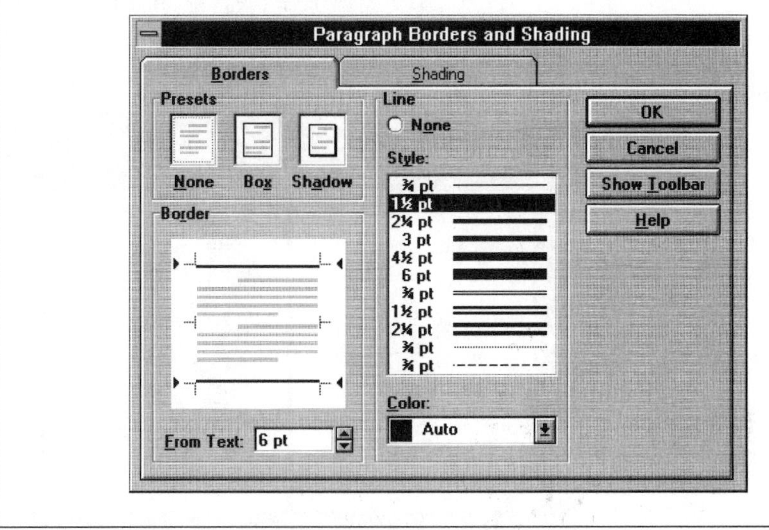

toggle case. You make your choices in an easy-to-understand dialog box. See Chapter 9.

►► Shrink to Fit

Ahh, technology. How many times have you had a document with one of those mostly empty pages at the end like the one shown in Figure 1.31?

With a whir and a buzz, Word tightens up your document just enough to make those last few lines fit on the preceding page. Very nice! See Chapter 4.

►► More Automatic Bullet and Numbered List Options

Geez, list makers. Check out all of the bullet options in Figure 1.32. See Chapter 9.

FIGURE 1.31

Shrink to fit eliminates bare-looking last pages like the one at the end of this document.

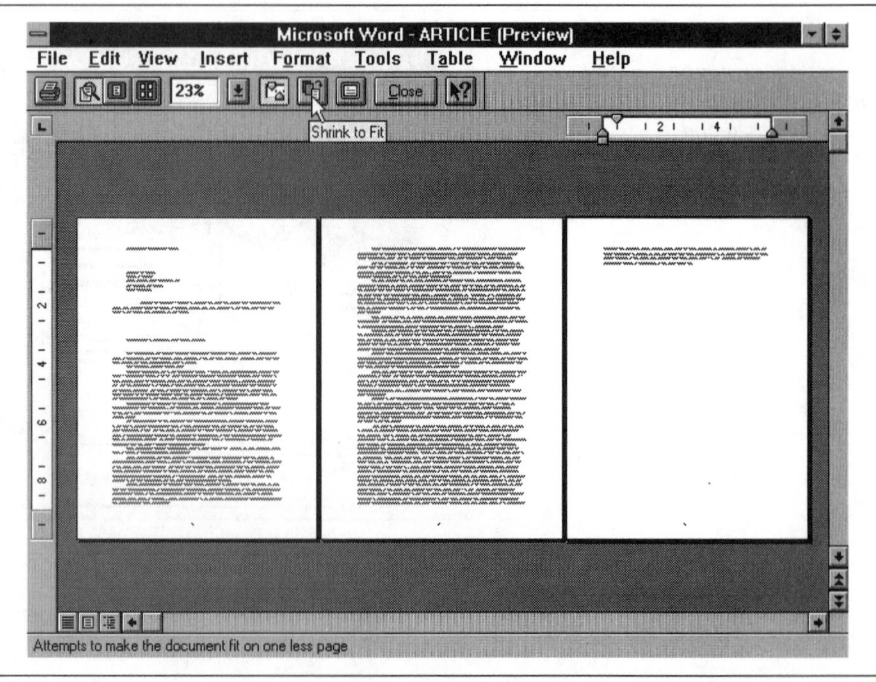

FIGURE 1.32

Word 6 offers a plethora of bullet choices.

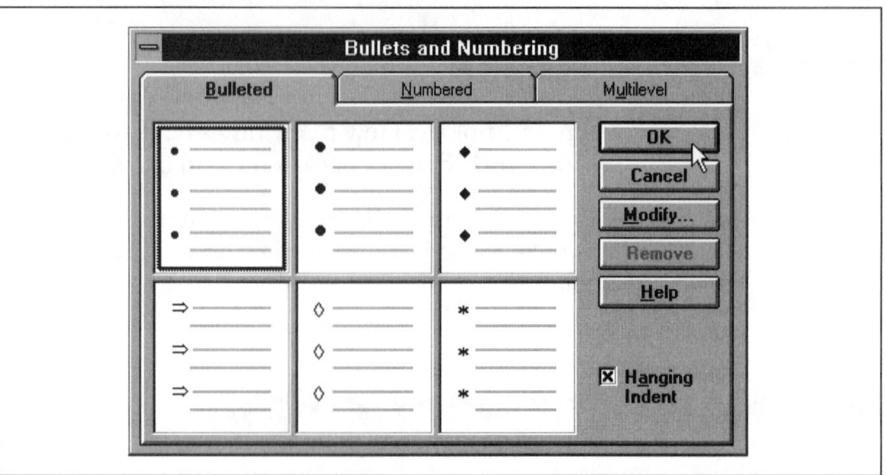

The Number and Multilevel tabs offer even more options. Pick paragraph numbering options like 1., a), i); or 1, 1.1, 1.1.1—you get the picture. See Chapter 12.

▸▸ Improved Hyphenation

Word's new hyphenation features are easier to use and more useful. Check them out in Chapter 9.

▸▸ Word Counts and Other Statistics

Word 6 offers a more robust Word Count command that also displays other statistics, as you can see in Figure 1.33. See Chapter 19.

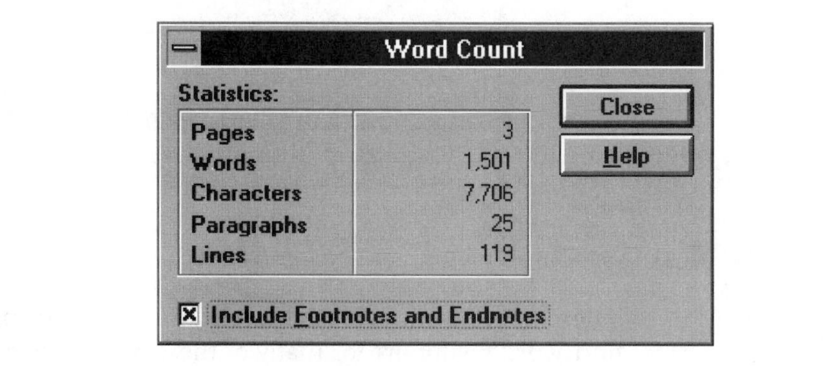

FIGURE 1.33 ▸

You want how many words in three weeks?

▸▸ Improved Document Protection

There are new document-protection options in Word 6, including several layers of password protection. Figure 1.34 gives you a glimpse. See Chapter 7.

▸▸ Improved Formulas

There are more formulas for performing mathematical computations now, and they can be used in more places. Word 6 formulas even facilitate number formatting conventions like dollar signs and commas. See Chapter 34.

FIGURE 1.34

Word 6 offers multiple levels of password protection.

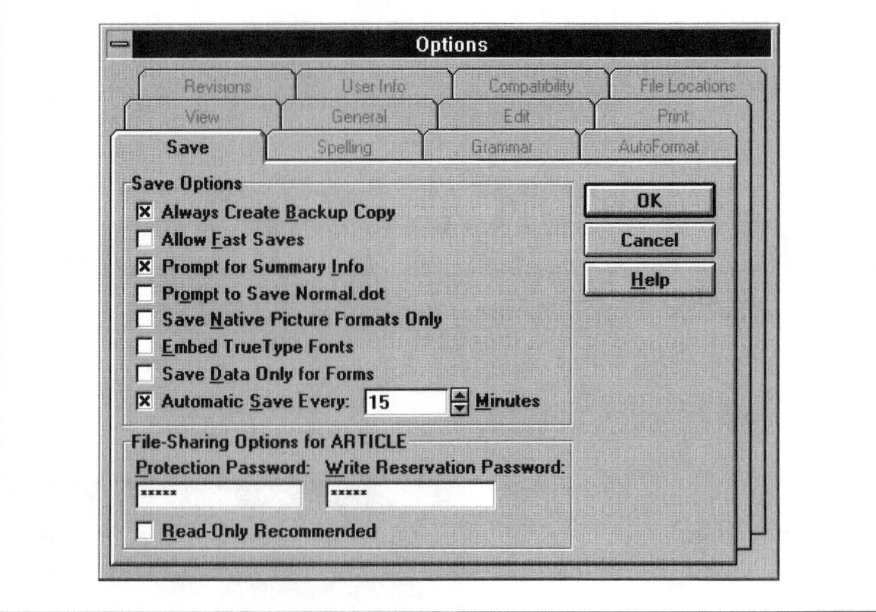

▸▸ Voice and Pen Support

Those of you with pen computers and voice-capable computers will find Word 6 support for many of these new hardware features.

▸▸ Lots of Menu Changes

You will find many menu changes in Word 6—most of them good. For example, Word 6 has its own Table menu, as shown in Figure 1.35.

A few of the changes may annoy you, but Word lets you reconfigure menus by using the Tools ➤ Customize command, so you can have it your way, whatever your way might be. See Chapter 36.

FIGURE 1.35

The menu bar has changed a bit.

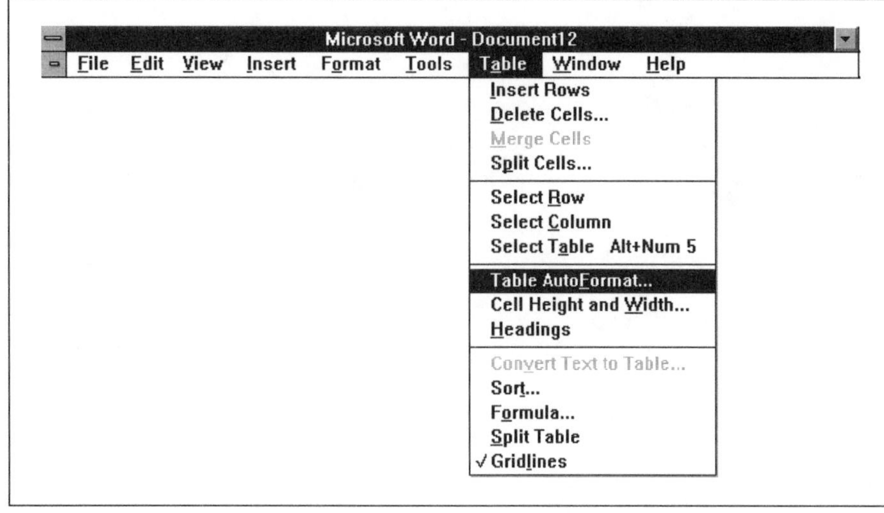

►► Many Keyboard Command Changes

Just as there have been menu changes, there have been keyboard shortcut changes. Again, you can override one or all of these by using Word's Customize command. See Chapter 36.

►► Improved Specifications

Many of Word's earlier restrictions (number of open windows, maximum file size, etc.) have been removed or greatly improved. For instance, you can now have up to 10,000 words in your spelling checker's user dictionary.

►► Just Do It

Buy this book. Buy the software. Install it, and let's get started. There's a lot to know if you plan to *master* Word 6. You're gonna love it.

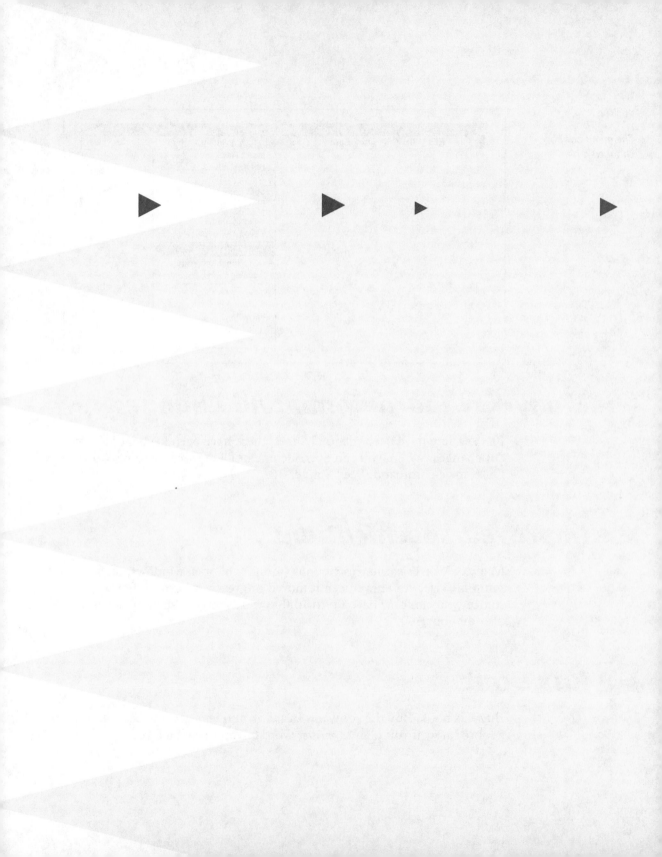

CHAPTER 2

Creating Your First Document

▸▸ FAST TRACK

To save yourself time and effort later on **_36_**

start each new project by thinking about your document's overall design and final appearance. It is always a good idea to input (at least preliminary) printer, paper, margin, and other document-design decisions before you start typing.

To start Word for Windows **_38_**

double-click on its program icon in Windows. An equally handy way to start Word is to double-click on a Word for Windows *document* icon.

To speed up and simplify your work **_40_**

use the key combinations (often called *hot keys*) that are assigned to many commands. These keyboard shortcuts are usually listed next to command names in menus. If a command doesn't have a shortcut, you can always assign one.

To delete unwanted text **_48_**

highlight the undesired text and press the **backspace** key.

To enter text **_52_**

click to place the insertion point where you want the text to appear and start typing.

To save documents 57

use the File ➤ Save (**Ctrl+S**) command. If you are saving a document for the first time, you will see the Save As dialog box. Give the file a meaningful name and be sure you are storing it in a useful place, then click the **OK** button (↵).

To completely quit Word 62

choose File ➤ Exit or double-click on the Control box in the upper-left corner of the main Word window. If you haven't saved changes, you will be given the chance to do so now. To save changes, click **Yes** (↵); to lose changes, click **No**.

To open a new, untitled document 74

choose File ➤ New or use the **Ctrl+N** keyboard shortcut.

To see a list of commands that you can issue with your mouse 79

click the nonprimary mouse button (usually the right).

To get help 79

use any of Word for Windows' three kinds of online help: topic-specific help (Help ➤ Search for Help on…), screen-element help, or WordPerfect help (Help ➤ WordPerfect Help…). If all else fails, contact Microsoft Product Support Services.

▸▸ In this chapter we'll explore Word's basic text-editing features, using default settings and a Mark Twain quote. You'll type, edit, save, close, and reopen your first Word for Windows project. It's a long chapter, but worth the effort. Chapter 2, along with the two chapters that follow it, will give you the essential foundation you need to master Word for Windows.

▸▸ Document Setup

Although we'll use Word's standard settings for this first exercise, it is worth noting that many experienced users start each new project by thinking about the document's overall design and final appearance. Word for Windows gives you on-screen clues about how your document will look on paper. It can show you line endings, page endings, the relative size and placement of text, graphics, margins, and so on. In order to do this, Word needs some information from you—like the paper size you plan to use and the kind of printer you will be using. You may also have strong feelings about how much white space you want around the edges of your pages. Once you tell Word these things, it changes the on-screen appearance of margins, the ruler, and other settings to accommodate and reflect your design.

Thus, it is always a good idea to input (at least preliminary) printer, paper, margin, and other document-design decisions before you start typing. In Part Two, you will learn how to do this by using Page Setup and other tools. Word for Windows 6 also provides *templates* that contain settings for particular kinds of jobs, making setup quick and easy.

If you are lucky enough to have a simple life with only one printer, one paper size, and similar projects, you may be able to make your setup decisions once and forget about them or even use Microsoft's default factory settings and perhaps a few standard templates for every project.

If you do complex tasks, a variety of projects, or you're a perfectionist, though, you'll frequently change specialized printer and document settings.

▶▶ TIP

Get in the habit of thinking about which printer and paper size you plan to use, the orientation of pages, and other design elements right when you start a new project. Visit Page Setup before you start typing.

▶▶ Typing Habits to Break

If you learned to type on a typewriter or even an old word processor, chances are you have established habits that will be counterproductive in your use of Word for Windows. Here are a few habits you should try to break:

- Do not use the Tab key or the spacebar to indent paragraphs. Instead, use the indent control in Word's ruler (the top "handle" at the left side of the ruler). You'll learn more about this in Chapter 10.
- Never use the spacebar to center or otherwise position text. Use the center-alignment button on the Formatting Toolbar instead. You'll learn about Toolbars later in this chapter.
- Don't use the spacebar to make columns. Instead use tabs, Word's multicolumn features, or tables. See Chapter 11.
- Do not manually space paragraphs with carriage returns. Use Word's paragraph spacing instead, as explained in Chapter 10.
- Do not hit ↵ repeatedly to start a new page. Instead, use Word's Insert Page Break command.

▶▶ Your First Word for Windows Project

With those preliminaries out of the way, you're ready to roll. We'll use Word's default settings for this first example in order to simplify things.

► Starting Word from within Windows

The preferred method of starting Word for Windows is to double-click on its program icon in Windows. An equally handy way to start Word is to double-click on a Word for Windows *document* icon. This will launch Word and immediately open the document itself so that you can get right to work on it. Or, you can start Word from the DOS prompt along with Windows. For now, let's use the program icon:

1. Locate the Word 6 icon, as shown in Figure 2.1.
2. Point to the Word for Windows program icon using your mouse (or trackball), then double-click (click on it twice quickly) to launch the program. Unless you've reconfigured your mouse for left-handed use, do all of your clicking with the *left* button. This is often referred to as the *primary* mouse button.
3. Unless someone has turned off this feature, you'll see a "tip of the day" each time you start Word. Take a moment to read them. They are often helpful and entertaining. Click OK to dismiss the tip. You'll be left with a new, untitled Word document window, as shown in Figure 2.2.

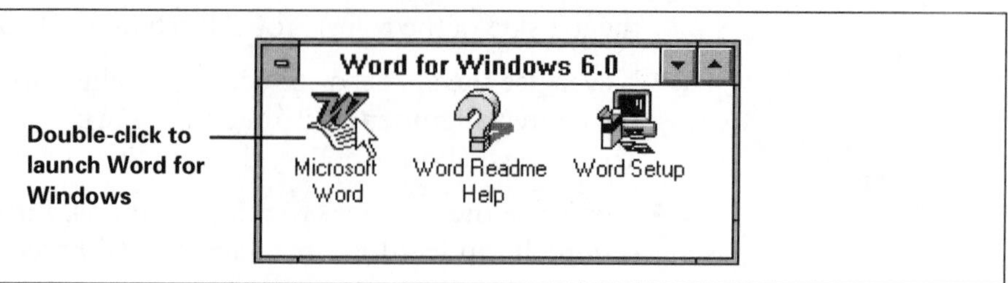

FIGURE 2.1 ►

You can start Word by double-clicking on the Word 6 icon. If you like, you can see a tip of the day each time you start.

► The Parts of a Word Window

An active Word window has standard Windows scroll bars, a title bar, zoom boxes, a menu bar, and so on. (If you are unfamiliar with these terms and concepts, take a moment to review your Windows manuals.)

FIGURE 2.2

A new document window appears each time you start Word.

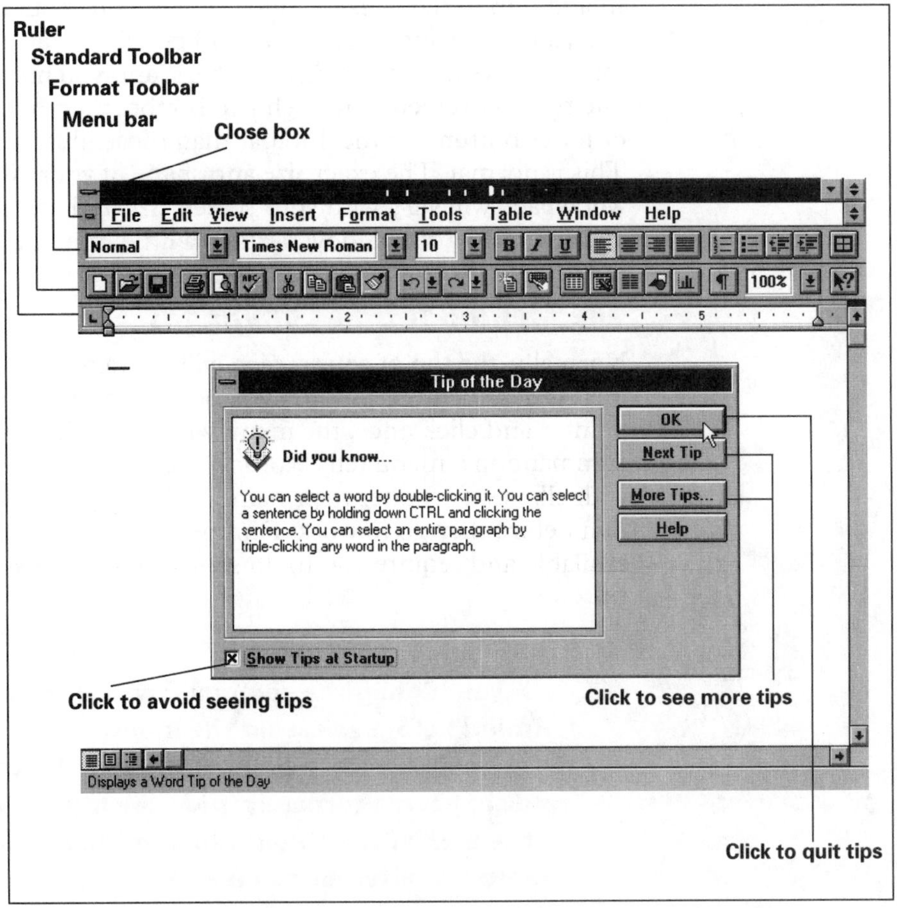

Ruler
Standard Toolbar
Format Toolbar
Menu bar
Close box
File Edit View Insert Format Tools Table Window Help
Normal Times New Roman 10
100%
Tip of the Day
Did you know...
You can select a word by double-clicking it. You can select a sentence by holding down CTRL and clicking the sentence. You can select an entire paragraph by triple-clicking any word in the paragraph.
OK
Next Tip
More Tips...
Help
Show Tips at Startup
Click to avoid seeing tips
Click to see more tips
Displays a Word Tip of the Day
Click to quit tips

NOTE

It is good to distinguish between the *document* window and the *application* window. The document window is where individual Word files appear, while the application window will be open even if there are no files open, as long as Word for Windows is running. Some of the items we talk about below are specific to the document or application window, but it is not crucial to know what belongs where. The important thing is to know which items are which.

In addition to the usual Windows tools, you should see a ruler, Toolbars, a flashing insertion point, and possibly a few other things. Word for Windows now has many Toolbars, and you may see up to eight at one time on-screen (although two is more common). You may see more or fewer buttons on the Toolbar than those illustrated in Figure 2.2. This is normal. The exact size and shape of your Word for Windows workspace will vary with your screen size and other factors. Let's look at a few of Word's window parts in a little more detail.

The Menu Bar and Commands

Normally, the top of your screen will contain traditional Windows-style menus in a menu bar. When you point to a menu title with the mouse pointer and click once, the menu will drop. Clicking on the desired command in a menu tells Word to execute that command. Commands with ellipses (...) after their names will ask you for additional information before they go to work. Dimmed commands are not currently available and require you to do something else first.

▸▸ TIP

If you highlight a command and then change your mind before releasing the mouse button, simply slide the pointer off the menu to make the command list disappear; alternately, slide the highlight up or down the menu list without releasing the mouse button to select a different command.

Many commands can also be executed by holding down specific key combinations (often called *hot keys*). These keyboard shortcuts are usually listed next to command names in menus. For instance, holding down the Ctrl key and pressing the P key is the same as choosing File ➤ Print.... You'll learn more about this later.

The Mouse Pointer

Your mouse pointer should look like an I-beam and move freely about the screen. The pointer will change shapes when it passes over certain parts of the Word for Windows workplace. For instance, it turns into a large arrow at the edges of Word windows. You'll soon learn how these changes in the pointer's appearance tell you what you can do next.

The Insertion Point

The *insertion point* or cursor denotes where text, graphics, and other things will be placed when you type or insert them. The insertion point is a tall, skinny, blinking vertical stick. Don't confuse it with the mouse pointer. The I-beam mouse pointer and insertion point are two very different devices. Take a moment to locate them both in Figure 2.2 and on your own screen.

NEW

Word for Windows now provides eight Toolbars that can be moved, edited, enlarged, and hidden as needed. You can even create your own buttons and button art!

Toolbars

Word for Windows provides eight different Toolbars, although you'll normally display only two or three at any one time. Microsoft's "factory settings" display only the Standard and Formatting Toolbars. Here are the names of all eight:

- Standard
- Formatting
- Borders
- Database
- Drawing
- Forms
- Microsoft
- Word for Windows 2.0

Toolbars contain buttons, drop-down menus, and other controls that help you quickly alter the appearance and arrangement of documents by executing a variety of Word for Windows commands.

For example, you can use the Formatting Toolbar's Bold button to make text bold, or its drop-down font menus to pick a font and size. Point to the buttons containing arrows (next to the font and type-size menus) to see drop-down lists of choices. You can also type font names or sizes directly into the font and size boxes.

The button containing the paragraph mark (¶) alternately shows and hides paragraph marks, tab marks, space marks (the little dots), and other nonprinting items.

We'll explore Toolbar buttons in-depth throughout the book. To display or hide Toolbars, choose View ➤ Toolbars....

▸▸ TIP

Word's new ruler is much easier to use, particularly when adjusting indents. There's also a new vertical ruler visible in Page Layout view.

The Ruler

new

The ruler lets you quickly change margins and indents. It serves additional roles when working in columns and tables. The ruler lets you alter the appearance of multiple paragraphs or just the paragraph containing the insertion point. You'll learn more about the ruler later in this chapter.

To display or hide the ruler, choose View ➤ Ruler.

▸▸ TIP

Word for Windows offers many formatting capabilities not found on the ruler or one of the Toolbars. For instance, while there is only one underline choice on the Toolbar, you can specify four types (single, words only, double, and dotted) by choosing Format ➤ Font. Think of the Toolbars and ruler as mini-formatting features. If you want to master Word, you should get to know the more robust menu commands, as well.

Status Area

The bottom of your Word window gives additional information about your work in a place called the *status area*. It's always present unless you choose the Full Screen view.

new ▶▶ NEW

You'll now see much more information in the status area than in previous versions. Get in the habit of watching the status area while you work.

As you'll read later, there are occasions when you might be asked to type things or click in the status area. Right now, let's start a document and put some of this horsepower to work. If it's not already running, start Word for Windows now.

▶▶ Typing Text

Type the following quotation (intentionally type **The the** rather than simply *The* at the beginning). Don't worry if you also make other typing mistakes; you'll learn how to fix them in a moment.

> The the difference between the right word and the almost right word is the difference between lightning and the lightning bug.

Watch the screen as you type. Notice that Word for Windows automatically moves text down to the next line when it runs out of room near the right edge of the screen. This is called automatic word wrap, a common and useful word processing feature. For this exercise, do not press ↵ until you've typed the period after the word *bug*.

Finish by typing Mark Twain's name then press ↵ again. When you are done, your screen should look something like Figure 2.3.

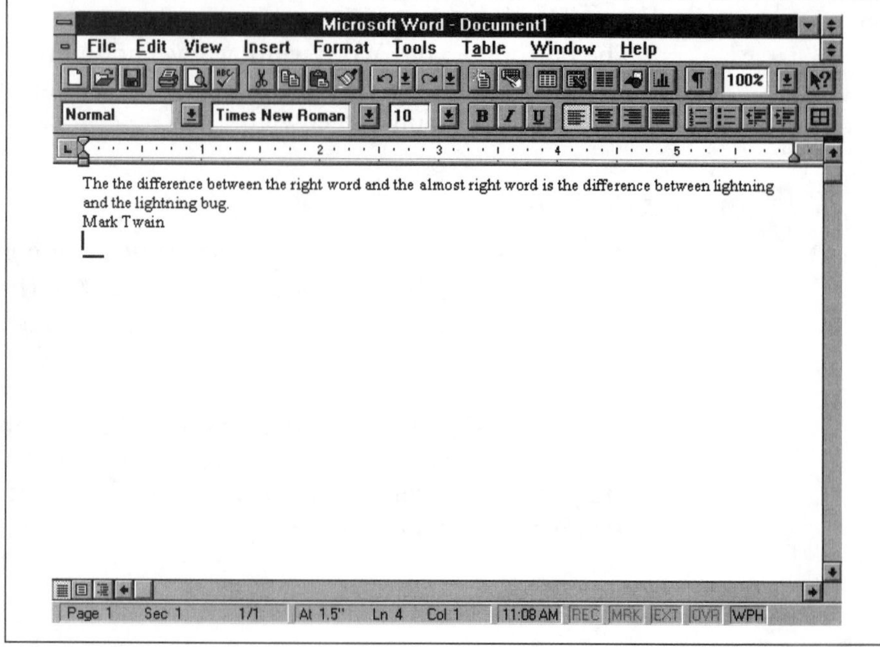

FIGURE 2.3 ►

Type in Mark Twain's unembellished quote.

►► Selecting Text

Word lets you do a lot with text after you've typed it. You can change its appearance, move it around, delete it, and copy it. The first step is *always* to tell Word which text you want to work with. This is done by *selecting* it. Word has many, many ways to select text. For instance, you can drag your mouse pointer over the text while holding down the primary mouse button. There are shortcuts for selecting individual words, lines, sentences, and paragraphs, which you will read about in a moment.

Depending on your system configuration, selected text will either change color or be surrounded by a gray or black background. That's how you know what you have selected, as you can see here.

The·the·difference·between·
and·the·lightning·bug.¶

If you are a new Windows user, practice selecting other words, sentences, and single characters with the mouse. It might be frustrating at first, but you'll soon find yourself reaching for the mouse even when using a computer that doesn't have one!

▶▶ TIP

If you have selected text and changed your mind, click anywhere outside of the selected area or press an arrow key to cancel the selection.

▶ Selecting Specific Blocks of Text with a Mouse

Here is a summary of text selection shortcuts for specific units of text, such as words, sentences, and graphics. Practice them all until they become second nature.

▶▶ NOTE

For purposes of selecting, graphics are treated the same as text.

Selecting Entire Words

Double-click anywhere on a word to select the entire word and the space that follows it. To select adjacent words, drag after double-clicking on the first word of interest. Entire words will be selected when you drag this way.

Selecting Entire Lines

To select entire lines, follow these steps:

1. Move the mouse pointer to the *selection bar* (an invisible strip running down the extreme left edge of the document window). The mouse pointer will change from the I-beam to an arrow.
2. Click the primary mouse button only once. The entire *line* to the right of where you've clicked will be selected.

Continue dragging down to select additional lines.

Selecting Entire Sentences

Hold down the Ctrl key while you click anywhere in the sentence of interest. This also selects the sentence's punctuation mark (period, question mark, etc.) and the space following the sentence, if there is one. Dragging after you click this way selects additional sentences.

Selecting Entire Paragraphs

The quickest way to select a paragraph with your mouse is to *triple-click* anywhere in a paragraph. That is to say, point anywhere in the paragraph and quickly press and release the mouse button three times in succession. You can also select paragraphs using the selection bar by following these steps:

1. Move the mouse pointer to the selection bar (the invisible strip running down the extreme left edge of the document window). The pointer will become an arrow.
2. Double-click. The adjacent paragraph will be selected.

Selecting Your Entire Document

To select the entire document, follow these steps:

1. Move the mouse pointer to the selection bar at the left edge of the document and the pointer will become an arrow.
2. Hold down the Ctrl key and click. The entire document will be selected. Alternately, you can triple-click to select the whole document.

Selecting Graphics and Other Objects

Click anywhere within the graphic or other object. You'll see a border—usually with *handles* (small black boxes) surrounding the selected object.

► Selecting Variable Units of Text

Sometimes you'll want to select just a single character or parts of a text string. Here are some techniques to use.

Automatic Word Select

Word for Windows now features an option called Automatic Word Select to help in selecting text. You select as many or as few characters of the first word you want to change. Then when you drag over to the next word, the *entire* second word is selected. You must hold down Alt to select partial words when Automatic Word Select is on (and it is on by default). You can turn this option off in the Edit tab in the Options dialog box.

Dragging to Select

To select adjacent bits of text, follow these steps:

1. Point to the place where you want selection to begin.
2. Hold down the primary mouse button and drag in any direction.
3. When the pointer hits a screen boundary (top, bottom, or side) the document will scroll as highlighting continues.
4. Release the mouse button when you've selected the desired area.

Shift-Clicking to Select Large Areas

To select large blocks of continuous text, follow these steps:

1. Point to the place where you want selection to begin.
2. Click to place the insertion point there.
3. Point to the end of the desired area (scroll if necessary) and hold down the Shift key while you click.
4. Release the mouse button.

Selecting Rectangular Areas

To select rectangular areas (like columns in a tabbed list), hold down the Alt key while you drag the mouse.

Selecting in Tables

There are many specific tools you can use to select items in tables. See Chapter 11 for details.

►► Deleting Text

There are several ways to delete unwanted text like that extra *the* you typed in the sample Twain quote. If you had spotted your mistake right after typing it, pressing the backspace key four times would have removed the unwanted characters and space.

Even if you did not make the correction earlier, it is easy to go back now, select the undesired text, and remove it. Follow these steps:

1. Double-click on the word to be deleted (*the* in this example).
2. The entire word and the space following it become highlighted.
3. Press the Delete key once.
4. You can use "Undo Clear" (discussed in a moment) if you accidentally delete something of value.

Later, you will learn other ways to delete text and numerous strategies to reuse deleted text (move it) elsewhere. If you haven't already done so, delete that unwanted *the*.

►► Undo, Redo, and Repeat

Do you know what a damnosecond is? It's that fleeting instant when you realize you've done something really stupid on your computer—like accidentally deleting or reformatting twenty pages of text.

Everyone makes choices they wish they could undo. Like few other things in life, Word often lets you rewrite history. You can even undo an Undo by *redoing* it.

And, for tasks that are repetitive and complex, it is nice to have your computer handle some of the drudgery. That's where Word's Repeat command can help. The combination of Undo, Redo, and Repeat can be both powerful and perplexing. Let's begin by looking at Undo.

▶ Undo

Word watches as you work. With surprising attention to detail, it remembers which steps you last took. When asked, it can frequently undo your errors. The exact name of the Undo choice on the Edit menu changes as you work. Sometimes it says Undo Typing. Other times it says Undo Formatting or Undo Sort, or some such.

Here are some examples of things Word can undo if you ask soon after you discover a problem:

- Editing changes (typing, cutting, pasting, etc.)
- Most formatting actions (changing styles, fonts, etc.)
- Most projects done with tools (for example, replacing Bill with Bob, etc.)
- Most drawing actions (dragging, filling, etc.)

There are three ways to undo:

- Edit ➤ Undo reverses just your last action.
- If you press Ctrl+Z repeatedly, it will reverse previous actions.
- The Undo Toolbar button and its associated drop-down list menu let you undo multiple actions in sequence.

new ▶▶ NEW

Word for Windows now lets you undo more than one previous action. To see a list of your prior actions, click on the arrow next to the Standard Toolbar's Undo button. You can undo one or more selected actions by picking them from the list.

▶ Using Undo

To undo your last action only, choose Edit ➤ Undo. The Ctrl+Z keyboard shortcut will reverse previous actions. Clicking the Undo button on the Toolbar will also work.

To undo multiple actions or selected actions, use the drop-down list reached with the arrow button next to the Toolbar's Undo button.

1. Reveal the list by pointing to the Undo list arrow. The last thing you've done will be on the top of the list.
2. Click on an item to undo it or drag to select and undo a sequence of actions.
3. If you accidentally undo the wrong things, use the Redo list to the right of the Undo list to "undo your Undo."

▶ Redo

Yes, it *is* possible to undo an Undo. To redo just your last action, choose Edit ➤ Redo, press the keyboard shortcut (F4), or click the new Redo button on the Standard Toolbar.

To redo multiple actions or selected actions, use the drop-down list reached with the arrow button next to the Toolbar's Redo button.

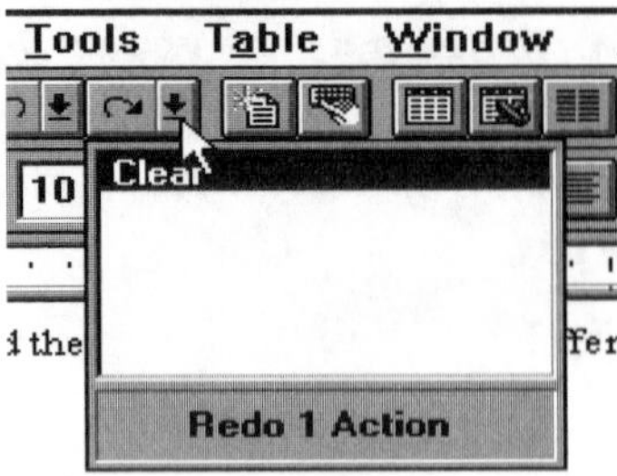

1. Reveal the list by pointing to the Redo list arrow. The last thing you've undone will be on the top of the list.
2. Click on an item to redo (undo the Undo) or drag to select a sequence of actions.

If you accidentally redo the wrong things, use the Undo list to the right of the Redo list to "undo your Redo."

▶ Whadaya Mean I Can't Undo?

Occasionally, you will see a "Can't Undo" message indicating that your most recent action cannot be undone. That's why it is a good idea to save your work early and often. Then, when such a message appears, you can close the messed-up document either by saving it under a different name (with File ➤ Save As...) or close the document without saving the changes (i.e., without saving your mistakes). Then open the earlier version that is (we hope!) in better shape. Sometimes you can save time by cutting and pasting between the earlier version and portions of the new (messed-up) work if you've saved it under a different file name.

▶▶ TIP

The best approach is to stop and think immediately after you notice a big, potentially time-consuming mistake. Get help. Sometimes more experienced Word for Windows users or Microsoft's telephone support staff can talk you through time-saving repair techniques. The less you fiddle after noticing a big mistake, the better your chances of salvation. If you are a new user, don't be embarrassed to ask for help right away when you notice a problem!

▶ Repeat

Sometimes, after you've done something repeatable (like formatting or typing) you will find a *Repeat* command on Word's Edit menu. The new shortcut is the F4 function key. Repeat watches you work and attempts to remember and recreate your actions on demand. Suppose, for instance, you change the width of a paragraph. If you have several other paragraphs scattered around your document that also need to be reformatted the same way, you could select each paragraph and use the Repeat feature to reformat them.

Like Undo, Repeat's name changes based on what you have last done, and it works with most Word for Windows actions immediately after you take them. Experiment.

Incidentally, there are often better ways to repeat actions. For instance, Word provides a format "paintbrush" you'll learn about in Chapter 14 that you may find easier to use when repeating format changes.

►► Inserting Text

Word offers several ways to insert new text into an existing document. The most straightforward approach is to move the insertion point to the desired location, then start typing. Word accommodates the new text by pushing the existing text to the right and down as necessary.

Suppose you wanted to add the word *obviously* between *the* and *right* in the first line of Mark Twain's quote. You would start by placing the mouse pointer (the I-beam) where you want to begin inserting text—between the space and the *r* in *right* for this example. Next, you'd press and release the mouse button to move the insertion point to the desired position.

►► **WARNING**

Beginners sometimes forget to press the mouse button after pointing with the I-beam. Don't confuse the I-beam with the insertion point! First you use the I-beam to point to where you want the insertion point placed. Then you must press and release the mouse button to move the insertion point.

Try it. Position the insertion point and type the word **obviously**, including the space that follows it. Your screen should look something like Figure 2.4.

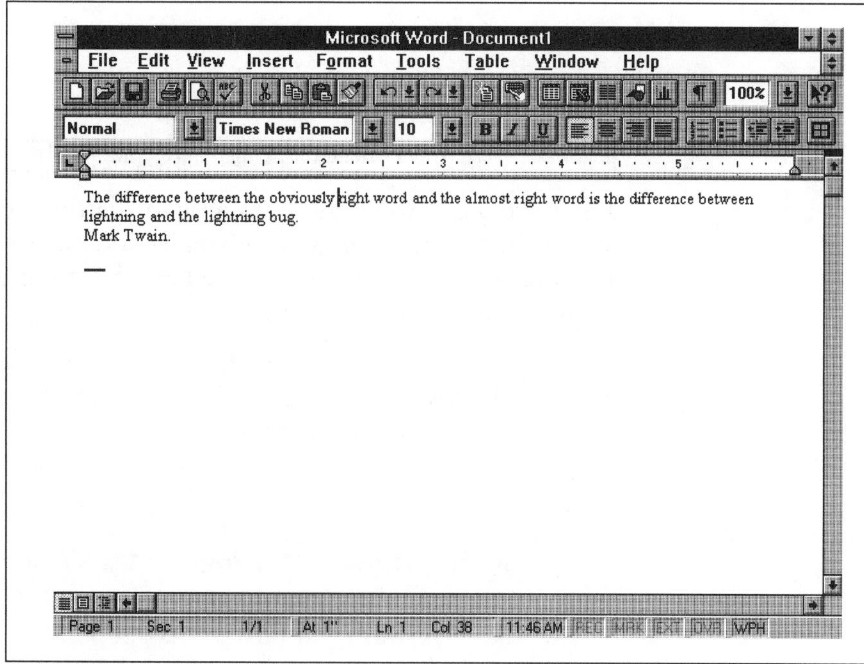

FIGURE 2.4 *You must position the I-beam and then insert the text.*

Replacing Text

Word also makes it easy to replace text. It combines the steps of deleting unwanted text, positioning the insertion point, and inserting replacement text. Simply highlight the unwanted text and start typing. The old text disappears and the new text snakes across the screen as you type it.

For example, watch the screen while you highlight the word *almost* (double-click on it) and type **nearly**. See how easily you can turn great prose into drivel? Because we'll be using this text for some future exercises, take a moment now to restore Mark Twain's actual words using the text-editing tricks you've learned so far.

Simple Formatting Tricks

Let's take a quick look at a few of Word's most often used ways to modify the appearance of text. They include Toolbars, menus, and keyboard shortcuts.

▸ Toolbars

Word's *Formatting Toolbar* is shown here.

There are other Toolbars containing formatting buttons, as you'll see later. Among other things, Toolbars let you make style changes by clicking buttons or pulling down single level menus, rather than going to the more crowded menu bar.

As always, you must select text before working with it. For this exercise, select all the text either by dragging, choosing Edit ➤ Select All, or by using the keyboard shortcut Ctrl+A.

▸▸ **TIP**

Get in the habit of using the Ctrl+A shortcut when you want to select your entire document. It can save you a lot of scrolling in large documents.

Let's start by increasing all of the type from 12 to 24 points. The third arrow in the upper-left corner of the Toolbar reveals a list of type sizes, as shown here.

10
11
12
14
16
18
20
22
24

To reveal the type sizes, point at the triangle, then press and hold the mouse button. Slide the pointer down to highlight *24* and release the mouse button. Your screen should look something like Figure 2.5.

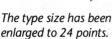

FIGURE 2.5 

The type size has been enlarged to 24 points.

The difference between the right word and the almost right word is the difference between lightning and the lightning bug.
Mark Twain

TIP

You can also *type* font names or sizes directly into their respective Toolbar boxes. Simply click in the box to highlight the old size (10 in our example) and type the desired size (24 in our exercise). When you're finished typing, press ↵ to change the size.

Regardless of which technique you use to change the size of text, you can change as much or as little as you like. For instance, you could highlight just the first letter *T* in the quote and make it 48-point type, creating a large initial cap effect.

TIP

You can accomplish better-looking versions of this and other "drop cap" effects automatically using Word's Drop Caps feature. Read about it in Chapter 9.

To change the appearance of characters (making them bold or italicized, for instance), first select them, then click the appropriate button on the Formatting Toolbar. Try italicizing the word *almost* in your Twain quote now:

1. Double-click to select the word *almost.*
2. Click on the Italic button in the Toolbar, as illustrated in Figure 2.6. Word will italicize the selected text.

FIGURE 2.6

Select words you wish to format and click on the desired button (Italic in this example).

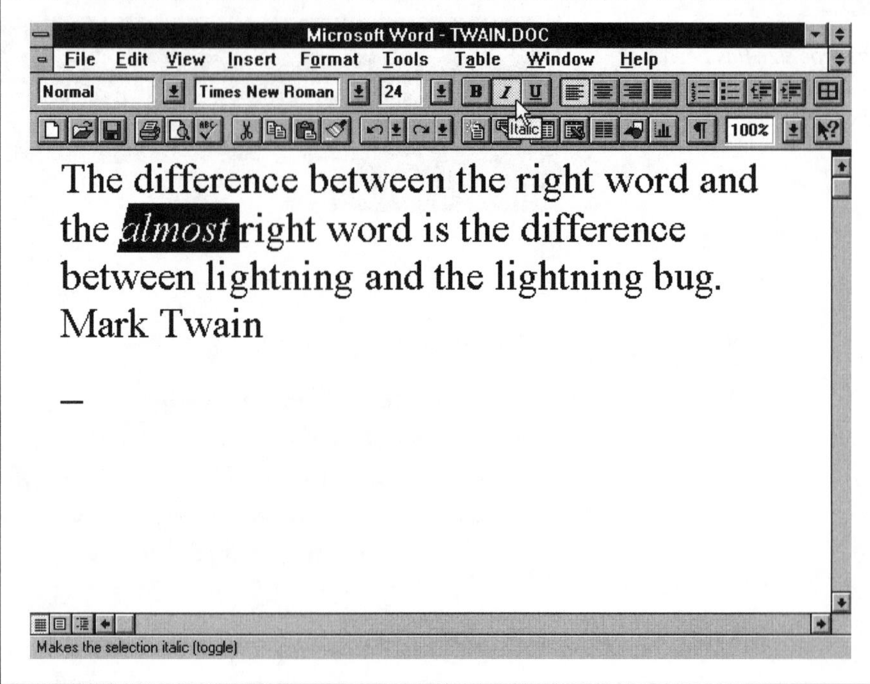

Next, use the same basic techniques to make Mark Twain's name appear in boldface. Start by selecting his first and last names by double-clicking or dragging. Then press the Bold button on the Format Toolbar (the uppercase B).

As you know, the button to the right of the Bold button italicizes text. The Underscore button is next to the Italic button.

▸▸ Aligning Text with the Formatting Toolbar

Notice the group of four buttons to the right of the Underline button in the Format Toolbar. They contain horizontal lines. These let you specify left-aligned, centered, right-aligned, or fully justified text.

These "paragraph formatting" buttons and similar formatting tools work on entire paragraphs. They can be used on a single paragraph by simply placing the insertion point in the paragraph to be affected before using the button. For instance, to right-align Mark Twain's name:

1. Place the insertion point anywhere in Mark Twain's name (point and click), as shown in Figure 2.7.
2. Click on the Right-align button. The text will move to the right, as illustrated in Figure 2.8.

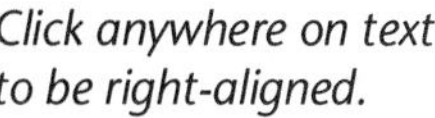

FIGURE 2.7

Click anywhere on text to be right-aligned.

The difference between the right word and the *almost* right word is the difference between lightning and the lightning bug.
Mark Twain

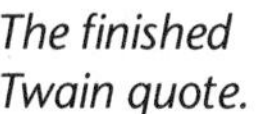

FIGURE 2.8

The finished Twain quote.

The difference between the right word and the *almost* right word is the difference between lightning and the lightning bug.
Mark Twain

To change multiple paragraphs simultaneously, select them first. Remember how plain the initial document looked? With a few mouse clicks you've changed its appearance considerably.

There's much more to learn about formatting, as you'll see throughout this book. You are probably itching to print by now, and you will in a moment, but it would be a good idea to save your work first. That way if you have a printer or system problem, you won't need to redo the entire exercise.

►► Saving Documents the First Time

The words that you have typed and stylized so far exist only on your screen and in your computer's volatile RAM (random-access memory).

If you were to switch off the computer or experience a power failure or other malfunction, your work would be forever lost. By saving your work to disk as you go, you can pick up where you have left off without losing your changes.

TIP

Many experienced computer users save every fifteen minutes or whenever they are interrupted by phone calls or visitors. That's a good habit to establish. Word for Windows will even do the saving for you automatically, if you wish, as described in Chapter 7.

Once you are happy with the appearance of the Mark Twain quote, select File ➤ Save. You will see the Save As dialog box, illustrated in Figure 2.9.

FIGURE 2.9

You see the Save As dialog box the first time you save a file.

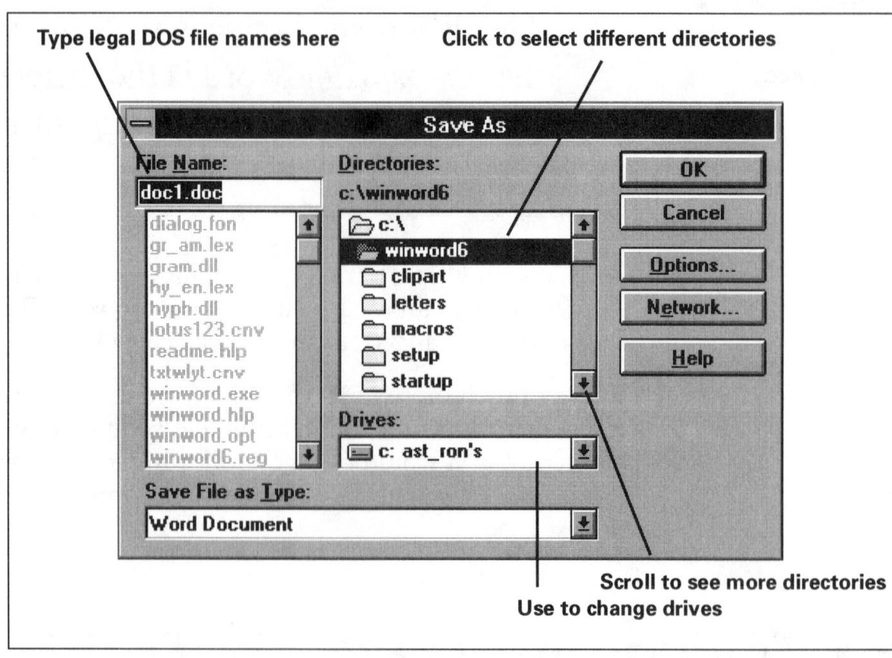

TIP

The Ctrl+S keyboard shortcut is a convenient way to save without visiting the File menu. Some folks use it exclusively. The Standard Toolbar includes a button that looks like a floppy disk, which will also start the Save process.

The Save dialog box tells you where Word for Windows plans to store your work and requests a name for the file. It also gives you many other Save options, which are discussed in Chapter 7.

Let's keep things simple for now and use Word's default save options. Start by noticing where Word proposes to put your document. This is a very important habit to establish.

WARNING

If you do not get in the habit of thinking about where you and Word for Windows save documents, you will misplace them. When saving to a floppy disk or your own small, uncluttered hard disk, this can be a minor annoyance. If you work on a far-flung network with multiple servers and gigabytes of storage space, it can take hours or days to locate lost files.

In Figure 2.9, Word for Windows is proposing to store our new document in the directory containing Word itself—called wordwin6. You can tell this from the picture of a folder next to its name (wordwin6) near the top of the dialog box.

TIP

It's not a good idea to clutter up your Word for Windows directory with a lot of documents, so in Chapter 7 we'll create some directories specifically for Word documents. If you are an experienced Windows user, you might want to do that now.

Look at your screen. Take a moment to see where Word for Windows plans to save your work. Chances are you will see something slightly different from the folder location shown in Figure 2.9.

▸ Telling Word Where to Save Your Document

Like any good Windows program, Word lets you specify save locations. You do this by picking the desired location from the scrolling directory list located just to the right of the scrollable file list shown in Figure 2.9. Use the Drives list to switch drives, if necessary. (For more information see Chapter 7.)

▸ Naming Word Documents

Type a name for your document in the File Name: box, then simply click the Save button. Names can be up to eight characters and must conform to the DOS file-naming rules (no spaces, asterisks, etc.). It's a good idea to use the extension .DOC for all of your Word documents unless you understand and know how to use the Windows Associate feature. Read more about this feature in your Windows documentation.

▸▸ TIP

Instead of clicking on the Save button, tap ↵. This will have the same effect as clicking Save. With Word, like most Windows programs, pressing ↵ will execute the button with the bold border in the active dialog box.

One way or the other, Word for Windows will save your document and, if the Summary Info feature is turned on (see Chapters 7 and 36), you will see a Summary Info dialog box similar to the one shown here,

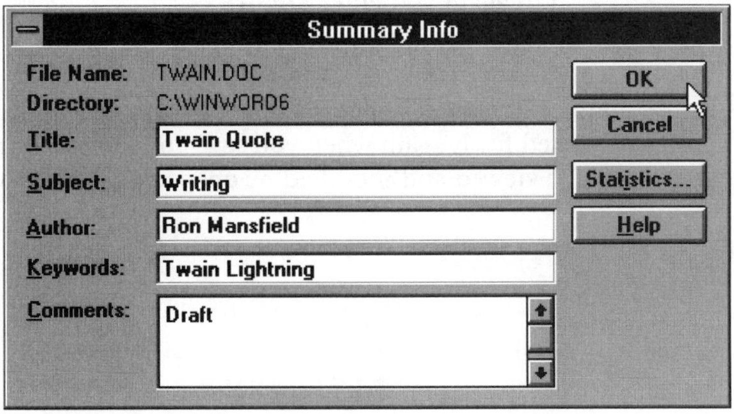

with blanks in many places. Don't be alarmed if you don't see the Summary Info dialog box right now. The information it collects is optional and can be added later, if you like.

▶ Summary Information

You needn't type anything in this dialog box, and you can prevent it from even appearing. But if you plan to keep many documents on your hard disk, and particularly if you will be storing things on a crowded network server, it is a good idea to use this handy feature. As you'll see in Chapter 7, it will help you quickly locate projects with the File ➤ Find File… command when you want to round them up for later use. Another useful aspect of Summary Info is that you can type in long file names.

Because we'll be using this document to explore the File ➤ Find File… feature later, take a moment to enter summary information:

1. If you don't see the Summary Info dialog box, choose File ➤ Summary Info… to bring it into view.
2. Type **Twain Quote** as the document title. Do not press ↵ yet.
3. Press the Tab key or point with the I-beam and click to move the insertion point to the next blank.
4. Type **Writing** as the subject.
5. Tab or point and click again and enter your name if it does not already appear in the author box.

6. Tab once more and enter some keywords (such as *Twain* or *lightning*).
7. Tab again and enter **Draft**.
8. Click the OK button or, quicker still, press ↵.

Once you have saved a document's summary information, you will not be asked for it again when you save your work. Summary information can be viewed and modified by choosing File ➤ Summary Info.

►► TIP

To prevent the Summary Info dialog box from appearing when you initially save a new document, turn it off via the Save category of the dialog box brought up by choosing Tools ➤ Options… (Chapter 36).

►► Saving as You Work

Once you've named a document and specified a place to save it, you won't see the Save As… or Summary dialog boxes when you save unless you request the. A quick trip to File ➤ Save or better still, the key combination Ctrl+S, will save your work whenever you desire. So will clicking the Save button on the Standard Toolbar. Save early, save often, and *always* save before you print or make major changes.

If you need help remembering to save regularly, Word can even save automatically at time intervals you specify. This feature is described in Chapter 7.

►► Quitting and Restarting Word

There are several ways to completely quit Word. You can choose File ➤ Exit or double-click on the Control box in the upper-left corner of the main Word window, both of which are shown in Figure 2.10. Try one or the other method now.

If you have made any changes since the last time you saved, Word will ask if you want them saved. Select Yes to save changes, No to ignore the

FIGURE 2.10

Quit by choosing File ➤ Exit or by double-clicking the control box in the Word for Windows application window.

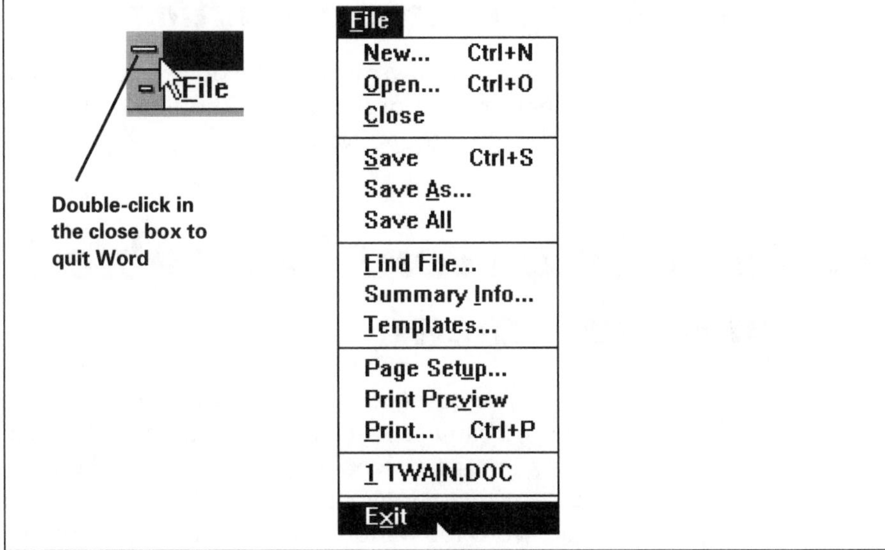

most recent changes, or Cancel to abort your exit request and return to word processing.

After you have satisfied Word that you have saved everything of value, Word will quit.

WARNING

Word needs to do some housekeeping when you exit. For instance, Word updates its settings files and asks if you want to save last-minute changes to your documents. When you use Word's Exit command, or attempt to quit Windows, this housekeeping will proceed smoothly. But if you use the power switch on your computer (or simply unplug it) without first executing a Word Exit or Windows Shut Down command, you may damage a document file or lose valuable changes to your Word settings (described in Chapter 34).

► Minimizing Instead of Quitting

Like other Windows programs, you can run Word *minimized*, which gets the program "out of the way" without actually exiting it. See your Windows documentation for details.

►► Launching Word by Double-Clicking on a Document

Once you've quit (exited) Word, you will need to restart the program before you can use it again. You could double-click on the Word for Windows program icon as you did before, then tell Word to load the document that you want to revise. But there is a shortcut. It is possible to load Word for Windows by double-clicking on a Word document icon. Try this by double-clicking on your Twain Quote document icon in the Windows File Manager window.

1. Switch to the Windows File Manager (launch it if necessary).

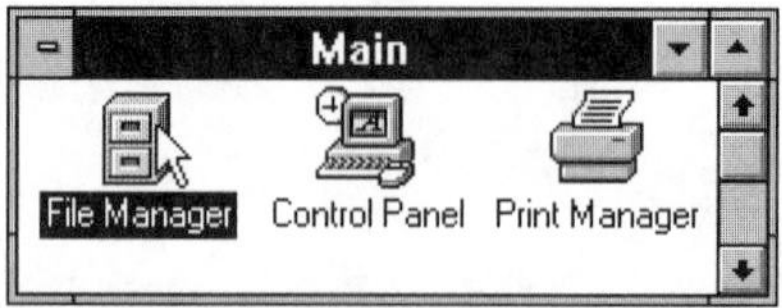

2. Find your Twain document (in your winword6 folder), as shown in Figure 2.11.
3. Double-click on the Twain Quote document icon.
4. After a moment, Word for Windows should be on your screen, along with the Twain document, ready for you to edit.

It is even possible to launch Word for Windows, version 6, by double-clicking on documents created with earlier Word versions. Word 6 will convert them for you automatically. See Chapter 35 before doing this.

FIGURE 2.11

Locate the Twain document.

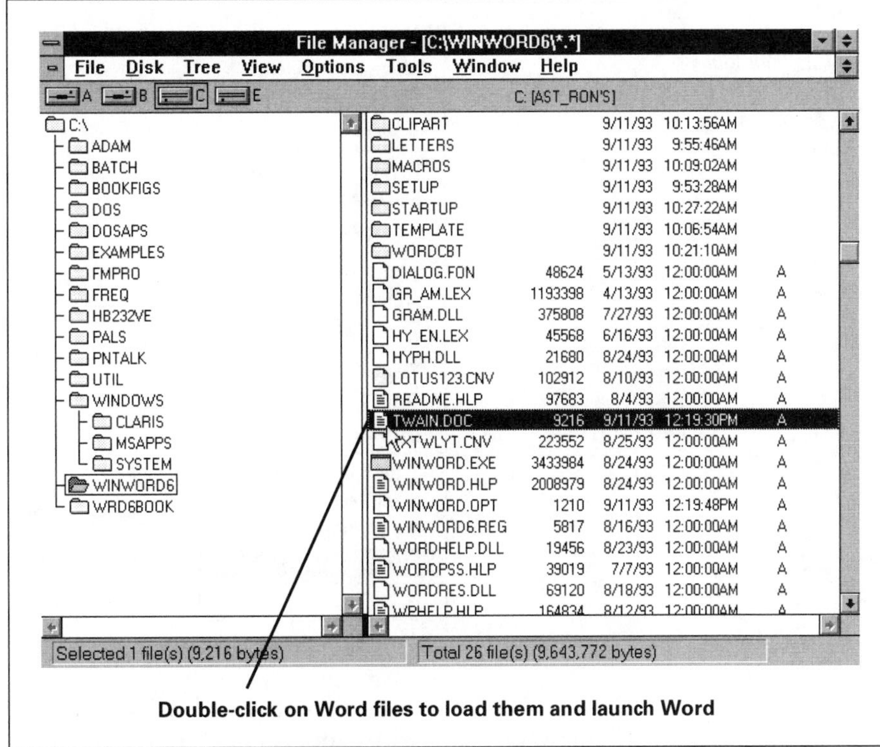

►► Loading Windows, Word, and a Document from the DOS Prompt

While cumbersome to do so, it *is* possible to launch Windows, Word, and a document with a single command from the DOS prompt. You'll need to include the necessary file names and paths:

```
c:\>win \winword6\winword twain.doc
```

►► Quick Access to Recent Projects

Once you have saved some Word for Windows documents, Word remembers their names and locations and lists them at the bottom of your File menu, as shown in Figure 2.12.

FIGURE 2.12 ►

Word lists your four most recent projects at the bottom of the File menu.

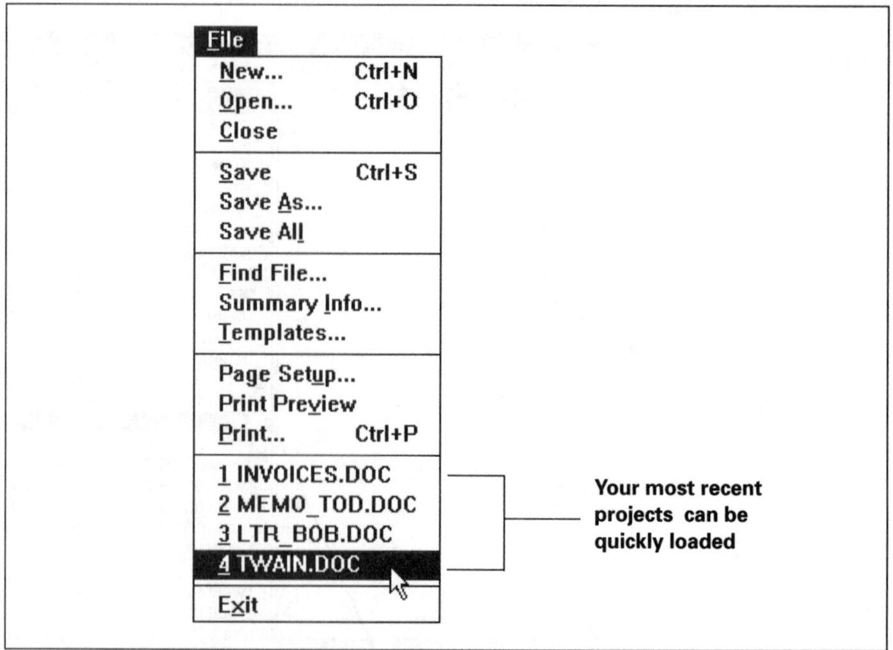

Choose the file of interest and Word will attempt to locate and load it. If you have changed the document's name or moved it since your last Word session, Word may ask for help locating it.

By default, Word lists your last four documents. You can specify longer or shorter lists in the General category of the dialog box reached with the Tools ➤ Options... command (discussed in Chapter 36).

►► Copying and Moving

Word for Windows supports all of the usual Windows techniques for copying and moving information. It also provides a feature called *drag and drop*, a handy one-step, mouse-assisted mover.

► Cut, Copy, and Paste

The traditional way to move or duplicate things in Windows programs is to select the items of interest, cut or copy them to the Clipboard, move the insertion point to the new position, and paste them in. For example, suppose you wanted to move the word *almost* so that it came before the first *right* in the Twain quotation.

1. Start by selecting the desired text (you could simply double-click on *almost*, as shown in Figure 2.13).

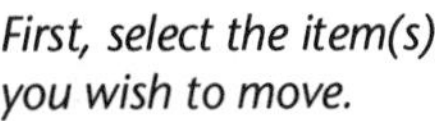

FIGURE 2.13

First, select the item(s) you wish to move.

The difference between the right word and the *almost* right word is the difference between lightning and the lightning bug.

Mark Twain

2. Choose Edit ➤ Cut or press the Ctrl+X shortcut. You can also click the Cut button on the Toolbar.
3. The selected text will disappear from the screen and will be placed on the Clipboard.
4. Now place the insertion point at the desired location (point and click). In this example, place it to the left of the first occurrence of the word *right*, as illustrated in Figure 2.14.

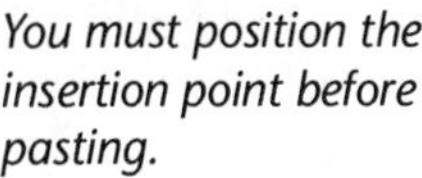

FIGURE 2.14

You must position the insertion point before pasting.

The difference between the right word and the right word is the difference between lightning and the lightning bug.

Mark Twain

5. Paste, using Edit ➤ Paste or the Ctrl+V shortcut. Text will flow to the right and down as the Clipboard's contents move into place. In our example, the resulting move would look like Figure 2.15.

FIGURE 2.15

The pasted (inserted) material forces the other material to the right and down.

The difference between the *almost* right word and the right word is the difference between lightning and the lightning bug.

Mark Twain

►► **TIP**

You can also use the Toolbar's Cut and Paste buttons instead. They look like a pair of scissors and a clipboard respectively.

► Copying from One Word Document to Another

Because you can open and work on multiple Word documents at the same time, it is easy to move things from one document to another. For example there are two legal documents open in Figure 2.16.

With a large screen, it is easy to size and position multiple windows in plain sight and quickly move back and forth simply by clicking in the window of interest. You can arrange your workspace by clicking and dragging the size boxes in the lower-right corners of windows to adjust their size and shape. You can move windows around by pointing to their title bars and dragging them.

While it is possible to have many windows in view at the same time, you can have only one active window. It is easy to tell which is the active window—it's the top one with the highlighted title bar in Figure 2.16.

There are several ways to activate a window. The easiest is simply to click in it. Even if only a small portion of an inactive window is showing, clicking on it will activate it and bring it forward.

1. Locate any portion of the desired window.
2. Click in it.
3. Resize and/or move windows if necessary to make it easier to work.

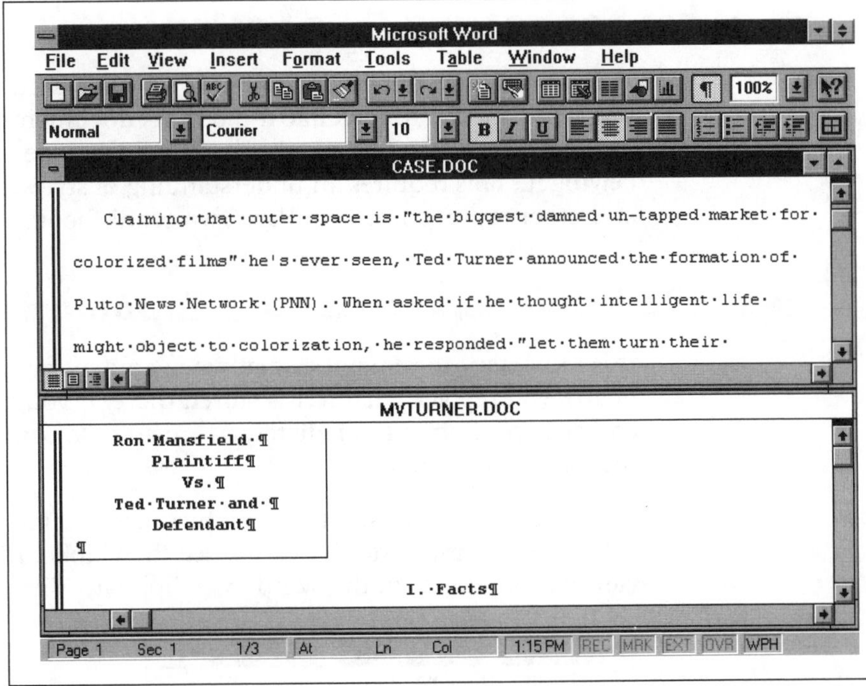

FIGURE 2.16

You can open several documents simultaneously.

Word's Window Menu

Sometimes your screen may not be big enough to display multiple Word documents in useful sizes. Word provides the Window menu for these instances. As you can see in Figure 2.17, the Window menu lists the open documents and lets you switch between them. A checkmark indicates the active window. Using this menu, you can activate one window to copy information, go back to the Window menu to activate and display another window, and then paste.

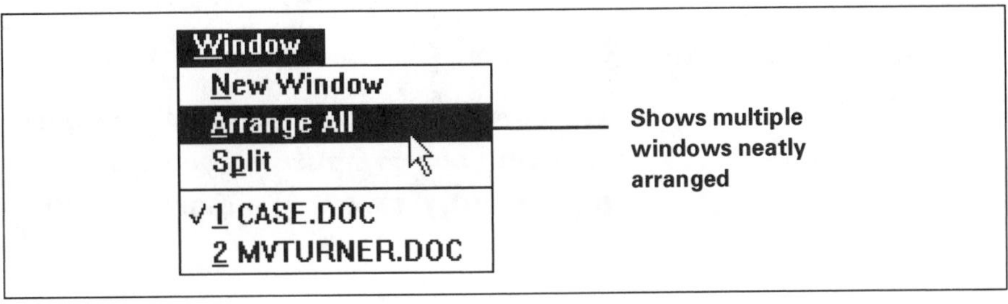

FIGURE 2.17

The Window menu allows you to switch between documents.

▶ What Formatting Gets Pasted?

When pasting from one document to another, sometimes you want the text being pasted to look like it did in its document of origin. Other times you want the text to take on the appearance of the document receiving it. This requires an understanding of styles, section formats, and other topics covered in Part Two of this book.

▶ Some Reminders about the Clipboard

It is important to remember that when you cut or copy to the Clipboard, you replace whatever is stored there. If you do this by accident and spot your error immediately, Word's Undo command will restore the Clipboard's contents.

The Clipboard can store text, graphics, even sound and animation. While you normally don't need to see the Clipboard to use it, you can view its contents with the Windows Clipboard Viewer, shown here.

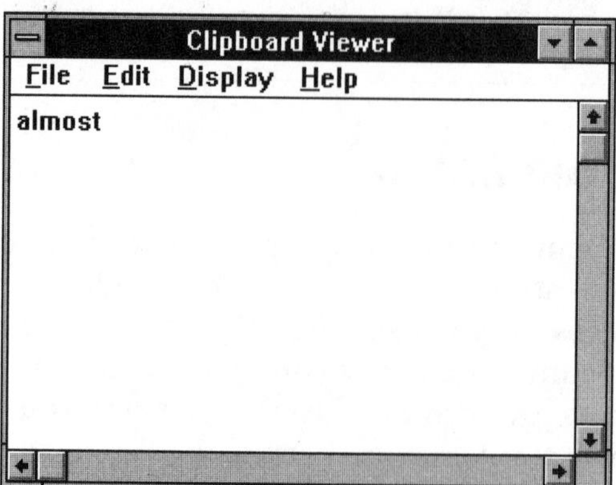

See your Windows documentation for details.

▶▶ **WARNING**

The contents of the Clipboard disappear when you turn off your computer. If you want to save something permanently, save it in a Word document.

The contents of your Clipboard usually stay the same when you switch from program to program, as long you do not turn off or restart your computer. Thus, you can copy items from a spreadsheet, quit the spreadsheet program, launch Word, and paste the spreadsheet information into your Word document. Or, you can run more than one program at once and use the Clipboard to pass information back and forth without quitting any of the programs.

For example, suppose that you have created invoices using a spreadsheet and you want to copy a customer's mailing information from the spreadsheet to a letter you are writing. Assuming you have enough RAM to run both programs, you might open the customer's invoice spreadsheet and a new Word document. You could then copy the customer's address from the spreadsheet onto the Clipboard, then paste it into the Word document.

You may find your computer will respond more quickly if you minimize one of the programs while working with the other. For instance, when copying from the spreadsheet, run Word "minimized," then minimize the spreadsheet and reactivate Word. If you are unfamiliar with this concept, consult your Windows documentation.

TIP

Advanced users will also want to explore other pasting options including Linking and Embedding (described in Chapter 30). These advanced techniques make it possible to keep multiple documents up-to-date when things change.

Collecting Information with The Spike

A Word tool called the *Spike* lets you collect multiple items from within the same document, then paste them all at once. See Chapter 17 for details.

Drag and Drop

Word's drag-and-drop move feature lets you highlight text or other movable objects and drag them to a new location. For instance, in Figure 2.18 the word *almost* has been highlighted with drag and drop enabled. With the primary mouse button depressed, the mouse pointer changes appearance slightly. Notice the small rectangle near the arrow. Notice also the long pointer. The arrow, box, and pointer move as one when you move the mouse with the button held down. Once you release the mouse button, the selected items will be moved to the drag-and-drop insertion point. In Figure 2.18, the word *almost* would be inserted between *the* and *right*. If you use drag and drop while holding down the Ctrl key, you will move a copy of the highlighted text, leaving the original untouched.

FIGURE 2.18

The pointer and insertion point change when drag and drop is enabled.

The selected word will be moved to the insertion point
The difference between the right word and the almost right word is the difference between lightning and the lightning bug.
Mark Twain

NOTE

If you've held down your primary mouse button while selecting things (while dragging or double-clicking, for instance), you'll need to release the mouse button and press it again before you'll see the drag-and-drop pointer. Practice will make this second nature. Start by dragging and dropping the word *almost* to restore the Twain quote.

Steps for Moving with Drag and Drop

To move text with drag and drop, follow these steps:

1. Select the desired text or other item(s).
2. Release the mouse button, if necessary, then point to the selected item(s), and press and hold down the mouse button. Watch the mouse pointer.

3. When you see the pointer change to its drag-and-drop shape, drag the pointer while holding down the mouse button until the insertion point is at the desired new location.
4. Release the mouse button. The selected item(s) should move.
5. Undo immediately (Ctrl+Z) if things didn't go right.

Steps for Copying with Drag and Drop

Drag-and-drop copying works just like drag-and-drop moving, with one exception. You hold down the Ctrl key while you work.

1. Select the desired text or other item(s).
2. Press and hold down the Ctrl button.
3. Release the mouse button, if necessary (while still holding down the Ctrl key), then point to the selected item(s) and press and hold down the mouse button. Watch the mouse pointer.
4. When you see the drag-and-drop pointer, drag the pointer while holding down the mouse button until the insertion point is at the desired new location.
5. Release the mouse button and the Ctrl key. The selected item(s) should be copied.
6. Undo immediately (Ctrl+Z) if you had a problem copying.

TIP

From time to time, you might accidentally drag and drop something when you intend to simply select by dragging. An immediate Undo (Ctrl+Z) will make things right. If you really hate drag and drop (and some people do), you can shut it off. Chapter 36 has details.

►► Creating New Documents if Word is Running

Whenever you start Word for Windows, it opens a new, untitled document so you can begin a new project from scratch. If you want to start a new project with Word already running, simply choose File ➤ New or use the Ctrl+N keyboard shortcut. Word will open a new, untitled document window. Each new window opened this way in a session is sequentially numbered (Document1, Document2, and so on). You'll be given a chance to use templates and Wizards (described in Part Two) when opening new document windows with the New command. When in doubt, start with Word's default—the NORMAL template, shown here.

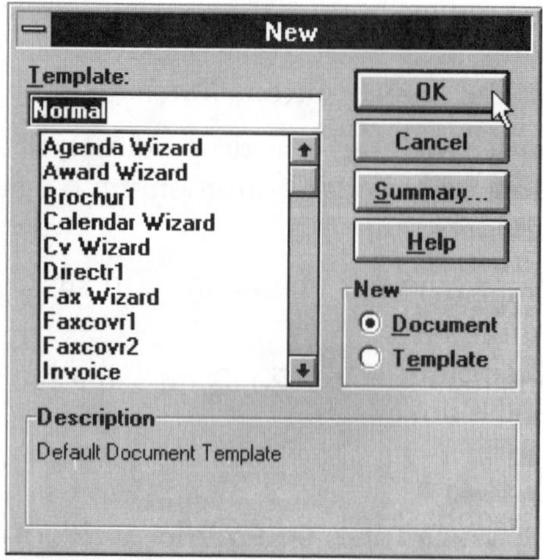

►► TIP

You can also open a new, untitled document window by clicking on the dog-eared document icon located on the Standard Toolbar.

▶▶ Keyboards and Word

The first computers were like Ford's Model T—simple and utilitarian. You had no choice of keyboards. Today, manufacturers provide keyboards with a variety of layouts and features. For instance, there are international keyboards labeled with accent marks and configured with special characters for a variety of languages. Some portable computers have unique space-saving keyboard layouts and keys.

Fortunately, Word accommodates most of these differences. To use international keyboard layouts, visit the Program Manager control panel. Double-click on the International icon. See your Windows documentation for details.

▶ Keyboard Shortcuts

Touch-typists often dislike taking their hands off of the keyboard, so, as you've already seen, Word for Windows offers a variety of keyboard shortcuts, such as Ctrl+X for Cut. These shortcuts make it unnecessary to reach for the mouse. Keyboard shortcuts are mentioned throughout this book, and many are shown on Word's menus. The Customize dialog box (Tools ➤ Customize…) will help you explore all of Word's keyboard shortcuts. It is possible to change or delete shortcuts or add your own new ones, as you will learn in Chapter 36.

▶ Key Combinations for Special Characters

Your computer and Word for Windows can work together to display and print special characters that aren't shown on your keyboard. Examples include the copyright symbol and international characters with diacritical marks (umlauted letters, for instance). In general, you either specify these characters by using key combinations or with the Insert ➤ Symbol… command. For instance, you can type the copyright symbol (©) by holding down the Alt key and pressing the Ctrl and c keys simultaneously.

The available special characters and the procedures used to create them vary depending on which fonts you are using. That's why it's often easier to use the Insert ➤ Symbol… command. Chapter 9 shows you how to get the characters you need. Figure 2.19 gives you a glimpse of this feature.

FIGURE 2.19

The Insert ➤ Symbol… command lets you see and type special symbols.

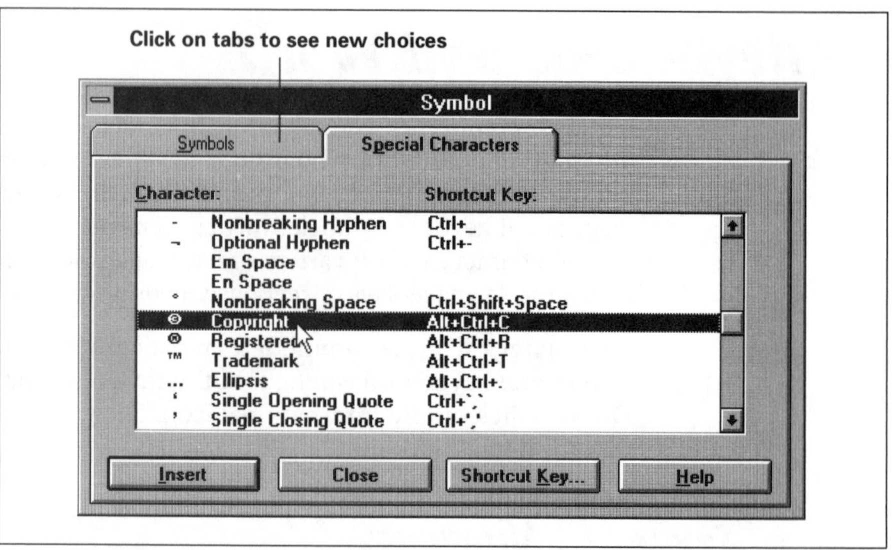

► Numeric Keypads and Word

Most newer keyboards have numeric keypads and screen-editing keys (Home, Page Up, and so on). Word for Windows uses many of these keys if you have them.

Numeric keypads serve two functions in Word. With the Num Loc feature enabled, you can use the keypad to enter numbers. With Num Loc off (the default) you use the numeric pad to navigate through your documents. Pressing 9 (PgUp) on the numeric pad scrolls the screen up, 3 (PgDn) scrolls down, and so on.

The key in the upper-left corner of the numeric keypad toggles Num Lock on and off. Newer keyboards contain both the word *Clear* and the abbreviation *Num Lock*. On some keypads it is labeled just *Clear*.

Some keyboards have a light that tells you when Num Lock is enabled, others do not. The status area at the bottom-left corner of your active Word window will also indicate Num Lock status.

A few keyboard shortcuts are unavailable to users without numeric keypads. For example, the Unassign Keystroke command shortcut is unavailable without a numeric keypad. If you don't have a numeric keypad, and you want to assign your own keyboard shortcuts to replace the ones you are missing, that is possible. Appendix B lists all of Word's standard shortcuts and numeric-keypad shortcuts.

▶ Repeating Keys

Most of the character keys and many of the navigational keys (like arrows) will repeat if you hold them down. This is an easy way to type a series of keystrokes.

You can change the speed of this feature from the Windows Keyboard settings of Windows Control Panel. The speed at which identical keystrokes are issued is called the Repeat Rate. A slider lets you pick anything from Slow to Fast. The length of time your computer waits between your first key depression and the rapid-fire insertion of identical keystrokes is called the Delay Before First Repeat setting. See your Windows documentation for details.

▶ Using Word's Menus without a Mouse

Beginners may want to skip this topic and revisit it at a later time. If you really hate to reach for your mouse when typing, or if your mouse dies in the middle of a project, you can use Word's Keyboard Menus feature. It lets you use → and ← to flip from menu to menu and ↑ and ↓ to make menu choices. Beginners—give yourself a week or two to get your eyes, hands, and brain working together before abandoning the mouse or trackball. If you must work sans mouse, here's how:

1. Activate the Keyboard Menu feature by pressing the Alt key.
2. Press the underlined letter of the desired menu, usually the first letter (*V* for View, *W* for Window, etc.) or you can use ← and → to display the desired menu. Menus drop down and stay down as you pick them.
3. Because two of Word's menu choices start with the letter *F* (File and Format), you must remember that the shortcut for the Format menu is *O*.
4. Pressing ↵ is equivalent to releasing the mouse button. Your choice will be carried out. To cancel the Keyboard Menu feature without taking any action, press the Esc (escape) key.

▶ Keyboard Tricks in Dialog Boxes

Word supports the usual Windows navigating tricks in dialog boxes. For instance, in dialog boxes where you are asked to type text or dimensions, you can tab from box to box. Holding down the Shift key will move you backwards when you press Tab. Anytime you see a button with a dark border, pressing ↵ will work in place of clicking on the button. If you are unfamiliar with tricks like these, consult your Windows manuals or try the tutorial programs that came with Windows.

►► Hotspots

Even experienced users are sometimes unaware that you can bring up dialog boxes, windows, and other tools of interest by double-clicking at appropriate areas (called *hotspots*) in Word for Windows. There may even be some undocumented hotspots you can discover on your own.

Beginners may want to just skim this topic for now. As you gain experience with Word, you'll want to try some of these hotspot tricks and explore to find others.

Paragraph Dialog Box Any indent marker.

Page Setup Dialog Box Hotspot If you click on the small square box at the right end of the Ruler, you'll see the Document dialog box used to control header, footer, and other measurements precisely.

When in Page Layout view, if you double-click in the margins at the corners of your document, you will also see the Document dialog box.

Footnote Window Hotspots To reveal a footnote window, simply double-click on a footnote reference mark.

The Go To Dialog Box Hotspot To bring up the Go To dialog box, useful for navigating in big documents, double-click on a page or section number in the status area at the lower-left portion of the document window.

Cell Height and Width Dialog Box The space on the ruler that separates cells.

Section Hotspot Double-click on section break marks to reveal the Page Setup dialog box. It contains section break information.

▶▶ New Mouse Command Shortcuts

Word for Windows now offers a nifty new mouse feature that employs the nonprimary (usually the right) mouse button. Frequently, when you point to items on the screen and press the nonprimary mouse button, you'll see a list of commands that you can issue with your mouse. For instance, in Figure 2.20, Word is telling you that you can cut, paste, change fonts, change paragraph settings, and more, simply by dragging to pick a choice from the list.

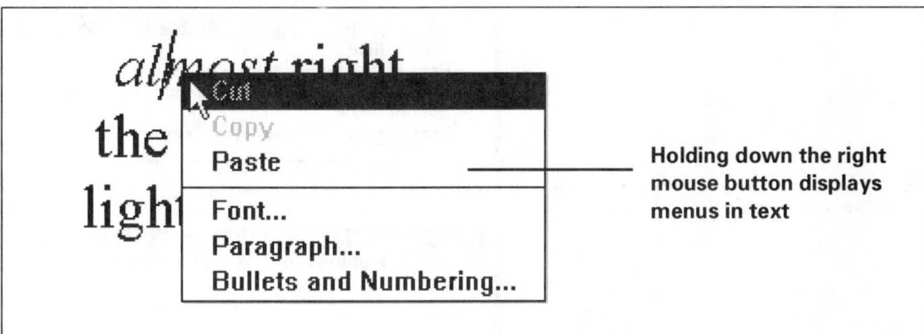

FIGURE 2.20

Use the nonprimary mouse button to view and pick commands without visiting menus or Toolbars.

▶▶ Getting Help with Word

It's a little ironic that Word for Windows has so many online help features that it takes several pages of a book to describe them. Word has three kinds of online help—topic-specific help, screen-element help, and (for WordPerfect users) WordPerfect help. In addition, Microsoft offers product support over the telephone, via fax, and through CompuServe and other bulletin board services (BBS). There is also TTY assistance for the hearing impaired.

Because Word's Help feature does a good job of explaining itself, we'll just touch on it here.

▶ Searching for Specific Words of Wisdom

The Help ➤ Search for Help on… command lets you enter specific words and phrases that Word uses to pull up help information. For instance, to find out more about printing, you might:

1. Choose Help ➤ Search for Help on....
2. Type the search word or phrase of interest (*print*, for example). Word will show you a list of possible topics, as illustrated in Figure 2.21.

FIGURE 2.21

Searching Help files for specific words or phrases.

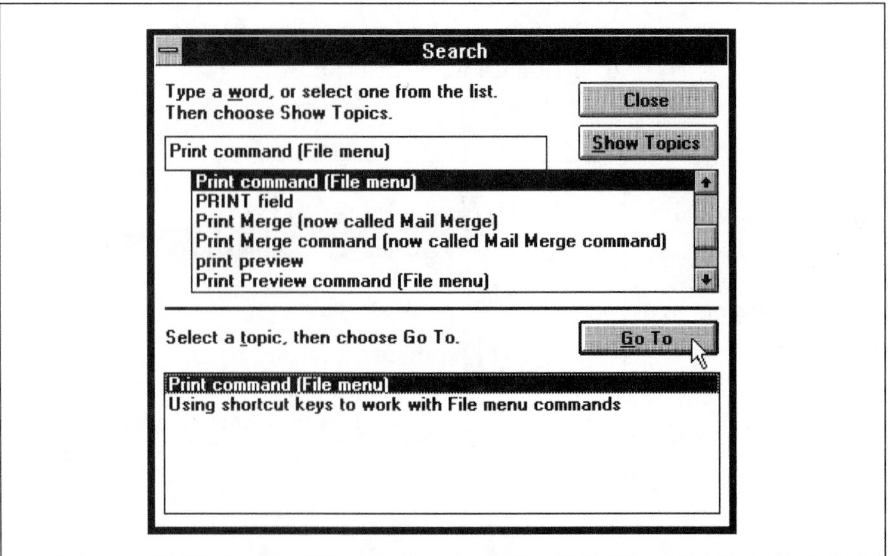

3. Clicking the Show Topics button will list possible hints.
4. Double-click on a listed topic or click once to select it and then click the Go To button.

► The Help Contents Window

To see an overview of Word's online help, choose the Help ➤ Contents... command. You'll see a scrolling list, as shown in Figure 2.22.

► Getting Different Kinds of Help

Click on an icon corresponding to the type of help you desire. For example, to see demonstrations of Word at Work, click on the *Examples and Demos* icon. To get step-by-step instructions, select the *Using*

FIGURE 2.22

Use this Help window to select topics and read more about them.

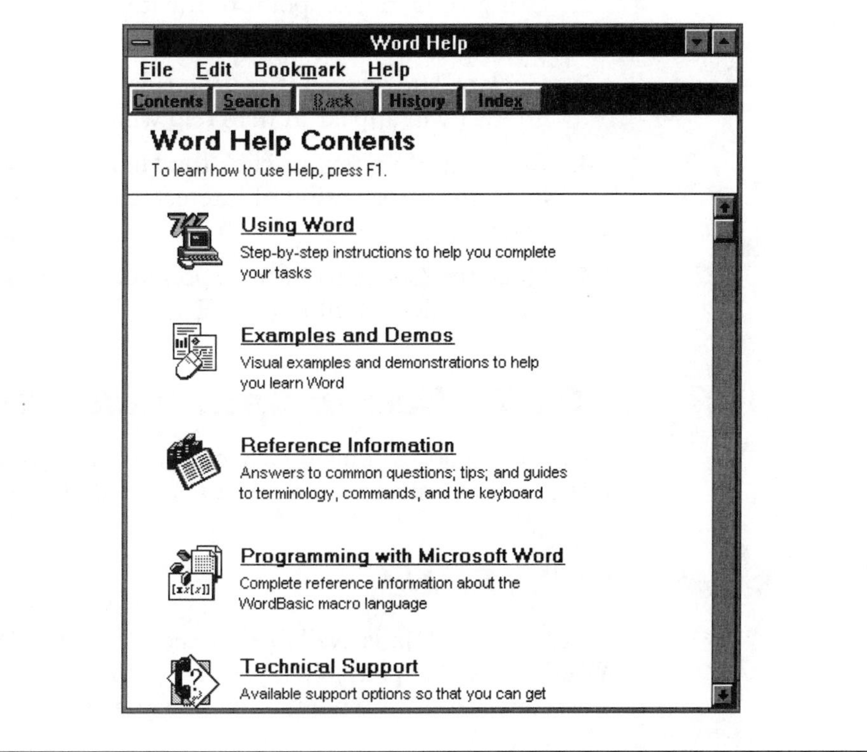

Word icon, and so on. Scroll to review all of the choices in the Contents window's list.

▶ Pointing to Get Online Help

You can often use your mouse to point to things on your screen and get help. For instance, pointing to a button on the Toolbar will reveal its function.

You can also use Word's Help button on the Standard Toolbar. It changes the pointer into an arrow with a question mark. When you point and click with that pointer, you get online help. Here's an example:

1. Press the Help button on the Standard Toolbar. (It looks like an arrow and a question mark.) Your mouse pointer will become a giant question mark with an arrow. (Press Esc if this happens by mistake.)

2. Using your mouse, point to the item of interest. (The ruler, for instance.)
3. Click on the desired item (the ruler in this case). The topic of interest will appear in the Help window.
4. Read the Help text or click the Help window's buttons to narrow in on the information of interest. Scroll, if necessary, to read the entire text.
5. Click the Contents button, press C to see the topics list again, or choose File ➤ Exit to quit Help.

► To Get Online Help in Open Dialog Boxes

Many dialog boxes contain Help buttons. Use them when you get stumped or when you want to learn more about a dialog box's capabilities.

► WordPerfect Help

WordPerfect Help is available for reformed WordPerfect users. With WordPerfect Help enabled, you'll see brief descriptions of items and their functions as you point to them with your mouse pointer. Figure 2.23 illustrates this.

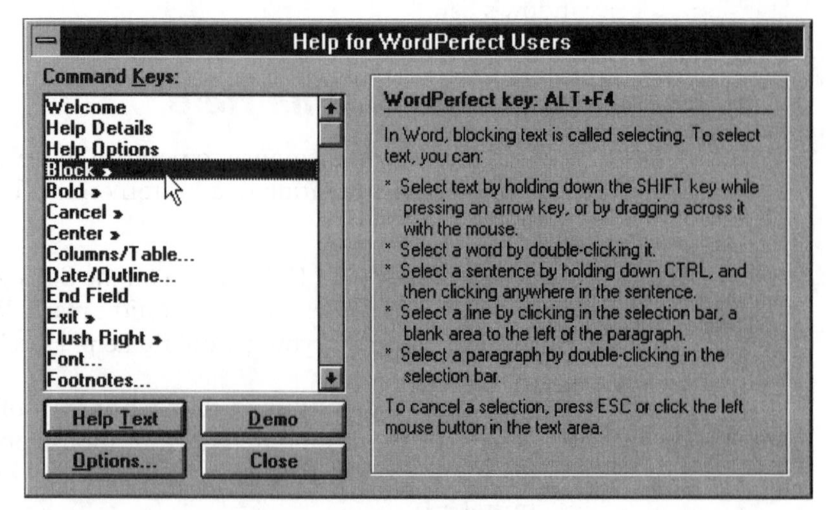

FIGURE 2.23 ►

WordPerfect Help in action.

To access WordPerfect Help, follow these steps:

1. Make sure WordPerfect Help has been installed and enabled.
2. Choose Help ➤ WordPerfect Help....
3. Pick the topic of interest from the scrolling list, as illustrated in Figure 2.23.
4. Point and click on a topic to read about it.
5. Use the buttons at the bottom of the window to see demos and explore other Help options.
6. Press Esc or use the Close button to quit.

►► TIP

Double-click on the WPH button in the status area for WordPerfect help.

► Printing Online Help

You can often print online help topics by using the Print Topic choice in a Help window's File menu. Be sure your printer is set up and ready first. For more information on printing, see Chapter 3.

► Quitting Online Help

Pressing Alt+F4 closes the Help window. So does clicking in the Help window's close box, found in the upper-left corner of the window.

►► Microsoft Product Support Services

When you really get stuck, Microsoft's huge technical support staff can be a big help. They provide technical note downloading services, CompuServe forums, prerecorded support messages and even real live people to answer your questions.

The first step, as they say in tech-support circles, is to "Read Your Friggin' Manuals." People who don't read are referred to as RYFMs. If you can't find the answers you need in Word's online help, or your manuals, or books like this one, it is time to call out the big guns.

▶ To Find Out More about Tech Support Options

Microsoft is changing the way it supports users, and things that were once free are now often quite expensive. To read more about available support options, use the Technical Support command on Word's Help menu. It will show you a list of topics something like the one in Figure 2.24. Click on topics to learn more.

▶▶ **WARNING**

Microsoft technical support is not always free. Be sure you understand the costs before obtaining support.

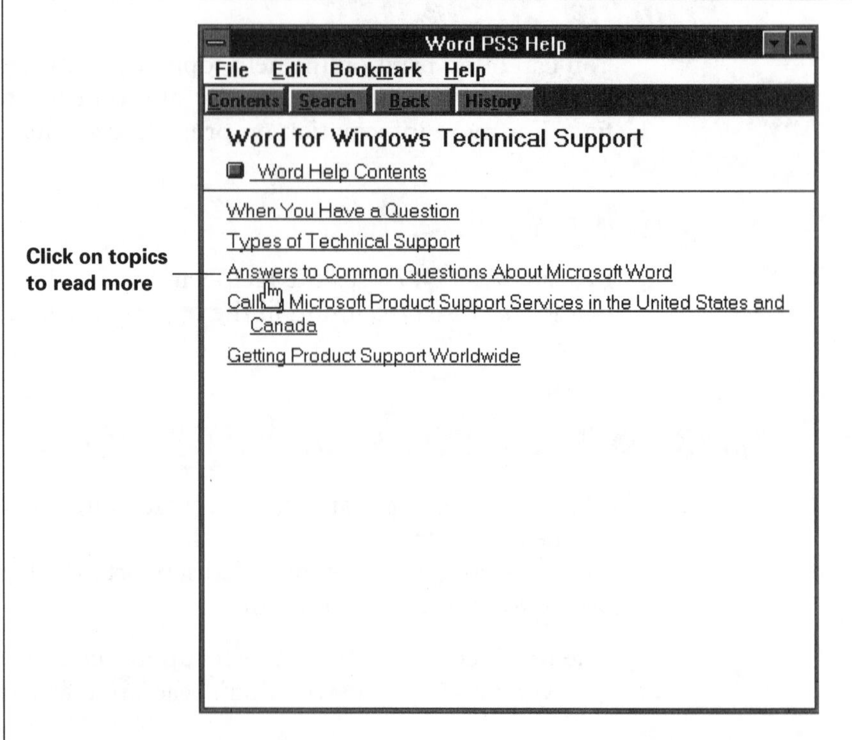

FIGURE 2.24 ▶

Click on a topic to read more about Microsoft technical support options.

CHAPTER 3

Viewing and Navigating

▸▸ FAST TRACK

To return to the last three places you've edited **97**

use the Go Back command (**Shift+F5** or **Ctrl+Alt+Z**).

To locate text quickly **97**

use the Edit ➤ Find... command (**Ctrl+F**—see Chapter 20 for details).

To switch quickly from one view to another **100**

use the view buttons in the lower-left corner of the status area.

To see text as it will print (almost!) **100**

use Print Preview (fairly accurate) or Page Layout view (very accurate).

To see widely separated parts of a document **103**

use the split-screen feature. You can split the screen by double-clicking the Split-bar rectangle in the upper-right corner of the document window. Alternately, you can drag the Split-bar pointer down to show Word how to size the panes. To unsplit the document window, double-click the Split-bar rectangle or use the **Alt+Ctrl+S** shortcut.

To entirely clear the screen of everything but text **108**

choose View ➤ Full Screen. To return to the prior view, click on the little Full button.

▶▶ You do your work in Word for Windows in *document windows*, which you can position and resize for your convenience. Word for Windows offers navigational tools that let you move quickly to the desired part of even huge documents. Several views make it easy to see what your document will look like without printing it. Other views are available to simplify and speed up the creation of rough drafts and outlines. In addition, you can hide and show elements such as paragraph marks (¶) and the little dots between words that denote spaces. Let's take a look.

▶▶ Scrolling in a Window

Most documents are too big to be displayed in their entirety on your screen. You reveal unseen portions of your document by scrolling to bring parts of the document into view while temporarily hiding other parts. Usually, you'll scroll up and down to see long documents, but you will sometimes need to scroll left and right to see different parts of wide documents. There are many ways to scroll.

▶ Scrolling with the Scroll Arrows

When you click on a scroll arrow you will see a different part of your document. For instance, suppose you are looking at page 2 of a three-page document. If you click on the up scroll arrow (located near the top-right of the active window), you will move a little nearer to the beginning of the document. Clicking on the down-pointing arrow will take you closer to the end of the document. (Typically, one click moves you up or down about one line.) The right- and left-pointing arrows let you see corresponding portions of wide documents.

▶▶ TIP

If you click and hold down the mouse button while pointing to any of the four scrolling arrows, your document will scroll continuously until you reach the end of the document or release the mouse button. But there are better ways to scroll long distances. Read on.

▶ Scrolling by Clicking in the Scroll Bars

Clicking in the shaded areas of scroll bars (as opposed to clicking on the scroll arrows themselves) scrolls approximately one screen's worth. The exact scroll distance will vary with your screen and document window size. Experiment.

▶ Scrolling with the Scroll Boxes

The square boxes in the horizontal and vertical scroll bars can be used to move great distances quickly. For instance, if you are looking at page 1 of a 100-page document, the scroll box will be at the top of the vertical scroll bar. Dragging it with your mouse exactly half way down the scroll bar will bring page 50 into view; dragging it three-quarters of the way will take you to page 75; and so forth. Horizontal scroll boxes can be used the same way to scroll wide documents quickly.

Obviously it is difficult to drag to the exact middle or three-quarters position on the scroll bar. Use the scroll boxes to get you in the neighborhood, then use other scrolling tools to fine-tune, as shown in Figure 3.1.

▶▶ WARNING

It's easy to forget to move the insertion point when you bounce from place to place in a document by scrolling or using the navigational tricks discussed in this chapter. Get into the habit of repositioning and then looking for the insertion point before you type, paste, or do other potentially destructive things!

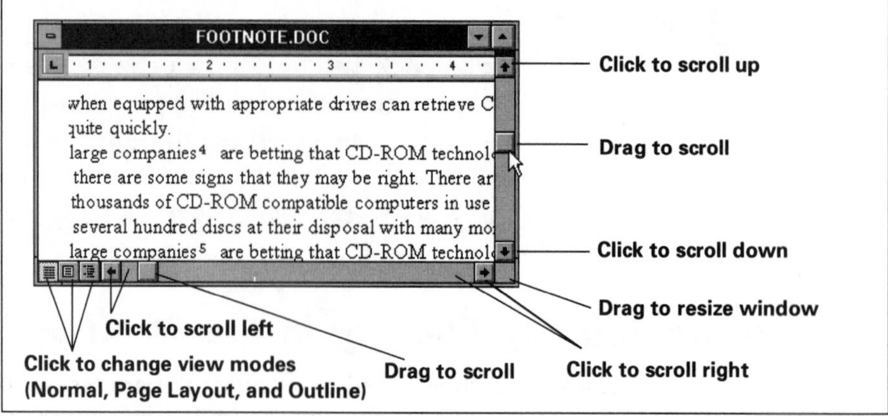

FIGURE 3.1 *Use the scroll tools and your mouse to see different parts of your document.*

►► Navigating with Your Keyboard

Word for Windows offers many, many keyboard shortcuts for navigating. You can just scroll using keyboard commands, or you can scroll and move the insertion point at the same time. Be sure you understand the difference!

Moreover, frequently if you hold the Shift key down while using keyboard shortcuts, you will select text in addition to scrolling and moving the insertion point. For example, pressing the Ctrl+→ key combination moves the insertion point to the beginning of the next word; while Ctrl+Shift+→ selects the current word starting at the insertion point and the space following it.

There should be a keyboard shortcut that lists all of Word's keyboard-navigation shortcuts, but there isn't. Table 3.1 is the next-best thing.

TABLE 3.1: *Keyboard Shortcuts for Moving, Scrolling, and Editing*

SCROLLING	
TO MOVE TO...	**PRESS...**
Up	↑ or 8 (keypad)
Down	↓ or 2 (keypad)
Left	← or 4 (keypad)
Right	→ or 6 (keypad)
Previous Word	Ctrl+← or Ctrl+4 (keypad)
Next Word	Ctrl+→ or Ctrl+6 (keypad)

TABLE 3.1: *Keyboard Shortcuts for Moving, Scrolling, and Editing (continued)*

SCROLLING	
TO MOVE TO...	**PRESS...**
Beginning of line	7 (keypad)
End of line	End or 1 (keypad)
Next page	Ctrl+Alt+Page Down
Previous page	Ctrl+Alt+Page Up
One page up	Ctrl+↑ or Ctrl+8 (keypad)
One page down	Ctrl+↓ or Ctrl+2 (keypad)
Top of window	Ctrl+Page Up
Bottom of window	Ctrl+Page Down
Start of document	Ctrl+Home
End of document	Ctrl+End
Scroll up one screen	Page Up or 9 (keypad)
Scroll down one screen	Page Down or 3 (keypad)
IN TABLES OR PAGE LAYOUT VIEW	
TO MOVE TO...	**PRESS...**
Next cell in table	Tab
Previous cell in table	Shift+Tab
Next page element	Ctrl+Alt+3
First cell in row	Alt+Home
Top cell in column	Alt+Page Up
Last cell in row	Alt+End
Last cell in column	Alt+Page Down
Up or down in row	↑, ↓, ←, →
EDITING	
TO...	**PRESS...**
Select the entire document	Ctrl+A
Delete character to left of cursor or selected text	Delete (Backspace)

TABLE 3.1: *Keyboard Shortcuts for Moving, Scrolling, and Editing (continued)*

EDITING	
TO...	**PRESS...**
Delete character after cursor or selected text	Ctrl+Alt+F or Del
Delete previous word	Ctrl+Backspace
Delete next word	Ctrl+Delete
Copy text	Ctrl+C
Copy formats	Ctrl+Shift+C
Paste formats	Ctrl+Shift+V
Insert Spike contents	Ctrl+Shift+F3

Use the numbers on the numeric keypad (with Num Lock off) for the tasks listed in Table 3.1. Home, End, Page Up, and Page Down keys are not available on all Ctrl keyboards. If you ever memorize all of Word's keyboard shortcuts, you are spending too much time with Word for Windows. Take a very long vacation.

▸▸ WARNING

Be careful when using the numeric keypad to navigate. For instance, if you select some text, then press the asterisk key (*) by accident when you meant to hit the Pg Up key on the keypad, your text will be replaced with an asterisk! Or, if Num Lock is accidentally turned on, when you press the ↑ key (or any other arrow key), the selected text will be replaced with the number corresponding to the key you've pressed. Some users avoid the numeric pad navigation shortcuts for these reasons.

▸▸ The Go To... Command

When editing big documents, particularly when you have a marked-up paper copy in your hand, it is useful to be able to scoot quickly to a particular page or to a specific page within a certain section. If you know page (and section) numbers, Word for Windows makes this easy. Word can also take you to specified lines, bookmarks, annotations, footnotes, endnotes, fields, tables, graphics equations, and objects. This is all accomplished in the Go To dialog box (see Figure 3.2), reached with the Edit ➤ Go To... command or the F5 function key.

FIGURE 3.2 ▸

The Go To dialog box.

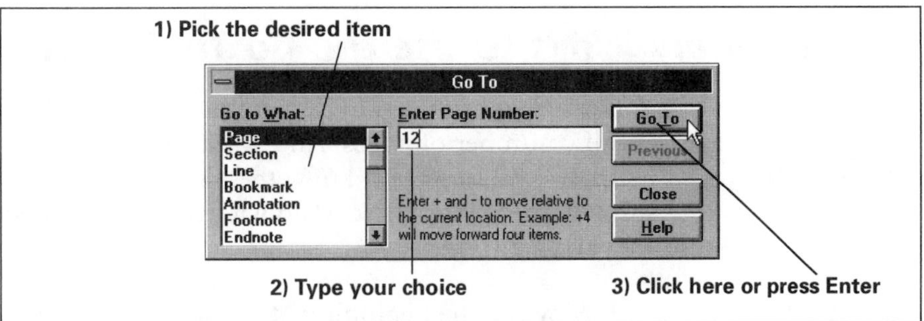

In single-section documents or documents where page numbers do not restart in each section, just type the desired page number and press ↵ or click the Go To button. Quicker than you can say *amen*, Word will take you to the requested page and place the insertion point at the beginning of the first line on the page. Here are the steps:

1. Press the F5 function key or choose Edit ➤ Go To....
2. Type the desired page number when you see the dialog box.
3. Press ↵. Word will take you to the requested page.
4. Close the Go To dialog box with the Close button or close box or press Esc.
5. Get back to work.

▸ Section Numbers and the Go To Command

If your document is broken into sections with page numbers that restart in new sections, you must specify section numbers in the Go To dialog box. (See Chapter 13 for more about sections.) To specify a section number in the Go To dialog box, type an **S**. For instance, typing **S4** would take you to the beginning of Section 4, (assuming your document has a Section 4).

To specify a particular page and section, type **P**, the page number, **S**, and the section number. Thus, **P3S5** would take you to the third page in the fifth section. **S5P3** will do the same thing.

You can also go to a particular section by selecting Section in the scrolling list and then typing the desired section number. Once in the desired section, you can use Go To… again to get to the appropriate page within the section.

▸ *Many Ways to Use the Go To Command*

You can also use the Go To command to move forward or backward a specific number of pages. And you can use it to go to the end of a document, even if you don't know the last page number. Here's a list of some of the things you can do with the Go To dialog box and samples of typical entries:

- Move to the beginning of the document (0)
- Move to the next page (+ or leave blank)
- Move to the last page (enter any number greater than the number of pages in the document)
- Move to a specific page number (4 or P4)
- Move to a specific page within a specific section (P4S3)
- Move to the first page of a specific section (S3)
- Move forward a specified number of pages—3 for example (+3)
- Move back a specific number of pages—5 for instance (-5)
- Move to other specific document elements like graphics, tables, bookmarks, annotations, etc.

▸▸ **TIP**

Double-clicking on the Page Number portion of the status area will bring up the Go To dialog box.

▶▶ Go Back

Here's a handy but often confusing gizmo. When you are editing, it is sometimes necessary to bounce from one part of a document to another part of the same document. Or, if you have two different documents open, you may find yourself repeatedly moving from one document to the other.

Word for Windows remembers the last three places you have edited plus the current insertion-point location. The Go Back feature lets you quickly move to those edit points. Simply press Shift+F5 (or Ctrl+Alt+Z) repeatedly to cycle you through the last three insertion-point locations. The Go Back command is not on Word's standard menus, but you can add it or even create a Toolbar button for it. See Chapter 36.

Incidentally, simply moving the insertion point somewhere in a document does not necessarily add that point to the places in the Go Back list. Generally, you need to edit something there.

▶▶ Using Find to Navigate

Word's Find… command is a great way to move to an area needing work. For instance, if you are looking at a printout containing a typo you want to fix, use the Find… command to get to the corresponding spot on your screen. Here are the basics (Chapter 20 has the details):

1. Press Ctrl+F or choose Edit ➤ Find… to bring up the Find dialog box.
2. Enter the text you wish to find, then press ↵. Word will search (usually down from the insertion point) and show you the first occurrence of the specified text.
3. Click on Next or press ↵ to move to the next occurrence, if that's not the occurrence you want.
4. If necessary, answer Yes (press ↵) when Word asks if it should search from the beginning of the document.
5. When you find what you need, close the Find dialog box or click in the document window to activate it.
6. Edit away.

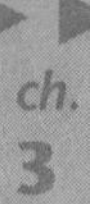

There is much, much more to know about Find… and its companion, the Replace… command. Be sure to read Chapter 20.

►► Views

Word for Windows can show you your document with varying levels of detail to make things easier to visualize or quicker to work with. These different display options are called *views*. Word provides six different views:

- Normal view
- Page Layout view
- Outline view
- Print Preview
- Split screen
- Master Document

► Normal View

Unless you are very patient, or have a very fast computer with a large screen, use Normal view for most of your heavy-duty text entry and editing. Word's other views respond noticeably slower to typing, editing, and scrolling.

Normal view (illustrated in Figure 3.3) keeps repagination and screen redraw delays to a minimum. It shows your text as you have typed it and displays graphics where you've inserted them (which is not necessarily where they'll print).

In earlier versions of Word for Windows, Normal view was called Galley view, a somewhat inaccurate homage to the typesetting profession. It was the default view. Normal view depicts things like type sizes, line spacing, indents, and so on with reasonable accuracy. It does not show side by side column positioning, footers, headers, nor the printing position of framed items. Columns are shown at their actual width, but not side by side. Automatic page breaks are shown as dotted lines. Manual page breaks, if you've defined any, are shown as darker lines containing the words *Page Break*, while section breaks are double dark lines with the words *End of Section*, and so on.

FIGURE 3.3

Normal view is the best for ordinary editing and text entry.

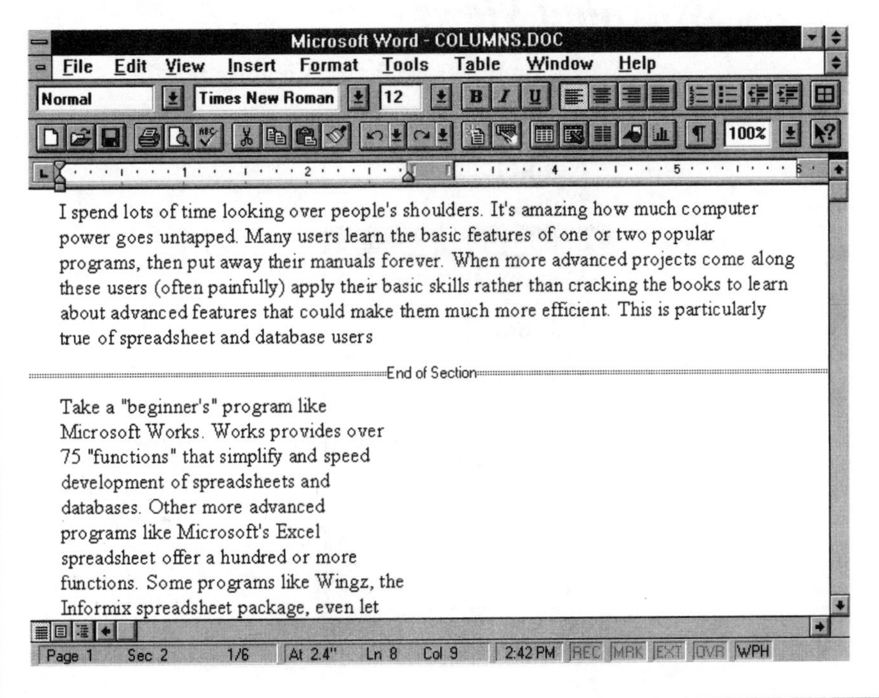

NOTE

If you have instructed Word for Windows to number lines, the numbers will not appear in Normal view. Use Page Layout view or Print Preview to see line numbers.

Editing in Normal View

You can create and edit text, columns, and graphics as usual in Normal view. To work on headers or footers, though, you must open Header or Footer windows from the View menu. For more detail, see Chapter 12.

► Switching Views

Word for Windows has a View menu

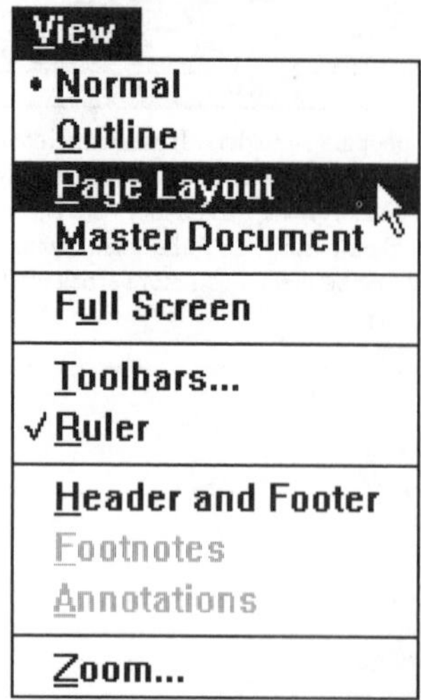

that you can use to select Normal, Outline, or Page Layout views.

Three buttons in the bottom-left corner of Word's status area let you quickly switch views. They are (from left to right) Normal view, Page Layout view, and Outline view.

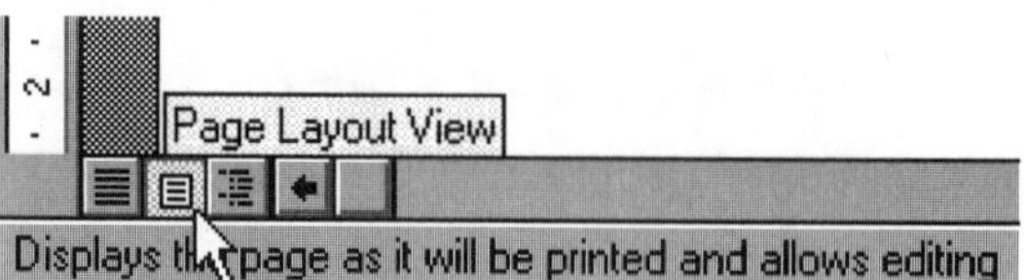

Switching to Print Preview either requires a trip to the File menu or use of a not-so-intuitive keyboard shortcut (Alt+F+V).

► Page Layout View

Figure 3.4 shows what happens to the text from Figure 3.3 when it is displayed in Page Layout view. In this view, the screen resembles a white sheet of paper, or at least a portion of a sheet.

Look closely at the top and left edges of the screen in Figure 3.4. You will see a dark background that Word for Windows places behind the

FIGURE 3.4

In Page Layout view, you can see text as it will print.

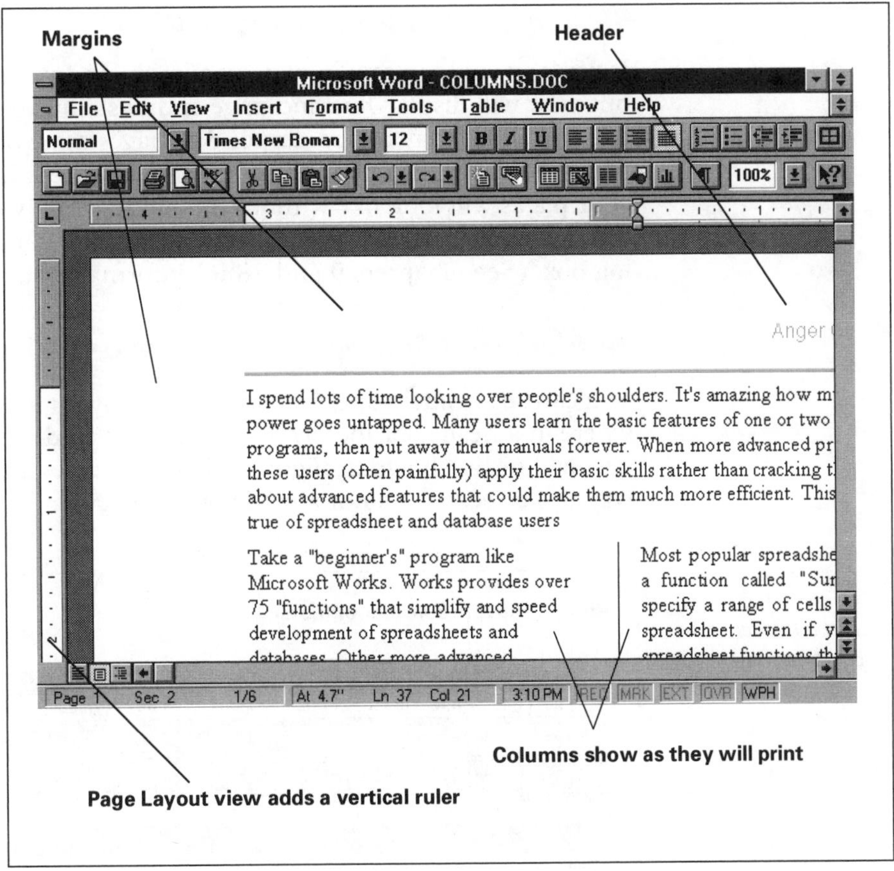

"paper." On a large-enough screen, you will see the whole page. On smaller screens or when using a large paper setting in Page Setup, you may need to scroll to see these representations of the paper's edges.

▶ Editing in Page Layout View

Generally, you edit as usual in Page Layout view. Text and graphics are positioned where they will print. Headers and footers can be both seen and edited. Click in a header, footer, or body text to position the insertion point. Page breaks, be they automatic or forced, are represented by new pages on the screen rather than by dashed lines in the text. You can scroll from page to page, as you'd expect.

Hidden Text in Page Layout View

If you have hidden text in your document and you reveal it, Page Layout view will display line and page endings adjusted to include the hidden text. This may not correspond to pages that you print if the Print dialog box's Print Hidden Text box is unchecked. In order to see what your pages will look like without the hidden text, you must hide the text by unchecking the Show Hidden Text box in the Preferences dialog box. (See Chapters 9 and 28 for information about hidden text.)

Headers and Footers in Page Layout View

You can see headers and footers in Page Layout view. To edit, click anywhere in a header or footer. It will "undim" and be surrounded by a dashed line, as shown in Figure 3.5. The Header and Footer Toolbar will also appear if it's not already on your screen.

FIGURE 3.5 

Click in a header or footer to edit it.

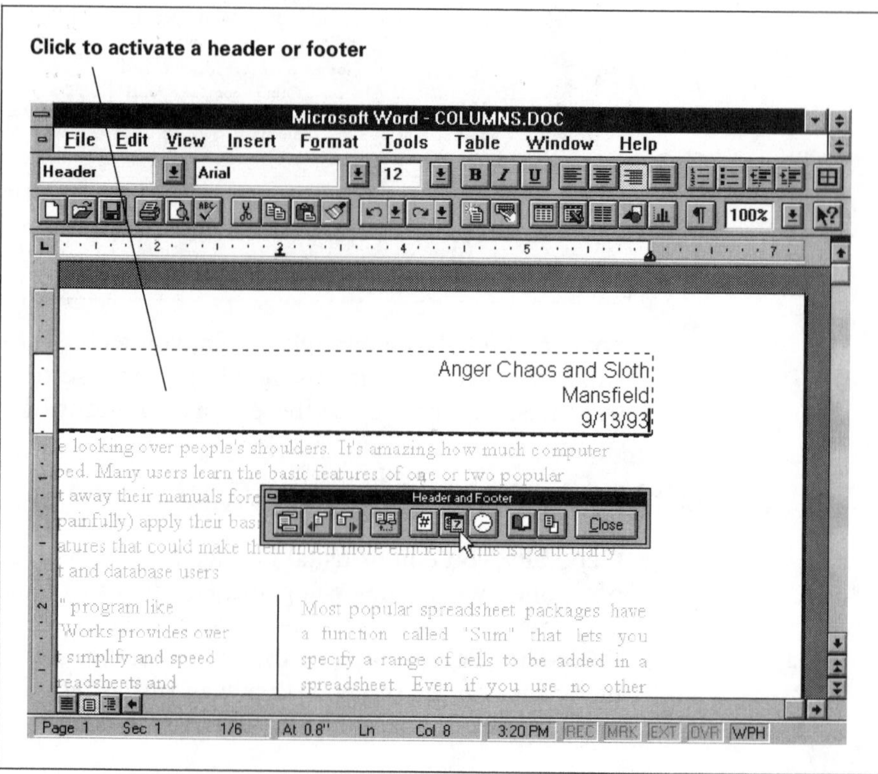

To add date or time entries and page numbering to headers and footers, use the buttons on the Header and Footer Toolbar. You can format text in headers just as you would anywhere else in a Word for Windows document. For instance, to right-align header text, place the insertion point in the text (or select multiple lines in the header and use the Format menu's Right-align button.

Even Line Numbers Show in Page Layout View

Unlike earlier versions of Word for Windows, if you have requested numbered lines, the numbers will appear in Page Layout view as shown here:

```
Harvy Herzmycard
Herzmycard, Soreneck and Numb
425 Hurtz Drive
Teaneck on the Hudson, NY  12345
Telephone: (800) 555-4321
Fax: (123) 456-9876


Attorney For: Ron Mansfield
```

► Split Screen View

Regardless of which view you prefer, you can profit from using Word's split-screen feature. You can use the split-screen to keep two widely separated portions of a document in view at the same time. To split the screen, simply point to the small black rectangle in the upper-right corner of your Word document window. The pointer will change to the Split-bar pointer, as shown in Figure 3.6. Drag the Split-bar pointer down to divide the screen.

FIGURE 3.6 ►

The pointer will change shape.

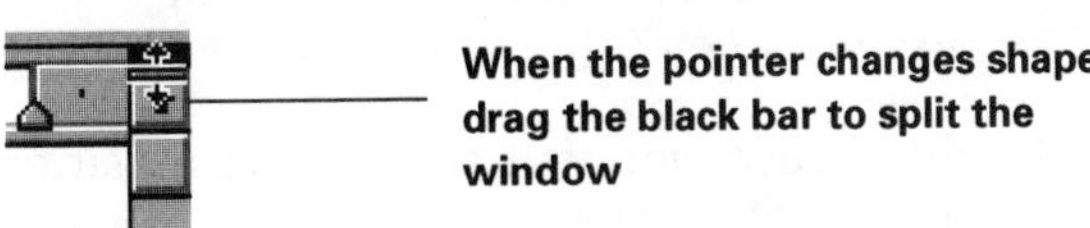

When the pointer changes shape, drag the black bar to split the window

When you release the mouse button, your screen will split into two independent windows, each with its own scroll bar. To return to a single screen, double-click the Split bar or drag it to just below the title bar. This takes some practice. Alternately, you can use the keyboard shortcut Alt+Ctrl+S.

►► **TIP**

When you unsplit the screen, the portion that the insertion point was in becomes the only screen. This can be a nuisance if you actually wanted to be in the other portion of text! So be sure that the insertion point is in the correct pane before you unsplit.

Why Split Screens?

With the screen split you can see two parts of your document at once. Use this feature to refer to different portions of a document as you write or to speed copying, cutting, and pasting. But there's another powerful reason to use split screens.

Split Screen and Different Views

You can use a different view in each portion of the split screen. For instance, you might want to speed scrolling and editing by working in a window pane set to Normal view while watching the effects of your changes in a Page Layout view pane, as shown in Figure 3.7.

► Print Preview

Print Preview is more than just another way to view documents. Choose File ➤ Print Preview or use Ctrl+Alt+I or Ctrl+F2.

Depending on your screen size and settings, you will see either an unreadable bird's-eye view of a page or two (like the one in Figure 3.8), or you will see a full, readable page.

In either case, you will be able to reposition margins in Print Preview. Notice that line numbers are displayed in Print Preview. You cannot edit text or headers and footers in Print Preview. You also will not be able to see certain Page Setup printer tricks, such as image flips.

FIGURE 3.7

You can arrange the document with Normal view in the top pane and Page Layout view in the bottom.

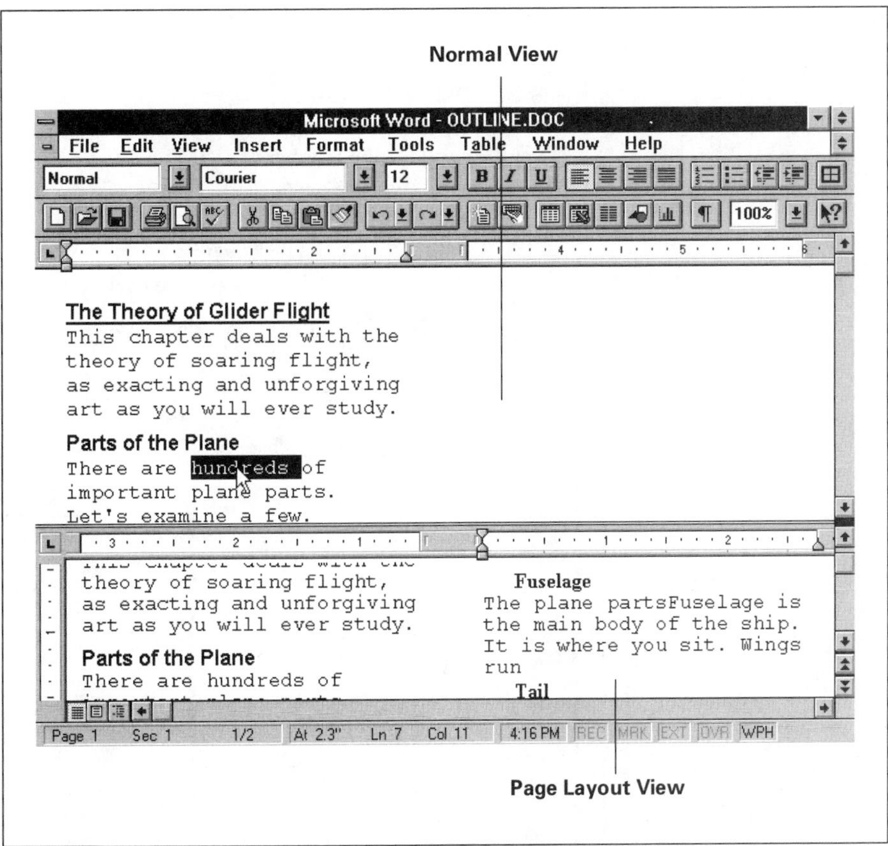
Normal View
Microsoft Word - OUTLINE.DOC
File Edit View Insert Format Tools Table Window Help
The Theory of Glider Flight
This chapter deals with the theory of soaring flight, as exacting and unforgiving art as you will ever study.
Parts of the Plane
There are hundreds of important plane parts. Let's examine a few.
theory of soaring flight, as exacting and unforgiving art as you will ever study.
Parts of the Plane
There are hundreds of
Fuselage
The plane partsFuselage is the main body of the ship. It is where you sit. Wings run
Tail
Page 1 Sec 1 1/2 At 2.3" Ln 7 Col 11 4:16 PM REC MRK EXT OVR WPH
Page Layout View

TIP

The button that looks like a magnifying glass and a piece of paper on the Standard Toolbar will switch you to Print Preview mode. Use the Close button in Print Preview to bring you back to whatever view you were in previously.

Outline View

A complete description of Word's Outline feature can be found in Chapter 21. For now it is enough to know that if your document is properly formatted, switching to Outline view lets you quickly navigate and reorganize even large, complex documents. Outline view allows

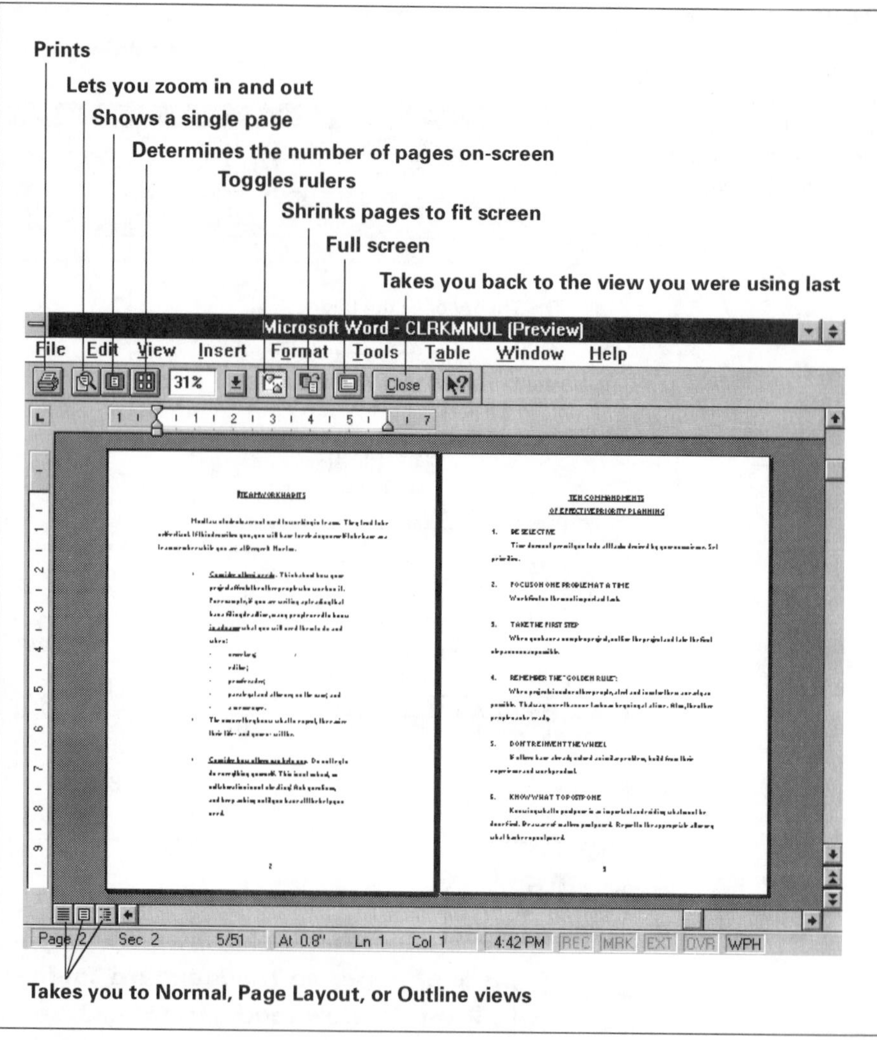

FIGURE 3.8

Print Preview gives you a bird's-eye view of one or two pages at once.

you to see the entire contents of the document, just chapter headings, just section headings, and so on. For instance, Figure 3.9 shows part of a book outline down to paragraph headings, but does not include the text of the book itself.

If you wanted to move all of the Landing Gear information to before the Tail information, you might ordinarily use Normal or Page Layout view to scroll through and select the complete text of all of the Landing

FIGURE 3.9

Part of a book outline viewed at paragraph-heading level.

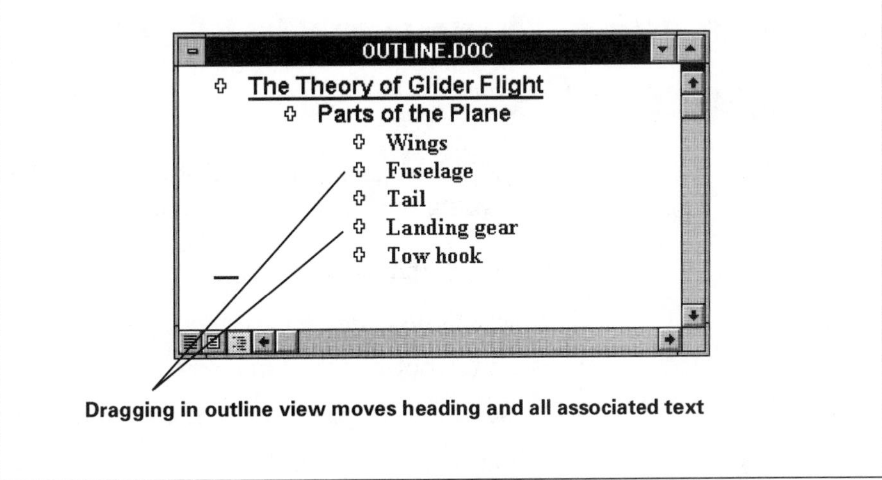

Gear information; then you would cut and paste it into the new position. But by using Outline view, you could simply “collapse” the view, as shown in Figure 3.9, and drag the +*Landing gear* heading up. All of its associated text would follow.

You need not begin projects by creating an in-depth outline, as you will see later when you read about styles and outlines. But by creating and applying appropriate styles for various heading levels, you can quickly create a document that can be expanded or compressed for viewing and editing with Outline tools.

▶ Document View

This view is used when working on large documents. See Chapter 24.

▶ View Defaults

Normal view is the default for new documents unless you change the default to Page View by using the View tab of the Preferences dialog box (see Chapter 34). Word for Windows remembers the view you were using when you last saved a document and opens the document in that view. If you opened a new document in Normal view, did some work, switched to Page Layout view, saved, and exited, the next time you opened the document it would appear in Page Layout view.

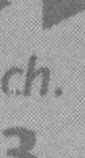

▸▸ Showing Paragraph Marks, Spaces, Etc.

Word for Windows can display helpful nonprinting characters to let you see what's going on. Examples include:

- Paragraph marks (¶)
- Dots denoting spaces
- Arrows denoting tab characters
- Dashed lines for page, section, and column breaks
- Text and graphic boundaries

I like to leave these on, although turning them off can sometimes help you better visualize the final appearance of a document. To toggle the display of these items, use the button that looks like a paragraph mark (¶) on the Standard Toolbar. (It's near the right edge.)

▸▸ Zooming

The little drop-down list near the right end of the Format Toolbar is called the Zoom Control. It lets you zoom in and out to see bigger or smaller on-screen representations. It does not affect printing size. Figure 3.10 shows it in use, magnifying the text 200 percent.

The View ➤ Zoom… command gives you even more control over on-screen character size.

▸▸ Full Screen—Seeing Just Your Work

The View ➤ Full Screen command, or the corresponding button that you'll find in Print Preview, removes all the usual workspace clutter and fills your screen with your current document. You'll also see a very small window containing a button, as shown in Figure 3.11.

FIGURE 3.10

Use the Zoom Control to increase or decrease the size of on-screen images.

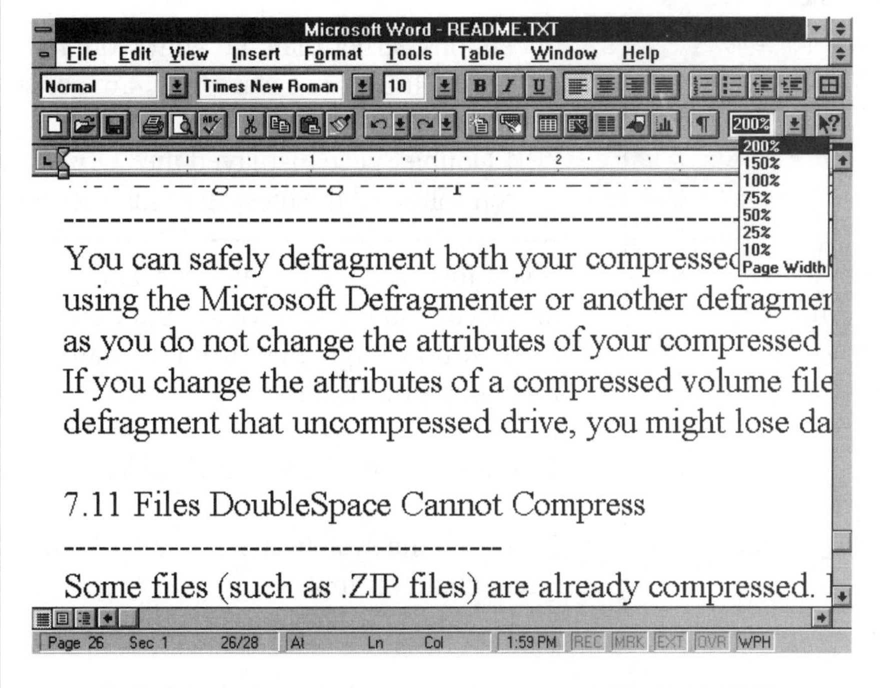

Edit as usual. Navigate with Page Up, Page Down, and the rest of the keyboard tools. To return to the prior view, click on the little Full button or use the Alt+V+U keyboard shortcut. Incidentally, the Full button's window can be dragged out of the way.

►► Speeding Up Screen Scrolling

If you find scrolling and other screen actions somewhat sluggish, here are some suggestions.

- Add more RAM and try the other usual Windows speed-up tricks well-documented elsewhere. Word for Windows runs best in 6 MB or more.
- Work in Normal view whenever possible.

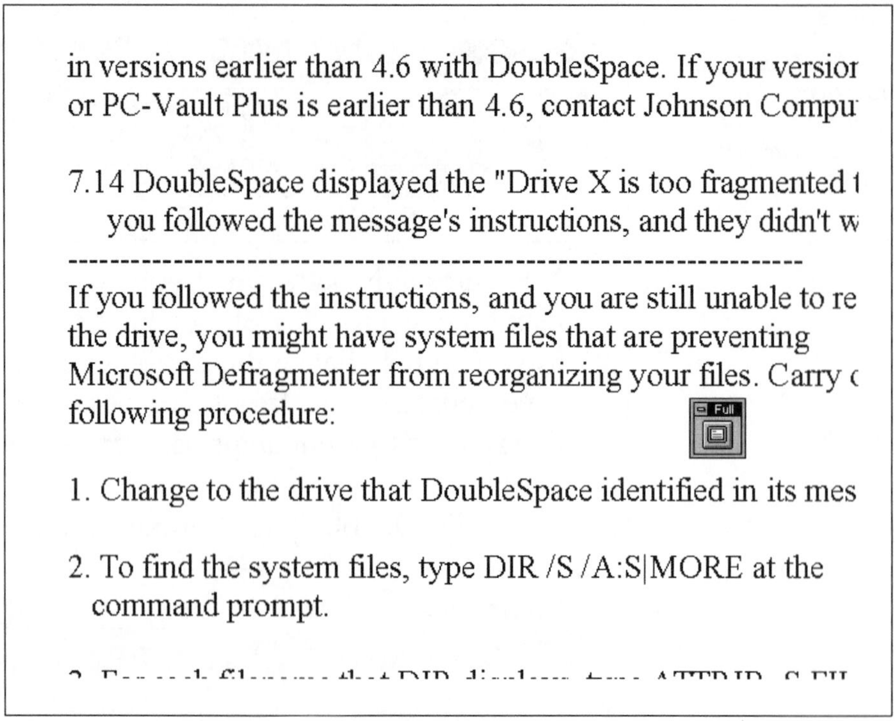

FIGURE 3.11

Full Screen removes everything but your work and a small button window.

in versions earlier than 4.6 with DoubleSpace. If your versio
or PC-Vault Plus is earlier than 4.6, contact Johnson Compu

7.14 DoubleSpace displayed the "Drive X is too fragmented
you followed the message's instructions, and they didn't w

If you followed the instructions, and you are still unable to re
the drive, you might have system files that are preventing
Microsoft Defragmenter from reorganizing your files. Carry
following procedure:

Full

1. Change to the drive that DoubleSpace identified in its mes

2. To find the system files, type DIR /S /A:S|MORE at the
command prompt.

- Close unwanted windows and applications that you are not using.
- Consider breaking one very large document into several smaller ones (books into chapters, for instance).

CHAPTER 4

Previewing and Printing

▸▸ FAST TRACK

To print one copy of the current document with the default settings **115**

click the Print button on the Standard Toolbar.

To ensure (relatively) smooth printing **117**

check to be certain of the following before you do anything else: the printer is cabled properly; you have set up your printer in Windows (see your Windows documentation for details); your printer is turned on and loaded with supplies (paper, toner, etc.); it is warmed up, if necessary, and the ready light is on.

To choose a printer **118**

choose File ➤ Print... or use the **Ctrl+P** shortcut. Click on the Printer... button to reach the Printers dialog box. Point and click in the scrollable list to select the desired printer. Click the Close box twice.

To print from more than one paper source **123**

choose the desired source under the Paper Source tab in the Page Setup dialog box.

To choose other print options, such as Draft Output, Update Fields, or Background Printing ***123***

choose the Print tab in Word's Options dialog box (reached by choosing Tools ➤ Options… or by pressing the Options button in the Print dialog box).

To see onscreen how your printed pages will look ***125***

choose File ➤ Print Preview (or use the keyboard shortcut **Ctrl+Alt+I**).

To print documents while you work ***131***

enable the Background Printing option: choose Tools ➤ Options…; click the Print tab, if necessary, to reveal printing options; make sure there is an X in the Background Printing box (click if necessary); click OK and print as usual.

To cancel printing ***132***

press the Esc key repeatedly until the printing status information disappears from your screen. If you are using background printing, you will probably need to visit the Print Manager and cancel the job there.

▶▶ ***P**rinting* can be quite simple or relatively involved, depending on what you're trying to do. First, be certain that: the printer is cabled properly; you have set up your printer in Windows (see your Windows documentation for details); your printer is turned on and loaded with supplies (paper, toner, etc.); it is warmed up, if necessary, and the ready light is on.

▶▶ **TIP**

It is always a good idea to *save before you print!* Occasionally, printing problems can lock up your computer, and you might lose any unsaved changes if you are forced to reboot or power-down. Get in the habit of clicking the Save button (the one that looks like a floppy disk on the Standard Toolbar) or using the Ctrl+S keyboard shortcut before you print.

▶▶ *Simple Printing*

If you only have one printer and it is properly installed and ready to go, and you just want to print a single copy of the current document, just press the Print button on the Standard Toolbar. Logically enough, this button looks like a printer, as shown in Figure 4.1. Try this now with your Twain Quote.

FIGURE 4.1

Use the Printer button on the Standard Toolbar to get a quick single copy of the current document.

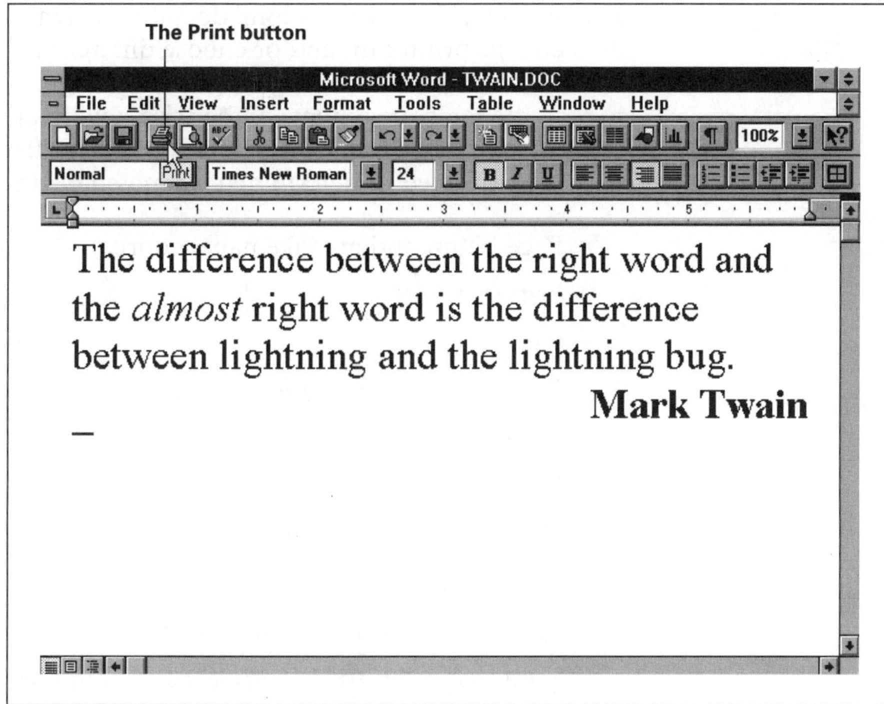

The status area will chart Word's progress as it prints. Page numbers and a little animated printer icon will tell you how many pages have been sent to the printer or to the Windows background printing feature.

▶▶ Printing as an Interactive Process

While printing can be as simple as previously described, it is a good idea to get into the habit of visiting the Page Setup dialog box, and possibly the Print dialog box, whenever you begin to create a new document—particularly if you work with a variety of printers, paper sizes, and document designs. If you wait until you have finished working on your document to choose a printer, your page and line endings may change considerably from those you initially saw on your screen. This can be a minor annoyance or a major disaster.

For example, if you write a long document, create a table of contents, then change printer models or choose different printing features, you will find that line and page endings may change. This will require you to redo the table of contents. Otherwise it will not agree with the printed pages. The following printer decisions affect pagination and should be selected or determined when you begin a project:

- Page Setup options (like paper source)
- Printer model
- Paper size
- Reduction/enlargement (scaling)
- Page orientation
- Margins
- Gutters
- Larger print area
- Printing/not printing hidden text
- Printing/not printing footnotes and endnotes
- Font substitution options

►► **NOTE**

These options and decisions will all be discussed in depth elsewhere.

Other changes affect the appearance of printed pages but have little impact on pagination.

If you have only one printer and it works properly, you can skip ahead to the section Choosing Print Dialog Box Options later in this chapter.

► Choosing a Printer

To choose a printer:

1. Choose File ➤ Print… or use the Ctrl+P shortcut. You will see a dialog box like the one in Figure 4.2.

FIGURE 4.2

Use the Print dialog box to reach the Print Setup dialog box.

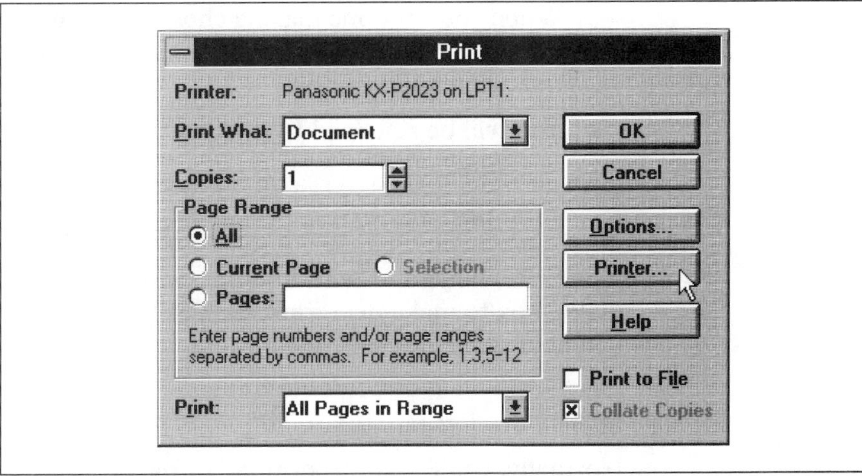

2. Click on the Printer… button to reach the Printer Setup dialog box, shown in Figure 4.3. (Yours will list your printer models.)

FIGURE 4.3

Use the Print Setup dialog box to pick a printer.

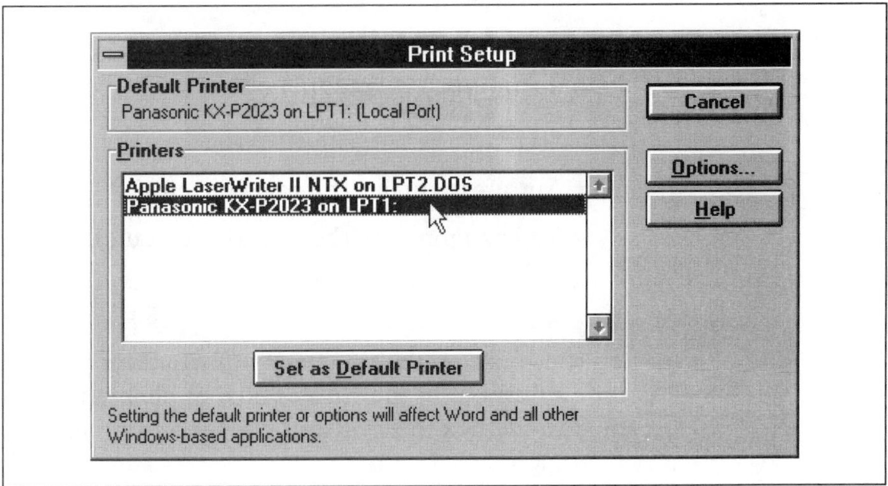

3. Point and click in the scrollable list to select the desired printer.
4. If the printer you've chosen has options (lighter/darker, letter quality vs. draft, etc.), you can usually reach them by clicking the Options… button.

5. When you are done making choices, return to the Print Setup dialog box (if you aren't already there) and click the Close box to select the printer and options.
6. You will be returned to the Print dialog box.

► Choosing Print Dialog Box Options

The Print dialog box will show you which printer is selected. Use this dialog box to make decisions, such as how many copies of which pages you need.

What to Print

Normally, you'll want to print all or part of your document. But sometimes you'll want to print other things, such as the document's annotations or other settings information. Use the drop-down list to pick any of the following options:

- Document
- Summary Info
- Annotations
- Styles
- AutoText entries (typing shortcuts)
- Key assignments (keyboard shortcuts)

Copies

To specify more than one copy of whatever you intend to print, either type a number in the Copies box, or click on the up or down arrows next to the box to scroll and choose a number.

Page Range

To print the entire page range, make sure the All button is darkened (the default). Click on the little button next to All, if necessary.

To print just the page in your document currently containing the insertion point, click on the Current Page button.

To print selected text, first select it, then bring up the Print dialog box and use the Selection button in the Page Range area. This choice will be dimmed unless you've selected something in your document.

To print a range of pages (pages 6–10 in a 50-page document, for instance), type the first and last desired page number in the Pages text box. Separate the numbers with hyphens (*6-10*, for instance).

To print specific pages, list them separated by commas (*3,5,8* for example). Ranges and single pages can be combined, so *6-10,13,19,83* will work as well.

Print All, Odd, or Even

Normally, Word prints all pages in order, but if you are planning to do "manual" two-sided printing, or you have other reasons to separate odd and even pages, use the drop-down Print list at the bottom of the Print dialog box to specify Odd Pages or Even Pages. For example, you might first print all odd-numbered pages, then put those pages back in the printer to print the even-numbered pages on the other side.

Print to File

It's possible to print to disk files instead of to a printer. This technique is sometimes used when you want to take a document to a service bureau for typesetting or other special services. It is a very good idea to do a test run before trying this technique for rush work, as there are many land mines. Consider providing your service bureau copies of the actual Word document files instead of (or in addition to) print files. Here are the steps for printing to a file:

1. Edit and polish your document as usual.
2. Consider creating a paper copy by printing normally.
3. Open the Print dialog box with File ➤ Print… or Ctrl+P.
4. Place an *X* in the Print to File box in the Print dialog box.
5. Click OK. You'll see the Print to File dialog box, illustrated in Figure 4.4.
6. Pick a drive from the Drives list.
7. Pick a directory as needed.

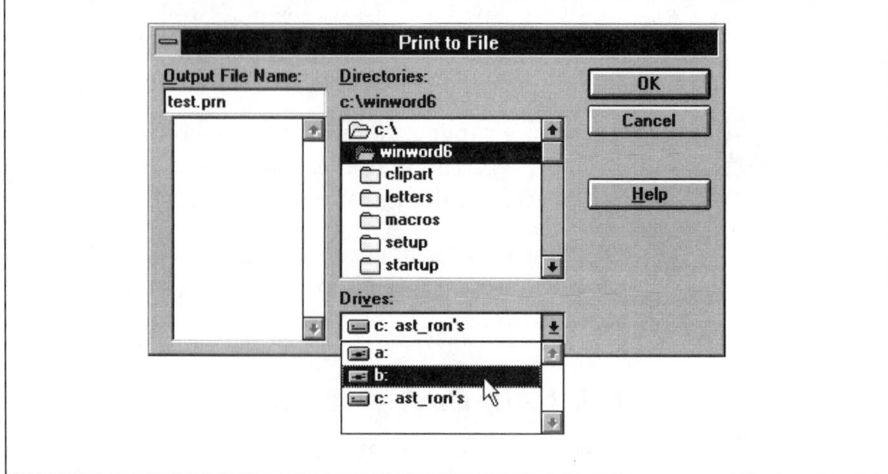

FIGURE 4.4

Enter a file name and drive destination for your print file.

8. Name the file in the Output File Name box.
9. Click OK to create the file.

TIP

Print files can get pretty big, particularly if they contain graphics. Consider printing small ranges of pages to multiple files if you need to transport print files on floppies. You'll need to experiment, since the actual number of bytes per page can vary widely, even between several pages in the same document.

Collate Copies

If you request multiple copies (five copies of a ten-page document, for instance) and you don't choose the Collate Copies option, Word will print all five page 1's, then all five page 2's and so on. You'll need to hand-collate them to make orderly sets.

The Collate Copies option prints five "books," each one complete and in order. This may or may not increase overall printing time depending on your printer and a number of other factors. Experiment.

▶ Letterheads, Second Sheets, and Two-Tray Printers

If your printer has two paper sources (two trays or a tray and a "pass-through," for instance), Word can switch sources as needed. Use the *First Page*, *Other Pages*, and perhaps *Apply To* choices found under the Paper Source tab in the Page Setup dialog box, as shown in Figure 4.5.

FIGURE 4.5 ▶

The Page Setup dialog box.

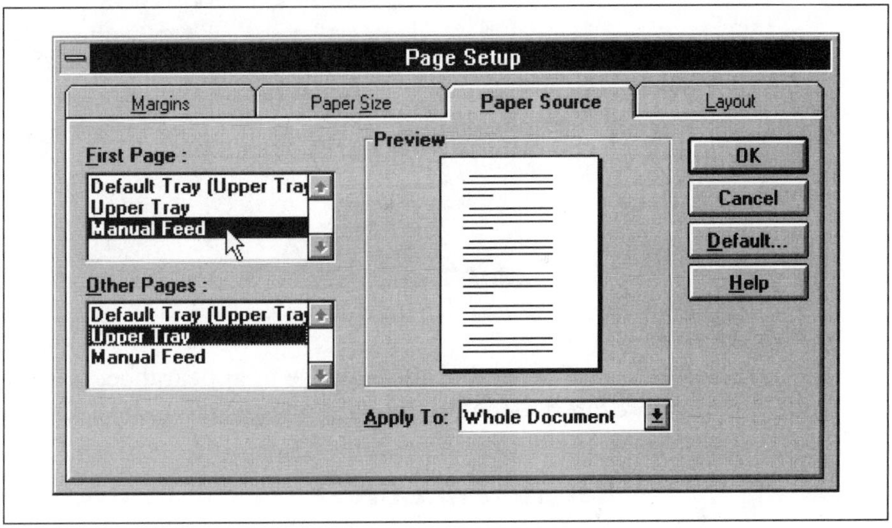

▶ Other Printing Options

There are other printer options available. They can be reached by choosing the Print tab in Word's Options dialog box, are shown in Figure 4.6, and are discussed in the following section.

You can display the Options dialog box either by choosing Tools ➤ Options… or by pressing the Options button in the Print dialog box. Most of these settings remain in place once you change them and are used for each new printing job until you change them.

Draft Output

This option can speed up printing. Its effect varies from printer to printer. Usually everything is printed in a single font, as efficiently as

FIGURE 4.6

The Print Options tab.

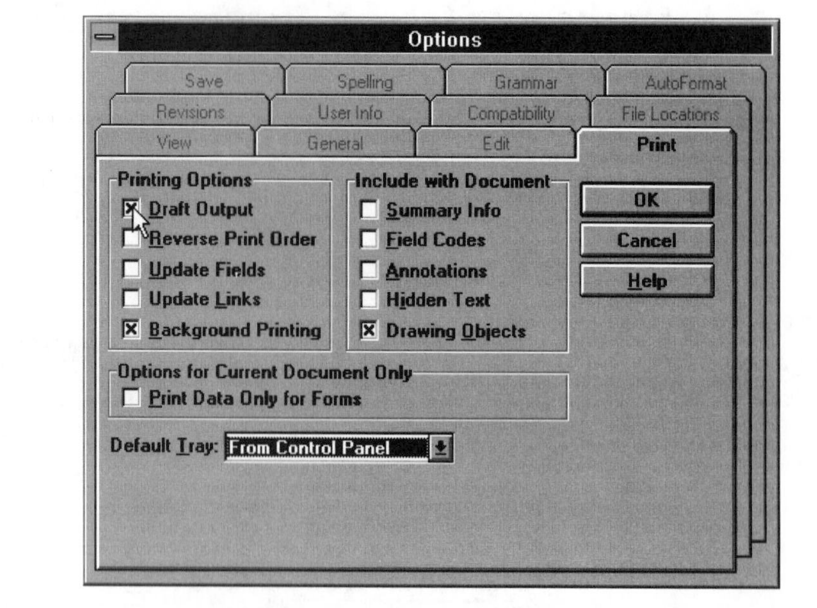

possible, and at the expense of appearance. It is often faster to print draft dot-matrix copy than fancy laser copy.

Reverse Print Order

Use Reverse Print Order when you want pages to come out last-to-first. This is handy for printers that "stack" pages in the wrong order.

Update Field and Update Links

As you'll see when you learn about linking and fields in Part Three, this is how you determine when and if things get updated before printing.

Background Printing

An X in this option box causes Word to use the Windows Background printing feature. Theoretically, it lets you work on other things while your document prints in the background. In real life it often makes your computer so sluggish that you'll end up taking a break anyway. If you keep getting printing errors or low memory messages while printing, try turning off background printing.

Include with Document

The Include with Document choices in the Print tab of the Options dialog box are pretty self-explanatory. An X causes things to be delivered with the printed pages (summary info, annotations, etc.). Click on an X to remove it and prevent the item from printing.

Current Document Options

The options that will appear here vary with the contents of your document. For instance, you may be given the option to print data without printing forms. See Chapter 33 for more about forms.

Tray Choice

Use this choice to force something other than the standard tray choice for special printing jobs (e.g., a cover letter on your business letterhead). Obviously the selected printer must have more than one paper source for this to be useful.

►► Print Preview

You can bypass the Print Preview and print immediately to hard copy, but previewing is advised. It lets you see a screen representation of one or more entire pages before you print them, often saving paper and time.

If you didn't try Print Preview on the Twain quote when you read about it earlier, this would be a good time to experiment. Choose File ➤ Print Preview (or use the keyboard shortcut Ctrl+Alt+I or Ctrl+F2).

new

This will give you an excellent idea of where the text will print on the paper. Unlike in previous versions of Word for Windows, you can now edit this text. You will be able to see margins as well. If your document contains headers, footers, line numbers, and other embellishments, you will see them, too, as illustrated in Figure 4.7.

Notice the buttons along the top of the screen. They let you control many of Print Preview's functions. As always, if you forget a button's function, simply pointing to it without clicking will reveal button help. Here is a general description of each button.

FIGURE 4.7 ►

Use Print Preview to get an overview, adjust margins, and even edit before printing.

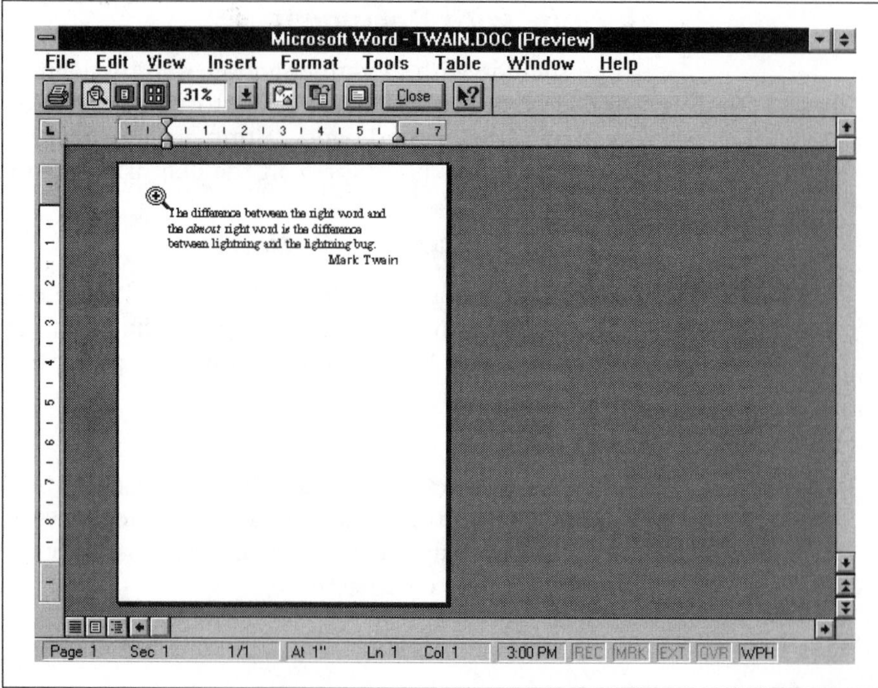

Print Preview's Print Button

The left-most button prints a single copy of the document without taking you to the Print dialog box. (If you really want to visit the Print dialog box, choose File ➤ Print… or use the Ctrl+P shortcut.)

Magnifier

The Magnifier button (with the magnifying glass) lets you zoom in to better read small portions of the page and zoom out to get a bird's-eye view of one or more pages. It also toggles you in and out of the edit mode, as you will see momentarily.

One Page

The next button (called One Page) displays a single page even if you are working with a multipage document.

Multiple Pages

The Multiple Pages button looks like four little pages. It lets you specify the number of miniaturized pages you'll see on-screen. Pressing this button reveals a matrix that you drag across to design your screen display. Choices range from a single page to 3 × 6 (18) pages, as shown in Figure 4.8.

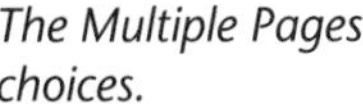

FIGURE 4.8

The Multiple Pages choices.

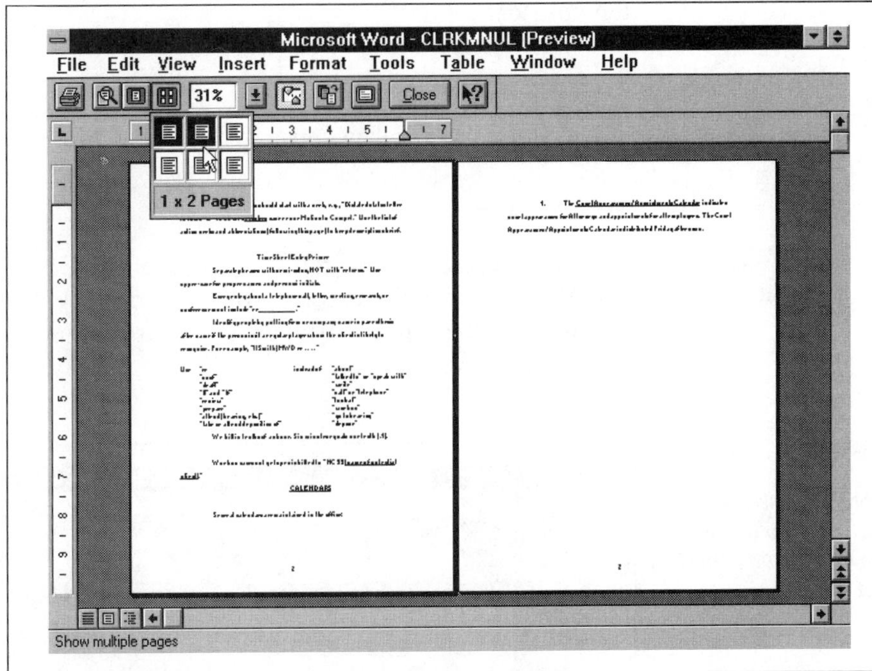

Zoom Control

The Percentage text box and related zoom list are called the *Zoom controls*. They tell you the current zoom percentage and let you pick a variety of zoom options from a drop-down list.

View Ruler

Next you'll see a View Ruler button. It is used to toggle the rulers that you use to see and change margin settings.

Shrink to Fit

When you press the Shrink to Fit button (to the right of the View Rulers button), Word attempts to tighten up documents that end with a mostly white page. For example, Figure 4.9 shows how Word proposes to tighten up the two pages shown in Figure 4.8.

To undo proposed changes, use the Ctlr+Z shortcut or Edit ➤ Undo Shrink to Fit. Occasionally, Word can't shrink your document and will tell you so.

Close Button

The Close button takes you back to the previous view.

Full Screen

The Full Screen button removes most of the Print Preview clutter (menu bar, status line, etc.) so that you can see a bigger version of your document. Pressing the Full Screen button a second time returns the hidden controls.

FIGURE 4.9 

Word's Shrink to Fit button can often remove those ugly short last pages.

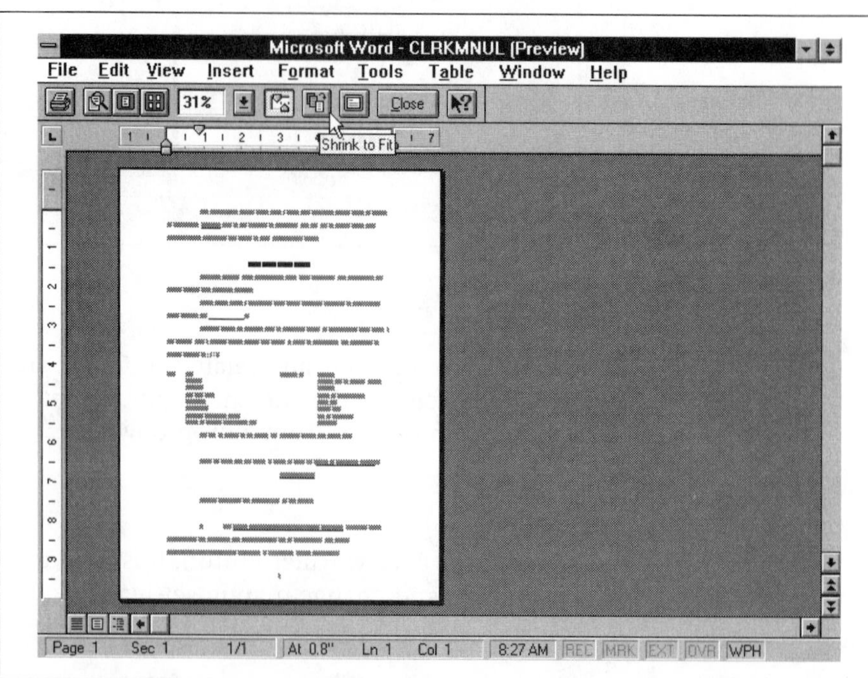

Help Button

The Help button will turn your pointer into a question mark. Point to the item of interest (the vertical ruler, for instance) to read any available help. Double-click on the Help window's Close box to quit help.

▶ Leaving Print Preview

Use the Close button to leave Print Preview and return to your previous view. The three standard view buttons (Normal, Page Layout, and Outline) are also available in the lower-left corner of the status area of Print Preview.

▶ Moving Margins in Print Preview

While a complete explanation of margins will have to wait until Chapter 8, here is a quick trick you can try on your Twain quote in Print Preview.

1. Display the rulers if they are not already on-screen by clicking on the View Rulers button.
2. Point to the vertical ruler on the left edge of your screen. Notice how the pointer gets smaller and has an up-and-down-pointing head, as shown in Figure 4.10.
3. Hold down the primary (usually the left) mouse button and notice the dashed margin line.
4. While holding down the mouse button, drag down to specify a new top margin while watching the dashed line.
5. Release the mouse button and Word will adjust the margin, moving the text down, as illustrated in Figure 4.11.

▶▶ Printing Labels and Envelopes

See Chapters 15 and 28 for envelope and label-printing tricks. Be sure to check out the new envelope printing feature discussed in Chapter 15!

FIGURE 4.10

Drag the margin handle to adjust the margins.

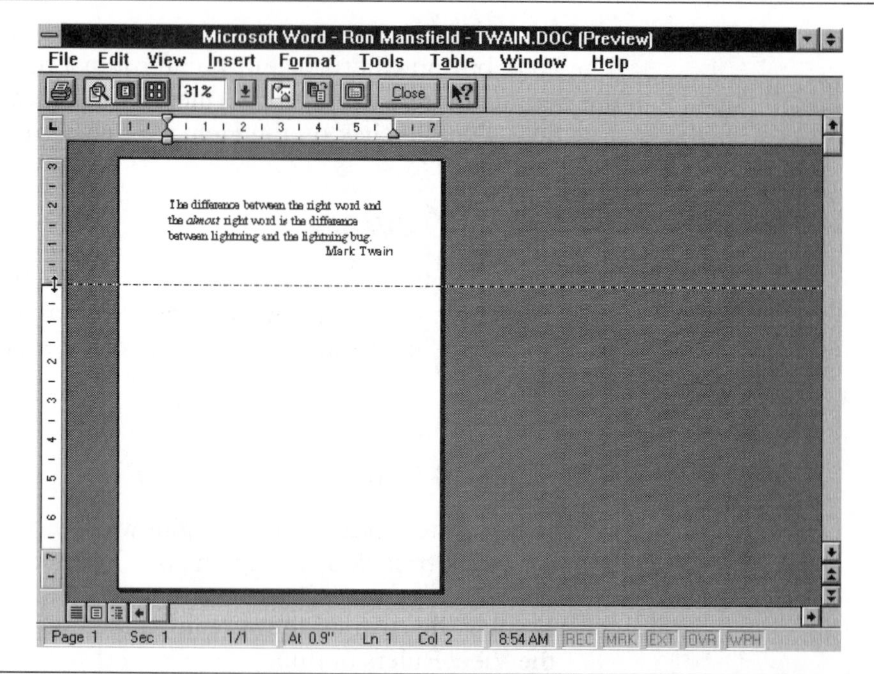

FIGURE 4.11

The Twain quote after dragging to increase the top margin.

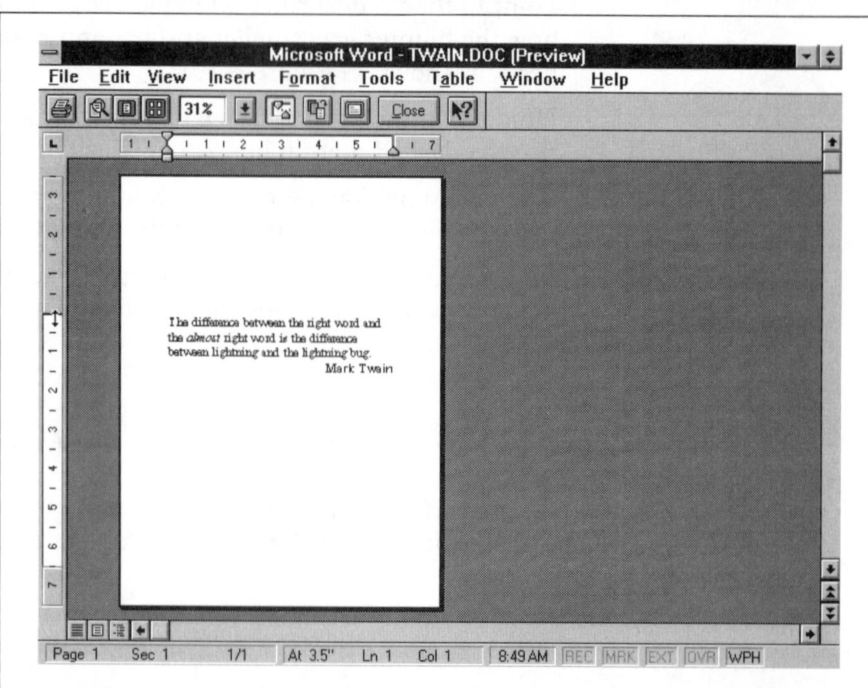

▶▶ Background Printing

Because some printing jobs can take many minutes or even hours, background printing can be a real productivity booster—at least in theory—as it supposedly lets you do other things while the printer prints "in the background." Moreover, you can use the Windows Print Manager application to check and control the status of multiple print jobs.

Your system does all of this by quickly sending print jobs to a file on your hard disk rather than directly to the printer. It then spools the work to your printer in the background.

▶ Enabling Background Printing

Turn on background printing from the Print tab in the Options dialog box.

1. Choose Tools ➤ Options....
2. Click the Print tab, if necessary, to reveal printing options.
3. Make sure there is an X in the Background Printing box (click if necessary).
4. Click OK and print as usual. Your documents will print in the background while you're working on other things.

▶ Checking the Status of a Print Job

▶▶ TIP

A great Windows shortcut to know is Alt+Tab. If you hit this key combination, Windows switches you to the next open application. If you have several open applications, repeatedly pressing Alt+Tab will cycle through them.

With background printing at work, you can use the Print Manager to check and change the status of multiple print jobs. Follow these steps:

1. Switch to the Print Manager window (hold down the Alt key and press Tab as many times as necessary to display the Print Manager name in the center of your screen, then release the keys).
2. Click to select the job or jobs you wish to cancel or reschedule.
3. Click on the appropriate button (Pause, Resume, or Delete).
4. Use Print Manager's menus for other options.
5. To return to Word for Windows, hold down the Alt key and press Tab as many times as necessary.

For more information about background printing with the Windows Print Manager, use the Print Manager's online help and see your windows documentation.

►► Aborting Printing

To stop printing prematurely, try pressing the Esc key repeatedly until the printing-status information disappears from your screen. Even after the print-status information disappears, your printer may print a few pages that were sent before print cancellation, as many printers contain their own memory (called a *buffer*). Check your printer manual for ways to quickly clear the printer's memory if this annoys you.

If you are using background printing, you will probably need to visit the Print Manager, as described earlier in this chapter, and cancel the job there.

CHAPTER 5

Working with Graphics

▸▸ FAST TRACK

▶▶ Word for Windows lets you draw, place, resize, reposition, and embellish graphics. You can work with your own drawings, charts from spreadsheet packages, photos from scanners, and just about any other computer-compatible art form. In fact, Word for Windows even comes with some clip art you can use to get your graphics library started.

You can simply *paste* graphics or place them in *frames*. As you'll soon see, the use of frames makes it easier for you to reposition and work with graphics.

There are plenty of new graphics-related buzzwords and standards to learn. In fact, another book the size of this one could be written just on those subjects. But this chapter contains all you'll need to start creating your own art and using free or low-cost clip art.

▶▶ Importing Graphics

Like text, computer art can be stored in disk files. Unfortunately, different drawing packages, scanners, and other graphic tools create files in their own unique formats. Word for Windows can use some graphic formats as is; the program comes with a number of built-in translation utilities (called *filters*) that can convert graphics from many sources, allowing you to insert them in Word for Windows documents. At a minimum, you will be able to work with the following graphic formats (their usual file extensions are listed after their names):

AutoCAD 2-D (DXF)
Computer Graphics Metafile (CGM)
CompuServe GIF (GIF)
CorelDRAW (CDR)
DrawPerfect (WPG)

Encapsulated PostScript (EPS)
HP Graphic Language (HGL)
Kodak Photo CD (PCD)
Lotus 1-2-3 (PIC)
Macintosh PICT (PCT)
Micrografx Designer 3/Draw Plus (DRW)
PC Paintbrush (PCX)
TIFF (Tagged Image File Format—TIF)
Windows Bitmap (BMP)
Windows Metafile (WMF)

If you don't see the format you need here, contact Microsoft technical support. They may be able to provide you with new filters, give you some workaround tips, or they can refer you to makers of graphics-conversion programs.

► Other Sources of Clip Art

If you don't have the time or inclination to draw your own art, you can purchase compatible clip art disks from mail-order firms and retail software dealers like Egghead. Many companies and nonprofit groups also distribute low-cost or free shareware and public domain clip art. Check local computer user groups and online art libraries like the ones provided by America Online and CompuServe. If you have a scanner, you can convert printed images to Word-compatible art. Be sure you understand and honor any copyright restrictions when you use other people's art.

► Using the Insert Picture Command

The easiest way to get hooked on graphics is to import a picture or two. Let's try it.

1. Start by opening your Twain document.
2. Place the insertion point where you want the picture to appear (on a new line after Mark's name, perhaps).
3. Choose Insert ➤ Picture… to bring up the dialog box in Figure 5.1.
4. You'll see a dialog box something like Figure 5.2. Click Preview Picture to enable the preview option.

FIGURE 5.1

Use the Insert ➤ Picture… command to insert disk-resident graphic files.

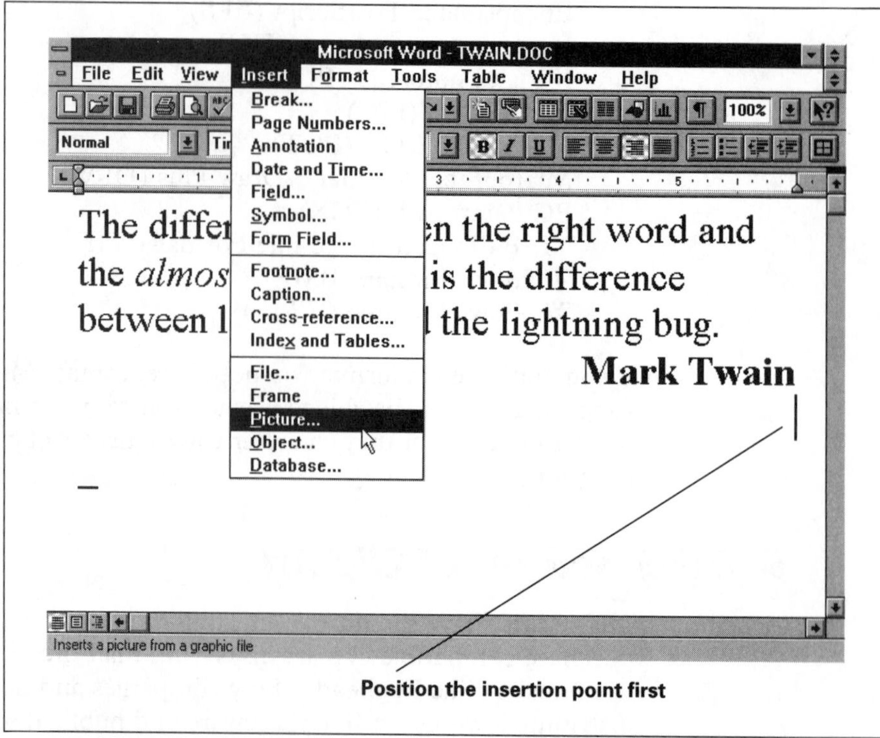

FIGURE 5.2

Enable the Preview Picture feature to browse.

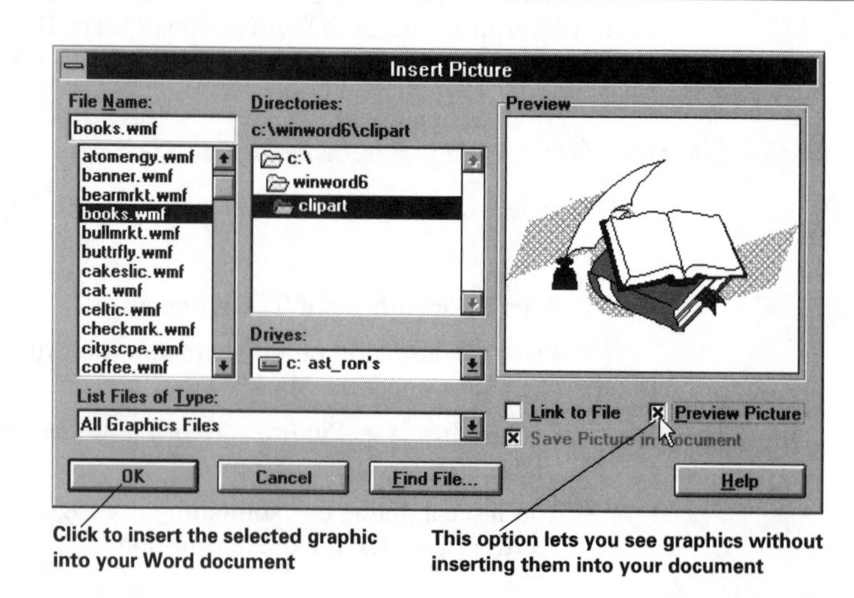

5. Browse by clicking on directories and files until you see something you like.
6. When you find your favorite graphic, click OK to insert it. (Figure 5.3 shows books.wmf from the c:\winword6\clipart directory.)
7. Reposition and perhaps resize or otherwise embellish the image as described later in this chapter.

The difference between the right word and the *almost* right word is the difference between lightning and the lightning bug.
Mark Twain

FIGURE 5.3
Graphics are placed at the insertion point.

In addition to the Word for Windows clip art folder, chances are you have other graphic images on your hard disk. For instance, your Windows directory probably has a dozen or so bitmap files (files ending in BMP). Use the scrollable lists to find files of interest. When you see one, click on the name to highlight it, then click the Preview Picture button to get an idea of what it will look like, as before.

Using Your Clipboard to Insert Art

If you already have a drawing program that you use to create and edit artwork, it is possible to copy your work to the Clipboard, then paste it into a Word for Windows document.

1. Switch to or run the drawing program.
2. Select the art of interest.
3. Copy it to the Clipboard (Ctrl+C).

4. Switch to or start Word (quit or minimize the drawing program if you like—this may be necessary to run Word for Windows).
5. Move the insertion point to the desired location in your Word document.
6. Paste the graphic with Edit ➤ Paste command or Ctrl+V.

▸▸ Resizing Graphics with Your Mouse

When you click on a graphic in a Word for Windows document to select it, the picture will be surrounded by a box containing eight handles—one in each corner and one on each side of the outline box. The mouse pointer will turn into a two-headed arrow.

▸▸ NOTE

When you hear someone talk about sizing something (a graphic, for example) *proportionally*, what that means is that as the size changes, the width and height retain the same proportions, relative to each other. That is, if the height gets three times larger, the width will get three times larger as well.

To increase or decrease the size of the entire graphic *proportionally*, drag a *corner* handle diagonally, releasing it when you are happy with the proposed size.

To distort a dimension, use the handles on the *edges* of the graphic outline to stretch (distort) the graphic, as shown in Figure 5.4. Undo works if you act promptly.

▸▸ Cropping Graphics with Your Mouse

To crop a document (hide part of it), hold down the Shift key while you drag any of the handles to create the desired effect (see Figure 5.5). The mouse pointer will turn into a square with a line through it.

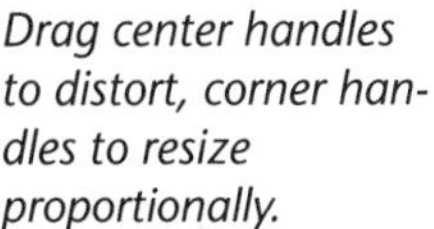

FIGURE 5.4

Drag center handles to distort, corner handles to resize proportionally.

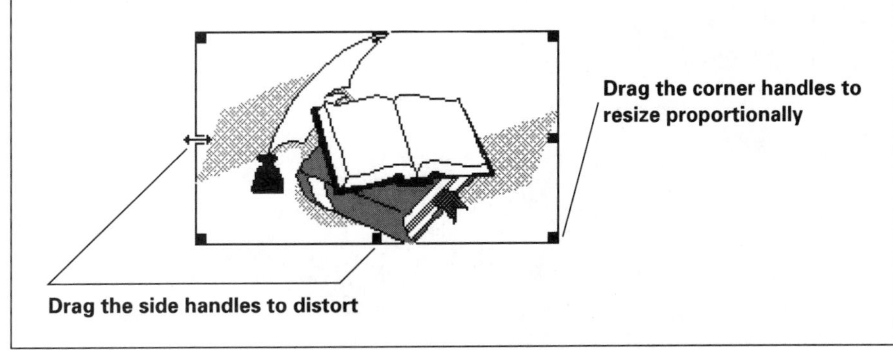
Drag the corner handles to resize proportionally
Drag the side handles to distort

FIGURE 5.5

Hold down the Shift key when dragging to crop (hide) part of a graphic.

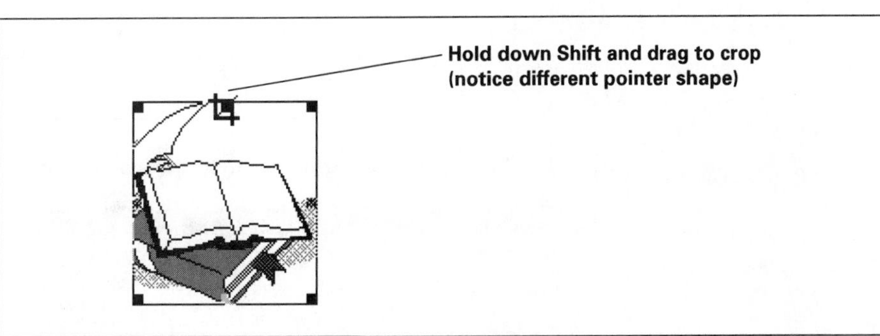
Hold down Shift and drag to crop (notice different pointer shape)

►► Adding White Space around Graphics

To add white space around a graphic, hold down the Shift key and drag handles away from the graphic (see Figure 5.6). Undo can restore the original size.

►► Sizing and Cropping Graphics with the Picture Command

The Format ➤ Picture… command reveals the Picture dialog box, shown in Figure 5.7. It contains information about a selected picture's original size and any cropping or resizing that's been done.

You can also use this box to specify new size and cropping dimensions. The Reset button returns a graphic to its original size and uncrops it.

FIGURE 5.6

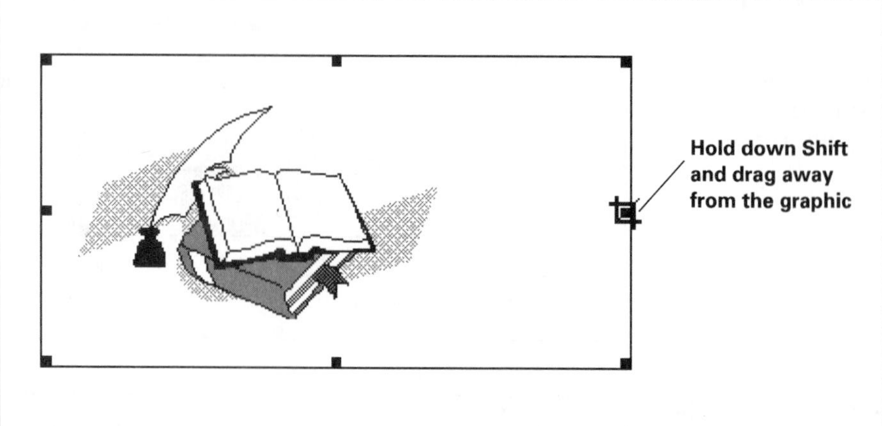

Hold the Shift key and drag handles away from the graphic to add white space.

FIGURE 5.7

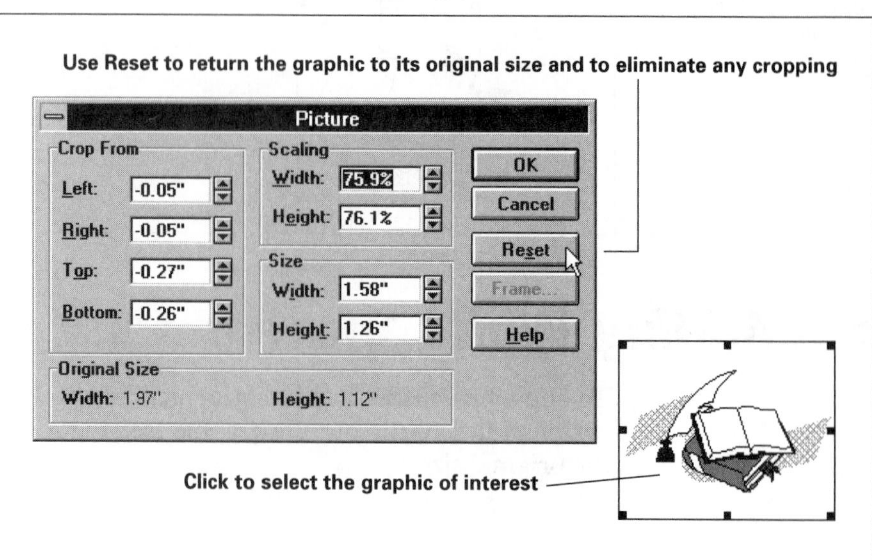

Use the Picture dialog box to see what you've done; you can modify or undo resizing and cropping settings here.

▸▸ Using Word's Drawing Features

To create a new drawing using the Word for Windows drawing features:

1. Open a new or existing Word document.
2. Place the insertion point where you want your new art to be inserted.

3. Click on the Standard Toolbar's Draw button—the button with the square, circle, and triangle. (Or, if you have a Word document containing a graphic you want to modify, double-click on the graphic.)
4. You'll see the Drawing Toolbar, illustrated in Figure 5.8.

You'll use a series of buttons, menu commands, and your mouse to draw, resize, and rearrange shapes lines and text.

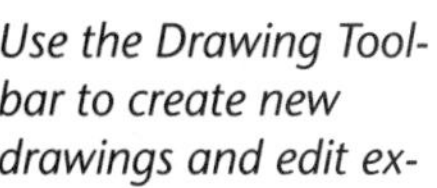

FIGURE 5.8

Use the Drawing Toolbar to create new drawings and edit existing ones.

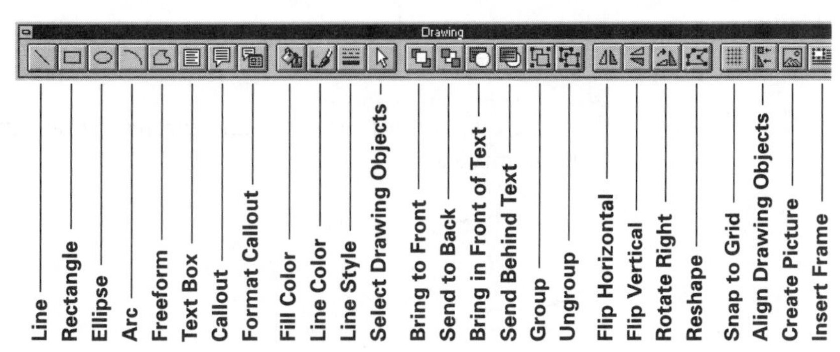

TIP

You might want to reshape the Drawing Toolbar to make it easier to move it around and keep it out of the way. Drag an edge of the Toolbar to change its shape from wide and short to tall and skinny, for instance, as shown in Figure 5.9.

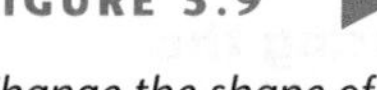

FIGURE 5.9

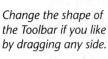

Change the shape of the Toolbar if you like by dragging any side.

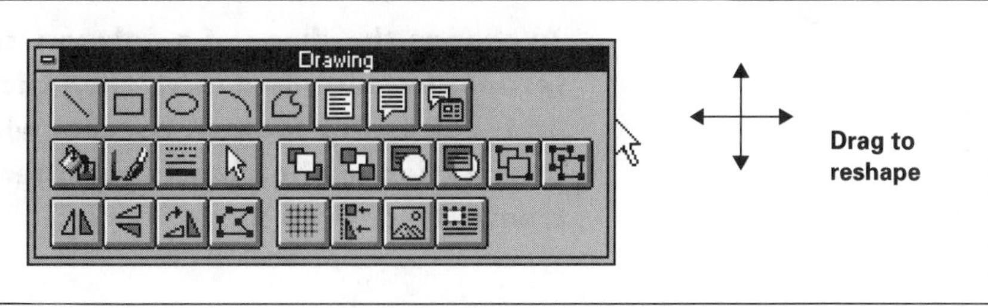

▸▸ Drawing Things

First click on a shape button or line button (line, ellipse, circle, etc.) in the Drawing Toolbar, then use your mouse to create lines or shapes. For instance, to create rectangles for an organizational chart, you would click on the rectangle button and drag with your mouse to create a rectangle of the desired shape and size. (Holding down the Shift key while you do this creates squares.)

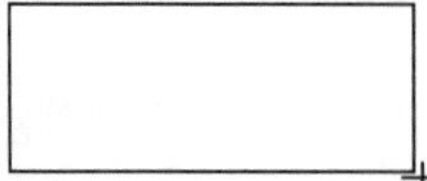

Use the ellipse tool for ovals and circles. (The Shift key helps you make precise circles.)

To create polygons, choose the free-form tool, then click and drag repeatedly until you are done. For example, to make a triangle, you would click once to anchor the first point and drag for the first side. Click again to anchor the second point and drag again. Click to anchor the third point, then drag back to the starting point and click one last time to complete the triangle.

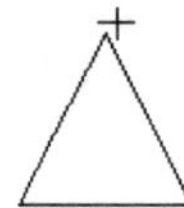

To change the shape of a polygon, select it using the techniques described next, then click the Reshape tool on the Drawing Toolbar. Handles will appear at each intersection of the shape. Drag them as necessary to create the desired shape.

▶ Selecting Objects

To select rectangles or other drawing elements (lines, text, etc.), click on the arrow button at the top of the drawing tool stack, then point to the item you want to move. This selects it.

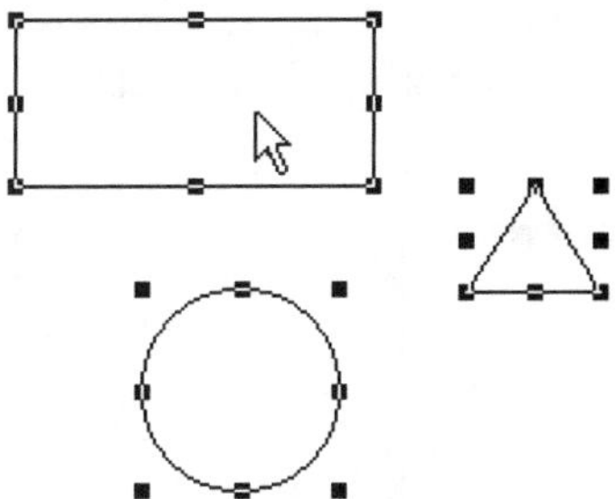

Holding down the Shift Key lets you select multiple objects. The Edit ➤ Select All command selects all text and pictures. Selected objects are surrounded by small handles. Click outside of any selected object to deselect all selected objects.

▶▶ Text in Drawings

You can create text for drawings either in *text boxes* or in *frames* (covered in Chapter 6). To create a text box, use the Drawing Toolbar's Text Box button, which looks like ragged lines of text. Text in boxes is automatically surrounded by black lines unless you eliminate them.

1. Click on the Toolbar's Text Box button.

2. Drag the text box to its desired size and shape. Make it big if in doubt.

3. Type the word **Marketing** (the insertion point's already in the box, so there's no need to position it).

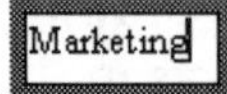

4. If necessary, you can increase the size of a text box by dragging, just as if it were any other graphic object.

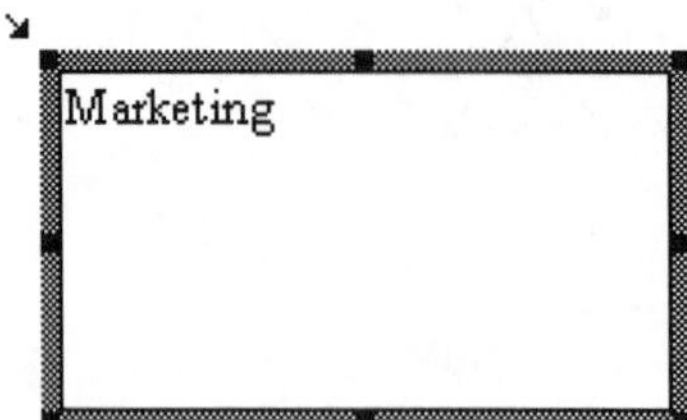

▶ Embellishing Text in Drawings

You can embellish text (make it bold, center it, change type styles, and so on), and you can combine the effects using most of Word's formatting tools. For example, here's a box with two typefaces, some bold characters, and a bulleted list, created with the Bullets Toolbar on the Format Toolbar.

Marketing Department

- Sandra Lexington
- William Johnson
- Karin Danialson
- Bobbi Wrightwood

▶ More or Less Space between Text and Box Lines

To increase or decrease the white space between the text and text box lines:

1. Select the text box.
2. Choose Format ➤ Drawing Object.

3. Select the Size and Position tab. You'll see the choices illustrated in Figure 5.10.
4. Specify a new internal margin by typing a new setting in the appropriate box or using the up and down arrow buttons. For instance, here's the marketing text box with 6 points (6pt) of internal margin:

Marketing Department
- Sandra Lexington
- William Johnson
- Karin Danialson

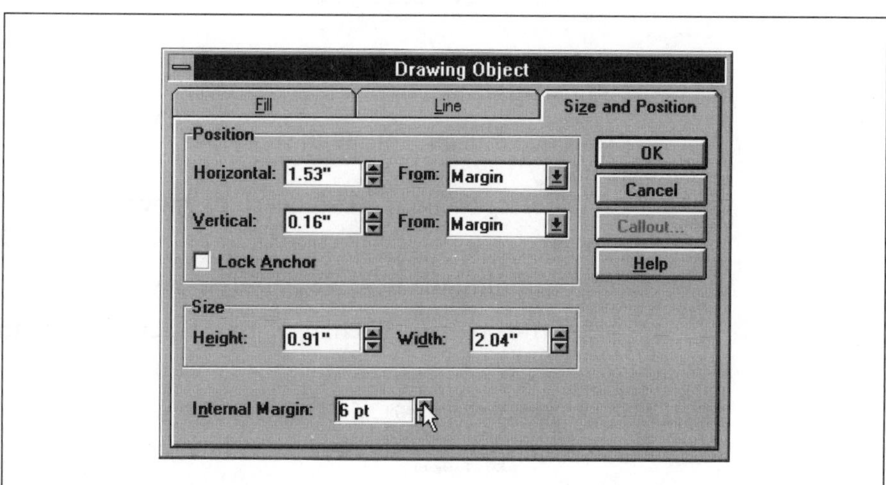

FIGURE 5.10

Use the Drawing Object dialog box to add white space in a text box.

Eliminating Text Box Lines

To eliminate the lines surrounding the text box, follow these steps:

1. Select the box or boxes by clicking or shift-clicking.
2. Use the Drawing Toolbar's Line Color button to reveal the line color palette.

3. Click on the None choice (at the top), as shown here:

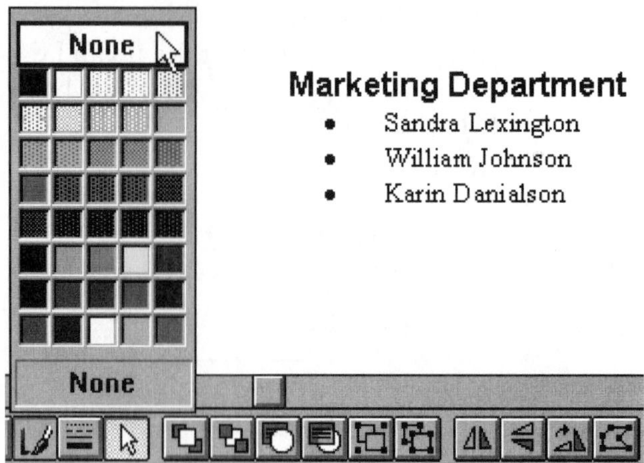

▶ Moving Objects

To move objects, follow these steps:

1. Select the item or items to be moved.
2. Point to one of the selected items with your mouse pointer, avoiding the object's handles.
3. The pointer will change, now looking like an arrow with four heads.

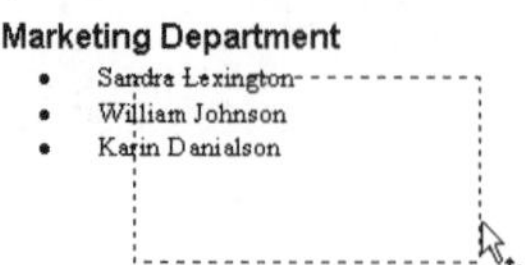

4. Drag with your mouse and watch as an outline of the object(s) proposes a new location.
5. Releasing the mouse button completes the move.

▶ Grid Lines

Word's drawing feature has optional *invisible gridlines* that make it easy to align things. This makes dragging a little jerky when the Snap To Grid feature is enabled. The gridlines act like magnets and moved objects migrate to them no matter how hard you try to prevent this. For precise, smooth moves, turn the Snap to Grid feature off. You can also change the spacing and origin of grids. Do all of this with the Snap to Grid dialog box. Reach it with the Snap to Grid button near the right end of the Drawing Toolbar. It looks like a window screen.

The button reveals the Snap to Grid dialog box, shown in Figure 5.11.

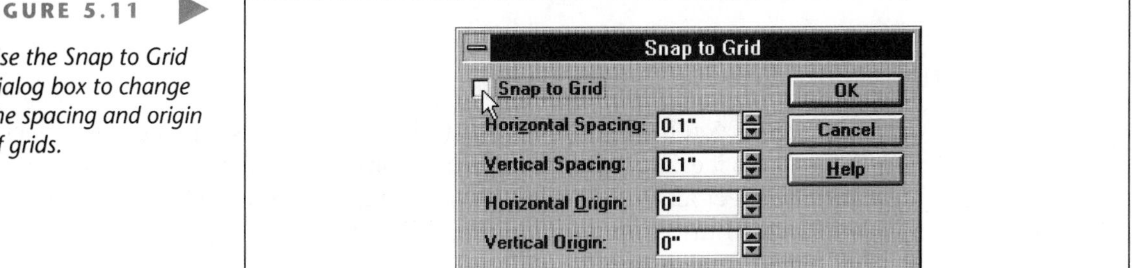

FIGURE 5.11 ▶

Use the Snap to Grid dialog box to change the spacing and origin of grids.

To turn off the snap feature, remove the *X* from the Snap to Grid box by clicking, as shown in Figure 5.11. Even if the grid is turned off, you can still use it whenever you wish by holding down the Alt key while you drag.

Use the other tools in the dialog box to change the grid's dimensions and starting point with respect to the upper-left corner of the window.

▶ Layers

You can construct objects from multiple elements placed near, on top of, or beneath each other. For instance, the books illustration in your

Twain quote contains a number of separate elements.

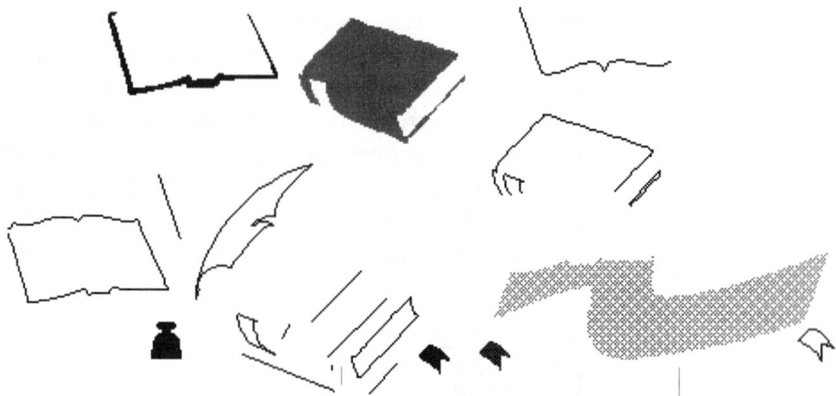

Things piled on top of each other are said to be *layered*. You can select items and use the Bring to Front or Send to Back buttons on the Drawing Toolbar to arrange layers to your liking.

▶ Grouping and Ungrouping

Sometimes you'll want to turn multiple drawing parts into a single object. This makes it easier to move and resize complex elements (see Figure 5.12). Simply select all of the elements of interest by shift-clicking, then use the Group button on the Drawing Toolbar.

Henceforth, all of the items will act as a single item, as you can see here,

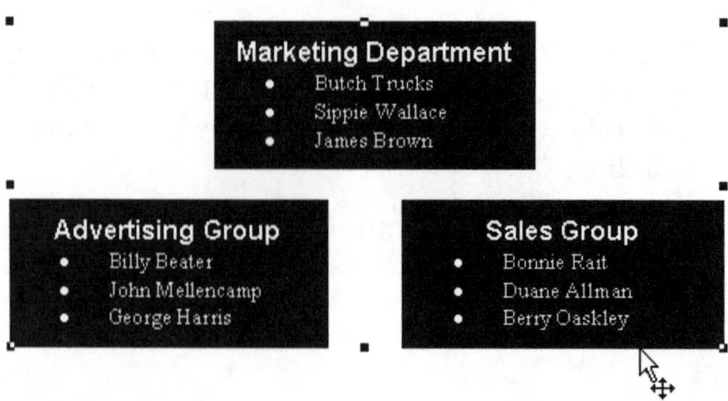

until you select the group and choose Draw ➤ Ungroup.

FIGURE 5.12

Grouping objects makes them easy to keep together.

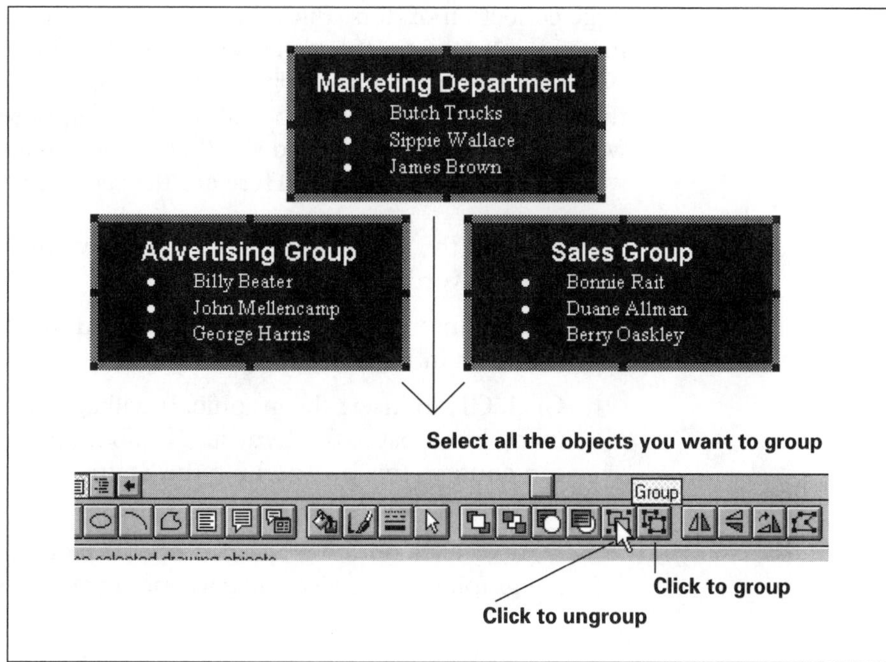

▶ Reorienting Objects

To flip objects, select them and choose Draw ➤ Rotate/Flip. Choose one of the three Flip and Rotate buttons on the Drawing Toolbar.

▶ Duplicating Objects

Once you've created an object (an "org chart" box, for instance), you can select, copy, and paste it to save time. Consider grouping complex collections of lines and shapes and text before duplicating them.

▶▶ Pictures vs. Drawing Objects

There are two general types of graphic images—drawings like the ones created and discussed in this chapter and "pictures" or "painted" images created with paint programs. Drawings are made up of individual elements—lines, circles, etc. Paint images are generally treated as one large collection of dots. Files that end with the extension .BMP are bitmap "paintings." So are many Windows Metafiles (.WMF). Word for Windows can use both drawings and bitmaps, but if you want to edit them, you must do so in a special window. Suppose, for instance, you want to change the color and shading of the ornamnt1.wmf file in the winword6/clipart directory. Here are the required steps:

1. Position the insertion point where you want the graphic to appear in your Word document.
2. Choose Insert ➤ Picture and locate the desired file (ornamnt1.wmf) as shown in Figure 5.13.
3. Click OK to insert the graphic. It will appear in the Word document, but most of the Drawing Toolbar buttons won't work. You can confirm this by watching the Status area as you point to the various buttons.
4. Double-click on the graphic to open a picture window. You'll see the graphic, a *picture boundary,* and a small dialog box:

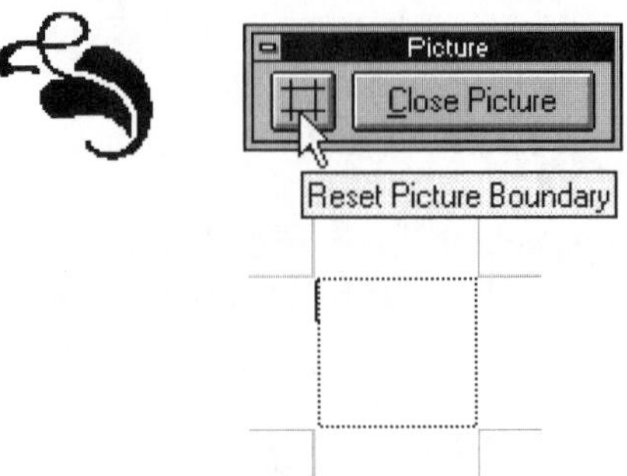

5. Click on the Reset Picture Boundary button to move the picture into the boundary as shown here:

FIGURE 5.13

Find the graphic file you wish to edit.

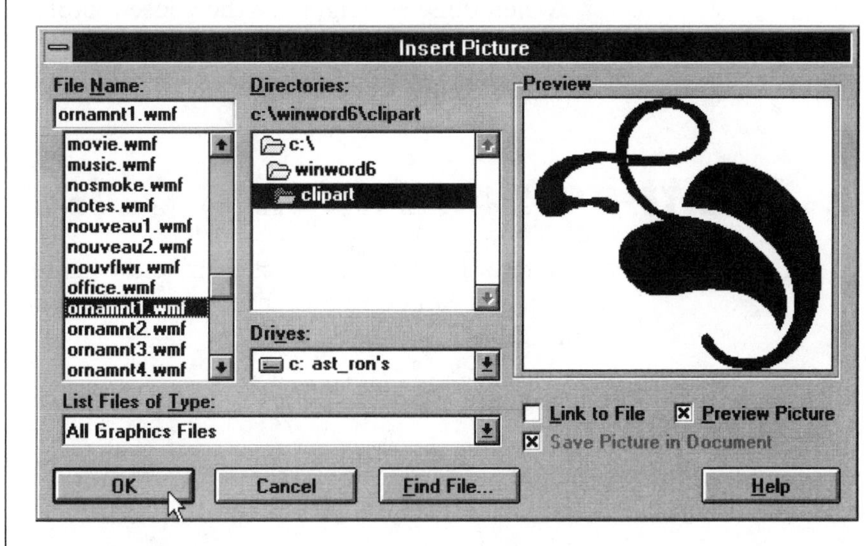

6. Edit the picture (shift-click to select all elements and use the Fill Color button on the Drawing Toolbar to choose a 20 percent gray, as illustrated here):

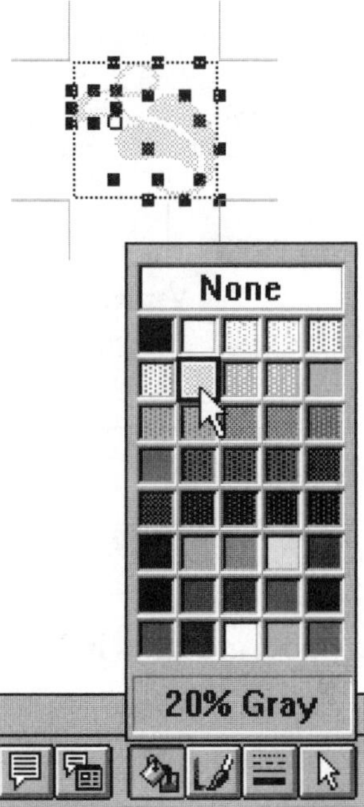

7. When done editing, click the Close Picture button in the little Picture window. The edited graphic will be placed in your Word for Windows document at the insertion point.

▸▸ Rotating and Flipping Objects

To rotate or flip objects, select them and use the Flip Horizontal, Flip Vertical, and Rotate Right buttons on the Drawing Toolbar, shown in Figure 5.14.

▸▸ **NOTE**

These buttons won't work on Text boxes. Use WordArt, described in Chapter 6, to manipulate the orientation of text.

FIGURE 5.14

Use these buttons to rotate and flip objects.

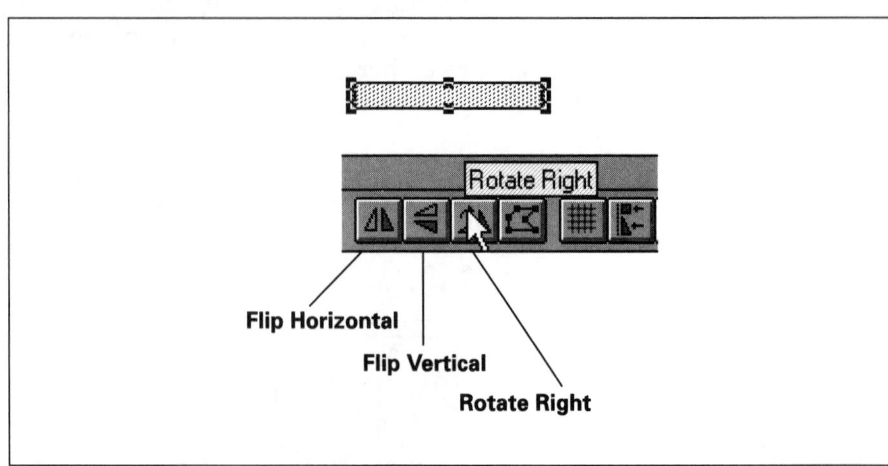

▸▸ Callouts

You can use callouts to label graphics in Word for Windows documents. Here are the steps:

1. Create or import a graphic.

2. Click the Callout button on the Drawing Toolbar:

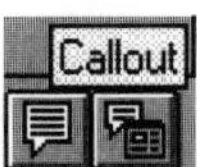

3. Click where you want the callout arrow to point.
4. Drag to where you want to position the text, then release the mouse button. The callout will appear.

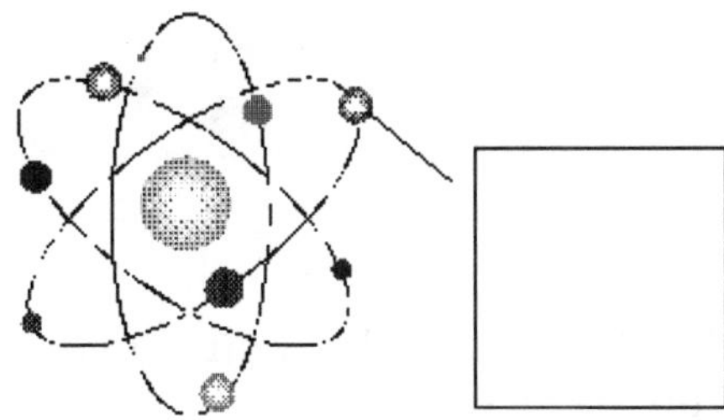

5. Type any text you want to show in the callout, then select the text and change its appearance if you like.
6. Select the callout box and resize it if you wish.
7. Drag the box and line as desired to reposition them.
8. To change the design of the callout box, use the Callout Defaults dialog box shown in Figure 5.15. Reach it with the Format Callout button (to the right of the Callout button).

NOTE

If you select a callout and then click on Format Callout, changes you make will affect that callout and the defaults, but not any other existing callouts.

Filling

To fill drawn items with different colors or shades of gray, follow these steps:

1. Select the desired item(s).

FIGURE 5.15

Use the Callout Defaults dialog box to change the design of the callout box.

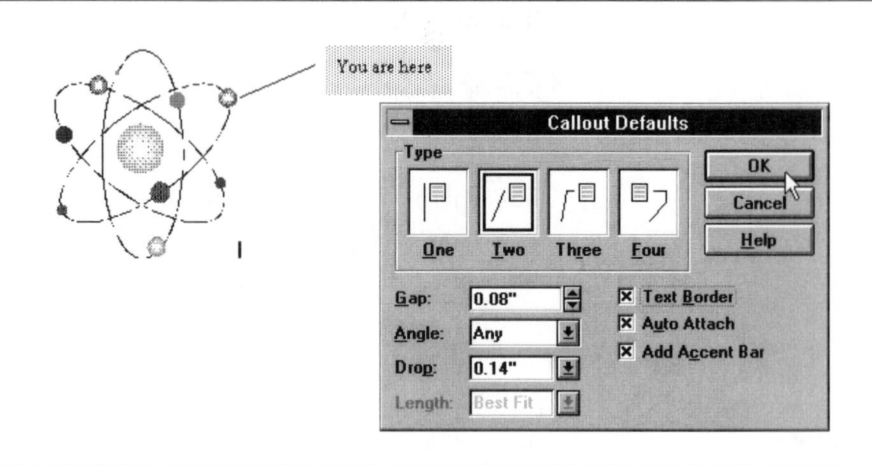

2. Use the Drawing Toolbar button that looks like a paint can to bring up the fill palette.
3. Click to select the desired fill color.

▸▸ Line Colors and Shades of Gray

To change the color or shade of lines:

1. Select the desired item(s).
2. Use the Drawing Toolbar button that looks like a paintbrush to bring up the line palette.
3. Click to select the desired line color.

▸▸ Line Sizes and Arrowheads

To change the size of lines and any arrowheads:

1. Select the desired line(s).
2. Use the Drawing Toolbar button that looks like a collection of various line thicknesses and styles to bring up the line palette.

3. Click to select the desired line type.
4. Choosing More brings up the Line tab in the Drawing Object dialog box, illustrated in Figure 5.16.

FIGURE 5.16

The Drawing Defaults dialog box gives you more control over line appearance.

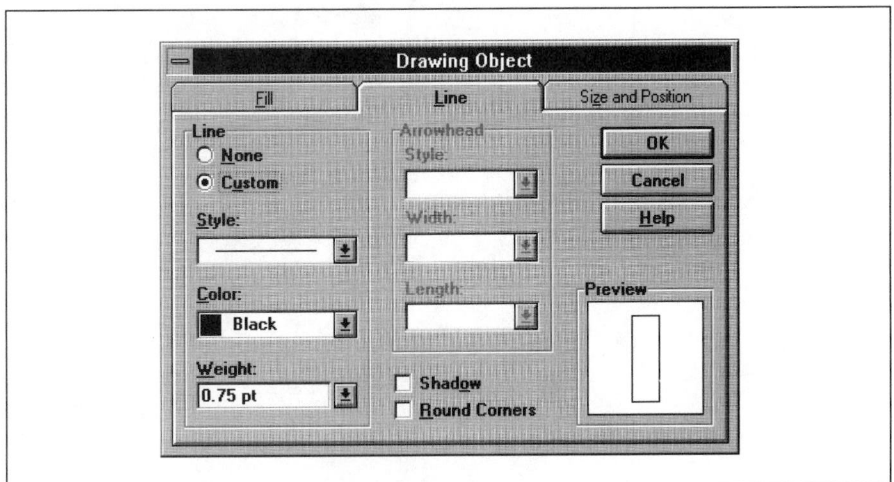

►► Time to Practice

If you have some free time, this would be a good place to stop and try some of your newfound skills. Type, edit, save, draw, print, and so on. At this point you know all the basics.

But don't put away the book just yet. There's lots more to know if you plan to *master* Word for Windows.

CHAPTER 6

Using Frames to Position and Anchor Things

▸▸FAST TRACK

To abort the framing process — 168

press Esc.

To reposition frames — 168

place the mouse pointer anywhere in the frame. Then press and hold down the mouse button and drag the frame to where you want to reposition it. When you are satisfied, release the mouse button.

To position frames precisely — 170

use the Frame dialog box (Format ➤ Frame…).

To place text in a frame (captioning) — 172

select the frame and press ↵. Then just type away, stylizing the text as you like. The caption will stay with the frame when you move it.

To delete a frame and its contents — 172

select the frame and press **Ctrl-X** or hit the **backspace** key.

To remove a frame from an object — 172

select the frame and choose Format ➤ Frame to reach the Frame dialog box. There, click the Remove Frame button.

▶▶ **F*rames*** are a sure source of confusion. Push on, though. It is worthwhile to understand them! Part of the confusion comes from the fact that the word *Frame* appears twice in the Word for Windows workplace—there's the Insert ➤ Frame command and the Format ➤ Frame… command. They do different things, so try to keep them straight.

If you simply paste a graphic into a Word for Windows document (without framing it), it is treated like a character. You can place the graphic between characters, move it from one line to another, copy it, delete it, and so on. But it is a slave to things like line and paragraph specifications, margins, indents, and such. To have maximum control over graphics and other document elements, you should place them in *frames*.

Frames can contain either graphics, text, or both. Frames let you precisely position objects virtually anywhere in your document. And you can tell Word for Windows to flow your unframed text around frames if you like. See Figure 6.1. Frames can contain graphics, Excel charts, Word text, or any combination thereof. In fact, it may be helpful to think of frames as pages within a page that you can move, resize, and embellish.

To use frames, you create them, insert things into them, then size and position them either with your mouse or with the Frame dialog box. Normally, you'll want to work with framed items in Page Layout view or Print Preview so that you can easily see and move them.

▶▶ **TIP**

It's a good idea to turn on hidden paragraph marks when working with frames. If they are not visible, click on the Show/Hide ¶ button in the Standard Toolbar. It looks like a ¶ mark.

FIGURE 6.1

Use frames to contain and position both text and graphics. Notice how frames "make room for themselves" in text.

Frame graphics, and text will wrap around them

Frame text, and it will span columns

A Business Lesson at 2,000 Feet

Ron Mansfield

I recently started learning how to fly gliders, a longtime ambition of mine. In the process, I've learned something that is very relevant to the art of small business computing.

While Hal, my flight instructor and I walked to the plane last week the talk turned to emergency procedures. "What's the first thing to do if you are solo and discover a rattlesnake in your glider at 2,000 feet?" He asked.

I blurted out something about avoiding quick leg movements and making a radio request for a precautionary ambulance. Hal ticked-off three or four more nightmares that had occurred at or near our desert airport. "What if you hear a loud clunk in the tail section? What if the rear canopy blows off?" And so-on.

Each time I had a different opinion–a reaction, I suppose, to the stated problem. Each time I was wrong.

"You should do the same thing immediately and continuously in each situation.", Hal said more firmly than I'd ever heard him before.

"Fly the plane, Ron Fly the plane."

The answer sounds too obvious at first, since "flying the plane" is something that you would expect pilots to do automatically. But, consider this. There have been several disastrous commercial jet crashes apparently because entire crews have focused on relativity small distractions while their *planes* flew *themselves* straight into the ground.

In one case, three seasoned pilots appear to have simultaneously wrestled with the same burned-out indicator lamp. They were all completely oblivious to audible low altitude warnings from their cockpit instruments; and ignored inquiries from puzzled air traffic controllers. Investigators believe that none of the flight crew members even looked outside!

That busy CEO had no business spending three *hours*, much less three *days* on programming a computer, but that's what he had done.

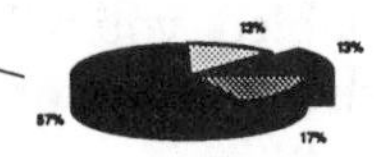

We do the same thing in business. Just today I got a call from the CEO of a nine-month old, multi-million dollar startup manufacturing company. We talked for ten minutes about the rapid growth of his business, the challenges of managing far-flung offices, and so on. Then he got to the real purpose of the call–what he thought was the rattlesnake in his cockpit. He had personally spent three days trying to integrate an order entry program from one software vendor with a general ledger program from another maker. It would save his company about $3000 since they could avoid buying the complete set of accounting modules that included his favorite order entry program. He wanted to know if he should keep trying to force the two dissimilar products to work together. He also talked about using a complex database management package to personally program a new order entry program from scratch. He never once mentioned spending the extra $3000 for a complete set of compatible accounting modules, or hiring someone else to do the programming.

You see, executives, like pilots are problem solvers at heart. We enjoy mental challenges, and computers provide them. They appear seductively easy to use, and their problems draw us in as they unfold. Solutions that seem moments away often elude us for days.

So, next time you find yourself caught-up in an intriguing computer challenge–somewhere between the second and third cup of coffee, ask yourself "Who's flying the plane?" Maybe someone else should change the light bulbs while you get back to the controls. Thanks, Hal for reminding me of that.

Place frames in headers and footers, and they'll print on each page

►► Inserting Frames and Framing Things

You can either insert an empty frame, then place something in it, or you can select something and frame it. In either case, you use the Insert ➤ Frame command *or* the Insert Frame button on the Drawing Toolbar (it looks like an American flag).

Inserting Empty Frames

Here are the steps for creating a new, empty frame:

1. Start by switching to Page Layout view, if you are not already in it. (If you forget to do this, Word for Windows will ask if it can switch views for you.)
2. Click the Drawing Toolbar's Insert Frame button or choose Insert ➤ Frame.
3. Your pointer will change to a crosshair. Drag to create a frame of the approximate size and shape you desire, located about where you want it to be placed.
4. Shortly after you release the mouse button, you'll see a frame surrounded by a border. If you have the Show/Hide Paragraph feature enabled, you will see a paragraph mark within the frame and an anchor outside of it, as shown in Figure 6.2.
5. You can either type text in the resulting frame (you'll learn how in a moment), paste things from the Clipboard, or use one of the Insert menu commands, such as the Picture… and Object… commands.

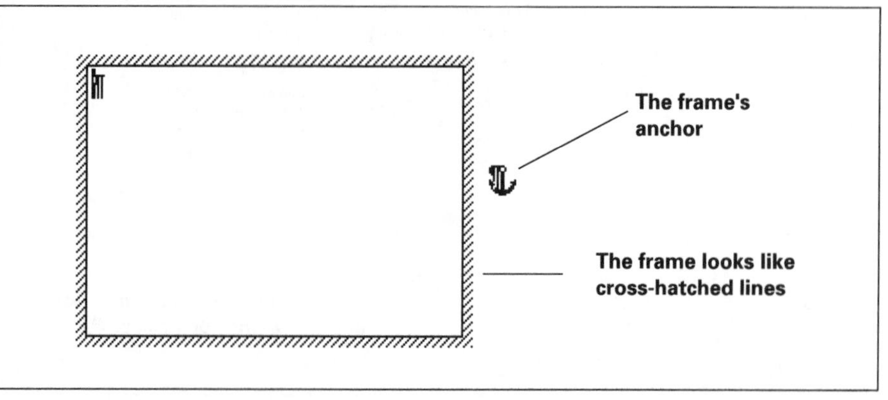
The frame's anchor
The frame looks like cross-hatched lines

FIGURE 6.2 ►

The new frame will appear, surrounded by a cross-hatched border, along with a little anchor.

Framing Existing Objects

If you already have something in your document that needs framing, you can frame it by following these steps:

1. Switch to Page Layout view if you are not there already.
2. Select the item or items to be framed.

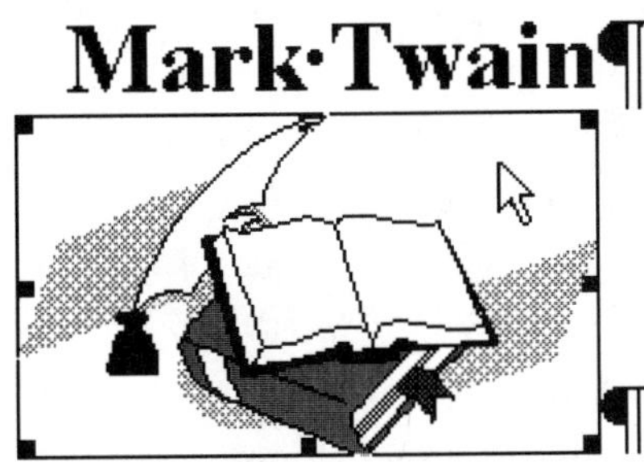

3. Use either the Frame button on the Drawing Toolbar or choose Insert ➤ Frame.
4. Your selected item(s) will be surrounded by a frame, and you'll see a paragraph mark and an anchor, as illustrated here, if you have clicked the Show/Hide ¶ button.

the·*almost*·right·word·is·the·difference·
between·lightning·and·the·lightning·bug.¶

Mark·Twain¶

¶

Framed items and their frames can be resized just as you resize graphics. Drag their handles. If you accidentally frame the wrong thing or too many or too few things, or accidentally distort the size or shape of a graphic, Undo should work.

▸▸ TIP

If you start the framing process (choose Insert ➤ Frame) and change your mind, cancel it by pressing Esc.

▸ Try It

Try framing the picture in your Twain quote. Follow these steps:

1. Load the Twain Quote document.
2. If you don't have a picture in your Twain document, use the Insert ➤ Picture… command to add one. (c:\winword6\clipart\books.wmf, perhaps.)
3. Switch to Page Layout View if you are not already there.
4. Select the picture by clicking on it.
5. Choose Insert ➤ Frame.
6. Reduce the size of the graphic to 50 percent of its original size by dragging the lower-right corner of the frame while watching the statistics in the status area:

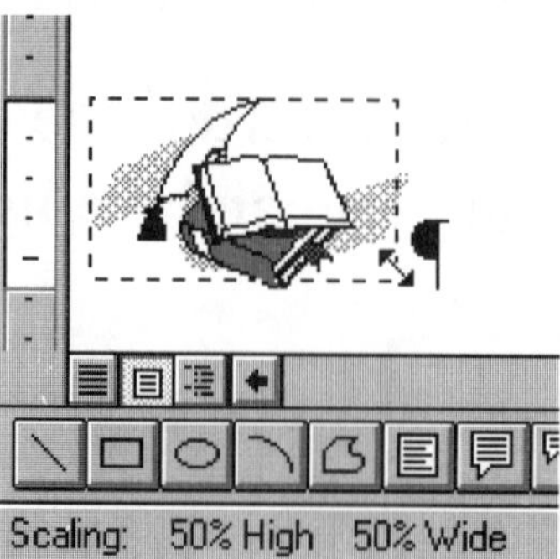

▸ Positioning Framed Items with a Mouse

The dirt-simple way to position frames is to drag them with your mouse while in Page Layout view or Print Preview. Follow these steps:

1. Place the pointer anywhere within the frame and watch the pointer.
2. The pointer will change to include a four-headed arrow.

3. Press down on the primary mouse button and drag the frame to the upper-left corner of the text.
4. Release the mouse button.
5. Soon after you release the mouse button the frame will take up residence in its new location. Text will move out of the way for the frame and the little anchor icon will move as well.

The·difference·between·the·right· word·and·the·*almost*·right·word·is· the·difference·between·lightning·and·the· lightning·bug.¶

You can continue to drag the framed graphic around to suit yourself. Switch to Print Preview and try moving it there too. Remember—you'll need to click on the Magnifier button in Print Preview before you can edit the document.

A frame is always anchored to a paragraph. When you position a frame by dragging it, it is initially anchored to its closest paragraph. When you move it, the anchor moves to the next nearest paragraph. To see where a frame's anchor is, select the frame. There'll be a little anchor icon like the one in Figure 6.3.

As you add or delete text in your document, the framed item stays with its paragraph. A frame always appears on the same page with its paragraph.

FIGURE 6.3

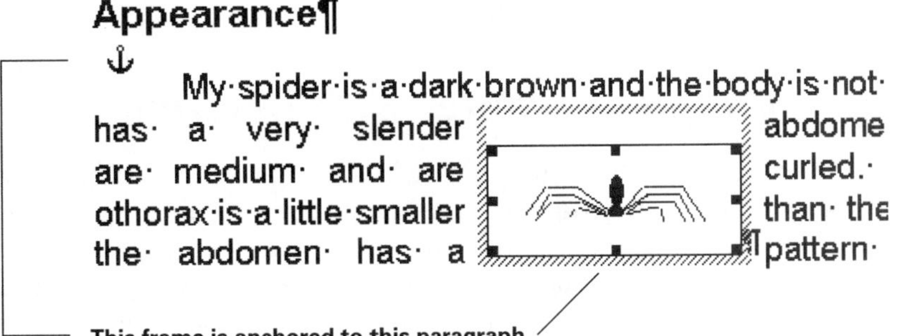
Appearance¶
My·spider·is·a·dark·brown·and·the·body·is·not·
has· a· very· slender
abdome
are· medium· and· are
curled.·
othorax·is·a·little·smaller
than· the
the· abdomen· has· a
¶pattern·
This frame is anchored to this paragraph

Normally, frames are anchored to nearby paragraphs.

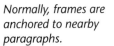

Using Frames to Position Things
ch. 6

This is often the desired effect. But what if you want to keep a framed item on a particular page, or a specific distance from a particular paragraph?

► Positioning Framed Items with the Frame Dialog Box

When you want to position frames precisely or force a frame to position itself relative to other things that might move, use the Frame dialog box reached by choosing Format ➤ Frame.... Figure 6.4 shows it.

FIGURE 6.4 ►

Use the Frame dialog box for precise frame sizing and positioning.

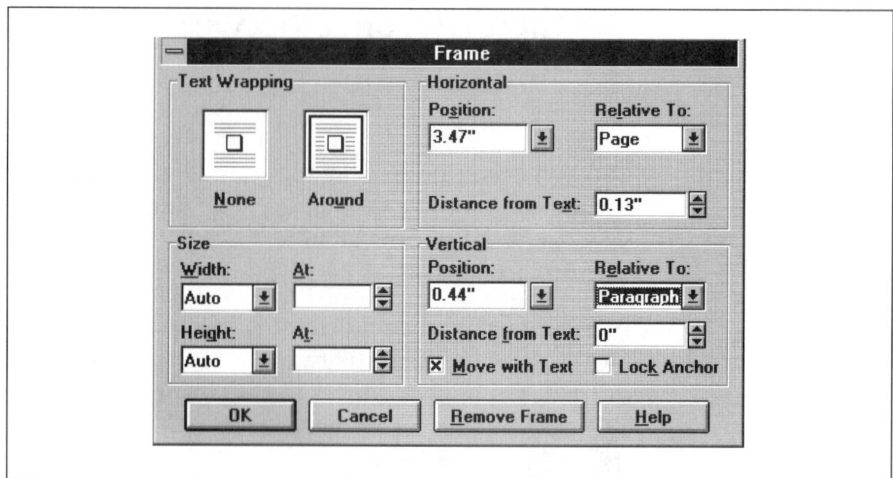

When you select a frame and open this dialog box, you will see the current size and position of the frame. You can specify new size and position settings for the frame in inches (in), centimeters (cm), points (pt), or picas (pi). You change the units of measurement by using the General tab in the Options dialog box, (reached by choosing Tools ➤ Options...).

► Aligning Frames with Reference Points

The Frame dialog box also provides a mind-boggling array of positioning and reference options. For instance, you can force a frame to always remain in the exact horizontal and vertical center of a page, even when you change margins or page sizes. Or, you can tell Word for Windows to keep a frame a specified distance from margins or columns. Finally, you can anchor a frame to text, so when the text moves, the frame accompanies it. Place a check mark in the Move with Text box to accomplish this.

▶ Text and Frames

Frames and text can be used together several ways. Besides framing text, you can position frames relative to text or have text flow around frames. Here are a few ways to work with frames and text.

Placing Text in Frames

You can use frames as small text windows that can be moved anywhere in your document. For instance, in Figure 6.5, Adam's paragraph headings are being framed and moved into his document's margin. (You may want to remove the frame borders when you do this.)

By checking the Move with Text option in the Frame dialog box, you can make sure the headings will stay with their paragraphs when you edit the document.

A quick way to create a lot of marginal headings like Adam's is to create one, then *redefine the document's heading style(s)* based on the example. All of your headings will be framed and placed in the margin quicker than you can say "arachnid." When framing existing *text*, Word for Windows will make the frame big enough to accommodate all of the text you've selected. If you paste text into an existing *frame*, make sure the frame is big enough to prevent "weird word wrap," a problem that

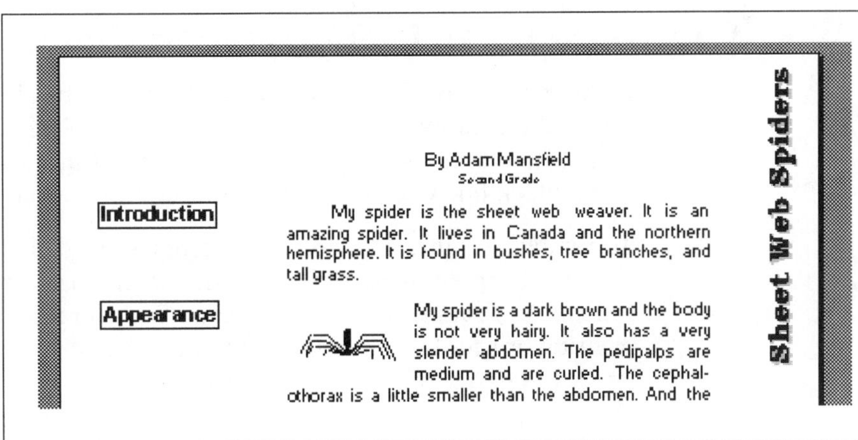

FIGURE 6.5 ▶

Framed text can be used to place headings in margins, among other things.

arises when you specify large line indents or place long words in narrow frames. If the text you insert changes into a long vertical string of characters, try resizing the frame to make the text legible. Feel free to use all of Word's text formatting tools in Frames. You can have multiple paragraphs in frames.

Word's Formatting Toolbar and ruler work in frames. You can change type sizes and styles, center, justify, and otherwise fool with text in frames. Even Word's spelling checker peeks into them.

Inserting Text in Framed Graphics (Captioning)

new

If you want to add a caption to a framed graphic, select the frame, then press ↵. You'll see a new paragraph mark in the frame. Type the caption. Stylize the text, if you like. The caption will stay with the frame when you move it.

►► How Framed Items Appear in Different Views

You can see where framed items will print by displaying them in Print Preview or Page Layout view. When you switch to Normal or Outline views, framed items will appear within the page boundaries where they will print but not necessarily in their printing positions. You can easily spot framed items in Normal and Outline views.

► Selecting and Deleting Framed Items

It's possible to delete frames *and their contents* by simply selecting the frame, then cutting (Ctrl+X) or pressing the Delete key. (Select a frame by pointing and clicking with your mouse.) Eight dark black handles and a black line will appear around the frame when you've selected it.

To remove a frame, but not its contents, select the frame, then use the Remove Frame button in the Frame dialog box (reached by choosing Format ➤ Frame). If you use this method to remove a frame that has a printing border but not its contents, the frame's *border* will remain. Delete it or change it as described next.

▶ Deleting or Changing Frame Borders

Frames are created without printing borders, but these can be added and altered.

1. Select a framed object in Page Layout view by clicking on the object.
2. Use the Format ➤ Shading… command to add, change, or remove the border. For instance, clicking on the None icon in the Preset area of the Border dialog box removes a frame's border.

See Chapter 10 for more information about borders and shading.

▶▶ **TIP**

There is also a border button on the Standard Toolbar. It's on the right end and looks like a four-pane window.

▶▶ Special Effects with WordArt

There's an intriguing little program installed with Word for Windows called WordArt. You can use it to create unusual-looking text objects. Choose Insert ➤ Object…, then scroll to Microsoft WordArt 2.0 and double-click on it. You'll see a dialog box like the one in Figure 6.6.

Try it out on your Twain quote. Here's how:

1. Open the Twain Quote in Page Layout view.
2. Place the insertion point on a new line after Mark's name.
3. Choose Insert ➤ Object….

FIGURE 6.6 

Use WordArt to create text containing special effects, then paste it into your Word for Windows document and frame it.

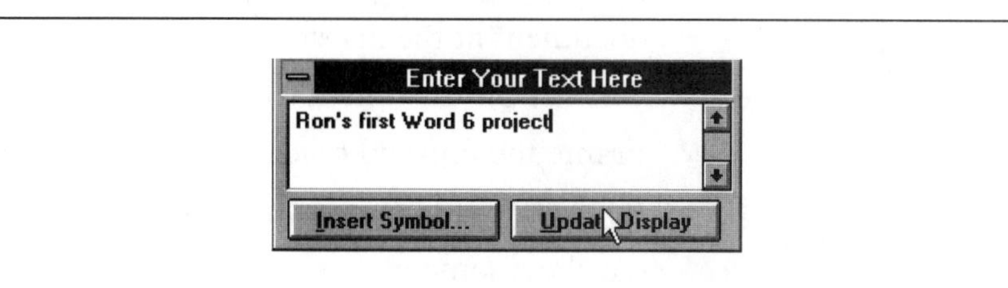

4. Pick MS WordArt from the scrolling list in the Create New tab by double-clicking, as shown here:

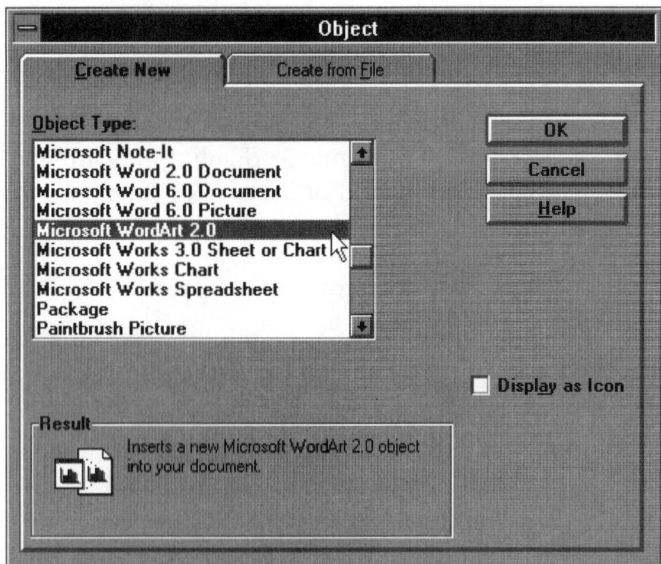

5. Either type new text or paste text from your Clipboard in the resulting dialog box. Then click Update Display to insert it into your document.
6. Notice that the menu bar has changed. It has a drop-down list of special effects. Experiment with the fonts, sizes, styles, alignment, and other options. You'll see a preview as you work, but it will take a moment for the screen to update fully. Don't panic if you see gnarly-looking "interim" images. The fonts supplied with WordArt are bitmap and may be hard to read in small sizes or appear jagged if they get too big. Figure 6.7 shows Footlight MT Light and the Arch Up effect.
7. When you are happy with your concoction, click on Update Display, and WordArt will paste it into your active Word for Windows document at the insertion point.
8. Click in the document to close WordArt.
9. Frame the finished object to make it easier to move.
10. Reposition it like any other framed item.
11. Go show someone!

FIGURE 6.7

Experiment with Word-Art to create special text effects.

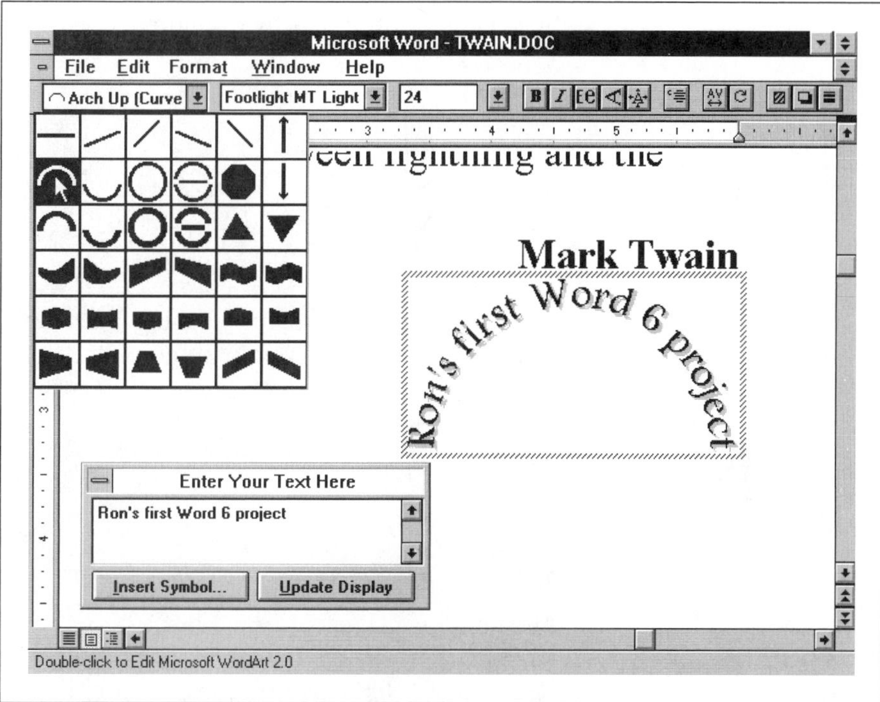

▸▸ Creating Vertical Text

WordArt is the tool to use if you want to run an occasional piece of vertical text. Follow these steps:

1. Open the Twain quote in Page Layout view.
2. Place the insertion point on a new line after Mark's name.
3. Choose Insert ➤ Object....
4. Pick MS WordArt from the scrolling list in the Create New tab, as before.
5. Either type new text or paste text from your Clipboard in the resulting dialog box, then click Update Display to insert it into your document.
6. Choose a font (Arial in this example).
7. Rotate the text 90 degrees by using ↑.
8. Click in the Word for Windows document itself to close WordArt.

9. Select the rotated text by dragging.

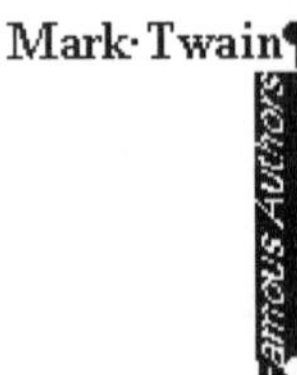

10. Frame the selected object by using Insert ➤ Frame. The frame will move to the left of your screen:

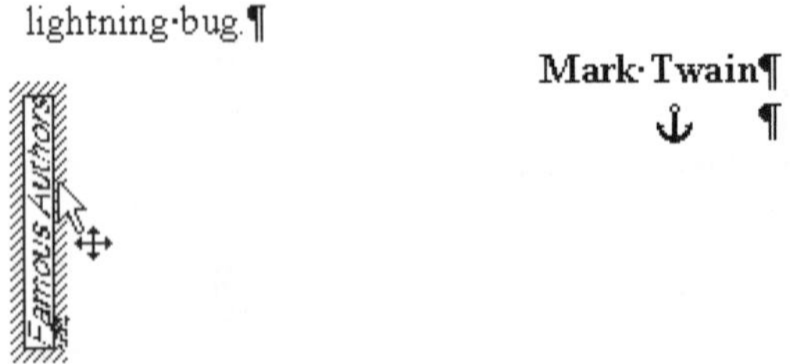

11. Reposition it like any other framed item—in the upper-right corner of the page, for instance. Remember that if you drag it too close to the edge of a page, your printer may not be able to print it.

▸▸ Repeating Framed Items on Multiple Pages

To repeat the same framed object on multiple pages, create or anchor it in headers or footers. You'll learn more about headers and footers in Chapter 12.

▸▸ Experiment

It's time to put down the book and grab your mouse. Try a few of the techniques in this chapter. When you're done frittering—err, I mean *learning,* check out the next chapter, where you'll see how Word for Windows can help you organize your documents.

CHAPTER 7

Managing Your Files

FAST TRACK

To help organize and locate files 182

use Word's Find File... and Summary Info... commands, both found on the File menu.

To open a previously saved document 183

pick File ➤ Open... (**Ctrl+O** or the Open Toolbar button) to get to the Open dialog box. Then show Word for Windows the path to your document by opening successive directories until the file that you desire is visible in the scrollable document list. Double-click the document to open it.

To find files that don't have the Word (.DOC) extension 184

pick the appropriate field type from the List Files of Type drop-down list or choose All Files (*.*) to show all non-hidden files.

To open a non-Word document 185

try opening it just as you would open a Word document (you may have to specify its file extension in the List Files of Type drop-down list). If Word has the necessary conversion filter, it will open it. If not, you may have to convert it with a third-party program before opening it in Word for Windows. Either way, don't expect absolute perfection.

To avoid changing an original document file 186

open the document as read only. You do so by clicking to enable the Read Only option in the Open dialog box.

To find a lost file **186**

choose File ➤ Find File... or click the Find File... button in the Open dialog box to reach the Search dialog box, where you can specify criteria for searching for the file.

To sort a list of found files **189**

choose Sorting... from the Commands menu in the Find File dialog box and specify your preferences in the Options dialog box.

To set more sophisticated restrictions on a search **190**

click the Advanced Search button in the Search dialog box. Another dialog box will appear, where you can specify a number of different restrictions on the search.

To speed up searches with Find File... **191**

be sure to always fill out the Summary Info box (which appears each time your save a new document) and be consistent in how you spell your name, name your files, etc.

To delete files from Word **193**

use Find File... to find the file to be deleted, then, in the Find File dialog box, choose Delete from the Commands menu.

To prevent your files from being opened or tampered with **198**

assign important documents passwords in the Save As dialog box.

Your hard disk can contain hundreds or even thousands of files. If you work in a large, networked organization, you may have access to ten times this many documents. If you've ever misplaced a file, you know how frustrating and time-consuming it can be trying to find it.

Word for Windows provides two features to help you organize and locate files. They are called Find File… and Summary Info…, both found on the File menu. For those of you new to the computer, we'll start with a quick review of the concept of files and directories, and something related, called a *path*.

Files, Directories, and Paths

Your computer lets you arrange your files in a hierarchical structure. Files (Word for Windows documents, for instance) can be stored in *directories*. Directories can also be stored within directories. Figure 7.1 shows an example of this.

FIGURE 7.1

A hierarchical directory arrangement contains directories within directories.

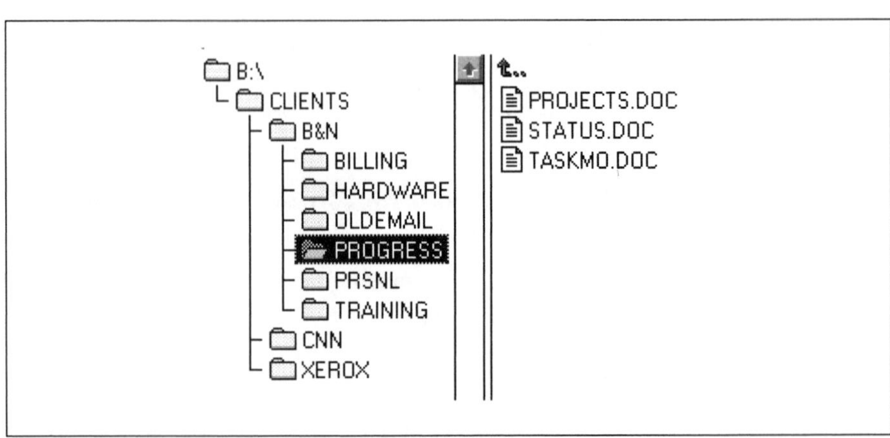

In the example, there is a directory called Clients. It contains all of the client-related directories and files for this computer. Within the Clients directory there are three client subdirectories, one for each client (B&N, CNN, and Xerox). Each of these client directories contains additional subdirectories and files relating to the particular client. For instance, the B&N directory contains the B&N Progress directory, in which project-related memos, lists, and reports are stored. The B&N subdirectory also contains other directories with billing and contract information, hardware information, etc. If you were to open the Xerox subdirectory, you might find a similar arrangement of Xerox-specific files.

This hierarchy makes it easy to store and find things. It also provides good hiding places for lost files. For instance, you'd need to open three directories to find the Projects file.

The steps that you take to find a file take you down a path. To get to the Projects or the Task List Memo (TASKMO.DOC), for example, you would start by choosing the hard disk containing the directories, then you would open the Clients directory. Next you would open the B&N directory, and finally the B&N Progress subdirectory. You can do this from the Windows File Manager by double-clicking on directories, or you can do it from within Word for Windows itself by using File ➤ Open... (Ctrl+O).

►► Opening Previously Saved Documents

When you pick File ➤ Open..., you will be presented with a dialog box. It will look something like the one in Figure 7.2.

You show Word for Windows the path to your document by opening successive directories until the file that you desire is visible in the scrollable document list. To open directories, scroll through the drop-down Directories list, double-clicking to open directories. In cases where you have directories within directories, you will need to double-click on more than one folder.

If you open one directory too many, revisit the list and choose the directory above the one you last opened.

FIGURE 7.2

From the Open dialog box, use the Drives drop-down menu to open to the drive containing the document you need, then choose subdirectories and files from scrolling lists.

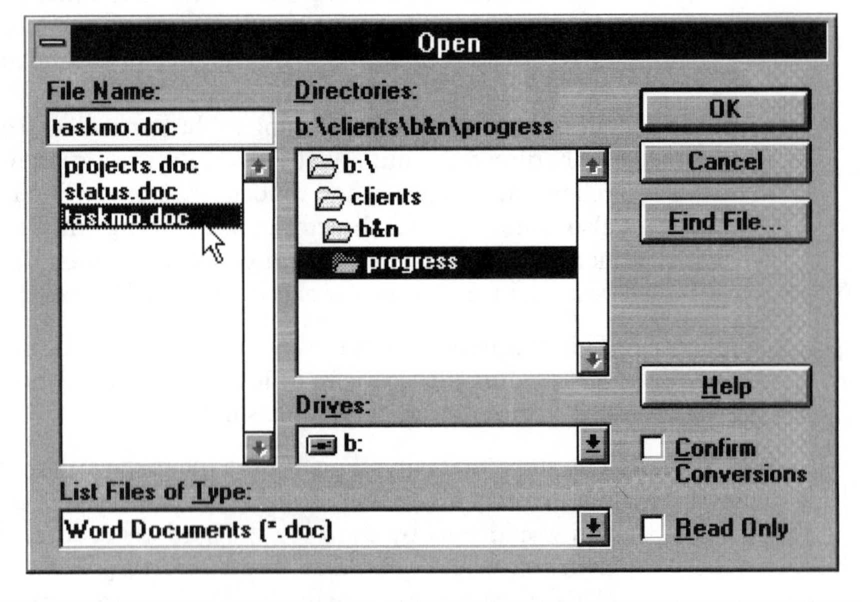

When you see the file (the document) that you want to work with, double-click on the document's name or just click on it and press ↵. Your Windows manuals and Windows disk-based tutorials contain more information on this subject and practice exercises if you need additional help. If you click Read Only, you will not be able to make any changes to the file; you will be asked to save any edits to a new file.

▸▸ **TIP**

If the documents you are looking for don't end with the extension .DOC, pick the appropriate field type from the List Files of Type drop-down list. All Files (*.*) will show all non-hidden files.

Notice that Word's Open dialog box has two devices you may not have seen in the Open dialog boxes of other Windows programs. The first is a drop-down menu called List Files of Type. This menu lets you restrict the types of files that you will see in the scrollable list. For instance, you can ask to see only text files that end with the extension .TXT, or only

Word documents ending in .DOC, or only Rich Text Format documents, and so on.

The other unique choice in the Open dialog box is a button labeled Find File.... This takes you to a Word for Windows feature that helps find lost files and round up collections of files meeting specific criteria.

▶▶ Steps for Opening Documents from within Word

Here are the general steps for opening Word documents with Word for Windows running:

1. From within Word, choose File ➤ Open... or Ctrl+O.
2. Use the drop-down list below the scrollable list to open the appropriate disk or scroll through the directory list.
3. Double-click on the desired file name to load the document.

▶▶ TIP

You can click on the Toolbar button that looks like an open file directory (second from the left on the Toolbar), to reach the Open dialog box.

▶ Opening Non-Word Documents

Each different word-processing program (Ami Pro, WordPerfect, etc.), creates document files containing unique control codes for things like character attributes, margins, and so forth. Frequently, if you use one word-processing program to open a document created by a different program, you will see these codes that look like unintelligible gibberish intermixed with the document's text. Margins may be different. Fonts and line spacing will often change.

There are third-party file-conversion programs that can minimize these problems (such as Word for Word, by Mastersoft). Word also has some file-conversion capabilities of its own. See Chapter 35.

Don't expect perfection when moving documents from one program or computer to another. You will probably need to make some formatting changes, deal with line-ending differences, and so on. Here are the general steps for loading non-Word documents:

1. From within Word, choose File ➤ Open… or Ctrl+O.
2. Point to the List Files of Type drop-down list to pick the kind of files you wish to view and open or specify *.* to see a list of all files.
3. Use the drop-down Drives list and scrollable Directories list to open the appropriate disk and directory (by double-clicking).
4. Double-click on the desired file name in the scrollable File Name list.
5. Word will convert and load the document or alert you to the fact that it cannot do the necessary conversion.
6. Inspect and clean up the document.
7. Save it as a Word for Windows document if you plan to use it with Word in the future, or use the Save As… command to save it in the originating program's format, if that's where you will be working on the document in the future.

▸ Opening Documents as Read Only

If you wish to open a document as read only to prevent yourself from accidentally making changes to the disk file, click on the Read Only option box on the Open dialog box.

Template documents are always opened as read only. When you open a template document, then make changes and save them, you will be automatically prompted for a different file name. Templates are discussed in more detail later in Chapter 16.

▸▸ Find File…

Word's Find File (reached by choosing File ➤ Find File…) is a powerful tool that helps you locate, list, sort, examine, open, and print documents based on simple or complex search criteria. You can examine your computer's hard disk(s) or even search a server or shared drive over a network. Both Word and non-Word files can be located using this feature. You can find files by file name, creation date, and much more. For instance, if you enter Summary information when saving Word for Windows documents, you can round up files based on their authors, keywords, and so on.

Let's start with a simple search. Suppose, for instance, that you've lost your Twain Quote document. Start by choosing File ➤ Find File... or by clicking the Find File... button in the Open dialog box. You will see a Search dialog box that looks something like Figure 7.3.

FIGURE 7.3

Word's Find File... can help you locate documents using a variety of search criteria.

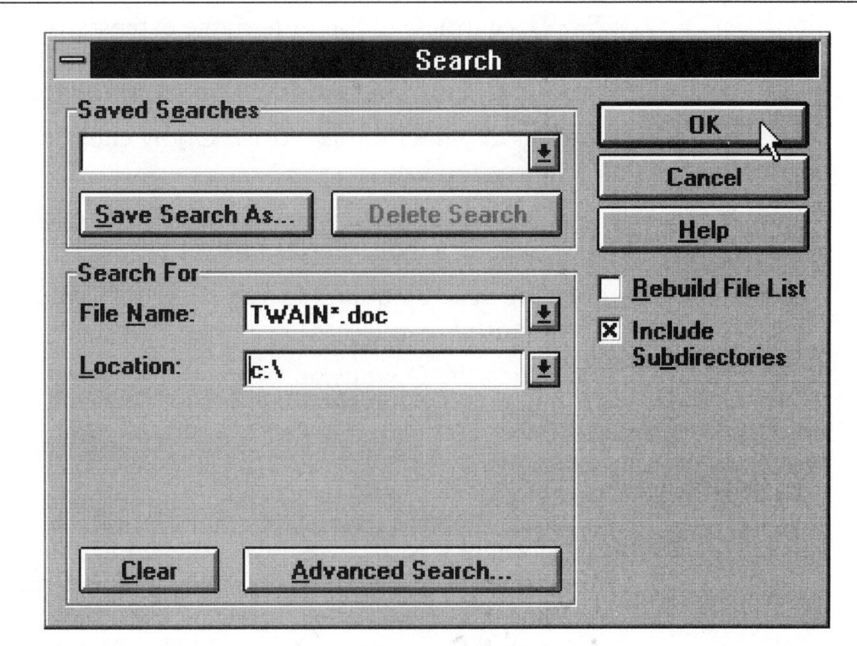

This dialog box gives you a number of places to type restrictive search criteria, an area to specify restrictive date and time ranges, plus three drop-down menus. In general you need to tell the Find File command:

- Which drive to search
- Which directory or directories to search
- What to look for
- Optional, advanced criteria to narrow the search (Summary info entries, for example)

► Searching by File Names

Continuing with the case of the missing TWAIN.DOC file, you know the file name contained the word *Twain*. But typing "Twain" alone in the File Name entry area of the Search dialog box and clicking OK or pressing ↵ will *not* find your file.

You will need to add wildcards to make the search fruitful. The string *Twain**.* is a good way to start. It will find things like Twain.DOC, Twain2.bak, etc. With that strategy in mind, here are the steps for searching your entire C: drive for file names containing the word *Twain*, regardless of their file-name extensions, if any.

1. Open Find File with the File ➤ Find File… command.
2. Specify the location (drive C:) by choosing it from the drop-down Location list.
3. Tell Word to search subdirectories by clicking to place an X in the Include subdirectories box.
4. Type the file-name search criteria (**TWAIN*.***) in the File Name box.
5. Click the OK button (if it is dimmed, you probably haven't specified a location) or press ↵.
6. In a moment, you'll see a list of potential matches like the one shown in Figure 7.4.

…And there it is. By clicking on the name of a found file, you can examine it more closely. The View drop-down menu lets you see (preview) the contents of the file or review its statistics (creator, last saved, size, and such). The window then displays available info. If you have entered Summary information or added comments using your computer's Get Info feature, you can read that information here as well.

Clicking the Open button at the bottom of the dialog box will open the document as usual. Clicking Search… will take you back to the Search dialog box. Print… opens the document and presents the Print dialog box. If you click on the directory name above the list of files, you can use the path menu to view additional files. The Sorting… option on the Commands menu is one of several devices designed to help you deal with long lists of documents meeting your criteria.

FIGURE 7.4

Find File creates a list of potential matches to your critera.

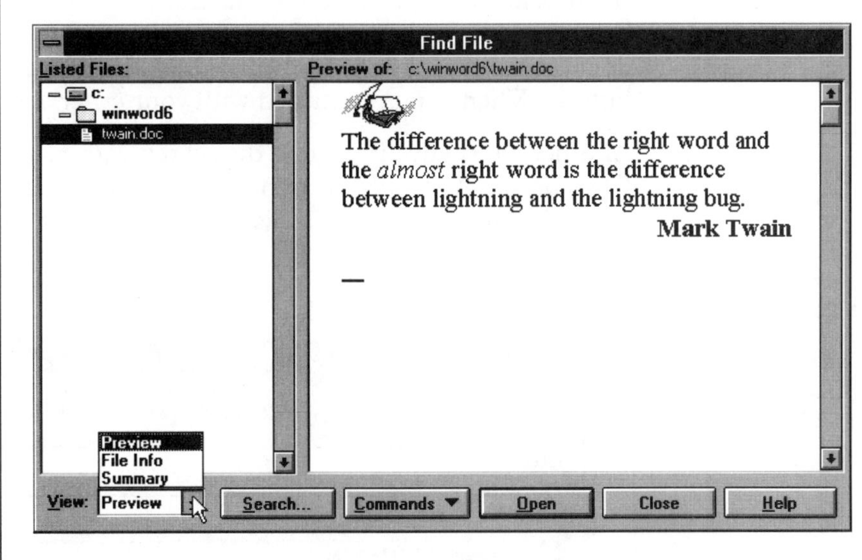

▶ Dealing with Large Lists

Long lists of found files can be handled in a number of ways. You can use the Sorting... option on the Commands menu in the Find File window to bring up the Options dialog box, which lets you sort your list (see Figure 7.5).

FIGURE 7.5

Find File's Sorting... option (on the Commands menu) brings up the Options dialog box, where you can arrange long file lists many ways.

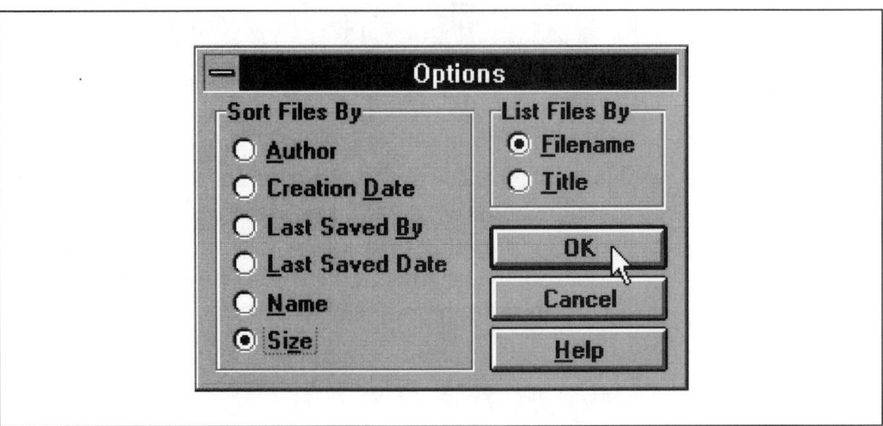

If you know the approximate time frame of a project, date sorts will help you narrow down the list to examine. If you knew this was a big document, a sort by file size might help. Click the appropriate radio button. When you are satisfied with your criteria, click OK or press ↵.

Another alternative is to redo the search with more specific criteria. Click on the Advanced Search... button in the Search dialog box to reach the Advanced Search dialog box, shown in Figure 7.6.

FIGURE 7.6 ►

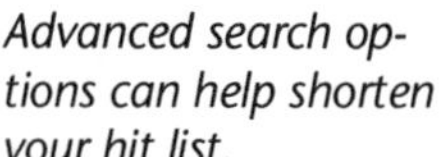

Advanced search options can help shorten your hit list.

new

There are three tabs in this dialog box designed to let you specify Summary information, time and date restrictions, and locations. For instance, you can list only files that contain specific words or phrases, or you can list just files of a specific type. If you've entered Summary information, you can use it to restrict searches.

► Searching Inside Documents

Searches on file names alone are the quickest and are recommended as the starting point for searches of any but the smallest disk drives. But if you cannot find a file with a file-name search, or if you find too many files containing the search word, it is possible to ask Word for Windows to look *inside* each file on the disk being searched and list only those files containing the word or words meeting your criteria. Find File... searches entire Word documents including headers, footers, and hidden text.

new

You place the search string in the Containing Text box in the Summary tab of the Advanced Search dialog box (see Figure 7.6). You need to use the same care when specifying search text that you use with Word's Find... and Replace... commands. If you are too specific, you may miss the file you are looking for. Use too vague a search string, and you will get excessively long file lists.

Suppose, for instance, you want to round up everything you've written about DAT (Digital Audio Tape). If you use *DAT* as your search text, Word for Windows will also list files containing the words *database*, *date*, and *Datsun*. Placing a space after *DAT* in the search string solves that problem. (This example illustrates a subtle point about search text: casing is irrelevant.)

Several wild cards work here. You will type them from the keyboard. For example, *Sm?th* will find both *Smith* and *Smyth*. The wild card ^W searches for white space. See Chapter 20 for more about Find and Replace wild cards that can be used here too.

new

Once you've entered search criteria in the Containing Text section of the Advanced Search dialog box and started the search by clicking OK or pressing ↵, Word for Windows will start examining the contents of your disk. This can take a while.

Eventually a list will appear and you can preview the hits or use the other buttons to open, sort, and so on.

▶ *Find File... and Summary Info...*

If you and your colleagues have been religious about entering consistent Summary information, you can use the Find File... feature to search for those entries. That's the purpose of the Title, Author, Keywords, and Subject entries in the Advanced Search dialog box.

Just remember that if you've created documents and failed to put your name in the author box when creating Summary info, or if you sometimes type your whole name and other times use your initials, you run the risk of missing documents when your Find File... search criteria includes Summary info search restrictions.

Naturally, documents created with programs that do not collect Summary info (such as WordPerfect) will be ignored.

Written policies and procedures regarding file naming and Summary information entries can be a big help in law firms, publishing houses, and other organizations with networks and thousands of files.

▸ Try It, You'll Like It

If you haven't already done so, search for your Twain Quote using some of the Summary info you entered when you initially saved the document.

▸ Multiple Searches

There are times when you will want to do multiple searches. For instance, in our earlier example, you may discover that sometimes you referred to DAT in documents by the complete name and not the acronym. You might think you would need to search once for *DAT* and a second time for *Digital Audio Tape* to find each relevant document. Similarly, you might think that if you use multiple disk drives you will need to perform multiple searches. Fortunately, you can *combine* search criteria. This means you can do all of the above in a *single* search. Read on....

Combining Searches

The classic combined search works like this. Search for the first criteria of interest (Any Text: = DAT for instance). Review the list.

Then reveal the Options list in the Summary tab of the Advanced Search dialog box. From the Options menu, choose Add Matches to list. Change the search criteria (to *DigitalAudio Tape*, for example). Then run the new search. The resulting list will contain documents meeting either criteria.

You can combine the results of different types of searches. For example, you can search first by file name, then by author, and so on.

Searching Multiple Disks

new

If you have more than one disk drive on your computer, or if you want to search both your computer's disk and other drives on a network, you can instruct Find File to look more than one place. Do this in the Location tab of the Advanced Search menu as illustrated in Figure 7.7.

FIGURE 7.7

The Location tab of the Advanced Search menu.

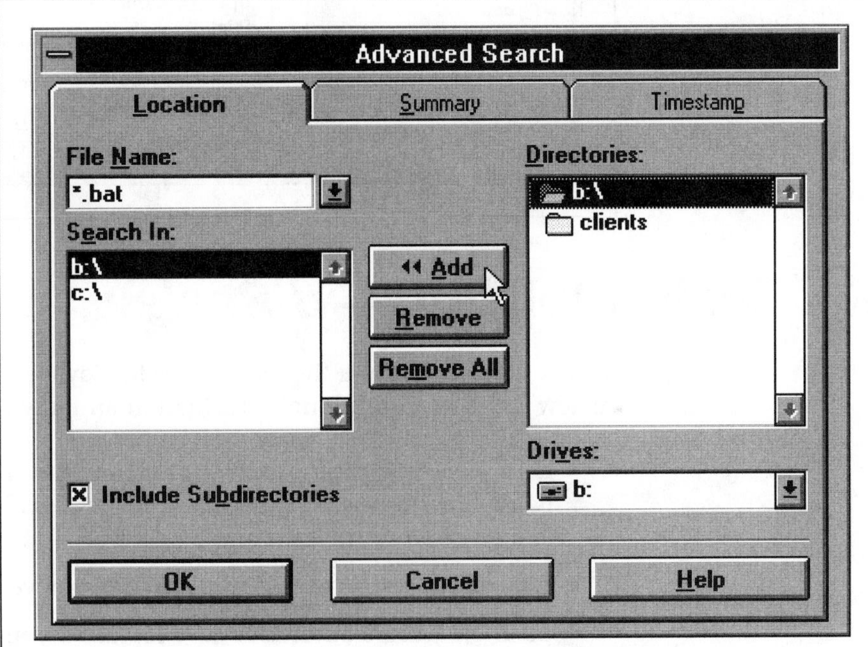

Deleting Files in Word

Here's a really useful feature tucked away in Find File: It's the ability to delete files from within Word for Windows. Simply select the file to be deleted in the Find File list and choose Delete from the Commands drop-down (often drop-up) list, as shown in Figure 7.8.

FIGURE 7.8

Delete selected files with the Delete command revealed with the Commands button in the Find File dialog box.

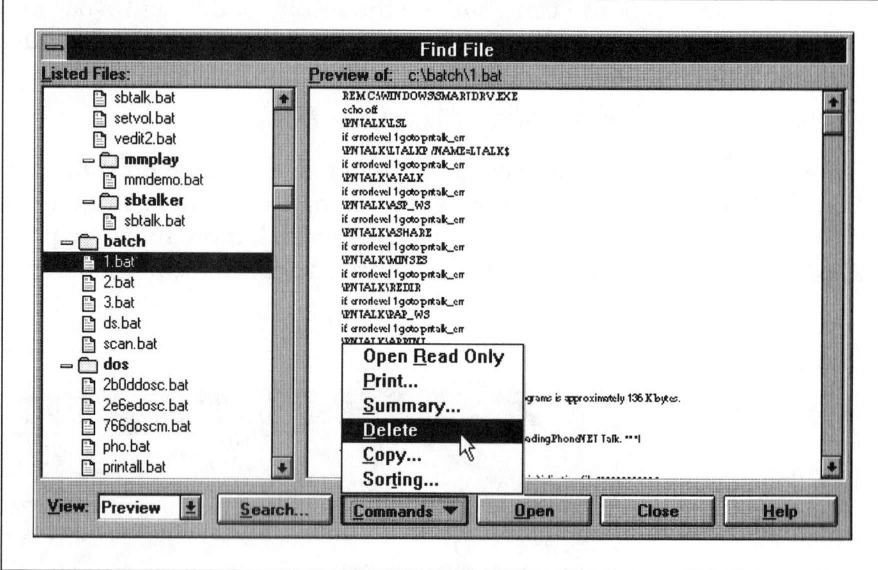

▸▸ Saving Initially—a Review

You've already learned the basic steps for saving in Chapter 2. Here's a review and some additional information and advice about saving.

- Until you save your document for the first time, it resides only in RAM (random-access memory) and will be lost if there is a power failure or other malfunction.
- Save about every fifteen minutes or whenever you are interrupted.
- Turn on Word's automatic save feature if you have trouble remembering to save. (Use the Save tab in the Options dialog box to enable automatic saves.)
- Always save before printing.
- Save before you do complex tasks that might drastically alter your document, such as replacing or hyphenating.
- To save initially, select File ➤ Save or use the Ctrl+S keyboard shortcut. (The Toolbar has a button that looks like a floppy disk. It will also start the Save process.)

- Pay attention to the part of the Save dialog box that tells you *where* Word plans to store your work.
- To specify a different drive, use the drop-down list located just below the scrollable file list.
- Type a name for your document in the File Name box, then click the OK button or press ↵. File names must meet the usual filename DOS requirements (a maximum of 8 characters, no spaces, and so on). Do not include colons (:) in your file names.
- You needn't type anything in the Summary Info dialog box, and you can prevent it from even appearing. But if you plan to keep many documents on your hard disk, and particularly if you will be storing things on a crowded network server, it is a good idea to use this feature.
- Once you have saved a document's Summary information, you will not be asked for it again when you save your work. Summary information can be viewed and modified by picking File ➤ Summary Info....
- A quick trip to File ➤ Save, or better still the key combination Ctrl+S, will save your work whenever you desire. So will clicking the Save button on the Toolbar. Save often.

▶▶ TIP

As you learned in Chapter 2, to prevent the Summary Info dialog box from appearing when you initially save a new document, turn it off via the Save tab in the dialog box brought up by the Tools ➤ Options command. For more information on this subject see Chapter 36.

▶▶ Save Options

It's worth exploring Word's save options, even though the default choices will work well for most people. Reach the save options with the Options... button in the Save As dialog box or via the Save tab in the Tools ➤ Options... command. It looks like Figure 7.9.

FIGURE 7.9

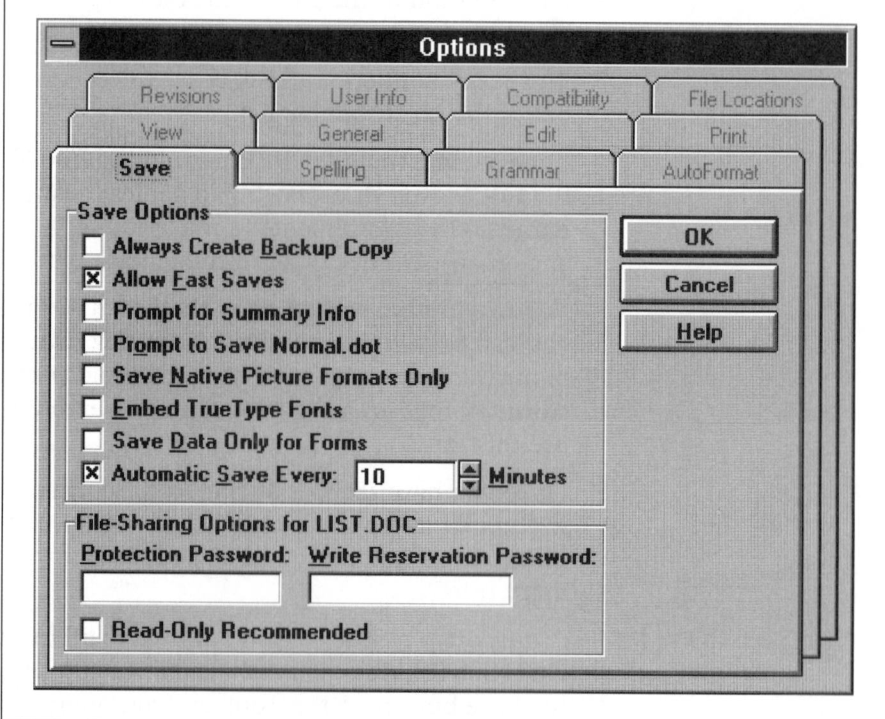

Word's save options can be found in the Save tab of the Options dialog box (Tools ➤ Options...).

Here is a list of the options you'll see in the Save As dialog box and some information about their use, followed by examples of typical save operations.

Always Create Backup Copy

Beware the Create Backup Copy option! With this option selected, Word for Windows makes a copy of the most recent disk-resident version of your file (giving it the extension .BAK) before saving your current changes to the original file. This is *not* a true backup for reasons described later in this chapter.

Allow Fast Save

The Allow Fast Saves option instructs Word for Windows to save just your changes most of the time rather than making you wait while it rewrites your entire document to disk each time you save. While this option can let you get back to typing and editing more quickly, it consumes extra RAM, uses more disk space, and can create real recovery problems if you have trouble with your disk while working on a big project.

TIP

Many experienced Word for Windows users leave Allow Fast Saves off.

Prompt for Summary Info

An *X* here interrupts you the first time you save a new document and prompts for author name, document title, keywords, and other information.

Save Native Picture Formats Only

This option saves only the Windows versions of graphics, thereby reducing file sizes when you've imported a graphic from another platform (a Macintosh, for instance). Leave it off if you plan to swap Word for Windows documents between platforms.

Prompt to Save Normal.dot

This choice displays a message when you exit Word (File ➤ Exit). It asks if you want to save changes made to default settings in the Normal.dot file.

Embed TrueType Fonts

This option instructs Word for Windows to save any TrueType fonts you've used with the document file so that other users can read your documents, even if they don't have the same TrueType files installed on their machines. Leave this feature off unless *all* of the following are true:

- You exchange files with others
- You use TrueType fonts
- The users you share with do not have the fonts installed

Save Data Only for Forms

When creating forms and collecting data on forms, Word for Windows can be instructed to save the data to disk without saving the forms. See Chapter 34 for details.

Automatic Save every N Minutes

This can be a blessing or a curse. If you are one of those people who never remembers to save early and often, Word for Windows can do it for you. Place an *X* in the appropriate box and tell Word the desired save interval (10 minutes is the default). Thereafter Word will save every 10 minutes or whatever without even asking.

On the other hand, if you are one of those people who works for an hour on a project, then decides not to save the changes (and revert to the old version), this automatic save feature can be a problem.

The File-Sharing Options

These options let you protect documents that are shared with others. If you password protect a document, you and others must use the password each time you reopen the document. Document passwords can be up to 30 characters long. Upper- and lowercase matters, so use care when assigning and entering passwords.

Protection Passwords This type of password prevents opening a document without knowing its password. If you use protection passwords, don't forget them.

Write Reservation Passwords Documents saved with only Write Reservation Passwords let users open them without knowing the password. Only users that know the Write reservation password can save changes, though.

Read-Only Recommended An *X* in this option box instructs Word to recommend that users not modify the document. It will *not*, however, prevent modification or deletion.

▸▸ Saving under a Different File Name

Normally, once you've named a document, Word for Windows will keep saving the document under the same name. Use the File – Save As... command to save a document under a different file name. Follow these steps:

1. If necessary, make the document you wish to save the active document, then choose File ➤ Save As... or use the F12 shortcut.
2. Type a new file name in the File Name area of the dialog box. Because this area is already highlighted, you can just start typing.
3. Specify a new directory and disk location if you wish, then click the OK button or simply press ↵.
4. Future saves will use this new name and location.

▸ Saving to Floppy and Other Disk Drives

Normally, once you've saved a document, Word will keep saving the document to the same disk and into the same directory you initially specified. Again, you use the File ➤ Save As... command (or F12) to save a document to a different disk or directory. Follow these steps:

1. If you plan to save to a floppy, insert it into your computer's floppy drive. If you plan to save to a different hard drive, be sure it is turned on and available. If you plan to save on a server, be sure your network connection has been established and that the desired server drive is mounted. (See your computer manuals or contact your network manager for assistance.)
2. If necessary, make the document you wish to save the active document, then choose File ➤ Save As... or use the F12 shortcut.
3. Specify the desired disk drive in the Save As dialog box by selecting a drive from the Drives drop-down list. When you've chosen the appropriate disk (or a directory on that disk), click the OK button or press ↵.
4. Future Saves will use this new location.

► Saving in Non-Word Formats

Just as you can open non-Word files with Word for Windows, you can save your work in non-Word formats. Use the drop-down Save File as Type list in Word's Save As... dialog box to specify the desired file format.

►► When Your Disk Gets Full

Occasionally, when you attempt to save, Word will tell you that there is not enough room for your project on the current disk. You may even get an insufficient disk space message seemingly out of the blue. This is because Word for Windows sometimes creates temporary files that need disk space of their own. There are several things you can do in this situation.

- Use the Save As command to save to a different hard drive on your computer or perhaps to a different hard drive elsewhere on your network.
- Use the Save As command to save to a floppy disk.
- Switch to the File Manager, delete old unwanted files, then switch back to Word and attempt to save again.

►► Making Backup Files for Safekeeping

It's a fact of life: Hard disks fail. Floppy disks are easily damaged. Fires, floods, winds, and earthquakes destroy computers and the files stored on their disks. Punks walk off with them. Nice people like you and me accidentally delete important files. Computers and software have a mean-spirited habit of trashing your important work-in-progress, usually when you are in a big hurry.

You need to make regular backup copies of your important Word for Windows documents, and you need to store those files far enough away from your computer so that they will survive a neighborhood disaster.

The easy way to save small, simple files is to copy them to floppies. Use File ➤ Save As... (F12) to place copies of important documents on separate disks, which should be stored away from your computer.

Or you can save entire directories to floppies with the Windows Backup program.

For big Word files and large collections of documents, consider backing up to removable portable hard disks or look into tape-backup systems.

Whatever you do, don't rely upon Word's automatic-backup feature as your only backup method! Backup files created with this automatic feature will almost never contain the most recent changes you've made. Many experienced users leave this automatic backup feature turned off and take active responsibility for backups themselves. (Turn it off in the Save tab of the Options dialog box, reached by choosing Tools ➤ Options…. See Chapter 36 for details.) If your organization has a computer support person or network manager, ask about backup policies and procedures.

►► Recovering Damaged Files

If, while you're working in Word for Windows, there is a power failure or other gremlin that causes your computer to lock up or otherwise misbehave, you may find yourself with a damaged document that will either refuse to load or be missing information. Word may be able to recover most of your recent work by loading the appropriate temporary file that Word has probably created. Restart Word.

►► **WARNING**

Never delete or rename temporary files when Word is running. Exit Word first.

Formatting Fundamentals

PART TWO

CHAPTER 8

Margins and Page Breaks

FAST TRACK

To get a better grasp of the page count and overall look of a document as you work ***208***

define your dimensions right when you begin a new project.

To ensure accurate margins on pages that will be bound as a two-sided document ***208***

use the Mirror Even/Odd margin feature.

To change a document's margins ***210***

use the Page Setup dialog box File ➤ Page Setup…); drag the margins using the rulers in Print Preview; or drag margins using the rulers in Page Layout view.

To change margins with the Page Setup dialog box ***211***

choose File ➤ Page Setup… and then enter the Top, Bottom, Right, and Left settings individually into these boxes.

To set different margins for different pages ***212***

click on the page you want to affect and choose This Point Forward in the Apply To box (Page Setup dialog box, Margin tab). If you want to return to old settings (or use new ones) somewhere later in the document, go to the page where you want them to take effect and repeat this process.

To roughly adjust your margins in Print Preview ***213***

click the View Rulers button if necessary, then place the insertion point in the page you want to affect and drag the ruler ends. The guidelines will show you the changing margins.

To roughly adjust your margins in Page Layout view **215**

choose View ➤ Ruler if necessary and drag the edge of the ruler where gray becomes white. Be sure you don't drag the pointed handles, because that will change the indents.

To avoid having your text cut off in the margins **216**

be sure you don't set the margins to smaller than the capabilities of your printer. Many printers, including most laser printers, cannot print right to the edge of the page.

To turn off automatic repagination (speeding things up) **219**

choose Tools ➤ Options… and click on the General tab if it's not already in view. Clear the *X* from the Background Repagination check box and close the Options dialog box.

To force a manual page break **219**

position the insertion point where you want the page break to appear and then choose Insert ➤ Break…(**Ctrl+↵**). Click OK in the dialog box that appears and a page break will be placed in your document.

To move or delete a manual page break **221**

move or delete it just as you would text in Normal or Outline view.

To keep selected lines, paragraphs, or tables together **221**

choose Format ➤ Paragraph… and click on the Text Flow tab. Then click the option you desire: Keep Lines Together or Keep With Next.

▶▶ The white space around the edges of a Word for Windows page are determined primarily by margin and optional gutter settings. (Gutters add extra white space for bound documents.) One set of margin and gutter settings can be used for an entire document, or you can define different settings for different pages in your document. Your choice of paper size, paper orientation (portrait vs. landscape), margin, and gutter settings work together to determine the size and shape of the text area of pages.

Larger margins and gutter settings decrease the available text area while increasing the surrounding white space on each page. Figure 8.1 shows the Word default margin and text-area dimensions for both portrait and landscape orientations when creating U.S. letter-size documents without gutters.

▶▶ Get Off to a Good Start

Because margin settings (and Page Setup information) all affect pagination, it is a good idea to define these dimensions right when you begin a new project. This will give you a better grasp of the page count and overall look of the document as you work. You can always fine-tune margin settings just before final printing.

Margins need not all be the same width. It is possible, for instance, to have a 1½" left margin and a 1.0" right margin, a ½" bottom margin and a ¾" top margin, or just about any combination you desire.

When printing two-sided documents, you may want to use Word's Mirror Even/Odd margin feature and possibly add gutters to place extra white space near the center of your book. (Note that it is convention to have odd-numbered pages on the right and even on the left—just look at any book!) If you plan to have different left and right margins in a two-sided

FIGURE 8.1

Margin settings, paper size, and orientation are three of the many factors that affect the available text area.

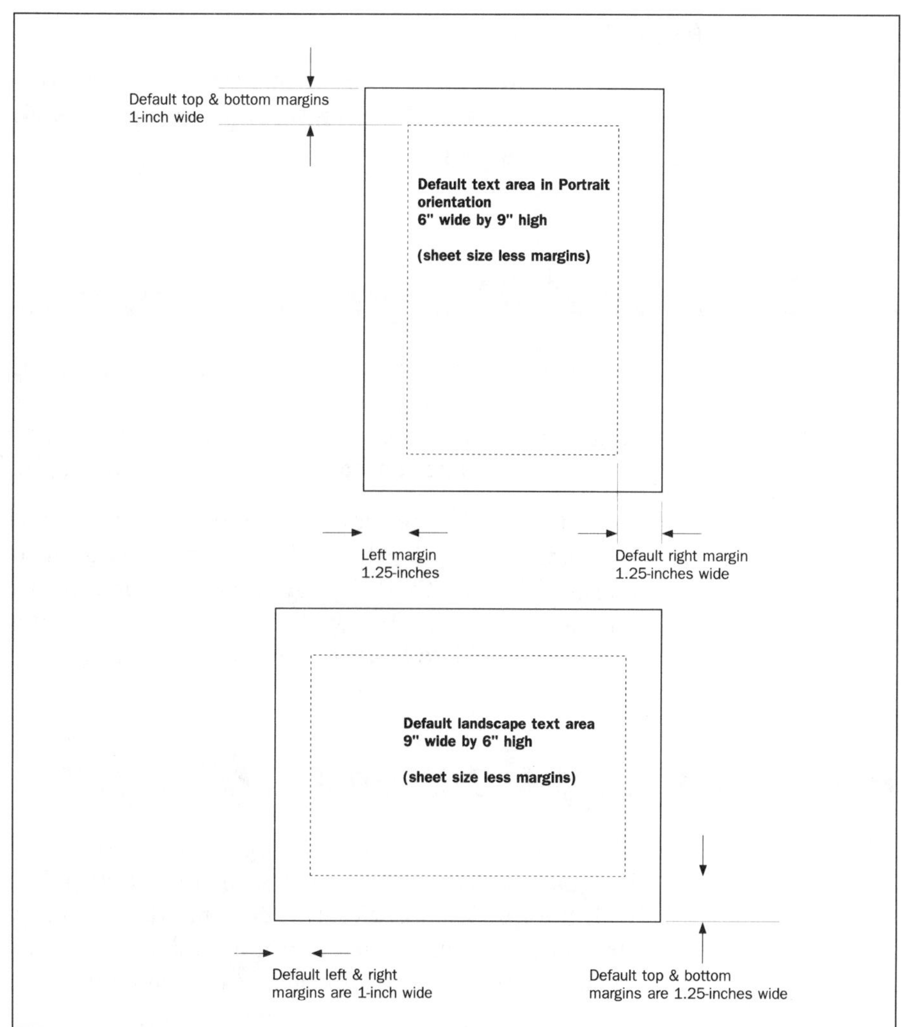

document (a wide left and narrow right, for instance), it is useful to think of these as *inside* and *outside* margins rather than left and right margins, as the wide margin will be on the left side of odd-numbered pages but on the right of even-numbered pages. You'll learn how in this chapter.

If you use headers and footers, you will want to know how they interact with margin settings. Word makes this all fairly painless.

▸▸ **NOTE**

Some printers cannot print at the extreme edges of a page. This can be a consideration when setting margins.

▸▸ Document Margins vs. Indents

Don't confuse Word's margin settings with its paragraph-indentation feature. A Word *page* can have only one user-specified left *margin* setting and only one user-specified right margin setting, but each *paragraph* on the page can have a different left and right *indentation* setting.

Indents are *added* to margin settings. That is to say, if you specify a 1.0" left margin and a ½" left indent, your text will print 1½" from the left margin. If you set a 1.0" right margin and indent the right edge of a paragraph 1.0", the text will stop 2.0" from the right edge of the page. See Chapter 11 to learn more about indenting.

▸▸ Changing Document Margins

There are three ways to set margins. The most straightforward method is to use the Margins portion of the Page Setup dialog box, reached with the File ➤ Page Setup… command. Curiously, there is neither a standard keyboard shortcut nor a Toolbar button for this oft-visited dialog box. You can add your own as described in Chapter 36.

It is also possible to drag margins using the rulers in Print Preview. This lets you see the results of margin changes after a slight repagination delay.

Finally, you can drag new margins with the rulers in Page Layout view. The margin brackets are located on the ruler. Let's look at all three techniques, starting with the dialog box.

Document margins are affected by your printer choice, page orientation, and other decisions made in the four tabs in the Page Setup dialog box (Layout, Paper Source, Paper Size, and Margins). Therefore, you should choose your printer, if you have more than one, *then* use the other tabs in the File ➤ Page Setup command to make any necessary changes before adjusting margins. Double-clicking on a dark-gray part of the ruler will bring up the Page Setup dialog box.

▶ The Page Setup Dialog Box Margin Settings

Figure 8.2 shows the Margins tab in the Page Setup dialog box (File ➤ Page Setup...). You are invited to enter new Top, Bottom, Left, Right, and Gutter margins.

The From Edge settings tell Word how close to the edges of the page you want headers and footers to print. For instance, a Header setting of 0.5" means that the top of a header will be 0.5" from the top edge of the paper, while the same setting for a footer means the bottom of a footer will be 0.5" from the paper's bottom edge.

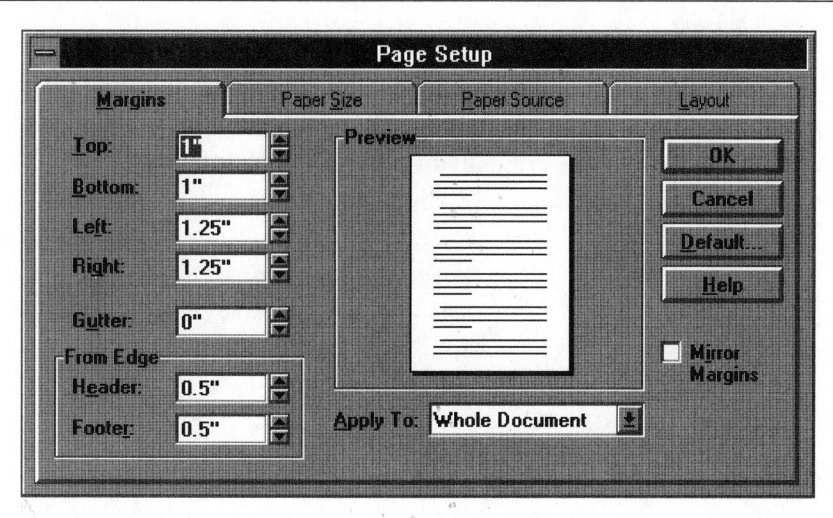

FIGURE 8.2 ▶

You have complete control over margins in the Margin tab of the Page Setup dialog box, reached by choosing File ➤ Page Setup....

new

It is important to note that settings can be uniform document-wide, or different on any and all pages. Be sure to check the setting in the Apply To box. Choices are Whole Document or This Point Forward. This Point Forward means from (and including) the page containing the insertion point.

The Preview will change to show you a miniature representation of the new settings as you adjust them. After you type in each new setting, press Tab to move to the next box. As with other Word dialog boxes, enter fractions as decimals $\frac{1}{4}$" would be 0.25, and so on).

Follow these general steps to change margins from within the Document dialog box:

1. Place the insertion point on the page where you want margin settings to be changed (unless you plan to use the Whole Document choice).
2. Choose File ➤ Page Setup....
3. Change paper size and orientation, if required, by using the Paper Size tab.
4. Switch to the Margins tab if it is not already displayed.
5. Current settings are shown in the various margin dimension boxes.
6. Type the dimensions you desire, or click in the little triangles to increase and decrease settings. The Preview will change as you work.
7. When satisfied, click OK.

►► TIP

Dimensional settings in most Word dialog boxes can be expressed in inches (in), points (pt), centimeters (cm), picas (pi), and, frequently, lines (li). For instance, to set a top margin's height to 12 points, you would type 12pt in the Top margin box. A one-and-one-half line top margin would be 1.5li, etc. It is worth noting that, while you can type other measurements, Word will convert them to the default measurement when you close the dialog box. You change the default measurement in the General tab of the Options dialog box.

▶ Dragging Margins in Print Preview

It's easy to change a document's margins while in Print Preview. Drag on the ruler ends, as shown in Figure 8.3, then wait a moment for your computer to redisplay the page with your new margin settings. Watch the ruler markings as you work. They will give you a good idea of the dimensions. For more precise settings, however, use the dialog box.

▶▶ **TIP**

> **If you don't see the rulers in Print Preview, click the fifth button from the *right* at the top of the Print Preview window as shown in Figure 8.4. This will display the rulers.**

When displaying multiple pages in Print Preview, you will need to click in a page before adjusting margins. The ruler(s) and guidelines will

FIGURE 8.3 ▶

Drag ruler ends in Print Preview to change your margins.

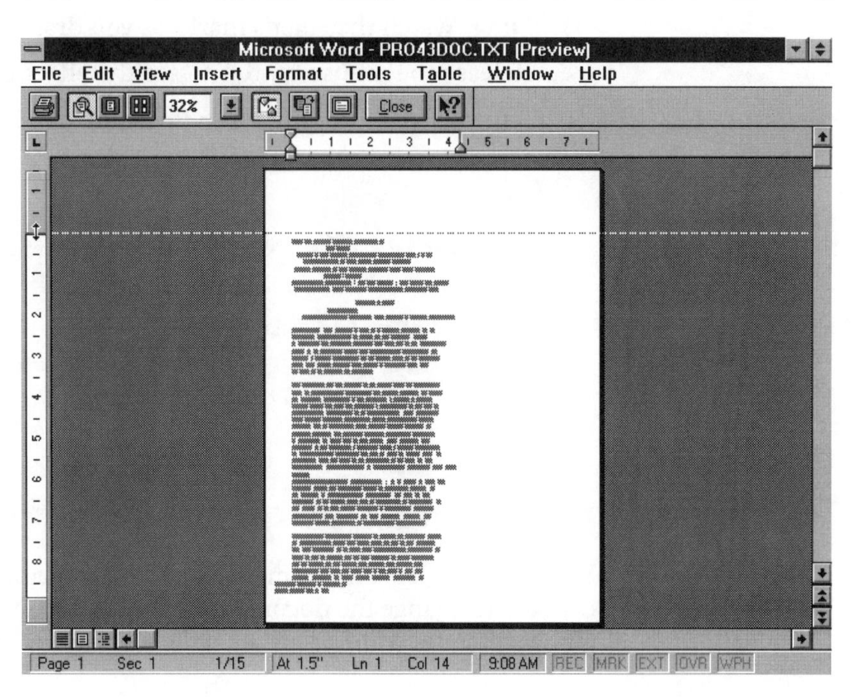

FIGURE 8.4 

Click here if necessary to reveal margin guidelines and handles.

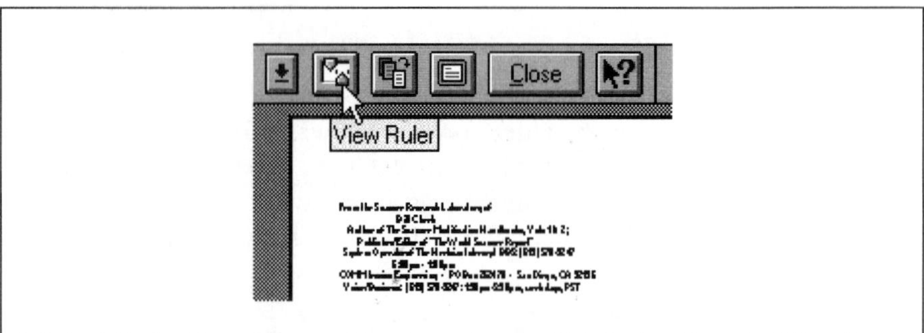

move to the page where you click. This lets you work with different left, right (or inside/outside), top, and bottom margin combinations. The general steps for changing margins in Print Preview are:

1. Choose File ➤ Print Preview.
2. If the rulers are not visible, click on the ruler icon.
3. If necessary, click in a page.
4. Point to a ruler's edge. The pointer will change to a two-headed arrow.
5. Drag. Watch the ruler's marks as you drag.
6. Release the mouse button to see the effect of the margin changes.
7. Repeat steps 3 through 6 to fine-tune, if necessary.

►► TIP

If you've chosen Mirror margins in the Margins tab of the Page Setup dialog box, be sure to display at least two pages in Print Preview to see the effect on facing margins as you drag. Odd pages (pages 1, 3, etc.) are always displayed on the right.

► Dragging Margin Brackets on the Ruler

Word's new rulers display margins as dark gray areas. These can be dragged to change the document's margins. Don't confuse margin dragging techniques with indent dragging techniques, which are similar, but have a very different effect. Follow these steps:

1. Change to Page Layout view if you're not there already.
2. If the ruler is not displayed, choose View ➤ Ruler.
3. Point to the transition area on the ruler where gray becomes white as shown in Figure 8.5.
4. The mouse pointer will become a two-headed arrow.
5. Drag the margin to the desired position with your mouse. Watch the ruler's dimensions change as you drag.

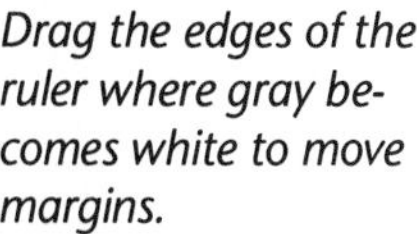

FIGURE 8.5

Drag the edges of the ruler where gray becomes white to move margins.

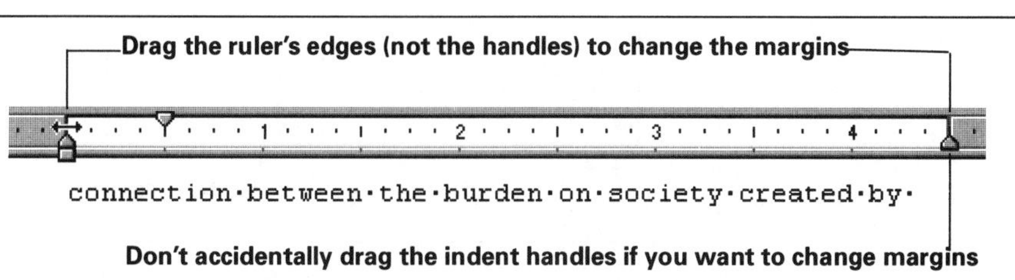
Drag the ruler's edges (not the handles) to change the margins
connection·between·the·burden·on·society·created·by·
Don't accidentally drag the indent handles if you want to change margins

►► Alternate Facing (Mirror) Margins

Select the Mirror Margins feature in the Margins tab of the Page Setup dialog box (File ➤ Page Setup...) when you want different left and right margin widths and your final output will be two-sided. Word makes inside margins of odd- and even-numbered pages the same size and does the same with the outside margins of odd and even pages, as illustrated in Figure 8.6. This is how you get white space on the appropriate side of even and odd two-sided pages.

When adjusting margins in Print Preview, if you've chosen the Mirror Odd/Even feature, be sure you display two pages in Print Preview. Otherwise you won't know if you're working with an odd or even page.

►► Gutters Facilitate Binding

Here's one of those features that apparently exists simply because other products have it. Gutter margins compensate for the paper tucked

FIGURE 8.6

Mirror Margins compensates for two-sided documents with dissimilar left and right margins.

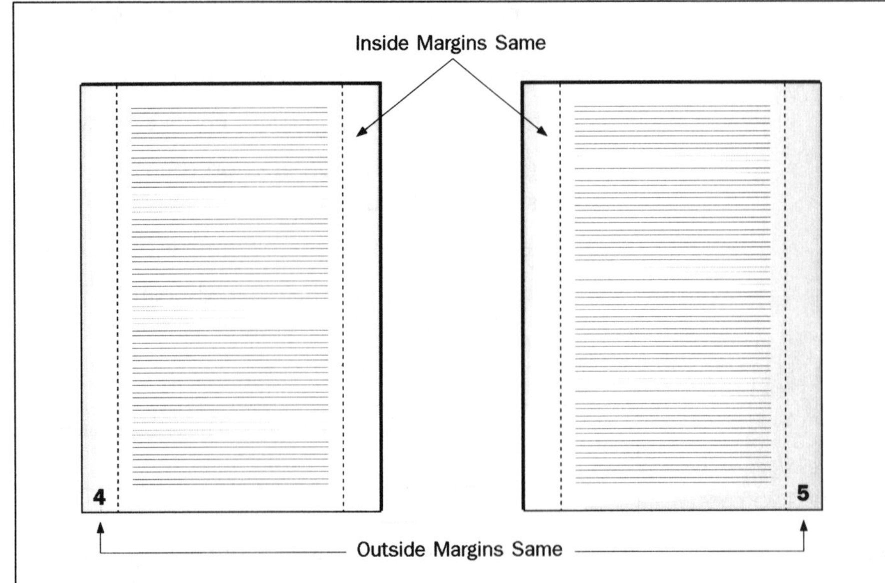

away in the binding of a two-sided book that would be unreadable. Gutters are additional white space in the inside margins. The gutter width, which you specify in the Margin tab of the Page Setup dialog box, reduces the text area, as shown in Figure 8.7.

In Print Preview, you can see the effect of gutter margins, but you cannot adjust them. To adjust the gutter, leave Print Preview and visit the Margin tab in the Page Setup dialog box (File ➤ Page Setup…).

►► **TIP**

Instead of using gutters, simply increase the size of the inside margins to accommodate binding.

►► Printer Capabilities Limit Margins

Many printers, including most laser printers, are incapable of printing all the way to the edge of the paper. Keep this in mind when setting margins. If, for instance, your printer cannot print past the last half-inch of a page, any margin of less than $^1/_2$" will result in cropped (chopped-off) text.

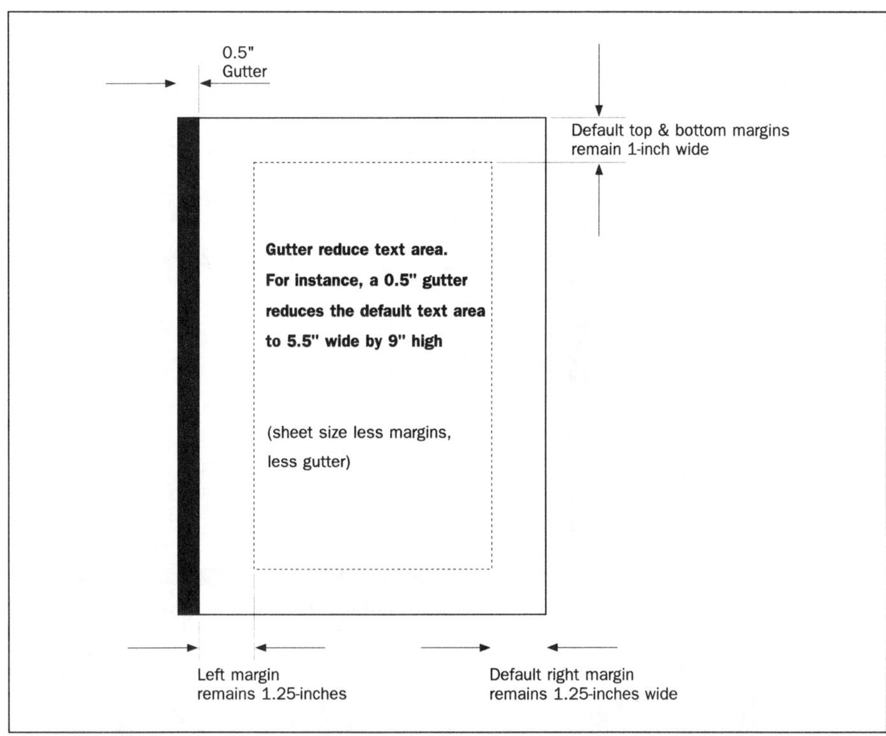

FIGURE 8.7

Gutter space compensates for paper used in the binding process by adding space to inside margins in two-sided documents.

Some printers offer ways to increase printing area. For instance, some laser printers let you trade font memory for larger printing areas. See your printer manual for details.

▶▶ Printing in the Margins

As you can see from Figure 8.8, it is possible to place text, graphics, and page numbers in margins by using indent markers. You can drag indent markers into margins, and text or graphics will follow. You can also use the Insert ➤ Frame command to place things in margins, as described in Chapter 6. Page numbers can also be positioned in margins, as you will learn in Chapter 12.

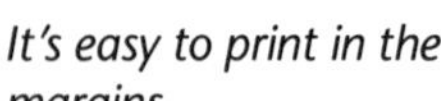

FIGURE 8.8

It's easy to print in the margins.

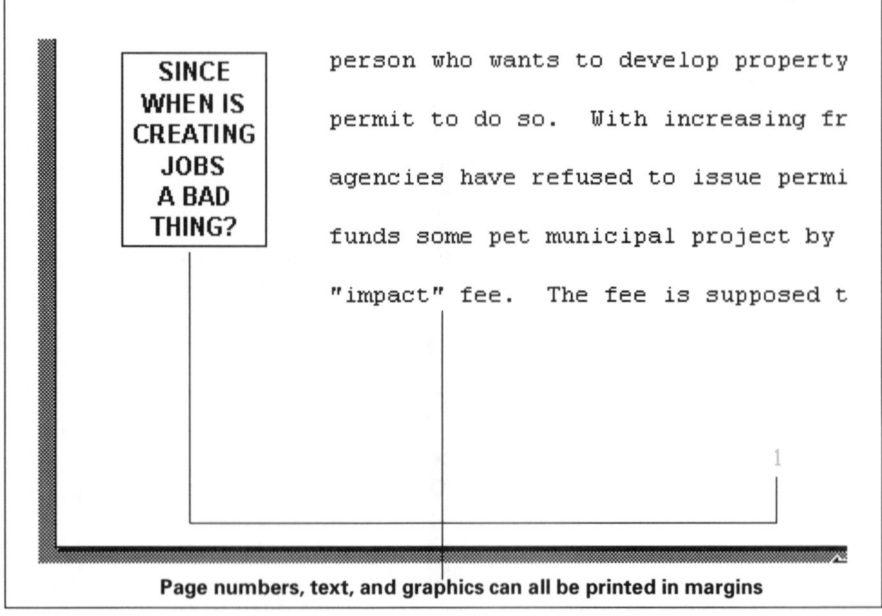

▸▸ How Headers and Footers Affect Margins

Headers and footers print in the top and bottom margins. The inclusion of headers and footers causes Word to automatically adjust top and bottom margins when necessary. For instance, if you use the Margin tab of the Page Setup dialog box to specify a minimum top margin of ½", then create a header that is 1.0" high, Word will increase the top margin size to make room for the big header. You can override this feature by specifying exact top or bottom margins in the Margin tab of the Page Setup dialog box. This will force Word to limit top and bottom margins, headers and footers be damned! This can create some interesting effects, desired and otherwise. Read about headers and footers in Chapter 12.

►► Page Breaks

Page breaks are the places in your document where one page ends and a new page begins. Many things affect where page breaks will occur. Factors include the size of your paper, margin settings, paragraph formats, and section breaks. Word automatically computes and displays page breaks as you add and delete information. You can visualize page breaks in all views before printing. Breaks appear as dotted lines in Normal and Outline views. Because both Page Layout view and Print Preview simulate sheets of paper, page breaks are easy to see in those views as well.

You can force your own page breaks. For instance, if you always want new chapters to start on a new page, you can force this by inserting manual page breaks at the beginning of each chapter.

►► Repagination

In order to display and print page breaks properly, Word must recalculate page endings after you've made changes. Normally this is done automatically in the background whenever Word can steal some otherwise unused computer time. This process is called *automatic repagination*. Because page endings affect certain other features, Word always repaginates when:

- You ask it to print
- You are in Print Preview or Page Layout view
- You compile a Table of Contents or Index

To turn off automatic repagination (and speed up slower computers when working on large documents), follow these steps:

1. Choose Tools ➤ Options....
2. Click on the General tab if it's not already in view.
3. Clear the *X* from the Background Repagination check box. (You won't be able to do this if you are in Page Layout view.)

4. Close the Options dialog box.
5. Word will repaginate only when you are in a view that requires it. To force repagination, switch to Page Layout, Print Preview, or issue a Print request.

▸▸ TIP

Word 6 does not have a Repaginate Now command like its predecessors.

▸ Forcing Page Breaks

When you want to force a page break, you can insert manual page breaks. In Normal and Outline views they look thicker than Word's automatic page breaks and contain the words *Page Break*.

▸▸ TIP

Generally speaking, forcing a page break is not a great idea. If you must do it, wait until you have done all of your other formatting, spell checking, and so forth.

To insert a manual page break:

1. Move the insertion point to where you want to place the break.
2. Choose Insert ➤ Break. You'll see this dialog box:

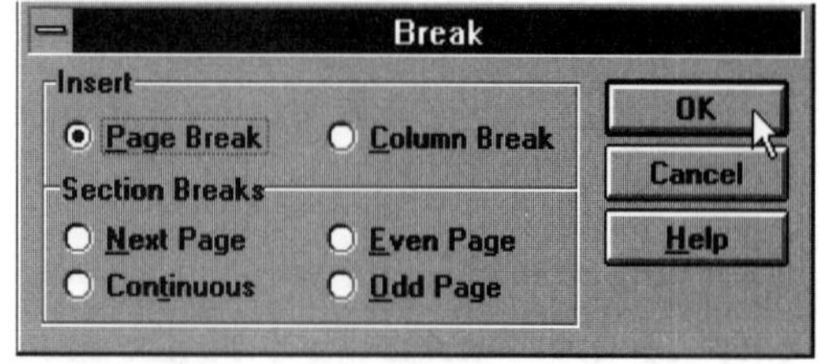

3. Make sure the Page Break button is selected (the default).

4. Click OK or tap the ↵ key.
5. The dialog box will disappear and you'll see a thick manual page break line on your screen. Text or graphics below the manual page break will appear on the next page of your document.

► Moving and Deleting Page Breaks

Manual breaks can be highlighted and deleted like text in Normal and Outline views. (You cannot delete automatic breaks placed by Word.) Select a manual break line and press Delete.

The Replace… command will also let you search for and delete manual breaks. You do this by searching for manual breaks and replacing them with nothing. See Chapter 20 to learn more about replacing.

►► Keeping Things Together on a Page

Sometimes automatic page breaks occur where they shouldn't, such as just after paragraph headings or in the middle of lists or tables. Word offers several ways to keep things together.

► Keeping Lines Together

To keep lines together and prevent a page break from separating them, do the following:

1. Select the lines you wish to keep together (this is often easiest in Normal view).
2. Choose Format ➤ Paragraph….

3. If necessary click on the Text Flow tab to reveal the options shown here.

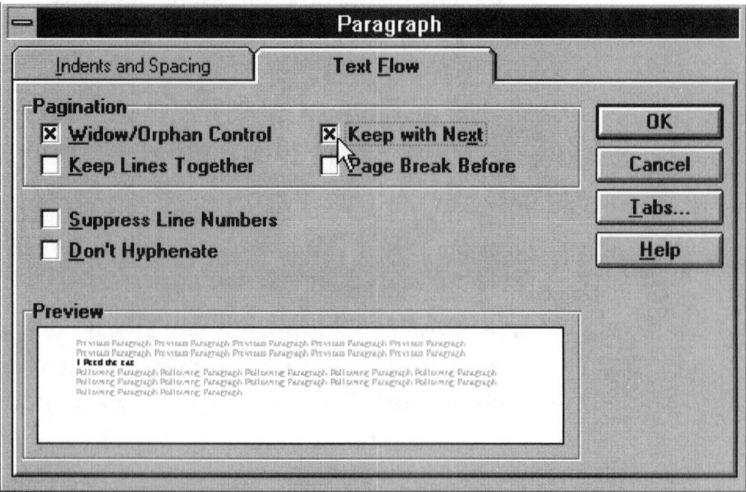

4. Enable the Keep Lines Together option by clicking to place an X in the appropriate box.
5. Click OK.
6. Small black, nonprinting blocks will appear next to the lines indicating that these lines have special formatting that may not be obvious in some views.
7. The lines will stay together on the same page with each other (sometimes causing very early page breaks).

► Keeping Paragraphs or Graphics and Labels Together

To keep paragraphs together, or to keep graphics and related text together on the same page, do the following:

1. Select the paragraphs (possibly including graphics) you wish to keep together.
2. Choose Format ➤ Paragraph… and reveal the Text Flow tab's options, if they are not already visible.
3. Enable the Keep With Next option by clicking to place an *X* in the appropriate box.

4. Click OK.
5. Small black, nonprinting blocks will appear next to the lines, indicating that these lines have special formatting that may not be obvious in some views.
6. The designated items will stay together on the same page with each other (sometimes causing very early page breaks).

▶ Keeping Parts of Tables Together

As you will learn when you read more about tables in Chapter 11, Word treats each row in a table as a separate paragraph. Select all the rows of a table and use the Keep With Next paragraph option to keep a table intact.

▶▶ Forcing Paragraphs to Start on a New Page

To force paragraphs to start a new page (chapter headings, for instance), do the following:

1. Select the paragraph you want to place at the top of a new page.
2. Choose Format ➤ Paragraph… and reveal the Text Flow tab's options.
3. Select the Page Break Before option.
4. Click OK.

▶▶ Removing Keep With Next and Similar Paragraph Options

To remove special paragraph and line options like Keep With Next, Keep Lines Together, and Page Break Before, follow these steps:

1. Select the paragraph(s) you want to change.

2. Choose Format ➤ Paragraph… and switch to the Text Flow tab if it's not already visible.
3. Click to remove *X*s from unwanted options.
4. Click OK.

▸▸ Controlling Widows and Orphans

Widows are short lines (typically a single word) at the end of paragraphs. Orphans are the first lines of paragraphs that print by themselves at the bottom of a page. While both can be distracting to readers, some editors will tell you to eliminate orphans and live with widows (pun intended). The choice is yours, unless you work somewhere with policies about such style issues.

Word automatically eliminates both widows and orphans unless you tell it to do otherwise. You may find it helpful to turn off this feature if you are having trouble making things fit, particularly in multicolumn documents. Here's how to turn off automated widow and orphan suppression:

1. Choose Format ➤ Paragraph….
2. Remove the *X* from the Widow/Orphan Control option box in the Text Flow tab.
3. Click OK.
4. Widows and orphans may occur, and you can deal with them manually or choose to ignore them.

▸▸ TIP

Sometimes Print Preview's Shrink to Fit can help with widows too.

CHAPTER 9

Characters and Fonts

▸▸ FAST TRACK

To add emphasis to your documents **230**

use different fonts for headlines, paragraph headings, and text.

To take best advantage of the space you have for text **233**

use *proportionally spaced* fonts.

To have the most control over the formatting of text **236**

choose the Format ➤ Font command and use its two tabs, Font and Character Spacing, to make exact specifications.

To see what character formats are at work **238**

click the Help button on the Standard Toolbar, point to the characters of interest, and an informational balloon box will appear.

To increase or decrease the size of selected text from the keyboard **243**

use the keyboard shortcuts **Ctrl+] and Ctrl+[** (changes the size one point at a time) or **Ctrl+Shift->** and **Ctrl+Shift-<** (changes the size by the standard increments listed in Word's various Font size lists).

To boldface selected text **243**

click the Bold button on the Formatting Toolbar, use one of the keyboard shortcuts—**Ctrl+B** or **Ctrl+Shift+B**, or enable Bold in the Font Style list in Word's Font dialog box.

To italicize selected text 244

click the Italic button on the Formatting Toolbar, use one of the keyboard shortcuts—**Ctrl+I** or **Ctrl+Shift+I**, or enable Italic in the Font Style list in Word's Font dialog box.

To underscore the selected text 244

click the Underline button on the Formatting Toolbar (for single, continuous underline), use the keyboard shortcut—**Ctrl+U**, or choose one of the options in the Underline list in Word's Font dialog box.

To make the selected text super- or subscript 247

either use the shortcuts **Ctrl+=** and **Ctrl+Shift+=**, click the Superscript or Subscript buttons on the Formatting Toolbar, or bring up the Character Spacing tab of the Font dialog box (Format ➤ Font…) and choose either Raised or Lowered.

To change the casing of the selected text 250

use the Format ➤ Change Case… command.

To copy character formatting from the selected text to other text 254

double-click on the Format Painter button in the Standard Toolbar and drag across the text you want to format. Release the mouse button and the text should reformat.

To make the selected text into a bulleted list 259

click the Bulleted List button on the Standard Toolbar. To have greater control over the bullets, use the Format ➤ Bullets and Numbering command.

▶▶ **S*pecialists*** called *typographers* spend their whole lives studying and improving the appearance of printed words. It is a complex profession steeped in tradition and romance. Computers have added to the trivia and mystique surrounding typography. Word for Windows provides considerable typographic prowess. For instance, you can:

- Specify fonts (type designs)
- Specify character size (in points)
- Embellish text (bold, italics, and underline)
- Adjust inter-character spacing (kerning)
- Specify colors for characters
- Change the case of text (e.g., lowercase to uppercase)
- Super- or subscript characters
- Copy and repeat character formatting
- Insert international accent marks and special symbols
- Hide and reveal text selectively (annotations)
- Use Word's typeset commands for equation and technical typing

For many, it may be enough to know how to print desired characters in appropriate sizes and styles. Other readers will want to know how to get just the right look. Some will need to know about various font technologies. You may need to be aware of compatibility issues when moving documents from one computer or printer to another.

This chapter progresses from simple, nontechnical techniques to fairly complex issues. Feel free to jump from topic to topic as the need arises.

If you always use the same computer and a single printer, and you are happy with your choice of fonts and effects, you may be able to completely ignore the technology and typesetting information found near the end of this chapter.

There are very few hard-and-fast rules where the art of typography is concerned. But there are plenty of rules where the technology of computer fonts is concerned. The best way to learn is to experiment.

▶▶ Terminology

People often use the terms *font* and *typeface* synonymously. The terms are not really synonyms, but because the world seems to be treating them that way these days, we will too. With apologies to professional typographers, let's start with some slightly oversimplified definitions.

▶ Characters, Fonts, and Typefaces

Characters are the letters, numbers, punctuation marks, and special symbols that you type from the keyboard. For our purposes, we'll define a font or typeface as a collection of characters and symbols with a common appearance, or design. Courier is an example of a font. It will remind you of old electric typewriters. Times is a different font (or typeface) that will remind you of newspaper and magazine copy.

Different fonts contain different collections of characters and symbols. Some fonts are designed to be used for specific purposes like headings or drop caps. Sometimes these have only uppercase letters and may not even contain punctuation. There are scientific and math fonts that contain the necessary Greek and other symbols for technical typing. Other fonts are used for adding decorations to your document. Wingdings is an example. Instead of numbers and letters, it contains tiny pictures of airplanes, boxes, check marks, and so on.

▸ Font Families

A collection of all of the variations of a font is called a *family*. For instance, you can purchase a font family from Adobe called Lucida. This family includes Lucida Roman, Lucida Italic, Lucida Bold, and Lucida Bold Italic.

One way to add emphasis to a document is to use different fonts for headlines, paragraph headings, and body copy. Sometimes you'll decide to pick different fonts from the same family, other times you'll mix fonts from different families. The headings and body type used in this book illustrate both techniques.

▸ Character Formatting

When you use Word for Windows, you need not purchase entire font families to use effects like bold and italics. Word has features that can often embellish the appearance of single plain fonts to create bold, italics, shadow, and other effects. The techniques used to do this are usually referred to as *character formatting*. Figure 9.1 shows many of the character formatting variations possible when using Word's character format tricks on the NewCenturySchlbk (schoolbook) font.

FIGURE 9.1 

With Word's formatting capabilities, you can enhance a font in many ways.

Normal (a.k.a. Plain text), **Bold,** *Italic*
Standard underline Word Underline
double underline Dotted underline
~~Strike-thru~~
all caps off, ALL CAPS ON
Small Caps Off, SMALL CAPS ON
^{Super}Normal$_{\text{Subscript}}$
Condensed character spacing Off
Condensed character Spacing On
Expanded character spacing Off
Expanded character spacing On
Black Blue Cyan Green Magenta Red Yellow
Bold + ***Italic*** + Outline + Shadow + Condensed

Don't confuse the character formatting tricks shown in Figure 9.1 with true bold, italics, and other fonts. Purists often prefer the real thing, and these character formatting effects can sometimes look downright awful when applied to certain fonts—including many of the low-cost shareware typefaces in common use.

Incidentally, not all font vendors provide identical-looking fonts, even when the font names are the same. The Courier installed in Apple's LaserWriters looks slightly different from the Courier in Pacific Data's PostScript products, for instance. Occasionally (but rarely) this can cause differences in line endings. And, once in a while, you'll find different special characters in fonts from various manufacturers. (You won't always find the little apple character in some non–Apple-provided fonts, for instance.)

Monospaced vs. Proportionally Spaced

Some fonts are said to be *monospaced* or fixed-pitch; others *proportionally spaced* or variable-pitch. Monospaced fonts like Courier use the same amount of horizontal space on a line for each character, regardless of the width of a character. With a monospaced font like Courier a letter *i* takes the same amount of horizontal space as the letter *W*. Thus, if, you can fit seventy *W*'s on a line in Courier, you can only fit seventy *i*'s in the same space. Obviously, this is an inefficient use of space and sometimes causes sloppy-looking words. Since people like lawyers, art directors, and publishers usually want to fit as many words as possible on a page, they turn to proportionally spaced fonts that tuck narrow letters in closer to their neighbors.

In Figure 9.2 the same word is printed first in 72-point Courier, a monospaced font, and then in 72-point Times and Helvetica, both proportionally spaced fonts. Notice the ocean of white space on either side of the letter *i* in the Courier example. A long base has been added to the bottom of the *i* in an attempt to distract you from this untidiness. Compare the white space on either side of all three *i*'s in Figure 9.2.

Ironically, the monospaced Courier font uses less horizontal space on the line than either of the proportionally spaced fonts, due mainly to the much wider *W*'s and *m*'s in the proportional faces. Generally, though, proportionally spaced fonts will be more economical with space than their monospaced brethren and sistren.

FIGURE 9.2

Notice that Courier (top) is much less elegant than Times (middle) or Helvetica (bottom).

Wimp

Wimp

Wimp

Point Sizes

The various sizes of type (9 point, 10 point, 12 point, etc.) are referred to as *point* sizes. You should know that 9-point type is smaller than 10-point type, and that there are 72 points to an inch. Thus, 72-point type will take 1 vertical inch of space, 36-point type will require $^1/_2$ inch of vertical space, and so on.

Point size is measured from baseline to baseline. For instance, in Figure 9.2 you would measure from the bottom of the *W* on one line to the bottom of the *W* above or below it. Sometimes different fonts of the same point size appear to be taller or shorter than each other, due to the amount of space the designer has allowed for the parts of characters that go below the baseline and above the tops of caps (called *ascenders* and *descenders*) and for white space above and below the characters (called *leading*). Notice how the 72-point Courier looks shorter than the 72-point Helvetica in Figure 9.2.

Your choice of point size affects the amount of space between lines (the leading), as well as the height of the characters. You can have more than one point size on a line, but Word for Windows will adjust the line spacing to accommodate the largest character on the line. You can override this feature, as you will see in the next chapter.

▶ Serifs vs. Sans Serifs

The horizontal cross lines on the *W*, *i*, and *p* in Figure 9.2's Courier and Times examples are called *serifs*. (The fonts themselves are called serif fonts.) Popular computer fonts with serifs include Courier, Bookman, Palatino, and Times. Fonts without these embellishments are said to be *sans serif*. Avant Garde, Modern, Arial, and Helvetica are examples of sans serif fonts.

▶▶ Character Formatting Tools—An Overview

There are many ways to tell Word for Windows to make characters bold, italicized, bigger, or smaller. Tools for character formatting include the Toolbar, menu choices, dialog boxes, and keyboard shortcuts. You can change the formatting of single characters, entire words, or whole documents. Let's start with an overview of the tools Word for Windows provides for character formatting, then we'll look at typical examples of the tools in use.

▶▶ TIP

You can either specify the desired appearance of characters before you type them, or you can type first, then select text and change its appearance. Virtually all of the character formatting techniques described in this chapter can be accomplished either before or after you keyboard text.

▶ Character Formatting Choices on Word's Menus

Word's various menus contain a number of character-related formatting choices. These let you:

- Pick fonts

- Pick font sizes
- Pick underline styles
- Add effects like superscript, subscript, etc.
- Change the color of displayed or printed characters
- Change default characters
- Preview changes in a preview window
- Change character spacing
- Insert special characters and symbols
- Change case (make words all uppercase, all lowercase, etc.)
- Create drop caps and similar effects

The Font... Command

Word's Format ➤ Font command opens a two-tab dialog box. The Font tab lists all of the fonts installed on your computer and their standard sizes, as illustrated in Figure 9.3. (Yours may list different fonts.)

FIGURE 9.3

The Font dialog box lists and demonstrates all fonts installed on your computer.

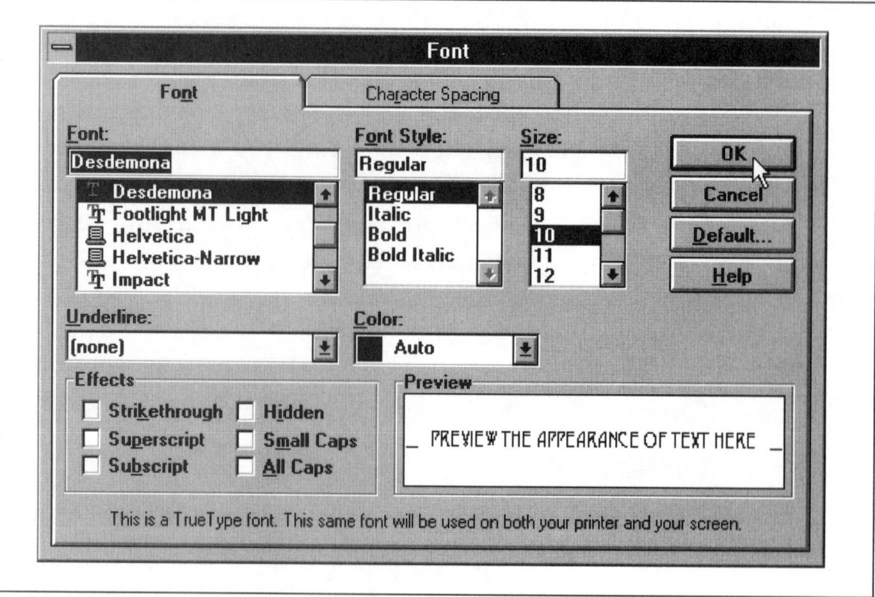

The Font tab also offers some underline and effects choices and a preview area that lets you see the results of your selections. An information line at the bottom of the screen often provides other clues about how the font will look on your screen and how it will print.

Text boxes display the current font, size, and font style. The up and down arrows scroll through the standard sizes available for the selected font. You can type in the Size box to specify nonstandard font sizes not found in the list.

Changing Word's Default Character Formatting The Default... button in the Font tab of the Font dialog box gives you the opportunity to make the current selections the new default settings used by Word.

▶ *Character Formatting with the Formatting Toolbar*

The most immediately visible way to modify character appearance is to use the buttons and font menus on the Formatting Toolbar, illustrated in Figure 9.4.

If the Formatting Toolbar is not in view, choose the View ➤ Toolbars... command. Choose the Formatting Toolbar by placing an *X* in the appropriate box, as illustrated in Figure 9.5. Then click OK.

From the Formatting Toolbar you can pick a font, change to a different point size, toggle bold, italic, and simple underline. Just click on the appropriate Toolbar button or pick the desired menu item from the Toolbar's drop-down lists. Clicking a second time on a Toolbar button removes or *toggles* the effect.

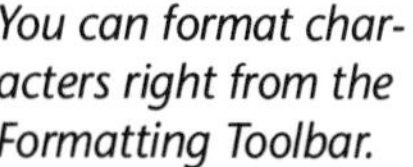

FIGURE 9.4 ▶

You can format characters right from the Formatting Toolbar.

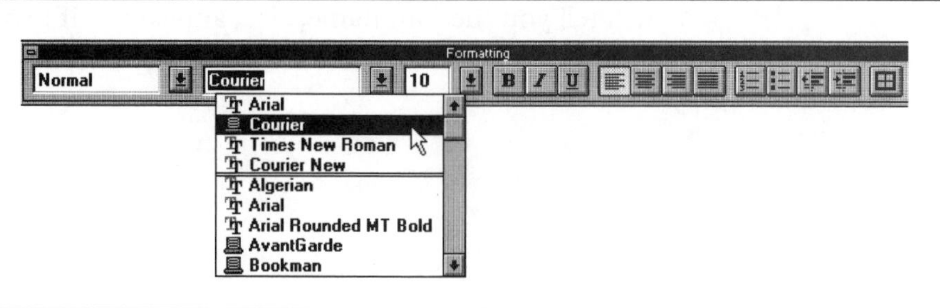

FIGURE 9.5

Use the View ➤ Toolbars… command to bring up the Toolbars dialog box.

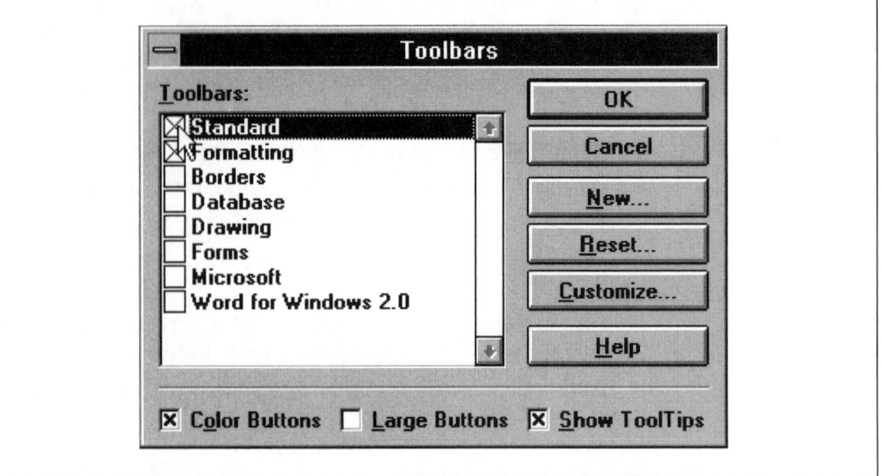

►► TIP

No, you are not seeing double. Word for Windows places the names of your most recently used fonts at the top of the font list in the Toolbar for quick access. The font names are also available in their normal locations.

►► Seeing Which Character Formats are at Work

You can see most of the information regarding character formatting by selecting characters and looking carefully at the Formatting Toolbar. It will tell you the font name, size, and so on. If text is bold, the Toolbar's bold button will be depressed, etc.

TIP

If the text you select is not identically formatted, some or all of the information areas in the Toolbar will be blank or incomplete. For instance, if you select text where some of the characters are different sizes, the Font size area of the Toolbar will be blank. If some of your selected text is bold and some not, the Bold button will not be depressed.

Here's a great new feature. Use the Help button on the Standard toolbar along with your mouse to see which character-formatting tools have been used on characters of interest. Follow these steps:

1. Click once on the Help button in the Standard Toolbar. The pointer changes shape.
2. Point to the character of interest. A cartoon-balloon-like box appears containing information about the paragraph and character styling at work, as shown in Figure 9.6.
3. Press Esc when you are done reading.

Because this new feature will tell you about one character at a time, it solves the mixed formatting problems mentioned earlier. Just move your mouse pointer from character to character to learn about each one.

FIGURE 9.6 

The Standard Toolbar's Help button will reveal character- and paragraph-formatting information when you point to text.

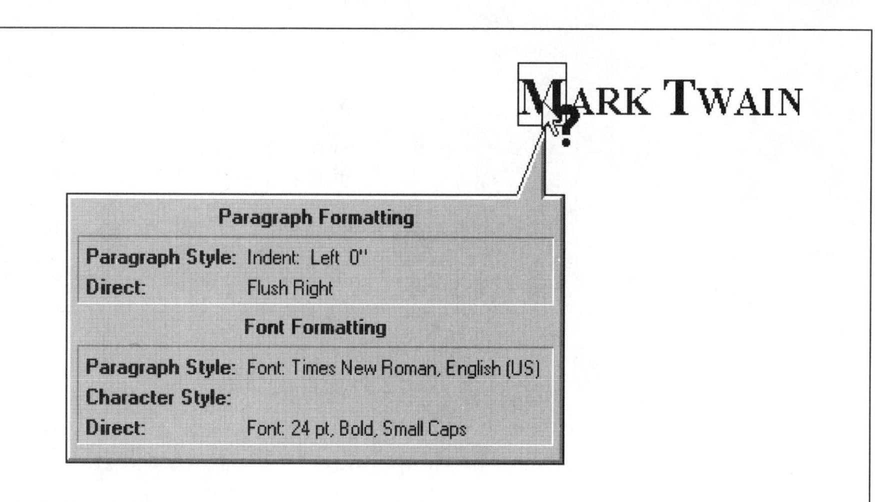

► What Happened to the Character Dialog Box?

"Progress"—that's what happened to the Character Dialog box. It's now called the Font dialog box, and is reached with Format ➤ Font… command. It still contains the most comprehensive collection of character-formatting options available in Word for Windows.

The Font dialog box lets you specify and combine a potentially gaudy array of character effects. It also presents yet another way to pick fonts, and it lets you fiddle with inter-character spacing. Drop-down menus provide you with underline and color choices. You can even enter nonstandard font sizes in the Size box. It also shows which character-formatting options have been enabled from the Toolbar, menu, and keyboard shortcuts. This is one busy box! Take a good look at Figure 9.7.

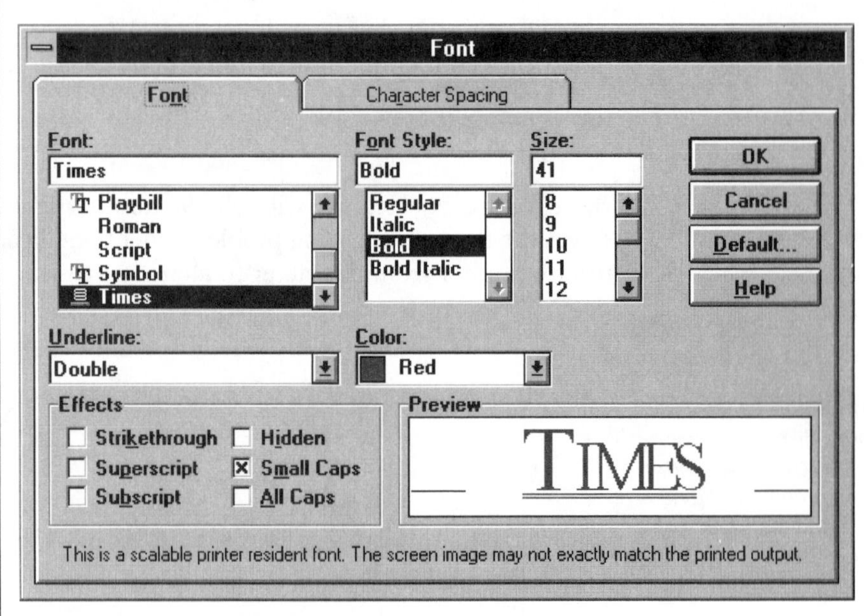

FIGURE 9.7 ►

The Font dialog box gives considerable control over character-formatting options.

Using the Font Dialog Box

Notice the Font Style section of the Font dialog box. It contains four choices—Regular, Italic, Bold, and Bold Italic. Other fonts offer more or fewer choices. For example, Bookman Old Style only offers Bold and Bold Italic:

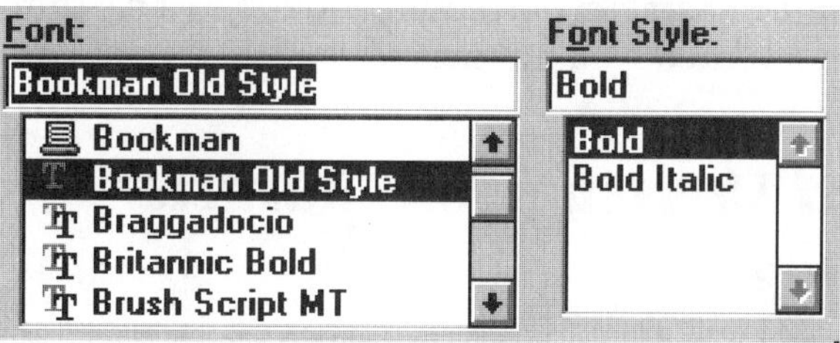

You can apply one or more of these choices to selected characters and to subsequently typed text. Simply click on the desired style. You can remove effects by clicking on Regular.

Effects can often be combined. For instance, it is usually possible to have text that is bold, italicized, and underscored. (Not all fonts accept all formatting options though, and occasionally you will see combinations on screen that will not print.) Click OK when you have selected the desired effects.

In Figure 9.7, the chosen options are Times, Bold, 41 points, Underline: Double, Small Caps, and Red.

About Effects Boxes

If you select text, then open the Font dialog box and see gray boxes next to the formatting options, it simply means that you have selected text with a variety of character-formatting options. For instance, some of your selected text may be Small Caps, other parts not:

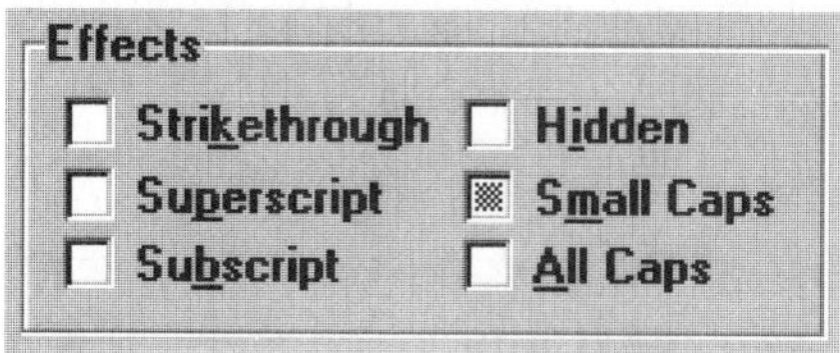

This is an important concept, as you will learn when you work with the Replace command in Chapter 20. An *X* in a character format box means *all* the selected text exhibits that particular attribute. A completely clear box (no *X* and not gray) means that the selected text definitely does not exhibit the specific attribute anywhere within it. A gray box means that some of the text may or may not exhibit some or all of the character-formatting options. (This third condition must have been invented by a politician.)

▸ Keyboard Shortcuts for Character Formatting

Many of Word's character-formatting tools have keyboard shortcuts. They are mentioned throughout this chapter and summarized in Appendix B.

▸▸ How to Specify Everyday Character Formatting

Now that you've seen an overview of the formatting tools, let's look at some specific everyday tasks.

▸ Choosing Fonts and Sizes

Word for Windows can use any font installed in your system. Theoretically at least, you can print any font in any size from 1 point to a whopping 1,638 points. This corresponds to character heights ranging from approximately 1/72nd of an inch to about 22 inches! In reality, you'll probably work with type sizes ranging from about 7 to 72 points most of the time, as they are easy to read and look good on traditional page sizes.

▸▸ **WARNING**

The type of printer you use, the system version you are running, the fonts you've chosen, and other factors affect the final printed appearance of fonts at various sizes. There is more information about this at the end of the chapter.

Word for Windows offers almost too many ways to pick fonts and sizes. Here's a summary of the various techniques:

- Use the drop-down Font and Size lists on the Formatting Toolbar.
- Type the name and size of the desired font directly into the font name and size boxes on the Toolbar, then press ↵. For instance, click in the font name on the Toolbar, then type all or part of a font name like Av for AvanteGarde. (You need type only enough to differentiate the desired font from other installed fonts.) Next click in the size box, if necessary, and type a new point size from 1 to 1,638. Press ↵.
- Select fonts from within the Font dialog box reached with the Format ➤ Font... command.
- To increase or decrease a font size one point at a time (from 10 to 11, for instance), use the keyboard shortcuts Ctrl+] and Ctrl+[.
- To increase or decrease font sizes by the standard increments listed in Word's various Font size lists (10 point, 12 point, 14 point, etc.), use the keyboard shortcuts Ctrl+Shift-> and Ctrl+Shift-<.
- Assign fonts and sizes as part of styles. (See Chapter 14 for details.)

► Creating Bold Characters

There are a number of ways to add bold character formatting to characters you've selected or to characters you are about to type. Here are four choices:

- Click the Bold button on the Formatting Toolbar. It looks like a bold B. (A "depressed" button indicates that bold character formatting is enabled.)
- Use either of the two keyboard shortcuts for bold character formatting—Ctrl+B or Ctrl+Shift+B.
- Enable the Bold option in the Font Style list in Word's Font dialog box.
- Assign bold formatting as part of styles. (See Chapter 14 for details.)

▸ Creating Italicized Characters

Create italicized characters in much the same way you create bold ones:

- Click the Italic button on the Toolbar. It looks like an italicized letter I. (A "depressed" I button indicates that italic character formatting is enabled.)
- Use either of the two keyboard shortcuts for italic character formatting—Ctrl+I or Ctrl+Shift+I.
- Enable the Italic style in the Font dialog box's Font Style menu.
- Assign italic formatting as part of styles. (See Chapter 14 for details.)

▸ Underlining

You can apply simple, single, continuous underlining with the Underline button on the Formatting Toolbar or with the Ctrl+U or Ctrl+Shift+U keyboard shortcuts. If you want different underline formats, you'll need to use the Font dialog box.

There are five choices on the Underline drop-down menu in the Font dialog box:

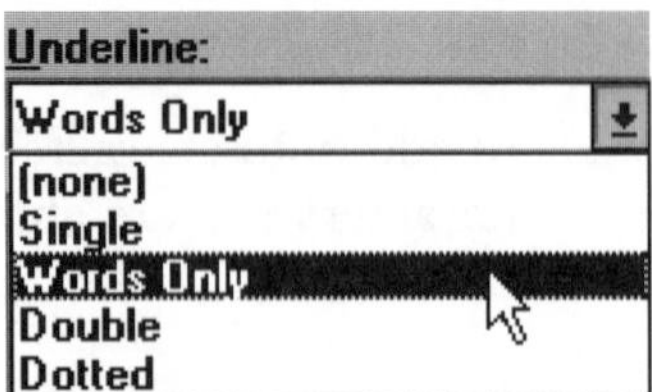

The choices are (none), Single, Words Only, Double, and Dotted. The effects of these choices are self-evident and illustrated in Figure 9.1. Unfortunately, underline choices cannot be combined; it is not possible to choose double words-only underline, for instance.

▶▶TIP

If you routinely use different underline styles like Double or Word, you can add commands for them to your Word for Windows menus or Toolbars. See Chapter 36 to learn how. There are keyboard shortcuts for various underline styles. They are listed in Appendix C.

▶ Strikethru

If you write contract drafts or work with other important documents, you may wish to use Word's Strikethru feature. It is a way to indicate text that will be deleted in the final copy. Choose the Strikethru option in the Font dialog box to overlay text with a horizontal line.

▶▶TIP

Use the Strikethru feature to format both the text and the spaces that you plan to delete in the final copy. When it comes time to delete, you can use Word's Replace... command to find text containing Strikethru text and replace it with nothing, thereby deleting the text. See Chapter 20 for more about the Replace... command.

▶ Expanding and Condensing Character Spacing

Word for Windows lets you override the standard spacing between characters defined by their designers. You can either move characters closer together with the Condensed character-formatting option, or move characters farther apart with the Expanded option. The default for expanding and condensing is 1 point.

▶▶ **NOTE**

Kerning **is a typesetter's term meaning to adjust the space (increase or decrease) between two letters. Usually this is done for reasons of aesthetics, but sometimes it is necessary simply to make a work fit in the space allotted it.**

Condensing can help you fit extra words on a line while Expanding can create interesting effects for headlines and other workspace publishing tasks. You'll see many examples of this in Chapter 23. To expand or condense, follow these steps:

1. Select the text of interest.
2. Choose Format ➤ Font....
3. Open the Character Spacing tab (click on it).
4. Choose Expanded (or Condensed) from the Spacing list, as shown in Figure 9.8.
5. Choose a new setting by typing in the By box or clicking on the increase and decrease triangles. The Preview will change as you work.
6. Click OK to save your changes or Cancel to revert to the original size.

FIGURE 9.8 ▶

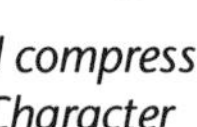

Expand and compress text in the Character Spacing tab of the Font dialog box.

You can condense characters a maximum of 1.75 points and expand them a maximum of 14 points. Word for Windows will remind you of this if you try to exceed the limits.

▶ Automatic Kerning and Manual Character Spacing

You can use the Condensed option to tuck pairs of letters closer to each other to tighten them up and improve the appearance of some awkward-looking combinations of wide and narrow letters. Simply select the letters you want to cozy up, then use the Condensed option in the Character Spacing tab of the Font dialog box. Or you can ask Word for Windows to automatically kern by enabling the Kerning option. Frequently you'll want tighter spacing than the automatic feature offers and you'll have to do it yourself.

For instance, here's how to tighten up the *T* and *W* in *Twain*.

1. Select just the characters *T* and *W*.
2. Open the Character Spacing tab of the Font dialog box (choose Format ➤ Font).
3. Choose Condensed spacing.
4. Choose a point value (1.8, perhaps).
5. Watch the preview and adjust spacing if you like.
6. Click OK to make the changes or Cancel to abort them.

▶ Creating Superscripts and Subscripts

Normally, any characters that you type are placed on an invisible line called the *baseline*. Superscripted characters are moved above the baseline; subscripted characters are placed below the baseline. While the obvious use for this is in equations and chemical formulas (H_2O, for instance), there are many other ways to use super- and subscripting. For example, if you abbreviate numbers like *2nd*, superscripting the letters and reducing them a point size or two (like this: 2nd) gives them a typeset look.

You can also use super- and subscripting to line up odd-sized bullets with adjacent text. As you'll soon see, it's possible to tweak the appearance of drop caps by super- or subscripting them (look ahead to the section called Large Initial Caps, Drop Caps, and Dropped Words).

There are two basic ways to super and subscript. You can use Word's Super and Sub features or you can raise and lower the *position* of characters with Word's Position option in the Character Spacing tab of the Font dialog box. The first method changes the size of super- and subscripted characters in addition to their position. The dialog box method keeps the character size.

Using Superscript and Subscript

The Font dialog box lets you super- and subscript. There are also keyboard shortcuts. Ctrl+= causes superscripting. The shortcut Ctrl+Shift+= subscripts. Both of these shortcuts apply "automatic" spacing decisions made for you by Word. Incidentally, the Font tab of the Font dialog box has choices (Superscript and Subscript) that do the same things as the aforementioned keyboard shortcuts.

To gain manual control over spacing:

1. Select the characters you wish to super- or subscript.
2. Choose Format ➤ Font....
3. Click, if necessary, to see the Character Spacing tab.
4. Choose Raised (or Lowered) from the Position list.
5. Specify the amount by which you want characters raised or lowered by using the By box or buttons.
6. Click OK to apply the changes or Cancel to lose changes.

Figure 9.9 shows an example of this. Characters are being raised (superscripted) 3 points.

▸▸ TIP

Sometimes line heights are not sufficient to display the tops and bottoms of super or subscripted characters, making them appear cut off. Adjust the line spacing as described in Chapter 10 if this happens.

FIGURE 9.9

These settings superscript characters 3 points without changing the size of the characters.

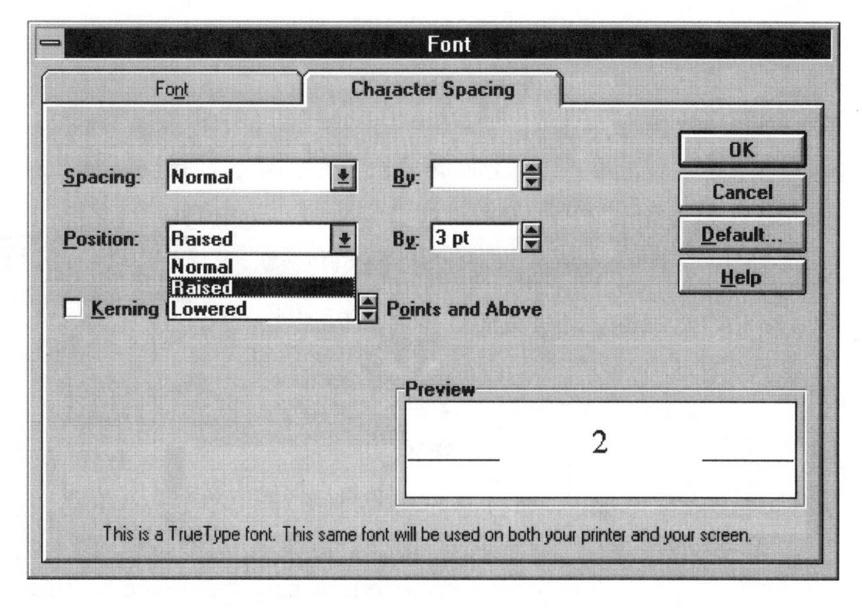

Character Color Choices

Even if you cannot display or print color, Word for Windows lets you specify six character colors plus black or white. You can then take copies of your disk files to color-capable hardware for display and printing. To specify a color follow these steps:

1. Start by selecting text or positioning the insertion point where you want to type colored text.
2. Choose the desired color from the drop-down Color menu in the Font tab of the Font dialog box. If your monitor supports color, you will see color characters in the Preview area. If your monitor supports shades of gray, colors will be converted to grays.
3. Click OK to close the character dialog box.
4. When you print, enable your printer's color or gray scale features if it has them.

Remember, not all computers can display grays or colors, but you need not display color to print it. To see which color you've assigned to text when using a black-and-white monitor, select the text and visit the

Font dialog box or use the Help button "cartoon" trick to read the name of the assigned color.

► Using the Change Case Command

The Format ➤ Change Case… command opens a dialog box that offers five choices:

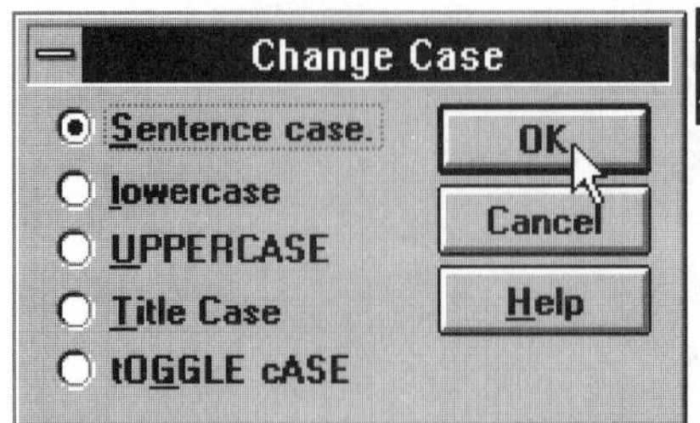

MARK TWAIN

Look closely at the dialog box. It demonstrates the results of the five choices in use. For instance, UPPERCASE changes all selected characters to uppercase letters, and the choice UPPERCASE itself appears all uppercase in the dialog box. Title Case changes the first letter of each selected word to uppercase as illustrated in the dialog box.

Alas, the Title Case feature is not context-sensitive, so it capitalizes prepositions and articles, including *of*, *the*, and so on. To change case with this feature, follow these steps:

1. Select the text you wish to change.
2. Choose Format ➤ Change Case….
3. Choose the desired case option.
4. Click OK.

When you change case using this dialog box, the characters themselves change to the specified case. It is just as if you had retyped them using the new capitalization scheme. Undo works here.

► Using the All Caps Option

The All Caps feature is found in the Font dialog box. It changes only the appearance of letters without actually changing the letters themselves. Unlike the Format ➤ Change Case… command, the All Caps option lets you type in lowercase and see uppercase letters as you work. Follow these steps:

1. Select the text you wish to change or position the insertion point for typing.
2. Choose Format ➤ Font....
3. Choose All Caps.
4. Click OK.

Selected and/or subsequently typed case will appear in uppercase, but the underlying text will retain its actual capitalization.

► Using the Small Caps Option

The Small Caps option in the Character Dialog Box can create some very interesting effects. Figure 9.10 shows some examples of Small Caps at work.

►► TIP

Remember that applying the Small Caps formatting option to text containing dingbats like those shown in Figure 9.10 will usually capitalize the dingbats, thereby changing the character that appears and prints. Select dingbats and remove Small Caps formatting. Use Word's Replace... command (described in Chapter 20) to do this if you have many changes to make.

►► Removing Character Formatting

Removing character formatting can be a simple or confusing task, depending on the situation. The six general ways to remove character formatting include:

- Toggling Toolbar buttons, menu commands, and keyboard shortcuts
- Using the Remove Formats keyboard shortcut (Ctrl+Spacebar)

FIGURE 9.10

These four samples of Small Caps character formatting show how easy it is to add punch and visual interest.

ASK MR. FOSTER AMERICAN INDUSTRIAL REAL ESTATE ASSN. FIRSTOURS CARLSON CORPORATION BEAR STERNS BERGER & NORTON CABLE NEWS NETWORK (CNN) CHILDRENS HOSPITAL LOS ANGELES SYBEX

SOUTHERN EXPOSURE

WRITTEN BY

GUY WIRE

DIRECTED BY

PHIL R. UPP

PRODUCED BY

MS. TAKE

CENTRAL VALLEY	10
SIERRA NEVADA	12
SACREMENTO AREA	14
MARIN COUNTY	22
CONTRA COSTA COUNTY	34

- Changing to a different style
- Using the Font dialog box
- Using the Replace command to automate removal
- Choosing the Regular font style in the Font dialog box

Unfortunately, not all approaches work under all circumstances, and there are some land mines, particularly when styles are involved. Removing character formatting is easiest if you are not using Word for Windows styles other than Normal. See Chapter 14 to learn about Styles.

▶ Toggling to Remove Character Formatting

You can use the Edit ➤ Undo command (Ctrl+Z) to undo formatting immediately after you've changed it. And you can remove most character formatting by applying it a second time. This process is called *toggling* (you've already encountered the toggling concept with Toolbar buttons). For instance, if you select a bold word and click on the Bold Toolbar button, the selected text will no longer be bold.

▶ The Regular Font Style

The Regular font style in the Font tab of the Font dialog box will remove most character formatting. Simply select the text, then execute the choice.

Limitations of Toggling and Regular Font Style

The toggling and Regular font style techniques just described will remove formats and many combinations, such as bold or bold with underlines. In fact, toggling and the Regular font style should work with the following character-formatting features in any combination:

- Bold
- Italic
- Underline
- Double underline
- Word underline
- Dotted underline
- Strikethru
- Outline effect
- Shadow
- Small caps
- All caps

- Hidden text
- Colors

However, the tricks will *not* tighten up characters that have been expanded, nor will it spread out characters that have been condensed. You cannot change fonts or their sizes this way either. You'll need either to visit the Font dialog box or use other specific controls.

▸▸ Copying and Repeating Character Formats

The Format Painter button is a slick new way to apply formatting to characters. To apply character formatting, do this:

1. Select only the characters of interest (but not the paragraph marker at the end of the paragraph) whose format you wish to copy.
2. Double-click on the Format Painter button in the Standard Toolbar. The pointer will turn into a paintbrush and the status area will display instructions.
3. Drag across the text you want to format.
4. Release the mouse button and the text should reformat.

▸▸ Typing Special Characters

Word for Windows makes it easy to type special characters and symbols not listed on your keycaps but available in most fonts. Let's look at the Symbol… feature and then review the old reliable keyboard shortcuts.

▸ The Symbol Command

The dialog box shown in Figure 9.11 appears whenever you choose Insert ➤ Symbol…. It has two tabs.

The dialog box shows you all available characters in the current font. Clicking on a symbol shows you a magnified, more readable version. Double-clicking inserts the character at the insertion point in your document. (Alternately, you can click on a character then click on the Insert button, but that's more work.)

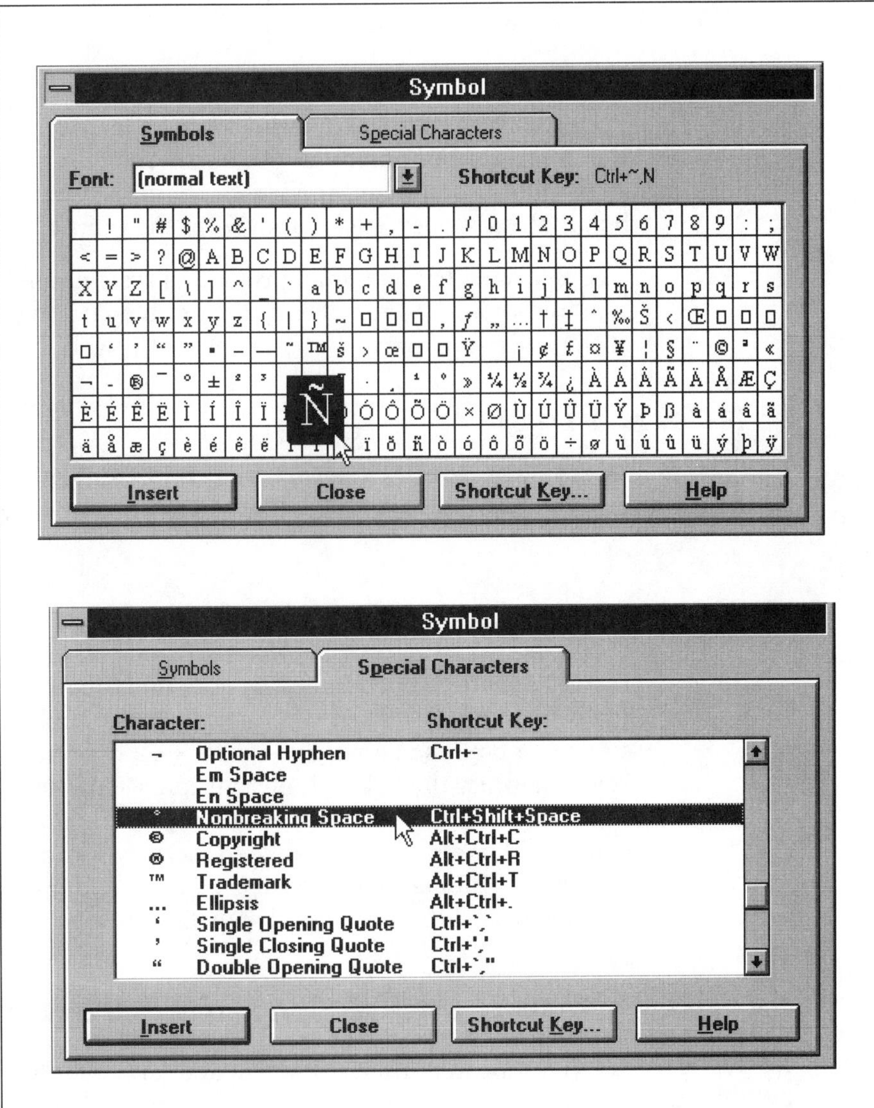

FIGURE 9.11

The two tabs in the Symbol dialog box (reached by choosing Insert ➤ Symbol…).

Once you've clicked to magnify a character in the Symbol dialog box, you can see magnified views of others by navigating with the arrow keys. This can eliminate the need for a lot of precision clicking. Also, once a character is highlighted, you can insert it by hitting ↵.

To see which symbols are available in different fonts, simply choose a font from the Font menu in the Formatting Toolbar and use the Insert ➤ Symbol… command to view the choices. Or, if the Symbol dialog box is already open, pick a font from the Font list in the dialog box.

The Special Characters tab provides a scrolling list of commonly used symbols and characters. Here too, double-clicking inserts the character at the insertion point.

The Special Characters tab in the Symbol window also lets you see (and change) keyboard shortcuts.

▸ Typing Symbols from the Keyboard

If you know the appropriate key combinations, you can enter them directly from the keyboard without using the Symbol… feature. For instance, to type the copyright symbol (©), hold down the Alt and Ctrl keys and press the C key. Different fonts sometimes have different key combinations, so you will need to consult the documentation that comes with your fonts or use the Insert ➤ Symbol… command to learn the combinations. Figure 9.12 shows commonly used special characters and their keyboard shortcuts.

▸ International and Accented Characters

To type accented international characters (like the ñ in La Cañada) you use three keys. First you hold down the Ctrl key plus a key to tell

FIGURE 9.12

Some of Word's commonly used special characters and their keyboard shortcuts.

Name	Sample	Keys	Notes
Angstroms	Å	Ctrl+@+A	
Bullet	•	Alt+0149	
Copyright	©	Alt+Ctrl+C	
Dagger	†	Alt+1034	
Degrees	°	Shift+Alt+1086	
Ellipsis	…	Alt+Ctrl+.	
em dash	—	Alt+Ctrl+Num-	Usually longer than hyphens
en dash	–	Ctrl+Num-	
Function, f-stop	ƒ	Alt+0131	
Logical not	¬	Alt+0172	
Mu (lowercase)	µ	Alt+0181	a/k/a Micro
Much greater than	»	Ctrl+`,>	Also European close quote
Much less than	«	Ctrl+`,<	Also European open quote
Cent sign	¢	Ctrl+/,c	
Paragraph mark	¶	Alt+0182	
Plus or minus	±	Alt+0177	
Pound (currency)	£	Alt+0163	Top row not keypad
Registered	®	Alt+Ctrl+R	
Section Mark	§	Alt+0167	
Single closed quote	'	Ctrl+','	
Single open quote	'	Ctrl+`,`	
Trademark	™	Alt+Ctrl+T	Top row not keypad
Yen (currency)	¥	Alt+0165	Top row not keypad

your computer which accent to apply, then you press the character key for the character you wish to accent. For example, to umlaut an o, do the following:

1. Hold down the Ctrl key and press the colon (:) key (don't forget to hold down the Shift key).
2. Release all three keys.
3. Press the o (or Shift+O) key to get a small (or capitalized) umlauted o (ö).

Incidentally, you can't accent just any old characters. Figure 9.13 shows you the possibilities and their key combinations.

FIGURE 9.13

Some of Word's accented characters and their keyboard shortcuts.

Name	Samples	Keys
Acute accent	áéíóú ÁÉÍÓÚ	Ctrl+'(apostrophe), letter
Circumflex	âêîôû ÂÊÎÔÛ	Ctrl+^ , letter
Dieresis	äëïöüÿ ÄËÏÖÜŸ	Ctrl+:, letter
Grave accent	àèìòù ÀÈÌÒÙ	Ctrl+`, letter
Tilde	ãñõ •ÃÑÕ	Ctrl+~, letter

▸▸ TIP

The keystroke combinations listed in Figure 9.13 are shortcuts. If you forget them, you can always locate and insert accented characters with the Insert ➤ Symbol... command.

▸ Wingdings and Dingbats

Add some spice to your life. Use the little pictures found in the Wingdings font instead of plain old bullets. Wingdings are also great as list separators and as border decorations. You've already seen examples back in Figure 9.10, and you'll see others in later chapters. Consider purchasing and installing other "dingbat" fonts, which are often found in shareware packages at very low cost. Use the Insert ➤ Symbol... command to see and insert them.

▸▸ Bulleted List Command

There's a button on the Standard Toolbar that looks like a bulleted list. It places plain old bullets in front of selected paragraphs and creates hanging indents (read about hanging indents in Chapter 10). The feature uses the current font.

▸ Bulleting Existing Paragraphs

To bullet existing paragraphs, follow these steps:

1. Select the paragraph or paragraphs you wish to format.
2. Click the Bulleted List button (it looks like three lines with boxes to their left). Word will create hanging intents and insert bullets in front of each selected paragraph.

Typing New Bulleted Lists

To type new bulleted lists, follow these steps:

1. Click the Bulleted List button on the Standard Toolbar or choose Format ➤ Bullets and Numbering. A bullet appears.
2. Type an entry and press ↵. A new bullet appears on the next line.
3. Repeat step 2 and continue until you've finished the list.
4. When finished, click the bullet button to deactivate the feature.

Changing Bullet Styles

Word for Windows offers an astonishing array of bullet list options. You can even choose your own, nonstandard bullet characters. Here are the general steps. Experiment to find combinations you like. Use the Bullets and Numbering dialog box shown in Figure 9.14.

1. Select your list if you've already typed it.
2. Choose Format ➤ Bullets and Numbering.
3. Click to pick a style you like.
4. Click OK to change the style of the selected list.
5. Type additional list items or a new list, as necessary.

FIGURE 9.14

Use this dialog box to modify the appearance of bulleted lists.

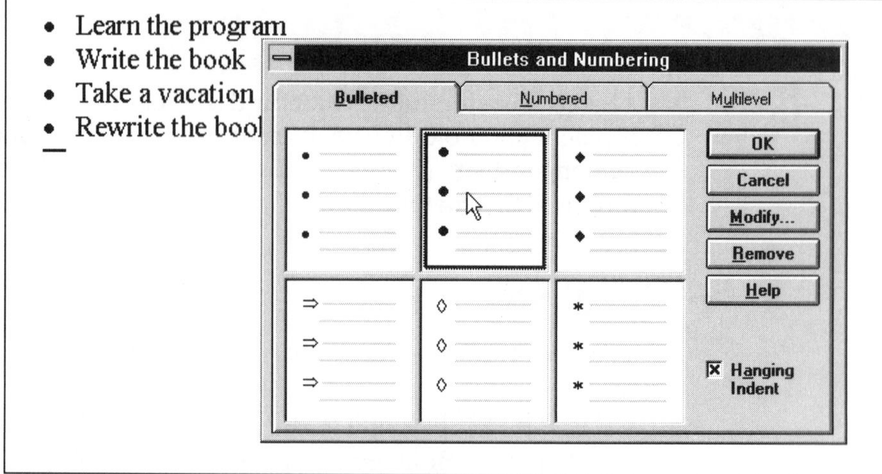

▸▸ Specifying Custom Bullets

Here's a nice way to spice up a dull list. Use Wingdings or other decorative characters instead of standard bullets:

1. Select your list if you've already typed it.
2. Choose Format ➤ Bullets and Numbering.
3. Click to pick a list style you like.
4. Click the Modify… button to reveal the Modify Bulleted List dialog box, shown in Figure 9.15.

FIGURE 9.15

Use this dialog box to change spacing and pick new bullet shapes.

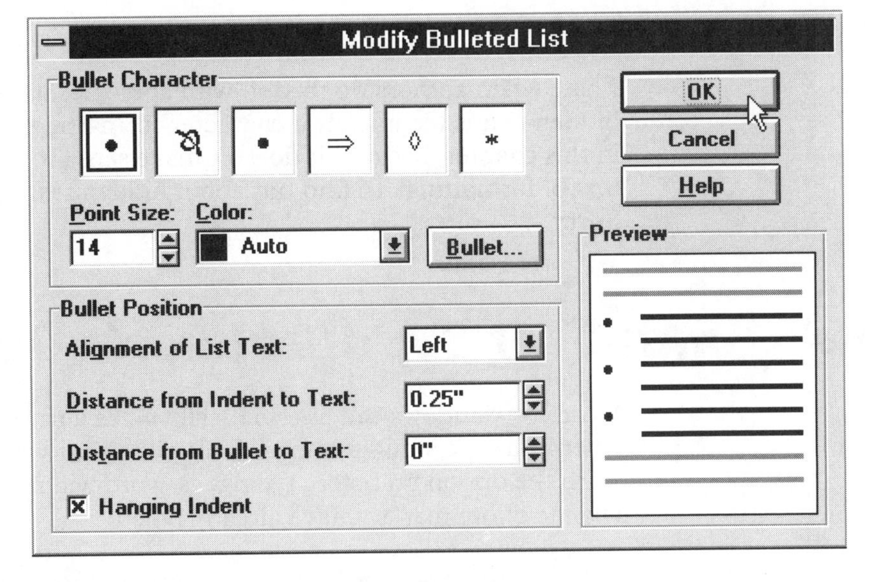

5. Change bullet positioning if you like by altering the dimensions in the Bullet Position area.
6. Pick a different type of bullet from the Bullet Character list.
7. To use bullets not shown in the Bullet Character box, click on the Bullet... button.
8. When you see the Symbol dialog box, pick a Font that has interesting characters (Symbol or Wingdings for instance).
9. Double-click to select the desired character to use as a bullet. Here are some examples from the Wingdings font:

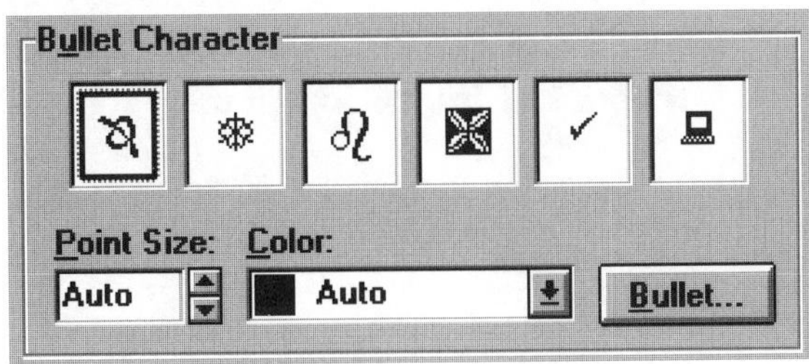

►► Hidden Text

I hate when authors do this, so with apologies, here goes. Even though hidden text is technically a character-formatting topic, it's not covered in this chapter, because it doesn't make sense to discuss it in the context of formatting. To find out about hidden text, see Chapter 28. Sorry....

►► "Smart" or Typographer's Quotes

Word for Windows can automatically place curly quotes in documents when you type straight quotes. This gives your work a typeset look. Turn the option on before typing, as Word will not automatically change quote marks you've already typed.

1. Use the Tools ➤ Options... command to display the Options dialog box.
2. Click on the AutoFormat tab to display the AutoFormat options.
3. Enable Smart Quotes by clicking to place an *X* in the option box.
4. Subsequently, when you type quotes, Word will convert them to curly opening and closing quotes (assuming that your chosen font has these characters).

►► TIP

If you are creating a document that you plan to export (for use with different word-processing software, perhaps), turn off the Smart Quotes feature before creating documents containing quotes. Otherwise you'll risk confusing the other folks with strange codes instead of quotation marks.

▶▶ Large Initial Caps, Drop Caps, and Dropped Words

Large initial caps are just what their name implies—big letters at the beginning of paragraphs. They are used as decorative flourishes. Drop caps are large initial caps that are dropped into a paragraph or into the margin next to a paragraph. They are often placed at the beginning of chapters and major topic transitions to catch your reader's eye. Dropped words are a variation on this technique. You create drop caps or dropped words by placing large initial caps or words in frames and positioning them to get the desired effect. Graphics can also be used as drop caps.

▶▶ **TIP**

You can use Word's Drop Cap... command to automate the process of creating drop caps and dropped words. Read about it in the following section.

Figure 9.16 shows a few examples. Read the text in each example to get an overview of how the effect was accomplished.

new

The process almost always looks easier than it is. It is very easy to fritter away the better part of a day lining up drop caps and the text they sit in. You'll often need to fiddle with paragraph formatting (line height and spacing settings), superscripts, subscripts, frame sizes, and font sizes. The new Drop Cap feature does a pretty good job of minimizing this, but there will still be times when you will be tearing your hair out.

▶ Using the Drop Cap Feature

You control drop caps from the dialog box shown in Figure 9.17. Reach it with the Format ➤ Drop Caps... command.

The Drop Cap... command is designed to work with single-spaced text only. It won't work in tables, headers, or footers. You won't be able to see the position of drop caps or create them in Outline view. You can't place drop caps in the margins of multicolumn documents, but you can place them within text in multicolumn documents. Narrow indents

FIGURE 9.16

Large initial caps and dropped words created using Frames, and character and paragraph formatting.

Word 's Drop Cap feature automatically creates frames, increases the size of the initial text and switches to Print Preview. It will place drop caps in the text or in the margin as shown here.

Drop caps can be created in a number of ways. This one was made by selecting just the letter D in 12 point New Century Schoolbook text and increasing it to 25 points. The D was framed with the Format menu's Frame... command. The Frame width was adjusted in the Frame dialog box. The D was then superscripted 6 points.

Large initial caps

Create these by choosing a larger type size for the first character. Minimize the resulting extra white space between the first and second lines by setting the lines' Space Before and Space After options to 0 points. You can use Frames to create similar effects.

Graphics can be used as drop caps too. This butterfly was pasted from the scrapbook, reduced in size, framed, then dragged into place from Print Preview. The From Text option was set to 0 in the Frame dialog box to tighten things.

Entire words can be dropped. This example was created with the Frame command on Word's Insert menu. First the word Entire was selected.

When you can't resist the urge to be decorative, consider using specialty fonts like Colonna MT shown here.

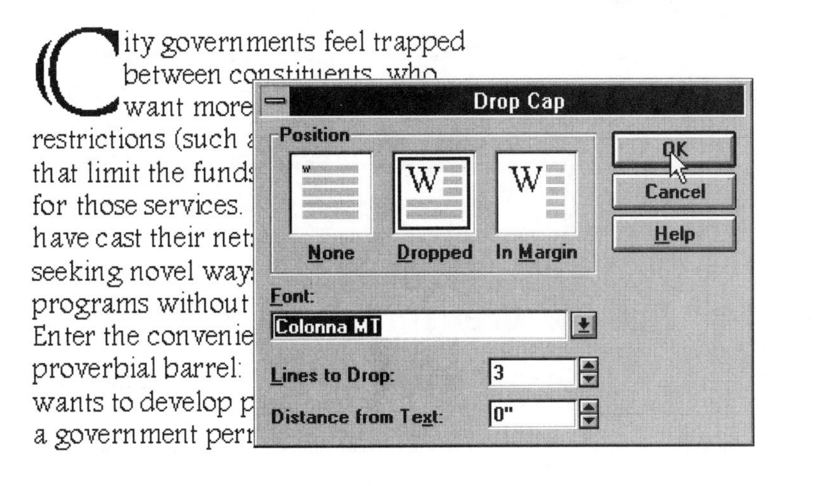

FIGURE 9.17

Automatic drop cap options are specified in the Drop Cap dialog box.

sometimes screw up the automatic drop cap feature. That said, here are the general steps:

1. Format the body text the way you like it. Be sure you are happy with things like margins, fonts, and so on. Single space the text.
2. Select the character or characters you want to drop and choose the Format ➤ Drop Cap… command. If you are not in Page Layout view, Word will prompt you to switch. You'll see the Drop Cap dialog box illustrated in Figure 9.17.
3. If you want to use a different font for the drop cap, choose it from the drop-down Font menu.
4. The Height box proposes the number of lines the cap will drop. For instance, 3 li means that the drop cap will be three lines tall and drop alongside the first three lines of text. Pick the desired number of lines from the drop-down line list, or alternately, type in an exact point size for the drop cap (36 pt, for instance).
5. Choose the Dropped Position option for traditional-looking drop caps or choose the In Margin choice to place drops in the margin.
6. When you click OK, Word places the specified text into a frame and positions the frame for you.
7. Use the character, frame, and paragraph tools, if you dare, to modify Word's settings.

▸▸ TIP

You can use the Format ➤ Drop Cap... command to drop graphics as well. Paste a graphic at the beginning of a line of text, drag, and if necessary, make it reasonably small. Then, with the graphic selected, use Format ➤ Drop Cap....

▸ Tips for Creating Drop Caps

When creating drop caps, keep the following in mind:

- Do text formatting, make font decisions, and spell check before you create drop caps.
- When using the Format ➤ Frame... command, remember to specify a frame width so that text can flow around your drop cap.
- To remove the excess space that often appears beneath a drop cap frame, use negative line spacing (space less than the point size of the type being dropped) and subscripting, as you saw in the preceding example.
- To remove excess space to the right of frames, use the From Text option in the Frame dialog box.

▸▸ Deleting Drop Caps

If you've just created a drop cap with the automatic Drop Cap... command, Edit ➤ Undo will delete it. Otherwise you'll need to take the following general steps:

1. With paragraph marks displayed, delete the paragraph mark just to the right of the drop cap. This will unframe the letter and place it back with the rest of its partners.
2. Change the letter's size, font, and other characteristics to match the rest of the text.

▶▶ Typing Nonbreaking Spaces

In order to keep multiple words on the same line (someone's title and first and last name, for instance), you can use special spaces called *nonbreaking* spaces. To do this, simply hold down the Ctrl and Shift keys when you press the Spacebar.

▶▶ Typing Hyphens and Dashes

To type hyphens, simply use the minus key (to the right of the zero key at the top of your keyboard). Hyphens typed this way will always print.

▶ Typing Nonbreaking Hyphens

Nonbreaking hyphens keep hyphenated words together on the same line. Never press the minus key (-) to enter a nonbreaking hyphen! Instead, hold down the Ctrl and Shift keys and press the hyphen on the main keyboard.

▶ Typing Em and En Dashes

Em dashes are used to indicate an abrupt change of thought—or did you know that already? People often confuse hyphens and dashes. Type the longer em dashes by holding down Alt+Ctrl+- (the minus key on the numeric pad). In some fonts em dashes are very long and obvious. That's not always the case, though.

Incidentally, em dashes get their name from their width. In most fonts an em dash is the length of a letter *m*. That's an easy way to remember what it's called. Shorter en dashes can be created with Ctrl+- (the minus key on the numeric pad).

▶▶ TIP

While dashes should always be longer than hyphens, in a few fonts they are not. You are not losing your mind after all. It's a feature.

► Typing Optional Hyphens

An optional hyphen will always be displayed whenever you have the Show Paragraph feature enabled, but it will print only if the word it is in sits on the right margin. Most people use Word's automatic hyphenation feature to enter optional hyphens, but you can enter them from the keyboard. Hold down the Ctrl key and press the minus key (-) on the main keyboard (not the one on the numeric pad).

►► TIP

If you still have trouble remembering what's where, use the Special Characters tab in the Symbol dialog box, reached with the Insert ➤ Symbol… command.

►► Automatic Optional Hyphenation

Word for Windows has an automatic feature that will work with you to place optional hyphens in words, based on certain built-in rules and a hyphenation dictionary. You can supervise the process or let Word for Windows take things into its own hands. If you use it, there are some things you will want to do first.

►► WARNING

Optional hyphenation is one of the last things you want to do when preparing a document. Finish *everything* else that affects line endings first. Otherwise, you will need to rehyphenate repeatedly.

► Preparing to Hyphenate

Be sure that your document is complete and properly organized. Do the spelling check. Polish the appearance of your text (fonts, sizes, character expansion, etc.). Remove extra spaces. Apply justification, if that's part of your plan. Break the document into sections if you need them. Set up columns. Have someone else proofread your work one last time.

You may, however, want to hold off on final page-break decisions until after hyphenation.

▶ Entering Optional Hyphens

Word for Windows will hyphenate an entire document or just selected text. When you choose Tools ➤ Hyphenation…, Word will open a small dialog box like the one in Figure 9.18. Choose automatic or manual hyphenation.

Working from the insertion point, Word for Windows will move through your document (or selected text) looking for a possible word to hyphenate. In Figure 9.19 it has found the word *reminded*.

If you've chosen manual hyphenation, you will see a dialog box offering several alternatives. The Yes button will place an optional hyphen between the *e* and *m*. The No button tells Word not to hyphenate this word and to continue. Cancel exits the hyphenation.

Optionally, you can move the hyphenation point yourself. Use your mouse to point to where you want to place the hyphen. Press the mouse button once. A nonblinking pointer will appear between the characters you've chosen. Click on the Yes button to place the optional hyphen and continue the automatic search.

FIGURE 9.18 ▶

The hyphenation dialog box.

Those priceless few moments before the sun sets always remind him of fine brandy or New England in the fall. Everything and everyone around the two of them was bathed in orange and red and hues without names. Photographers call it *magic light.*

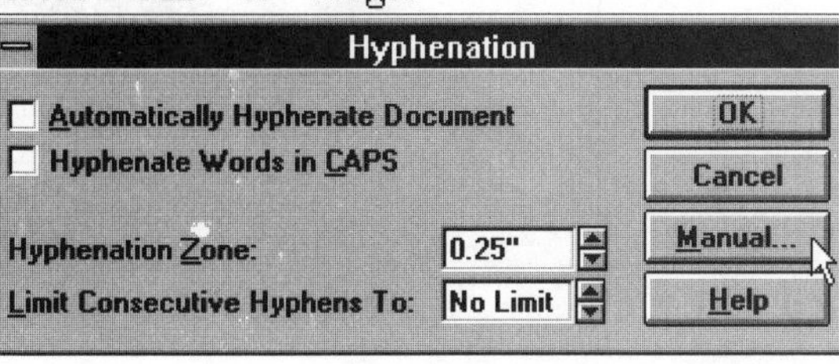

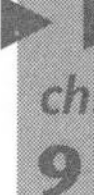

FIGURE 9.19

Word is suggesting that reminded be hyphenated between the e *and the* m.

Those priceless few moments before the sun sets always re-
mind him of fine brandy or New England in the fall. Everything and everyone around the two of them was bathed in orange and red and hues without names. Photographers call it *magic light.*
Manual Hyphenation: English (US)
Hyphenate At: re-mind
Yes
No
Cancel
Help

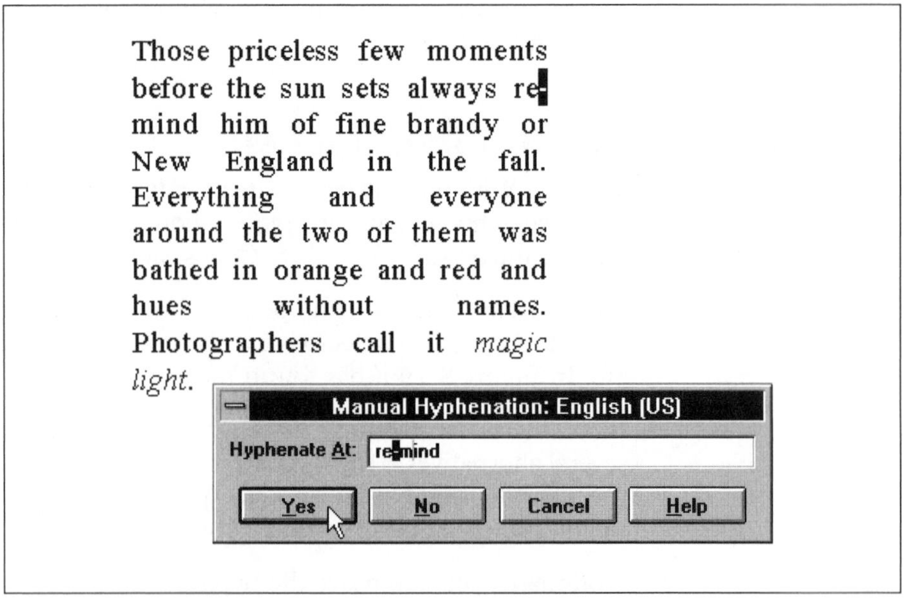

As you can see from Figure 9.20, Word suggested several hyphenation points in our example. It is proposing an awkward hyphenation.

FIGURE 9.20

Word's automatic hyphenation may not solve all your problems.

Those priceless few moments before the sun sets always re-
mind him of fine brandy or New England in the fall. Every-
thing and everyone around the two of them was bathed in or-
ange and red and hues without names. Photographers call it *magic light.*
Manual Hyphenation: English (US)
Hyphenate At: or-ange
Yes
No
Cancel
Help

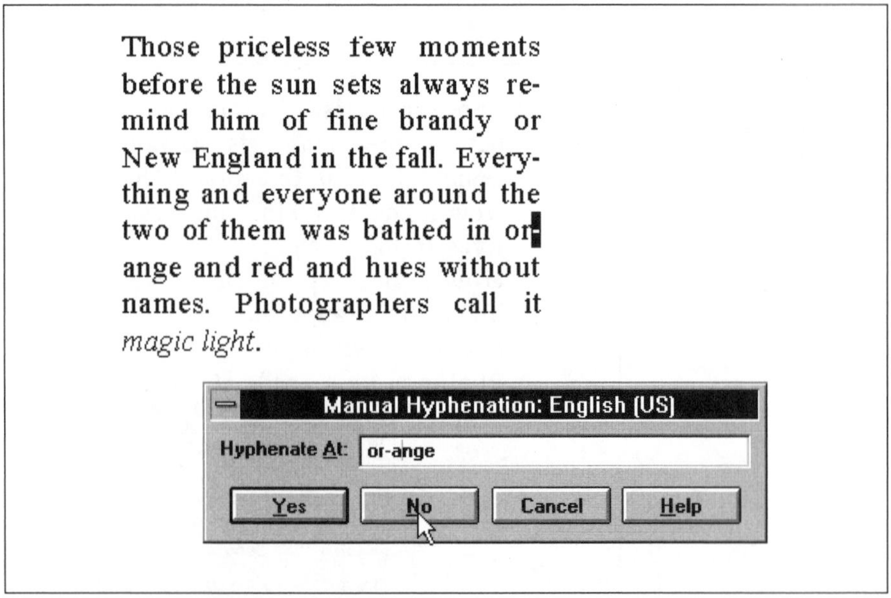

Some editors and style manuals will tell you not to hyphenate words in ways that leave only one syllable on a line, yet Word has done just that. There are few hard-and-fast hyphenation rules.

Rejecting the suggested hyphen in *orange* creates a much nicer-looking paragraph, as you can see in Figure 9.21. The combination of manual and automatic hyphenation even found a home for the widow.

FIGURE 9.21 

Adding a few hyphens really improves the final appearance of the paragraph.

Those priceless few moments before the sun sets always re-mind him of fine brandy or New England in the fall. Every-thing and everyone around the two of them was bathed in orange and red and hues with-out names. Photographers call it *magic light.*

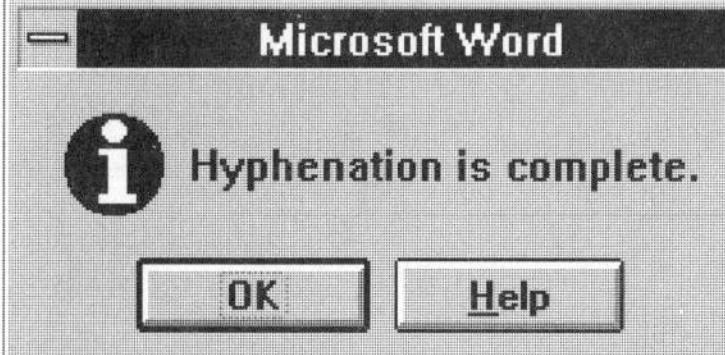

▶▶ TIP

If you like tight copy, you may want to run the auto-hyphenation feature and then fine-tune a bit by hand.

▶ Removing Automatic Hyphens

The Edit ➤ Undo Hyphenation (Ctrl+Z) command will be available to remove optional hyphens if you use it immediately after you run the auto-hyphenation feature. You can delete hyphens like any other charac-ter. Select them and cut or delete. Word's Find and Replace features will also help you delete hyphens of all sorts. See Chapter 20 for details.

▶ ▶ CHAPTER 10

Paragraphs, Line Spacing, Borders, and Shading

▸▸ Fast Track

To create a paragraph **_276_**

press the ↵ key.

To split a long paragraph into two or more smaller paragraphs **_277_**

position the insertion point where you want to break the paragraph and press ↵. Watch out for extraneous spaces!

To join two paragraphs together into one **_278_**

select the paragraph mark that separates them and press the **spacebar**. Look out for extra spaces or tabs.

To force a new line without creating a new paragraph **_278_**

press **Shift+↵**. This inserts a *new line* mark, pushing text down to the next line, but does *not* create a new paragraph. This can be important when you are working with sophisticated styles.

To delete a paragraph **_279_**

double-click in the left margin to select the doomed paragraph and press the **Backspace** key. This will delete the paragraph *and* its ¶ mark. Alternately, you can select all text in the paragraph except the ¶ delete it, which will leave the ¶ mark with its formatting information.

To modify the appearance of paragraphs **_279_**

use the ruler, the Formatting Toolbar, and the Paragraph dialog box.

To quickly modify the appearance of paragraphs **284**

use one of Word's paragraph-formatting shortcut key combinations.

To indent paragraphs automatically **284**

drag the top half of the triangular indent marker to the right to the desired position (**Ctrl+M**) or enter a setting in the First Line indent box in the Paragraph dialog box.

To increase or decrease the indents on selected paragraphs by one tab stop **287**

use the Increase Indent and Decrease Indent buttons on the Formatting Toolbar.

To create hanging indents **289**

drag the top half of the triangular indent marker to the left to the desired position (**Ctrl+Shift+M**), or enter a setting in the First Line indent box (in the Paragraph dialog box) that is *farther* left than the indent of the paragraph as a whole. Alternately, click the Numbered (list) button or the Bullets (list) button on the Formatting Toolbar, which automatically creates a hanging indent.

To specify the alignment of selected paragraphs **290**

use one of the four paragraph alignment buttons on the Formatting Toolbar.

To apply borders and shading to paragraphs **296**

use the Borders and Shading dialog box (Format ➤ Borders and Shading…) or the Borders Toolbar.

▶▶ In this chapter we'll explore Word's paragraph-formatting tools, which you will use for adjustable line spacing, indentation, and text alignment. You'll see how to use Word's border features to create boxes and lines. Paragraph numbering, shading, and sorting are also discussed. You can save complex sets of formatting decisions as styles, as you'll see in Chapter 14.

▶▶ Word's Paragraphs

Your English teachers taught you that paragraphs are collections of sentences on a related topic. Word for Windows uses a somewhat more liberal definition. A Word paragraph can be a single text character, a graphic, or even a blank line consisting only of the paragraph mark (¶), which appears in your document when you press the ↵ key. Paragraph-formatting features are an important part of Word's arsenal. Figure 10.1 contains five Word for Windows paragraphs, each ending with a paragraph mark. Can you find them all?

Each Word for Windows paragraph in your document can be uniquely formatted and need not contain text. For instance, the first paragraph in Figure 10.1 is single spaced with the first line indented about 1/2". The next paragraph is right-justified. The third paragraph is a blank line created by pressing just the ↵ key. The fourth paragraph is centered. The final paragraph is a graphic (without text), followed by a paragraph mark. Notice that this last paragraph (the graphic) has been centered.

▶ Creating Paragraphs

Each time you press the ↵ key you create a new paragraph. It's that simple. When you open a new document, Word for Windows applies

A·Word·paragraph·can·be·a·single·text·character,·a·graphic,·or·even·a·blank·line.¶
They·can·have·different·formats¶
¶
There·are·five·paragraphs·in·this·example·Can·you·find·them·all?¶
¶

FIGURE 10.1 *Word paragraphs always end with a paragraph mark (¶).*

the default paragraph settings stored as a style called Normal. It formats each new paragraph the same way until and unless you tell it to do otherwise.

Splitting Text into Multiple Paragraphs

If you want to split a lengthy section of text into two or more paragraphs, follow these steps:

1. Place the insertion point where you want the new paragraph to begin. (Be careful not to include unwanted spaces when splitting text.)
2. Press ↵. The text will split, and you'll see a paragraph mark if the Show ¶ feature is enabled. Note that the new paragraph will take on the characteristics of the one above. For instance, if the original big paragraph had a first line indent, the two little ones will too.

Notice how, in Figure 10.2, the new paragraph takes on the same indentation characteristics as the preceding one.

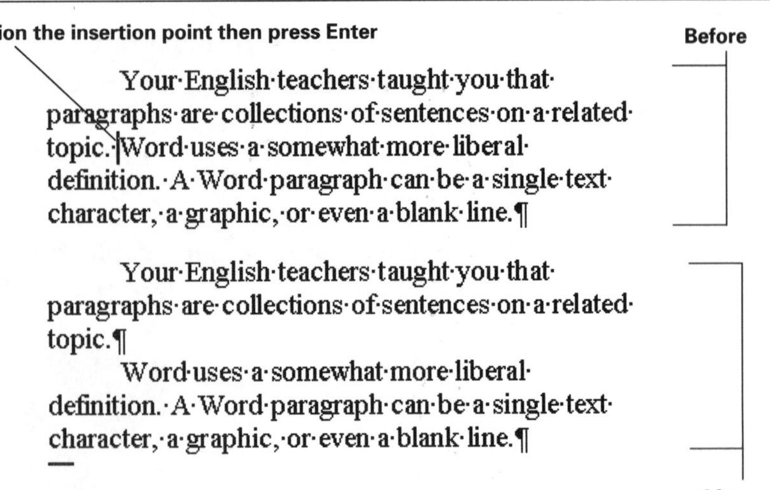

FIGURE 10.2 ▶

To split one paragraph into two or more paragraphs, position the insertion point (watching for unwanted spaces) and press ↵.

▶ Joining Paragraphs

It's easy to turn two paragraphs into one. Just delete the interceding paragraph mark and add any necessary space to separate the new neighbors. For instance, to rejoin the two short paragraphs in Figure 10.2, you'll need a space between the period after the word *topic* and the *W* in *Word*. The quick way to join these two paragraphs would be to select the unwanted paragraph mark and type a space to replace it. Follow these steps:

1. Turn on the Show ¶ feature to make things easier.
2. Delete the paragraph mark between the two paragraphs, adding space if necessary. Text above will take on the appearance of text below if the two paragraphs originally had different paragraph formatting.

▶ Forcing New Lines without Using Paragraphs

Sometimes you'll want to force a new line without creating a new paragraph. The reasons will become more apparent as you start to use advanced Word for Windows features like paragraph numbering and styles with Next Style options, so tuck this trivia nugget away. To force new lines without creating new paragraphs, use the Shift-↵ key combination. Instead of a paragraph symbol, you'll see arrows like the ones in Figure 10.3.

FIGURE 10.3 

Use the Shift-↵ feature to force new lines without starting a new paragraph.

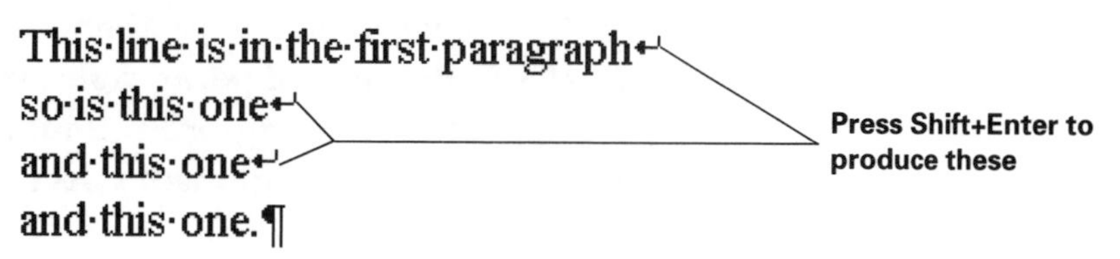

Deleting Paragraphs

Think twice when deleting paragraphs. You can delete just the contents of a paragraph or delete the contents and the paragraph marker. If you delete the marker, text above the old paragraph will take on the characteristics of the remaining paragraph below it. This is by design and is not a bug. If you accidentally delete a paragraph mark and create a problem, Undo (Ctrl+Z) will usually return your heart rate to normal.

Adding Blank Lines between Paragraphs

You can create blank lines, typewriter style, by just mashing on the ↵ key all day. But hey, it's almost the year 2000. Instead, create white space between paragraphs, rather than adding blank lines. Use the Paragraph dialog box. As you'll soon see, this will give you better control over spacing between paragraphs and make it easier to keep paragraphs together. Read on.

Paragraph Formatting

You modify the appearance of paragraphs using the ruler, the Formatting Toolbar, and the Paragraph dialog box. The ruler and Formatting Toolbar are easy to use and readily available. When precise formatting is required, consider using the Paragraph dialog box rather than the ruler. Some formatting features have keyboard shortcuts.

If you want to reformat only one paragraph, simply place the insertion point anywhere within the paragraph, then make formatting changes. There is no need to select the text in a single paragraph. To alter multiple paragraphs, select them first. Your changes will affect all selected paragraphs, including any partially selected paragraphs. Double-clicking at the left edge of a paragraph will select it.

As we did in the previous chapter, let's start with a quick tour of the paragraph-formatting tools, then we'll look at some everyday paragraph-formatting tasks.

▸ Formatting with the Formatting Toolbar

The Formatting Toolbar contains a number of handy paragraph-formatting tools. If it is not showing, bring it into view with the View ➤ Toolbars… command. Figure 10.4 shows you the location and function of the ruler's paragraph-related features.

You must tell Word for Windows which paragraph or paragraphs you wish to format before using the Formatting Toolbar's tools. If you have only one paragraph selected, or if all of the selected paragraphs have identical paragraph-formatting options, activated paragraph options

FIGURE 10.4 ▸

The Formatting Toolbar places paragraph-formatting tools at your fingertips and also shows many paragraph settings options.

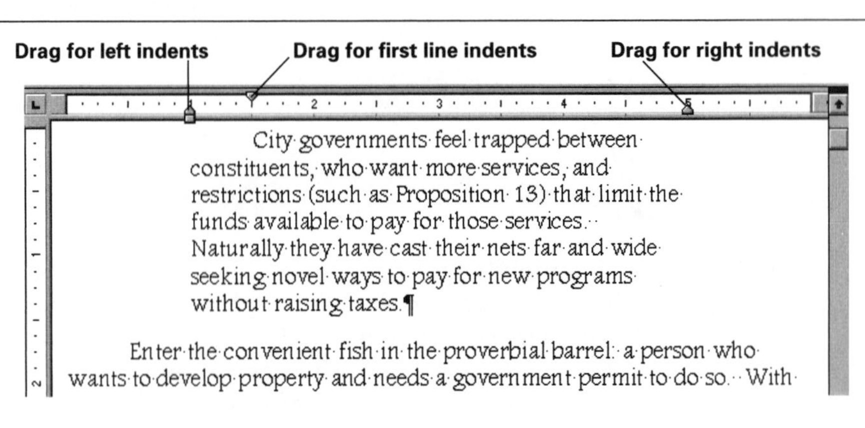

(like center) will be indicated with depressed buttons. But if you select dissimilar paragraphs, these indicators will not be accurate.

Moreover, if you select two dissimilar paragraphs (like those in Figure 10.4), you'll see subtle changes on the ruler. Indent handles will have dim outer edges, for instance. This is Word's way of saying it can't display two different settings at once.

▶ Formatting with the Toolbar

Paragraph buttons on the Formatting Toolbar include Align Left, Center, Align Right, Justify, Numbering (lists), Bullets (lists), Decrease Indent, Increase Indent, and Borders. Figure 10.5 shows the buttons. You've seen some examples of these buttons at work already.

FIGURE 10.5 

Paragraph-formatting buttons on the Toolbar.

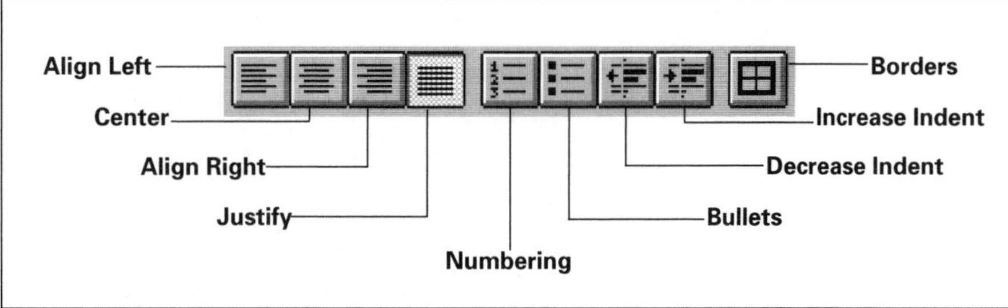

▶ Formatting with the Paragraph Dialog Box

The Paragraph dialog box shown in Figure 10.6 is reached by choosing Format ➤ Paragraph....

 **TIP**

Double-clicking on any indent marker will bring up the Paragraph dialog box!

FIGURE 10.6

Reach the Paragraph dialog box from the Format menu or via hotspots. Both tabs are shown here.

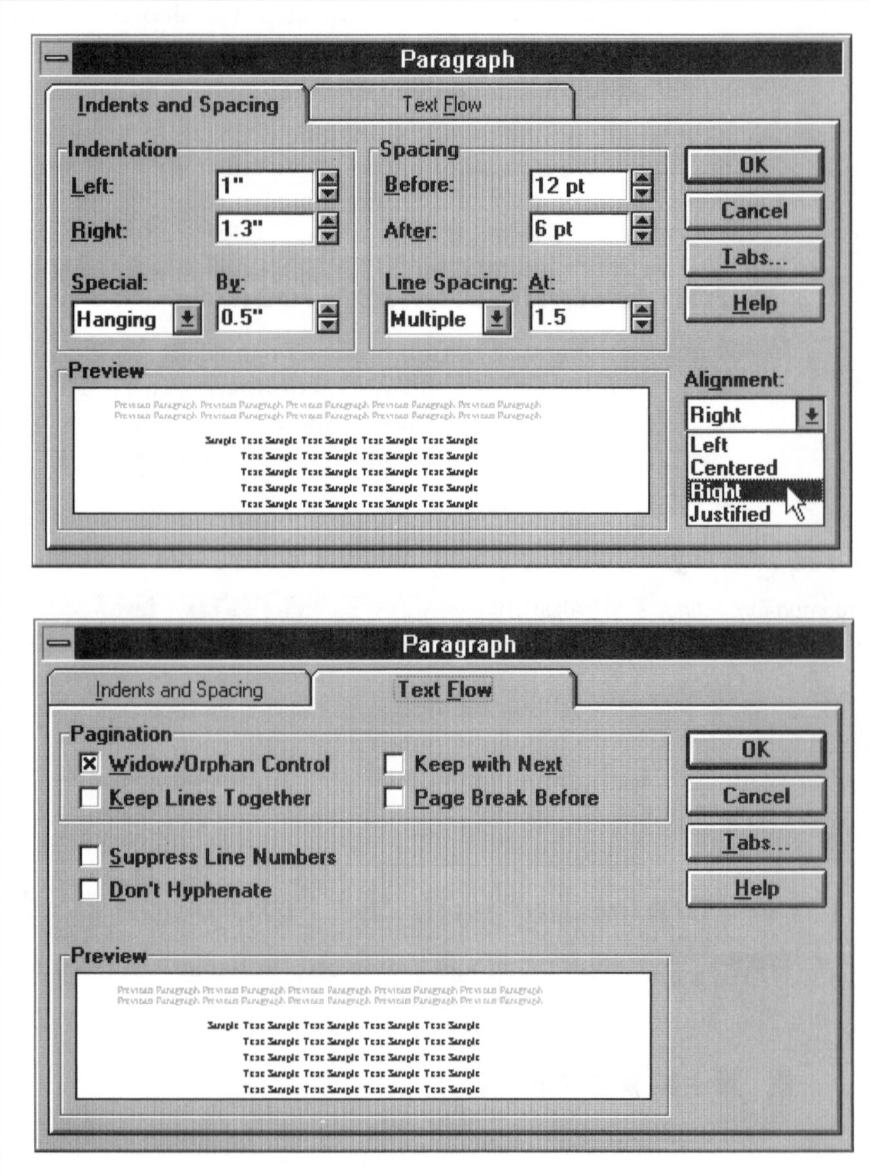

The Paragraph dialog box lets you:

- Precisely specify inter-line spacing (single, double, etc.)
- Precisely specify inter-paragraph spacing (space before and after paragraphs)
- Dictate exact indentation measurements
- Turn off line numbering for specific paragraphs
- Specify text alignment (left, centered, right, or justified)
- Specify text-flow guidelines (widows, orphans, etc.)
- Suppress hyphenation

When you enter measurements in the Paragraph dialog box, you can often use different units of measure for the same specification. For instance, you can specify line height in points (pt), lines (li), inches (in), picas (pi), or centimeters (cm). Each possible numeric entry in the Paragraph dialog box has a default unit of measure, which is shown in each entry box.

NOTE

Line Spacing shows a unit of measure when you select At Least or Exactly. When you select Multiple, you can enter a number and Word will assume you mean *li*.

WARNING

It is possible to make entries in the Paragraph dialog box without specifying units of measure if you know the default unit of measure for each type of entry. For instance, the default for line spacing is points. Here's the rub. If you enter *2*, Word for Windows will assume you mean 2 points, not double spacing. To specify double spacing, you'd need to enter *2 li*. When you are uncertain about the default unit of measure for a paragraph specification, to play it safe, always enter the abbreviation for the unit of measure.

In United States Word versions, the default for horizontal measurements, such as indents, is inches. The default unit of measure for line and paragraph spacing is points. (There are 72 points per inch.)

► Keyboard Formatting Shortcuts

There are numerous keyboard shortcuts for paragraph formatting. They are mentioned throughout this chapter and summarized in Appendix C.

A few keyboard shortcuts are additive. That is to say, instead of toggling, when you press them more than once, they increase their effect. For example, pressing Ctrl+M indents a paragraph ½" from the left; pressing it twice indents the paragraph 1"; and so on.

► Specifying Paragraph Formats

As promised, here are the steps for applying paragraph formats and everyday examples. Don't forget that it is possible to store and quickly recreate complex paragraph formats using Styles, as described in Chapter 14.

►► Indenting Paragraphs Automatically

There are a number of ways to indent paragraphs. Indents are *added* to margins, thereby increasing the white space and decreasing the text area for specific paragraphs. Thus, if you have a 1.0" right margin and specify a right indent of 1.0", your text will print 2.0" from the right edge of the paper.

►► **WARNING**

Don't confuse indenting with aligning. Aligning paragraphs is covered later in this chapter. Also, don't confuse indenting with margins.

The first line of each paragraph can be indented differently from other lines in the paragraph. First lines can be shorter than the others, creating regular indents, or longer than the others, creating *hanging* indents (sometimes called outdents). Once you change indents, each new paragraph you start by pressing ↵ will maintain the same indentation settings until you change them. Indented paragraphs can have other paragraph formatting as well. Figure 10.7 shows several indenting examples.

TIP

Whenever you place the insertion point in a paragraph, the indent markers on the ruler move to show you the setting for the current paragraph.

FIGURE 10.7

Several examples of paragraph indenting.

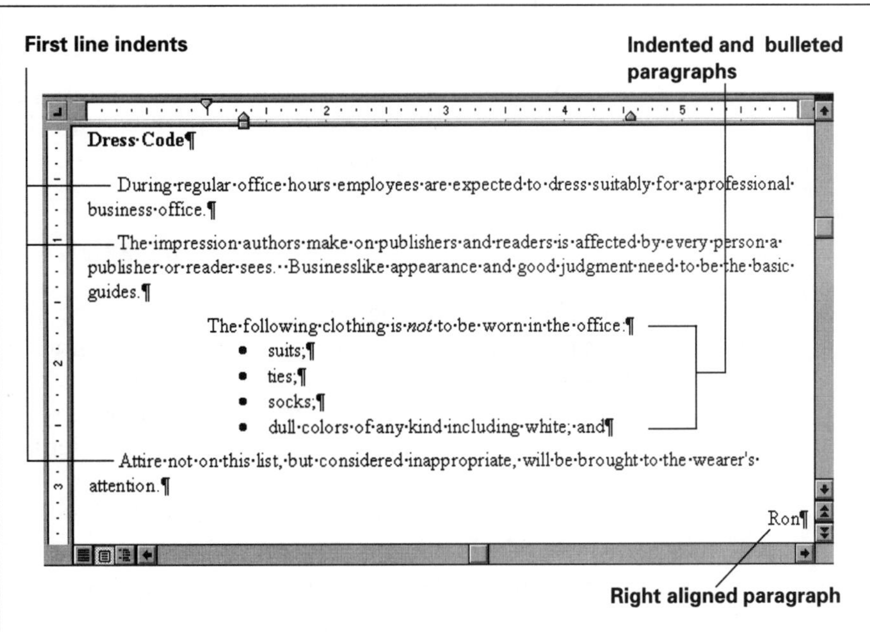

► Indenting with the Ruler

The quickest way to indent is to drag indent markers on the ruler. To adjust left and right paragraph indents from the ruler:

1. Place the insertion point in a paragraph or select multiple paragraphs.
2. Point to and then drag the appropriate triangular indent markers to the desired locations. (Drag on the bottom part of the left marker to set the overall left indentation.)

3. Watch the ruler's scale as you drag. It shows the position of the indent mark in relation to its respective margin. The bottom part of the left marker is divided by a black line. Click on the upper portion of the bottom part to move it independently of the other part.
4. You will see the text move when you release the mouse button.
5. Whenever you place the insertion point in a paragraph, the indent markers on the ruler move as necessary to show you the setting for the current paragraph.

► Indenting with the Paragraph Dialog Box

The Paragraph dialog box lets you type in specifications for right, left, first line, and hanging indents. The default dimension in the United States is inches (in). By including the appropriate unit of measurement with your entry, you can specify points (pt), picas (pi), or centimeters (cm) instead. To adjust left and right paragraph indents from the dialog box:

1. Place the insertion point in a paragraph or select multiple paragraphs.
2. Open the Paragraph Dialog box with the Format ➤ Paragraph… command or double-click on a hotspot.
3. Enter specifications for right, left, and/or first line indents.
4. You will see the effects of your changes in the Preview box. Click OK when you are happy with the indentation.

5. Once you move indent markers, each new paragraph you start by pressing ↵ will maintain the same indentation settings until you change them.

Indenting with Keyboard Shortcuts

There are keyboard shortcuts that move the left indent marker. These are additive commands and can create nested paragraphs.

Center	Ctrl+E
Justify	Ctrl+J
Left align	Ctrl+L
Right align	Ctrl+R
Left indent	Ctrl+M
Remove left indent	Ctrl+Shift+M
Create hanging indent	Ctrl+T
Reduce hanging indent	Ctrl+Shift+T

Indenting with the Toolbar

new

The Increase Indent Toolbar button moves the left indent marker to the right the distance of one standard tab stop, and the Decrease Indent button moves it back the same distance. These are additive commands. Pressing Increase Indent twice indents farther than pressing it once. There are no Toolbar buttons for the right indent marker.

Indents in Margins

It is possible to specify indentations that print in the right and/or left margins. Specify negative margin settings in the paragraph dialog box (-0.5 in for instance) or drag indent markers into margins. Be patient. Horizontal scrolling is required when you drag indent markers into margins, and the process can sometimes be slow.

► Indenting First Lines

You can indent the first line of a paragraph with the ruler, the Paragraph dialog box, or tabs. Tabs are generally the least efficient method.

First-Line Indenting with the Ruler

To set up automatic first-line indenting with the ruler, follow these steps:

1. Place the insertion point in a paragraph or select multiple paragraphs.
2. Drag the top half of the left indent marker. The text moves when you release the mouse button, and subsequently typed paragraphs will indent the same way.

First-Line Indenting with the Paragraph Dialog Box

To set up automatic first-line indenting with the Paragraph dialog box, follow these steps:

1. Place the insertion point in a paragraph or select multiple paragraphs.
2. Open the Paragraph dialog box (choose Format ➤ Paragraph... or double-click on an indent marker in the ruler).
3. In the Special box, select First Line from the drop-down list and specify a first-line indent dimension in points (pt), inches (in), picas (pi), or centimeters (cm). Watch the preview to see the effect without closing the dialog box.
4. Click OK when you are happy with the indent.

First-Line Indenting with the Tab Key

You can create first-line indents with the Tab key. But it's extra work, because you'll need to remember to tab each time you start a new paragraph. Use the ruler trick instead. You'll like it.

▶ Hanging Indents

Sometimes it is desirable to have the first line in each paragraph stick out. This is particularly useful for creating bulleted lists, numbered paragraphs, bibliographies, and so forth. The first line in a hanging indent is called (cleverly) a *hanging indent*. The subsequent lines beneath are called *turnover* lines. Figure 10.8 shows some examples.

FIGURE 10.8

Some examples of hanging indents.

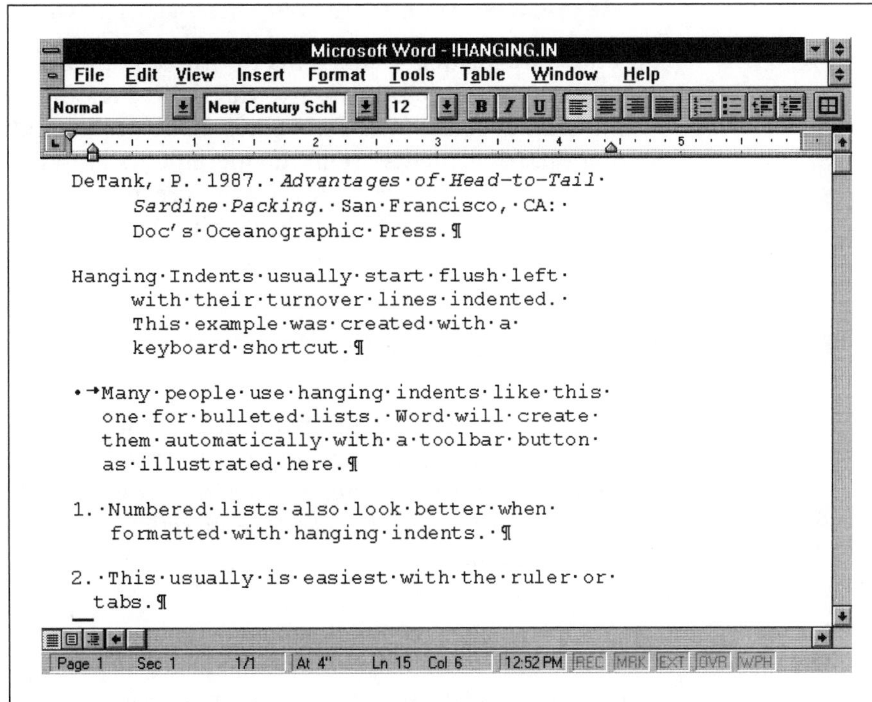

Hanging Indents with the Ruler

When creating hanging indents from the ruler, follow these steps:

1. Place the insertion point in the paragraph you need to format, select multiple paragraphs, or place the insertion point where you plan to begin typing hanging-indented paragraphs.
2. Set the position of the left (indented) edge of the turnover lines. To do this, with the ruler in view, drag the bottom half of the left indent marker to the right.

3. If you plan to indent the right edge of your paragraph(s), drag the right indent marker either now or later.
4. To create the hanging indent, drag the top half of the left indent marker to the left, past the turnover indent, and release the mouse button when you reach the desired point. The ruler will scroll to show you the hanging indent's position with relation to the rest of the paragraph.

Keyboard Shortcuts for Hanging Indents

There are keyboard shortcuts for moving the left indent. Use Ctrl+M to move the left tab marker to the right. Pressing Ctrl+Shift+M moves the marker to the left. Ctrl+Shift+N moves the indent back to the left margin. Movements are in the increments used for default tab settings (usually $^1/_2$"). This is a great way to create nested indents! (Note that neither Ctrl+Shift+N nor Ctrl+Shift+M will go past the left margin.)

▸▸ Aligning and Justifying Text

The four Formatting Toolbar buttons that look like lines of text let you quickly justify, center, and right- and left-align. The lines in the buttons demonstrate the expected results. As always, you must first either select multiple paragraphs or place the insertion point in the paragraph you want to align.

▸ Left Alignment

Left alignment is Word's default. Text sits right up against the paragraph's left indent position. If you have specified a first-line indent, the left alignment feature does not override it. Instead, it uses the specified first-line setting, then left-aligns the remaining text.

▸ Centering

Clicking the Center button places the text or graphics smack dab between the indent markers for the paragraph being centered. If you want to center things between document margins, be sure the left and right indent markers are sitting on their respective document margins.

Moving the first-line indent marker will affect centering.

Never use spaces to center. Always type words at the left margin then click the Center button.

▶ Right Alignment

Clicking on the Align Right button places selected items flush against the right indent position for the paragraph. Use this feature for correspondence dates, inside addresses, and for added impact.

If you want to right-align things with the document's right margin, be sure the paragraph's right indent marker is sitting on the right document margin.

The first-line indent feature works in conjunction with right-aligned text. That is to say, text can be both right-aligned and have the first line indented.

▶ Justifying Text

Clicking on the Justify button causes Word for Windows to add space between words in the selected paragraphs. This results in what some people consider to be a typeset look.

With the exception of the last line in a paragraph, all of the justified lines will have exactly the same length and will all be flush left *and* right with the paragraph's left and right indent markers. Justified text can also have the first line indented.

If the uneven spacing and rivers of white space caused by justification annoy you, consider inserting hyphens to tighten up the text. See Chapter 9 for details.

►► Adjusting the Space between Lines

The Indents and Spacing tab of the Paragraph dialog box provides a drop-down list for simple but effective control of the space between lines under most circumstances. The preview area demonstrates the relative effect of single, one-and-a-half, and double line spacing. Single spacing causes 12-point line spacing, $1\frac{1}{2}$-line spacing is 18 points, and double-spaced lines will be 24 points apart. (There is little or no effect for text larger than 24 points.)

When you use these choices, Word for Windows will compensate for graphics, superscripts, and large or small type sizes. To force exact line spacing, use the At Least or Exactly choices described in a moment.

► Single Spacing Text

To single space text, follow these steps:

1. Single spacing is Word's default spacing. To reapply it to text spaced some other way, place the insertion point in a paragraph or select multiple paragraphs.
2. Press Ctrl+1 or choose Single in the Paragraph dialog box's Line Spacing menu. Selected text and subsequent typing will be single spaced.

► Double Spacing Text

To double space text, follow these steps:

1. To apply double spacing to text spaced some other way, place the insertion point in a paragraph or select multiple paragraphs.
2. Press Ctrl+2 or choose Double in the Paragraph dialog box's Line Spacing menu. Selected text and subsequent typing will be double spaced.

▶ Line-and-a-Half Spacing

To apply line and a half spacing to text spaced some other way, follow these steps:

1. Place the insertion point in a paragraph or select multiple paragraphs.
2. Press Ctrl+5 or choose 1.5 lines in the Paragraph dialog box's Line Spacing menu. Selected text and subsequent typing will be one-and-a-half line spaced.

▶ Specifying Exact Line Heights

Word for Windows automatically sets the appropriate amount of white space between lines for you unless you tell it to do otherwise. It even compensates for different-size characters on the same line by setting line spacing to the largest character.

But sometimes, you'll want to specify exact line spacing for one or more paragraphs. Increasing the spacing by a nonstandard amount can help you fill unused space when your copy runs a little short. Or, specifying slightly less than normal space between lines can help keep that last lonesome line from printing on its own page.

It's the Paragraph dialog box you need to visit. Here you tell Word for Windows you want At Least or Exactly a specified amount of space.

1. Place the insertion point in a paragraph or select multiple paragraphs.
2. Open the Paragraph dialog box (choose Format ➤ Paragraph... or double-click on any indent marker).
3. Choose Exactly or At Least from the drop-down list.
4. Enter a specification and a unit of measure (2.5 li, 26 pt, 1.5 in, 22 cm, etc.) in the At box. Watch the preview as you work.
5. Click OK to make the specified spacing change.

▶▶ TIP

If the tops or bottoms of characters are cut off, you may have set a line height that is too small. Revisit the Paragraph dialog box and increase the height.

▸▸ Space before and after Paragraphs

Many people place white space between paragraphs by pressing the ↵ key several times—typewriter style. While this works just fine, there is a preferred method.

new

The Paragraph dialog box (Format ➤ Paragraph…) has an area in the Indents and Spacing tab called *Spacing*. It lets you define the amount of white space Word places before and after paragraphs. You can enter spacing settings in points (pt), inches (in), centimeters (cm), or lines (li). Thus, 12 points would be entered as *12pt*, 25 centimeters would be entered as *25cm*, and so on.

Each paragraph can have unique before and after spacing if you wish. One advantage to adding space this way is that the spacing before and after paragraphs does not change when you change the point size of your text. Another advantage is that you can use different spacing combinations for different purposes.

Headings often have different spacing requirements from body text, for instance. You may wish to create different before and after spacing designs for figures and figure captions as well.

As you will learn in Chapter 14, you can save unique spacing specifications as part of a style, making it easy to keep the look of your documents consistent.

▸▸ TIP

When adding space, remember that if a paragraph has space added after it, and the paragraph beneath it has space added before, the white space between them will be the *combination* of the two settings. For example, if one paragraph has 12 points of spacing after it and its successor has 6 points of spacing before, the white space between will be 18 points.

Adding White Space before Paragraphs

To add a single line of white space before a paragraph, follow these steps:

1. Place the insertion point in a paragraph or select multiple paragraphs.
2. Press Ctrl+0 (zero).

To enter a specific amount of space before a paragraph:

1. Place the insertion point in a paragraph or select multiple paragraphs.
2. Double-click on any indent marker to open the Paragraph dialog box.
3. Enter new Before dimensions in the Spacing area in lines, inches, picas, etc. Selected paragraphs and subsequent ones will have additional amounts of white space before them.

To remove single lines of white space (originally created with Ctrl+0), press Ctrl+0 a second time.

Fine-Tuning Paragraph Spacing

new

While the ruler buttons are fine for most occasions, you may need to visit the Paragraph dialog box occasionally to get just the right look. Enter appropriate specifications in the Spacing Before and After boxes to fine-tune. You can observe the effect of your changes in the Preview box. Click OK when you are satisfied.

Space before at Page Tops

When you print, Word for Windows ignores the Space Before setting in paragraphs that automatic pagination places at the top of a page. If you force a page or section break, however, Word retains this extra space. It will also retain the additional space if you check the Page Break Before option in the Pagination section of the Paragraph dialog box.

▸▸ Borders and Shading

Word for Windows bristles with paragraph border and shading features. You can apply various border treatments and shading to single paragraphs or groups of paragraphs. For instance, all of the paragraphs in Figure 10.9 are surrounded by a common double-line border, while the last paragraph has a single line top border and shading.

FIGURE 10.9 ▸

You can apply borders and shading to one paragraph or multiple paragraphs.

You can have it fast.
You can have it cheap.
You can have it done right.
Pick any two of the above.

▸ Creating Lines with the Border Command

Don't be fooled by the boxy-sounding name of this command. Format ➤ Borders and Shading... can be used to create lines as well. Check out the samples in Figure 10.10.

You adjust the horizontal *length* of borders or lines by adjusting a paragraph's width with indent markers or the Paragraph dialog box. It's also easy to control the distance between text and border lines. You can use borders to surround paragraphs, framed objects (like graphics), and tables.

▸ The Borders Toolbar

The Borders button on the Formatting Toolbar brings up a handy Borders Toolbar. (You can also display the Borders Toolbar from the View menu by choosing View ➤ Toolbars....) You will see the changes in your document as you work. Here are general steps for using it:

1. Place the insertion point in the paragraph of interest or select elements to be formatted—multiple paragraphs, graphics, etc.

FIGURE 10.10

By leaving off parts of borders, you can create lines.

Borders needn't be *boxes*. Use them to create *lines* like this one.

Lines *above* attract attention

Make thick lines from thin, shaded paragraphs...

Lines below set things off

Consider leaving off left & right sides

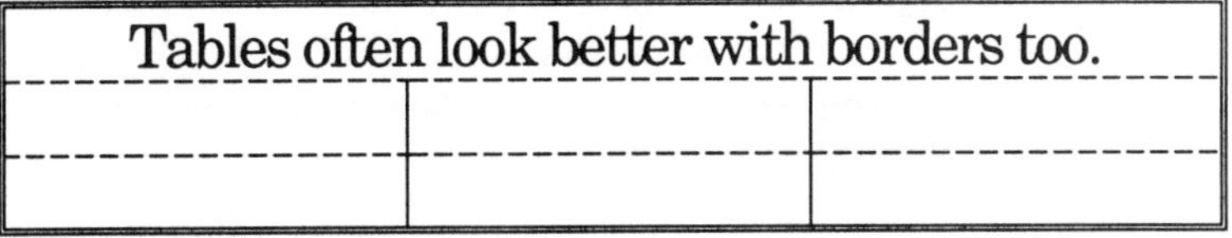
Tables often look better with borders too.

2. Adjust indents if necessary to define the desired width for the borders.
3. Reveal the Borders Toolbar (use the Borders button or View menu), shown in Figure 10.11.
4. With the Borders Toolbar open, choose the desired line thickness from its drop-down list.

FIGURE 10.11

The Borders Toolbar.

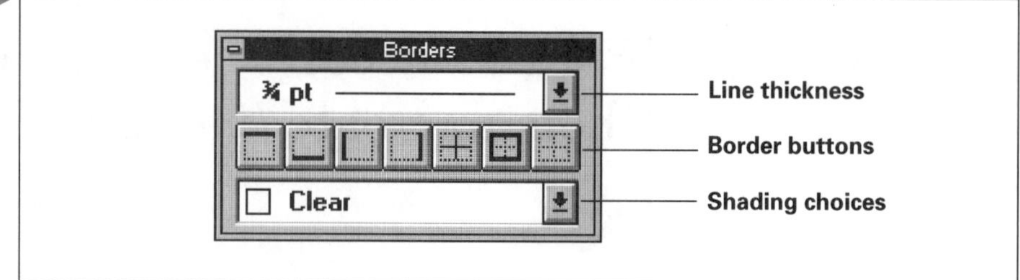

5. Click on the button corresponding to the desired border (No Border, Outside, Inside, Right, Left, Bottom, or Top).
6. Pick shading, if you like, from the drop-down shading list.
7. Admire your work.

▸▸ TIP

You can mix line thicknesses and shading by reselecting different parts of the project and using different settings. Read on.

▸ Custom Borders and Lines

Border and line play can be great rainy day entertainment. Just don't get carried away on busy days or with a deadline looming. Before you can effectively create custom borders, you must understand the Border sample part of the Borders and Shading dialog box, highlighted in Figure 10.12.

The border sample changes to represent the border you are creating. For instance, in Figure 10.12, the border specifications call for a thick black line around the entire border and a 1.5-point magenta line separating the two paragraphs. You specify lines (add and remove them) by clicking on border guides. They look like dotted *T*'s and *L*'s. Two of them are labeled in Figure 10.12. Clicking on any of the three horizontal guides toggles horizontal lines. Clicking on vertical guides—well, you know.

The little triangles that appear and disappear are called *selection markers*. They show you which border lines will be affected when you click a

FIGURE 10.12

The Border sample portion of the Borders and Shading dialog box.

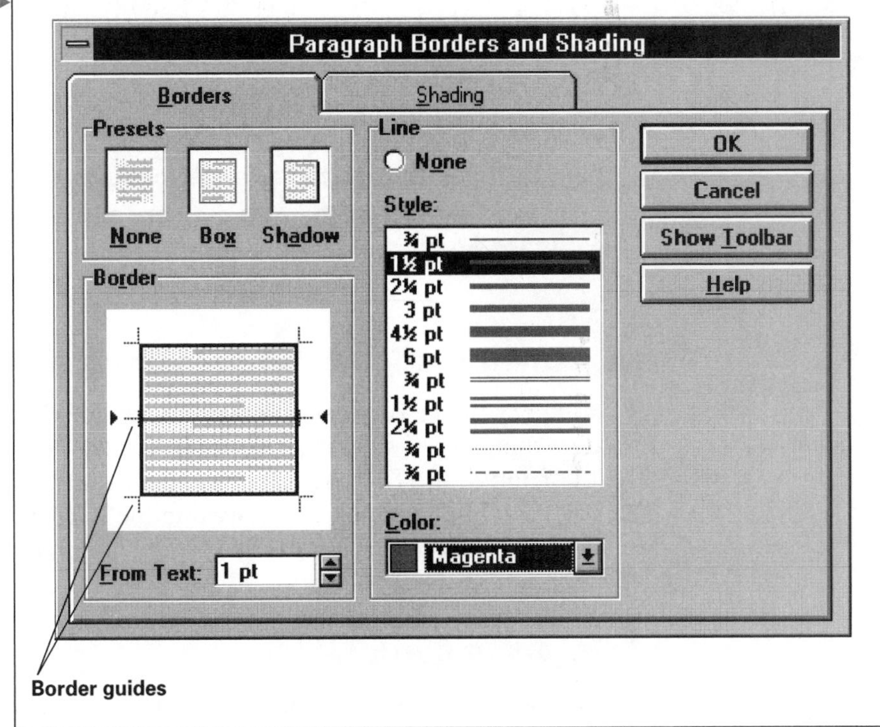

border guide. Don't worry, this will begin to make sense when you experiment on your own.

If you've selected multiple paragraphs (or tables) you'll be able to place lines between the different paragraphs (or table rows) thanks to those center border guides. And, as you've seen in the examples, it is possible to specify the line widths used for borders. It's even possible to combine different line styles in the same project. Here are the general steps for custom borders:

1. Place the insertion point in the paragraph of interest, or select elements to be formatted—multiple paragraphs, graphics, etc.
2. Open the Border dialog box (shown in Figure 10.12).
3. Click on the appropriate border guides in the sample to turn them on or off.

4. Click on the line type(s) you wish. Watch your document change as you work.

TIP

Once you've created some favorite border combinations, consider saving them as glossary entries or styles. See Chapters 14 and 17 for details.

Increasing the Space between Borders and Text

To add extra space between the text contained within borders and the borders themselves, specify a measurement (in points) in the From Text portion of the Borders tab of the Borders and Shading dialog box. You can do this when you are designing the border, or you can select an existing border and change the spacing later by visiting the Borders and Shading dialog box.

Controlling Border Width

A paragraph's indents (and the document's margins) control the width of a border. To change the border, select the paragraph(s) containing the border formatting and change the indents.

► Shading

Shading can be added to paragraphs with or *without* borders. Use shading to create forms or just to add decoration. Be aware, however, that shading can look pretty raggedy on many printers. Test print some samples before spending hours shading your favorite form or resume.

You can use either the Borders Toolbar or the Borders and Shading dialog box to add and change shading. To add paragraph shading, pick a shading percentage from the drop-down Shading menus or enter the first number of a percentage in the entry box.

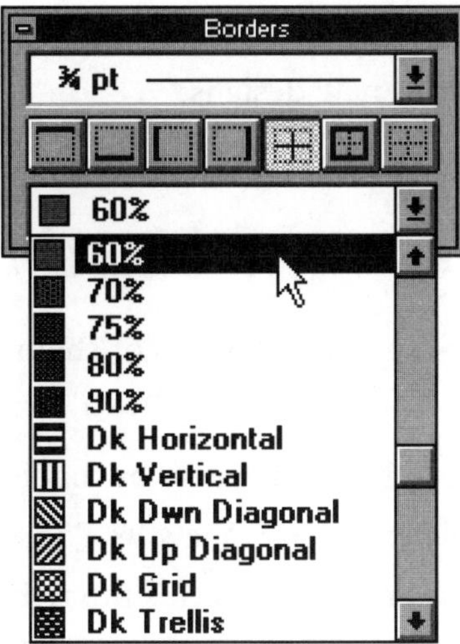

For example, to choose a 40 percent shading, type **4** in the shading list box and press ↵. The smaller the percentage, the lighter the shading—100 percent is solid black.

For settings that begin with the same number (e.g., 5 and 50), typing the number acts as a toggle. For example, typing 5 once selects 5; typing it a second time selects 50.

While you can remove borders and shading either with the Borders Toolbar or the Borders and Shading dialog box, the Toolbar's easier. Here are the general steps for using the Borders and Shading dialog box:

1. Place the insertion point in the paragraph of interest or select elements to be shaded—multiple paragraphs, graphics, etc.
2. Open the Paragraph and Borders and Shading dialog box with the Format ➤ Borders and Shading… command.
3. Click on the Shading tab.
4. Scroll through the Shading list and select a percentage.
5. You will see the effects of your work in the Preview box.

6. Click OK.
7. Be sure to test print new designs.

►► Removing Borders and Shading

Here are the steps for removing borders or shading with the Borders Toolbar:

1. Select the objects with the borders or shading you wish to remove.
2. Display the Borders Toolbar (View ➤ Toolbars…).
3. Click on the No Border button (it's the right-most button).
4. If shading has been applied, choose Clear from the Shading list, or type **c** in place of the displayed percentage and press ↵.

►► NOTE

Each paragraph can have its own tab settings. Read about tabs in the next chapter.

►► Tables and Paragraphs

As you'll see in the next chapter, tables can contain paragraphs. Generally, paragraphs in table cells behave like ordinary paragraphs.

CHAPTER 11

Tabs, Tables, Math, and Sorting

▸▸ FAST TRACK

To place a custom tab stop **308**

with the ruler in view, click the button at the left edge of the horizontal ruler repeatedly until it shows the icon for the desired tab-stop type. Then click on the ruler where you want to place a tab stop.

To create tab leaders **313**

select the paragraphs you want to pretty up and double-click on the tab where you want the leaders. Then choose the leader style you desire from the Tabs dialog box and click OK.

To create a table **316**

use the new and improved Table button or the new Table menu.

To move the insertion point backwards one tab at a time in tables **320**

hold down the **Shift** key and press **Tab**.

To enter tab characters in cells **320**

hold down the **Ctrl** key while pressing **Tab**.

To select an entire column in a table **322**

hold down the **Alt** key while clicking anywhere in the column.

To properly select an entire table **323**

hold down the **Alt** key and double-click anywhere in the table. There is also a new Select Table command on the Table menu (**Alt+5** on the keypad).

To add a new row at the end of an existing table **324**

place the insertion point anywhere in the last cell (the one in the lower-right corner of your table) and press the **Tab** key.

To delete a row or rows of cells **328**

select the row(s) to be deleted, then use the Table ➤ Delete Rows command. To delete the *contents* of cells but leave the cells intact, use Word's usual text deletion tricks (select text or graphics and press the **delete** key, for instance).

To automatically make cells snugly surround their contents **332**

use the new AutoFit feature.

To automatically have cell settings that make a presentable table **334**

use the Table ➤ Table AutoFormat command.

To create tables automatically **341**

use the new Table Wizard.

To easily rearrange rows **344**

use Outline view.

To create complex formulas **350**

use Equation Editor.

Word for Windows novices often either under- or overuse tabs. Primarily a quick way to position text or graphics, tabs have a lot of competition in Word for Windows. Some people use the spacebar instead of tabs. Lovers of Word's table features often abandon tabs altogether in favor of tables. This is probably a mistake too. Moreover, your typing teacher may have told you to use tabs to indent the first line of each paragraph. You may prefer Word's split left indent marker. Word's first-line indent feature is probably a better choice for that task.

This chapter also shows you how to have Word for Windows do simple math calculations (a great way to compute and proof totals and subtotals in tabular typing). And you'll see how Word can sort things like phone lists. Finally, Word comes with a separate program called Equation Editor, manufactured by Design Sciences, Inc. It will be of particular interest to scientists and academicians. Microsoft ships a customized version of the program designed specifically for use with Word for Windows. This chapter introduces you to the Equation Editor and tells you how to obtain additional information or an even more robust version of the program.

Tabs

Tabs are great for creating quick, relatively simple lists, and tabs do some things in Word for Windows you can't do on a typewriter. For instance, they can help you exchange Word data with spreadsheets, databases, and other programs. Each paragraph in a Word document can have the same or different tab settings. So turn off that "Gilligan's Island" rerun, and let's explore the wonderful world of tabs and tab stops!

Word for Windows offers five specialized tab-stop types. They each work with tabs to help align text and are particularly useful for making simple columnar lists like the one in Figure 11.1.

FIGURE 11.1

Word for Windows provides left, center, right, decimal, and bar tabs.

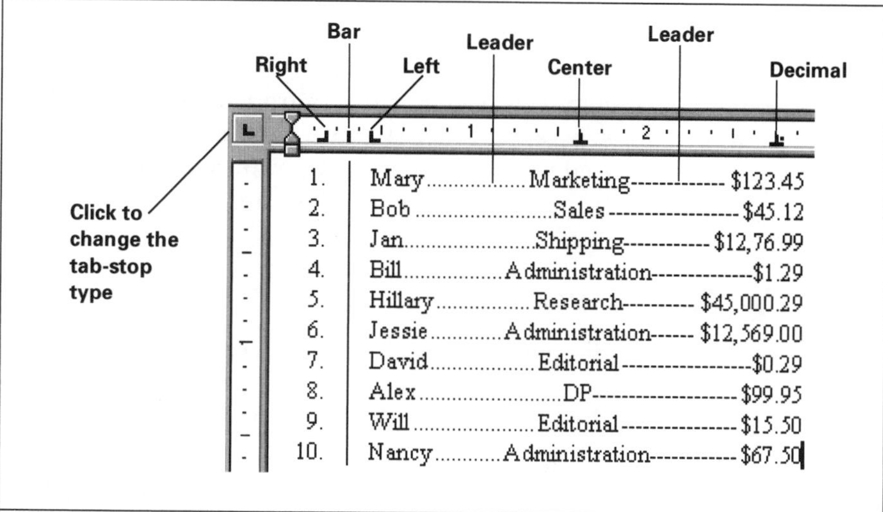

Left Tab Stops

Left tab stops are like the plain vanilla ones you find on your old Smith Corona. Text typed at these tab stops bumps up against the left edge of the stop. A left tab was used to align the peoples' names (the third tab stop) in Figure 11.1.

Center Tab Stops

A center tab stop centers your text around the tab stop. In Figure 11.1 the department names (at the fourth stop) are aligned with a center tab stop.

Right Tab Stops

Right tab stops position whatever you type to the left of the tab. As you can see in the first column of Figure 11.1, this is a great way to type long lists of numbers and have them line up.

Decimal Tab Stops

Decimal tab stops behave as you'd expect. They align columns of numbers on the decimal point and are perfect for simple financial reports.

Bar Tabs

Don't you wish you had had these in college? (On second thought, perhaps you do.) The Bar button creates nice, thin vertical lines you see separating the first and second columns in Figure 11.1. They aren't actual tab stops (that is, you cannot use them to align text), but they can be placed and moved like stops.

▸ Tables vs. Tabs

Simple tabular columns are great if you have items that always fit on one line. But suppose that one of the departments in Figure 11.1 was the Department of Redundancy Department, for instance. If you use tabs, the title won't automatically wrap to fit the format. You would need to redesign the tab layout, shorten the department title, or cobble things up with a carriage return. Ugh. Long items like these give tab typists fits. As you will see later in this chapter, tables make it easy to deal with this and other problems.

Serious typists will probably choose table solutions over tabs most days. The price is speed and complexity. Word's table features can be slow at times, and you may scratch your head in the beginning. Tables require an understanding of tabs, too. So, for simple projects like the example here, you might want to stick with tabs alone, at least until you've mastered them.

▸▸ Setting Custom Tab Stops

In the United States, at least, Word for Windows starts out each new document with tabs set at ½" intervals. You can create custom tab locations to replace these.

Tab stops are always stored with the paragraph mark for each paragraph, thus all of the rules about paragraph markers apply. If, for example, you set tab stops once and type ↵ at the end of each typing line, each new paragraph (line) will use the same tab stops as the preceding one until you tell Word otherwise.

▶ Setting Tab Stops with the Ruler

You can set custom tabs as you type or use the standard tabs initially then go back to fine-tune. Here are the general steps.

1. With the ruler in view, click the button at the left edge of the horizontal ruler repeatedly until it shows the icon for the desired tab-stop type (they are Left, Right, Decimal, and Center).

2. Click on the ruler where you want to place a tab stop. If you make a mistake, drag the stop off the ruler and try again.
3. When you type, press the Tab key to move the insertion point to the new tab positions. With Show ¶ turned on, you'll see fat arrows indicating each tab character you type.

   →1. → Mary........→........Marketing------→----- $123.45¶
   →2. → Bob............→............Sales--------→-------- $45.12¶

▶ Moving Tab Stops on the Ruler

To move tab stops before you've entered text, simply point to the stop of interest and drag away. If you have already entered text that uses the tab stops you want to move, first select all of the text before moving the tab stop.

For instance, if you had already typed the ten lines in Figure 11.1 and wanted to move the left tab stop for all of the lines, you would need to highlight *all ten* lines before moving the tab stop. Otherwise, some lines (paragraphs) would have different stops than others. Incidentally, you'd want to also highlight the paragraph mark *beneath* the last line too if you plan to enter more items. Otherwise the last paragraph marker won't know about the change and subsequent entries would be off.

If you highlight paragraphs with different tab-stop settings, the tab stops will be dimmed. Only the stops for the top paragraph will be displayed.

▸ Setting Tab Stops with the Tabs Dialog Box

While using the ruler is easy, you may want to use the Tabs dialog box for some projects. It provides ways to precisely set tab stops and it offers some additional tab-related options. Figure 11.2 shows the Tabs dialog box at work.

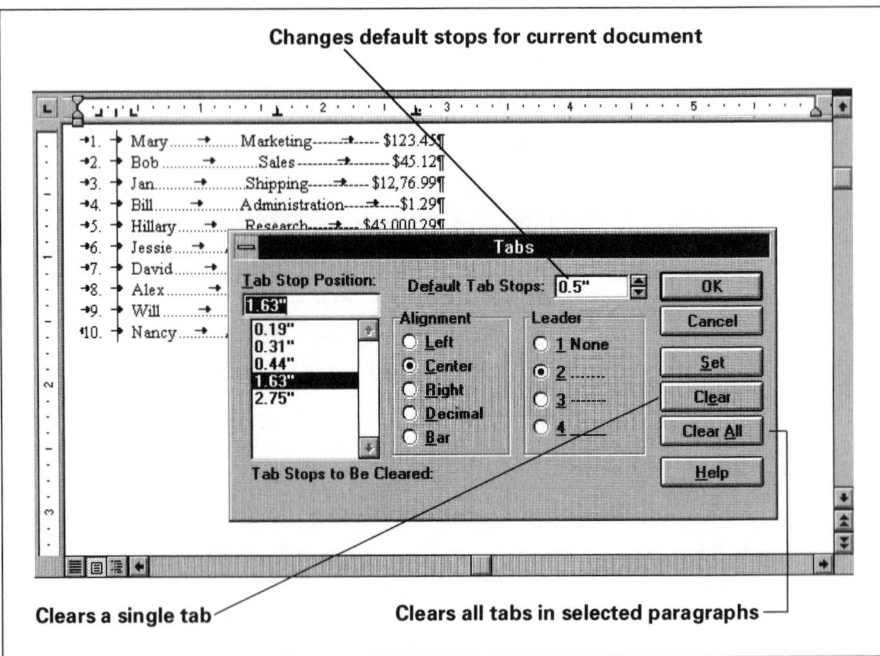

FIGURE 11.2 *The Tabs dialog box gives you precise control and additional tab-related features.*

You can reach the Tabs dialog box in any of these ways:

- Double-click any tab stop on the ruler.
- Choose Format ➤ Tabs….
- Click the Tabs… button in the Paragraph dialog box.

- Double-click in the tab-stop area of the ruler to place a new left tab stop where you have clicked *and* bring up the Tabs dialog box. The position of the new tab stop will be shown in the Position area of the dialog box and will change as you move the tab stop.

WARNING

Remember to select all affected text and paragraph markers before moving tab stops. Undo (Ctrl+Z) will save you when you forget.

Units of Measure in the Tab Dialog Box

Measurements in the Tabs dialog box are assumed to be in inches unless you type another legal abbreviation (*cm* for centimeter, *pt* for point, or *pi* for pica). As an example, *5 cm* would position a tab stop five centimeters from the left margin.

There is also an alignment section in the Tabs dialog box, where you can change current tab-stop types. This is the only place where you can select a bar tab.

Leading Characters for Tabs

Word for Windows' *leader* characters are dots, dashes, and solid lines. These leaders precede tabbed entries, producing the effect demonstrated in Figure 11.3. You set them in the Tabs dialog box. They make it easy to read wide, sparsely populated lines without losing your place.

FIGURE 11.3

Word provides tab leaders that make it easy to read lines without losing your place.

```
              Leader 1
..............Leader 2
--------------Leader 3
______________Leader 4
```

To create leaders, follow these steps:

1. Select the paragraphs you want to pretty up.
2. Click on the tab where you want the leaders.
3. Choose the leader style you desire from the Tabs dialog box.
4. Click OK.

You can apply this effect when defining new tab stops or by double-clicking on existing stops to bring up the Tabs dialog box as an afterthought.

▸▸ Default Tab-Stop Positions

The Word for Windows standard settings specify tabs every ½" (0.5 in). You can change this for a single document by changing the setting in the Tabs dialog box. To forever change default tabs, change and save stops in the Normal template, as described in Chapter 16.

▸ Clearing Tab Stops

You can drag the occasional tab off the ruler if you don't need it. The Tabs dialog box provides facilities for clearing multiple tabs at once. If you do choose a specific tab, the Clear button in the Tabs dialog box will still remove it.

▸▸ When Your Tabs Don't Line Up

Select all of the paragraphs that you want to conform and set identical tabs or correct the first paragraph, then copy the paragraph format.

You might also consider using the Clear All button. It removes all custom tabs. Defaults remain. This can make an absolute mess of your pride and joy. Undo should work if you accidentally clear all custom tabs, but it is always a good idea to save your work before experimenting with major changes like these. Remember, these features work only on paragraphs you have selected.

▶▶ Entering and Editing Tabular Data

Once you have set up tab stops, simply press the Tab key to reach the stop and begin typing. Word for Windows will position the text as you type. If you are typing at a center or right stop, text will flow appropriately as you type. When you type at decimal stops, the insertion point sits to the left of the decimal position until you hit the period key; then it hops to the right side. To leave an entry blank, simply tab past it by pressing the Tab key.

▶▶ Tabs and Data Exchange

Tabs and carriage returns are often used by databases and spreadsheets, particularly when exchanging data with Macintosh computer users. Tabs usually separate fields in records and carriage returns usually separate the records themselves, as illustrated in this radio frequency database in Figure 11.4.

FIGURE 11.4 ▶

Many computers can use tab-separated data created with Word. Save files like these as text.

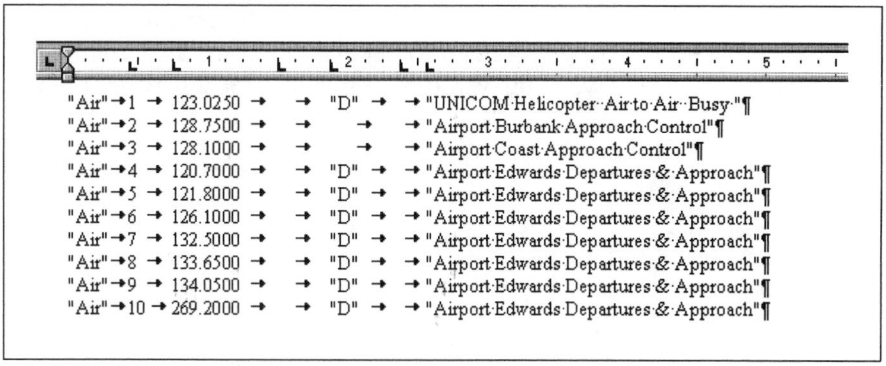

```
"Air"→1 → 123.0250 →  →  "D" →  → "UNICOM Helicopter Air to Air Busy "¶
"Air"→2 → 128.7500 →  →      →  → "Airport Burbank Approach Control"¶
"Air"→3 → 128.1000 →  →      →  → "Airport Coast Approach Control"¶
"Air"→4 → 120.7000 →  →  "D" →  → "Airport Edwards Departures & Approach"¶
"Air"→5 → 121.8000 →  →  "D" →  → "Airport Edwards Departures & Approach"¶
"Air"→6 → 126.1000 →  →  "D" →  → "Airport Edwards Departures & Approach"¶
"Air"→7 → 132.5000 →  →  "D" →  → "Airport Edwards Departures & Approach"¶
"Air"→8 → 133.6500 →  →  "D" →  → "Airport Edwards Departures & Approach"¶
"Air"→9 → 134.0500 →  →  "D" →  → "Airport Edwards Departures & Approach"¶
"Air"→10 → 269.2000 → →  "D" →  → "Airport Edwards Departures & Approach"¶
```

If you use Word for Windows to type a list of tab-separated names, addresses, and phone numbers, for instance, you might be able to export the list to your favorite database or time-management program by saving it as a text-only file. Check out the importing sections of your other program manuals.

▸▸ Tables

Tables help you organize complex columnar information. Use them to create such diverse documents as forms, television scripts, financial reports, parts catalogs, and resumes. You can insert tables anywhere you need them in Word for Windows documents. Word's table feature and the terminology used to describe it will remind you of a spreadsheet.

Word tables consist of horizontal *rows* and vertical *columns*. You do the typing in areas called *cells*. Cells can contain text, numbers, or graphics. Text in cells is edited and embellished as usual with Word's Formatting Toolbar and ruler.

A number of table-specific features let you control the size, shape, and appearance of cells. Border and shading features are available. It is also easy to insert and delete rows and columns.

Tables can be created from existing text without needless retyping. Or you can use the table feature to organize information and then convert your table to text. You can even import and export spreadsheet data. A new feature called the Table Wizard helps you automate table creation, but we'll wait to discuss it until after you understand the manual process. That's because you will often want to fine-tune the Wizard's results, so you'll need to become a wizard also. Figure 11.5 shows a typical Word for Windows table and its constituent parts.

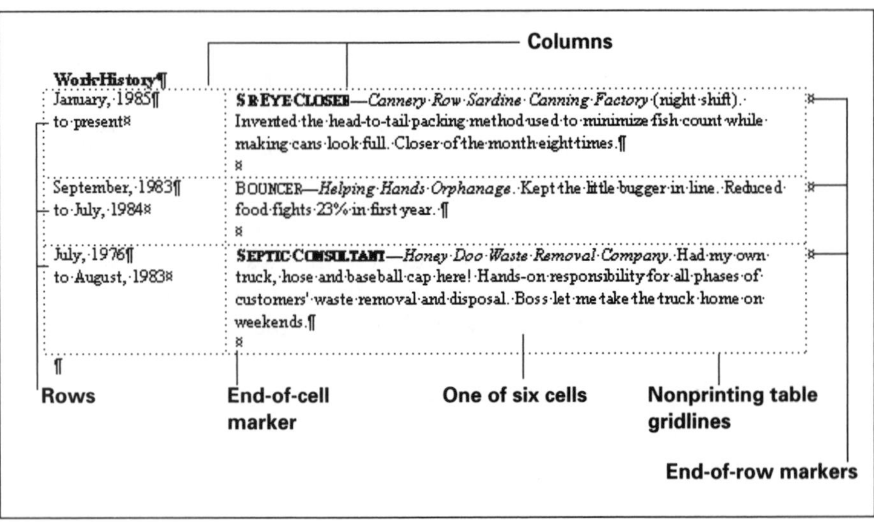

FIGURE 11.5 ▸

A typical table consisting of three rows, each containing two columns, for a total of six cells. The dotted cell gridlines will not print.

The dotted lines around each cell represent *nonprinting table gridlines*. You can add printing borders with the Format ➤ Borders and Shading... command. The larger dots are end-of-cell and end-of-row marks. Click the Show ¶ button in the Standard Toolbar to reveal them.

▶▶ Creating a Simple Table

Word for Windows has several new table features that you will love almost immediately. The first is the new and improved Table button, the second is an entire Table menu. Then, of course, there's the Table Wizard. Let's start with the button.

▶▶ TIP

If you plan to add regular (non-table) text above a table in a new document, press ↵ once or twice *before* inserting a table. This will make it *much* easier to insert text above the table later. Then, if you haven't already, make any preliminary formatting decisions including the printer you plan to use, page orientation, margins, font, and so on. Word will consider these factors when inserting your new table. You can always change your mind later, but this step can greatly simplify things.

▶ Using the Table Button

To create a table with the Table button, follow these steps:

1. Place the insertion point where you want to insert a table (ideally, *not* at the very beginning of a new, otherwise-empty document).
2. With the Standard Toolbar in view, click the Table button, then drag while holding down the mouse button to highlight the desired number of rows and columns.
3. When the displayed grid represents the desired number of rows and columns, release the mouse button.

4. Word will insert an empty table when you release the mouse button.

TIP

Generally, it is best to guess at least how many columns there will be. Because Word determines the width of each column based on the number of columns and the space available, adding columns and getting them just the right width later on can be more difficult than simply adding rows.

Don't worry if you are uncertain about the exact number of columns or rows you'll need. You can always add or delete them later. Figure 11.6 shows the grid for eight two-column rows. Try to make your own 8×2 table with the button.

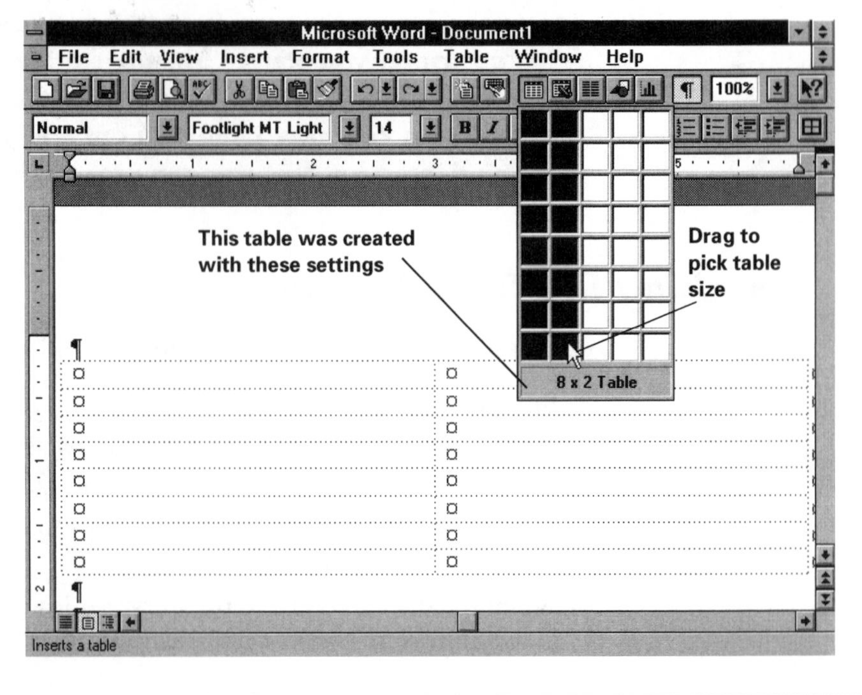

FIGURE 11.6

The Insert Table menu box and the resulting table it creates.

▶ Using the Table Menu to Create a Table

new

You can use the Table ➤ Insert Table... command to create tables. Here's how:

1. Position the insertion point where you want the table (ideally, not at the very beginning of a new, otherwise-empty document).
2. Choose Table ➤ Insert Table....
3. You'll see the dialog box shown in Figure 11.7.

FIGURE 11.7 ▶

You can use the Insert Table dialog box to define new tables or launch the Table Wizard (discussed later).

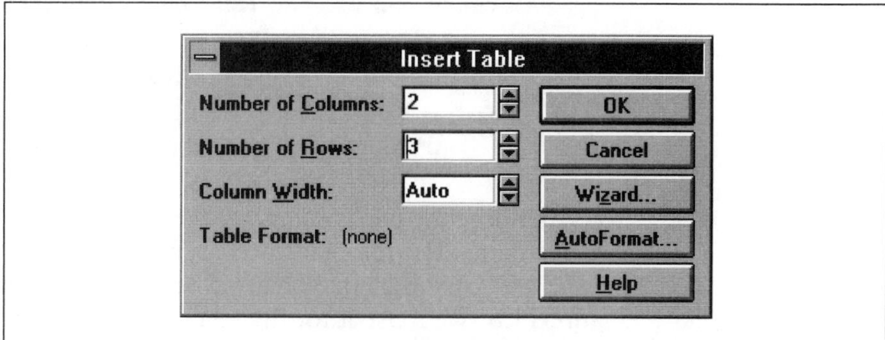

4. Enter the desired number of columns and rows for your table.
5. Click OK.

Unless you specify a column width in the Column Width box, Word for Windows computes a column width automatically, taking into consideration the available text area in your document and the number of columns you've specified. Initially, all table columns are the same width, but you can change column widths using techniques described later in this chapter.

▶ Entering and Editing Text in a Table

With only the few exceptions noted in this chapter, you navigate, enter, and edit table text just as you do any other Word for Windows text. Use your mouse or arrow keys to position the insertion point, then type normally. Think of the cell borders as margins. Word will automatically wrap text within the cell as you reach the right edge. Rows will automatically grow taller as necessary to accommodate your typing.

To move from cell to cell within a table, either use your mouse or use the Tab key to go forward and Shift+Tab to go backward. The insertion point will move left and down to the next row when you press Tab in the last column on the right side of a table, and it will move right and up one row when you Shift+Tab past the last column on the left. If you press Tab in the last cell of the last row, you will create a new row.

TIP

Because you use the Tab key to navigate in tables, you cannot simply press Tab to enter tab characters in cells. Instead, you need to hold down the Ctrl key while pressing Tab.

You can apply the usual character formatting to all or selected characters in a table. The familiar Toolbar, ruler, and menu features all work here. Try recreating a personalized version of the to-do list shown in Figure 11.8. We'll use it for the rest of the exercises in this chapter.

► Paragraphs in Cells

First-time table users are sometimes unaware of the important role paragraphs play in tables. *A cell can contain more than one paragraph.* Create paragraphs in the usual way. While typing in a cell, press ↵. If necessary, all of the cells in a row will increase in height to accommodate the extra paragraphs you create in a cell. Try adding the words *Home* and *Office* to all of the cells in the second column. Create two paragraphs in the process. Copy and paste if you like:

Tuesday¤	Home¶ Office¤
Wednesday¤	Home¶ Office¤

You can apply all of Word's paragraph formats to paragraphs in cells. Because cells can contain multiple paragraphs, they can also contain multiple paragraph formats. Thus, within a single cell you can have several different indent settings, tab settings, line-spacing specifications, styles, etc. For instance, the text in this cell was selected by double-clicking and dragging, made bold with the Formatting Toolbar's Bold button, and centered using the Formatting Toolbar's Center button:

¶
Ron's·To-Do·List¤

Try it.

FIGURE 11.8

Try to add text to your first table.

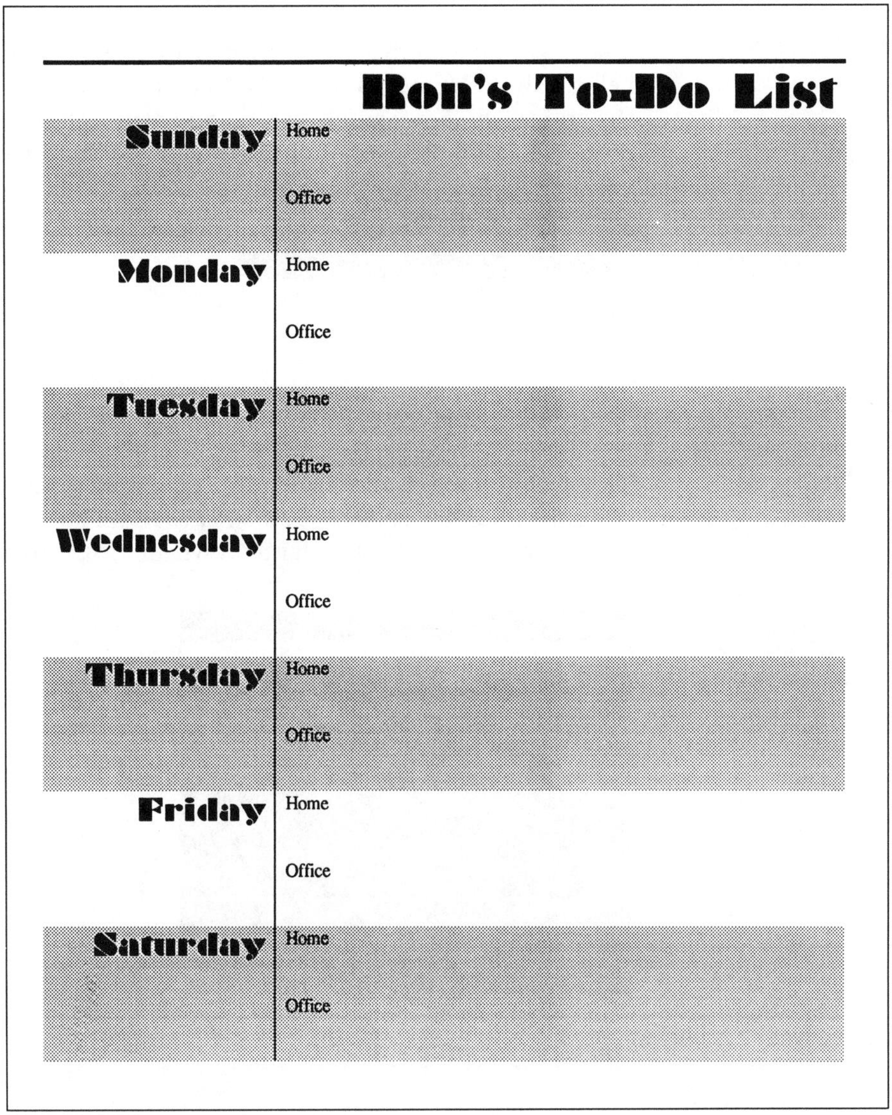

Ron's To-Do List

Sunday	Home Office
Monday	Home Office
Tuesday	Home Office
Wednesday	Home Office
Thursday	Home Office
Friday	Home Office
Saturday	Home Office

▸▸ Selecting in Tables

As you've just seen, you can select characters, words, and other items in table cells using Word's usual mouse and keyboard features. In addition, Word also provides *table-specific* selection tools enabling you to choose whole cells, entire rows, columns, or areas.

▸ Selecting Single Cells

The area between the first character in a cell and the left edge of the cell is called the *cell selection bar*. Clicking on it selects the contents of the entire cell. You can also select an entire cell by dragging with the mouse. Just be sure you include the end-of-cell mark in your selection:

▸ Selecting Columns

To select a column, move the mouse pointer to the area at the top of a column called the *column selection bar*. You'll know you've arrived when the pointer changes into a large down-pointing arrow.

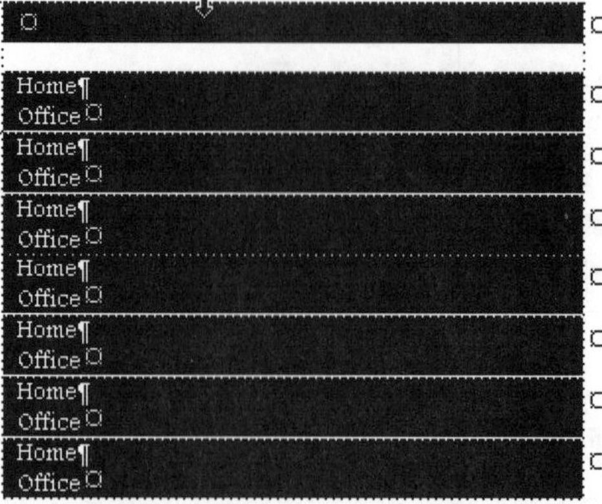

Click to select the entire column.

Holding down the Alt key while clicking anywhere in a column will also select the entire column. Selecting the bottom or top cell in a column and dragging up or down is somewhat tedious but will also work.

▶ Selecting Rows

Double-clicking any cell-selection bar will select the entire row. Selecting the left-most or right-most cell in a row and dragging will also work.

▶ Selecting Adjacent Groups of Cells

To select groups of adjacent cells, either drag through the cells or click in one cell and Shift+click in the others. For instance, to select all the "weekday" cells you could click in the Monday cell then Shift+click in the cell to the right of Friday. The 10 weekday cells would be selected:

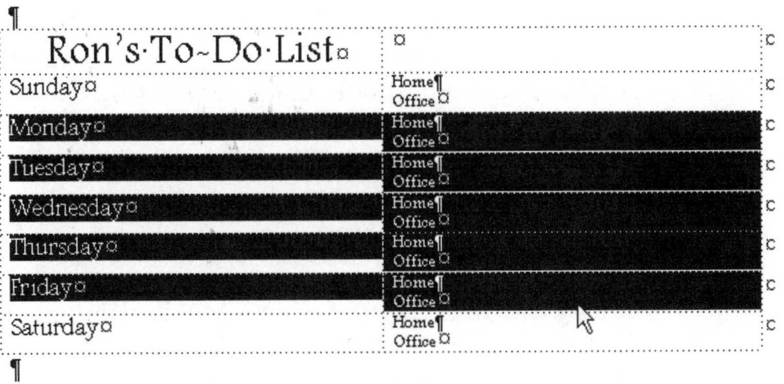

▶ Selecting the Whole Table

To properly select an entire table, hold down the Alt key and double-click anywhere in the table. If your document contains multiple tables and they are not separated by paragraph marks, this technique will select all adjacent tables.

Do *not* use Word's Select All command to select a table, as this will also select paragraph marks and other things *outside* of the table.

new ►► NEW

Word for Windows has a new Select Table command on the Table menu. Its corresponding keyboard shortcut is Alt+5 on the numeric keypad (Num Lock has to be off for this to work).

►► Modifying Table Designs

While Word's default table settings may be fine for simple typing tasks, you will eventually want to change column widths, overall table width, cell spacing, and so on. You'll want to insert, delete, and move rows and columns. As you can see from Figure 11.9, it is even possible to create professional-looking forms by modifying Word's standard tables.

Creating complex tables like this can be a little frustrating at first. It is a good idea to save your work before you experiment with new table formats. Beginners should consider working on copies of important documents. That said, let's look at a number of ways to modify standard table designs.

► Table Borders that Print

An easy way to dress up a table is to add printing borders. The form in Figure 11.9 is an example of this. Select the cell or cells you wish to surround, then use the line-thickness portion of the Borders Toolbar. Pick the desired combination of line thicknesses and apply the borders just as you would add them to Word for Windows paragraphs.

► Adding Rows at the End of a Table

To add a new row at the end of an existing table, place the insertion point anywhere in the last cell (the one in the lower-right corner of your table) and press the Tab key. Word for Windows will insert a new row using the styles of the cells immediately above.

FIGURE 11.9

Create professional-looking forms by adding borders and adjusting row and column sizes.

SALESPERSON	P.O. NUMBER	DATE SHIPPED	SHIPPED VIA	F.O.B. POINT	TERMS

QUANTITY	DESCRIPTION	UNIT PRICE	AMOUNT
			$ 0.00
			$ 0.00
			$ 0.00
			$ 0.00
			$ 0.00
			$ 0.00
			$ 0.00
		SUBTOTAL	$ 0.00
		SALES TAX	
		SHIPPING & HANDLING	
		TOTAL DUE	$ 0.00

Adding Rows in the Middle of a Table

To insert a single row in the middle of a table:

1. Place the insertion point in the row *below* where you want the new row.
2. Click on the Table ➤ Insert Rows... command.
3. To add multiple rows, either repeat the Insert Rows command or try the alternate approach in the next step.
4. Select as many existing rows as the number of new ones you want to insert before making the insertion. In other words, if you want to add three rows, select the three existing rows beneath the desired insertion point, then use the Table ➤ Insert Rows... command. Word will insert three new rows.

► Changing Row Heights

Normally, Word for Windows sets the height of each row automatically to accommodate the cell containing the tallest entry. For instance, if one cell in a row needs 2.0" to accommodate the text or graphic it contains, all of the cells in that row will be 2.0" high. All cells in a row must be the same height, but different rows can have different heights.

Dragging a Row to New Heights

To adjust the height of a row, follow these steps:

1. Click anywhere in the row you wish to resize.
2. Move the pointer to the vertical ruler at the left edge of the screen, watching the pointer as you move it.
3. When it becomes an up-and-down arrow, use it to drag the row to the desired height.

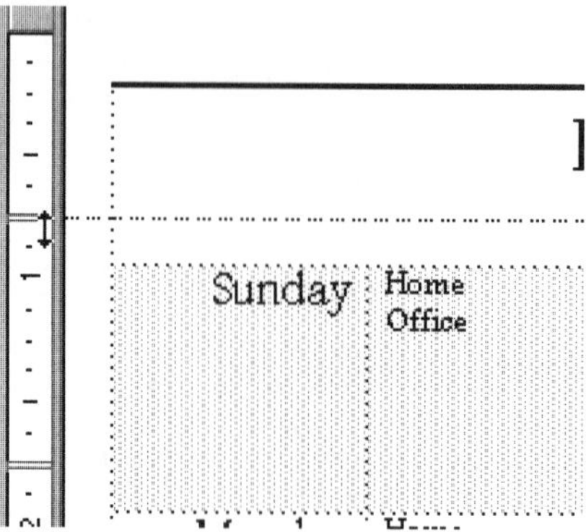

4. Release the mouse button.

► Resizing Rows with Cell Height and Width...

You can also overrule Word's automatic row-height (and column-width) settings via the Table ➤ Cell Height and Width... command. This is one way to create forms with fixed-sized entry areas.

There is no standard keyboard shortcut for this command, but experienced table typists often add their own. Figure 11.10 shows the Cell Height and Width dialog box.

FIGURE 11.10

Specify table row heights and Column widths with the Table ➤ Cell Height and Width... command.

To resize cells, follow these steps:

1. Place the insertion point anywhere in the row whose height you wish to specify. If you want multiple rows to share the same height, you can select all of them.
2. Choose the Table ➤ Cell Height and Width... command.
3. Click on the Row tab, if necessary, to reveal its choices.
4. Use the drop-down list to choose Auto, At Least, or Exactly.
5. Enter the desired dimension in points, inches, centimeters, and so on. (The default is points.)
6. To change settings for previous or next rows, click the Previous or Next buttons.
7. Click OK to make the change and close the dialog box.

TIP

If the exact height you specify is too small to accommodate the biggest entry in a row, the excessive text or a portion of the too-tall graphic will be cropped when printed. Simply increase the row height if this is undesirable.

▸ Deleting Rows

To delete a row or rows of cells, select the row(s) to be deleted, then use the Table ➤ Delete Rows command. This will delete both the rows themselves (the cells) and their contents (text or graphics or whatever). To delete the *contents* of cells but leave the cells intact, use Word's usual text-deletion tricks (select text or graphics and press the delete key, for instance).

▸ Changing the Spacing between Rows

To change the amount of white space between rows, you must change the before and after spacing of the first or last paragraphs in the cells. (Don't confuse this with changing the *height* of rows, which is something else entirely.) Use the same techniques you use to add space between non-table paragraphs (see Chapter 10). Select the paragraph of interest, choose the Format ➤ Paragraph... command, and specify before and after spacing.

▸ Inserting Columns in the Middle of a Table

To insert a single column in the middle of a table:

1. Select the column to the *right* of where you want the new column to appear.
2. Click the Table button in the Standard Toolbar (notice how its name has changed to Insert Columns) or choose Table ➤ Insert Columns.
3. Word will add a new column but will not change the width of the earlier columns to accommodate it. In order to make the enlarged table fit on your page, you will probably need to adjust margins, column widths, (described in a moment) or change page orientation. New columns retain the format of the old right-most columns, but borders will not transfer.

▶▶ TIP

To insert multiple columns, select as many existing columns to the right of the desired location of the new columns as the number of new ones you want to insert. In other words, if you want to add three columns, select the three existing columns to the right of the desired insertion point, then click on the Table button. Word for Windows will insert three columns.

▶ Inserting Columns at the Right Edge of a Table

To insert a column at the right edge of a table:

1. Select an end-of-row marker.
2. Click on the Table button in the Standard Toolbar (notice how its name has changed to Insert Cells).
3. You'll be visited by the Insert Cells dialog box, illustrated in Figure 11.11.
4. Pick Insert Entire Column.
5. Click OK.

▶ Deleting Columns

To delete columns, follow these steps:

1. Select the column or columns to be removed. The choices on the Table menu change to include column-related commands.
2. Choose Table ➤ Delete Columns.

▶ Changing Column Widths

You can change the widths of entire columns or selected cells within columns. Most changes can be made by dragging column markers on

FIGURE 11.11

Use the Insert Cells dialog box to insert columns, rows, or cells.

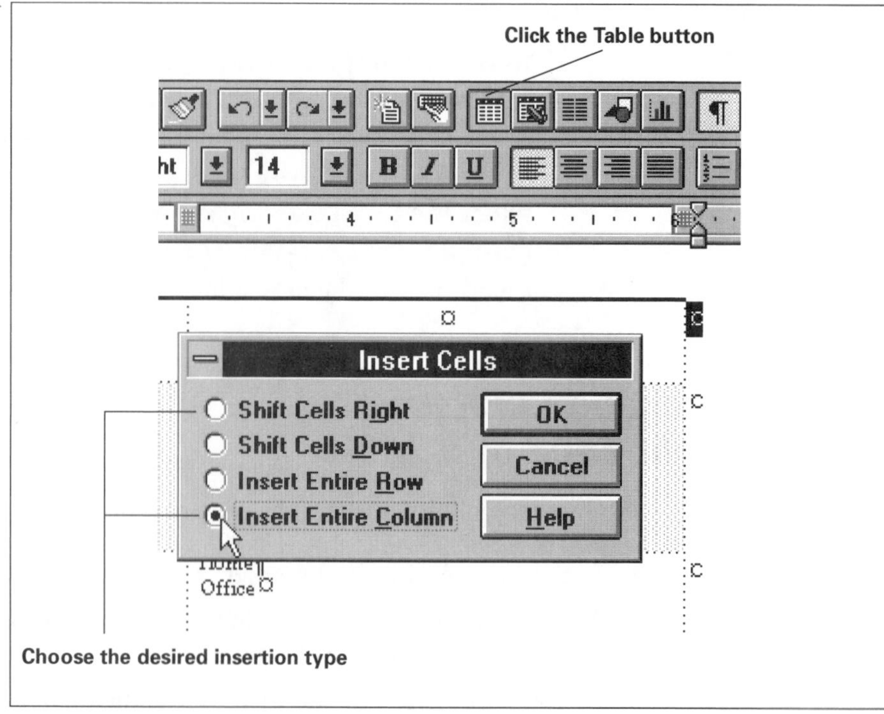

the table scale in the ruler. But you can make precision adjustments in the Table Cells dialog box.

Changing Column and Cell Widths with the Ruler

new

To change the width of an entire column, follow these steps:

1. Point to a column boundary.
2. The pointer will change shape.

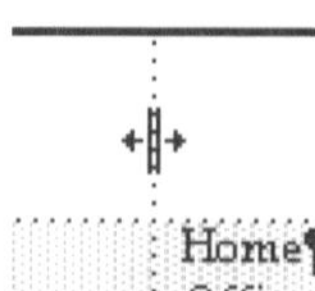

3. Drag the column-width marker.

4. Watch the dotted line and ruler settings, then release the mouse button when it reaches the desired width.

If you hold down the Shift key while dragging, the column to the right changes size while the table's overall width remains unchanged. (Note that this affects two columns: the one being dragged and the one whose width is encroached upon.)

If you hold down Ctrl while dragging, all columns to the right change size, but the table's overall width does not.

TIP

You can also drag the column markers on the ruler to change column widths. Just don't accidentally drag the cells' indent markers instead, as illustrated in Figure 11.12.

As you can see in Figure 11.13, it is possible to change the width of one or more cells by selecting them and visiting the Cell Height and Width dialog box. Specify a new width in the Columns tab.

FIGURE 11.12

You can also change column widths by dragging these markers.

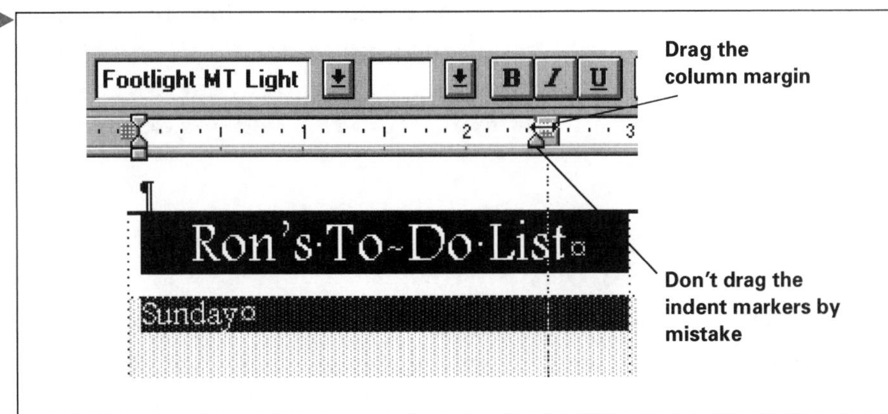

FIGURE 11.13

You can change individual cell widths or groups of cells with the Column tab in the Cell Height and Width dialog box.

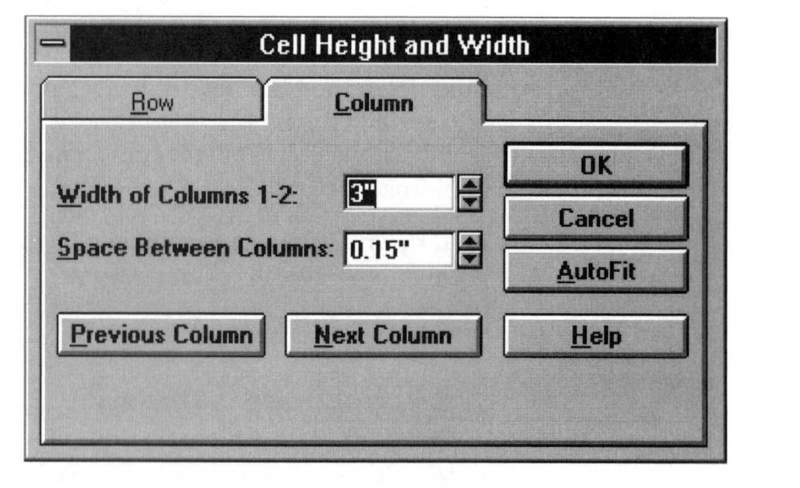

▸▸ TIP

When you are just learning, it's pretty easy to mess things up while dragging cell and column borders around this way, particularly if you change individual cell widths when you meant to change column widths. If multiple undos can't fix the problem, and you don't have a better, previously saved version, perhaps the AutoFit button can help. It's described next.

Changing Table Cell Widths with AutoFit Button

The AutoFit button attempts to make cells snugly surround their contents. Therefore, it is best to use it after you've entered all of the information in your table or after you are done adding or deleting items. Follow these steps:

1. Select the cells you wish to resize or, more often, the entire table.
2. Choose Table ➤ Cell Height and Width….
3. Reveal the Column tab if it is not already in view.

4. Click on the AutoFit button.
5. Word will snug up the selected cells.

▶ Merging Cells

Use the Merge Cells feature to combine the contents of multiple cells. This is a common way to make a heading in one cell span an entire table or selected group of columns. For example, you could merge the two cells in the top row of your To-Do list to form a heading like this that spans both columns.

As shown in Figure 11.14, you select the cells to merge, then choose Table ➤ Merge Cells, and the contents of the designated cells will merge. You may need to reformat text merged this way.

FIGURE 11.14 ▶

The contents of several cells can be merged together with the Table ➤ Merge Cells… command.

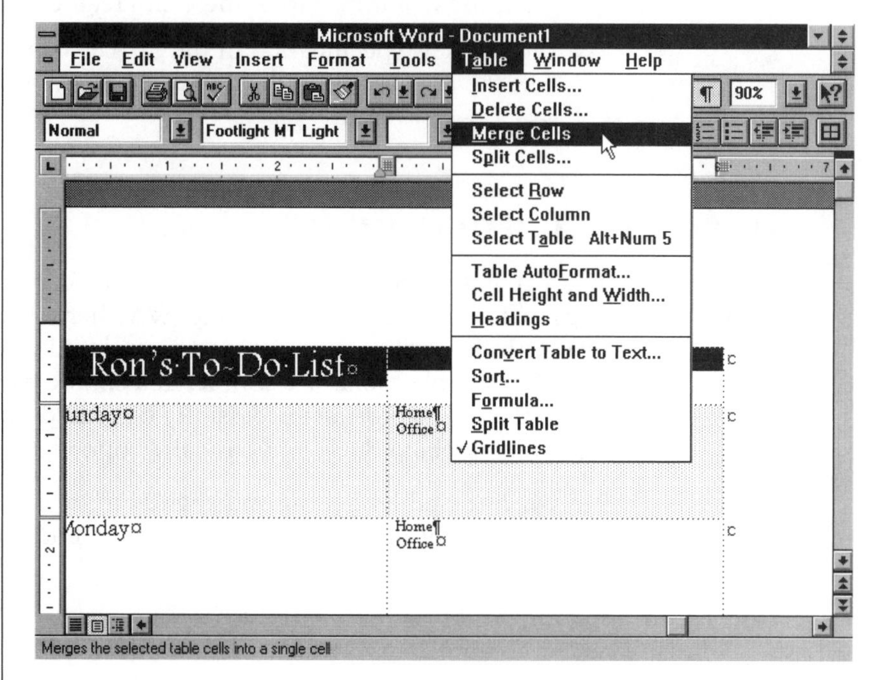

▶ Unmerging Cells

To split (unmerge) cells, follow these steps:

1. Place the insertion point in a merged cell.
2. Choose Table ➤ Split Cells. You'll be asked how many cells you want after the split.

▶ Changing the Space between Columns

Word for Windows assigns cell widths based on the available text area and the number of columns you request. In the process, it sets aside a small amount of unprintable space between (actually within) each cell. This space takes away from the usable cell space. For instance, a 1½" column with ¼" column spacing would have 1¼" of usable space in the middle of each cell.

To change the space between columns, follow these steps:

1. Select the columns of interest.
2. Visit the Columns tab of the Cell Height and Width dialog box.
3. Type a new specification in the Space Between Columns box or use the arrows to flip through suggested choices.
4. Click OK.

▶ AutoFormatting Tables

The Table ➤ Table AutoFormat... command attempts to pick cell settings that make a presentable table. Whether it succeeds or not will vary with the project it's given and your definition of success. Personal taste plays a role too. For example, in a simple case like the one in Figure 11.15, Auto-Format successfully tightened up the table, added some nice-looking lines, and basically yupped it up.

But when the tables get big and slightly more complicated (containing merged cells for instance), things can get a little unpredictable.

FIGURE 11.15

Before and after AutoFormatting a simple table.

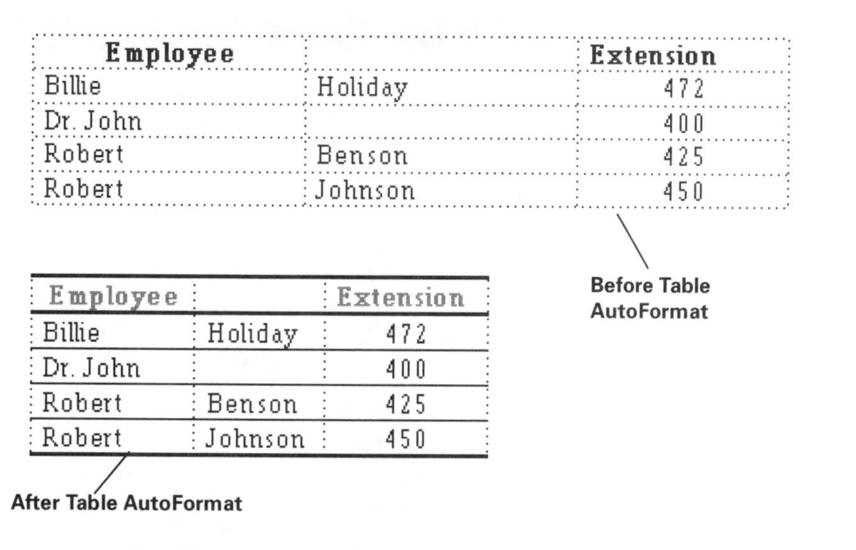

Employee		Extension
Billie	Holiday	472
Dr. John		400
Robert	Benson	425
Robert	Johnson	450

Employee		Extension
Billie	Holiday	472
Dr. John		400
Robert	Benson	425
Robert	Johnson	450

WARNING

Before using the Table AutoFormat... command, save your work to disk. That way if you get one of those "Insufficient memory to undo..." messages somewhere along the line, you'll at least have a disk copy of your "before" table.

Thus forewarned, here are the basic steps for using Table AutoFormat...:

1. Enter, edit, spell check, reorganize, and otherwise finish with your table.
2. Save your document to disk.
3. Select the entire table (Alt+5 on the numeric keypad with Num Lock off).
4. Choose Table ➤ Table AutoFormat....
5. Preview the format choices from the scrolling list, as shown in Figure 11.16, by highlighting their names one at a time. ↑ and ↓ are handy here. Pay particular attention to how Word handles row and column headings in the preview examples.

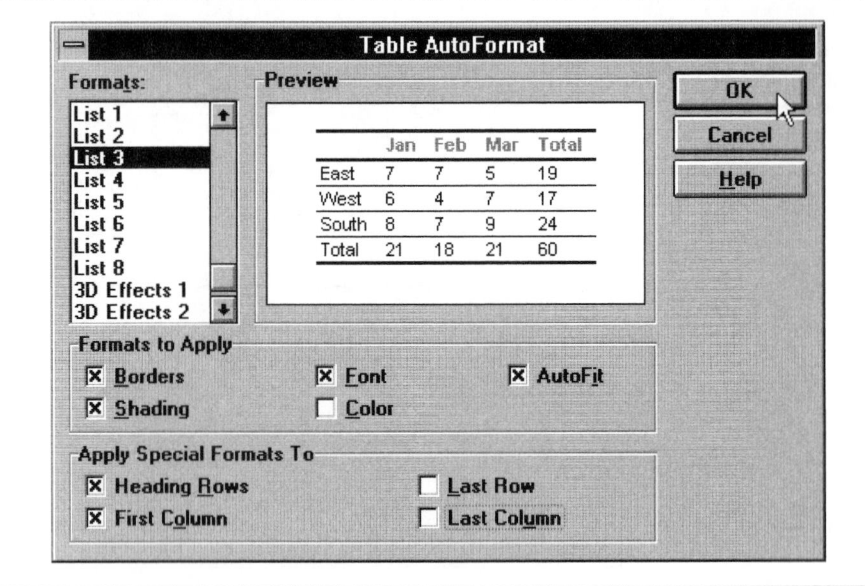

FIGURE 11.16 *Watch the previews of headings carefully when previewing automatic table style options.*

6. Pick a style by highlighting it and click OK.
7. Behold—then undo and try again, if necessary.

Some (but not all) styles can add special effects to last columns or rows. This is a good way to highlight grand totals. Turn these effects on and off with their corresponding check boxes in the Apply Special Formats To area of the Table AutoFormat dialog box. You can also turn off many of the AutoFormat effects (borders, shading, etc.) the same way.

▸▸ **TIP**

Word's Format ➤ AutoFormat... command does not format tables. Use the Table ➤ Table AutoFormat... command instead.

▸▸ Graphics in Tables

Tables aren't just for bean counters and resume writers. Check out Figure 11.17.

FIGURE 11.17

This is a two-column, one-row table!

Make Big Money from  Tiny Sea Creatures ! Now you can turn a worldwide labor shortage into a real career opportunity. There are big bucks to be made in sardine eye closing.	Did you know that there are always openings in the canning industry? We need experienced eye closers now! Day and night positions are available. Benefits include all the fresh sardines you can eat, and a free oil cloth apron... **Phone** **1-800-EYE-SHUT**

Figure 11.17 is a two-column, one-row table with a graphic and a half-dozen different paragraph formats. Think of table cells as text and graphic containers, then set your imagination on turbo.

Importing Excel Worksheet Data as Tables

If you took offense at the bean-counter remark a moment ago, here's a tip designed to make your life easier and put me back in your good graces. You can import Excel worksheets as tables, then edit and reformat them as necessary. The results can be pretty impressive, as you can see in Figure 11.18.

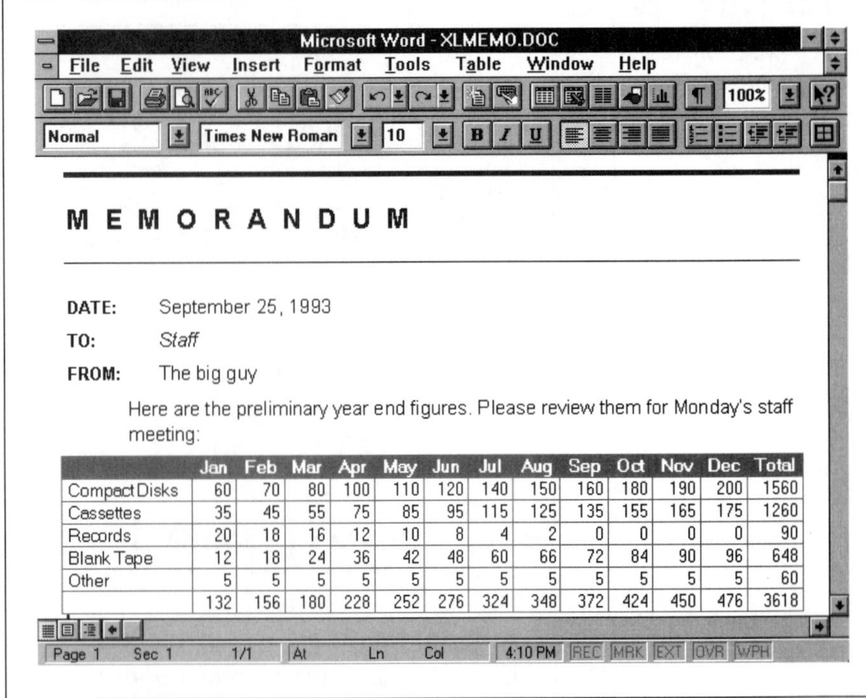

MEMORANDUM

DATE: September 25, 1993

TO: *Staff*

FROM: The big guy

Here are the preliminary year end figures. Please review them for Monday's staff meeting:

	Jan	Feb	Mar	Apr	May	Jun	Jul	Aug	Sep	Oct	Nov	Dec	Total
Compact Disks	60	70	80	100	110	120	140	150	160	180	190	200	1560
Cassettes	35	45	55	75	85	95	115	125	135	155	165	175	1260
Records	20	18	16	12	10	8	4	2	0	0	0	0	90
Blank Tape	12	18	24	36	42	48	60	66	72	84	90	96	648
Other	5	5	5	5	5	5	5	5	5	5	5	5	60
	132	156	180	228	252	276	324	348	372	424	450	476	3618

FIGURE 11.18 *Either paste Excel cells, which become a Word table as shown here, or use Word's linking and embedding (described in Chapter 30).*

You can either copy and paste Excel worksheet cells (at which point they are converted to Word tables), or you can use more powerful tools like Link and Embed. See Chapters 30 and 36 for details.

►► Converting Tables to Text and Vice Versa

Sometimes you'll start a project using tabs and wish you'd created a table—or a coworker will give you some tabbed text. Other times, you will want to export things you've typed using Word's table feature for use with database and other programs that expect tab- or comma-separated (delimited) input. Word for Windows has solutions for all these contingencies.

Word makes it quite easy to convert back and forth from tables to text. You may need to do some cleanup before or after conversion, though. Always work on copies of your documents when you do this!

▶ Converting Text to Tables

Highlight the text in your document that you want to turn into a table. Choose Table ➤ Convert Text to Table... and click the appropriate option button in the resulting dialog box, shown in Figure 11.19.

FIGURE 11.19 ▶

Word offers a number of conversion options. Pick the right one for your situation.

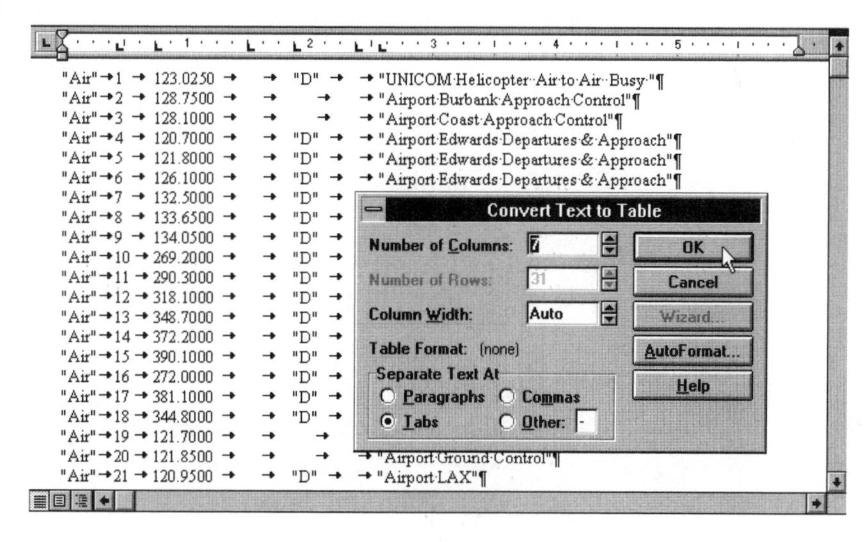

Tab-Delimited Text

Click the Tabs button in the Concert Text to Table dialog box. Lines of text separated by paragraph marks or line breaks will become rows in your table. Tab-separated strings of text within those lines will become cell entries in the row. Word for Windows will automatically create the necessary number of columns based on the maximum number of tabs in a line.

For instance,

> Sony Corporation [Tab] 800-222-7669 [↵] SYBEX, Inc. [Tab] 415-523-8233 [Tab] Publisher [↵]

would create two rows with three columns, even though the last cell in the first row would be empty.

Comma-Delimited Text

Click the Commas button in the Convert Text to Table dialog box. Lines of text separated by paragraph marks or line breaks will become rows in your table. Comma-separated strings of text within those lines will become cell entries in the row. Word for Windows will automatically create the necessary number of columns based on the maximum number of commas in a line.

For instance,

> Sony Corporation [Comma] 800-222-7669 [↵] SYBEX, Inc. [Comma] 415-523-8233 [Comma] Publisher [↵]

would create two rows with four columns, even though the last two cells in the first row will be empty.

►► **WARNING**

> **Notice how *SYBEX, Inc.* created an unintentional column. While many database programs let you use quotation marks to solve this problem, Word does not.**

Figure 11.20 shows part of the comma-separated text after conversion to a table, editing, and formatting. Notice that the quotes surrounding the imported text have *not* been removed by Word's Text to Table feature. Use Replace... to do this. See Chapter 20 for details.

Converting from Paragraphs

Click the Paragraphs button in the Convert Text to Table dialog box. If you ask Word for Windows to convert paragraphs to tables, it will propose a single column and create as many rows as you have paragraphs. Changing the number of columns will distribute paragraphs among the columns from left to right. In a two-column layout, the first paragraph would end

FIGURE 11.20

Once you convert text to tables, you may need to clean it up.

"Air"	1	123.0250	"D"	"UNICOM Helicopter Air to Air Busy "
"Air"	2	128.7500		"Airport Burbank Approach Control"
"Air"	3	128.1000		"Airport Coast Approach Control"
"Air"	4	120.7000	"D"	"Airport Edwards Departures & Approach"
"Air"	5	121.8000	"D"	"Airport Edwards Departures & Approach"
"Air"	6	126.1000	"D"	"Airport Edwards Departures & Approach"
"Air"	7	132.5000	"D"	"Airport Edwards Departures & Approach"
"Air"	8	133.6500	"D"	"Airport Edwards Departures & Approach"
"Air"	9	134.0500	"D"	"Airport Edwards Departures & Approach"
"Air"	10	269.2000	"D"	"Airport Edwards Departures & Approach"

up in the top-left cell of the new table, the second paragraph in the top-right cell, the third in the left cell of row two, and so on.

▶ Converting Tables to Text

Select the table cells you wish to convert or use the Alt+double-click trick to select the whole table. Choose Table ➤ Convert Table to Text.... Word will bring up a Table to Text dialog box, which asks if you want the table converted to paragraphs, tab-delimited text, or comma-delimited text. Pick one. If you pick the comma or tab options, Word will convert each row of your table into one line (a paragraph, actually). Cells in your old tables will become tab- or comma-separated items on the lines.

Remember that in-text commas will confuse Word for Windows. It would treat *SYBEX, Inc.* as two distinct entries. If you choose tab text, you will probably need to set new tabs after the conversion.

Choosing the paragraph option will convert each old table cell into at least one paragraph. If cells contain multiple paragraphs, the paragraph marks are retained during the conversion, so some cells will create more than one new paragraph.

▶▶ The Table Wizard

Okay. I promised, so here goes. The Wizard will ask you some questions and format your table. Let's s'pose you want to make a ten-row table with a column for each month. Here are the basic steps:

1. Place the insertion point where you want the table. Tap ↵ once or twice if you've just opened a new document.
2. Choose Table ➤ Insert Table.
3. Click the Wizard button in the resulting dialog box.
4. You will be presented with a number of screens like this one, asking you questions:

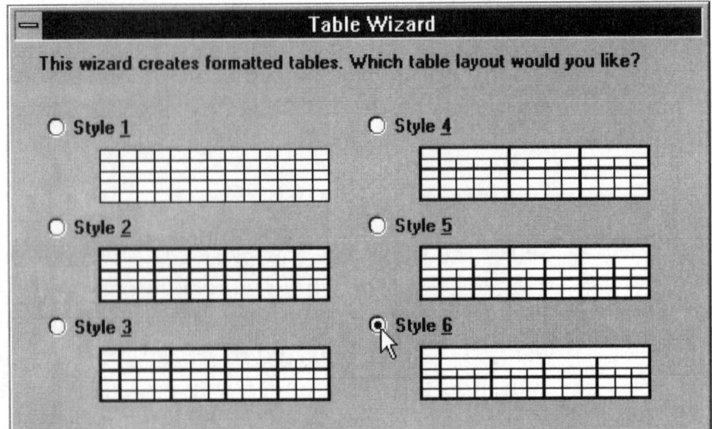

5. Look at each choice *carefully* and study the examples if they are given. Don't confuse *rows* and *columns* when the Wizard gives you choices. Try to imagine *your* data in the sample table formats.
6. Click on the Next button after each choice or Back to back up one screen.
7. When the Wiz runs out of questions, click Finish.
8. You'll be presented with the Table AutoFormat dialog box (which you read about earlier).
9. Cruise the format samples until you find just the right mood.
10. Click OK, wait a moment, and see what develops. Figure 11.21 shows the results of these requests:
    - Style 6
    - No heading, just 13 columns, Year 1993, quarters, then months
    - Repeat headings, center column headings in cells

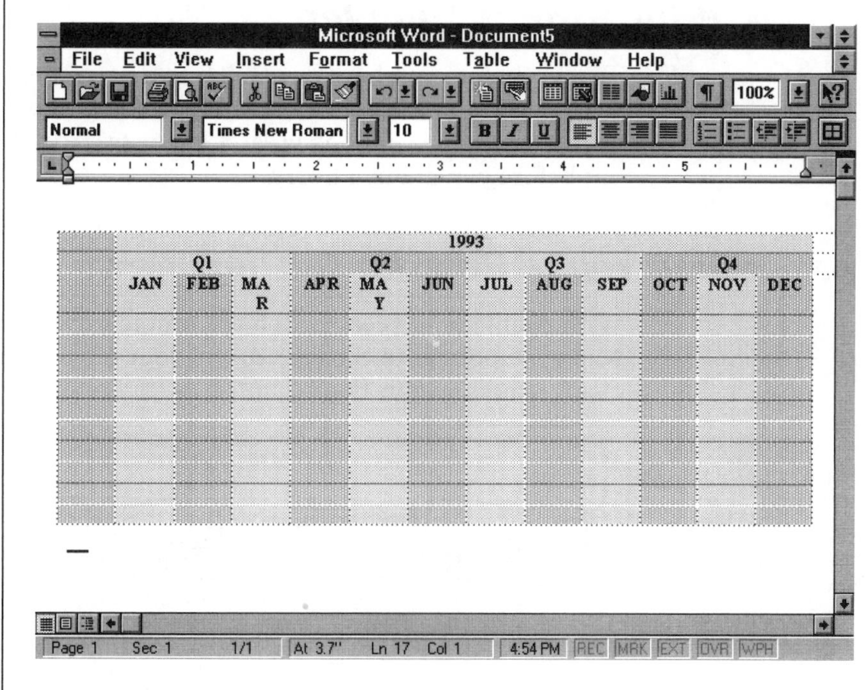

FIGURE 11.21

The Table Wizard at work.

- No headings, just ten rows
- Numbers: aligned on decimal
- Portrait
- Finish
- 3-D Effects 3

And that's why *manual* table skills were covered first in this book. At a minimum, you'll need to increase the width of the first column and tidy up a few things before using the Wizard's creation. Fortunately, it's easy to do. Press on....

▶▶ Table Tips

Here are some tips to help make you a more productive table editor. They cover a variety of subjects.

▸ Print Format Samples

Today—before you have a rush job to do—create some sample tables using the automatic formats that appeal to you *and print them* on your printer(s). Some will look great. One or two may be unreadable. Find out before you are in a hurry.

▸ Rearrange Rows in Outline View

With a table on-screen, switch to Outline view (View ➤ Outline). Move the pointer to the left edge of your table. The pointer shape will change, as shown in Figure 11.22.

FIGURE 11.22

Drag rows in Outline view to rearrange tables.

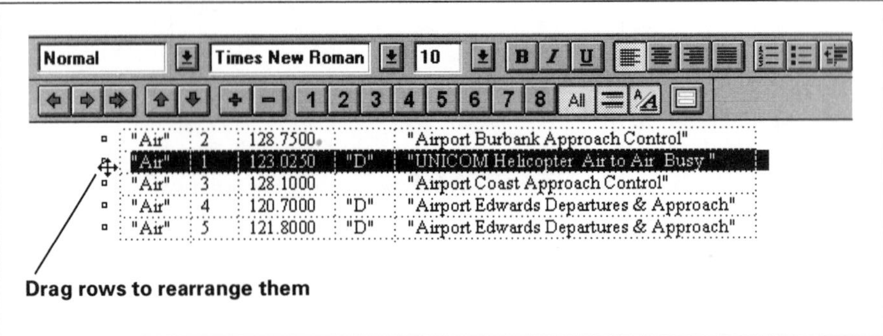

You can drag rows to new positions using Word's Outline features. See Chapter 21 for more information about Outline view.

▸ Moving Cell Contents

To move the contents of cells, follow these steps:

1. Find or create empty destination cells in the appropriate quantity and configuration to hold the items you plan to move. For instance, if you plan to move a four-row-by-six-column collection of cells, you will need the same number of available cells in the same configuration (4×6) to receive the moved items.
2. Copy or cut the items of interest by highlighting them and using Edit ➤ Copy or Edit ➤ Cut or the keyboard shortcuts Ctrl+C and Ctrl+X.

3. Now you can either select the same cell configuration at the destination (four rows of six columns each in our example) or you can try a shortcut. Simply place the insertion point in the upper-left destination cell. (If you use this shortcut, do *not* select the cell.) Be sure to place the insertion point before the end-of-cell mark, then paste. All of the cells will flow into their new destinations, bringing their formatting information with them.
4. Delete unused columns using the Table ➤ Delete Columns command if necessary.

▶ Styles and Tables

Word for Windows will use the current style (at the insertion point) when creating a new table. You can change the style of the whole table or apply different styles to different portions of the table.

Consider creating multiple styles if you plan to play with table formatting. For instance, you might have a style for table headings, another for standard text, another for decimal-aligned numbers, and so on. See Chapter 14 for more detail on styles.

Apply the new style to all appropriate paragraphs in your table by selecting the paragraphs and using the Formatting Toolbar's Style menu. From then on, simply changing a style will change all table text formatted with the changed style.

▶ Create AutoText Entries and Templates for Tables

If there are complex table setups that you reuse regularly, save them as Templates or AutoText entries. See Chapters 16 and 17 for details.

▶ Repeating Headings on Multipage Tables

To repeat column headings on each page of a multipage table, tell the Wizard or follow these steps:

1. Select the row or rows you wish to use as headings (typically the top one or two).

2. Choose T<u>a</u>ble ➤ <u>H</u>eadings.
3. When a table spills over onto a new page, the headings will repeat.

►► **TIP**

If you insert manual page breaks, the heading will *not* repeat.

► Use Tables to Create Forms

When you get good at manipulating tables, you can use them to create forms like the one shown in Figure 11.23. It's simply a combination of cells, borders, shading, and paragraph formats.

FIGURE 11.23 ►

Use tables to create forms like this one.

User Survey

Fill this out while at the user's desk			*Network information (confidential)*	
External Monitor?	Yes No	Screen size (diag):	User ID	Password
Color?	Yes No	Bits (8, 24, etc.): Grays:	Mail Name	Password
Printer	Laser Dot matrix		Groups	Sec Level
Please list software installed on this machine:			Interface type (Ethernet, etc.)	
			Zone & Port	
			Network User Training? Yes No	Date:

►► Sorting in Word

Have you ever created something like an alphabetical list of employees and their phone extensions, then needed a list of phone-extension assignments sorted by extension number? Most of us have small lists like these, and they always seem to be in the wrong order.

You could retype the old list or cut and paste, but the Table ➤ Sort… command or the Sort Text button on the Database Toolbar might be a better solution.

Word for Windows can sort lines of tabular text, items you've entered in tables, or even paragraphs in a document. The Sort command can be helpful when preparing data files for Word's Print Merge feature (discussed in Chapter 28).

▶▶ **WARNING**

As with some other Word features, Sort can make substantial changes to your document (read: ruin your hard work), so it is best to save before you sort. Consider practicing on copies of important files.

▶ Sorting with the Database Toolbar

There's a new Toolbar that contains some sorting buttons among other things. It's called the Database Toolbar, and it looks like Figure 11.24.

FIGURE 11.24 ▶

The Database Toolbar, while used mostly for Mail Merge products, can help with simple sorts too.

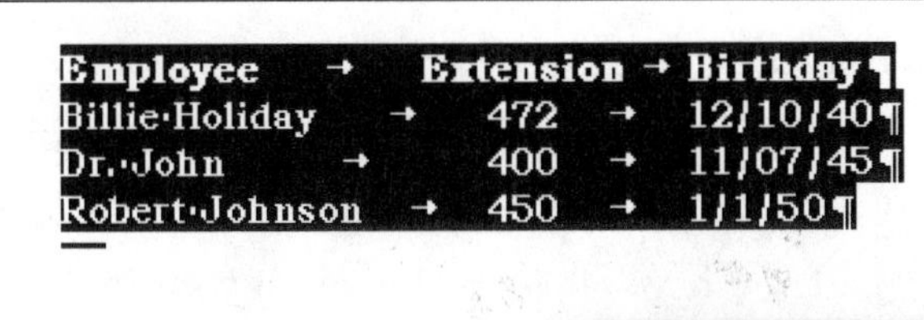

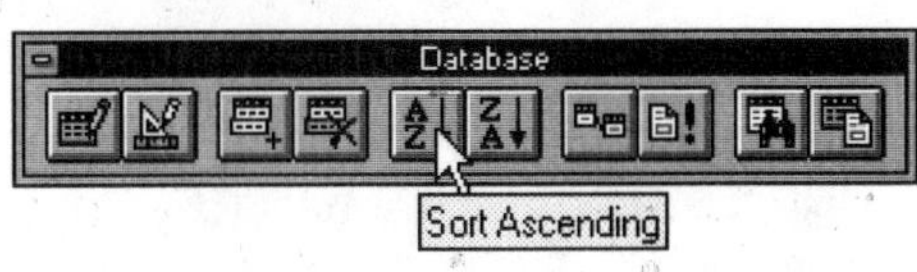

To sort rows of text, select them and click on either the Sort Ascending or Sort Descending button. Word for Windows will sort based on the first letter(s) at the left of each line. Remarkably, if the first row (line) of text is bold or otherwise "looks" like labels, Word will not move it.

To sort items in a table with the Database Toolbar, follow these steps:

1. Save your work, just in case.
2. Place the insertion point in the column that you want to use as the "sort by" column.
3. Click the Ascending or Descending sort button.
4. Word will sort the entire table (all columns), leaving labels untouched.

To learn more about the database capabilities and the rest of the buttons on the Database Toolbar, read Chapter 33.

▸ Sorting with the Sort Text… Command

Word's Table ➤ Sort Text… command will attempt to sort selected text alphabetically, numerically, or chronologically at your request. Sorts can be up to three levels "deep" (see Chapter 33). It can be used in free-form text but is much more powerful when used with a table. To sort a table with this command, follow these steps:

1. Save your work, just in case.
2. Place the insertion point in the table you wish to sort.
3. Pick Table ➤ Sort Text….
4. Word will highlight (select) the entire table.
5. You will see a dialog box like the one in Figure 11.25.
6. If you have labels at the top of your table, choose the My List Has Header Row option.
7. There will be up to three drop-down lists containing the column labels (if you have them) or column numbers (1, 2, and 3).
8. Specify the sort order by choosing the desired column for each sort level.
9. Choose a sort order for each column.
10. Tell Word if the data in each column are text, numbers, or dates by choosing from the drop-down Type lists.
11. Click OK and Word will sort.

FIGURE 11.25

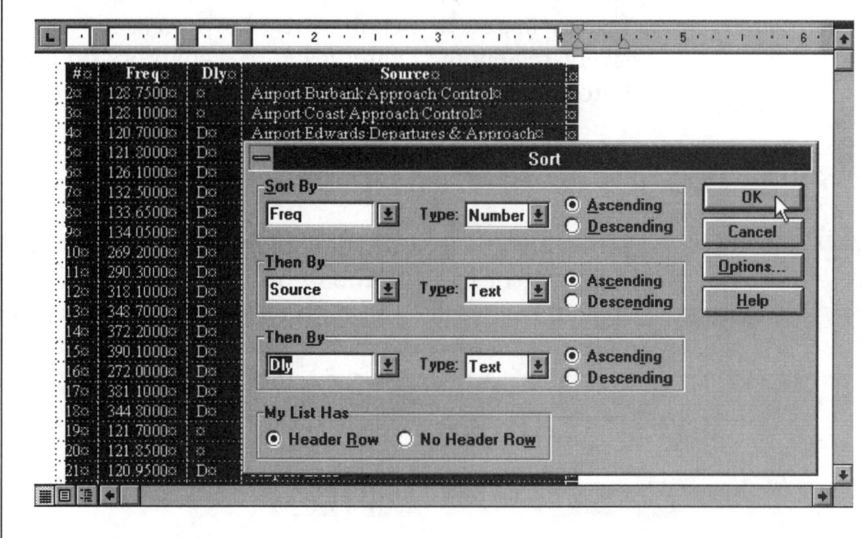

Word lets you sort tables up to three levels deep.

If you want the sort to be case-sensitive, or if you are sorting things not in a table, click the options button in the Sort dialog box and make the appropriate choices in the Sort Options dialog box. It is shown in Figure 11.26.

FIGURE 11.26

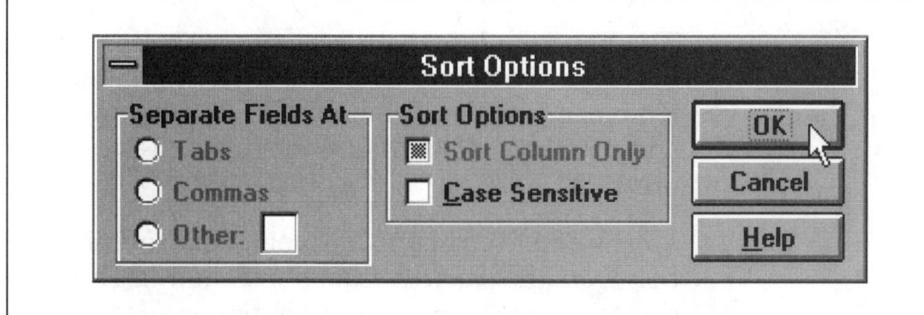

The Sort options dialog box.

►► Adding, Subtracting, Multiplying, and Dividing

Word's Table ➤ Formula command will add, subtract, multiply, and divide numbers you've typed in your documents. It is perfect for creating simple financial reports or for proofreading columns of numbers. The feature has some peculiarities, however, so if you plan to use it extensively, review the examples in this chapter and create some of your own before your next rush project.

▸ Word's Built-In Math Capability

How often have you typed an important memo and made a math or typing error in a column of numbers? Word's Formula feature can minimize mistakes like these. In its simplest capacity, the command adds columns or rows of numbers in tables, but it can do much more. Read all about it in Chapters 32 and 33.

▸▸ The Equation Editor

The Equation Editor is a more elegant way to create complex formulas. It helps you build formulas using palettes of math symbols and templates. The feature understands formula-typesetting rules and conventions, and will do much of the formatting for you.

▸ Starting the Equation Editor

The Equation Editor is a separate program that runs under Word's supervision. The program and related help file should be installed in your Commands folder. Choose Insert ➤ Object, go to the Create New tab, and double-click on Microsoft Equation 2.0 to start it, as shown in Figure 11.27.

You assemble equations by typing text and picking templates and symbols from the palettes. Equation Editor has a number of keyboard shortcuts, which are detailed in the program's context-sensitive help screens. Create equations by choosing elements from drop-down lists, as shown in Figure 11.28.

To receive online help about a particular palette or symbol, visit the Equation Editor's online Help menu.

FIGURE 11.27

Starting the Equation Editor.

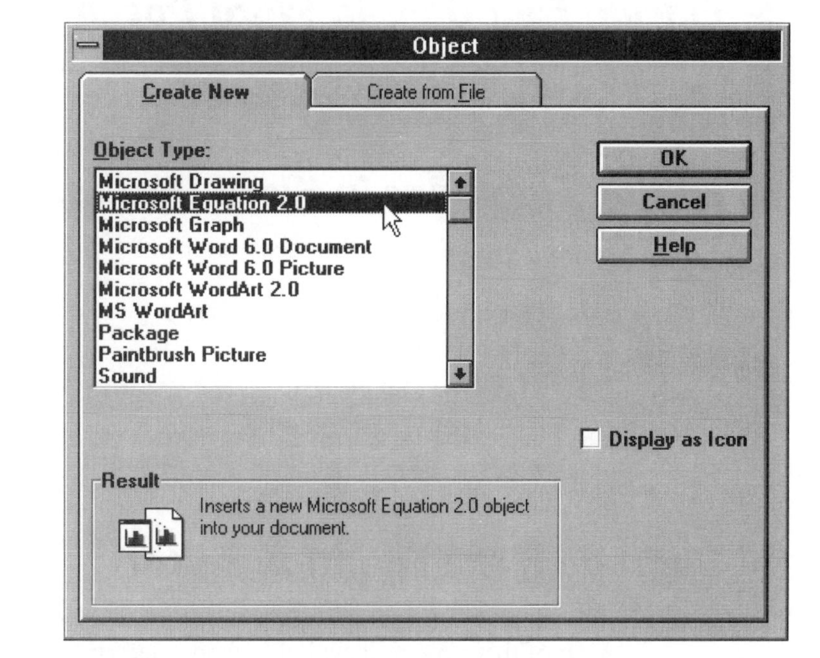

FIGURE 11.28

Choose elements for your equations from the drop-down lists.

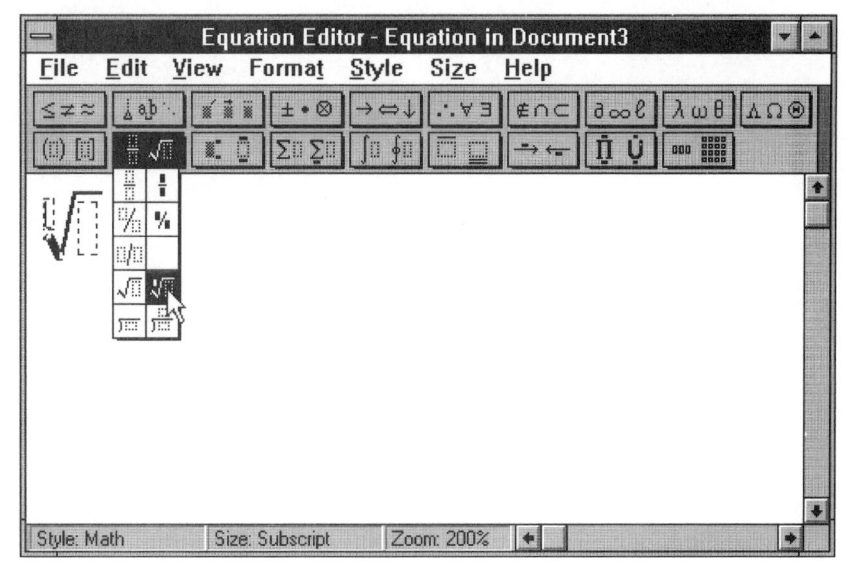

► Placing Equations in Word Documents

Closing the Equation Editor window pastes the equation you've created into your Word for Windows document at the insertion point.

► Editing Equations in Word Documents

To edit equations, follow these steps:

1. Double-click on the equation in your document to open the Equation Editor window.
2. Make the changes.
3. Close the Equation Editor window to replace the old equation with the new.

► Upgrading the Equation Editor

If you work a lot with equations, there is an even more powerful version of this program available from Design Sciences, Inc. Their address is 4028 Broadway, Long Beach, CA, 90803. Or you can phone them at (800) 827-0685.

CHAPTER 12

Headers, Footers, Page Numbers, and Footnotes

▶ ▶ FAST TRACK

To create unique headers and footers for the first page of your document **363**

place the insertion point in the section where you want the different first page effect to begin and open the Page Setup dialog box (double-click in a blank part of a ruler or choose File ➤ Page Setup…). Then choose the Layout tab and check the Different First Page choice in the Headers and Footers area.

To add page numbers to your document **364**

use the new Insert ➤ Page Numbers… command, which provides a wider variety of numbering options than the button in the Header and Footer Toolbar.

To delete all of the page numbers in a multi-section document **369**

open a header or footer containing page numbers and choose Edit ➤ Select All or use the **Ctrl+A** shortcut. Delete a page number; the rest will disappear.

To add a footnote **369**

place the insertion point where the footnote marker is needed and choose Insert ➤ Footnote…

▶▶

Word's *headers* and *footers* are places to put repetitive information in a document's top and bottom margins. Logically enough, headers print at the top, footers at the bottom. (Don't confuse footers with *footnotes*, which are different.)

You can use headers and footers to print something simple on each page, such as your name, or something complex, such as a graphic. Stylized text, dates, and automatic page numbering can all be included in headers or footers.

Headers and footers can be identical on all pages in your document, or you can specify different contents for each section of the document. Odd and even pages can have different designs if you wish. The first page of each document or each section can be unique.

new

Now in Word for Windows, header and footer editing always takes place in Page Layout view. You work right in the header and footer area of your document after double-clicking to undim it.

It is possible to apply virtually any paragraph or character style using the Formatting Toolbar and rulers in headers and footers. You can also place framed items and frame anchors in headers or footers. They will repeat on all pages thereafter.

Once headers and footers have been added to a document, it is possible to see and edit them in the Page Layout view. They are also displayed in Print Preview, but when you attempt to open a header or footer in Normal view or Print Preview, Word for Windows switches you to Page Layout view and displays the Header and Footer Toolbar.

Word's footnote features are equally powerful and easy to use. You can enter, edit, and view footnote numbers in a variety of formats. Word for Windows simplifies inserting, deleting, and moving footnotes by automatically numbering and renumbering them as necessary.

►► Entering Basic Headers and Footers

To enter a header that repeats on all pages in your document:

1. Choose View ➤ Header and Footer or double-click in the header area of the first page to be modified in Page Layout or Print Preview.
2. Word will switch to Page Layout view if it is not already there and display the Header and Footer Toolbar.
3. Create and edit header text as you would any other. You can paste graphics, apply styles, and otherwise format your work normally. Figure 12.1 shows an example.
4. Use the automatic page number, time, and date features described later in this chapter.
5. Double-click in the main document to return to work there.

FIGURE 12.1 ►

A header window can contain stylized text, borders, shading, and graphics.

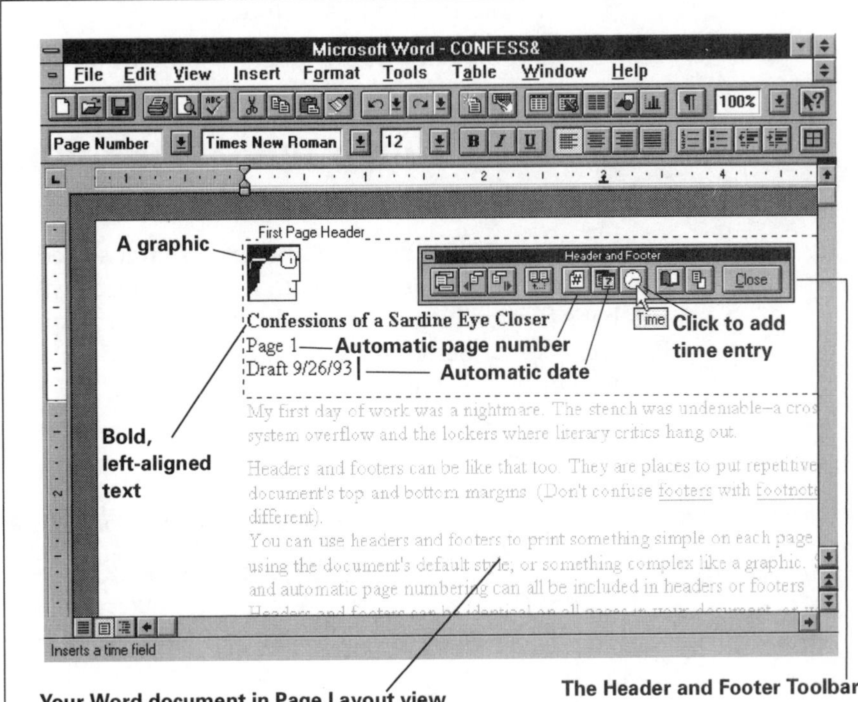

TIP

Unless you already have a header, double-clicking can be cumbersome. So, until you have a header, it's probably best to use the menu command.

Footers are entered the same way as headers, except that you work in a Footer window:

1. Choose View ➤ Header and Footer or double-click in the footer area of the first page to be modified in Page Layout or Print Preview.
2. Word will switch to Page Layout view if it is not already there and display the Header and Footer Toolbar.
3. Create and edit footer text as you would any other. You can paste graphics, apply styles, and otherwise format your work normally.
4. Use the automatic page number, time, and date features described later in this chapter.
5. Double-click in the main document to continue working there.

▶ Adding Dates, Times, and Simple Page Numbers

In Figure 12.2 a page number has been inserted in a footer by clicking on the page-numbering icon. It was centered with the Formatting Toolbar's Center button. You could use other formatting tricks as well—adding some space before the page number with the Paragraph tab's Space Before option, for instance.

FIGURE 12.2 

Use Toolbars to enter and position things like page numbers.

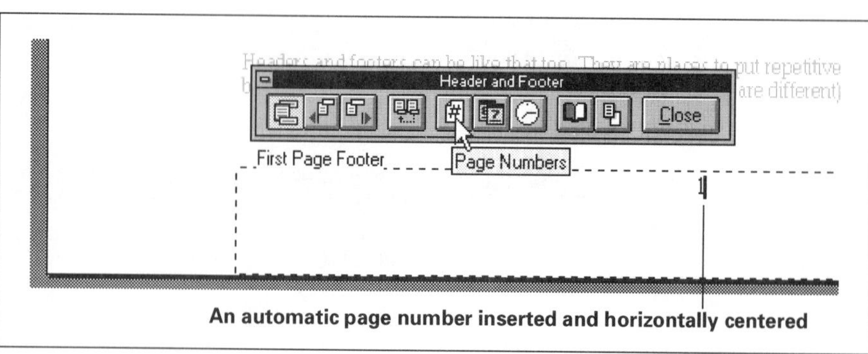

TIP

You can place *fields* in headers or footers so that things like authors' names, file names, date last saved, and other information can appear automatically. See Chapter 33 for details.

Rulers and Toolbars in Headers and Footers

Use your regular document ruler or Formatting Toolbar when working in header and footer windows. Margins, indents, tabs, and all the other tools work as you'd expect. The Header and Footer Toolbar's functions are shown in Figure 12.3.

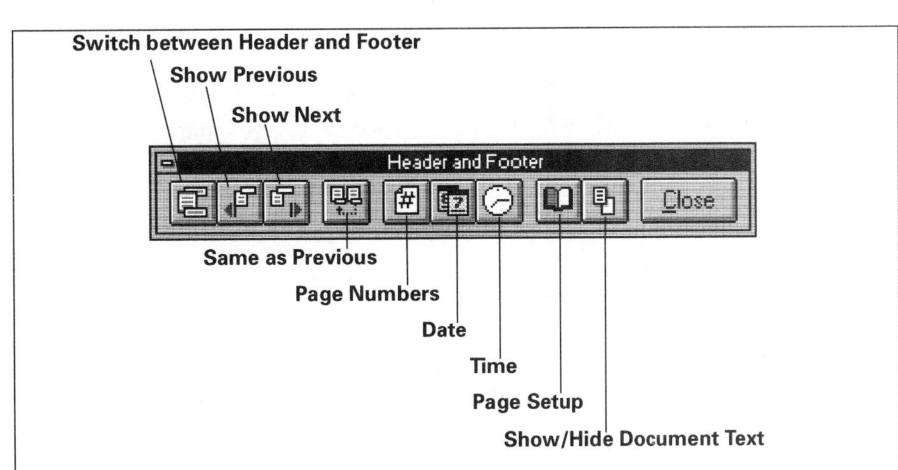

FIGURE 12.3

The Header and Footer Toolbar functions.

Headers and Footers in Print Preview

It is a good idea to switch to Print Preview occasionally when designing headers and footers. You can get a good approximation of how headers and footers will print and spot potential problems (like the footer that appears only on odd pages in Figure 12.4).

FIGURE 12.4

Use Print Preview to view your work. This can help you spot potential problems so you can fix them before printing.

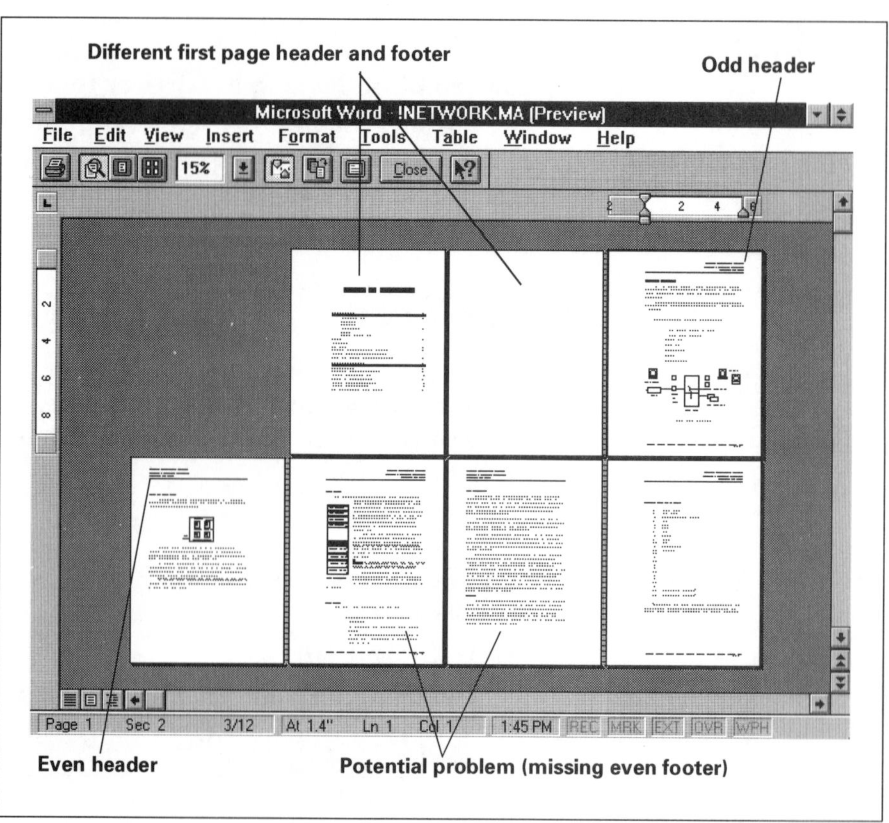

►► TIP

Remember that many printers cannot print at the very edges of the paper and that it is possible to position a header or footer in nonprinting areas. If you have selected the correct printer at the start of the project, Word does a pretty good job of showing you when a header or footer will be cut off by your printer.

Take another look at Figure 12.4. Because this document will be printed two-sided and then bound, mirrored margins and odd/even headers and footers have been specified. Notice too that the table of contents page does not have a header or footer and the back side of that page (the even page) is blank. Read on to learn how to accomplish these effects.

▶▶ Even and Odd Headers and Footers

To create different even and odd headers or footers:

1. Place the insertion point in the section where you want the odd/even effect to begin (read more about sections in Chapter 13).
2. Open the Page Setup dialog box (double-click in a blank part of a ruler or choose File ➤ Page Setup...).
3. Visit the Layout tab.
4. Check the Different Odd and Even choice in the Headers and Footers area.

   Headers and Footers
   [X] Different Odd and Even
   [X] Different First Page

   Odd Page Header
   Odd Page Footer
   Even Page Header
   Even Page Footer

   You now have four header and footer areas in Page Layout view. Their names will change from page to page.

▶▶ Different First Page Headers and Footers

The Layout tab in the Page Setup dialog box contains a choice called Different First Page. (Chapter 13 goes into more detail about sections.) To create unique headers and footers for the first page of your document:

1. Place the insertion point in the section where you want the different first page effect to begin (read more abut sections in Chapter 13).
2. Open the Page Setup dialog box (double-click in a blank part of a ruler or choose File ➤ Page Setup…).
3. Choose the Layout tab.
4. Check the Different First Page choice in the Headers and Footers area. You'll have different header and footer areas on the first page. Their names will be visible in Page Layout view:

First Page Header

First Page Footer

5. Create different headers and footers for the first page in Page Layout view.

▸▸ Page Numbering

Word for Windows offers a variety of tools to help you automatically number pages. You are given many page-numbering format and style choices. It's possible to position page numbers nearly anywhere that pleases you. Let's explore these features and discuss the effects of document sections and pagination on page numbering.

TIP

If you plan to break a document into multiple sections, you may want to insert page numbers *before* you split the document into sections. Otherwise, you will have to repeat the page-numbering process for each section of your document. That said, let's dig right in.

Word for Windows provides two page-numbering techniques. Both have advantages and disadvantages. Normally, you will use only one for a particular document. Otherwise, you might end up with two or more sets of page numbers!

▶ The Header and Footer Toolbar Method

As you've seen already, Word for Windows makes it easy to place page numbers in headers and footers. To add page numbers using the header/ footer method:

1. Open a header or footer by double-clicking on it in Page Layout view.
2. Click on the page-numbering button in the Header and Footer Toolbar.
3. A number will be inserted for you in your header or footer at the insertion point.
4. Like anything else placed in headers and footers, page numbers can be stylized, repositioned, surrounded with borders, accompanied by text, and otherwise embellished.

Word for Windows uses the standard header or footer style to format page numbers placed therein. You can override this by applying additional character and paragraph formats or by changing the standard header or footer style (see Chapter 14).

Headers and footers have tab stops, which you may find useful for page-number positioning.

▶ The Page Numbers... Command

The new Insert ➤ Page Numbers... command provides a wider variety of numbering options. It reveals the Page Numbers dialog box and lets you quickly reach the Page Number Format dialog as shown in Figure 12.5.

1. Start by placing the insertion point in the section you want to number.
2. Display the Page Numbering dialog box by choosing Insert ➤ Page Numbers....

FIGURE 12.5

The Page Number Format dialog box.

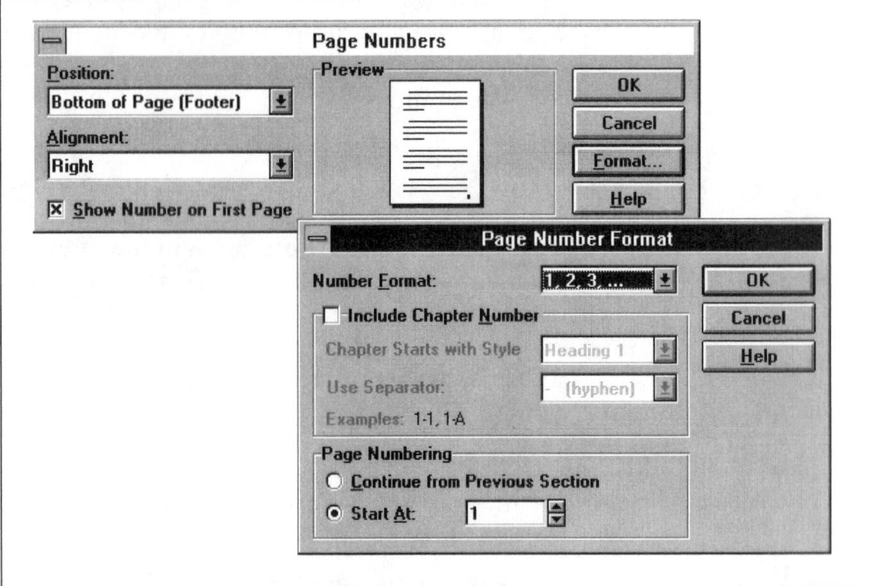

3. Word suggests page numbers in the bottom-right corner of your document (½" from the bottom and right edges of the paper), but you can specify different positions with the Position and Alignment drop-down menus. Watch the Preview area as you work.
4. Choose to place a page number on the first page or not by clicking to add or remove the corresponding *X*.
5. Either click OK or click on the Format… button to review other page-numbering options.

▸▸ Page-Numbering Formats and Styles

Word for Windows supports four page-number formats. Standard Arabic numbers (1, 2, 3…) are the default. It is also possible to number with capital Roman numerals (I, II, III…) or with capital letters (A, B, C…). Lowercase formats are also provided (i, ii, iii… and a, b, c…).

Specify number formats in the Page Number Format dialog box reached by clicking the Format… button in the Page Numbers dialog box (Insert ➤ Page Numbers…), shown in Figure 12.5. All of these formats are available, regardless of which page-numbering technique you choose.

You can use Word's many character- and paragraph-embellishment features to spruce up page numbers. Pick the font of your choice, make numbers bold, align them, put boxes around them. Text can appear next to the numbers (*Page-1*, for instance).

After inserting page numbers, switch to Page Layout view and change their appearance.

TIP

Documents containing multiple sections can have different formats in each section. That's both good and bad news. If you want all sections to have the same format, you will want to pick a format before you break up the document. Otherwise, you must place the insertion point in each section and pick the same format for every one. Plan ahead.

Chapter Numbers in Page Numbers

If you use Word's standard heading Styles, and if you use one of the headings for chapter titles, you can have Word for Windows include chapter headings with your page number (*2-36*, for instance). You can specify one of four separators—hyphens, periods, colons, or em dashes.

TIP

Don't confuse hyphens and em dashes. Em dashes (—) are much longer than hyphens and are used to show breaks in thought.

You set up chapter page numbering in the Page Number Format box, in the section called Use Separator:

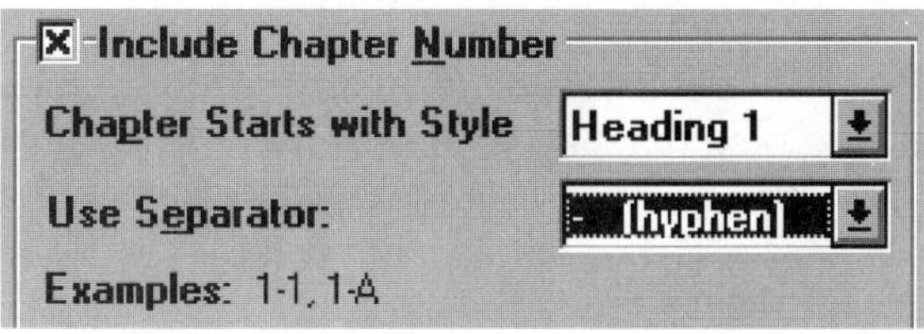

▸ Managing Starting Page Numbers

Usually you will want Word for Windows to place the number 1 on your first printed page, but not always. For example, many people prefer their multipage letters to be printed without a 1 on the first page. They still want the second page to be numbered 2, the third 3, and so on. Let's call this *first page number suppressed.*

Or you may wish to start each new section in a multisection document with 1. Let's call this *restart sections with 1.*

Sometimes you may want your first page to be printed without a number (a cover page, for instance) and then the next page to contain the number 1. Let's call this *begin second page from 1.*

Finally, you might want to use some other number for the first page, like 25 or 100. This is helpful when you are combining your work with other documents. Let's call that *starting page other than 1.*

Note that in all the following examples, we assume that your document does not already have page numbers.

First Page Number Suppressed

This one's easy.

1. Place the insertion point in the desired section.
2. Open the Page Numbers dialog box with the Insert ➤ Page Numbers... command.
3. Remove the *X* from the Show Number on First Page box:

   ☐ Show Number on First Page

4. Click OK.

Restart Sections with 1

To restart each section at page 1, follow these steps:

1. Place the insertion point in any section. Open the Page Number dialog box, reached with the Insert ➤ Page Numbers... command.

2. Click on the Format... button to reach the Page Number Format dialog box.
3. Check the Start At box.
4. Specify the number each section will start with (1 in this example).

▶ Removing Page Numbers

Simply open the header or footer containing unwanted page numbers and delete one. The rest of the page numbers in the section will disappear. To delete all of the page numbers in a multi-section document, follow these steps:

1. Open a header or footer containing page numbers.
2. Choose Edit ➤ Select All or use the Ctrl+A shortcut.
3. Delete a page number. The rest will disappear.

▶▶ Footnotes

Word for Windows lets you create simple *footnotes* and personalize their appearance. Here are the various techniques.

▶ Easy Automatic Footnotes

Figure 12.6 shows an automatic (default) Word for Windows footnote. It should take you less than ten seconds to add your first footnote to existing text.

Follow these steps:

1. Start by placing the insertion point where the footnote marker is needed (after the words *data lines* in our example).
2. Choose Insert ➤ Footnote....

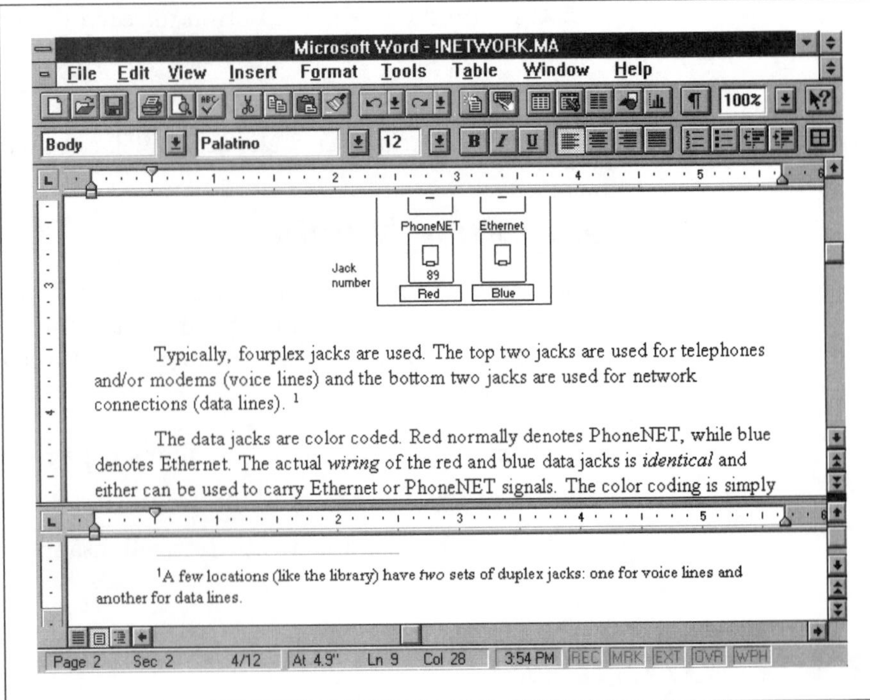

FIGURE 12.6

Standard footnotes like these require very little effort.

3. You can dismiss the Footnote and Endnote dialog box by clicking OK, because Word's defaults are fine for this project.
4. If you are in Normal view, a second window pane opens where you do the footnote typing:

In Page Layout view you type right where the footnote will print—usually between the text and footer:

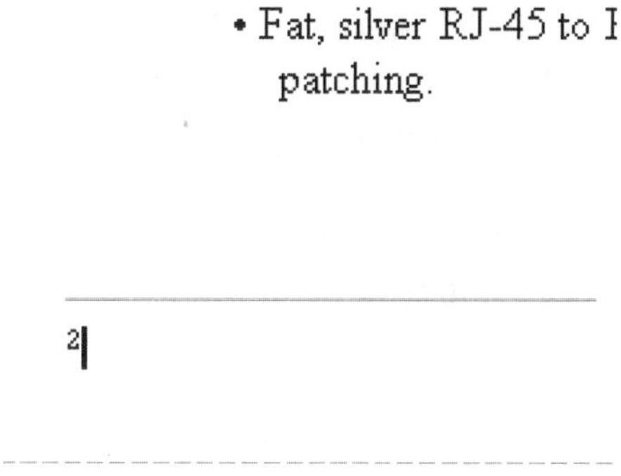

• Fat, silver RJ-45 to I
patching.

2|

5. In either case, the insertion point automatically moves to the proper place for you to type the footnote. Type it.
6. To return to the main document, move the insertion point with the mouse or press Ctrl+Alt+Z.

▶ Viewing Footnotes

Footnotes are always displayed in Page Layout view and Print Preview. If they are not visible in Normal or Outline view, choose View ➤ Footnotes. Word for Windows will switch to Page Layout view.

If you are constantly entering or referring to footnotes in Normal view, you can leave the footnote window visible while you work. Scrolling in your document will cause corresponding scrolling in the footnote window. Use the footnote scroll bars if necessary to view notes. Feel free to resize the footnote window to suit your taste and screen size. Drag the bar separating the two windows the same way you resize other Word for Windows split screens (point to the Splitbox and drag).

To hide the footnote window, choose View ➤ Footnotes or click the close button and remove the check mark next to the command.

►► TIP

Double-clicking on a footnote marker in your document will display the footnote pane and place the insertion point at the beginning of the footnote. If necessary, Word for Windows will open the footnote pane and scroll to the appropriate note. Also, moving the insertion point in the footnote pane will cause the main document to scroll to the reference.

► *Inserting Footnotes ahead of Existing Ones*

Whenever you insert (or delete) footnotes, Word for Windows renumbers the existing ones properly. Just position the insertion point and choose Insert ➤ Footnote.... Word for Windows will take it from there. To delete a footnote, just delete its number in the text. Again, Word will do the dirty work.

►► *Editing and Personalizing Footnotes*

You can copy, move, or delete entire footnotes as easily as you would a single character.

1. Select the footnote marker of interest in the document text. (This might take a steady hand, particularly if you have drag-and-drop enabled.)
2. Cut, copy, paste, or drag-and-drop the footnote mark.
3. Word does the rest. If you have Numbering turned on, Word will update the numbers in your text and in the corresponding footnotes. If you copy and paste a mark, a corresponding new footnote will magically appear in the right spot in your footnotes. Deletion works as you would expect.

► *Editing Footnote Text*

Visit the footnote pane in Normal view or the footnote itself in Page Layout view. Cut, paste, and drag-and-drop away to your heart's content. (Note that you cannot cut a footnote's entire text; you must cut the footnote mark in text if you wish to delete or move it.)

▶ Personalizing Footnotes

Word for Windows lets you modify many footnote parameters via the Insert ➤ Footnote... command and the Note Options dialog box.

1. Choose Insert ➤ Footnote....
2. Use the Symbol button to change the footnote symbol character.
3. Click Options... to bring up the Note Options dialog box, shown in Figure 12.7.

FIGURE 12.7 ▶

Personalize footnote appearance using the Footnote choices in the All Footnotes tab of the Notes Options dialog box.

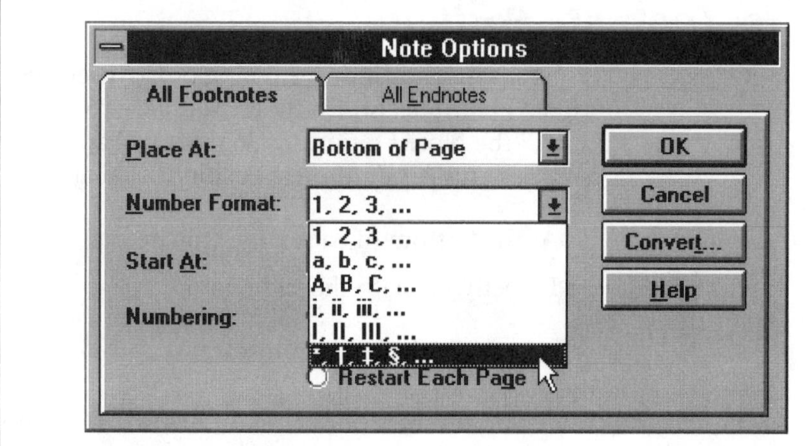

4. Click to switch to the All Footnotes tab, if necessary.
5. Specify note placement, number formats, starting numbers, and starting points.
6. Click OK.

▶ Controlling Footnote Numbering

You can specify the starting number for footnotes in the Footnotes area of the Format menu's Document dialog box. The same choices are available here as before. Footnote numbering can restart on each page if you check the Restart Each Page button in the Footnotes area of the All Footnotes tab of the Notes Options dialog box.

▸ Footnote Text Style

You can embellish selected footnote text as you would expect. Highlight the text of interest, then use the ruler, Formatting Toolbar, or format-related menu choices (bold, italic, and so on).

To change the size or font or other footnote style elements for all footnotes, modify the Microsoft standard footnote text style. (Footnote text is based on the Normal style.) To change the footnote-reference marks, modify the footnote-reference style.

▸ Footnote Position

The Footnote and Endnote dialog box (Insert ➤ Footnote…) has two options: Footnote and Endnote. You have to click on the Options button, and the Note Options dialog box will appear. It has two tabs: All Footnotes and All Endnotes. Positions available for Footnote are:

- At the bottom of each page (the default)
- Directly beneath the last text on a page

Positions available for Endnote are:

- At the end of a section in multi-section documents
- At the end of your document

Specify footnote position by using the drop-down Place At list in the corresponding tab of the Note Options dialog box. Phew!

Incidentally, in multicolumn sections, footnotes print below each column.

▸ Footnote Separators

The little black lines that separate document text from the footnotes themselves are cleverly called *footnote separators*. Edit them as follows:

1. Switch to Normal view.

2. Display footnotes.
3. Choose Footnote Separator from the drop-down list.

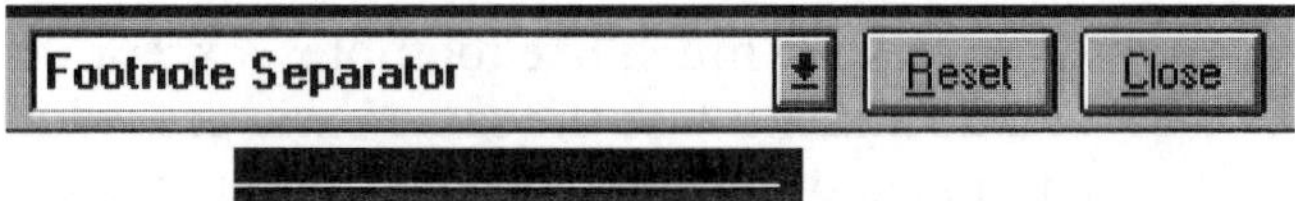

4. This is just like any other Word window. You can edit the length of the line (it's a paragraph). Insert a graphic, if you like. You can even use Word's drawing tools here. Double lines look nice. Use Word's Paragraph Border feature to create them. It is possible to use a ruler and Formatting Toolbar in the separator window.
5. Click Close (or Reset to restore the standard separator).

When you are happy with your creation, close the separator window and view the results in Print Preview or Page Layout view.

▶ Footnote-Reference Marks

Footnote-reference marks appear wherever you place them in your document's text area and at the beginning of each footnote in the footnote area itself.

By default, Word for Windows uses numbers for reference marks. If you turn off the Numbering feature, Word for Windows defaults to an asterisk as the footnote-reference mark. You can type any character of your choosing in the Custom Mark portion of the All Footnotes tab of the Note Options dialog box. In fact, it is possible to use as many as ten characters for a footnote-reference mark.

▶ Footnote Continuation

Continuation separators appear whenever footnotes carry over onto the next page. These notices can be modified the same way you change regular separators as described in the previous section on Footnote Separators.

►► Endnotes

Endnotes are much like footnotes, except that they appear at the end of a document. Use the same basic procedures as you do for entering, editing, and moving footnotes. When working in the Note Options dialog box, choose the All Endnotes tab.

►► Footnote Tips and Cautions

Here are some tips and caveats on using footnotes:

- Word does not automatically spell check footnotes, but you can select footnotes and run the spellchecker.
- Do not place index or table-of-contents entries in footnotes. They will be ignored.
- Word's new Find and Replace features can help you search for and reformat footnotes. See Chapter 20.
- Save frequently used footnote entries and use AutoText to eliminate tedious retyping. See Chapter 17.

▶ ▶ CHAPTER 13

Organizing Your Work with Section Breaks

FAST TRACK

To do any of the following within a single document, you must use a section break: ***382***

change page orientation within a document; change margins in part of a document; turn line numbering on or off; change footnote appearance or suppress notes; change the appearance of headers and footers; change the format, position, or progression of page numbers.

To insert a section break ***383***

position the insertion point where you want the break to go, then choose Insert ➤ Break.... Double-click Section to insert the break.

To have text from preceding sections occupy the same page as the designated section ***385***

select the Continuous printing strategy.

To print text at the top of a new column in multicolumn format ***385***

choose the New Column printing strategy.

When you think of *sections*, you probably imagine traditional book sections—collections of several related chapters, for instance. Word's section features can help you organize large projects this way, of course, but they do much more. Word for Windows sections are designed to let you change major formatting features at places you decide in your document.

Sections need not be used only for books or reports. It is a shame sections aren't called zones or something less ambiguous.

You must start a new section whenever you need to:

- Change page orientation within a document
- Change margins in part of a document
- Turn line numbering on or off
- Change footnote appearance or suppress notes
- Change the appearance of headers and footers
- Change the format, position, or progression of page numbers

While the exact sequence of events will vary with your project and needs, in general you will:

1. Place the insertion point where you want a new section to begin.
2. Use the Insert ➤ Break… command to create the new section.
3. Make the desired formatting and other changes for that section.
4. Perhaps create other sections farther down in the document.

You'll see practical applications of sections in a moment. There are no hard and fast rules about *when* to create new sections. Experienced Word for Windows users often create ten or twenty sections in a one-page document. Others use a single section for an entire 100-page report.

Occasionally, Word for Windows will insert section breaks for you—when creating an automatic table of contents, for instance. Mostly, you'll insert them yourself.

▶▶ Inserting Section Breaks

new

To insert a section break, follow these steps:

1. Prepare to create a new section by placing the insertion point where you want the break to occur.
2. Next, choose Insert ➤ Break.... Choose Section in the resulting dialog box and click OK.
3. This places a double-dotted, nonprinting line containing the words *End of Section* at the insertion point on your screen (see Figure 13.1). The status area reflects section numbers as you move the insertion point or scroll to pages in the new section.

FIGURE 13.1 ▶

Sections are marked with double-dotted, nonprinting lines; the section number appears next to the page number in the status area.

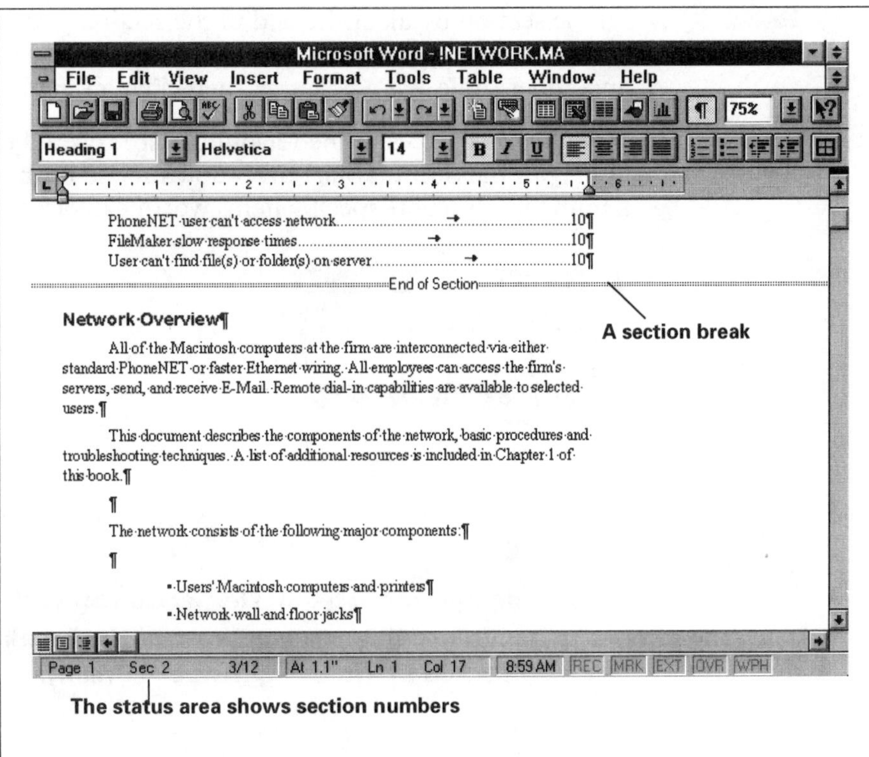

▶ Sections as Chapter Elements

It is very common to create a new section for each chapter in a large publishing project, such as a manuscript or report. This makes it possible to change header and footer information like chapter names. If you were creating an employee handbook, Chapter One's header might contain the words *Welcome new employees,* while the headers in Chapter Two might say *Your health plan explained,* and so forth.

Sections also make it possible to customize page numbers within chapters. Your document's front matter might be numbered in lowercase Roman numerals (i, ii, iii, etc.). Pages within chapters might contain chapter-related numbers that restart at the beginning of each chapter (1-1, 2-1, and so on). As you'll recall, you can use different page-numbering styles in each section of your document, and you can restart page numbering at the beginning of any new section.

▶ The Layout Tab in Page Setup

You reach the Layout tab in the Page Setup dialog box by double-clicking on the section break at the end of the section you wish to change. It is also possible to place the insertion point in the section being designed and choose File ➤ Page Setup, then click on the Layout tab.

Many of the choices in the Layout tab are covered elsewhere in this book, but the Section Start drop-down menu of the dialog box contains a number of section-specific items worth exploring. It is shown here:

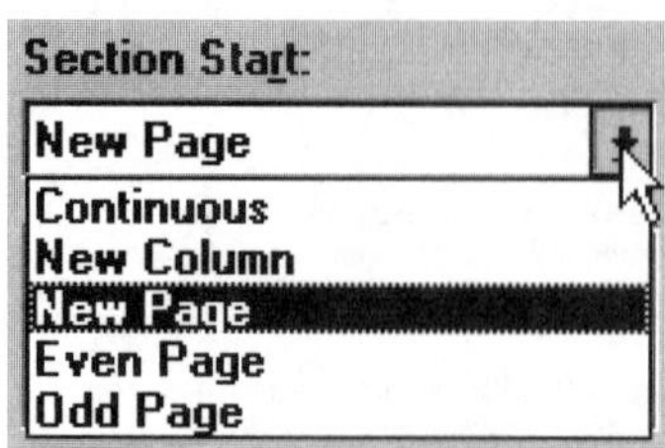

▶▶ NOTE

The options listed in the Section Start drop-down menu are the same as those in the Break dialog box (reached by choosing Insert ➤ Break).

This is how you tell Word for Windows where you want it to start printing the various sections of your document. You can make a different choice for each section. Here are explanations of your options.

Continuous

Continuous is Word's default section printing strategy. Text from preceding sections will occupy the same page as the designated section, if there is enough room for the text from both sections.

New Column

In multicolumn formats, Word for Windows breaks a column when it encounters a section mark. It prints the subsequent text at the top of a new column. (See Chapter 22 for more about columns.)

New Page

Word for Windows will always start new sections on new pages with this choice.

Even Page

Word for Windows starts printing the new section on an even-numbered page, even if it means leaving an odd-numbered page blank.

Odd Page

Word for Windows will start the new section on an odd-numbered page. This is a great way to ensure that new sections start on right-hand pages when designing documents for two-sided printing.

▶ Apply To

Another area worth scrutinizing is the Apply To portion of the Layout tab. It lets you tell Word how far to go with your requested changes.

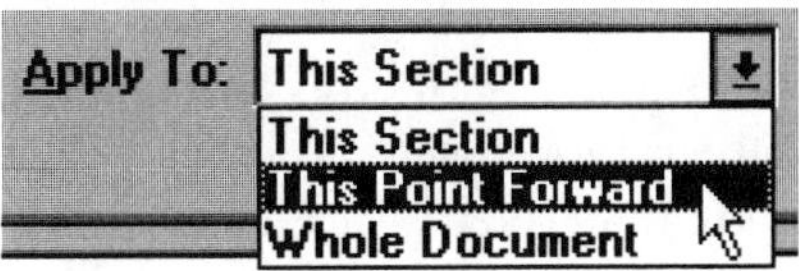

This Section

If you check This Section, the changes will affect only the section containing the insertion point.

This Point Forward

This Point Forward makes the changes effective from the insertion point to the end of the document.

Whole Document

This choice makes the changes document-wide.

▸▸ Copying Section Breaks

Section-formatting information is stored with section breaks much the same way paragraph formatting is stored with paragraph marks. And you can copy section information by copying and pasting section breaks. It is even possible to place section breaks as AutoText items. See Chapter 17 for details.

Like paragraph marks (¶), a section break controls the information above it.

Click on a break to select it. A thick insertion point will straddle the break line. You may find it easiest to do this in Normal view. Once selected, you can then copy, cut, etc.

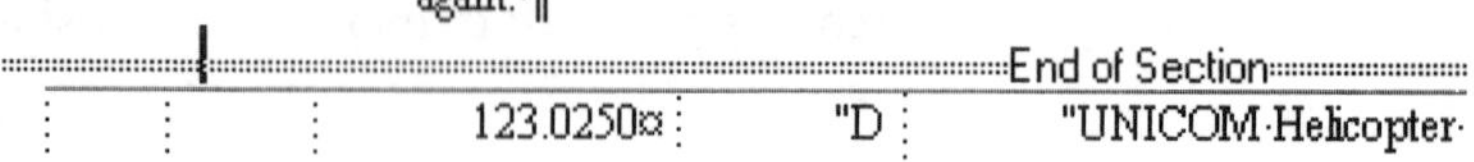

▸▸ Deleting Section Breaks

Select a section break as just described. Then press the backspace or Delete key. Text before the removed section break will take on the characteristics of the following material. It may take a moment for Word for

Windows to reformat and repaginate the document. Watch the status line and be patient.

Changing Page Orientation with Breaks

Section Breaks make it possible for you to mix portrait and landscape page orientations in the same document. For instance, you could have a three-page memo with pages one and three in portrait mode (the text, perhaps) and the middle page in landscape mode (a wide spreadsheet, perhaps). Figure 13.2 illustrates the general concept with an article example.

NOTE

Word for Windows flips headers, footers, page numbers, and other marginalia for you unless you override this. Therefore, if you've placed page numbers at the bottom of your pages, the landscape page(s) will have numbers at the right edge of the paper so that they read like the rest of the (flipped) text on the page(s).

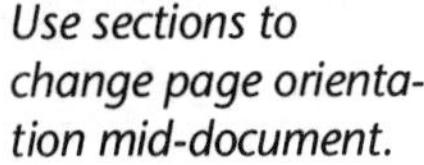

FIGURE 13.2

Use sections to change page orientation mid-document.

Today· had· started· out· normally· enough.· Piloting· an· engine-less· airplane· requires· thousands·of·decisions--some·technical,·others·personal;·each·potentially·life-threatening.·¶
For·me·at·least,·the·process·always·starts·during·the·ninety-minute·drive·from·home·to·the· gliderport.·¶ End of Section

It·was·already·nearly·75·degrees·at·8·AM· when· I· pulled· onto· our· quiet· suburban· street.·Even·knowing·that·it·would·be·ten· degrees·cooler·in·the·mountains,·with·a· flick,· a· tap,· and· a· twist· the· electric· convertible·top· went· down,· the· Metal-SR· cassette· in,· and· the· volume· up.· Surging· LEDs· on· the· graphic· equalizer· and· protests· from· the· neighbor's· dog· cumulus·clouds·with·their·puffy·tops·and· sexy,· anvil-flat· bottoms· were· already· forming·in·the·desert·on·the·other·side·of· the·mountains.¶
These· surrealistic· sky· sculptures· are· a· soaring·pilot's·friends.·They·signal·rising· air· and· the· miracle· called· lift.· On· exceptional· days· like· this· one,· there· would· sometimes· be· row· after· row· of·

Here are the general steps:

1. Position the insertion point where you want the break to occur.
2. Choose Insert ➤ Break....
3. Choose the Next Page Option.
4. Click OK.
5. Move the insertion point to where you want the orientation to change again (if you do)—the beginning of page 3 in our example.
6. Insert another page break there.
7. Position the insertion point in the new section you've created.
8. Visit the Layout tab in Page Setup (double-click in an unmarked part of the ruler or choose File ➤ Page Setup...).
9. Make other page layout choices in the other Page Setup tabs.
10. Preview, then print your work.

▸▸ TIP

You can center a spreadsheet between the top and bottom margins of its page with the Vertical Alignment setting in the Layout tab of the Page Setup dialog box. Choose Center to create this effect.

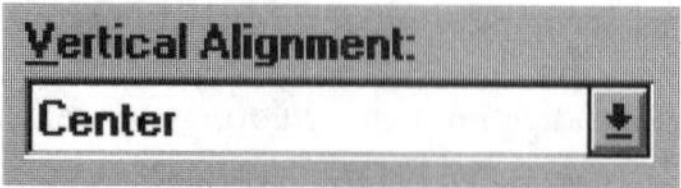

▸▸ Time-Saving Section Tips

Here are some time-saving section tips:

- Documents start out as one big section, and it is often best to wait until you are nearly finished with a document before breaking it into smaller sections. Do, however, think about the divisions in your document early on.

- Section formatting done when there is only one section affects the *entire* document. For instance, header and footer choices will be applied throughout.

new

- Set up templates and AutoText entries for complex section designs. See Chapter 17.

▶ ▶ CHAPTER 14

Using AutoFormat and Styles

▸▸ FAST TRACK

To reuse complex paragraph formats without laboriously recreating them each time ***394***

use *styles*.

To use one of the built-in Word for Windows styles ***395***

either place the insertion point in a paragraph or select several paragraphs and then scroll through the drop-down style list on the Formatting Toolbar. Click on the desired style.

To quickly apply commonly used styles ***397***

select the text to be affected and choose one of the keyboard combination shortcuts.

To create your own style ***398***

display the Formatting Toolbar. Place the insertion point in the formatted paragraph whose style you'd like to capture. Then click *once* on the style box (the name portion of the drop-down style-name list). Type a meaningful style name and press ↵.

To create legal style names ***398***

do not use: backslashes (\), braces ({}), or semicolons (;). Also, Word distinguishes between uppercase and lowercase.

To define new styles and rename, explore, list, or delete existing ones (among other things) ***399***

use the Styles dialog box (Format ➤ Style…).

Word's *style* features are responsible for much of its power and popularity. They also confuse and initially frustrate most new users. It is possible to plug along in Word for Windows for the rest of your life without knowing a whit about styles. That would be a shame, though. Learning about Word's standard styles, custom styles, and concepts like Normal style and base styles can save you hundreds or even thousands of hours.

new

As if things weren't complicated enough, Word for Windows now has two kinds of styles—Paragraph styles, as always, and new *character styles*. These are collections of character-formatting decisions (bold, italic, etc.).

When you couple your knowledge of styles with Word's AutoText, Auto-Correct, AutoFormat, and template features (covered elsewhere in this book), Word for Windows can make you a dramatically more efficient author and typist. If you work with other people on large, complex projects, or if your organization wants a uniform look for all of its printed documents, styles are essential.

Some styles do more than just change the appearance of text. For example, Heading styles make it easier to create a table of contents.

I think it's important to understand what styles are and how to modify them before you turn Word's AutoFormat feature loose on your documents. That way you can fine-tune things. Consume this chapter a little at a time. Try a few style experiments when you are not working on a rush project. Play with noncritical documents or on copies of important documents. If your eyes begin to glaze over or you find yourself pounding the desk with your fist, take a break. It will all make sense sooner than you think.

►► What Are Styles?

Styles are collections of paragraph- and character-formatting decisions that you or others make and save using meaningful names. Styles make it easy for you to reuse complex paragraph formats without laboriously recreating them each time. There are "built-in" styles available in all Word documents. And each document can have its own collection of custom styles. The sales letter shown in Figure 14.1 illustrates nine different styles.

FIGURE 14.1 ►

This letter uses many different styles.

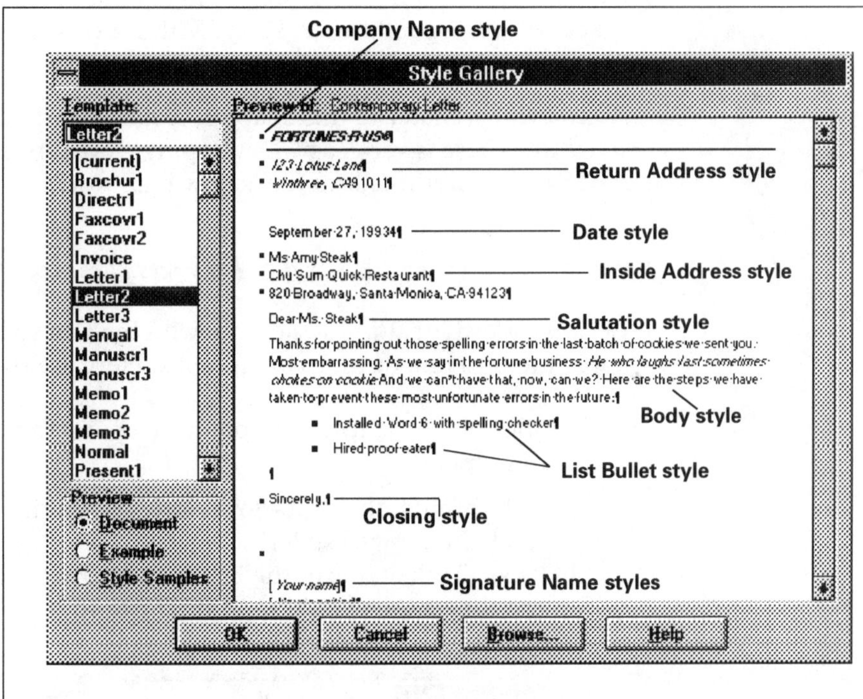

►► **NOTE**

Templates are simply collections of styles and boilerplate text designed to get you quickly working on everyday tasks.

All of the styles in Figure 14.1 are from Word's standard "gallery" of styles. In fact, the letter was created using one of the letter templates provided by Word. (*Templates* are simply collections of styles and boilerplate text designed to get you quickly working on everyday tasks.)

Some styles in the example are very simple. For instance, the style used for the body of the letter is called Body. It's just like the default text you use for typing except that Word for Windows adds six points of white space at the end of each paragraph. This separates paragraphs from each other without your needing to type extra carriage returns.

The Company Name style is more complex. It is body text plus bold character formatting, all caps, a hanging indent of 0.25", 6 points of space before, 3 points after, Keep With Next is enabled, Keep Lines Together is enabled, and a single bottom border will print. Phew!

As you will see later in this chapter, creating and naming your own styles like these is very easy. Developing clever style *strategies* takes much more forethought. Here's how it all works.

► Applying Styles from the Formatting Toolbar

Because Word for Windows comes with built-in styles, you can easily apply them to one or more paragraphs. Here are the general steps.

1. Either place the insertion point in a paragraph or select several paragraphs.
2. Scroll through the drop-down style list on the Formatting Toolbar to pick the desired style.
   The available items in the list will vary from document to document for reasons you'll soon understand.

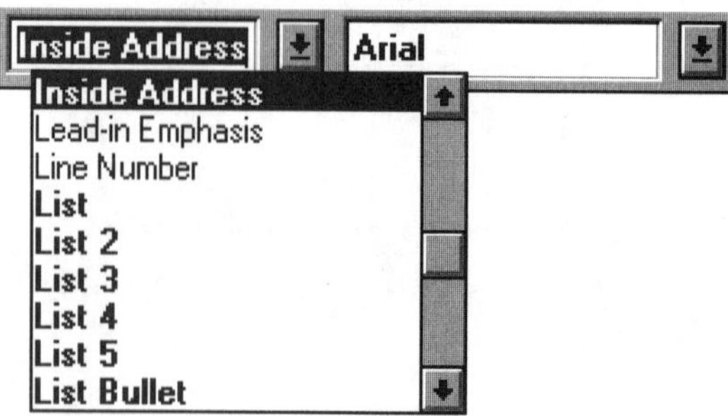

3. Click on a style name to apply it to the selected text. Your text will be reformatted using the selected style.
4. Use Edit ➤ Undo if you don't like the results.

▶▶ TIP

When the drop-down list is long, type the first letter of the style's name. The list will scroll to the proximity of your desired style.

▶ Applying Styles from the Keyboard

A few of the commonly used styles have their own keyboard shortcuts. To use them, select text or place the insertion point in the paragraph to be stylized and use one of the following key combinations:

STYLE	PRESS
Normal	Ctrl+Shift+N
Heading 1	Alt+Ctrl+1
Heading 2	Alt+Ctrl+2
Heading 3	Alt+Ctrl+3
List Bullet	Ctrl+Shift+L
Style Shown in Toolbar	Ctl+Shift+S

▶▶ TIP

The Edit ➤ Repeat keyboard shortcut (Ctrl+Y) works when applying styles. After you apply a style once, you can move the insertion point to other paragraphs and press Ctrl+Y to apply the new style where needed.

▶ Defining Your Own Styles from the Formatting Toolbar

You can define your own styles, and many experienced users do that. But before spending hours reinventing the wheel, check out the styles already provided by Word. When you have satisfied yourself that you need something that doesn't exist, try the following steps:

1. Display the Formatting Toolbar if it is not already in view.
2. Place the insertion point in the formatted paragraph whose style you'd like to capture. Make any last-minute changes in style.
3. As shown here, click *once* on the style box (the name portion of the drop-down style-name list). The style box will be highlighted, indicating that you can type a new style name.

4. Type a meaningful style name and press ↵.
   Word will save the style information and add the new name to the drop-down style list for the current document.

new ▸▸ NEW

You can no longer type the first few characters of a style name to apply it as you could in earlier Word versions.

▸▸ Style Name Considerations

Style names can be up to 253 characters long, but shorter is often better. Names can contain any legal characters except backslashes (\), braces ({}), or semicolons (;).

▶▶ **WARNING**

Word cares about capitalization in style names. For example, *Figure* and *figure* are two different names. Try to be consistent when naming similar styles in different documents. You'll learn why later in this chapter.

▶▶ The Style Dialog Box

For styles, as is often the case with Word for Windows features, there is a dialog box that contains powerful options not found on the Formatting Toolbar. Reach the Style dialog box by picking Format ➤ Style.... You will see something like Figure 14.2.

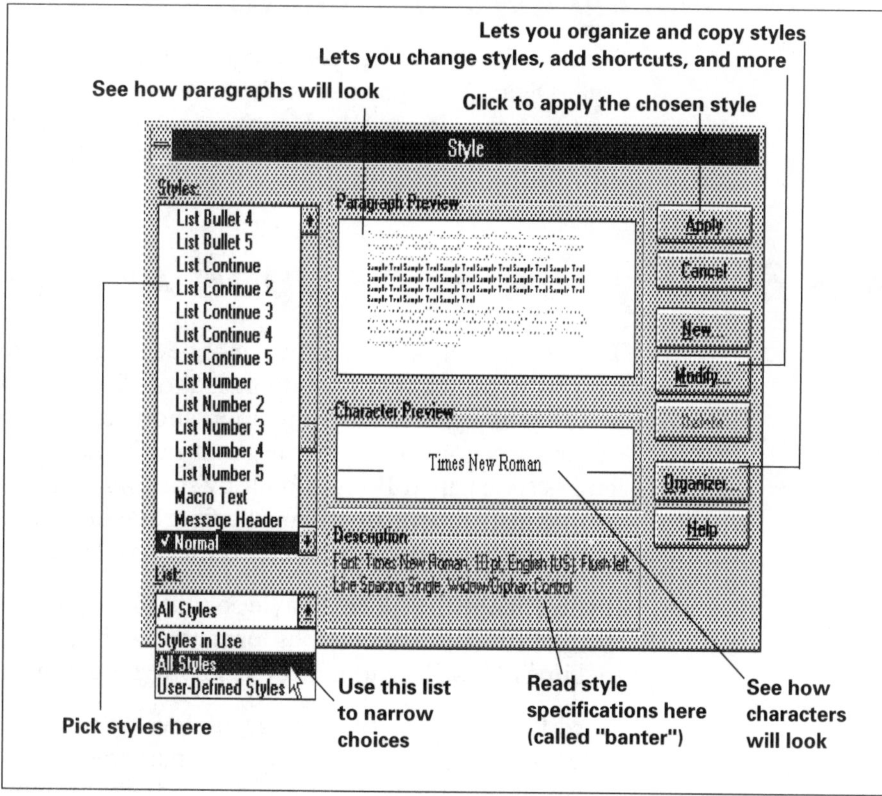

FIGURE 14.2 *The Style dialog box, reached by pressing Ctrl+S+S (i.e., S twice) or choosing Format ➤ Style....*

This dialog box lets you define new styles and rename, explore, list, or delete existing ones. It serves other purposes, as you will soon see.

► Defining Styles in the Style Dialog Box

To define a style via the Style dialog box, follow these steps:

1. Place the insertion point in or select a paragraph containing the desired format.
2. Open the Style dialog box.
3. Click on the New... button.
4. Type a legal style name in the box provided.
5. Click on OK to record the style.

► Defining Keyboard Shortcuts for Styles

Word for Windows lets you assign keyboard shortcuts from the Modify Style Dialog box (reached with the Modify... button in the Style dialog box) You can also use the Keyboard tab of the Customize dialog box (reached with Tools ➤ Customize...). See Chapter 36.

►► Basing One Style Upon Another

This time saver is often a source of bewilderment for newcomers. It occasionally catches old pros off guard too. Word for Windows lets you build upon styles or base one upon another. You've seen examples of this in the sample customer letter at the beginning of the chapter. The letter's style called Body is built by starting with the Normal style and adding instructions to indent the first line of each paragraph. In other words, the style Body is based on the style Normal.

If you change the Normal style so that it uses Times New Roman instead of Arial, any paragraphs formatted with the Body style will change to Times New Roman too. That's both good news and bad news.

Word for Windows watches as you develop new styles and bases new styles on the styles you modify. For instance, if you type the last paragraph of a letter in a style that produces indented paragraphs and decide when you get to the end of the last paragraph in your letter that you want to create a new closure style, you might be tempted to press ↵ to start a new paragraph, then drag the left indent marker to the left before typing *Sincerely*. If you then create a closure style based on the *Sincerely* line, Word will base the new Closure style on the indented body style, because that's the style you modified to create the Closure. No problem at the moment, but wait.

If you ever change the distance that the Body style indents first lines, the Closure paragraph will move too.

Unless you are careful, you can create quite a chain reaction this way. Experienced users try to create one or two base styles and tie most of the rest of their styles to those base styles, rather than basing each new style on the previous style.

The Modify Style dialog box, shown in Figure 14.3, lets you force specific styles to be based upon other styles of your choosing.

FIGURE 14.3

Word lets you specify which style each style is based upon.

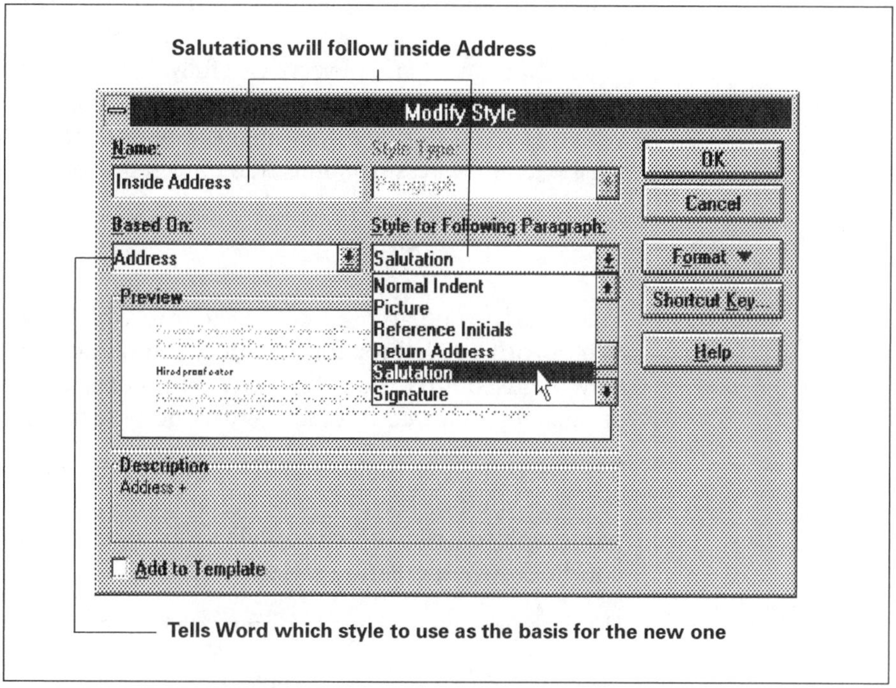

To base styles, follow these steps:

1. Choose Format ➤ Style....
2. Select the style you plan to base on another.
3. Click the Modify... button.
4. When you see the Modify Style dialog box, choose a base style from the Based On list.
5. Make any other necessary changes in the Modify Style dialog box.
6. Click OK when you're done.

►► TIP

To add a style you've created to the template upon which the document you are working on is based, enable the Add to Template option in the Modify Style dialog box.

What's the appropriate base style? That will vary with your project. At first, you may find it less confusing to base all of your styles upon Normal. Then experiment and observe carefully. You will soon learn from experience which combinations work best for you. Newcomers, beware. Play with *copies* of important documents, especially if it is ten minutes before the Federal Express person is due to pick up your document.

► Next Style

Frequently, you can predict the order in which styles will be used. When you type letters, for instance, you know that the To style will always be used after the From style. In reports and manuals, headings are usually followed immediately by body text, and so on.

The Modify Style dialog box lets you specify which style Word will flip to when you finish typing a paragraph and press ↵. Often, you want a paragraph to be in the same style as its predecessor. This is the default condition when creating styles.

But it is possible to specify different next styles. Follow these steps:

1. Choose Format ➤ Style....
2. Select the style you plan to modify.

3. Click the Modify… button.
4. When you see the Modify Style dialog box, choose a "next" style from the Style for Following Paragraph list, shown in Figure 14.3.
5. Make any other necessary changes in the Modify Style dialog box.
6. Click OK when done.

▶▶ Finding Out Which Styles Have Been Used

The obvious way to sniff out styles is to place the insertion point in the text of interest and look at the Formatting Toolbar indicators (the style list, which buttons are depressed, and so on). But there are several ways besides the obvious to see which styles and character formatting have been applied. The first is to print out a style list.

▶ Printing Out a Style List

It is often useful to have a printed list of styles and their descriptions. This can help you keep things consistent in a large organization, and it can help you troubleshoot formatting problems in complex documents. To print style information:

1. Open the document of interest.
2. Choose File ➤ Print… or use the Ctrl+P keyboard shortcut.
3. Choose Styles from the drop-down Print What list.

4. Click OK.

Open a document and print out a style list of your own. Take a moment to examine it. Pretty slick, eh?

▶ The Style Gallery

This new feature is a little like the Smithsonian Institute. You can spend days exploring it and learn something new each visit. It's an excellent place to see the seemingly endless collection of styles provided with Word's templates. The first figure in this chapter showed one use of the Style Gallery (previewing the effect of a template style on your document). Figure 14.4 shows another way to use the Gallery.

By clicking the Style Samples button in the Style Gallery, shown in Figure 14.4, you can see examples of all of the styles for a document or

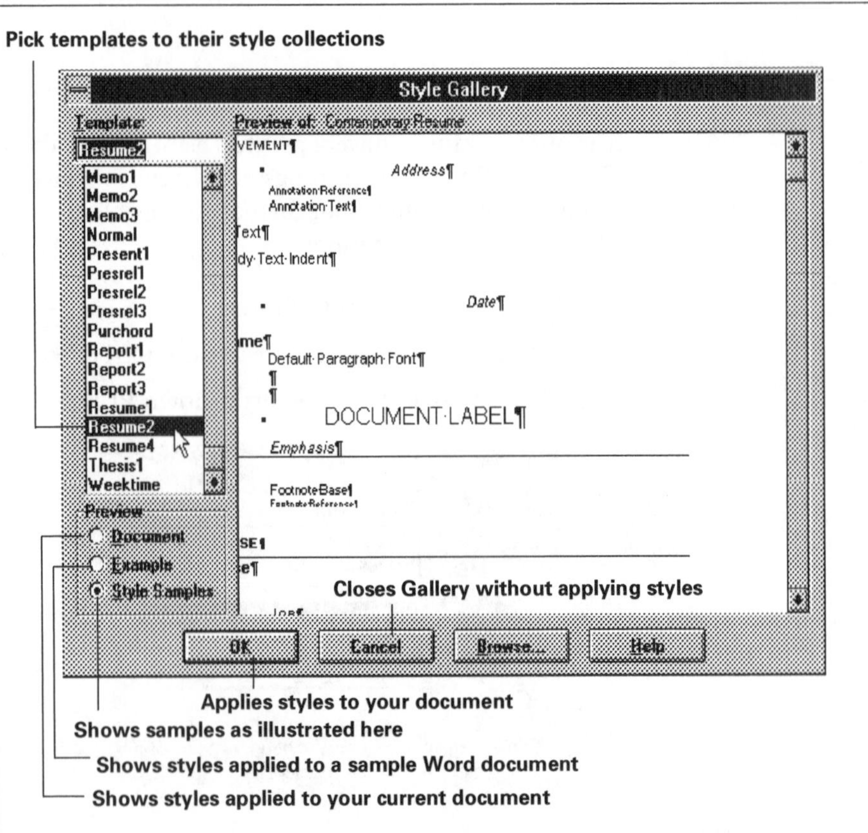

FIGURE 14.4 ▶

The Style Gallery showing you examples of a template's predefined styles.

template. If you are currently working on a project, you can also see how the project would look if you applied styles from various templates. If you like what you see, you can even have Word for Windows automatically apply the styles to your current project. You do not need to have a project in the works to visit the Gallery, but if you think you might want to reformat something, open it first and make it the active Word project before you begin. Here are the general steps.

1. Open a Word project if you think you might want to reformat it.
2. Open the Gallery with the Format ➤ Style Gallery… command.
3. Click the Style Samples button.
4. Pick a style from the Template list.
5. Wait a moment while Word displays the samples.
6. Choose different template names if you wish to see samples of other style collections.
7. Click the Document button if you want to see the styles automatically applied to the current document you have open (your current project).
8. Click OK to close the gallery *and apply the new styles* or Cancel to close the gallery without changing your document.

▶ Reveal Formats—the Cartoon Balloon

Another way to see style settings is to use Word's new Reveal Formats command, or what I call the style "cartoon balloon." Here's how it works.

1. Click once on the Standard Toolbar's help button.
2. The mouse pointer gets a big question mark.
3. Point to a paragraph of interest and click to read about formatting, as illustrated in Figure 14.5.

▶ Displaying Format Names On-Screen

Here's another interesting trick. You can display style information at the left edge of the screen in something called the *style area*, illustrated in Figure 14.6.

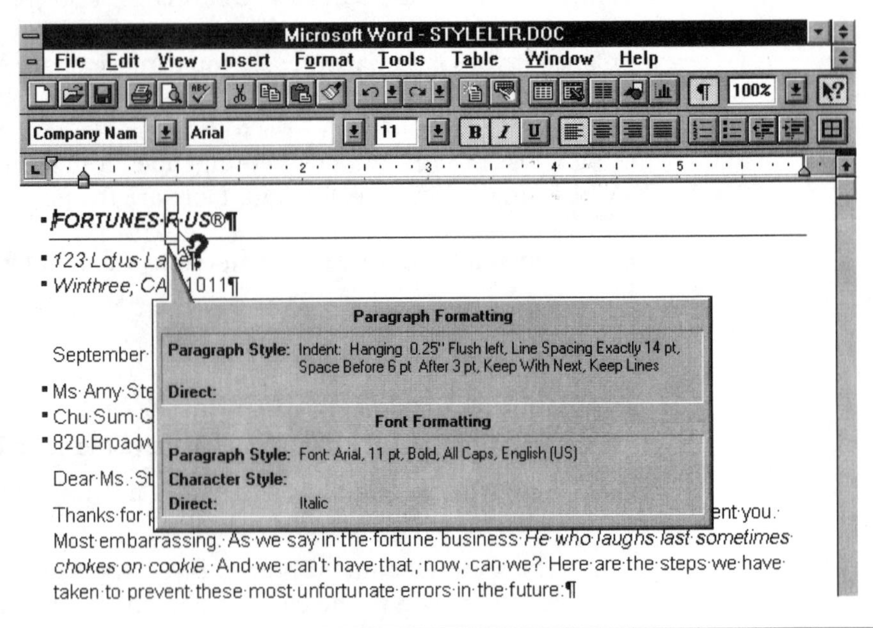

FIGURE 14.5

The Style "cartoon ballon" in use.

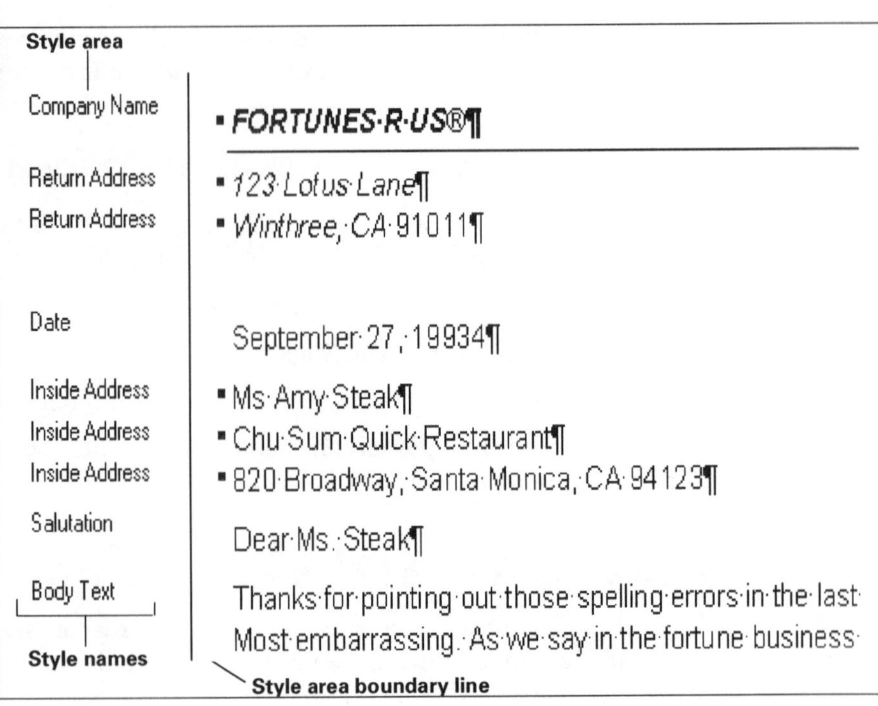

FIGURE 14.6

You can see format names in the style area if you enable it.

Here is how it works:

1. Switch to Normal or Outline view.
2. Choose Tools ➤ Options....
3. Visit the View tab.
4. Pick a style-area width (1", perhaps) from the Style Area width section of the View tab. Figure 14.7 shows where to do this.
5. Click OK.
6. Style names will appear at the left of the screen in Normal and Outline views.
7. To remove them, repeat steps 1 through 5, choosing 0 (zero) for the Style Area Width.

FIGURE 14.7

Specify the width of the style area in the View tab of the Options dialog box (Tools ➤ Options).

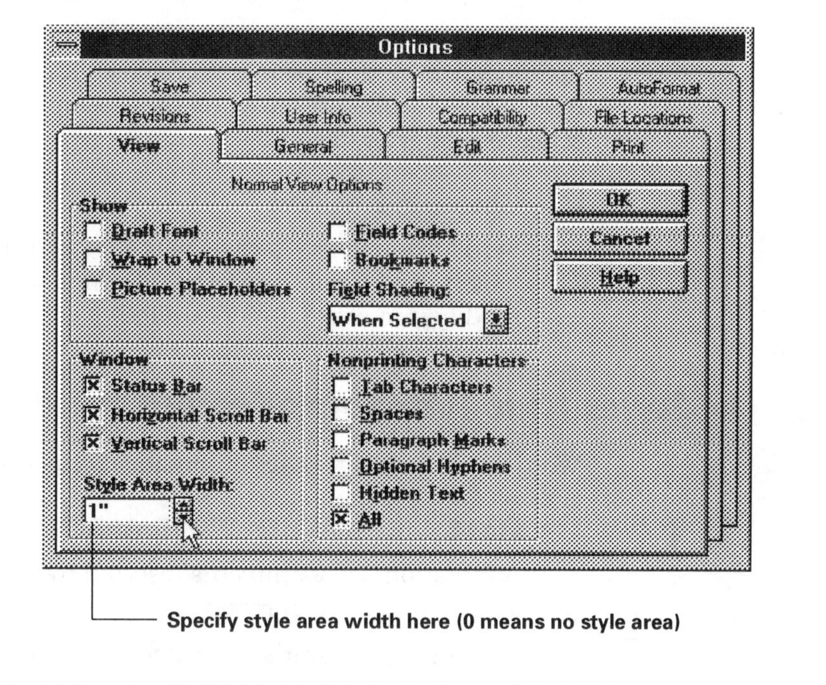

▸▸ When and Where Styles Are Saved

Styles are saved with your document and they are saved only when you save the document. This is yet another good reason to get in the habit of saving early and often. If your computer crashes after you've spent several hours setting up a complex collection of new styles, or if you accidentally click No to the Save Changes? prompt when you close a document, you will not be happy.

▸▸ Word's Standard Styles

Word's designers have created hundreds of standard styles that are used by its footnote, outline, index, table-of-contents, page-numbering, header, and footer features.

Many of the templates for letters, brochures, newsletters, and other documents have their own predefined styles. Take some time now to open a few documents based on these templates and explore their styles. As a starter, try this:

1. Choose File ➤ New.
2. Scroll through the list and pick Report.1 Take a few moments to look it over. Could you use this template as is? How might you modify it to make it more useful?

▸ Styles that Word Applies Automatically

Word applies certain styles automatically, as listed here:

STYLE	WHEN WORD APPLIES
Annotation Text	Comments inserted by the Annotation command
Annotation Reference	Initials of person who inserted the comment
Caption	Captions and table and figure titles
Footer	In footers

STYLE	WHEN WORD APPLIES
All Footnotes	Text in a footnote
All Endnotes	Text in an endnote
Footnote Reference	Numbers and characters used as reference marks
Endnote Reference	Reference marks
Header	Header info
Index 1–Index 9	Index entries created with the Index And Tables
Line Number	Automatic line numbers
Macro Text	Text of a WordBasic macro
Page Number	Automatic page numbers
TOC 1–TOC 9, Table of Contents	TOC entries
Table of Figures	Automatic figure numbering

▶ Additional Formatting and Styles

It is possible to override or embellish styles with additional character formatting. But there are some caveats.

You already know how to make character-based changes from the Formatting Toolbar, and the changes will work in stylized paragraphs. But they interact with formatting elements in your styles. Read on.

► Reapply/Redefine Styles

If you ask Word for Windows to apply a style to a paragraph that already uses that style (applying Normal to an already Normal paragraph, for instance); you will be visited by this strange and powerful dialog box:

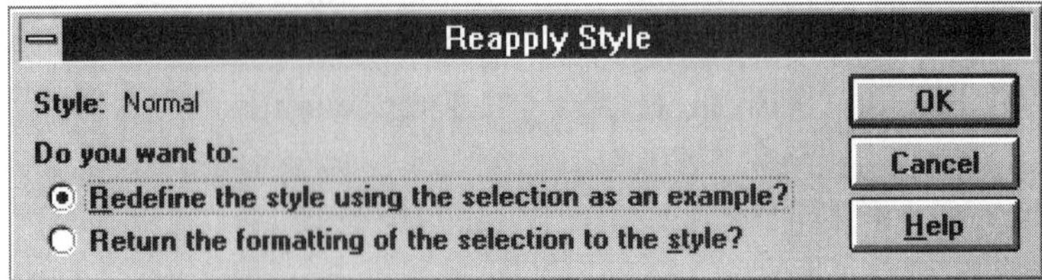

To Restore Styles

This box serves two purposes. First it lets you reapply a style to a paragraph that you have inadvertently messed up. Suppose you accidentally dragged the first-line indent marker in a Body paragraph and the paragraph no longer looks like the others. By choosing the Body style again from the Formatting Toolbar you will get a chance to reapply your Body style and repair the errant paragraph. Follow these steps to restore a style:

1. Select the paragraph, paragraphs, or characters you wish to restore.
2. Choose the desired style from the Formatting Toolbar's list.
3. If asked to reapply or redefine, pick Reapply.
4. Click OK.

To Redefine a Style

The second use of this dialog box is to let you quickly redefine a style. Suppose you hate the first-line indent you've used for body text. Change the indent in any one Body style paragraph, then pick Body from the Style list. Click on the Redefine button and click OK. Word for Windows will redefine the Body style using the new indent from your sample paragraph. All of your Body paragraphs will be changed. To redefine a style, follow these steps:

1. Select any paragraph or character formatted with the style to be changed.

2. Make the desired appearance changes (indents, underlining, etc.).
3. From the Formatting Toolbar's list, choose the style *originally* used for the formatting.
4. When you see the Redefine/Reapply choice, choose Redefine.
5. Click OK.

Strange things sometimes happen when you redefine or reapply styles to manually embellished paragraphs, however. While the interaction of manually applied formatting and styles may seem almost random sometimes, it is not. Read about it at the very end of this chapter.

▶▶ Deleting Styles

You cannot delete Word's built-in styles (headings and Normal, for instance), but you can remove custom ones you've created and many of the fonts provided with Word's templates. Unwanted styles can be deleted by selecting them in the Style dialog box and clicking the Delete button, as shown in Figure 14.8.

FIGURE 14.8 ▶

Deleting unwwanted styles.

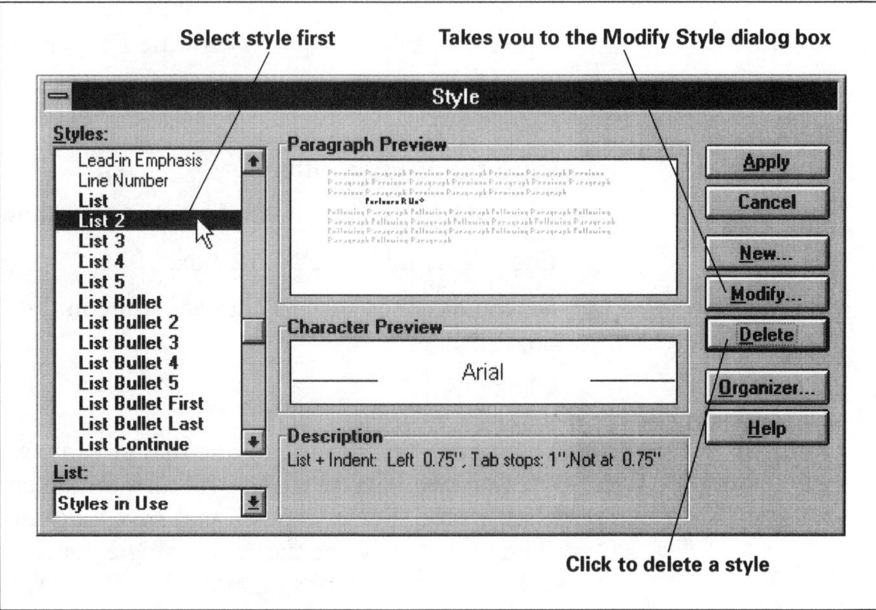

You will be asked to confirm; press OK. All paragraphs formatted with a deleted style will revert to the document's Normal style. Follow these steps:

1. Open the Style dialog box with Format ➤ Style....
2. Click on the style you want to delete in the Styles list (scroll, if necessary).
3. Click Delete.
4. Click OK to confirm the deletion.
5. The style will be deleted from the current document

►► NEW

You can use the Undo list pulled from the Standard Toolbar to replace accidentally deleted styles.

►► Renaming Styles

Styles can be renamed in the Style dialog box. Follow these steps:

1. Open the Style dialog box with the Format ➤ Style... command.
2. Click on the style you want to rename in the Styles list (scroll, if necessary).
3. Click the Modify button.
4. You will see the Modify Style dialog box, shown in Figure 14.9.
5. Edit the name in the Name box.
6. Make any other desired changes while in the Modify Style dialog box.
7. Click OK.

If you change a style's name to one that already exists in the document, the style that you have renamed will take on the characteristics of the pre-existing style. For instance if you have a double-spaced style called Draft and you change the name of a single-spaced style from Body to Draft, all of the paragraphs formatted as Body will be double-spaced

FIGURE 14.9

The Modify Style dialog box.

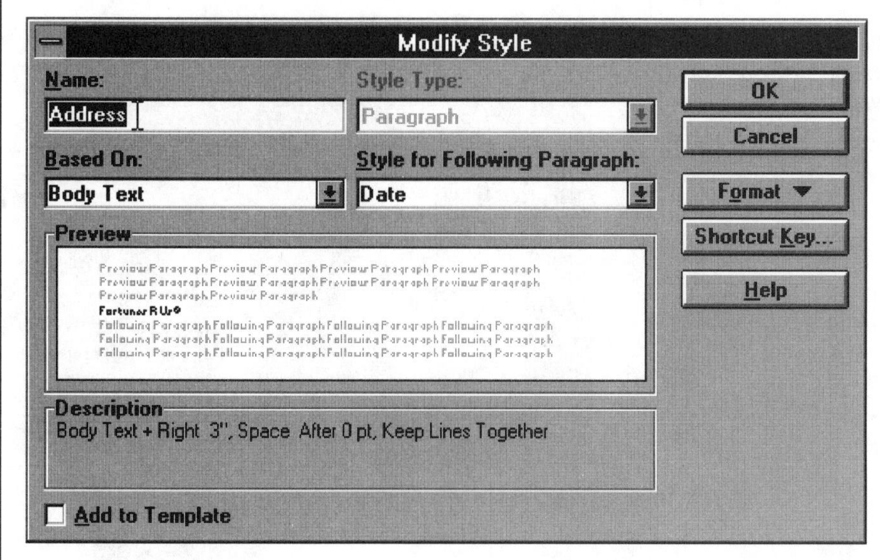

and take on any other style characteristics associated with the original Draft style.

Remember—Word for Windows cares about capitalization when you name styles. The names *Salutation* and *salutation* are not the same.

►► Finding and Replacing Styles

Style-change junkies rejoice. Word for Windows now lets you search for and replace styles. While Word's vastly improved replace feature is fully described in Chapter 20, here's a quick style replacement how-to:

1. Open the Replace dialog box with the Edit ➤ Replace command or use the Ctrl+H keyboard shortcut (see Figure 14.10).
2. Place the insertion point in the Find What box.

FIGURE 14.10

The Replace feature lets you locate or swap styles.

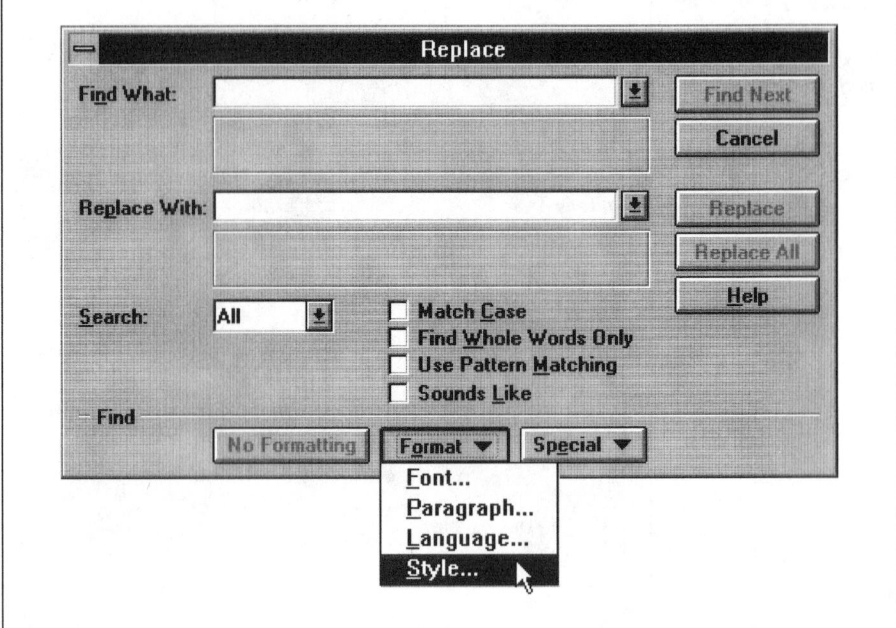

3. Choose Style… from the drop-down Format menu. You will be presented with a list of possible styles in the Find Style dialog box:

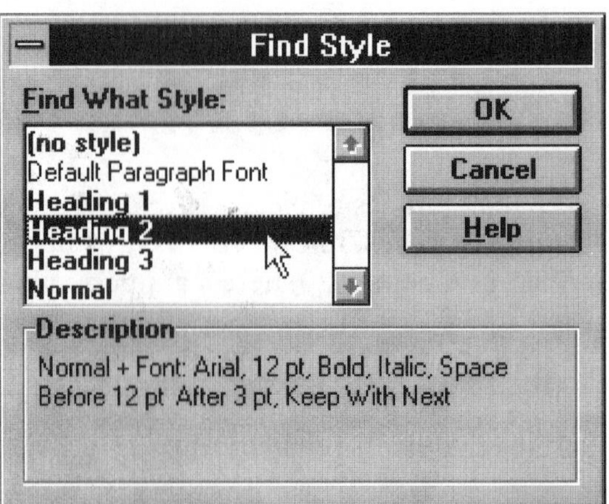

4. Pick the style you wish to replace (Heading 2, for instance) and click OK. The name of the style will appear in the format portion of the Find What area.

5. Move the insertion point to the Replace With portion of the dialog box.
6. Choose Style… from the drop-down Format menu again.
7. Choose the new style from the resulting Replace Style dialog box list (Heading 1, for example):

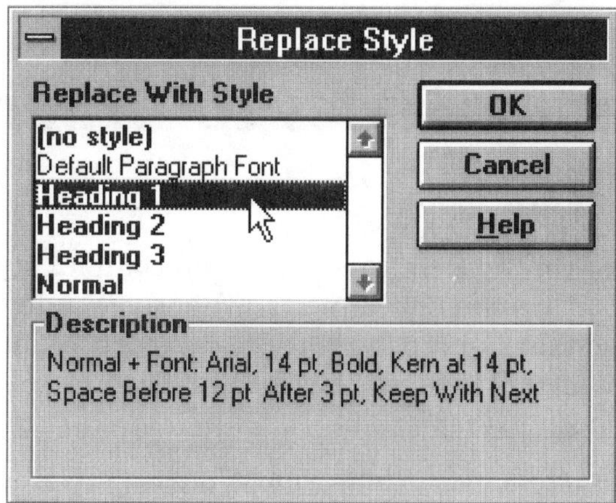

8. Click OK.
9. Tell Word if you want to search the whole document (All), up from the insertion point or down from the insertion point.
10. When you are ready, Click Find Next and Replace, or Replace All, as appropriate. For instance, to replace all Heading 2 style occurrences with Heading 1 styles, you'd pick Search: All and Replace All:

Find What:
Format: Style: Heading 1
Replace With:
Format: Style: Heading 2
Search: All
Match Case
Find Whole Words Only
Find Next
Cancel
Replace
Replace All
Help

▸▸ **NOTE**

Chapter 20 covers finding and replacing in detail. If you can't wait, experiment on copies of important documents rather than the real things.

▸▸ Transferring Styles to Other Documents

After you've spent time setting up complex styles, it would be nice to re-use them in new projects. Word for Windows provides several ways to do this. For repetitive tasks, consider setting up Template documents containing styles, as described in Chapter 16, and AutoText entries, described in Chapter 17.

If you have just a style or two you want to copy from one document (the source) to another (the destination), follow these steps:

1. Select some text from the source document containing the style of interest and paste it into the destination document needing the style.
2. Word will bring over the style with the text.

▸▸ **WARNING**

Remember that if the destination document has a style name identical to the style being copied from the source, the destination document will reformat the incoming text rather than take on the new style. Moreover, if you copy more than fifty styles at once, the source document's entire style sheet will be automatically copied to the destination document.

It is also possible to merge different style sheets, which copies unique styles from one document to another and modifies styles with identical names.

Think of the document containing styles you want to copy as the *source* document and the document receiving the new styles as the *destination* document. Here's how to merge style sheets:

1. With styles properly named and saved, work in the destination document.
2. Open the Style dialog box with the Format ➤ Style… command.
3. Click on the Organizer… button to open the Organizer dialog box shown in Figure 14.11.
4. Pick the Styles tab if it is not already foremost.
5. The name of the source file should appear in the In list at the left side of the dialog box, and probably the file NORMAL.DOT will be specified as the destination or To file on the right of the dialog box. This is telling you that Word wants to copy new styles to the NORMAL.DOT template so that it will be available in each new document that you open.

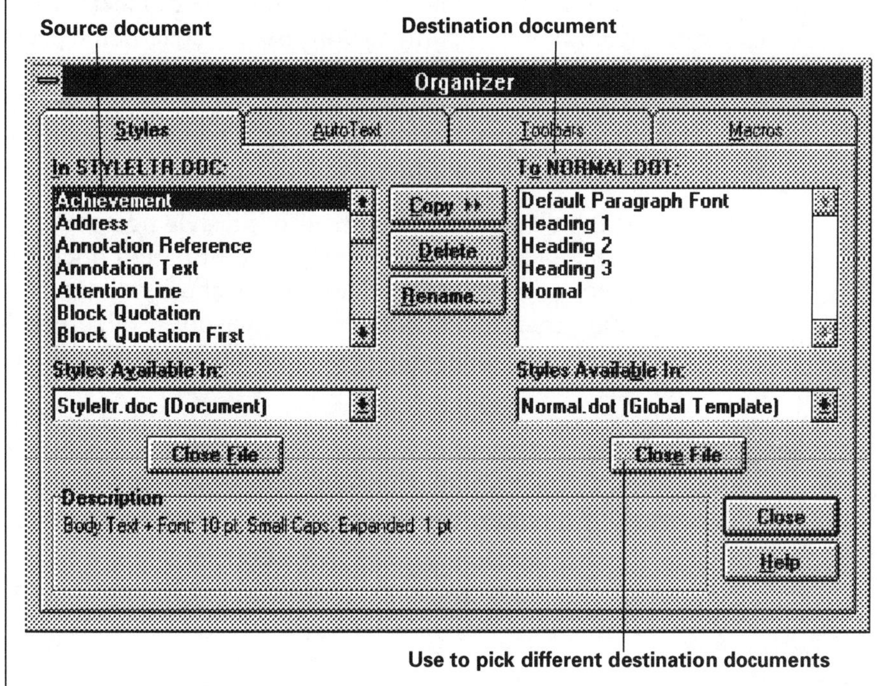

FIGURE 14.11

The Organizer dialog box.

6. If you want to make the style or styles you are copying globally available, leave the To setting as NORMAL.DOT. If you want to add the style(s) to just a selected document or template, click the *right* Close File button (note that there are two). It will change to an Open File button. Choose the desired destination file using standard Windows file-opening techniques.
7. When the source and destination files have been properly identified, pick the styles you wish to copy in the left-hand scrolling list. Click to choose a single style, Shift+click to select ranges, or hold down the Ctrl key while you selectively click on noncontiguous styles.
8. With the desired styles selected, click Copy.
9. Use the Delete or Rename… keys as necessary.
10. Open other source or destination files as necessary, then click Close when you're done.

Here are a few tips worth noting. First, you should save any changes to the source document before attempting to copy styles. This records the current styles for the source document. Next, inspect the source and destination documents for possible style-name problems. Remember that Word for Windows styles are case sensitive—*body* and *Body* are different style names. As you may have guessed, this can work for or against you. Consider printing out style sheets for both the source and destination documents and comparing them *before* you copy styles.

If the destination document has a style name identical to the style being copied from the source, the destination document will reformat the incoming text rather than take on the new style. Moreover, if you copy more than fifty styles at once, the source document's entire style sheet will be automatically copied to the destination document.

Other Word commands that exchange style information will bring over styles as necessary. For instance, Subscribe, Link, AutoText, and Paste Special all attempt to bring styles with them.

▶▶ A Few More Style Tips

Here are a few tips on using styles:

- Get to know the styles provided in Word's templates before creating your own.
- Establish organization-wide style sheets and style-naming conventions. This will make it easy for groups of people to work on projects together.
- When experimenting with styles, work on document copies. This is particularly important for new users working on complex documents containing interrelated styles.
- Establish one or two base styles for complex documents. They need not be based on Word's Normal style, particularly if the look of the document is radically different from your normal work.
- Because Word's new AutoFormat feature (described shortly) works only on text that has been formatted with styles, you'll want to get in the habit of using at least the Normal style when you type. Fortunately, this happens automatically unless you tell Word for Windows to do otherwise, as Word always formats typing in your new documents as Normal. If you import documents from other programs or import plain ASCII text, however, you'll probably need to select it and apply at least Normal style.

▶▶ AutoFormat

AutoFormat inspects your document and suggests formatting changes that you can accept or reject. Consider this "before" glimpse at a report that was formatted entirely in Normal.

What's·Wrong·Here?¶
Introduction¶
City·governments·feel·trapped·between·constituents,·who·want·more·serv
Proposition·13)·that·limit·the·funds·available·to·pay·for·those·services..¶
With·increasing·frequency,·government·agencies·have·refused·to·issue·pe
some·pet·municipal·project·by·paying:¶
→ linkage¶
→ impact··fees¶
→ other·payments¶
The·fee·is·supposed·to·beruth·is·that·the·only·connection·some·of·these·fe
planned·buildings.··The·tproject·is·that·the·property·developer·is·standing
created·by·the·proposed·wrong·time·(when·the·City·is·looking·for·funds).·
planning·counter)·at·the·

Word for Windows can locate and reformat headings, change straight quotes to curly quotes, and more. Here are the general steps and an example of AutoFormat at work:

1. Open the document you wish to reformat.
2. Choose Format ➤ AutoFormat. You will see this dialog box:

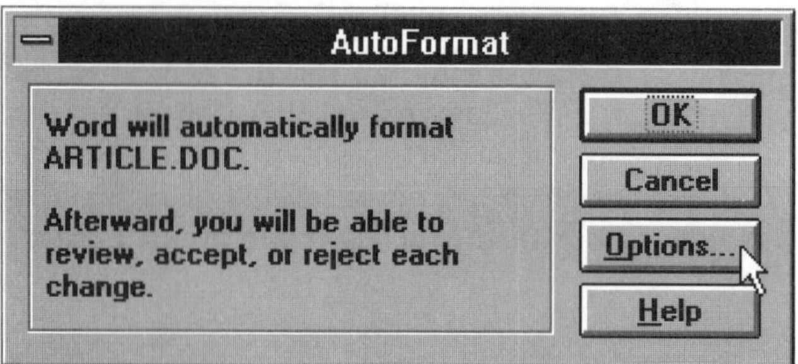

3. If you wish to change the way AutoFormat works, click the Options… button. Click to tell which formatting tasks you don't want it to perform. For instance, if you don't want Word to preserve any Styles you've already applied, click to remove the *X* from the appropriate box.
4. When you have specified any necessary changes to Word's usual AutoFormatting habits, click OK to be taken back to the AutoFormat dialog box.

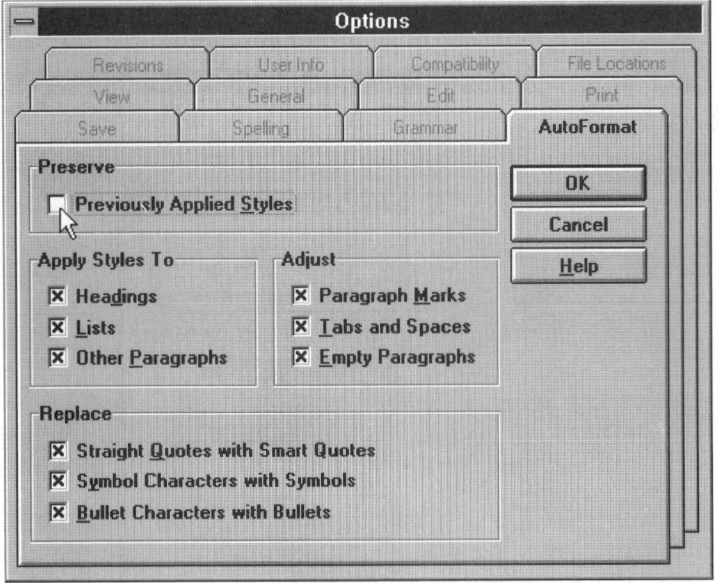

5. Click OK in the AutoFormat dialog box.
6. Word will go to work. In a few moments, you'll see this dialog box:

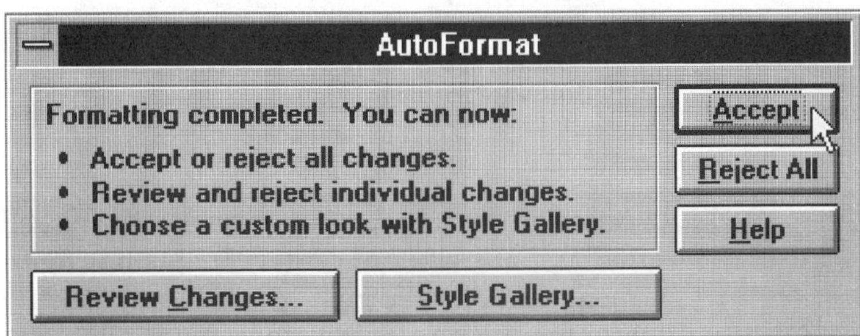

7. To see and review each proposed change, choose Review Changes. To apply further formatting via the Style Gallery click the Style Gallery… button; otherwise, simply accept or reject all changes.
8. Inspect your finished product carefully to be sure that you got what you wanted.

Typically, you'll want to polish Word's work. For instance, take a look at two of the pages in our sample document (see Figure 14.12).

FIGURE 14.12

The effects of AutoFormatting a typical "all Normal" document.

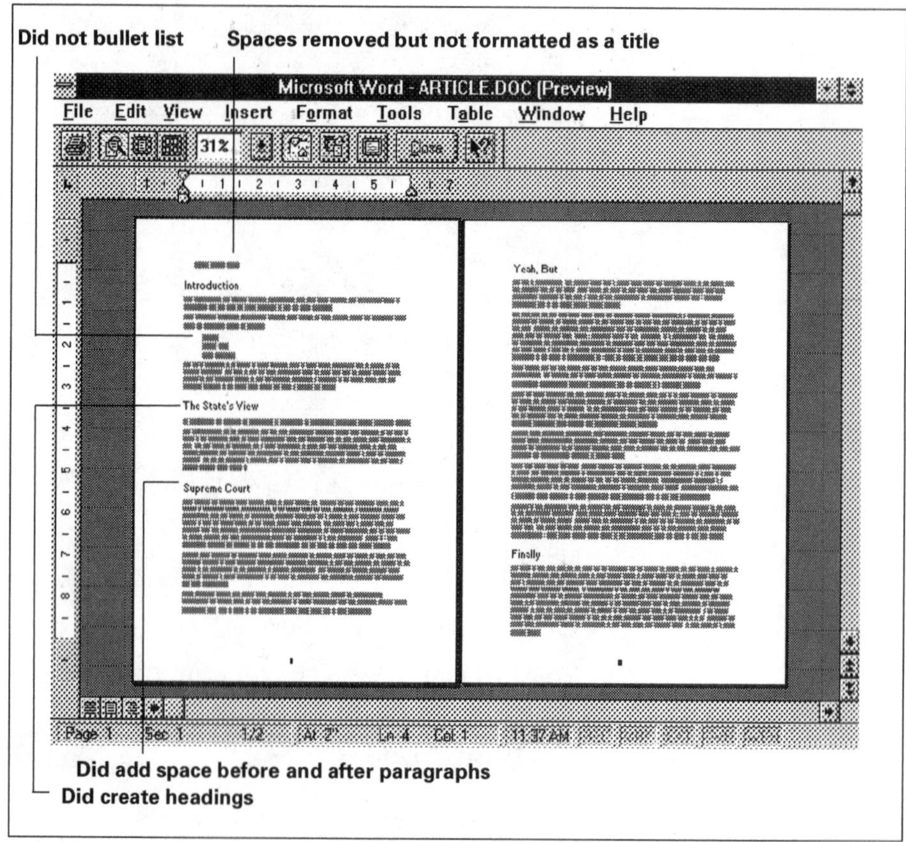

AutoFormat removed all those spaces in the first line designed to "center" it, but it did not center the line nor figure out that it was a document title. AutoFormat spotted likely paragraph headings, increased their point sizes, change their fonts, and added paragraph spacing nicely. It did not recognize a tabbed list as a candidate for bulleting and therefore did not add bullets.

So, as you can see, while AutoFormat does a nice job considering that this whole document was formatted as Normal text, you can still add some polish to all but the simplest projects.

▶▶ Manual Formatting and Styles

As promised, here's an explanation of how styles and manual formats interact (although, perhaps *collide* is a better word). Don't feel bad if this seems confusing. It is. First, there are some important concepts to review:

- By now, you should know the difference between character and paragraph formatting. Paragraph formatting describes things that happen to all of the characters in a paragraph—like indenting and line spacing. Character formatting can be applied selectively to all, or to just a few, characters in a paragraph.
- You'll probably remember that some character-formatting choices toggle. Specifying bold twice, for instance, turns bold character formatting on then off. Other character-formatting features don't toggle. Choose Helvetica twice, for example, and nothing interesting happens.

new

Now for the new stuff. When you use menu choices, the Formatting Toolbar buttons, or keyboard shortcuts to specify formatting, you are doing something called *manual* formatting. When you use a style to format text, that's called (yep) *style* formatting. There's a difference, as you will soon see.

When you initially define a new style, Word for Windows looks at any paragraph and character formatting you've done and memorizes a collection of your manual-formatting decisions. If all of the text in the sample paragraph(s) is identical, that's a no-brainer.

But what if you ask Word to a create a style from a sample paragraph or paragraphs containing inconsistent formatting? What should it do, for instance, about bold if some of the text in the sample paragraph is bold and some isn't—ignore bold formatting, make everything bold, lock up your computer? And what if some of the lines you've selected for the sample are single-spaced and others double-spaced? Or how about inconsistent spacing before and after selected paragraphs, or wacky indents? (Variety has its price.)

Word for Windows needs to come to some conclusions about these inconsistencies, because, when you apply styles, they must format all of the specified text consistently.

Sooooo, Word looks at the first 255 characters in your sample text and decides whether or not to include manually applied formatting as part of the style. If a particular manual format (bold, for instance) appears in at least half of the first 255 characters of your sample, it becomes part of the style. Suppose, for example, you have a 600-character paragraph and at least 128 of the first 255 characters (more than half of the first 255) are bold. The style will include bold as one of its formatting features.

Any text you subsequently apply this style to will receive bold formatting. However, if at least 128 of the first 255 characters are not bold, the style will not contain bold formatting, even if the last 300 characters in the text sample are bold. So far so good? Read on.

Once you've defined a style (1" left and right indents, plus all bold text, for instance), selecting unformatted, plain vanilla text, and applying the new style will make the text conform to the style's formatting definitions (indented, bold text, in our example).

But what if the text you apply this style to already has other manual formatting like bold or italic—or what if you later try to apply manual formats to text you've formatted with your indented bold style? "Well," as President Clinton says, "that depends."

Let's take it one situation at a time—but first, a word or two about formatting *layers*, as Microsoft likes to call them.

► Formatting Layers

Suppose you use a style to format otherwise plain vanilla text. You would be applying something Microsoft refers to as the *style-formatting layer*. The once-plain text would take on the formatting characteristics defined by the style (indented, bold Times, let's say).

Then, suppose you manually format some of those same characters—italicize a word or two, increase the point size of the first character, and so on. You've added something called the *manual-formatting layer*.

▶▶ Format Layers and the Replace... Command

What's that? You wonder about Word's Replace... command and format layers? 'Tis sad but true. When you run around globally replacing styles or manually applied formatting with the Replace... command, described in Chapter 20, you'll need to keep in mind Word's behavior when it encounters combinations of manual formatting and styles. The Replace command causes the same toggling and other behavior problems as do human intervention.

▶▶ Removing Styles and Retaining Formats

Occasionally you might want to remove all of the styles in a document without affecting the appearance of the document. You'll want to remove the Bold Indent style you've created, for instance, but you want the text to remain bold and indented. Some people do this before sharing Word for Windows documents with WordPerfect DOS users, for example. Here are the steps:

1. Save your document with the Rich Text Format choice in the Save As dialog box. (It's in the Save File as Type scrolling list.)
2. Word will save the document. The resulting document can be used by Word for DOS, WordPerfect for DOS, and many other DOS word-processing programs.

Time Savers

PART THREE

CHAPTER 15

Envelopes, Labels, and Simple Mailing Lists

▸▸ FAST TRACK

To avoid envelope printing altogether **432**

use window envelopes whenever possible and set up letterheads, invoices, and similar documents with the inside address properly positioned for standard window envelopes.

To print a lot of envelopes from your printer **432**

purchase an envelope tray or feeder.

To reach the Envelopes and Labels dialog box **433**

use the Tools ➤ Envelopes and Labels command.

To have Word print your return address in the upper-left corner of envelopes **433**

choose the printer you plan to use (if you have more than one) and open the Envelopes and Labels dialog box (Tools ➤ Envelopes and Labels). Click on the Envelope tab if it is not foremost. If Word finds an address in the current open Word document, you will see it in the Delivery Address portion of the dialog box. Type your return address in the large box labeled Return Address and click Print.

To suppress the printing of return addresses (for preprinted envelopes) **435**

either leave the Return Address area blank, or, if you have a return address typed there, click to place an *X* in the Omit box.

▶▶ It's ironic that expensive computers make the simple task of envelope and label printing more difficult. Many offices keep typewriters around just for this reason. Sound familiar? Computerized envelope printing is not so bad once you get the hang of it, and you can set up documents that remember the recipe for you. In Word, there are envelope, label, mail, and list-management features that you'll find quite useful. Before we get into the details, here are some general tips:

- Use window envelopes whenever possible to avoid envelope printing altogether. Set up letterheads, invoices, and similar documents with the inside address properly positioned for standard window envelopes.
- Ask your letterhead designer to take your computer printer into consideration when picking paper stocks and envelope designs.
- Pick envelopes designed for your printer. These supplies are easier to find now, and many office-supply stores and mail-order paper sellers stock them. (Try Paper Direct, for instance—800-272-7377.) Laser-friendly envelopes have special flaps and flap glue that minimize jamming. Ink-jet–savvy envelopes are made of paper stock that won't fuzz up your characters.
- Purchase an envelope tray or feeder for your envelopes if you print a lot of them.

▶▶ Printing Envelopes

Word can print addresses on envelopes by looking for the addresses in your documents (the inside address of a letter for instance), or you can type an address in the Envelopes and Labels dialog box, as illustrated in Figure 15.1.

FIGURE 15.1

Word can find addresses in your documents, or you can type them.

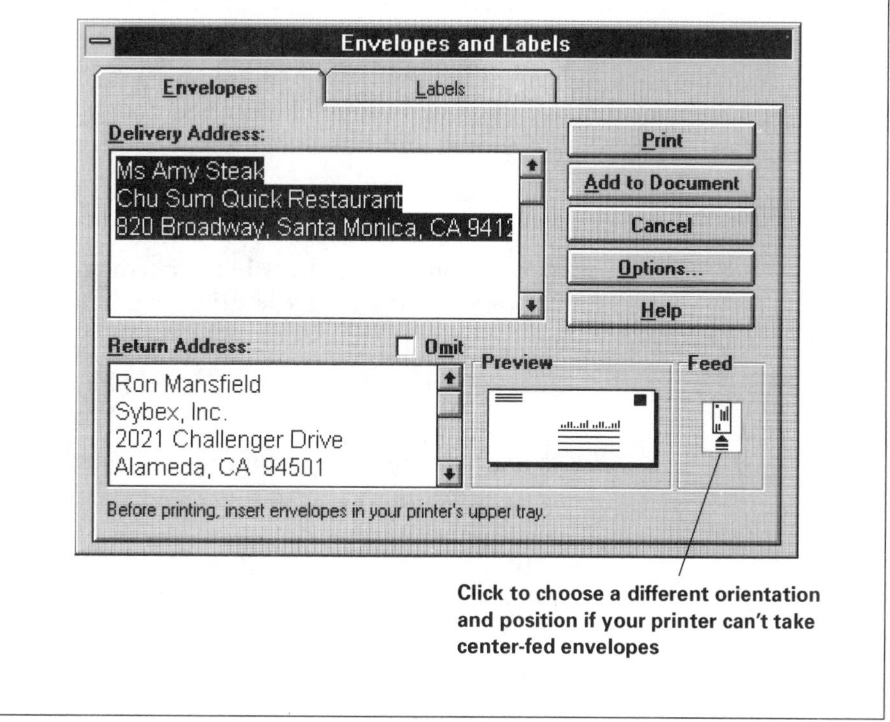

You reach the Envelopes and Labels dialog box with the Tools ➤ Envelopes and Labels command. The dialog box lets you:

- Print envelopes containing onetime addresses that you type into the dialog box itself.
- Copy an address from your document for envelope printing.
- Type envelope addresses then insert them into your letters or other Word documents.

▶ Setting Up a Return Address

If your envelopes have preprinted return addresses, you can skip this task. But if you want to use plain envelopes and have Word print your return address in the upper-left corner of envelopes, do this:

1. Choose the printer you plan to use if you have more than one.
2. Open the Envelopes and Labels dialog box by choosing Tools ➤ Envelopes and Labels.
3. Click on the Envelopes tab if it is not foremost. You'll see the dialog box shown in Figure 15.1.
4. If Word finds an address in the current open Word document, you will see it in the Delivery Address portion of the dialog box.
5. Type your return address in the large box labeled Return Address. (Part of the address may be already filled out automatically, based on your Word User Info.)
6. When you are happy with the spelling and appearance of your return address, try test printing on a plain #10 ($4\frac{1}{8} \times 8\frac{1}{2}$) envelope. Word assumes that you can center-feed envelopes in your printer. If that's not possible, click on the envelope in the Feed section of the dialog box to bring up the Envelope Options dialog box, shown in Figure 15.2.

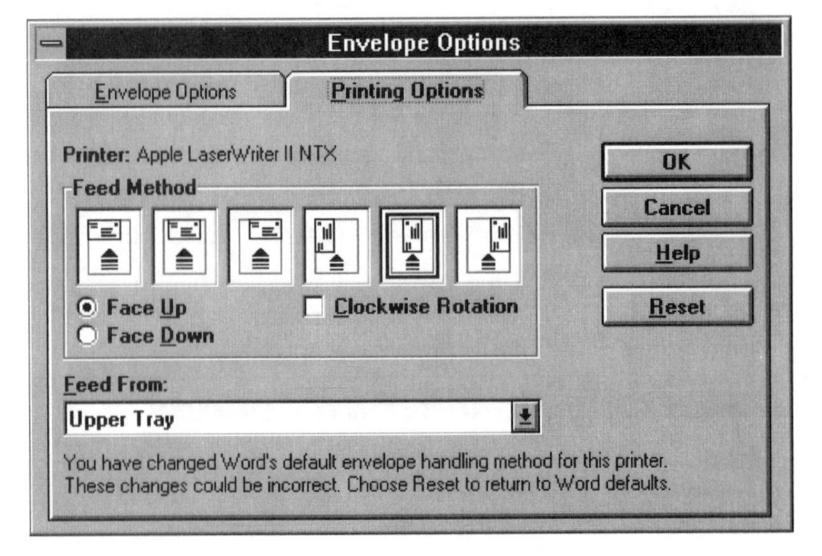

FIGURE 15.2

You can change the envelope-printing options in the Envelope Options dialog box.

7. Select a combination that will work with your printer, then click OK.
8. Place an envelope in your printer.
9. Back in the Envelopes tab of the Envelopes and Labels dialog box, click Print.

▶ Suppressing Return Addresses

If you always plan to use envelopes that contain preprinted return addresses, you can make sure that nothing prints by making the Return Address area blank. Or you can have a return address typed there and suppress its printing by clicking to place an *X* in the Omit box.

▶ Printing Envelopes with New Addresses

You can either type an envelope address directly into the Envelopes and Labels dialog box or select an address in your letter or other Word document, then open the Envelopes and Labels dialog box. Here are the general steps for envelope printing:

1. Select the address in your document if there is one.
2. Open the Envelopes and Labels dialog box by choosing the Tools ➤ Envelopes and Labels command.
3. If you selected an address in step 1, you'll see it in the dialog box; if not, type an address in the Delivery Address box.
4. Insert an envelope in your printer.
5. Click on the Print button.

▶▶ TIP

Word will often make a guess as to what it thinks should be the delivery address. Generally, it makes pretty good guesses, but if you don't have an address, or if it is ambiguous where you want the correspondence sent, select the address or place the insertion point in it to help out.

► Adding an Envelope Page to Documents

Clicking on the Add to Document button in the Envelopes and Labels dialog box adds an envelope page to the beginning of your document. Word takes care of all the details. You can see what it does by switching to Print Preview with two pages showing, as illustrated here in Figure 15.3.

► Changing Addresses

Once you've inserted an envelope page in your document, you can change the envelope and inside address at any time. Here's how:

1. Open the document.
2. Make the address change in the inside address.

or

3. Open the Envelopes and Labels dialog box (Tools ➤ Envelopes and Labels).

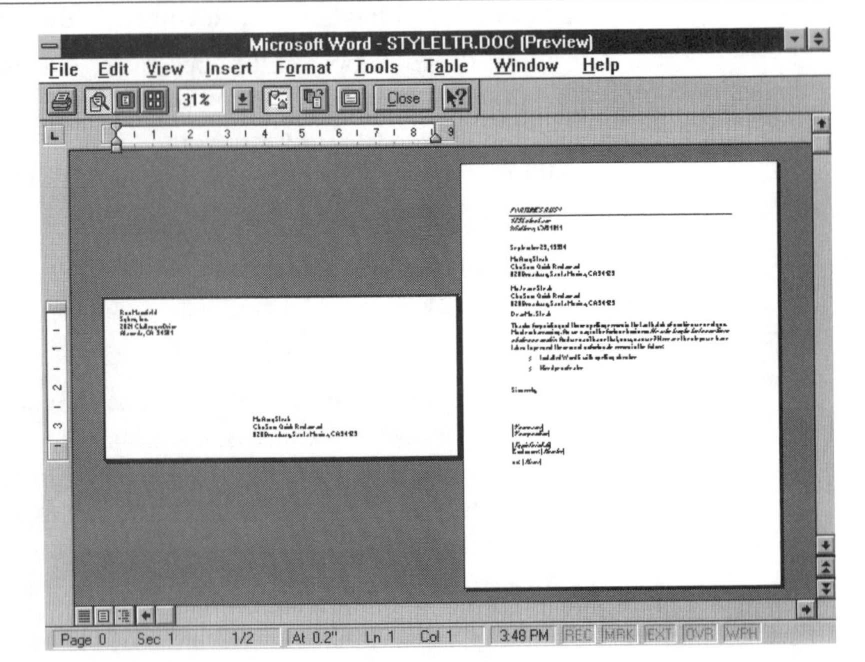

FIGURE 15.3 ►

Word will add an envelope to your document file if you like.

4. Click the Change Document button. The envelope will be changed.

▶▶ **WARNING**

If you change the Delivery Address in the Envelopes and Labels window, then click the Change Document button, Word will update the envelope but not the inside address, so be careful. It's better to make the change in the document, not the Envelopes and Labels window.

▶ Envelope Sizes, Fonts, and Other Options

new

Word lets you specify envelope sizes (both standard and custom), fonts used for delivery, return addresses, and more. The options are selected in two tabs located in the Envelope Options dialog box. Let's look at the Envelope Options tab first. It is illustrated in Figure 15.4.

Envelope Size

Choose from any of the standard sizes listed in the drop-down list or specify a custom size by typing dimensions or selecting Custom Size…

FIGURE 15.4 ▶

The Envelope Options tab.

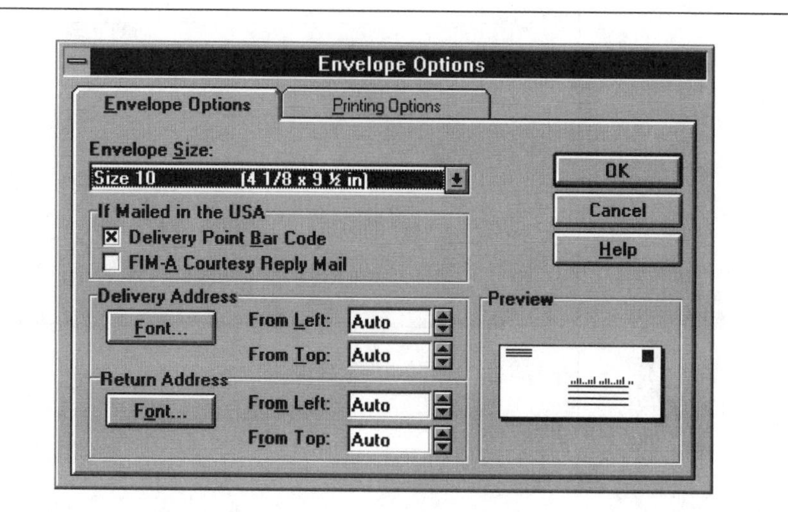

in the drop-down list in the Envelope Size dialog box:

Obviously you'll need to specify dimensions that your printer can handle.

Bar Codes to Speed Postal Delivery

If you are planning to send mail within the United States, you can ask Word to print bar codes on your envelopes. These will speed automated mail sorting. Two coding techniques are provided—POSTNET for regular mail and FIM-A for "courtesy reply" mail. Both types of codes are illustrated in Figure 15.5.

Place an X in the box or boxes you desire. Word will do the rest.

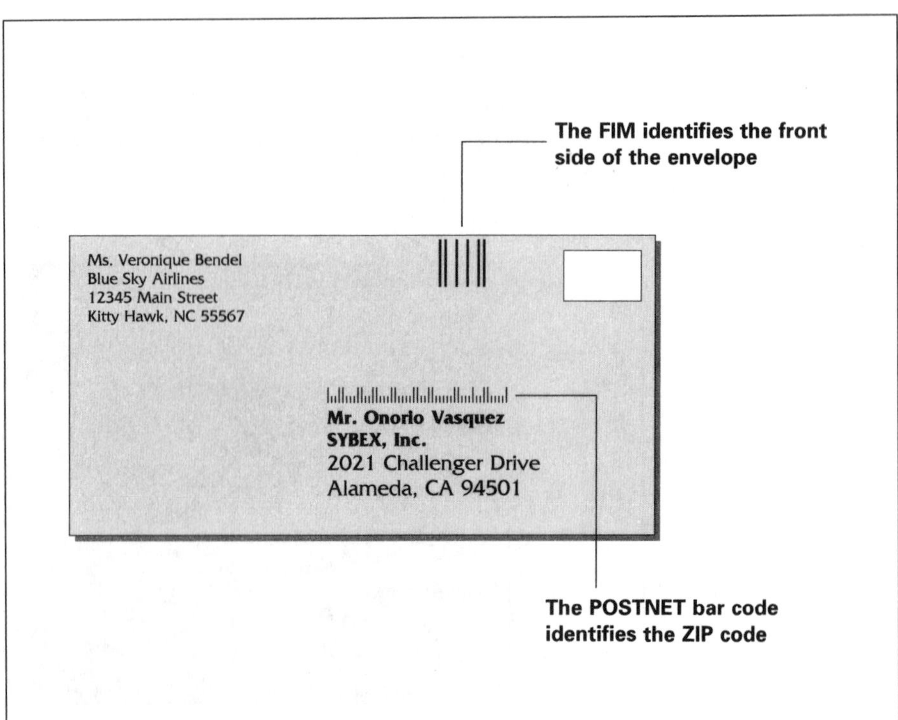

FIGURE 15.5

There are the two types of bar codes.

Fonts and Address Positioning

Use the Font buttons to choose the desired fonts for the delivery and return addresses. They bring up the Envelope Address Font tab, which lets you specify fonts, font sizes, colors, character formatting, etc.

The dimension boxes in the Delivery Address and Return Address sections of the Envelope Options tab let you specify address spacing. Auto makes Word do all of the work. You can type new dimensions or use the triangles to change dimensions. Watch the preview as you work.

▶▶ The Care and Feeding of Envelopes

You've already seen the Printing Options tab in the Envelope Options dialog box, but it deserves a second look. As you can see in Figure 15.6, this is where you tell Word how you plan to feed envelopes.

The choices vary with the chosen printer. If you have multiple trays, you specify the tray containing envelopes (upper, lower, etc.). Click Reset to return to the default settings for the chosen printer.

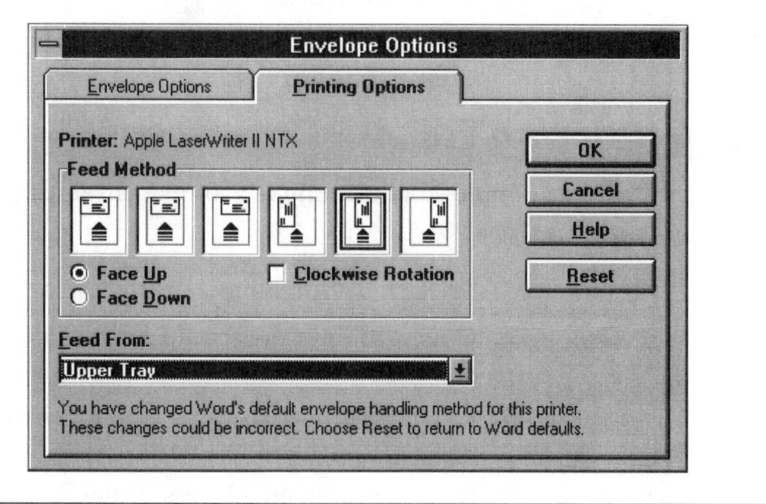

FIGURE 15.6 ▶

Pick envelope-feed options here in the Printing Options tab of the Envelope Options dialog box.

▸▸ Labels

Label printing is a lot like envelope printing except you have even more options. For instance, you can print single labels or sheets of labels. Word "knows" the dimensions for many different industry-standard stocks from Avery and others. For instance, you'll find Word knows how to print:

- Audio tape labels
- Business card perf stock
- Diskette labels
- File folder labels
- Mailing (address) labels
- Name tags
- Postcards
- Ready indexes
- Rotary (Rolodex) cards
- Shipping labels
- Videotape labels
- WorkSaver tabs

▸ Printing Labels

Simple label printing is a lot like envelope printing. Here are the general steps:

1. Select the address in your document if it has one.
2. Open the Envelopes and Labels dialog box with the Tools ➤ Envelopes and Labels command.
3. Click on the Labels tab if it is not already foremost. You'll see the options illustrated in Figure 15.7.
4. If you selected an address in step 1, or if Word finds one on its own, you'll see it in the dialog box; if not, type an address in the big box.

FIGURE 15.7

The Labels tab.

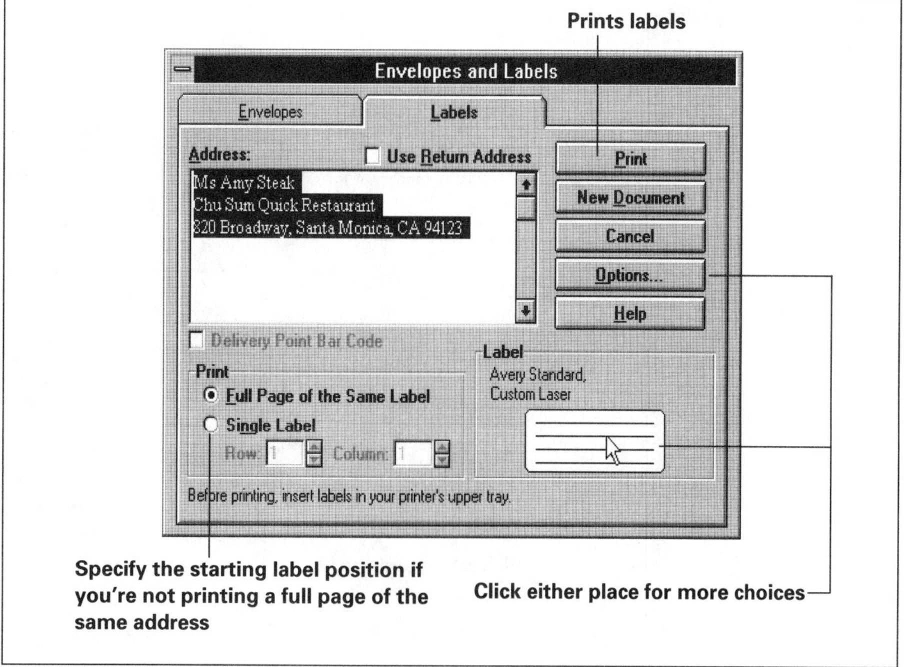

5. Choose the desired options in the main Labels tab. To print a single label on a multi-label sheet, click on Single Label and specify the row and column location of the label. Choose to print or not print the bar code and return address.
6. To select different label sizes, click either on the picture of a label or the Options button. You'll see the choices illustrated in Figure 15.8.
7. Pick the label maker, label product number, and printer type. For more detailed options, press the Details… button to see the choices in Figure 15.9.
8. Fine-tune Top and Side margins here if your printer prints *all* of the labels of the current type too high or too far left or right. The other settings are probably correct if you selected the correct label type back in step 6. When you have made all of your choices, click OK once or twice as necessary to return to the Label tab of the Envelopes and Labels dialog box.
9. Insert a label or sheet of labels in your printer. (Make sure the label isn't too small for your printer.)
10. Click on the Print button.

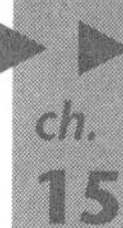

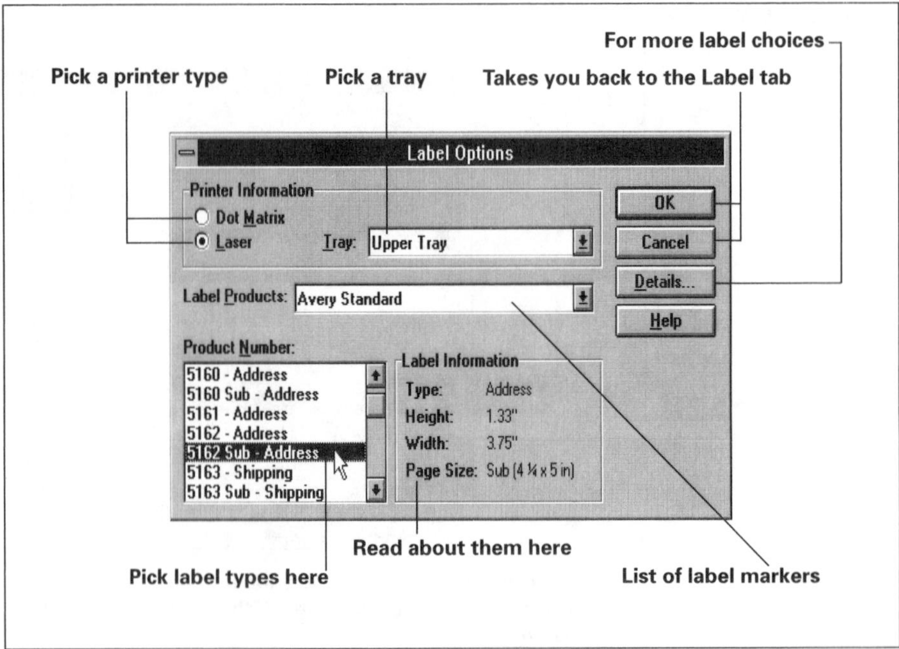

FIGURE 15.8

The Label Options dialog box.

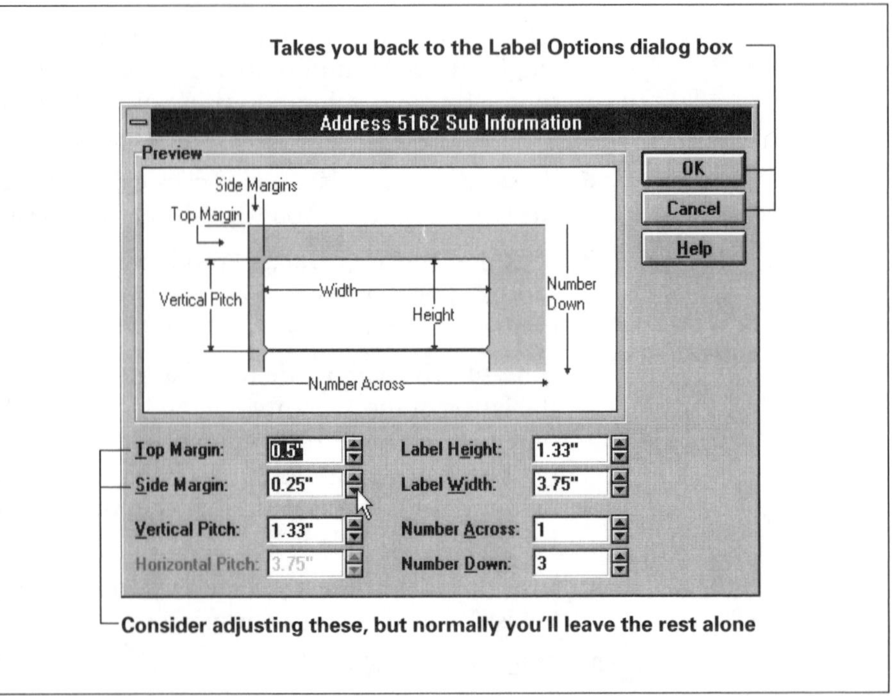

FIGURE 15.9

Additional Label details.

TIP

Normally, you can put partially used sheets of laser labels through your printer once or twice more, but you run the risk of jamming and possibly damaging your printer. It's often better to print full sheets and file the unused labels for the next time you mail something to the same recipient.

▶ Including Graphics on Envelopes

You can print graphics on envelopes. It's a great way to add logos, special messages, business reply art, and so on. Here are the general steps:

1. Select the Envelope tab in the Envelopes and Labels dialog box reached with Tools ➤ Envelopes and Labels.
2. Click on either the Add To Document or Change Document button.
3. Switch to Page Layout if not already there.
4. Paste or create a graphic and frame it (using the Insert ➤ Frame command), then move it into position as you would any other framed item:

5. Make any other changes that you like (rearrange or reformat lines of text in the inside address, for instance).

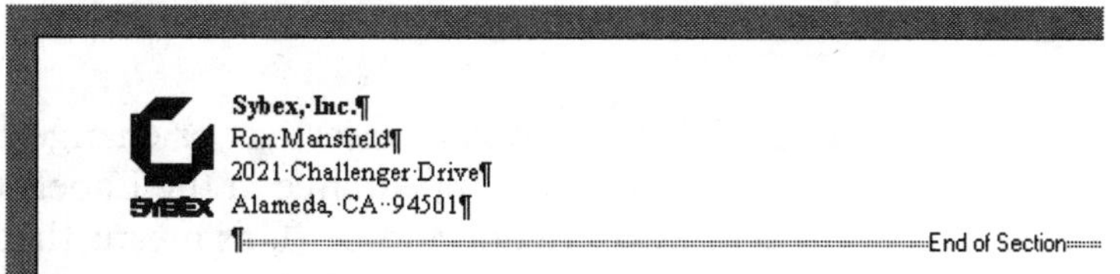

At this point, the envelope is one-of-a-kind, and in a separate section at the top of your current document. You can either save the document and print the envelope along with the rest of the document, or save the document as a template for repeated use. But there's one other possibility. If you want the artwork to appear on *all* of your envelopes, you can select the art and create a special AutoText entry called EnvelopeExtra 1 or EnvelopeExtra 2. Use the techniques described in Chapter 17 to create AutoText entries.

▸▸ Envelopes, Labels, and Long Mailing Lists

When mailing to many different addresses, consider using Word's Mail Merge feature. It is described in Chapter 28.

To preview envelopes, follow these steps:

1. In a document, type the name, address, etc., that you want on the label.
2. Format the information, adding graphics if you wish.
3. Select label, including the graphic.
4. Open the Envelopes and Labels dialog box.
5. Select the right label size and make any other appropriate changes.
6. Click on New Document on the Labels tag, and your labels will appear in a document, which you can preview.

It is a good idea to practice on plain white paper and hold test pages up to the light in front of a sheet of labels or an envelope to see how things will line up.

▸▸ Wish List

There is no easy way to insert art or change the font, size, or other elements of character appearance in the Labels tab (although you can do these things with envelopes). This means that Name tags, video-spine labels, and similar specialty labels are going to look pretty boring.

There is a workaround to this problem (use the Add to Document button, then edit the individual labels in the document), but it probably isn't appropriate if you're running big jobs.

CHAPTER 16

Templates, Wizards, and Sample Documents

▸▸ FAST TRACK

To quickly create or restyle your own documents **_450_**

use the *template* documents that come with Word to get you started.

To have Word create documents for you from scratch **_450_**

use the new Wizards that come with Word.

To see examples of documents created by Microsoft **_450_**

use the sample documents that come with Word.

To give documents different moods **_452_**

choose the template type (choose any one of the four different types) that will work best with the project you are working on.

To give your work a consistent look **_452_**

always use templates of the same type.

To quickly preview templates **_454_**

use the Style Gallery, reached with the Format ➤ Style Gallery… command.

To browse through templates in the Style Gallery **454**

open a new document with the File ➤ New... command and choose Normal (the Default template). Then choose Format ➤ Style Gallery... and pick the template that you want to see from the scrolling list. Click the Example button in the Preview area to see a preview of the template's appearance and scroll to make sure you see the entire template (they are often several pages long). When done, click Cancel. Clicking OK copies the styles to your current document but does not load the other template elements (boilerplate text, etc.).

To use a prewritten letter template **457**

locate the one you want in the Letters subdirectory within your Word directory. Replace the underlined phrases with your own information, then delete the underlining.

To speed the task of changing repeating information in a template **457**

consider using Find and Replace.

To create a document with the Wizard **459**

start Wizards with the File ➤ New command, then pick the desired Wizard from the scrolling list. You'll be asked questions about your hopes and dreams for the new document. All the while, Word shows you a preview, making changes as you answer questions. Eventually the Wizard tires of this and, when you click the Finish button, it works its magic.

Word's templates are read-only documents containing styles and other design elements that you can use to create or restyle your own documents. *Wizards* are like computerized assistants. Like you, Wizards also use templates to create documents, after asking some questions and making a few design decisions on their own. *Sample documents* are examples created by Microsoft to show you what can be done. They are great learning tools. Table 16.1 shows a list of the template, Wizard, and sample files supplied with Word.

TABLE 16.1: *Word's Templates, Wizards, and Sample Documents*

TEMPLATES	WIZARDS	SAMPLE DOCUMENTS
BROCHUR1.DOT	AGENDA.WIZ	CLASSIC1.WZS
DIRECTR1.DOT	AWARD.WIZ	CLASSIC2.WZS
FAXCOVR1.DOT	CALENDAR.WIZ	CLASSIC3.WZS
FAXCOVR2.DOT	CV.WIZ	CLASSIC4.WZS
INVOICE.DOT	FAX.WIZ	MODERN1.WZS
LETTER1.DOT	LETTER.WIZ	MODERN2.WZS
LETTER2.DOT	MEMO.WIZ	MODERN3.WZS
MANUAL1.DOT	NEWSLTTR.WIZ	MODERN4.WZS
MANUSCR1.DOT	PLEADING.WIZ	
MANUSCR3.DOT	RESUME.WIZ	
MEMO1.DOT	TABLE.WIZ	
MEMO2.DOT		

TABLE 16.1: *Word's Templates, Wizards, and Sample Documents (cont.)*

TEMPLATES	WIZARDS	SAMPLE DOCUMENTS
MEMO3.DOT		
NORMAL.DOT		
PRESENT1.DOT		
PRESREL1.DOT		
PRESREL2.DOT		
PRESREL3.DOT		
PURCHORD.DOT		
REPORT1.DOT		
REPORT2.DOT		
REPORT3.DOT		
RESUME1.DOT		
RESUME2.DOT		
RESUME4.DOT		
THESIS1.DOT		
WEEKTIME.DOT		

These files are all located in their own subdirectory called TEMPLATE, if you did a complete installation.

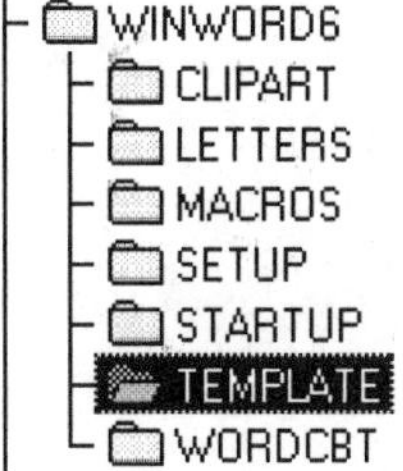

Look for the TEMPLATE subdirectory in your Word for Windows directory. Let's begin our tour with Templates.

►► Templates

There are at least four different ways to use templates:

- Start new projects based on templates shipped with Word
- Modify existing projects by choosing templates and *completely reformat* your work in the template's styles
- Copy *selected* styles from templates for use in your projects
- Create and save new templates of your own creation

► Template Types

Word's standard templates come in up to four different "flavors." Microsoft refers to these as *Template Types*:

- Classic (type 1)
- Contemporary (type 2)
- Typewriter (type 3)
- Elegant (type 4)

The different types give documents different "moods." For instance, a Classic Letter template uses Times Roman while a Contemporary letter uses Arial. The Company Name style in the Contemporary letter template includes a border, while the Classic type does not, and so on.

By always using templates of the same type, you can give your work a consistent look. And when creating your documents based on templates, you can copy the existing styles using the tricks you learned in Chapter 14.

Not all templates come in all types. For instance, there is only one Elegant document, which is titled RESUME4.DOT. Here's a summary of the rest:

TEMPLATE TYPE	CLASSIC	CONTEMPORARY	TYPEWRITER
Brochure	BROCHUR1.DOT		
Directory	DIRECTR1.DOT		
Fax cover sheet	FAXCOVR1.DOT	FAX-COVR2.DOT	

TEMPLATE TYPE	CLASSIC	CONTEMPORARY	TYPEWRITER
Letter	LETTER1.DOT	LETTER2.DOT	LETTER3.DOT
Manual	MANUAL1.DOT		
Manuscript	MANUSCR1.DOT		MANU-SCR3.DOT
Memo	MEMO1.DOT	MEMO2.DOT	MEMO3.DOT
Normal	NORMAL.DOC		
Presenta-tion	PRESENT1.DOT		
Press release	PRESREL1.DOT	PRESREL2.-DOT	PRESREL3.-DOT
Purchase order	PURCHORD.DOT		
Report	REPORT1.DOT	REPORT2.DOT	REPORT3.DOT
Resume	RESUME1.DOT	RESUME2.DOT	
Thesis	THESIS1.DOT		
Timesheet	WEEKTIME.DOT		

▶ Using Templates

Once you know what each template looks like, you can quickly start projects by picking a template whenever you start a new project. Just pick it by name from the Template list in the New dialog box:

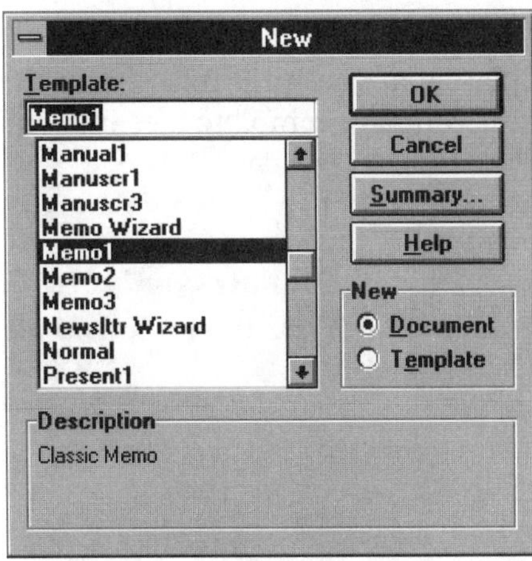

Then you simply add your own text by clicking on the appropriate areas of the template and replacing the labels with your own words.

Memorandum¶

DATE: → September·30,·1993¶

TO: → John,·Paul,·George·and·Ringo¶

FROM: → *[Names]*¶

RE: → *[Subject]*¶

CC: → *[Names]*¶

[Type·your·memo·text·here]¶

But first, it's helpful to know what the various templates look like. You could load each one and take a look, but there's an easier way.

► Exploring Templates

Use the Style Gallery, reached with the Format ➤ Style Gallery… command, to preview templates. Here are the general steps.

1. Open a new document with the File ➤ New… command.
2. Choose Normal (the Default template).
3. Choose Format ➤ Style Gallery… You will see a window like the one in Figure 16.1.
4. Pick the template that you want to see from the scrolling list. Click on Browse… if you have template files in a different directory.

►► NOTE

Remember: Classic templates end in *1*, Contemporary templates end in *2*, Typewriter *3*, and Elegant *4*.

5. Click the Example button in the Preview area to see a preview of the template's appearance.
6. Scroll to make sure you see the entire template. They are often several pages long.
7. Click Style Samples to see the names of styles displayed in the styles themselves. Unfortunately, these are often too small to read.
8. When you are done, click Cancel. (Clicking OK copies the styles to your current document but does not load the other template elements [boilerplate text, etc].)

FIGURE 16.1

You can preview templates in the Style Gallery.

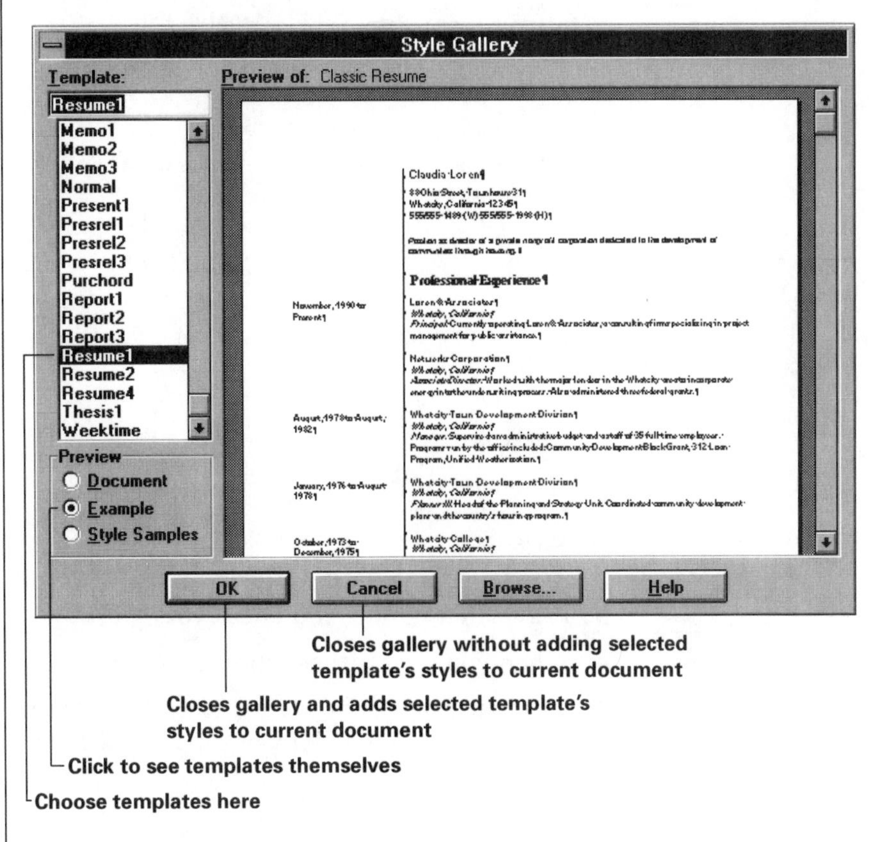

► Modifying Templates

You can change templates just as you would any other Word documents. The only difference is one additional step you must take when saving your work. Suppose you wanted to update the Classic letter template to include your company logo. Follow these steps to see how:

1. Use the File ➤ New… command to open the Letter1 template:

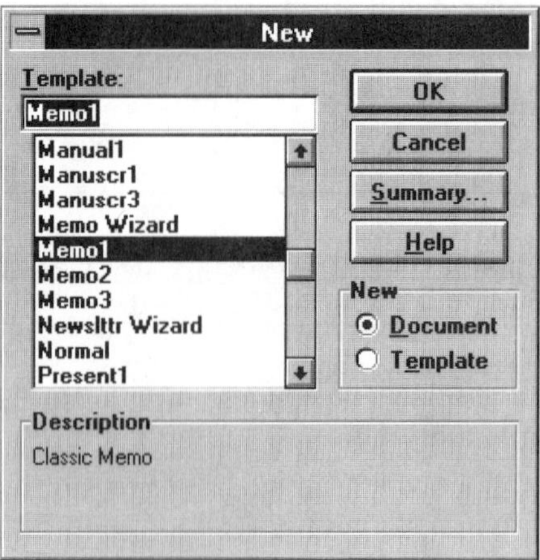

2. Make the changes, such as adding your logo and other embellishments.

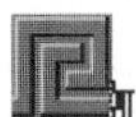

[*Company·Name*]¶
▪ [*Street·Address*]¶
▪ [*City,·State/Province·Zip/Postal·Code*]¶

3. Print out a sample and check your work.
4. When you are satisfied, choose File ➤ Save As….
5. Type the exact same file name as the old template if you want to replace the old template, or type a new file name if you want to

keep *both* the old and new (make sure to type the extension .DOT if you choose a new file name):

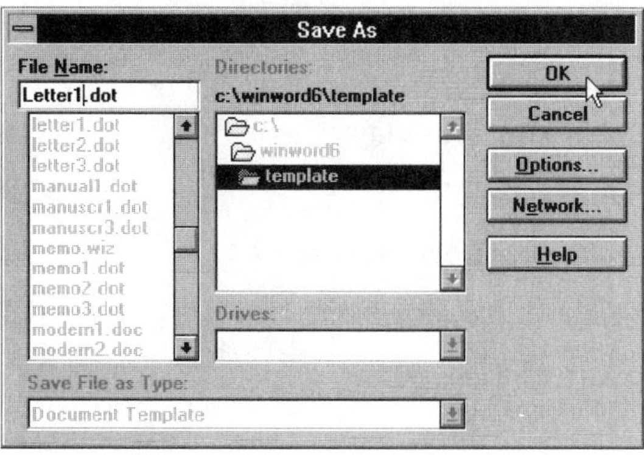

▶ Prewritten Business Letters

Word comes with a number of prewritten letters for various occasions. They all end with the file extension .DOT, and you can find them in the Letters subdirectory within your Word directory. Whether the letters will work for you is a matter of taste and circumstance.

141·Kinsford·Avenue¶
Anytown,·WA··6999¶

Dear·Mr·Picard,¶

What·could·be·better·than·Word·version·2?·That's·easy·—·Word·version·6!¶

Although·you·might·find·it·hard·to·believe,·we·have·significantly·improved·Word,·adding·safety·and·operating·features·that·make·it·faster·and·easier·to·prepare·potatoes.¶

The·new·Tater·Dicer·Mark·II*plus*·offers·the·following:¶

To use the letters, replace the underlined phrases with your own information, then delete the underlining.

▶▶ **TIP**

Use Find and Replace to speed the task of changing things like product names that repeat many times in the same document. To remove underlining, consider using the Select All command (Ctrl+A) and toggling all underlining off at one time by clicking the Underline button in the Formatting Toolbar.

Here's a list of form letters provided with Word:

LETTER DESCRIPTION	FILE NAME
Price increase announcement	CSTMRR03.DOT
Apology for delay	CSTMRC03.DOT
Collection letter	CRED01.DOT
Credit report request	CRED11.DOT
Customer complaint	CSTMRC01.DOT
Direct mail	MKTG07.DOT
Lease expiring	SPACE03.DOT
Letter to Mom	OTHER10.DOT
Press release	ADPR01.DOT
Resume cover letter	EMPRL02.DOT
Returning product letter	SUPPL13.DOT
NSF check (request for payment)	CRED04.DOT
Thanks for inquiry	MKTG02.DOT
Thanks for job application	EMPRL03.DOT
Thanks for the suggestion	CSTMRR05.DOT

▸ Tips for Using Templates

Word often gets information from the User Information entered with the User Info tab in the Options dialog box (reached with the Tools ➤ Options… command). Make sure your info is up to date by visiting that tab.

In templates with inside addresses, signature blocks, and other multi-line items, consider the Shift+↵ trick to keep lines all in the same paragraph. This eliminates unwanted "space before" in each address line, for example.

Switching types (from typewriter to Classic, for instance) can give your documents a whole new look. And you can mix and match styles by copying selected styles from other documents.

Some of the more complex templates (like Manual1.dot) use a wealth of Word features including table of contents, index entries, etc.

Don't forget other time savers such as the Tools ➤ Envelopes and Labels command. They work with templates too.

▶▶ Wizards—The Computer Wants Your Job

You've seen Wizards at work elsewhere in this book, but because they often use templates, they are worth mentioning here, as well. Wizards ask you questions, then use your responses to design documents for you. Take the Calendar Wizard, for instance. You start Wizards with the File ➤ New command. Pick the Calendar Wizard from the scrolling list, and it will appear:

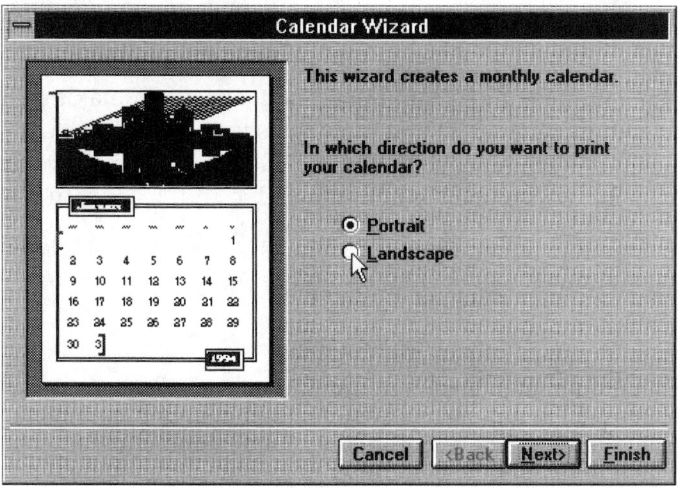

▶▶ TIP

Turn off the Show ¶ feature for better-looking previews.

You'll be asked questions about your hopes and dreams for the new document. Do you want portrait or landscape orientation? Would you like to leave room for a picture or other graphic? Do you want fries with that? You get the idea.

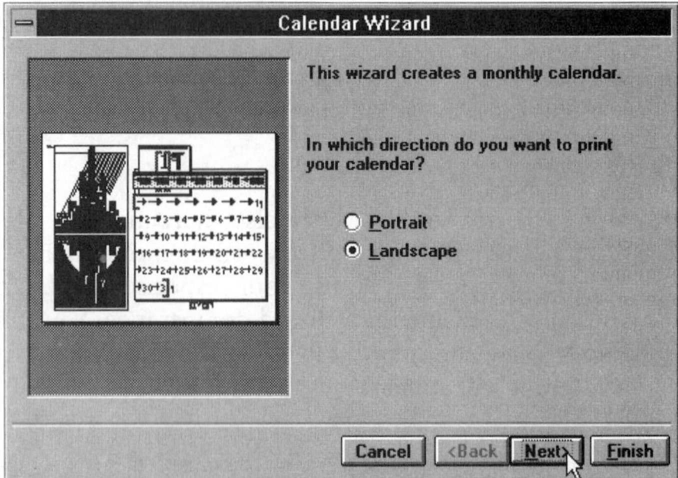

All the while, Word shows you a preview, making changes as you answer questions. The preview is very useful because you can try several different settings in each window to see which you prefer. Eventually the Calendar Wizard tires of this and, when you click the Finish button, it works its magic (see Figure 16.2).

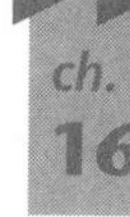

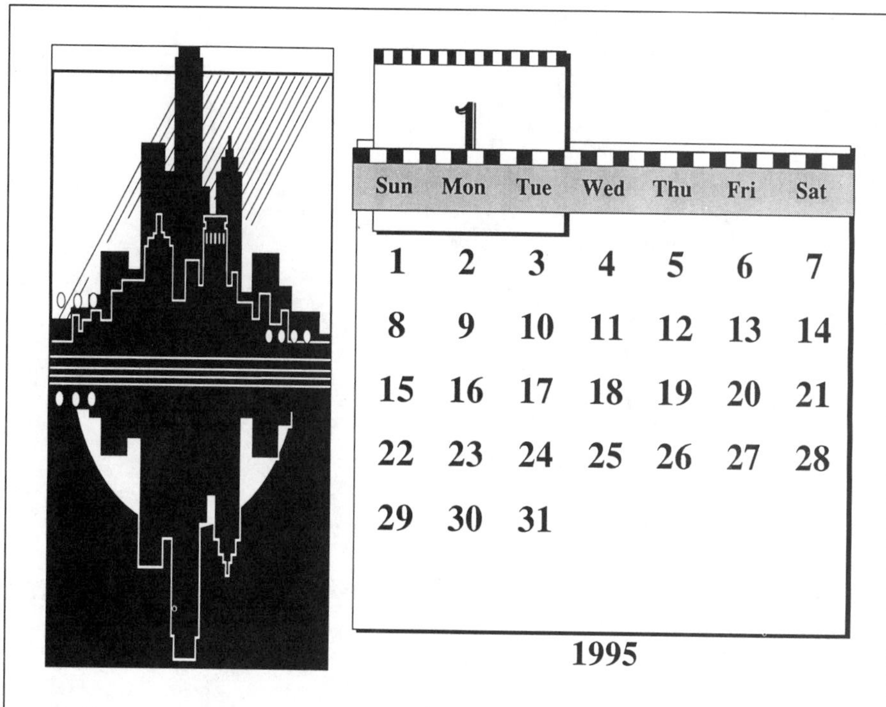

FIGURE 16.2

The Wizard's work.

For more on Wizards, see Chapter 27.

CHAPTER 17

End Monotony with AutoText, AutoCorrect, and Insert

FAST TRACK

To store text as an AutoText entry — 466

simply select whatever it is you wish to memorialize, then choose Edit ➤ AutoText… (or click the AutoText button on the Standard Toolbar). If you want to store the paragraph formatting with the entry, be sure to include paragraph marks in your selection. (Even if you store an entry *with* paragraph formatting, you can later insert the entry *without* formatting if you wish.)

To save AutoText entries — 467

review the automatic entry name Word for Windows has assigned. To change the name, just type a new one in the name box. If you want an entry to be available whenever you use Word, leave the default choice All Documents (Normal.dot) in the drop-down "availability" list. To attach an entry to a different template, pick one from the drop-down list. Click the Add button.

To insert an AutoText entry — 468

place the insertion point where you want the entry to go and do one of the following: Type all or part of an AutoText entry's name, then click the AutoText Toolbar button, press the **F3** function key, or type **Alt+Ctrl+V**; or, choose Edit ➤ AutoText… (you'll see a preview), then pick an entry from the scrolling name list by either double-clicking or clicking once and then clicking the Insert button or pressing ↵.

To edit an AutoText entry — 469

insert the entry in a document. Edit and reformat it as necessary. Select the corrected entry and any necessary punctuation, paragraph marks, spaces following, etc. Visit the

AutoText dialog box (Edit ➤ AutoText…). Rename the entry, if necessary, and click the Add button. Answer Yes to the "Do you want to redefine" question.

To delete an AutoText entry **469**

open the AutoText dialog box (Edit ➤ AutoText…). Select the doomed item from the scrolling list. Look in the Preview box or insert the entry and check to be *certain* that this is the entry you wish to delete. Click Delete.

To create your own AutoCorrect entries **474**

open the AutoCorrect dialog box with the Tools ➤ AutoCorrect… command. Type the "name" (the text string you wish to replace) in the Replace box. Type the replacement in the With box (or see the tip that follows).

To delete an AutoCorrect entry **475**

open the AutoCorrect dialog box (Tools ➤ Auto Correct…). Select the victim. Click the Delete button. The entry will be deleted.

To cut a selcetion to the Spike **479**

press Shift+F3.

To insert and clear the Spike **479**

press Ctrl+Shift+F3.

To insert without clearing the Spike **479**

type **spike** and then press F3.

▶▶ **W***ord* for Windows offers three convenient ways to store, retrieve, and insert frequently used text, graphics, and other document elements. The techniques employ Word's AutoText, AutoCorrect, and Insert commands. Each has strengths and weaknesses. Read about all three approaches before you develop a strategy and spend hours personalizing your computer.

▶▶ AutoText

AutoText is the replacement for Word's old Glossary… command. It's an easy way to store and retrieve "boilerplate" text, graphics, addresses, letter closings, memo distribution lists, tables, logos, and just about anything else that you can create with Word for Windows.

You can store AutoText entries with the NORMAL template so that they are always available or with other templates for specialty projects.

Users of earlier Word for Windows versions will notice that there are no Microsoft "standard" AutoText entries analogous to those in the old Glossaries. These functions (inserting dates and times, for instance) are now handled in other ways described elsewhere in this and other chapters.

▶ Creating AutoText Entries

Simply select whatever it is you wish to memorialize, then choose Edit ➤ AutoText…. You'll see a dialog box like the one in Figure 17.1.

If you want to store the paragraph formatting with the entry, be sure to include paragraph marks in your selection. (Even if you store an entry *with* paragraph formatting, you can later insert the entry *without* formatting if you wish.) Click Add.

FIGURE 17.1

Name and store AutoText entries with the Edit ➤ AutoText… command.

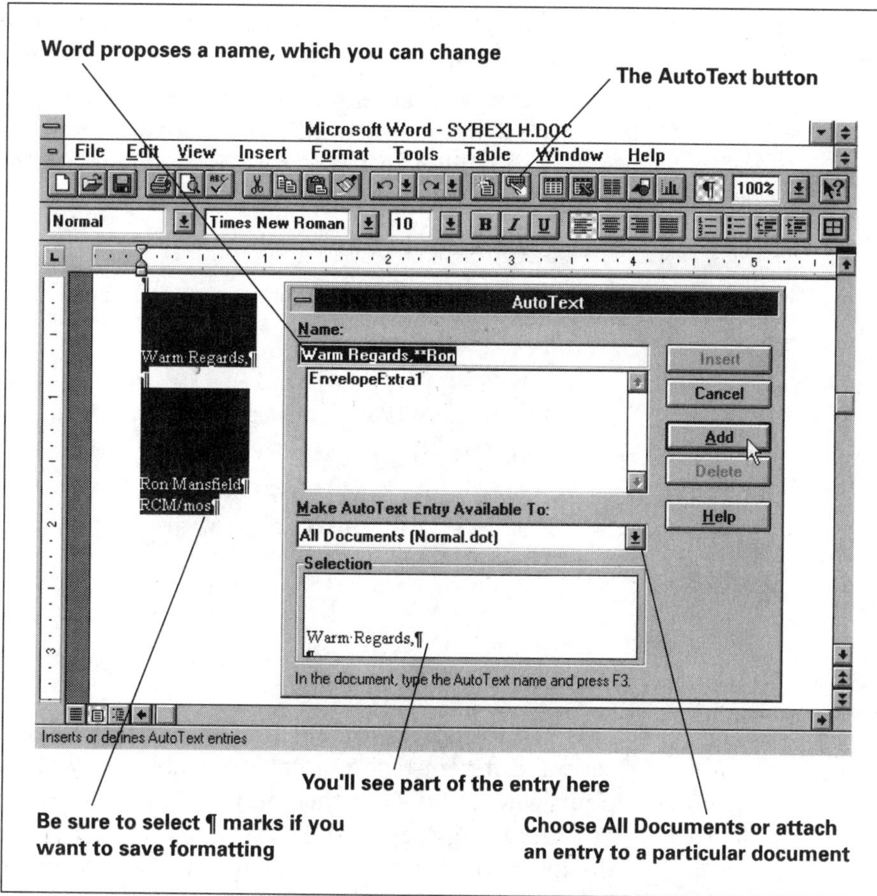

TIP

There's a Toolbar button for AutoText on the Standard Toolbar. It looks like a keyboard with a finger pointing at it.

▶ Saving AutoText Entries

To save AutoText entries, follow these steps:

1. Before saving an entry, you are given a chance to review and change the automatic entry name Word for Windows assigns. To

change the name, just type a new one in the name box. Names can be up to 32 characters long, and spaces are permitted.

2. If you want an entry to be available whenever you use Word, leave the default choice All Documents (Normal.dot) in the drop-down "availability" list. To attach an entry to a different template, pick one from the drop-down list.
3. Click the Add button.

▸▸ TIP

It is often good to select the space *after* text being memorialized when creating an AutoText entry (that is, the single space created by the spacebar, not the blank line created by the paragraph return). This will save you from typing a space each time you insert the entry later.

▸ Using AutoText Entries

Once you've saved some AutoText entries, you can insert them using several different techniques. Always begin by placing the insertion point where you want the entry to be placed. If you need spaces or tabs or other things before the entry, it is easiest to type them first. When the insertion point is properly positioned, do one of the following:

- Type all or part of an AutoText entry's name, then click the AutoText Toolbar button.
- Type all or part of an AutoText entry's name, then press the F3 function key.
- Type all or part of an AutoText entry's name, then type Alt+Ctrl+V.
- Choose Edit ➤ AutoText... (you'll see a preview), then pick an entry from the scrolling name list by either double-clicking or clicking once and then clicking the Insert button or pressing ↵.

In any event, Word for Windows will insert the entry. Edit it as you would any other text or graphic or other document element.

Forcing Plain Text

You can have an AutoText entry take on the appearance of the text at the insertion point in the current document, even if you saved it with its own formatting. To do so, choose Plain Text in the Insert As box of the AutoText dialog box:

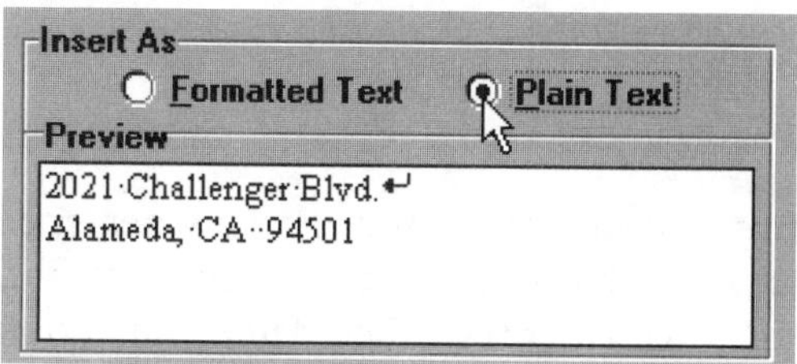

▶ Editing AutoText Entries

To edit an entry, follow these general steps:

1. Insert the entry in a document.
2. Edit and reformat it as necessary.
3. Select the corrected entry and any necessary punctuation, paragraph marks, spaces following, etc.
4. Visit the AutoText dialog box (Edit ➤ AutoText).
5. Rename the entry, if necessary.
6. Click the Add button.
7. Answer Yes to the "Do you want to redefine" question.

▶ Deleting AutoText Entries

Deleting AutoText entries is as simple as you'd expect (and hope). Follow these general steps:

1. Open the AutoText dialog box (Edit ➤ AutoText).
2. Select the doomed item from the scrolling list.
3. Look in the Preview box or insert the entry and check to be *certain* that this is the entry you wish to delete.
4. Click Delete.

►► **WARNING**

Word does not ask if you *really, really* want to delete AutoText entries, and Undo *will not work* here, so stay awake, particularly if you have a lot of similar-looking entries or entries with similar names.

► Shortcuts for Frequently Used Entries

You need not type an entire entry name when specifying it. You need only type enough characters to uniquely identify the entry. For instance, if you have an entry called *Mansfield* and another called *Manhole*, typing **Mans+F3** would insert the *Mansfield* entry while **Manh+F3** would get you *Manhole*.

►► **TIP**

If you like the previously described AutoText entry shortcut, keep it in mind when *naming* Entries. Make the first few characters in an entry name as unique as possible.

It is also possible to assign keyboard shortcuts (hot keys) and to create Toolbar buttons for your favorite AutoText entries. See Chapter 36 for details.

► Converting Old Glossaries to AutoText

Glossary entries in old templates will work with the new version of Word for Windows. Simply open documents using the old templates.

► EnvelopeExtra Entries

Word for Windows normally lets you use any names you like for AutoText entries. There are two exceptions. Word reserves the names EnvelopeExtra1 and EnvelopeExtra2 for a special purpose (see Chapter 15). If you give items these names, they will appear on envelopes each time you print them. For example, you might select a logo, and perhaps return address text, then name it EnvelopeExtra1, as shown Figure 17.2.

Thereafter, whenever you use Word's Envelope and Labels command, it will insert the contents of EnvelopeExtra1 and EnvelopeExtra2, if they exist. Figure 17.3 shows the results of including the EnvelopeExtra1 entry shown in Figure 17.2.

To delete these entries forever, delete them as you would any other entry. To temporarily defeat them, rename them. Remember, you can create different entries for different templates, so you can have multiple EnvelopeExtra1 and EnvelopeExtra2 entries for different projects. For instance, you could have one template with an entry like *Your newsletter is enclosed* and another that says *Here is the literature you've requested* and so on.

▶ Printing Lists of AutoText Entries

To see printed examples of all AutoText entries and their full names, follow this procedure:

1. Open a new document using the template of interest (NORMAL, for instance).
2. Open the Print dialog box (Ctrl+P or File ➤ Print).

FIGURE 17.2

Word reserves the AutoText entry names EnvelopeExtra1 and EnvelopeExtra2 for envelope printing.

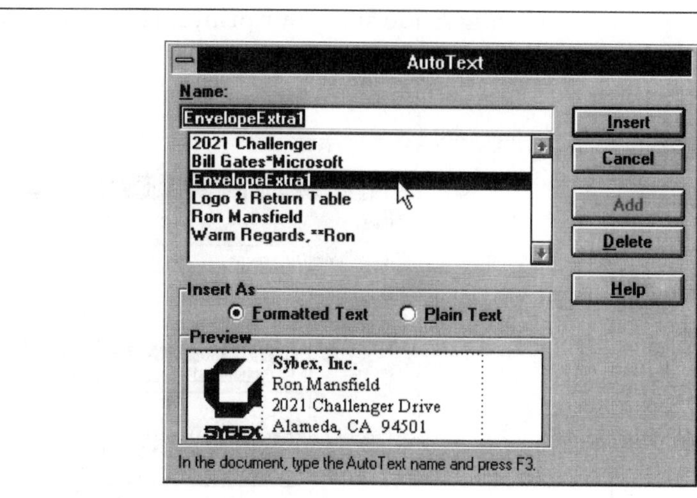

FIGURE 17.3

An EnvelopeExtra1 entry in an envelope.

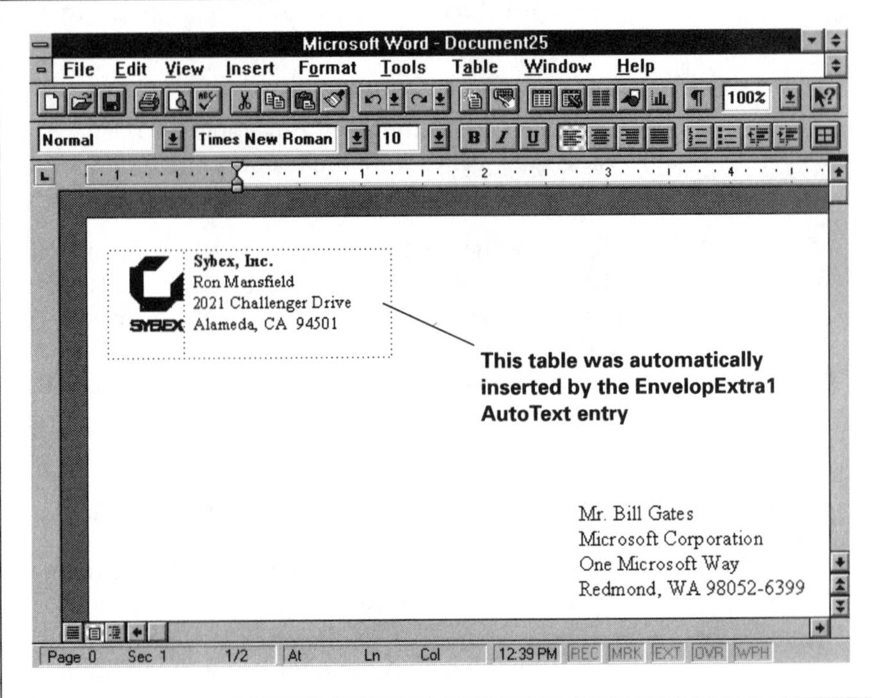

3. Choose AutoText Entries from the Print What list, as shown in Figure 17.4.
4. Having made sure your printer is ready, click OK or press ↵.
5. The list will present itself.

FIGURE 17.4

Choose AutoText Entries to print out a list.

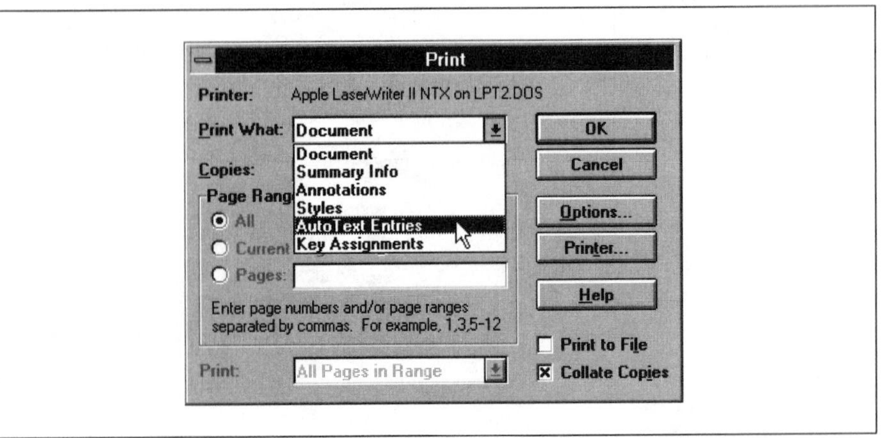

►► AutoCorrect

I suspect that *AutoCorrect* started out with one purpose in life, then someone discovered a second use for it. (I call these discoveries "hey lookits," as in "Hey look at what this can do!")

The primary reason for AutoCorrect is to fix typos like *teh* when you meant to type *the*. Word for Windows will watch you type and change things for you.

You can create your own entries, and there are some predefined entries. For instance, if you type **(r)** or **(R)**, Word will replace those characters with the Registered symbol.

To use the built-in entries, you just type along as usual. Word for Windows will make changes when it thinks they are needed. You can see a list of the current auto corrections by scrolling in the AutoCorrect dialog box (reached with the Tools ➤ AutoCorrect… command), shown in Figure 17.5.

FIGURE 17.5 ►

See and change AutoCorrect entries in the Autocorrect dialog box. Reach it with the Tools ➤ AutoCorrect… command.

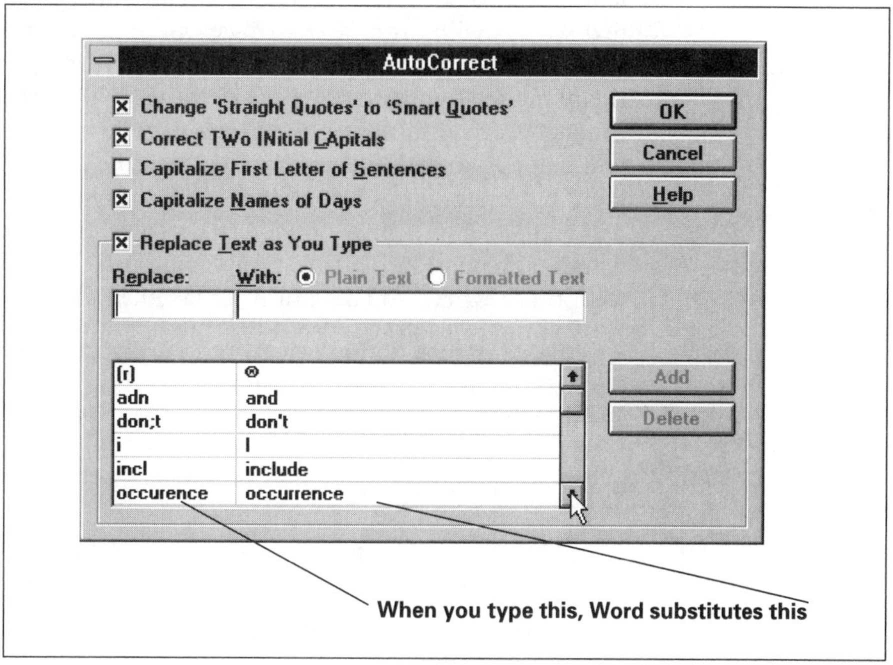

▶ Other Uses of AutoCorrect

Here's the hey lookit. In addition to correcting typos, you can use Auto-Correct to convert "shorthand" into longer text strings. For instance, you could tell Word for Windows that you want it to replace *aka* with *also known as*, or replace *mwg* with *Mr. William Gates*, and so on. You can even insert text and graphics this way. Type *sylogo,* for instance, and insert the Sybex logo (see Creating Your Own AutoCorrect Entries, next). Sound familiar? Isn't that what *AutoText* is for? Yeah. Does Auto-Correct have the wrong name if we're gonna use it for replacing things that are already correct? Sure, but hey, lookit!

The primary difference here is that *AutoCorrect* will *always* make the replacement when you type a defined string of characters followed by a space. *AutoText* waits for you to press the F3 key or click on the Toolbar button before it takes over.

▶ Creating Your Own AutoCorrect Entries

When creating your own AutoCorrect entries, there is one potential landmine, which is that AutoCorrect will always blindly replace certain text strings with other text strings. For example, if you want to change each occurrence of *add* with your inside address, and you assign *add* as the name for this auto correction, things will work fine until the first time you type a sentence like *Please add my name to the carpool list.* Then you'll get your address smack in the middle of an otherwise perfectly good sentence. So use care when defining the text that AutoCorrect will react to (the name for each entry) and give some thought to whether the text string you're replacing is likely to occur in cases other than those where you'd want it replaced.

Try to use names that are uncommon, yet easy to remember. If you get hooked on AutoCorrect, consider preceding all of your many entry names with some unusual character that will never appear in normal text, like a backslash (*\add* for instance). Names can be up to 31 characters long. That said, here are the steps:

1. Open the AutoCorrect dialog box with the Tools ➤ AutoCorrect… command.
2. Type the "name" (the text string you wish to replace) in the Replace box.

3. Type the replacement in the With box (or see the tip that follows).
4. Click Add.
5. Make any other entries or changes.
6. Click OK when done.

☒ Replace Text as You Type
Replace: With: ◉ Plain Text ○ Formatted Text
commnad | command

▶▶ TIP

If you select the text (or graphics and other things) you want to use as the replacement item before you open the AutoCorrect dialog box, it will appear in the With portion of the box when it opens. If the items are formatted, you'll be given the choice of pasting the items as formatted or not.

▶ *Editing AutoCorrect Entries*

To modify an AutoCorrect entry, follow these steps:

1. Correct the entry in a document.
2. Open the AutoCorrect dialog box (Tools ➤ AutoCorrect…).
3. Type the old Replace name.
4. When the Replace button undims, click it.
5. Answer Yes to the "Do you want to redefine" question.
6. The entry will be updated.

▶ *Deleting AutoCorrect Entries*

To delete an AutoCorrect entry, follow these steps:

1. Open the AutoCorrect dialog box (Tools ➤ AutoCorrect…).
2. Select the victim.

3. Click the Delete button.
4. The entry will be deleted.

▶ Automatic Correction

In addition to fixing things as you type them, you can run the Auto Correct feature at any time to inspect and clean up documents. Use the AutoCorrect dialog box to choose the options you wish Word to use, as shown here:

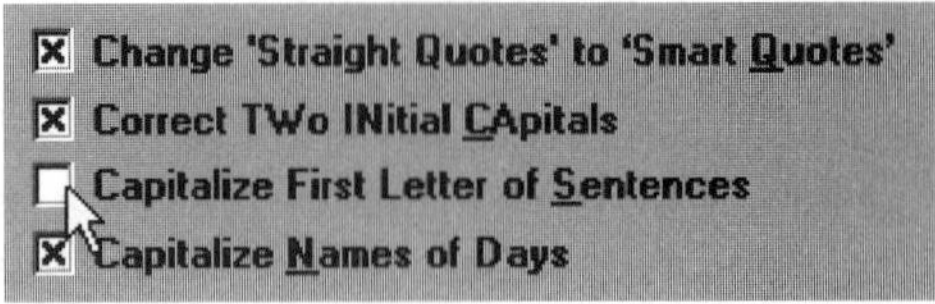

▸▸ Insert Commands

Word's Insert menu has a number of useful choices that can do things similar to AutoText, AutoCorrect, and the now-defunct Word Glossary command. While you'll find more about this topic in Chapter 32, let's take a quick look at a few of the commands here.

▶ Insert ➤ Date and Time...

The Insert ➤ Date and Time... command gives you a wide choice of date and time formats, as shown here.

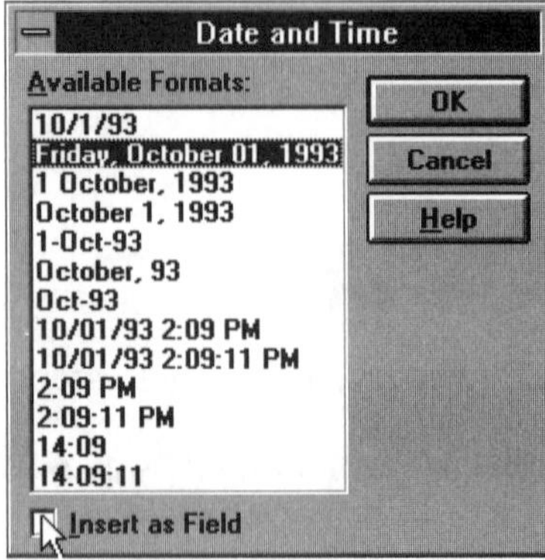

If you check the Insert as Field box, Word for Windows will place a date or time field in your document. Then Word for Windows will update the date and time whenever you *print* your document. See Chapter 32 for details.

▶ Insert ➤ File...

The Insert ➤ File... command lets you place the entire contents of any file into the open document. It places the file at the insertion point. Word for Windows can insert other Word documents, documents created by many other word processors, graphic files, plain text files, and more. When in doubt give it a try.

The Insert ➤ File... command brings up the File dialog box. Just pick the file of interest and click OK. Word will insert it. You may need to reformat it after insertion.

▶▶ TIP

Save your work before inserting files, just in case....

▶ Insert ➤ Picture...

The Insert ➤ Picture... command brings up the Insert Picture dialog box, shown in Figure 17.6.

Use the Insert Picture dialog box to preview pictures. When you click OK, a full-sized version of the selected graphic will be pasted at the insertion point in your current Word document.

Crop, resize, and move the graphic if necessary using the techniques you learned in Chapter 5.

▶ Insert ➤ Field...

The Insert ➤ Field... command lets you insert fields that can automate many aspects of document preparation. For instance, the

FileName field will insert the file's name in your document.

You'll learn a lot more about fields in Chapter 32.

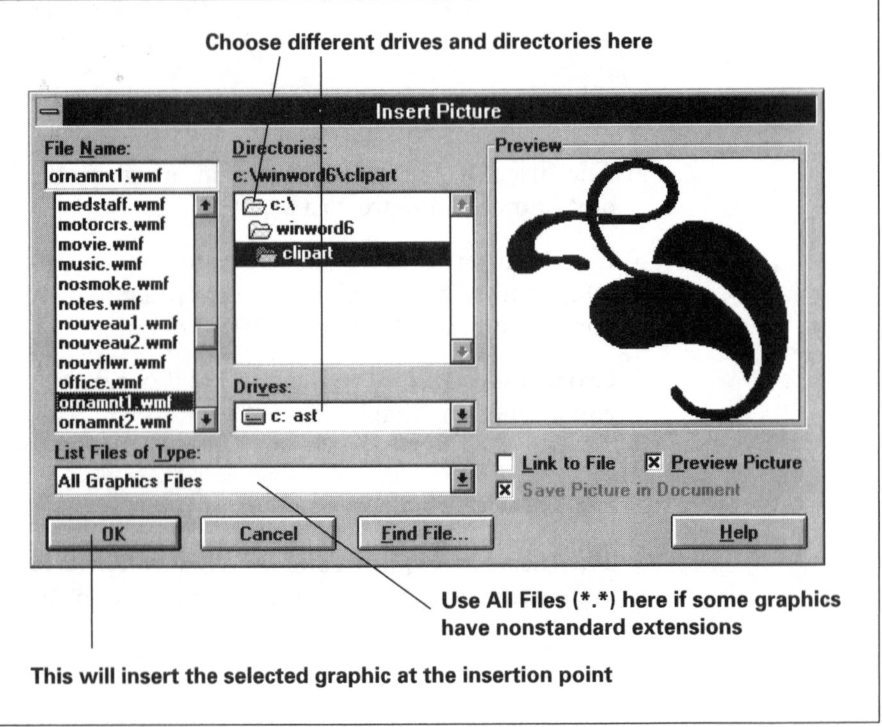

FIGURE 17.6

Preview and choose the picture you wish to insert.

▶▶ The Spike

Word has one other built-in tool for cutting and pasting, called the Spike. The Spike is a special, preset AutoText entry. You use it to collect a series of selections into a list and then insert them all in one place, in the order that you "spiked" them.

To cut something (text or graphics) to the Spike, first select it in any of the normal ways. Then press Ctrl+F3. The selection will disappear. Repeat this process as often as you like to stack up a series of selections in the Spike.

There are two ways to insert the Spike's contents in a document. You can insert the contents and clear the Spike at the same time, or you can insert the contents without clearing the Spike. Use the latter method when you want to insert the Spike contents elsewhere or continue adding items to the Spike.

▶ Insert and Clear the Spike

To insert the contents of the Spike and clear it out at the same time, first place the insertion point where you want the contents to appear. Then press Ctrl+Shift+F3. The contents will appear in the order that you spiked them, each as a separate paragraph (separated by paragraph marks).

▶ Insert without Clearing the Spike

To insert the contents of the Spike without clearing it, place the insertion point at the beginning of a line or between two spaces. Then type **spike** and then click the AutoText button on the Standard Toolbar, press F3, or press Alt+Ctrl+V. The contents will appear in the order you spiked them, each as a separate paragraph.

▶ Spike Summary

So, just to review:

TO DO THIS	TYPE THIS
Add a selection to the Spike	Ctrl+F3
Insert and clear the Spike	Ctrl+Shift+F3
Insert but don't clear the Spike	**spike** *and then* F3

▸▸ Tips and Strategies

Here are some tips for using the time-saving features discussed in this chapter:

- In my humble opinion, you should use AutoText, the Insert commands, and Templates for inserting things; use AutoCorrect only for its named function—correcting typos. If you *do* use AutoCorrect for heavy-duty boilerplate insertions, be certain that the names are uncommon and distinct.
- Set up keyboard shortcuts for regularly used AutoText entries.
- Consider adding buttons to a Toolbar for the really frequent entries. Visit the Toolbars tab in the Customize dialog box (Tools ➤ Customize…), and scroll to the AutoText category. (See Chapter 36 for details.)

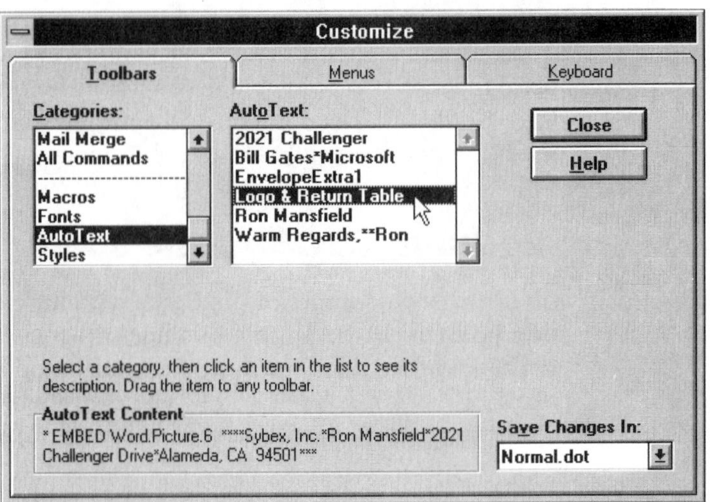

Next stop, Word's Thesaurus, where you'll learn how to find just the *right* word.

CHAPTER 18

Using the Thesaurus to Find the Right Words

▸▸ FAST TRACK

To add interest and texture to your prose **_486_**

use Word's thesaurus, accessed via the Tools ➤ Thesaurus... command or **Shift+F7**.

To look up words in the thesaurus **_486_**

highlight the word or phrase you wish to replace, or position the insertion point in a word, and then choose Tools ➤ Thesaurus.... If you haven't chosen a word, Word for Windows will choose the closest one. Clicking on a meaning in the Meanings list displays related synonyms in the Synonyms scrollable list. Clicking on a particular synonym places it in the editable Replace with Synonyms area of the Thesaurus dialog box. If you don't like any of the choices, clicking Cancel will close the thesaurus window and take you back to your unchanged document.

To replace the word in your document with a word in the Thesaurus dialog box **_488_**

highlight the word you like best. It will appear in the Replace with Synonyms box. Click the Replace button in the thesaurus window. Word will replace the highlighted text in your document with the contents of the Replace with box; then the thesaurus window will disappear. If you don't like the results, the Edit ➤ Undo Thesaurus command is available, provided you act immediately.

English is a rich language. There are many ways to say the same thing, yet we all tend to use a few words and phrases repeatedly. Word's *thesaurus* can help you add interest and texture to your prose. It gives you lists of synonyms (words that mean the same thing), then lets you quickly replace your original word with the alternative of your choice. Sometimes Word for Windows can offer antonyms (words with opposite meanings). Word's thesaurus also contains common phrases like *in consideration of* and *at rest.*

The Thesaurus… command lives on the Tools menu and has a new keyboard shortcut—Shift+F7.

TIP

If you frequently use the thesaurus, consider adding a Thesaurus *button* to your Toolbar. It's easy. Chapter 36 shows you how.

Looking Up Words and Phrases

Highlight the word or phrase you wish to replace or position the insertion point in a word and then choose Tools ➤ Thesaurus…. A dialog box will appear, similar to the one shown in Figure 18.1.

FIGURE 18.1

Word's thesaurus suggests synonyms and antonyms for highlighted words or phrases.

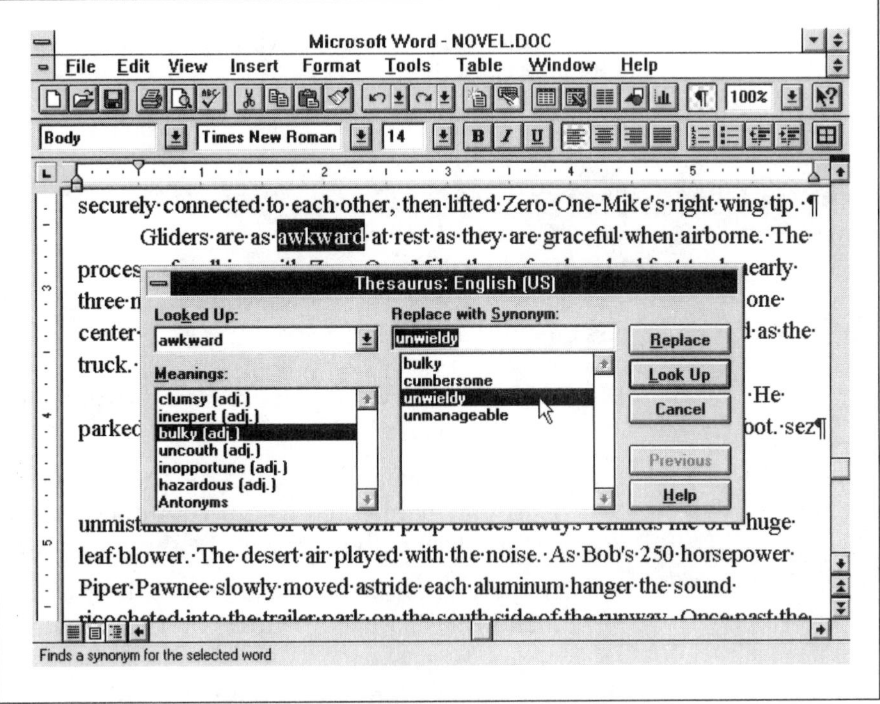

TIP

If you don't select a word and the insertion point is not in a word, the thesaurus feature will pick the word closest to the insertion point.

If you haven't done so already, Word for Windows will highlight the word in your document and place it in the Thesaurus dialog box next to Looked Up. This word (or phrase) is referred to as the *original* word.

If your original word has more than one meaning, the various meanings and their parts of speech will appear in the Meanings scrollable list. Clicking on a meaning in the Meanings list displays related synonyms in the Synonyms scrollable list. In Figure 18.1 the thesaurus offers six meanings for *awkward*. Clicking on *bulky* displays its synonyms.

Clicking on a particular synonym for *bulky* (*unwieldy*, for instance) places the synonym in the editable Replace with Synonym area of the

Thesaurus dialog box. If you don't like any of the choices, clicking Cancel will close the thesaurus window and take you back to your unchanged document.

►► Replacing Words and Phrases

After exploring the various potential replacement words or phrases suggested by Word for Windows, you can replace your original word by following these steps:

1. Highlight the word you like best. It will appear in the Replace with Synonym box.
2. Click the Replace button in the thesaurus window. Word will replace the highlighted text in your document with the contents of the Replace with box; then the thesaurus window will disappear.
3. If you don't like the results, the Edit ➤ Undo Thesaurus command is available, provided you act immediately.

Sometimes if you highlight a phrase, Word for Windows can suggest synonyms. Try it by highlighting the words *at rest*, for example. Watch carefully whenever you highlight phrases and replace them using the thesaurus, as it does not always do what you'd expect.

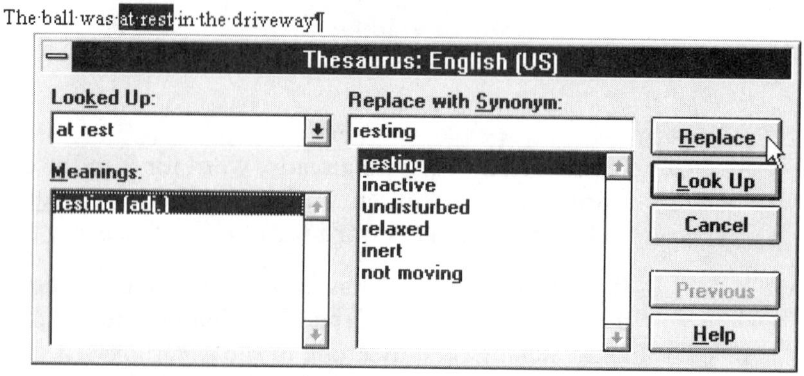

► Related Words and Phrases

Frequently, Word's thesaurus will not contain an exact match for your original word. This can happen if you've misspelled a word. In that case, you will probably see an alphabetical list of words in place of the Meanings list. Pick the correct word from the list or return to your document and correct the spelling error and then try the Tools ➤ Thesaurus... command again.

You will also have trouble matching certain tenses of words. For instance, if you attempt to replace *ambled*, Word for Windows will tell you to seek related words, as shown in Figure 18.2, because it contains the word *amble* but not ambled.

Clicking on a related word in the scrollable Related Word list will place it in the Replace with box. For instance, double-clicking on the Related Words choice in the list on the left will reveal a list of related words on the right, as shown in Figure 18.3. Once you have the related word in the Replace with box, click on the Look Up button to find synonyms and antonyms.

FIGURE 18.2

You may need to use a related word in the thesaurus and then edit it.

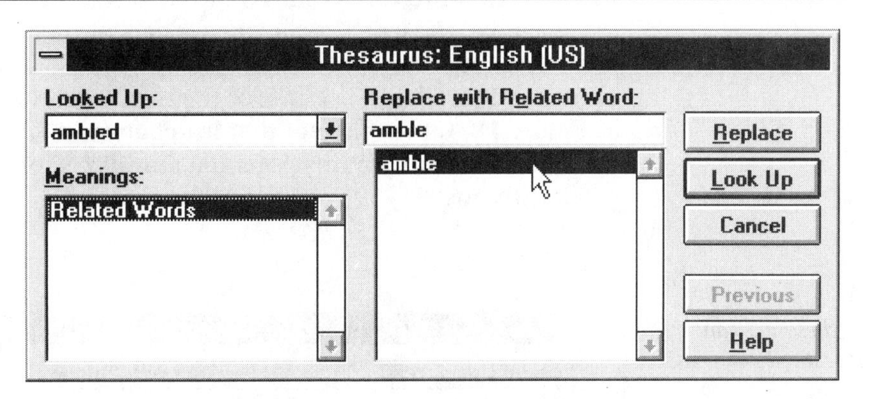

FIGURE 18.3

With the related word moved to the Replace with box, click Look Up, and you'll be able to peruse a list of synonyms for the related word.

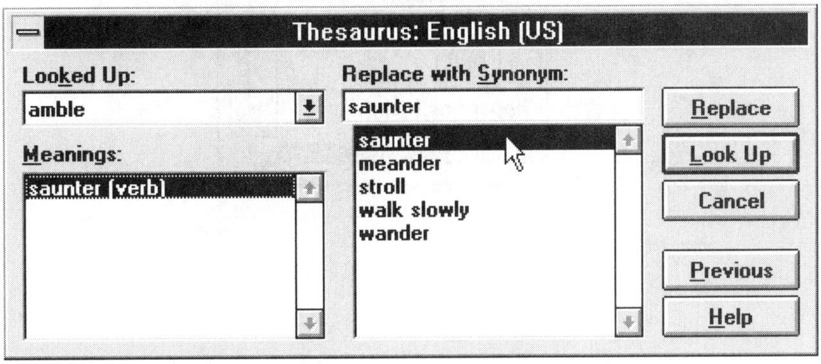

When you find a related word (*saunter*, for instance), click on it to move it to the Replace with box, then edit the word to suit your needs before clicking Replace. For instance, you'd probably want to add *-ed* to *saunter* in our example.

▸ Restoring the Original Word

Clicking on the Looked Up list in the Thesaurus dialog box will let you go back to earlier choices. The top of the list contains the original word. Click to restore it. You can also use Undo to restore your original word.

▸▸ Finding Antonyms

Frequently, Word for Windows can help you find antonyms. When they are available, the word *Antonyms* appears at the bottom of the scrollable Meanings list. Click on Antonyms to display a list of them in the right-hand scrollable-list area of the thesaurus window. As you can see in Figure 18.4, the name of that list changes from Synonym to Antonym, and the list contains potential antonyms for the word in the Replace with box.

FIGURE 18.4 ▸

The thesaurus can suggest antonyms too.

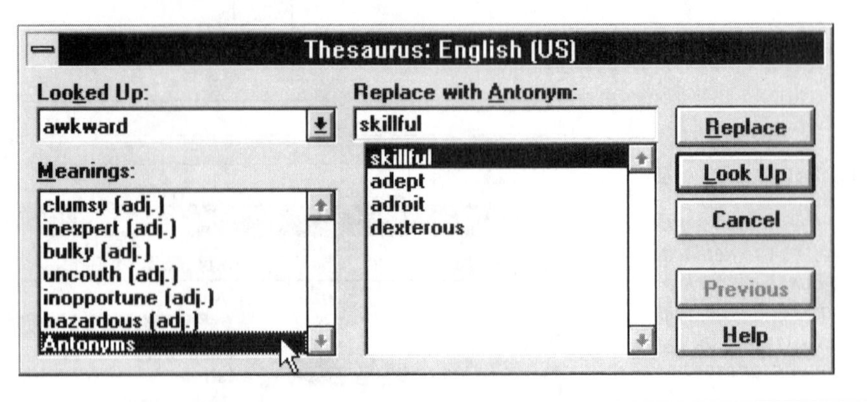

►► Spelling Help from the Thesaurus

While Word's thesaurus doesn't actually contain definitions, you can sometimes use it to help pick the appropriate spelling of confusing words like *which* and *witch* or *weather* and *whether*. Look up the words in question and compare synonyms to help you pick the right spelling. Figure 18.5 illustrates this.

FIGURE 18.5 ►

Use the thesaurus to eliminate confusion over words like weather and whether.

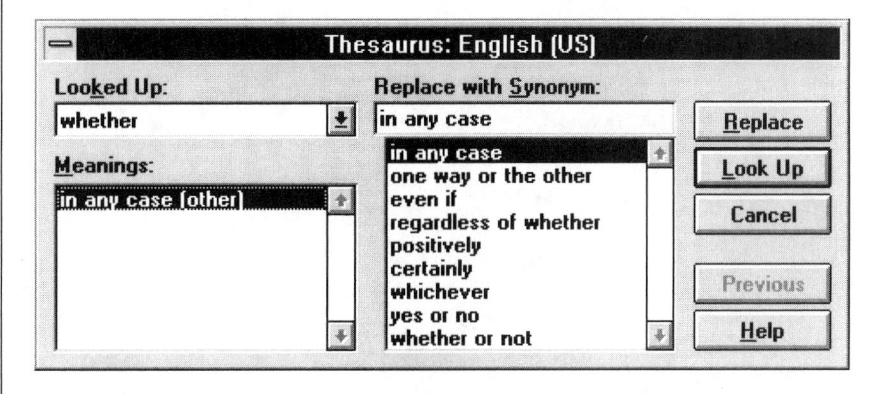

►► Exploring the Thesaurus

Here are some guidelines for exploring the thesaurus.

- It is possible to really meander around in the thesaurus! A single click on any word (either in the left or right lists) places a new word in the Replace with box. Then you can click on Look Up and go from there.
- Double-clicking on a synonym places that word in both the Replace with and Meanings spaces.
- Double-clicking on a Meanings word places just that word in the Replace with space.

CHAPTER 19

Checking Spelling, Word Counts, and Grammar

▸▸ FAST TRACK

To check the spelling in your document **498**

start the Spelling checker with the **F7** shortcut or by picking Tools ➤ Spelling.... Unless you've selected only a portion of your document to check, Word for Windows scans down, beginning at the insertion point, and will ask if you want to go back to the top of the document to continue checking, if necessary. The Spelling checker looks for words that it cannot find in its open dictionaries. When it spots a word that it can't match, Word highlights the questionable characters, scrolls the document so that you can see the problem word in context, and offers you a number of choices.

To change a misspelled word **499**

type a replacement in the highlighted Change To box and press ↵ or click the Change button. Word will replace the problem text with the new text you have typed in the Change To box and then continue spell checking. To change the word throughout the document that you are checking, click Change All instead of pressing ↵ or clicking Change.

To create a new custom dictionary **502**

visit the Spelling tab in the Options dialog box either by choosing Tools ➤ Options... or by clicking the Options... button in the Spelling dialog box. Click New... to create a new dictionary. You will be prompted for a dictionary name. Type a new name containing up to 32 characters. Open the folder where you want to store the dictionary (it is best to keep custom dictionaries with the main dictionary). Click Save.

To count the number of words in your document **505**

choose the Tools ➤ Word Count... command. Word will scan an entire document or just text you've selected, counting pages, words, characters, paragraphs, and lines. If you place an X in the appropriate box, it will include footnote and endnote text when counting.

To check grammar and style **506**

choose Tools ➤ Grammar.... Unless you select a portion of your document, Word will attempt to check the whole thing. Working from the insertion point, Word will highlight a portion of your prose (usually a sentence) and evaluate it. There may be a slight delay. If Word spots questionable spellings, you will be given the opportunity to correct them or tell Word to ignore them. Once spelling issues have been dealt with, Word will use its Grammar dialog box to point out questionable style and grammar issues. The text being considered is listed in the scrolling Sentence box.

To accept Word's suggested changes **507**

double-click on its suggestion or click the Change button to apply the change. When Word is unable to make changes by itself, the Change button will be dim. When the Grammar checker finishes, it will tell you so. Use the Cancel button to exit sooner. If you have the statistics option turned on, you'll see a readability report.

▶▶ **W*ord*** for Windows provides a powerful Spelling checker that lets you check the spelling of an entire document, including headers, footers, and hidden text. You can also use the feature to check a single word. Unlike the printed dictionary on your desk, Word's checker does not contain definitions. It does not consider words in context. While it knows that *two*, *too*, and *to* are all proper spellings, it cannot warn you of their improper use. For instance, Word's Spelling checker would not object to the sentence *She went two the bank too get a to dollar bill.*

What it *can* do is offer suggested spellings with uncanny accuracy. Misspellings are usually replaced with just a mouse click or two. You can add and edit your own custom dictionaries, which might contain proper nouns, technical terms, and other specialized words or numbers. You'll learn how to use all of these features in this chapter.

We'll also explore the Tools ➤ Word Count… command. It's a way for authors to quickly determine the number of characters, words, lines, and paragraphs in documents and footnotes.

Finally, we'll look at the Grammar checker. It can help you spot many common writing errors and evaluate your document's readability.

▶▶ *Setting Up the Spelling Checker*

The first time you use the Spelling checker it's a good idea to ensure that it is set to use the proper dictionary—English (US) in the United States. Here are the steps:

1. Choose Tools ➤ Language….

2. Scroll to the desired language—probably English (US)—and select it by double-clicking or clicking once on the name and once on OK.

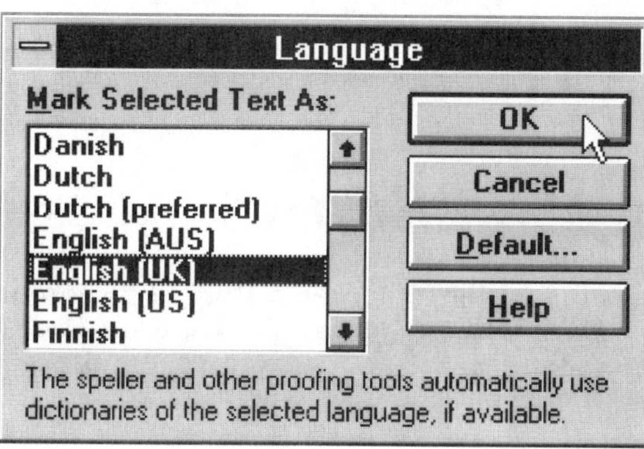

3. Click the Default button.
4. Answer Yes to the confirmation.
5. Click on OK.

WARNING

You can format certain text (foreign language or technical, for example) as "no proof" text, which means Word will skip it during spell checks. If you don't instruct Word for Windows to use a dictionary, you might think Word has spell checked your document and found nothing wrong. Your only clue will be a casual note about text being formatted with "no proofing."

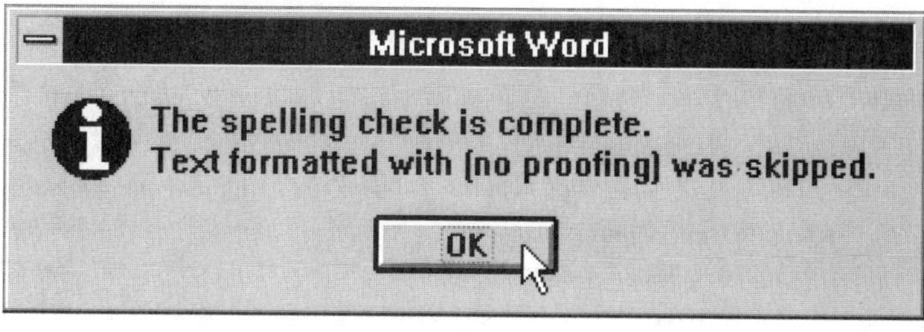

▸▸ TIP

You can assign different languages to different templates if you frequently use more than one language.

▸▸ Checking Spelling

Start the spelling checker with the F7 shorcut or by picking Tools▸ Spelling.... The Spelling dialog box appears, as shown in Figure 19.1.

FIGURE 19.1 ▸

The Spelling checker lets you pick suggested replacement words, type your own corrections, ignore unrecognized words, or add them to custom dictionaries.

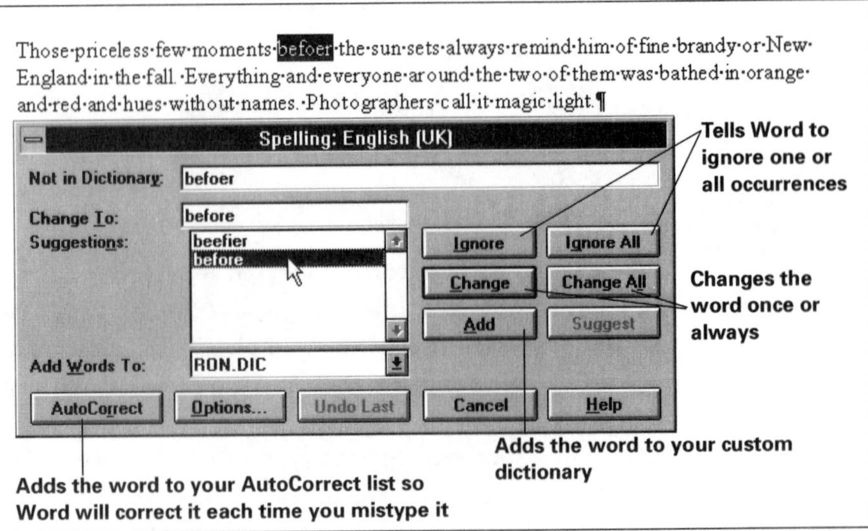

▸▸ TIP

There's a Spelling button on your Standard Toolbar. It contains a check mark and the letters *ABC*.

Unless you've selected only a portion of your document to check, Word for Windows scans down, beginning at the insertion point, and will ask if you want to go back to the top of the document to continue checking, if necessary.

The Spelling checker looks for words that it cannot find in its open dictionaries. When it spots a word that it can't match, Word highlights the questionable characters, scrolls the document so that you can see the problem word in context, and offers you a number of choices.

▶▶ TIP

The checker will confine itself to single words or phrase if you select items of interest before issuing the Spelling command.

▶ Typing Your Own Changes

If you want to change a misspelled word only once:

1. Type a replacement in the highlighted Change To box.
2. Press ↵ or click the Change button. Word will replace the problem text with the new text you have typed in the Change To box and then continue spell checking.

To change the word throughout the document that you are checking, click Change All instead of pressing ↵ or clicking Change. If the new word you've typed is something you want Word for Windows to recognize in all of your documents, see the section Custom or User Dictionaries, later in this chapter.

▶ Word's Suggested Changes

If you have suggestions enabled (check the Always Suggest option in the Spelling tab of the Options dialog box), Word for Windows will usually list one or more possible spellings, placing what it thinks is the best guess in the Change To box. If the default is not enabled, you can always ask for suggestions by clicking Suggest. Other suggestions, if any, will be listed in the scrollable Suggestions box. This may take a moment. You'll know Word is finished looking for alternative suggestions when you see either (End of Suggestions) or (No Suggestions) in the Suggestions list.

If you agree with Word's best guess, simply click the Change button to change this occurrence or use the Change All button to change this and all succeeding occurrences of the word. The Spelling checker will replace the word and continue examining your document.

Word's best guess is usually, but not always, right, as you can see in Figure 19.1. If one of the alternative suggestions is correct (the word *before* in Figure 19.1), simply double-click on the desired word to replace the misspelled word or click once on the desired word in the list to move it to the Change To box, then click the Change or Change All button as necessary. Sometimes, however, Word's guesses will be bizarre or comical (e.g., *broccoli* for *Berkeley*), so be sure you read the replacement text carefully.

► Overruling Suggestions

Sometimes Word won't make correct suggestions, or you might want to correct the problem yourself without retyping the entire word or phrase. For instance, Word for Windows may spot two run-together words like the ones shown in Figure 19.2.

FIGURE 19.2 ►

Problem text can be edited right in the Change To box.

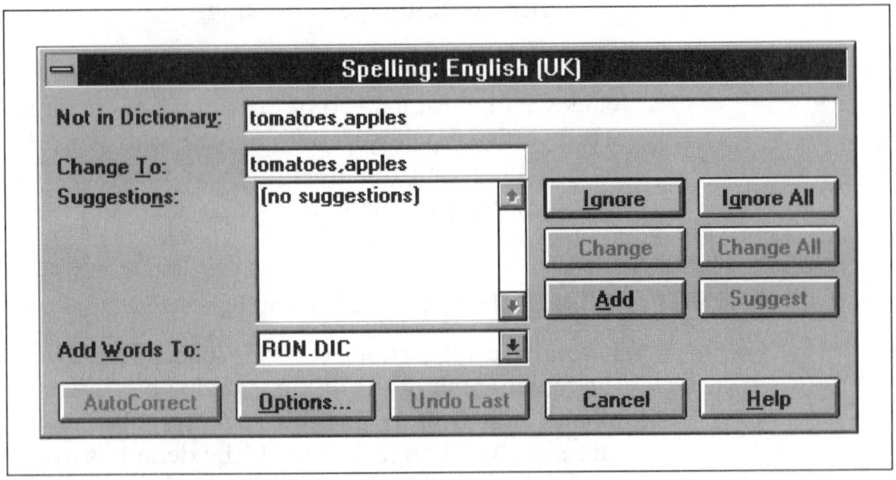

When it has no suggestions, Word for Windows moves the problem text to the Change To box where you can edit it yourself (place a space between the two words, for instance).

▶ Ignoring Flagged Words

Sometimes Word for Windows will spot a word that is properly spelled, but that isn't in its open dictionaries. Proper nouns, technical jargon, and typesetting codes are examples.

If you want Word for Windows to ignore the text only once, click the Ignore button. Word will leave the word or other text string as you typed it and continue spell checking. To ignore the word throughout the document you are checking, click Ignore All. (If the word is something you want to ignore in all of your documents, you may want to add it to a custom dictionary.)

▶▶ NOTE

The Spelling checker's Ignore All button ignores words for your *entire* Word session. That is to say, if you tell Word to ignore a word in the morning, it will ignore the word all day in each document you check, unless you exit Word or use the Reset Ignore All... button in the Spelling tab (of the Options dialog box), as shown in Figure 19.3.

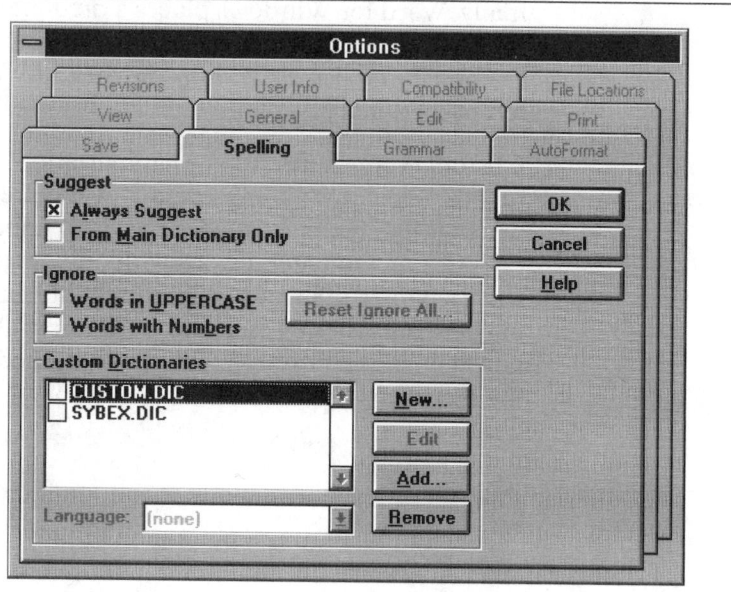

FIGURE 19.3 ▶

Reach the Spelling tab either by choosing Tools ➤ Options... or by clicking the Options... button in the Spelling dialog box.

►► Custom or User Dictionaries

Most of the words used by the Spelling checker are located in a dictionary that comes with your Word for Windows program. In the United States, Word is shipped with a dictionary called the US English Dictionary. It is kept in the Commands folder. You cannot make changes to this dictionary.

You can, however, maintain one or more of your own *custom* dictionaries. Word checks only open dictionaries. The more dictionaries you have open, the slower spell checking will be.

► The Standard Custom Dictionary

When you install Word for Windows, the installation program places an empty Custom Dictionary in your Commands folder. The default name for the dictionary is CUSTOM.DIC. It is opened and used whenever you spell check unless you instruct Word otherwise. This is where you will want to keep most proper nouns, trademark names, etc.

Word for Windows will place words in the Custom Dictionary whenever you click the Add button while spell checking. (The first time you add a word, you may be asked to create a custom dictionary.) Normally, Word for Windows places a dictionary called CUSTOM.DIC in the Proof subdirectory. You can overrule this default use of the Custom Dictionary by using the drop-down Add Words To list to specify a different dictionary.

Custom dictionaries handle capitalization as follows. If you add a word to a dictionary as all lowercase, it will be recognized later, regardless of whether it is typed as all lowercase, all uppercase, or with an initial capital letter. If you enter a word with only the first letter capitalized, Word will recognize the word when it later appears in all caps or with a leading cap, but will question the word if it is all lowercase. Unusual capitalizations, like VisiCalc, will be questioned unless they are stored in the dictionary exactly as they should be.

▶ Creating Additional Custom Dictionaries

If you work on unusual projects that involve technical jargon, typesetting codes, etc., you might want to create one or more additional specially named custom dictionaries, which you can turn on or off in the Spelling tab of the Options dialog box. (Back in Figure 19.3, a new dictionary called SYBEX.DIC has been added.) To create a new custom dictionary, follow these steps:

1. Visit the Spelling tab in the Options dialog box either by choosing Tools ➤ Options... or by clicking the Options... button in the Spelling dialog box. Figure 19.3 shows the Spelling tab.
2. Click New... to create a new dictionary. You will be prompted for a dictionary name.
3. Type a new name containing up to 32 characters.
4. Open the folder where you want to store the dictionary (it is best to keep custom dictionaries with the main dictionary).
5. Click Save.

▶ Opening and Closing Custom Dictionaries

To make a dictionary available to the Spelling checker, it must be open. Place checkmarks next to both custom dictionaries in Figure 19.3 to make both open and available for the Spelling checker to use. Click in the box next to the desired dictionary to open or close it. A checkmark means it's open.

To open dictionaries that are not in the folder containing the main dictionary, click the Add... button. Show Word for Windows where the desired dictionary is, using standard Windows directory-navigation techniques.

▶ Editing Custom Dictionaries

To add items to a custom dictionary, click Add when the Spelling checker encounters a word of interest or type a Word for Windows document containing all of the words you want to add. Spell check this document, adding each unrecognized word.

If you accidentally add a word to a custom dictionary, it is a good idea to delete it, as extra words mean more searching time during your spell checks. And if you add misspelled words, they will no longer be challenged by the checker. Removing words from a custom dictionary is slightly more involved than adding them.

1. Choose the dictionary you wish to edit from the Spelling tab in the Options dialog box (reached by choosing Tools ➤ Options...).
2. Click the Edit... button.
3. A dialog box will appear, as shown in Figure 19.4, offering to let you edit the dictionary as a regular Word document. Click Yes.

FIGURE 19.4 ►

Word lets you edit custom dictionaries as Word documents. Click Edit... in the Spelling tab of the Options dialog box to get started.

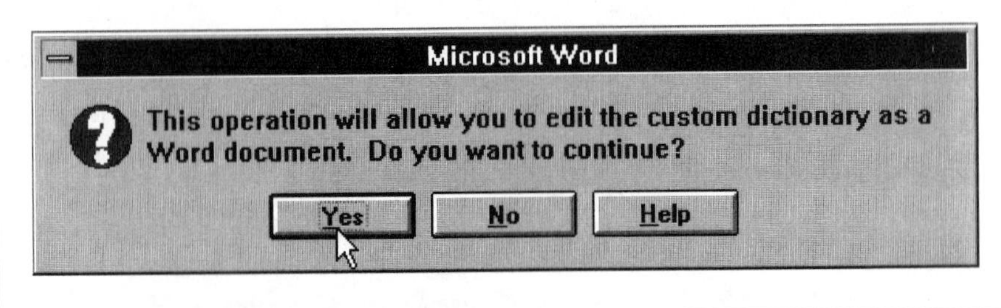

4. Close the Options dialog box.
5. Edit the dictionary.
6. Save it with the Save command (Ctrl+S).

►► **TIP**

The Spelling tab provides other spelling options, which should be self-explanatory. Choose Help to learn more from Word's online help feature.

► Speeding Up the Spelling Checker

Here are some tips for speeding up your spell checking:

- Place the insertion point at the beginning of your document (Ctrl+Home) and check in Normal view.

- If you are a good speller with a slow computer and are mostly looking for typos, consider turning off suggestions to speed checking. (Visit the Spelling tab in the Options dialog box reached with Tools ➤ Options….)
- Keep custom dictionaries fairly small (a hundred or two hundred words, perhaps).
- Split larger custom dictionaries into smaller ones by categories that match different kinds of work you do (legal, technical, etc.). Open just the one(s) you need.

►► The Word Count Command

The Word Count… command is found in the Tools menu. Simply choose the command to start the process. Figure 19.5 shows typical results.

FIGURE 19.5 ►

The Word Count feature also counts characters, lines, paragraphs, pages, both in the main text and in footnotes.

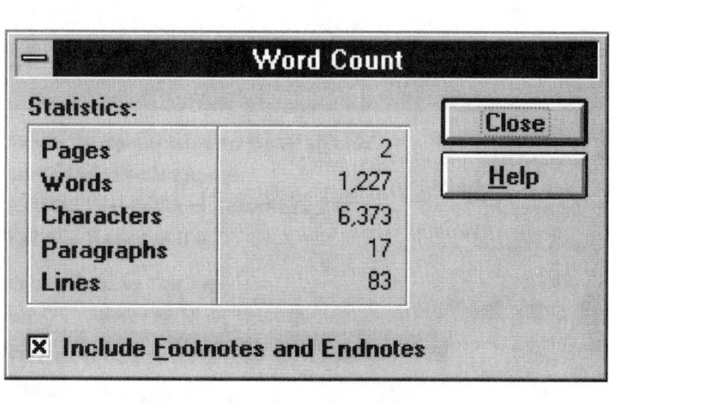

Tools ➤ Word Count… will scan an entire document or just text you've selected. It counts pages, words, characters, paragraphs, and lines. If you place an X in the appropriate box, it will include footnote and endnote text when counting. It does *not* count words in headers and footers. You must display invisible text to count it.

►► Checking Grammar and Style

Word's Grammar checker evaluates style and points out many, but not all, grammatical errors. It can often suggest changes and even make some of them for you. Word for Windows uses collections of rules when analyzing your documents. You can turn off specific rules that annoy you or cramp your style. Word will explain and demonstrate the rules for you.

Statistics and readability indexes are created at the end of a grammar-checking session. These help you determine if the writing style is appropriate for your audience.

Because the Grammar checker needs to work with properly spelled documents, it sometimes activates Word's Spelling checker when it encounters unfamiliar words.

Word for Windows is not a complete replacement for a human editor. For instance, it will not catch things like missing periods at the end of sentences or double spaces between words.

The fact that Word considers parts of speech when checking grammar might make you believe that it understands what you've written. This is not the case. For instance, the nonsense phrase *Eye sea sum tins knot write hear* passes the grammar check successfully.

None the less (oops, Word prefers *Nonetheless*), the checker will help you spot many common problems and can help you polish your style.

►► TIP

If you never use the Grammar checker, save some disk space and RAM by reinstalling Word for Windows without it. See Appendix A.

You may want to save your document just before grammar checking or run the check on a copy of your masterpiece. While grammar and style changes are often reversible with Undo, this is not always the case. Also be sure that you've specified a language for proofing as described at the beginning of this chapter.

To check grammar and style:

1. Save your work and move the insertion point to the beginning of your document.
2. Choose Tools ➤ Grammar.... Unless you select a portion of your document, Word will attempt to check the whole thing.
3. Working from the insertion point, Word will highlight a portion of your prose (usually a sentence) and evaluate it. There may be a slight delay. If Word spots questionable spellings, you will be given the opportunity to correct them or tell Word to ignore them.
4. Once spelling issues have been dealt with, Word will use its Grammar dialog box to point out questionable style and grammar issues. The text being considered is listed in the scrolling Sentence box. Suggestions and observations are made in the scrolling Suggestions box. For example, in Figure 19.6, the Grammar checker doesn't like *doesn't*.

FIGURE 19.6

Word finds this document not wordy enough.

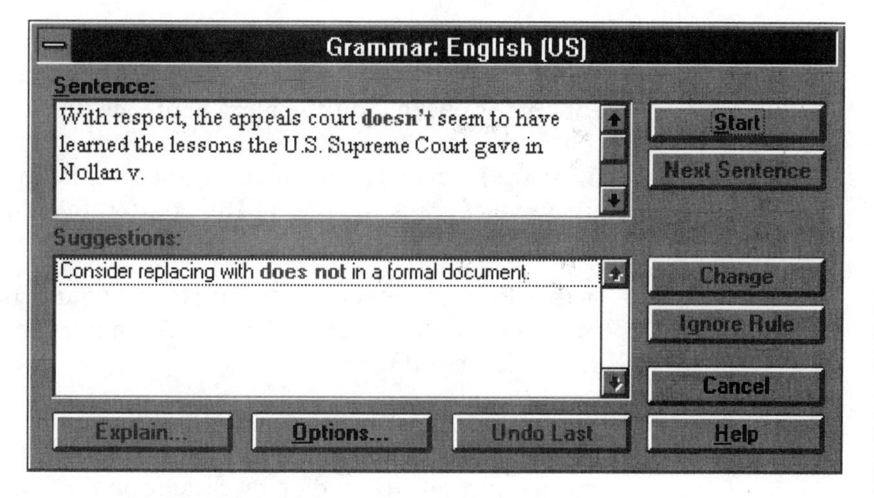

▶ Accepting Word's Suggestions

In Figure 19.6, Word for Windows is suggesting does not as a replacement for *doesn't*. When Word makes specific suggestions like this, you can double-click on its suggestion or click the Change button to apply the change. When Word is unable to make changes by itself, the Change button will be dim.

When the Grammar checker finishes, it will tell you so. Use the Cancel button to exit sooner. If you have the statistics option turned on, you'll see a readability report.

► Making Manual Changes

Many of the problems the checker spots need your intervention. To make manual changes, type right in the Grammar window's Sentence box. Click the Change button when done. The Grammar checker will make the change and continue checking.

► Ignoring Suggestions

The Ignore button in the Grammar dialog box instructs Word for Windows to ignore the current occurrence of a problem but will not prevent the Grammar checker from pointing out similar problems in the future.

You can skip to the next sentence without making changes to the current one by clicking on the Next Sentence button. Clicking Ignore Rule in the Grammar dialog box tells Word to stop using the current rule with the current document. For example, to stop reminders about passive voice, click the Ignore Rule button the first time Word points out a passive construction.

To turn off passive-voice checking for all your projects, turn off the rule (called Passive Verbs Usage) in the Grammar tab of the Options dialog box, as described next.

Changing Preferences

You can turn rules on and off by clicking on the Customize Settings… button in the Grammar tab in the Options dialog box, shown in Figure 19.7.

Here you can fine-tune Word's grammar pickiness. Rules are listed in two categories—Style and Grammar. Pick a list to scroll by clicking on

FIGURE 19.7

Reach the Grammar tab of the Options dialog box with Tools ➤ Options... or by clicking Options... in the Grammar window.

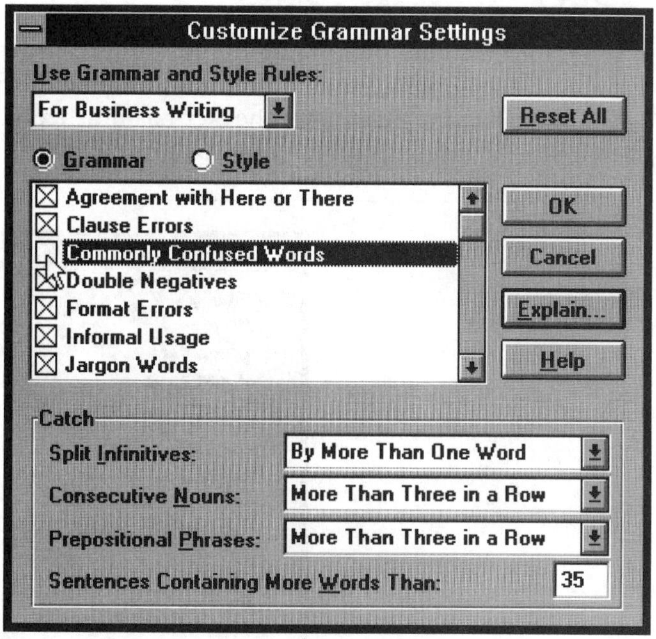

Customize Grammar Settings

Use Grammar and Style Rules:

For Business Writing

Reset All

Grammar Style

- [x] Agreement with Here or There
- [x] Clause Errors
- [ ] Commonly Confused Words
- [x] Double Negatives
- [x] Format Errors
- [x] Informal Usage
- [x] Jargon Words

OK

Cancel

Explain...

Help

Catch

Split Infinitives: By More Than One Word

Consecutive Nouns: More Than Three in a Row

Prepositional Phrases: More Than Three in a Row

Sentences Containing More Words Than: 35

the appropriate button. Checkmarks next to a rule mean the rule will be enforced. Clicking near a checkmark toggles it on and off. For more information about a rule, highlight it and click on the Explain... button.

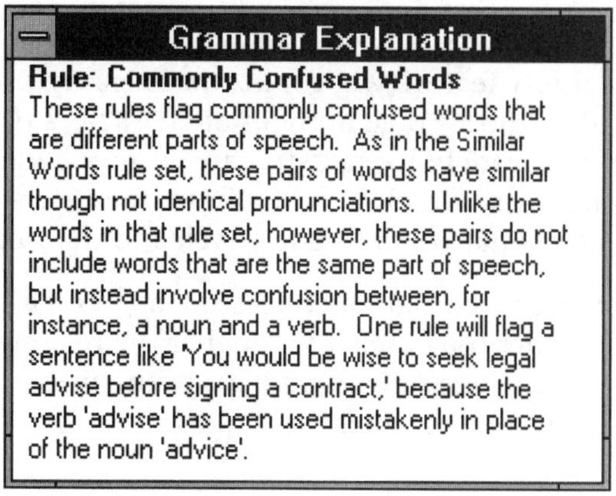

Grammar Explanation

Rule: Commonly Confused Words

These rules flag commonly confused words that are different parts of speech. As in the Similar Words rule set, these pairs of words have similar though not identical pronunciations. Unlike the words in that rule set, however, these pairs do not include words that are the same part of speech, but instead involve confusion between, for instance, a noun and a verb. One rule will flag a sentence like 'You would be wise to seek legal advise before signing a contract,' because the verb 'advise' has been used mistakenly in place of the noun 'advice'.

► Document Statistics

There are liars, damned liars, and statistics. Word for Windows can provide the latter, as illustrated in Figure 19.8. Document statistics appear after the Grammar checker has finished scanning your document.

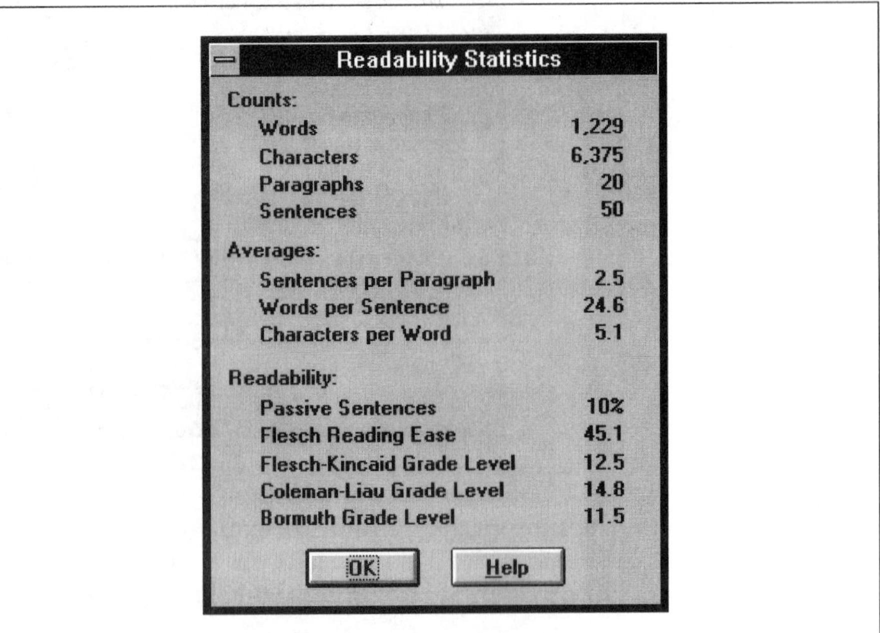

FIGURE 19.8 ►

Word can try to quantify your writing style.

The Readability feature will count words, paragraphs, and sentences, then calculate the average number of characters per word and similar trivia. Several readability statistics are computed, including a count of passive sentences, Flesch Reading Ease, the Flesh-Kincaid Grade Level, the Coleman-Liau Grade Level, and the Bormuth Grade Level.

The Grade Level measurements assign a (US public school) grade level. The higher the index, the tougher the reading. Imagine how much better Shakespeare might have been, given tools like these. To write passively, or not. That is the question.

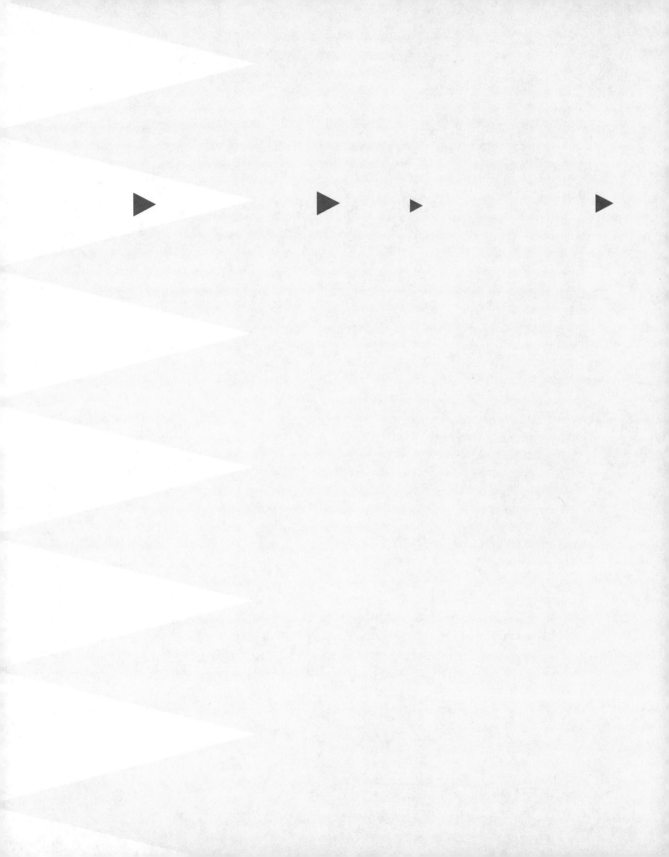

CHAPTER 20

Finding and Replacing

▸▸ FAST TRACK

To find things in your document **_517_**

choose Edit ➤ Find... (**Ctrl+F**). Specify text and special characters (if any) to find. Specify formatting characteristics (if any) to find. Tell Word where to search and in which direction. Use the Special menu to search for things like section breaks, paragraph marks, etc. Check off any special search requests like Match Case or Find Whole Words Only. Click Find Next to start the search. When Word finds what you want, return to the document. To find again, press = (the equals sign) on the numeric pad (if you're still in the document) or click the Find Next button in the dialog box.

To enter certain special characters like tab marks, nonbreaking spaces, etc., when constructing a search request **_520_**

place the insertion point in the Find What box where you want the special character to go and choose the desired character from the drop-down list.

To find spaces, nonbreaking spaces, and page breaks **_521_**

insert Word's White Space special character in your search string.

To perform advanced searches for combinations of things **_523_**

use Word's *operators* (they are a lot like wild cards).

To replace text in your document 524

choose Edit ➤ Replace… (**Ctrl+H**). Create search criteria. Specify the desired replacement text, formats, etc. Tell Word where to search and in which direction. Click Find Next or Replace All to start the replacement. Confirm the replacements.

To replace formatting 527

specify the character attributes you want Word to find. You can do this by pulling down the Format menu in the Replace dialog box. From there, choose Font, then click in the option or options you wish to change in the Font dialog box. Next go to the Replace With box and specify the new format the same way. Let 'er rip! Either tell Word to Replace All, or you can supervise each change.

To replace styles in the Replace dialog box 528

click on the Format button. Choose Styles. You will see a list of your document's styles and descriptions. Pick styles for both the find and replace criteria, then proceed as usual.

To paste long passages or obscure characters like umlauted letters or math symbols when replacing 531

copy the text, graphics, etc., from your document to the Clipboard, then paste it into the Find What or Replace With boxes.

To enter special characters (paragraphs, tabs, etc.) 533

enter their two-character codes into Find and Replace boxes from the keyboard. It's often the quick way to go.

▶▶ **E***very* contemporary word-processing product has a way to quickly locate and replace specific text strings (collections of words, numbers, and other characters). Lawyers use these features (sometimes called *global replace features*) to do things like finding each occurrence of *Marion Morrison* in a contract and replacing it with *John Wayne*.

Some typists enter shorthand or acronyms for lengthy items when they draft. Then, while polishing the document, they replace the shorthand with the actual text. For instance, you might initially type *DRD* in the draft of a government document, then have Word find and replace each occurrence of *DRD* with *Department of Redundancy Department*.

▶▶ **TIP**

If you do a lot of this, consider using Word's AutoCorrect feature instead. It will replace acronyms as you type them.

Word provides two separate commands, called Edit ➤ Find... (Ctrl+F) and Edit ➤ Replace... (Ctrl+H). Find... is really just an evolutionary predecessor to Replace. In fact, if you are careful, you can use Replace... instead of Find... for everything.

With Word you can search for and then replace or remove special characters like paragraph marks, optional hyphens, or footnote-reference marks.

A form of wild-card searching is permitted, letting you insert question marks in search requests to work-around minor spelling variations. Asking Word to find **Sm?th**, for instance, would find both *Smith* and *Smyth*. You can search for ranges of numbers using a similar technique. Word's designers refer to this process as searching for *unspecified letters* and *unspecified digits*.

Occasionally, Word's find and replace features can be used to reformat documents. You might, for instance, search for all occurrences of two consecutive spaces and replace them with a single space. But Word can do much more than that. The find and replace commands can do the following:

- Help you find all or selected paragraphs formatted with a particular style and apply a different style.
- Remove things simply by telling Word to search for the item you wish to delete and replace it with nothing.
- Search your entire document or selected portions. You specify the direction of the search (up or down).

►► The Art of Finding

The Find... feature helps you quickly locate text, formats, special characters, and combinations thereof. It lets you search selected parts of your document or the whole enchilada. Simple find requests can locate text regardless of format.

new

New Word 6 features make it easy to ask Word to search for very specific things, like occurrences of the word *Liberace* formatted in bold, blue, 24-point Playbill.

You need not limit your searches to text. You can look for section marks, graphics, paragraph marks, and more. When using the Find... command (as opposed to Replace...), Word finds what you've requested, then scrolls to the found item and its surrounding text without modifying anything.

You must click in the document window to work with the found item. You can leave the Find dialog box out on your screen as you work, flipping between it and your document window. Figure 20.1 shows the Find dialog box.

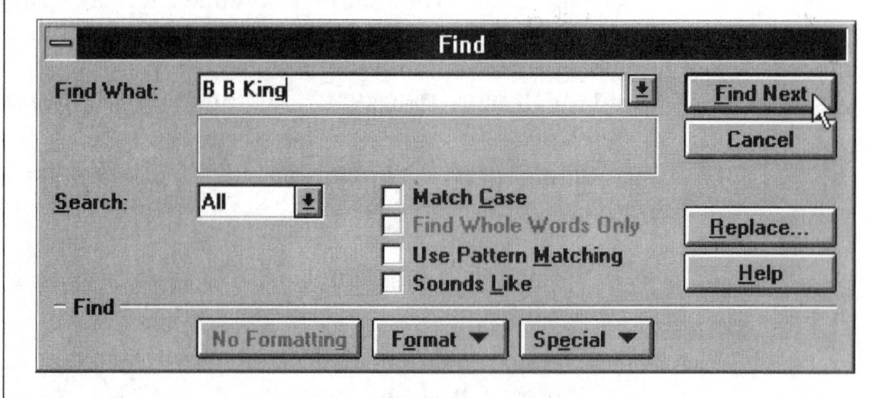

FIGURE 20.1 *The Find dialog box (reached with the Edit… Find command) lets you specify search criteria.*

Here's a general overview of the Find dialog box. (Details will follow.) To do a search:

1. Choose Edit ➤ Find….
2. Specify text and special characters (if any) to find.

3. Specify formatting characteristics (if any) to find.

4. Tell Word where to search and in which direction.

5. Use the Special menu to search for things like section breaks, paragraph marks, etc.

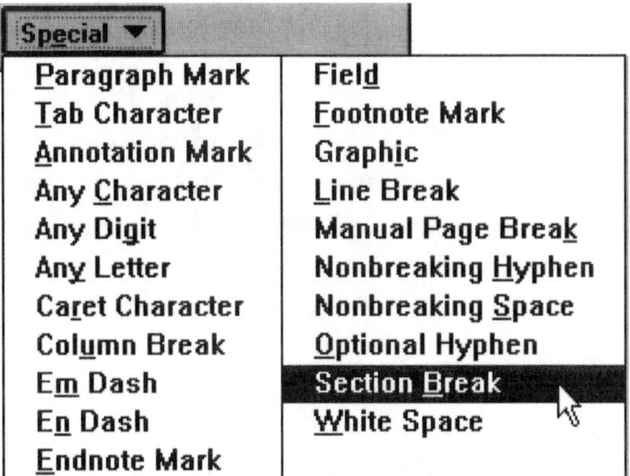

6. Check off any special search requests like Match Case or Find Whole Words Only.

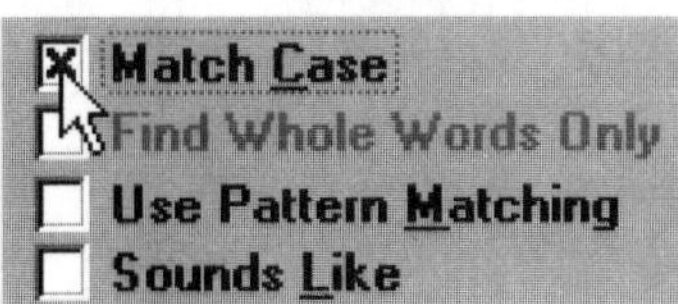

7. Click Find Next to start the search.
8. When Word finds what you want, return to the document.
9. To find again, press = (the equals sign) on the numeric pad (if you're still in the document) or click on the Find Next button in the dialog box.

Like any good computer program, Word takes your requests quite literally, so you will need to understand each Find… option fully to locate exactly what you want.

For example, if Word searches using the criteria specified in Figure 20.1, it will find *B B King*, but not *B.B. King*, *BB King*, or *Burger King*.

There are ways to get Word to find each of these text strings, of course. Just realize that you may need to carefully formulate and test your search strategy. In some cases, you will need to perform multiple searches to find similar but subtly different text strings.

Word will automatically search in headers and footers. For multi-section documents, you may need to open and search headers and footers in each section. If your search plans include things like paragraph marks or hidden text, the hidden text must be visible on the screen.

Consider proofing your document or at least running the Spelling checker before important, major searches. If you spell *banana* correctly six times and incorrectly once, Word will find only six of your seven bananas....

► Finding Text

Choose Edit ➤ Find... or use the Ctrl+F shortcut. Move to the text area of the Find What box and type enough text (a maximum of 255 characters) for an accurate, unambiguous search. For instance, suppose you wanted to find the word *man*. Entering **man** in Find What would cause Word to find the words *man*, *Man*, *Mansfield*, *reprimand*, *manhole*, and *man* at the end of a sentence (followed by a period, question mark, etc.).

Placing a space after **man** in your find request would eliminate the unwanted *Mansfield*, *reprimand*, and *manhole*, but would also prevent you from finding *man* at the ends of sentences because periods, question marks, and such are not spaces.

That's the reason for the Match Whole Word Only checkbox in the Find dialog box. If you type **man** (no space) in the Find What area and check Find Whole Words Only, Word will locate only *man*, *Man*, and *man* at the end of sentences.

The Match Case checkbox instructs Word to look for exact capitalization matches. If you type **postscript** in the Find What area and check Match Case, Word will not find *POSTSCRIPT*, *PostScript*, or even *Postscript* at the beginning of sentences.

Extra spaces, nonbreaking spaces, and forced page breaks can also get in the way of searches. See the section White Space later in this chapter to see how to work around this.

► Finding Special Characters

The Special drop-down list is a convenient way to enter certain special characters like tab marks, nonbreaking spaces, etc., when constructing a search request. Place the insertion point in the Find What box where you want the special character to go, and choose the desired character from the drop-down list.

Find… requests can combine regular text and special characters. For instance, you could ask Word to search for occurrences of *Bob* followed by two tab marks. Many of the special characters in the drop-down list are self-explanatory. Let's look more closely at the ones that are not. Some are extremely useful.

White Space

Here's one to keep you awake nights. Suppose that you are searching for two words together like *Microsoft Corporation*. Suppose further that sometimes you used nonbreaking spaces to separate the two words. Other times you've just typed regular spaces. Occasionally, you typed two spaces between the words by mistake. Unless you use Word's White Space feature, you will not find the occurrences of *Microsoft Corporation* containing nonbreaking spaces or two spaces!

So, to do it right, insert Word's White Space special character in your search string. In our example, you'd start by typing **Microsoft** in the Find What box. Then, without touching the spacebar, choose White Space from the Special menu. The White Space code (^w) will appear next to *Microsoft*. Type **Corporation**. Your finished search string would be *Microsoft^wCorporation*. That should do it.

Any Letter

The Any Letter character lets you overcome some nasty problems too. Suppose you've used accented characters sometimes but not always. *La Cañada* and *La Canada* are not the same thing to Word when it searches. A search for *La Ca^*ada* will find both. Enter the Any Letter character from the Special drop-down menu the same way you entered the White Space character.

Any Digit

This special character will sometimes help you find numbers within ranges. It might be helpful for finding specific groups of part numbers or zip codes.

▸▸ NOTE

When using Any Digit once with the Replace feature, Word will find all occasions but only highlight the first two digits. So, when you use Replace, you must handle this differently. With the Find feature, it doesn't matter.

For instance, the search string **99^#** would find any number between 990 and 999. The specification **1^#** would find the combinations *101* and *11* in *111*. It would also find *1000*, but not *1,000*, because Word treats numbers as text, not numeric values, in searches like these. Commas confuse things. Ah, computers....

▸ Finding Sound Alikes

Word can attempt to locate words that sound alike but are spelled differently (*smith*, *smyth*, *but*, and *butt*, for instance). This is an imprecise art at best, because even things that are *spelled* the same *sound* different in various parts of any country. (If you doubt this, ask a Bostonian, New Yorker, and Chicagoan to pronounce the word *car*.)

At any rate, the Sounds Like option can sometimes round up useful word variations and misspellings.

It is difficult to predict whether a soundalike will match the word you're looking for, as Word is less than forthcoming about how it applies criteria. Presumably, it distinguishes consonants from vowels and then compares parts of the word in question to a table of equivalent sounds. Search for *kerection* and you'll find *correction*, but search for *cerection* and you won't. Go figure.

The real purpose of this option is to cut you some slack if you're not absolutely sure about how to spell a word. If you're searching and finding nothing, when you're sure that word is in there somewhere, check Sounds Like and try again. (Then note how to spell the word for future reference.)

►► Pattern Matching

To perform advanced searches for combinations of things (such as both *bet* and *bat*), you use things called *operators*. They will remind you of wild cards. For instance, to find either *bet* or *bat*, you would place **b?t** in your Find What box and check Use Pattern Matching. If you forget to check Use Pattern Matching, the results will not be what you expect. Here's the list of operators you can use with Word and what they help you do:

OPERATOR	LETS YOU FIND
?	A single character: **b?t** finds *bet* and *bat*
*	Any string of characters: **b*d** finds *bed*, *befuddled*, and *blood*
[characters]	Any of the characters in brackets: **b[eo]d** finds *bed* and *bod* but not *bid*
[character-character]	Any character in the range: **b[a-i]d** finds *bed* and *bid* but not *bod*
[!character]	Any single character except the one in brackets: **b[!i]d** finds *bed* and *bod* but not *bid*
[!characters]	Any single character except the ones in brackets: **b[!ie]d** finds *bad* and *bud* but not *bid* or *bed*
[!character-character]	Any single character *except* those in the specified range: **b[!a-i]** finds *bud* and *bod* but not *bad* or *bid*
character{*n*}	Any *n* occurrences of the preceding character: **ble{2}d** finds *bleed* but not *bled* (or for that matter, *bleeeeed*). What's the purpose of this? Well it only makes sense if you're looking for a long string of a repeated character. In that case it would save you some typing. Otherwise, it seems silly: ble{2}d requires more typing (not to mention unusual characters) than bleed does!
character{*n*,}	At least *n* occurrences of the preceding character: **ble{1,}d** finds *bled* and *bleed*

OPERATOR	LETS YOU FIND
character{*n*,*m*}	At least *n* occurrences of the preceding character and no more than *m*: **1{1,2}5** finds both *15* and *115* but not *1115*
character@	One or more occurrences of the preceding character (thus, @ is equivalent to {1,}): **ble@d** finds *bled* and *bleed*
<text	The beginning of a word: **<man** finds *manhole* and *manage* but not *human*. (This works better than putting a space in front of the text, as it deals with exceptions such as the beginning of a paragraph.)
text>	The end of a word: **in>** finds *in* and *herein* but not *interfere*. (Likewise, this works much better than putting a space after the text, as it covers words that end at a period or other punctuation.)

To search for characters used as operators ({, ! *, etc.), separate them with a backslash. For instance, to find the asterik, search for *.

Notice that the ? symbol with Pattern Matching is equivalent to the ^? special character without it, just as the * symbol with Pattern Matching has the same effect as the ^* symbol without it.

All of the above operators can be combined, so, for example, **<ble@d** finds *bleeding-heart*, but not *nosebleed* or *doubled*. If you combine several of these operators, you can use brackets to clarify which operations Word must evaluate first. Brackets can also go inside other brackets, though I hope for your sake that it is never necessary!

▸▸ The Art of Replacing

To replace, follow these general steps:

1. Save your work.
2. Choose Edit ➤ Replace… or press Ctrl+H.

3. Create search criteria using the techniques discussed in the previous section.
4. Specify the desired replacement text, formats, etc.
5. Tell Word where to search and in which direction.
6. Click Find Next or Replace All to start the replacement.
7. Confirm the replacements.

WARNING

It is a good idea to save your work before using the Replace... feature. If you are working on a complex, important project, you might want to use a copy rather than the original document as it is much easier to screw up a document with Replace... than it is to repair it.

As you can see from Figure 20.2, the Replace dialog box looks like the Find dialog box, with additional features. Word lets you confirm each replacement before it happens, or it will find and replace without your intervention.

FIGURE 20.2

The Replace dialog box resembles the Find box, with added features.

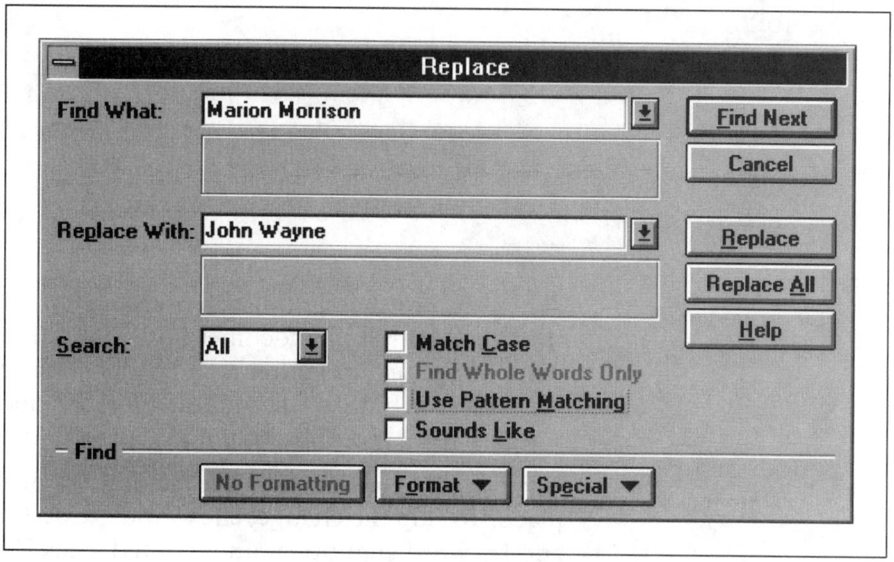

Just as you can search for text, formats, styles, and special characters, you can also replace them. For instance, you could replace *Marion Morrison* with *John Wayne*. (Don't you wish the Duke had kept his given name?)

Or you could change each occurrence of two consecutive paragraph marks to a single end-of-line marker, or change the style of certain paragraphs from chapter-heading style to appendix style. It is even possible to replace text with graphics. Here are examples of each technique.

► Replacing Text with Text

To simply replace text (like changing *Marion Morrison* to *John Wayne*) without altering formats or styles, start by entering the text to find and the desired replacement text. For instance, you might enter *Marion Morrison* in the Find What box and *John Wayne* in the Replace With box. Follow these steps:

1. Save your work.
2. Choose Edit ➤ Replace (Ctrl+H).
3. Visit the Search drop-down menu to tell Word if you want it to search the entire document, a selected portion, and so on.

►► **WARNING**

If there are any formats or styles listed under the Find What or Replace With boxes, click No Formatting with the insertion point in the appropriate place (Find What, Replace With, or both). This way, Word will not alter the style or format of the document.

4. When the replacement instructions are complete, click Find Next. Word will search the document (or selected portion) for things matching your Find criteria and propose the next replacement. The Replace button will undim, and your document screen will scroll to reveal the first potential replacement point.
5. If you want Word to make the change it is proposing, click Replace. To skip the change, click Find Next. To make the change and let Word continue uninterrupted, click Replace All. Word will

make the rest of the replacements nonstop, probably too quickly for you to even see them. The status area in the lower-left corner of your document window will briefly flash the number of replacements made.

6. Check your work. Undo will work here.

▶ Replacing Formatting

Suppose you have italicized words scattered throughout your text and decide to change all of them to underlined words. Start by removing any text from the Find What and Replace With boxes. (This is because you want Word to find all italicized text, not just words in the Find What box that are italicized.) Then follow these steps:

1. Specify the character attributes you want Word to find (italics for example). You can do this in one of several ways. Always start by placing the insertion point in the Find What entry box. Then specify the Italic format either from the Standard Toolbar, or pull down the Format list in the Replace dialog box. From there, choose Font, then click in the Italic option of the Font dialog box.

▶▶ TIP

You can use keyboard shortcuts or Toolbar buttons to specify formatting as well. It is often much quicker.

The word *Italic* (or whatever) will appear beneath the Find What box.

2. Next go to the Replace With box and choose a new format (Underline in this example). To prevent Word from changing italic to italic underline, double-click the Italic button on the Formatting Toolbar so that the Format information under the Replace With box reads **Not Italic, Underline.** Figure 20.3 shows how your dialog box should look after this maneuver.

3. Let 'er rip! Either tell Word to Replace All or you can supervise as before.

You can also change the formatting of specific text only for specific text or combine the replacement of text and formatting. To change the formatting of specific text, type the text you want to change in both the

FIGURE 20.3

This combination will change all italicized text to underlined text.

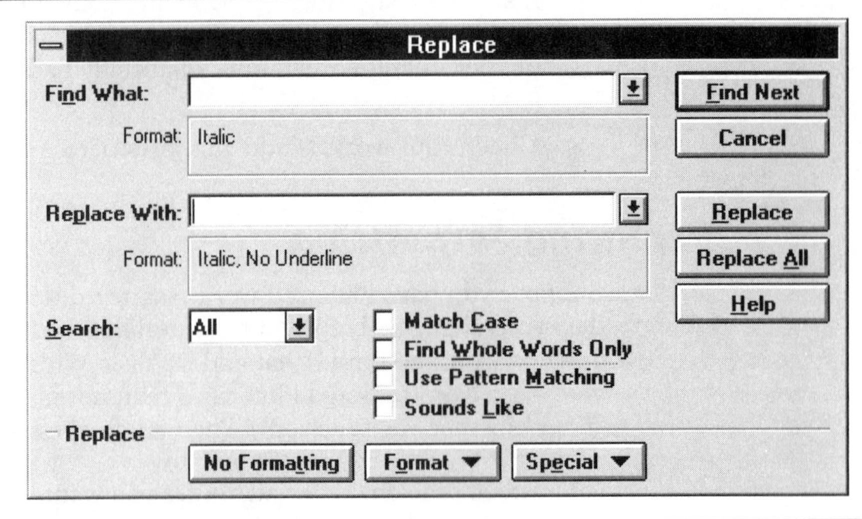

Find What and Replace With boxes. Click on the Find What format box and select the type of formatting the text has now. Then click on the Replace With format box and select the type of formatting you want to give to the text.

Changing both text and formatting at the same time is just as easy. Suppose you want to replace every instance of the italicized word *ennui* with the unitalicized word **boredom**. That would be simple. Just type **ennui** in the Find What box and select Italic formatting. Then type **boredom** in the Replace With box and click the Italic button on the Formatting Toolbar twice to select Not Italic. Then proceed with Replace as normal.

▸ Replacing Styles

If you want to change the style of certain paragraphs, the Replace… command can help:

1. Click on the Format button.
2. Choose Styles.
3. You will see a list of your document's styles and descriptions, as shown in Figure 20.4.

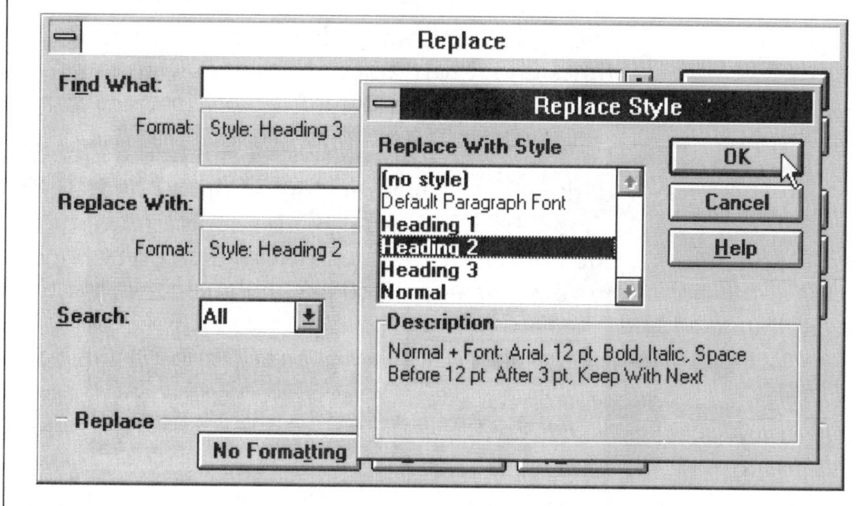

FIGURE 20.4 *Specify styles to find and replace with the Replace Style dialog box.*

4. Pick styles for both the find and replace criteria, then proceed as usual.

In this example paragraphs formatted with the Heading 3 style will be reformatted using the Heading 2 style.

Combining Replacement Tasks

Within reason, it is possible to combine search and replace instructions to restrict actions. For instance, assuming you had a document with appropriate styles, you could italicize all occurrences of *Gone With The Wind* in the body text of your report, while leaving the same words alone when they appear in headings, the table of contents, and the index.

You would do this by typing **Gone With The Wind** in the Find What box and restricting the find to the body text style. Then specify Italic as the format in the Replace With box. You could type **Gone With The Wind** again in the Replace With box, but you don't need to. Computers are very obedient but not very clever. Undo should help, but work on copies of important documents just in case.

With all the different possibilities of finding text or formatting or both and replacing it with other text or formatting or both, you might sometimes find it hard to think through what exactly will change. Table 20.1 outlines how the different choices interact with each other.

So, for example, if you type **ennui** in the Find What box, choose Underline formatting, then put nothing in the Replace With box and choose both Italic and No Underline (click the Underline button on the Formatting Toolbar twice), then every underlined instance of *ennui* in your document will become italicized, but the word won't change.

TABLE 20.1: *Combining Text and Format Options in Replace*

IF YOU FIND	AND REPLACE IT WITH	YOU GET
text	text	all Find text replaced with Replace text
text	format	all Find text formatted
text	text and format	all Find text replaced with formatted Replace text
format	text	all formatted text replaced with Replace text in same format
format	format	all formatted text given new format
format	text and format	all formatted text replaced with Replace text in new format
text and format	text	all formatted Find text replaced with Replace text in same format
text and format	format	all formatted Find text given new format
text and format	text and format	all formatted Find text replaced with Replace text in new format

▶ Search

You have several choices around how Word will search your document for words you wish to either find or replace. These options are found under the Search drop-down menu in the Find and Replace dialog boxes. Up searches back toward the beginning of the document, while Down searches toward the end. All searches the entire document, as you would expect.

If you choose Up or Down, Word will search until it gets to the beginning (or end) of the document, and then tell you it has reached the end of the document and ask if you want it to continue the search. If you choose Yes, it will continue in the same direction from the other end of the document until it reaches the place you started from. If you choose No, it will end the search. Why would you want to end the search? Well, you may know that the word you're searching for occurs several times in the beginning of your document, and you may not want to change any of those earlier instances.

Another way to limit the range of the search is to select a portion of the document before selecting Replace. Word will search just the selection first. Then it will ask if you want it to continue the search in the rest of the document. Choose No to end the search then.

If you stop in the middle of a Replace to, say, correct something else you've noticed, be sure to deselect the last found word before resuming the Replace. Otherwise, Word will begin the Replace again by searching just the selection (the last word found). This does no harm, but always having to click on Yes to continue the search gets boring.

Resume the Replace by clicking on the Find Next button.

▶▶ Using the Clipboard with Find and Replace

The Clipboard can be used for several interesting Find... and Replace... tasks. For instance, you can copy text from your document to the Clipboard, then paste it into the Find What or Replace With boxes. This is a great way to paste long passages or obscure characters like umlauted letters or math symbols. It is even possible to overcome the 255-character limitation this way.

Word also lets you replace text with graphics if you place the graphics on the Clipboard. Figure 20.5 illustrates how that is done.

FIGURE 20.5

It is possible to replace text with graphics on the clipboard.

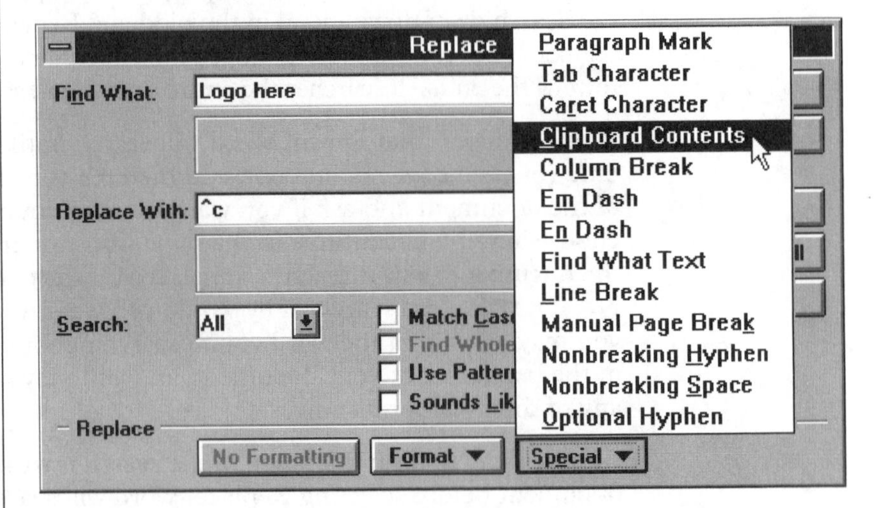

1. Copy a graphic to the Clipboard.
2. Visit the Replace dialog box.
3. Enter Find What criteria.
4. Click on the Replace With portion of the dialog box.
5. Choose Clipboard Contents from the Special list.
6. Replace as usual.

▸▸ Replacing Tips

Here are some tips for replacing:

- The Replace… command uses considerable memory if you make a lot of changes. It is a good idea to perform a normal save after assuring that your replacements are satisfactory.

- Undo will undo all changes if you use Replace All, but only your last change if you have been supervising with the Find Next button.
- If you've used styles in your document, you may find it easier to make wholesale style changes by redefining or reapplying styles rather than using Replace.
- You can specify any character in Find or Replace strings by typing **^n**, where *n* is the ASCII (decimal) code for the character of interest.
- Remember to click No Formatting when specifying new search criteria in the Find What and Replace With boxes.
- All of the special characters (paragraph markers, tabs, etc.) can be represented by caret codes that you can enter directly from the keyboard into the Find What box, the Replace With box, or both. This is often the quick way to go. Table 20.2 shows a handy reference list of special-character codes. Notice that they all require lowercase characters.

TABLE 20.2: *Special Characters and Their Find and Replace Codes*

CHARACTER	CODE	CAN GO IN FIND WHAT BOX?	CAN GO IN REPLACE WITH BOX?
Annotation mark	^a	Yes	No
Any single character	^?	Yes	No
Any single digit	^#	Yes	No
Any single letter	^$	Yes	No
ASCII character number *nnn*	^O*nnn*	Yes	Yes
Caret character	^^	Yes	Yes
Clipboard contents	^c	Yes	Yes
Column break	^n	Yes	Yes

TABLE 20.2: *Special Characters and Their Find and Replace Codes (continued)*

CHARACTER	CODE	CAN GO IN FIND WHAT BOX?	CAN GO IN REPLACE WITH BOX?
Contents of the Find What box	^&	No	Yes
Em dash (—)	^+	Yes	Yes
En dash (–)	^=	Yes	Yes
Endnote mark	^e	Yes	No
Field code	^d	Yes	No
Footnote mark	^f	Yes	No
Graphic	^g	Yes	No
Line break	^l	Yes	Yes
Manual page break	^m	Yes	Yes
Nonbreaking hyphen	^~	Yes	Yes
Nonbreaking space	^s	Yes	Yes
Optional hyphen (activated)	^-	Yes	Yes
Paragraph mark	^p	Yes	Yes
Section break	^b	Yes	No
Tab	^t	Yes	Yes
White space	^w	Yes	No

►► How Replace Interacts with Styles

Be aware that just as manually applied formatting and styles interact when you change styles or formatting yourself, they interact when the Replace... command makes changes.

As explained at the end of Chapter 14, Word makes a distinction between manual formatting (formatting you apply directly from the toolbar or Font menu) and style formatting (formatting that is applied to text as part of a style definition). When you define a style based on a manually formatted selection, Word tries to include in the style any kind of formatting that is appplied to the majority of the selection (actually the first 255 characters of it, to be pedantic). Any manual formatting applied intermittently is interpreted as just that, manual formatting layered on top of the style formatting.

Replace operations can include combinations of style formatting and manual formatting. Searches for boldface text, for example, will find text you've made bold manually as well as text that has been formatted with a style that includes bold. You can search for any combination of style formatting and manual formatting and replace with any other combination.

If you combine both types of formatting under the Find What box, Word will find any examples that have the style formatting and match the manual formatting. If you combine both types of formatting under the Replace With box, Word will apply the style formatting first, then layer the manual formatting on top of it. Of course, you can also use different combinations of either or both in the two boxes. Table 20.3 shows how the two types of formatting interact during the Replace operation.

To make matters worse, you additionally have the option of including text or not in either of the boxes, along with any combination of formatting. Realistically, you shouldn't need to get involved in such complicated, twisted operations.

TABLE 20.3: *Combining Manual and Style Formatting in Replace*

IF YOU FIND	AND REPLACE IT WITH	YOU GET
manual formatting	manual formatting	all formatted text given new format
manual formatting	style formatting	all formatted text given style formatting in addition to manual formatting
manual formatting	manual and style formatting	all formatted text given style formatting and new manual formatting layered on top
style formatting	manual formatting	all text in that style given manual formatting in addition to the style formatting
style formatting	style formatting	all text in the old style given the new style
style formatting	manual and style formatting	all text in the old style given the new style and the manual formatting layered on top

CHAPTER 21

Get Organized with Outline View

▸▸ FAST TRACK

To help you plan, create, and reorganize long documents **542**

use Outline view (View ➤ Outline or **Ctrl+Alt+O**).

To use Outline view **543**

your headings need to be formatted using Word's standard-heading styles (heading 1 through heading 9). If you didn't use these styles when you created a document, it is easy to reformat with them.

To promote or demote a heading **545**

place the insertion point in the heading you wish to promote or demote. Click the left arrow to promote or the right arrow to demote.

To outline existing documents **545**

open your document in Outline view. You will see the first line of each paragraph. Place the insertion point in each heading and promote or demote them as desired. Save your work. Use the viewing techniques described next to view, rearrange, and understand the organization of your document.

To expand or collapse body text **547**

click on the All Text or First Line icon.

To hide or reveal the levels of your document **548**

click on the numbers 1 through 8 in Outline view.

To work on large documents **548**

consider splitting the screen to show your document in Normal view in one half of the window and Outline view in the other.

To split your document window **548**

double-click on the Split-bar. Then drag it up or down to change the size of the two areas. Double-clicking on the Split-bar in a split window returns you to a single window.

To move all text below a heading **549**

simply move it up or down in Outline view.

To swiftly rearrange tables **550**

move rows by dragging them in Outline view.

To number headings in Outline view **551**

choose Format ➤ Heading Numbering.... Click on a sample to select the numbering format you desire or choose Modify for custom numbering choices. Click OK. Word will renumber immediately whenever you rearrange your outline. Whenever you add a heading it will automatically be numbered.

To print a document in Outline view **552**

collapse the document to the desired level, then use the File ➤ Print command or **Ctrl+P** shortcut.

Word's *Outline* view, located on the View menu (Ctrl+Alt+O), is really more than a view. It's a collection of tools designed to help you plan, create, and reorganize long documents. It does this by letting you expand or contract the amount of detail you see on your screen. Figure 21.1 illustrates this.

The top window in Figure 21.1 shows part of a document in Normal view. The bottom window shows the same document in Outline view with all of the body text collapsed (not revealed). Because only paragraph headings are visible in the bottom window, it's easy to see the overall organization (the outline) of the document. As you will soon see, Outline view lets you control how much detail you see. For instance, you can view the first line of text following each heading if you wish.

FIGURE 21.1

Outline view (bottom) lets you get a bird's-eye view of large documents (top).

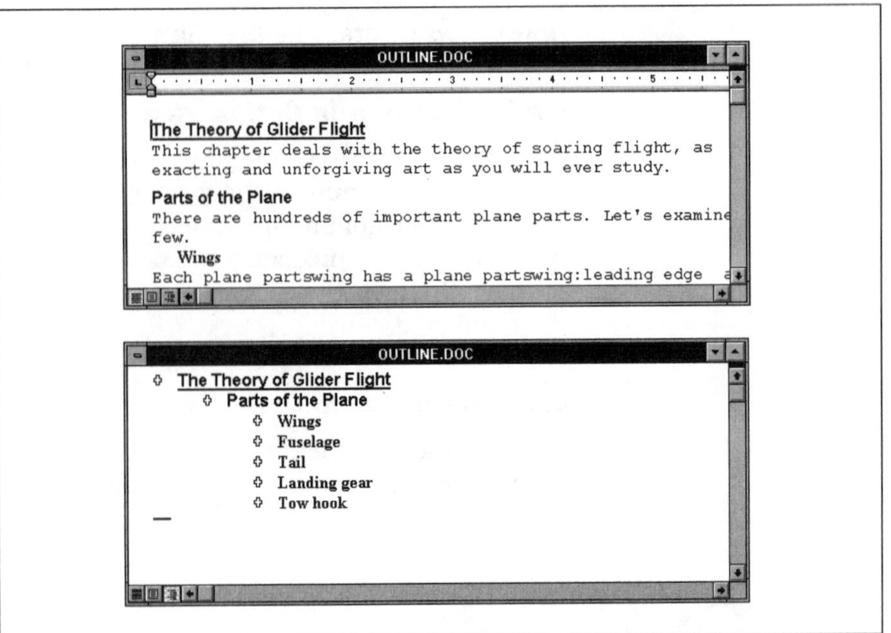

OUTLINE.DOC
The Theory of Glider Flight
This chapter deals with the theory of soaring flight, as exacting and unforgiving art as you will ever study.
Parts of the Plane
There are hundreds of important plane parts. Let's examine few.
Wings
Each plane partswing has a plane partswing:leading edge
OUTLINE.DOC
The Theory of Glider Flight
Parts of the Plane
Wings
Fuselage
Tail
Landing gear
Tow hook

Notice also that headings in Outline view are indented, giving you a better idea of the document's organization. Each new level is indented $^1/_4$" from the preceding one.

It's a snap to reorganize documents in Outline view. If you want to move all of the paragraphs having to do with Landing gear so they appear before Tail, simply drag the Landing gear heading using the Outline view's special pointer. This will move all corresponding paragraphs, called *subtext*.

Finally, you can quickly promote or demote portions of your document using the Outline view tools, found on the Outline bar.

►► Styles and Outlines

In order to use Outline view, your headings need to be formatted using Word's standard-heading styles (heading 1 through heading 9). If you didn't use these styles when you created a document, it is easy to reformat with them. And, as you probably know, you can change the appearance of standard headings if you don't like Word's standard styles. (See Chapter 14 for more about styles.)

►► The Outline View's Toolbar

Outline view provides a number of unique tools. They are found on the Out-line Toolbar at the top of the screen. There is a new pointer shape indicating the pointer's ability to move large collections of text. It looks like a compass.

As you can see in Figure 21.3, on-screen text is often underlined with an unusual line style. This does not indicate text that will be underlined when printed. Rather, it indicates that there is collapsed subtext beneath it.

► Plus Signs, Dashes, and Boxes

Large plus signs, boxes, and dashes appear next to many headings in Outline view. Boxes tell you that you are looking at body text; pluses indicate headings containing subtext; and minuses denote headings without subtext.

Finally, Outline view includes the Outline bar with its special heading and body-text symbols.

The Outline Toolbar's Tools

Figure 21.2 summarizes the Outline bar's unique tools. They promote and demote heading levels, hide or reveal body text, and turn formatting on and off.

The best way to understand the effect of these tools is to open a document containing standard Word for Windows headings in Outline view and experiment. If you don't have a document of your own, create one or use the Business Report from the Sample Documents folder. The rest of this chapter describes the various Outline view tools, offering tips on how to use them.

FIGURE 21.2

Tools on the Outline bar promote and demote headings and reveal and hide text and formatting.

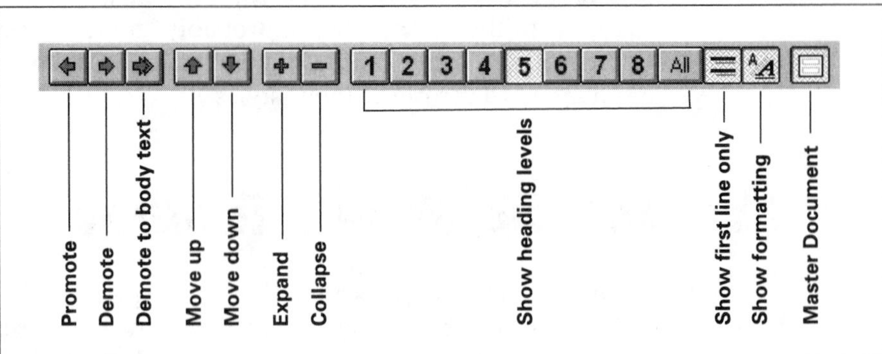

►► Creating and Editing Outlines

When you start typing a new document in Outline view, Word for Windows assumes the first thing you want to type is a level 1 heading. Each new paragraph you type will take on the heading level of the previous paragraph.

One strategy is to type all of your top-level headings first, and then go back and insert headings in progressively lower heading levels. Another approach is to type all your document's headings in sequence, promoting and demoting as you go. It is even possible to type the entire document (all headings and text) in Outline view without doing a traditional outline first.

The approach you choose is largely a matter of personal preference. In any scenario, you will need to know how to promote and demote headings and text.

▶ Promoting and Demoting

The two arrows at the left end of the Outline bar are used to promote and demote headings. Place the insertion point in the heading you wish to promote or demote. Click the right arrow to demote. Figure 21.3 shows this at work on a new outline originally typed with everything at level 1.

Here we placed the insertion point in the Parts of the Plane heading and clicked the right arrow once. Then we highlighted the headings Wings through Tow hook and clicked the right arrow twice, which demoted them two levels. The results are shown at the bottom of Figure 21.3. We have left the Theory of Glider Flight heading at the top level; Parts of the Plane is now the next level down, and Wings through Tow hook are at heading level 3. (You could confirm this by switching to Normal or Page Layout view.)

Promoting works as you'd expect. With the insertion point in a heading, click the left arrow to turn a level 3 heading into a level 2 heading, and so on.

▶ Outlining Existing Documents

To outline existing documents, follow these steps:

1. Open your document in Outline view.
2. You will see the first line of each paragraph.
3. Place the insertion point in each heading and promote or demote them as desired.
4. Save your work.
5. Use the viewing techniques described next to view, rearrange, and understand the organization of your document.

FIGURE 21.3

The right arrow demotes selected headings and the left arrow promotes.

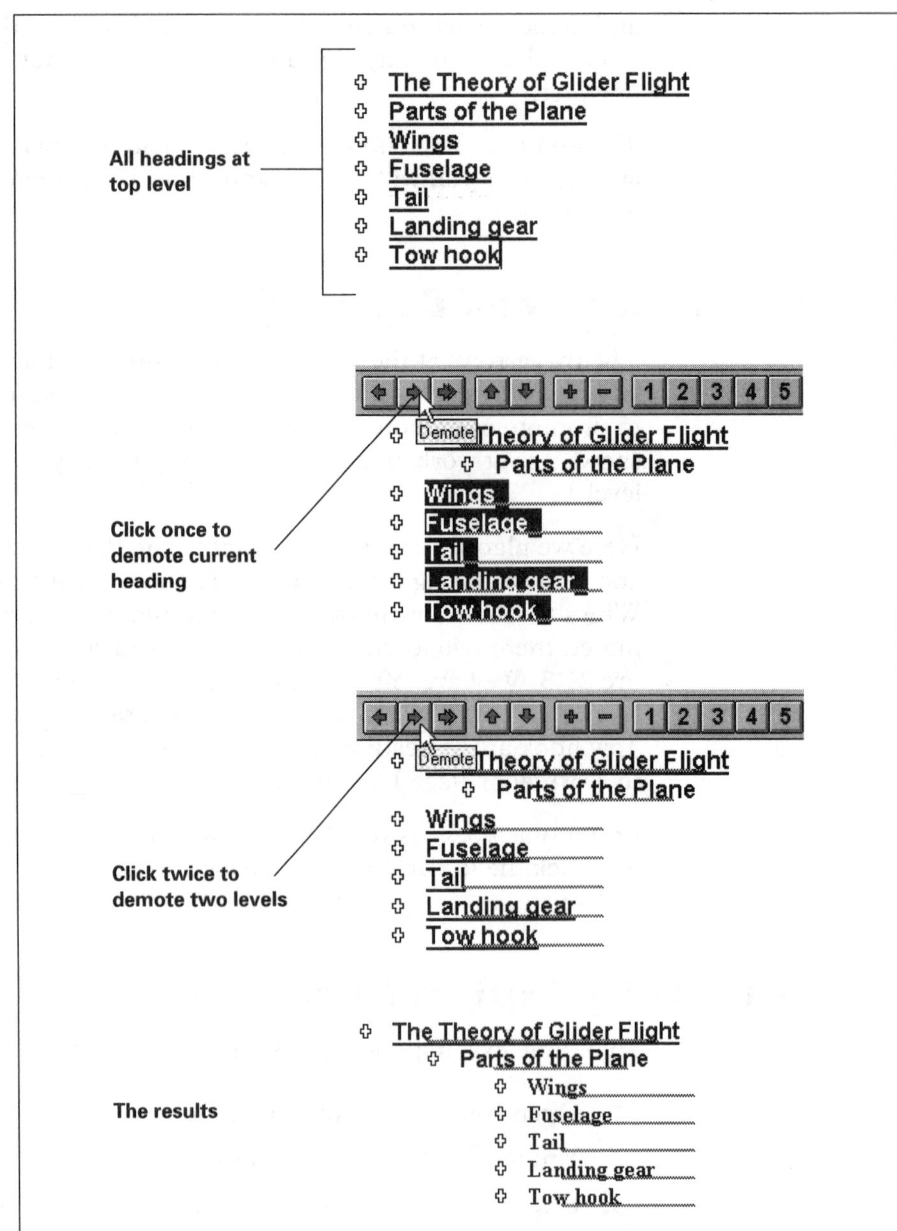

▶ Expanding and Collapsing Outlines

One of the main reasons to use Outline view is to get a collapsed overview of a document's contents. Do this by expanding and collapsing views with the numbers on the Outline bars and the buttons to their right.

For instance, Figure 21.4 shows our Glider book in a bit more detail than the view in previous figures. The first line of text beneath each heading has been revealed.

FIGURE 21.4 ▶

Click the All Text or First Line icon on the Outline bar to show the first line of text beneath each heading.

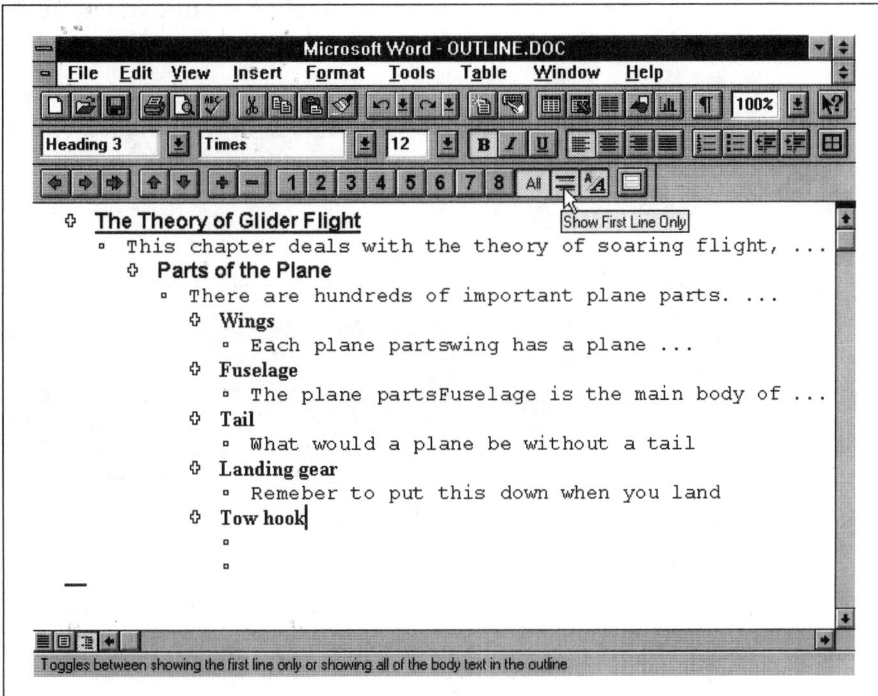

This was accomplished by clicking on the All Text or First Line icon (just to the left of the *ff* icon) on the Outline bar. (Clicking the Entire Document icon—just to the right of the number 8—reveals all the document text.)

The document's true heading styles are apparent in Figure 21.4. The *ff* button at the end of the Outline bar turns character formatting on and off.

Clicking on the numbers 1 through 8 in Outline view hides or reveals the levels of your document. For instance, in our sample document, clicking on 1 will reveal only level 1 headings (the Theory of Glider Flight). Clicking on the 2 would reveal both level 1 and level 2 headings (Parts of the Plane). Clicking the All button (just to the right of the number 8) shows all text.

▸ Split Views

Figure 21.5 illustrates a strategy for working on large documents. You can split the screen and show your document in Normal view in one half of the window and Outline view in the other.

To split a window this way, double-click on the Split bar. Then drag it up or down to change the size of the two areas. Double-clicking on the Split bar in a split window returns you to a single window. Each part of the screen has its own scroll bars.

FIGURE 21.5

Splitting the screen lets you work in Outline and Normal views at the same time.

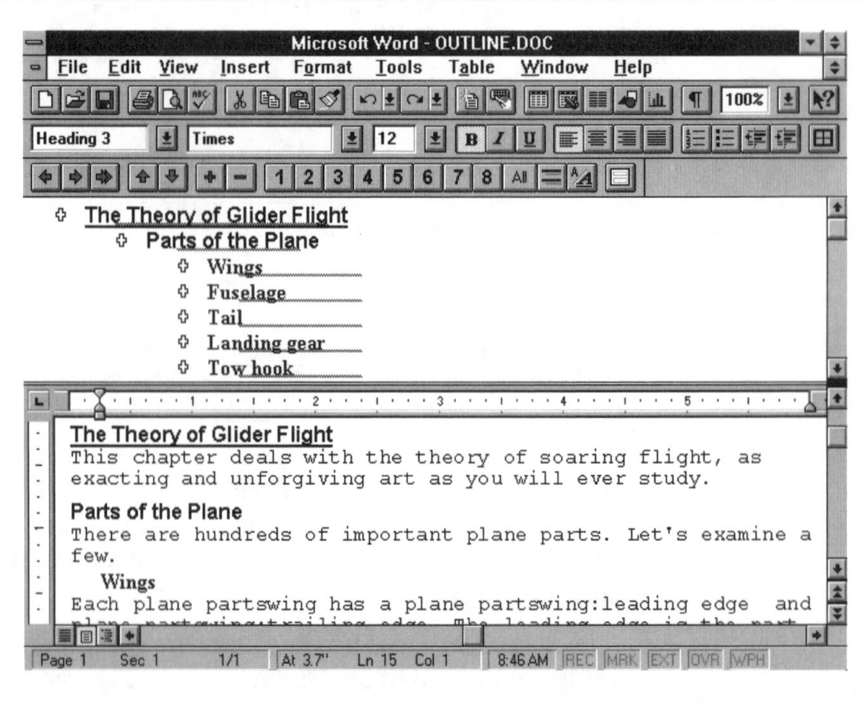

TIP

When you double-click the Split bar to unsplit a document divided into two panes, the pane that becomes the full page will be where you had the insertion point. So be careful! If you are taken away from where you want to work, pressing F5 (Go Back) might help.

▶ Moving Paragraphs

With the outline collapsed, you can move collections of paragraphs (also called *subtext*) by moving their associated headings. When you move a heading, *all* heads (i.e., those of lower head levels) and text below it will be moved along with it. This facilitates the movement of entire chapters without needing to highlight them. Think of this feature as drag-and-drop on steroids. Figure 21.6 shows how it works.

Placing the pointer over the left edge of a heading changes the pointer's shape. It will look like a compass. Click and drag, and a large right arrow will appear along with a dotted line, like the ones shown in Figure 21.6. Drag the line and the pointer to where you want to move the text. Release the mouse button and the document will be reorganized.

The up- and down-pointing arrows on the Outline bar will also move items up and down. Highlight the headings, then click on the appropriate arrow.

FIGURE 21.6 ▶

Drag outline headings to move them and all their related subtext.

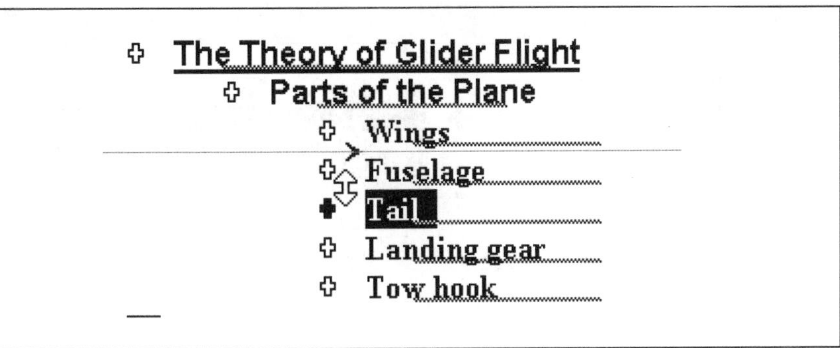

▸▸ Dragging to Change Levels

You can also drag to change the indent level in Outline view. When you do, the pointer arrow changes, and you'll see a guideline that indicates the pending indent level as shown in Figure 21.7.

FIGURE 21.7

You can drag to change indent levels in Outline view.

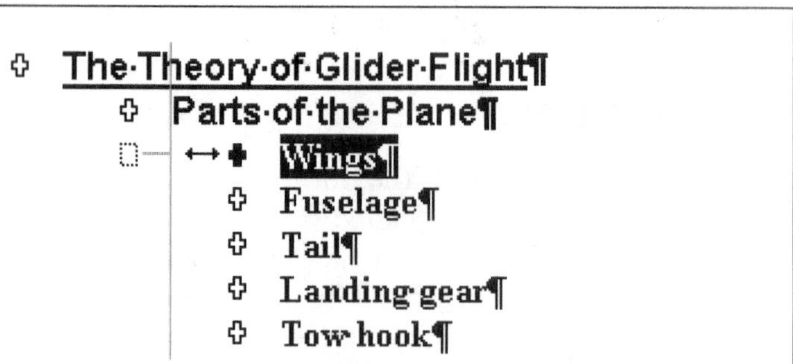

▸▸ Rearrange Tables by Dragging Rows

When you view a table in Outline view, it is possible to move rows by dragging them. This is illustrated in Figure 21.8.

FIGURE 21.8

Outline view is a handy place to rearrange Word tables by dragging rows.

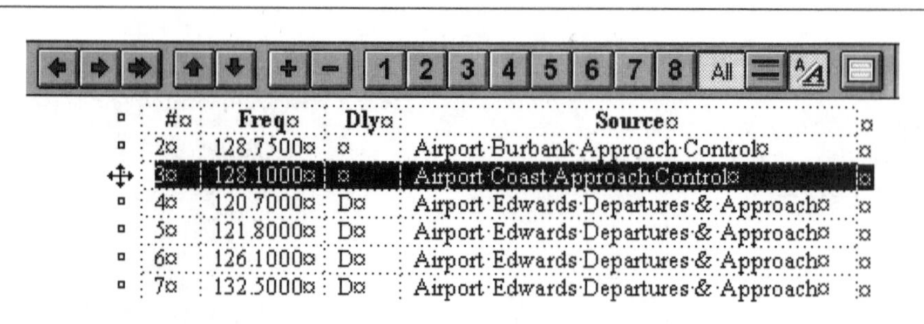

#	Freq	Dly	Source
2	128.7500		Airport Burbank Approach Control
3	128.1000		Airport Coast Approach Control
4	120.7000	D	Airport Edwards Departures & Approach
5	121.8000	D	Airport Edwards Departures & Approach
6	126.1000	D	Airport Edwards Departures & Approach
7	132.5000	D	Airport Edwards Departures & Approach

▶▶ Numbering Headings in Outline View

You can number headings in Outline view just as you can in any other view. Figure 21.9 illustrates this.

The basic steps, as you may recall, are:

1. Choose Format ➤ Heading Numbering….
2. Click on a sample to select the numbering format you desire, or choose Modify for custom-numbering choices.
3. Click OK.
4. Word will renumber immediately whenever you rearrange your outline. Whenever you add a heading it will automatically be numbered, as shown in Figure 21.10.

FIGURE 21.9

You can use the Format ➤ Heading Numbering… command in Outline view, too.

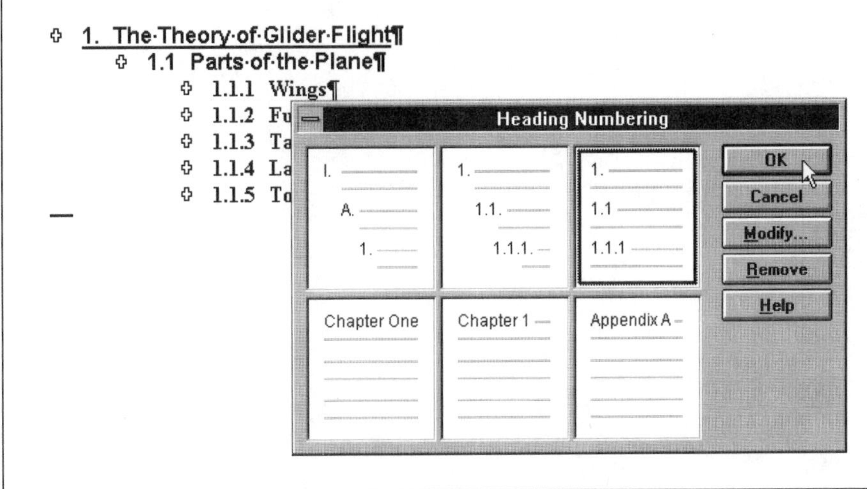

FIGURE 21.10

When you add headings, they will be numbered as you have specified.

1.1.4 Landing·gear¶
1.1.5 Tow·hook¶
1.2 Thermals—Rising·Hot·Air¶

▸▸ Outlines and Tables of Content

Because Outlines use (assign) standard Word for Windows Heading styles to headings, you can quickly create a table of contents based on your outline. The TOC will include each heading.

▸▸ Printing Outlines

Printing in Outline view creates a document containing only the levels you see on the screen. Collapse the document to the desired level, then use the File ➤ Print command or Ctrl+P shortcut. Even if just the first line of text appears, Word for Windows will print the whole paragraph.

Desktop Publishing

PART FOUR

CHAPTER 22

Multiple Columns

FAST TRACK

To quickly arrange your text into columns **558**

click the Columns button on the Formatting Toolbar and *drag* it to select from one to six columns. When you release the mouse button, Word automatically determines the appropriate width of columns and the amount of white space between columns based on the page and document settings.

To avoid odd column widths and spacing **559**

change margins, page size, orientation, indents, and related settings *before* you set your text in columns.

To have greater control over the look and number of columns **559**

use the Columns dialog box (Format ➤ Columns…), where you can preview the results of choices made.

To create different numbered columns (even on the same page) **560**

select the text to be "columnized" and specify column settings with the Toolbar button or the Columns dialog box. Word will apply the settings only to the selected text and insert necessary breaks automatically.

To drag columns to different widths using margin markers **561**

place the insertion point in the desired column and, in Page Layout view, display the rulers if they aren't already on-screen. Click on the Margin Marker button in the ruler to display the margin markers, then drag any marker, and the columns will adjust to their new width.

Most people find short lines of text easier to read than long ones. That's one reason newspapers and book designers frequently use side-by-side snaking *columns*. Text flows from the bottom of one column to the top of the next until a page is filled, then it flows onto the next page.

Creating Multicolumn Documents

Word for Windows makes it easy for you to arrange your text in columns like these. The Formatting Toolbar buttons let you choose from one to six columns (single is the default). Moreover, the Columns dialog box lets you specify up to forty-five columns. It also provides a way to adjust the amount of white space between columns.

TIP

When you start with a new document, the Toolbar button lets you choose up to six columns. When you get to the Columns dialog box and increase the number of columns, the Toolbar will show up to the highest number you've assigned.

In a single-section document, all of your pages will always have the same number of columns. But, by breaking a document into multiple sections, you can have as many different column designs as you have sections.

Word for Windows automatically adjusts column widths to accommodate your chosen page size, orientation, and document margins. You can overrule these decisions.

It is possible to use indents within columns. You can edit columnar text just as you do any other. When you work in Page Layout view, you will see side-by-side columns as they will print. When working in Normal view, you will see text in the appropriate column width, but you will not see the columns in position next to each other.

new

Word's new column feature no longer requires that all columns in a section be the same width. You can drag columns or specify their widths precisely from your keyboard.

▶ Simple Column Creation

Here's an easy way to create up to six columns if your document has only one section and if you want the same number of columns throughout the document:

1. Make any page setup, margin, and other design decisions that will affect the amount of text area on your page.
2. Click on the Columns button near the right edge of the Standard Toolbar. As you can see in Figure 22.1, you *drag* it to select the desired number of columns.
3. When you release the mouse button, Word automatically determines the appropriate width of columns and the amount of white space between columns based on the page and document settings. You can see the columns as they will print in Page Layout view and Print Preview. You will see a single column only in Normal view.

Changing margins, page size, orientation, indents, and related settings will cause corresponding changes in column widths and spacing. The zero point on the ruler is always at the left edge of the column containing the insertion point. Clicking in the left column would move the zero point of the ruler to the left edge of the left column. Indents work as you'd expect within columns.

▶ Using the Columns Dialog Box

You can create more than eight columns (up to forty-five) and specify the desired amount of white space between columns by using the Columns portion of the Columns dialog box. You can also specify decorative

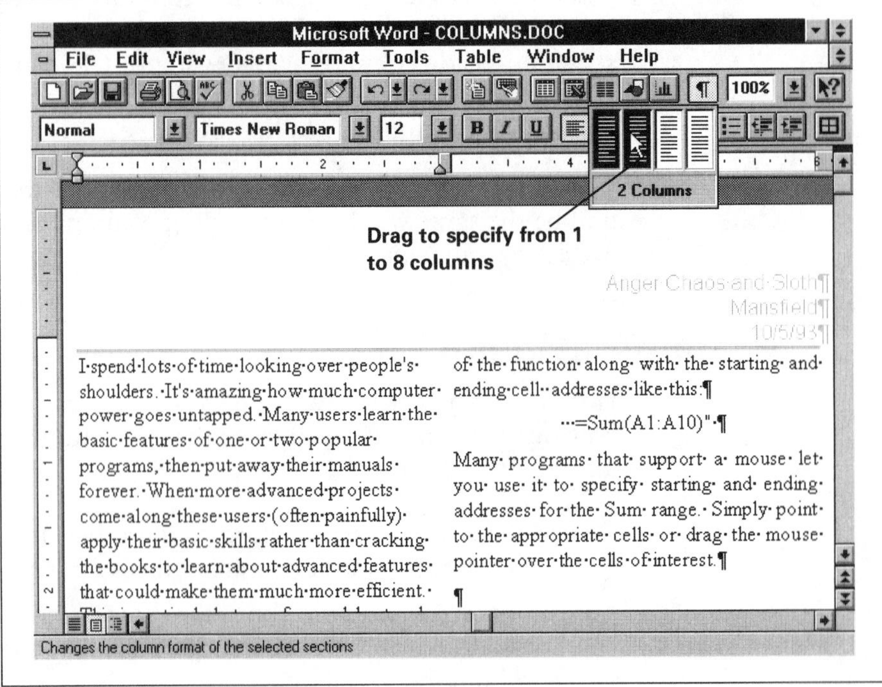

FIGURE 22.1

The Columns Toolbar button puts up to eight-column text a click and drag away.

lines between columns here. And you can create adjacent columns of differing widths.

Reach the Columns dialog box by choosing Format ➤ Columns.... Figure 22.2 shows the specifications for two columns with different widths. Notice that you can preview the results of choices made in this dialog box.

▸▸ Different Column Designs in the Same Document

You can have different column designs in different parts of a document. For instance, part of a page could be a single column with the rest two or three columns.

Word for Windows makes it easy to specify where new column settings should begin and end. Essentially, all you need to do is select text and

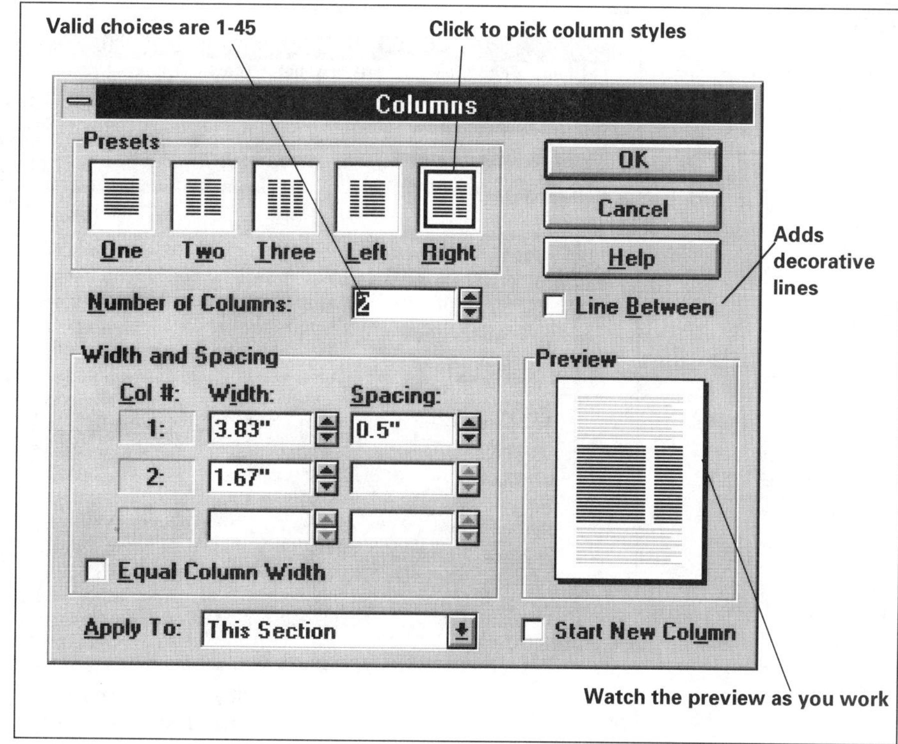

FIGURE 22.2

You can precisely specify the number of columns and the spacing in the Columns dialog box.

specify a column design for the selected text. Word will format the columns, insert necessary breaks, etc.

For example, to create the effect shown in Figure 22.3, you need to take the following steps:

1. Select the text to be "columnized."
2. Specify column settings with the Toolbar button or the Columns dialog box (described next). Word will apply the settings only to the selected text and insert necessary breaks.

Controlling Column Width

Word for Windows initially sets the widths and spacing for you. It's possible, however, to drag columns to different widths using margin markers. Here's how. Follow along in Figure 22.4.

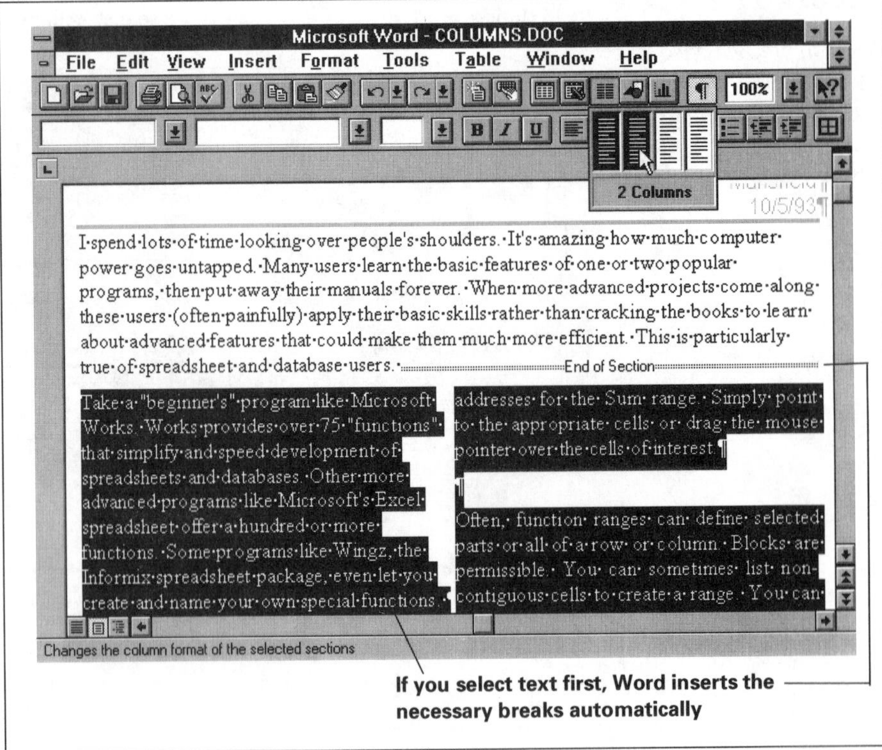

FIGURE 22.3

Select text then specify desired column settings.

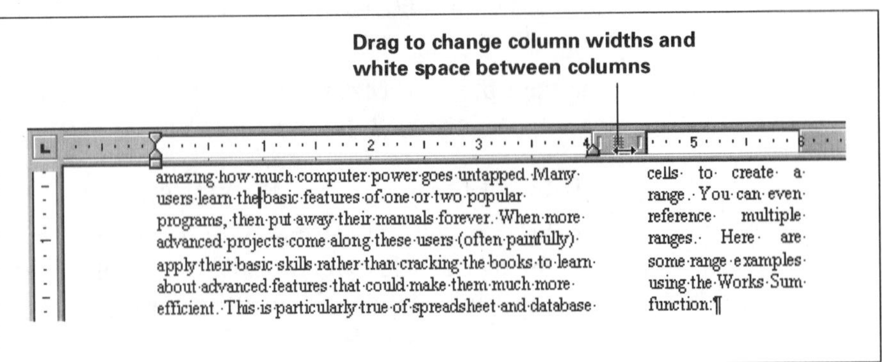

FIGURE 22.4

Drag margin markers to change column widths in Page Layout view.

1. Place the insertion point in the desired column.
2. From Page Layout view, display the rulers if they aren't already on-screen.

3. Click on the Margin Marker button in the ruler to display the margin markers.
4. Drag any marker, and the columns will adjust to their new width.

▶▶ TIP

When creating columns of justified type, things can get a little raggedy. Consider using unjustified text or optional hyphens to tighten up columns.

▶ Adding Decorative Lines between Columns

Use the Columns dialog box to add decorative lines between columns. There is only one line style.

1. Place the insertion point in a column that you wish to decorate.
2. Choose Format ➤ Columns....
3. Choose Line Between.

▶ Controlling Column Breaks

Use Word's Keep Lines Together and Keep with Next Paragraph features to prevent unwanted breaks. Sometimes, you will want to force breaks. For example, the last page of a two-column document may end with uneven columns because Word will completely fill the left column before putting text in the right column.

Use Word's Insert ➤ Break... command to force column breaks. Place the insertion point where you want the column break, then choose Insert ➤ Break..., specify Column, and click OK. You remove breaks by highlighting them and pressing Delete.

▶ Balancing Column Endings

Sometimes you'll have uneven column endings on the last page of a document or section. Figure 22.5 illustrates this problem (and no, you are not going blind).

If you wish to "even out" the columns, do the following in Page Layout view:

FIGURE 22.5

If uneven columns like this trouble you, insert a continuous break at the end of the text.

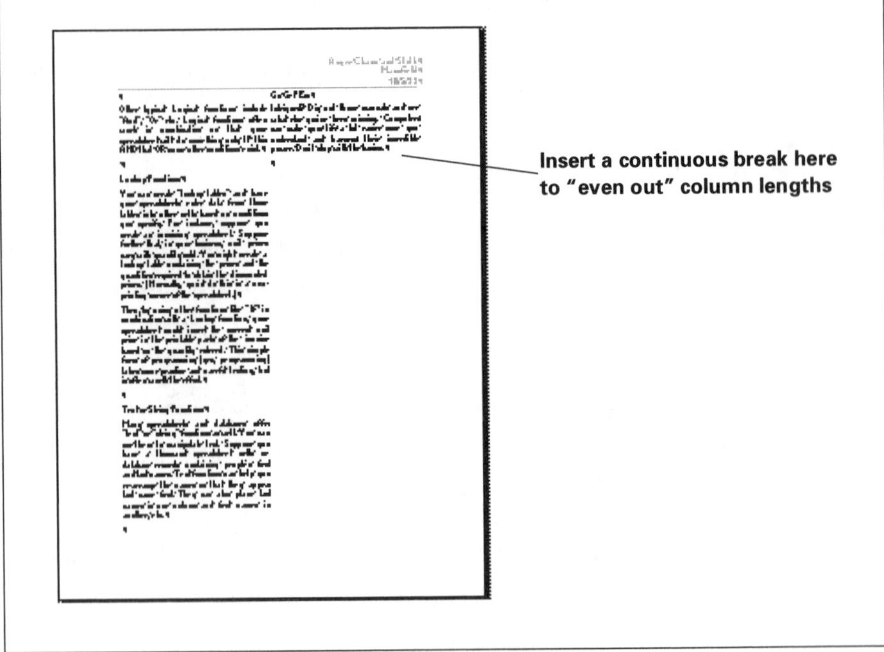
Insert a continuous break here
to "even out" column lengths

1. Place the insertion point after the last character in the text.
2. Choose Insert ➤ Break….
3. Choose Continuous in the Sections area.
4. Click OK. The column bottoms will align as shown in Figure 22.6.

FIGURE 22.6

Flush column bottoms.

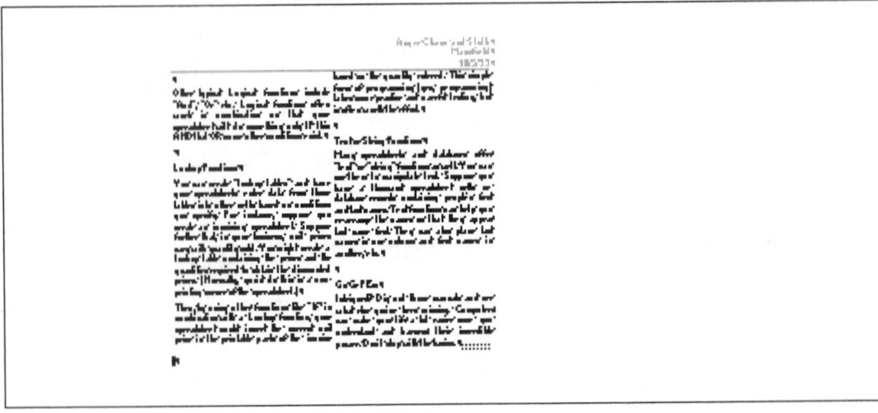

▶▶ Don't Forget Tables as an Alternative

While Word for Windows has made it easy to create and edit multiple columns, there are times when it will be easier for you to use tables instead of columns. This is particularly true for things like resumes and "television-style" scripts where you want side-by-side information to always maintain the same horizontal relationship.

▶▶ Removing Columns

To remove columns from an entire document, select all of the text and use the Toolbar's Columns button to specify a single column. To remove one of several column specifications in a multi-section document, place the insertion point in the unwanted column and then use the Toolbar button.

CHAPTER 23

Creating Tables of Contents and Indexes

▸▸ FAST TRACK

To create a table of contents — 570

begin by formatting your document's headings with Word's standard heading styles. When you have typed and proofed your document and are happy with margins, headers, footers, and other design elements (especially those that affect page breaks), pick Insert ➤ Index and Tables.... You will see the Index and Tables dialog box. Choose the Table of Contents tab if it is not already foremost. Preview the available formats by clicking in the Formats list and watching the Preview area. Pick one. Choose the number of levels you wish to include. If you wish to include a tab leader (dashes or dots, for instance), choose the style from the drop-down list. Click OK or press ↵. Word will compile the new TOC. It starts by repaginating your document. Then it will create a new section at the top of your document and place the TOC in it.

To turn levels on and off with the Table of Contents Options dialog box — 573

open the Index and Tables dialog box (reached with Insert ➤ Index and Tables...) and go to the Table of Contents tab. Click the Options button. Turn off headings by removing numbers from the Level box. Change levels by typing in the Level boxes.

To update a TOC after you've made changes to your document — 575

click in the TOC to highlight the entire TOC (it will turn gray). You'll see a dialog box, where you'll have a choice of whether to Update Page Numbers only or the Entire Table. Decide which you prefer and click OK.

To update (recompile) an index 578

click anywhere in the index to select it. Press the right button to see Word's mini-menu. Choose Update Field. Word will repaginate, then recompile and update the index.

To change the appearance of index entries 579

click anywhere in the index to select it, then visit the Index and Tables dialog box (Insert ➤ Index and Tables…) and choose the Index tab. Click on format names and watch the preview box. (Use ↑ and ↓ to speed selection of different format names if you like.) When you find one you like, click OK to apply the new format to the index.

To have Word for Windows automatically index a document 580

create a new document with the New command. Insert a two-column table (with the Table button, perhaps). Type all index entries in the first column. They must be identical to text Word will find in the document you intend to index. Capitalization counts. In the second column, type all index entries as you wish them to appear in the index. Open the document to be indexed. Choose Insert ➤ Index and Tables…. Visit the Index tab of the Index and Tables dialog box. Click the AutoMark button. Choose the concordance file from the resulting "Open" dialog box. Click OK.

▶▶ **W*ord*** for Windows will help you create a *table of contents* (TOC) for your documents. If you format your headings using Word's standard heading styles or Outline feature, the Insert ➤ Index and Tables… command will quickly compile (create) a simple but very usable table of contents and place it in a new section at the beginning of your document.

It is also possible to manually select items to appear in your table of contents. You do this by identifying words and phrases in your document using hidden text codes called *TOC Entry* codes. You can control the appearance of the table of contents as well. Your TOC can have one or multiple levels.

The Insert ➤ Index and Tables… command and the hidden *Index Entry* codes work together to produce equally simple or distinctive *indexes* at the end of your document.

▶▶ **TIP**

If you plan to create an index for your document, you may want to create it before you create the table of contents so that it will show up as an entry in your TOC.

▶▶ Creating a Table of Contents

Figure 23.1 shows a simple table of contents containing only paragraph headings, created using Word's standard heading 1 through heading 3 styles.

Notice that Word for Windows has placed the TOC in its own new section at the beginning of the document. It has automatically inserted tabs, leading dots, and page numbers. To format and indent the new

FIGURE 23.1

You can produce simple multilevel TOCs using Word's standard heading styles.

Network Overview 1
Wall and floor jacks 2
Patch panel 3
Patch cords 3
Star controllers 4
Servers 4
Ethernet users as of 3/3/94 5
Printers 6
Dial-in access 6
DAT Backup 6
Moving an existing computer along with its user 7
Giving an existing computer to a different user 7
Adding newly purchased computers to the network 8

Network Troubleshooting 9
User(s) can't print 9
All or part of job prints from wrong tray 9
User can't send and receive mail 10
Ethernet user can't access network 10
PhoneNET user can't access network 10
FileMaker slow response times 10
User can't find file(s) or folder(s) on server 10

End of Section

table of contents, it has used TOC styles corresponding to the standard heading styles. Thus, headings in the document formatted with standard heading 3 will appear in the TOC formatted with a standard style called TOC 3.

new

To create a table of contents, follow these general steps:

1. Begin by formatting your document's headings with Word's standard heading styles. (These styles can be added to your Formatting Toolbar's drop-down style list by visiting the Style dialog box. Be sure to hold down Shift when clicking on the Formatting Toolbar's drop-down style list. See Chapter 14 for more about styles.)
2. When you have typed and proofed your document and are happy with margins, headers, footers, and other design elements (especially those that affect page breaks), pick Insert ➤ Index and Tables.... You will see the Index and Tables dialog box, as shown in Figure 23.2.
3. Choose the Table of Contents tab if it is not already foremost.
4. Preview the available formats by clicking in the Formats list and watching the Preview area. Pick one.
5. Choose the number of levels you wish to include in the TOC.

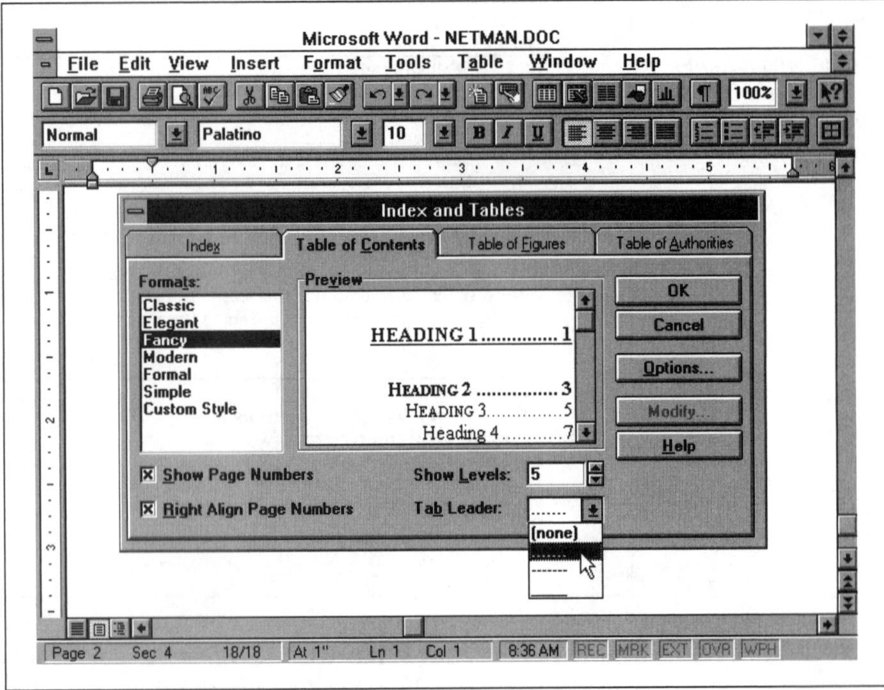

FIGURE 23.2

The Index and Tables dialog box with the Table of Contents tab foremost.

6. If you wish to include a tab leader (dashes or dots, for instance), choose the style from the drop-down list.
7. Click OK or press ↵. Word will compile the new TOC. It starts by repaginating your document. Then it will insert the TOC at the insertion point.

►► **NOTE**

If you've already created a TOC for the document, Word will ask if you want to replace it. If you choose "No," you will end up with *two* TOCs at the beginning of your document. This is a way to create two levels of content detail like the Contents at a Glance and regular TOC at the beginning of this book.

▶ Including Non-Heading Styles in Your TOC

Word for Windows now lets you easily specify non-heading heading styles for inclusion in your TOC. For example, suppose you create and define a style called Chapters, and you want it to be "above" Heading 1 in your TOC. You can use the TOC options to accomplish this.

1. Create and define styles for items you wish to include in the TOC.
2. Format the material using these styles.
3. Open the Table of Contents tab in the Index and Tables dialog box (reached with Insert ➤ Index and Tables…).
4. Click on the Options button.
5. You will see a scrolling list of all of the styles in the current document, as illustrated in Figure 23.3.

FIGURE 23.3 ▶

A list of styles.

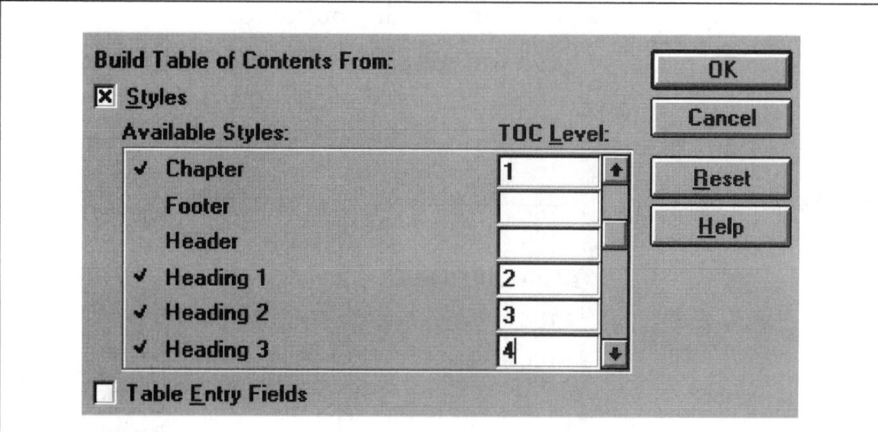

6. Assign "levels" to the styles you wish to include in the TOC, as illustrated in Figure 23.3, where Chapters will be the first level, Heading 1 the second, and so on.
7. Make any other formatting choices and create the TOC as usual.

▸ Changing a TOC's Appearance

Notice how some of the styles apply things like all caps and small caps formatting for different levels. Some styles include underlines. If it bothers you that some headings have both underlines and leader characters (like the top-level headings in Figure 23.2), remove one or the other format and redefine the style using standard Word techniques.

You can edit the resulting TOC as you would any other text in your document. Feel free to embolden characters, change line spacing, etc. As you'd expect, changing the style definitions for styles 1 through 9 will change the appearance of your TOC. There's an easy way to do this in Word:

1. Visit the Table of Contents tab in the Index and Tables dialog box (reached with Insert ➤ Index and Tables…).
2. Pick Custom Style from the Formats list.
3. Click the Modify button.
4. You will see the Style dialog box, illustrated in Figure 23.4.

FIGURE 23.4

The Style dialog box.

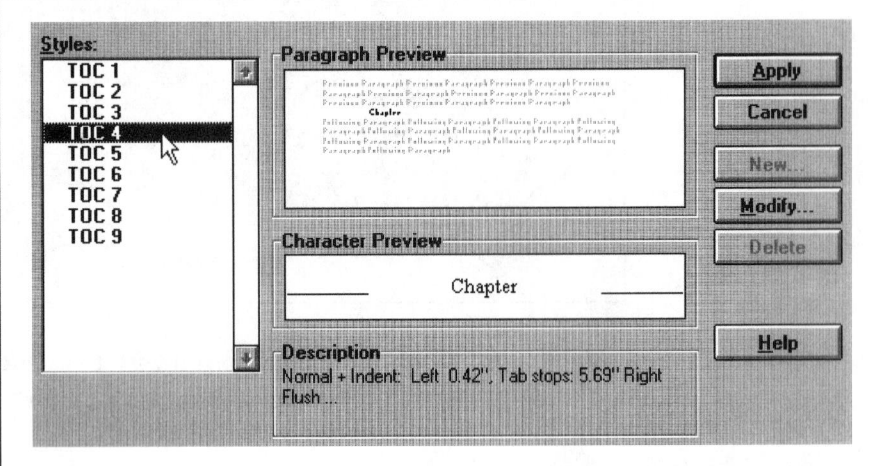

5. Pick the style you wish to modify by clicking on it in the scrolling list.
6. Click the Modify button.
7. You'll see the Modify Style box.

8. Make the desired changes to the style using the drop-down lists and the Format button (which takes you to familiar formatting dialog boxes).
9. "Back out" to the Index and Tables dialog box and click OK.

Restricting Levels

If you want to suppress the printing of all of the levels past a certain point (everything after 5, for instance), specify the levels you wish to print in the Show Levels portion of the Table of Contents tab:

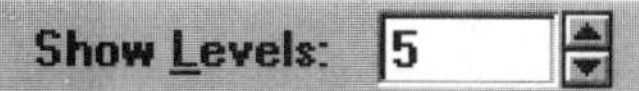

You can also turn levels on and off with the Table of Contents Options dialog box.

1. Open the Index and Tables dialog box (reached with Insert ➤ Index and Tables…) and go to the Table of Contents tab.
2. Click the Options button (for Custom Style only).
3. Turn off headings by removing numbers from the Level box.
4. Change levels by typing in the Level boxes. For instance, in this example Heading Level 3 will not print, and headings 4 and 5 will print as levels 3 and 4.

Available Styles:	TOC Level:
Header	
✓ Heading 1	1
✓ Heading 2	2
Heading 3	
✓ Heading 4	3
✓ Heading 5	4

▶ Updating a Table of Contents

You can update a TOC after you've made changes to your document. You'll be given the choice of just changing page numbers or updating the entire TOC. Here are the general steps:

1. Click in the TOC to highlight the entire TOC (it will turn gray). You'll see a dialog box like this one:

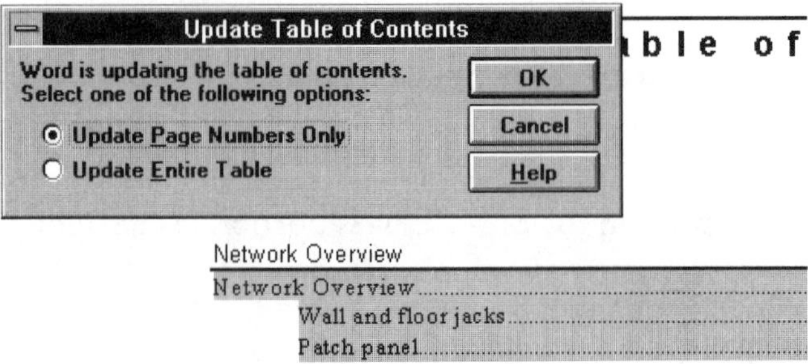

2. Click the right mouse button, then, from the drop-down menu, select Update Fields.
3. Choose Update Page Numbers Only or Update Entire Table.
4. Click OK.

►► Creating an Index

Automatic indexes are created using hidden codes sometimes called *XE* or *Index Entry* codes. Word for Windows compiles indexes on demand and places them at the end of your document in new sections that it creates for this purpose. Index entries can include the contents of headers and footers if you wish.

► Marking Index Entries

Word for Windows now makes it easy to create an index. Simple indexes can be created by selecting text, issuing the Alt+Shift+X keyboard shortcut, and choosing a few options. Word then compiles and stylizes an index and places it at the document's end. Here are the basic steps:

1. Start by making sure that you are done proofing, fiddling with margins, page endings, and the like.

2. Select (highlight) a word or phrase you want to use as an index entry.
3. Press Alt+Shift+X.
4. You'll see the Mark Index Entry dialog box, as illustrated in Figure 23.5.

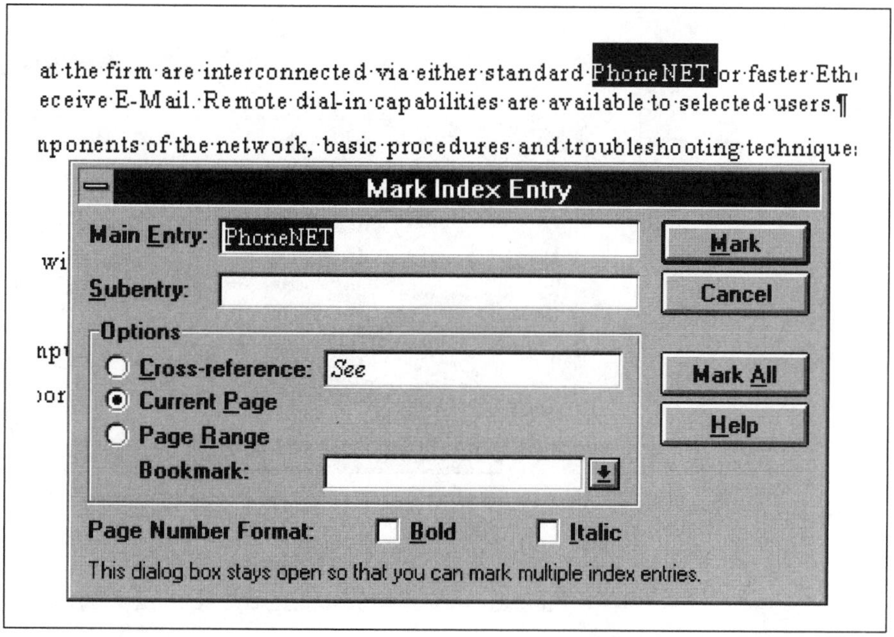

FIGURE 23.5

The Mark Index Entry dialog box can be reached with Alt+Shift+X.

5. Click Mark to mark just this entry, or Mark All to mark all occurrences. (Word will scan the document, marking all occurrences, and the status area will tell you how many were found.) Edit the entry and add a sub-entry. You can also include a cross-reference at this time (See…).
6. The Mark Index dialog box remains visible so that you can scroll to other text and mark it or simply type words to be indexed into the Main Entry section of the dialog box.
7. Repeat steps 2 through 6 until you have specified all desired entries.
8. Click on Close to close the dialog box.

9. Place the insertion point where you want the index (typically at the end of your document).
10. Choose Insert ➤ Index and Tables....
11. Visit the Index tab of the Index and Tables dialog box, as shown in Figure 23.6.

FIGURE 23.6

The Index tab of the Index and Tables dialog box.

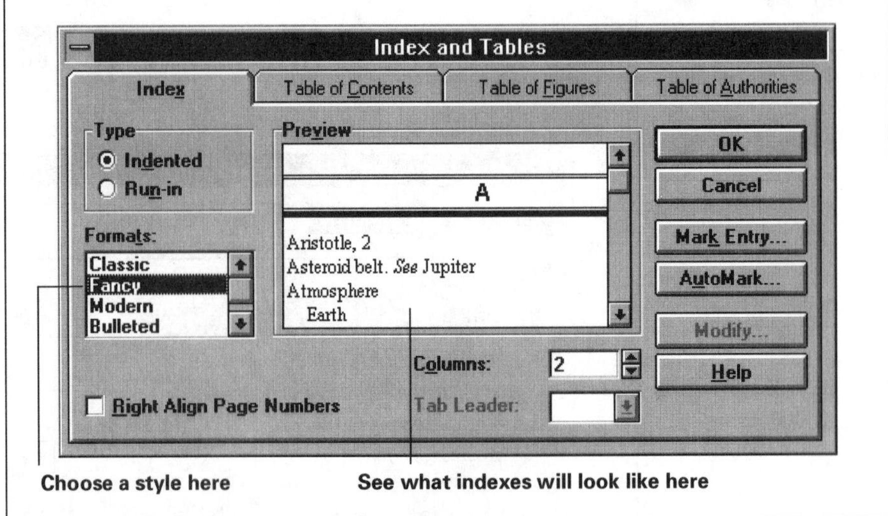

12. Pick an index style using the scrolling Preview area as your guide.
13. Double-click on the name of the desired style or click once on a style name and once on OK.
14. Word will repaginate the document, then create an index that will be placed at the insertion point.

▸ Updating Indexes

Each time you visit and close the Index tab in the Index and Tables dialog box, Word for Windows will ask if you want to replace (recompile) the selected index. Click Yes if you do (and you probably will want to). But there's also a shortcut worth knowing:

1. Click anywhere in the index to select it.

2. Press the right button to see the mini-menu:

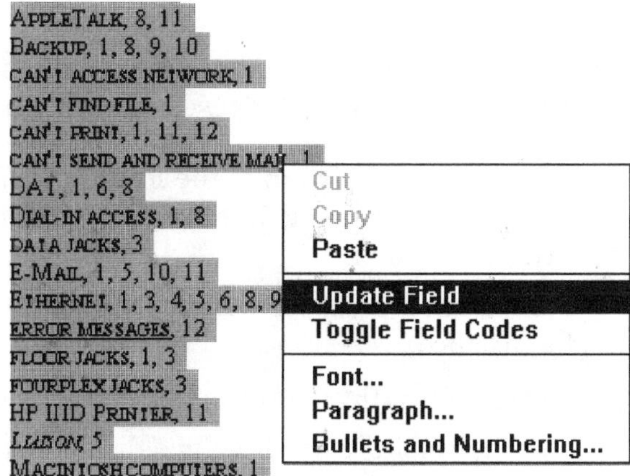

3. Choose Update Field. Word will repaginate, then recompile and update the index.

▶ Formatting Indexes

The easy way to change the appearance of index entries is to pick a different index format choice from the scrolling Formats list in the Index tab of the Index and Tables dialog box. Watch the Preview area of the dialog box as you shop.

1. Click anywhere in the index to select it.
2. Visit the Index and Tables dialog box (Insert ➤ Index and Tables…) and choose the Index tab.
3. Click on format names and watch the preview box. (Use ↑ and ↓ to speed selection of different format names if you like.)

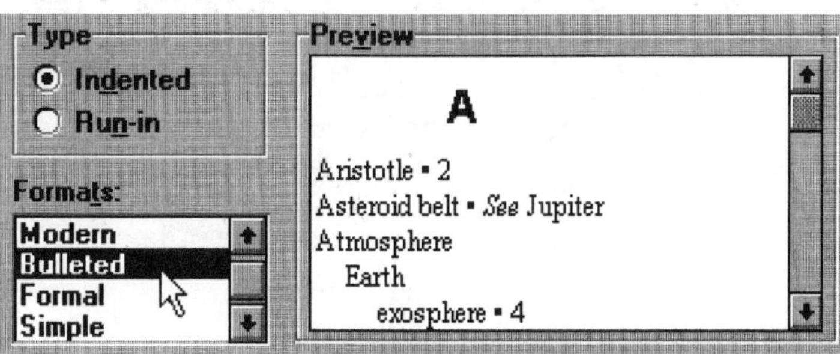

4. When you find one you like, click OK to apply the new format to the index.

It is also possible to change the standard index styles (Index 1–Index 9). Here are the general steps for customizing index styles:

1. While in the Index tab of the Index and Tables dialog box, select Custom Style and click the Modify… button, which reveals the Style dialog box.
2. Pick an index style you wish to modify from the Style list (Index 1, for instance).
3. Click the Modify… button in the Style dialog box.
4. Use the resulting Modify Style dialog box to change the appearance of the style. (For instance, to apply Small Caps formatting, pick Font… from the Format list revealed with the Format button.)
5. "Back out" by clicking OK as necessary (or press Esc).
6. Answer Yes to the "replace selected index" question. The index will be restyled. (Undo will work if you don't like the results.)

▸ Creating Automatic Indexes

It is possible to have Word for Windows automatically index a document without your needing to visit the text manually. You do this by creating a list of terms you wish to index (called a *concordance* list). Here are the general steps:

1. Create a new document with the New command.
2. Insert a two-column table (with the Table button, perhaps).
3. Type all index entries in the first column. They must be identical to text Word will find in the document you intend to index. Capitalization counts. (*Network Troubleshooting* might be a typical entry.)
4. In the second column, type all index entries as you wish them to appear in the index (*Troubleshooting: network*, for instance).
5. Save the document.
6. Open the document to be indexed.
7. Choose Insert ➤ Index and Tables….

8. Visit the Index tab of the Index and Tables dialog box.
9. Click the AutoMark button.
10. Choose the concordance file from the resulting “Open” dialog box.
11. Click OK.
12. Word will mark the entries for you.

►► Tables of Authorities

Word can help you automatically create tables of Authorities. It provides commonly used categories, including:

- Cases
- Statutes
- Other Authorities
- Rules
- Treatises
- Regulations
- Constitutional Provisions

You can control the appearance of the entries and the table itself. Word will even help you seek out items to be included in your table.

► Creating Entries

Always type a long citation as your first entry in a legal document—*Mansfield v. Newman*, 45 Wn 2d 412 (1994), for instance. Subsequent entries can be short versions like *Mansfield v. Newman*. Once you’ve typed all of the entries:

1. Scroll to the first long entry.
2. Select it.
3. Press Alt+Shift+I to bring up the Mark Citation dialog box, like the one in Figure 23.7.

FIGURE 23.7

The Mark Citation dialog box.

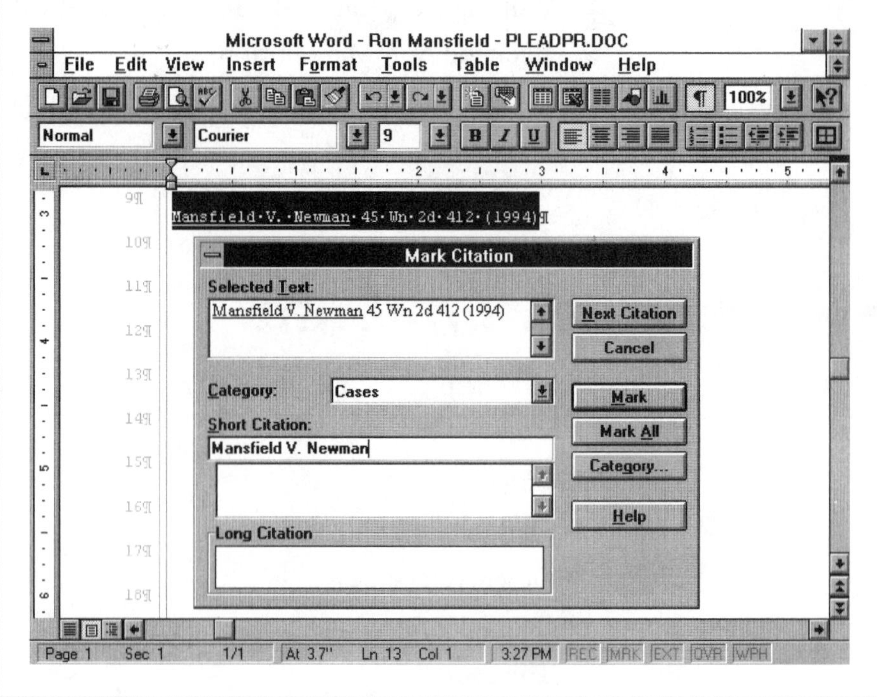

4. Type your selected text in both the Selected Text and Short Citation boxes.
5. Edit the long Citation and format it if you like; you may use only the keyboard shortcuts here (Ctrl+B, Ctrl+I, etc.).
6. Pick a category (Cases, for example).
7. Edit the short Citation so that it matches those in your document, Mansfield v. Newman, for instance.
8. Click the Mark button to visit each potential citation or Mark All to automatically mark them.
9. To find the next citation to mark, click Next Citation. Word will search for legalese (*v.*, *in re*, etc.) and display possible citations. When you find one, repeat steps 2 through 8.
10. When you've marked all the citations, click Close.

▶ Creating the Actual Table of Authorities

To format and compile the actual table, visit the Table of Authorities tab in the Index and Tables dialog box. Follow these steps.

1. Choose Insert ➤ Index and Tables….
2. You'll see a dialog box like the one in Figure 23.8.

FIGURE 23.8 ▶

The Table of Authorities tab.

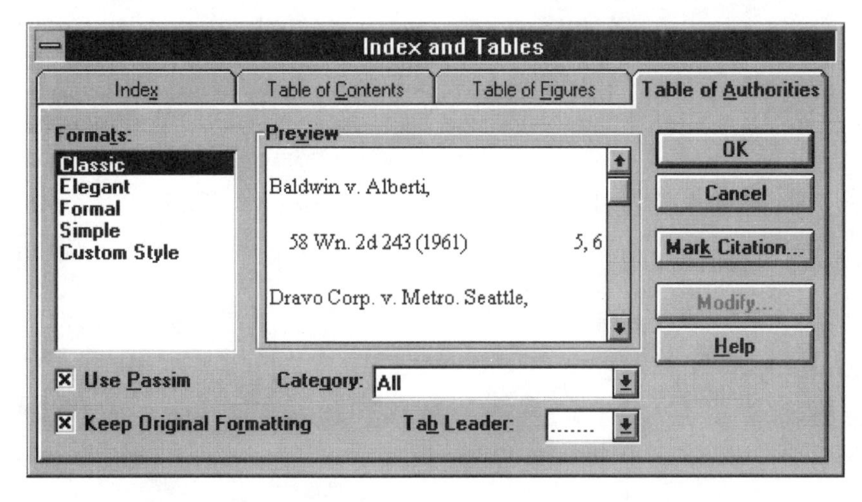

3. Pick a format from the Format list.
4. If you want Word to replace five or more page references with *passim*, choose that option.
5. Click OK. Word will compile the table.

▶ Updating a Table of Authorities

Place the insertion point anywhere in the table of authorities, then press F9. Word will update the table to include any recent insertions, deletions, etc.

▶ Custom Styles and Categories

Word lets you change the appearance of the styles used for TOAs. It also lets you create and edit category names. Consult the online help for details.

▸▸ Tables of Figures

Word will help you create tables of figures and other elements based on captions and bookmarks. Assuming you've captioned documents with the Insert ➤ Caption… command, the process is quite simple:

1. Place the insertion point where you want the table to appear.
2. Choose Insert ➤ Index and Tables….
3. Display the Table of Figures tab if it is not in view. It will look like Figure 23.9.

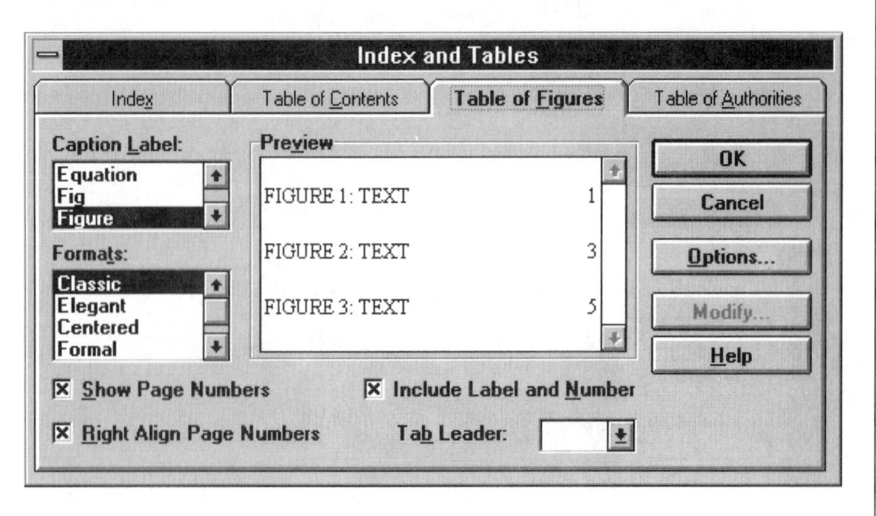

FIGURE 23.9 ▶ *The Table of Figures tab.*

4. Select the desired caption label from the scrolling list.
5. Select a format for the table.

6. Visit the Table of Figures Options dialog box if necessary to pick the style you want Word to use as the basis of the table.
7. Back in the Table of Figures tab, make other option choices (Show Page Numbers, etc.).
8. Click OK.
9. Word will compile a table and place it at the insertion point.

▶ Updating a Table of Figures

Place the insertion point anywhere in the table of figures, then press F9. Word will update the table to include any recent insertions, deletions, etc.

CHAPTER 24

Working with Large Documents

▸▸ FAST TRACK

▸ *To quickly round up multiple files to create a long document* **591**

use the Insert ➤ File... command.

▸ *To divide up a long document into shorter subdocuments* **592**

use a *master document* and *Master Document* view.

▸ *To rename a subfile* **596**

click on the subfile icon of interest and choose File ➤ Save As.... Pick a more fitting name. Click OK. Rename all the subdocuments this way before closing the main document.

▸ *To print an entire document* **599**

open the master document. Switch to Normal view. Print Preview if you like. Print.

▸ *To print the whole project's outline* **599**

switch to Master Document view, reveal the desired levels of detail as you would in Outline view (see Chapter 21 for details), then print.

▸ *To define text as hideable* **600**

select the desired text. Visit the Font dialog box (choose Format ➤ Font...). Check Hidden in the Effects area. Click OK to set. When printing, check the Print Hidden Text choice in the Print dialog box (File ➤ Print...) if you want the annotations to print.

To create annotations 602

place the insertion point in your document or select the item you wish to discuss. Pick Insert ➤ Annotation (*not* View ➤Annotations...). You'll see the annotation window pane. Word will insert initials as hidden text. Type the note. Either choose Close or leave the pane visible as you work.

To view annotations 602

double-click on the annotation mark of interest in your document or use the View ➤ Annotations command. (If you don't see marks, reveal them with the Standard Toolbar's ¶ button.) To view the next or previous annotations, scroll in the annotations window. To filter annotations so that you see only those from a particular author, pick the initials of interest from the annotation pane's drop-down list. Close the Annotations pane with the Close button.

To password protect a document 603

choose Tools ➤ Protect Document.... The Protect Document dialog box will appear. Choose the protection you desire (Annotations). Enter a clever password. Repeat it when Word asks. Click OK or press ↵. Remember it....

To have Word mark your revisions 606

start with a draft document and turn on revision marking by checking the Mark Revisions While Editing option box in the upper-left corner of the Revision Marks dialog box. As you work, Word marks your revisions using embellishments you specify by selecting Options... in the Revision dialog box. Print and distribute (or e-mail) your marked-up draft with the revisions.

▶▶ **One** person's large document is another's small one. Word for Windows has the ability to create documents of virtually any length. At some point, however, you will find that Word's performance degrades as your document size increases. This is particularly true of older, slower computers with limited RAM and slow hard disks.

Many people routinely work with documents containing hundreds of pages. But if performance (scrolling speed, spell checking, etc.) becomes disappointing, you might want to split a single document into multiple documents. Another reason to split documents is to have different people work on different parts of the project. After everyone is done, you'll probably want to print the whole body of work as if it were one document.

Sometimes people create parts of a long document at various sites and then combine them. Whether you start out with a bunch of small documents and combine them, or split a big document for whatever reason, chances are you'll want to print the completed work as a whole. You *can* combine all the parts and treat the resulting large document as a single entity. Or, you can keep the document broken into multiple sections and use Word's new *Master Document* feature.

Group work sometimes causes confusion, so Word for Windows offers a number of ways to annotate text and share your thoughts with other authors working on the project. You can even exchange voice notes with each other if you have the right gear.

There are two important things to watch whenever there's more than one "cook in the kitchen"—consistency of appearance and correct page numbering across document parts. This chapter discusses all of these techniques and problems.

▶▶ Planning for Large Documents

If you know you are going to create a large document, templates, AutoText entries, and possibly a set of author's instructions, then use these tools to create the multiple parts.

If other people will be working on parts of the document, provide them with copies of your templates, and possibly copies of your custom spelling dictionaries and special fonts. The more alike your computers are, the fewer problems you will have during the crunch.

Develop a strategy. Decide how you plan to number figures, tables, and other design elements. Test these strategies on "mini" versions of your document containing a few samples of each element you plan to use (headers, footers, page numbers, tables, figures, figure captions, paragraph headings, etc.). Work out the bugs with twenty or thirty pages before typing and formatting hundreds.

Consider making logical breaks at the beginning of chapters or sections. Use Word's standard styles and templates and the Style Gallery whenever possible. Put one person in charge of rounding everything up.

▶▶ Combining Documents with Insert ➤ File...

The obvious way to round up multiple files to create a long document is to use the Insert ➤ File... command. It places specified files at the insertion point in your document. You are presented with the familiar File dialog box where you pick the next file to be inserted. If necessary, Word for Windows will attempt to convert files coming from non-Word authors.

How Word for Windows handles things like headers, footers, styles, and other formatting issues will depend upon the source files. Here again, it's best to test before the crunch.

▸▸ Master Document Features Facilitate Teamwork

You can use a *master document* and *Master Document* view to divide up a long document into shorter subdocuments. This facilitates workgroup editing, and it makes it easier to format, organize, and number pages. Master documents facilitate other tasks like cross-referencing and creating an index or table of contents. Master documents handle many details for you, including the automatic naming of subdocument files. Master documents are perfect for workgroups sharing a file server. By placing the master document on the server, everyone can work on the entire document or its parts without worrying about the location or names of the subfiles.

▸ Creating a Master Document

You can either create a master document at the time you start a new project, or you can turn an existing document into a master document. It's also possible to combine multiple documents to create a master.

Creating a Master Document for a New Project

Here's an easy way (but not the only way) to create a new master document at the time you begin a project:

1. Open a new document using the template you desire to use as the starting point for your project.
2. Choose View ➤ Master Document. Your screen will look like Figure 24.1.
3. Word displays the Outline Tools described in Chapter 21 and the Master Document Toolbar, nestled at the right end of the Outline Toolbar. Figure 24.2 details the button names.
4. Create an outline for your master document using the techniques described in Chapter 21.

FIGURE 24.1

Master Document view and the Master Document Toolbar.

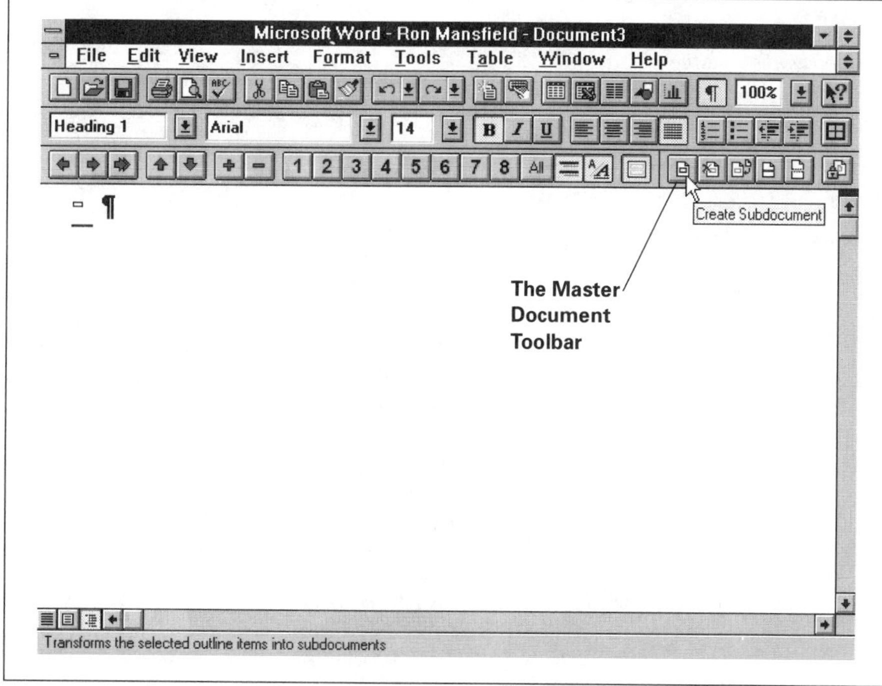

FIGURE 24.2

The Master Document Toolbar.

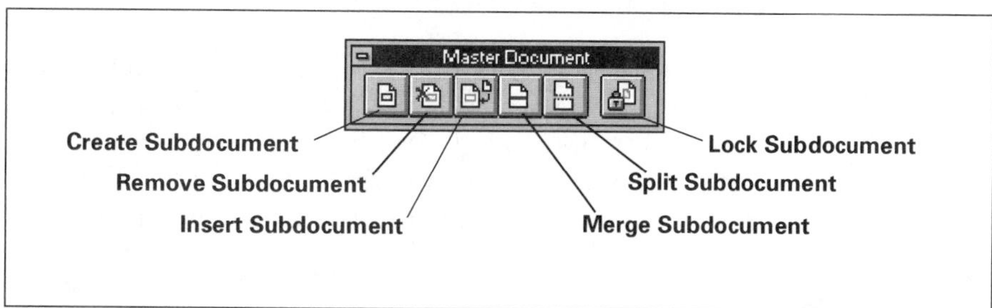

TIP

Assign Word's Heading 1 style *only* to the entry that you wish to use as the start of each subdocument. For example, if you wanted a subdocument for each chapter, apply the Word Style Heading 1 to chapter heads (and to chapter heads only) as shown in Figure 24.3.

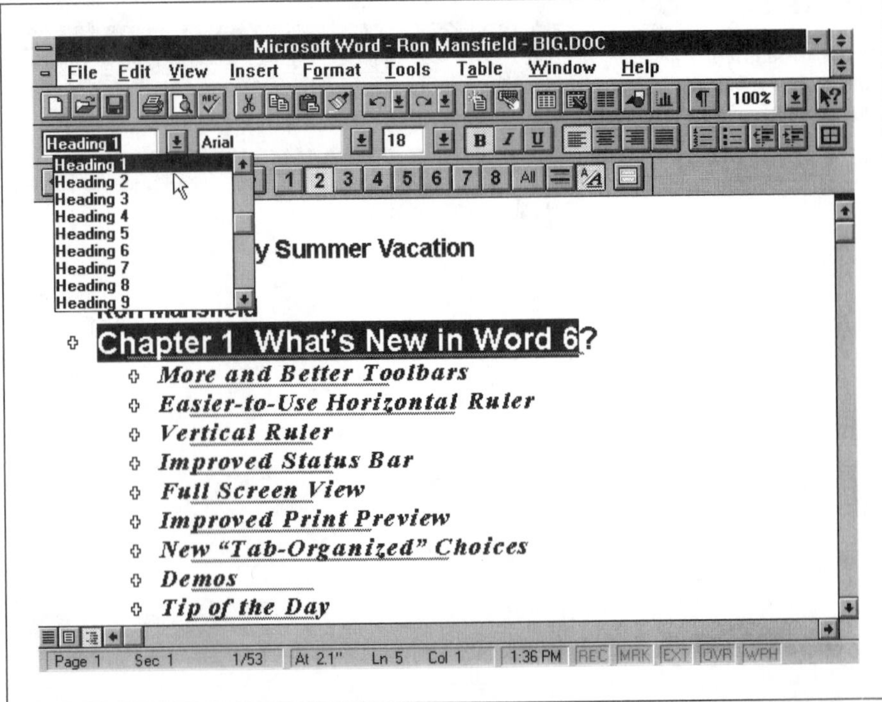

FIGURE 24.3 ▶

Assign Heading 1 only to those headings that you want to start a new subdocument.

5. Select *all* of the text and headings you wish to subdivide, being sure to include the heading you wish to use at the start of each subdocument (the first Heading 1 entry, for example). This heading should be the first item selected. Do not select things you don't want turned into a subdocument.

▸▸ **TIP**

Because you are working in an outline, consider collapsing the outline to the top level to make it easier to select the headings and their related text. Figure 24.4 illustrates this concept.

6. Click the Create Subdocument button on the Master Document Toolbar (the left-most Master Document Toolbar button).

FIGURE 24.4

Select only headings and text you wish to divide. Make sure the first thing selected is a "top-level" heading you wish to use as the starting point for each new subdocument.

How I spent my Summer Vacation
by
Ron Mansfield
Chapter 1 What's New in Word 6?
Chapter 2: Creating Your First Document
Chapter 3: Viewing and Navigating

7. Word will insert break lines and split the entire project up into subdocuments. You'll see little subdocument icons next to each subdocument break point as shown in Figure 24.5.

FIGURE 24.5

The master document now contains three subdocuments—one for each chapter. The book title and author name are saved in the master document.

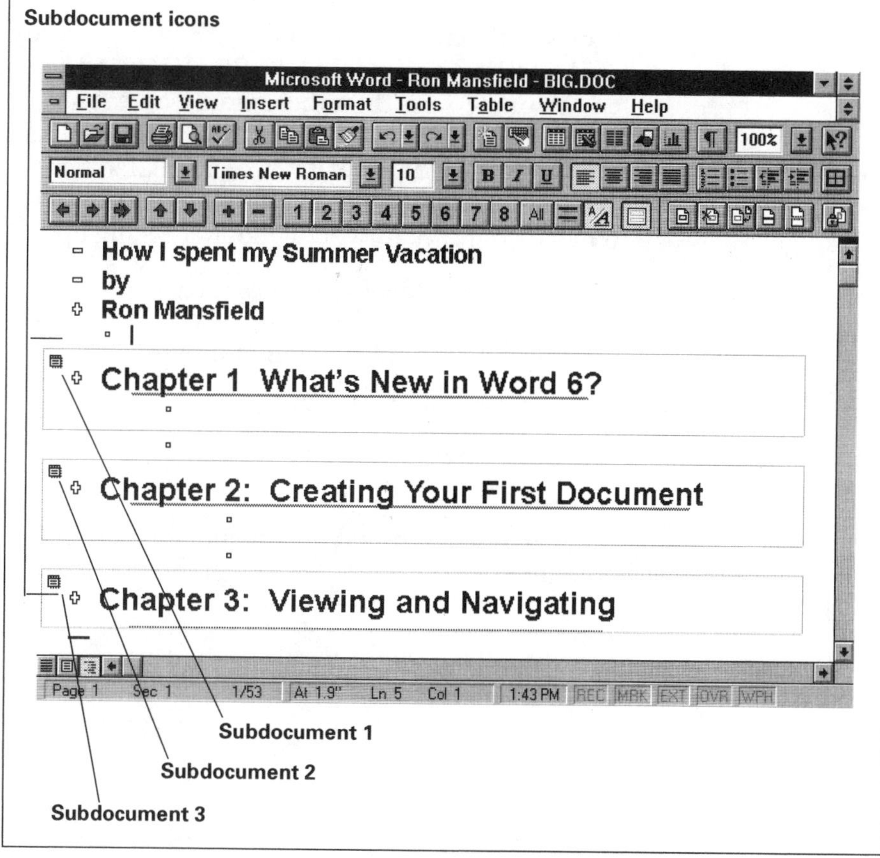

▶ Saving Masters and Subs

When you save your master document for the first time, Word for Windows assigns file names and locations to the subfiles as well. It does this by using characters from the first heading in each subdocument. When headings are similar, Word assigns numbers as part of the file name to differentiate the different subdocuments.

For instance, in our book example, all the first headings begin with CHAPTER(SPACE), so Word for Windows will assign numbers at the end of each file name. In a perfect world, that would mean that the subfile for Chapter 1 would be automatically named CHAPTER1.DOC, subfile 2 would be CHAPTER2.DOC, and so on. But that ain't necessarily so. Read on....

▶ A File-Naming Gotcha

If the subdirectory to which you are saving already *has* files named CHAPTER1.DOC, CHAPTER2.DOC, and so on, Word will use different numbers for the subchapters—and you've guessed it, haven't you? It is possible to end up with a subdocument containing Chapter 1 but named CHAPTER4.DOC, and a Chapter 2 subdocument called CHAPTER5.DOC, ad nauseam. Never (ever, ever) trust a computer to name your files for you without checking up on it.

To rename a subfile, follow these steps:

1. Click on the subfile icon of interest.
2. Choose File ➤ Save As....
3. Pick a more fitting name.
4. Click OK.
5. Rename all the subdocuments this way before closing the main document.

▶▶ WARNING

Don't ever change subdocument file names from the Windows File Manager or any other way except via the Save As... command as just described. You'll confuse Word for Windows and raise your blood pressure.

▶ Working with a Master Document

So, now what? All that work and what does it buy? Here's the deal. You can switch to Master Document view to get the big picture. Rearrange things just as you do in Outline view. Create cross-references for multiple subdocuments. You work on Chapter 1 while somebody at the other end of the network fiddles with Chapter 2. Spell check and reformat the whole mess at once. Make sweeping style changes. Save a tree; print preview all 200 pages.

You can make sweeping changes by working in Master Document view or change just a subdocument or two in Normal view. Remember to switch to Master Document view before attempting project-wide changes.

Don't forget that the section breaks Word for Windows inserts for each subdocument will play a part in things like header and footer designs. Give some thought to whether you want to design headers and footers before or after breaking a large document into subdocuments.

Incidentally, there are some things to remember when working with other people on the same project across a network. You may not be able to change subdocuments that you or others have currently opened elsewhere. You can tell when this will be a problem two ways. First, you'll see a little padlock beneath certain subdocument icons as shown here:

Chapter 1

The other surefire sign of trouble is an alert like this one:

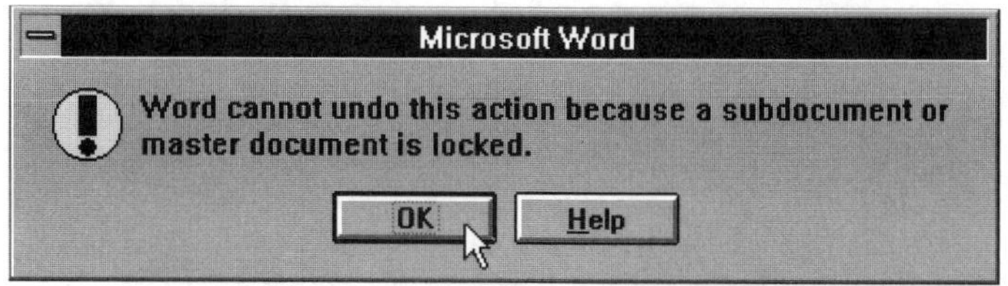

There are two possible reasons for this. Either you are not the original author of the subdocument, in which case it will need to be unlocked (with the appropriate password), or the subdocument is already in use by you or someone else.

If you are the culprit, close the window containing the subdocument or start the search for your partner in crime elsewhere on the network. Make sure that your network's and Word's file protection are set to give access to those with a need to know, read, and write. Learn any necessary passwords. Contact your network manager and the subdocument author(s) for assistance.

Turning an Existing File into a Master

Once you've created a master document it is easy to insert old Word (and many other) documents. Here are the general steps:

1. While in Master Document view, position the insertion point where you want the outside document to be placed.
2. Click the Insert Subdocument button on the Master View Toolbar. It's the third button from the left.
3. Use the resulting Insert Subdocument dialog box just as you'd use Word's Open dialog box—find the document of interest and click OK.
4. Word will add the document, converting it from another format (like WordPerfect) if necessary.
5. If the incoming document and master document were based on different templates, the incoming work will take on the characteristics of the master document.

►► NOTE

If you later open an external document without using Master Document view, the document will retain its old formatting (based on its original template instead of the master document's template).

▶ Printing Masters and Subs

To print an entire document:

1. Open the master document.
2. Switch to Normal view.
3. Print Preview if you like.
4. Print.

To print the whole project's outline, switch to Master Document view, reveal the desired levels of detail as you would in Outline view (see Chapter 21 for details), then print.

▶▶ TIP

You can open a subdocument by double-clicking on its icon.

To print just a subdocument, open it as you would any other document and print. Be advised however, that if you use any of Word's handy cross-referencing features (described in Chapters 23, 25, and elsewhere), the references will probably not be properly updated, and you may see error messages unless you print from the master document.

▶▶ Annotations

Are you one of those people like me with Post-it notes stuck all over your documents? Word for Windows offers several alternatives. Hidden text was available in earlier Word versions and remains in this one. It has been joined by *voice annotations*, a way to record and play back sounds attached to specific locations in Word for Windows documents if your computer is sound-capable.

Finally, Word's text annotation and Revisions features let you document changes as you work.

►► Using Hidden Text for Annotations

Hidden text might be better named *hideable* text, as it is not always hidden. In fact, many people leave hidden text in view most of the time. So, with apologies to Microsoft, let's call it hideable text here.

Authors often use hideable text to make notes to themselves or to colleagues. They leave the notes in view while working, then hide them when they print their work. Figure 24.6 shows an example of a hideable note.

FIGURE 24.6 ►

Hideable text has dotted lines under it unless you check the Hidden Text box in the View tab of the Options Dialog box.

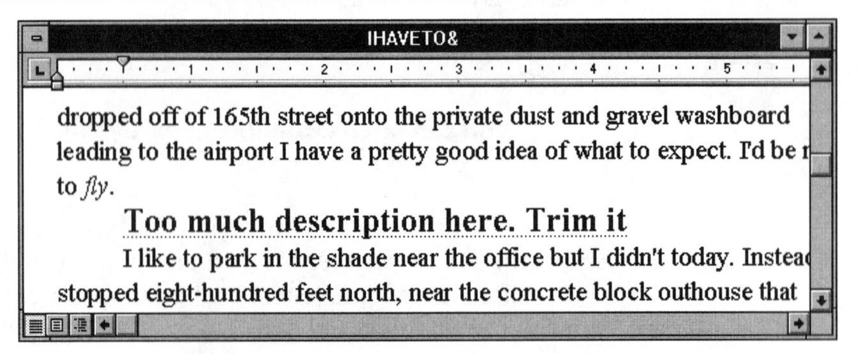

In the example, *Too much description here. Trim it.* is hideable text. As you can see, it is possible to embellish hideable text just as you can embellish regular text.

To define text as hideable:

1. Select the desired text.
2. Visit the Font dialog box (choose Format ➤ Font...).
3. Check Hidden in the Effects area:

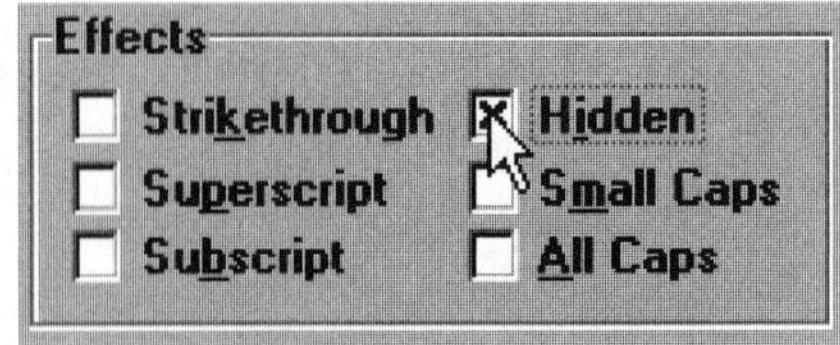

4. Click OK to set.

5. When printing, click on Options… in the Print dialog box (Edit ➤ Print) and check the Hidden Text option in the Include with Document section of the Options dialog box.

The keyboard shortcut to define text as hideable is Ctrl+Shift+H. This command toggles hidden text. If you use it with hideable text, the text will revert to non-hideable text.

▶ Showing and Hiding Text

To show or hide text, follow these steps:

1. Use the View tab in the Options dialog box (reached with Tools ➤ Options…).
2. Enable or disable the Hidden Text feature by clicking to add or remove an X.

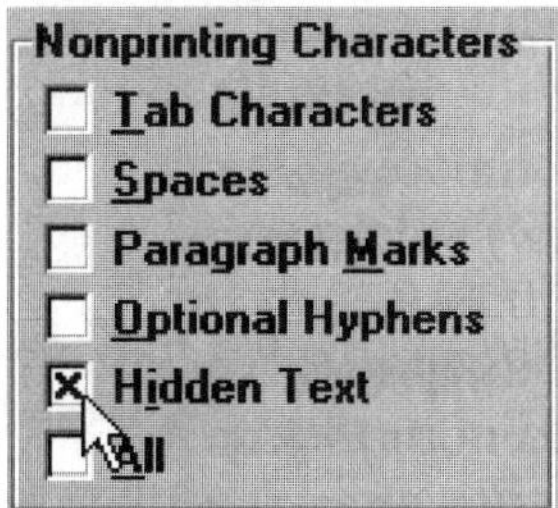

3. Click OK.

If you find yourself toggling hidden text frequently, add the Show Hidden Text command to a menu or the Toolbar. You may wish to define a keyboard shortcut as well. See Chapter 36 to learn how.

▸▸ Text Annotations

This feature lets you add reminders to yourself and notes to others collaborating on your document. The notes can be completely hidden, flagged, or displayed and printed. When you are done with them, they can be deleted or incorporated into your final document.

▸ Inserting Annotations

Creating annotations with Word for Windows couldn't be easier. Follow these steps:

1. Place the insertion point at the place in your document where you want to insert the annotation or select the item you wish to discuss.
2. Pick Insert ➤ Annotation (*not* View ➤ Annotations…).
3. You'll see the annotation window pane.
4. Word will insert initials (yours, assuming your initials are in the User info tab of the Options dialog box) as hidden text.
5. Type the note.
6. Either choose Close or leave the pane visible as you work.

▸▸ TIP

If you don't see your initials in the document or in the drop-down From list, visit the User Info tab in the Options dialog box and type your initials in the initials area. Click OK.

▸ Viewing Annotations

You view annotations with the View ➤ Annotations command. (Notice that *this* command is plural while the one on the Insert menu is singular, because you insert annotations one at a time but can view several at once.)

1. Double-click on the annotation mark of interest in your document or use the View ➤ Annotations command. (If you don't see marks, reveal them with the Standard Toolbar's ¶ button.)

2. To view the next or previous annotations, scroll in the annotations window.
3. To filter annotations so that you see only those from a particular author, pick the initials of interest from the annotation pane's drop-down list.
4. When you are done, close the Annotations pane with the Close button or leave it open while you work.

NOTE

If the author of an annotation highlights document text or other elements when creating the note, those items will be highlighted again when you read the annotation. This is not the same thing as selecting before editing. If you wish to edit highlighted things, you'll still need to select them.

▶ *Editing and Protecting Annotations*

You can change any existing annotation, even if you are not the author of the annotation. Hmmm... Startled?

Actually, it is possible for authors to password-protect annotations (and revision marks) with the Tools ➤ Protect Document command. If you work with the "ethically challenged," protect your annotations and revisions thusly:

1. Choose Tools ➤ Protect Document.... The Protect Document dialog box will appear:

Protect Document
Protect Document For
Revisions
Annotations
Forms
Password:
*****
OK
Cancel
Sections...
Help

2. Choose the protection you desire (Annotations).
3. Enter a clever password.
4. Repeat it when Word asks.
5. Click OK or press ↵.
6. Remember it....

▸▸ **WARNING**

Punctuation counts when entering passwords. *watergate, Watergate,* and *WATERGATE* are all different (and dumb) passwords. Beware of the Caps Lock key.

new ▸▸ **NEW**

Because Word no longer indicates in the status area whether Caps Lock is on or off, you have to be especially careful when creating passwords.

▸ *Incorporating Annotations*

You can copy and paste text from the annotation pane into the document. Drag and drop works here too!

▸ *Printing Annotations*

To print just the annotations, visit the Print dialog box (Ctrl+P) and choose Annotations from the Print What list:

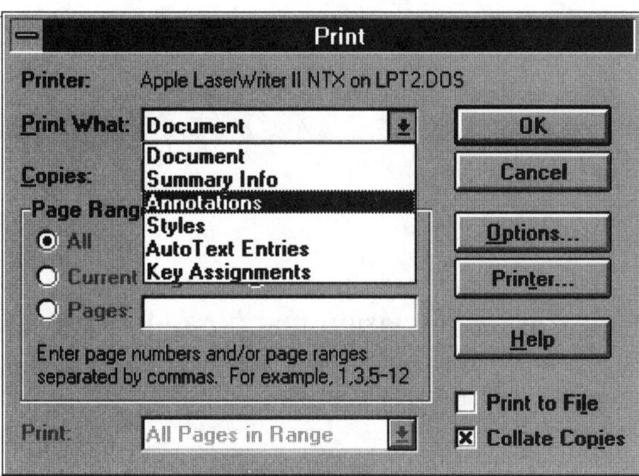

To print a document and its annotations, choose Document in the Print dialog box's Print What list, then click the Options… button to reveal the Print Tab. Choose Annotations from the options list:

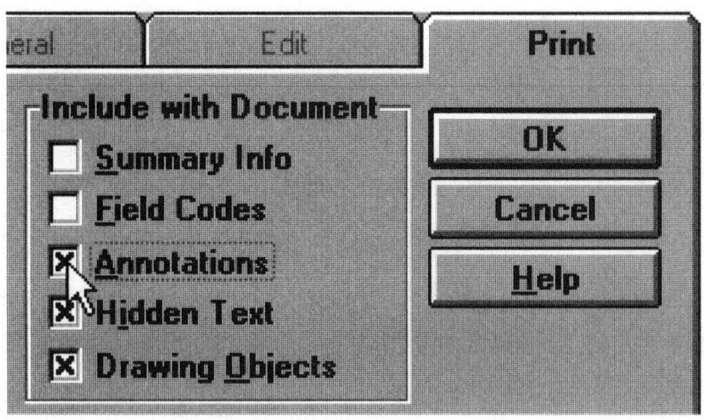

▶▶NOTE

This choice will be unavailable if you have selected Annotations in the Print What box back in the Print dialog box, which makes sense, if you think about it.

▶ *Moving and Removing Annotations*

Feel free to move and delete annotations by treating their annotation marks as you would any other character in a document. Select them, drag and drop, delete, copy, etc. This assumes of course that the document is not password-protected, unless you know the password.

▸▸ Using the Tools ➤ Revisions... Command

Revision marks show who did what, when, and where—an audit trail of changes, if you will. Revision marks can include strike-throughs, underlining, double underlines, bold characters, and so on. You get to decide how revisions will be marked.

When several people edit a document, Word for Windows assigns their reviewer's marks and labels different colors to help keep things straight. Revisions can be displayed and printed, protected, hidden, incorporated in the text, or deleted altogether. You can merge revisions from several copies of a document into one "consolidated" document file. Let's have a look.

▸▸ TIP

Word uses only eight colors for marking revisions, so if you have more than eight contributors, things can get a little confusing. Consider using one color for each workgroup (marketing, accounting, etc.) and specify colors on each group's machines by using the Revisions tab of the Options dialog box, described later in this chapter and in Chapter 36.

▸▸ Revision Marks

The Tools ➤ Revisions... command reveals the dialog box shown in Figure 24.7.

FIGURE 24.7

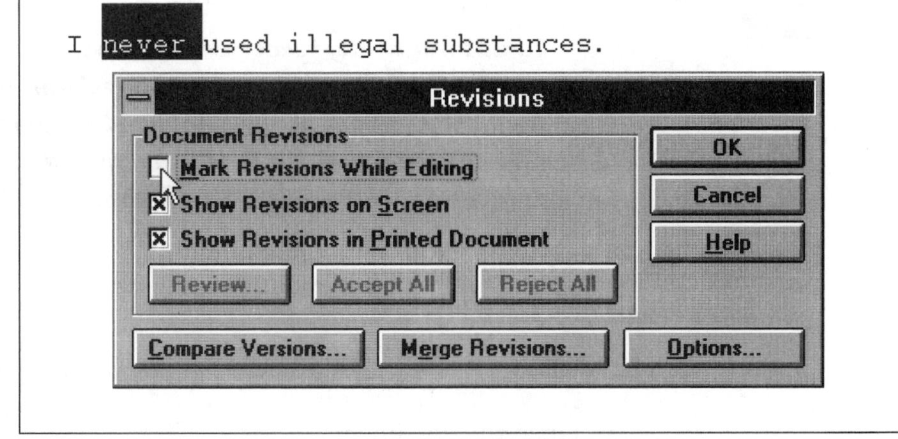

Turn on revision marking. Edit the draft, pass it around for review, then click Accept All to make all changes and remove the revision markings or use Review... to pick and choose.

Revision marks show readers where people have changed the document.

1. Start with a draft document and turn on revision marking by checking the Mark Revisions While Editing option box in the upper-left corner of the Revision Marks dialog box.
2. As you work, Word marks your revisions using embellishments you specify by selecting Options… in the Revision dialog box. At this point you will see old and new text whether you have deleted it or not. In Figure 24.8, newly inserted text is underlined and deleted text is marked with strike-through lines.

FIGURE 24.8

```
     To the best of my recollection, I never inhaledused
illegal substances while in this country.
```

Revisions are marked for review.

3. Print and distribute (or e-mail) your marked-up draft with the revisions.

TIP

To automatically force revision tracking, open the NORMAL.DOC template, enable revision tracking, and save the changes as NORMAL.DOC (replace the old NORMAL.DOC). If you work in a group, make sure everyone's NORMAL.DOC template is modified.

► Reviewing Revisions

Here's how to review revisions whether you or someone else created them:

1. Open the document.
2. Unmodified text, modified text, and revision marks will show. If you have a color display, revisions will be in one or more colors.
3. Choose Tools ➤ Revisions.... You'll see the dialog box shown back in Figure 24.7.
4. At this point you can click the Accept All button to accept all revisions, Reject All to reject all revisions, or Review... to consider revisions one at a time.
5. If you choose Review, you'll see a new dialog box illustrated in Figure 24.9.
6. You'll see who made the change and when. You can accept or reject the change, or procrastinate by moving on or closing without making a decision. When you accept, the related revision marks and deleted text will disappear. Inserted text will take its rightful place.
7. Move from revision to revision with the two Find buttons. A check in the Find Next box moves you to the next revision after accepting or rejecting a change. Undo—well, it undoes.
8. Cancel will close the dialog box for you.

FIGURE 24.9

Review, accept, and reject individual changes from here.

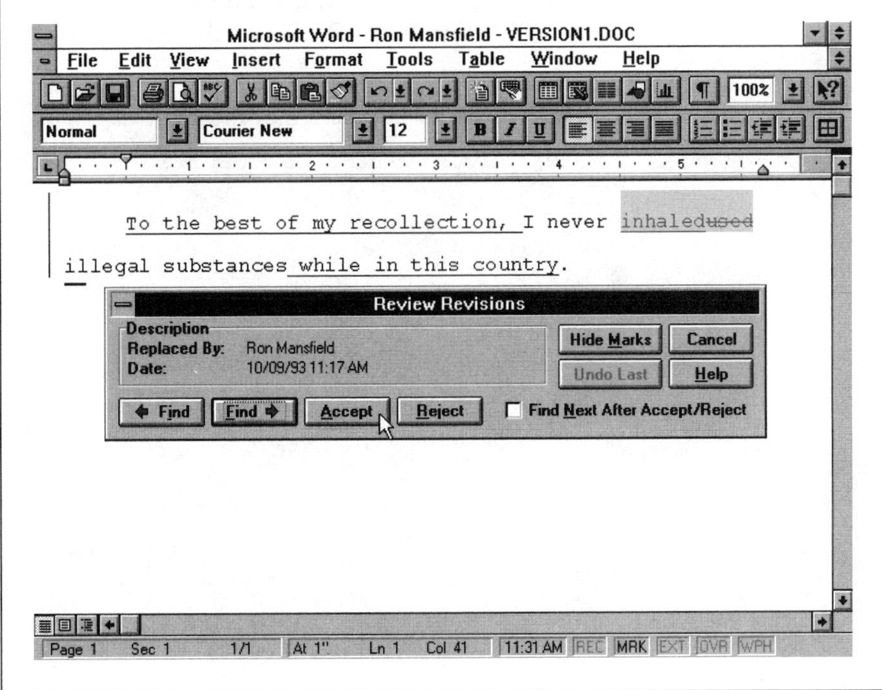

Comparing Documents

Sometimes it's helpful to compare two documents—an original and edited file, for instance. The files must either have different file names or reside in different directories. Here are the general steps:

1. Open the *edited* document.
2. Choose Tools ➤ Revisions....
3. Click Compare Versions....
4. Type or select the *original* file name and location.
5. Accept or reject revisions.

Customizing Revision Marks

Oh boy! New toys. Word for Windows lets you specify colors, revision-mark types, and more from the colorful Revisions tab of the Options

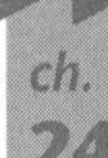

dialog box. Reach it with the Tools ➤ Options… command or with the Options button in the Revisions dialog box.

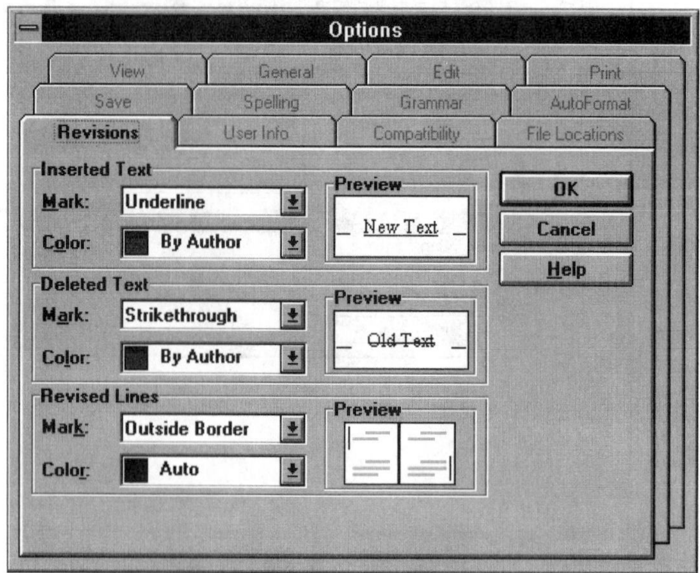

►► Voice-Annotations—Maybe

Some computers contain audio boards that let you record sounds to disk, then play them back. Word for Windows provides a built-in software feature to control the recording of voice annotations. It saves voice annotations with your Word documents. But before you toss out your pocket dictating machine, there are some things you should know. Sound files are pretty big. There are RAM considerations as well. Not all soundboards are Word-compatible. Once the appropriate sound-recording hardware is installed and configured (check your manuals for these things), if you give a file to others, they must also have properly installed, compatible soundboards to listen to your voice notes.

▶ Recording Voice Annotations

Word for Windows makes it easy to record voice annotations. Here are the steps for recording voice annotations on an audio-capable computer:

1. Place the insertion point where you want to attach a voice annotation (after a text annotation, perhaps) or select an item you wish to discuss.
2. Choose Insert ➤ Annotation.
3. The annotations pane will appear, complete with a button that looks like a cassette recorder. It's called the Insert Sound Object Button.

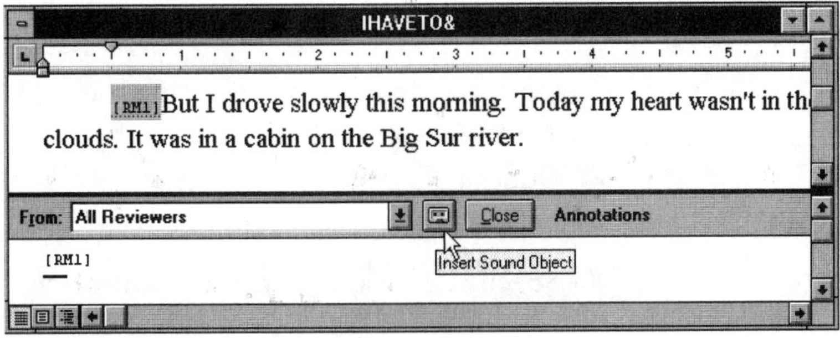

4. Click on the button to begin recording.
5. Follow the instructions that came with your soundboard regarding recording.
6. If asked if you want to update the sound object, answer Yes.
7. Either close the annotation pane or leave it open if you wish to add other annotations.

▶ Playing Voice Annotations

You must have a properly installed audio board to play sounds. Choose View ➤ Annotations. Double-click on the icon for the sound you wish to hear.

► Pen Annotations

You can write directly in the annotations window if you have a pen-equipped computer. Word treats the writings as graphic objects. Install the Pen Annotation button in one of your Toolbars so that you can click it before writing. See Chapter 36 to learn more about adding Toolbar buttons and consult your hardware manuals regarding pen features.

►► Merging Revisions and Annotations

Sometimes you will want to combine revisions or annotations from multiple authors playing pass the floppy or the network equivalent. Here are the general steps.

1. Open the document containing the revisions or annotations (from a coworker, perhaps).
2. Choose Tools ➤ Revisions....
3. Click Merge Revisions....
4. Specify the original document (the one that will be receiving the additions) in the Original File Name box.
5. Word will incorporate the changes.

►► **WARNING**

Word can sometimes make changes you won't like when you merge. It's a good idea to work with a copy of your "original" document when merging, particularly if you work with the Automatic Save feature enabled.

►► Routing Documents

While we are on the subject of teamwork, it is worth noting that if y'all are connected to a network, Word for Windows can help you play "pass the document." Check out the great new Routing feature discussed in Chapter 31.

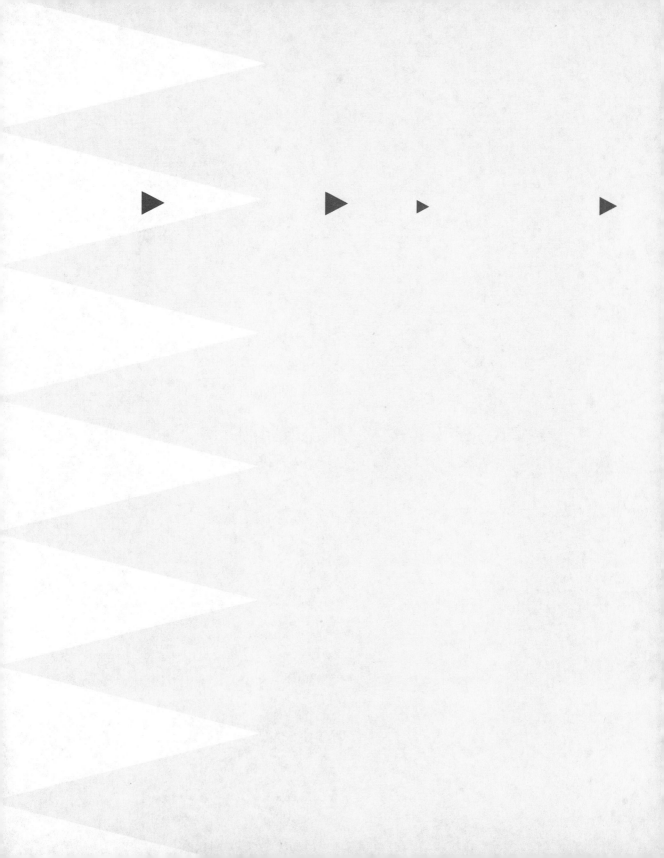

CHAPTER 25

Bookmarks, Captions, and Cross-Referencing

▸▸ FAST TRACK

To define bookmarks **_618_**

either move the insertion point to the item of interest or select the item. Choose Edit ➤ Bookmark… (Ctrl+Shift+F5). You'll see the Bookmark dialog box. Give the bookmark a unique name consisting of up to 40 characters. Spaces are *not* allowed, so use an underscore instead. Click Add. (If the button is dimmed, check to see that the name is less than 40 characters long and contains no spaces.) Create more bookmarks or close the box. Clicking the Add button will also close the dialog box.

To delete a mark but not the marked item(s) **_621_**

visit the Bookmark dialog box. Choose the desired bookmark name. Click the Delete key, then click Close. The bookmark disappears and the previously marked items remain.

To delete a bookmark and the items it marks **_622_**

turn on Bookmark markers in the View tab. Select the item and both bookmark markers. Delete as usual (Cut, press Delete, etc.). The mark and the items(s) will disappear.

To manually caption **_622_**

select the item to be captioned. Choose Insert ➤ Caption…. You'll see the Caption dialog box. Word proposes a caption label that you can accept as is or edit. For example, you can type descriptive text. Change the default appearance options, if you wish, by visiting the Position List and Numbering dialog box. Click OK to insert the label. Be patient, it takes a moment.

To automatically caption things — 624

choose Insert ➤ Caption... and click AutoCaption.... Pick a type of item to automatically caption. You can pick more than one type for the same caption label. Inserting either will have the same effect. Pick a label type from the Use Label list or create your own with the New Label button. Pick a position for the label (above or below the item). Change the numbering scheme if you like. Repeat these steps for each different type of caption you want. Click OK.

To create new label types — 625

use the New Label... button in the Caption and AutoCaption dialog boxes.

To include chapter and similar numbers in automatic captions — 625

format all of the Main headings (Chapters, for example) as Heading Style 1. Choose Format ➤ Heading Numbering.... Make sure a numerical numbering style is in use (not Chapter One, for instance). Visit either the Caption or AutoCaption dialog box. Choose the Numbering button. When you see the Caption Numbering dialog box, choose Include Chapter numbers. Back out by clicking OK as needed.

To update cross-references immediately — 626

press **F9**. They will also be updated when you switch to Print Preview or print.

►► **W***ord's* Bookmarks let you name specific points or areas of your document. Use bookmarks to identify the beginning of chapters, tables, spots that need work, the place where you left off, and so on. You can mark a place, a character, ranges of characters, graphics, or just about any other Word document element. You can then tell Word for Windows to go to those specific points without a lot of scrolling and searching.

Captions are the words that appear next to a figure in your text, explaining what the figure is supposed to be illustrating.

Cross-references let you refer to different places in your document and have Word for Windows keep track of references when things change. For example, if you're writing a book and you say *see Figure 3* in the body of your text, then add a new figure between the old figures 2 and 3, Word will automatically renumber the figures and the in-text references to those figures.

►► Bookmarks

To use bookmarks, you simply locate things of interest, define them as bookmarks, and visit them as necessary. Here are the general steps.

► Defining Bookmarks

To define bookmarks, follow these steps:

1. Either move the insertion point to the item of interest or select the item.
2. Choose Edit ➤ Bookmark... (Ctrl+Shift+F5). You'll see the Bookmark dialog box, shown in Figure 25.1.

FIGURE 25.1

Creating a bookmark.

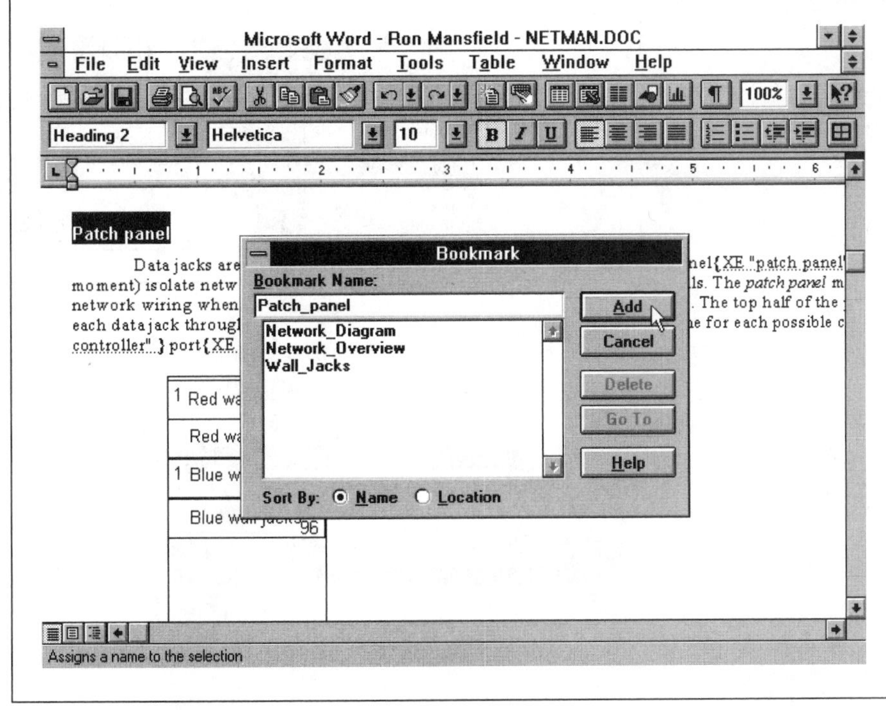

3. Give the bookmark a unique name consisting of up to 40 characters. Spaces are *not* allowed, so use an underscore instead, as illustrated in Figure 25.1.
4. Click Add. (If the button is dimmed, check to see that the name is less than 40 characters long and contains no spaces.)
5. Create more bookmarks or close the box. Clicking on Add also closes the dialog box.

▶ Going to a Bookmark

Once you've defined some bookmarks, you can go to them in one of two ways. If you select Edit ➤ Go To, you'll see a list of bookmarks in scrolling lists (as illustrated in Figure 25.2). Double-click on a bookmark's name to go there. If you click the Go To button in the Bookmark dialog box, however, Word will go to the selected bookmark without displaying the dialog box.

FIGURE 25.2 ►

Double-click on a bookmark's name either in the Go To or Bookmark dialog box to take you to it.

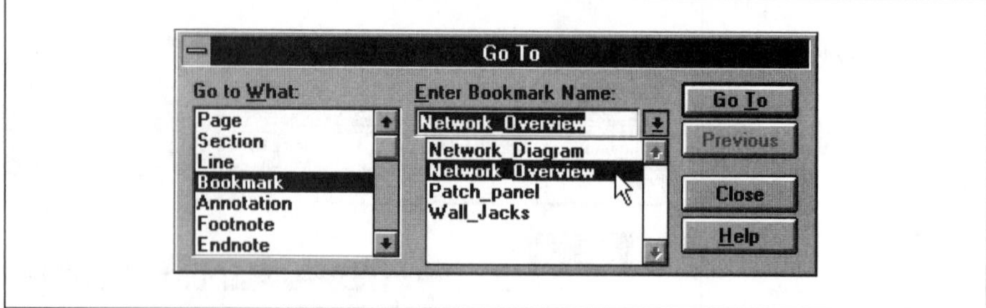

In the Bookmark dialog box, you can sort the list either by name or by the relative location of the bookmark in the document:

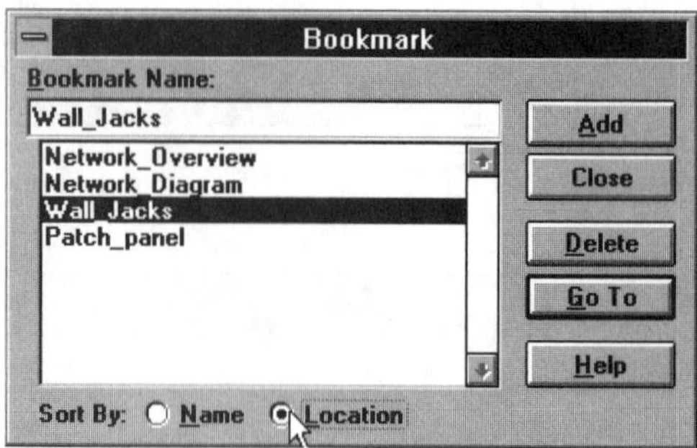

► *Viewing the Marks Themselves*

You can see little in-document markers that indicate the location of bookmarks. These large square brackets indicate the beginning and ending of a bookmarked area. For instance, the entire heading *Patch Panel* is a bookmark:

¶

[Patch·panel]¶

Data·jacks·are·

►► **NOTE**

If you select text before setting a bookmark, you'll get something that looks like [...]. If you don't select text, though, you'll get something that looks like a big *I*.

As you can see, these markers can get in the way of the text, so you can turn them on and off in the View tab of the Options dialog box:

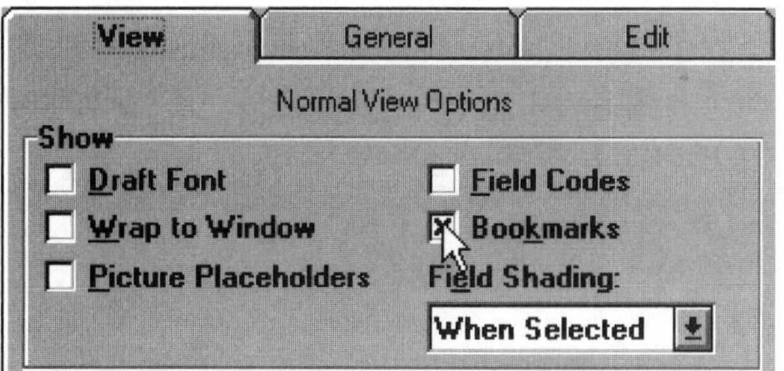

▶ Working with Bookmarked Items

It's often easiest to work with bookmarked items and see the effect of your work if you have the bookmark markers displayed.

If you move a bookmarked item, the mark moves with it, even to another document (as long as this won't create a duplicate bookmark name in the destination document).

Deleting the entire text or other items between two bookmark markers deletes the bookmark as well. (Say that five times fast.)

To add things and have them included with the bookmark, insert them within the bookmark marks. To insert things and not have them included, place the insertion point to the right of the bookmark marker.

You can use bookmark names in some field operations (described in Chapter 32), so it is even possible to perform computations and do other tricks with marked items.

▶ Deleting Bookmarks

To delete a mark but not the marked item(s), follow these steps:

1. Visit the Bookmark dialog box.
2. Choose the desired bookmark name.
3. Click the Delete key.
4. Click Close. The bookmark disappears and the previously marked items remain.

To delete a bookmark and the items it marks:

1. Turn on Bookmark markers in the View tab.
2. Select the item and both bookmark markers.
3. Delete as usual (Cut, press Delete, etc.). The mark and the items(s) will disappear.

►► Captions

If you write long documents with numbered figures, tables, and other elements, are you gonna love this new feature! It automatically numbers things, lets you label them, then renumbers them if you move them or otherwise change their sequence in a document. There are a variety of appearance options as well.

► Adding Captions

You can either manually caption the occasional item or turn on automatic captioning. To manually caption:

1. Select the item to be captioned.
2. Choose Insert ➤ Caption....
3. You'll see the Caption dialog box, illustrated in Figure 25.3.
4. Word proposes a caption label that you can accept as is or edit. For example, you can type descriptive text, as shown in Figure 25.3.
5. Change the default appearance options, if you wish, by visiting the Position List and Numbering dialog box.
6. Click OK to insert the label. Be patient, it takes a moment.

To automatically add captions to items of a particular type (all drawings, for instance), use the AutoCaption dialog box, reached with the AutoCaption... button in the Caption dialog box. The AutoCaption dialog box is illustrated in Figure 25.4.

FIGURE 25.3

Manually inserting a caption.

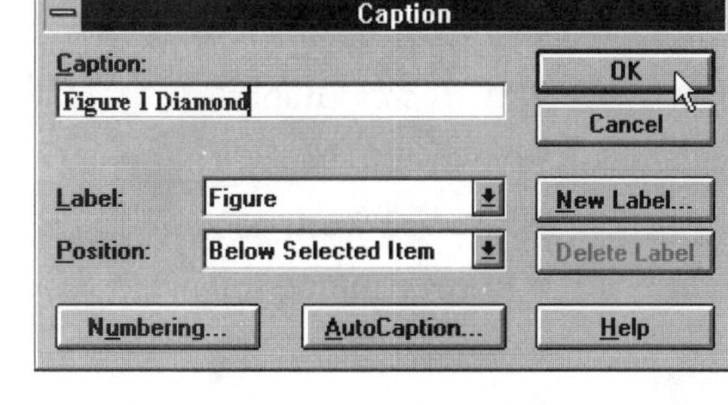

FIGURE 25.4

Autocaptioning.

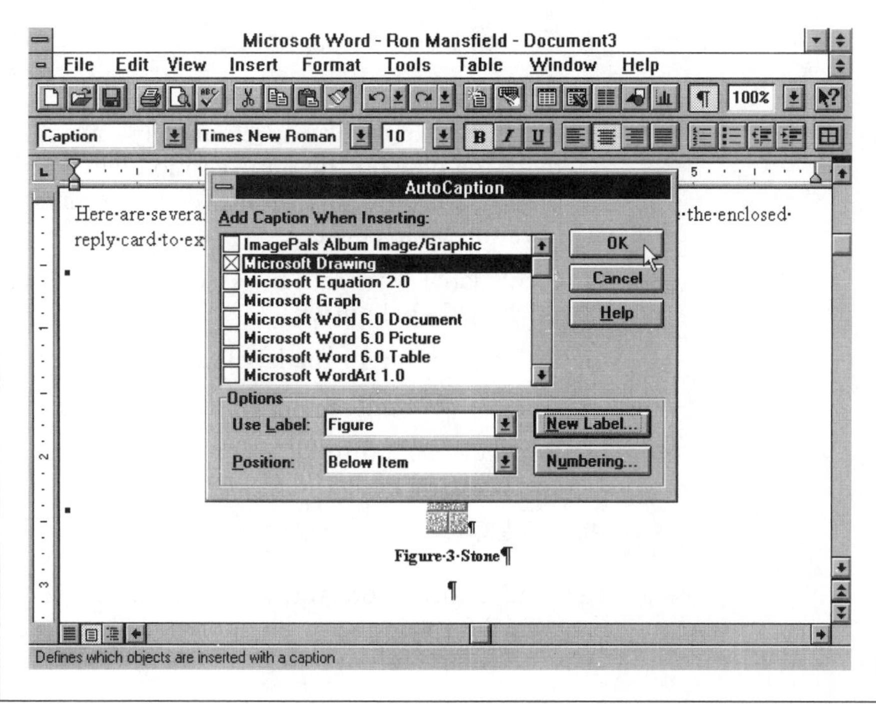

Word for Windows can recognize and automatically caption the following types of files:

- Most graphic files
- Microsoft drawings
- Microsoft equations
- Microsoft Graphs
- Microsoft WordArt
- Inserted Word documents
- Paintbrush pictures
- Sounds
- And much more

To automatically caption things, follow these steps:

1. Choose Insert ➤ Caption....
2. Click AutoCaption....
3. Pick a type of item to automatically caption. You can pick more than one type for the same caption label (for instance, you can pick Microsoft drawings and Word pictures). Inserting either will have the same effect.
4. Pick a label type from the Use Label list or create your own with the New Label button.
5. Pick a position for the label (above or below the item).
6. Change the numbering scheme if you like.
7. Repeat steps 3 through 6 for each different type of caption you want.
8. Click OK.

After you've turned on AutoCaption and defined the appearance options, Word for Windows will automatically label any insertion that meets the AutoCaption criteria.

If you move a figure and its label, Word for Windows will not immediately update the figure labels. But it *will* update figure numbers whenever you ask to print or switch to Print Preview. To force an immediate update, select all of your text (Ctrl+A) and press F9.

To revise a caption, just edit it like any other text. To change all of the captions of a given type (*Figure* to *FIG*, for instance), select a caption in text, visit the Caption or AutoCaption dialog box, and pick a different label from the Use Label List.

To create new label types (*FIG*, for example), use the New Label... button in the Caption and AutoCaption dialog boxes.

▶ Including Chapter and Other Numbers in Captions

You can include chapter and similar numbers in automatic captions if you like. Here are the general steps:

1. Format all of the Main headings (Chapters, for example) as Heading Style 1.
2. Choose Format ➤ Heading Numbering.... Make sure a numerical numbering style is in use (not Chapter One, for instance).
3. Visit either the Caption or AutoCaption dialog box.
4. Choose the Numbering button.
5. When you see the Caption Numbering dialog box, choose Include Chapter numbers.
6. Back out by clicking OK as needed.

▶▶ Cross-References

Cross-referencing lets you say things like *see Chapter 9 for details*, then have Word for Windows automatically update the reference if you change the chapter number. Cross-references are not limited to chapter numbers; they can refer to just about anything, including headings, footnotes, endnotes, captions, etc. You can cross-reference things in different documents, as long as they are in the same Master Document (see Chapter 24).

▸ Creating Cross-References

Here are the general steps for creating cross-references:

1. Begin by typing the in-text reference followed by a quotation mark (**See** ", for example).
2. Choose Insert ➤ Cross-reference.... You'll see the Cross-reference dialog box, illustrated in Figure 25.5.
3. Pick the Reference Type that will tie the in-text reference to the item you wish to reference. (Figure, for instance.)
4. Choose the item you wish to reference in the scrolling For Which list.
5. Click Insert. You'll see some new information at the insertion point. This is actually a field. (See Chapter 32 to learn more about fields.)
6. Click Close or make other cross-references first, then close.

Once you've created cross-references, they will be updated when you switch to Print Preview or print. To update immediately at any time, select the entire document and press F9.

If you delete an item that is referenced, Word will alert you.

FIGURE 25.5 ▸

The Cross-reference dialog box.

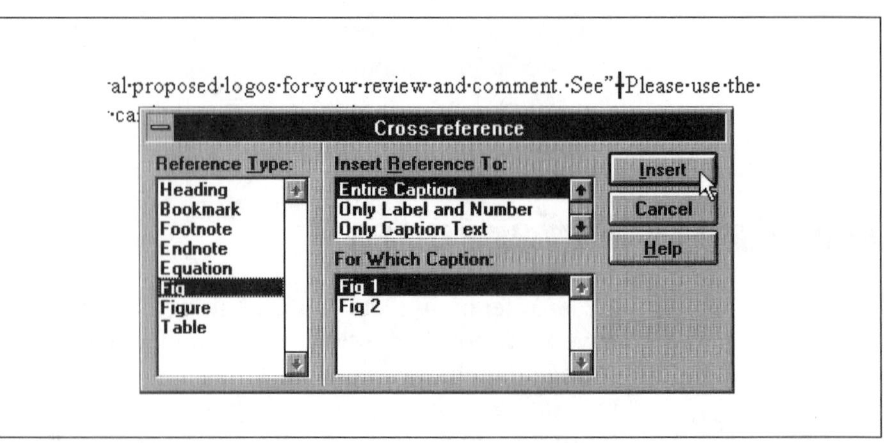

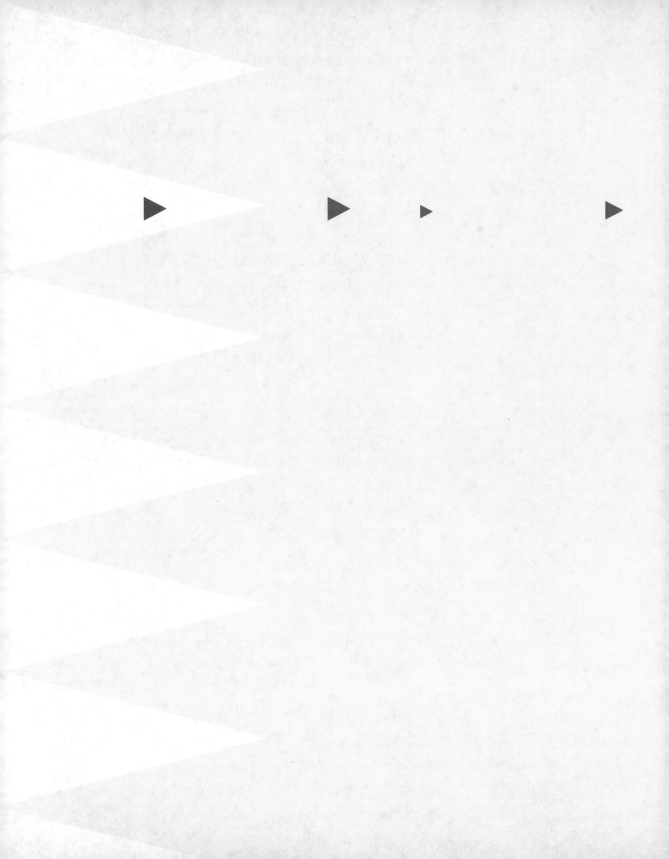

CHAPTER 26

Using Specialty Paper Stock

FAST TRACK

To select a standard paper size **632**

select File ➤ Page Setup and choose the Paper Size tab. Select a paper size from the Paper Size drop-down list box and click OK.

To change the orientation of your paper **633**

select File ➤ Page Setup and choose the Paper Size tab. Select Landscape (or Portrait) in the Orientation box and click OK.

To specify a paper source **635**

select File ➤ Page Setup and choose the Paper Source tab. Select a paper source in the First Page and Other Pages list boxes. If you want the whole document printed from the same source, select that source in both boxes. Then click OK.

To apply a paper size, orientation, or source to a section **636**

first create the section. Put the insertion point within the section. Select File ➤ Page Setup and choose the settings you want. Make sure This Section is selected in the Apply To drop-down list box and click OK.

To create a section break as you apply your new settings **636**

place the insertion point where you want the break to appear and then select File ➤ Page Setup and choose the settings you want. Select This Point Forward in the Apply To drop-down list box and click OK.

To create two section breaks before and after your new settings ***637***

first select the text you want to get the new settings. Then select File ➤ Page Setup and choose the settings you want. Make sure Selected Text is showing in the drop-down list box and click OK.

To change the normal paper size, orientation, or source ***639***

select File ➤ Page Setup and choose the settings you want. Then click the Default button. Click Yes on the dialog box that appears. Then click OK.

To create a custom paper size ***640***

select File ➤ Page Setup and choose the Paper Size tab. Enter the measurements of your special paper in the Height and Width boxes and then click OK.

To maintain several custom sizes ***641***

create each size in a different new document and save each document as a template.

►► *Special* documents often require special printing stock and unusual kinds of paper. If you lay out a three-fold brochure, you may decide that you'd rather print on thicker card stock instead of the usual paper. With the right kind of paper stock, you can print your own rolodex-style cards or produce odd-sized mailings.

Word doesn't offer too many built-in choices. They're all variations on standard letter, legal, or European page sizes, or typical envelopes. Fortunately, Word allows you to customize the paper-size settings, so you can just measure your paper stock and enter the correct dimensions manually.

Before we get into designing your paper size, let's first run through the basic procedures for choosing a different paper size (or orientation).

►► Selecting a Paper Size and Orientation

You choose your paper size and orientation setting from the Page Setup dialog box. To get there, select File ➤ Page Setup.

►► **TIP**

It's best to make your paper size and orientation selections, along with your other page-setup choices, before you start typing up your document. (It's easy to change these settings at any point, but why not get started with the correct dimensions?)

This brings up the Page Setup dialog box. Select the Paper Size tab (see Figure 26.1).

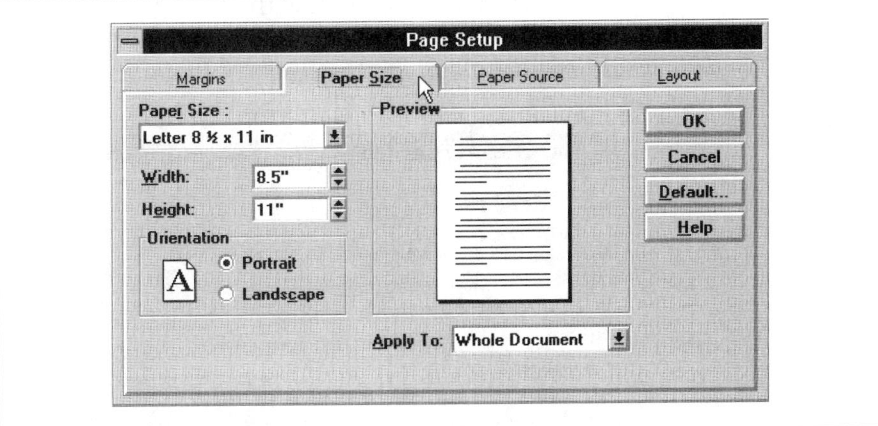

FIGURE 26.1 *The Page Setup dialog box with the Paper Size tab showing.*

The Paper Size box and the Width and Height boxes are interconnected. The Orientation setting also affects the Height and Width boxes. If you choose Letter $8^1/_2 \times 11$ in (the default choice), the Width will automatically set itself to 8.5" and the Height to 11" (as long as the Orientation is Portrait).

Choosing a Different Orientation

The Orientation indicates the way the paper is turned relative to the text on it. (Of course, the paper doesn't actually turn in a different direction in your printer—the printer turns the text instead.) Portrait is the usual vertical orientation of a letter page. Landscape is the alternative, wider than it is high.

If you click the Landscape radio button in the Orientation area, the Width and Height figures will do a switcheroo. The numbers stay the same, because the paper size has not changed, but they switch places.

Look also at the Preview area. It's more than a simple, static picture of a dummy page. It responds and changes to reflect the choices you make in the other boxes. When you click Landscape, the picture changes and the dummy text spreads out to fill the new shape.

Choosing a Different Paper Size

Choosing a built-in paper size is as simple as clicking the Paper Size drop-down list and choosing one of the options listed there. Try selecting Legal

$8\frac{1}{2} \times 14$ in and notice how the Preview changes. Then try selecting Envelope # 10 4 1/8 × 9 and look at the Preview. It looks kind of weird doesn't it? Click the Landscape button. Now that's better, isn't it?

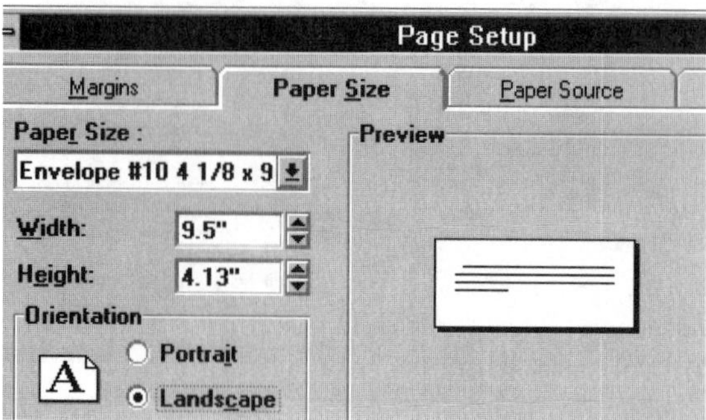

Now try selecting Custom Size in the Paper Size list box (it's the last choice). Look, nothing happens—whatever Height and Width went along with your last Paper Size choice are still there. Custom Size doesn't mean any specific Height and Width. It means you can specify the size you want.

Now try this: select the Letter Paper Size (and Portrait) again. Now change the Height and Width to anything different. Either type new measurements in the Height and Width boxes or click the tiny little arrow button to increase or decrease the measurements by .1" at a time:

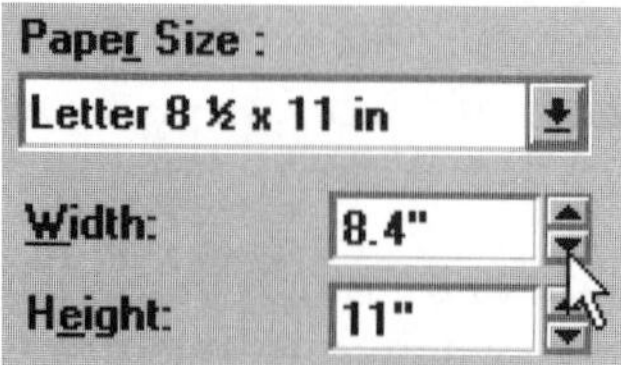

If you stick within .2" of the normal measurement for letter-size paper, then the Paper Size entry will stay the same. As soon as you change it any more than that, the Paper Size choice jumps to Custom Paper.

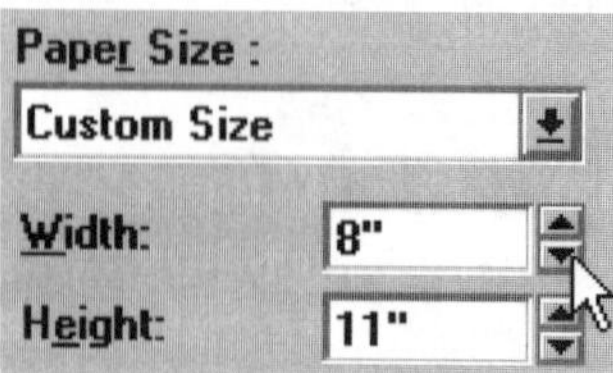

When you've chosen the Paper Size and Orientation that you want, click OK. Depending on the size or orientation you've chosen, the zoom percentage might change. You can change it back if you prefer.

▶ Specifying the Paper Source

If you're planning to print on a nonstandard paper stock, then you might want to select a different option for the paper source. By default, all the pages of your document will be printed from the default tray (usually the upper tray, if there's more than one) of your printer. To choose a different source, select File ➤ Page Setup and select the Paper Source tab (or just click the Paper Source tab if the Page Setup dialog box is already on the screen), as shown in Figure 26.2.

If the first page is going to be treated as different from the rest (printed on different paper, for example), then you can select a different option in the First Page list box. Otherwise, select the same options in both the First Page and the Other Pages list boxes.

The available options will vary depending on your printer. For a standard, HP Laserjet II-type printer, the options are:

- Default Tray (Upper Tray)
- Upper Tray
- Envelope Manual Feed

FIGURE 26.2 ▶

The Paper Source tab of the Page Setup dialog box. Specify a source for the first page and the rest of the document here.

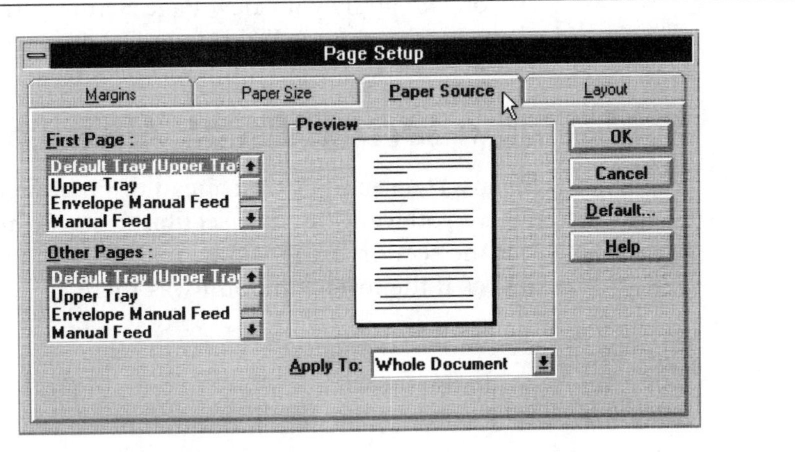

- Manual Feed
- Lower Tray
- Envelope

Select Upper Tray only if you have both a lower and upper tray, the lower tray is the default, and you want to use the upper tray. The two manual feed options are there so that you can feed in a different kind of stock (envelope or other) while keeping your normal paper in the default tray. Choose Envelope if you have a special envelope feeder.

▸▸ Applying a Different Paper Size to Part of a Document

If you need part of a document to be printed on a different type of paper or on paper fed from a different source, you can break your document into sections and then choose different Page Setup options for each section.

▸▸ NOTE

Sections are covered in Chapter 13.

There are two ways to do this. You can create your section breaks first, or you can apply your new Page Setup settings to just part of your document and force Word to create section breaks for you.

▸ Making a Section Break Ahead of Time

To insert a section break ahead of time, first place the insertion point where you want the new section to start. (You can make a selection, but the section break will be inserted at the beginning of the selection just as if the insertion point was there.)

Then select Insert ➤ Break. This brings up the Break dialog box:

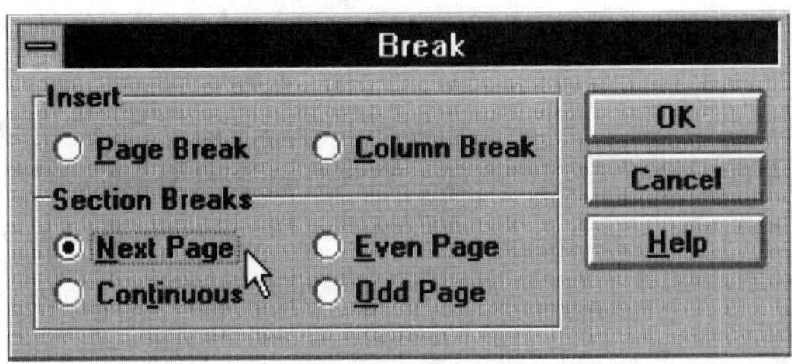

Select Next Page in the Section Breaks area and then click OK. If you're going to want another section break, either to go back to the original settings or, to apply a third set of Page Setup options, move the insertion point to the next breaking place and repeat this process.

▶▶ **TIP**

If you want one section in the middle of a document to get a different page setup and the rest to stay the same, use the method described in Applying New Page Setup Settings to a Selection, coming up.

Now put the insertion point in the section you want to change (if you've just added a single section break, then it should already be in the right place) and follow the instructions in Selecting a Paper Size and Orientation (a previous section of this chapter).

▶ *Applying New Page Setup Settings from "This Point Forward"*

If you know that you'll want different Page Setup settings to apply from a certain point through the end of a document (or up to the point where you next make some changes), then you don't need to make your section break first.

Instead, just put the insertion point where you want your new settings to take hold. Then select File ➤ Page Setup. This brings up the Page Setup dialog box shown in Figures 26.1 and 26.2. Choose the settings that you want in whatever tabs you want and then select This Point Forward in the Apply To drop-down list box. Then click OK. Word inserts a section break where the insertion point was and applies your settings in the new section.

▸▸ **NOTE**

If you select This Point Forward in any tab of the Page Setup dialog box, your selections in all the other tabs will also be applied from this point forward when you click OK. However, if you want to apply one setting to the entire document and settings from another tab just from this point on, select File ➤ Setup and choose your universal settings, making sure to apply them to the Whole Document, and click OK. Then select File ➤ Setup again and choose your local settings, making sure to apply them from This Point Forward.

▸ Applying New Page Setup Settings to a Selection

If you know for sure that you want your special Page Setup settings to apply to a limited portion of your document, then you don't need to make the section break first. Instead, just select the text that will constitute your new section and then select File ➤ Page Setup. This brings up the Page Setup dialog box shown in Figures 26.1 and 26.2. Choose the settings that you want in whatever tabs you want and make sure Selected Text is showing in the Apply To drop-down list box. Then click OK. Word inserts a section break before and after your selection, applying your settings to the section in between while keeping the old settings in sections before and after the new breaks.

▶▶ NOTE

If you select Selected Text in any tab of the Page Setup dialog box, your selections in all the other tabs will also be applied to the selection when you click OK. However, if you want to apply one setting to the entire document and settings from another tab just to selected text, select File ➤ Setup and choose your universal settings, making sure to apply them to the Whole Document, and click OK. Then select File ➤ Setup again and choose your local settings, making sure to apply them to Selected Text.

▶ What Happens When You Delete Section Breaks?

If you delete a section break, then the settings for the following section get applied to the preceding section. This is because the Page Setup settings are stored in the section break character. If you delete that character, the sections before and after the break are joined into one, and the settings for the latter apply.

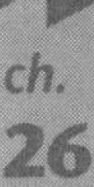

▶▶ Changing the Normal Paper Size or Orientation

If, for whatever reason, you plan to use a different paper size or orientation most of the time, you can make those settings the default so that all new documents (at least all new ones based on the NORMAL.DOT template) will have that paper size and orientation.

To do this, select File ➤ Page Setup and choose the settings that you want to be the default (in whichever tabs you want). Then click the Default button, on the right.

This will bring up the following dialog box:

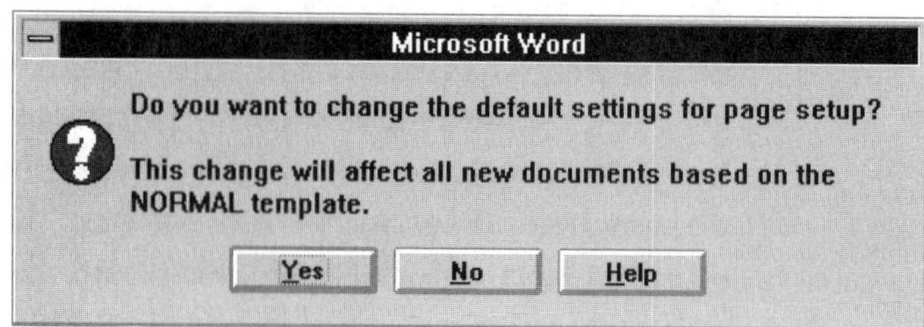

Click Yes if you're sure, No to change your mind, or Help to get more information.

▸▸ **NOTE**

All you've really done if you click the Default button is saved your Page Setup settings in the NORMAL.DOT template. You could achieve the same effect by opening NORMAL.DOT, selecting File ➤ Page Setup there, choosing your settings, clicking OK, and then saving the changes. The Default button is just a shortcut.

▸▸ Creating Custom Paper Sizes

If none of the built-in paper sizes are appropriate for your desktop publishing project (such as if you plan to use any kind of nonstandard size), then you'll just have to roll up your sleeves and create a custom size. It's actually remarkably easy.

First of all, measure the paper stock you'll be using. (Perhaps the measurement is given on the packaging, but it never hurts to measure it for yourself.) Jot down the height (the long dimension) and the width.

Then select File ➤ Setup and click the Paper Size tab (see Figure 26.1). Select Custom Size in the Paper Size box or just go ahead and change the Height and Width settings. You can enter your measurements directly or click the little arrow buttons to inch (actually tenth of an inch) your way to the correct dimensions. It's usually easier just to type them in. The

Preview will adjust as you change the measurements, and it's a good idea to eyeball it and make sure that it looks proportional to the paper you're using (just to avoid gross errors).

Click OK, and you're done. See the previous sections for how to choose a different paper source, apply your custom size to just part of a document, or make your new size the default.

►► TIP

For rotary card (Rolodex-style) stock or other specialty paper sizes with more than one unit to the page, you'll find it easier to pretend you're making custom mailing labels. You still have to measure your basic unit size. Mailing Labels are explained in Chapter 15, but here's the quick-and-dirty run-through: Select Tools ➤ Envelopes and Labels, click the Labels tab, and click the Options button. Select Custom Laser in the Product Number box and then click the Details button. Enter the measurements for your paper stock and then click OK, OK, and Print.

►► Maintaining Several Different Custom Paper Sizes

The Page Setup dialog box will only allow you to establish one kind of Custom Size (per section), so if you want to have more than one preset Custom Size available, you'll have to create a different template for each one. Just start a new document, select File ➤ Page Setup, and choose the settings you want. Then select File ➤ Save to save the document. In the Save As dialog box, choose Document Template in the Save File as Type drop-down list box. Give the template a name and click OK.

Then, when you want to use that kind of paper stock, just create a new document based on the template you saved. You can create as many templates as you need.

CHAPTER 27

The Document Shop

▸▸ FAST TRACK

To make an award 647

use the built-in Award Wizard, found in the New dialog box.

To make a three-fold brochure 653

use Word's Brochur1 template, found in the New dialog box.

To make a calendar 656

use the built-in Calendar Wizard, found in the New dialog box.

To make a fax cover sheet 659

use the built-in Fax Cover Sheet Wizard and the two templates that the Wizard uses, found in the New dialog box.

To make an invoice 662

customize and use the invoice template that Word provides, found in the New dialog box.

To make a letter 666

use the built-in Letter Wizard and the three templates that the Wizard uses, found in the New dialog box.

To make a memo 671

use the built-in Memo Wizard and the three memo templates that the Wizard uses, found in the New dialog box.

To make a newsletter 675

use the built-in Newsletter Wizard, found in the New dialog box.

▶▶ **This** chapter includes some quick and easy instructions for constructing useful documents in minutes. Some of the "recipes" use Word's built-in templates and wizards; other templates you'll make from scratch.

For each one, just follow the instructions step by step. Of course, you'll need to personalize the recipes with your own particular information, but that's the easy part.

The ready-made documents in this chapter include:

- Award
- Three-Fold Brochure
- Calendar
- Fax cover sheet
- Invoice
- Letter
- Memo
- Newsletter
- Organizational chart
- Phone list
- Press release
- Purchase order
- Resume
- Time sheet

Here Goes.

▶▶ Award

Word provides a built-in Award Wizard. Here's how to create an award with it:

Select File ➤ New (but don't click the New Document button). This will bring up the New dialog box (see Figure 27.1).

FIGURE 27.1 ▶

The New dialog box. Select the Award Wizard template here to create an award.

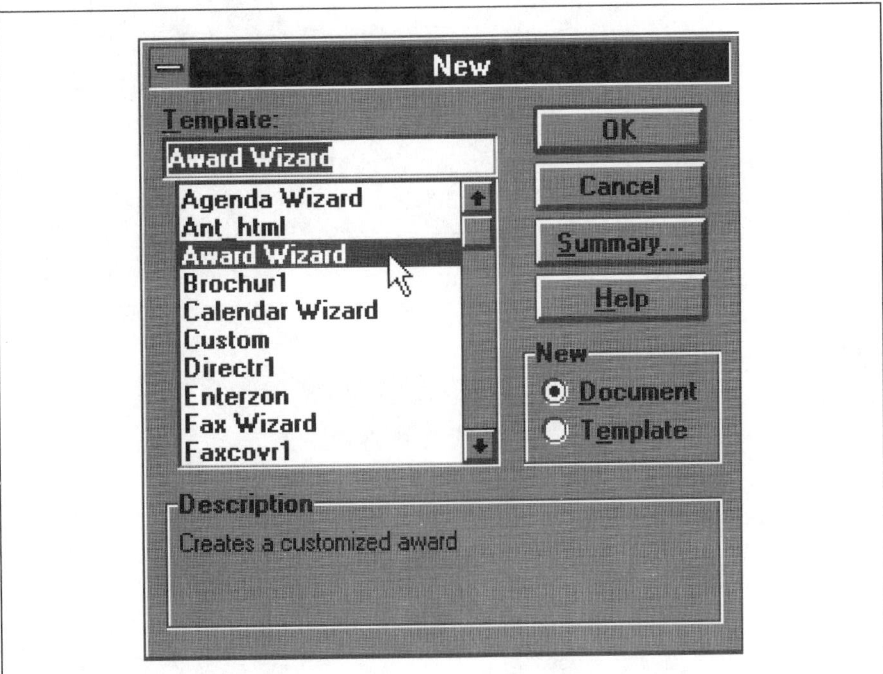

2. Select Award Wizard.
3. Click OK. This opens a new document based on the Award Wizard template. The Wizard displays a dialog box (see Figure 27.2).
4. Select one of the four different styles for your award. To preview the different styles, click on them one after another and wait for the sample to update itself.
5. When you've chosen the style you want, Click the Next> button. The dialog box changes to ask you some more questions (see Figure 27.3).

FIGURE 27.2 ►

The Award Wizard dialog box. Select the type of award you want to make.

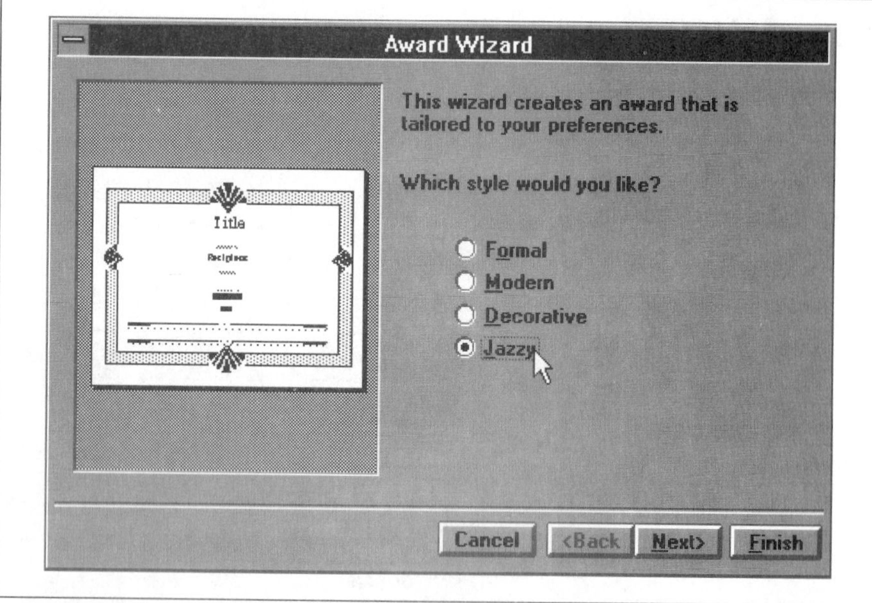

FIGURE 27.3 ►

Decide if you want the award to have Portrait orientation (higher than it is wide) or Landscape, the default.

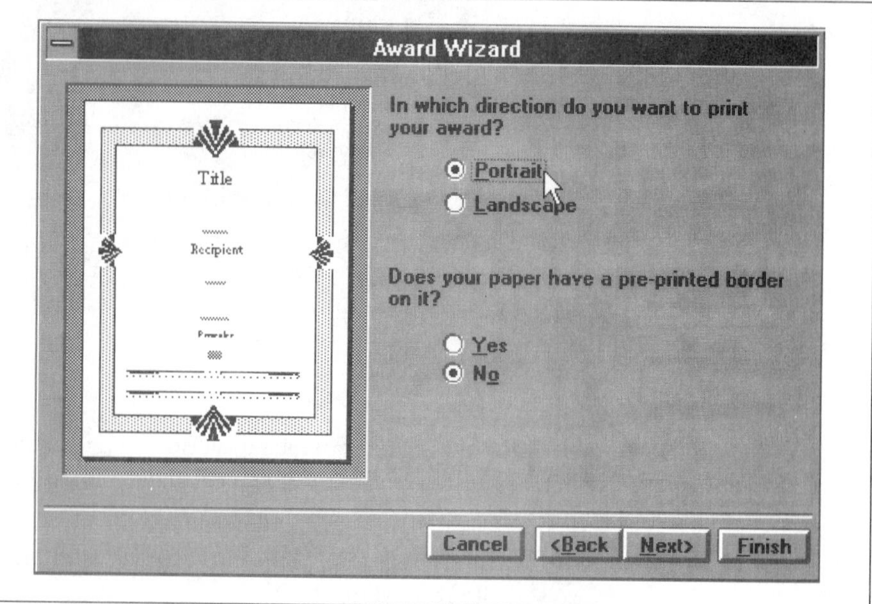

6. Select Portrait if you want that sort of orientation or leave the first question's answer as Landscape if you prefer.

7. Click Yes to the second question if you have special bordered paper to print your award on. (If you do, you'll still want to do a test print on normal paper to see if the layout fits.)
8. Click the Next> button. The dialog box changes again (see Figure 27.4).

FIGURE 27.4

Enter a name and a title.

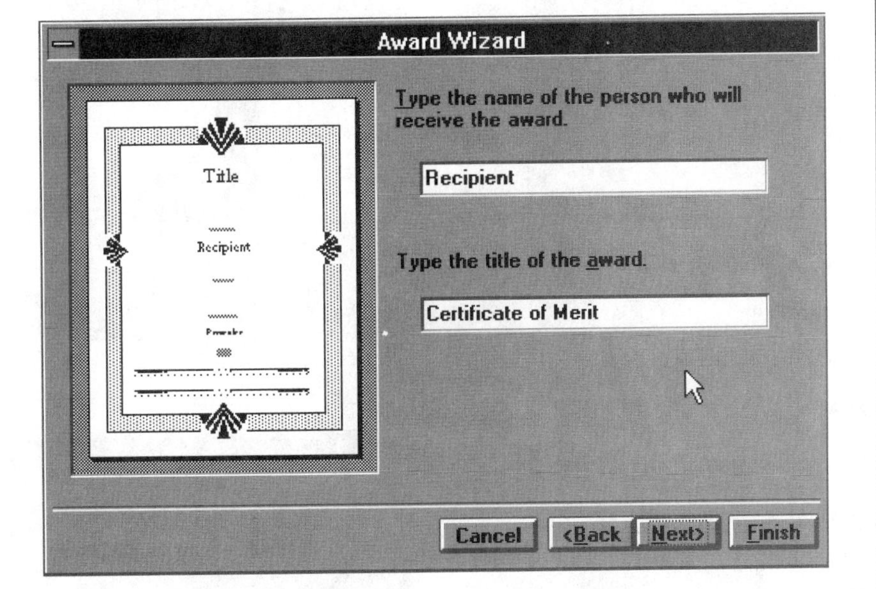

9. Type the name of the recipient in the first text box and the title of the award in the second.
10. Click the Next> button (see Figure 27.5).
11. If you want your name to be first among the presenters of the award, click the Add button. Otherwise, type a different name and then click the Add button. Repeat as often as necessary. If you add a name by mistake, highlight the wrong name and click the Remove button.
12. Click the Next> button (see Figure 27.6).
13. If you want to enter a name for the presenting organization, click Presented by and then type an organization name in the text box.
14. Click the Next> button (see Figure 27.7).

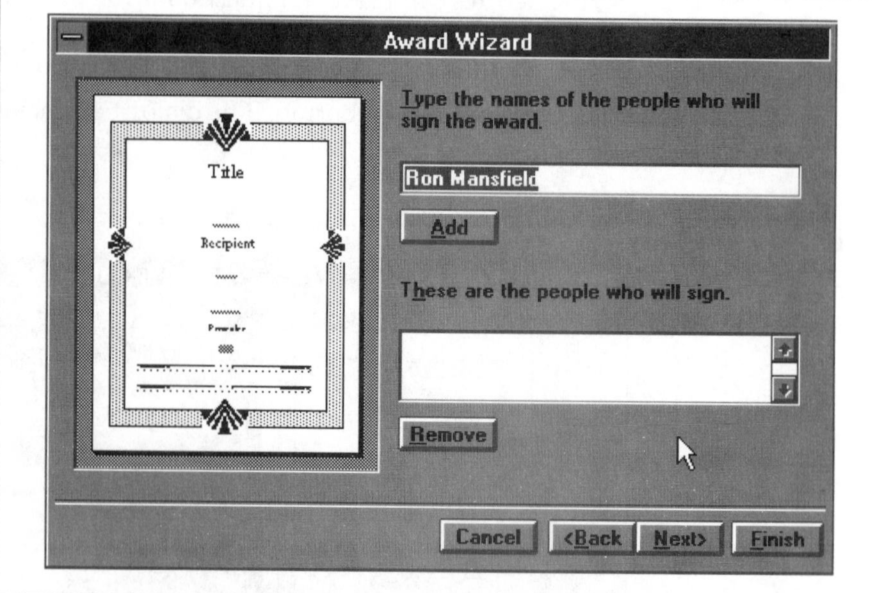

FIGURE 27.5

Add signature lines to the award.

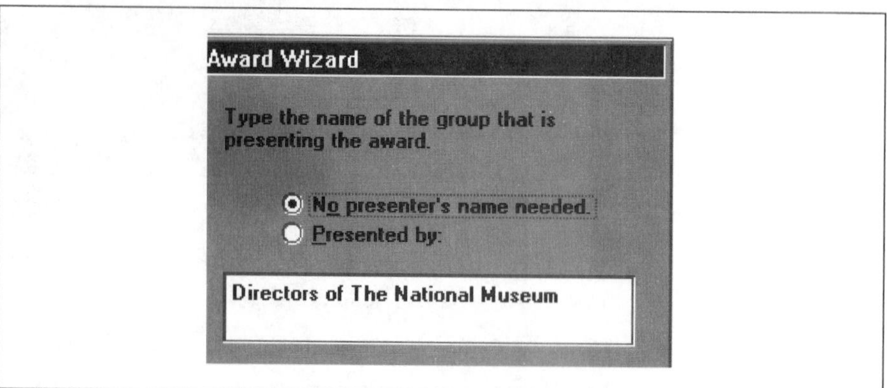

FIGURE 27.6

Enter a presenting organization if you want.

15. Type the date of the award in the first text box (or accept today's date, the default, if that's appropriate).
16. If you want additional text on the award, type it in the second box. If you want none, delete the dummy text suggested by the Wizard. (If, by some amazing coincidence, "For extraordinary work" is exactly what you would have added yourself, then just leave it.)

FIGURE 27.7

Type a date and any additional text you might want.

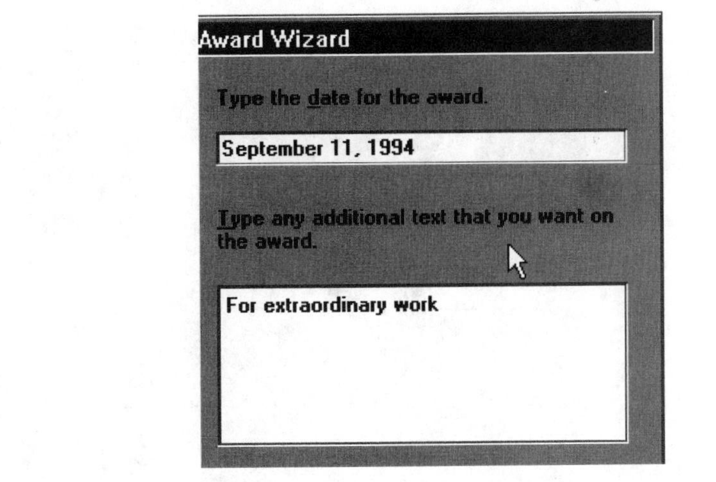

17. Click the Next> button. Your hard work is done! The Wizard lets you know you're finished (see Figure 27.8).
18. If you want the Wizard to display Help on the screen after creating your award, click Yes, display Help as I work.
19. Click Finish. The Wizard creates your award (see Figure 27.9).
20. Click the Print button to print the award:

TIP

If you *do* have bordered paper of your own, print the award on plain paper first and then hold the sample up to the light with the bordered paper as an overlay. If the text does not fit the border properly, play around with the margins of the award document and print it out again. Repeat until it fits and *then* print the award on your special paper.

FIGURE 27.8

The Wizard tells you you're done and offers continued help.

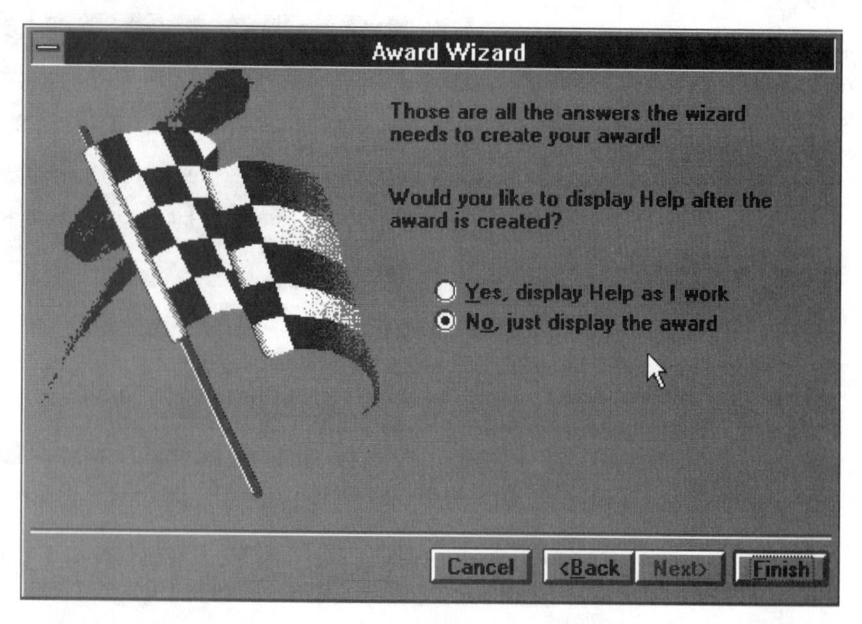

FIGURE 27.9

My finished award, ready for printing.

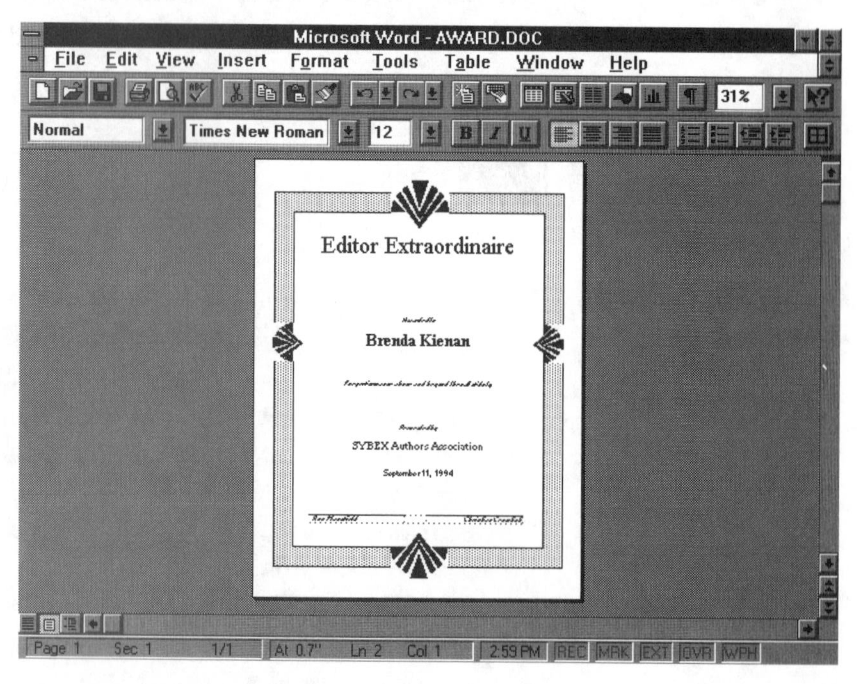

▸▸ Three-Fold Brochure

Before starting to make your three-fold brochure in Word, you should first plan it out on scratch paper. There are six panels to a three-fold brochure, three per side of the paper stock. One the outside, there's the inner flap, the back, and the outer flap. There are also three panels on the inside (see Figure 27.10).

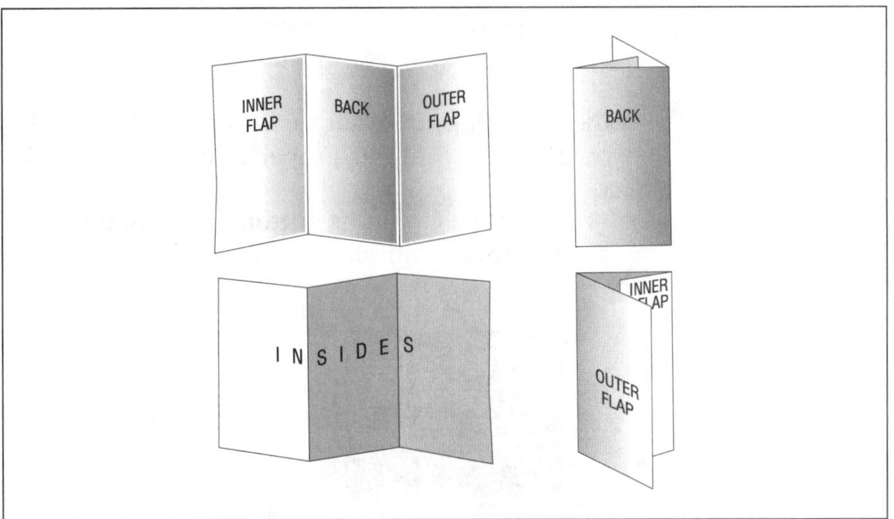

FIGURE 27.10

Before trying to create your brochure with Word, first plan it out on paper. Think about what's going to be on each side.

Then use Word's Brochur1 template to actually create the three-fold brochure:

1. Select File ➤ New (but don't click the New Document button or press Ctrl+N). This will bring up the New dialog box (see Figure 27.1).
2. Select Brochur1.
3. Click OK. This opens a new document based on the Brochur1 template.

You won't notice much at first, although if you switch to Page Layout View (View ➤ Page Layout, naturally), you'll see that the page has a landscape orientation. The main thing this template provides is a set of preset styles and some style gallery settings.

TIP

To get some ideas of how to lay out a three-fold brochure, select Format ➤ Style Gallery, click the Brochur1 in the Template box, and then click the Example radio button in the Preview box. This will show you a sample brochure that uses the built-in styles from this template. (After you enter your text, you can try out the Preview in this dialog box with your actual content.)

The first thing you want to do is set up three columns, which will help you place the contents properly on the three folds of the brochure.

1. Click the Columns button on the Standard Toolbar and drag to select three columns:

2. Click the Zoom box on the Standard Toolbar and type in 100 to zoom in (now that you're only dealing with one column at a time).
3. Now enter the text for the inner first-page flap. Try out the different preset styles that Word provides to see if any suit your needs.

▶▶ **TIP**

If what you type for the inner flap spills past the first column and runs into the second, play around with the font size and line spacing to make it fit.

From time to time, switch to Page Layout View to see how your contents are fitting on the page as a whole. If your text ends too high on the panel, go back to the top and press Enter a few times to move it down.

4. When you have completed the text for the inner first-page flap, press Ctrl+Shift+Enter to insert a column break.
5. Enter the text for the back first page of the brochure.
6. Press Ctrl+Shift+Enter when you are done.
7. Enter the text for the outer first-page flap. Figure 27.11 shows a Page Layout View of three panels of a brochure.

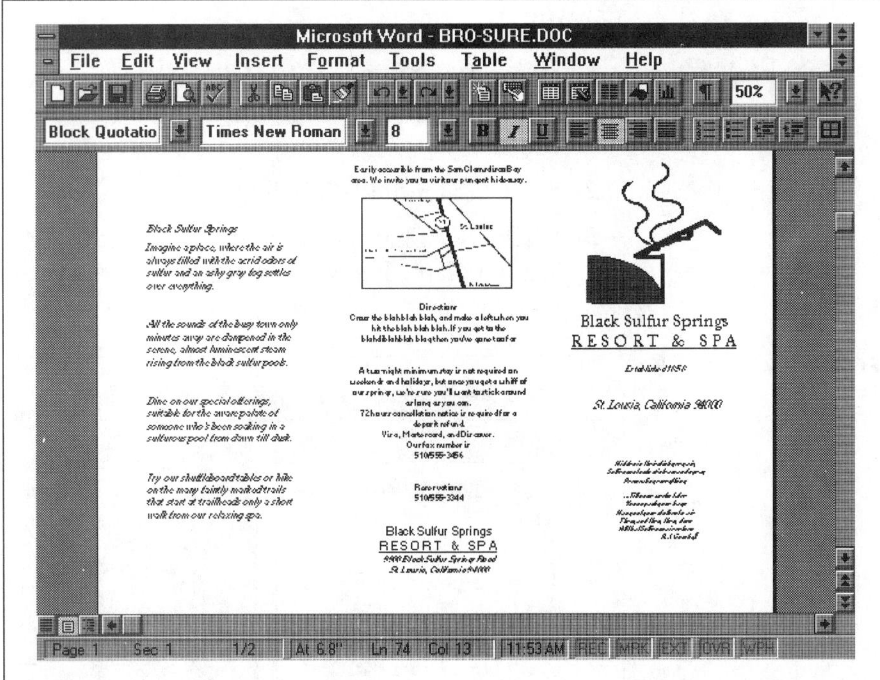

FIGURE 27.11

This brochure uses a combination of built-in styles and some custom formatting, along with a scanned map for the back and some Microsoft Draw art for the outer flap.

8. Now press Ctrl+Shift+Enter again, this time to go to the second page.
9. Enter the text for the first second-page panel and press Ctrl+Shift+Enter when you are done.
10. Enter the text for the middle second-page panel and press Ctrl+Shift+Enter when you are done.
11. Enter the text for the last second-page panel.
12. Save your brochure.

There you have it. You should print the two pages and then take them to a copy shop or service bureau to produce the actual brochures on card paper, fold them, and have them stapled if necessary.

▸▸ Calendar

Word provides a built-in Calendar Wizard. Here's how to create a calendar with it:

1. Select File ➤ New (but don't click the New Document button or press Ctrl+N). This will bring up the New dialog box (see Figure 27.1).
2. Select Calendar Wizard.
3. Click OK. This opens a new document based on the Calendar Wizard template. The Wizard displays a dialog box (see Figure 27.12).

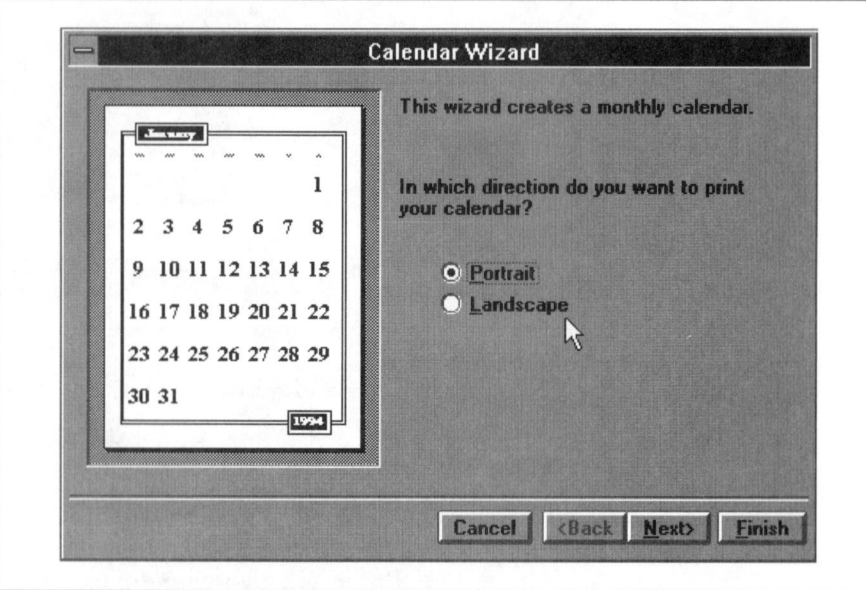

FIGURE 27.12

The Calendar Wizard dialog box. Use the default Portrait (higher than wide) layout or select Landscape.

4. Select Landscape if you want that sort of orientation or leave the first question's answer as Portrait if you prefer.

5. Click the Next> button. The dialog box changes again (see Figure 27.13).
6. Select a style from the three choices. The preview will show you what they look like.
7. Click the Next> button (see Figure 27.14).

FIGURE 27.13

Choose a style.

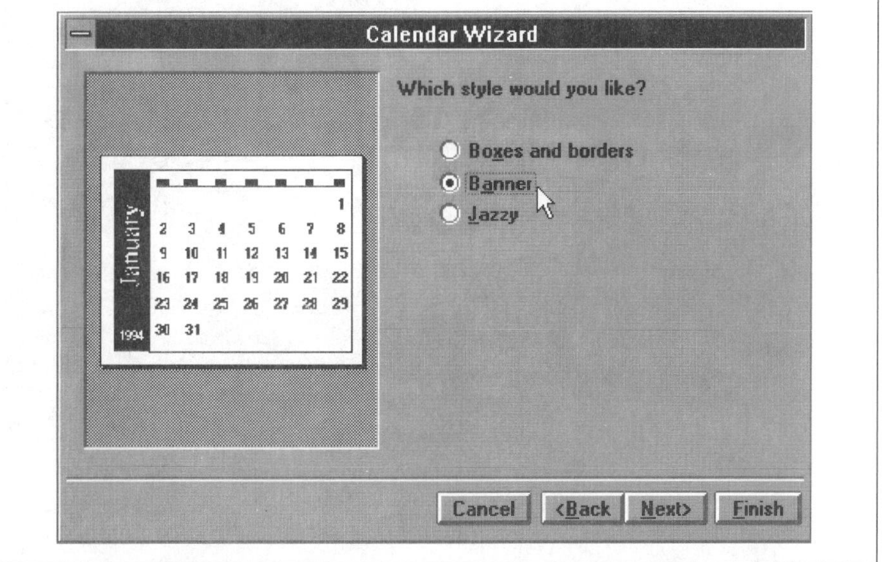

FIGURE 27.14

Decide if you want to personalize your calendar with a picture.

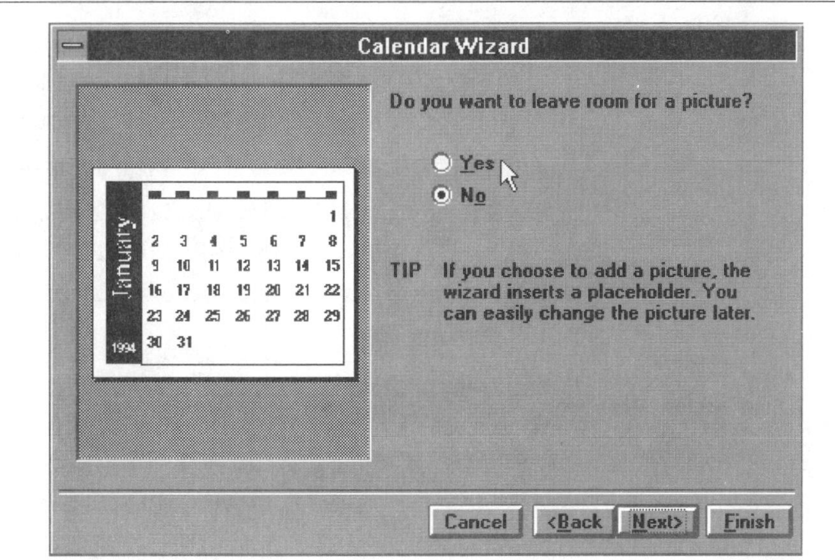

8. If you want to add a picture to your calendar, click Yes.
9. Click the Next> button (see Figure 27.15).

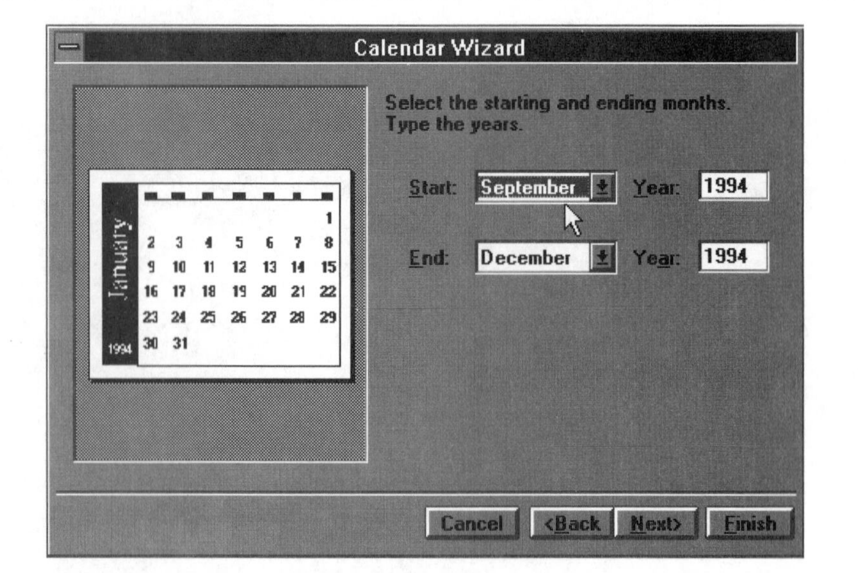

FIGURE 27.15

Choose a starting and ending month and year for your calendar (or enter the same month in both places to print just one).

10. Select a Starting month for your calendar from the drop-down list.
11. Enter a year (or accept the current year).
12. Select an Ending month (use the same month as the Starting month to print just that month).
13. Enter an ending year (or leave it as the current year).
14. Click the Next> button. The Wizard lets you know you're finished.
15. If you want the Wizard to display Help on the screen after creating your calendar, click Yes, display Help as I work.
16. Click Finish. The Wizard creates your calendar (see Figure 27.16).

FIGURE 27.16

The first month of my finished calendar, ready for printing.

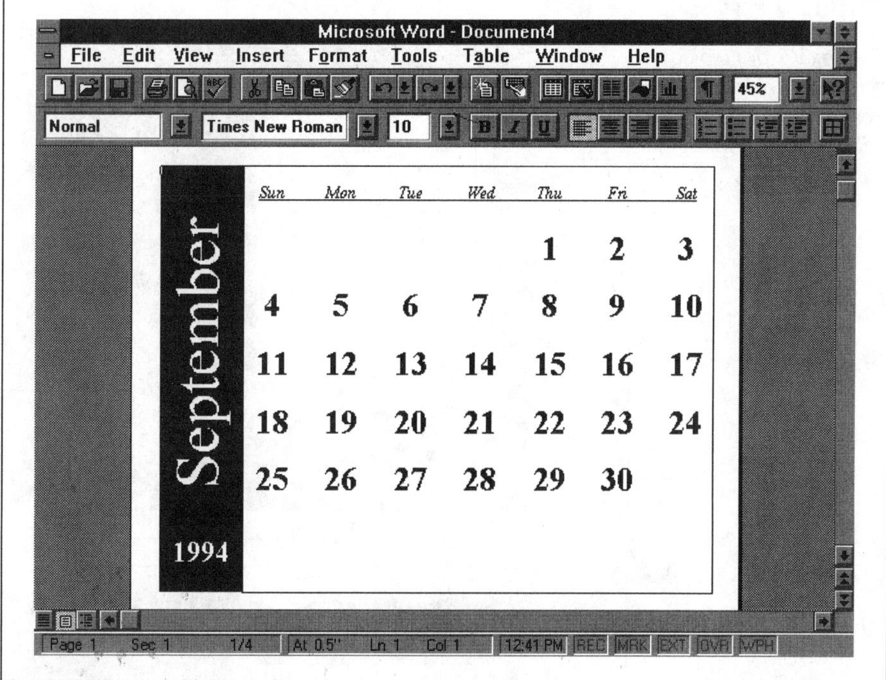

►► Fax Cover Sheet

Word provides a built-in Fax Cover Sheet Wizard and two templates that the Wizard uses. Here's how to create a fax cover sheet with the Wizard:

1. Select File ➤ New (but don't click the New Document button or press Ctrl+N). This will bring up the New dialog box.
2. Select Fax Wizard.
3. Click OK. This opens a new document based on the Fax Wizard template. The Wizard displays a dialog box (see Figure 27.17).
4. Select Landscape if you want that sort of orientation or leave the first question's answer as Portrait if you prefer.
5. Click the Next> button. The dialog box changes again (see Figure 27.18).

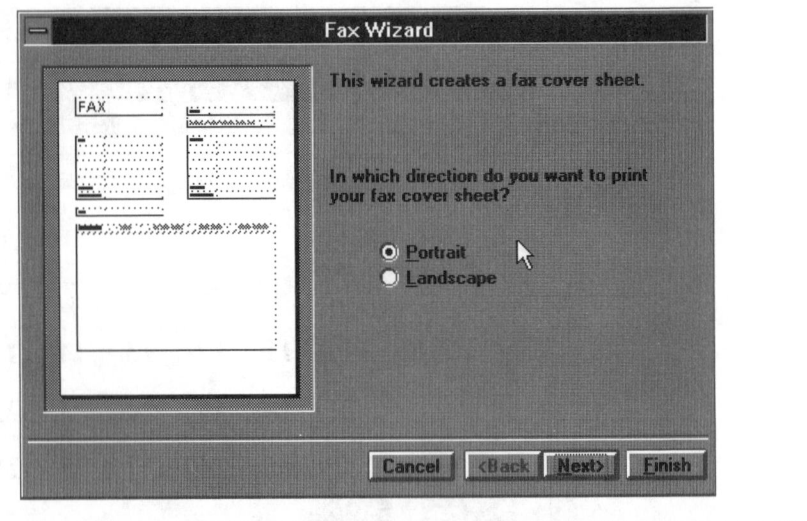

FIGURE 27.17

The Fax Wizard dialog box. Use the default Portrait (higher than wide) layout or select Landscape.

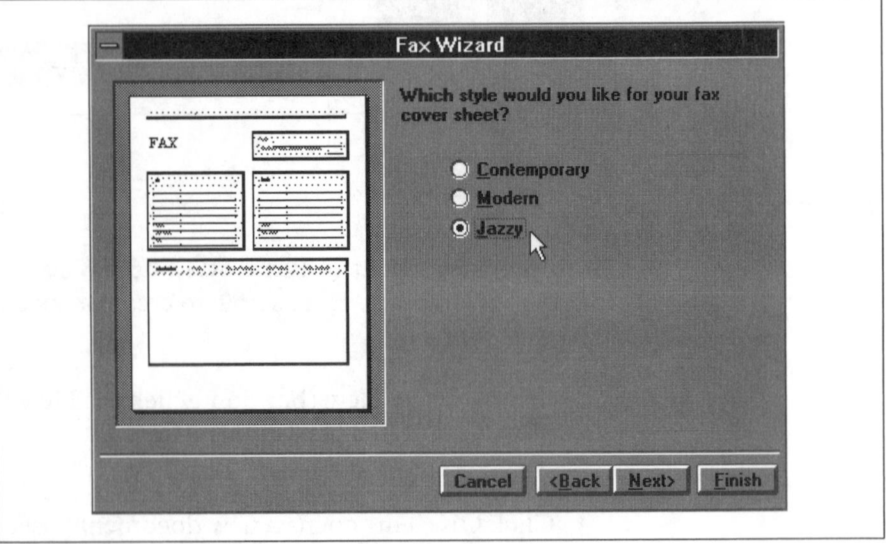

FIGURE 27.18

Choose a style.

6. Select a style from the three choices. The preview will show you what they look like.
7. Click the Next> button (see Figure 27.19).

FIGURE 27.19

Enter a name, company name, and address, if you like.

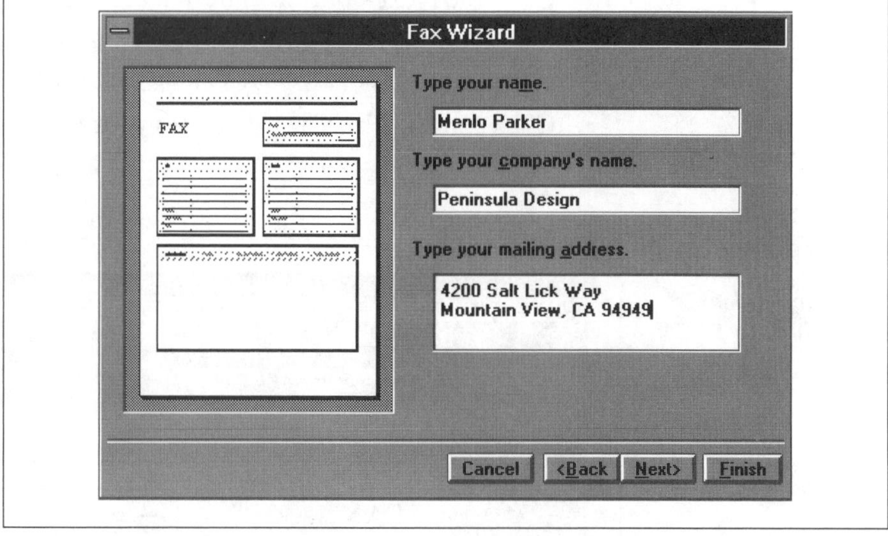

8. Enter your name, your company's name, and its address, if you want to include that information.
9. Click the Next> button (see Figure 27.20).

FIGURE 27.20

Enter your voice and fax phone numbers.

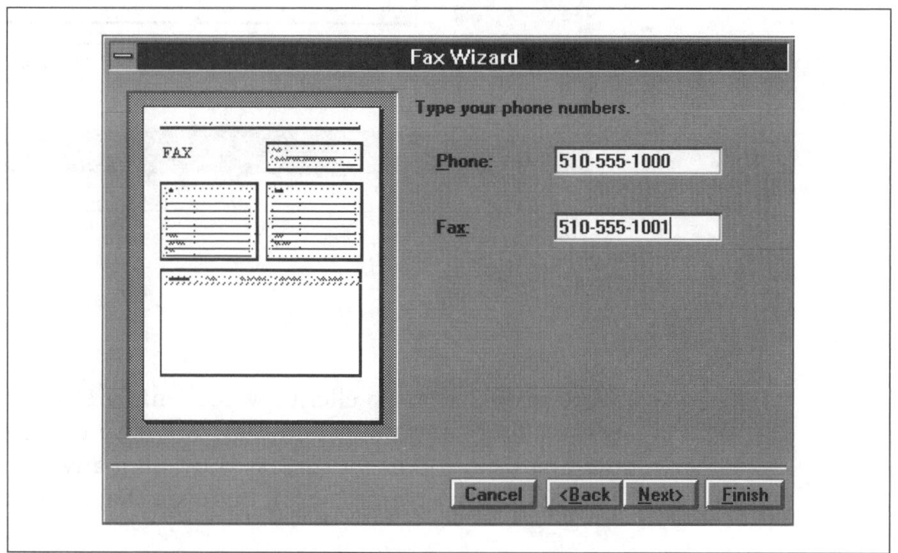

10. Enter your voice phone number and your fax phone number.

11. Click the Next> button. The Wizard lets you know you're finished.
12. If you want the Wizard to display Help on the screen after creating your fax cover sheet, click Yes, display Help as I work.
13. Click Finish. The Wizard creates your fax cover sheet (see Figure 27.21).

FIGURE 27.21 ►

The completed fax cover sheet.

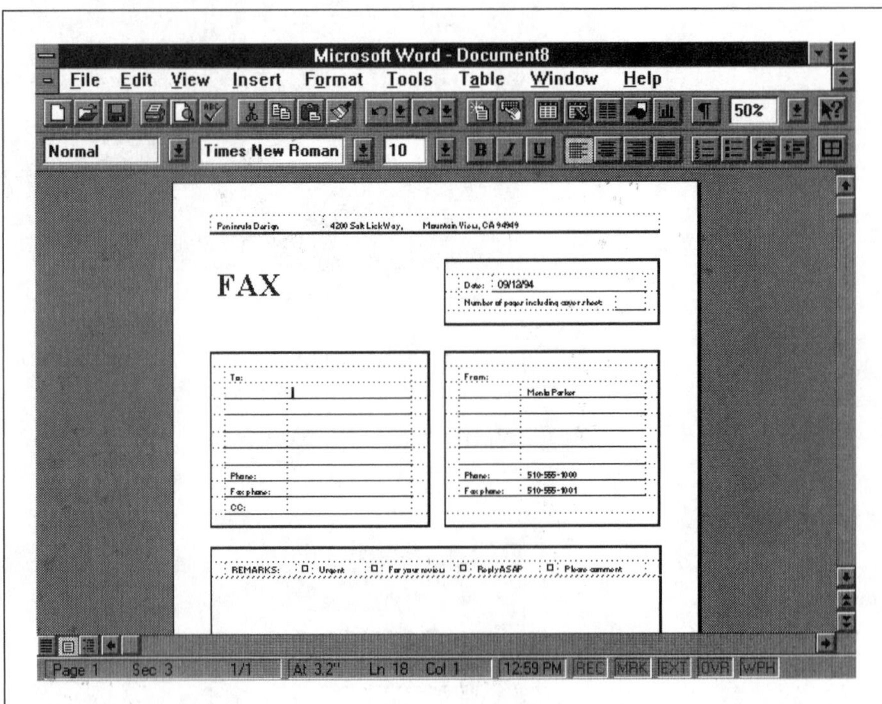

►► Invoice

Word provides an excellent invoice template that uses form fields to make filling it out quick and easy. You have to customize the template the first time you use it (unless your company happens to be called Your Company Name Here), but even that's not too rough.

1. Select File ➤ New (but don't click the New Document button or press Ctrl+N). This brings up the New dialog box (see Figure 27.22).

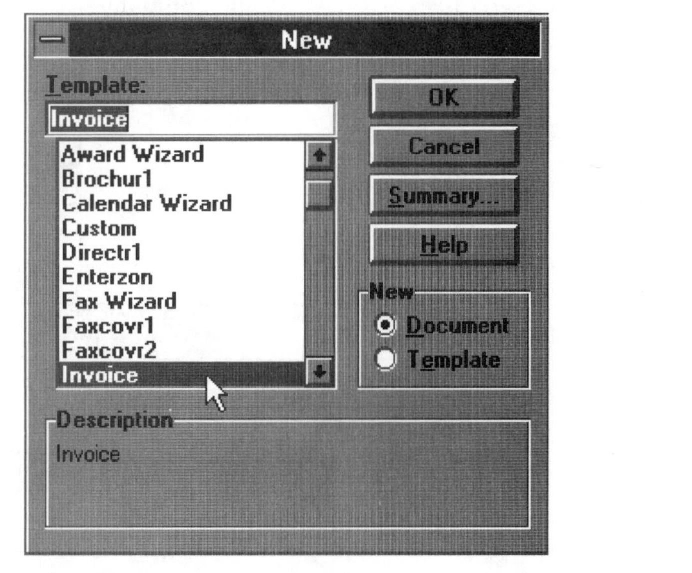

FIGURE 27.22

The New dialog box. Select the Invoice template and click OK.

2. Select the Invoice template as shown in Figure 27.22 and click OK. This starts a new document based on the Invoice template.
3. The document is a protected form, so to change it, you need to unprotect it. Select Tools ➤ Unprotect Document..., as shown in Figure 27.23.
4. Replace the dummy text (Your Company Name Here, etc.) with your own information (see Figure 27.24).
5. Also personalize the information at the bottom of the invoice (see Figure 27.25).

FIGURE 27.23

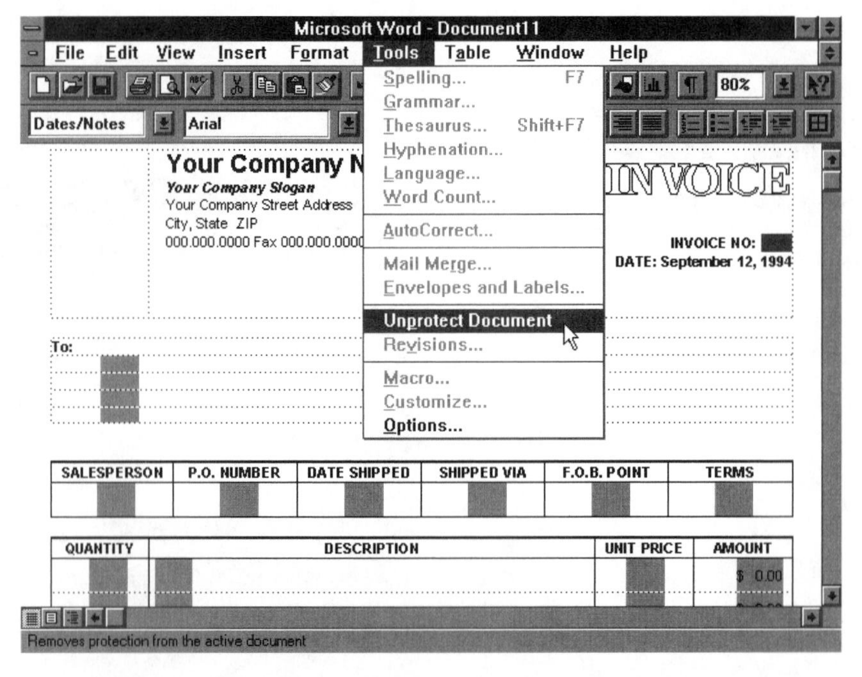

Select Tools ➤ Unprotect Document so you can customize the Invoice template.

FIGURE 27.24

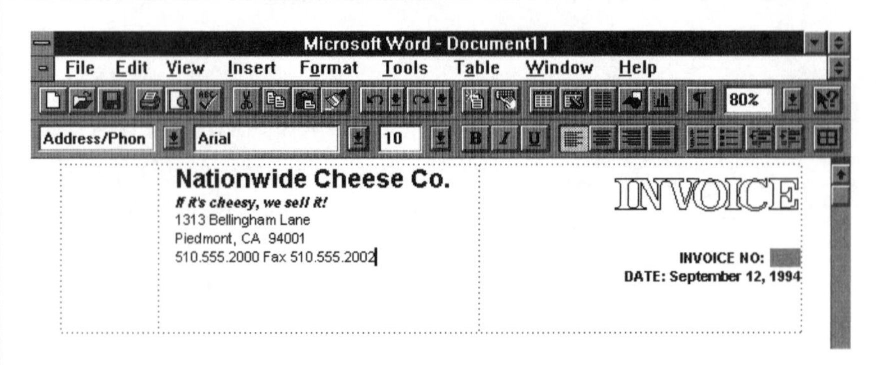

Type your own information in the company name, slogan, address, and phone number areas.

FIGURE 27.25

Make all checks payable to: Nationwide Cheeses
If you have any questions concerning this invoice, call: I. B. Cheezey, 510-555-2002

THANK YOU FOR YOUR BUSINESS!

Page 1 Sec 1 1/1 At Ln Col 1:46 PM REC MRK EXT OVR WPH

Enter your company name and the name of a contact at the bottom of the invoice.

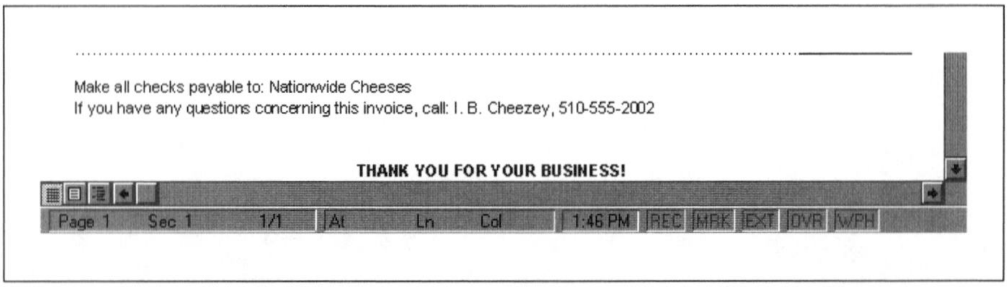

▶▶ TIP

Currently, the sales tax field near the bottom of the invoice is a straight text field for which you must calculate the sales tax separately and type it in. You can make it calculate the tax automatically if you want. Click the right mouse button over the field and select Form Field Options. Then select Calculation in the Type drop-down list box and enter E8*(*t*) after the = sign in the Expression box, substituting your local sales tax rate for *t*. Then click OK.

6. Reprotect the document by selecting Tools ➤ Protect Document… (see Figure 27.26).

FIGURE 27.26 ▶

Select Tools ➤ Protect Document to prepare the template for data entry.

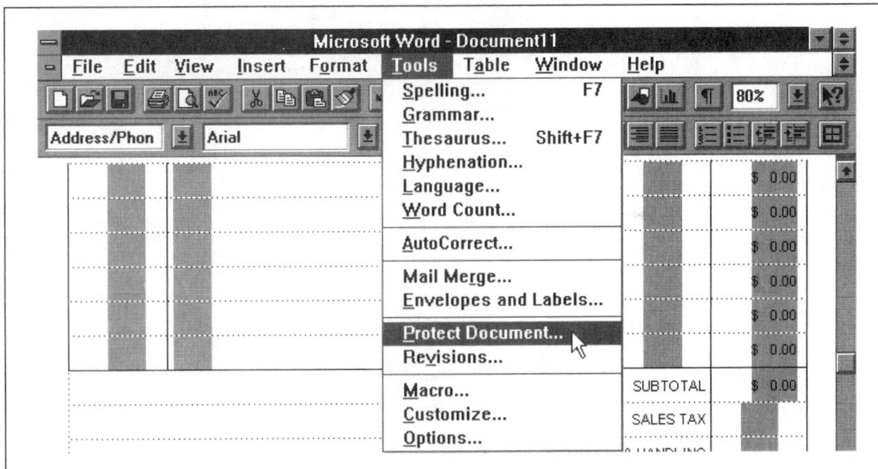

This brings up the Protect Document dialog box:

Protect Document
Protect Document For
Revisions
Annotations
Forms
OK
Cancel
Sections...
Help
Password:

7. Make sure Forms is selected and click OK.
8. Select File ➤ Save As. When the Save As dialog box appears (see Figure 27.27), type a new file name and select Document Template in the Save File as Type drop-down list box.

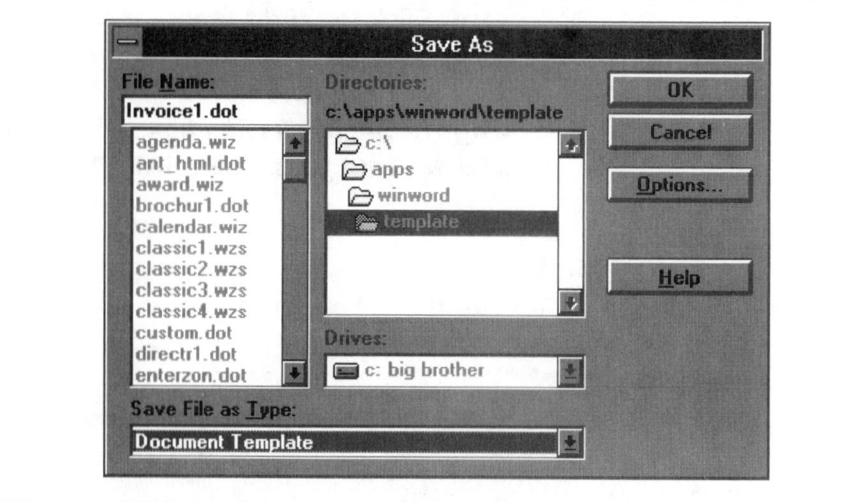

FIGURE 27.27

Save your modified template as a Document Template.

Now, whenever you want to fill out an invoice, select File ➤ New and choose your customized invoice template. Then enter the particular information required, such as the invoice number; charge-to and ship-to names; information about the sale; number of units, description, and price per unit; sales tax; and shipping costs. When your invoice is complete, save and print it.

▸▸ Letter

Word provides a built-in Letter Wizard and three templates that the Wizard uses. Here's how to create a letter with the Wizard:

1. Select File ➤ New (but don't click the New Document button or press Ctrl+N). This will bring up the New dialog box.
2. Select Letter Wizard.

3. Click OK. This opens a new document based on the Letter Wizard template. The Wizard displays a dialog box (see Figure 27.28).
4. Accept the *Select a prewritten business letter* choice to use one of the Wizard's prewritten stock letters (you'll have to modify it, naturally, but much business communication involves boilerplate and rote phrasing, so the prewritten letters can save you some time), or choose *Write a business letter* or *Write a personal letter* to start with just the built-in styles and the bare bones.

FIGURE 27.28

The Letter Wizard dialog box. Choose to work with a prewritten letter or to write your own business or personal letter.

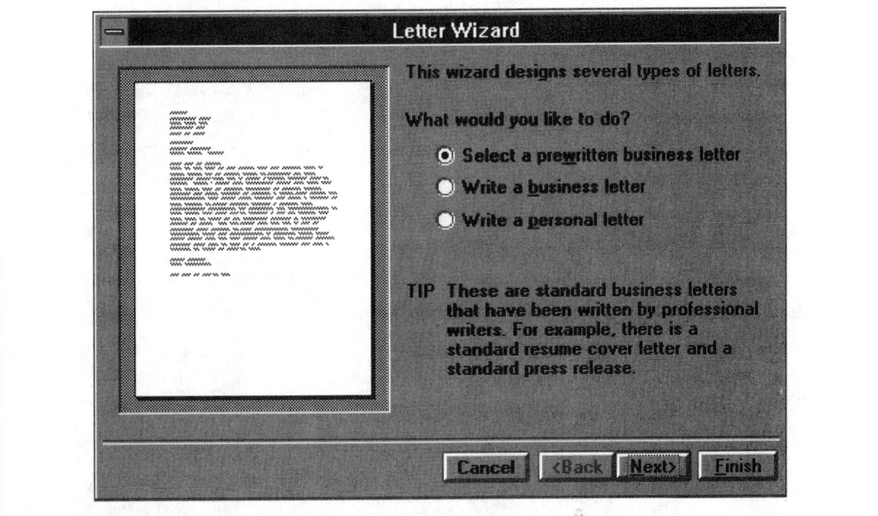

5. Click the Next> button. If you're making a prewritten letter, the dialog box will offer you a choice of letters (see Figure 27.29). Otherwise, skip to step 8.
6. Select a letter from the list shown.
7. Click the Next> button. The Wizard will ask you which elements to include in your letter (see Figure 27.30).
8. Check the letter elements you want to include in your letter.
9. Click the Next> button (see Figure 27.31).

FIGURE 27.29

Choose the standard letter you want from the list shown.

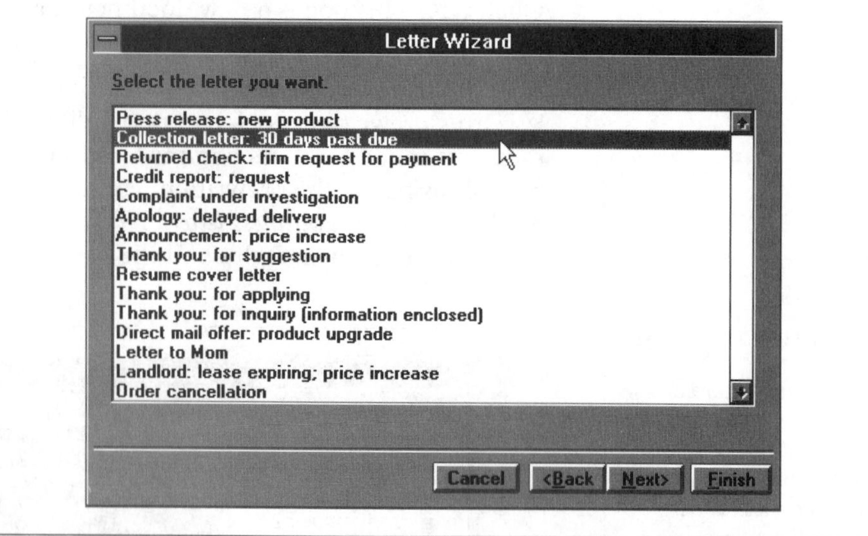

FIGURE 27.30

Choose the elements you want in your letter (for personal letters, only the first two choices are offered).

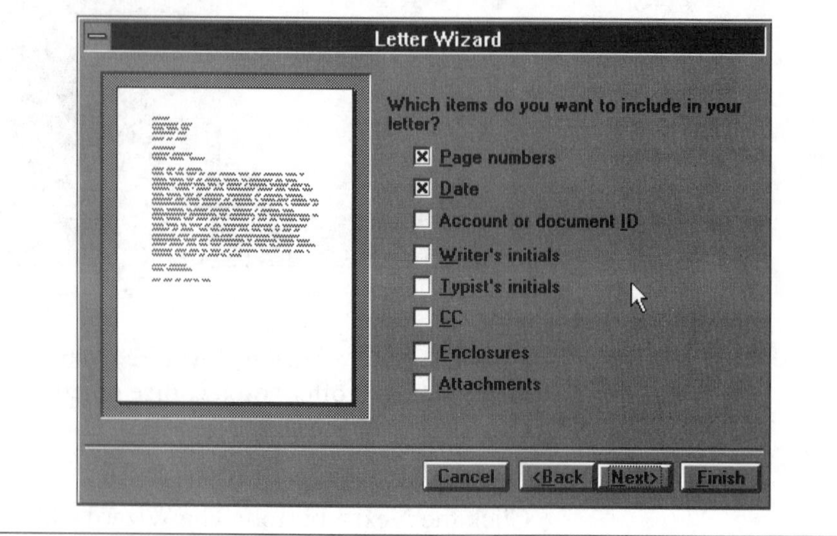

10. Check Letterhead stationery if that's what you're going to print on.
11. Click the Next> button. If you're making a personal letter, skip to step 13.

12. If you're making a business letter, you'll next have to enter the recipient's address and verify your own address. Then click the Next> button again.

13. Choose a letter style from the three choices (see Figure 27.32).

FIGURE 27.31

Check off Letterhead stationery if you plan to print on letterhead.

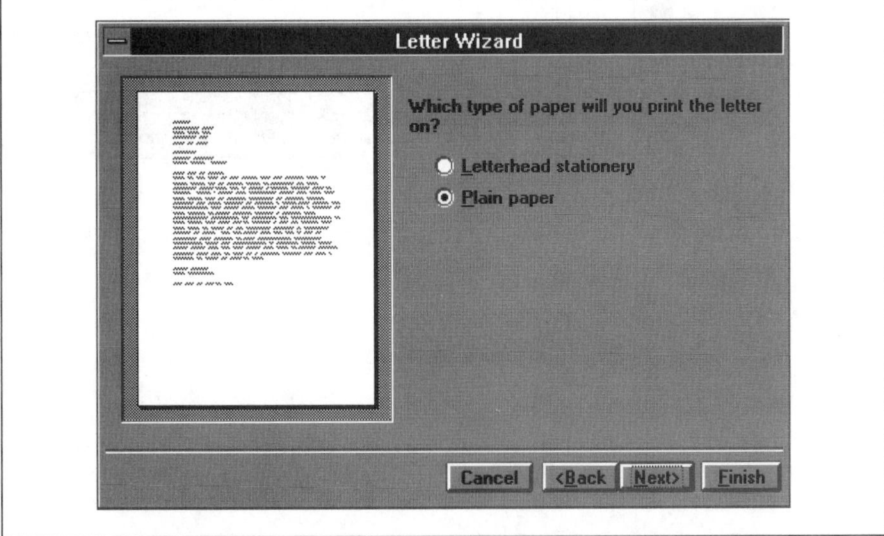

FIGURE 27.32

Choose a letter style.

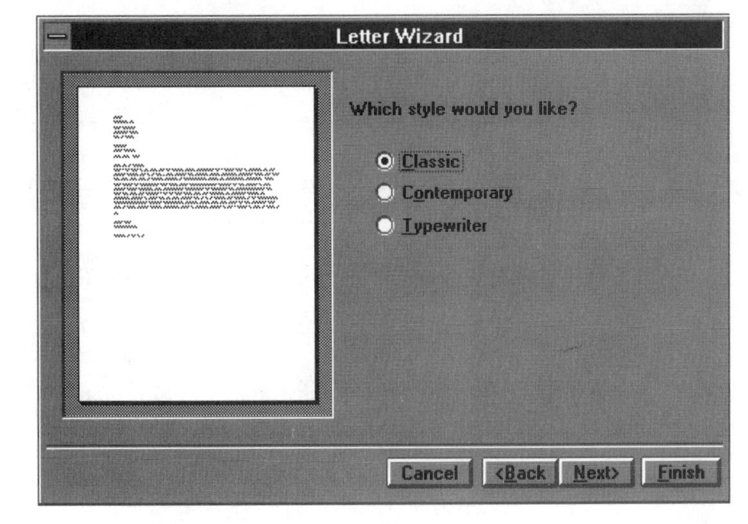

14. Click the Next> button. The Wizard lets you know you're finished.
15. If you want the Wizard to display Help on the screen after creating your letter, click Yes, display Help as I work.
16. Click Finish. The Wizard creates your letter (see Figure 27.33).

FIGURE 27.33

A completed prewritten letter.

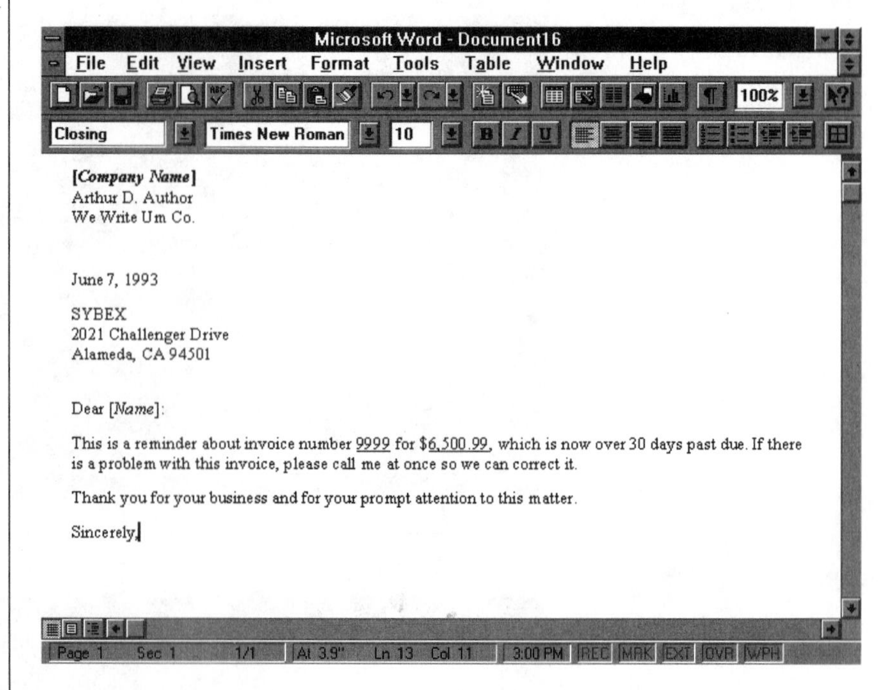

If you've chosen to write your own letter, only the skeleton of a letter will be there (see Figure 27.34).

17. Enter any further personalizing information you need.

FIGURE 27.34

The bare bones of a personal letter.

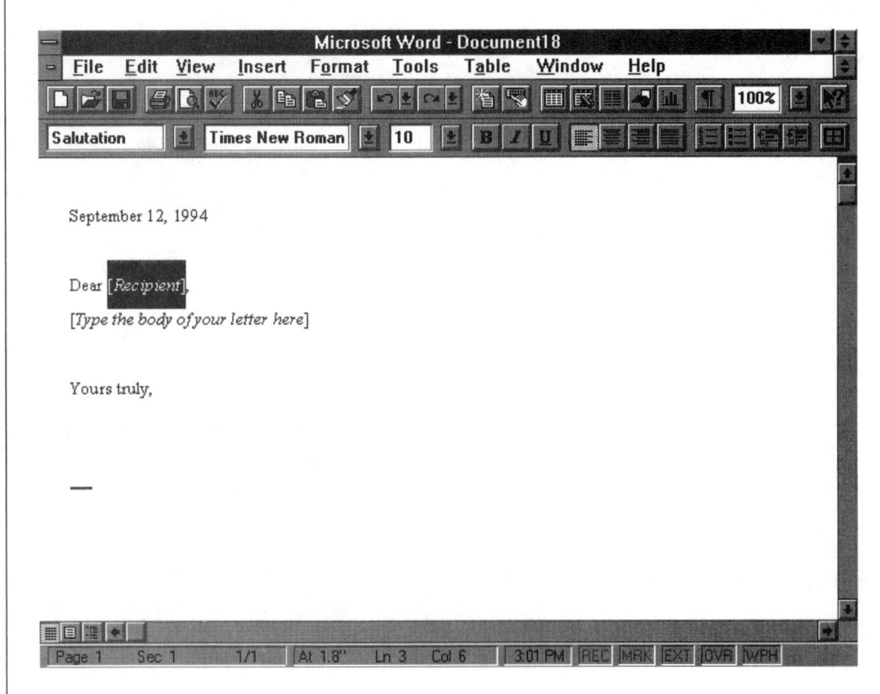

▶▶ Memo

Word has a built-in Memo Wizard and three memo templates that the Wizard uses. To make a memo using the Wizard:

1. Select File ➤ New.
2. Select Memo Wizard in the New dialog box and click OK.
3. This starts a new document and displays the Memo Wizard dialog box (see Figure 27.35).
4. Type text or accept Interoffice Memo, or click No, etc., to have no header text.
5. Click the Next> button (see Figure 27.36).

FIGURE 27.35

The Memo Wizard dialog box. Enter heading text or choose No, etc.

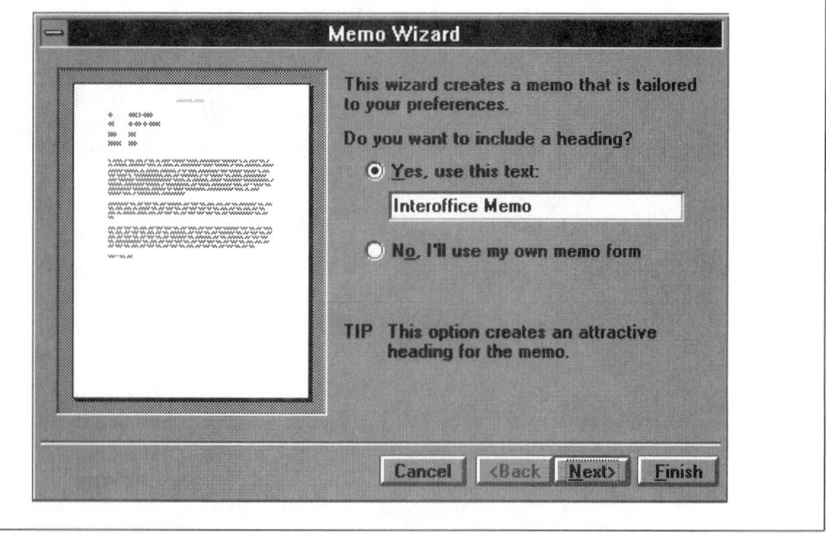

FIGURE 27.36

Click Yes if you want a distribution page.

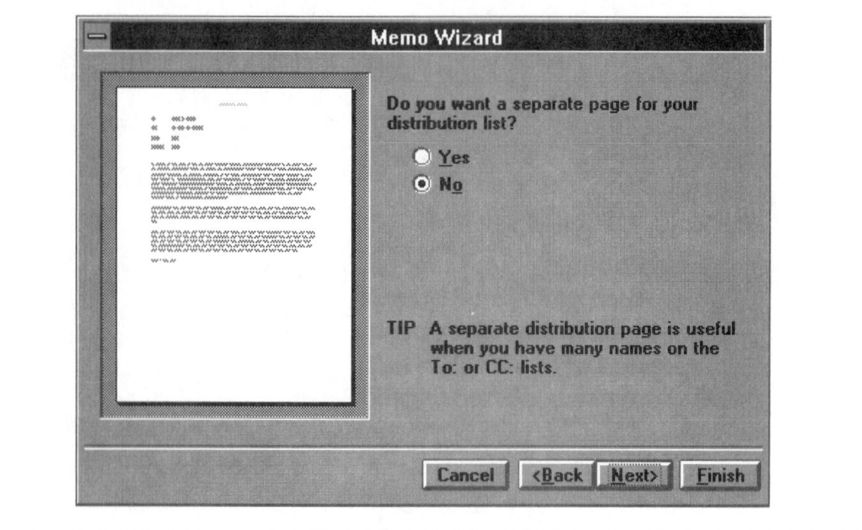

6. Click Yes for a distribution page if you want one.
7. Click the Next> button (see Figure 27.37).
8. Check any elements you want at the top of your memo. Change the date or From name if you want.
9. Click the Next> button (see Figure 27.38).

FIGURE 27.37

Check any elements you want to include at the top of your memo.

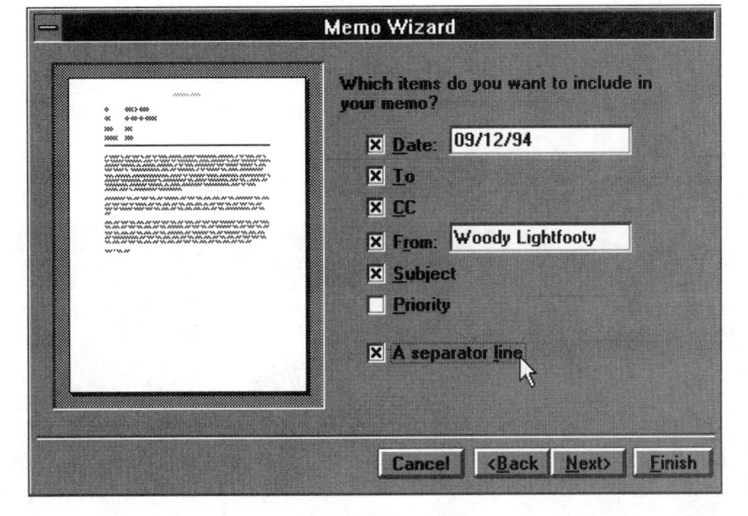

FIGURE 27.38

Check any elements you want to include at the bottom of your memo.

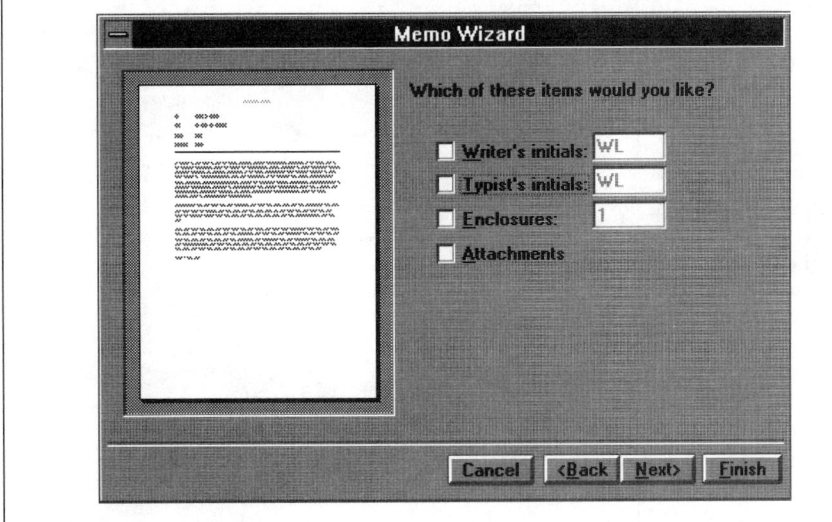

10. Check any elements you want at the bottom of your memo. Change any of the text boxes if need be.
11. Click the Next> button (see Figure 27.39).

12. Check any elements you want in the header or footer of pages after page one (if there are any), or just skip this stuff if you know the memo is a one-pager.
13. Click the Next> button (see Figure 27.40).

FIGURE 27.39

Check any elements you want in the header or footer of subsequent pages, if any.

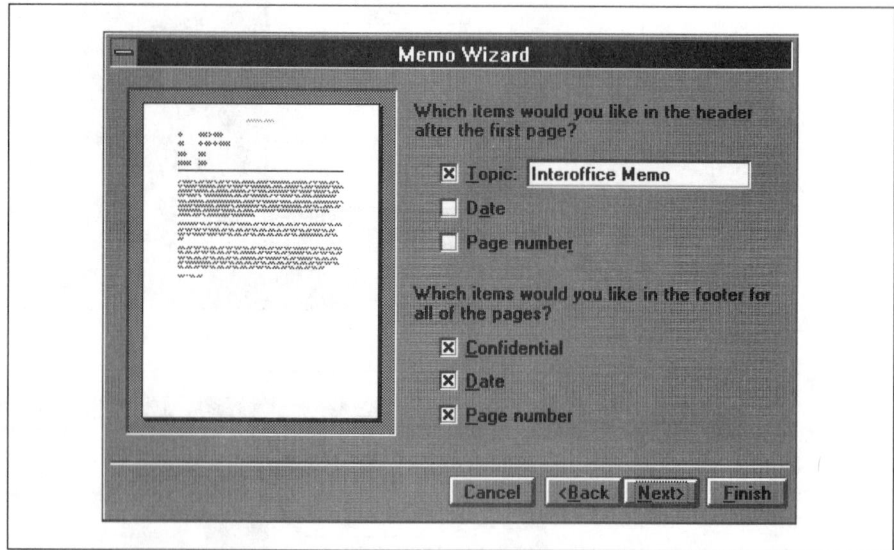

FIGURE 27.40

Choose a style for your memo.

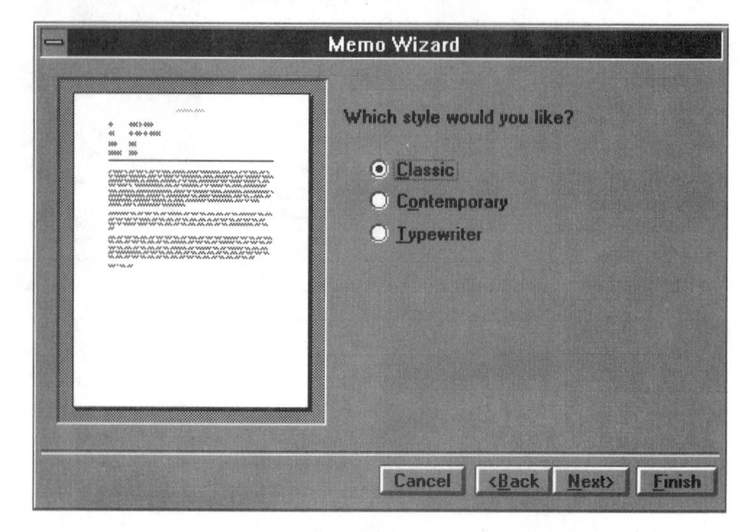

14. Choose a style for your memo.
15. Click the Next> button. The Wizard lets you know you're finished.
16. If you want the Wizard to display Help on the screen after creating your memo, click Yes, display Help as I work.
17. Click Finish. The Wizard creates your memo.
18. Write the memo.
19. Customize the contents any way you like.

▶▶ Newsletter

Word provides a built-in Newsletter Wizard. It simplifies the process of planning and laying out a newsletter, but, of course, it still leaves a lot of hard work in your lap, writing the articles and making them fit into the layout. Here's how to use the Wizard:

1. Select File ➤ New, but don't click the New Document button or press Ctrl+N. This brings up the New dialog box (see Figure 27.41).
2. Select Newsletter Wizard and click OK. Word opens a new document and displays the Newsletter Wizard dialog box (see Figure 27.42).

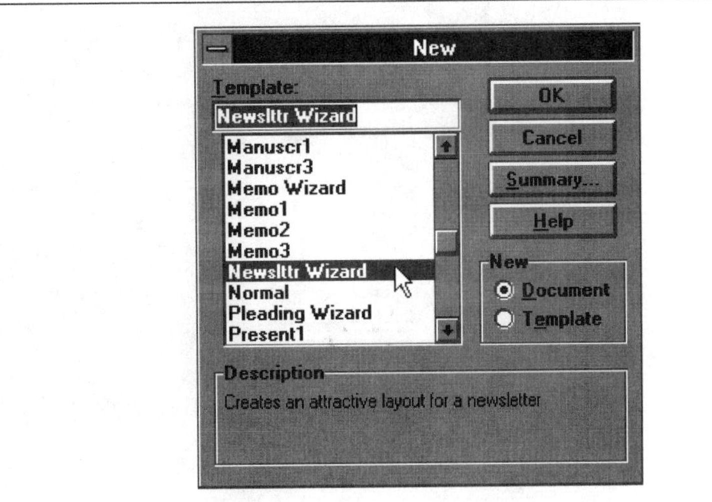

FIGURE 27.41 ▶

Select the Newsletter Wizard and click OK.

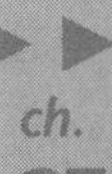

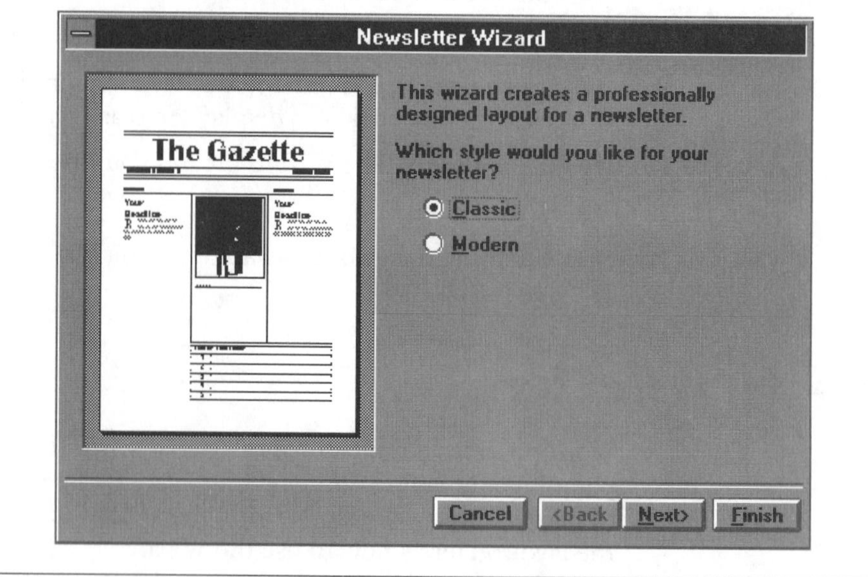

FIGURE 27.42

The Newsletter Wizard dialog box. Select a style for your newsletter.

3. The Wizard offers two styles for your newsletter. Choose one.
4. Click the Next> button (see Figure 27.43).

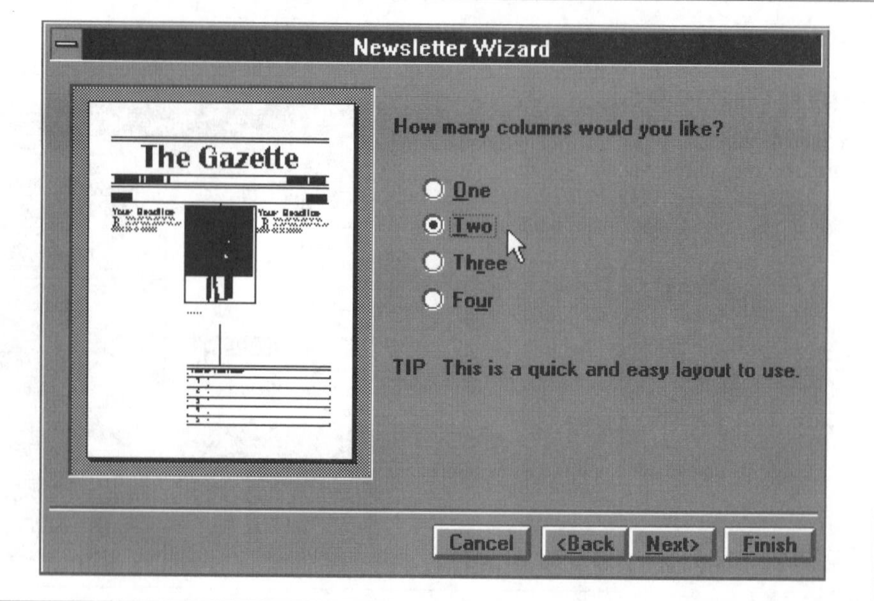

FIGURE 27.43

Choose a number of columns for your newsletter's layout.

5. The Wizard suggests three columns for your newsletter's layout, but it can also do one, two, and four. Choose a number of columns.
6. Click the Next> button (see Figure 27.44).

FIGURE 27.44

Type a name for your newsletter.

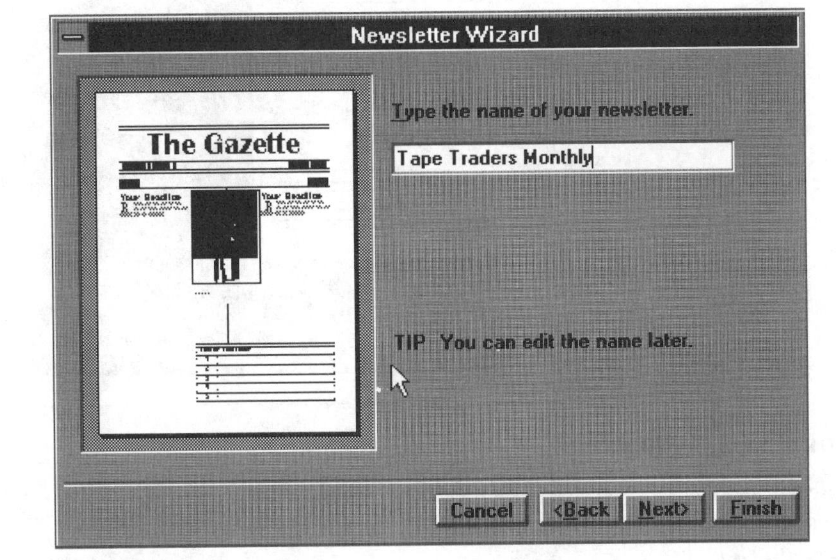

7. Type a name for your newsletter (unless you were planning to call it *The Gazette* anyway).
8. Click the Next> button (see Figure 27.45).
9. Enter a number of pages for your newsletter.
10. Click the Next> button (see Figure 27.46).
11. Check whichever elements you'd like to use in your newsletter design.
12. Click the Next> button. The Wizard lets you know you're finished.
13. If you want the Wizard to display Help on the screen after creating your newsletter, click Yes, display Help as I work.
14. Click Finish. The Wizard creates the basic layout of your newsletter (see Figure 27.47).

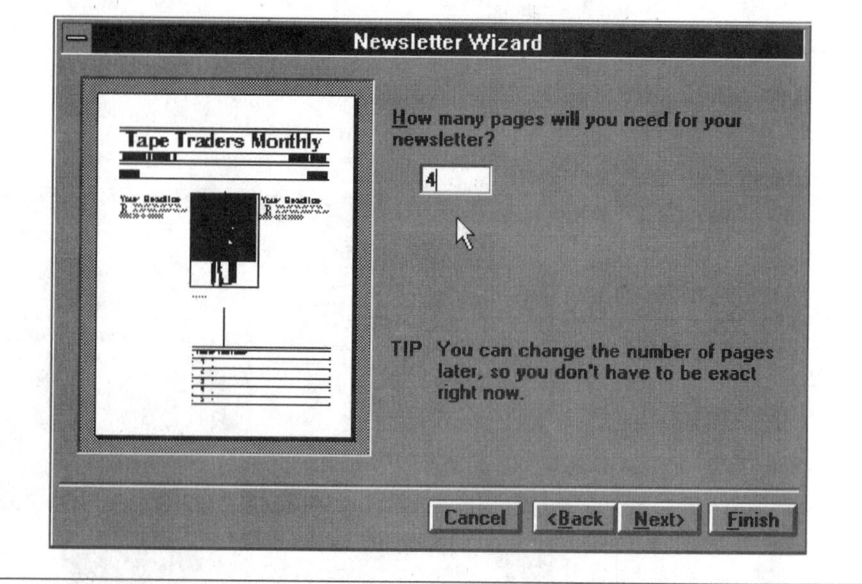

FIGURE 27.45

Guess how many pages you'll need for your newsletter (you can always change this later).

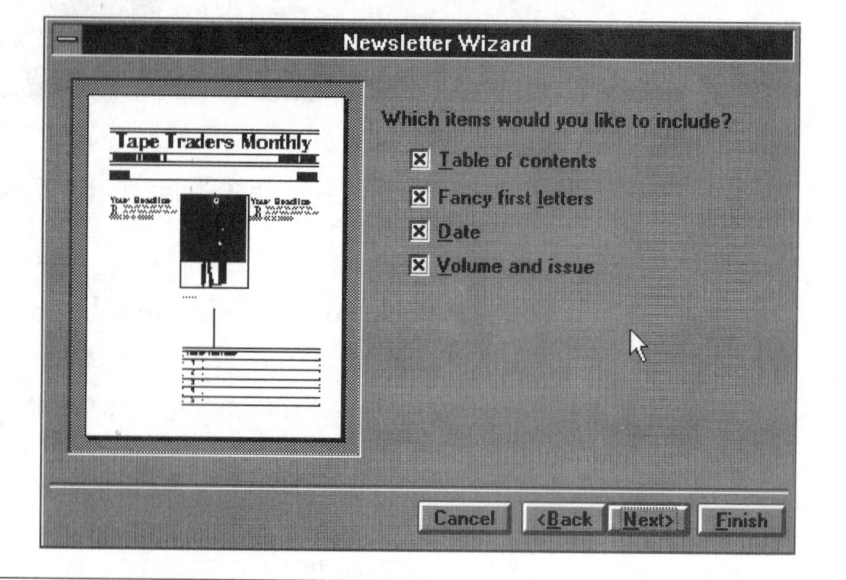

FIGURE 27.46

Choose which of the optional items you want to include in your newsletter design.

FIGURE 27.47

The skeleton of your newsletter. You may have to tweak it a little bit. Type your articles or insert prewritten articles into this shell.

15. You may have to play around with the placement of the design elements a bit.
16. Type your articles into the space provided or insert prewritten files.
17. Continue tweaking the layout to make your articles fit.

►► Organizational Chart

Word doesn't provide a Wizard or template for making an organizational chart, but they're pretty easy to do by hand. Here's how:

1. First sketch out a rough approximation of the organizational chart, so you can get an idea of the number of boxes you'll need in the bottom row and the number of levels in the chart.

▶▶ **TIP**

If the chart is going to be wide, choose Landscape in the Page Setup dialog box.

2. Multiply the number of boxes in the bottom row by three and subtract one (so if there will be four boxes, 4×3=12–1=11). This is the number of columns you'll need to start with.
3. Multiply the number of rows by three and subtract two (so if there are three rows, 3×3=9–2=7). This is the number of rows you'll need to start with.
4. Start a new document (click the New Document button).
5. Select Table ➤ Insert Table. This will bring up the Insert Table dialog box (see Figure 27.48).

Word inserts the table you specified (see Figure 27.49).

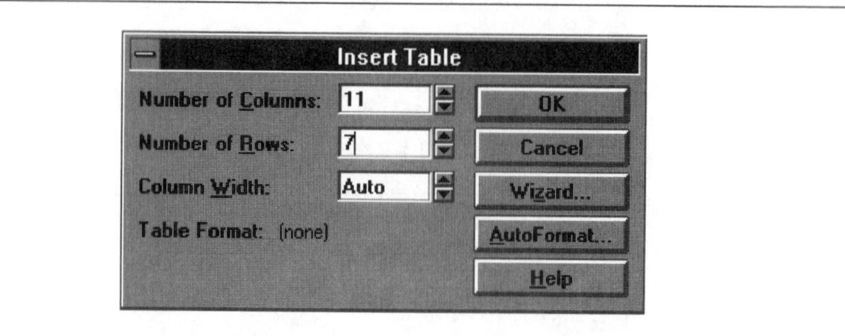

FIGURE 27.48

The Insert Table dialog box. Enter the number of rows and columns you determined in steps 2 and 3.

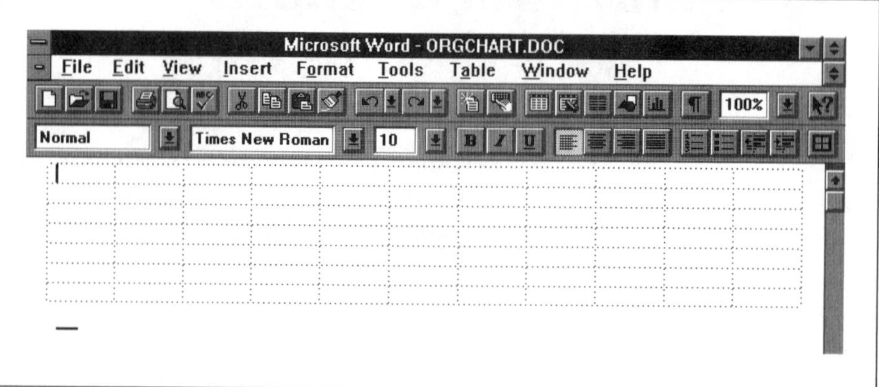

FIGURE 27.49

The empty table.

6. Select the entire table (or the whole document even), and choose a nice large font size (at least 12 points), and center alignment (click the Center button on the Formatting Toolbar).
7. Join the first two cells in the bottom row of the table by selecting them both and then selecting Table ➤ Merge Cells.
8. Skip a cell and then do the same thing for the two after the one you skipped. Repeat this process until the bottom row consists entirely of double-width cells separated by single cells.
9. Enter the titles of the people represented by the boxes in the bottom row (see Figure 27.50).

FIGURE 27.50

The bottom row of the organizational chart.

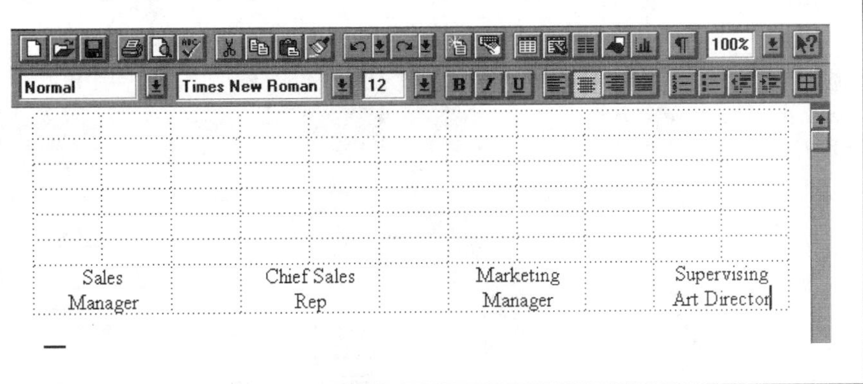

10. Leaving *two* blank rows above the boxes you've already entered, merge together cells in the next row up. You'll need to center the relevant boxes over the boxes that relate to them and include at least two cells in each box.
11. Enter titles in this next row up (see Figure 27.51).
12. Repeat this process as many times as necessary until you have created the single box at the top of the chart.
13. Now select a box containing a title (select the entire cell, not just the paragraph of text inside it).
14. Select Format ➤ Borders and Shading. This brings up the Cell Borders and Shading dialog box (see Figure 27.52).

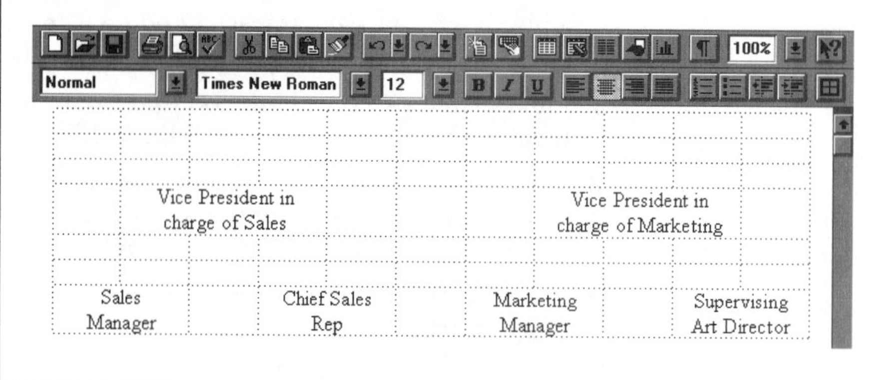

FIGURE 27.51

The next row up of the organizational chart.

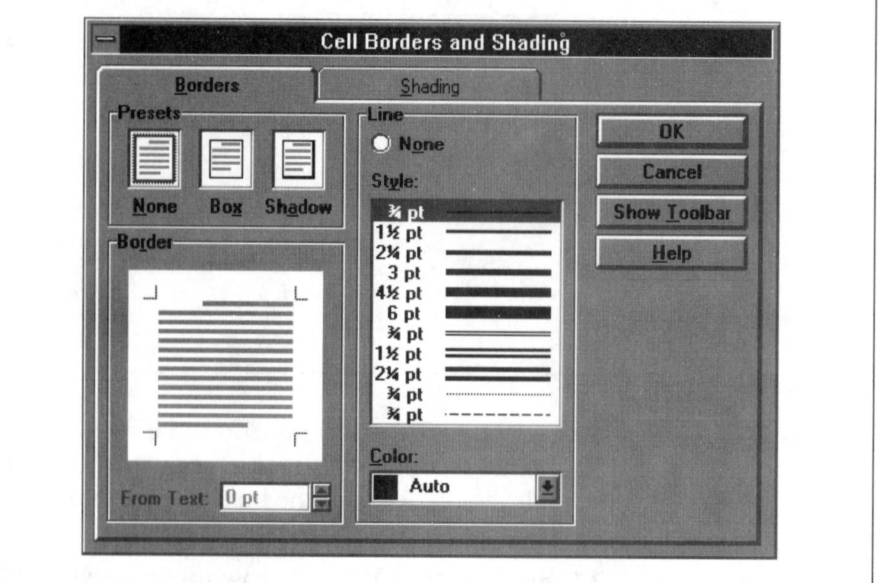

FIGURE 27.52

The Cell Borders and Shading dialog box. Choose a border style for your box.

15. Choose a border style for the box and then click OK.
16. Repeat this process for all the other boxes (See Figure 27.53).

This next part is tricky.

17. For each box without an empty table cell edge directly below its middle, select the empty cell directly below the middle of the box and one of the empty cells next to it.

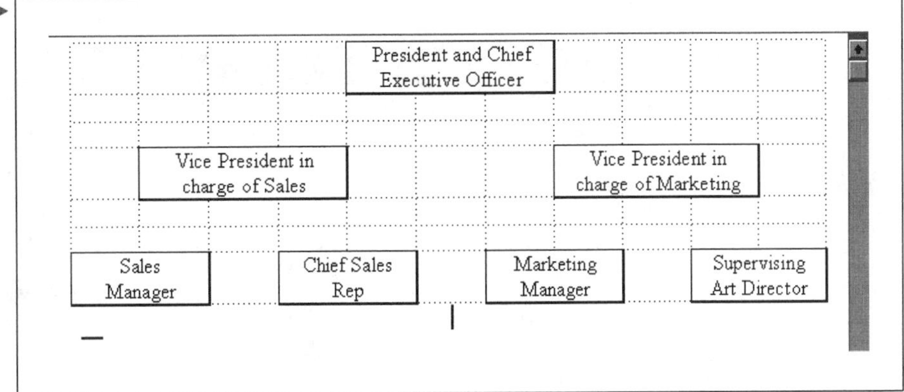

FIGURE 27.53

Put borders on all your boxes.

18. Then drag the divider between those two empty cells to a point directly below the middle of the box, as shown:

19. Repeat as often as necessary.
20. Do the same to center cell dividers above boxes.
21. Now click the Borders button at the right edge of the Formatting Toolbar:

This brings up the Borders Toolbar:

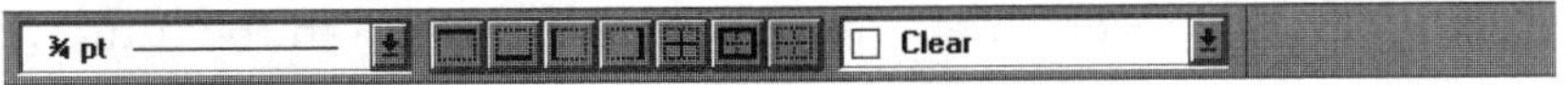

22. Now select cells and add borders to them using the partial-border buttons in the Borders Toolbar to add the lines between the boxes, as shown in Figure 27.54.

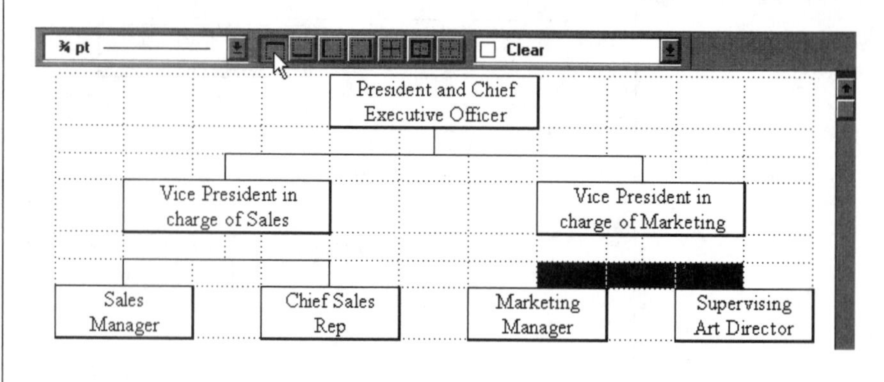

FIGURE 27.54

Select cells and add borders to them to create the lines of authority between the boxes.

▸▸ **TIP**

Place the horizontal lines first, selecting rows of cells and adding partial borders above or below them as appropriate. Then select single cells to add the vertical lines.

23. Click the Borders button again to remove the Borders Toolbar. Your organizational chart is complete (whew!). Figure 27.55 shows a completed organizational chart with table gridlines not showing.

▸▸ Phone List

One nice thing about making a list of phone numbers on your computer is that you can easily update it in the future, changing numbers, adding new people, and so on. Word has no template or Wizard for making a phone list, but it's pretty easy.

1. Start a new document (click the New Document button).
2. Type **Phone List** and format it in some nice large size and clear font.
3. Press Enter and then select the blank line below the words *Phone List*.

FIGURE 27.55

My completed organizational chart.

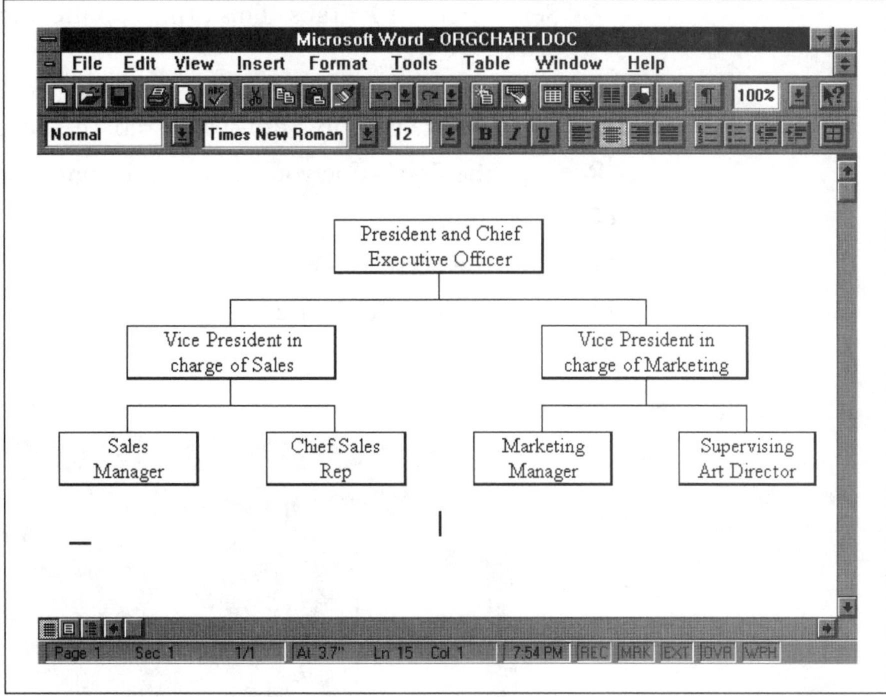

4. Click the Columns button on the Standard Toolbar and create two columns with it:

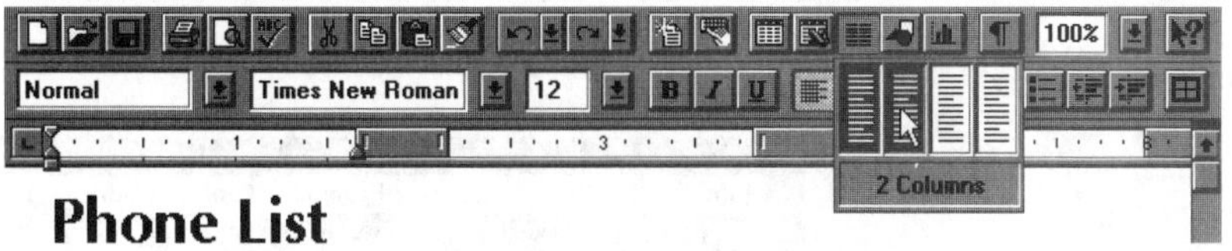

This creates a section break and then a two-column layout thereafter.

5. Click the square at the left end of the Ruler twice to change the symbol in it to the right-aligned tab symbol.
6. Click in the Ruler above the first column and drag the tab symbol to the right edge of the first column:

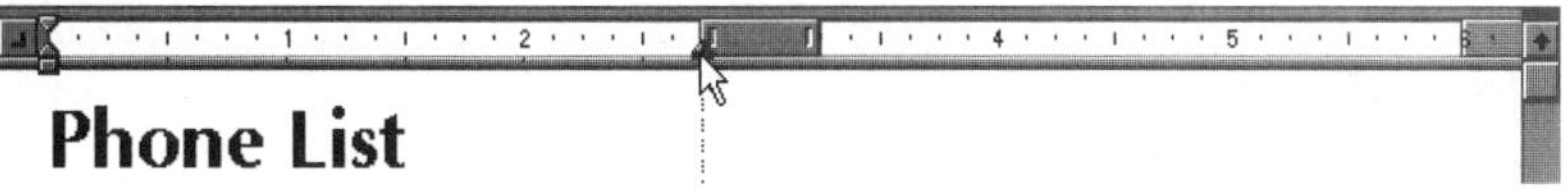

7. Select Format ➤ Tabs. This brings up the Tabs dialog box (see Figure 27.56).
8. Click the number 2 option in the Leaders area of the Tabs dialog box to make the tab a dot-leader tab, then click OK.
9. Type the first name you want in your phone list.
10. Press Tab.
11. Type the person's phone number.
12. Press Enter (see Figure 27.57).

FIGURE 27.56

The Tabs dialog box. Make the tab you just created a "dot-leader" tab.

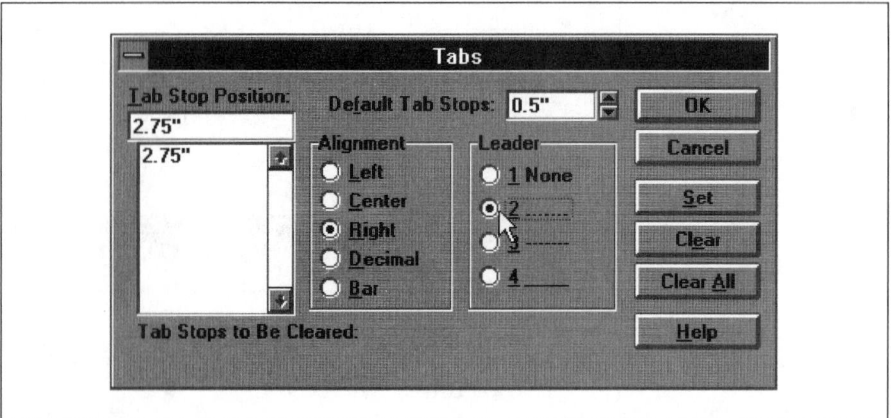

FIGURE 27.57

The first entry in my phone list.

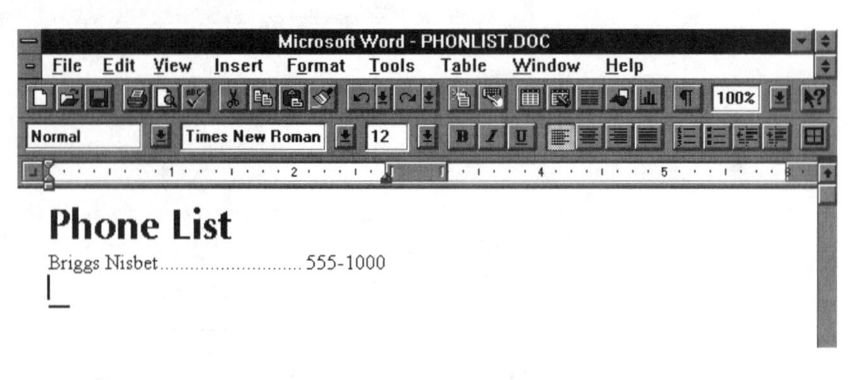

13. Repeat Steps 9 through 12 as often as you like (you might want to collect all your teensy-weensy scraps of paper first) to complete your phone list for now. Figure 27.58 shows a filled phone list.

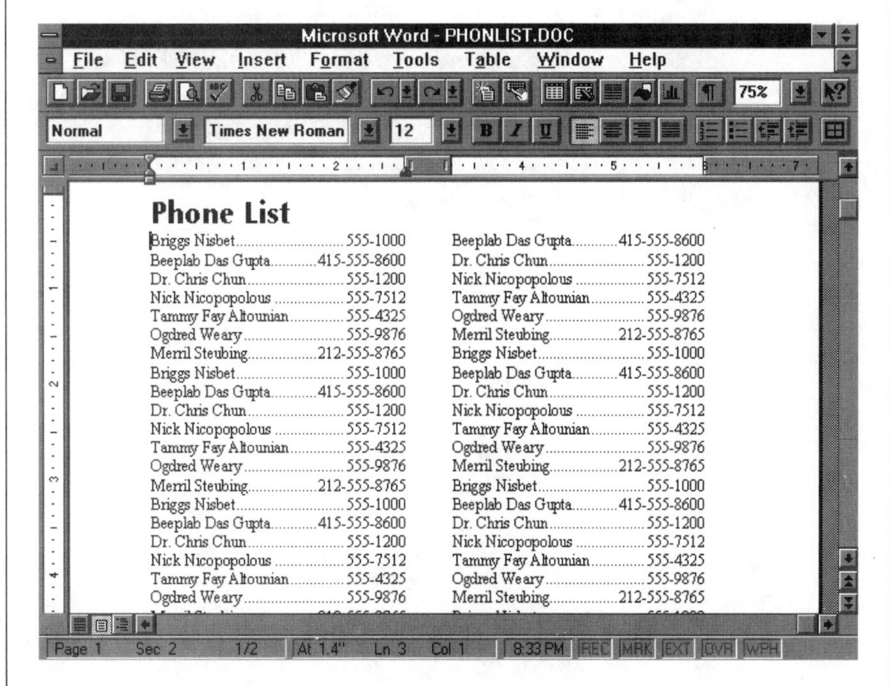

FIGURE 27.58

A filled phone list.

Press Release

Word supplies three press-release templates, one each in its "Classic," "Contemporary," and "Typewriter" styles. I guess there's no call for a "Jazzy" press release. Here's how to make a press release based on one of the templates:

1. Select File ➤ New (but don't click the New Document button or press Ctrl+N).
2. Select Presrel1 if you want to make a classic press release, Presrel2 for a contemporary press release, or Presrel3 for a press release that looks typewritten.

3. Click OK. Word starts a new document based on the template you chose. It has all kinds of preset styles with dummy text already in place (see Figure 27.59).

FIGURE 27.59

A document based on the contemporary press release template (I've decreased the zoom a tiny bit to fit it all on the screen).

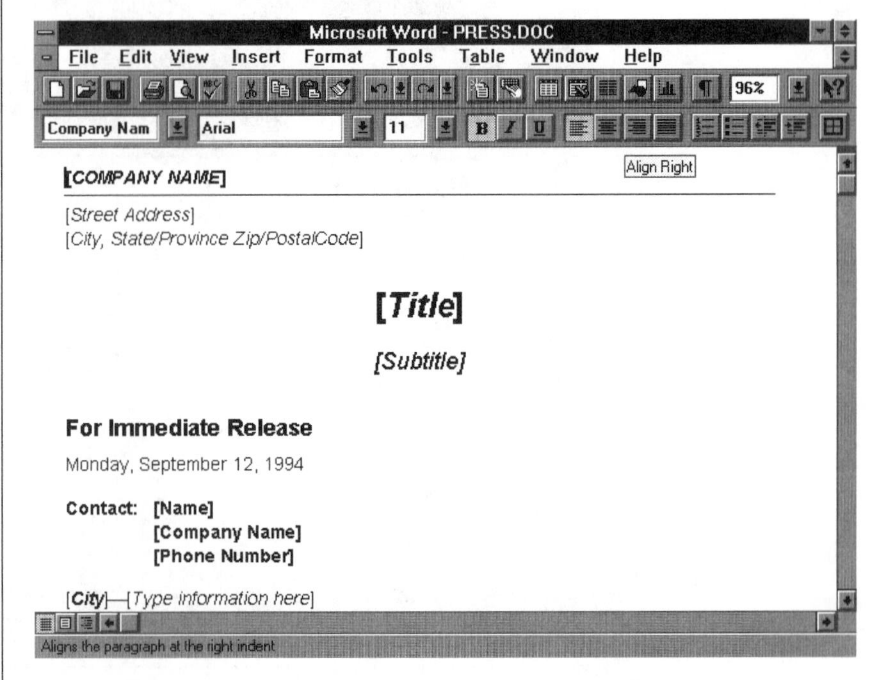

4. Replace [*COMPANY NAME*], [*Street Address*], and [*City/State*/etc.] with the correct information.
5. Replace [*Title*] and [*Subtitle*] with recommended headlines for your news release.
6. Change the date if necessary.
7. Enter information for a contact who can verify the information in the release to reporters.
8. Replace [*City*] with the name of the city or locale in which the newsworthy event is taking place.
9. Now replace [*Type information here*] with the actual news you intend to release to the press. Figure 27.60 shows a completed press release.

FIGURE 27.60

My press release is ready to print and send out (or fax) to reporters everywhere.

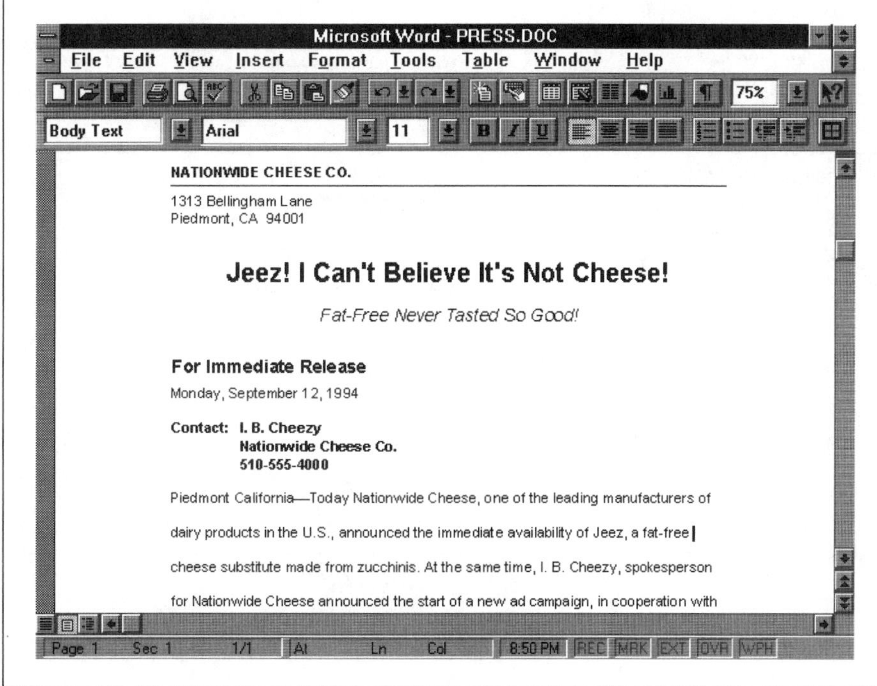

►► Purchase Order

Word provides a nice purchase-order template that uses form fields to make filling the order out quick and easy. (It's very similar to the invoice template that's covered earlier in this chapter.) You have to customize the template the first time you use it, but even that's not too bad, and you never have to do it again.

1. Select File ➤ New (but don't click the New Document button or press Ctrl+N). This brings up the New dialog box.
2. Select the Purchord template and click OK. This starts a new document based on the Purchase Order template.
3. The document is a protected form, so to change it, you need to unprotect it. Select Tools ➤ Unprotect Document.
4. Replace the dummy text (Your Company Name, etc.) with your own information (see Figure 27.61).

FIGURE 27.61

Type your own information in the company name, slogan, address, and phone number areas.

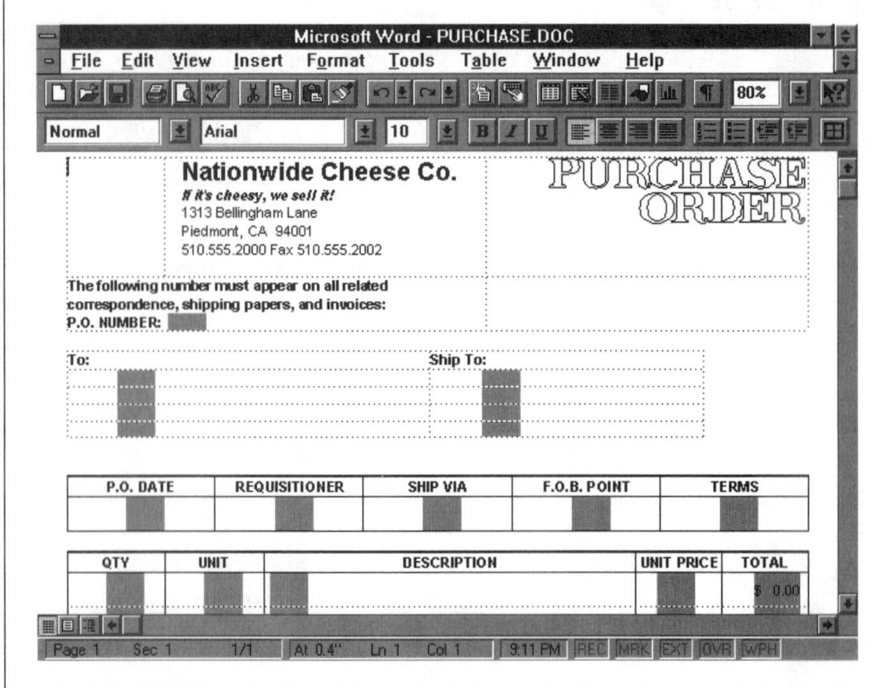

5. Also personalize the information at the bottom of the purchase order.
6. Then reprotect the document by selecting Tools ➤ Protect Document. This brings up the Protect Document dialog box:

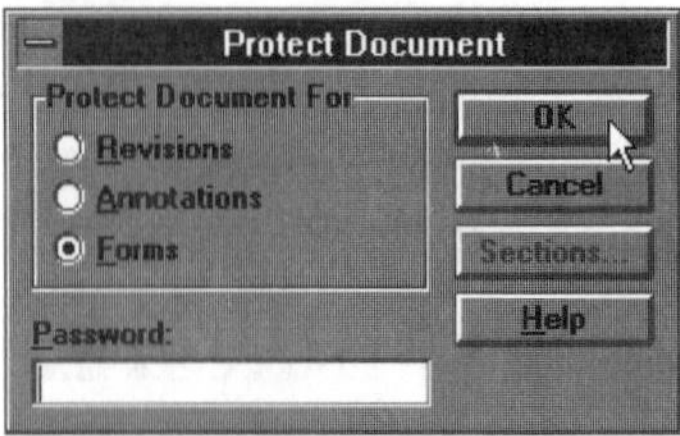

7. Make sure Forms is selected and click OK.
8. Select File ➤ Save As. When the Save As dialog box appears, type a new file name and select Document Template in the Save File as Type drop-down list box.

Now, whenever you want to fill out an purchase order, select File ➤ New and choose your customized purchase-order template. Then enter the particular information required, such as the PO number; charge-to and ship-to names; information about the purchase; number of units, description, and price per unit; sales tax; and shipping costs. When your purchase order is complete, save and print it.

►► Resume

Word provides a Resume Wizard (and three resume templates that the Wizard uses) to automate the process of creating a clean, well-designed resume. Here's how to create a resume using the Resume Wizard:

1. Select File ➤ New (but don't click the New Document button or press Ctrl+N).
2. Select Resume Wizard.
3. Click OK. Word starts a new document based on the Resume Wizard template and starts you off with the Resume Wizard dialog box (see Figure 27.62).

FIGURE 27.62 ►

The Resume Wizard dialog box. Choose the type of resume you want.

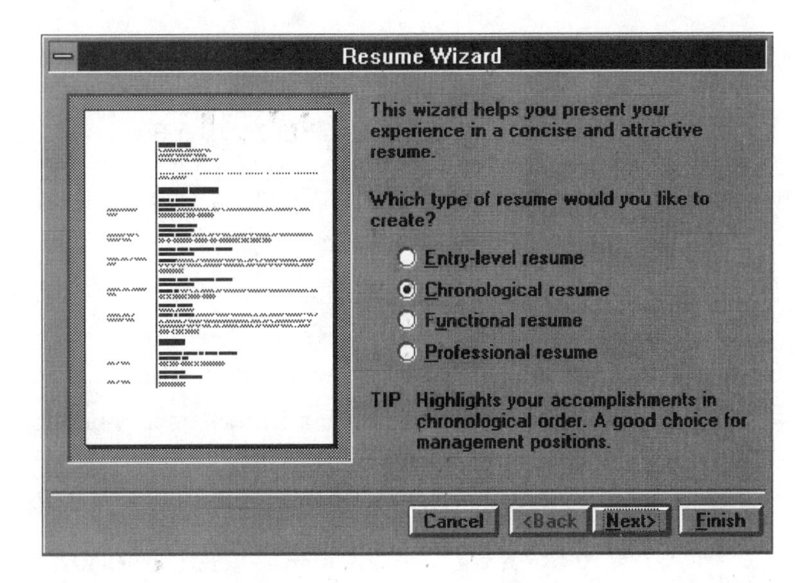

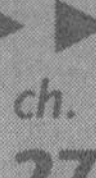

4. Choose a resume type, depending on your career objectives. Read the TIP information for each one to see which one suits you best.
5. Click the Next> button (see Figure 27.63).

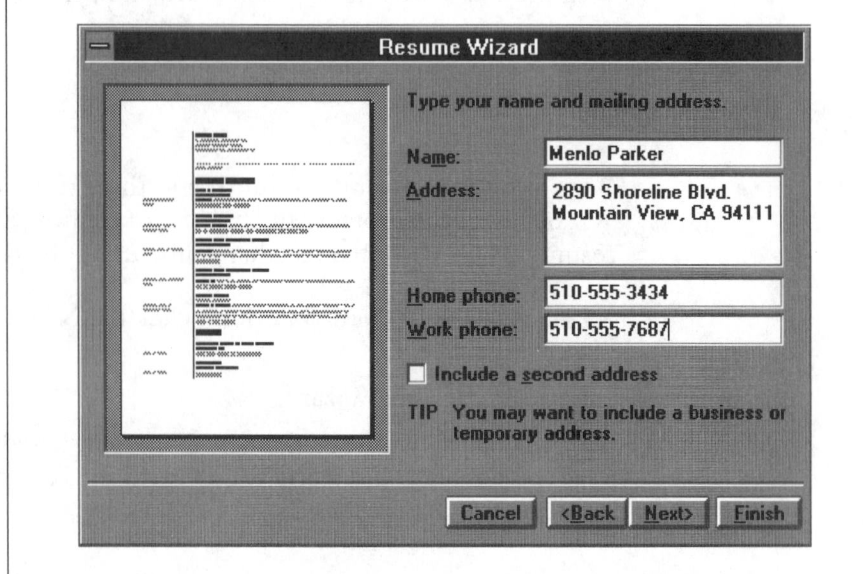

FIGURE 27.63

Type your name, address, and phone number.

6. Type your name, address, and phone number. If you want to add a second address, check Include a second address and enter it.
7. Click the Next> button (see Figure 27.64).

If you chose the Functional resume, your list will be shorter (see Figure 27.65).

8. The Wizard suggests the headings you'll probably want in your resume. Uncheck any that don't apply.
9. Click the Next> button (see Figure 27.66).
10. The Wizard offers a further set of possible headings. Check any that suit your experience.
11. Click the Next> button (see Figure 27.67).
12. If you want to include headings that the Wizard has not suggested, type the first one and click the Add button.

FIGURE 27.64

Choose the headings you want in your resume.

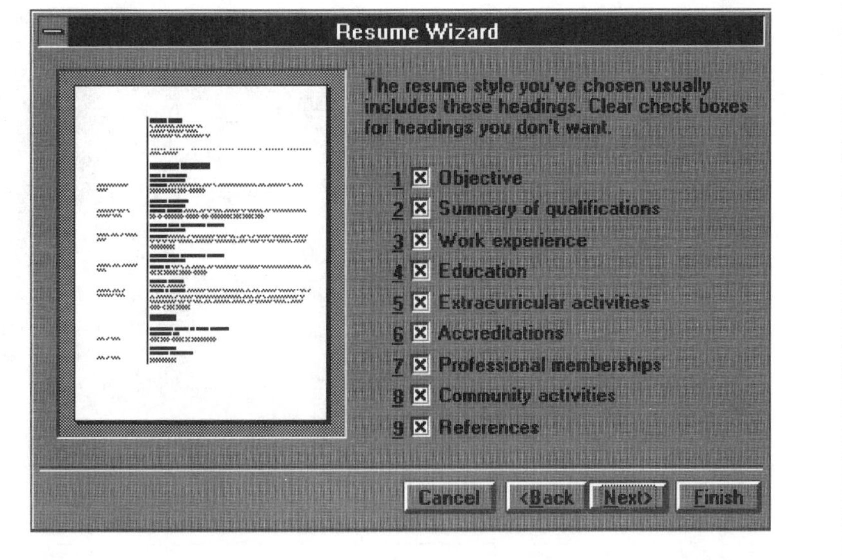

FIGURE 27.65

The heading list for a functional resume.

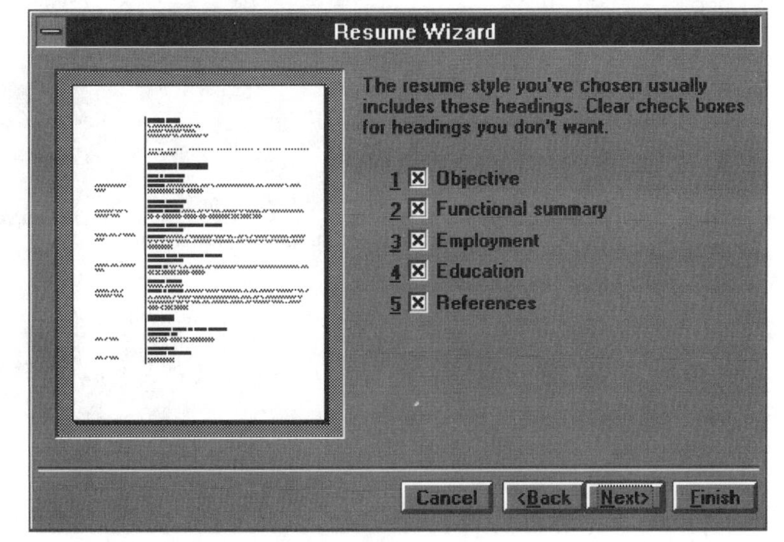

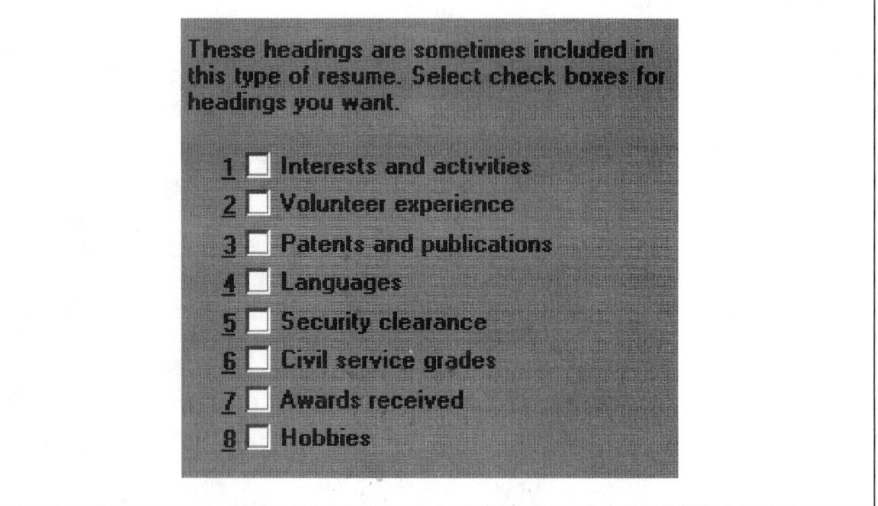

FIGURE 27.66

Check any additional headings you want.

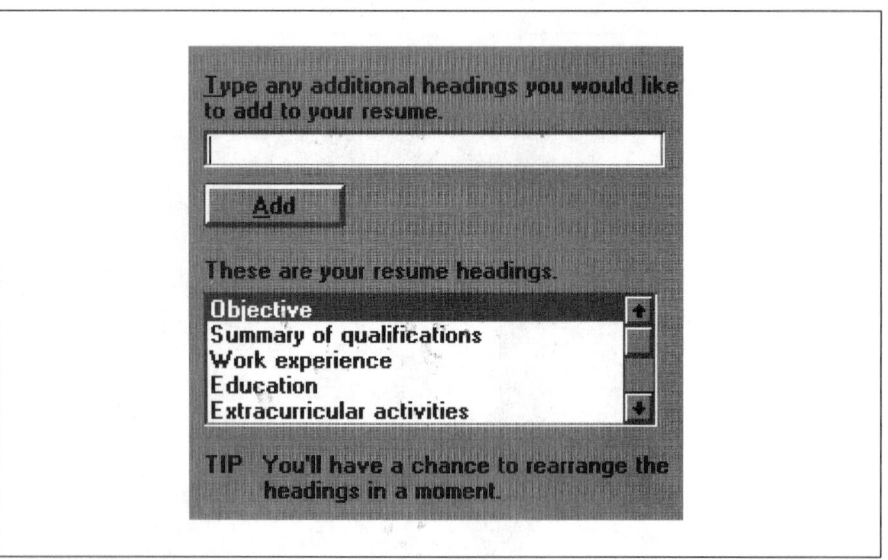

FIGURE 27.67

Add any new headings you want.

13. Repeat step 12 as often as necessary, if at all.
14. Click the Next> button (see Figure 27.68).

FIGURE 27.68

Highlight a heading and click Move Up or Move Down to change its position.

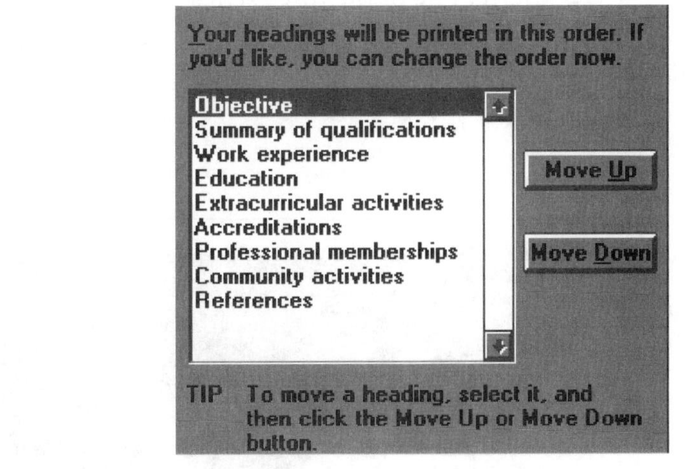

15. To rearrange your headings, highlight the one you'd like to move and then click Move Up or Move Down to change its position.
16. Repeat step 15 as often as necessary, if at all.
17. Click the Next> button (see Figure 27.69).

FIGURE 27.69

Choose a style for your resume.

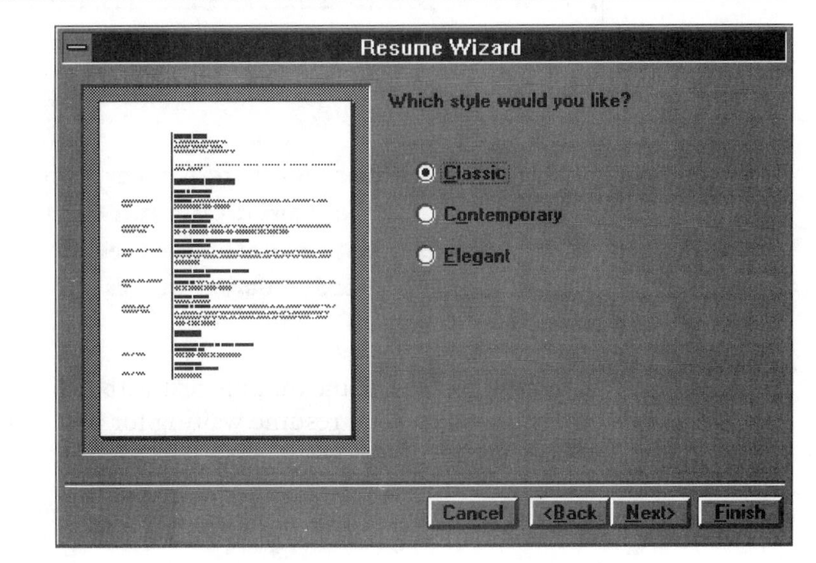

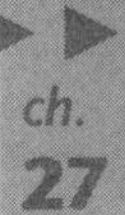

18. Select one of the three styles offered.
19. Click the Next> button. Your resume is done (see Figure 27.70).
20. If you want to make a cover letter now as well, click Create a cover letter.

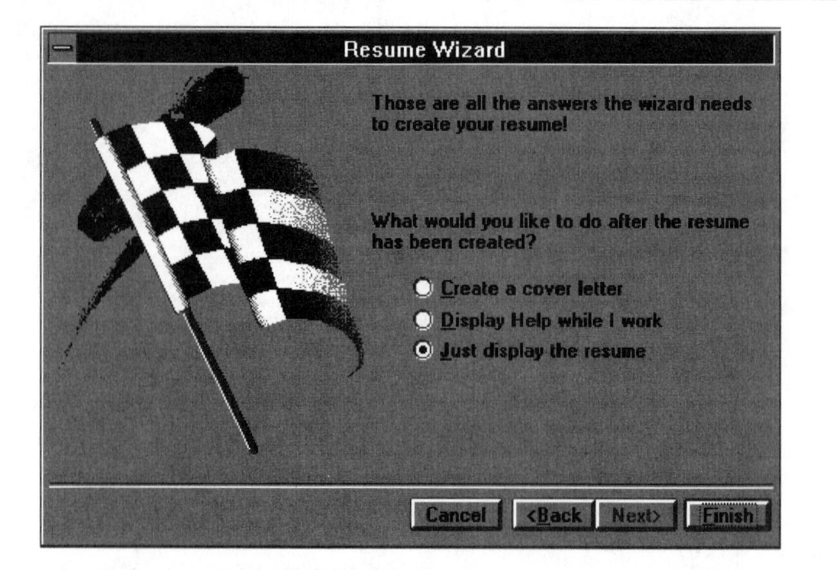

FIGURE 27.70

Click Create a cover letter if you want to make a cover letter to go with your resume.

▸▸ NOTE

If you choose to create a cover letter, the Resume Wizard will automatically run the Letter Wizard and suggest the prewritten Resume cover letter choice. See the Letter section earlier in this chapter for more details.

21. Now replace all the dummy text with real information. Figure 27.71 shows a skeletal resume waiting for real experience.

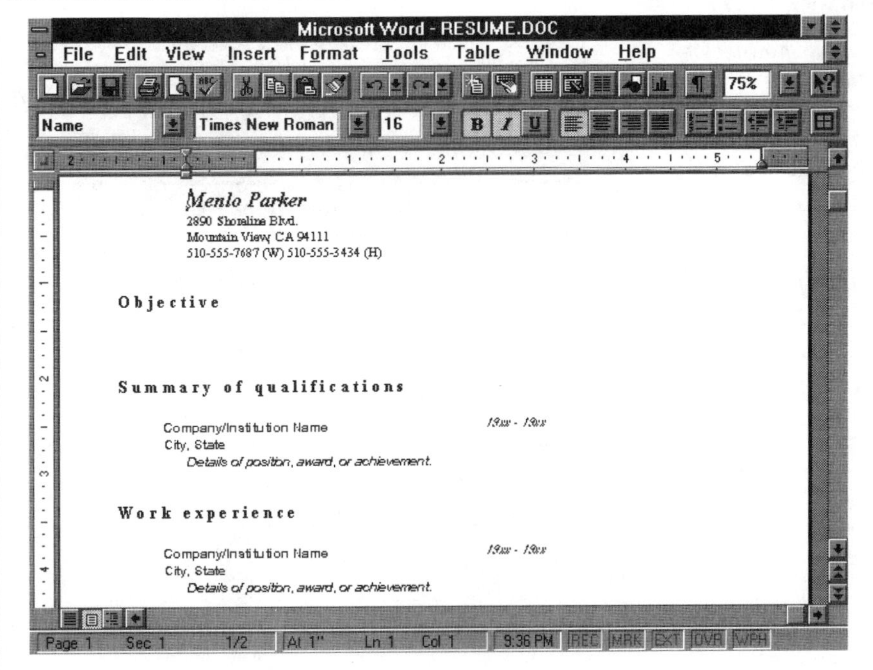

FIGURE 27.71

The elegant resume layout before actual information has been entered.

▸▸ Time Sheet

Word provides a weekly time-sheet template that uses form fields. You have to customize the template the first time you use it, but that's not too hard. It uses a layout similar to that of the Invoice and Purchase Order templates explained earlier in this chapter. Here's how to set it up:

1. Select File ➤ New (but don't click the New Document button or press Ctrl+N). This brings up the New dialog box.
2. Select the Weektime template and click OK. This starts a new document based on the Weekly Time Sheet template.
3. The document is a protected form, so to change it, you need to unprotect it. Select Tools ➤ Unprotect Document.
4. Replace the dummy text (Your Company Name, etc.) with your own information (see Figure 27.72).

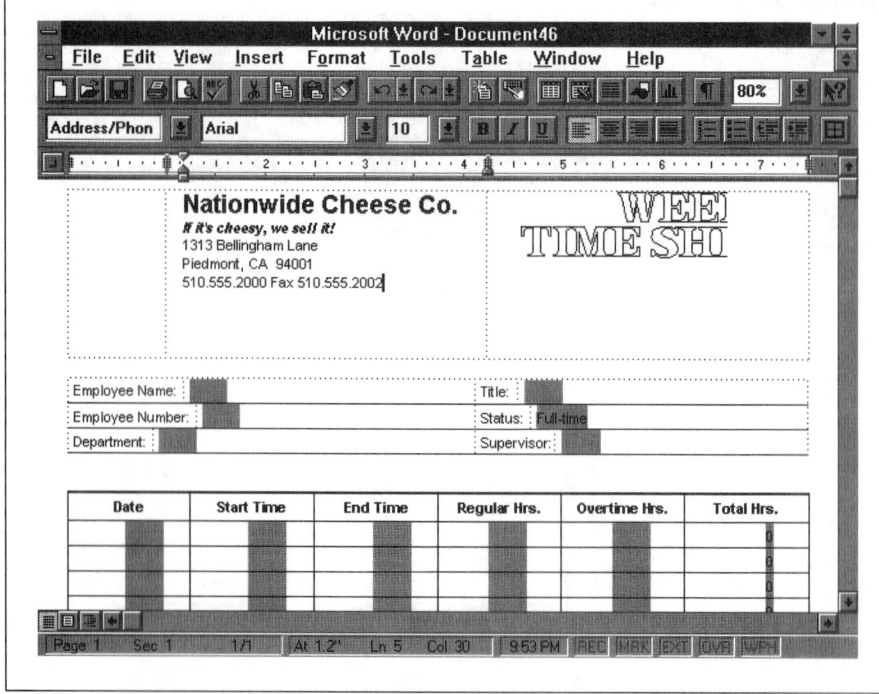

FIGURE 27.72

Type your own information in the company name, slogan, address, and phone number areas.

5. Then reprotect the document by selecting Tools ➤ Protect Document. This brings up the Protect Document dialog box:

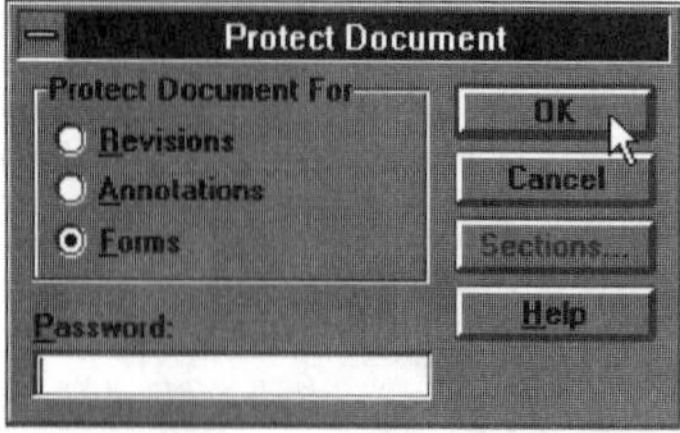

6. Make sure Forms is selected and click OK.
7. Select File ➤ Save As. When the Save As dialog box appears, type a new file name and select Document Template in the Save File as Type drop-down list box.

Now, whenever you want to fill out a time sheet, select File ➤ New and choose your customized time-sheet template. Then enter the particular information required, such as the employee name, number, department, and title; employment status (you get to choose from a drop-down list form field); name of supervisor; and the dates, starting times, ending times, regular, and overtime hours for the week. When your time sheet is complete, save and print it.

Power Tools

PART FIVE

CHAPTER 28

Mail Merge: Creating Custom Documents

▸▸ FAST TRACK

▸ ***Word for Windows' new Mail Merge Helper*** **706**

greatly simplifies the creation of merged documents. You can use it to produce form letters, mailing labels, envelopes, and catalogs.

▸ ***To perform a merge*** **706**

you need a *main document*, which contains the text of the document to be generated and fields in which to insert information, and a *data source*, which contains the records that will be inserted into the fields in the main document.

▸ ***To start the Mail Merge Helper*** **712**

select Tools ➤ Mail Merge....

▸ ***To start your main document for the merge*** **713**

select the Create button in the Mail Merge Helper dialog box and choose the type of document to create from the drop-down list.

▸ ***To specify the data source for the merge*** **715**

click the Get Data button in the Mail Merge Helper dialog box and choose whether to open an existing data source or create a new data source.

▸ ***Prepare your data source for the merge*** **716**

by adding, removing, and arranging fields using the Field Names in Header Row box.

▸ ***Enter records in your data source*** **718**

by using the Data Form dialog box.

▶▶ **W*ord*** for Windows' Mail Merge feature lets you quickly create personalized correspondence and other documents by combining (*merging*) information from two different files. For instance, you could merge a list of names and addresses from one file (your *data document*) with a form letter in another file (your *main document*) to produce a number of personalized form letters.

Never going to do a mail merge? What about producing a catalog, a form, or an invoice—or even a whole bunch of labels? Mail Merge can help with all these tasks. You could even personalize a Christmas letter to all your relatives, tailoring the news to what each one would be interested in. That beats a business letter for entertainment any day, so we'll use that as an example in this chapter.

You insert data instructions (*fields*) in the main document wherever you want data from the data source to appear in your merged documents. For instance, for this Christmas letter to your friends and relatives, you could use fields to create suitable salutations for each one. Instead of writing plain old boring "Dear" to each victim, you could have a salutation field containing any number of greetings. Then you could have a name field for the hapless recipient of the letter. And then, if you wanted, you could have a third field (to appear on the same line) of further greeting. This way, you could produce such salutations as "Hi, Joe Bob, how's it going?" and "My darling little Rosemary, how much you've grown this year!" as well as the staid "Dear Aunt Edna." How's that for variety?

Once the main document and the data source are prepared, you're ready to merge them. The Mail Merge Helper lets you send merged documents directly to your printer or save them to a file for editing and later printing.

In either case, Word will automatically take care of things like word wrap and pagination for each new document. Figure 28.1 shows an overview of the elements in a mail-merge project.

FIGURE 28.1

Mail-merge projects require a data source (top) and a main document (bottom) to produce new documents that contain information from both.

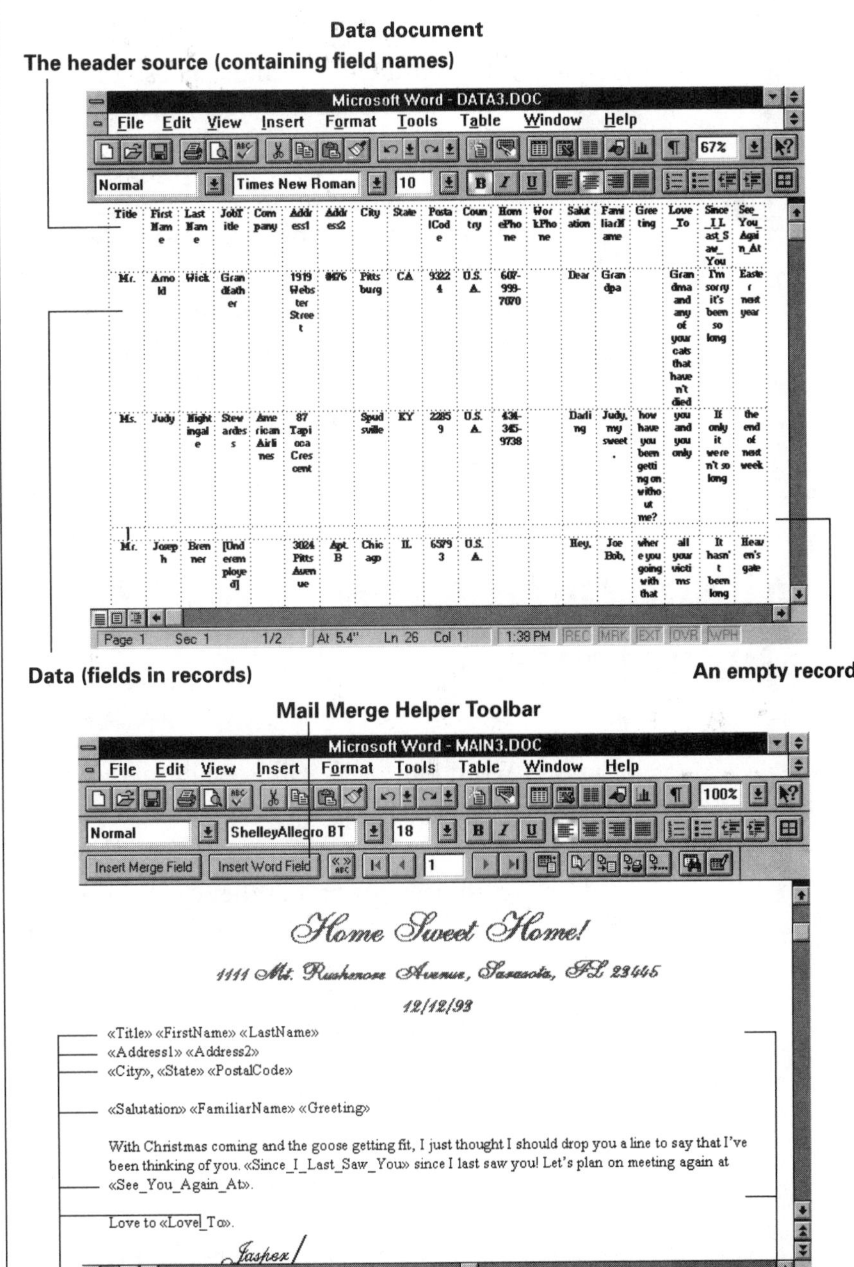

Thanks to Word 6's new Mail Merge Helper, merging is relatively painless, though you still need to pay plenty of attention to what you're doing. Some planning beforehand doesn't hurt either, but it's not absolutely essential. That said, let's get into it.

►► **NOTE**

Unfortunately, a book this size cannot cover all the variables involved in mail merges. Sometimes you'll find it easier to copy a form letter a few times and paste in the names and addresses of the recipients rather than perform an entire mail merge. Take a quick reality check before turning blindly to the Mail Merge Helper.

►► About Data Sources and Main Documents

Data sources are organized collections of information—databases—stored as Word tables. As you'll see in this chapter, Word 6's Mail Merge Helper leads you step by step through the creation of a new data source.

Word can also use data from other applications, such as Microsoft Excel or Microsoft Access. All data sources, no matter where they come from, contain *records* and *fields*. For instance, an employee data source would usually contain one record for each employee. This record would contain multiple fields—one field for the employee's first name, one for the middle initial, one for the last name, one for each part of the address, and so on.

Main documents, as mentioned above, contain the text of your project (the body of a letter, for instance), fields, and merge instructions.

▶ Using Main Documents from Earlier Versions of Word

You can use main documents from earlier versions of Word for Windows—for example, version 2.0*x*—with no problem. Simply open the document in Word for Windows 6 and proceed as normal.

▶▶ NOTE

When you open a main document in Word 6, it will bring with it the association (to its data source) with which it was last saved. If you use a previously created main document, remember to attach to it any new data source that you want to use.

▶ Using Main Documents from Other Applications

You can use a main document from other applications by opening that document in Word 6 and converting its contents to Word for Windows. However, field names and formatting from some applications may not translate well into Word for Windows format. Check the fields in your main document and adjust them if necessary before completing the merge.

If you experience problems, try pasting the main document into Word for Windows as plain text then applying the formatting and entering the field names.

▶ Using Data Sources from Other Applications

You can use data sources from other applications in your Word for Windows merges. For example, if you have data in a Microsoft Excel spreadsheet, you can insert either the whole worksheet or just a range of cells. If you have Microsoft Access, you can open a database and insert records from a table or a selection of records defined by a query.

After opening a data source in another application, make sure that the merge fields in your main document match those in the data source.

▸▸ Creating Your First Mail-Merge Project

The best way to learn how to create a print merge document is to try one. Consider working along as you read the rest of this chapter.

▸ Project Overview

For each new mail-merge project, you'll need to:

- Create a new data source
- Enter information into the data source
- Create and proof the text of your main document
- Insert fields into your main document
- Check for design and data-entry errors
- Merge the data source and main document and print the merge documents

For your first mail-merge project, Word's Mail Merge Helper runs you through the process of creating your data source and main document in a given order. If this feels like wearing a straitjacket, don't worry—on subsequent projects you can vary the order in which you complete the steps. For instance, you can create the main document first and then create a data source, or vice versa.

Because data sources in Word are simply documents containing tables, you can add information and edit them at any time before doing the actual merge. Once you get comfortable with merging and its possibilities, feel free to do things in any workable order that pleases you.

While you don't need to type your main document first, it's often helpful to make a draft to get a sense of which information you will need from your data sources and where to insert it.

▶▶ NOTE

If you already have a data source, simply open it or adapt it for the new project.

▶ Planning Your Data Document

Designing a useful and easy-to-maintain data source is one of the most important parts of a new mail-merge project. With a little ingenuity, you can use the same data sources for a number of projects.

For instance, if you plan to use an employee data source to send letters or memos, you might want one field for the employee's full legal name and another for an informal salutation. That way you could address mailing envelopes to Dr. Tyler Z. Gradgrinder and have the salutation of the letters or memos read *Dear Ty* or *Dear Doc*.

At first glance, it might seem a good idea to create a single field for all the address information needed for letters and labels. Then you could type everything—the recipient's name, company name, street address, city, state, and zip code—in that single field, insert that field in your main documents for form letters and envelopes, and merge merrily away. The problem with this comes when you need to break up the information you put in that field—for example, to produce a quick list of employees (without their full addresses) who live in a particular city who might appreciate ride-sharing.

It's far better to break your data up into multiple fields. Create separate fields for recipients' first and last names. Then you can use Word's Sort feature to produce alphabetized lists or labels sorted by last name. Break addresses down into five or six fields, as Word's Mail Merge Helper encourages you to do: street address, apartment number (if any), city, state, country (if you're international), and zip code. Putting city, state, country, and zip code in their own fields gives you enormous flexibility—you can easily find out who all your customers are in, say, Anaheim, Colorado, or Mexico.

►► TIP

Test your new design with small data documents containing a dozen or so representative records. Try your sample data source with a number of different main documents, or have an experienced print-merge user look over your new design before you spend hours entering data into your first data source. Consider keeping sample main documents and data sources at hand in a test directory so you can perform quick tests on new merge projects you put together.

►► Using the Mail Merge Helper

Word 6's Mail Merge Helper guides you through the steps of merging documents. The process seems a little convoluted the first time, but it works well. Once you've tried it once or twice, you'll be merging merrily with the best of them.

►► NOTE

In the following sections, we'll discuss how to perform the different stages of a mail merge by using the Mail Merge Helper, because this is the easiest way to merge. We'll indicate parenthetically how you can proceed without using the Mail Merge Helper.

To start the Mail Merge Helper, select Tools ➤ Mail Merge.... The Mail Merge Helper dialog box appears, as shown in Figure 28.2. Note the instructions in the box at the top telling you to click the Create button to set up the mail merge. Watch these instructions as you proceed with subsequent stages of the mail merge. If you're ever confused about what to do next, consult this box.

The first step in the mail merge is to create your main document, as the type of main document governs the subsequent choices you can make in the Mail Merge Helper. Form Letters, Mailing Labels, Envelopes,

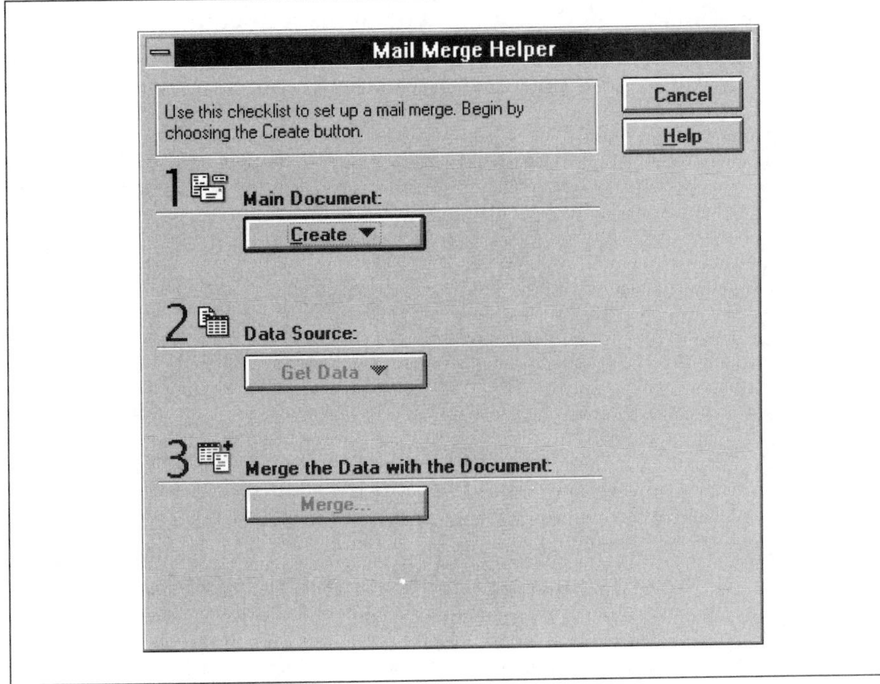

FIGURE 28.2

The Mail Merge Helper dialog box. Watch the instructions in the top left corner.

and Catalogs have different components, so the Mail Merge Helper offers you different choices of data source.

▶▶ Starting Your Main Document

To start your main document, follow these steps:

1. Select the Create button to start creating your main document. A list will drop down offering you four choices—Form Letters, Mailing Labels, Envelopes, and Catalog:

2. Select the type of main document you want. (In the example, I've chosen Form Letters....) A dialog box will appear offering you the choice of the active window or a new main document:

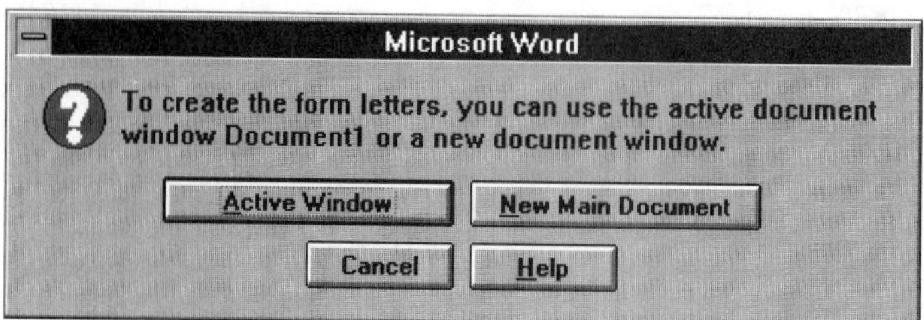

3. Select the window you want to use. If you're starting from a new document, as in the example, or if the active window contains information for your main document, choose the Active Window button. If your active window contains valuable information that has nothing to do with the mail merge, choose the New Main Document button.

   - If you choose the New Main Document button, Word will open a new document. The previously active document stays open—Word does not save or close it.

Regardless of which button you chose, Word will return you to the Mail Merge Helper dialog box for the next stage of the mail merge, arranging the data source. You'll see that the space below the Create button now lists the information you've entered so far—the type of merge and the main document to use:

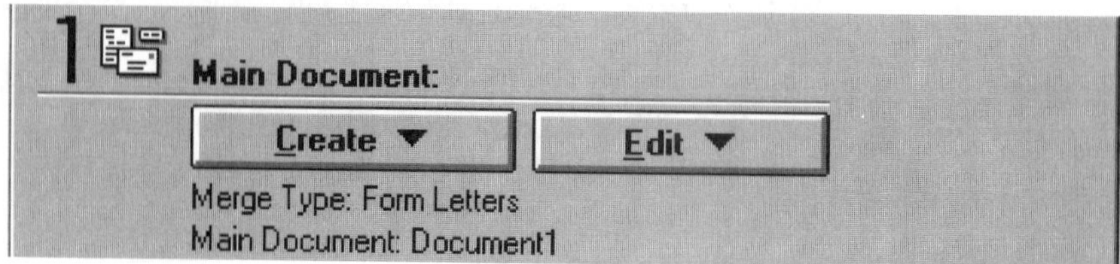

The information box at the top of the Mail Merge Helper dialog box tells you that the next step is to specify the data source. Let's do it.

▶ Specifying the Data Source

Next, you need to specify the data source and arrange in it the fields that will be available to your main document for the merge.

1. Click the Get Data button to display a list of options for your data source:

2. If you already have a data source that you want to use, select Open Data Source.... If you want to create the data source, select Create Data Source....

If you chose Open Data Source..., skip ahead a section. If you chose Create Data Source..., read the next section.

▶ Creating a Data Source

The Create Data Source dialog box that appears when you choose Create Data Source... contains a list of commonly used field names for the type of mail merge you're performing. Figure 28.3 shows the Create Data Source dialog box for form letters.

FIGURE 28.3 ▶

The Create Data Source dialog box offers a list of commonly used field names. Chop and change these at will.

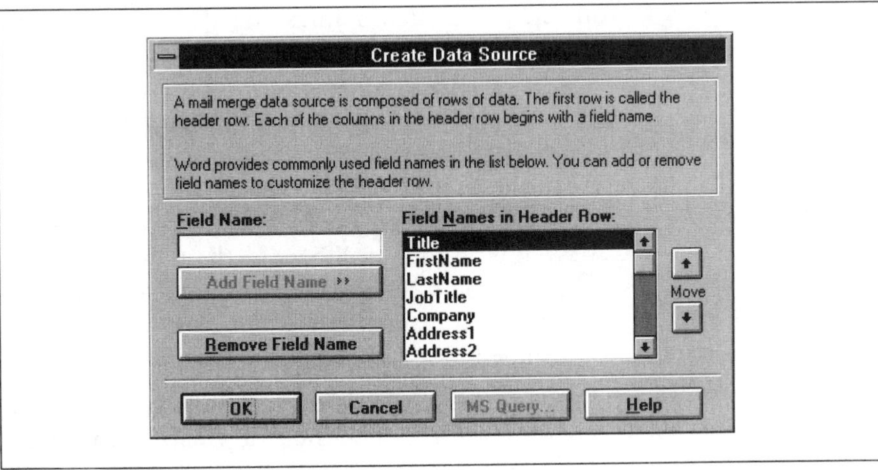

Adding a Field Name

Here's how to add field names to the list in the Field Names in Header Row box:

1. Type the name in the Field Name box.

▸▸ NOTE

Field names can be up to 40 characters long and can contain letters, numbers, and underscores (_). Field names *cannot* contain spaces and must start with a letter (not a number or an underscore). For example, What_We_Discussed_At_Yesterday's_Meeting is an acceptable field name (and might remind you better of the field's purpose than MeetingTopic), but 1994_May_15_Meeting is not. Bear in mind that the ends of very long field names may not show in the Field Names in Header Row box, so it can be confusing to have long field names that differ only at their ends.

2. Click the Add Field Name button. The new field name is added at the bottom of the list.
3. To move the new field name to a different position in the list, make sure it's highlighted and click the Move arrow buttons.

You can see the field names that I've entered for my Christmas mail merge at the bottom of the list in Figure 28.4.

Removing or Modifying a Field Name

1. In the Field Names in Header Row box, highlight the field name you want to remove by clicking it with the mouse or by scrolling to it with the scroll bars or the down arrow. Then click the Remove Field Name button. The field name will be removed from the Field Names in Header Row list and will appear in the Field Name box.
2. To modify the field name, make your changes in the Field Name box and then click the Add Field Name button.

FIGURE 28.4

New field names for my sample mail merge.

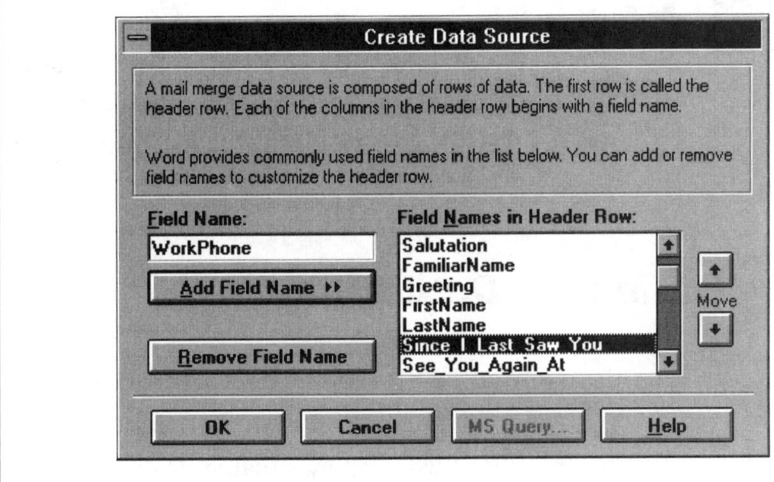

Rearranging Field Names

To rearrange the field names in the Field Names in Header Row box, highlight the field you want to move and click the Move up and down arrows beside the Field Names in Header Row box to move the highlight field up or down.

Saving Your Data Source

When you've finished adding, removing, and arranging fields, click OK to save your data-source. In the Save Data Source dialog box that appears, enter a name for your data-source file and select OK to save the file.

Word will save the data-source file under the name you give and then return you to the Mail Merge Helper dialog box.

Opening a Data Source

To open an existing data source, select Open Data Source... from the Get Data drop-down list. The Open Data Source dialog box works just like the File Open dialog box: Select the document you want to use and click OK. Word will open the document and return you to the Mail Merge Helper dialog box.

▸▸ NOTE

If you want to use a data source from another application, such as Microsoft Excel or Microsoft Access, simply choose it at this point and select the data records you want to use.

▸ Editing the Data Source

Back in the Mail Merge Helper dialog box, you'll see that Word displays the name of the data source document beneath the Get Data button.

Word now checks your data source to see if it contains records. If it doesn't, Word will display a dialog box informing you of this and inviting you to edit the data source or the main document, as shown below. Choose the Edit Data Source button to edit your data source.

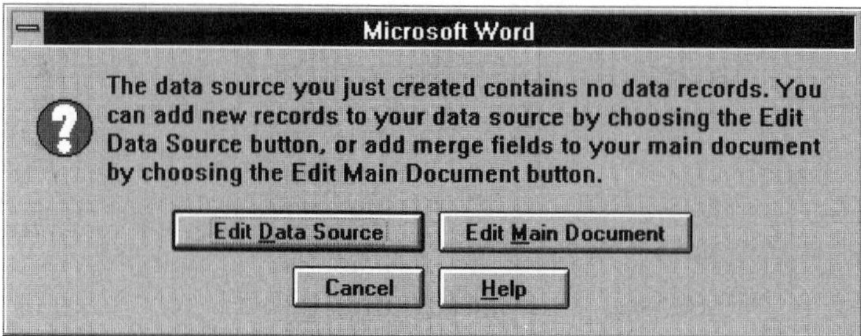

Entering Your Records

In the Data Form dialog box that Word displays (see Figure 28.5), enter the details for each of your records by typing text into the boxes. Press Tab or ↵ to move from field to field. To move backwards, press Shift+Tab.

Here's how to alter the records in the Data Form dialog box:

- To add a new record, choose the Add New button.
- To delete a record, choose the Delete button.
- If you realize you've trashed a record (by entering data in the wrong place or whatever), click the Restore button to return its entries to their previous state.

FIGURE 28.5

Entering data in the Data Form dialog box.

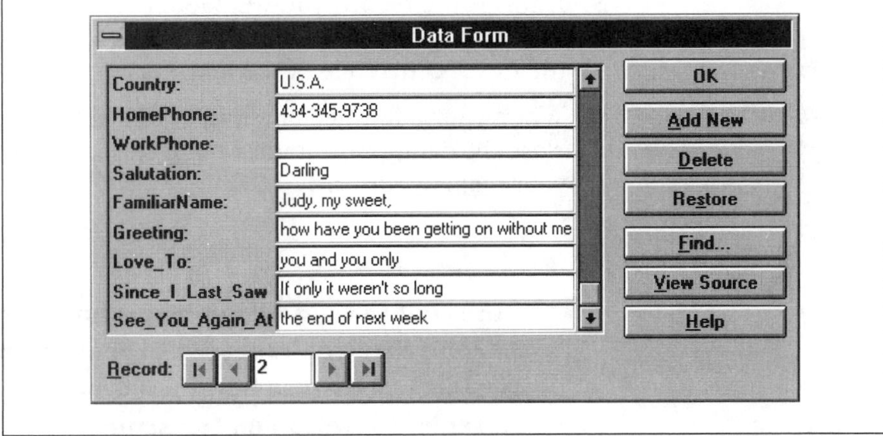

To Find a Record

Word's database functions offer great flexibility in searching. You can search for any word or part of a word in any of the fields.

To find a record, follow these steps:

1. Click the Find... button. The Find in Field dialog box will appear:

2. Type the word or words you want to find in the Find What box.
3. Click the arrow at the right end of the In Field box to drop down the list of field names and select the name of the field you want to search.
4. Click the Find First button. Word will search for and display the first record it finds containing the word or words in the selected field.

5. If this is the record you were looking for, click Close to close the Find in Field dialog box. If not, click the Find Next button to find the next occurrence of the text.
6. When you've finished entering or updating your records, click OK to close the data source and save the changes. Now you're ready to edit your main document.

TIP

If the Find in Field dialog box is hovering annoyingly over the field you're trying to read, grab it by clicking anywhere in its title bar, then drag it to a more convenient location on the screen.

You can also edit your data file directly (if the Data Form dialog box is on the screen, click OK to close it). You can simply type in the cells of the table as you would normally. (Don't worry about word wrap—or anything cosmetic for that matter.)

You'll also notice that Word automatically includes the Database Toolbar in any data-source document. Here it is:

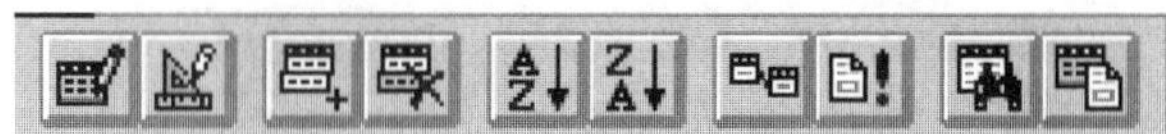

Here's what the buttons on the Database Toolbar do:

ICON	NAME	FUNCTION
	Data Form	Brings up the Data Form dialog box (the one that appeared when you first created the data source)
	Manage Fields	Lets you add, remove, or rename fields
	Add New Record	Inserts a new record (row) in the data-source table
	Delete Record	Removes the current record (row) from the data-source table

ICON	NAME	FUNCTION
	Sort Ascending	Sorts all the records (rows) in the data source in ascending order, based on the current field (column)
	Sort Descending	Sorts all the records (rows) in the data source in descending order, based on the current field (column)
	Insert Database	Inserts records from a data source
	Update Fields	Updates the contents of selected *field codes* (such as links to database documents)
	Find Record	Searches for a record with specified text in a specified field
	Mail Merge Main Document	Switches you to the main document

▶ *Sorting the Data Source*

If your data source grows large, you might find it useful to sort the records. This makes it easier to search through the data source manually, it gives you a way to keep tabs on the progress of a large print job, and some deals from the US Post Office require that your bulk mail be sorted by ZIP code.

Sorting a data source is easy.

1. Put the insertion point in the field (column) you want to sort on. It doesn't matter which record (row) you put it in.
2. Click either the Ascending Sort or Descending Sort button on the Database Toolbar. (For normal alphabetical order, click Ascending Sort.)

▸ Finding a Record in the Data Source

If your data source is very large and you don't feel like sifting through it manually to find a particular record, click the Find Record button on the Database Toolbar. This will bring up the Find in Field dialog box, as shown:

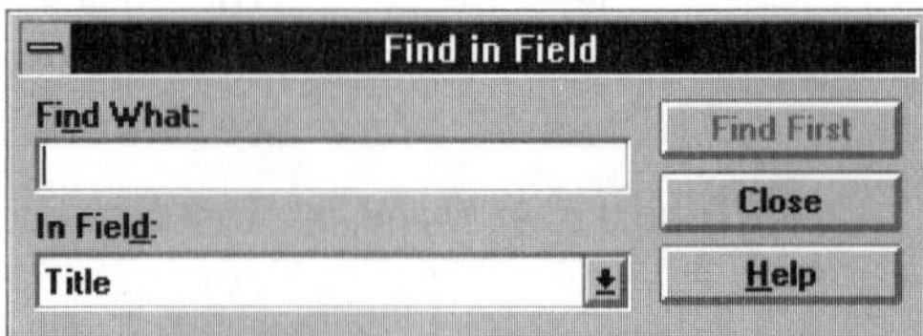

1. Type the text you're looking for in the Find What box.
2. Press Tab.
3. Select the field where the text will be found in the In Field drop-down list box.
4. Click Find First. Word highlights the first record it finds with the text you entered in the field you selected.
5. If necesary, click Find Next.
6. If necessary, repeat step 5.

▸ Inserting or Removing Fields or Records in a Data Source

If you maintain a data source long enough, you're going to have to make changes to it from time to time. The Database Toolbar gives you easy shortcuts for managing your fields and records.

Inserting, Removing, or Renaming Fields

Before fooling around with your fields, save a backup copy of your data source in case things go seriously awry. Then, to make changes to the fields in your data source, click the Manage Fields button on the Database Toolbar. This brings up the Manage Fields dialog box:

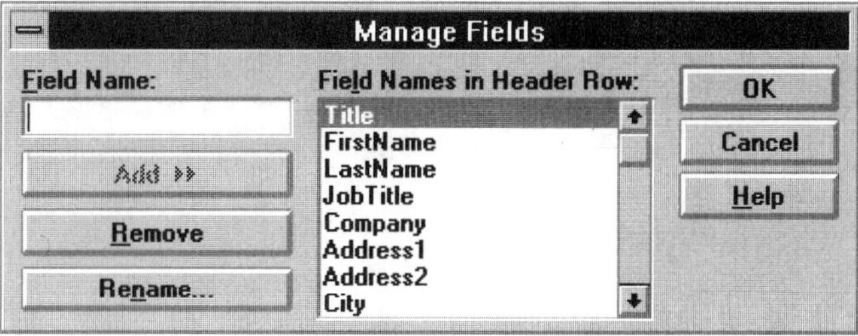

You can make all your field changes from this one dialog box.

- To insert a new field, type the field name in the Field Name box and then click the Add >> button. (The field will be added at the end of the list—at the right side of the data table. There's no shortcut for moving a field after you've created the data source, though you can move it by selecting the entire column and dragging it to a new location in the table.)
- To remove a field and all the data in it, highlight the name in the Field Names in Header Row list box and then click the Remove button. Then click Yes to confirm that you *really* do want to do this.
- To rename a field, highlight the old name in the Field Names in Header Row list box and then click the Rename button. This brings up the Rename Field dialog box:

  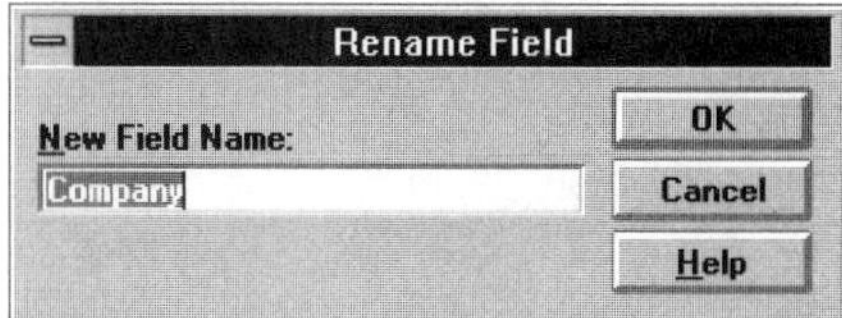

  Type a new field name and then click OK.

When you are done, click OK in the Manage Fields dialog box. If you'd like to undo your changes, click Cancel (or press Esc) instead.

►► NOTE

You can also make any of these changes directly simply by editing the table in the data source. Somehow, though, it seems easier and less risky to use the Manage Fields dialog box to make these changes.

Inserting or Removing Records

Data sources inevitably grow (though you occasionally need to prune them back as well) as new names are added to your mailing list or new records in general. The Database Toolbar makes it easy to add or remove records when the time comes to make these changes.

You can always add a new record to the end of a data-source table simply by pressing Tab in the last field of the last record. Also, the Data Form dialog box (Figure 28.5) has an Add New button. Click it to add a record to the end of the data-source table.

- To add a record to the end of the data-source table, click the Add New Record button on the Database Toolbar.
- To delete a record, first select it. Then click the Delete Record button on the Database Toolbar. To delete several records at once, select them all and then click the Delete Record button.

► *Inserting Data from Another File*

If you've already got the data you need for your merge in an existing file—a word-processing, database, or even a spreadsheet document—then you can insert this data into your data source. There are two ways you can do this. You can simply insert the data directly into your data source, or you can insert field codes that link your data source to the database file. (Chapter 30 explains links and Chapter 32 fields.)

The benefit of inserting field codes is that you can update the information automatically when it changes in the original database file. If you know you'll never need to update it, you can simply insert the data directly. Either way, do this:

1. Click the Insert Database button on the Database Toolbar. This brings up the Database dialog box:

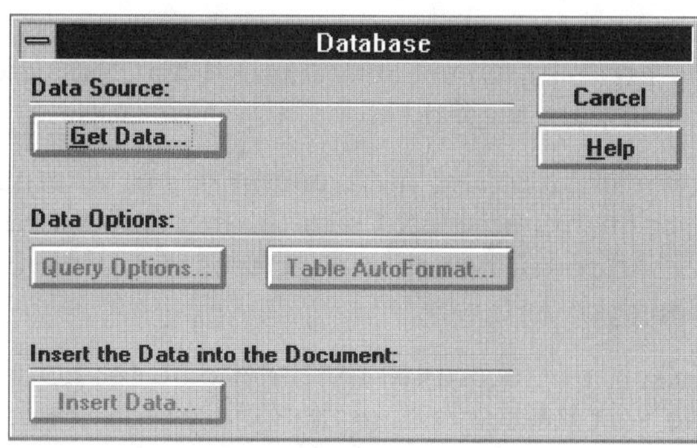

2. Click the Get Data button. This brings up the Open Data Source dialog box, which works just like the Open File dialog box. Select the document you want to use and click OK.

For some types of files, such as spreadsheets and databases, Word will display a dialog box that allows you to select just part of the data from the other file for insertion.

3. If you want to limit the data from the other file in some way, click the Query Options button on the Database dialog box. This brings up the Query Options dialog box:

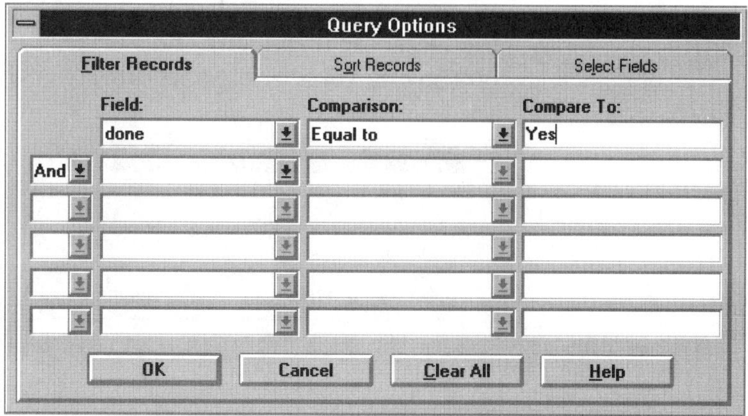

From this dialog box, you can filter the records, sort the records, and select which fields to import:

To limit the records imported into your data source, choose a field from the Field drop-down list box (or just type the first letter of the field you want, repeatedly if necessary). Then press Tab and choose a comparison in the Comparison box (such as Equal to, Greater than—b is greater than a—and so on). Then press Tab again and Enter a value to compare the field with.

If you want to add more conditions to your query, accept And as the relationship or select Or in the little unnamed box to the left of the second row. Then repeat the process for the Field, Comparison, and Compare To boxes.

To sort the records in the other data file before importing them, click the Sort Records tab in the Query Options dialog box. Choose a field to sort on in the Sort by drop-down list box and then accept Ascending order or select Descending. If you want to add secondary and or tertiary sort criteria, select fields and sort order in the next two boxes.

To select fields to import, click the Select Fields tab in the Query Options dialog box. Word starts you off with all the fields selected. To remove one, highlight it and click the Remove button. To remove them all and start over, click the Remove All button. That will change the buttons to Select and Select All. Then highlight and select the fields you want. If you don't want a header row of field names in the imported data, uncheck Include Field Names.

When you are done with the Query Options dialog box, click OK.

4. When you are ready, click the Insert Data button at the bottom of the Database dialog box. This brings up the Insert Data dialog box, giving you one more control over the import procedure:

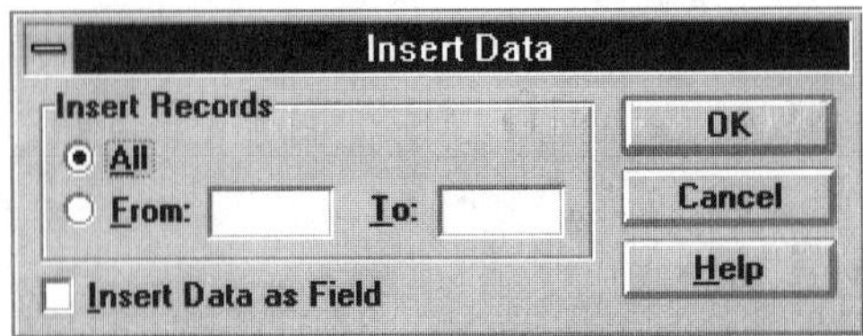

5. If you want to import only certain records from the data file (and you know which ones they are by number), enter the numbers of the first and last records you want in the From and To boxes of the Insert Data dialog box. (You can always remove records after importing, as explained above in Inserting and Removing Records.)
6. If you want to insert linked data into your data source instead of straight text, check Insert Data as Field.
7. When you are ready, click OK.
8. If you already had data in your data source and the insertion point was in the table, then Word will warn you that the data table will be replaced with the imported data. If you want this, click Yes. If not, click No and then move the insertion point past the original table (or start over with a new data document).

If you chose to insert linked data, then you can update any entry by selecting it and clicking F9. To unlink the data and turn it into regular text, select the entire table and press Ctrl+Shift+F9.

►► Editing the Main Document

Main documents contain the following:

- Text and punctuation
- Merge instructions and field names that Word uses to merge data

Figure 28.6 shows a main document for our sample mail merge. We'll discuss the various elements in detail.

► Text in Main Documents

Use Word 6's word-processing and graphics features to create the text and design elements for your main document. In the sample, a suitably sickly letterhead was created by typing the return address in Shelley-Allegro and centering it. (The first line was increased to 26 points, and the second to 16 points.)

FIGURE 28.6 ▶

The main document for the Christmas mail-merge letter.

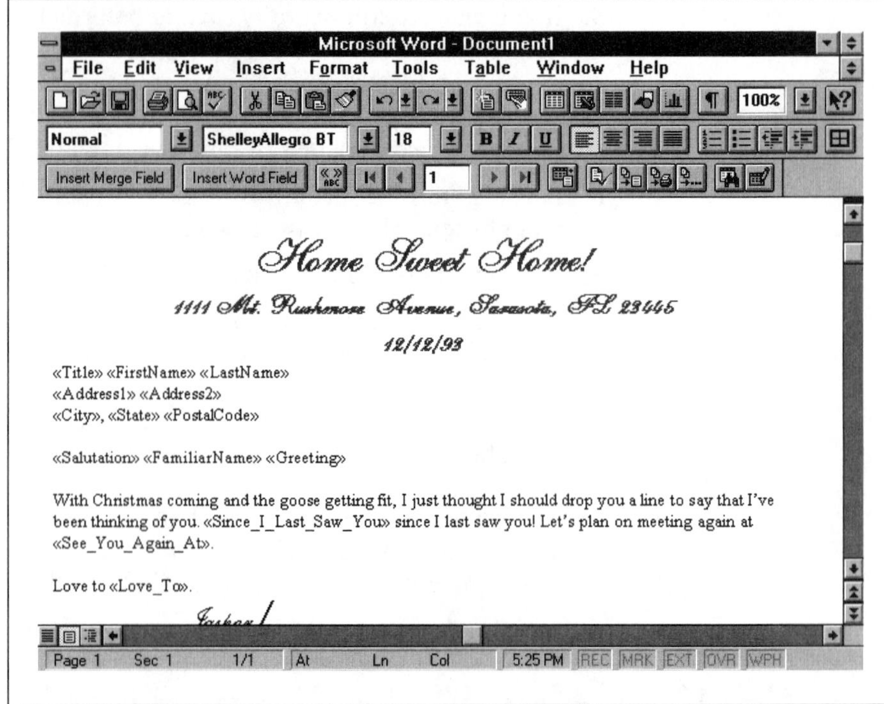

The body of the letter was typed (in 10-point Times New Roman) using regular Word techniques, with data instructions containing field names and other merge devices inserted as needed, as explained below.

▶ Inserting Data Instructions

The Mail Merge Helper makes it easy to insert field names and other data instructions in your main documents. Just place the insertion point where you want to insert a data instruction, then pull down the appropriate list from the Mail Merge Toolbar and pick the item to insert.

For example, to insert the title field name shown in Figure 28.6, you would place the insertion point on a new line at the beginning of the document (below the header). Then click the Insert Merge Field button on the Mail Merge Toolbar to display the list of field names available in the associated data source. Next select the appropriate field name to insert it into the document. (The guillemets—<< and >>—come free with the field name.)

When preparing the text of a main document, remember to include things like spaces between field names and any required punctuation following them. Running people's first and last names together will spoil the effect of your carefully personalized letters. You know the feeling if you've ever been insulted by Publishers' Clearing House.

As you'll see in a moment, you can use combinations of merge fields from the Insert Merge Field button and Word fields from the Insert Word Field button (both on the Mail Merge Toolbar) with text typed from the keyboard to put together powerful merge instructions.

▶ Try It

Take a moment to create a main document for a merge yourself. The steps below refer to the sample letter in Figure 28.6. Use these instructions for general guidance.

1. Create a header for your letter by selecting View ➤ Header and Footer, typing the return address, and applying such formatting as you see fit. If you want to include the date, click the Date button on the Header and Footer Toolbar.
2. Close the header by clicking the Close button on the Header and Footer Toolbar.
3. With the insertion point at the beginning of the document, insert the Title field by clicking on the Insert Merge Field button and selecting Title from the drop-down list. Don't press ↵ yet—the Title, FirstName, and LastName fields all belong on the same line.
4. Type a space to separate the Title and FirstName fields.
5. Use the Insert Merge Field drop-down list to insert the FirstName field.
6. Add a space and insert the LastName field.
7. Now press ↵ to start a new line.
8. Add the Address1, Address2, City, State, and PostalCode fields, together with whatever punctuation and spacing they need.
9. On a new line, insert the Salutation field, a space, the FamiliarName field, another space, and the Greeting field.
10. Type the body of your letter, including any merge fields that you need.

11. Save your main document.
12. If you didn't enter any data in your data source earlier, switch to it (if necessary, crank up the Mail Merge Helper by choosing Tools ➤ Mail Merge...) and add a few names and addresses. Try leaving the Address2 field blank in at least one record so you can see how Word 6 handles blank lines.

If your main document does not contain merge fields, Word will display this dialog box, inviting you to edit it and insert merge fields:

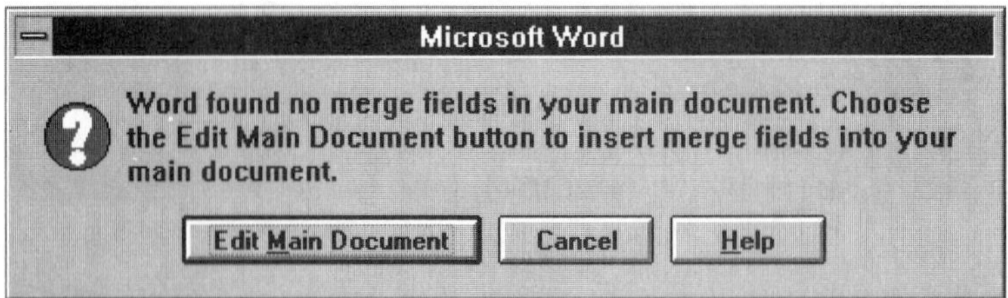

Choose the Edit Main Document button if you want to edit your main document. The Mail Merge Helper dialog box disappears, leaving your main document on-screen, ready for editing.

► Testing and Proofing

Before firing up the Mail Merge Helper and churning out a whole batch of letters, proofread your work. Use Word's spell checker and grammar tools (see Chapter 19 for more information on these). Make any necessary corrections. Remember that Word will faithfully copy every error in your main document into every single copy it merges.

Next run the Mail Merge Helper's error-checking program. Choose the Check Errors button from the Mail Merge Toolbar. The Checking and Reporting Errors dialog box will appear:

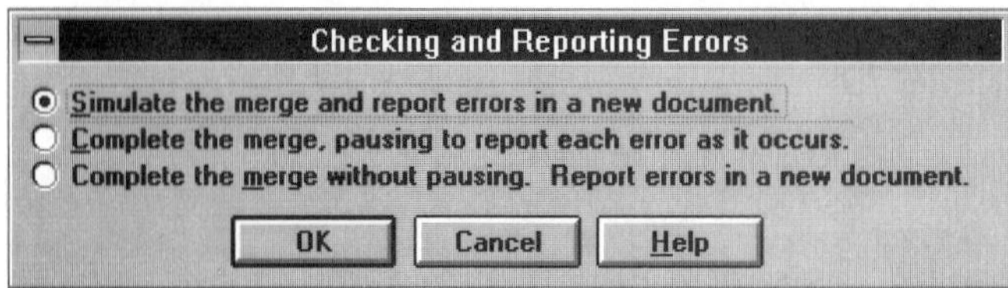

For now, choose the first option, *Simulate the merge and report errors in a new document.* Word will check your data source and main document for errors (such as missing data fields in the data source and misspelled field names in your main document). If Word finds no errors, you will see a happy dialog box telling you that no mail merge errors have been found. If errors are found, correct them.

As a final check, consider merging some or all of your documents to a file and inspecting them, rather than printing them all at once. We'll look at how to do this in just a moment. First, let's look at Word's sorting and filtering features.

►► Sorting Merged Documents

Usually, records are merged in the order they occur in your data source, but Word 6's Mail Merge Helper lets you sort the records during the merge. In addition, Word lets you use filters to restrict merging to records containing certain data. (Filtering is discussed in the next section.)

To sort records before you perform a merge, follow these steps:

1. Open the Mail Merge Helper dialog box and choose the Query Options... button. The Query Options dialog box will appear (see Figure 28.7).

FIGURE 28.7 ►

The Query Options dialog box. Here's where you choose sorting and filters for the merge you're about to perform. I'm going to sort my relatives by FamiliarName and then LastName. That way I'll be able to work out which aunt is which. I hope.

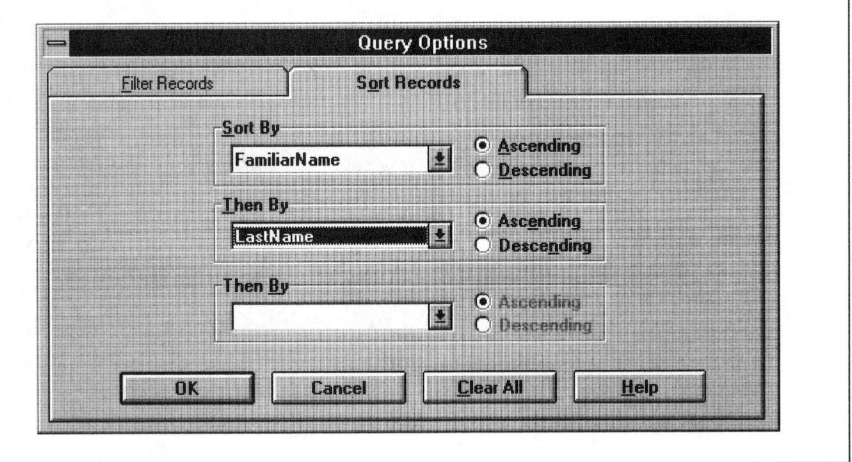

2. Click the Sort Records tab to enter your sorting preferences.
3. In the Sort By field that you want to use, click the down arrow, then select a field to sort by from the list that appears.
4. Select a field for one or both Then By fields if you want to refine your sort further.
5. When you've defined the sort to your satisfaction, click OK. If you mess things up, click the Clear All button to clear the fields and start again or click Cancel to escape from the dialog box.

▸▸ Filtering Merged Documents

If you're not content with sorting your records, you can filter them as well. Filtering gives you a lot of flexibility in removing entries from the merge records that for one reason or another you don't want to use. For instance, if I thought that my sister would never speak to me again if I sent her a form letter for Christmas, I could exclude her record from the merge to safeguard myself.

Here's how to set up filtering:

1. Pull up the Mail Merge Helper dialog box and choose the Query Options… button. The Query Options dialog box will appear.
2. Select the Filter Records tab.
3. In the Field column of the first row, choose the field you want to use as a filter.
4. In the Comparison column of the first row, drop down the list of filtering comparisons. This is what they do:

COMPARISON	EFFECT
Equal to	The contents of the data field you chose must match those of the Compare To box.
Not Equal to	The contents of the data field you chose must not match those of the Compare To box.

COMPARISON	EFFECT
Less than	The contents of the data field you chose must be less than those of the Compare To box.
Greater than	The contents of the data field you chose must be greater than those of the Compare To box.
Less than or Equal	The contents of the data field you chose must be less than or equal to those of the Compare To box.
Greater than or Equal	The contents of the data field you chose must be greater than or equal to those of the Compare To box.
Is Blank	The merge field must be empty.
Is Not Blank	The merge field must not be empty.

5. In the second row, choose And or Or in the first column to include additional or complementary criteria for filtering.
6. Repeat steps 3, 4, and 5 for further rows as necessary to refine your criteria further.
7. When you've defined the filtering criteria to your satisfaction, select OK. If you mess things up, select Clear All to start again or Cancel to escape from the Query Options dialog box.

NOTE

When you compare a data field that contains text, Word compares the sequence of characters based on the ANSI sort order. Because antelope precedes zebra alphabetically, Word considers it "less than" zebra. So if you wanted to retrieve data records for only the second half of the alphabet, you could specify LastName Is Greater Than M. If you mix numbers with letters, Word compares the numbers as though they were a sequence of text characters.

▸▸ Printing Merged Documents

When you've specified any filtering and sort-ordering that you want, you're ready to run the mail merge.

1. Start the merge process by making your main document the active document (click in it if necessary).
2. Click the Merge… button in the Mail Merge Helper dialog box to bring up the Merge dialog box (see Figure 28.8).
3. You can either merge directly to your printer by selecting Printer in the Merge To: box, or you can have Word merge to a new, untitled document that will contain all of the merge documents by selecting New Document.
4. Select the Records to Be Merged by choosing All or From: and To:. If you choose From: and To:, specify the record numbers for the merge to start and stop at.
5. The default is not to print blank lines when data fields are empty. If you *do* want to print blank lines when the fields are empty—perhaps you have a reason, like to show gaps in your data source—choose the *Print blank lines when data fields are empty* option.
6. When all is set to your liking, click OK. The mail merge will finally take place.

When the mail merge is finished, close the Mail Merge Helper dialog box. If you merged to a new document, it should be on-screen now. If you merged to a printer, the printer will be churning out your merged documents. Either way, check your output carefully before inflicting it on your victims. The law of mass mailing clearly states that you'll only notice an egregious error *after* you've mailed the whole batch.

If you have unsaved changes in your main document, Word will invite you to save them.

▸▸ Specifying Header Options

The header row is the row of fields at the top of a data source that identifies each kind of information in the data source—the Title, FirstName, and LastName fields and so on.

FIGURE 28.8

The Merge dialog box—the culmination of your quest. Choose your final options here.

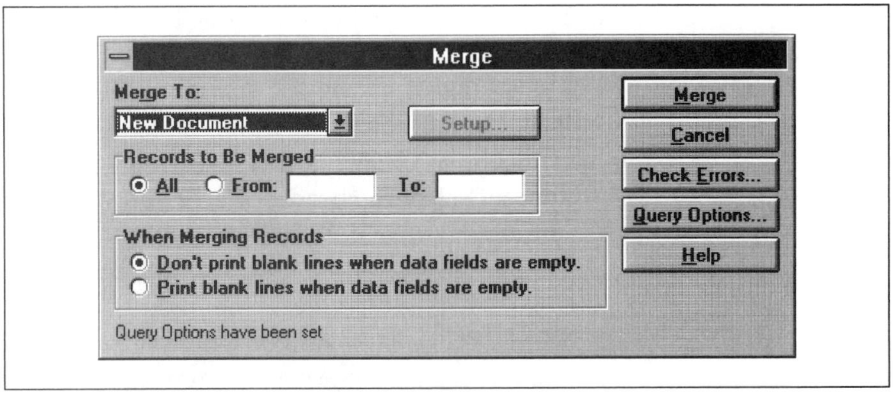

Why would you want to reuse a header? Well, you could then use the same header source with more than one data source. If you can't change the merge fields in a data source to match the names of the merge fields in a main document (the file might be read-only), you can use a header source that contains matching merge fields.

To specify a header source:

1. Choose the Get Data… button in the Mail Merge Helper dialog box and select Header Options…. The Header Options dialog box will appear (see Figure 28.9).
2. In the Header Options dialog box, choose Create… to create a new header source. Or choose Open… to open an existing header source, then skip ahead to step 5.
3. If you chose Create…, the Create Header Source dialog box will appear. This works just like the Create Data Source dialog box we discussed under "Creating a Data Source," earlier in the chapter. Add, remove, and rearrange the fields to your satisfaction, then click OK.

FIGURE 28.9

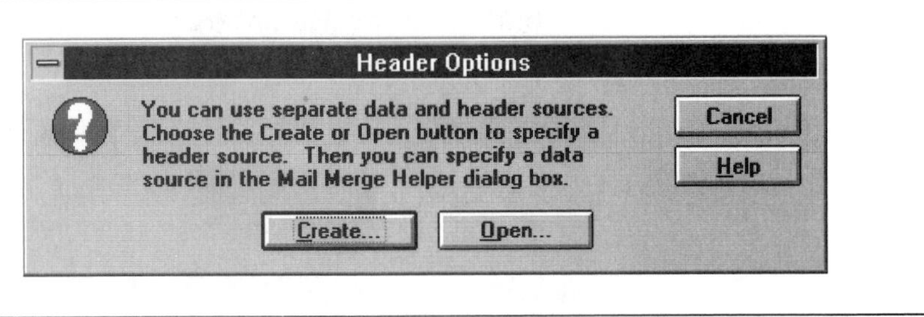

The Header Options dialog box. To open an existing header source, choose Open…. To create a new header source, choose Create….

4. In the Save Data Source dialog box that appears, give your header source a name and click OK. You'll be returned to the Mail Merge Helper dialog box, and the header source you created will now appear under the Get Data… button.
5. If you chose Open…, the Open Header Source dialog box will appear. Select the header source you want to use and click OK. You'll be returned to the Mail Merge Helper dialog box, and the header source you created will now appear under the Get Data… button.
6. Word will check the header source against the data source and warn you if the data source contains too many data fields, as shown below. The Merge… button on the Mail Merge Helper dialog box will be dimmed, indicating that you cannot yet run the merge.

7. If the data source contains too many fields, edit the data source or header source.

►► Checking for Errors in Your Data Source

To check your data source for errors (such as inconsistencies between the fields in the source and fields in the main document), click the Check Errors button on the Mail Merge Toolbar (the one with the checkmark on it). If you can't find it, maybe you're looking in the wrong document. Open the main document. Then click the Check for Errors button on the Mail Merge Toolbar. This brings up the Checking and Reporting Errors dialog box:

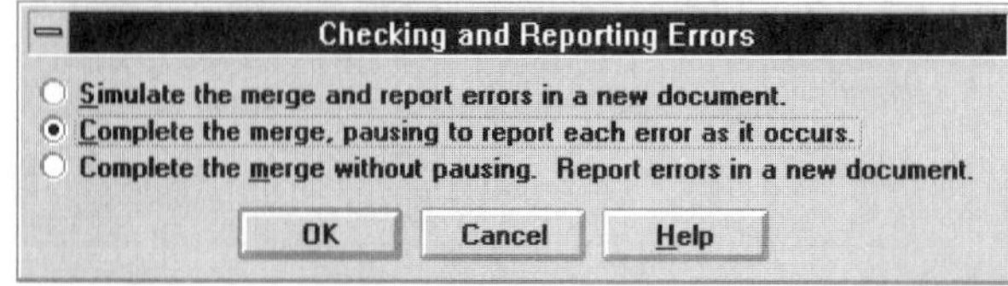

There are three options. Choose the first if you don't want to actually do the merge yet, just see what might go wrong if you did. Word will list any errors in a new document. The second option, the default, merges the data and main documents and reports errors to you in a dialog box as they occur. The third option proceeds with the merge and lists the errors in a new document.

If Word encounters no errors, it will report that fact to you when it's done. Correct any detected errors when the check is completed. The most common problems involve different numbers of fields in different records. All records must have the same numbers of fields, and that number must match the number of field names.

►► Merging onto Letterhead

If you want to print your form letters on letterhead, you have to make allowances for the first page of the letter so that the text begins low enough on that page to leave room for the letterhead itself. It's easy, though:

1. Go to the top of your main document.
2. Select File ➤ Page Setup.
3. Click the Margins tab.
4. Type a new top margin, large enough to clear the letterhead contents.
5. Click OK.
6. Go to the bottom of the first page.
7. Select Insert ➤ Break.
8. On the Break dialog box, click Next Page.
9. Click OK.
10. Select File ➤ Page Setup.
11. Reenter the original top margin.
12. Click OK.

If you don't have letterhead stock, you could skip steps 5 and 6 and then select View ➤ Header and Footer and create a letterhead (by typing and formatting text and inserting graphics such as a logo, if necessary) in the header area. When you're done, click Close.

►► Using Different Data Sources with a Single Main Document

You can create a master main document and merge different data sources into it. The procedure for attaching a new data source to a main document is essentially the same as the original procedure. Click the Mail Merge Helper button on the Mail Merge Toolbar. This brings up the Mail Merge Helper dialog box (see Figure 28.2). Click the Get Data button and select Open Data Source (or Create Data Source if you want to create the new data document on the fly).

That's it. The new data source is attached to the main document. Check the new data source for errors right away, in case the fields don't match up perfectly. Repeat the procedure to reattach the original data source at any time.

If you need to use different database documents as data sources, then you might want to attach a header file to your main document. A header file only needs to contain the field names (though it can be a complete data source in its own right and still function as a header file for another source). The new data source must have the same number of fields as there are in the header file, *but* it does not need to have a header row of its own to identify the fields.

To attach a header file, click the Get Data button in the Mail Merge Helper dialog box and choose Header Options. This brings up the Header Options dialog box:

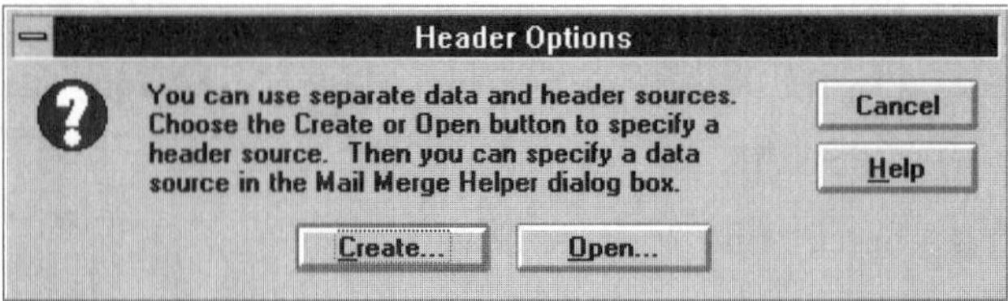

Click the Open button to open an existing data source as a header file or click the Create button to create a new one.

If you click Open, this will bring up the Open Header source dialog box (which looks uncannily like the Open Data Source dialog box). Select the file you want to use and click OK.

If you click Create, this brings up the Create Header Source dialog box:

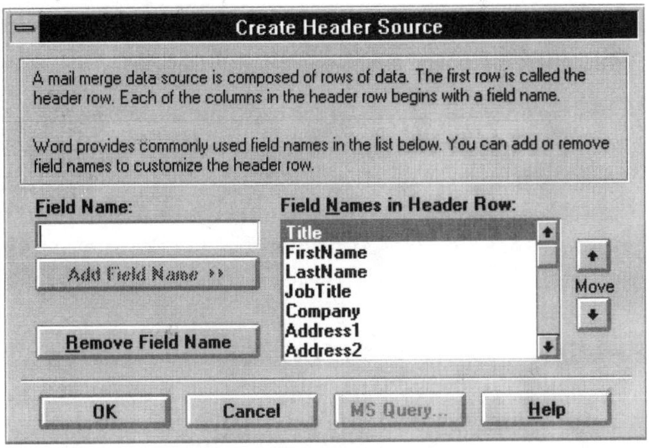

This looks about the same as the Create Data Source, and it works the same way too. Type field names and click Add Field Name to add them to the field-name list. Highlight existing field names and click Remove Field Name to delete them.

When you are done, click OK. The Save Header Source dialog box (much like the Save Data Source dialog box, of course) will appear. Type a file name and click OK.

After you attach a header source, you must still attach a data source (and it should not have a header row of its own, as it will be misinterpreted as a record).

▶▶ Using Word's Merge Instructions

Word 6 provides a number of ways to change its behavior based on the contents of individual records in your data source. As you've just seen, it can eliminate unwanted blank lines in merged documents. It can insert special text if certain conditions are met or stop during each merge to let you enter unique text from the keyboard. If you decide to use these features, be prepared to spend some time experimenting and troubleshooting.

► ASK...

The ASK feature causes Word to stop during the merge each time a new record is merged to prompt you for keyboard input to be printed.

ASK is normally used to include data in merged documents that has not been stored in the data document. Suppose, for example, that you were creating ten welcome letters to bungee jumpers, like the one in Figure 28.10, and that you wanted to enter a date and time for each jumper's first lesson. Suppose further that your data document does not contain a field for first lesson dates and times.

Setting Up an ASK Entry

When designing your main document, move the insertion point to where you want the information entered for the ASK field to appear. Then pick ASK... from the Insert Word Field drop-down list on the Mail Merge Toolbar. Word displays the Insert Word Field: Ask dialog box (see Figure 28.11).

Use this dialog box to create a new field unique to the main document (not the data source). In the Bookmark field, type a name for the bookmark. This gives you quick access to the field. In the Prompt box, enter the text that you want to appear on-screen during the merge to prompt the operator to enter appropriate information. In the Default Bookmark Text box, you can enter default text that will appear to guide the operator. When you're done, click OK.

Word gives you a preview of the dialog box that will appear:

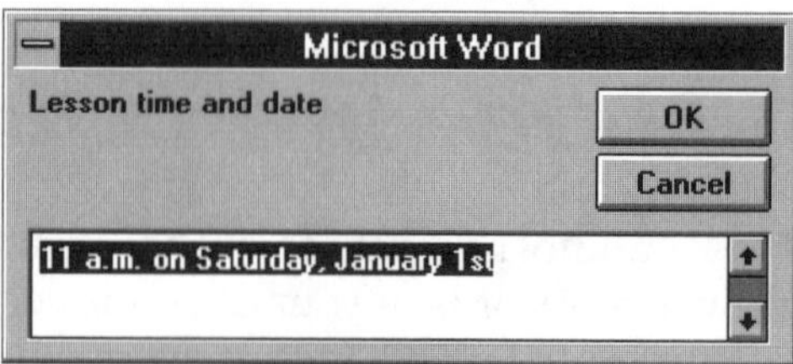

Choose OK if it's all right; otherwise, choose Cancel and make your corrections.

Word inserts the ASK instruction at the insertion point. To view the ASK field, display field codes (select Tools ➤ Options, choose the View tab, check the Field Codes box, then click OK).

FIGURE 28.10

This form letter (top) uses merge instructions to ask the operator for information from the keyboard, as you can see when Field Codes are revealed (bottom).

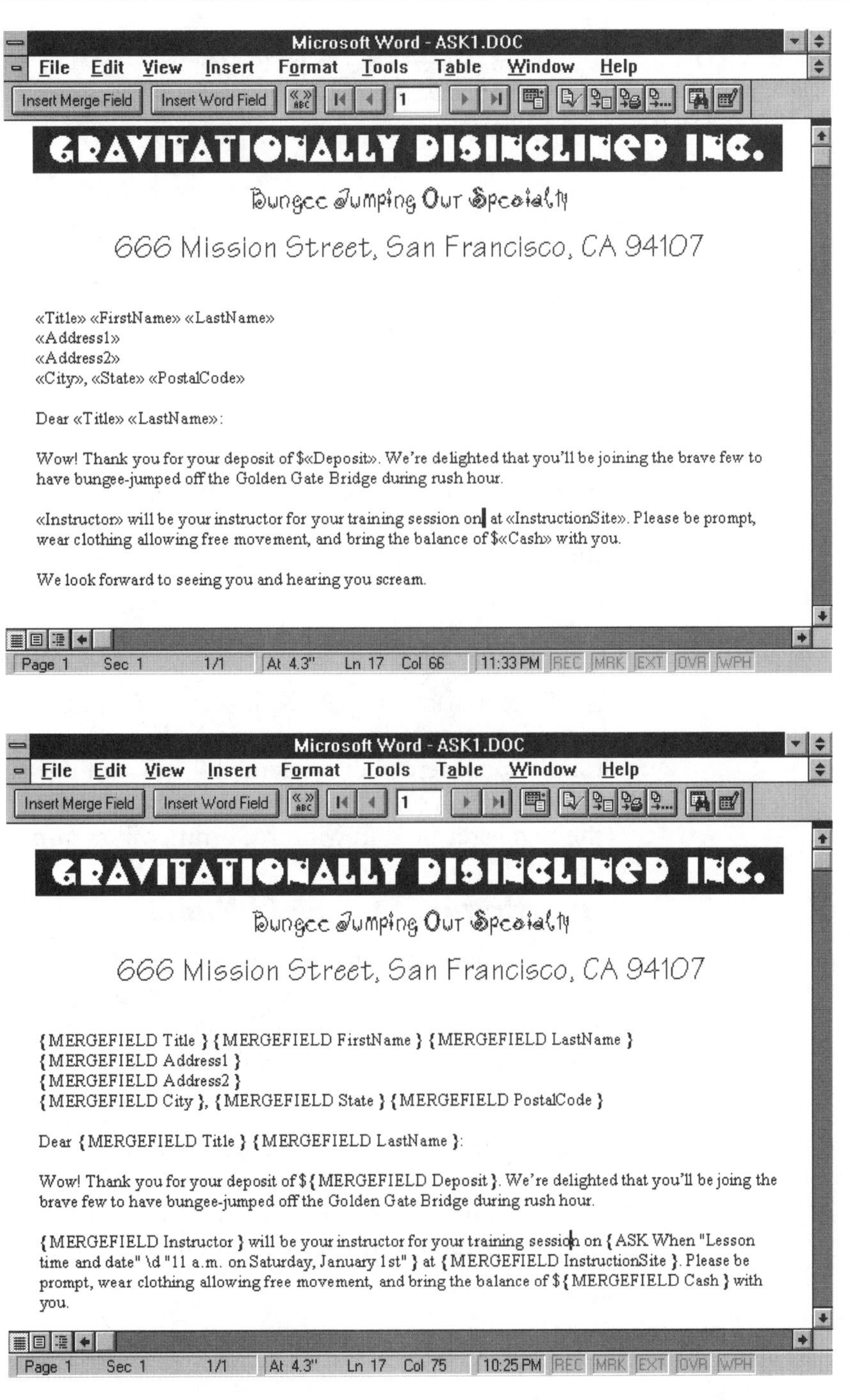

FIGURE 28.11

The Insert Word Field: Ask dialog box creates prompts for keyboard entries when you merge.

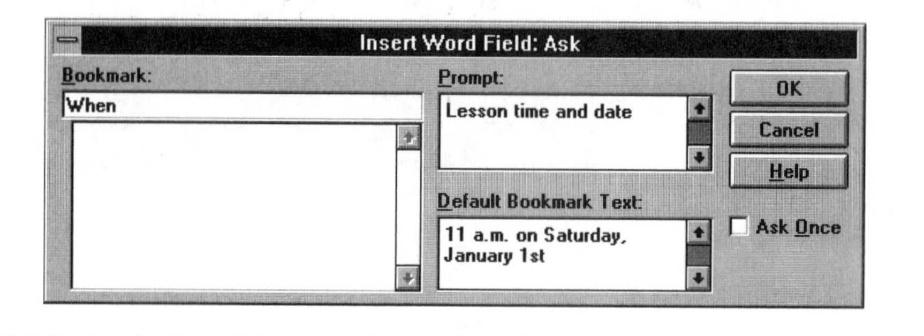

Using ASK

When you actually merge your ten letters (to continue the bungee jumping example), you'll see a dialog box like the one shown above for each letter. In it you enter the date and time for each bungee jumper, then click OK or press ↵.

► Set Bookmark...

Set Bookmark..., like ASK, inserts a field unique to the main document (i.e., not in the data source). The value you define for it is used for all documents being merged—you don't get to enter a different value for each one. For instance, you could use it to insert Winter in the Semester field in winter, Summer in summer, and so on.

Inserting a SET... Field Name

When designing your main document, move the insertion point to where you want the SET information to appear. Pull down the Insert Word Field list on the Mail Merge Toolbar and choose the Set Bookmark... command. Word displays the Insert Word Field: Set dialog box, as shown in Figure 28.12.

In the Bookmark box, type the name of the bookmark you want to create. If you want to specify a default value, enter that in the Value box. Click OK to accept the bookmark name and value. Word inserts the SET information in your document at the insertion point.

FIGURE 28.12

The Insert Word Field: Set dialog box.

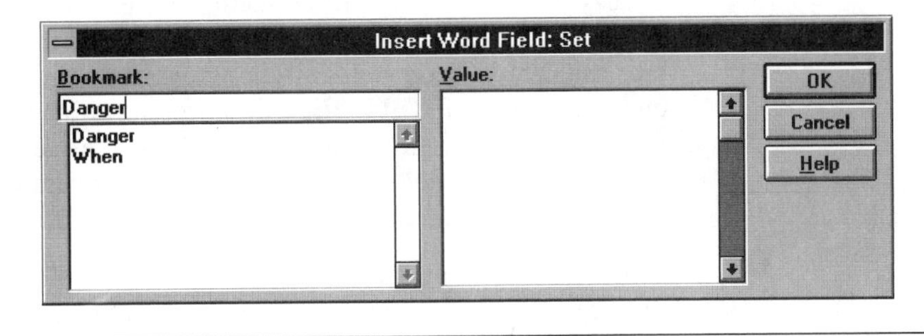

Using SET...

When you actually merge your documents (ten letters, for instance), Word automatically prints the defined SET value in each letter at the points where you've inserted the field names.

▶ *IF...THEN...ELSE...*

You can use IF...THEN...ELSE... to make Word do different things based on conditions it finds in fields in your data sources. For example, you could enter a field in the bungee-jumping letter to check whether the would-be jumper had paid a deposit. If the condition was met, you could have THEN make Word thank the jumper for the deposit and request the balance of the fee; otherwise, ELSE would cause Word to request the full fee.

To insert an IF...THEN...ELSE... field, click on the Insert Word Field drop-down list on the Mail Merge Toolbar.

This brings up the Insert Word Field: IF dialog box:

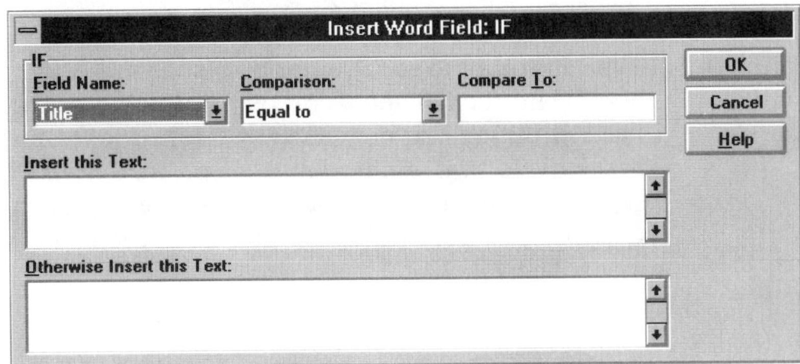

So, say you're sending out collection letters and you want to vary some of the language you use, depending on how overdue your invoices or bills are. You'd need to maintain an age field for overdue bills and then include an IF…THEN…ELSE expression that IF the overdue bill's age was greater than 90 days, THEN a sentence containing strong language would be included, ELSE a more conciliatory sentence would be included instead.

This means that in the Insert Word Field: IF dialog box, you'd select the Age field in the Field Name box, select Greater Than in the Comparison box, and enter **90** in the Compare To box. Then you'd type something like "Please remit immediately to protect your credit rating!" in the Insert this Text box and something like "Did you forget?" in the Otherwise Insert this Text box. Then click OK.

► *Fill-In…*

Fill-in… prompts for text to be inserted at the location of the field in one document. For more than one document, use ASK instead. To insert a Fill-in… field, click on the Insert Word Field drop-down list on the Mail Merge Toolbar.

This brings up the Insert Word Field: Fill-in dialog box:

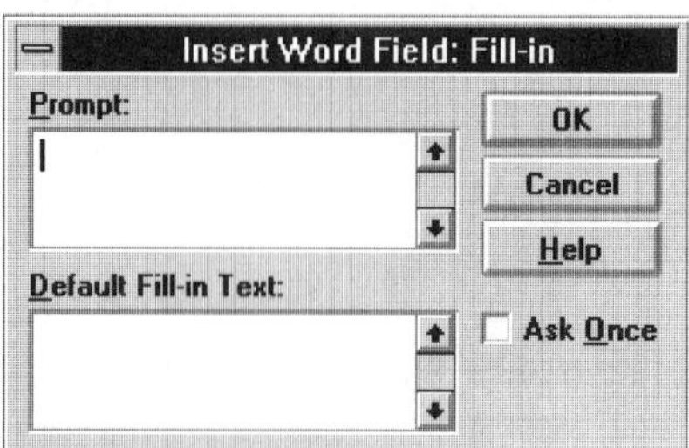

Type a prompt in the Prompt box (such as "Add a friendly message here") and then, if you want, type a suitable example sentence in the Default Fill-in Text box (such as "Hope the weather is nice in your part of the world"). If you'll want to be prompted only once so that your answer is printed in all the merged documents, check the Ask Once box. Otherwise, you'll be able to personalize each and every merged document. Then click OK.

Word will show you the prompt as it will appear when you merge the document:

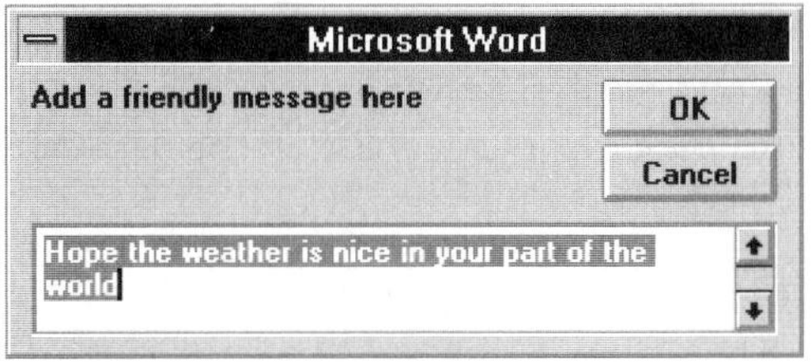
Microsoft Word
Add a friendly message here
OK
Cancel
Hope the weather is nice in your part of the world

Click OK. Word will insert a field code into your main document (field codes are explained in Chapter 32). It will appear as your default text unless you choose to view field codes in the Option dialog box (Tools ➤ Options, View tab). Then it will look something like this:

{ FILLIN "Add a friendly message here" \d "Hope the weather is nice in your part of the world" }

When you merge the document, you'll be prompted for a personalized message.

▶ Merge Record # and Merge Sequence

Merge Record # inserts the merge record number in the merge document. You might use it for keeping track of the records you print—for example, for invoice numbers.

Merge Sequence # inserts the merge-sequence number in the merge document. This can differ from the merge-record number if only some of the data records in the data source are used for a merge. For example, if you used only data records 157 to 300 for a merge, the Merge Record # for the first one would be 157, but the Merge Sequence # would be 1.

Insert these fields from the Insert Word Field drop-down list on the Mail Merge Toolbar.

▶ Next Record and Next Record If...

Next Record merges the next record into the current merge document rather than into a new merge document. Next Record If... does the same if the comparison between two expressions is true. Insert these fields from the Insert Word Field drop-down list on the Mail Merge Toolbar.

▶ Skip Record If...

Skip Record If... skips the current document and moves to the next record if the comparison between two expressions is true. Insert a Skip Record If... field from the Insert Word Field drop-down list on the Mail Merge Toolbar.

▶ Try It

Try applying some of these tricks and fields on a few practice merge documents of your own. The best way to learn how the fields work is to play around with them.

▶ Using the Mail Merge Toolbar

As I mentioned before, the Mail Merge Helper can feel like a strait-jacket at first—it may seem to be pushing you all over the place, opening up this document and that, with little rhyme or reason. As you get used to it though, you'll probably find that it offers more flexibility than it at first appears to.

But if you don't get along with the Mail Merge Helper, put together your mail merge using the Mail Merge Toolbar. We've looked at it briefly along the way, but here it is in all its glory:

Here's what the buttons on the Mail Merge Toolbar do:

ICON	NAME	FUNCTION
Insert Merge Field	Insert Merge Field	Inserts a merge field at the insertion point

ICON	NAME	FUNCTION
Insert Word Field	Insert Word Field	Inserts a Word field (e.g., ASK…) at the insertion point
« » ABC	View Merged Data	Toggles between viewing merge fields and the data that will appear in them
	First Record	Displays the first record in the data source
	Previous Record	Displays the previous record in the data source
1	Go to Record	Enter the number of the record you want to go to in this box
	Next Record	Displays the next record in the data source
	Last Record	Displays the last record in the data source
	Mail Merge Helper	Displays the Mail Merge Helper
	Check for Errors	Displays the Check for Errors dialog box
	Merge to New Document	Merges the main document and the data source to a new document
	Merge to Printer	Merges the main document and the data source to a printer
	Mail Merge	Displays the Merge dialog box
	Find Record	Displays the Find Record dialog box
	Edit Data Source	Displays the Data Form dialog box

▸▸ Merge-Printing Labels and Envelopes

You can also use Word 6's Mail Merge Helper to merge labels and envelopes. Because the procedures for merging labels and envelopes are very similar to those for form letters, we'll discuss them only briefly here.

▸ Printing Labels on Laser Printers

The Mail Merge Helper makes merging labels on a laser printer dead simple. You use the Mail Merge Helper to create a main document containing a table with fixed-size cells and cell spacing that match the size and position of your blank labels. Then insert merge instructions in each table cell. Here's how to do it:

1. Select Tools ➤ Mail Merge... to fire up the Mail Merge Helper.
2. Click the Create... button to drop down a list of options.
3. Select Mailing Labels... from the drop-down list.
4. Arrange your data source as usual. Word will then invite you to set up your main document. In the Label Options dialog box that appears (Figure 28.13), make the appropriate choices for your printer and labels:
    - In the Printer Information box, select Laser or Dot Matrix as appropriate. If necessary, click the arrow to drop down the Tray list and select a different tray.

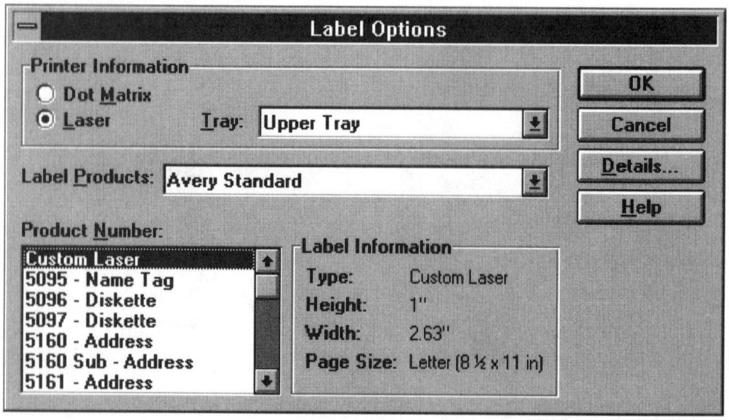

FIGURE 28.13 ▸

The Label Options dialog box. Select the type of printer and labels you're using here.

TIP

Consider selecting a different Tray option when printing labels on a network. That way, you might be able to avoid having someone else print a 90-page report on your precious disk labels.

- In the Label Products box, select the brand of labels you want: Avery Standard, Avery Pan European, or Other. (Other includes brands such as Inmac and RAJA.)
- In the Product Number box, select the number for the labels you're using. If you don't know the number, consult the Label Information box to find out the size of the labels listed in the Product Number box. If you're still no wiser, measure your labels carefully and choose the closest match.
- For precise layout information on the labels, choose the Details... button. In the dialog box that appears, make any necessary adjustments in the labels' margin, pitch, dimensions, and layout, then click OK.

5. When you've chosen the labels to use, choose OK to close the dialog box.
6. The Create Labels dialog box will appear (see Figure 28.14). Enter the fields here by pulling down the Insert Merge Field list and selecting them in turn. Remember to include any necessary spaces and punctuation.

   - To include a postal bar code, click the Insert Postal Bar Code... button. In the Insert Postal Bar Code dialog box (shown below), enter the Merge Field with ZIP Code and Merge Field with Street Address in the appropriate boxes, then click OK.

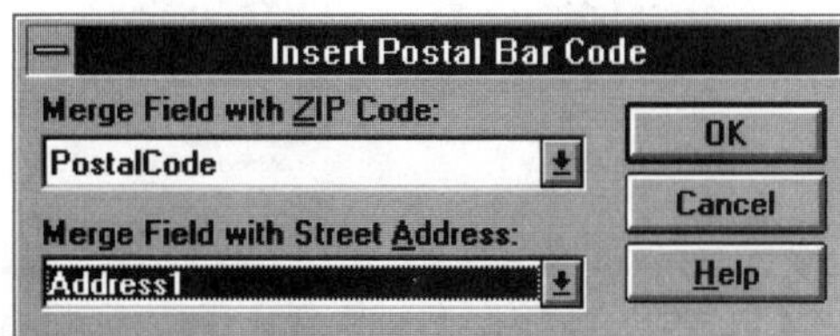

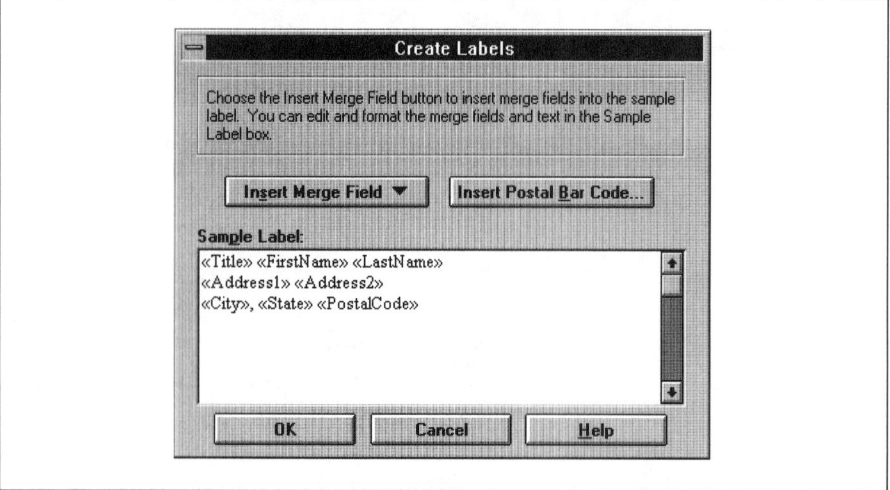

FIGURE 28.14

The Create Labels dialog box. Add the fields here for your labels.

Click OK when you're finished making choices in the Create Labels dialog box. Word will then enter your label fields into the main document, as shown in Figure 28.15.

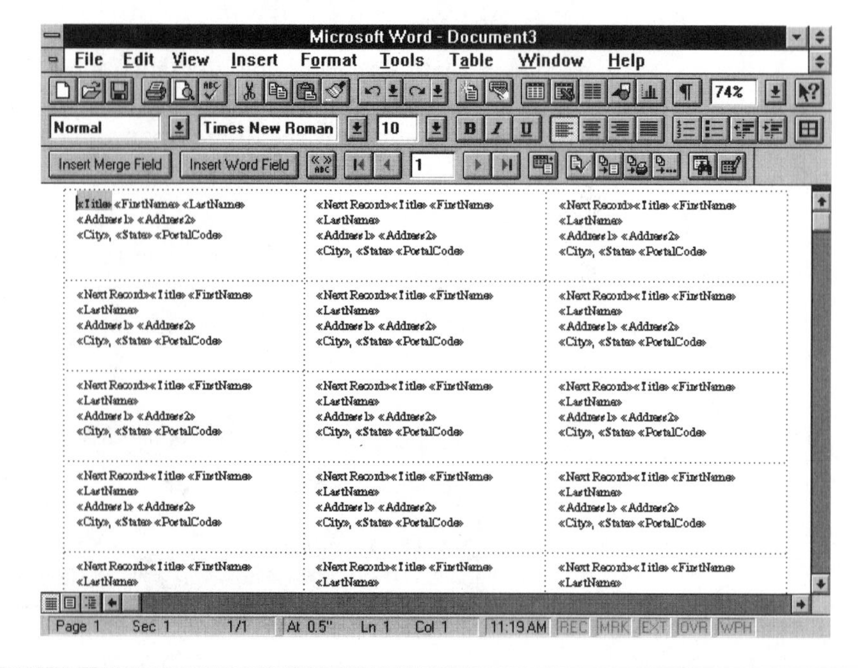

FIGURE 28.15

The labels merged into the main document. Note the NextRecord field that appears in each label but the first, instructing Word not to print each label on a separate page.

7. Make any necessary adjustments to your main document (for example, adding ASK or FILL-IN fields).
8. Open the Mail Merge Helper dialog box and choose the Merge... button to merge your data source with the main document. Choose whether to merge to a new document or to the printer. (You can also use the Merge to New Document and Merge to Printer buttons on the Mail Merge Toolbar here.)
9. Save your documents with meaningful names.

▶ Making Custom Mailing Labels

If you can't find mailing labels in the Label Options dialog box that match the ones you have, you can always create your own. To do so,

1. In the Label Options dialog box, find a label format that's close to the dimensions that you need and select it.
2. Click the Details button. This brings up an Address Information dialog box, such as this one:

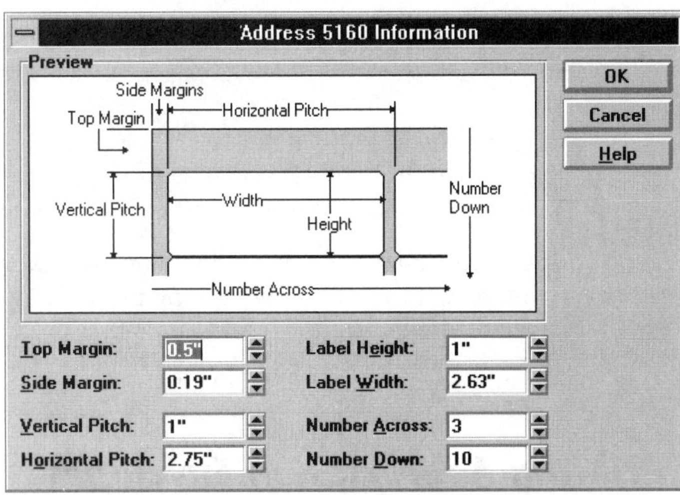

Either type in new dimensions to match your mailing labels or play with the little arrow buttons to zero in on the correct dimensions.

The diagram will change to reflect the information you enter. When you are satisfied, click OK three times and then continue with step 6 in the previous section.

▸ Printing a Label for a Single Piece of Mail

Labels are great for mass mailings, but you may also want to use individual labels for single pieces of mail every now and again. With your main document on the screen, select Tools ➤ Envelopes and Labels. This brings up the Envelopes and Labels dialog box:

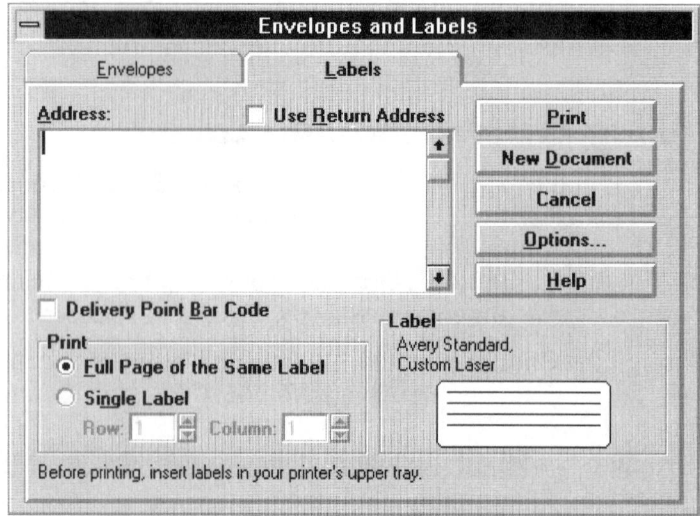

Correct the address, if necessary, or check Use Return Address to print a return-address label. If you want to print a single label and not a full page of the same label over and over, check Single Label.

If the upper-left label is available on your label sheet, leave Row and Column set to 1. Otherwise, type in the Row and Column of the first available label.

When you are ready, click Print.

▸ Printing Addresses on Envelopes

Word 6 offers the ability to print addresses on envelopes. This can be convenient for small numbers of envelopes; but as most laser printers require you to feed envelopes in by hand, printing large numbers of envelopes can be a slow business. Take a quick reality check before you arrange to print a whole slew of envelopes and consider using mailing labels on the envelopes instead.

TIP

Before starting to prepare envelopes, make sure your return address is correct. Choose Tools ➤ Options to display the Options dialog box. Click on the User Info tab to view (and if necessary change) the name and mailing address. Click OK when you're finished.

1. Select Tools ➤ Mail Merge… to fire up the Mail Merge Helper.
2. Click the Create… button to drop down a list of options.
3. Select Envelopes… from the drop-down list.
4. Arrange your data source as usual. Word will invite you to edit your main document. In the Envelope Options dialog box that appears (Figure 28.16), make the appropriate choices for your envelopes:
   - On the Envelope Options tab, click the Font… button in the Delivery Address box or the Font… button in the Return Address box to change the font in which the addresses appear. If necessary, adjust the position of the delivery address or return address by entering From Top and From Left measurements in their boxes.

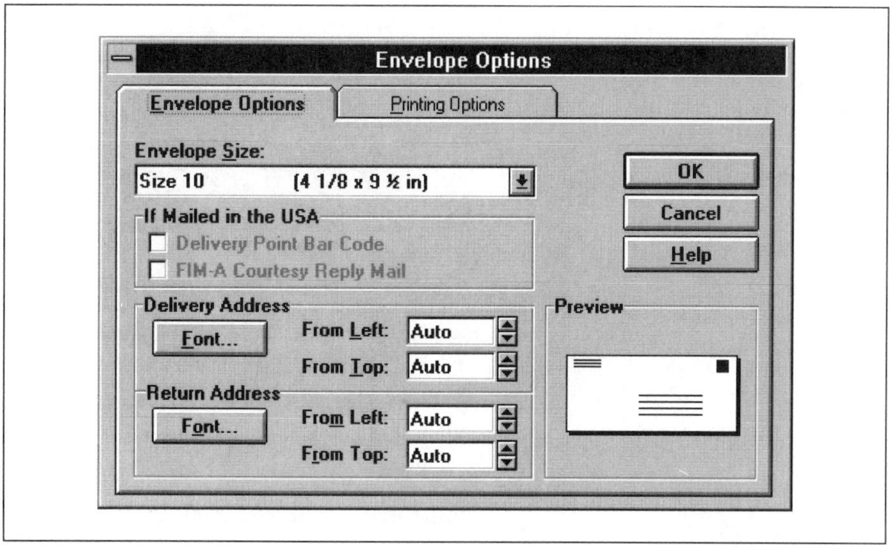

FIGURE 28.16

The Envelope Options dialog box. Choose your envelopes here.

- On the Printing Options tab, select the Feed Method and the tray to Feed From. Note that the default Feed From option is manual. For large numbers of envelopes, you'll be spending half the afternoon chez the printer.

▶▶ NOTE

Word displays the name of your currently selected printer in the Printing Options tab of the Envelope Options dialog box. If need be, change the printer using File ➤ Print… and then choosing the Printer… button. If necessary, click the arrow to drop down the Tray list and select a different tray.

5. When you've chosen the envelope options and printing options, choose OK to close the dialog box.
6. The Envelope Address dialog box will appear (see Figure 28.17). Enter the fields here by pulling down the Insert Merge Field list and selecting them in turn. Remember to include any necessary spaces and punctuation.
    - To include a postal bar code, click the Insert Postal Bar Code… button. In the Insert Postal Bar Code dialog box,

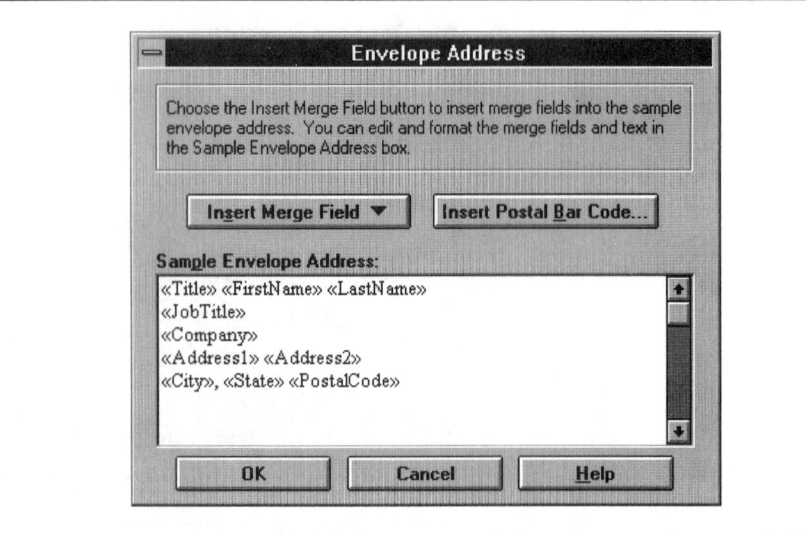

FIGURE 28.17

The Envelope Address dialog box. Enter fields here as for mailing labels.

enter the Merge Field with ZIP Code and Merge Field with Street Address in the appropriate boxes, then click OK.

Click OK when you're finished making your choices in the Envelope Address dialog box. Word will then enter your label fields into the main document, as shown in Figure 28.18.

7. Make any necessary adjustments to your main document.
8. Open the Mail Merge Helper dialog box and choose the Merge... button to merge your data source with the main document. Choose whether to merge to a new document or to the printer. (You can also use the Merge to New Document and Merge to Printer buttons on the Mail Merge Toolbar.)
9. Save your documents with meaningful names.

TIP

See Chapter 15 for more information on envelopes.

FIGURE 28.18

The envelope main document.

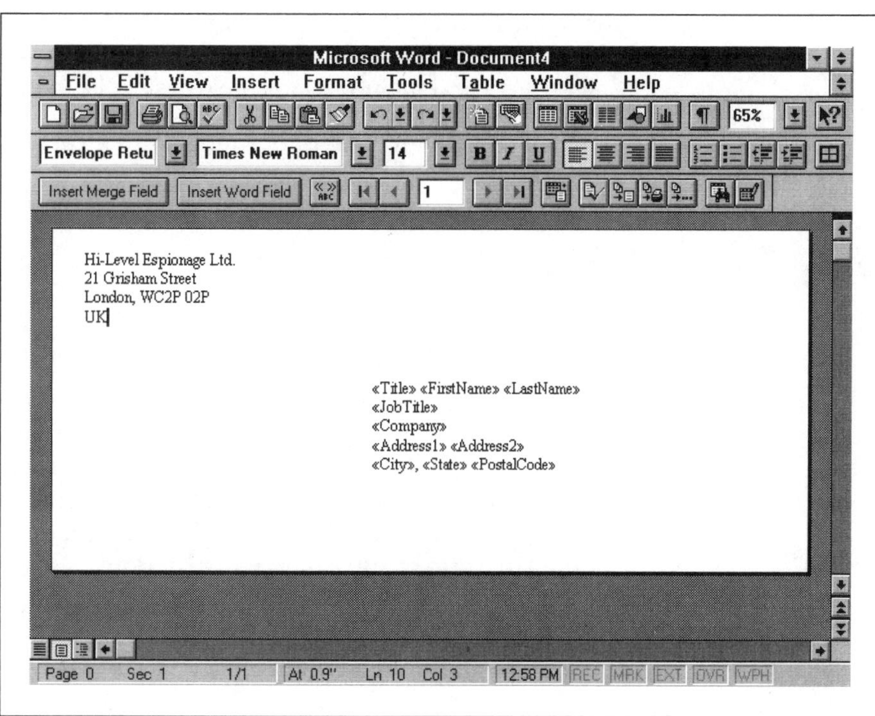

►► Creating Catalogs with Mail Merge

If you need to create a document with variations on the same information repeated throughout, you can use the Catalog option with Mail Merge. When you designate your main document as a catalog instead of as a form letter, each record from the data source is merged into a single document. (With form letters, each record creates a distinct resulting document.)

This enables you to create a document with a series of similar entries by only typing the basic information once. Then, as you merge the records from the data source into the catalog file, the contents of the main document will be repeated once for each record without any automatic section or page breaks between entries.

To perform a catalog merge, start with a fresh document. Select Tools ➤ Mail Merge. This brings up the Mail Merge Helper dialog box (Figure 28.2). Click the Create button and select Catalog. Click the Active Window button to use the new document as the main document.

Now click the Edit button and select Catalog. This will drop you into the main document with the the Mail Merge Toolbar across the top of the screen. Type into this document any information you want to repeat for each record and include merge fields as explained earlier in this chapter.

You can use any normal data source with a catalog document.

►► Tips, Techniques, and Troubleshooting

Here are some tips for working with Word's mail-merge feature:

- To change the appearance of merged characters—to make them bold or italic, or a larger point size—format their merge instructions in the main document. Merged characters take on the formatting of their merge instructions.
- If you move your data-source files, Word will ask you to relocate them before you can merge.

- To print selected items from a longer data file, sort them and print just the range containing the desired records (from 10 to 30, for instance).

▶ Shortcut Key Combinations for Merging Documents

The following shortcut key combinations are available when merging documents using the Tools ➤ Mail Merge… command:

KEY COMBINATION	EFFECT
Alt+Shift+K	Preview a mail merge
Alt+Shift+M	Merge a document
Alt+Shift+N	Print the merged documents
Alt+Shift+E	Edit a mail-merge data source
Alt+Shift+Q	Sort and filter records

▶▶ Restoring a Mail-Merge Document to a Normal Word Document

You can restore a mail-merge main document to a normal Word document when you've finished merging with it. This removes the association between the main document and its data source and header source (if it has one). The text of the main document does not change.

To restore a main document to a normal Word document, follow these steps:

1. Open the Mail Merge Helper dialog box by selecting Tools ➤ Mail Merge….
2. In the Main Document section, choose the Create… button to display the list of options.
3. Choose the Restore to Normal Word Document… option.
4. In the Restore to Normal Word Document dialog box that appears, choose Yes. The association between the main document and its data sources will be removed.

CHAPTER 29

Using Charts and Graphs

▸▸ FAST TRACK

▶▶ **Microsoft** Graph is a supplementary application included with Word for Windows that you can use to create, import, and edit charts and graphs. These charts and graphs are *embedded* objects; not only can you insert them into any application that supports Object Linking and Embedding (more on this in the next chapter), but you can simply double-click them to open them (and Microsoft Graph) for editing.

You can create the following using Microsoft Graph:

- Area charts
- Bar charts
- Column charts
- Line charts
- Pie charts
- Scatter charts
- Combination charts
- 3-D variations on many of the above

To give you some idea of the possibilities Microsoft Graph offers, Figure 29.1 shows a chart created with Microsoft Graph and then inserted in a Word for Windows document.

▶▶ Making Sure Graph Is Installed

First, make sure that whoever installed Word for Windows on your PC included Graph in the installation. A complete installation of Word includes Graph, a minimum installation doesn't include Graph, and a Custom installation lets you choose whether to install Graph.

FIGURE 29.1

A chart created with Microsoft Graph and inserted in a Word for Windows document.

1

In any project, tight deadlines can cause a lot of stress for all concerned. Stress can lead to a phenomenon press psychologists know as *sense of humor failures*. These generally appear to occur spontaneously but are in fact connected closely to the surreptitious approach of a deadline.

Press Psychology sponsored a special study of sense of humor failures by Professor E. Nostrums of the College of Applied Lunatic Science in Doonesville.

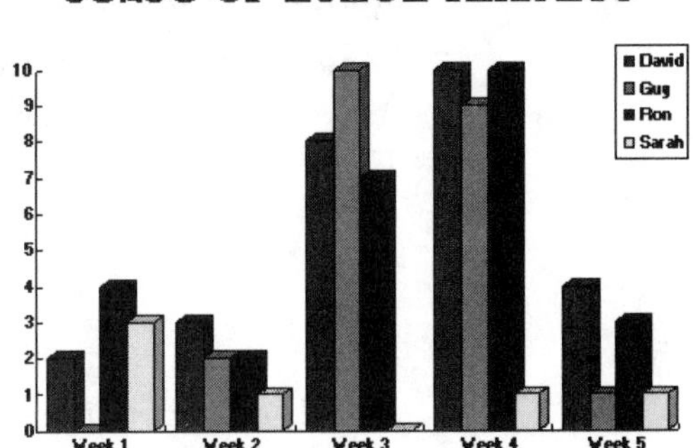

In carefully controlled experiments, Professor Nostrums applied calculated doses of stress to his subjects (these had volunteered for the experiment and understood the risks to their health and sanity). With each subject, maximum sense of humor failure was achieved by moving the

If Graph isn't installed on your PC, dig out those Word for Windows installation disks and install it. Run the Setup program by double-clicking the Microsoft Word Setup icon in your Word for Windows or Microsoft Applications group in the Program Manager. (If you can't find the Microsoft Word Setup icon: From the Program Manager, choose File ➤ Run…, type **a:setup** [or **b:setup** if the disk is in your B: drive], and press ↵.) When Setup appears, choose the Custom option and follow the instructions for installing Graph.

NOTE

For more information on installing Word for Windows on your PC, turn to Appendix A.

►► Getting Started with Word Graphs

The general steps for creating a graph are so simple that you can be up and running in a flash.

1. Open a Word document and place the insertion point where you want the new graph to appear.
2. Make sure the Formatting Toolbar is displayed (if it isn't, select View ➤ Toolbars…, check the Formatting Toolbar check box in the Toolbars dialog box, and click OK). Click the Chart button:

3. Graph will open in its own window, displaying a *datasheet window* that looks like a small spreadsheet, together with a *chart window* (aka a *graph window*—take your pick). Enter your data and labels into the datasheet window.
4. You'll notice that Graph has its own menu bar with the following menus:

   File Edit DataSeries Gallery Chart Format Window Help

   We'll look at how to use these menus in the following sections.
5. Use Microsoft Graph's menu commands to embellish the graph with text, arrows, different typefaces and type sizes, and so on. Resize the graph by dragging the size box in the lower-right corner of its window.
6. When you're ready to insert the graph into your Word for Windows document, select File ➤ Exit and Return to *WhateverDocumentYou'reWorkingOn*.
7. Microsoft Graph will ask if you want to update the graph. Click Yes. Your Word for Windows document will appear, now containing the graph.
8. Caption, resize, reposition, frame, apply a border, and otherwise embellish the chart and its surrounding area as you would when dealing with any other graphic object.

9. To make changes to the content and appearance of the chart itself, double-click it in your Word for Windows document to launch Microsoft Graph and make the necessary changes.
10. Save your Word for Windows file when you've finished editing the graph.

▶▶ NOTE

If all you see in your Word document is EMBEDMSGRAPH, you've got field codes turned on. Select Tools ➤ Options..., click on the View tab, and uncheck the Field Codes check box.

▶▶ Parts of a Graph Project

There are three parts to any Graph project—the datasheet window, the chart window, and the Graph object that you embed in your Word for Windows document. In the following sections, we'll look at each separately.

Figure 29.2 shows the datasheet window and the chart window.

▶▶ TIP

If the Datasheet or Chart window appears in an awkward position—for example, if one's blocking your view of the other—grab the offender by clicking in its title bar and drag it to somewhere more convenient in the Microsoft Graph window. Maximize the Microsoft Graph window to give yourself more space.

▶ Datasheet Window

The datasheet window, which works much like any other window, is where you enter all the numbers and much of the text that you want to graph. As you can see in Figure 29.2, it's similar to a spreadsheet.

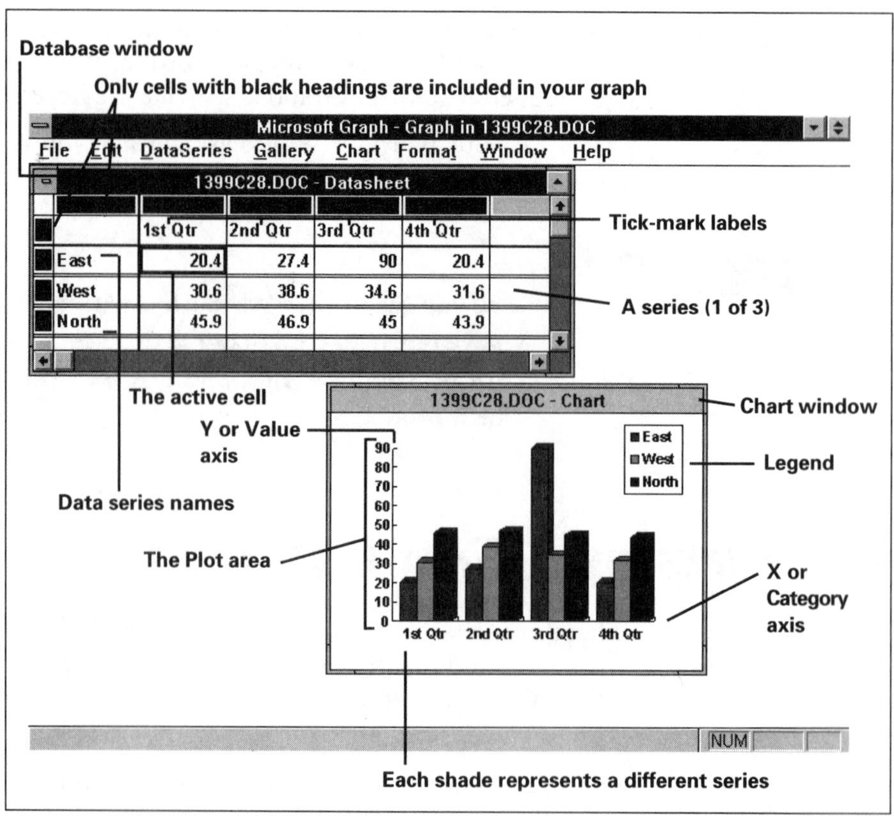

FIGURE 29.2 *Microsoft Graph's Datasheet and Chart windows.*

When you start Microsoft Graph, you'll see a datasheet complete with sample data.

The following sections describe the parts of the datasheet window.

Cells

The individual rectangles containing numbers and text are called *cells*, just as they are in a spreadsheet. You can type and edit in cells as you'd expect. Enter each data item for your graph in a separate cell.

The Active Cell

To work in a cell, you must first make it active by clicking in it or moving to it with the arrow keys. The active cell is indicated by a dark border. In Figure 29.2, the active cell contains the number 20.4. Any data that you enter will appear in the active cell.

Rows and Columns

Cells are arranged in horizontal rows and vertical columns. A datasheet can contain a maximum of 1,024,000 cells (4,000 cells by 256 columns). You can select a row or column by clicking its heading.

Row and Column Headings

Those black boxes at the top and along the left of the datasheet in Figure 29.2 are row and column headings. When they are solid black, their corresponding data will be included in a chart. When they are gray (dimmed), their corresponding data will not appear in your graph. Double-click on headings to toggle them on and off.

Data Points

Each cell containing a value is a *data point*. The datasheet in Figure 29.2 has 12 data points.

Data Series and Double Lines

A collection of related cells is called a *data series*. In Figure 29.2 there are three series—East, West, and North. Each series contains four data points.

A data series plots one line or piece of pie or one set of columns or bars in the chart.

Double Lines

Double lines are used to separate the data series in the datasheet. When the double lines appear between columns, each column is a distinct data series; when the double lines appear between rows, each row is a distinct data series.

In Figure 29.2, the double lines are horizontal, indicating that the data series consist of rows rather than columns.

Series Names

Series names are in the leftmost cells when a data series is plotted in horizontal rows. Series names are at the top of vertical columns when your graph will be plotted in columns. (In Figure 29.2, the series names are East, West, and North.)

Tick-mark Labels

Tick-mark labels are the names that appear along the horizontal axes of area, column, and line charts, or along a bar chart's vertical axis. In Figure 29.2, the tick-mark labels are 1st Qtr, 2nd Qtr, and so on.

▸ Chart Window

The chart window has its own terminology. Here are the basics.

The Chart

Everything inside the chart window is considered to be part of the chart. This includes the bars, pie slices, labels, arrows, and so on.

Data Markers

Data markers come in various shapes, depending upon the graph type. For example, the data markers are bars in bar charts, lines in line charts, pie slices in pie charts, and dots or symbols in line or scatter charts. Each marker represents the value of a single data point or value.

Data Series

Just as a data series in the datasheet represents a group of data points, so does a data series in the chart window. Figure 29.2 has three data series represented by three different shades of data markers.

Axis

An *axis* is a line along which data are plotted. Two-dimensional graphs like line and bar graphs usually have a horizontal axis (or X-axis) and a vertical axis (or Y-axis). 3-D charts have a third axis, called the Z-axis.

Tick Marks

Tick marks are the intersections of X and Y axes. They are usually labeled with tick-mark labels.

Gridlines

Gridlines are those optional vertical and horizontal lines that make it easier to judge values on a graph. Gridlines begin at tick marks and continue through the chart either horizontally or vertically.

Chart Text

Microsoft Chart text comes in two flavors—*attached text*, used for things like data and axes markers; and *unattached text*, which you can add by typing it. Use unattached text to point things out and make your chart intelligible and meaningful. You type unattached text directly into the chart, and you can move it or size it.

Legends

Legends are little reference boxes that tell you which shades (or colors) are used to represent each data series. You can hide legends if they are unnecessary or get in the way. Look back to Figure 29.1 to see how useful legends can be to make things clear.

▶ Graph Objects in Word Documents

When you quit Microsoft Graph, it embeds a graph object in your Word for Windows document. You can resize objects, crop them, add borders to them, and so on. Treat graph objects as you would any other embedded object. See Chapter 30 for more information on object linking and embedding (OLE).

▶▶ Getting Online Help

You can get online help by pressing F1 at any point (the easy way) or by choosing either Help ➤ Index or Help ➤ Keyboard. (If you *really* need help, try Help ➤ Using Help. Yup, it gets existential here.) Figure 29.3 shows what you get by pressing F1 at the beginning of a graph project.

Click a topic of interest to read about it. Often, you'll have to go through several levels of help screen to reach your topic. Use the Contents, Search, Back, History, ≤, and ≥ buttons to navigate.

FIGURE 29.3

Get help by pressing F1 at any point (here, I pressed it at the beginning of a graph project) or selecting Help ➤ Index or Help ➤ Keyboard. Click the item you want to get help with. For help with Help, press F1 again.

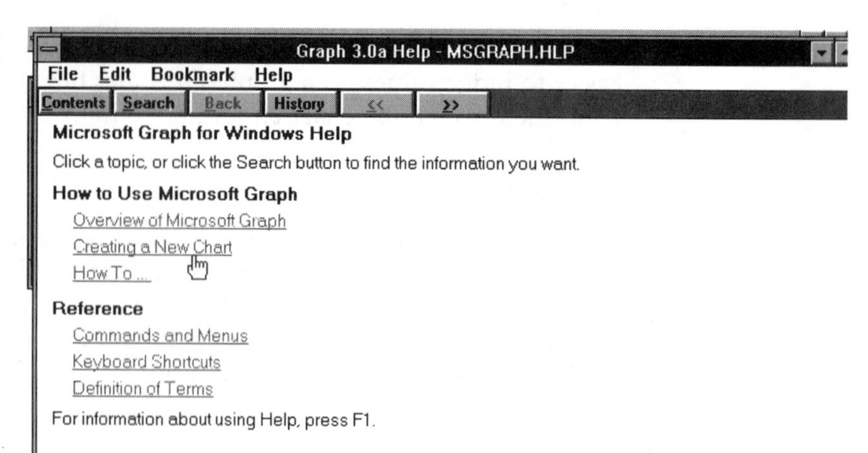

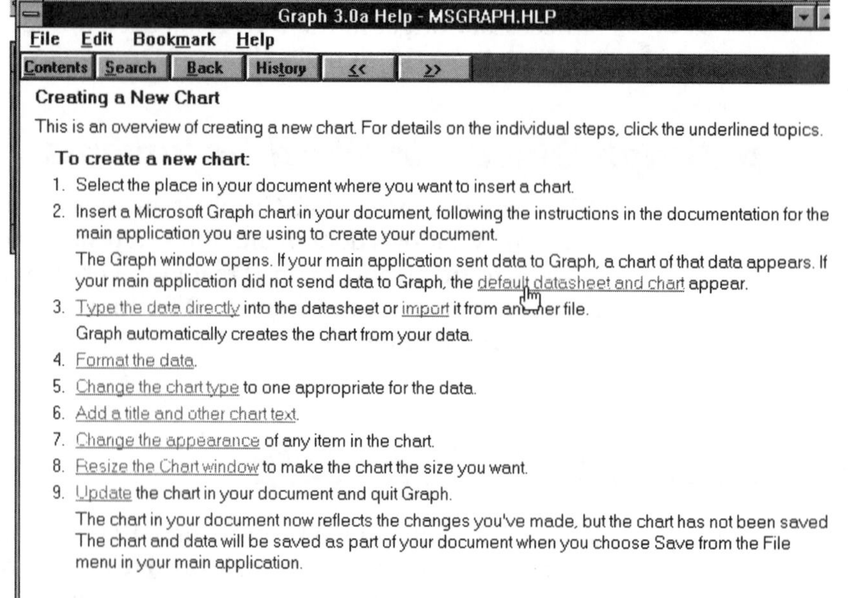

▶▶ TIP

Some key words and phrases, like the one the cursor is pointing to in Figure 29.3, can be expanded by clicking them. Those with a solid underline contain hypertext jumps that will take you to a new help screen. Those with a dotted underline will pop up a box on the same screen explaining the word or phrase you clicked.

▶▶ Working in the Datasheet Window

Use the datasheet window to enter data. It behaves so much like a Word table that we won't go into it in exhaustive detail here. The next section offers some pointers.

▶ Entering and Editing Cell Data

Here are some tips for entering and editing data:

- Click in the datasheet window to activate it, then click in a cell to edit its contents.
- Always type data-series labels in the first column of a datasheet and category names in the first row.
- Changes to cell formatting (fonts, sizes, bold, etc.) are not reflected in the graph. (See Formatting Chart Text later in this chapter.) You apply formatting to all the cells in the datasheet at the same time.

- You can use the Edit ➤ Clear… command in datasheets to clear the data, cell formatting, or both. Just click the appropriate choice in the Clear dialog box:

Importing Data

If you select a table in your Word for Windows document before clicking the Insert Chart button, Microsoft Graph will import your selection into the datasheet when it opens.

You can import data from other places using Graph's File ➤ Import Data… command. In the Import Data dialog box (Figure 29.4), select the file you want to import.

▸▸ **NOTE**

If you throw Microsoft Graph a curveball by asking it to import something it can't, it'll tell you it "Cannot read this file." Try opening the application that created the file and using the Clipboard to transfer the data (we'll discuss this in a minute).

To import an existing chart from Microsoft Excel, use File ➤ Open Microsoft Excel Chart…. In the Open Microsoft Excel Chart dialog box (see Figure 29.5), select the chart you want to open and click OK.

FIGURE 29.4

The Import Data dialog box. Select the file from which you want to import data, select All or Range (if you choose Range, specify the range in the text box), and click OK.

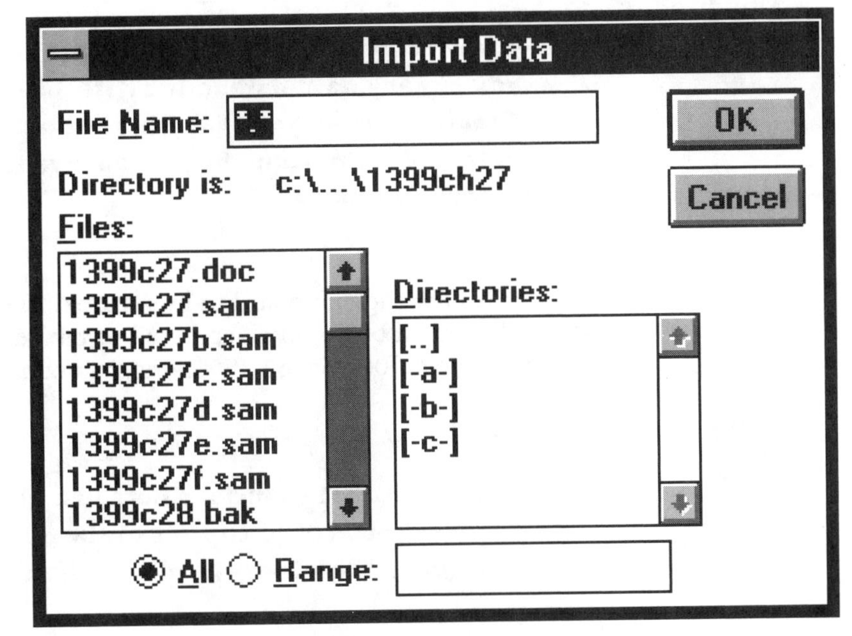

FIGURE 29.5

The Open Microsoft Excel Chart dialog box. Does just what it says.

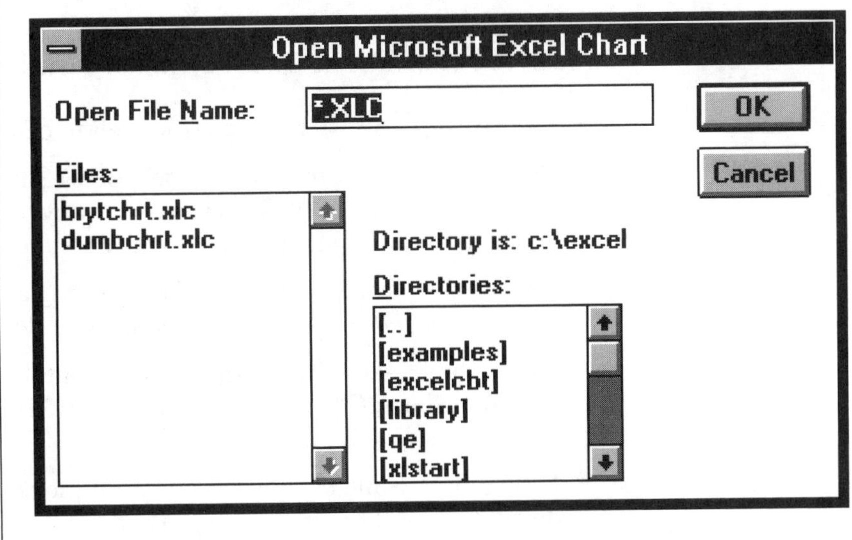

▶▶ **WARNING**

If you choose File ➤ Open Microsoft Excel Chart... when you already have data in the datasheet, Microsoft Graph will warn you that you're about to lose your data and formatting. Be sure you want to do this before clicking OK.

You can also use the Clipboard to import text. Bear in mind that incoming data must be comma-separated or tab-separated text and must not exceed the 4,000-row by 256-column maximum.

▶▶ **NOTE**

Remember that to include data in a graph, the data heading above or to the left of the data must be black (not gray). Click these headings to toggle them.

▶ Navigating in Datasheets

Navigating in datasheets is so easy that you'll hardly have to read through this section. The usual navigational tricks work:

- Use →, ←, ↑, and ↓ to move from cell to cell.
- Press Tab to move from cell to cell; press Shift+Tab to move backwards from cell to cell. This is a quick way to change the active cell location, though clicking in the target cell is even quicker.
- Home takes you to the first cell containing a data point in the row; End takes you to the last cell in the row.
- Ctrl+Home takes you to the first cell containing a data point in your datasheet; Ctrl+End takes you to the last cell containing a data point.
- Dragging or Shift-clicking selects multiple cells, as does holding down Shift and pressing →, ←, ↑, or ↓.
- Clicking at the left edge of a row or the top of a column selects the entire row or column.

- To speed entry, select multiple cells before entering data, then tab from one to the next to move left to right or ↵ to move up and down. The active cell will never leave the selected area. For example, select a three-by-four block of cells. Make your entry in the first cell and press ↵—Graph will make the next cell down the active cell. When you reach the bottom of the block, Graph will take you to the first highlighted cell in the next column. (With Tab, you move sideways and go down a row when you reach the right-most selected cell.)
- Minimize, maximize, and restore your datasheet window by using the minimize, maximize, and restore buttons. Or click and drag the borders of the window to resize it.
- Scroll up and down your datasheet as you would in any window.

▶ Number Formats in the Datasheet

Microsoft Graph allows you to format numbers in a variety of commonly accepted ways:

- Numbers too long to be displayed in cells will be stored as you typed them but displayed in scientific notation. For example, 1234567890 would be displayed as 1.235E+09.
- You can apply predefined number formats by selecting Format ➤ Number… and choosing a Number Format in the Number dialog box (see Figure 29.6). If you don't like the predefined formats, select one as a victim and edit it in the Format box. When you're done, click OK.
- Inspect the sample formats or read online help for assistance. Excel users will find the process and formats familiar. For instance, use dollar signs ($), pound signs (#), commas, decimal points (.), percent signs, parentheses, and colors to specify custom formats. Thus, **$#,###.;[Red]($#,###.)** would display and print dollars with commas and no pennies. Negative dollar amounts would be shown in parentheses and red. The custom format **0.0%** would display percentages to one decimal place.

FIGURE 29.6 ▸

The Number dialog box. Choose a number format that tickles your fancy. If you don't like any of them, edit one of them in the Format box and then click OK.

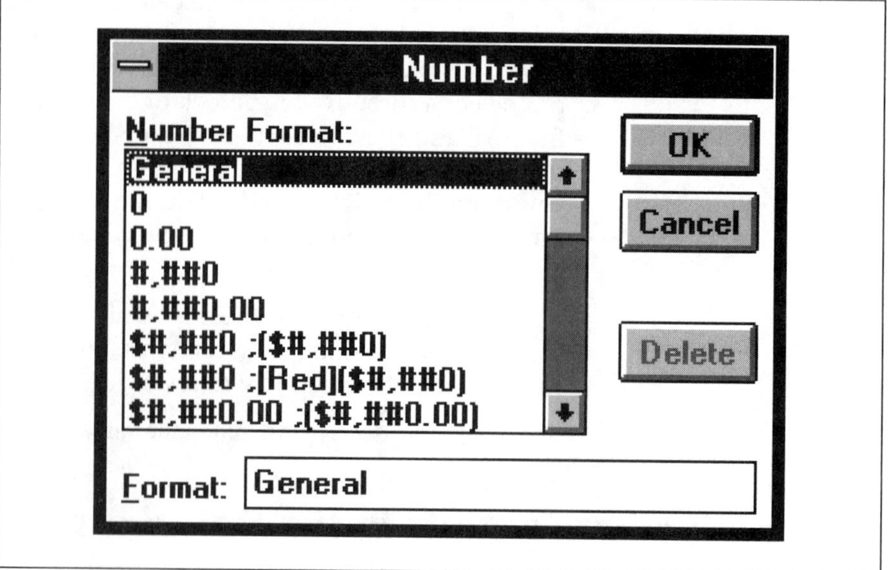

▸ Column Widths

Columns can be up to 255 characters wide, but 9 characters is the standard column width. You can change column widths by dragging the right edge of columns or use Format ➤ Column Width… to specify column widths in characters.

▸ Inserting and Deleting Rows and Columns

Inserting rows works the way it does in Word tables. Select the row beneath the point where you want to see a new one and choose Edit ➤ Insert Row/Col…. If you first select multiple rows, you'll insert a like number of new ones.

To insert a column, select the column to the right of the place where you want to see a new one, and choose Edit ➤ Insert Row/Col…. If you first select multiple columns, you'll insert a like number of new ones.

To delete rows and columns, select them and choose Edit ➤ Delete Row/Col….

NOTE

If you select a cell rather than a row or column, you'll get the Insert Row/Col or the Delete Row/Col mini-dialog box. Select Row or Column.

TIP

You can insert and delete rows and columns even more quickly by using the keyboard shortcuts. To insert rows or columns, press Ctrl++ (that's Ctrl and +); to delete rows and columns, press Ctrl+- (Ctrl and -). Again, you can first select the number of rows or columns to delete.

Working in the Chart Window

Use the Chart window to specify the appearance and size of the chart object you want to insert into your Word for Windows document. (To activate the Chart window, just click in it.)

The next few sections offer some tips for working in the Chart window.

Pick the Right Chart Type

Use the Gallery menu to pick the desired chart type for each project. The right chart can convey your information clearly and powerfully; the wrong chart can smother it. Below are descriptions of the types of charts available and the uses of each type.

Area

Area charts show changes in relative values of multiple series over time. Use area charts to emphasize differences and amount of change (for example, changes in various presidents' approval ratings at various stages of their terms). Figure 29.7 shows some of the available area formats.

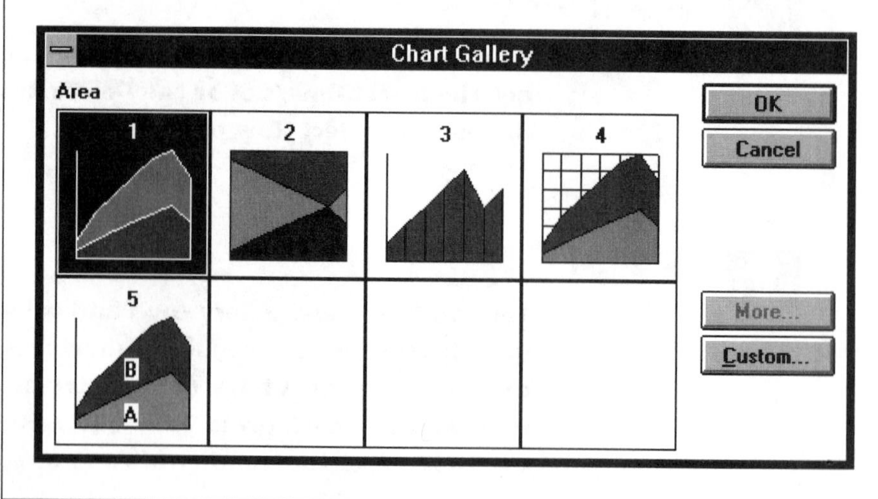

FIGURE 29.7

Some area chart formats.

Bar

Bar charts organize categories vertically and show comparisons between items (speeds of various disk drives, for instance). Figure 29.8 shows some of the available bar formats.

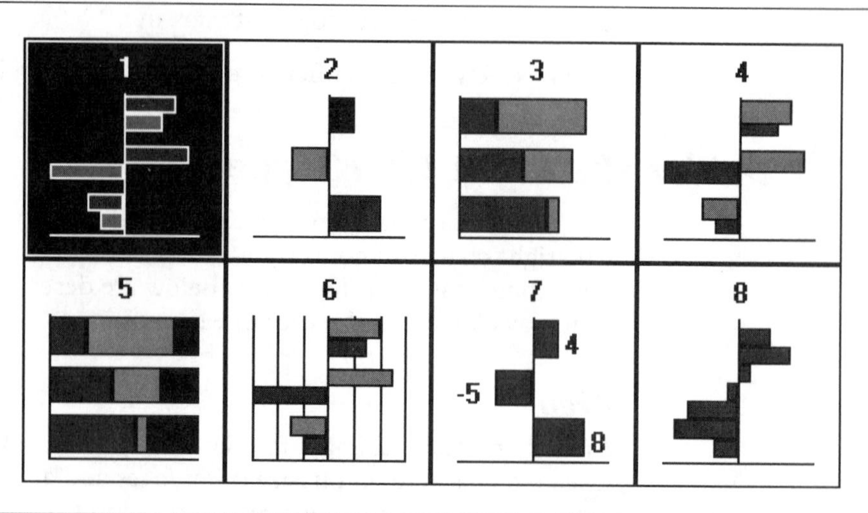

FIGURE 29.8

Some bar formats.

Column

Column charts organize the same types of information as bar charts, but they display it with vertical bars (columns). Figure 29.9 shows some of the available column formats.

Line

Line charts emphasize time and rate of change—such as sales growth over a twelve-month period. Figure 29.10 shows some of the available line formats.

FIGURE 29.9

Some column chart formats.

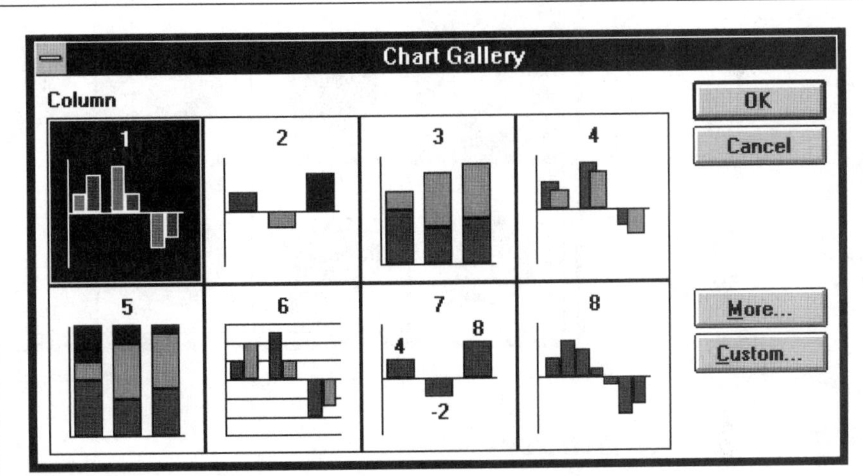

FIGURE 29.10

Some line chart formats.

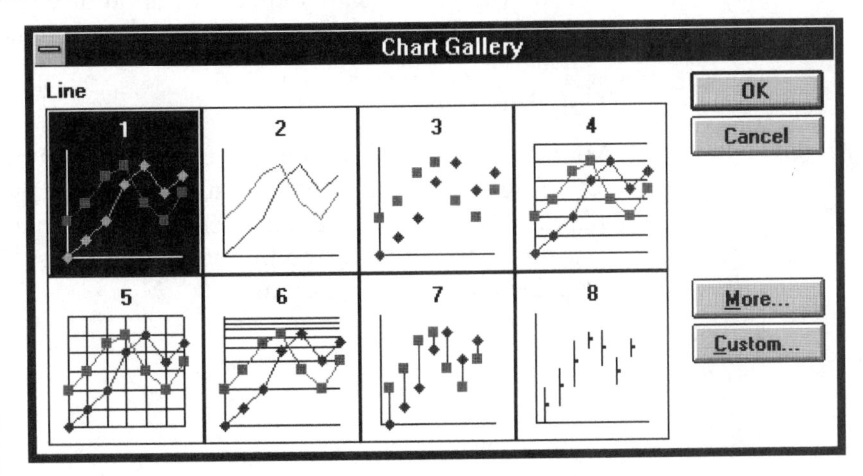

Pie

Pie charts show the relationships of parts to the whole—each department's contribution to the firm's total expense budget, for instance, or the number of arguments each member of the household causes. You can include only one data series in a pie chart, so it's not suited to a wide variety of uses. Figure 29.11 shows some of the available pie formats.

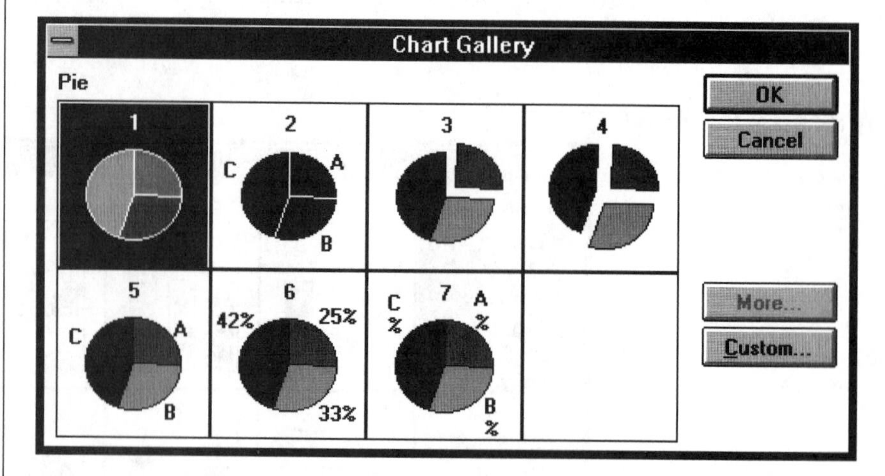

FIGURE 29.11

Some pie chart formats.

Scatter

Scatter charts are useful for demonstrating trends and patterns. They can show if variables are dependent upon or affect each other. Figure 29.12 shows some of the available scatter formats.

Combination

Microsoft Graph's combination charts can contain up to four axes representing data in different formats (lines and columns for instance). It's a great way to overlay actual versus projected data or loosely related items like temperature and humidity. Figure 29.13 shows some of the available combination formats.

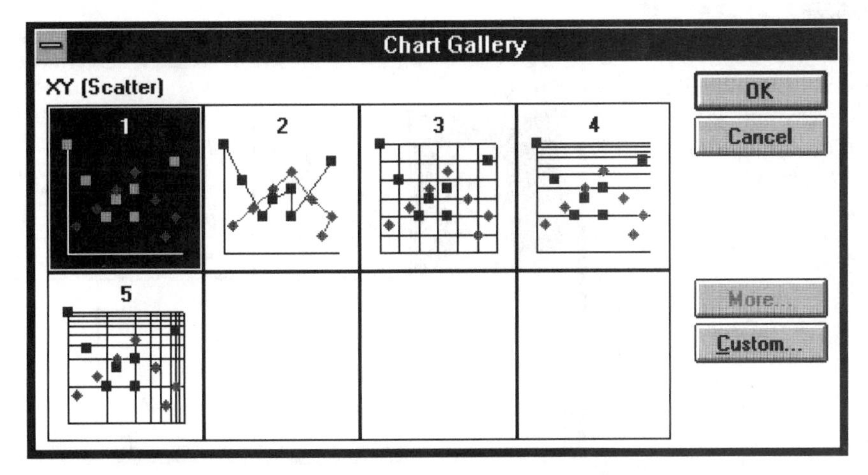

FIGURE 29.12

Some scatter chart formats.

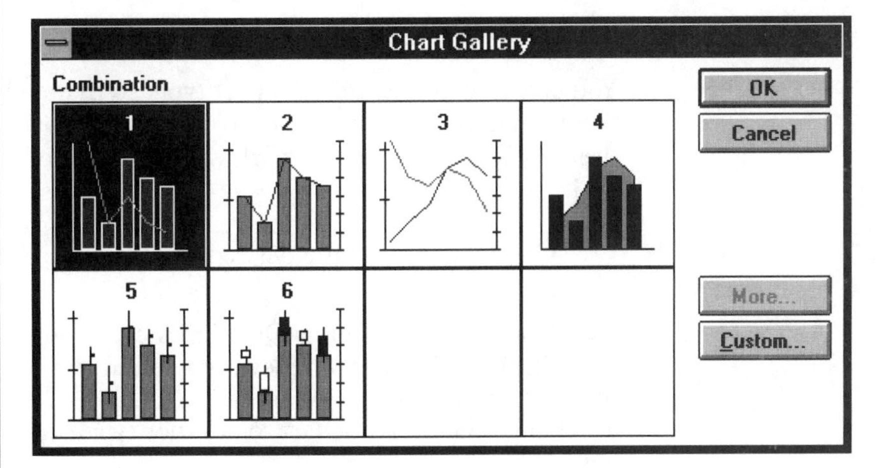

FIGURE 29.13

Some combination chart formats.

3-D

Microsoft Graph's 3-D variations give perspective to data representations. 3-D graphs can be rotated to change the bird's-eye view (this can sometimes emphasize or even distort relationships of related data—an effect I'll leave you to work out how you can). Figure 29.14 shows just a few of the many, many 3-D variations.

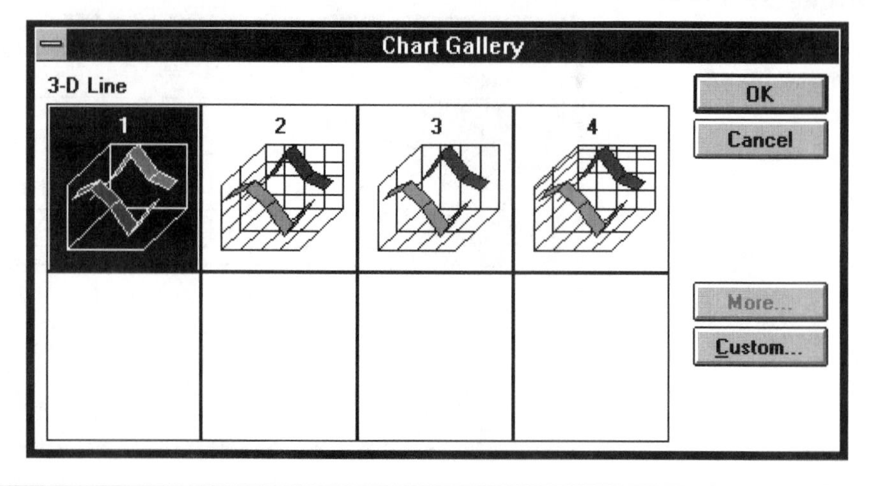

FIGURE 29.14

Some 3-D formats. These 3-D line graphs produce a satisfyingly bizarre effect even for mundane data.

► Changing the Default Chart Type

You can change the default chart type, so that a chart other than the column chart greets you when you open Microsoft Graph. This can be useful when you regularly work with one type of chart. Here's how to do it:

1. Create a chart of the desired appearance (chart type, formats, and so on).
2. Choose File ➤ Set as Default Chart. Now Microsoft Graph will display this chart whenever you open it.

To change the default chart to another type, repeat steps 1 and 2.

► Changing the Chart Size

Dragging a chart window's size box (in its lower-right corner) changes the size of the chart. Text and chart parts are automatically resized to fit the new window size. This new size will be reflected in your Word for Windows document when you quit the Chart window and update the Word for Windows document. (Don't confuse this feature with Chart Window View, described next.)

▶▶TIP

Remember that you can change the size of a chart in Word for Windows if you embed the chart at an unsuitable size. Simply click and drag the sizing handles or select Format ➤ Picture... and change the size in the Picture dialog box.

▶ *Viewing Graphs in Different Sizes*

If you wish to change the size of a chart in the chart window without affecting the size of the chart in your Word document, pull down the Window menu and choose a view percentage (33% View, 50% View, 66% View, 100% View, 200% View, or 400% View). This changes the screen view but not the actual chart size and is useful for working on small chart elements or stepping back to get the big picture.

▶▶NOTE

Microsoft Graph will only offer you view sizes that will fit on the screen. If your chart takes up the whole screen at 100%, Graph won't let you choose 200% View.

▶ *Editing Parts of a Chart*

You can select various chart parts, then edit, move, and embellish them. Click to select a single item; Shift-click to select multiple items. Selected items are surrounded by handles. Solid black handles indicate that the selected item can be formatted with commands and moved or resized with your mouse. White handles mean you must use commands to make changes. (See Figure 29.15.)

For example, you can select the legend box or chart title and drag them to new locations. You can format selected text (change fonts, apply italics, etc.). However, you can't move selected axes with a mouse, but you can modify them using Microsoft Graph's menu commands.

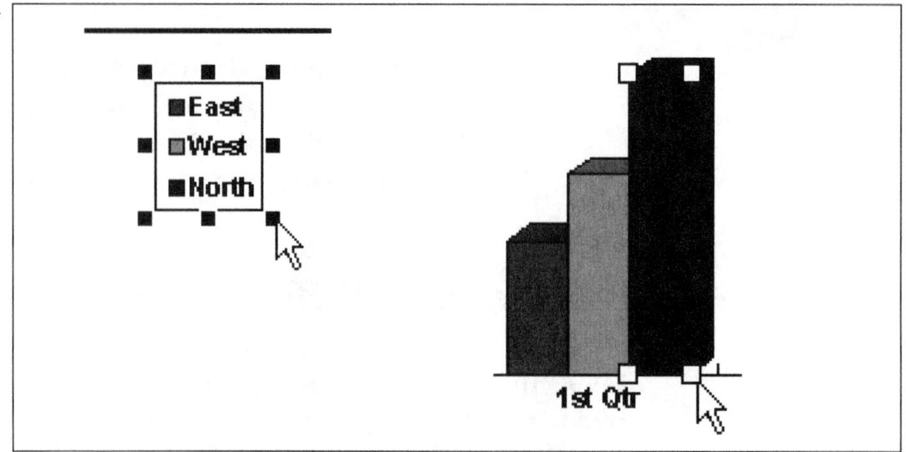

FIGURE 29.15

Black handles indicate that a selected object can be moved and resized with the mouse. White handles (right) indicate that the selected object can only be changed using commands.

The following items can be selected and altered:

- 3-D floor
- 3-D walls
- Arrows
- Axes
- Charts
- Data series (any)
- Drop lines
- Gridlines
- Hi-lo lines
- Legends
- Plot areas
- Series lines
- Text
- Up/Down bars

Here's a hot tip. Frequently, double-clicking on an object in the chart window brings up a dialog box containing the available formatting options. For instance, double-clicking on an axis brings up the Axis Patterns dialog box. Double-clicking a pie wedge brings up the Area Patterns dialog box, and so on. Explore!

▶ *Dragging to Change Data*

You can drag data points and thereby change the appearance of a chart and the underlying numbers in the datasheet! Yep. Read it again. For example, you can drag a column up or down and see the changes visually in the chart and numerically in the datasheet.

Try it. Hold down Ctrl, then click the ends of bars and columns, the selection boxes on lines, etc. This will produce white selection handles around the object and a single black handle at the draggable extremity. Drag this handle in the appropriate direction, as illustrated in Figure 29.16.

FIGURE 29.16

Changing data can be a real drag. Do it the easy way—hold down Ctrl and click to select an object, then drag the black handle to change its values in both the chart and the datasheet.

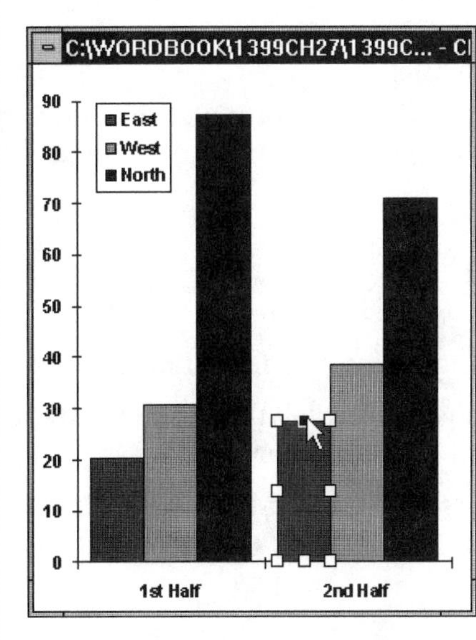

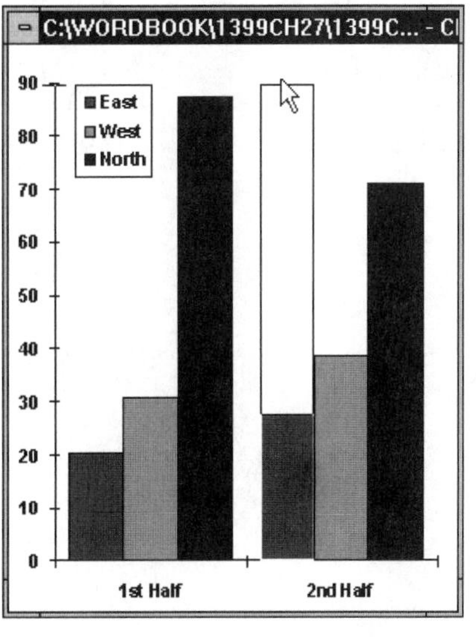

▸▸ NOTE

You can't drag to change data in some chart types. In others you can Ctrl-click until the cows come home, but you won't get a draggable black handle. Don't expect *too* much.

▸ Typing Attached Title Chart Text

Here's how to type or edit attached text (titles):

1. Choose Chart ➤ Titles… to display the Attach Title dialog box.
2. In the Attach Title dialog box, choose the object to which you want to attach the titles (the chart, an axis, etc.), then click OK:

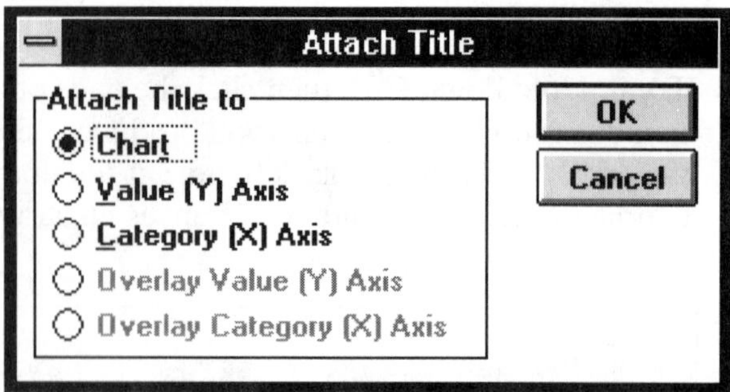

3. Chart opens a tiny text object surrounded by white selection squares within easy commuting distance of the object you chose:

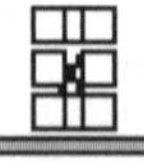

4. Begin typing. Press ↵ to force new lines without ending the entry.
5. When you've entered all the desired text, press Esc. The object will expand to reveal your typing.
6. Pick a new font, style, and so on, but forget about moving attached text. For text you can move, see the next topic.

▶ *Typing Unattached Chart Text*

If you want to add to your chart unattached text notes that you can easily move, follow these steps:

1. Simply start typing in the active chart window. The text first appears in the center of your chart window. Press ↵ to force new lines without ending the entry.
2. When you've completed the entry, press Esc. The object will expand to reveal your typing.
3. Pick a new font, style, and so on.
4. Position the text by clicking on it and dragging it to its new location.

Figure 29.17 shows a chart with a title and text added.

FIGURE 29.17

A chart with a title and text added.

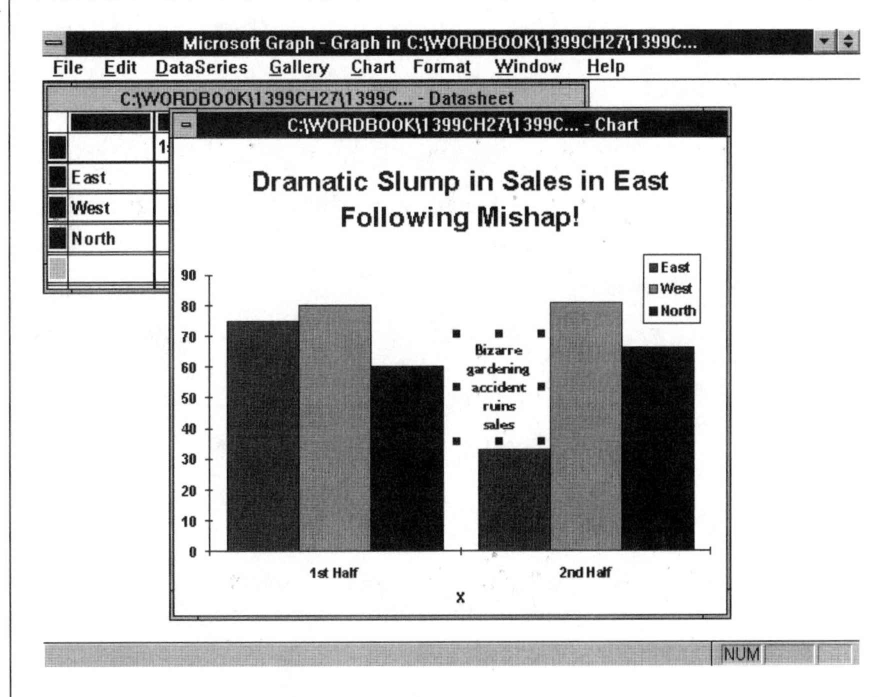

► Editing Chart Text

To edit chart text, first click to select it. Move the pointer into the text so that it changes to an I-beam, then use the I-beam cursor to select and edit the desired text.

► Formatting Chart Text

To format chart text, click it so that it is surrounded by handles. Then use Format ➤ Patterns…, Font…, and Text… to change the appearance of the text.

- Patterns… displays the Area Patterns dialog box, which offers you a choice of patterns for borders and areas.
- Font… displays the Chart Fonts dialog box, which offers you a choice of typefaces and sizes.
- Text… displays the Chart Text dialog box, which offers you the following options:

  Horizontal text alignment: Left, Center, and Right

  Vertical text alignment: Top, Center, and Bottom

  Text orientation: horizontal, vertical, upwards, and downwards

►► NOTE

The Chart Fonts, Area Patterns, and Chart Text dialog boxes each contain two buttons that lead to the other two dialog boxes.

► Gridlines on Charts

To specify gridlines, select Chart ➤ Gridlines… and specify the gridlines you want in the Gridlines dialog box. You can choose Major Gridlines and/or Minor Gridlines for each of the axes.

Double-click on gridlines to pick different line patterns for them from the Line Patterns dialog box.

▶ Rotating 3-D Charts

The 3-D View… command is available on Chart's Format menu when you are working with a 3-D chart. It reveals the Format 3-D View dialog box (see Figure 29.18).

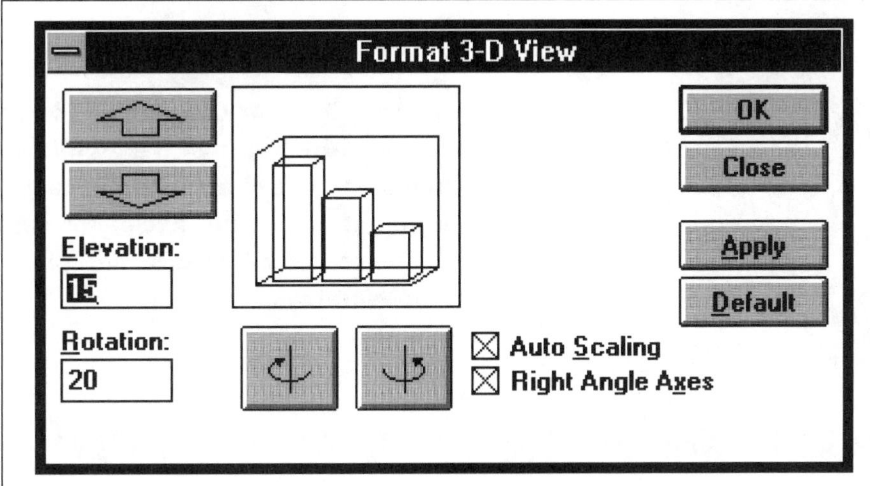

FIGURE 29.18

Control the orientation of 3-D charts with this dialog box, reached by selecting Format ➤ 3-D View….

You can control elevation, perspective, rotation, axes orientation, and height by clicking on boxes that demonstrate these functions. The Right Angle Axes option forces right angles. Auto Scaling sometimes helps with the conversion of 2-D charts to 3-D charts.

▶▶ **WARNING**

Use caution when changing a 3-D graph's orientation, particularly perspective. You can give misleading impressions of the relative size or importance of data this way. Now, of course, if you're doing it deliberately…

►► Saving Charts and Their Data

The only way to save charts and chart data is to embed them into a Word document by answering Yes to the Update Graph question when you quit the Chart. You must then save the Word document to preserve the chart and data.

►► TIP

To embed a Microsoft Graph chart in an Excel spreadsheet, select Edit ➤ Copy Chart while you're in Graph and then paste the chart into the target spreadsheet. Then again, if you've got Excel, you might be better off using it to create charts and then pasting them into Word for Windows.

►► Positioning Graphs in Word Documents

You can use normal paragraph-formatting techniques to position embedded graphs. For instance, to center a graph:

1. Select the embedded graph in your Word document by clicking on it.
2. Remove first-line indenting (if there is any) from the paragraph containing the graph.
3. Use the Center button on the Formatting Toolbar or choose Format ➤ Paragraph and choose Center... in the Alignment box on the Indents and Spacing tab of the Paragraph dialog box.

▶▶ TIP

For fancy positioning, you can put graphs in a frame, then use Format ➤ Frame... to position them. The advantage to this is that you can use text wrapping around the frame, as in Figure 29.1 at the beginning of this chapter. See Chapters 5 and 6 for more information.

▶ Resizing and Cropping Graphs

To resize and crop graphs, follow these steps:

1. Select the embedded graph in your Word document by clicking on it. Small handles appear around the edges and in the bottom-left corner.
2. Move the mouse pointer over one of the corner handles so that it changes into a double-headed arrow, click, and drag the corner handle to resize the graph. If you want to crop (cover up) portions of the graph, hold down the Shift key when you do this; the mouse pointer changes shape to overlapping L-shapes to indicate that you're cropping.

▶▶ TIP

For more precise resizing and cropping of graphs, choose Format ➤ Picture... and enter exact measurements or scaling percentages in its boxes. To leave white space around your graph—for example, between the graph and its border or the surrounding text—enter negative numbers in the Crop From boxes.

▶ Editing and Updating

To update a graph, follow the steps below:

1. Double-click on the graph in your Word document or right-click the graph and select Edit Microsoft Graph from the shortcut menu. The graph will open in a Microsoft Graph window.

2. Make the desired changes in the graph.
3. Choose File ➤ Exit and Return.
4. Answer Yes to the Update question. You will be returned to Word, and the updated graph will be in position.
5. Save your Word document to save the changes.

▸▸ TIP

If you accidentally answer Yes to the Update Graph question when you shouldn't, and insert a graph containing unwanted changes into your Word document, choose Edit ➤ Undo Object.

▸ Other Ways to Incorporate Graphs in Your Word Documents

You can create graphs with other programs (Excel, for instance) and either copy and paste them via your Clipboard or link them to your Word document using Object Linking and Embedding. Read more about these techniques in Chapter 30.

CHAPTER 30

Linking and Embedding to Keep Things Current

▸▸ FAST TRACK

To lock and unlock links ***812***

select Edit ➤ Links… , select the link or links that you want to lock or unlock and check the Locked check box to lock them or uncheck it to unlock them. To lock links quickly, select the links and press **Ctrl+F11**. To unlock links, press **Ctrl+Shift+F11**.

To reconnect lost links ***812***

choose Edit ➤ Links..., choose the link to reconnect, choose the Change Source button, and select the file to which you want to reconnect the link.

To embed objects in your documents ***814***

open in the source application the file containing the object, then select the object and copy it to the Clipboard. Switch back to Word, and paste in the object.

To edit an embedded object ***816***

double-click the object to open the application in which the object was created. Edit the object, then select File ➤ Exit and Return to quit the source application and return to Word.

To remove an embedded object ***820***

select the object and press Delete.

▶▶ With Word 6 for Windows' Object Linking and Embedding (OLE), you can include in your Word for Windows documents information created in other applications. For example, you could create a picture in a drawing program like CorelDRAW! or Micrografx Designer and then insert it in your Word document. You could include in a Word document a table from a spreadsheet in Microsoft Excel or data from a Microsoft Access report. In each case, you could choose to have the information updated automatically whenever the source was changed, updated only when you wanted it updated, or left forever as it was when you inserted it.

Big deal, I hear you say, but what does this mean to *me*? So you're a financial hotshot; you could insert in your annual report figures linked to your profit-and-loss statement in a spreadsheet or database, and then have Word update the report automatically whenever the spreadsheet or database changes. So you're a design whiz; you could keep your brochure up to date with your latest designs. As a crude example of this, Figure 30.1 shows a CorelDRAW drawing paste-linked into a Word document with automatic updating on. Every time I change the drawing in CorelDRAW, it'll be updated in the Word document.

Before Object Linking and Embedding, I would have had to reopen the source application, change the source data, and then copy and paste it into my Word document to bring it up to date. Believe me, this gets tedious fast.

new Word 6 implements several new features that are sure to interest old hands at OLE:

- You can display an embedded or linked object as an icon instead of at its full size. As the icon takes less memory to display than the full object, scrolling in your document is faster.

FIGURE 30.1

This CorelDRAW drawing is linked to the Word document in which it appears. Whenever the drawing is changed in CorelDRAW, it'll be updated in Word automatically.

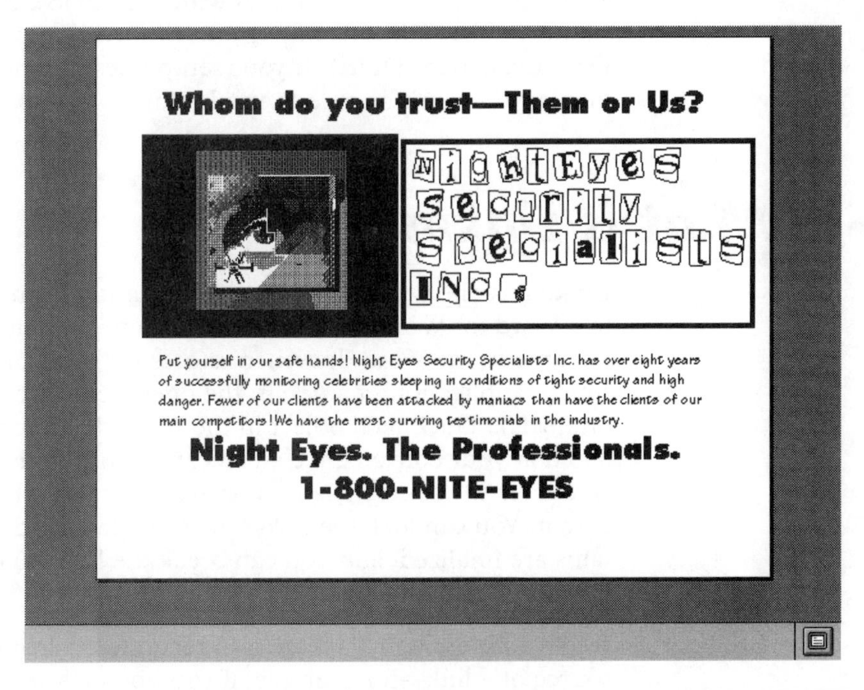

- You can convert an embedded or linked object to a different application. For example, say I need to update the document in Figure 30.1 on a computer that doesn't have CorelDRAW installed: I can convert the linked object to a similar format and then update it. Clearly this offers welcome flexibility.

After a quick peek at the technical requirements for linking information between applications, we'll look at exactly what linking and embedding mean. Then we'll consider what each is for. Finally, we'll discuss how to link and embed.

▸▸ Technical Requirements for Linking Information

For you to be able to link an object created in another application to a Word file, you need to be running both applications in the same environment (e.g., in Windows with MS-DOS). Both applications must support either Object Linking and Embedding (OLE) or Dynamic Data Exchange (DDE). If your setup doesn't match these requirements, you won't be able to use Linking.

▸▸ What Is Linking?

Linking is one way of attaching information from another application to a Word for Windows document. When you link an object to a Word document, the Word document stores the location of the object and its source application in a *field* in the document (see Chapter 32 for more on fields). The linked object in the Word document can then be updated at your convenience—you can choose to update it automatically whenever the source changes or manually just when you want to update it. You can lock the links when the document and the object it contains are finalized, and you can break the links so that objects cannot be updated any further.

If that isn't enough, you can also reconnect a lost link or change the source of a link—for example, if you update a source in a different file in the source application.

▸▸ What Is Embedding?

Embedding is an alternative way to attach information from another application to a Word for Windows document. When you embed information, it becomes part of the Word document and is stored in it. You can double-click the information in Word to open the source application with the information displayed ready for editing.

▸▸ NOTE

Having a touch of *déjà* viewed? As discussed in the last chapter, graphs created with Microsoft Graph are embedded in your document. When you double-click one of them, Microsoft Graph opens with the chart and datasheet ready for editing.

You've no doubt worked out the corollary to this—embedding an object in a Word file increases the size of that file. Considerably. If you embed a whole bunch of big objects (TIFF true-gray files, for example), your Word for Windows files will grow to Brobdingnagian proportions. Time to dust off your wallet and buy a fistful more RAM. But seriously, don't embed too many objects in a file and expect your computer to run like Roger Bannister.

If you can't get around embedding masses of objects in your file, you can do a few things to improve matters. See the section later in this chapter, Converting an Embedded Object to a Graphic.

►► Why Link or Embed?

If you've read the above paragraphs, the reasons to link or embed should be pretty obvious. If you link objects in documents to their sources, you can update the objects either whenever the source objects change or whenever suits you. When your document is finalized, or ready for distribution, you can lock or break the links and freeze it in that state.

Another advantage of linking is that it keeps your documents from getting too large. No matter how large the linked information is, you only have to store it once: in the original file. The link itself increases the size of the document by only a few characters.

One major disadvantage of linking is that when you give your Word document that's linked to other files to someone else, they must have the source files and the applications those other files were created in to maintain the links. Another disadvantage is that making changes to linked data requires opening up the source file in the original application and changing the information there, then manually updating the links.

If you embed objects in documents, you can enjoy the quality of the originals in Word documents and the convenience of being able to edit them in the original application by double-clicking on them. No need to remember which object came from which source application—Word keeps track of that information for you.

The major disadvantage of embedding is that it can make your documents enormous when they contain embedded data from bulky sources, such as graphics files. If you don't need an active link and you're concerned about the size of your document, consider simply pasting in the data or image instead of embedding it. This will require less storage space.

Another disadvantage of embedding is that it does not allow you to change a series of linked documents by changing just the information in a single source to which all the other documents are linked. Changing the original source of embedded information has no effect on the document with the embedding.

▸▸ The Risks of Automation

If all of the above sounds wonderful and you've decided to link all the information you've imported into Word with its sources and have it updated automatically, do me a favor and pause for a minute. Now consider the dangers of automatic updating.

For example, you're writing the report that's going to send your career into the stratosphere. The report's in Word, and it contains figures drawn from your company's financial database in Microsoft Access. To keep the figures in the report up to date, you link the Access object in the Word document to its source. All well and good; next stop, the head office across from Le Parc. Time for the Accounting department to chuck a wrench in the works. The day before you present your report, some fool over there runs a test program on the database to track down a ten-cent overpayment on a shipment of widgets. Like a faithful dog, Word fixes up an instant update on your figures, your report is way off target, and you find yourself reporting to the branch office in Alpha Centauri instead.

Even if you're not connected to a network, and nobody but you can change your data, I'd recommend thinking carefully before using automatic updating. If you decide to go for it, keep a backup file with manual links just to humor me.

▸▸ Link or Embed?

To link or to embed, that is the sixty-four-million–dollar question, as Rosenstern or Guildenkrantz once said. Which is it going to be, and why?

You'll remember from the previous sections that embedded information becomes part of the Word document (and is stored in it), while linked information is stored in the source file in the source application. When you link, Word records the location of the information in the source file and displays a picture of the information in the Word document.

Here's the bottom line: *Link* when you will need to share information with another file. *Embed* when you know you will not need to share information with another file.

Keep a couple of other considerations in mind:

- Linking is a complicated operation, even with the improvements in Object Linking and Embedding that Word 6 implements. Even if your computer's a thundering 486DX-66 with twin overhead cams and more megs of RAM than you have fingers, updating large linked files will take a while. If you have a slow computer, plan a few coffee breaks.
- Linking creates a number of temp files (you know, the ones that look like they've been named by dogs—~wrf0001f.tmp and so on). Reckon to have a little space available for these; more importantly, check your computer every now and then for stray temp files and erase them (see the note below about this). You're most likely to have them if your computer crashes while working with linked files.

TIP

Temp files (~dft064f.tmp and the like) are files created by Windows applications for temporary storage. They're supposed to be deleted automatically when you exit the application that produced then or when you quit Windows (depending on what produced them). Every now and then, check your disk for stray temp files *after* loading Windows and *before* running any Windows applications—i.e., before your applications get a chance to create new temp files—by running File Manager, selecting File ➤ Search, and specifying ~*.tmp. This will round up the usual suspects ready for deletion at dawn.

▸▸ How to Link

Now that you've decided to link (brave soul!), how do you go about it? I'd recommend starting off by learning to link the easy way, then graduating to the more sophisticated way if need be.

▸ Establishing a Link the Easy Way

You can choose either to link an existing object or to create a new object and then link it.

The simplest way to link an object to a Word file is as follows:

1. Fire up the source application for the object you want to link.
2. Create or open the file containing the object.
3. Select the object and copy it to the Clipboard (select Edit ➤ Copy, hit Ctrl+C or Ctrl+Ins, or click any Copy button the application offers).
4. Switch back to Word for Windows by pressing Alt+Tab or hauling down the Task List (press Ctrl+Esc or click the control box in the northwest corner of your screen and select Switch To…), selecting Microsoft Word, and clicking the Switch To button.
5. Put the insertion point at a suitable place in your Word document and select Edit ➤ Paste Special... to open the Paste Special dialog box (see Figure 30.2).
6. In the Paste Special dialog box, select the Paste Link option button to link the object to your Word file. (The Paste Link option button description will be dimmed if it's not available—i.e., if the object copied to the Clipboard is in an application that doesn't support OLE.)
7. In the As: box, select the form in which you want the linked object to appear. The Result box explains the effect of the option selected in the As: box.
8. Check the Display as Icon check box if you want to display the object as an icon in your Word document.
9. Click OK. The object will be paste-linked into your Word document.

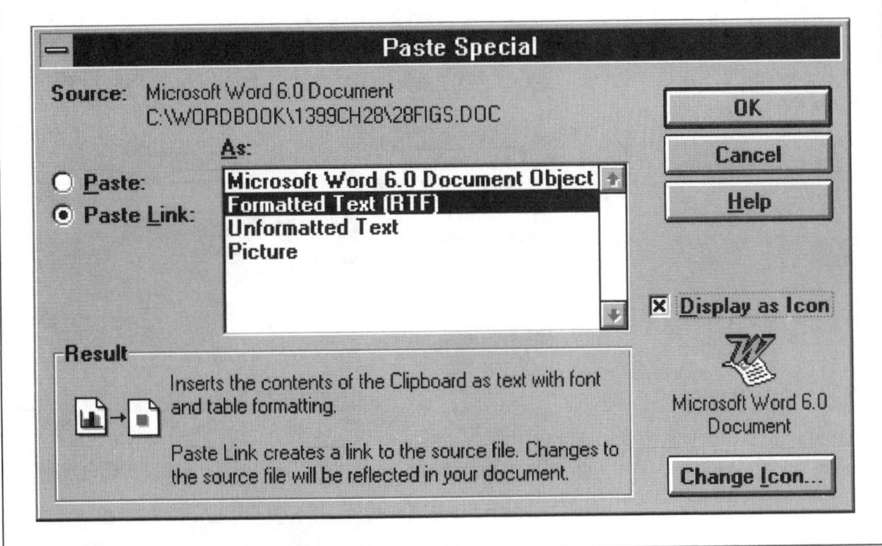

FIGURE 30.2

The Paste Special dialog box. Select the form in which you want the linked object to appear, select Paste Link or Paste, and click OK.

Linking for the More Sophisticated

In case you're interested, here's a slightly more complicated way of linking an object to your Word document.

Linking an existing object and creating a new object to link take you down different avenues of Word, so let's look at them separately to keep the dialog boxes straight.

To Link an Existing Object

Here's how to link an existing object to a document:

1. In your Word document, put the insertion point where you want to insert the linked object.
2. Choose Insert ➤ Object. The Object dialog box will appear.
3. As you're linking an existing object, choose the Create from File tab (see Figure 30.3).
4. Enter the name of the file from which you want to insert a linked object.

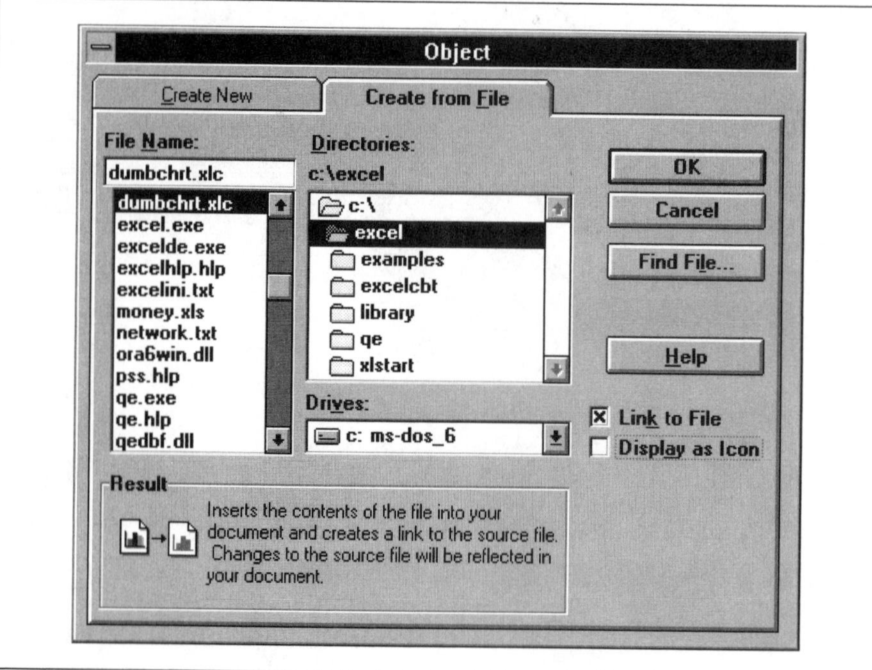

FIGURE 30.3

The Object dialog box with the Create from File tab selected. You're now ready to insert an existing object.

5. If you want to display the linked object as an icon in Word, check the Display as Icon check box. The standard icon for the application you chose will appear below the check box with a Change Icon... button.

   - If you want to display a more exciting icon for your object—heck, you see the same boring old icon *all the time* in the Program Manager—select the Change Icon... button. In the Change Icon dialog box, either select one of the icons the application offers, or click the Browse button to chick out the icons from different applications. When you're done browsing, click OK to return to the Change Icon dialog box, and OK again to accept the icon you've chosen. It'll now appear in the Object dialog box.

6. Check the Link to File check box and choose the OK button. The selected object will be inserted and linked to your Word file.

▶▶ **NOTE**

"Well, Ron, what's the point of this procedure compared to the other one? Frankly, the only advantage that I can see is that you don't have to open up the source application for the object and get your hands dirty mucking around with it. The whole business is often so slow that you hardly save any time over opening the source application yourself and fixing things up manually." Watch this space for further news.

Create a New Object and Link It

To create a new object and link it to your Word document, follow these steps:

1. In your Word document, put the insertion point where you want to insert the linked object.
2. Choose Insert ➤ Object.... The Object dialog box will appear. The Create New tab should be displayed by default (see Figure 30.4.) If it isn't, select it.
3. In the Object Type box, select the application in which you want to create the new object. Check the Display as Icon check box if you want the new object to appear as an icon in your Word document. Change the icon if need be (see To Link an Existing Object, above, for details).
4. Choose OK. The application you chose will open.
5. Create the object you want, then select File ➤ Exit and Return to return to Word. The object will be inserted and linked to your document.

▶ When Are Linked Documents Updated?

You can choose for links to be updated in any of three ways:

- *Automatically.* This is the default. Links are created with automatic updating, so you'll have to change it if you want something else.

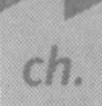

FIGURE 30.4

The Object dialog box with the Create New tab displayed.

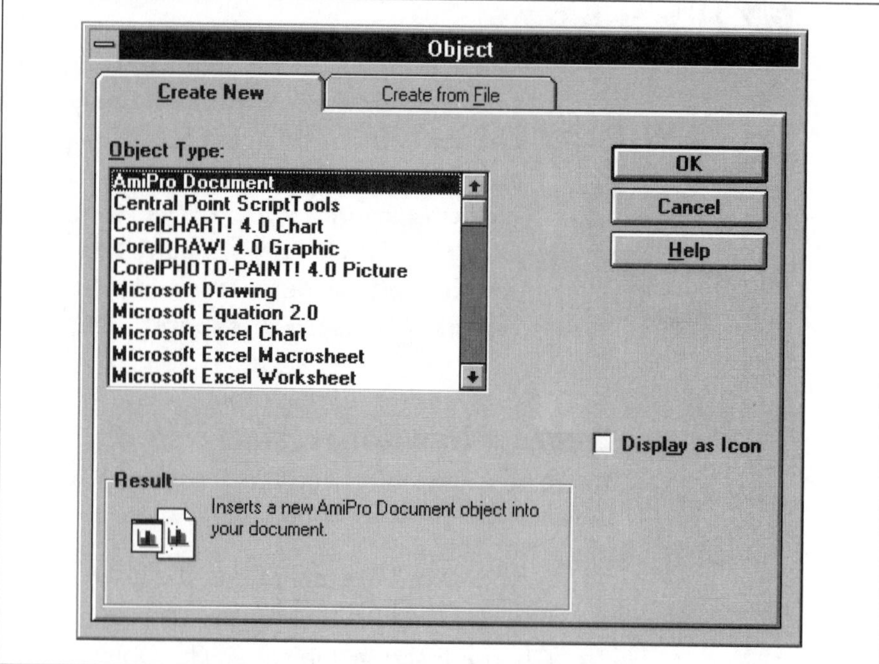

- *Manually.* You update any or all links whenever you want to.
- *On printing.* Whenever you print the document, all links will be updated.

See the following sections for details on these three options.

▶ Updating a Link

Updating a link is straightforward and intuitive:

1. Select Edit ➤ Links....
2. In the Links dialog box (see Figure 30.5), select the link or links that you want to update.

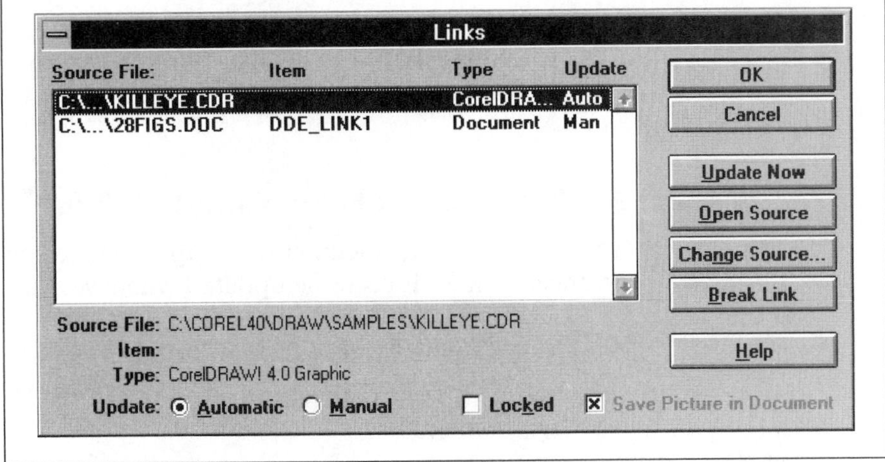

FIGURE 30.5

The Links dialog box. Here's where you select the links to update, lock, or break.

- To update several links, hold down Ctrl while you click on each link, or hold down Shift and click on the first and last links of the desired range to select all the links between the two.

3. Choose how you want the selected links to be updated:
    - Choose the Automatic option button to update linked information every time the source file is changed.
    - Choose the Manual option button to update links only when you choose to do so.
4. Choose OK to close the Links dialog box and accept the changes you've made.

To Update a Link Manually

Update your links manually to retain the most control over your document and its linked objects. Here's how:

1. Select Edit ➤ Links…
2. In the Links dialog box, select the link or links that you want to update.
3. Choose the Update Now button to update the links.

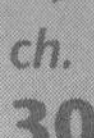

►► TIP

To update links quickly, select the links you want to update and press F9.

To Update Links Every Time You Print

To make sure your documents are up to date whenever you print them, arrange for their links to be updated whenever you print. Here's how:

1. Select Tools ➤ Options....
2. In the Options dialog box, select the Print tab by clicking on it or by pressing P.
3. In the Printing Options box, check the Update Links check box (see Figure 30.6).

FIGURE 30.6 ►

Check the Update Links check box in the Printing Options area of the Options dialog box to have links updated whenever you print documents.

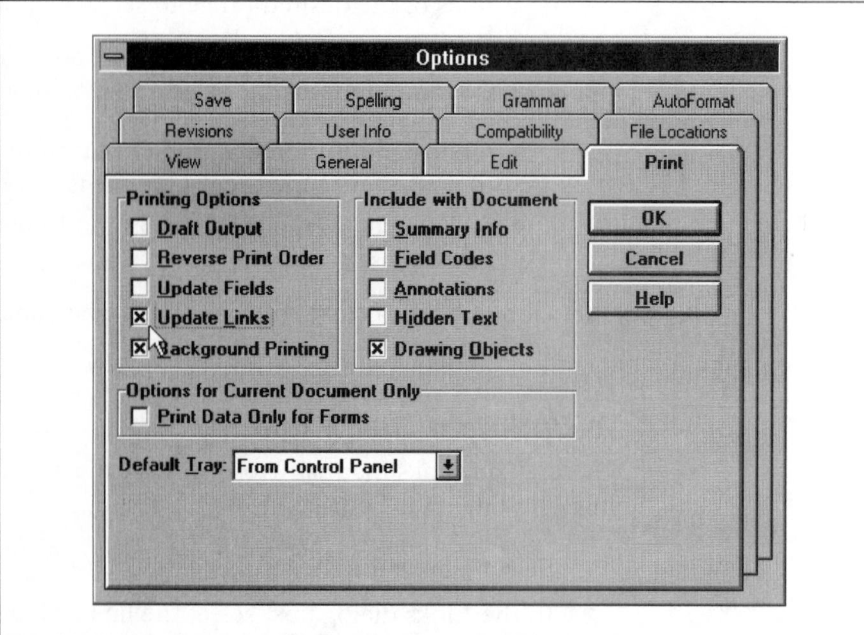

4. Click the OK button to close the dialog box. Links in your documents will now be updated whenever you print.

▶ Editing Linked Information

You'll find you're best off editing linked information in its source file so that your changes are reflected in both the source file and the destination documents.

To edit linked information:

1. Select the linked information to edit. For example, click the linked object in your Word document.
2. Select Edit ➤ Object… (this menu item will vary depending on what kind of object you have selected—e.g., Picture Link) and choose Edit from the mini-menu that appears. Word will open the source application with the selected information displayed.
3. Make the edits you want in the source file.
4. Select File ➤ Exit and Return to get back to your Word document, which will now reflect the edits you made in the source file.

▶ Breaking Links

If you want to prevent linked information from being updated ever again, you can break a link. Once you've broken a link, though, you cannot reconnect it other than by using Undo *pronto*. If you want to *temporarily* prevent linked information from being updated, you can *lock* a link—see the next section for details.

Here's how to break a link:

1. Select Edit ➤ Links…
2. In the Link dialog box, select the link or links that you want to break.
3. Choose the Break Link button. Word will display a dialog box asking if you are sure:

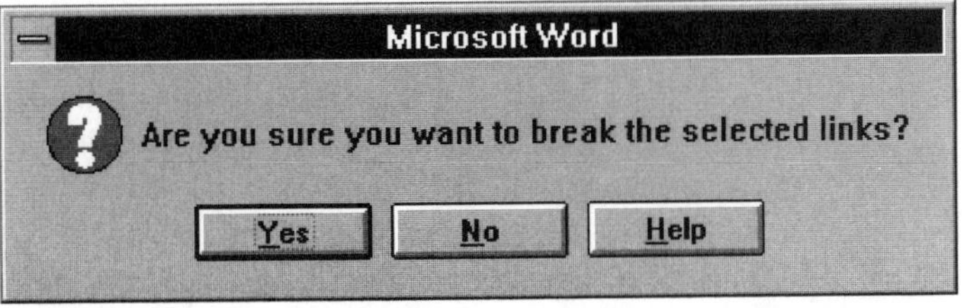

4. Choose OK. The link or links will be broken.

▸▸ TIP

To break a link quickly using the keyboard, press Ctrl+Shift+F9.

▸ Locking and Unlocking Links

You can *lock* links to temporarily prevent linked information from being updated. When you want to be able to update them again, you unlock the links. Here's how to do both:

1. Select Edit ➤ Links....
2. In the Link dialog box, select the link or links that you want to lock or unlock.
3. To lock a link or links, check the Locked check box. To unlock a link or links, uncheck the Locked check box.
4. Choose OK to leave the Link dialog box and save your changes.

▸▸ TIP

To lock links quickly using the keyboard, select the links and press Ctrl+F11. To unlock links, press Ctrl+Shift+F11.

▸ Reconnecting Lost Links

If you lose links in a document, blame yourself rather than the dog, but don't despair—you *can* reconnect lost links. (Sorry. You must have been wondering, is Ron going to make it through a chapter on links without slipping in a joke about sausages? Clearly not.)

How would you lose links? Well, you might rename or move the source file, forgetting that information in it was linked to a Word file. Someone else might even do this for you.

Here's how to reconnect lost links:

1. Choose Edit ➤ Links....
2. In the Links dialog box, choose the link you want to reconnect.
3. Choose the Change Source button.
4. In the File Name box of the Change Source dialog box, select the file to which you want to reconnect the link, then click OK.
   - If your document contains other links to the same source file, Word will ask you whether you want to change all links from the previous source file to the new source file. Choose Yes or No.

So how will you know if your links have become lost? Well, the next time you update the links in your file, any lost links will generate an error message:

Error! Not a valid Filename.

If you no longer have the original source file, you can delete the linked data. If you've got a new source file, simply create a new link to the new source.

You could also lock the link to preserve the most recent data and the information in the link. Then, if you can locate or replace the source file, you can unlock the link and reconnect it to the source. (Locking and unlocking links are explained in the previous section.)

Another stopgap solution would be to break the link (as described in Breaking Links, earlier in this chapter). This would preserve the information but sever the faulty link.

►► Eliminating Graphical Representations of Links to Save Space

As I explained at the beginning of this chapter, a link takes up a lot less "space" than embedded data does because it stores information about where to find the data but it does not import all the data itself into the

Word document. However, links do include graphical representations of the data or image linked, and these graphics do take up some space. With enough of them, you can bog down your document almost as badly as you could with embedded data or images. (Either way, you'll eventually have to sit through the loading of the graphical images into your document.)

To store links without their graphical images:

1. Select Edit ➤ Links.
2. Select a link to be stored without its image.
3. Uncheck Save Picture in Document.
4. Click OK.

▸▸ How to Embed

You can choose either to embed an existing object or to create an object and then embed it.

There's a dead simple way to embed objects, and then there's a more formal and more complicated way. Which would you like to learn first? Right. Here we go.

▸ Embedding the Easy Way

Here's the easy way to embed objects in your documents:

1. Crank up the source application for the object you want to embed.
2. Create or open the file containing your victim object.
3. Select the object and copy it to the Clipboard (select Edit ➤ Copy, hit Ctrl+C or Ctrl+Ins, or click any Copy button the application offers).
4. Switch back to Word for Windows by pressing Alt+Tab or hauling down the Task List (press Ctrl+Esc or click the control box in the northwest corner of your screen and select Switch To…), selecting Microsoft Word, and clicking the Switch To button.

5. Put the insertion point at a suitable place in your Word document and paste in the object from the Clipboard by selecting Edit ➤ Paste, pressing Ctrl+V or Shift+Ins, or clicking the Paste button. Word will embed the object in your document.

▶▶ TIP

If you want Word to do any of its fancy new OLE tricks on your object, follow the above procedure through step 4 and then switch to step 5 in the following section, Embedding an Existing Object.

▶ Embedding the Formal Way

If the way to embed described in the previous section is too easy for you or you want to get a little more sophisticated with your object than simply pasting it in, use this method instead. Or combine the two.

Embedding an existing object and creating a new object to embed are a little different. Let's look at embedding an existing object first.

Embedding an Existing Object

Here's how to embed an existing object in a document:

1. In your Word document, put the insertion point where you want to embed the object.
2. Choose Insert ➤ Object. The Object dialog box will appear.
3. As you're inserting an existing object, choose the Create from File tab.
4. Enter the name of the file from which you want to embed an object.
5. If you want to display the embedded object as an icon in Word, check the Display as Icon check box. The standard icon for the application you chose will appear below the check box with a Change Icon… button.
6. Choose OK. The selected object will be embedded in your Word file.

Creating a New Object and Embedding It

To create a new object and embed it in your Word document, follow these steps:

1. In your Word document, put the insertion point where you want to embed the object.
2. Choose Insert ➤ Object.... The Object dialog box will appear. The Create New tab should be displayed by default. (If it isn't, select it.)
3. In the Object Type box, select the application in which you want to create the new object. Check the Display As Icon check box if you want the new object to appear as an icon in your Word document. Change the icon if need be (see To Embed an Existing Object, above, for details).
4. Choose OK. The application you chose will open.
5. Create the object you want, then select File ➤ Exit and Return to return to Word. The object will be embedded in your document.

▸ Editing Embedded Objects

You edit embedded objects just like you learned to edit graphs in Chapter 29:

1. Click the object to select it. Selection handles and a frame will appear around it, and "Double-click to Edit" will appear in the status area.
2. You guessed it. Double-click the object. Your computer will chug and whir for a while (quite a while if your object is something complicated, like the Corel drawing here—go get a jar of java or bug your office mate for a minute). Then the application in which the object was created will open with the object ready for editing.
3. Edit the object.
4. Select File ➤ Exit and Return to quit the source application and return to Word. Word will reappear with the object updated to reflect your changes, as shown in Figure 30.7.

new

You can use a shortcut menu to carry out common commands such as Cut, Copy, and Paste on an embedded object. Right-click on the

FIGURE 30.7

When you select File ➤ Exit and Return in the source application, Word reappears with the object updated to reflect your changes.

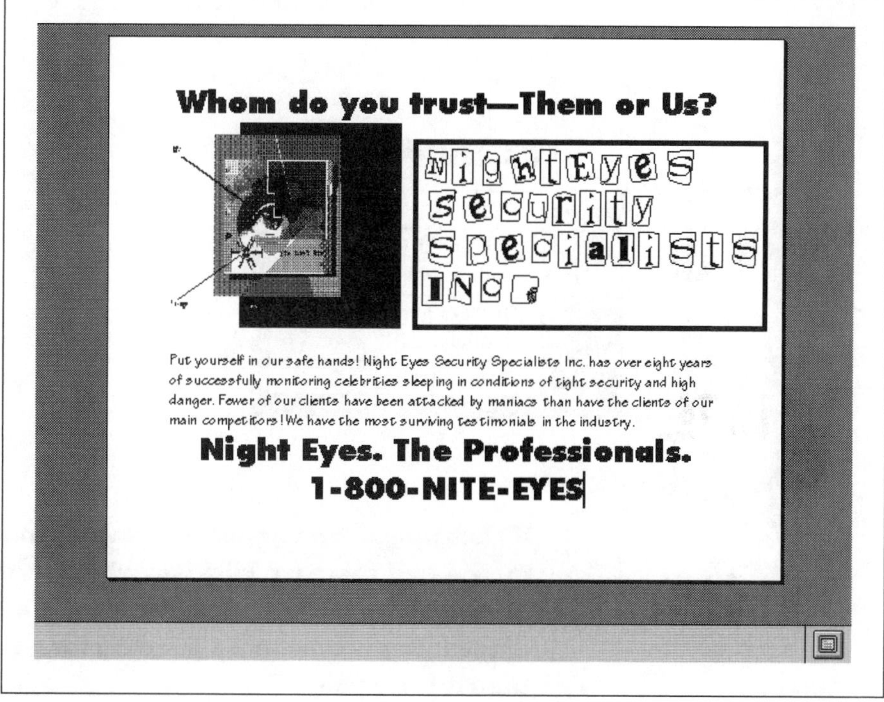

offending object and select the command from the shortcut menu. The shortcut menu will vary depending on the source application for the embedded object. For example, here's the shortcut menu for WordArt:

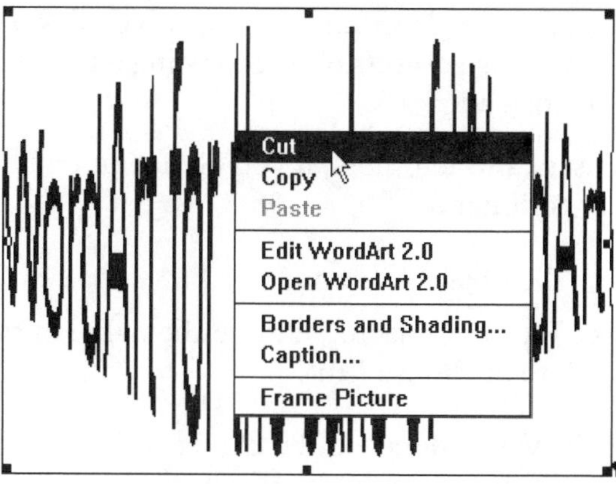

And here's the one for a CorelDRAW object:

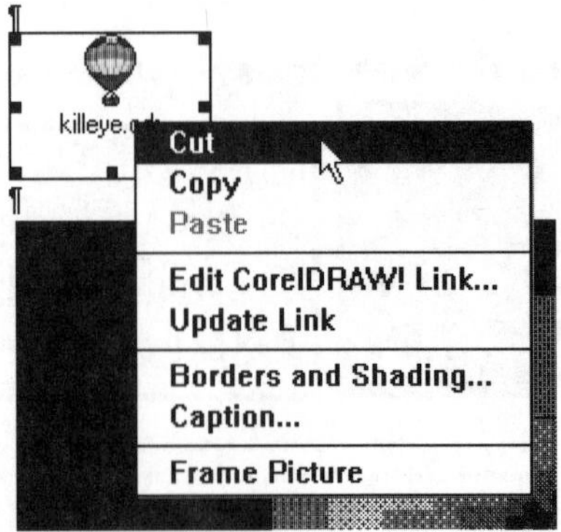

►► NOTE

If the application temporarily trashes some of the Word menus and toolbars, click anywhere in the Word document to restore them. Bear in mind that embedding is even more puzzling for your computer than it is for you.

► Editing Sound and Video Clips

If you've been using sound and video clips, you'll have spotted the fallacy in the preceding section. If you double-click a sound or video clip, you'll run it. These objects object to being edited this way. They just wanna play instead.

In such cases (and in others, if you like), edit embedded objects using the Object command:

1. Select the object you want to edit.
2. Select Edit ➤ Object..., choose the name of the object you want to edit, then choose Edit.
    - If Word offers you the choice of Edit or Open, choose Edit to edit the object in the Word window or choose Open to open the application to which the object belongs and edit it there.

3. When you're finished editing the object, select File ➤ Exit and Return to get back to Word. Word will reappear with the edited object in place.

▶ Converting an Embedded Object to a Different Format

If necessary, you can convert an embedded object to a different format. You might want to do this if you receive a file containing an embedded object created in an application you do not have or if you take a file created on your computer and containing embedded objects to a colleague's computer that does not have the relevant application.

To change an embedded object's source application:

1. Select the object to change.
2. Select Edit ➤ Object, choose the object you want to convert, and select Convert from the extension menu.
3. In the Convert dialog box, specify the application to which you want to convert the file.
    - Select the Convert To button to permanently convert the embedded object to the format you specify.
    - Select the Activate As button to temporarily convert the embedded object to the format you specify. You can then edit the object in that format, but when you save it, it will be saved in its original format.
4. Click OK.

▶ When Are Documents Containing Embedded Objects Updated?

Trick question. Answer: When you choose to update them.

Remember that when you update embedded objects, you need to have the application or applications that created them loaded on the computer you're using.

▸ Converting an Embedded Object to a Graphic

If you've been embedding objects like a maniac and your file is doing a Charles Atlas and splitting its shirt, you can reduce the file's size by converting the objects to graphics.

Before you do this, there's one little disadvantage you must know about:

- You can't convert the graphic back to an embedded object.

Still want to do it? Here's how:

1. Select the object you want to convert.
2. Select Edit ➤ Object… and select the object in the Object dialog box.
3. Choose Convert.
4. In the Object Type box, select Picture. Click OK. The object will be displayed as a picture.

▸▸ NOTE

If you have field codes displayed, you will see the field {Embed Word Drawing}.

▸ Removing Embedded Objects

Removing an embedded object is easier than winking. Select it and hit Delete.

To remove an object the fancy way, right-click on the object to pop up the shortcut menu and choose Cut (as shown in Figure 30.8). Bear in mind that this will copy the object to the Clipboard. Anything else you've got on the Clipboard will get hosed.

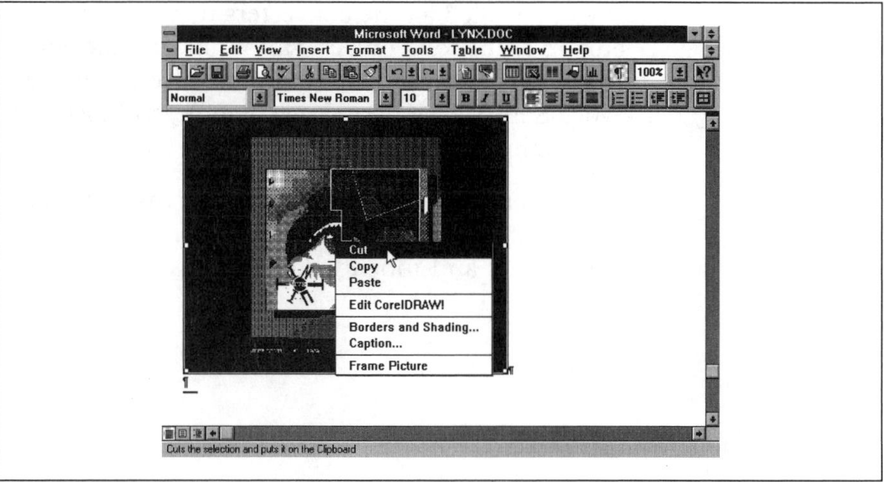

FIGURE 30.8

The second-easiest way to get rid of an embedded object: Right-click it to pop up the shortcut menu, then select Cut. (The easiest way is to select the object and hit Delete.)

Editing Embedded Objects on Other People's Computers

As intimated above, you cannot edit embedded objects on a computer that does not have the source applications installed. For instance, you might create a Word document with a linked Excel spreadsheet on your computer and take it in to your boss to show it to her. All goes well until you double-click the Excel object, only to find that your boss doesn't have Excel on her computer—she has Quattro Pro for Windows instead. *Bzzzzzzz!* Word for Windows won't like this.

WARNING

When you take a file containing embedded objects to someone else's computer, make sure that that computer has all the necessary applications available before attempting to edit the embedded objects.

If you installed all the converters that come with Word, then you can edit an embedded object without having the source application available. If you did not install the converters, you can still run Microsoft Word Setup, do a partial installation, and install the converters from the original disks.

To convert an embedded object to a different file format so that you can use it on a computer without the source application loaded, see Converting an Embedded Object to a Different Format earlier in this chapter.

CHAPTER 31

E-Mail and Other Network Features

▸▸ FAST TRACK

Word 6's File ➤ Add Routing Slip… and File ➤ Send… commands ***828***

allow you to send and return copies of your Word documents to others on a network using Microsoft Mail or a compatible mail program.

To send a Word document via electronic mail ***829***

open the document you want to send and select File ➤ Add Routing Slip…. Click the Address button to add addresses. Add any Subject and Message Text you want, choose routing options, and click the Route button.

You can route a message to recipients in two ways: ***831***

Choose the One After Another option button to send a single copy around (to each addressee in turn), or choose the All at Once option button to send multiple copies (one to each addressee).

To revise and return a document mailed to you ***832***

retrieve the document from your mail program and open it in Word, revise the document using annotations or revisions (depending on how the sender protected the document), and choose File ➤ Send… to send the document on its way.

To merge revisions and annotations 833

into your original document, open the document containing the revisions you want to merge, select Tools ➤ Revisions..., and click the Merge Revisions button. Select the original file in the Merge Revisions dialog box and click OK. Repeat the process for other revised copies of your document.

When using Word on a network 836

take precautions: Protect your documents from changes, save and back your documents up frequently, and be careful about whom you give access to your documents (if necessary, make them read-only).

If you're sharing documents a lot 836

remember a few basic points: Don't use templates that the other people in the group don't have; don't redefine built-in key combinations in shared templates; don't use fonts that the other people in the group don't have; and never, never, *never* lose your file-protection password.

▶▶ **C*hances*** are, these days, that your place of work has a network. If it has, you'll know that networks add exciting new dimensions to working with computers: Not only can you screw up your documents, but someone else can access them from another workstation and screw them up for you. If you guard against that, the network can strike back by crashing while you're in the middle of a project and trashing all of your unsaved work.

The benefits of networks include access to files and applications that you haven't got on your workstation—other people's work, applications that simply won't fit on your PC, etc.—and instant communications with others on the network. (You can also install Word on a network rather than on an individual workstation, but that's beyond the scope of this book.) In this chapter, we'll look at Word's features for sending and sharing files on a network.

When you are on a network and your organization uses Microsoft Mail or a compatible mail program for in-house electronic communications, you can use the File ➤ Add Routing Slip… and File ➤ Send… commands to send and return copies of your Word documents to others.

You and the recipients must have Word and Microsoft Mail (or a compatible mail program) installed on your computers in order to use these features. Oh, and your network needs to be running… but you'd probably guessed that already.

Sending Word Documents via E-Mail

WARNING

Before we get into how easily you can propagate your Word documents all over the place, remember the importance of protecting them. You'll remember that we discussed this a bit in Chapter 7; we'll look at it again briefly later in this chapter in the Network Considerations section.

Sending Word documents via electronic mail is pretty simple:

1. Open the document you want to send.
   - If the document's already open because you've just created or altered it, make sure it's saved. Thanks.
2. Select File ➤ Add Routing Slip…. The Routing Slip dialog box will appear, as shown in Figure 31.1.
3. Click the Address button. In the Address dialog box (see Figure 31.2), select the names of the people you want to send the document to and choose the Add button.
   - To route the document to one recipient after another (we'll get into this in a minute), arrange the names in the appropriate order by using the Move up- and down-arrow buttons.
4. Click OK to return to the Routing Slip dialog box. The names you entered will appear in the To box.
   - If the To box shows you that you've added someone you shouldn't have, click the Remove button and remove them from the list. Click OK again to get back to the Routing Slip dialog box.
5. Type the subject of your communiqué in the Subject box and any message in the Message Text box. Each recipient will get the same subject and message, so don't get too personal.

FIGURE 31.1

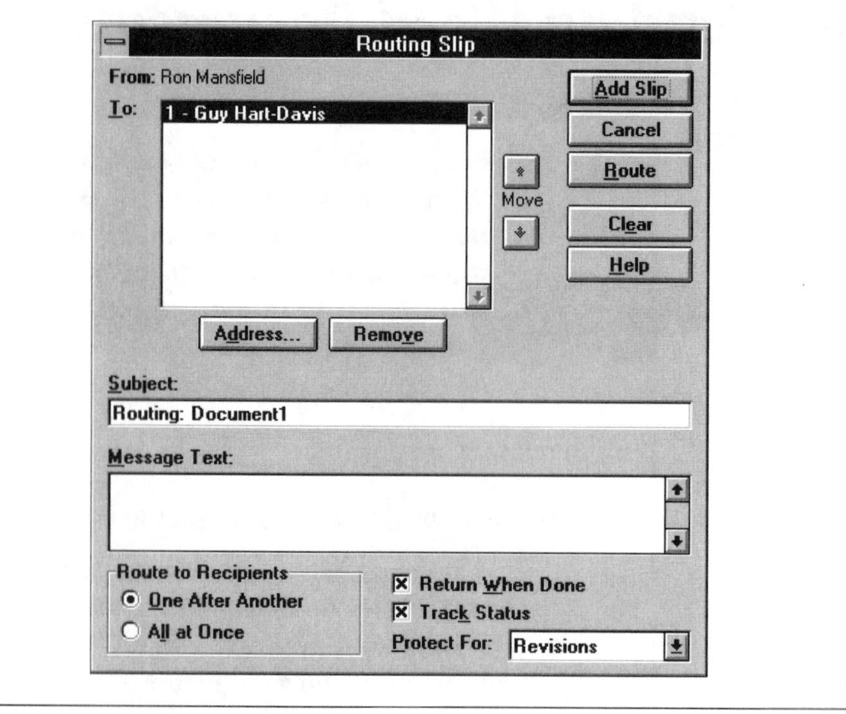

The Routing Slip dialog box.

FIGURE 31.2

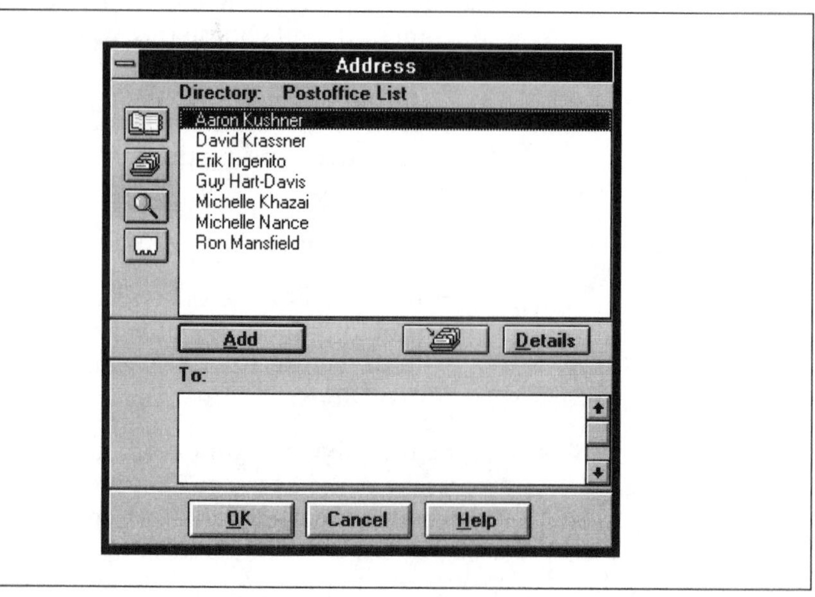

The Address dialog box. Choose your victims here.

- Word will automatically add to your message instructions that tell the recipients to select File ➤ Send... when they are finished with the document you send them, so you don't need to write that in your message.

6. In the Route to Recipients area, choose whether you want the document to be sent to the recipients One After Another or All at Once.

▶▶ TIP

If you send a document to the recipients One After Another, each successive recipient will see his or her predecessors' comments. This way, you may be able to avoid duplicate comments. If you send multiple copies to All At Once, everyone's comments will be between them and you (until you put them in the ultimate document and attribute them to their maker!). You'll probably also get quicker answers this way.

7. If you're ready to send your document, choose the Route button. The document will be sent to your chosen recipients as an attached Word file.

   - To further edit your document before you send it, click the Add Slip button again, do your editing, and then select File ➤ Send... to send the document. Click Yes in the confirmation dialog box.

Let's look quickly at three further options in the Routing Slip dialog box: Return When Done, Track Status, and Protect For.

Return When Done	Check the Return When Done check box to have the document sent back to you when the last recipient finishes with the document and chooses File ➤ Send....

Track Status	Check the Track Status check box to keep track of where your document has been routed. Word will send you a message each time the document is sent on to the next person in the To list.
Protect For	Select protection for your document from the drop-down list: **Annotations** allows recipients to add only annotations to the document; **Revisions** allows them to make changes (forcibly marked with revision marks) and add annotations; and **Forms** lets recipients enter information only in form fields (see Chapter 33 for more on forms).

▸▸ Revising and Returning a Mailed Document

If you're the target of an e-mailed Word document, here's how you do your bit:

1. Retrieve the document from your mail program in the usual way for that program and open the document in Word.
2. Revise the document depending on how the sender has protected it:
    - If the document allows annotations only, select Insert ➤ Annotation, type your annotation into the annotation pane, and click Close when you're done. (See Annotating Documents in Chapter 24 for more details.)
    - If the document allows both revisions as well as annotations, just go ahead and make your revisions. Friendly Word will mark the revisions for you using revision marks (look back to Chapter 24 to refresh your memory if need be)—in fact, you won't be able to turn them off.
    - If the document is protected as a form, you're wearing a straitjacket. Fill in the fields (*all* the fields; be good) and don't try to do anything else.

3. Choose File ➤ Send.... The Send dialog box will appear (see below), asking if you want to use the routing slip or send the document without using the routing slip. To wing the document on its merry way, choose the Route Document option and click OK.

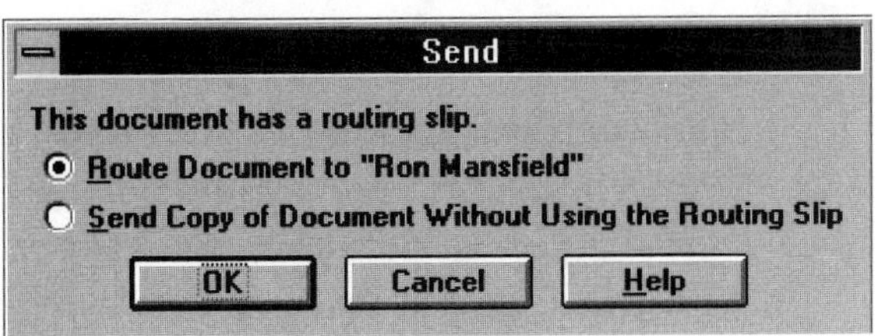

- If the original sender chose to route the document to recipients All At Once, this will return the document to the sender.
- If the original sender chose to route the document to recipients One After Another, this will pass the document on to its next victim—unless you're the last, in which case the document will be returned to the sender.
- If the original sender checked Track Status, Word will let the sender know when you send the document on to its next recipient. Yup, Big Brother is e-mailing about you.

▶▶ NOTE

If you choose the Send Copy of Document Without Using the Routing Slip option, all protection the original sender chose remains in effect.

There, that was painless, wasn't it?

▶▶ The Fun Part—Merging Annotations and Revisions

So you sent out—all at once—seven copies of your latest marketing proposal for industrial-strength deodorant, *Hang-Gliding off Power Pylons,* and everyone got back to you with helpful comments. Well, sort of helpful. Most of them, anyway. Bunch of cynics, the lot of them. Now you need to merge the annotations and revisions into one copy so that you can pick out the best and trash the rest.

▸▸ **WARNING**

You can't merge annotations and revisions back into the original document unless they're marked. Makes sense if you think about it. This is another good reason for protecting your document for revisions or annotations before sending it out. If you forget to protect your document, try using Tools ➤ Revisions… and using the Compare Versions… feature.

To merge all those pesky revision marks and annotations:

1. Retrieve your returned document from your mail program. Word will automatically ask you if you want to merge revisions with the original document.

2. Click OK. The Merge Revisions dialog box will appear (well, what did you expect?), as shown in Figure 31.3.
3. Select the original file and click OK. The original document will open and the revisions will be merged into it.
4. Repeat as necessary with the other six copies of the report.

FIGURE 31.3

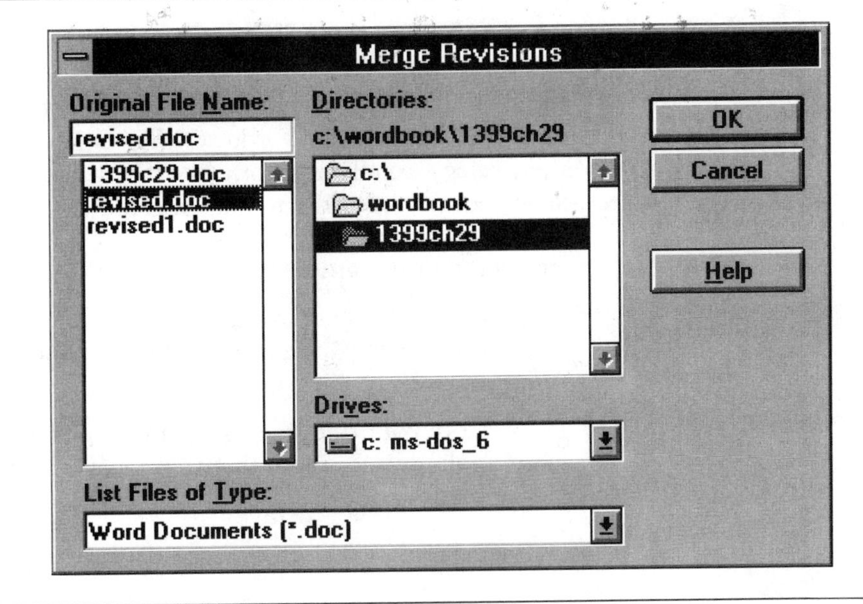

The Merge Revisions dialog box. Select the original file here and click OK. Change drives and directories just as you would in the Open dialog box.

▶▶ NOTE

When you merge revisions or annotations from multiple documents into the original, Word will use a different color for each reviewer (up to eight; after that, Word will cycle through the colors again).

▶▶ For Additional Help with Mail

Mail and network connections can be confusing, particularly on the complex networks that have been proliferating recently. Read your mail program's user guide to glean further information or go harass your friendly network administrator or hallway guru.

▸▸ Network Considerations

As I hinted at the beginning of this chapter, networks can be a source of grief as well as of joy to the Word user. While there's no way that you can absolutely safeguard all your work (short of sealing yourself and it in a lead-lined room), remember to take the following obvious precautions:

- Protect your documents from changes (see Chapter 7).
- Save your documents frequently and back them up to a safe medium as often as you're prepared to lose them—that should be pretty frequently.
- If you store your documents on a network drive, be careful about whom you give access to them. If necessary, make your documents read-only.

If you're sharing documents a lot, here are a few things to think about first:

- Don't use templates that the other people in the group don't have.
- If you share templates, keep them clean. Don't redefine built-in key combinations—you may confuse your coworkers, or worse.
- Don't use fonts that the other people in the group don't have. (But remember that you can embed TrueType fonts in shared documents so that other users who don't have the fonts installed can see the fonts and print them. Select Tools ➤ Options£, click the Save tab in the Options dialog box, and check the Embed TrueType Fonts check box. See Chapter 9 for more information about this kind of thing.)
- Don't lose your file-protection password(s).

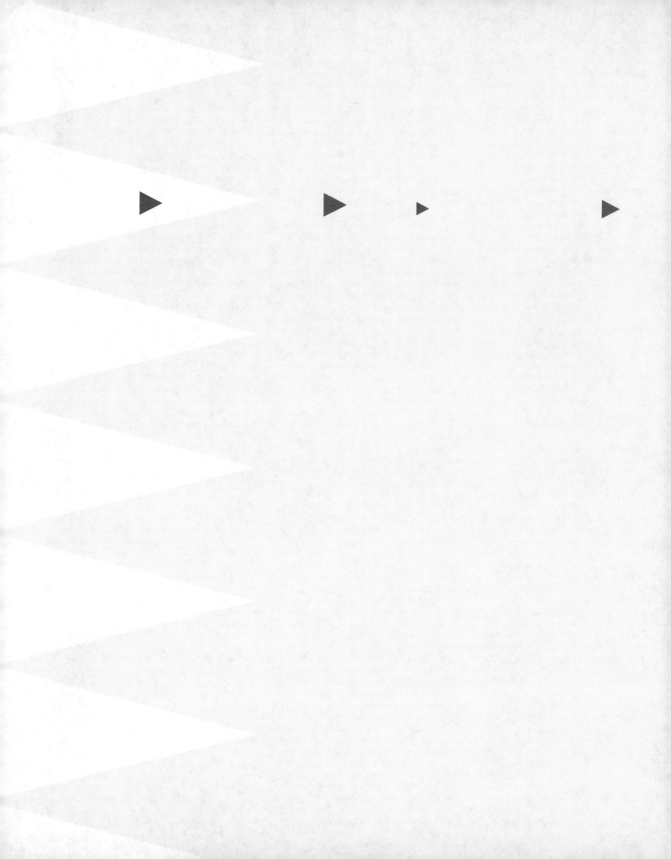

CHAPTER 32

Creating and Using Fields

▸▸ Fast Track

Fields are special codes **842**

you use to tell Word to insert information in your documents. You can insert codes to add and automatically update text, graphics, and so on.

To insert a field in a document **846**

select Insert ➤ Field…, select the category of field you want, and select the field you want. Choose the Options… button to add switches or formatting to the field you selected and then select OK.

To display the field code for a single field **850**

place the insertion point in the field, click the right mouse button to display the pop-up shortcut menu, and choose Toggle Field Display.

To display all the codes in a document **850**

select Tools ➤ Options…, choose the View tab, and check the Field Codes check box.

To view field codes and results at the same time **851**

split the document window into panes and set different view options for each pane.

To display field results shaded **851**

select Tools ➤ Options…, choose the View tab, pull down the Field Shading list, and choose Always.

To format fields **853**

format either the field result itself or the field code.

▶▶ **U*mmm...field.*** There. Now I've said it. If you're one of the people who runs screaming into the next jurisdiction whenever anybody mentions the word "field"—and if you're still reading this—take heart. You don't actually have to use fields. Not now, not ever. You could go through your whole life without using a single Word for Windows field. It might be tough, but you *could* do it.

On the other hand, if you *do* use fields, you can save yourself a tremendous amount of work. You can keep your documents up to date more easily, include material from a bunch (dare I say plethora? Perhaps not) of different sources with the stab of a finger, and automate your life to a large extent.

First, let's take a squint at what fields are. Then we'll look at what you might want to use them for. Finally, we'll get into examples and check out the new fields in Word 6. If you find fields interesting (and let's face it, most people don't), you should find Word 6's new fields stimulating. Don't worry—it's quite legal, and it's almost harmless.

▶▶ What Are Fields?

Fields are special codes you use to tell Word to insert information into your documents. You can insert codes to add and automatically update text, graphics, and so on. For example, you could use codes like these:

```
{ AUTHOR \* MERGEFORMAT } {DATE \* MERGEFORMAT } {TIME
\* MERGEFORMAT } {TITLE \* MERGEFORMAT } Page {PAGE \*
MERGEFORMAT } of {NUMPAGES \* MERGEFORMAT }
```

to create a footer that looks like this:

> Janice Horsefly 04/01/94 8:33 AM The Impact of Ultraviolet Lasers on the Cerebral Cortex Page 291 of 316

Author, date and time, title, and the page number out of the total number of pages—not bad for a few seconds' work with half a dozen codes. If you formatted the codes, the result would look even better. But the best thing is that you can have these fields updated instantly at any time, either automatically or at the punch of a key. (Yes, the page-number and number-of-pages codes update themselves automatically, adjusting for each page of your document.)

If you don't want fields to be updated, you can lock them and then unlock them again when you need to update them.

As in the preceding example, Word usually displays the *result* of the field—the text or graphics the field will produce when printed. To indicate which text in your document is actually a field, you can have field results displayed shaded. You might want to do this if you find yourself hosing field codes accidentally. (See Viewing Fields and Their Contents later in the chapter.)

▶ Where Do the Fields Get Their Information?

At this point, you might well be wondering where these fields get their information from. Out of thin air? By psychic transmission?

Unfortunately, it ain't quite so, Joanna. We're not talking Newtons and radio PC-to-PC communications here. Your copy of Word (viz., the copy of Word you're using, whomever it's actually licensed to; I'm assuming the one and the other are the same) already knows a whole bunch of stuff about you. Whatever you entered for the user name and address when you first installed Word is stored for use in your documents; you can access it by selecting Tools ➤ Options… and clicking the User Info tab in the Options dialog box. Word uses the Name field there for the Author name in the Summary Info dialog box, the Initials for use in annotations, and the Mailing Address for the return address in any envelopes you print. Sure, you can change all of these, but remember, Word is storing information about you.

When you save a file and fill in the Summary Info dialog box, Word stores that information for retrieval in fields. The Author information Janice Horsefly used in her footer came from this dialog box, as did the Title information. The Date and Time information comes from the system clock that you set in Windows or DOS. The page-information fields—the page number and the number of pages—Word itself generates from your document.

There isn't space here to go into all the different fields and where they get their information, but I think you get the idea: Some fields draw on permanent or semipermanent information (such as the user name), some draw on information you enter for any given document (title, keywords), and others are generated by Word (number of characters in a document, etc.).

►► Typical Uses of Fields

You can use fields in Word 6 to

- Insert text, graphics, and other information in your documents
- Keep changing information updated
- Perform calculations

Most people's introduction to fields in Word for Windows comes when they put dates, times, and page numbers in their documents. Clicking the buttons for these fields on the Header and Footer Toolbar is a pretty intuitive way of inserting fields. In fact, you might not even know they are fields unless you turn field codes on.

As you saw in Chapter 28, Word's mail-merge features make extensive use of fields. As you learned in Chapter 29, embedding charts from Microsoft Graph in Word documents also involves fields—as does Object Linking and Embedding, which we discussed in Chapter 30. Boy, you can hardly get away from the little buggers! In case you're wondering, the next chapter, Creating and Using Forms, will feature further fields. They've got you surrounded. You might as well make the best of it.

That said, let's look at how you insert fields in your documents to produce these wonderful results.

►► The Different Types of Fields

There are three types of fields—result fields, action fields, and marker fields.

- Result fields are the most common. They display information. This information can come from within the document, from Word, from other documents, or from Windows itself.
- Action fields prompt the user to do something and then perform some action in response. There are only four: ASK, FILLIN, GOTOBUTTON, and MACROBUTTON.
- Marker fields simply mark a location without displaying anything in the document or "doing" anything.

►► The Basic Parts of a Field

Unless you specifically choose to see field codes, you will only see the images or information that the result fields display, the prompts from the action fields, and no sign at all of the marker fields. If you display fields (by selecting Tools ➤ Options and checking Fields on the View Tab of the Options dialog box), however, you will see neither results nor prompts. Instead you'll see the field *code*.

Field codes consist of three elements:

- Fields always begin and end with { and }, but these are not the simple curly-brace characters { and } that you can type in from the keyboard. They are called *field characters*.
- The first part of a field after the opening field character is the *field name* (for example, AUTHOR or TITLE, both of which refer to entries in the Document Summary dialog box). The field name identifies the field and the result, action, or marking it performs.
- One or more optional *field instructions* (such as * MERGEFORMAT) modify the basic field result or action in some way, supplying default text, selecting an option among several choices in a Word command, giving the file name of a linked file, and so on. (MERGEFORMAT causes the field to retain its formatting when updated, but that's getting a little ahead of ourselves.)

Field instructions themselves come in several flavors:

- *Bookmarks*, as elsewhere, refer to locations or selections in documents. Fields with bookmark instructions can make use of the contents of the bookmark as well as its page number.

- *Expressions* are instructions used with the = field. They are all mathematical or logical operations, values, or references to values stored or inherent in the document.
- *Text*: Enclosed in quotation marks (though this is not necessary for single words) or passed to the field as variables, text instructions simply supply text to a dialog box, prompt, or default box entry. (References to graphics are also considered text instructions, ironically enough.)
- *Switches* are instructions that further modify the result or action of a field. They all begin with the \ (backslash) character. They can take further instructions. There are four general switches:

  * (format)

  \# (numeric picture—that is, numeric format)

  \@ (date-time picture—or format)

  \! (lock result)

  and myriad field-specific switches. A field can have a maximum of ten general switches and ten field-specific switches, though let's hope you never feel limited by this cap!

All of these types of field instructions can be represented by variables as well as by their literal names.

▸▸ Inserting Fields

Some Word processes insert fields automatically. The Word commands for creating tables of contents and indices, the Page Number command on the Insert menu, many of the Mail Merge commands: all insert codes automatically.

There are two ways to insert fields manually. The easiest is to use the Field command on the Insert menu, but it is also possible to type field codes directly into the document (and there are a number of keyboard shortcuts for some of the most useful fields).

▶ Inserting Fields with Insert ➤ Field

To insert a field in a document:

1. Put the insertion point where you want the field to appear.
2. Select Insert ➤ Field.... The Field dialog box will appear (see Figure 32.1).
3. In the Categories list, select the category of field you want.
    - Select [All] to see all the fields in alphabetical order.

FIGURE 32.1 ▶

The Field dialog box.

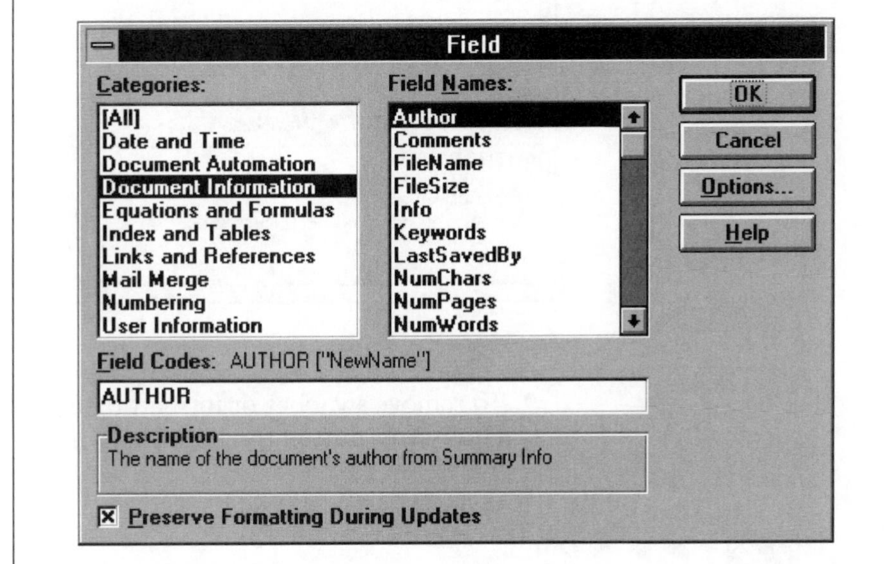

4. Select the field you want.
5. Choose the Options... button to add switches or formatting to the field you selected. In the Field Options dialog box (shown in Figure 32.2), select the switch or formatting you want in the box (its name varies depending on the options available for the selected

field), and hit the Add to Field button. When you're finished adding formatting and switches, choose OK to return to the Field dialog box.

FIGURE 32.2 

The Field Options dialog box. Select switches or formatting for your fields here.

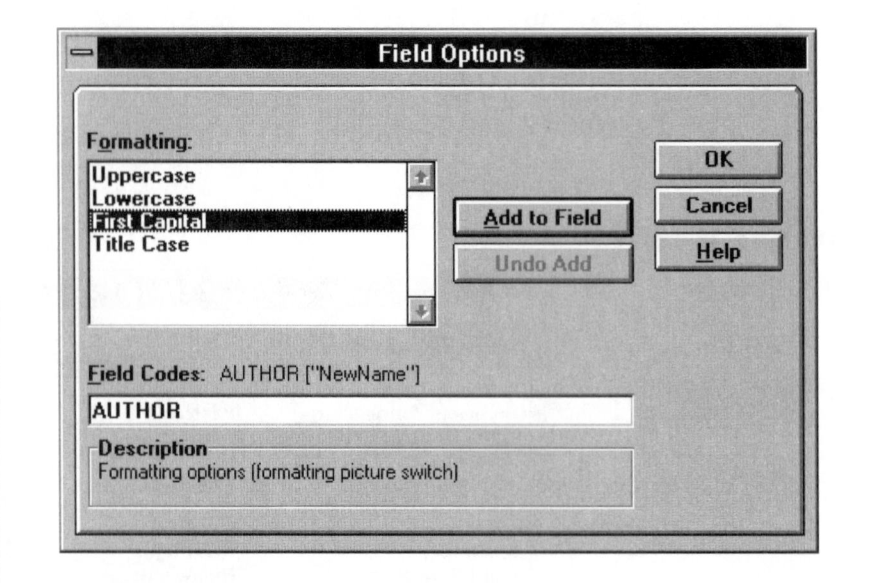

- To remove switches or formatting from the field, select the Undo Add button (great use of English) in the Field Options dialog box.

▸▸ **NOTE**

General field code switches are explained in great detail later in this chapter under Adding Switches to Fields.

6. Back in the Field dialog box, click OK to insert the selected field in your document.

▶ Inserting Field Codes Directly

If you know what you're doing, you can type field codes directly from the keyboard. Here's how:

1. Put the insertion point where you want to insert the new field.
2. Press Ctrl+F9. This inserts the field character, like so—{ }—and leaves the insertion point in the middle, between the two field characters.
3. Type the field name followed by a space.
4. Type the field instructions you want, if any.
5. Press F9 to update the field immediately.

▶▶ **NOTE**

The above procedure works just as well if you do steps 3 and 4 before step 2 (type the field name and instructions and then press Ctrl+F9).

If you have mistyped, the field will display an error message, such as:

Error! Unknown switch argument.

If this happens, press Shift+F9 to display the field code again and correct your error.

▶▶ Viewing Fields and Their Contents

You can view codes either as field results or as field codes. As discussed earlier, field results consist of the text or graphics that will be printed; field codes are the instructions to Word that will produce said text or graphics.

By default, Word displays field results, so you can see how your document will appear when printed. But when you are working with fields, you can display field codes instead of field results. You can display codes for a single field or for all fields at once.

▶ To Display Field Codes for a Single Field

You display the field code for a single field like this:

1. Place the insertion point in the field.
2. Click the right mouse button to display the pop-up shortcut menu.
3. Choose Toggle Field Display from the shortcut menu to turn on the codes for the field.

To turn the codes off again, repeat the procedure. The toggle will return the codes to their result display.

▶ To Display Field Codes for All Fields

When inserting or adapting field codes, you may want to display all the codes in a document so you can better see them. Here's how:

1. Select Tools ➤ Options….
2. In the Options dialog box, choose the View tab.
3. Check the Field Codes check box, and then click OK.

Your fields will now appear as codes—{TITLE * MERGEFORMAT } and so on. To return them to text, repeat steps 1 through 3 but uncheck the Field Codes box.

▶▶ WARNING

Some field codes—the RD (Referenced Document), TA (Table of Authorities), TC (Table of Contents), and XE (Index Entry) fields—do not appear when other field codes are displayed; these field codes are formatted as hidden text. To reveal them, select Tools ➤ Options… select the View tab, and check the Hidden Text check box. To hide them again, uncheck the Hidden Text check box.

▶ To View Field Codes and Results at the Same Time

Sometimes you may find it helpful to view both field codes and their results at the same time so you can see what effect changing the field codes has on their results. To do so, split the document window into panes (by dragging the Split bar down from the top of the vertical scroll bar or by selecting Window ➤ Split and dragging the Split bar to an appropriate place) and set different view options for each pane.

▶ To Display Field Results Shaded

You can choose to have field results displayed shaded so you don't delete or alter them by mistake. Here's how:

1. Select Tools ➤ Options....
2. In the Options dialog box, choose the View tab.
3. Pull down the Field Shading list (see Figure 32.3) and choose Always, then click OK.
   - You can choose When Selected in the Field Shading drop-down list to have fields shaded when they are selected or choose Never (the default) to avoid having any shading at all.

▶▶ NOTE

Field shading is only a convenience for working on-screen; it is never printed.

▶▶ Printing Field Codes

Regardless of whether fields are shown as results (and prompts) or as field codes, they will not print as field codes unless you specifically request that they do when you print your document. It's not a bad idea to print

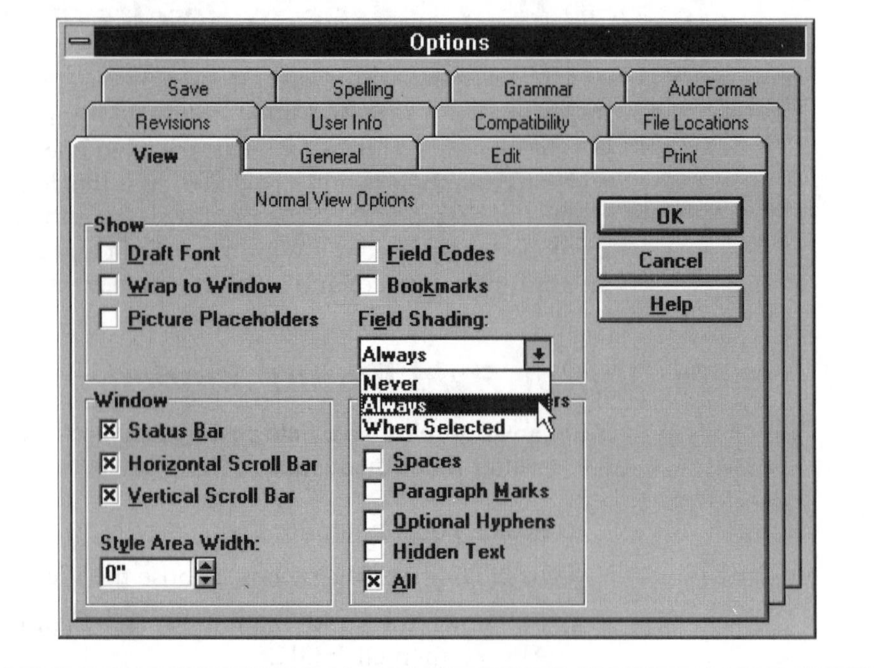

FIGURE 32.3 *Display field results shaded so you don't delete or alter them by mistake.*

out a document with its field codes showing for reference. To do so:

1. Select File ➤ Print.
2. In the Print dialog box, click the Options button. Make sure the Print tab is selected (it should be).
3. Check Field Codes in the Include with Document box.
4. Click OK. This returns you to the Print dialog box.
5. Click OK again to print your document.

That's all there is to it.

►► **TIP**

Field Codes will stay selected in the Print tab of the Options dialog box until you uncheck the box, so be sure to do that before printing again (unless you want field codes to print again next time).

▶▶ Formatting Fields

Fields are simple to format: You can format either the field result itself or the field code, so with its field codes looking like *this:*

{ **AUTHOR * MERGEFORMAT** } {DATE * MERGEFORMAT } {TIME * MERGEFORMAT } *{TITLE * MERGEFORMAT}* Page {PAGE * MERGEFORMAT } of {NUMPAGES * MERGEFORMAT }

the example header from the beginning of the chapter could look like *this*:

Janice Horsefly 04/01/94 8:33 AM *The Impact of Ultraviolet Lasers on the Cerebral Cortex* Page **291** of **316**

Yes, I know that's hideous. I was just trying to make the point. OK? Good.

You can also format field results by adding switches to the field codes. This is a little esoteric and is mainly useful for very sophisticated projects. We'll take a quick look at adding switches to field codes in the next section, but I suggest you format your field results the easy ways outlined earlier unless you've got a compelling reason to use switches instead. Save this for making minor adjustments to field codes you formatted slightly incorrectly.

▶▶ Adding Switches to Fields

By adding *switches* to fields, you can customize the format of a field's result or lock the result. There are four general switches for fields, each of which has a plethora (yes, we *can* use the word here) of permutations.

Here are the general switches:

SWITCH	EFFECT
Format(*)	Arabic or roman numberals. Adds formatting (for example, capitalization) to the field's result
Numeric Picture (\#)	Controls the number of decimal places, literal characters, and so on for a numeric result

SWITCH	EFFECT
Date-Time Picture (\@)	Formats a date or time (or both) result—for instance, to produce *April 1, 1994* or *11:59 PM*
Lock Result (\!)	Prevents fields included in the result of a BOOKMARK, INCLUDE-TEXT or REF field from being updated

▸▸ NOTE

Formatting created by switches takes precedence over manual formatting of the type demonstrated in the previous section.

Again, many field codes also have field-specific switches available in addition to the general switches. When you insert a field code with the Insert ➤ Field command, click the Options button to see the field-specific switches available for that field code, if any.

If you want to enter field-specific switches manually, you'll have to consult Appendix E.

▸ Switches That Preserve Manual Formatting

If you can stand to learn a thing or two about switches, you can actually make it easier on yourself to format fields and keep them from reverting to other formats when updated. There are two switches that preserve the manual formatting of a field after updating. They are:

```
\* MERGEFORMAT
```

and

```
\* CHARFORMAT
```

* MERGEFORMAT preserves whatever manual formatting was applied to the *field result*, including both character formatting (such as boldface) and paragraph formatting (such as line spacing). * CHARFORMAT applies whatever character formatting there is on the first character of the *field name* to the entire field result.

WARNING

*** MERGEFORMAT applies the formatting of the previous field result word by word to the updated field result. If the formatting is complicated and various and the new field result has a different number of words, the formatting may "slip" and get screwed up. If this happens, reformat the field result manually.**

* MERGEFORMAT also preserves picture formatting such as scaling and cropping dimensions.

Specific Format Switches

There are two other types of * format switches—those used for case conversion and those used for numeric conversion.

Case-Conversion Switches

The case-conversion options are as follows:

SWITCH	WHAT IT DOES
* caps	Capitalizes the initial letter of *each* word in the result
* firstcap	Capitalizes the initial letter of the *first* word in the result
* lower	Makes all the letters in the result lowercase
* upper	Capitalizes all the letters in the result

Here are some examples:

A FIELD WITH THIS SWITCH AND INSTRUCTION	DISPLAYS THIS RESULT
{ AUTHOR * caps }	Ron Person
{ AUTHOR * lower }	ron person

A FIELD WITH THIS SWITCH AND INSTRUCTION	DISPLAYS THIS RESULT
{ AUTHOR * upper }	RON PERSON
{ ***A***UTHOR * lower * firstcap * CHARFORMAT }	***Ron person***

Numeric Switches

And the numeric-conversion options are the following:

SWITCH	WHAT IT DOES
* alphabetic	Converts the resulting number to the corresponding letter of the alphabet—10 becomes j, 27 becomes aa
* Alphabetic	Converts the resulting number to the capitalized corresponding letter of the alphabet—10 becomes J, 27 becomes AA
* arabic	Converts the resulting number to arabic (standard) form, which is the default anyway, but it overrides any manual change to the numeric form (such as a different option in the Page Number Format dialog box)
* cardtext	Spells out the resulting number (card text stands for *card*inal number—such as "one," as opposed to the ordinal "first"—*text* form) in lowercase letters
* dollartext	Spells out the resulting number with initial letters capitalized, adds "and", and then displays the first two decimal places of the number (rounded off, if necessary) as an arabic numerator over 100, suitable for payroll checks.
* hex	Converts the resulting number to hexidecimal form
* ordinal	Converts the resulting number to arabic ordinal form (1st, 2nd, 10th, etc.)

SWITCH	WHAT IT DOES
* ordtext	Spells out the resulting number in ordinal form (first, second, tenth, etc.)
* roman	Converts the resulting number to lowercase roman numerals
* Roman	Converts the resulting number to uppercase roman numerals

Here are some examples:

A FIELD WITH THIS SWITCH AND INSTRUCTION	DISPLAYS THIS RESULT
{ =2+2 * cardtext }	four
{ =7*5 * cardtext * caps }	Thirty-Five
{ =99/2 * dollartext * firstcap }	Forty-nine and 50/100
{ *P*AGE * ordinal * CHARFORMAT }	*2nd*
{ PAGE * ordtext }	second
{ PAGE * roman }	ii

▶ Specific Numeric Picture Switches

Numeric picture switches control the appearance of the number displayed by the field code by demonstrating the "picture" or pattern that the number's display should follow using dummy characters. Numeric picture switches can add characters such as $ or % to the number. They can also control the number of digits displayed, the way negatives are displayed, whether commas are used to separate digits in the thousands place, and so on.

The numeric-picture-switch instructions (they can be combined in many ways) are as follows:

SWITCH INSTRUCTION	WHAT IT DOES
any character	includes that character in the number display

SWITCH INSTRUCTION	WHAT IT DOES
'multiple words'	includes the words between apostrophes in the number display
"*several numeric picture instructions*"	combines the instructions between the quotation marks and preserves spacing
#	optional digit placeholder, displays as a space if no digit is required
0	required digit placeholder, displays as a zero if no digit is required
x	truncating digit placeholder, eliminates any digits to the left unless placed after a decimal point, in which case it eliminates any digits to the right
.	decimal point, holds the place of the decimal point in relation to digit placeholders
,	thousands separator, used to group numbers by thousands to make them easier to read (compare 100000 to 100,000)
–	uses minus sign as indicator for negative numbers
+	uses plus sign for positive numbers *and* minus sign for negatives (and a space for zero)
;	separates custom positive and negative numeric pictures, or positive, negative, and zero numeric pictures

Here are some examples:

A FIELD WITH THIS SWITCH AND INSTRUCTION	DISPLAYS THIS RESULT
{ =10 \# $##.00 }	$10.00
{ =10 \# "## 'dollars'" }	10 dollars
{ =(1/2)*100 \# ##% }	50%
{ =10^5 \# #,### }	100,000
{ =10 \# –## }	10
{ =–10 \# –## }	–10
{ =3255.5–10000 \ # $##,###.00;($##,###.00) }	($ 6,744.50)

▶ Specific Date-Time Picture Switches

Date-time picture switches control the appearance of the date or time displayed by the field code by demonstrating the "picture" or pattern that the date or time's display should follow using instructions that are simple abbreviations for the parts of a time or date (h for hours, m for minutes, M for month, d for day, etc.).

The date-time–picture-switch instructions (they can be combined in many ways) are as follows:

SWITCH INSTRUCTION	WHAT IT DOES
any character	includes that character in the date display
'multiple words'	includes the words between apostrophes in the number display (put quotation marks around the entire instruction)
"*several date-time picture instructions*"	combines the instructions between the quotation marks and preserves spacing

SWITCH INSTRUCTION	WHAT IT DOES
h	hours of the twelve-hour clock without a leading zero for single-digit hours
hh	hours of the twelve-hour clock with a leading zero for single-digit hours
H	hours of the twenty-four–hour clock without a leading zero for single-digit hours
HH	hours of the twenty-four–hour clock with a leading zero for single-digit hours
m	minutes without a leading zero for single-digit minutes
mm	minutes with a leading zero for single-digit minutes
s	seconds without a leading zero for single-digit seconds
ss	seconds with a leading zero for single-digit seconds
AM/PM	AM or PM as appropriate
am/pm	am or pm as appropriate
A/P	A or P as appropriate
a/p	a or p as appropriate
M	month number without a leading zero for single-digit months
MM	month number with a leading zero for single-digit months
MMM	three-letter abbreviation for the month
MMMM	full name of the month
d	day of the month without a leading zero for single-digit days

SWITCH INSTRUCTION	WHAT IT DOES
dd	day of the month with a leading zero for single-digit days
ddd	day of the week as a three-letter abbreviation
dddd	full name of the day of the week
yy	year as a two-digit number with a leading zero for years ending in 01 through 09
yyyy	year as a four-digit number

Here are some examples:

A FIELD WITH THIS SWITCH AND INSTRUCTION	DISPLAYS THIS RESULT
{ DATE \@ "dddd, MMMM d, yyyy" }	Thursday, September 1, 1994
{ DATE \@ dd/MM/yy }	01/09/94
{ DATE \@ d-M-yy }	1-9-94
{ TIME \@ h:mm:ss am/pm }	10:02:15 am

Don't forget that the month instruction is a capital M and the minute instruction is a lowercase m.

Using Bookmarks in Fields

Bookmarks that only indicate a location in the document can still return a page number or other information about that location. Bookmarks that refer to selections can supply the contents of the selection (text or numerical) to another field code instruction, switch, or mathematical expression. In expressions, bookmarks play the role of variables.

To include a bookmark in a field, simply type its name. A field may consist of only a bookmark.

You can also use the SET field to store a value in a bookmark, such as:

{ SET Title "Sales Coordinator" }

▸▸ Changing the Contents of Fields

You can change field codes so they produce the results you're looking for. For example, you might have an =(Formula) that multiplies the bookmark TaxThemAll by 31 percent:

{=TaxThemAll*31%}

But if you find that 31 percent isn't giving you the revenue you need, you need to up it to 46 percent. Here's how:

1. Put the insertion point in the field.
2. If the field is showing its result, display the field codes by pressing Shift+F9 or by right-clicking the field and choosing Toggle Field Display from the shortcut menu.
3. Edit the field. Change 31 to **46**: {=TaxThemAll*46%}
4. Display the field result again by pressing Shift+F9 or by right-clicking the field and choosing Toggle Field Display from the shortcut menu.
5. Update the field by pressing F9 or by right-clicking the field and choosing Update Field from the shortcut menu.

▸▸ Nesting One Field inside Another

In addition to text, switches, and other instructions, field codes may also contain other fields. It's easier to nest a field inside a field than you may think. To do so,

1. Insert the first field, either with the Insert Field command (in which case, press Shift+F9 afterward to display the field code) or

by pressing Ctrl+F9 and entering the code manually.

2. Move the insertion point inside the field code to where you want the nested code to appear.
3. Insert the nested field, again either with the Insert Field command or by pressing Ctrl+F9 and entering the code manually.
4. Press F9 to display the field result or prompt.

So, for example, if you want to prompt someone for their title and store that text as a bookmark called JobTitle, you could press Ctrl+F9, type **SET JobTitle** and a space, press Ctrl+F9 again, type **FILLIN "Enter your title"**, and press F9. This would display the following dialog box:

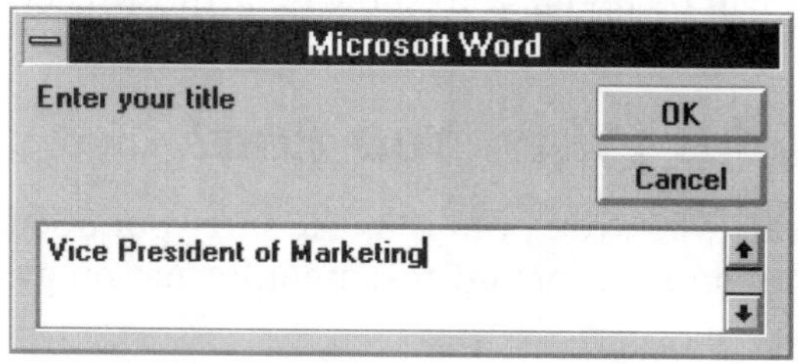

If you enter a title and click OK, the title you typed will be stored as the bookmark JobTitle. If you then make the following field code:

{ JobTitle }

and press Ctrl+F9, you will see the title you entered.

▶▶ Updating Fields

As you'll have gathered by now, the whole point of inserting fields in your document rather than inserting straight information is that the fields are easy to update.

You can choose to update all fields at once or update them one at a time. Further, you can choose to update all fields whenever you print a document to ensure up-to-date information for your printouts.

► Updating Fields One at a Time

To update fields one at a time, place the mouse pointer in the field in question and click the right mouse button to pop up the shortcut menu. From the shortcut menu, choose Update Field. The field will be updated and will show its most recent result.

► Updating All Fields Simultaneously

To update all fields in a document at once, choose Edit ➤ Select All and then click the right mouse button to pop up the shortcut menu. From the shortcut menu, choose Update Field. All the fields in the document will be updated to show their most recent results.

► Updating Fields When You Print

Update fields when you print to make sure your documents, forms, and reports contain the most up-to-date information available. Here's how:

1. Select Tools ➤ Options....
2. In the Options dialog box, select the Print tab.
3. In the Printing Options area, check the Update Fields check box, then click OK.

All the fields in your documents will now be updated each time the documents are printed. To stop this updating, repeat steps 1, 2, and 3, but uncheck the Update Fields check box.

►► **WARNING**

Like other options in the Options dialog box, Update Fields is sticky—its setting will stay the same until you change it again.

▶ Undoing or Halting Updates

If you've just updated fields and want to undo it, simply select Edit ➤ Undo Update Fields (or press Ctrl+Z). If you start updating a document and then realize that you don't want to update the whole thing or wait for it to finish, press Esc to cancel the process.

▶▶ Locking the Contents of Fields

When you want to keep the result of a field from being updated and changed, you can either *lock* the field or *unlink* it. Locking a field prevents the field from being updated until the locker unlocks the field, while unlinking a field permanently replaces the field with its current result.

▶ To Lock a Field

To lock a field to prevent it from being updated:

1. Place the cursor in the field you want to lock.
2. Press Ctrl+F11 or Ctrl+3 to lock the field.

▶ To Unlock a Field

To unlock a field so it can once again be updated:

1. Place the cursor in the field you want to unlock.
2. Press Ctrl+Shift+F11 to unlock the field.

▶ To Unlink a Field

To unlink a field so it can never again be updated:

1. Place the cursor in the field you want to unlink.
2. Press Ctrl+Shift+F9 or Ctrl+6 to unlink the field.

▸▸ NOTE

You can use Undo to restore fields you just unlinked, but only until *Unlink Fields* drops off the bottom of the Undo button's drop-down list.

▸▸ Examples of Fields at Work

The more you use Word 6, the more chances you'll get to use fields to enhance your documents and minimize your work. Word uses fields for many of its specialized functions, and chances are you'll find yourself using fields without having consciously made the decision to do so. For example, in Chapter 29 you learned how to insert graphs into Word documents using Microsoft Graph, and in Chapter 30 you learned how to link and embed objects in Word documents. In either case, select Tools ➤ Options... and check the Field Codes check box, and you'll find that you've been using field codes—your graph turns into a field code that reads { EMBED MS Graph }, and your link to a different application turns into something a little more esoteric. The mail-merge documents you learned about in Chapter 26 use all sorts of fields—some defined by Word and some by you, the user—to produce the form letters.

Chapter 33 further illustrates the many uses of fields in Word for Windows.

▸▸ Moving Quickly between Fields

You can move quickly between fields by using Edit ➤ Goto... and selecting Field in the Go to What area of the Go To dialog box. You can choose to move between particular fields, between any fields, or simply search for the previous or next field. Here's how:

▸▸ TIP

To pop up the Go To dialog box quickly, press F5 or double-click some blank space in the status area.

1. Select Edit ➤ Goto....
2. In the Go to What box (see Figure 32.4), select Field.

FIGURE 32.4 

You can use the Go To dialog box to move rapidly between fields.

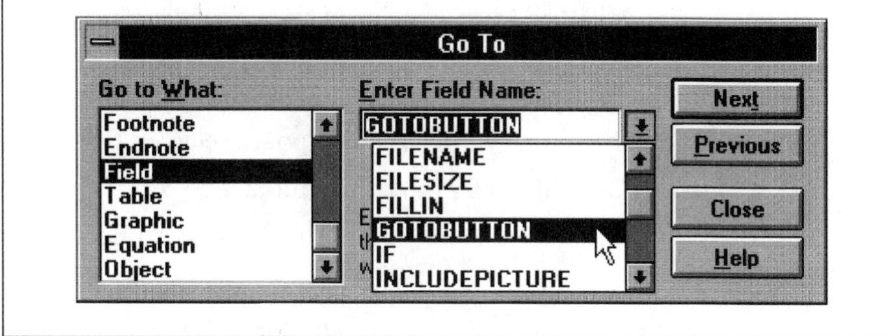

3. In the Enter Field Name box, select the name of the field or accept Any Field.
4. Choose the Next button to find the next occurrence of the chosen field or the Previous button to find the previous occurrence.
5. Click the Close button when you get where you want.

TIP

To go to the next field, press F11; to go to the previous field, press Shift+F11.

Shortcut Keys for Working with Fields

There is a bunch of shortcut keys for working with fields in Word. Some we've touched on in this chapter; some we've met (or will meet) in other chapters. Here they all are, for your reference:

KEY COMBINATION	EFFECT
Alt+Shift+D	Insert a date field

KEY COMBINATION	EFFECT
Alt+Shift+P	Insert a page field
Alt+Shift+T	Insert a time field
Ctrl+F9	Insert a blank field
Ctrl+Shift+F7	Update linked information in the source document
F9	Update selected fields
Ctrl+Shift+F9	Unlink a field
Shift+F9	Toggle between field codes and results
Alt+F9	View field codes
Alt+Shift+F9	Perform the action in the field when the insertion pointis position in the field
F11	Go to the next field
Shift+F11	Go to the previous field
Ctrl+F11	Lock a field
Ctrl+Shift+F11	Unlock a field

▸▸ Using Fields to Assign and Display Bookmarks

As you've already seen in this chapter, field codes can use bookmarks as variables, as ways to store and transmit information. In addition to the field codes that can take bookmarks as instructions, there are a couple that are specifically designed to store and display bookmark contents. They are SET and REF.

▸ Storing Bookmark Contents with SET

The SET field code is used to assign a value to a bookmark. SET fields take the following form:

{ SET *bookmark "text"* }

The field assigns the text inside the quotation marks to the bookmark. You can also nest another field inside the SET field to prompt for the text to assign to the bookmark. Such a field would look something like this:

{ SET Zodiac { FILLIN "What is your sign?" * "Scorpio" } }

This field displays a prompt on the screen asking the user to type in a sign of the zodiac. The text entered is assigned to the bookmark called Zodiac.

▶▶ NOTE

The ASK field, described later in this chapter, can also be used to assign a value to a bookmark.

▶ Displaying Bookmark Contents with REF

The REF field code is used to display the value contained in a bookmark. REF fields take the following form:

{ REF *bookmark* *optional switches* }

The field displays the text associated with the bookmark named.

The field-specific switches for REF are:

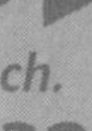

\f	Includes a footnote, endnote, or annotation number, incremented if necessary
\n	Inserts paragraph numbering (if any) from the paragraph marked by the bookmark

▶▶ Working with Action Fields

In this section, I'll explain how to use the four action fields—ASK fields, FILLIN fields, GOTOBUTTON fields, and MACROBUTTON fields.

▶ ASK Fields

ASK fields take the following form:

{ ASK *bookmark "prompt text" \optional switches* }

The field displays a dialog box that includes the prompt text and a text box. Whatever is entered into the text box is assigned to the bookmark.

The field-specific switches for ASK are:

\d "*default text*"	Used to supply default text (highlighted) in the text box
\o	Prompts only once during a mail merge (instead of once for each resulting document)

▶ FILLIN Fields

FILLIN fields take the following form:

{ FILLIN *"optional prompt text" \optional switches* }

The field displays a dialog box that can show a prompt. Whatever text you enter into it is inserted at the insertion point (as the field result, not as regular text).

The field-specific switches for FILLIN are:

\d "*default text*"	Used to supply default text (highlighted) in the text box
\o	Prompts only once during a mail merge (instead of once for each resulting document)

▶ GOTOBUTTON Fields

GOTOBUTTON fields take the following form:

{ GOTOBUTTON *destination display-text* }

The field shows the display text on the screen as a clickable field result or button (you can also insert a graphic into this field to have the button display as a graphic). Double-clicking the button jumps the reader to the destination, which can be any acceptable Go To destination (Go To is explained in Chapter 3) such as a bookmark, page number, table, and so on.

▶ MACROBUTTON Fields

MACROBUTTON fields take the following form:

{ MACROBUTTON *macro display-text* }

The field shows the display text on the screen as a clickable field result or button (you can also insert a graphic into this field to have the button display as a graphic). Double-clicking the button executes the macro.

You can format the display text and add the * MERGEFORMAT switch to preserve the formatting through subsequent updates.

▶▶ **TIP**

If you insert the MACROBUTTON field with the Insert ➤ Field command, you can click the Options button to see a list of available macros to choose from.

The field { MACROBUTTON FileSave **Click Here to Save the File** } would look like this:

Click Here to Save the File

Clicking there would be equivalent to selecting File ➤ Save.

▶▶ Getting Field Code Help

Word has extensive online help for each field code with complete syntax and switches. To see this help for a specific field code, select Help ➤ Index, click the letter button for the first letter of the field, and then click the index entry for complete information.

You can also get context-sensitive help directly when the insertion point is on a field code name. Just press F1 to jump directly to the help entry for that field.

►► NOTE

See also Appendix E for complete field and switch information.

The last section in this chapter looks at the main changes in fields in Word 6 for Windows.

►► What's New in Fields in Word 6?

There are three main things new in fields in Word 6. First, some fields from previous versions of Word for Windows have been renamed, though they have the same result. For example, the field =(expression) from Word 2 is called =(formula) in Word 6. Second, some fields with the same names now behave differently or need different field codes. For example, the FILENAME field now has a \p switch that returns the path with the file name—a significant improvement on the Word 2 field. Third, there are new fields to go along with the new features of Word. We'll look briefly at these changes in the following sections.

►► NOTE

When you open a document containing field names from an earlier version of Word, those field names will work even if they have been renamed in Word 6.

► Fields That Have Been Renamed

Here's a quick rundown on the fields that have been renamed in Word 6:

OLD NAME	NEW NAME	COMMENT
=(Expression)	=(Formula)	Used for calculating mathematical formulas
EQ(Formula)	EQ(Equation)	Used for mathematical equations

OLD NAME	NEW NAME	COMMENT
FTNREF	NOTEREF	Can now reference footnotes as well as endnotes
GLOSSARY	AUTOTEXT	Used for automatically inserting predefined text
IMPORT	INCLUDE-PICTURE	Used for importing a picture into a document
INCLUDE	INCLUDE-TEXT	Used for including text in a document

▶ *Fields That Have Been Modified*

The following fields from previous versions of Word have been modified:

FIELD	CHANGE
=(Formula)	You can now use logical operators to compare strings. You can specify table cells and ranges using Excel's style (for example, **A1:C3**).
Filename	\p switch returns the path with the file name
INCLUDEPIC-TURE	\d switch prevents storing graphic data in a document
INDEX	\c switch builds an index with up to four columns on a page. \f switch builds an index using only XE fields with the specified entry type
INFO	Can now return the size of the document in bytes, using information from the Document Statistics dialog box
NOTEREF	Result of this field is formatted with an endnote or footnote reference style

FIELD	CHANGE
REF	\n switch inserts the number of the paragraph marked by a bookmark instead of the bookmarked text. \f switch includes and increments footnote, endnote, and annotation numbers
STYLEREF	Can now search for character styles as well as paragraph styles. \n switch inserts the paragraph number instead of the paragraph itself
SYMBOL	\h switch overrides the Auto setting for line spacing in the Paragraph dialog box
TC (Table of Contents entry)	\n switch suppresses the page number for an entry
TEMPLATE	\p switch includes the path with the template name
TOC (Table of Contents)	\a switch excludes labels and numbers from a table of contents. \c switch uses SEQ fields to build a table of captions. \I switch uses the entry level specified by TC fields. \n switch excludes page numbers. \p switch specifies a separator character between the table entry and the page number. \t switch employs user-defined style names for entry levels
XE (Index Entry)	\f switch specifies an entry type you can use to customize the result of the INDEX field

► New Fields in Word 6

Word 6 includes a number of useful new fields:

FIELD	COMMENT
ADVANCE	Offsets text to the left or right, up or down, or to a specific position on the page

FIELD	COMMENT
BARCODE	Adds a postal bar code to your document
COMPARE	Compares two values and returns 1 for true or 0 (zero) for false
DATABASE	Inserts the result of a database query in a Word table
FILESIZE	Inserts the number of bytes in the document (using the statistics you can reach using File ➤ Summary Info... and then choosing the Statistics... button)
FORMTEXT	Inserts a text box in a form
FORMCHECKBOX	Inserts a check box in a form
FORMDROPDOWN	Inserts a drop-down list in a form
MACRO	Runs the specified macro when updated
MERGESEQ	Inserts a number based on the order in which data records are merged (see Chapter 29)
PRIVATE	Stores data for documents converted from other file formats
SECTION	Inserts the number of pages in the current section
SECTIONPAGES	Inserts the number of pages in the current section
TA (Table of Authorities entry)	Defines the text and page number for a table of authorities entry
TOA (Table of Authorities)	Builds and inserts a table of authorities

CHAPTER 33

Creating and Using Forms

▸▸FAST TRACK

▶▶ **You** can use the features of Word for Windows that you've learned about in the preceding chapters of this book to create your own business forms. You can create forms that you print and then fill in by hand or forms to be filled in online, saved as a file, and then printed.

For online forms, Word 6 lets you protect areas against being filled in or changed; for example, you might have some *form fields* (areas of a form) that should not be filled in by an employee, and you almost certainly don't want anyone filling in the form to change the basic structure of the form itself. You can specify that certain form fields have specific data types, formatting, or default text, and you can create check boxes and drop-down lists to help the user fill in the form. You can add macros that run automatically to a form and attach help messages to fields to further assist the users.

You may be thinking that protecting a form is an extreme measure, but the way Word arranges forms, you need to protect them to be able to fill them in properly. Until you protect a form, the fancy features like drop-down lists and help text attached to fields are set up to be edited rather than to be used.

new You can add AutoText entries to a form you save as a template. You can also add macros, customized Toolbars, customized menus, and the other features associated with templates.

Designing most forms involves using Word's table features (discussed in Chapter 11) to lay out the form and then applying character, paragraph, and table formatting to give the form a satisfactory appearance.

TIP

When you create a form, save it as a *template* (discussed in Chapter 16) rather than as a document so you can open any number of copies based on it without altering its contents and then save them as documents. If you protect the template, that protection will also apply to all new documents based on that template. (When you need to change the form, you can edit the template directly.)

Designing and Creating Forms

When designing a form, you'll probably want to start with a rough draft or sketch of what you're trying to produce. While you *can* just type into your computer everything you think you'll need to include in the form and then hack it into shape, you may wind up with a beautifully designed form lacking just one crucial component.

If you can't be bothered to make a sketch, get a similar form from somewhere and scrawl your main items in its boxes. That'll give you a head start.

Figure 33.1 shows a job log I created for Unincorporated, Inc., a deconstruction firm that deals with special projects. The job log illustrates some of the main features of forms in Word 6. In the coming sections, we'll look at how to insert these elements, using the job log as an example.

Starting a Form

To start a form, first open a new document to work in. The job log is to be an online form, so select the Template option button rather than the Document option button in the New dialog box.

Using normal keyboard procedures, enter your new template text that doesn't need to be in a table—for example, the main headings.

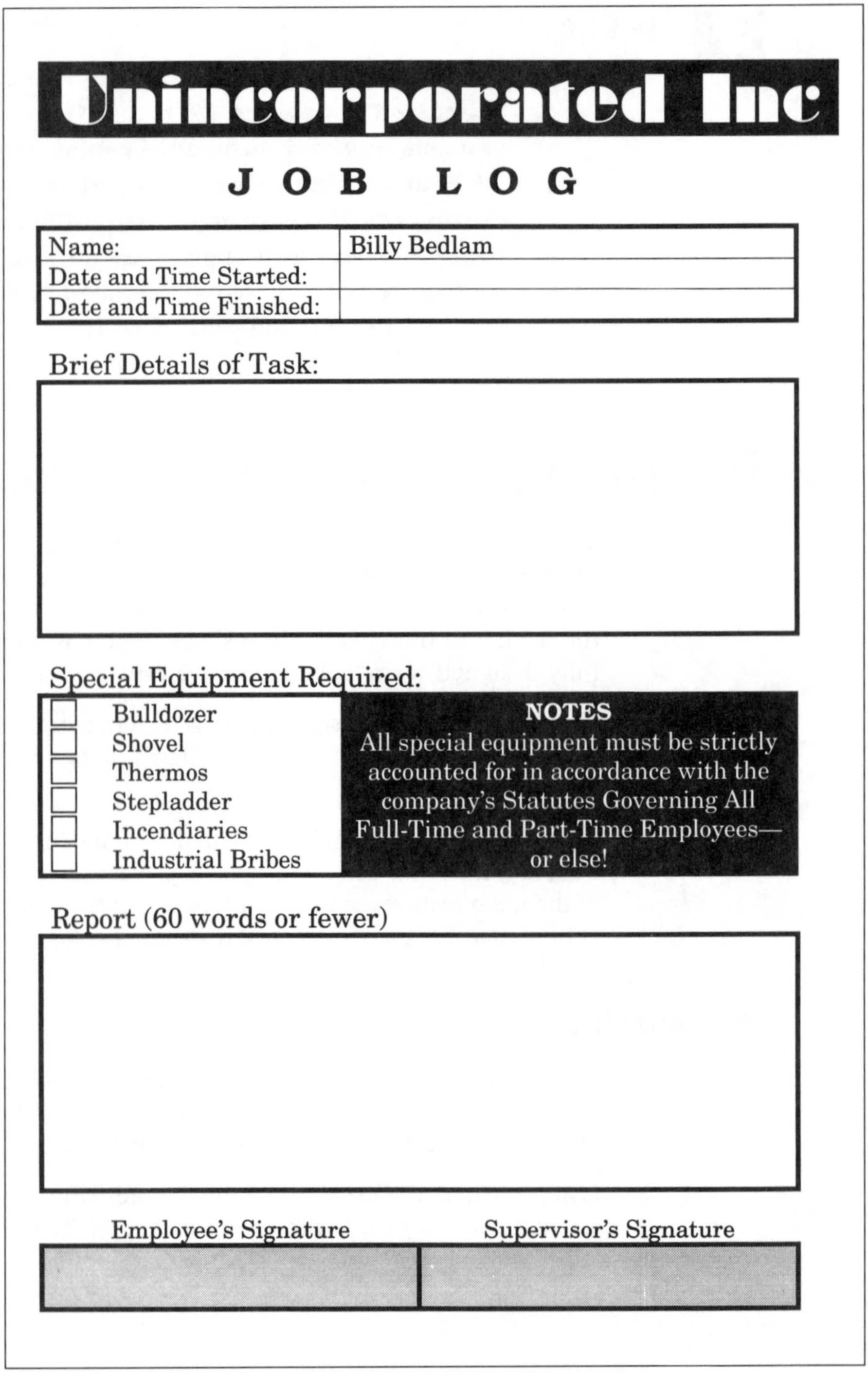

FIGURE 33.1

Unincorporated, Inc.'s Job Log form.

Unincorporated Inc

J O B   L O G

Name:	Billy Bedlam
Date and Time Started:	
Date and Time Finished:	

Brief Details of Task:

Special Equipment Required:

- ☐ Bulldozer
- ☐ Shovel
- ☐ Thermos
- ☐ Stepladder
- ☐ Incendiaries
- ☐ Industrial Bribes

NOTES
All special equipment must be strictly accounted for in accordance with the company's Statutes Governing All Full-Time and Part-Time Employees—or else!

Report (60 words or fewer)

Employee's Signature	Supervisor's Signature

▶ Displaying the Forms Toolbar

When working on forms, you can use either menu commands or the buttons on the Forms Toolbar. We'll discuss how to use both throughout this chapter.

If you want to use the Forms Toolbar, display it: Either select View ➤ Toolbars... and click the Show Toolbar button in the Form Field dialog box. If you do the former, the Forms Toolbar will appear at the top of the screen; if you do the latter, it will appear where you last positioned it, as shown in Figure 33.2.

FIGURE 33.2 ▶

The Forms Toolbar. Drag it to wherever you want it or double-click it to display it at the top of your screen.

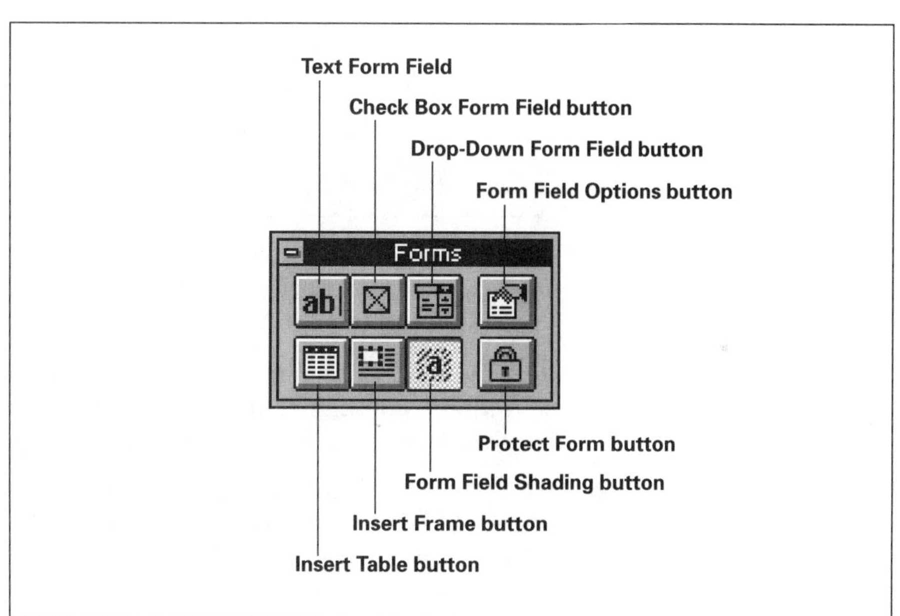

▶ Adding a Table to the Form

Much of the Job Log form consists of tables, the cells of which contain the form fields and their descriptions. Here's how to insert a table in which to enter text or a form field:

1. Place the insertion point where you want the table to start.

2. Click the Insert Table button on either the Standard Toolbar or the Forms Toolbar to display the table-insertion grid:

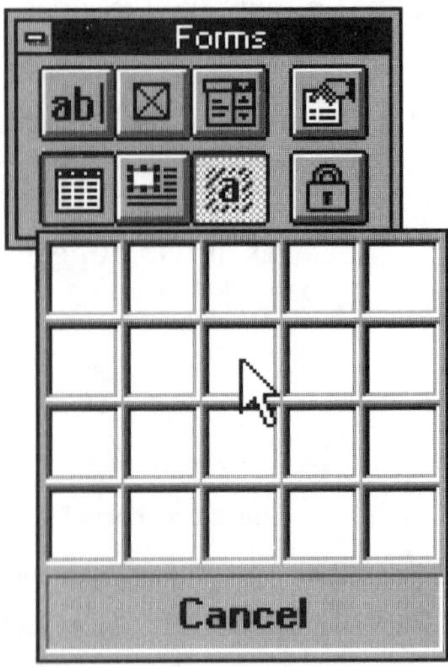

- You can also select Table ➤ Insert Table... and specify the number of rows and columns in the Insert Table dialog box.

3. Click the square that shows the number of rows (counting from the top) and columns (counting from the left) that you want in the table. Word will insert the table in your document.
4. Size the table by dragging its gridlines or by selecting Table ➤ Cell Height and Width... and specifying measurements in the Cell Height and Width dialog box.

▸▸ **NOTE**

By default, Word inserts tables as wide as your page with all cells the same width.

Type text into the table cells as usual (look back to Chapter 11 for information on working in tables) and format it in the normal ways.

▶ Adding Borders and Shading to the Form

To add borders to a table, as in the Job Log form, select the table or the cells to which you want to add the border or shading; then select Format ➤ Borders and Shading... and specify borders and shading in the Paragraph Borders and Shading dialog box.

▶▶ Inserting Form Fields into Your Form

There are three types of form fields you can insert into your form automatically. They are check boxes, text boxes, and drop-down list boxes. The following sections detail how to insert each type of box.

▶ Adding a Check Box to the Form

Word 6 gives you the option of adding check boxes to your forms. (With previous versions, you had to create a check box in another application, such as Microsoft Draw, and then paste it in—very tedious.) Here's how to do it:

1. Place the insertion point where you want the check box to appear.
2. Select Insert ➤ Form Field... to display the Form Field dialog box (see Figure 33.3).
3. Select Check Box.

FIGURE 33.3 ▶

The Form Field dialog box.

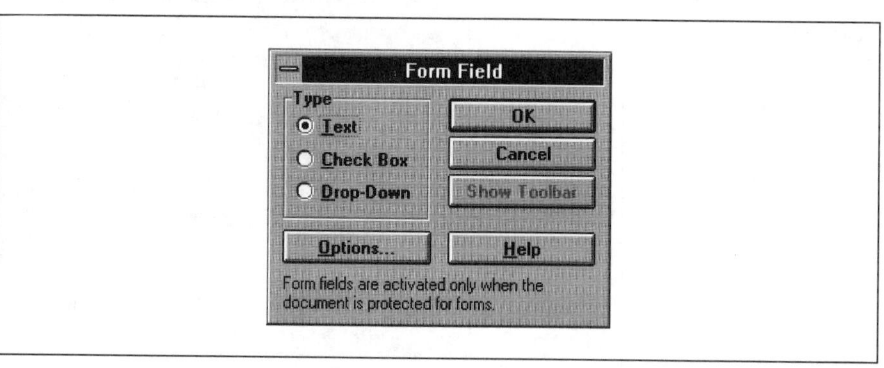

4. Select the Options... button to specify more details about the check box. The Check Box Form Field Options dialog box will appear (see Figure 33.4.)

5. The following options are available:

   - **Check Box Size:** Use Exactly to specify a fixed point size for the check box.
   - **Default Value:** Choose Not Checked or Checked as the default value for the check box—that is, whether it should be checked or unchecked when the user opens the form.
   - **Run Macro On:** To run a macro when the user enters or exits the form field, specify the macro in the Entry or Exit box.
   - **Bookmark:** Type a bookmark name to be associated with the field. Macros reference bookmark names.
   - **Check Box Enabled:** Clear this check box to make the form field read-only for users.
   - **Add Help Text:** Click this button to display the Form Field Help Text dialog box so you can enter help messages.

6. When you've chosen your options, click OK to close the Check Box Form Field Options dialog box. Click OK again to close the Form Field dialog box and insert the selected field into your document.

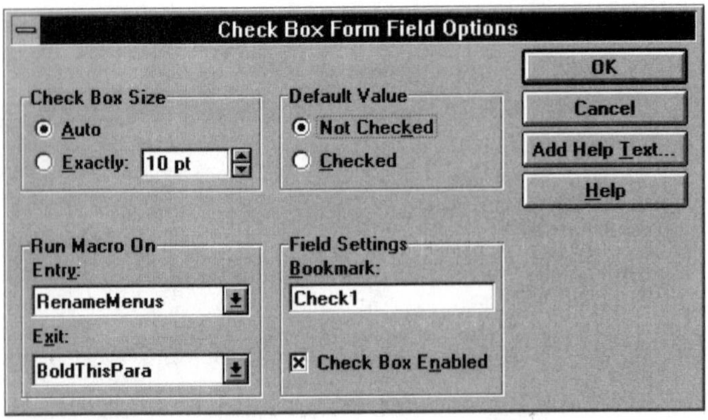

FIGURE 33.4

The Check Box Form Field Options dialog box.

▶ Adding a Text Box to the Form

A *text box* is a form field in which the user enters text. You can limit the text entry to a certain number of characters, and you can provide default text to show the user the type of text (or indeed the answer!) that you are expecting.

Here's how to insert a text box:

1. Place the insertion point where you want the text box to appear.
2. Select Insert ➤ Form Field... to display the Form Field dialog box.
3. Select Text Box.
4. Select the Options... button to specify more details about the check box. The Text Form Field Options dialog box will appear (see Figure 33.5).
5. The following options are available:
   - **Type:** Select the type of text form field you want—Regular Text, Number, Date, Current Date, Current Time, or Calculation.
   - **Default Text:** Enter any text you want to be displayed by default when the user opens the form. (This field changes to Expression when you choose Calculation in the Type box.)
   - **Text Format:** Select the format for the data in the form field.

FIGURE 33.5 ▶

The Text Form Field Options dialog box.

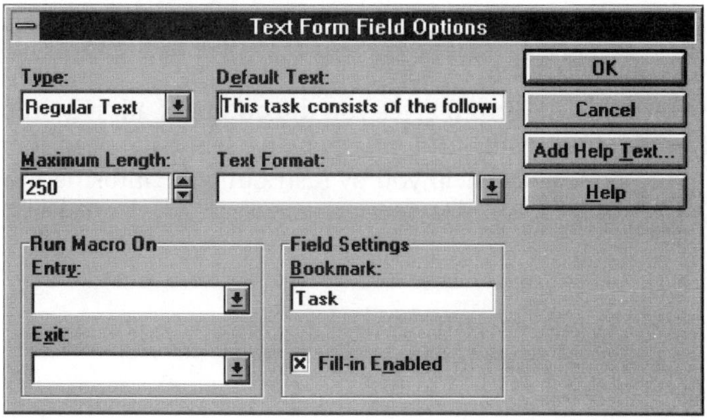

- **Maximum Length:** Enter the number of characters you want the form field to accept (255 is the maximum allowed).
- **Run Macro On:** To run a macro when the user enters or exits the form field, specify the macro in the Entry or Exit box.
- **Bookmark:** Type a bookmark name to be associated with the field. Macros reference bookmark names.
- **Fill-in Enabled:** Clear this to make the form field read-only for users.
- **Add Help Text:** Click this button to display the Form Field Help Text dialog box so you can enter help messages.

6. When you've chosen your options, click OK to close the Check Box Form Field Options dialog box. Click OK again to close the Form Field dialog box and insert the selected field into your document.

For the Type box, choose *Regular Text* when any type of text entry will be acceptable (when you don't need to limit the type of text entry in any way).

Choose *Number* when you want only numeric entries in that particular text box. Choose *Date* when you want only date entries in that text box.

Choose *Current Date* or *Current Time* to have the current date or time entered automatically into that text box. The user will be unable to enter any text there.

Choose *Calculation* to add a column or row of numbers or to perform a more complex calculation. Like the Current Date and Current Time types of text boxes, a Calculation text box cannot be altered by the user.

▸ Adding a Drop-Down List to a Form

Word 6 gives you the option of adding drop-down lists to your forms, which can greatly help users and speed their input. Drop-down lists can also help you by restricting the information users can enter in the fields.

The Unincorporated, Inc. job log contains a drop-down list of employee names:

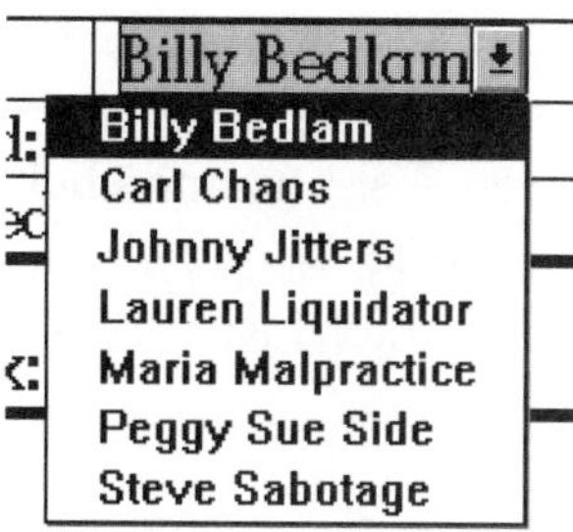

To add a drop-down list to your form:

1. Place the insertion point where you want the drop-down list to appear.
2. Select Insert ➤ Form Field… to display the Form Field dialog box.
3. Select the Drop-Down option.
4. Select the Options... button to specify more details about the drop-down list. The Drop-Down Form Field Options dialog box will appear (see Figure 33.6).

FIGURE 33.6

The Drop-Down Form Field Options dialog box.

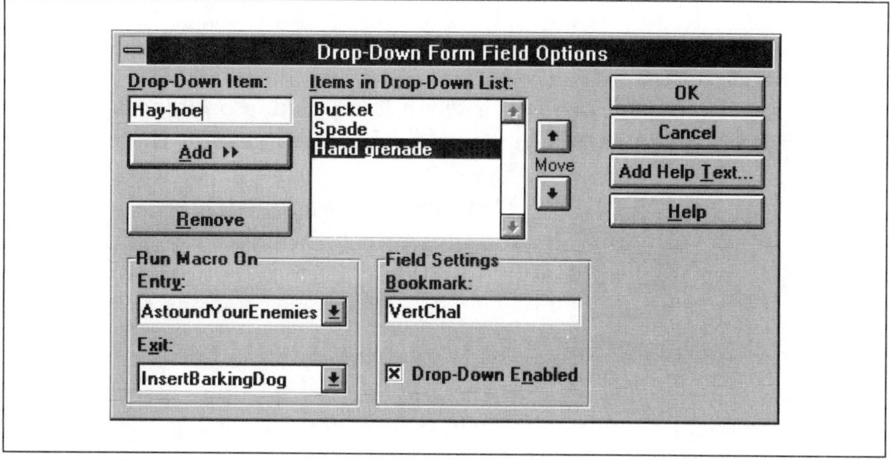

5. In the Drop-Down Item text box, add items for the drop-down list to its right.
   - Click the Add button to add each new item to the list.
   - To remove an item from the drop-down list, select it in the Items in Drop-Down List box and click the Remove button.
   - To rearrange the items in the drop-down list, highlight the item to move and use the Move arrows to move it up or down.
6. Choose options in the dialog box:
   - **Run Macro On:** To run a macro when the user enters or exits the form field, specify the macro in the Entry or Exit box.
   - **Bookmark:** Type a bookmark name to be associated with the field. Macros reference bookmark names.
   - **Drop-Down Enabled:** Clear this check box to make the form field read-only for users.
   - **Add Help Text:** Click this button to display the Form Field Help Text dialog box so you can enter help messages.
7. When you've chosen your options, click OK to close the Check Box Form Field Options dialog box. Click OK again to close the Form Field dialog box and insert the selected field into your document.

► Naming Form Fields

When you insert a form field, a bookmark is automatically created that names the form field and refers to it. By default, Word will choose sequential names for your form fields—Text1, Text2, Text3; Check1, Check2; Dropdown1, Dropdown2; etc. You can override this default, though, and give your form fields any names (any bookmarks) you want. Why would you want to do this? To make them easier to keep track of, especially if you are referring to your bookmarks with field codes or macros.

You can name a form field as you're inserting it or at any later time. To name the form field while inserting it, click the Options button on the Form Field dialog box (see Figure 33.3), then enter a name in the

Bookmark text box in the Field Settings area of the Options dialog box that appears. Proceed as usual.

To name a form field after you've already inserted it,

1. Unprotect the document if it's protected already.
2. Position the mouse pointer over the form field and click the right mouse button. A dialog box will drop down:

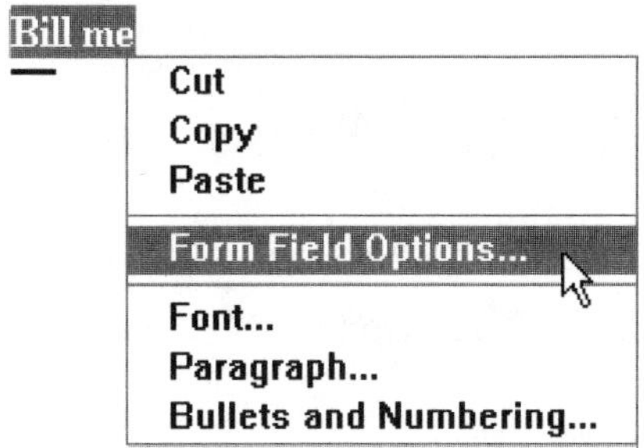

3. Select Form Field Options. This will bring up the appropriate Options dialog box (see Figures 33.4, 5, and 6).
4. Type a name in the Bookmark box in the Field Settings area and click OK.

NOTE

You can also just double-click an unprotected form field to bring up the appropriate Options dialog box.

Finding a Form Field

To find a form field, you must know its name (the bookmark that refers to it). If you know the name, there are two ways to find (and go to) the form field. Here's the first way:

1. Unprotect the document if it's already protected.

2. Select Edit ➤ Bookmark. This brings up the Bookmark dialog box:

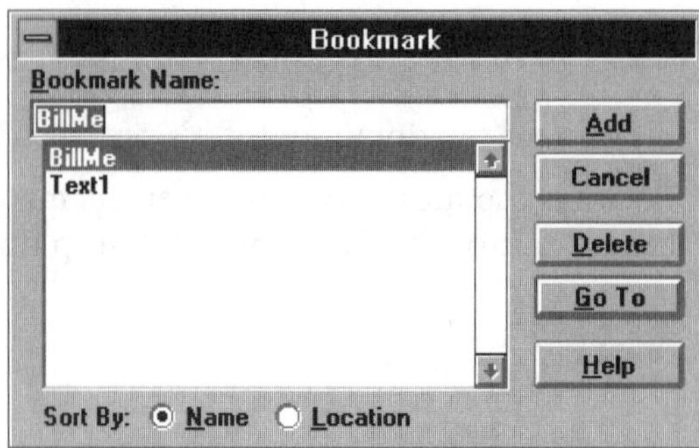

3. Select the bookmark (form field) you want to go to.
4. Click the Go To button.

Here's the second way:

1. Unprotect the document if it's already protected.
2. Select Edit ➤ Go To (Ctrl+G). This brings up the Go To dialog box:

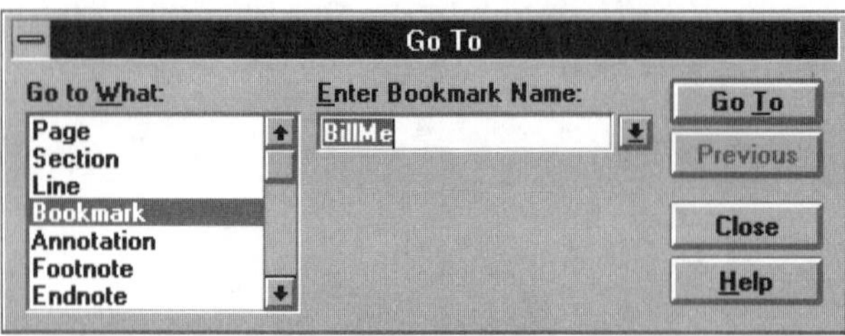

3. Select Bookmark in the Go to What list box.
4. Choose the bookmark (form field) you want from the Enter Bookmark Name drop-down list box.
5. Click the Go To button.

Take your pick.

▸▸ Formatting Form Fields

If you want the text entered or selected in a form field to be formatted, you have to format the fields yourself before protecting the document. Users will not be able to format the text they enter or select.

The best time to format a field is right after inserting it. You have all the usual methods available to you for character and paragraph formatting. You can:

- Pull down the Format menu, select a formatting choice, and choose the type of formatting you want (for example, Format ➤ Font, Bold, OK).
- Click the field with the right mouse button, select a formatting choice from the drop-down menu that pops up, and choose the type of formatting you want (for example, right mouse click, Font, Bold, OK).
- Click a formatting icon on the Formatting Toolbar (for example, click the Bold button).
- Press a keyboard shortcut (for example, Ctrl+B).

▸▸ Adding Help Text to a Form

As mentioned in the previous sections, you can add help text to your form fields to assist the user in filling them in. Here's how to do it:

1. Double-click the form field in question to display the Form Field Options dialog box. (Exactly *which* form field options dialog box will appear depends on the type of form field you select.)
2. Click the Add Help Text button. The Form Field Help Text dialog box will appear.

    - To add a status bar entry, select the Status Bar tab.
    - To add a help key entry, select the Help key tab.

Figure 33.7 shows the Form Field Help Text dialog box with the Status Bar tab selected. This is perhaps the more useful option for short entries because the help text will appear in the status bar when the user encounters the field. (With Help Key entries, the user must press F1 to display the help, which appears in a message box.)

3. Choose the entry you want:

   - **None:** Turns off the help text.
   - **AutoText Entry:** Lets you choose an existing AutoText entry from the drop-down list.
   - **Type Your Own:** Lets you do just that, up to 255 characters.

4. Select OK to close the Form Field Help Text dialog box and then click OK in the Form Field Options dialog box.

FIGURE 33.7

The Form Field Help Text dialog box. Decide whether you want to display help in the status bar or when the user presses F1.

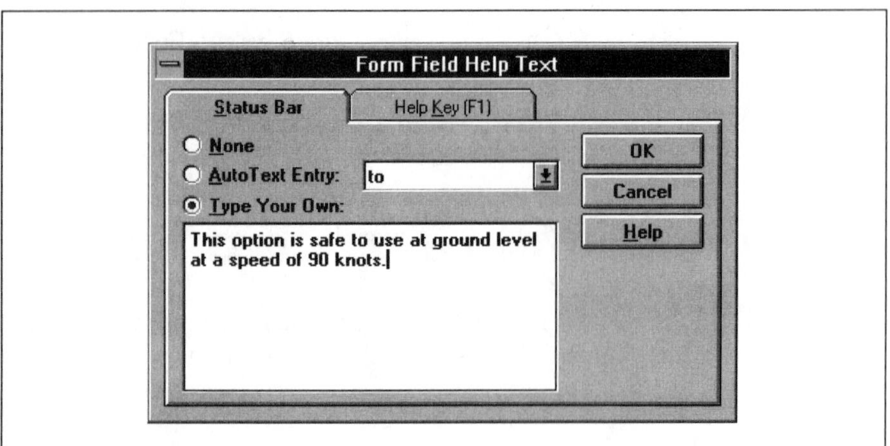

▸▸ Protecting a Form

Having unprotected forms these days can be a risk, given the high incidence of networks and file sharing. You'll probably want to protect or lock your templates to make sure nobody else can modify them accidentally or otherwise. When a template is protected, documents based on it will be protected too, and users will only be able to fill in form fields and unprotected areas. Users benefit too because pressing Tab will take them from form field to form field without stopping in table cells or text that they cannot modify.

WARNING

As mentioned at the beginning of this chapter, you need to protect a form before the check boxes, text boxes, drop-down lists, and help features will work.

Here's how to protect a form from changes:

1. Select Tools ➤ Protect Document....
2. In the Protect Document dialog box (see Figure 33.8), select the Forms option button.

FIGURE 33.8

The Protect Document dialog box. Choose the Forms option button here to protect your form. Enter a password if you like.

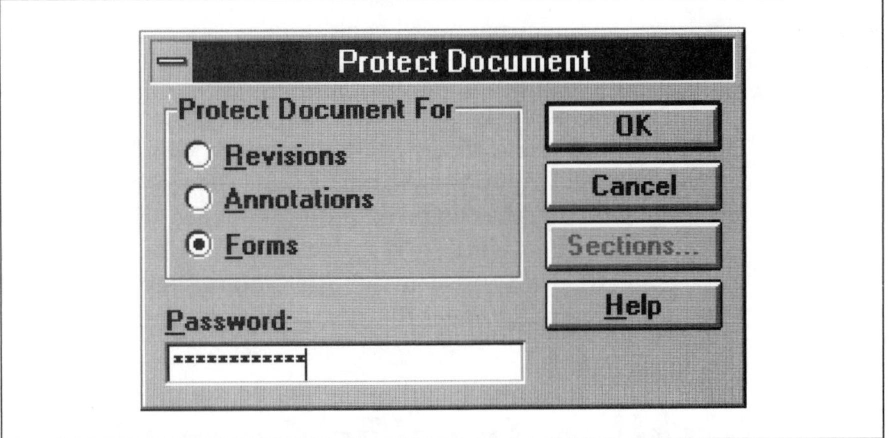

3. To protect some sections of forms but not others, select the Sections... button (which will be dimmed if unavailable—for example, if your document doesn't have sections) and, in the Section Protection

dialog box that appears (see below), check the check boxes for the sections you want to protect.

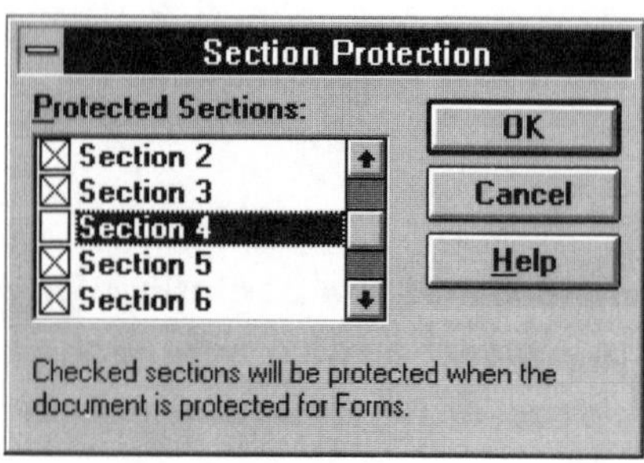

4. To assign a password to the form, type one into the Password box. Word will display asterisks (for the benefit of anyone reading over your shoulder) for each character you type, and when you select OK, Word will ask you to reenter the password in the Confirm Password dialog box.

    - Passwords can be up to 15 characters long and can contain letters, numbers, symbols, and spaces. They're case-sensitive —you must type upper- or lowercase letters correctly in the password each time.

To unprotect your form, select Tools ➤ Unprotect Document. If you entered a password when protecting the document, Word will pop up an Unprotect Document dialog box in which you have to enter the password. (If you get the password wrong, Word will pop up a dialog box telling you that this password is incorrect, whereupon you can try again. But don't worry—Word's not like one of those ATMs that retain your card "for your security" after you miskey your PIN three times. You can keep trying to get the password right until the cows come home.)

▸▸ Disabling Specific Form Fields

In addition to the document protection, which you must turn on to activate your form fields, you may also want to disable certain form fields to prevent the user from altering them. To disable a form field:

1. Unprotect the document if it's already protected.
2. Double-click the form field to bring up its Options dialog box (or click the right mouse button and choose Form Field Options).
3. Uncheck the Enabled (Check Box Enabled, Fill-in Enabled, Drop-Down Enabled) option in the Field Settings area.
4. Click OK.

►► Filling In an Online Form

When you've finished creating and editing your form, set protection as described in the preceding section, Protecting a Form, and save it as a template rather than as a document. You can then open copies of the form on any computer that can access the template and fill them in online.

With protection set, Word will prevent the user from accessing anything but the form fields; the user can move from one form field to the next by pressing Tab.

►► Printing a Form's Data without Printing the Form Itself

Word lets you print the data in a form without printing the form itself. You might want to do this to fill in a preexisting form, such as a government form. You would set up your form template in Word to match exactly the target form and print only the data in the form. The data would then be printed in the correct areas of the target form.

To print a form's data without printing the form itself:

1. Select Tools ➤ Options… to display the Options dialog box.
2. Select the Print tab by clicking it or by pressing P.
3. Check the Print Data Only for Forms check box in the Options for This Document Only area, then click OK.

►► Printing a Form Along with Its Data

To print the entire form, both its structure and contents, simply print the finished document the normal way. You can:

- Click the Print button on the Standard Toolbar.
- Select File ➤ Print (Ctrl+P) and click OK.

►► Printing a Blank Form

If you want to print out an empty form to keep a printed version of the blank form handy, simply open a new copy of the form from the template:

1. Select File ➤ New or press Ctrl+N, but don't click the New File button on the Standard Toolbar.
2. Select your form from the list in the Template dialog box that appears.
3. Click OK.
4. Click the Print button on the Standard Toolbar or select File ➤ Print (Ctrl+P) and click OK.

►► Saving a Form's Data without Saving the Form Itself

Similarly, you can save the data in a form without saving the form itself. This is useful for saving form data as a single record to use in a database. Here's how:

1. Select Tools ➤ Options… to display the Options dialog box.
2. Select the Save tab by clicking it or by pressing S. (If the Save tab is already displayed, pressing S again will display the Spelling tab.)
3. Check the Save Data Only for Forms check box, then click OK.

▶▶ **NOTE**

Of course, to save the form with the entered data, simply save the form as you would any Word document: Click the Save button on the Standard Toolbar or select File ➤ Save (Ctrl+S).

▶▶ Attaching Macros to a Form

As mentioned earlier in this chapter, you can attach both AutoText and macros to a form by making the original file a template rather than a document. We'll get into macros in the next chapter, but I should just mention here that forms are a classic place to use some of Word's auto-executing macros:

MACRO NAME	EFFECT AND USE
AutoNew	Runs whenever you open a new document based on the template to which it is attached
AutoOpen	Runs whenever you open an existing document based on the template to which it is attached
AutoClose	Runs whenever you close a document based on the template to which it attached

You might set up an AutoNew macro to arrange the form for filling in—you could display on the screen Toolbars the user might need and remove ones not needed, maximize the screen display, automatically update selected fields or the information available for them, or display a help message. You could write an AutoOpen macro that would advise users when the form was last updated and advise them to save a backup copy under a different name before they destroy your precious data. Finally, an AutoClose macro could back up the changes to the form to a different directory or drive, restore general screen preferences, display a message box advising the user to update other connected forms, and so on. You get the idea.

▸▸ Creating a Form with Fill-In Dialog Boxes

If you are creating a form that will reuse the same information in several different places, then you might want to use field codes to enter, store, and reuse text so that the text entered in one form field can be reused in all the other form fields that require the same information. Entries such as names and addresses are especially suited to this approach.

A FILLIN field displays a dialog box prompting the user for an entry. After the user types an entry and clicks OK, the FILLIN field passes the entry to a bookmark.

If you combine the FILLIN field with a SET field and some REF fields, then you can assign the text entered in response to the FILLIN field to a bookmark, then refer to that bookmark (and thereby its contents) in other places in your form.

To do this, you'll need to nest a FILLIN field inside a SET field, like so:

```
{ SET CustAdd { FILLIN "Type the customer's address" } }
```

▸▸ TIP

Fields in general, the FILLIN field, and nesting fields are all covered in much greater depth in Chapter 32.

Then you can reuse the bookmark value throughout the form with the REF field, like so:

```
{ REF CustAdd }
```

▸ Inserting the Field Codes

There are two ways to insert a field code. You can do it with Insert ➤ Field, or you can enter the field manually. Let's try it both ways with the nested field. To insert the SET field manually,

1. Press Ctrl+F9. This inserts the field characters { } and leaves the insertion point between the two field characters.

2. Type **SET** and a space.
3. Type the name of the bookmark you want to assign.
4. Normally, here you would type the value to be assigned to the bookmark. Instead, you can now insert the FILLIN field.

To insert a FILLIN field automatically,

1. Select Insert ➤ Field. This brings up the field dialog box:

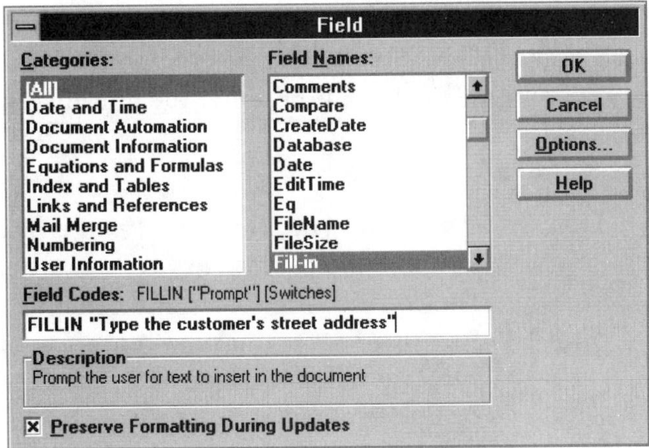

2. Select [All] in the Categories box if it's not already selected.
3. Select Fill-in in the Field Names box.
4. Type a space and then a prompt between quotation marks in the Field Codes box.
5. If you want default text, type a space, then **\d**, another space, then the default text you want between quotation marks.
6. Click OK.

Now, wherever you want to reuse that bookmark value, insert the REF field as described above.

▶ Testing the Fill-In Form by Updating the Fields

Once you have created (all or part of) your form, you can test your fill-in fields by updating them. First, of course, you have to save the template containing the form and then start a new document based on that template.

1. Select Edit ➤ Select All to select the whole document, all fields included.
2. Press F9 to update all selected fields.
3. One field at a time, enter the information requested and click OK.

▶▶ **WARNING**

When entering fields by hand and especially when nesting them, it is easy to make typographical errors that render the fields unworkable. While testing your form this way, you may therefore see an error message displayed in the place of a field, rather than a prompt or updated value. If this happens, select the field and press Shift+F9. Then check the field carefully for spelling and syntax.

▶ Setting Up an AutoNew Macro to Start the Updating Automatically

Because any time anyone opens a new document based on your form template they'll expect to fill in the fields in the form, you might as well attach an AutoNew macro to the form that starts the updating process. This way, as soon as the user opens the new document, the first prompt will appear, and the user will be taken field by field through the form automatically.

To do this,

1. Select Tools ➤ Macro. This brings up the Macro dialog box:

2. Type **AutoNew** in the Macro Name box.
3. Click the Record button. This brings up the Record Macro dialog box.
4. Click the Make Macro Available To drop-down list box and select the option Documents Based on your-template.
5. Click OK. The macro starts recording.
6. Press Ctrl+A (to select the whole document).
7. Press F9 to start the updating process. The first fill-in prompt will appear on the screen.
8. Press Esc repeatedly until all the prompts have come and gone.
9. Click the Stop Recorder button in the little floating Macro Record Toolbar.
10. Press Ctrl+S to save the template with the new macro.

To test your AutoNew macro, select File ➤ New to start a new document, choose the form template, and click OK.

CHAPTER 34

Creating and Using Macros

▸▸ FAST TRACK

A macro is **908**

a series of Word commands grouped together as a single command to make everyday tasks easier.

You can assign a macro to **908**

a Toolbar, menu, or shortcut keys and run it by simply clicking a button, selecting a menu choice, or pressing a key combination.

You can create a macro in two ways: **912**

either record a series of actions using the keyboard and mouse, or type commands directly into the macro-editing window.

To start the macro recorder **914**

double-click REC in the status area; or select Tools ➤ Macro…, then click the Record button in the Macro dialog box; or click the Record button on the Macro Toolbar.

To record a macro **915**

start the macro recorder, enter a name for the macro in the Record Macro Name box, enter a description, and decide where to assign the macro. Click OK to get rid of the Record Macro dialog box, then perform the actions you want to record. To stop recording the macro, double-click REC in the status area or click the Stop button on the Macro Record Toolbar.

To suspend and resume recording a macro **919**

click the Pause button on the Macro Record Toolbar to pause recording; click it again to restart recording.

Most people are afraid of macros, which is a shame. Macros aren't nearly as bad as people make them out to be, and they can simplify your life considerably. All right, your work life. Macros are much more fun than having your teeth drilled. Once you get them working, they're even quicker.

First, we'll discuss what macros are and what they can do for you. Second, we'll look at Word's tools for creating, recording, editing, and running macros. Third, we'll discuss five automatic macros that you really should consider trying, even if you don't care for anything else you read in this chapter. Finally, we'll throw out a couple of resources for those of you whom this chapter inspires to pursue macros further.

What Are Macros?

A macro is a series of Word commands grouped together as a single command to make everyday tasks easier. You can assign a macro to a Toolbar, menu, or shortcut keys (see Chapter 36 for more on this) and run it by simply clicking a button, selecting a menu choice, or pressing a key combination.

Macros are recorded as instructions in Word's macro language, WordBasic, so-called because it uses words and it's basic. Well, more like because it's the Basic language used by Word. Don't let WordBasic worry you; you can create macros without understanding a single word of it.

You can create a macro in two ways:

- Record a series of actions using the keyboard and mouse. This is the easiest way.

- Type a macro directly into a macro-editing window. This way you have more flexibility and can include WordBasic instructions that you can't record using the keyboard and mouse.

If you record a macro using the keyboard and mouse, you can then open it in the macro-editing window and edit it. Often the best way to create a macro is to record as much of it as possible using the keyboard and mouse, then edit it and add further WordBasic instructions in the macro-editing window.

▶▶ How You Might Use Macros

So what would you actually *use* a macro for? Well, several things: to perform routine editing and formatting tasks faster; to combine several commands that you always have to perform in sequence; to instantly adjust an option in a remote dialog box (for example, to change printers and set printer options with one keystroke); or to automate a complex series of tasks.

So, Ron, gimme a concrete example. OK; say you write your reports with the body text in double-spaced Courier 12-point with 1" margins all the way around your paper. You print out drafts like that—nice and easy to read, and you don't care how typewriterish it looks—but when you print out your final report, it needs to look completely different, single-spaced 10-point Times Roman for the body text, three levels of headings in different sizes of a display font like Braggadocio, 1½" margins. Oh, and you always forget to run a spelling and grammar check before you print it. You could write a macro to:

- Change the body text to 10-point Times Roman.
- Apply the three heading styles to the relevant paragraphs.
- Adjust the margins and line spacing.
- Force you to check the spelling and grammar.

You gotta admit that beats dentistry any day.

►► Things You Can Do without Using Macros

Far be it from me to discourage you from recording and running macros, but I should point out that macros are hardly the only form of automated convenience that Word offers. Before delving into the challenging process of recording a custom macro to create a shortcut, consider first whether you can achieve the effect you want with Styles, the Style Gallery, AutoFormat, AutoCorrect, Autotext, the Spike, Bookmarks, Field Codes, Form Fields, or even Find and Replace.

- Styles help automate the formatting process, allowing you to apply multiple character and paragraph formats to separate text elements in a single step. They also allow you to change formatting consistently throughout your document. Styles are covered in Chapter 14.
- AutoFormat takes a lot of the formatting decisions out of your hands but gives you a lot of control over accepting or rejecting its suggestions. AutoFormat is covered in Chapter 14.
- AutoCorrect is designed to fix your typos as you make them, but you can also add abbreviations to it that are automatically expanded into their full references as soon as you type them. AutoCorrect is covered in Chapter 17.
- AutoText is an even more sophisticated way to create abbreviations and store boilerplate text for reuse. AutoText is covered in Chapter 17.
- The Spike enables you to skim through a document and pull out specific pieces of it and then deposit them all in another location. The Spike is covered in Chapter 17.
- Bookmarks make it easier for you to navigate through your documents and can also play the role of variables with field codes and macros. Bookmarks are covered in Chapter 25.
- Field codes produce a result or start a macro somewhere in the document. They can interact with the user, taking and storing input or even producing varying results depending on the user's entry. Field codes are covered in Chapter 32 and Appendix E.

- Form Fields can automate the process of creating a document or filling out a form. They can also be combined with field codes to take user input and reuse it throughout a document. Form Fields are covered in Chapters 32, 33, and Appendix E.
- Find and Replace can automate some of your editing, particularly when you need to make identical or similar changes throughout a document. With advanced Replace features, you can carefully fine-tune what gets changed and what does not. Find and Replace are covered in Chapter 20.

▶▶ The Macro Toolbar

The Macro Toolbar contains twelve buttons and a name box, as shown in Figure 34.1.

FIGURE 34.1 ▶

The Macro Toolbar.

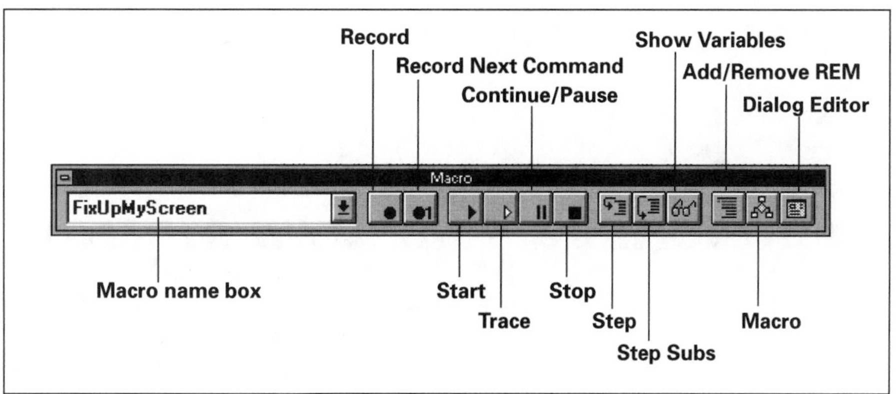

Here's what the different parts of the Macro Toolbar do. Don't worry about them too much at the moment but be prepared to come back to this section for reference when working on your macros.

TOOLBAR ITEM	WHAT IT DOES
Macro name box	Lists the name of the macro
Record	Turns recording a macro on or off
Record Next Command	Records the next command executed

TOOLBAR ITEM	WHAT IT DOES
Start	Starts running the current macro
Trace	Highlights each statement as the active macro executes it
Pause/Continue	Pauses or continues running the macro
Stop	Stops running the macro
Step	Runs the active macro one step at a time
Step Subs	Runs the active macro one step at a time, considering subroutines one step
Show Variables	Lists the active macro's variables
Add/Remove REM	Adds or removes a REM (remark) at the beginning of each selected line in the active macro
Macro	Runs, creates, deletes, or revises a macro
Dialog Editor	Launches the macro Dialog Editor, a mini-application that you can use to design dialog boxes

▸▸ Recording Your Own Macros

To record your own macros, you start the Word macro recorder and record a sequence of actions. You then stop the recorder and edit the macro if need be. Then you can run the macro whenever you need to perform the same sequence of actions.

▸ Things to Do before Recording a Macro

Before you actually start recording your macro, make sure that the Word workspace is in roughly the same shape it will be in whenever you run the macro. If you end up doing some "housecleaning" while recording the macro, all of those steps will be included in the macro as well and often won't make sense.

▶▶ NOTE

On the other hand, you can save things—like going to the top of the document—for the beginning of the macro, if they're going to be necessary every time the macro runs.

It's good to think about what position your documents will be in when you run your new macro on them. It helps clarify the steps that will be needed when you start recording the macro.

1. Make sure you've got open the kind of document you'll use your macro in. (Open a document from the Normal template if you'll want your macro available to all documents.)
2. Run through the procedure without recording it to notice all the steps (it's easy to forget the details!).
3. If the macro involves selecting something, decide if you want to make the selection before the recording (in which case the macro will work properly only after you've selected something), or after.
4. Think up a good name for the macro.
5. Decide if you'll want a keyboard shortcut for it (and think of one easy to remember), if you'll want it on a Toolbar, or if you'll want to slap it on a menu.

▶ Thinking through the Steps to Record Ahead of Time

Here's an example. Let's take a look at creating a simple macro to maximize the space available to you on the screen. We need to do the following:

- Maximize Word for Windows.
- Maximize the document window.
- Hide the horizontal ruler, the Toolbars, the scroll bars, and the status bar.

To do this with the mouse or keyboard would involve a series of simple actions staggeringly tedious to repeat, so this is a great candidate for a macro.

▶ Starting the Macro Recorder

There are three ways to start the macro recorder:

- Double-click REC on the status bar. This is the quick and easy way.
- Select Tools ➤ Macro..., then click the Record button in the Macro dialog box (see Figure 34.2). Easy but slower. You may want to save this for when you type in a macro rather than recording it.

FIGURE 34.2 

The Macro dialog box.

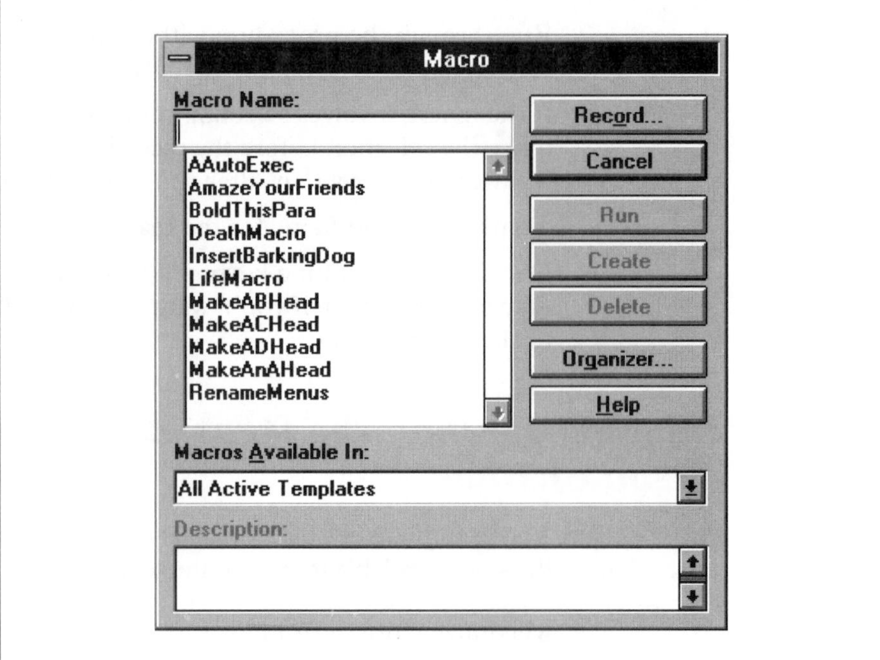

- Click the Record button on the Macro Toolbar. This involves having the Macro Toolbar displayed (it'll be displayed when you start recording a macro).

▶ Record the Macro

Let's look at the steps for recording a macro, then record the one proposed above.

1. Start the macro recorder by double-clicking REC on the status bar. The Record Macro dialog box will appear (see Figure 34.3).

FIGURE 34.3 ▶

The Record Macro dialog box. Give your macro a name here and choose whither to assign it.

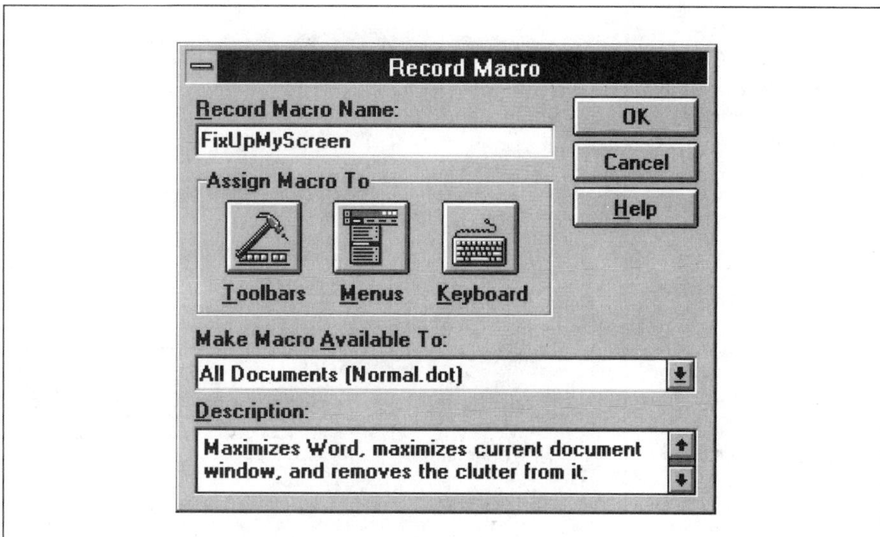

2. Enter a name for the macro in the Record Macro Name box.
    - If you don't give your macro a name, Word will name it Macro1, Macro2, and so on. This is all fine and convenient for the time being, but unless you rename your macros, they'll be most uninformative after a while.
    - No spaces, commas, or periods allowed in the name.
3. Enter a description of what the macro does in the Description box. This is optional but heavily recommended, even if it's only *Second try at infernal maneuver, 4/1/95. Delete tomorrow.* This description will appear on the status line for a macro you assign to a menu item or Toolbar button. You've got up to 255 characters, so get typing.

4. To assign the macro to a Toolbar, a menu, or a keyboard shortcut, click the Toolbars, Menus, or Keyboard button. This will fire up the Customize dialog box with the appropriate tab selected, as shown in Figure 34.4, where I've chosen to assign the FixUpMy-Screen macro to the Help menu. For details on assigning macros to the Toolbars and the keyboard, see Chapter 36 or follow your instincts.

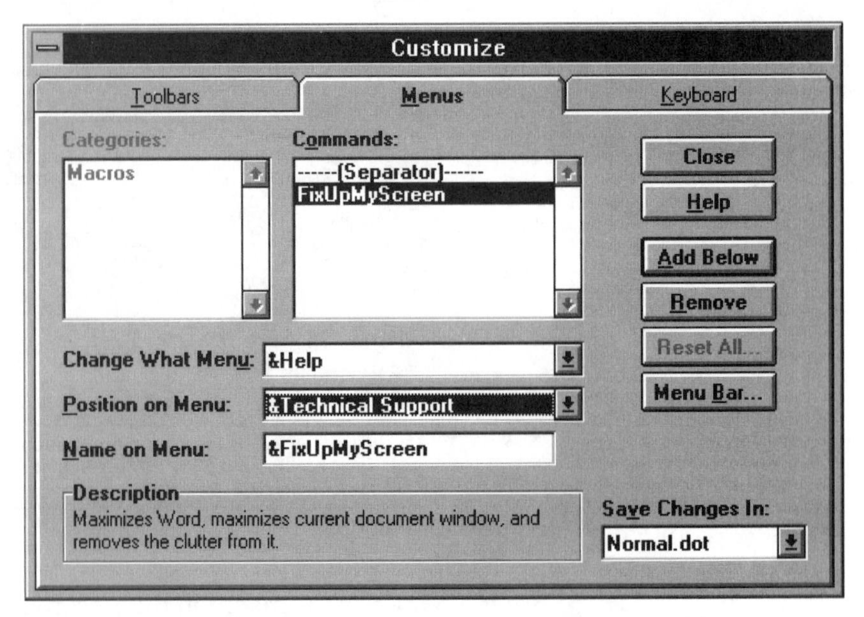

FIGURE 34.4

The Customize dialog box. Here I'm assigning the FixUpMyScreen macro to the Help menu.

5. If your current document is attached to a template other than NORMAL.DOT, drop down the Save Changes In list and select either that template or Normal.
   - If the current document is attached to NORMAL.DOT, Word will automatically store the macro there. As you can see, that's the case here.
6. Click OK. Now you can finally start recording your macro.

The Macro Recorder Toolbar will appear on the screen:

It has two buttons—from left to right, a stop button and a pause button (sort of like a tape recorder, right? so where's the fast forward?). The little mini–control menu in the upper-left corner of the Macro Recorder Toolbar just closes the Toolbar without stopping recording. If you click it by mistake, you'll need to select Tools ➤ Macro to pause or stop the recording.

Notice also that the mouse pointer gets a little cassette tape icon attached to it, to remind you that you're recording. (How embarrassing it would be a week later to realize you'd recorded everything you did!)

Notice also the REC box in the status bar becomes highlighted. This is also supposed to remind you that you're recording.

▶ Actually, Finally, Recording the Macro

Now, perform the actions you want to record. Here are the steps for recording the FixUpMyScreen macro:

1. Click Word's maximize button to maximize Word.
2. Click the document window's maximize button to maximize the document window.
3. Select View ➤ Ruler to turn off the ruler. (If that turns the ruler on rather than off, don't worry—we'll fix the problem when we edit the macro.
4. Select Tools ➤ Options... to display the Options dialog box, then choose the View tab. Uncheck the check boxes for Horizontal Scroll Bar, Vertical Scroll Bar, and Status Bar, then click OK.
5. Select View ➤ Toolbars... to display the Toolbars dialog box, then uncheck the Standard and Formatting check boxes.

6. To stop recording the macro, click the Stop button on the Macro Record Toolbar (or double-click the word REC in the status bar). The Macro Recorder Toolbar will disappear.

There, one macro recorded! No pain, lots of gain, and no novocaine. We'll open the macro up in a moment. But first, a brief intermission.

▸ What Gets Recorded and What Doesn't

Technically, the macro recorder does not record actions that you perform. It records the commands, the results of your actions. When you change something about your document while recording the macro, the macro remembers what you changed it to, not what it used to be.

▸▸ WARNING

Some Word commands simply toggle between two possibilities, such as Show/Hide ±. For commands of that sort, the macro recorder will only record that the status was changed. When played back, the macro will change the status without regard to which toggle position it starts in.

For commands chosen from a dialog box, you must click OK for the result to be recorded. And clicking OK in a dialog box records the selected state, including all defaults, of every option *in that tab* of the dialog box. To record commands in another tab of the same dialog box, you must open the dialog box again, switch to the other tab, make your selections, and click OK again.

The macro recorder generally does not record mouse motions. Well, that's not exactly right. You choose commands by pulling down menus and clicking Toolbar icons with the mouse, and those results will be recorded, but you can't select (and therefore also can't drag and drop, of course) text or other elements of your document with the mouse.

You can, of course, select text, copy it, paste it, cut it, and move it with the keyboard shortcuts. Select text by holding down Shift and pressing the arrow keys and other movement keys (or by using the Extend command—F8—and the arrow and movement keys). Use Ctrl+C to copy, Ctrl+V to paste, and Ctrl+X to cut. Use cut and paste together to move.

Because the macro recorder records results, not literal keystrokes, when you play back your macro, you won't see menus being pulled down and ghost mouse clicks like a player piano. You'll just see Word clinically and surgically executing your commands.

▶ Taking a Break from Recording the Macro

In Word for Windows 2.0*x*, once you started recording a macro, you had to go through with it to the end. If you screwed up or had to perform an unexpected maneuver in the middle of the macro because you hadn't thought the sequence through properly before starting, all your actions were recorded into the macro. Sure, you could edit them out later, but that involved learning something about WordBasic.

new

Word 6 improves upon this by allowing you to suspend and resume recording a macro as suits you. If you reach some impasse in the procedure that you don't want to record for posterity, or just want to record isolated actions here and there as the fancy strikes you, here's what to do:

1. Click the Pause button on the Macro Record Toolbar to pause recording.
2. Perform the actions you don't want to record.
3. Click the Pause button again to restart recording (just like a tape recorder!).

► Solving Problems Recording a Macro

If you make a mistake while recording a macro, you can pause the macro as explained in the previous section and put the document back to the way it should be before continuing, or you can stop recording the macro and then start over from the beginning. The latter may be easier if you are near the beginning of the recording process.

►► NOTE

If you pause the macro recording and fool around with the document, then you'll still need to edit the macro when you're done to eliminate the mistake from the recording. Editing macros is covered later in this chapter.

If you choose some incorrect settings in a dialog box and can't remember what the original choices were, you can simply click the Cancel button or press Esc to close the dialog box without recording your incorrect selections. (Remember, the macro recorder will only record your actions in a dialog box if you click OK when you are done.)

Another thing you can do is select Edit ➤ Undo, press Ctrl+Z, or even click the Undo drop-down menu button on the Standard Toolbar to undo your mistake. However, you must still check and edit the macro when you are finished, because the macro recorder will record both the incorrect action and the Undo. Not only is this confusing to anyone looking at the macro listing later (or watching it work), it may also give the wrong result, as the Undo may only undo the last result of your previous action, if, as with some Ruler, Toolbar, or dialog box commands, there is more than one result.

►► Running a Macro

Once you have recorded a macro, there are a number of ways to play it back. You should test your macro out on a saved document right away to make sure it's working correctly. If it isn't, either edit it, as explained in the next section, or record it again from scratch.

Here are the different ways to run a macro:

- Select Tools ➤ Macro, choose the macro, and click the Run button.
- Click a MACROBUTTON field code in a document (as explained in Chapter 32).
- Run another macro that itself runs this macro.
- Click the macro's Toolbar icon.
- Select the macro's menu command.
- Press the macro's keyboard shortcut.

If you can't find a macro later when you try to run it, chances are you assigned the macro to a specific template and now have a different template open.

▶ Assigning a Macro to a Toolbar, Menu, or Keyboard Shortcut After the Fact

Of course the last three options will only be available to you if, when you first started the recording process, you assigned the macro to a Toolbar, menu, or keyboard shortcut. If you did not do it then and wish you had, things get a little trickier.

1. Select Tools ➤ Customize. This brings up the Customize dialog box:

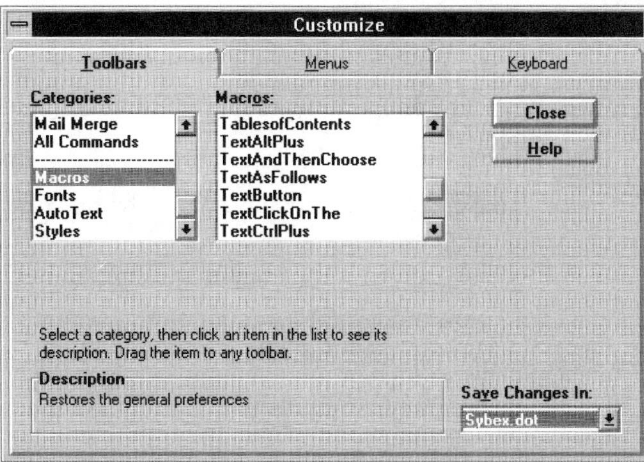

2. Click the appropriate tab (Toolbars, Menus, or Keyboard).
3. Select Macros in the Category box.
4. Choose the macro you want to assign.
5. Then drag the macro you want to a Toolbar, select a menu and position, or enter a keystroke combination.
6. For menus, click Add. For keystrokes, click Assign.

► Macros that Start Themselves

AutoNew, AutoOpen, AutoClose, and AutoExec macros (they are all explained later in this chapter) all run automatically when certain events occur. As you might imagine,

- AutoNew macros start when you start a new document based on the template the macro is stored in;
- AutoOpen macros start when you open a document containing them;
- AutoClose macros start when you close a document containing them;
- AutoExec macros start whenever you run Word.

You can also run Auto macros in all the other ways that you run normal macros.

► Running a Macro from the Macro Dialog Box

Whether or not you've assigned your macro to a menu, Toolbar, or keyboard shortcut, you may always run any macro from the Macro dialog box.

1. Select Tools ➤ Macro. This brings up the Macro dialog box (see Figure 34.2).
2. Select the macro you want to run. (If you don't see the macro you're looking for, change the selection in the Macros Available In box to the template containing the macro.)
3. Click the Run button.

▸▸ Editing Macros

Once you've recorded macros, you can edit them and run them. Often, you'll want to edit macros before running them, either to remove flaws recorded in the macro or to enhance the macro with WordBasic commands that you cannot record.

Here's how to edit a macro:

1. Select Tools ➤ Macro…. The Macro dialog box will appear.
2. Select the list of macros to choose from by dropping down the Macros Available In box.
3. Choose the macro you want to edit, then click the Edit button. The macro-editing window will appear, displaying the text of the macro you chose. Figure 34.5 shows the text of the FixUpMy-Screen macro.

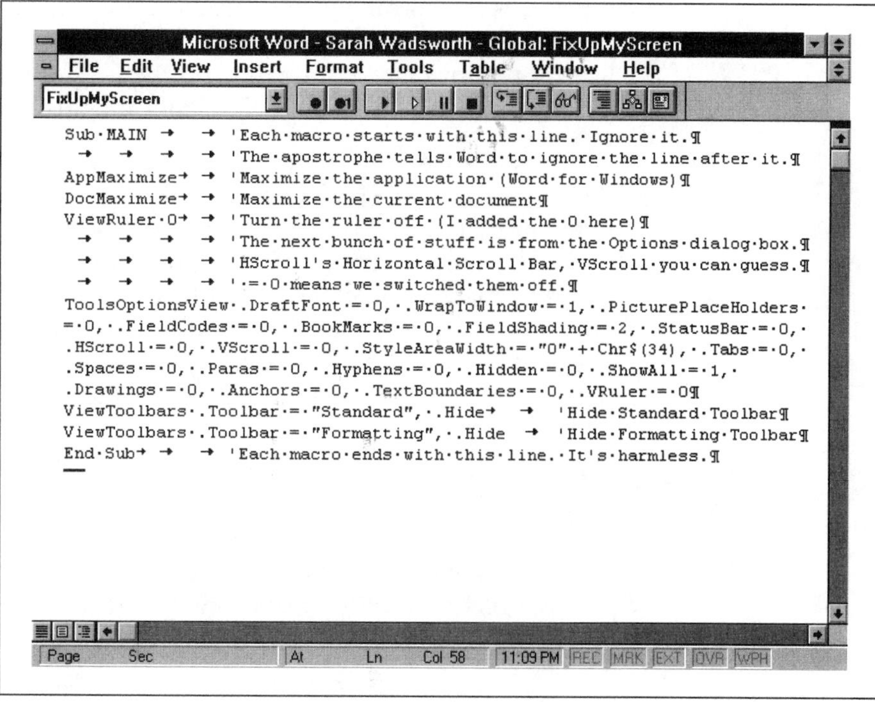

FIGURE 34.5 ▶

The macro-editing window, displaying the FixUpMyScreen macro with comments added to it. Edit the macro, close the file, and save changes.

4. Edit the macro.

   - If your ViewRuler line toggled the ruler on rather than switching it off, change it to **ViewRuler 0** to make sure the macro switches the ruler off.

5. Close the file and choose Yes when Word invites you to save changes.

►► NOTE

You'll notice that the macro appears in a window much like any normal Word document. For your purposes, it *is* a Word document, and you can edit it as you would any document.

As you look over the listing of a macro, notice what was recorded and what wasn't. The macro is not so much a recording of everything you did as it is a recording of the results of everything you did. If you made a mistake and then selected Undo, there will be at least one command line for the mistaken command and then an additional line for the Undo command. (You can delete both the mistake and the Undo line.)

Also, if you made selections from a dialog box, look at the commands that were recorded (for example, look at the ToolsOptionsView command in Figure 34.5). You'll see that every element of the dialog box registered some setting, whether you changed the default or not. When editing a macro, you can remove the extra parts of commands (the arguments) that are irrelevant to your purposes. It's not necessary to do that, but it does make the macro easier to read and interpret if you need to edit it again or see what it does later.

►► TIP

While editing a macro, be sure to save it every now and again. Select File ➤ Save All to save any open documents, including macros. (Word will automatically prompt you to save your macros—as changes to the templates they're in—when you quit, but it's safer to save them yourself while you're still working on them.)

Organizing Your Macros

Word 6's new Organizer dialog box greatly simplifies managing your macros. You can use it to move, copy, or rename a macro. By default, macros are stored in the Global Template in NORMAL.DOT and so are available for use with every Word document. However, you can store them in other templates if you wish. For example, if you have a macro that's only useful for annual reports, you might include it in your ANNUREPO template.

Copying Macros from One Template to Another

new

Word 6 lets you easily copy macros from one template to another. So, you can record or write a macro in the Normal template, then decide you only need it in your IMCLEVER template, and transfer it across.

Here's how to copy a macro from one template to another:

1. Select File ➤ Templates.... The Templates and Add-Ins dialog box will appear.
2. Click the Organizer... button to display the Organizer dialog box (see Figure 34.6).
3. Choose the Macros tab.
4. If necessary, close the open file, select the Open File button, and open the template or document containing the macro.
5. Select the macro you want to copy, then choose the Copy button.
    - To select a range of items, hold down Shift and click the first and last items. To select several individual items, hold down Ctrl and click each one.
6. Click the Close button when you've finished copying macros.

FIGURE 34.6 ▸

The Organizer dialog box, new in Word 6, lets you manage your macros with minimal effort.

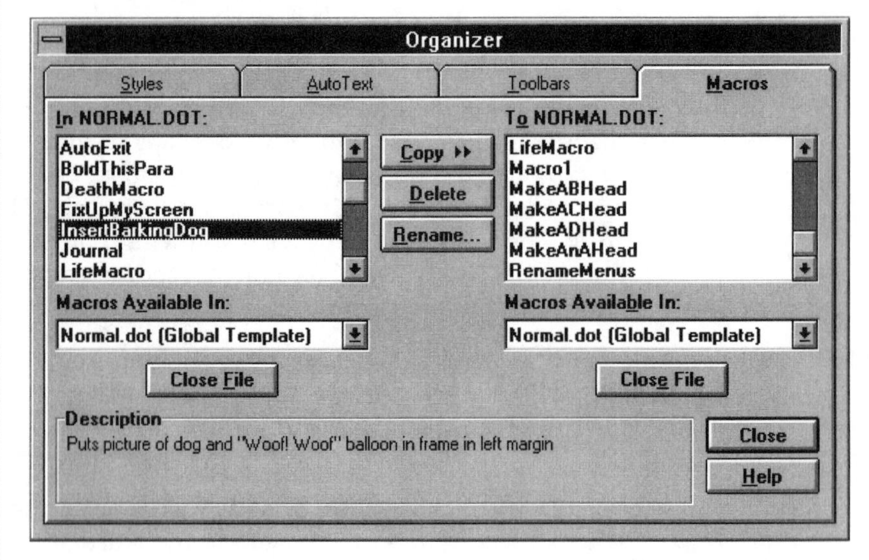

▸▸ **TIP**

You can also get to the Organizer dialog box by selecting Tools ➤ Macro… and clicking the Organizer… button in the Macro dialog box.

▸ Renaming a Macro

If you give several macros in different templates the same name, or if you record your macros as Macro1, Macro2, Macro3, and so on, you may want to rename macros at some point. Here's how to do it:

1. Select Tools ➤ Macro…. The Macro dialog box will appear.
2. Click the Organizer button. The Organizer dialog box will appear with the Macros tab selected.
3. In the left list box, choose the macro to rename. If necessary, choose a different template in the Macros Available In list box.

4. Click the Rename... button. The Rename dialog box will appear.

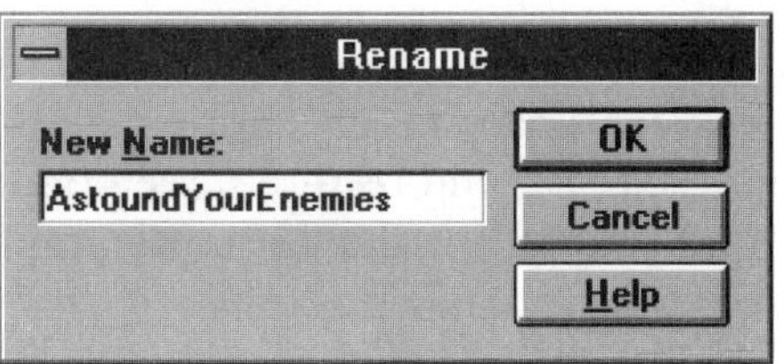

5. Enter the new name for the macro and click OK. The macro will be renamed.

▶ Deleting a Macro

Getting rid of a macro you no longer need is easy and intuitive:

1. Select Tools ➤ Macro.... The Macro dialog box will appear.
2. Highlight the macro to delete.
3. Click the Delete button.
4. Click the Close button to return to your document.

▶▶ Using the Sample Macros That Come with Word

Word supplies a bunch of sample macros that are built into sample templates stored in the TEMPLATE subdirectory. One way to learn more about macros and get some practice editing them is to check out these sample macros.

As described in the previous section, you can copy any of these macros from the templates they are associated with to a new template using the Organizer. Once you've done that, you can run the macros, open them up for editing, and change them, if you want, without harming the originals stored in the sample templates.

►► Word's Automatic Macros

Even if you never get deeply into writing and using macros, you should look briefly at Word's five autoexecuting macros. With only a little effort, you can use these to set and restore screen preferences, open a bunch of documents, and generally make life a little more pleasant for you.

The five automatic macros are:

MACRO NAME	WHAT IT DOES
AutoExec	Runs when you start Word
AutoNew	Runs when you open a new file
AutoOpen	Runs when you open a file you created before
AutoClose	Runs when you close a file (new or created before)
AutoExit	Runs when you exit Word

You can create automatic macros just as you do any other macros—by typing the commands into the macro-editing window (reached by selecting the Edit... or Create... button in the Macro dialog box), by recording a series of actions, or by a judicious mixture of the two. The sections below suggest a few uses for these automatic macros; no doubt you'll quickly come up with your own uses.

► Uses for an AutoExec Macro

If you don't like having Word automatically create a new document based on the Normal template whenever you start Word, you could write a brief AutoExec macro to specify a new document based on a different template, such as SPESHL4U.

```
Sub MAIN
    FileNew .Template = "SPESHL4U"
End Sub
```

Or you could arrange to have Word open the same file—for example, a journal—whenever you start Word and go to either your last edit or the end:

```
Sub MAIN
    FileOpen "C:\WINWORD6\JOURNAL\19940401.DOC"
If MsgBox("Click OK to go to the scene of the last crime; click Can-
cel to start a new entry at the end of the journal.", "OK, So
Whaddaya Wanna Do Widdya Journal?", 1 + 32) Then GoBack Else
Goto NewStuffLokiSaveUs
Goto Bye
NewStuffLokiSaveUs:
    EndOfDocument
Bye:
End Sub
```

Get your imagination to work on a good AutoExec macro—it can improve your life.

▶ Uses for an AutoOpen Macro

While you can have only one AutoExec macro for your copy of Word, you can have a different AutoOpen macro for each template. As a result, you may want to use AutoOpen macros to customize the screen for templates, to display a message box to greet the user, or both:

```
Sub MAIN
Print "Hang on a tick while yer favorite template customizes yer
screen..."
    ViewToolbars .ColorButtons = 1, .LargeButtons = 1, .ToolTips = 1
    ViewToolbars .Toolbar = "Standard", .Show
    ViewToolbars .Toolbar = "Formatting", .Show
    ViewRuler
MsgBox "Screen customized to your satisfaction—well, mine any-
way.", "Thank you! You are free to proceed!", 0 +48"
End Sub
```

▶ Uses for an AutoNew Macro

You can use an AutoNew macro in similar ways to an AutoOpen macro to set up the screen and options for a given template. But you might also want to ensure that the user saves the file immediately to prevent lost data and gives it the necessary summary information for you to keep track of things:

```
Sub MAIN
Dim SaveNow As FileSaveAs
Dialog(SaveNow)
Dim SumItAllUp As FileSummaryInfo
Dialog(SumItAllUp)
End Sub
```

Here the user is automatically asked to save the document. Other possibilities include setting up the screen to suit the user or document.

► Uses for an AutoClose Macro

The AutoClose macro is the perfect choice for either restoring screen preferences for documents using other templates or, as in the example below, backing up the file being closed to a file server or backup drive:

```
Sub MAIN
    ClosingFile$ = FileName$()
    FileClose 1
    Copyfile ClosingFile$, "f:\ronstuff\worddocs\backup"
    MsgBox "Backed up your file successfully!", "Backup", 0 + 64
End Sub
```

►► **NOTE**

As with the AutoOpen and AutoNew macros, you can have an AutoClose macro for each different template. This gives you great flexibility.

► Uses for an AutoExit Macro

An AutoExit macro runs whenever you quit Word, so that limits your possibilities a bit—there's not much point in having it open a new file! You might want to use it to reset any environment options that your other macros and templates are liable to change. That way, when you restart Word, all the settings will be as you like them.

Here's how you might turn off the Toolbars that the AutoOpen macro earlier turned on:

```
Sub MAIN
    ViewToolbars .Toolbar = "Standard", .Hide
    ViewToolbars .Toolbar = "Formatting", .Hide
MsgBox "Thank you for using your own copy of Word for Win-
dows. Please have a good day.", "Drive Safely and Be Nice to Your
Spouse", 0 +48
End Sub
```


►► Debugging Your Macros

If your macro is not working properly, you can use the Step button on the Macro Toolbar to debug it. *Debugging* is a programming term for finding the errors in a program. As the macro executes, you can step through it one command at a time and figure out exactly when it goes wrong. (After a macro fails, the offending command is highlighted in red, so that should help, too.)

If necessary, you may have to include special commands at various places in your macro to display the current contents of variables (see Macros That Talk Back later in this chapter).

►► Advanced Macros and WordBasic

To get any fancier with macros, you have to bite the bullet and learn a little bit about WordBasic. Look, it's not as bad as it sounds. Remember how to edit a macro you've already recorded. (See Figure 34.5.) Those commands shown in the macro listing are WordBasic commands. So you've been dealing with WordBasic already even if you didn't realize it.

Word macros consist entirely of WordBasic commands. The same is true for actual Word commands themselves. When you pull down the File menu and select Open, that action is equivalent to running the FileOpen command macro.

This is not a book for programmers, so I don't expect you to have a background in "writing code," and I'm not going to try to turn you into a software engineer. The rest of this chapter, however, will cover some of the more straightforward uses of WordBasic.

▶ The Structure of WordBasic Commands

WordBasic is itself based on a programming language called BASIC that was developed to teach beginners programming. BASIC requires less "housekeeping" on the part of the programmer (you don't have to declare variables, reserve memory, or anything like that) and is fairly easy to learn and use. BASIC commands are as close to plain English as is possible.

WordBasic is a tailored version of BASIC with all sorts of built-in commands relating to word processing and Windows standards (such as the format of dialog boxes, which is the same from program to program in Windows). It also contains the necessary commands for more complicated structures, such as subroutines, conditionals, and loops.

Subroutines are miniature programs that branch off from a main program. Conditionals are statements that execute actions only if some other condition is true. Loops are sets of statements that start over from the beginning and execute repeatedly until or unless some other condition occurs. (Infinite loops are poorly structured loops that continue repeating forever, unless interrupted, such as "Lather, rinse, repeat.")

The elements of any WordBasic command are its statements, functions, variables, constants, and arguments.

- Statements perform actions
- Functions return (produce) results
- Variables carry values that can be assigned and changed
- Constats are values that don't change
- Arguments modify statements and functions

The FixUpMyScreen macro shown in Figure 34.5 consists entirely of statements and arguments. The macro comprises a series of actions performed on the Word screen. The ViewRuler command includes an argument (0) to specify exactly what it should do (not just toggle the Ruler from its previous position, but actually turn it off no matter what). Actually, in a sense, the 0s and 1s used to switch various statements or arguments on and off are technically constants.

Variables can contain text (in which case they are called string variables) or numbers (numeric variables). String variables always ends in the symbol $ (which is, by association, pronounced string).

Both string and numeric variables can be manipulated. There are functions to pluck out specific parts of a string or concatenate two strings together. There are also basic mathematical operators (the familiar +, –, *, /, and so on) as well as mathematical functions that perform more complicated operations on numeric variables.

▶ Getting Advanced Macro Help

Beyond the basic macro information available from Word Help, there is also a wealth of WordBasic help. If you start fooling around with WordBasic or trying to do something tricky while editing a recorded macro and you run into trouble that you can't solve with my advice here, you should look into the WordBasic help. To do so, select Help ➤ Contents. This brings up the Word Help window (see Figure 34.7).

Click *Programming with Microsoft Word.* That brings up the WordBasic Help window (see Figure 34.8).

FIGURE 34.7 ▶

Word Help. Click the Programming with Microsoft Word icon or label to go to the WordBasic Help.

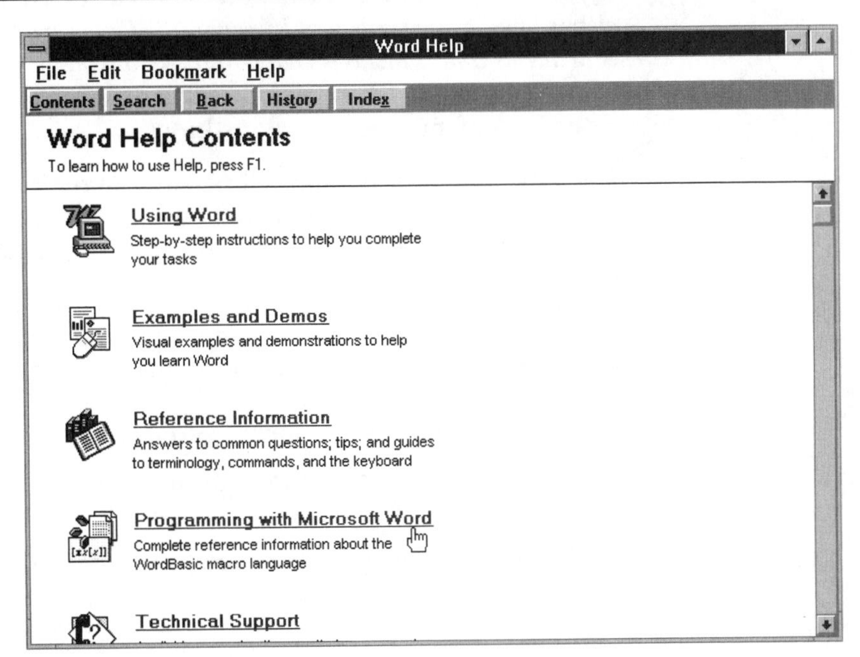

FIGURE 34.8

WordBasic Help. Here you can find complete syntax information for each WordBasic command, help in making dialog boxes, and all kinds of examples and helpful explanations.

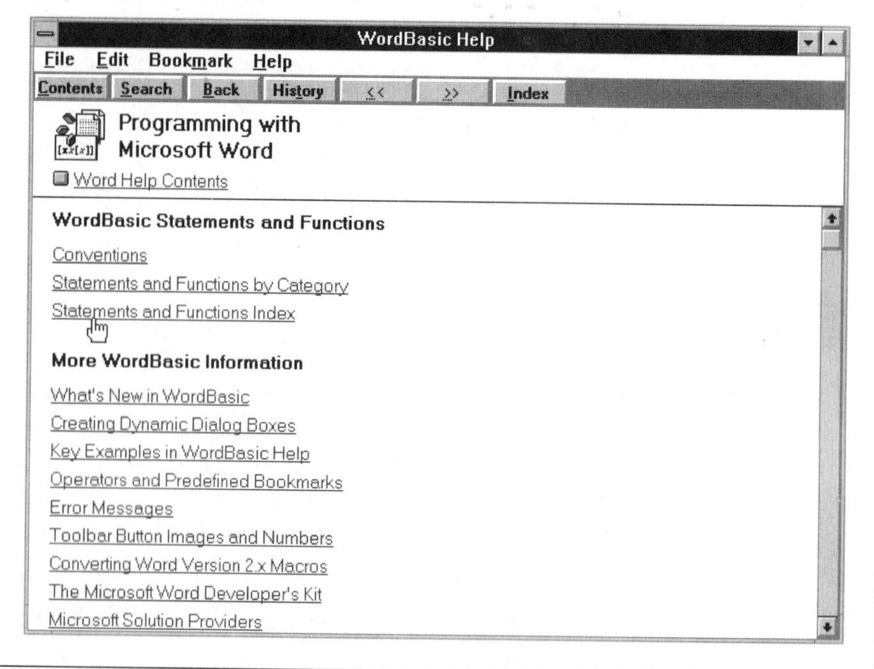

If you're looking for information on a specific command, you can either click *Statements and Functions by Category,* to zero in on it, or *Statements and Functions Index* to look for it alphabetically. (They both lead eventually to the same information.) Figure 34.9 shows the WordBasic Statements and Functions Index.

Click the letter button for the first letter of the command (statement or function) that you're looking for. Then click the entry itself to go to an informative Help entry. Figure 34.10 shows the entry for the EditReplace command.

All WordBasic entries start the same way, by giving the syntax of the statement or function. The conventions are as follows:

- The name of the command and its arguments are **bold**.
- Words in *italics* are dummy (example) words and must be replaced with specifics.
- Arguments between [brackets] are optional.

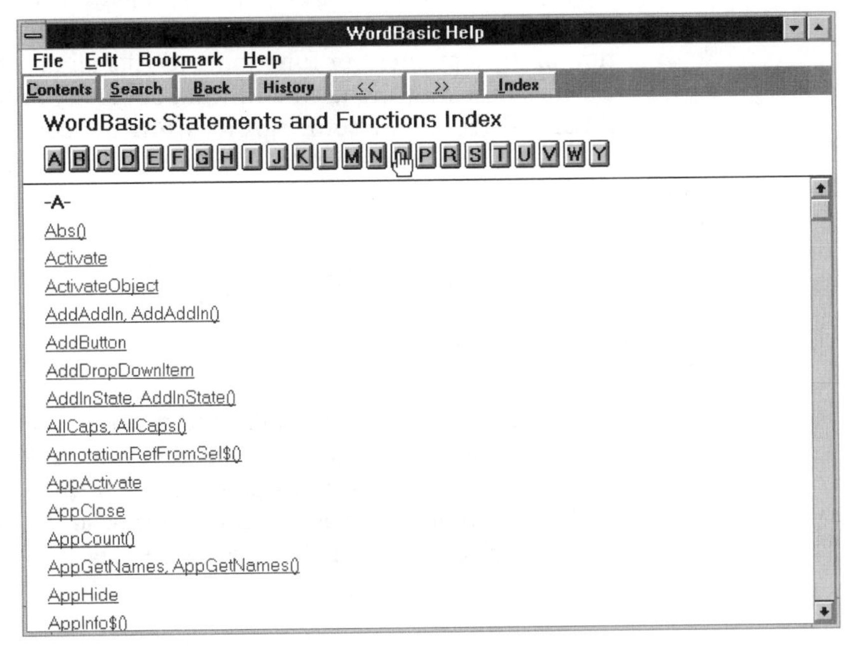

FIGURE 34.9

The WordBasic Statements and Functions Index. You can also get here by clicking the Index button below the menu bar after you've clicked Programming with Microsoft Word. It works like any other Help index. Click a letter button to skip to that part of the index. Click a command or function to see its syntax, explanations, and examples.

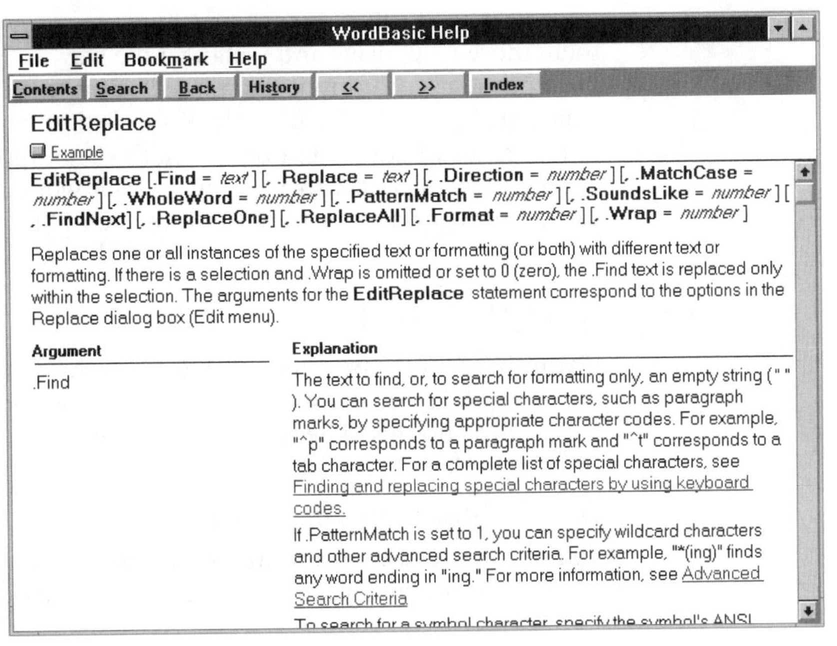

FIGURE 34.10

The EditReplace entry with complete syntax, information on each argument, some tips, and links to related entries.

After giving the syntax (don't worry, it gets easier to read that gibberish after you've done it a little while), the entry then gives a brief explanation of the statement or function and lists all of the arguments and clarifies how they are used and what choices you have to set them to. Finally, there will be some tips for using the command and then some hot (clickable) cross-references to related commands.

►► Not-Too-Hard WordBasic Programming

If you start creating more ambitious macros (go ahead, you can call 'em WordBasic programs!), you'll soon want to know how to prompt the user for input, how to display results, how to deal with multiple possibilities, and how to create subroutines or loops. In the next few sections, I'll give you a start in all of those areas.

►► Hello in There!—Talking to Macros

As your macros get more sophisticated, you're going to want to make them more responsive and flexible. One way to do this is to have them prompt the user for input and then do different things depending on what gets "put in." The flip side of this is that you'll want your macros to report on what they're doing—that's the output side of the coin. Recorded macros are taciturn. They do their work and disappear. But you can set up your macros to both "listen" and "talk."

► Getting User Input

If your macro is to be interactive, it has to be able to accept input from the user (and store the value of the input as a variable). There are several ways to do this. The simplest is to put a prompt in the status bar.

Simple Input on the Status Bar

To prompt the user on the status bar, use the Input command. With Input, you can prompt for the value of a string or numeric variable.

Input statements have the syntax

Input [*Prompt$*,] *Variable*[$]

So the statement:

Input "What is your title", Job$

will display the prompt in quotation marks on the status bar and store the user's input in a string variable called Job$:

What is your title?

Notice that WordBasic adds the question mark to your prompt.

TIP

You can prompt for numeric input just as easily.

To respond to this type of prompt, type an answer and press Enter.

User Input in a Box

For a more elaborate (and harder to miss) form of input, you can use the InputBox$ command to put a dialog box up on the screen. The InputBox$ statement has the syntax

*Variable$* = **InputBox$**(*Prompt$* [, *Title$*] [, *Default$*])

So the statement:

Job$ = InputBox$("What is your title?","Personnel")

will display the prompt in a dialog box with the title specified and no default answer in the text box, and store the response in a variable called Job$:

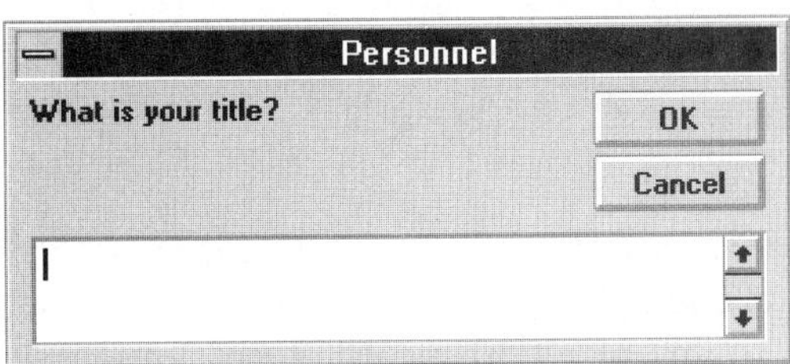

Notice that WordBasic does not automatically supply a question mark for the InputBox$ prompt. To respond to this sort of prompt, type an answer and click OK.

Just Yes or No, Please

If all you need from the user is a Yes or No answer, then you can use the MsgBox() command. The MsgBox() command has the following syntax:

Variable = **MsgBox**(*Message$* [, *Title$*] [, *Type*])

where *Type* can be any number from 0 to 5 and indicates the type of response buttons available:

0	OK
1	OK, Cancel
2	Abort, Retry, Ignore
3	Yes, No, Cancel
4	Yes, No
5	Retry, Cancel

If you don't specify a type, the default is 0. The statement

```
Answer = MsgBox("Do you have any additional comments?","Comments",4)
```

will display the prompt in a dialog box headed with the title string and containing Yes and No buttons.

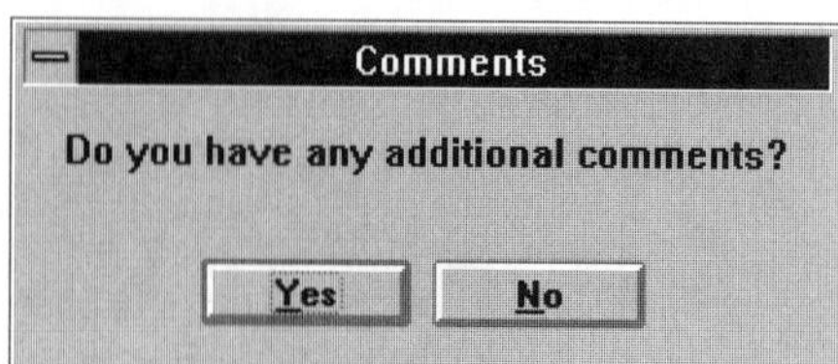

The response is stored in the variable Answer. With MsgBox(), if the first button is clicked, the value returned is –1. For the second button, it's 0, and if there are 3 buttons, the third returns 1.

NOTE

The button responses, such as Yes, No, and Cancel, don't do anything by themselves. Your WordBasic program must take the value returned and do something with it, depending on what it is. See If Statements later in this chapter for more on conditionals.

Macros That Talk Back

So now you know a couple of different ways to pass information to your macros. Now you'll also need to know how your macros can report information back to you. As with input, there's a simple way to do it that displays information on the status bar and another fairly easy way that displays a dialog box.

On the Status Bar

To display text on the status bar, use the Print command. Print statements have the syntax

Print *Variable*[$]

So the statement:

```
Print "Vice President of Marketing"
```

or

```
Print Job$
```

will display the string named:

Vice President of Marketing

TIP

You can print numeric values just as well.

In a Message Box

If you want your macro to really announce the information it has, you can use the MsgBox. The MsgBox statement has the syntax

MsgBox *Message$* [, *Title$*] [, *Type*])

So the statement:

MsgBox "Your title is "+Title$, "Personnel"

will display the message in a dialog box with the title specified and an OK button:

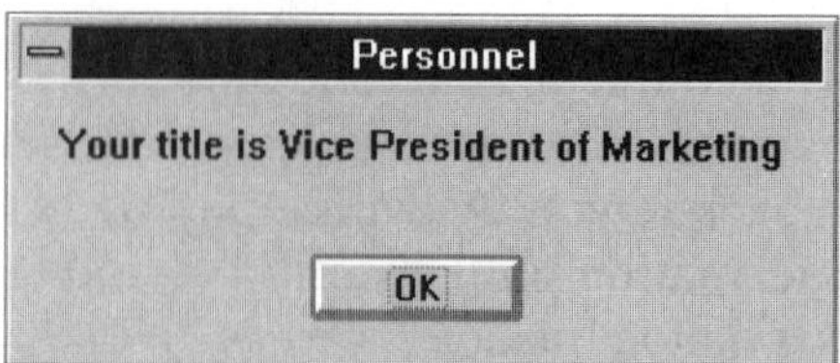

▸▸ NOTE

The type options for MsgBox are the same as for the MsgBox() input command explained earlier.

▸▸ Creating Dialog Boxes

You've already seen how to display simple dialog boxes and use them to get input or display output, but those dialog boxes are still fairly limited in what they can do. If you understand a little more about how dialog boxes work, you can modify existing dialog boxes or even create your own.

▸ Understanding Dialog Boxes

Word commands that call up dialog boxes translate into WordBasic macro commands with many parameters. You saw in the sample macro FixUpMyScreen earlier in this chapter how recording the selection of the View tab of the Options dialog box translated into a WordBasic Tools-OptionsView command with every option in that tab recorded as a parameter set to some value (see Figure 34.5).

This set of parameters recorded from the dialog box is known as an array. If you want to create a dialog box or modify an existing one, you have to first plan out the array that the dialog box command will use.

In recording that macro, I selected Tools ➤ Options, then turned off the horizontal and vertical scroll bars and the status bar, and clicked OK. That action was recorded as:

```
ToolsOptionsView .DraftFont = 0, .WrapToWindow = 0, .Picture-
PlaceHolders = 0, .FieldCodes = 0, .BookMarks = 0, .FieldShading =
2, .StatusBar = 0, .HScroll = 0, .VScroll = 0, .StyleAreaWidth = "0" +
Chr$(34), .Tabs = 0, .Spaces = 0, .Paras = 0, .Hyphens = 0, .Hidden =
0, .ShowAll = 0, .Drawings = 0, .Anchors = 0, .TextBoundaries = 0,
.VRuler = 0
```

Those parameters listed after the ToolsOptionView command are all *fields* in the command's array. Figure 34.11 shows the View tab of the Options dialog box.

FIGURE 34.11

The View tab of the Options dialog box. Notice how the different check boxes, text boxes, and drop-down lists correspond to parameters in the ToolsOptionsView command.

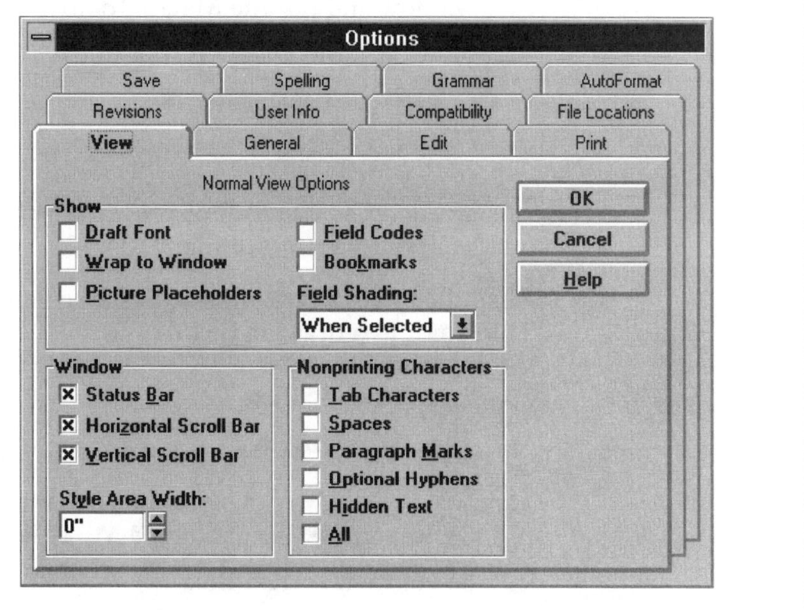

So each element of the dialog box (tab) corresponds to a field in the WordBasic command's array.

► Creating Your Own Dialog Boxes

Whether you realized it or not, Word came with another program called the Dialog Editor. You use the Dialog Editor to lay out your dialog box. You then copy and paste it into your macro, and it produces the skeletal WordBasic commands you'll need to display the dialog box. After that, you still have to add the instructions that use the information the dialog box can gather and store.

This process can become rather involved, and although there's fairly good support in the WordBasic section of Word Help, you really need the *Microsoft Word Developer's Kit*, available from Microsoft, if you plan to get serious about this level of WordBasic. Just to give you an idea, though, I'll take you through a simple example.

1. Select Tools ➤ Macro to bring up the Macro dialog box.
2. Type **Questionnaire.**
3. Click the Create button. This will open a new blank macro-editing window and put the Macro Toolbar on the screen.
4. Now click the Dialog Editor button:

This starts the Dialog Editor program with a generic dialog box in the middle of the screen (see Figure 34.12).

That dialog box in the middle of the screen is only a dummy, a picture. Think of it as a drawing board.

5. Select Item ➤ Text.
6. Type **My name is**.
7. Select Item ➤ Text Box.
8. Select Item ➤ Text and type **My title is**.
9. Select Item ➤ Text Box.

FIGURE 34.12

The Dialog Editor program. It makes assembling a dialog box a snap. (Making it do something is a little trickier.)

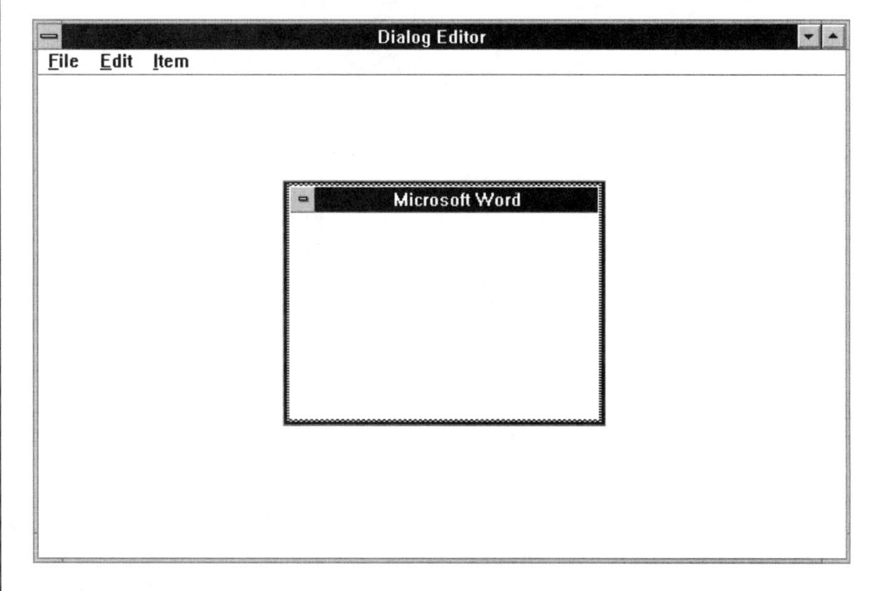

10. Select Item ➤ Text and type **My favorite color is**.
11. Select Item ➤ List Box. This brings up the New List Box dialog box:

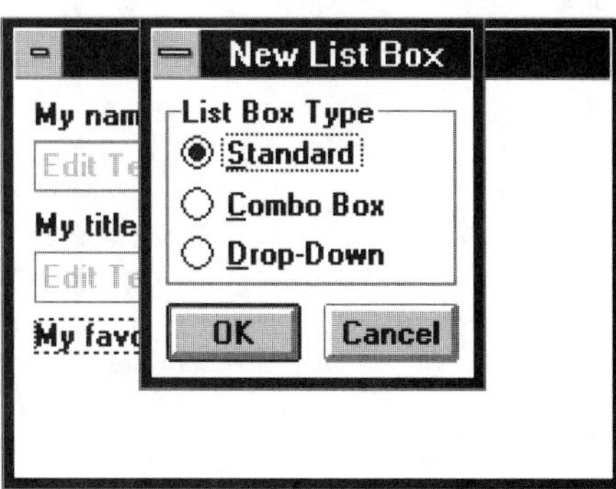

12. Click Drop-Down and then click the OK button.

13. Select Item ➤ Button. The New Button dialog box will appear:

14. Click Check Box and then click the OK button.
15. Type **I like ice cream**.
16. Select Item ➤ Button. Make sure the OK option is selected and then click the OK button.
17. Select the OK button and move it to the lower-right corner of the dialog box, as shown:

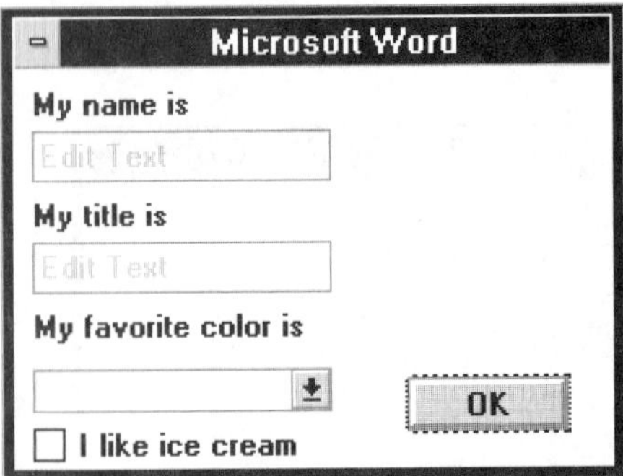

18. Double-click the title bar of the dummy dialog box. This brings up the Dialog Information dialog box.
19. Select the words *Microsoft Word* in the Text$ dialog box and type **Personnel Questionnaire**.
20. Click OK.

▶▶ TIP

To edit the text or variable names associated with any part of the dialog box you're working on, simply double-click the element or select it and then select Edit ➤ Info.

21. With the dialog box dummy still selected, press Ctrl+C (or select Edit ➤ Copy).
22. Select File ➤ Exit. This should put you back in the macro-editing window.
23. Press Ctrl+V (or select Edit ➤ Paste).

What gets pasted into your macro listing is the command equivalents of all the dialog box elements you selected:

```
Begin Dialog UserDialog 320, 144, "Personnel Questionnaire"
    Text 10, 6, 85, 13, "My name is", .Text1
    TextBox 10, 22, 160, 18, .TextBox1
    Text 10, 46, 73, 13, "My title is", .Text2
    TextBox 10, 62, 160, 18, .TextBox2
    Text 10, 86, 145, 13, "My favorite color is", .Text3
    DropListBox 10, 107, 160, 108, DropListBox1$(),
    .DropListBox1
    CheckBox 10, 126, 145, 16, "I like ice cream", .CheckBox1
    OKButton 209, 110, 88, 21
Dialog box height = 215
CheckBox = 185
OKButton = 185
End Dialog
```

Now, as I mentioned, there's more to using dialog boxes than creating their shells in the dialog box editor. If you added the commands for displaying a dialog box and ran your macro now, it would look pretty, displaying the dialog box you created, but it would not be "wired up" to anything inside.

To make your macro good for something, you might start by giving the variables descriptive names that you can understand later (though that's not necessary from Word's point of view—it will work just as well with the generic variables it supplied). Replace .TextBox1 with .Name, .TextBox2 with .Job, DropListBox1$() with Colors$(), .DropListBox1 with .Color, and .CheckBox1 with .IceCream. (You can get rid of the fields .Text1, .Text2, and .Text3.)

Next, you'd have to create an array variable for the drop-down list-box choices by inserting something like this before the Begin Dialog command:

```
Dim Colors$(3)
Colors$(0) = "Blue"
Colors$(1) = "Red"
Colors$(2) = "Yellow"
Colors$(3) = "None of the above"
```

▸▸ **NOTE**

You're dealing with computers here now, and they like to start counting at zero.

Now the generic dialog box is not going to be big enough for the drop-down list you've built into it, so you'll have to change the height dimensions. On the Begin Dialog box command line, change the number 144 (or the second number) to **215**. On the CheckBox command line, change the number 16 (the last number) to **185**. And on the OKButton command line, change the number 21 (the last number) to **185**.

You'll have to do something with the values that are stored—both the text entered in the text boxes and the results of the drop-down list and check-box responses (which are returned as numbers—0 or 1 for unchecked or checked, 0 through 3 for the drop-down list box choices). If your macro has *control structures*, things that make decisions based on conditions, then you need to pass the variables on to those structures.

Finally, you'll have to include the command to set up an array to hold the field variables of the dialog box:

```
Dim dlg As UserDialog
```

and then you need to include a command that will display the dialog box:

```
Dialog dlg
```

or

Variable = Dialog(dlg)

▶▶ Basic Programming Structures

For fully functioning WordBasic programs, you need control structures so that the macro can decide what to do in various situations. This means the macro needs to be able to recognize different conditions and respond differently to them, and to repeat certain processes under certain conditions.

▶ If Statements

The basic conditional command is the If statement. A basic If statement has the syntax

If *Condition* **Then** *Instruction* [**Else** *Instruction*]

So the statement:

```
If Job$ = "Vice President of Marketing" Then Goto Marketing Else
Goto End
```

will compare the value of Job$ to the text in quotes and then send the macro interpreter to one section of the macro if the variable matches the text or to another section if it does not.

▶▶ TIP

Goto is explained a little farther ahead.

You can turn a recorded command into an If statement easily by preceding what the macro recorded with the If command and following it with a Then statement.

► Loops

Most advanced macros require certain actions to be repeated until some condition is met. This is known in programming as looping. There are several different ways to create loops.

Goto

The simplest loop uses the Goto command. Goto is fairly straightforward. It sends the macro interpreter to the section named. Its syntax is

Goto *Label*

For it to work, you must label a part of the macro. Simply add a line before that section with the label name followed by a colon.

►► WARNING

If you use Goto by itself and the label it goes to precedes the Goto command, you'll create an infinite loop, with no alternative for the macro but to repeat the loop forever (until you stop it).

To be effective as a control structure, the Goto command must be combined with a conditional command, such as an If statement.

For ... Next

For ... Next statements give you more control over the looping. Their syntax is

For *Counter* = *Start* **To** *End* [**Step** *Increment*]
...
Next [*Counter*]

So the commands

```
For Decade = 10 To 100 Step 10
Print Decade
Next
```

would print 10, 20, 30, etc., up to 100 on the status bar (so quickly that you'll probably only see the 100 if you try it).

You need to specify the counter variable name in the Next statement only if you have more than one For … Next loop going at once.

While … Wend

While … Wend loops are a little more subtle. They allow you to have a loop running while some condition obtains. Their syntax is

> **While** *Condition*
> …
> **Wend**

While … Wend loops are flexible, as the conditions that govern how often they will repeat can change during the execution of the loop.

▶ ▶ CHAPTER 35

Using Word and Word Documents with Other Applications

▸▸ FAST TRACK

To open a document created in another application — 954

select File ➤ Open... and select the drive, directory, and document. Drop down the List Files of Type list and select the appropriate designation. Select the file and click OK. If Word asks you which converters to use, choose one in the Convert File dialog box and click OK.

To make Word 6 automatically display the Convert File dialog box — 957

when you open a file with a different format, check the Confirm Conversions check box in the Open dialog box.

If a document isn't converted correctly — 957

close it without saving changes and try converting it again using a different converter.

If Word refuses to recognize the file — 957

select the Text Only option Word offers you in the Convert File dialog box. If Word then trashes your file, try saving the source file in Word for Windows format in the source application and then opening it in Word.

To save the converted document — 958

select File ➤ Save... and choose Word 6 or the original format in the Save Format dialog box; or, to simply save the file under a new name in Word 6 format, choose File ➤ Save As... and give the file a new name in the Save As dialog box.

To save a Word document in another format ***959***

select File ➤ Save As…, select the format you want from the Save File as Type list, enter a new name for the file in the File Name box, and choose OK.

To convert several files at once ***960***

run the BatchConverter macro located in CONVERT.DOT and follow its instructions.

To exchange information with applications for which Word has no converters ***962***

select File ➤ Save As…, choose a text-only format from the Save File as Type list, and save the file under a different name.

To customize Word's conversions ***963***

run the EditConversionOptions macro in CONVERT.DOT and choose the appropriate options.

To improve Word's compatibility with other applications ***964***

select Tools ➤ Options… and click the Compatibility tab. Make the choices you want, then click OK.

To install further converters ***966***

run the Microsoft Word Setup program again by double-clicking the Word Setup icon or selecting File ➤ Run… and entering SETUP.EXE.

▶▶ **W*ord*** makes it easy to work with documents created in other applications. So if you used WordPerfect for all your documents before switching to Word for Windows, you'll still be able to open and work with your old documents. If you've just upgraded from Word 2.0*x* for Windows to Word 6, you'll have no problem at all.

Exactly which files created in other applications your copy of Word can open depends on the converters you installed with your copy of Word. See the Make Sure You've Got the Right Filters Installed section at the end of this chapter if you know that you don't have some necessary converters installed or if Word won't open documents you suspect it should be able to.

▶▶ Opening a Document Created in Another Application

With Word 6, you can easily open documents created in many other applications.

1. Select File ➤ Open… or click the Open button on the Standard Toolbar. The Open dialog box will appear (see Figure 35.1).
2. In the Drives box, select the drive the target document is on. In the Directories box, select the directory the target document is in. (Hey, Ron, this is real easy! Didn't we do this in Chapter 2?)
3. If your file has an extension other than .DOC, pull down the List Files of Type list and select the appropriate option. If your target document was created in an application other than Word, you'll probably want All Files (*.*).

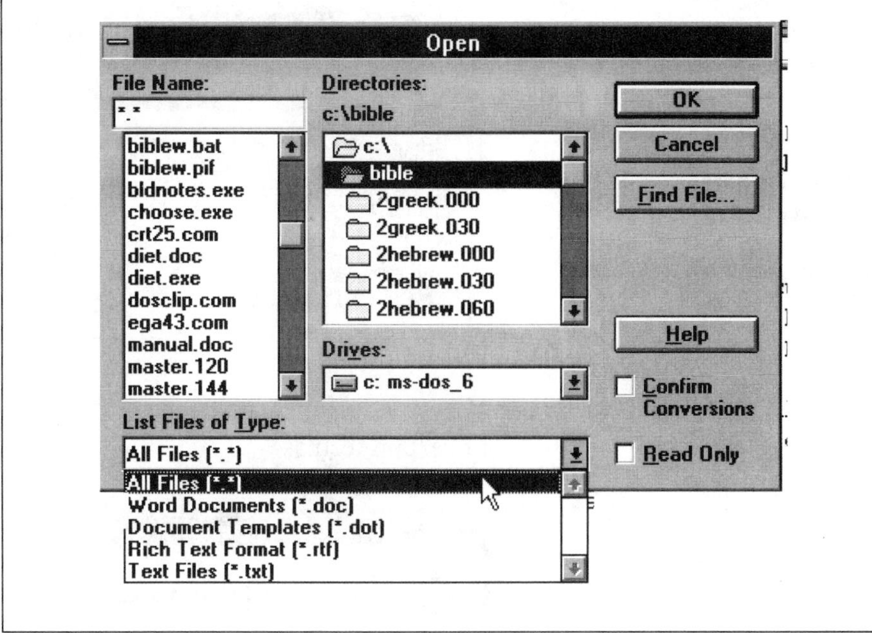

FIGURE 35.1

The Open dialog box. Drop down the List Files of Type list to display file names with extensions other than .DOC.

- If you know the extension of the file you want, type it into the File Name box and press ↵ for a finer sort—for example, ***.SAM** for Ami Pro documents or ***.XLS** for Excel spreadsheets (or ***.SAM; *.XLS** to see both). That way, you can get the type of file you want without having to sift through all the other junk that may be cluttering up the directory.

4. Select the name of the file you want to open and click OK. Word will open the file for you.

   - If Word doesn't recognize the contents of the file, it will try to use the converters suggested by the file's extension. If that doesn't work, Word will ask you to choose a converter, as shown in Figure 35.2. Choose the converter you think corresponds to the contents of the file and choose OK.

FIGURE 35.2

The Convert File dialog box. Word will pop this up at you if you ask it to open a file whose format it doesn't recognize. Make your best guess and click OK. Word will tell you if you're wrong.

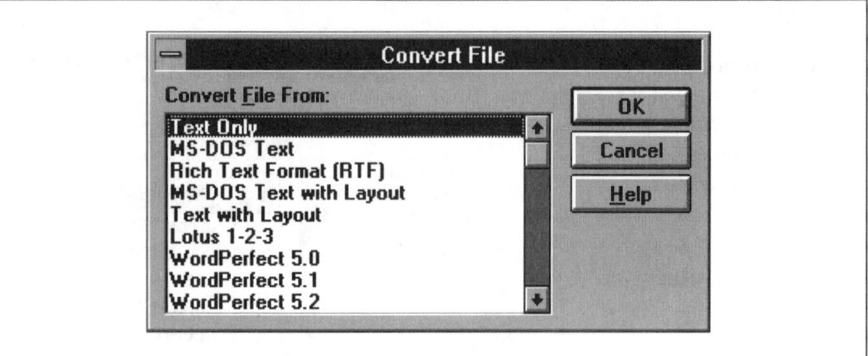

- If you choose the wrong filter, Word will tell you so in no uncertain terms:

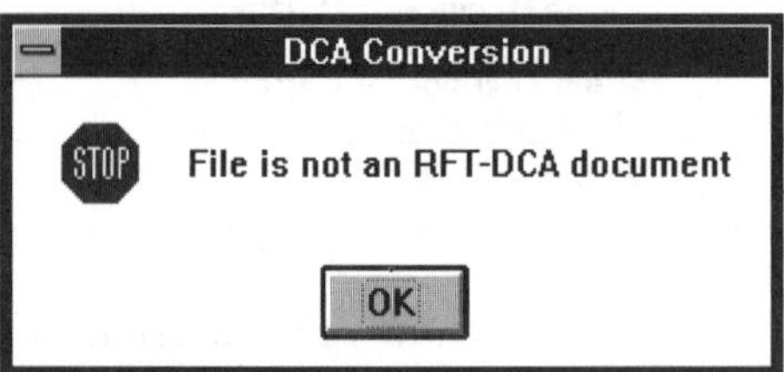

- Click OK (there ain't much choice). Now you get the good news:

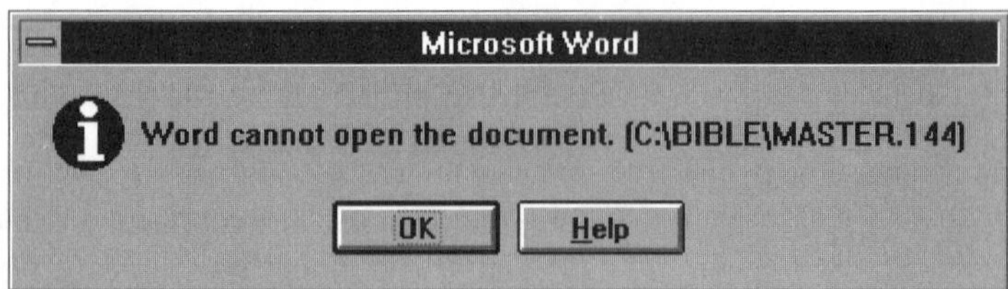

- Click OK to get out of this and try again. (Click Help to get a complicated online explanation of what I'm about to tell you.)

▶▶ **NOTE**

Remember that a file's extension may not correspond to its contents: You could take a TIFF file called ODDFACES.TIF and rename it ODDFACES.DOC or WOTISZIS.DOC, but it would still be a TIFF file, not a Word document. Similarly, IDIOTS.WS could be a WordPerfect 6 or XyWrite file rather than the WordStar file its extension suggests. It could even be CorelDRAW! Here's a quick tip for free: Save your files with the extensions you (or anyone else) would expect to find on that type of file. Life will be friendlier.

▶▶ **NEW**

To make Word 6 automatically display the Convert File dialog box (as Word 2.0 always used to, even when it *knew* what the file was) when you open a file with a different format, check the Confirm Conversions check box in the Open dialog box.

If a document isn't converted correctly, your best bet is to close it without saving changes and try converting it again using a different converter.

▶ *If Word Refuses to Recognize the File*

If Word can't get a handle on what format the file is, you have little option but to accept the Text Only option it'll offer you in the Convert File dialog box. Word will then display the file as if its contents had been text only. This conversion may mangle a file beyond all recognition. Figure 35.3 shows a short document in Ami Pro 3.0, a format that Word resolutely refuses to acknowledge (professional jealousy, no doubt), and what Word 6 pretends to think the document contains.

In cases like this, try saving the file in Word for Windows format in the source application and then opening it in Word. Failing that, you may have to resort to saving it as a .TXT file in the source application and then opening it as a (true!) text-only file in Word. This way, you'll get your text ungarbled, but you'll lose all the formatting.

FIGURE 35.3 ►

In the left corner, a short Ami Pro 3.0 file, and in the right corner, Word 6's brave attempt to translate it. If you look at Word's status bar, you'll see that there are twelve pages of garbage preceding this one—quite impressive for a six-word Ami Pro document!

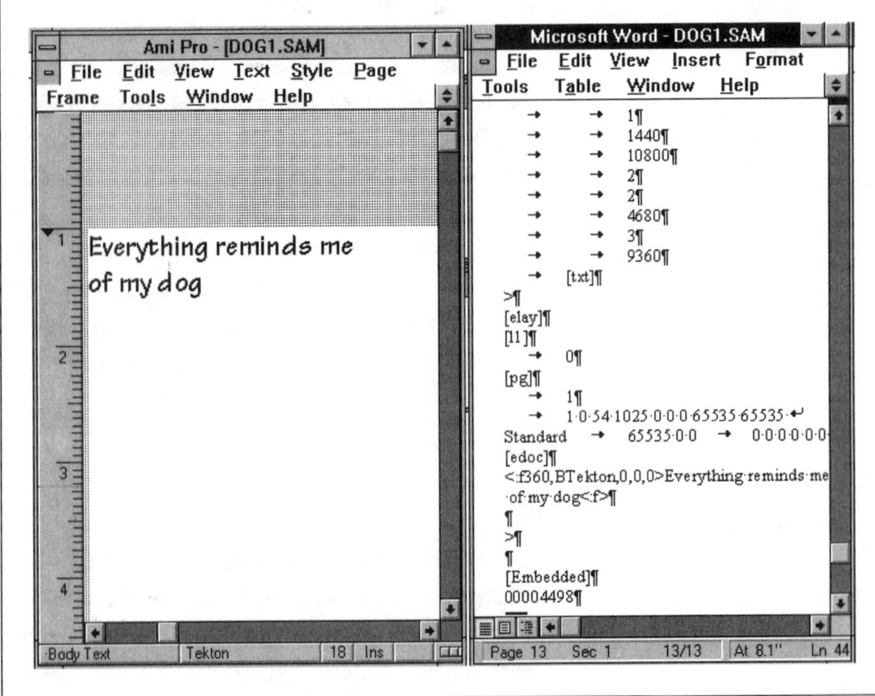

► Saving the Converted Document

The file you converted is now stored in your computer's memory. To keep it as a Word for Windows document, you need to save it as a Word file. If you select File ➤ Save, Word will display the Save Format dialog box asking if you want to save the file in Word 6 format or in its original format. Here's the Save Format dialog box you'll see if the file in question is a Word 2.0 for Windows document:

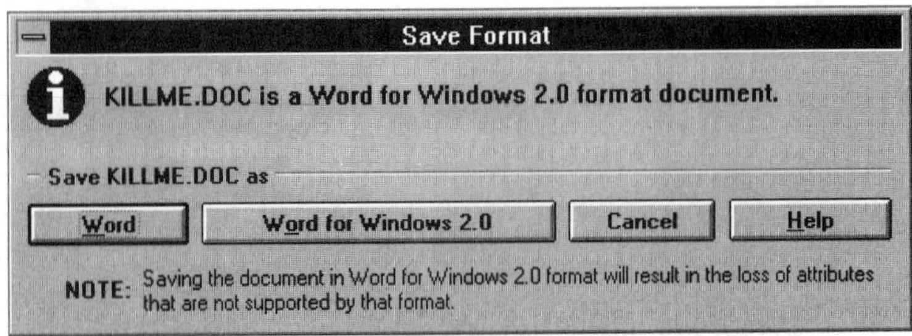

Note the warning in the Save Format dialog box that you may lose some formatting if you don't save the file in Word 6 format.

To simply save the file in Word 6 format, choose File ➤ Save As..., select Word Document in the Save File as Type drop-down list, and give the file a new name in the Save As dialog box.

▶▶ NOTE

The Save File as Type box will automatically show the format of the original document.

▶▶ Saving a Word Document in Another Format

What if you need to use a Word 6–format file in another application or in an earlier version of Word? Simply save the file in the file format for the other application:

1. Select File ➤ Save As.... The Save As dialog box appears.
2. Pull down the Save File as Type list and choose the format you want. (There's quite a list to scroll through, and it's not in alphabetical order.)
3. Enter a new name for the file in the File Name box, then choose OK.

▶▶ WARNING

Don't bank on a Word file's summary information (reached by selecting File ➤ Summary Info...) being carried to any format except Word and Rich Text Format (RTF).

▸▸ Saving Time by Converting Several Files at Once

To convert a whole bunch of documents at a time, either to or from Word format, run the BatchConverter macro located in CONVERT.DOT.

First make sure CONVERT.DOT is loaded as a global template:

1. Choose File ➤ Templates…. The Templates and Add-ins dialog box will appear (see Figure 35.4).
2. If CONVERT.DOT is shown in the Global Templates and Add-ins box, go to step 5. If CONVERT.DOT isn't shown, click the Add… button. The Add Template dialog box will appear (see Figure 35.5).
3. In the Add Template dialog box, change the directory to C:\WINWORD6\MACROS\, select CONVERT.DOT, and click the OK button. CONVERT.DOT will appear in the Global Templates and Add-ins box.
4. Make sure the CONVERT.DOT check box is checked (see Figure 35.4), and then click OK to close the Templates and Add-ins dialog box.

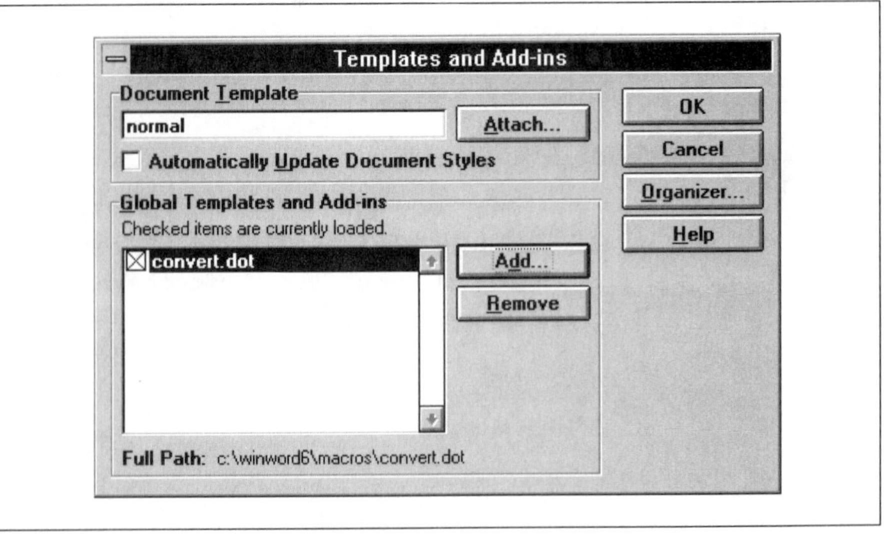

FIGURE 35.4 ▸ *The Templates and Add-ins dialog box. Make sure the CONVERT.DOT check box is checked.*

FIGURE 35.5

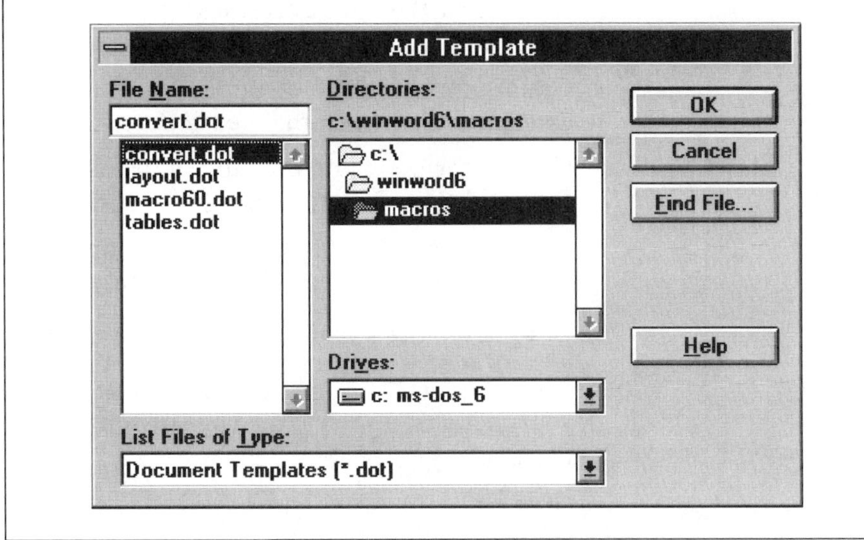

The Add Template dialog box. Select CONVERT.DOT from the C: WINWORD6 \MACROS subdirectory to add it.

Now run the BatchConverter macro in CONVERT.DOT:

1. Select Tools ➤ Macro…, choose BatchConverter from the list of macro names, and click the Run button.
2. In the Batch File Converter dialog box that appears (see Figure 35.6), choose "From another format to Word for Windows" or "To another format from Word for Windows," then click the Next>> button.

FIGURE 35.6

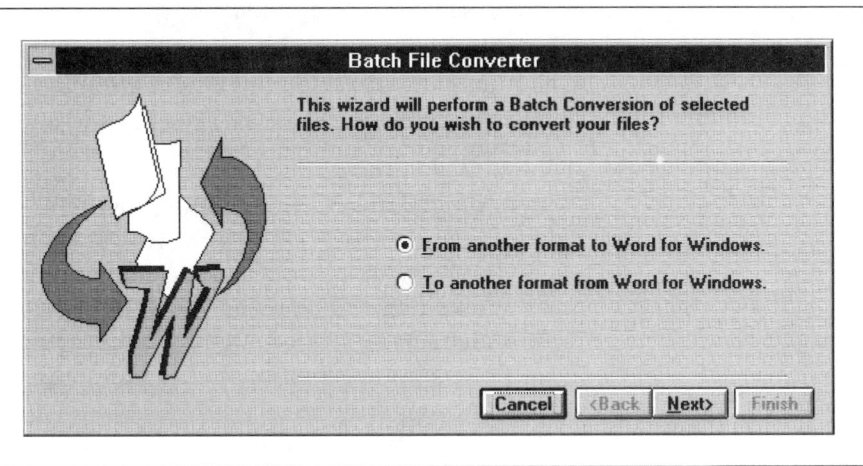

The Batch File Converter dialog box. Select the type of conversion you want and hit the Next>Button.

3. In the next Batch File Converter dialog box that appears, choose the format in the Convert From box and click the Next> button.
4. Choose the drive and directory where the files to convert are located, and then click the Next> button.
5. Choose the drive and directory in which to place the converted files, and then click the (you guessed it) Next> button.
6. Choose the files to be converted by double-clicking them one at a time or by choosing the Select All button to convert all.
    - To remove a file, double-click it in the Files to Convert List box.
7. Click the Next>button. The Batch File Converter will convert your files and display a message of congratulations when it's done.
8. Click the Next button to repeat the conversion with more files or click Finish to close the Converter. (Click Cancel if you didn't convert anything.)

▸▸ Exchanging Information with Applications for Which Word Has No Converter

If you need to use a Word file in an application for which Word has no converters, save the file as a plain-text file:

1. Select File ➤ Save As.... The Save As dialog box will appear.
2. Pull down the Save File as Type list and choose one of the text formats:
    - You'll get very similar effects with the two Text Only (Regular and MS-DOS) and the two Text Only With Line Breaks options unless you're doing something very sophisticated: Your text will be saved without formatting, and all line-break characters, section breaks, and page breaks will be converted to paragraph marks.
    - The two Text With Layout options will preserve the length of lines and the approximate spacing between them and

elements of the document. Section breaks and page breaks will be converted to paragraph marks.

- Rich Text Format saves all formatting, converting formatting to text instructions that other applications can read. You'll know if you want to use RTF.

3. Give your file a different name and the appropriate extension (.TXT or whatever).
4. Open the file in the other application and work on it there.

▶▶ **NOTE**

Many companies offer third-party conversion programs. For example, check out Design Software's Word for Word.

▶▶ Customizing Word's Conversions

If you don't always get the results you want when you convert a document created in another application into a Word file, you can customize Word's conversions to improve compatibility with the other application. For example, differences in fonts or printer drivers in the other application might cause lines and pages to break in unsuitable places.

To customize Word's conversions, run the EditConversionsOptions macro in CONVERT.DOT:

1. First, make sure CONVERT.DOT is loaded and active. (See the section Saving Time by Converting Several Files at Once earlier in this chapter for details on how to do this.)
2. Select Tools ➤ Macro.... The Macro dialog box will appear.
3. Select the EditConversionsOptions macro and click the Run button. The Edit Conversions Options dialog box will appear, as shown in Figure 35.7.
4. Pull down the Conversion list and select the conversion you want—in the figure, I've selected Word for MS-DOS 3.0–6.0, which has a decent list of conversion options.

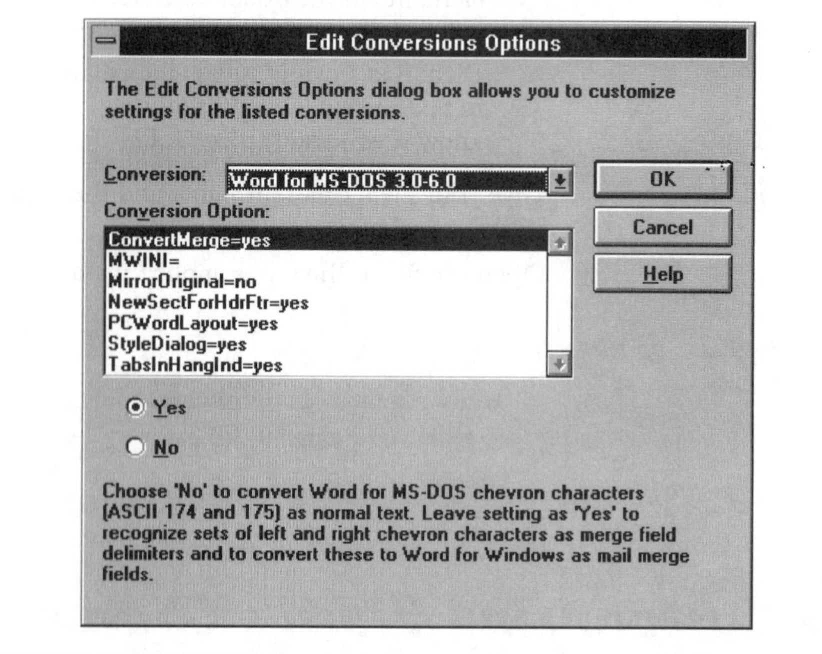

FIGURE 35.7

The Edit Conversions Options dialog box. Select the conversion you want and highlight the conversion option; the area at the bottom of the dialog box will display information on that option.

5. In the list of conversion options, highlight the one you're interested in (scroll if necessary). The area at the bottom of the dialog box will display information on that option.
6. Select Yes or No for each option you're interested in (or enter a setting in the Setting box and then click Set), then click OK to carry out your changes.

▸▸ Improving Word's Compatibility with Other Applications

Word 6 includes new options for improving Word's compatibility with the following word processors: WordPerfect, Word for Windows 1.0 and 2.0, Word for the Macintosh 5.*x*, and Word for MS-DOS. There's also a Custom choice for working with other word processors.

Word saves compatibility options with the document when you convert it. You can turn these compatibility options on or off at any time. These options affect only how the document behaves while you work with it in Word; it will still behave the same way in the other word processor if you convert it back to its original format.

To turn the compatibility options on or off:

1. Select Tools ➤ Options. The Options dialog box will appear.
2. Click the Compatibility tab to bring the compatibility options to the front (see Figure 35.8).
3. Drop down the Recommended Options For list and choose the file format you want.
4. In the Options box, check or uncheck boxes to turn the options on or off.
5. To use the compatibility options you're now setting for all new documents you create using Word, choose the Default button. Word will check that this is really what you want to do:

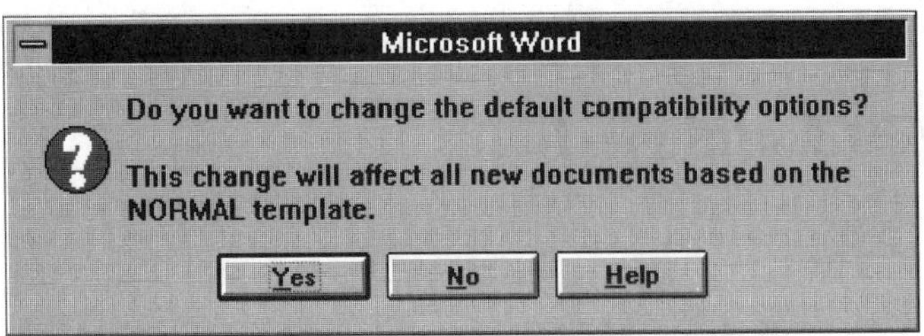

6. Click Yes if it is what you want; click No if it isn't.
7. To specify font substitution for documents that don't come through the conversion looking right, click the Font Substitution button in the Options dialog box. In the Font Substitution dialog box, select a font for which you want to change the substitution in the Missing Document Font box and then drop down the Substituted Font list and choose a suitable font. To convert fonts permanently, hit the Convert Permanently button and choose Yes in the confirmation dialog box. When you're finished assigning substitute fonts, choose OK.
8. Click OK to accept your choices and close the Options dialog box.

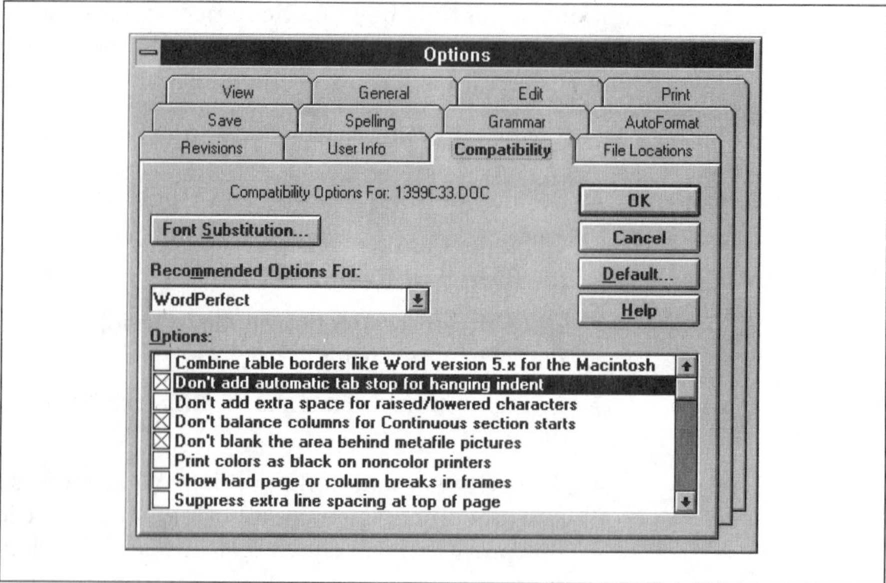

FIGURE 35.8 ▸

The Options dialog box with the compatibility options displayed.

▸▸ Make Sure You've Got the Right Filters Installed

As discussed earlier in this chapter, Word uses converters to convert documents from one file format (for example WordPerfect, Works) to another (for example, Word itself). The converters available to you depend on which ones you installed on your computer when you installed Word.

If you chose a complete installation of Word 6, all its converters and graphics filters should be available to you. But if you chose a laptop installation, a typical installation, or a custom installation, you may not have all the filters you need.

To install the filters, run the Microsoft Word Setup program again by double-clicking the Word Setup icon that should be reposing in your Program Manager. If you can't find the Word Setup icon, select File ➤ Run…, browse to find SETUP.EXE (usually in C:\WINWORD\SETUP\), and follow the instructions to install converters and filters. Bear in mind that each converter or filter you install takes up extra space on your hard drive, so if you're pressed for space, you may want to select only the converters and filters you know you'll need. (You can install further converters and filters by running Setup again at any point.)

CHAPTER 36

Personalizing Word

▸▸ FAST TRACK

You can customize Word's Toolbars **1004**

by adding and removing commands, macros, AutoText entries, fonts, and styles to them. You can create custom Toolbars and move Toolbars to different positions on the screen.

To display Toolbars **1004**

select View ➤ Toolbars... and mark the check boxes for the Toolbars you want to see.

To change Word's predefined Toolbars **1006**

select Tools ➤ Customize..., select the Toolbars tab, select a category in the Categories box, and then drag the button or item to where you want it on the Toolbar. To delete a button, drag the button off the Toolbar.

To move a Toolbar button quickly **1008**

hold down Alt and drag the button to where you want it. To copy a button, hold down Ctrl+Alt and drag the button to where you want it.

To assign an item to a Toolbar button **1013**

select Tools ➤ Customize..., choose the Toolbars tab, select the right template, select the category containing the item to add, and drag the item name from the box to the right of the Categories box to the Toolbar. Select a button, then click the Assign button.

To add a menu item 1017

select Tools ➤ Customize... and click the Menus tab. Select the template in which the item is stored, select the category to which the item belongs, and select the item you want to assign. Then choose the menu you want, choose a position for the new item, choose a name for the item, and click the Add or Add Below button.

To remove a menu item 1018

press **Ctrl+Alt+-** and click the menu item you want to remove.

To add a new menu 1020

select Tools ➤ Customize..., choose the Menus tab, and select the template for the new menu. Then select the Menu Bar button, enter the name for the menu with an ampersand (&) to designate a hot key, position the menu, and click the Add or Add After button.

To change your keyboard shortcuts 1021

select Tools ➤ Customize... and select the Keyboard tab. Then select the category containing the item you want, select the command, enter the new keyboard shortcut, and click the Assign button.

Features to assist physically challenged users 1023

are available from Microsoft and other sources.

▶▶ **T**his chapter discusses how to customize Word 6, which gives you even more flexibility than Word 2.0 did (and Word 2.0 was pretty customizable). You'll learn how to change Word's standard menu settings, Toolbars, and keyboard shortcuts. You'll learn how to add, delete, and rename menus. While reading this chapter, you might also want to refer to Appendix C, which contains a complete list of each Word command, a description of its function, some tips on use, and associated keyboard shortcuts.

▶▶ A Caution

Imagine living in a community where everyone made their own laws. One driver could decide that red traffic lights mean go and green lights mean speed (I know, some do this already). Your neighbor could decide to build a toxic-waste dump in his or her backyard (yes, likewise). Similarly, changing Word's look, feel, and functions carries risks and responsibilities.

Adding a couple of extra commands like PrevWindow and NextWindow (which take you to the previous window and next window, respectively, without your having to specify which number window you'd like) to the File or View menu won't usually harm anyone. Deleting menu items that you never use might also seem reasonable—if you never use tables, you could get rid of most of the Table menu and put something more useful in its place. But what if you substitute a tricky command like ExitWindows, which closes Word *without even giving you a chance to save changes* and then quits Windows, for File ➤ Exit? You could even give it the same hot key. Anybody who didn't know your machine wouldn't stand a chance and would probably lose unsaved work when they tried to exit Word.

Moving things from menu to menu or from Toolbar to Toolbar (or from menu to Toolbar to key combination—here's that flexibility we were talking about) may make life easier and more logical for you, but it may make life difficult for others who need to use your machine. Imagine being a temporary worker trying to figure out a completely reorganized set of Word menus, or even a copy of Word with no visible menus and most of the screen obscured by Toolbars that are not easy to remove (the menus have gone, remember). The training of new hires can be slowed by undocumented, department-wide changes to menus as well.

If you work in a large organization, your systems manager may have strong feelings about your changing Word's menus, Toolbars, and shortcuts. Check first. With that out of the way, let's look at ways to personalize Word.

What? Before we get on, you want to know what that ExitWindows command is for? When I asked that same question, I was told, "Don't ask." Perhaps if you were racing to the DOS prompt. Just watch out for someone putting an AutoExec macro (see Chapter 34 for more details) containing the command ExitWindows in your copy of Word!

►► Default Settings

Word's original settings are referred to as the *defaults.* Microsoft's designers have chosen settings they feel will work for the majority of people doing general typing and correspondence. For instance, they assume you will use standard letter-size ($8^1/_2 \times 11$") paper and have specified right, left, bottom, and top margins that should accommodate most binding, header, and footer needs. They have turned on popular Word features and turned off more esoteric ones that annoy some people. They have organized the menus for you and held back many potential menu choices.

Many of these defaults will not suit you perfectly. For instance, you probably won't want to type all your documents in Times New Roman 10 point, as Word's designers apparently would have you do. Maybe you want to use legal-size paper or print out all your documents on postcards. This is all quite natural and perfectly harmless. But rather than having to change one particular feature the same way every time you start a document, you'll probably want to change Word's default settings and save yourself time and temper.

►► Understanding and Changing Word's Options

Word gives you a great deal of control over its various features. For example, you can dictate default view settings, menu appearance, default font settings, and much more. Many of these choices are made using the Tools ➤ Options command and the tabs in the Options dialog box. These choices apply to all your Word templates.

Choices made using the Tools ➤ Customize… command and the tabs in the Customize dialog box are template specific—they apply only to the template in which you arrange them. This means you could have NORMAL.DOT and all documents based on it display the default Word menus, Toolbars, and so on, but have your CLEVERME and SPESHL4U templates and their documents display customized menus and Toolbars. This way, both you and your default temp can be happy.

► View (Show)

The View tab (see Figure 36.1) lets you control what you see in your document. For instance, if you want to see hidden text, check the Hidden Text check box. If you want a 3" style area, here's where you set it up. The following sections discuss these different options in more detail.

These are the default settings for the options on the View tab:

FEATURE	DEFAULT SETTING
Show	
Draft Font	Off
Wrap to Window	Off
Picture Placeholders	Off
Field Codes	Off
Bookmarks	Off
Field Shading	When Selected
Window	
Status Bar	On

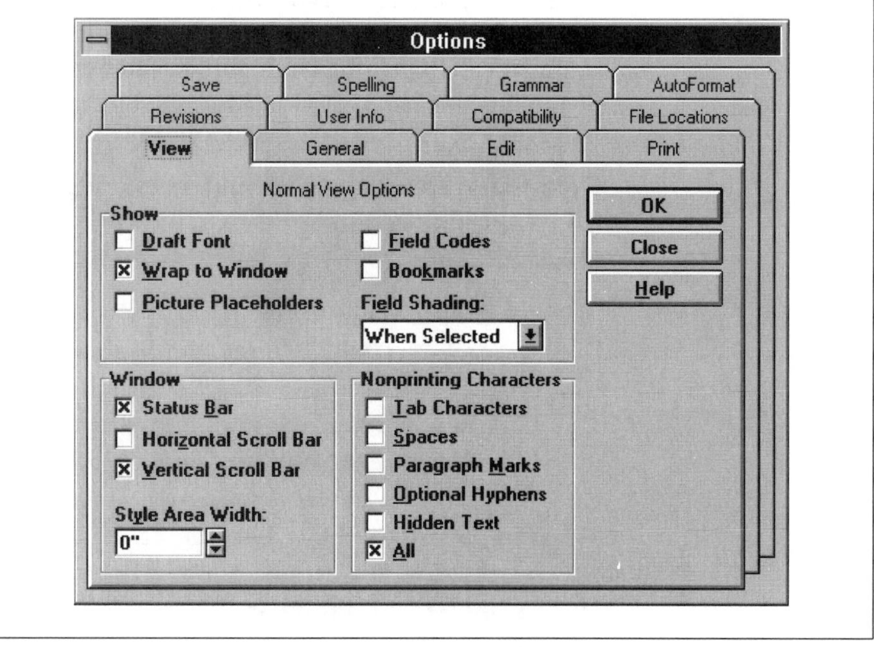

FIGURE 36.1 *The View tab on the Options dialog box. Here's where you decide what you want to see in the document. I've decided not to see the horizontal scroll bar.*

FEATURE	DEFAULT SETTING
Horizontal Scroll Bar	On
Vertical Scroll Bar	On
Style Area Width	0"
Nonprinting Characters	
Tab Characters	Off
Spaces	Off
Paragraph Marks	Off
Optional Hyphens	Off
Hidden Text	Off
All	Off

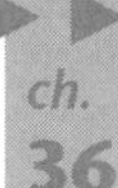

Draft Font

The Draft Font choice is for Outline and Normal views and determines whether Word displays your prose in the fonts you've chosen or in its draft font. The draft font is the font used in the menus, the message boxes telling you your system is about to crash, and so on. It's faster to use than your fancy fonts; it's also uglier. Use this option when you're hacking the text in large documents on a small-brained computer and you're not worried about how things look on-screen.

Draft font displays any character formatting as underlined and bold. All for speed.

▸▸ NOTE

When you're in Page Layout view, you'll get three different options: Draft Font will change to Drawings. Again, this speeds scrolling the document. You'll also get an Object Anchors option, which displays the anchor connecting an anchored object to a paragraph as a little anchor symbol. Text Boundaries displays dotted lines around page margins, text columns, objects, and formats.

Wrap to Window

Wrap to Window wraps the text from one line to the next within the document window. Use this when you need to work with several windows visible on your desktop at the same time and you don't want your text to be wider than the window.

Picture Placeholders

On slower PCs, Word can slow to a crawl if your document contains large graphics. To speed work in such documents, mark the Picture Placeholders check box to display graphics as empty boxes.

Field Codes

You'll probably want to view field codes rather than field results when you're inserting and editing fields. Simply check the check box. As you learned in Chapter 32, fields look like this:

```
{ EDITTIME \* MERGEFORMAT }
```

Bookmarks

Check the Bookmarks check box to display the bookmarks and links your document contains. Bookmarks appear in square gray brackets.

Field Shading

When you're working with a document that contains fields, you can choose to have their results shaded so you can avoid changing them by mistake—remember, the results may look like regular text. Choose from When Selected (when the insertion point is in the field), Always, and Never.

Status Bar

If you find the information on the status bar confusing, or if you simply need more space on your screen for displaying your immortal words in huge point sizes, uncheck this box to remove the status bar.

Horizontal Scroll Bar

If you never use the horizontal scroll bar—and why should you, if your documents fit in the width of the screen and you don't need the three buttons to flip between views—you can remove it by unchecking the check box. That'll give you a little more space on the screen.

Vertical Scroll Bar

If you always use the keyboard for moving through your documents, you may want to remove the vertical scroll bar from your screen to give yourself a bit more space. Simply uncheck the box, and it'll be gone.

Style Area Width

You'll recall that the style area is the area to the left of the text that shows the applied style names. By default, the style area width is 0", so you don't see it. To display it, enter a positive decimal measurement, such as 0.5." (That should be enough for most of the predefined style names; if you define styles with long names, enter a larger measurement.) To rid the display of the style area, enter 0 (that's an actual zero, not a capital O).

Tab Characters

Check the Tab Characters check box to display tabs as right-pointing arrows. You may want to do this if you're aligning things and can't be bothered to use tables.

Spaces

Check the Spaces check box to display spaces entered with the spacebar as dots about halfway up the height of the line. This helps you find double or triple spaces in proportional fonts.

Paragraph Marks

Check the Paragraph Marks check box to display hard returns entered with ↵ as ¶. This can be especially useful when you're editing a document that uses styles and deleting the wrong paragraph mark inadvertently will apply the wrong style to your text.

Optional Hyphens

Optional hyphens—the ones you insert to indicate where to break a word if it falls at the end of a line—are normally not displayed. To display them, check the Optional Hyphens check box.

Hidden Text

To view hidden text, check the Hidden Text check box. It will appear as text with a dotted underline. Bear in mind that while viewing hidden text will change the line breaks and pagination of your document, hidden text will not print unless you've selected the Hidden Text option in the Include with Document area on the Print tab in the Options dialog box. (Phew! That was a mouthful!)

All

Check this check box to display all the nonprinting characters—tabs, spaces, paragraph marks, optional hyphens, and hidden text. (If you don't always want these displayed, you can get the same effect by clicking the Show/Hide ¶ button on the Standard Toolbar.)

▶ General Options

The options on the General tab (see Figure 36.2) modify Word settings such as the default units of measurement and the display of three-dimensional effects. You can also choose how many of your last-opened files Word tacks onto the bottom of the File menu, whether Word repaginates your document in the background as you work, and whether Word beeps at you when you screw up. This is a good tab to mess around with.

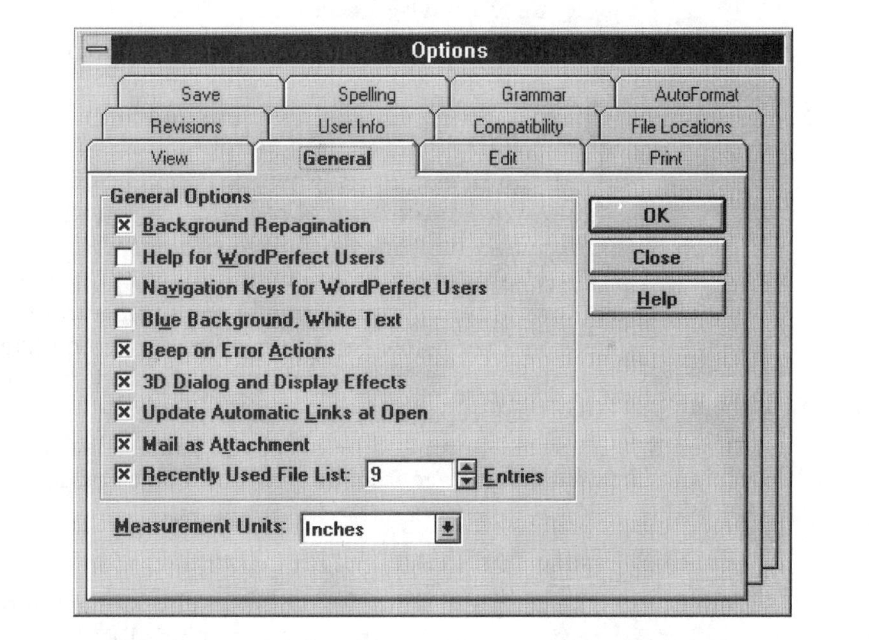

FIGURE 36.2 ▶

The General tab of the Options dialog box. Decide how many of your last-opened files Word tacks onto the bottom of the File menu. I've gone for the max—nine.

In the following sections we'll look briefly at each of the settings on the General tab. But first, a brief intermission, during which we bring you the default settings:

FEATURE	DEFAULT SETTING
Background Repagination	On
Help for WordPerfect Users	(User prompt at installation)

FEATURE	DEFAULT SETTING
Navigation Keys for WordPerfect Users	Off
Blue Background, White Text	Off
Beep on Error Actions	On
3D Dialog and Display Effects	On
Update Automatic Links at Open	On
Mail as Attachment	On
Recently Used File List	On; 4 Entries
Measurement Unit	Inches

Background Repagination

With the Background Repagination check box checked, as it is by default, Word automatically repaginates your documents as you work, computing new lines and page endings whenever you are not typing. There's not much wrong with that except it takes a bit of your computer's memory, so unless you're running an immensely complex project on a very slow computer or you're typing like an infinite number of monkeys, I suggest you leave this checked. If you uncheck the box, Word will repaginate only when you tell it to by running the ToolsRepaginate command or when you print. (Background repagination is always on in Page Layout view and Print Preview. Think about it.)

Help for WordPerfect Users

The Help for WordPerfect Users check box will be selected if you agreed to have it active when you installed Word. With this option selected, Word displays information or demonstrates a command when you press a WordPerfect for DOS key combination in Word. This sort of disables Word's own key combinations, so you'll have to make up your mind about which to use.

Navigation Keys for WordPerfect Users

Check the Navigation Keys for WordPerfect Users check box to change the functions of the Page Up, Page Down, Home, End, and Esc keys to their WordPerfect equivalents. Bear in mind that this disables those keys' regular functions for Word.

Blue Background, White Text

Check this check box to display the text as white characters on a blue background. Don't ask how this is supposed to help you.

Beep on Error Actions

Here's a good one. When the Beep on Error Actions check box is checked, as it is by default, Word will give you a subtle auditory admonition whenever you screw up. If this bugs you, uncheck the check box to get the sounds of silence.

3D Dialog and Display Effects

The 3D Dialog and Display Effects check box controls the appearance of the dialog boxes. If you prefer them plain and two-dimensional (for that flat-screen effect), uncheck it. They may also appear a tad more quickly.

Update Automatic Links at Open

The Update Automatic Links at Open check box is one you might seriously consider unchecking. When it's checked, any information in a document that's linked to other files is updated every time you open the document. If you're linked to something fancy, like a drawing-application figure or six, you'll be subjected to a few minutes of your hard disk grinding before you can use the document. Then again, keeping it checked will keep your documents up to date. Forcibly.

Mail as Attachment

Check the Mail as Attachment check box to attach documents to a mail message. You need to have an e-mail program installed on your computer to use this option.

Recently Used File List

The Recently Used File List box controls the number of your last-used files that appear at the bottom of the File menu. Choose between 0 and 9. Most people find this feature useful, but some consider it a threat to security. (The boss can find out about all those letters you were writing while ostensibly working on your report.) You decide. If you add any commands to the File menu and choose 9 for this list, the menu may not fit on your screen. Life's tough.

Measurement Units

Pull down the Measurement Units list and choose Inches, Centimeters, Points, or Picas as the default measurement unit for Word. You may want to choose Points or Picas if you're typesetting things.

► Edit Options

The Editing tab (see Figure 36.3) is where you control a whole bunch of important options that affect the way you work. This is where you control whether what you type will replace a selection or bump it along, how Word handles drag-and-drop editing, and whether Word worries about extra spaces when you use cut and paste.

FIGURE 36.3 ►

The Editing tab of the Options dialog box.

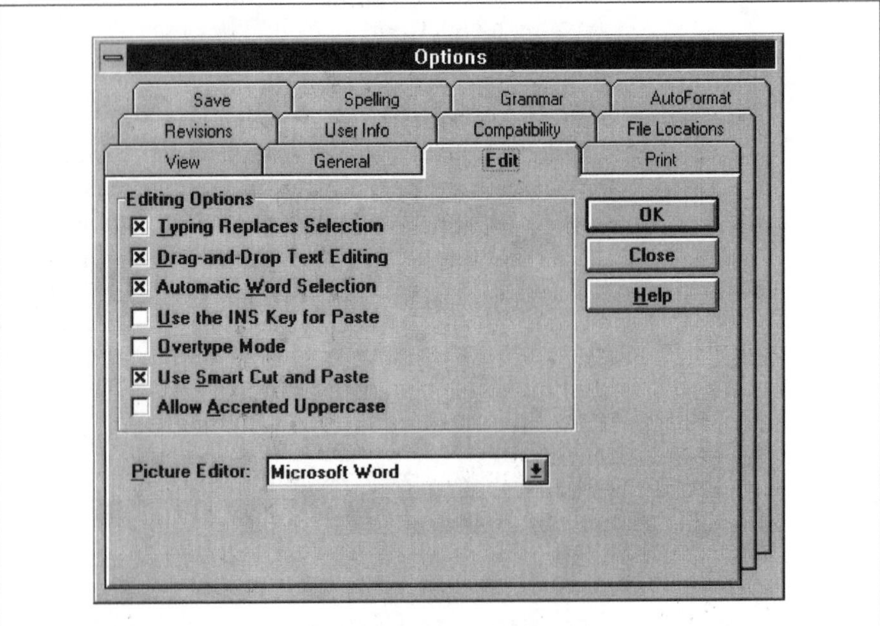

In the following sections, we'll look at each of the options on the Edit tab. But first, here are their default settings:

FEATURE	DEFAULT SETTING
Typing Replaces Selection	On
Drag-and-Drop Text Editing	On

FEATURE	DEFAULT SETTING
Automatic Word Selection	On
Use the INS Key for Paste	Off
Overtype Mode	Off
Use Smart Cut and Paste	On
Allow Accented Uppercase	Off
Picture Editor	Microsoft Word

Typing Replaces Selection

With the Typing Replaces Selection check box checked, any text you've selected gets deleted as soon as you start typing. This saves you the step of deleting a selection when you want to replace it, but if your mind doesn't work that way and you find this option awkward, uncheck the check box. Then selected text will be bumped along to the right when you type something.

Drag-and-Drop Text Editing

Drag and drop, as you'll recall from Chapter 2, lets you move or copy selected text without pasting it to the Clipboard. If you never use it, turn it off by unchecking the Drag-and-Drop Text Editing check box.

Automatic Word Selection

new

When the Automatic Word Selection check box is checked, Word selects the entire word (*including any trailing space at the end*) when you select any part of it by dragging the mouse pointer from the previous word. If this bugs you (it does me), uncheck the check box.

Use the Ins Key for Paste

Check the Use the INS Key for Paste check box if you get tired of pressing Shift+Ins to insert the contents of the Clipboard into your document. Needless to say, this stops you from using the Ins key to toggle between Insert and Overtype modes.

Overtype Mode

Check the Overtype Mode check box to have Overtype mode turned on by default when you use Word for Windows. Few people want this.

Use Smart Cut and Paste

Check the Use Smart Cut and Paste check box to have Word automatically remove extra spaces when you delete text or add spaces when you insert text. This isn't one hundred percent perfect, but it's pretty cool. If smart cut and paste offend thee, pluck it out.

Allow Accented Uppercase

Check the Allow Accented Uppercase check box if you're working with text formatted as French and you want to allow the spelling and grammar checkers to suggest that Word add an accent mark to an uppercase letter. If you're not working in French, leave this check box unchecked, as it is by default.

Picture Editor

Select the application you want to use as a picture editor from the drop-down list. Your choices will depend on what's loaded on your machine.

▸ Printing Options

The Print tab (see Figure 36.4) allows you to make some vital settings, so listen up for a minute. You can decide to print backwards (á la Merlin), you can make sure fields and links get updated before you print, and you can print stuff like annotations and hidden text with your document.

In the following sections we'll look at each option in turn. Before that, let's take a quick glance at their default settings:

FEATURE	DEFAULT SETTING
Printing Options	
Draft Output	Off
Reverse Print Order	Off

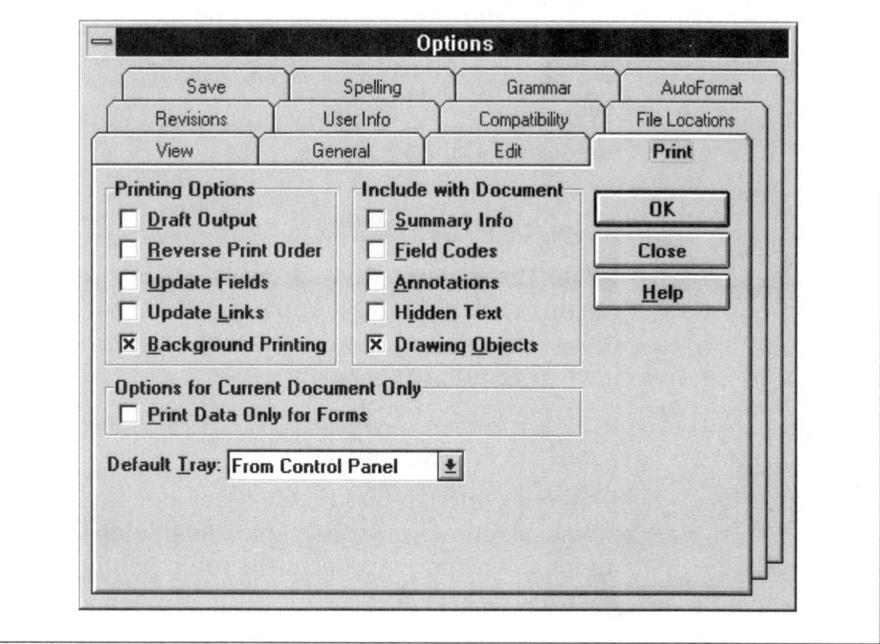

FIGURE 36.4 *The Print tab of the Options dialog box.*

FEATURE	DEFAULT SETTING
Update Fields	Off
Update Links	Off
Background Printing	On
Include with Document	
Summary Info	Off
Field Codes	Off
Annotations	Off
Hidden Text	Off
Drawing Objects	On
Options for Current Document Only	
Print Data Only for Forms	Off
Default Tray	From Control Panel

Draft Output

Check the Draft Output check box to print your documents with minimal formatting. The amount of formatting that will be printed depends on the printer. As its name implies, this option is intended for fast printing of drafts of documents.

Reverse Print Order

Check the Reverse Print Order check box to print your documents starting at the last page. You might want to use this if you've got one of those weird copiers that reverses the order of collated copies. Don't use it when printing envelopes.

Update Fields

Make sure the Update Fields check box is checked if you want all fields in your document (for example, date fields and page numbers) to be updated whenever you print. If you're aiming for special effects, uncheck this check box.

Update Links

Check the Update Links check box to have all links in your document updated every time you print. If the sources for your links are apt to change or be unavailable, leave this check box unchecked.

Background Printing

Check the Background Printing check box if you want to be able to continue working in Word while you print a document. Bear in mind that background printing takes up memory and is liable to slow down both your work and your printing, thus vexing you mightily. I'd recommend unchecking this check box.

Summary Info

Check the Summary Info check box to have Word print file-summary information on a separate page after printing the document.

Field Codes

Check the Field Codes check box to have Word print the field codes rather than the field results in the document.

Annotations

Check the Annotations check box to have Word print out a document's annotations on a separate page at the end of the document.

Hidden Text

Check the Hidden Text check box to have Word print out any hidden text the document contains. Hidden text will look like normal text when printed; Word doesn't print the dotted underline you see for hidden text on the screen. Bear in mind that printing hidden text will affect line and page breaks in your document; if that matters to you, view hidden text on-screen before printing it and do any necessary fiddling with line and page breaks.

Drawing Objects

Check the Drawing Objects check box to have Word print drawing objects (for example charts, graphics, and equations) created in Word with the document.

Print Data Only on Forms

Check the Print Data Only on Forms check box to print only the information entered in form fields in a form—not the form itself. You might want to use this for filling in preprinted forms. Note that this option applies only to the current document, not to all documents.

Default Tray

Choose a default paper tray from the drop-down list. The default setting is From Control Panel, as that's where you'll probably set printing options for all your Windows applications. If you want to use different paper sources for different sections of documents (for example, if you're printing an envelope and a letter), use File ➤ Page Setup….

▸ Options for Revision Marks

Word 6 lets different reviewers on the same document use different-colored revision marks. Choose Tools ➤ Options and select the Revisions tab of the Options dialog box (see Figure 36.5) to specify the revision options you want.

FIGURE 36.5

The Revisions tab of the Options dialog box.

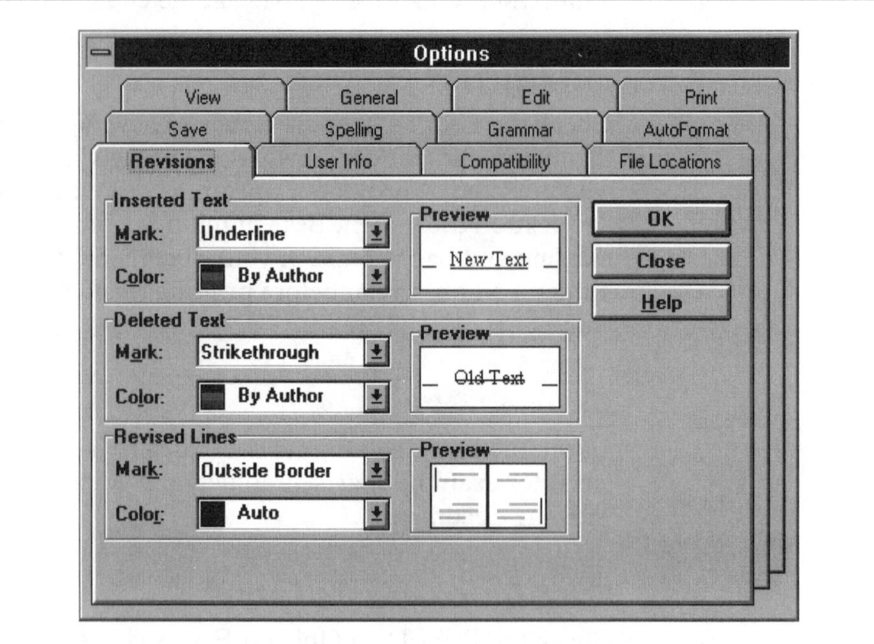

In the following sections we'll discuss each option in turn, but here are the default settings for the Revisions tab:

FEATURE	DEFAULT SETTING
Inserted Text	
Mark	Underline
Color	By Author
Deleted Text	
Mark	Strikethrough
Color	By Author

FEATURE	DEFAULT SETTING
Revised Lines	
Mark	Outside Border
Color	Auto

Inserted Text

Drop down the list for the Mark option and select the format with which you want mark new text. Choose from none, Bold, Italic, Underline, and Double Underline.

Color for Inserted Text

Drop down the list for the Color for New Text option and select the color with which you want to mark new text. Choose By Author for automatic choice of colors by Word for the first eight people to revise the document (after that, Word starts over with the colors), or choose one of the colors manually.

Mark Deleted Text

Use the Mark drop-down list to select how you want to display text you are deleting from the document. Choose Hidden or Strikethrough.

Color for Deleted Text

Drop down the Color list and select the color with which you want to mark deleted text. Choose By Author for automatic choice of colors by Word for the first eight people to revise the document (after that, Word starts over with the colors) or choose one of the colors manually.

Mark Revised Lines

Drop down the Mark list and select how to mark revised lines. Choose from None, Left Border, Right Border, or Outside Border (the default).

Color for Revised Lines

Drop down the list and select the color with which to mark revised lines. Choose By Author for automatic choice of colors by Word for the first eight people to revise the document (after that, Word starts over

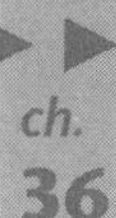

with the colors), or choose one of the colors manually. Consider using a different color for each group of authors when working on large projects with more than eight authors.

▶ User Info

The User Info tab (see Figure 36.6) specifies information about the primary user of the copy of Word for Windows you are using: the name, the return address for envelopes, and the initials to be used for annotations.

For a little change of pace, the User Info tab doesn't have default options worth listing. It takes its information from what you entered when installing Word.

Name

Type the name for Word to use as the author in the summary information (File ➤ Summary Info) for documents you create. The default setting is the name entered when installing Word.

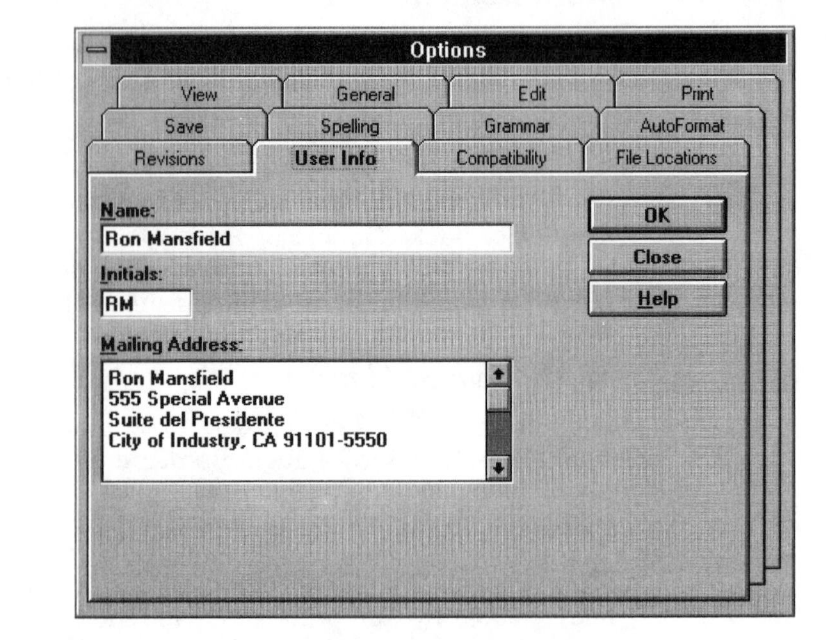

FIGURE 36.6 ▶

The User Info tab of the Options dialog box.

Initials

Enter the initials you want Word to use for annotation marks. The default setting is the initials entered for the name when installing Word.

Mailing Address

The Mailing Address area displays the return address used on envelopes once you've used the Create Envelope command. Until then, the default setting is the address entered when installing Word. Any address you enter here will be displayed as the return address in the Envelopes and Labels dialog box.

▶ Compatibility Options

The options on the Compatibility tab determine how Word displays documents created either in earlier versions of Word or in other word processing programs. Use these settings to make documents in Word 6 more closely match the original documents.

Figure 36.7 shows the Compatibility tab of the Options dialog box.

Font Substitution

Select the Font Substitution button to choose substitute fonts for fonts used in the active document that are not available on your computer.

Recommended Options For

Pull down the Recommended Options For drop-down list and select the word-processing application for which to set options. Select Custom to specify options for an unlisted application. In the list of Options, check the options you want to use.

▶ File Locations

The File Locations tab (see Figure 36.8) of the Options dialog box lets you define where your documents, templates, and other items are stored by default.

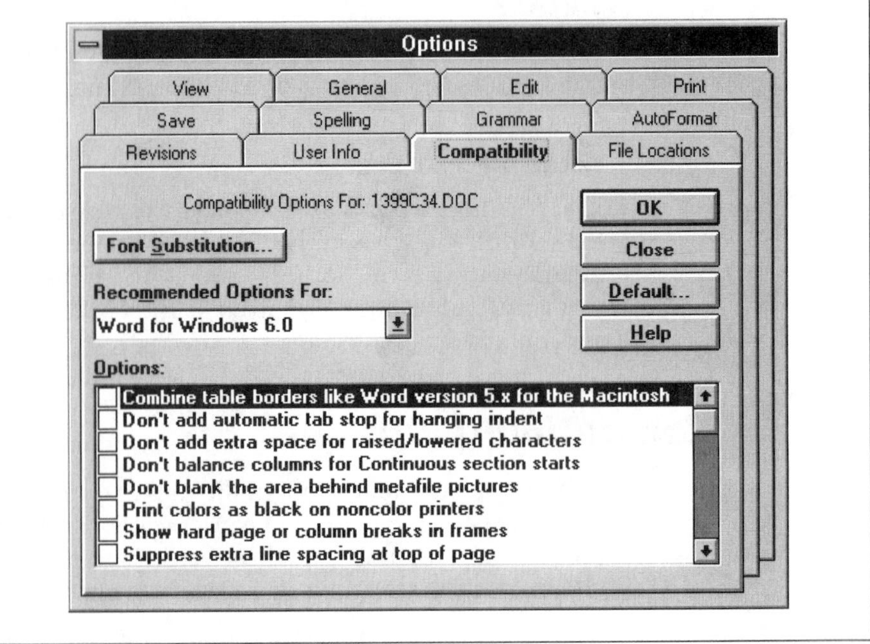

FIGURE 36.7

The Compatibility tab of the Options dialog box.

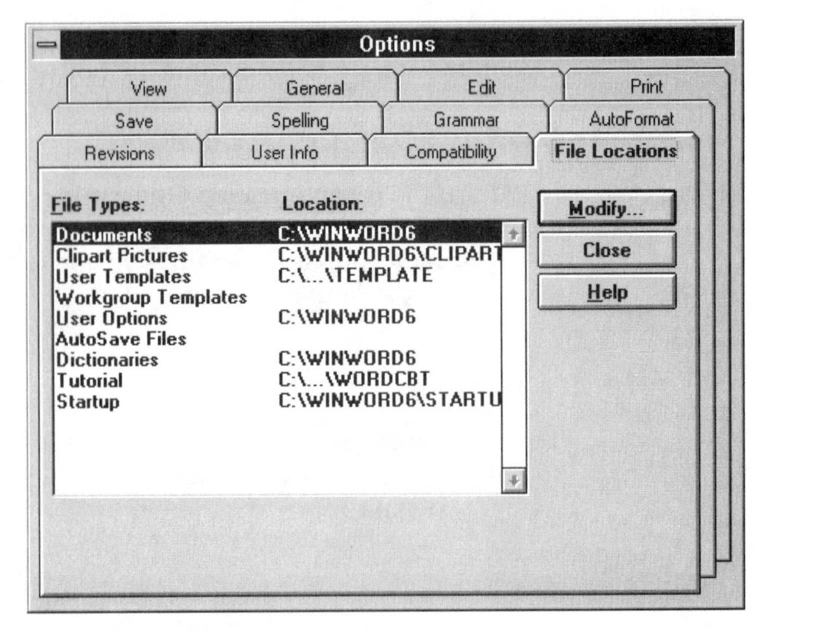

FIGURE 36.8

The File Locations tab of the Options dialog box. Here you can define where your documents, templates, and other items are stored by default.

Here are the default settings for options on the File Locations tab:

FILE TYPE	DEFAULT LOCATION
Documents	C:\WINWORD
Clipart Pictures	C:\WINWORD\CLIPART
User Templates	C:\WINWORD\TEMPLATE
Workgroup Templates	(Depends on workgroup selections)
User Options	C:\WINWORD
AutoSave Files	(Depends on system settings)
Dictionaries	C:\WINWORD
Tutorial	C:\WINWORD\WORDCBT
Startup	C:\WINWORD\STARTUP

To set a new default location for an item, select the item and choose the Modify button. In the Modify Location dialog box, select the drive and directory for the item, and then click OK. (You can create a new subdirectory by clicking the New button.)

TIP

Define a new default location for documents to keep them apart from your Word program files.

Save Options

The settings on the Save tab in the Options dialog box (see Figure 36.9) let you customize how and when you save your documents and choose protection for file sharing for the current document.

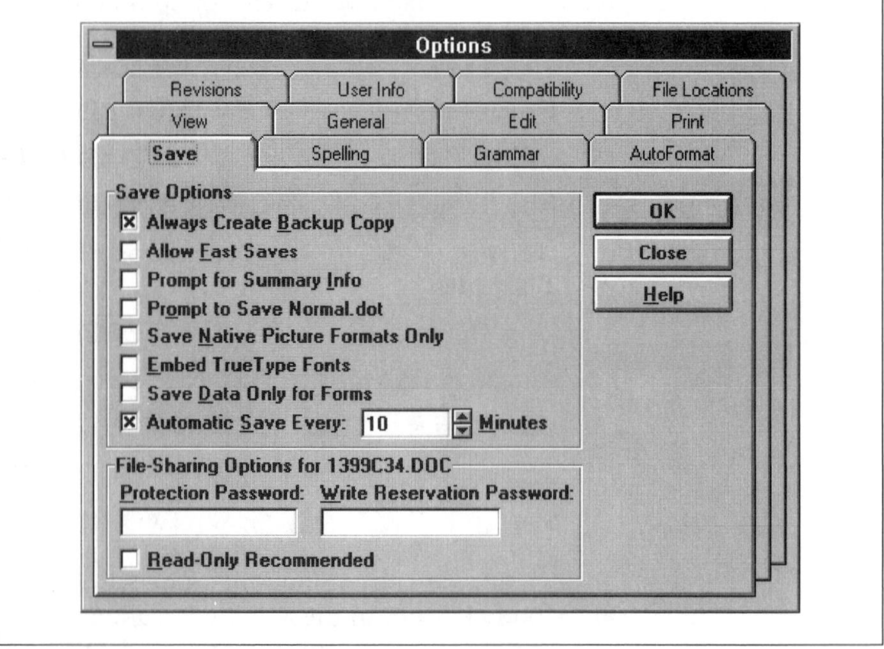

FIGURE 36.9

The Save tab of the Options dialog box. Here you can decide how and when you save your documents and choose protection for file sharing for the current document. I've chosen to always create a backup copy and not use the fast-save option.

In the following sections we'll look at each of the options. But first, here's a sneak preview of their settings:

FEATURE	DEFAULT
Save Options	
Always Create Backup Copy	Off
Allow Fast Saves	On
Prompt for Summary Info	Off
Prompt to Save Normal.dot	Off
Save Native Picture Formats Only	Off
Embed TrueType Fonts	Off
Save Data Only for Forms	Off
Automatic Save Every:	On; 10 Minutes
File Sharing Options	
Protection Password	Off

Write Reservation Password	Off
Read-Only Recommended	Off

Always Create Backup Copy

Check the Always Create Backup Copy check box to have Word make automatic backups for you. Each time you save a document, Word saves a duplicate with a .BAK extension. This is a useful option if you tend to bastardize your documents by mistake, but bear in mind that it doubles your disk-space requirements.

Allow Fast Saves

Check the Allow Fast Saves check box to speed up saving. Word then records only the changes to the document when you save it (rather than resaving the whole file).

NOTE

Fast saves take up more space than regular saves. It can also cause problems for some third-party conversion programs. If you're strapped for space, consider switching off fast saves.

Prompt for Summary Info

Check the Prompt for Summary Info check box to have Word display the Summary Info dialog box automatically whenever you save a new document. If you use the Summary Info dialog box to set up headers or footers in your document, you'll probably want to enable this option.

Prompt to Save Normal.dot

Check the Prompt to Save Normal.dot check box if you want Word to consult you before saving changes you made to the default settings in your Word session when you exit Word. This box is unchecked by default, so Word automatically saves changes to NORMAL.DOT when you exit Word.

Save Native Picture Formats Only

Check the Save Native Picture Formats Only check box if you want to save only the Windows version of imported graphics. If you bring graphics into Word from another platform (for example, from the Macintosh), you can reduce the size of the Word document by storing only the version of the graphics that is native to Word.

Embed TrueType Fonts

Check the Embed TrueType Fonts check box if you want others who read the document on PCs that do not have the fonts used in it to be able to view it with the right fonts. If you're not sharing documents, leave this box unchecked.

Save Data Only for Forms

Check the Save Data Only for Forms check box to save the data in a form as a record you can use in a database. To save the data with the form, leave this box unchecked.

Automatic Save Every nn Minutes

Check the Automatic Save Every *nn* Minutes check box to have Word provide a safety net for you in the event of a power failure or computer crash. When you restart Word after a power failure or a crash, Word will open all documents open at the time of the crash and display (Recovered) in the title.

Set the number of minutes between 1 and 120. While Word autosaves your document, you'll have to stop working for a few seconds.

Protection Password

Enter a password (up to 15 characters: letters, spaces, symbols, and numbers are all okay) in the Protection Password text box to prevent other users from opening the current document.

Write Reservation Password

Enter a password (up to 15 characters: letters, spaces, symbols, and numbers all OK) in the Write Reservation Password text box to prevent other users from saving changes to the current document. Reenter the password in the confirmation dialog box. You'll then need to enter the password to open the document normally, but you can open the document as read-only by choosing the Read-Only button in the Password dialog box.

Read-Only Recommended

Check the Read-Only Recommended check box to recommend that others open the current document as read-only. (It's only a recommendation—they can disregard it.)

▶ Spelling Options

The settings on the Spelling tab in the Options dialog box let you control the behavior of Word's spelling checker. You can instruct the spelling checker to ignore certain words, use up to ten dictionaries, and use a specific language. Figure 36.10 shows the Spelling tab of the Options dialog box.

FIGURE 36.10 ▶

The Spelling tab of the Options dialog box. I've added my custom dictionary from Word 2.0 for Windows.

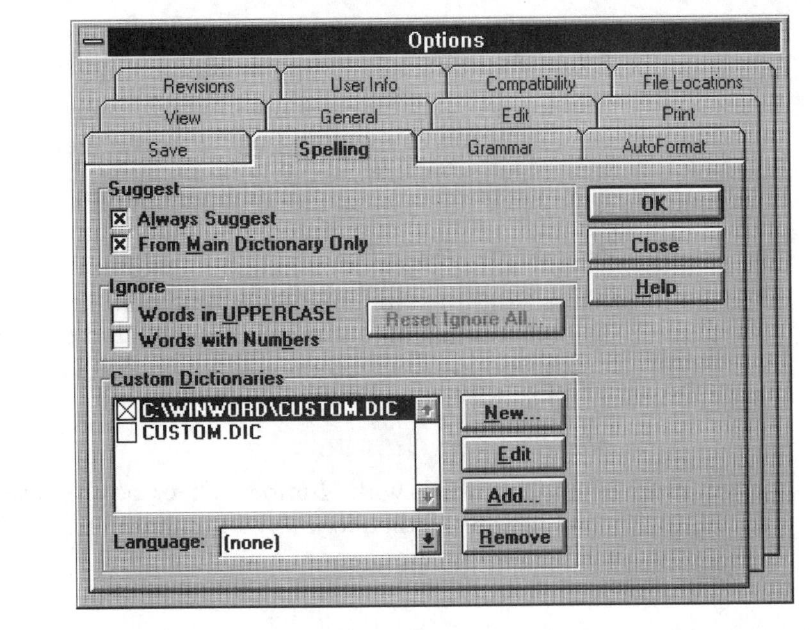

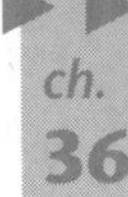

In the following sections, we'll look at each of the options. But first, here's a preview of their default settings:

FEATURE	DEFAULT SETTING
Suggest	
Always Suggest	On
From Main Dictionary Only	On
Ignore	
Words in UPPERCASE	Off
Words with Numbers	Off
Custom Dictionaries	
CUSTOM.DIC	On
Language	[None]

Always Suggest

Check the Always Suggest check box to have Word display suggested spellings for misspelled words it finds during a spelling check.

From Main Dictionary Only

Check the From Main Dictionary Only check box to have Word display suggested correct spellings from the main dictionary but not from any open custom dictionaries.

Words in UPPERCASE

Check the Words in UPPERCASE check box to have Word's spelling checker ignore words in which every character is uppercase. This is useful for working with technical terms, abbreviations, and so on.

Words with Numbers

Check the Words with Numbers check box to have Word's spell checker ignore any word that contains a number. This too is useful for working with technical terms and the like.

Reset Ignore All

Click the Reset Ignore All button to stop Word from ignoring the words you marked with Ignore All during the current Word session. This button isn't available till you've told Word to ignore all instances of a word.

Custom Dictionaries

Check any dictionary available here to activate it. You can then add words to it that aren't in the main dictionary when you run a spelling check.

New

Click the New button to display the Create Custom Dictionary dialog box and create a new custom dictionary that you can teach all the words that Word's main dictionary disagrees with. This way, you can have different dictionaries for different types of work.

Edit

Highlight a custom dictionary and then click the Edit button to open it as a Word document so you can edit it. This is useful for removing misspelled words that creep into your dictionaries over the course of time.

Add

Click the Add button if you want to add a custom dictionary to the list for checking spelling.

Remove

To remove a custom dictionary from the Custom Dictionaries list, select it and click the Remove button.

Language

Pull down the Language list and choose a language to apply its formatting to a custom dictionary. Then Word will use that custom dictionary only when checking text formatted in that language. Format the dictionary as None to have Word use that dictionary when checking text formatted in any language.

▸ Grammar

Here's where you get to choose which rules Word's grammar checker uses when critiquing your documents. Figure 36.11 shows the Grammar tab of the Options dialog box.

Here are the default settings for the options on the Grammar tab:

FEATURE	DEFAULT SETTING
Use Grammar and Style Rules	For Business Writing
Check Spelling	On
Show Readability Statistics	On

Use Grammar and Style Rules

Choose from Strictly (All Rules), For Business Writing, and For Casual Writing to define which rules Word uses when grammar-checking your documents. Choose Custom 1, Custom 2, or Custom 3 to set up your own rules without disturbing Word's preset offerings.

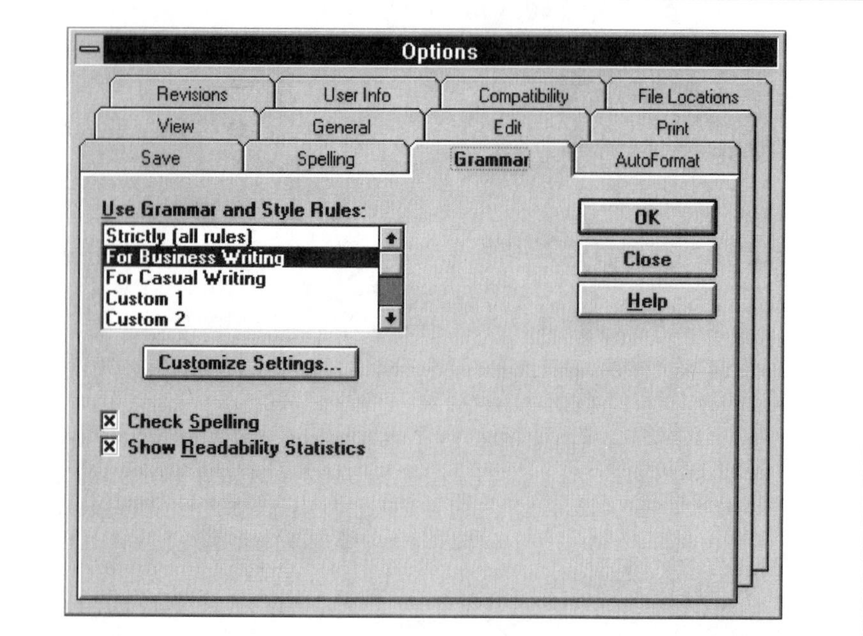

FIGURE 36.11 *The Grammar tab of the Options dialog box. Choose the rules you want Word to apply to your documents.*

Customize Settings

Click the Customize Settings button to produce the Customize Grammar Settings dialog box, in which you can choose which rules to apply by default to your documents.

Check Spelling

Uncheck the Check Spelling check box (checked by default) if you don't want to check spelling in your documents while checking the grammar—for example, if you've already run a spelling check on your document and don't want to have to click the Ignore button again fifty times.

Show Readability Statistics

Uncheck the Show Readability Statistics check box (checked by default) if you don't want to see the Readability Statistics dialog box after each completed grammar check. Microsoft has removed from Word 6 the Gunning Fog Index reading, which was the only fun statistic in the Readability Statistics dialog box in Word 2.0x.

▶ AutoFormat Options

The options on the AutoFormat tab (see Figure 36.12) let you set rules for Word to follow when it automatically formats text with the built-in styles. For example, you can instruct Word to replace straight quotes with smart quotes.

Here are the default settings for the options on the AutoFormat tab:

FEATURE	DEFAULT SETTING
Preserve	
Previously Applied Styles	On
Apply Styles To	
Headings	On
Lists	On
Other Paragraphs	On

FEATURE	DEFAULT SETTING
Adjust	
Paragraph Marks	On
Tabs and Spaces	On
Empty Paragraphs	On
Replace	
Straight Quotes with Smart Quotes	On
Symbol Characters with Symbols	On
Bullet Characters with Bullets	On

Previously Applied Styles

Check the Previously Applied Styles check box to have Word retain styles you applied when it automatically formats the document.

Headings

Check the Headings check box if you want Word to automatically apply Heading 1 through Heading 9 styles to headings.

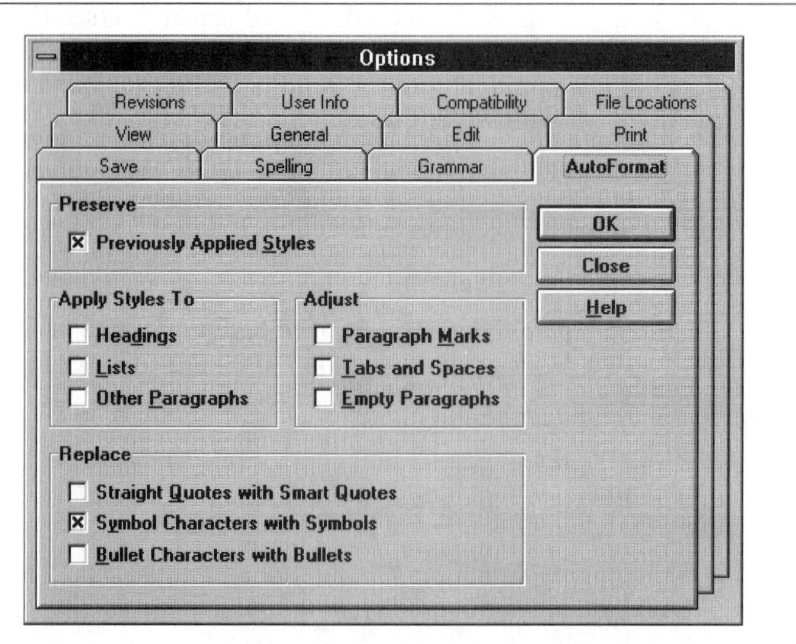

FIGURE 36.12 *The AutoFormat tab of the Options dialog box. As you can see, I've unchecked the options I don't like—most of them!*

Lists

Check the Lists check box if you want Word to automatically apply list and bullet styles to numbered, bulleted, and multilevel lists. Bear in mind that Word will automatically remove any manually inserted numbers or bullets in the process.

Other Paragraphs

Check the Other Paragraphs check box if you want Word to automatically apply paragraph styles other than the styles for headings and lists. For example, with Other Paragraphs checked, Word could apply Body Text style and so on.

Paragraph Marks

Check the Paragraph Marks check box if you want Word to standardize spacing in the document by removing paragraph marks it considers unnecessary (for example, a paragraph mark at the end of a line that would normally wrap) or adding paragraph marks it thinks your document is missing.

Tabs and Spaces

Check the Tabs and Spaces check box if you want Word to standardize spacing by replacing spaces with tabs and removing tabs and spaces it considers unnecessary. Be prepared for a few disagreements if you check this box.

Empty Paragraphs

Check the Empty Paragraphs check box if you want Word to standardize spacing by removing blank lines between paragraphs with certain styles—for example, between body text and body text.

Straight Quotes with Smart Quotes

Check the Straight Quotes with Smart Quotes check box if you want Word to replace ″″ with “” and ″ with ‘’ when it formats your document.

Symbol Characters with Symbols

Check the Symbol Characters with Symbols check box if you want Word to replace characters used in place of symbols with symbols—for example, (TM) with ™, (R) with ®, and (C) with ©.

Bullet Characters with Bullets

Check the Bullet Characters with Bullets check box if you want Word to replace characters used as bullets (for example, * or +) with •.

►► Customizing Word's Toolbars

You can customize Word 6's Toolbars to simplify the way you work. You can add and remove commands, macros, AutoText entries, and styles and move buttons from one Toolbar to another. You can even create custom Toolbars. You can move Toolbars to different positions on the screen or have them float freely above the document. You can move and resize a floating Toolbar as if it were a window. In the following sections we'll look at the different things you can do with Toolbars.

Figure 36.13 shows how zany you can get with Toolbars by illustrating the "text porthole" concept.

► Displaying Toolbars

To display Toolbars, select View ➤ Toolbars. In the Toolbars dialog box (see Figure 36.14), check the check boxes for the Toolbars you want to see and click OK.

►► NOTE

You can't display the Mail Merge Toolbar unless you're running a mail merge. (Select Tools ➤ Mail Merge to fire up the Mail Merge Helper.)

To remove a Toolbar from the screen, select View ➤ Toolbars and uncheck the check box for the guilty party.

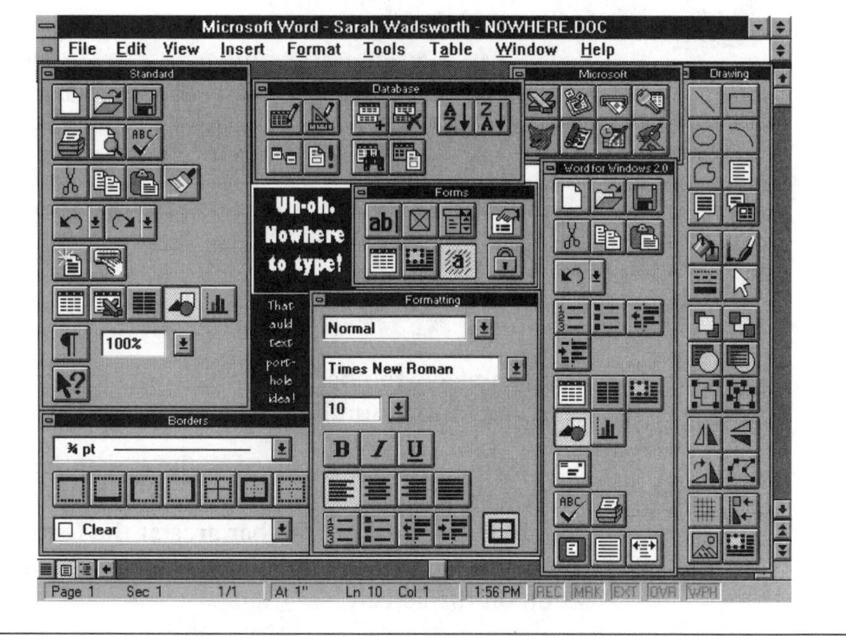

FIGURE 36.13

I've arranged my Toolbars for ease of access.

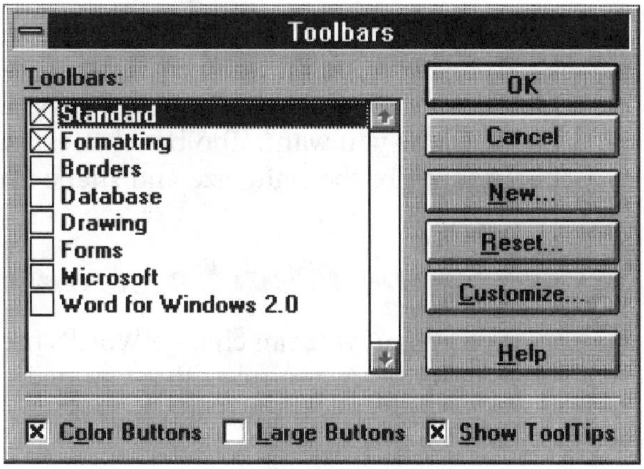

Toolbars

Toolbars:

- ☒ Standard
- ☒ Formatting
- ☐ Borders
- ☐ Database
- ☐ Drawing
- ☐ Forms
- ☐ Microsoft
- ☐ Word for Windows 2.0

OK | Cancel | New... | Reset... | Customize... | Help

☒ Color Buttons ☐ Large Buttons ☒ Show ToolTips

FIGURE 36.14

The Toolbars dialog box. Check the check boxes for the Toolbars you want to see.

▸▸ TIP

To display and remove Toolbars using the mouse, right-click on a displayed Toolbar to display a shortcut menu and click to display an unchecked Toolbar or to hide a checked Toolbar. Click Toolbars or Customize to display the Toolbars or Customize dialog box, respectively.

▸ Moving and Resizing Toolbars

You can place Toolbars anywhere on your screen that suits you and resize them to a number of shapes.

To move a Toolbar displayed at the top of the screen, click in the blank space and drag it to where you want it. It'll change shape as soon as you drag it out of the Toolbar area at the top of the screen. Alternatively, double-click in the blank space to display it in its last floating position on the screen.

To return a Toolbar to the top of the screen, click in the blank space and drag it to the top of the screen, where it'll revert to its long and wide shape. Alternatively, double-click in the blank space to flip it back up there.

To resize a Toolbar, move the mouse pointer over one of its borders so that a double-headed arrow appears, then click and drag the border to the shape you want. Toolbar shapes adjust in jumps, not smoothly, so that they're the right size and shape for their buttons.

▸ Changing the Predefined Toolbars

If you want, you can change Word's predefined Toolbars. You might want to remove buttons that you never use or change the command that an existing button runs. Here's how:

1. Display the Toolbar you want to change.
2. Choose Tools ➤ Customize. The Customize dialog box will appear.
3. Select the Toolbars tab (see Figure 36.15).

FIGURE 36.15

The Toolbars tab of the Customize dialog box.

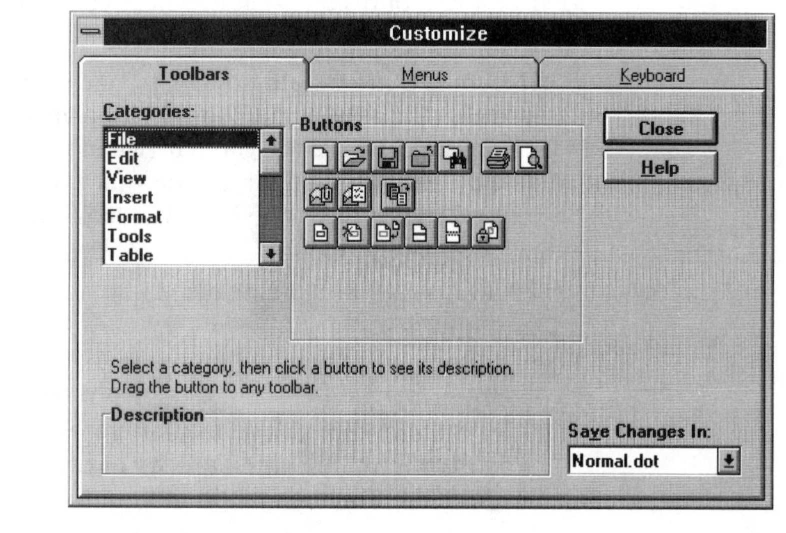

4. To add a button, select the correct category in the Categories box, then drag the button or item to where you want it on the Toolbar.
5. To delete a button, drag the button off the Toolbar and drop it in the dialog box (or anywhere else where no Toolbar is).
6. When you're done, click the Close button.

WARNING

When you delete a built-in Toolbar button, it'll still be available in the Customize dialog box. But when you delete a custom Toolbar button, it's gone for good. Consider creating a storage Toolbar for keeping unused buttons rather than deleting them permanently.

Moving or Copying a Toolbar Button

Here's how to move or copy buttons from one Toolbar to another:

1. Select Tools ➤ Customize. The Customize dialog box will appear.
2. Select the Toolbars tab.

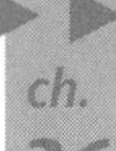

3. To move a button, drag it to where you want it on the same Toolbar or on another Toolbar.
4. To copy a button, hold down Ctrl and drag the button to where you want it on the same Toolbar or on another Toolbar. Word will automatically close the gap left (when you move a button) and shift the buttons along in the new location. So if you want fifteen smiley FoxPro faces on your Microsoft Toolbar, go right ahead.
5. Click the Close button.

▸▸ TIP

To move a Toolbar button quickly, without opening the Customize dialog box, hold down Alt and drag the button to where you want it. To copy a button, hold down Ctrl+Alt and drag the button to where you want it.

▸▸ NOTE

To add space before a button, go to the Toolbar tab in the Customize dialog box and drag a button a little way to its right. When you're done, close the dialog box. This seems pretty pointless unless you're *mega*-clumsy with your mouse, and even then you'd be better off recalibrating the mouse's movements in the Control Panel.

▸ Resetting a Built-In Toolbar

If you modify a built-in Toolbar and then regret it, here's how to restore it to its original settings:

1. Select View ➤ Toolbars. The Toolbars dialog box will appear.
2. Highlight the Toolbar you want to restore, and then click the Reset button.
3. In the Reset Toolbar dialog box (see Figure 36.16), select the template in which to make the change, and then choose OK.

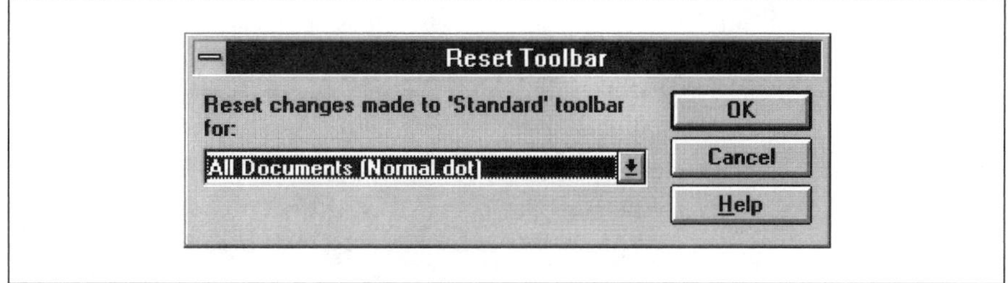

FIGURE 36.16

The Reset Toolbar dialog box.

4. Click OK to close the Toolbars dialog box.

▶ Creating a Custom Toolbar

If you find yourself using buttons on half a dozen different Toolbars in the course of the day's work, you may want to create a custom Toolbar with only the buttons you need on it. Here's how:

1. Select View ➤ Toolbars. The Toolbars dialog box will appear.
2. Click the New button. The New Toolbar dialog box will appear:

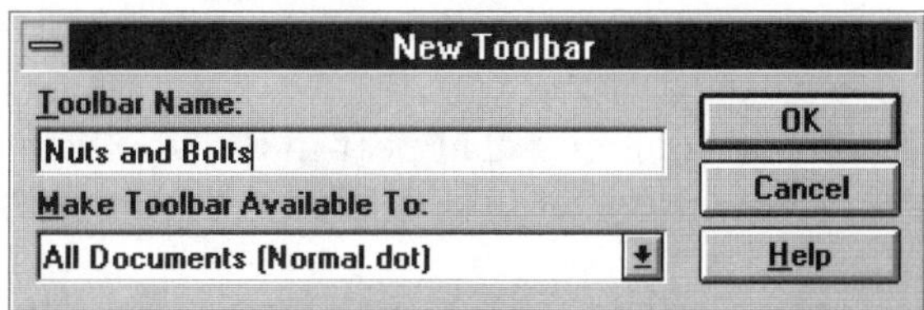

3. Type a name for the new Toolbar in the Toolbar Name: box.
4. Select the template in which to store the Toolbar in the Make Toolbar Available To: box, and then click OK. Word will display the Customize dialog box with the Toolbars tab selected and a new Toolbar without buttons in its own Toolbar window.
5. In the Categories box, select the category containing the first button to add to the new Toolbar.
6. Drag the appropriate button to the new Toolbar (see Figure 36.17).
7. Add further buttons as appropriate.
8. When you finish building your new Toolbar, click the Close button.

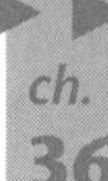

FIGURE 36.17 ►

Dragging a button to the new Toolbar.

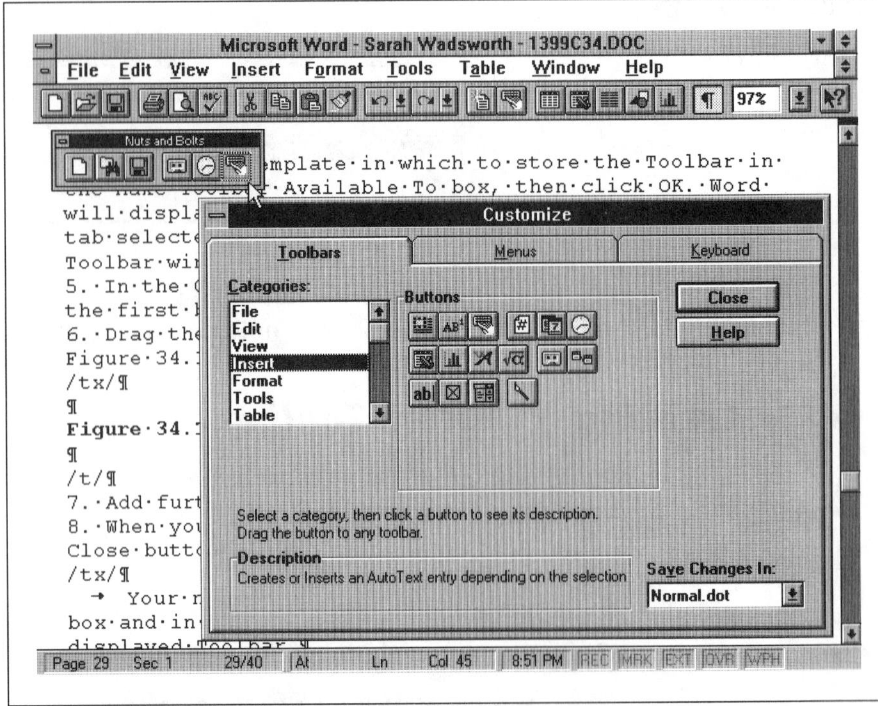

Your new Toolbar will appear in the Toolbars dialog box and in the shortcut menu produced by right-clicking a displayed Toolbar.

► Deleting a Custom Toolbar

When you get sick of your custom Toolbars, you can easily delete them:

1. Select View ➤ Toolbars to display the Toolbars dialog box.
2. Highlight the custom Toolbar you want to delete and click the Delete button.
3. Click Yes in the confirmation dialog box.

►► **NOTE**

Word won't let you delete the Toolbars it provides, only your custom Toolbars.

▶ Renaming a Custom Toolbar

You can rename a custom Toolbar at any point:

1. Select File ➤ Templates. The Templates and Add-Ins dialog box will appear.
2. Click the Organizer button. The Organizer dialog box will appear.
3. Select the Toolbars tab (see Figure 36.18).
4. In the left or right box, highlight the Toolbar to rename, then click the Rename button.
5. In the Rename dialog box (shown below), enter a new name and click OK.

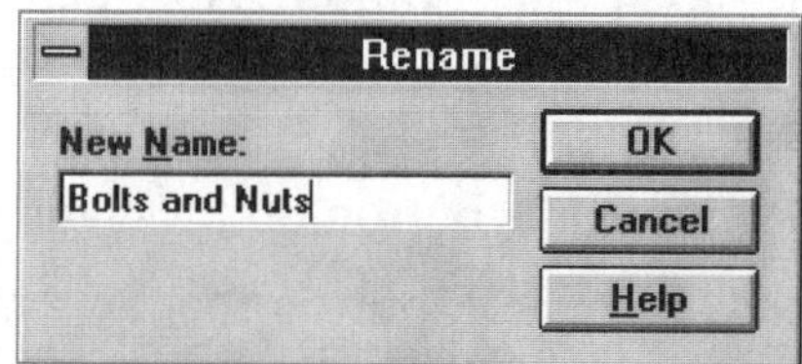

6. Click Close to close the Organizer dialog box.

FIGURE 36.18 ▶

The Toolbars tab of the Organizer dialog box. Select the Toolbar you want to rename.

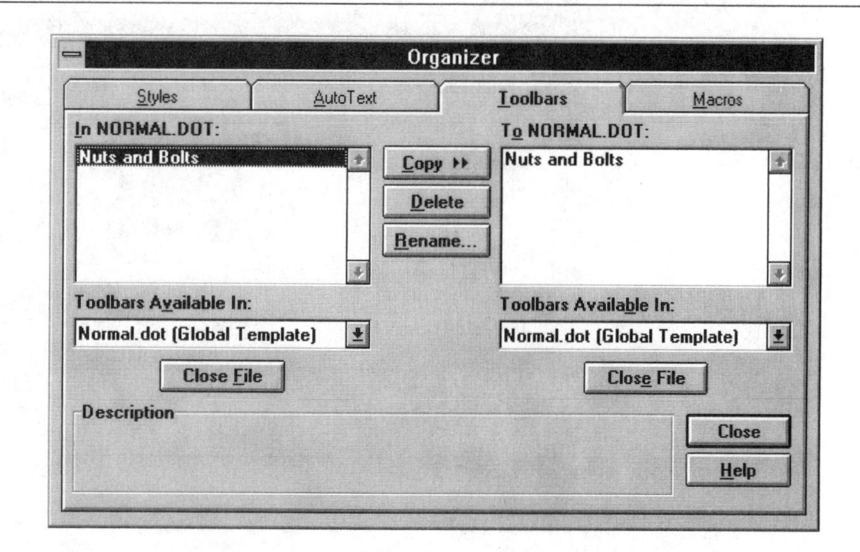

▶ Copying a Toolbar from One Template to Another

If you create a Toolbar in one template and you'd like to make it available in another, it's easy:

1. Select File ➤ Templates…. The Templates and Add-Ins dialog box will appear.
2. Click the Organizer… button. The Organizer dialog box will appear.
3. Select the Toolbars tab.
4. Click the Close File button on the left side of the Organizer dialog box. It turns into an Open File… button.
5. Click the Open File… button. An Open dialog box appears. Find and select the template you want to copy the toolbar *from*. Then click OK.
6. Click the Close File button on the right.
7. Click the Open File… button that appears in its place. In the Open dialog box that appears, select the template you want to copy the toolbar *to* (see Figure 36.19).

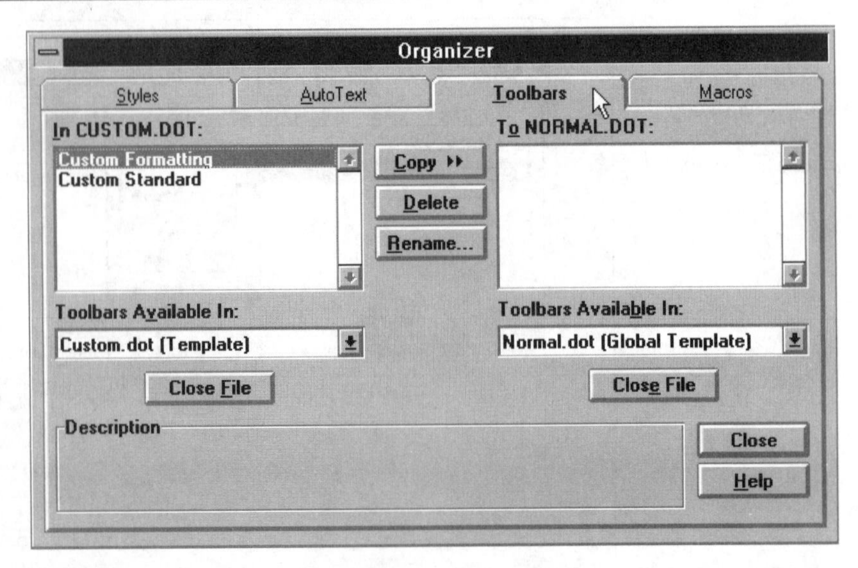

FIGURE 36.19 ▶

The Toolbars tab of the Organizer dialog box, ready to copy Toolbars from one open template to another.

8. Highlight the Toolbar or Toolbars to copy, then click the Copy >> button.
9. Click Close to close the Organizer dialog box.

The Toolbar (or Toolbars) you selected will be copied to the other template.

▶ Assigning an Item to a Toolbar Button

You can assign Toolbar buttons to run commands, macros, fonts, AutoText entries, or styles. You can attach Toolbars to specific templates, which gives you great flexibility.

To assign an item to a Toolbar button:

1. Open a document based on the template containing the item you want to assign—or open the template itself.
2. Display the Toolbar you want to change.
3. Select Tools ➤ Customize. The Customize dialog box will appear.
4. Choose the Toolbars tab (see Figure 36.20).
5. In the Save Changes box, select the template containing the item you want to assign to the Toolbar.
6. In the Categories box, select the category containing the command to add.
7. Drag the item name from the box to the right of the Categories box to the Toolbar.
    - When you choose an item without a built-in button, you'll get a blank button on the Toolbar, and Word will open the Custom Button dialog box. (See the section Creating a Custom Button, coming up in a moment.)
8. Select a button, then click the Assign button, and then click Close.

▶ Creating a Custom Button

You can create a custom Toolbar button in two ways: Either create a new image in the Button Editor dialog box or copy an image from a

FIGURE 36.20

The Customize dialog box with the Toolbars tab selected.

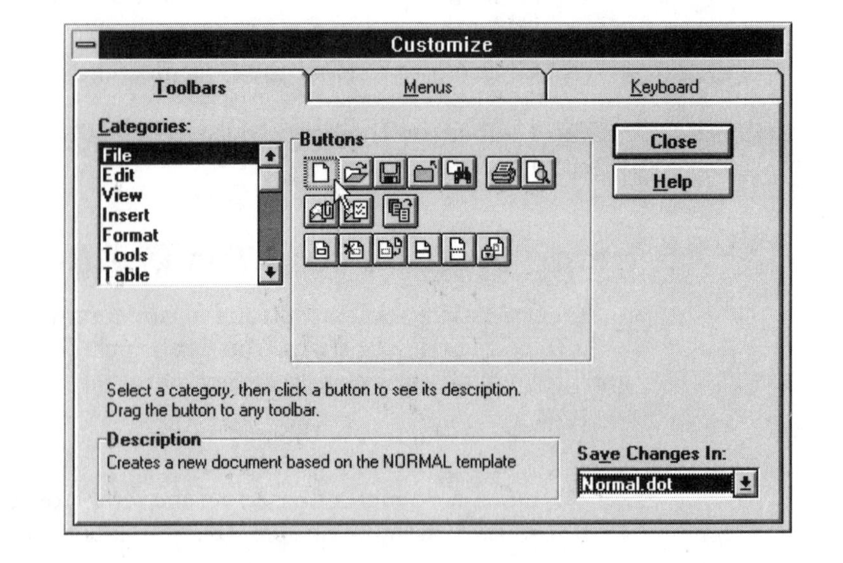

graphics application and paste it onto a button. The latter's more fun, so let's look at it first:

1. Create the image in your graphics application and copy it to the Clipboard, preferably in bitmap or picture format.
2. Switch to Word and display the target Toolbar.
3. Select Tools ➤ Customize.
4. In the Customize dialog box, select the Toolbars tab.
5. Right-click the Toolbar button to receive the image.
6. Choose Paste Button Image from the shortcut menu.
7. Click the Close button.

If you don't have a graphics application, here's how to create (from a blank button) or modify a Toolbar button:

1. Display the Toolbar whose button you want to modify.
2. Select Tools ➤ Customize. The Customize dialog box will appear.
3. Click the Toolbars tab.

4. Right-click the button you want to modify.
5. Choose Edit Button Image from the shortcut menu. The Button Editor dialog box will appear (see Figure 36.21).
6. Change the button image to your liking.
7. Choose Close.

▶ Restoring a Built-In Toolbar Button's Image

If you don't like the changes you made to the image on a button, you can easily restore it:

1. Display the Toolbar whose button you want to change.
2. Select Tools ➤ Customize. The Customize dialog box will appear.
3. Select the Toolbars tab.
4. Right-click the button you want to restore.

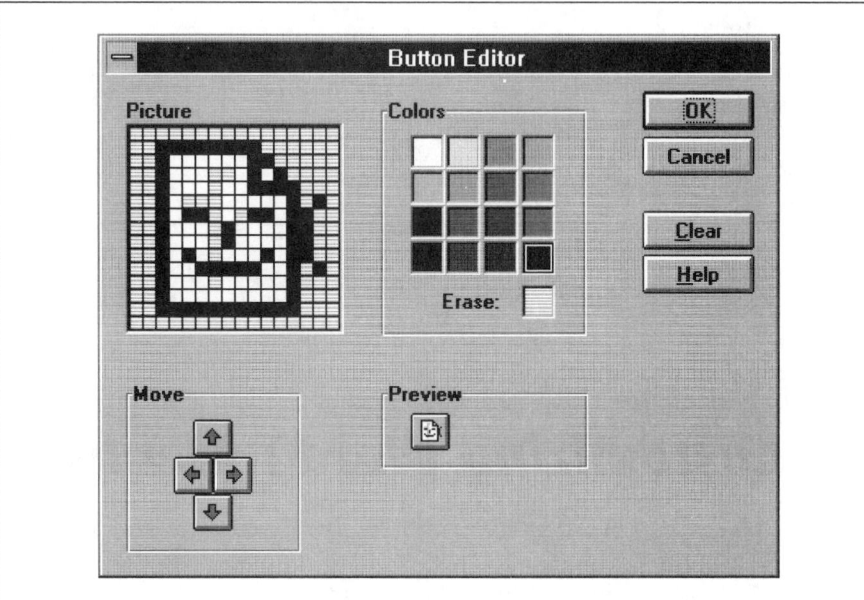

FIGURE 36.21

The Button Editor dialog box. Change or design your button here.

5. Choose Reset Button Image from the shortcut menu.
6. Choose Close.

▸ Enlarging Toolbar Buttons

If you're tired of peering at Word's Toolbar buttons, unable to make out one button from another, you may want to enlarge the Toolbar buttons. The only problem with doing this is that fewer buttons will fit across the width of the screen; you may want to remove unnecessary commands from the Toolbars so the necessary ones fit.

To display large Toolbar buttons:

1. Select View ➤ Toolbars to display the Toolbars dialog box.
2. Check the Large Buttons check box, then click OK. Your Toolbars will appear with large buttons, as illustrated in Figure 36.22.

To restore Toolbar buttons to their normal size, select View ➤ Toolbars and uncheck the Large Buttons check box.

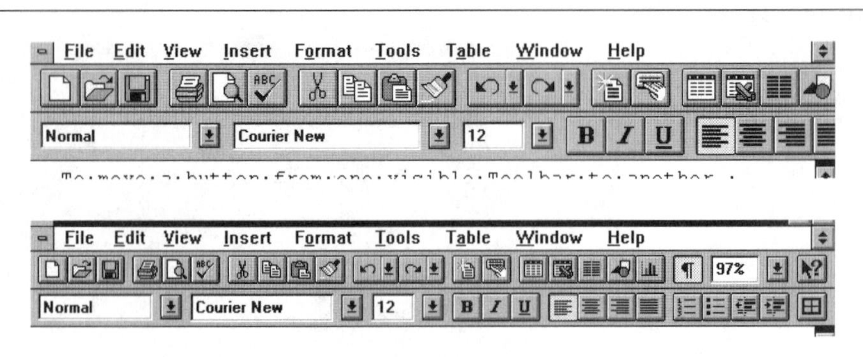

FIGURE 36.22

The difference between Toolbars with large buttons (above) and regular buttons (below).

▸▸ Customizing Word's Menus

Word lets you control the appearance and arrangement of its menus. You can add, delete, and reposition menu items. You can also change the keyboard shortcuts for most menu items. You can use this flexibility to make your copy of Word extremely easy to use or to deliberately restrict someone's options. For example, you could prevent your default temp from applying any formatting to your precious documents.

▶ Adding Menu Items

Here's how to customize Word's menus so they contain the commands, macros, fonts, AutoText entries, and styles you need most often:

1. Open a document based on the template containing the item you want to assign—or open the template itself.
2. Select Tools ➤ Customize. The Customize dialog box will appear.
3. Click the Menus tab (see Figure 36.23).
4. In the Save Changes In box, select the template in which the item is stored.
5. Select the category to which the item belongs in the Categories box.
6. Select the item you want to assign in the Commands box to the right of the Categories box.
7. Choose the menu you want in the Change What Menu box.

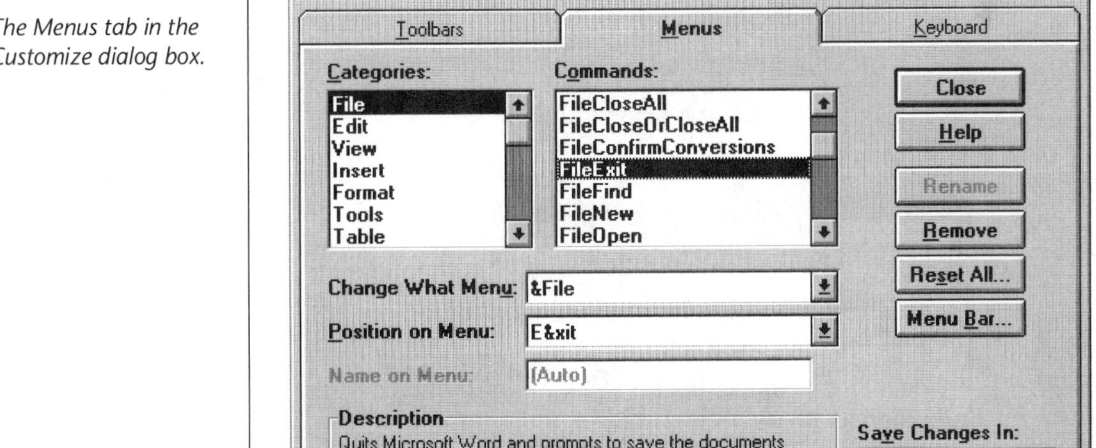

FIGURE 36.23

The Menus tab in the Customize dialog box.

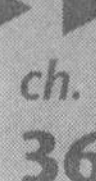

8. In the Position On Menu box, select (Auto) to let Word automatically position similar menu items together, select (At Top) or (At Bottom) to position the item at the top or bottom of the menu, or select the item below which to position the item if you want to position it within the menu list.
9. In the Name on Menu box, either accept the default name or type the name you want to appear. Put an ampersand (&) in front of the hot key letter.
10. Click the Add button or Add Below button. (Word will offer you one or t'other.)
11. To close the Customize dialog box, click the Close button.

▸▸ NOTE

To add a menu-item separator bar, choose (Separator) in the Commands area of the Customize dialog box, position it as described above, and click the Add or Add Below button.

▸ Removing Menu Items

Here's the quick way to remove items you don't need from menus:

1. Press Ctrl+Alt+- (that's Ctrl+Alt+minus). The mouse pointer will change to a heavy horizontal line:

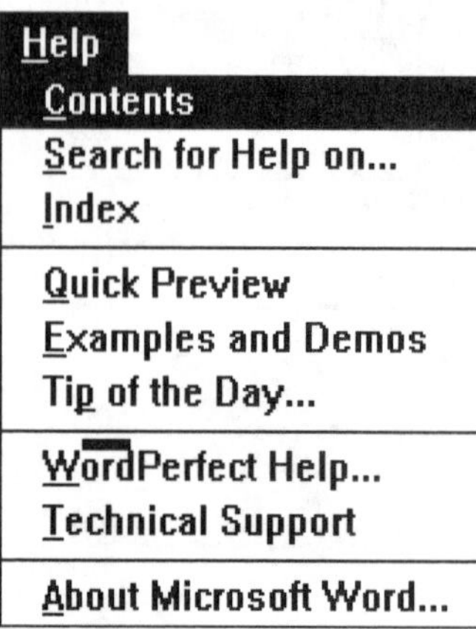

NOTE

If you change your mind, press Esc to return the mouse pointer to normal.

2. Click the menu item you want to remove. It'll disappear.

This method is much more fun than using the Tools ➤ Customize dialog box, selecting the command to remove, and then clicking the Remove button, but that way works, too.

NOTE

To remove a menu-item separator bar, choose (Separator) in the Commands area of the Customize dialog box and click the Remove button.

Restoring Built-In Menus to Their Original Settings

To quickly restore all built-in Word menus to their original state:

1. Select Tools ➤ Customize. The Customize dialog box will appear.
2. Choose the Menus tab.
3. Select the template to restore in the Save Changes In box.
4. Click the Reset All button.
5. Click Yes in the confirmation dialog box.
6. Click the Close button.

WARNING

Think twice before restoring all menus, especially if you've made any significant changes. Consider backing up any superb pieces of customization so you can't trash them in an instant with the Reset All button.

► Adding New Menus

Word 6 lets you add new menus—a great improvement over Word 2.0! You can add as many menus as you want, but they may not all fit on your screen.

To add a new menu:

1. Select Tools ➤ Customize. The Customize dialog box will appear.
2. Choose the Menus tab.
3. Select the template for the new menu in the Save Changes In box.
4. Select the Menu Bar button. The Menu Bar dialog box will appear:

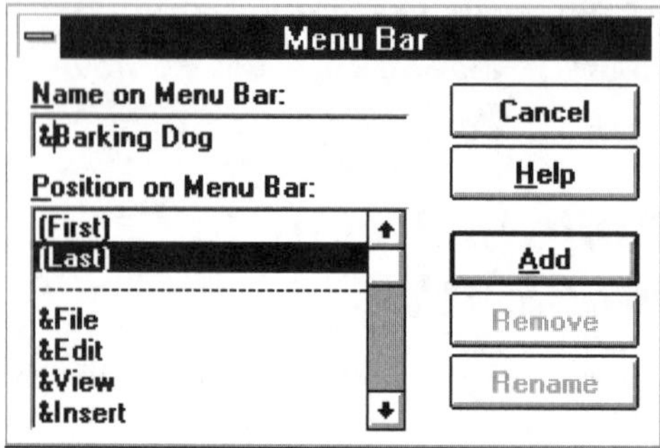

5. Enter the name for the menu in the Name on Menu Bar box. Use an ampersand (&) in front of a letter to designate a hot key.
6. Position the new menu using the Position on Menu Bar box:
   - To position it first, select First.
   - To position it last, select Last.
   - To position the menu after another menu, select the menu for it to appear after.
7. Click the Add or Add After button (Word will offer you one or the other, depending on your choice in step 6) to add the menu.
8. Choose the Close button to close the Menu Bar dialog box, add menu as described before, and choose the Close button again to close the Customize dialog box.

▶ Renaming Menus

You can rename a menu so it suits your purposes better. Perhaps Fail would be more appropriate than File, or Fools than Tools? Here's how:

1. Select Tools ➤ Customize. The Customize dialog box will appear.
2. Choose the Menus tab.
3. Select the template containing the menu you want to rename in the Save Changes In box.
4. Select the Menu Bar button. The Menu Bar dialog box will appear.
5. Select the menu to rename in the Position on Menu Bar box.
6. Type the new name in the Name on Menu Bar box.
7. Click the Rename button.
8. Click the Close button to close the Menu Bar dialog box and then click the Close button on the Customize dialog box to close that, too.

▶▶ Customizing Word's Keyboard Shortcuts

You can get the most use from your keyboard by customizing Word's keyboard shortcuts. You can assign shortcut keys to commands, macros, fonts, AutoText entries, styles, and special characters. You want Ctrl+A to change selected text to 40-point Kidnap? *No problemo.* You need Ctrl+Shift+T to type: "I was quite ecstatic to see you last night, darling!"? Read on, MacDuff!

▶ Changing Keyboard Shortcuts

Here's how to see what your current keyboard shortcuts are and change them:

1. Select Tools ➤ Customize. The Customize dialog box will appear.
2. Select the Keyboard tab (see Figure 36.24).

3. In the Categories box, select the category containing the items you want.
4. In the Commands box, select the command whose shortcut you want to view. The shortcut will appear in the Current Keys box.
5. Move to the Press New Shortcut Key box and press the keyboard shortcut you want to assign. Word will display the current assignation of that keyboard shortcut.
6. Click the Assign button to assign the shortcut key to the item.
7. Click the Close button to close the Customize dialog box.

▸▸ TIP

Here's a shortcut: Press Ctrl+Alt++ (that's Ctrl+Alt+plus). The mouse pointer changes to a command symbol. Choose a menu command or click a Toolbar button. Word will display the Customize dialog box showing the command you select. Follow steps 5 to 7 of the preceding list.

FIGURE 36.24

The Keyboard tab of the Customize dialog box.

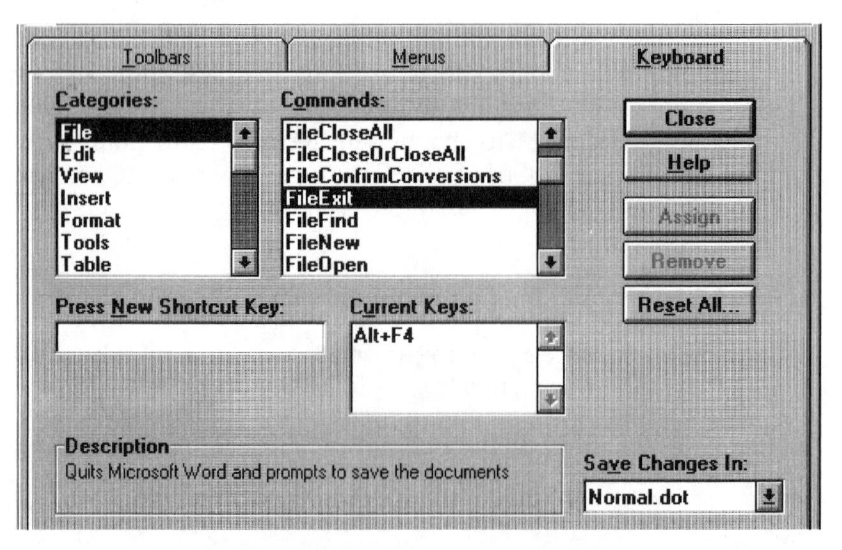

▶ Deleting Shortcuts

By deleting shortcuts, you can prevent yourself or another user of your computer from performing unwanted actions. Here's how:

1. Select Tools ➤ Customize. The Customize dialog box will appear.
2. Choose the Keyboard tab.
3. Select the template containing the item whose shortcut you want to remove in the Save Changes In box.
4. In the Categories box, select the category containing the item.
5. In the Commands box, select the item.
6. Select the shortcut key to delete in the Current Keys box.
7. Click the Remove button.
8. Choose the Close button to close the Customize dialog box.

▶ Reverting to Default Keyboard Shortcuts

Here's how to restore all shortcut key assignments to their original settings:

1. Select Tools ➤ Customize. The Customize dialog box will appear.
2. Choose the Keyboard tab.
3. Select the template containing the shortcut key assignments you want to restore in the Save Changes In box.
4. Click the Reset All button.
5. Choose Yes in the confirmation dialog box that Word throws at you.
6. Click the Close button to close the Customize dialog box.

▶▶ Features for Physically Challenged Users

Word 6 includes a number of features to assist physically challenged users. These are discussed in the following sections.

► Microsoft's Access Pack

For people with motion or hearing disabilities, Microsoft's Access Pack provides better access to computers running Windows. With the Access Pack, you can:

- Type Shift-, Ctrl-, and Alt-key combinations with one finger.
- Instruct applications to ignore accidental keystrokes.
- Adjust the repeat rate (the rate at which a key registers multiple presses when held down) or turn off character repeating.
- Use the keyboard to control the mouse cursor.
- Use an alternate input device to control the keyboard and mouse.
- Display visually when the computer beeps or makes sounds.

Getting Access Pack

You'll find Access Pack in the file ACCESS.EXE in the Microsoft Windows Driver Library. You can also download the Microsoft Windows Driver Library from network services—CompuServe, GEnie, Microsoft Online, and Microsoft Download Service (MSDL). MSDL's number is (206) 936-MSDL (that's 936-6735).

If you don't have a modem, you can order the Access Pack by calling Microsoft Product Support Services at (206) 637-7098 or (206) 635-4948 (text telephone).

► Single-Handed Keyboard Layouts

If you have difficulty using the standard QWERTY keyboard, you can get from Microsoft Dvorak keyboard layouts that make the most frequently typed characters on a keyboard more accessible.

There are three Dvorak keyboard layouts:

- Two-handed
- Left hand only
- Right hand only

The left-handed and right-handed layouts can be used by people who type with a single finger or with a wand. You don't need any special equipment to use them.

▶ Low Vision Aids

Users with low vision can customize the Word display to make it easier to see. In Chapter 3, we discussed how to zoom in and out to improve your view of Word, and in the Enlarging Toolbar Buttons section earlier in this chapter, we looked at how to display Word's large Toolbar buttons.

Further products available include screen-enlargement utilities and screen readers that provide output by synthesized voice or refreshable Braille displays.

▶ Audio Documentation

You can get Microsoft software documentation on audio cassettes and floppy disks. Contact Recording for the Blind, Inc., at this address:

Recording for the Blind, Inc.
20 Roszel Road
Princeton, NJ 08540
Phone: (800) 221-4792
Phone outside the U.S.: (609) 452-0606
Fax: (609) 987-8116

▶ TDD Product Support

Microsoft provides a text telephone (TT/TDD) service to give people who are hard of hearing access to product and support services.

Microsoft Sales and Service and Microsoft Product Support Services are open 6 A.M. to 6 P.M. Pacific time. Here are the numbers for the text telephones:

Microsoft Sales and Service: (800) 892-5236

Microsoft Product Support Services: (206) 635-4948

Microsoft will charge you for their support services. You have been warned.

► For More Assistance and Information

For more information on Microsoft products and services for people with disabilities, contact Microsoft Sales and Service at (800) 426-9400 (voice) or (800) 892-5234 (text telephone).

For general information on how computers can help you, consult a trained evaluator. To find one, contact the National Information System, Center for Developmental Disabilities, Benson Building, University of South Carolina, Columbia, SC 29208. Here are its numbers:

Voice/text telephone outside South Carolina: (800) 922-9234, ext. 301

Voice/text telephone in South Carolina: (800) 922-1107

Voice/text telephone outside the United States: (803) 777-6222

You can also get the *Trace ResourceBook* from the Trace R&D Center at the University of Wisconsin-Madison. The *Trace ResourceBook* describes and illustrates about 2,000 products to help people with disabilities use computers. Here is the address for the Trace R&D Center:

Trace R&D Center
S-151 Waisman Center
1500 Highland Avenue
Madison, WI 53705-2280
Voice telephone: (608) 263-2309
Text telephone: (608) 263-5408
Fax: (608) 262-8848

APPENDICES

APPENDIX A

Installing Word

▶▶ **Y***ou* can install Word on any machine that runs Windows 3.1 (including an 80286) that has a minimum of 4 MB of RAM. You cannot use Word 6 with Windows 3.0. You'll need a EGA or better display. You really should have a mouse or trackball, though this is not a requirement. Disk-space estimates vary with your needs.

A *Minimum* (also called a *Laptop*) installation requires five to six MB of disk space. You'll get just the bare bones—the program, Spelling checker, and Word Readme Help file (*not* online help). Travelers, listen up. You are gonna wish you had the online help at midnight in some hotel room. Read on.

A *Typical* installation requires 18 MB or more. It includes the program, Spelling and Grammar checkers, new online help (well worth the disk space!), and supplementary programs like WordArt and Graph.

A full installation requires twenty-five to thirty MB. If you have the room, do a full install, then go back later to remove things you never use, like the Grammar checker and Equation Editor. But at least try them and the many other tools provided in a full installation. After all, you paid for them, didn't you?

▶▶ **TIP**

Because Word 6 can use your old custom dictionaries, glossaries, styles, and templates, don't throw out these files when deleting Word version 2. When in doubt, make backup copies of things you might need some day.

Network users can choose a "Workstation" installation, which requires around 4 MB of local hard-disk real estate. Read more about network installations later in this appendix.

Word's installer will check to see if you have enough space, but you can save some time by assuring that there is room beforehand.

▶▶ Running the Installer from Floppies

The files on the installation floppies are compressed, thus they cannot simply be dragged onto your hard disk. You need to run the Installer program, which will walk you through the simple installation steps.

1. Start Windows.
2. Insert the first Setup disk in a floppy drive.
3. Choose the Run… choice on the Program Manager's File menu.
4. Type the disk-drive name (A: or B:) and **Setup**, as shown here:

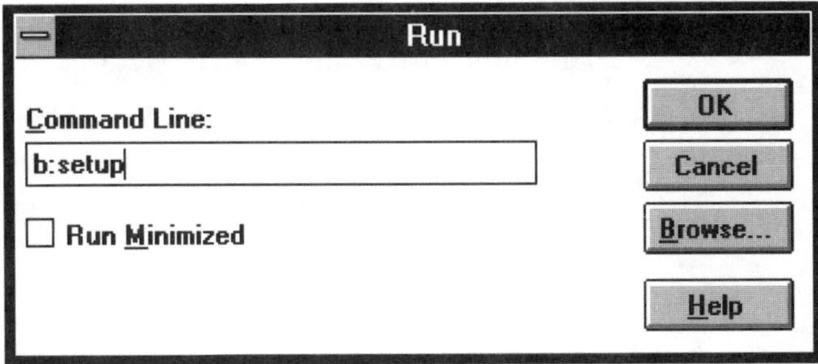

▶▶ **TIP**

You can also double-click on the Setup.exe file in File Manager to start the installation process.

5. In a moment, you will see a Setup dialog box similar, but not necessarily identical, to this one:

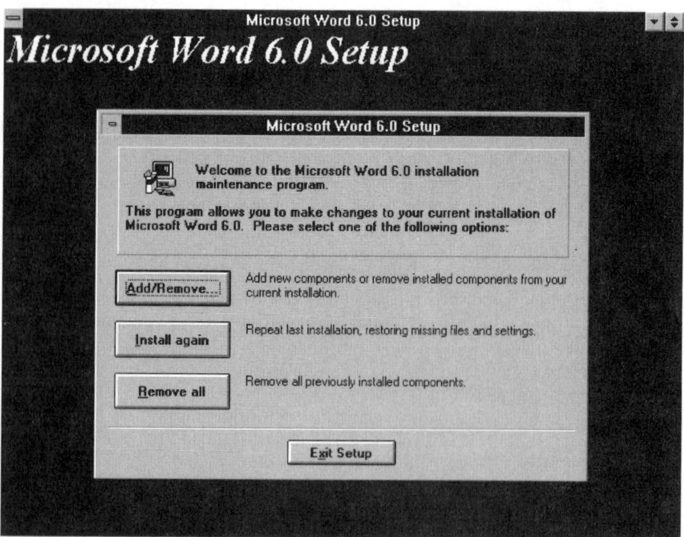

6. The choices you will be given will vary with your situation. Read each choice carefully before clicking the Continue button.
7. When asked if you want a Typical, Minimum (Laptop), or Complete installation, opt for Complete if you have the required disk space. You can always remove unwanted elements after you've had a chance to explore them.

▸▸ Running the Installer from a Server

If your company has a network and is licensed to do so, you may be able to install Word from the server (over the network) without the need for floppy shuffling. Contact your network administrator for details.

Running Word after Installation

You will need to restart your computer to use Word. The Installer will provide congratulations and a Restart button.

Custom Installation and Removing the Unwanted

If you choose not to do a complete installation, you can tell the Installer which items you want to install. And you can revisit the Setup program later to remove items you don't use. This is helpful if you have limited disk space or if one of your nonessential disks is damaged. In either case, you'll see a series of dialog boxes, each with lists of items that can be added or removed. Most of the dialog boxes also contain Change Options… buttons that give you more detailed control. For example, the first dialog box lets you add or delete all Proofing Tools, while the next level down lets you pick and choose from options like Spelling, Hyphenation, Thesaurus, and Grammar. As you add or remove checks in the various option boxes, Word revises its estimation of the required disk space and displays the statistics at the bottom of the dialog boxes.

The "top" dialog box looks like this:

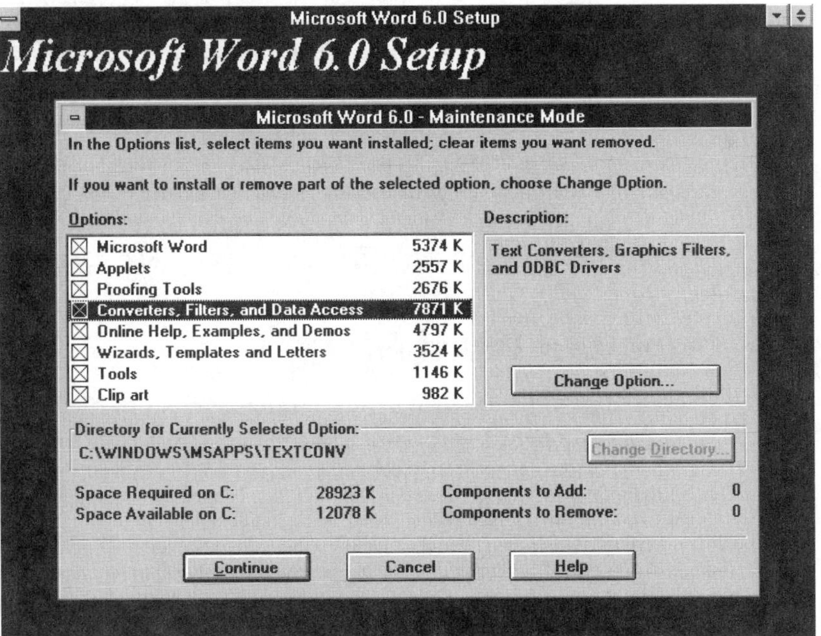

To reach the detailed choices, click the Change Option… button:

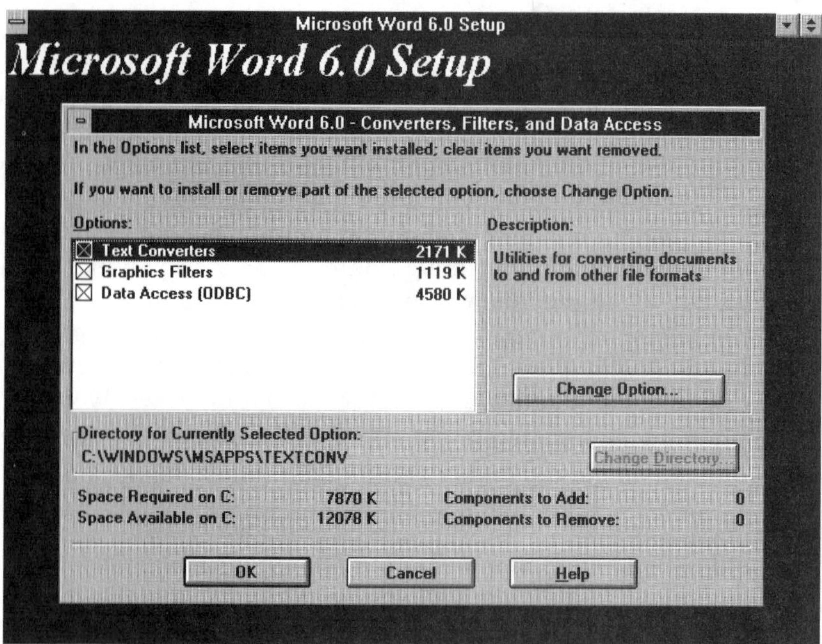

It's a good idea to install the templates and sample documents, as they contain helpful files and examples. If you choose not to install certain features, they will either not appear on your Word menus or will always be dimmed. You can always return to the Installer later and install just the items you left off when you last did a custom installation.

► Using Old Word Files

If you have old Word documents, custom dictionaries, and templates from Word version 2 scattered around your hard disk, you will be able to use them with Word 6. Word will convert them when you open them, and you can either save them as Word 6 files or save them as earlier version files. You can even use your old custom menu, Toolbar, and keyboard settings, although you may be better off personalizing the Word 6 tools from scratch.

If you have modified Word's Standard styles in earlier versions, the Installer tries to preserve these changes. Macros should work as well.

It goes without saying that you should explore the effects of the Installer's "automatic" conversions and accommodations before you start any large rush projects that depend upon them.

APPENDIX B

Word for WordPerfect Users

▶▶ If you're a former WordPerfect user, then you might find Word for Windows disorienting at first. In this appendix, I'll help ease your transition.

▶▶ How Word and WordPerfect Really Differ

First of all, if you've been using WordPerfect *for Windows*, then your transition to Word is going to be much easier. When Word users look at the Windows version of WordPerfect, it looks like a wannabe version of Word. That's not a completely fair assessment, as a lot of the similarities between the two word processors are direct consequences of Windows standards.

Most of the other similarities are the result of the intense competition between the two companies that make the products. Any new feature of one of the word processors that proves popular or gets good press is bound to show up somewhere in the other.

Nevertheless, even the Windows version of WordPerfect retains some of the flavor of the DOS version. For example, WordPerfect for Windows still uses the concept of hidden codes—codes that can be shown with the Reveal Codes command—which are used for hands-on control over formatting and other features. Word has nothing like that (except for hidden *text* and the Show/Hide hidden-characters button, which can make spaces, tabs, and paragraph marks visible).

If you're switching over from a "classic" version of WordPerfect (say, any of the versions 4.0 to 6.0 for DOS), however, then you are really in for some changes. First of all, everything looks different. Instead of WordPerfect's famous blank blue screen, you've got a Windows screen full of buttons and other gizmos. Instead of unadorned, simple text, you've got WYSIWYG (What You See Is What You Get), a fair approximation of what your document will look like when you print it.

Much of the terminology is different, even when it applies to essentially the same thing. You don't block text in Word, you select it. You don't use the Move/Copy command, you Cut and Paste text or drag and drop it. Instead of Search, you have Find. Instead of a Layout full-screen menu, you have a Format pull-down menu. And on and on.

►► Transition Strategies—Gradual or Cold Turkey

There are essentially two different ways to make your transition from WordPerfect to Word. You can make the change easier and more gradual by setting up Word to look or act as much like WordPerfect as possible, but then you might never really get the hang of how Word is organized, and you might end up handicapped by having to always think in terms of WordPerfect commands.

Or you can just use the vanilla, out-of-the-box Word configuration and just try to get used to it as quickly as possible. Word has some built-in WordPerfect Help features that can give you Word equivalents to WordPerfect commands so you won't be completely on your own. The choice is yours.

►► Word's Quick Preview for WordPerfect Users

Word has a built-in demo (demonstration) feature called Quick Preview to give beginners some orientation when they first use Word. Part of this demo is geared especially toward WordPerfect users. To check it out, select Help ➤ Quick Preview. This brings up the Quick Preview screen (see Figure B.1).

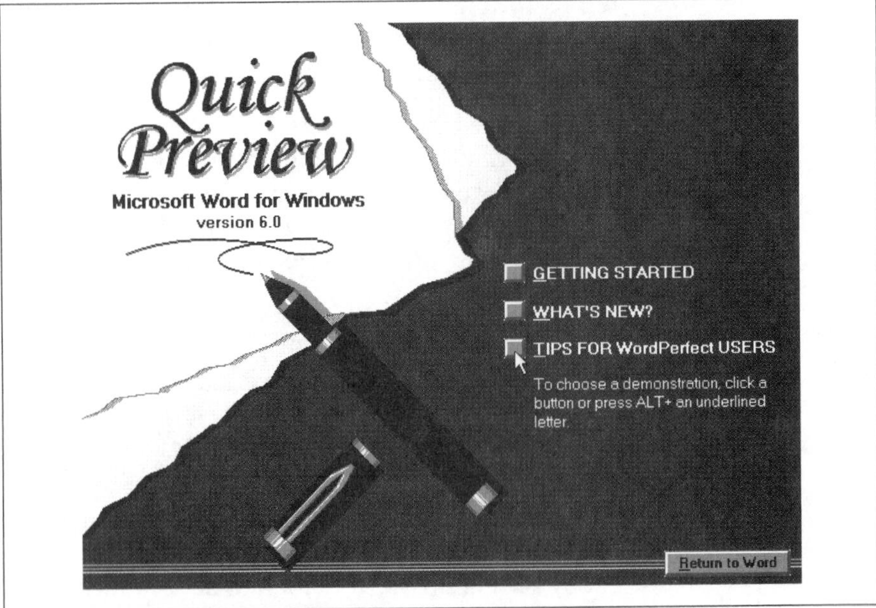

FIGURE B.1

The Quick Preview screen. This tutorial demonstrates how Word works.

Click the TIPS FOR WordPerfect USERS button to see a demonstration/tutorial explaining the basics of Word (such as how to select and format text) as compared with WordPerfect (see Figure B.2).

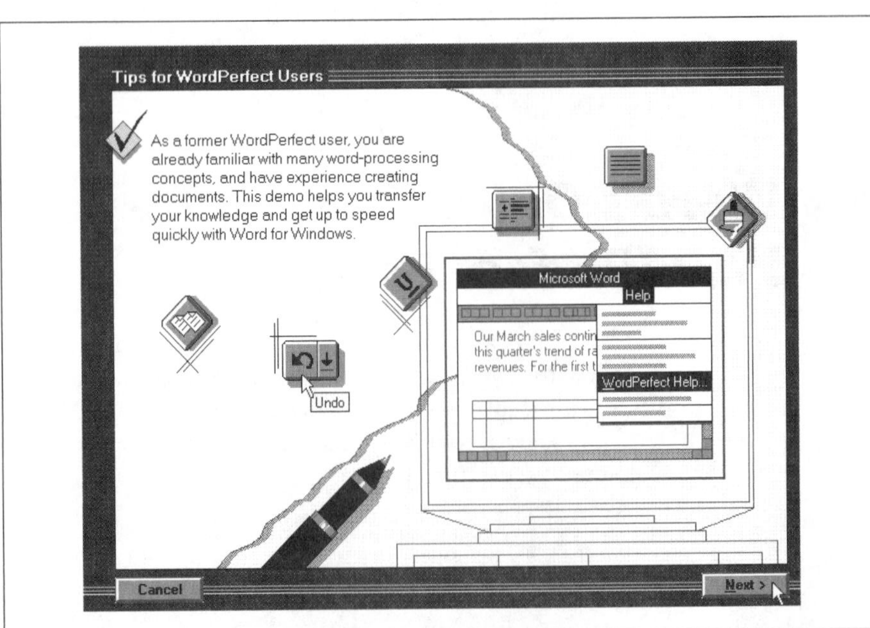

FIGURE B.2

Quick Preview's Tips for WordPerfect Users screen. Proceed through the demonstration by clicking the Next> button.

To work your way through the demo, just keep clicking the Next> button. (Quick Preview will even move the mouse pointer to the button for you.) Figure B.3 shows the beginning of the demo for WordPerfect users.

FIGURE B.3

This screen gives you a look at what the rest of the Preview will cover. Click Next> to continue or Cancel to return to the beginning.

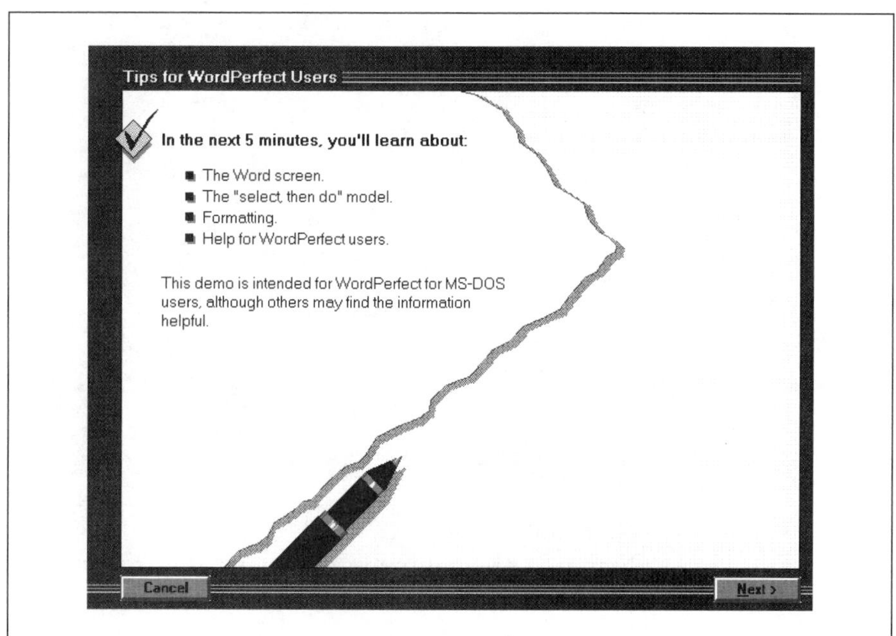

You can click Cancel at any point, then the Return to Word button to end the demo before it's through.

►► Denial Part One: Making Word Look Like WordPerfect

If you want to keep your environment looking as much like WordPerfect used to as possible, here's what you do. The first step is to remove all of the gooey buttons, sliders, and readouts from the screen.

1. Select Tools ➤ Options and click the View tab (see Figure B.4).
2. Uncheck Horizontal Scroll Bar and Vertical Scroll Bar. You've taken your first step toward freedom.

FIGURE B.4 ►

The View tab of the Options dialog box.

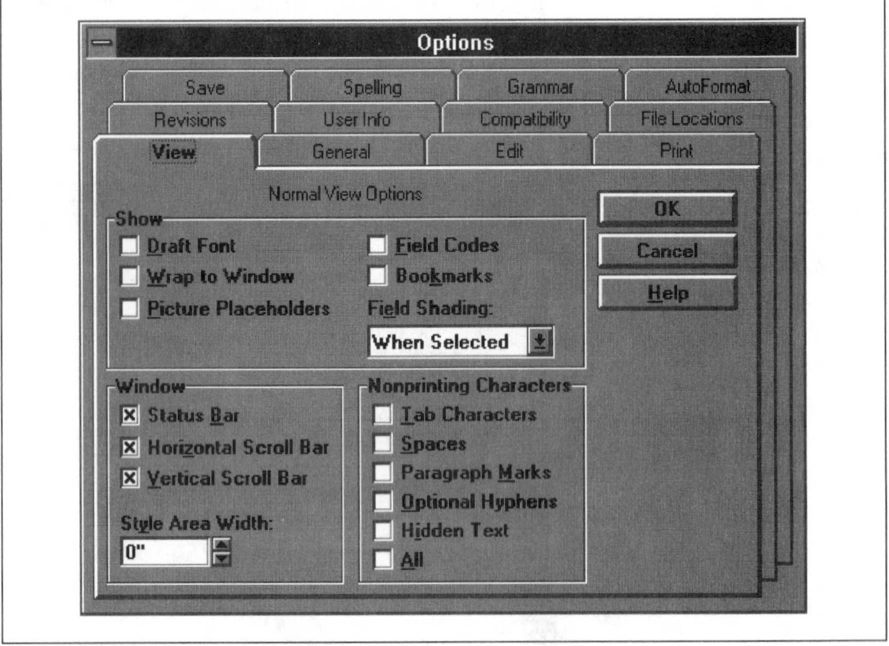

You might be tempted to uncheck Status Bar as well (and go ahead if you want to), but we'll take care of that in a minute.

Next, you'll want to change that harsh, glaring black-on-white screen to a nice, soothing white on blue, right?

3. Click the General tab in the Options dialog box (see Figure B.5).
4. Click Blue Background, White Text.
5. Click OK. We're halfway there.

Now you want to get rid of the rest of that stuff on the screen.

6. Select View ➤ Full Screen. The Menu Bar, Standard Toolbar, Formatting Toolbar, Ruler, and Status Bar disappear from the screen, leaving just the wide blue yonder (and a little one-button Toolbar escape hatch), as shown in Figure B.6.

FIGURE B.5

The General tab of the Options dialog box.

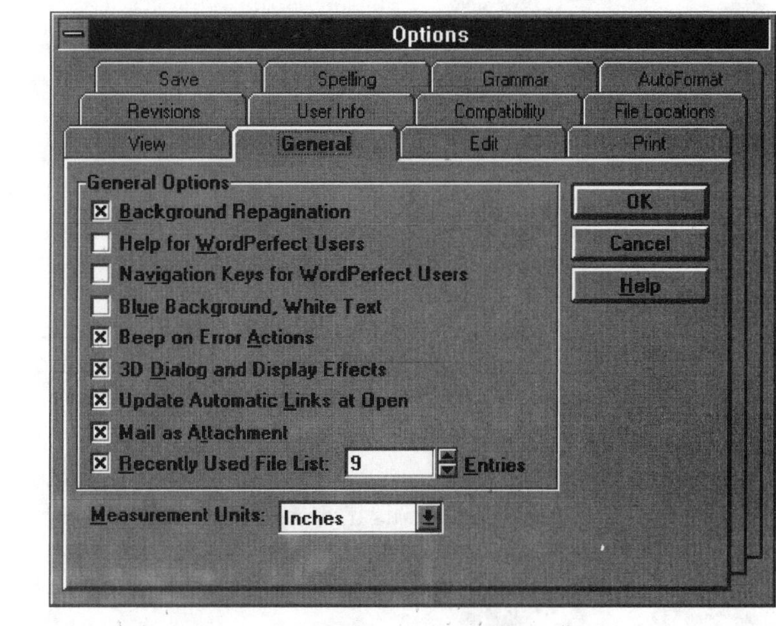

FIGURE B.6

About the closest you get to the classic WordPerfect screen in Word.

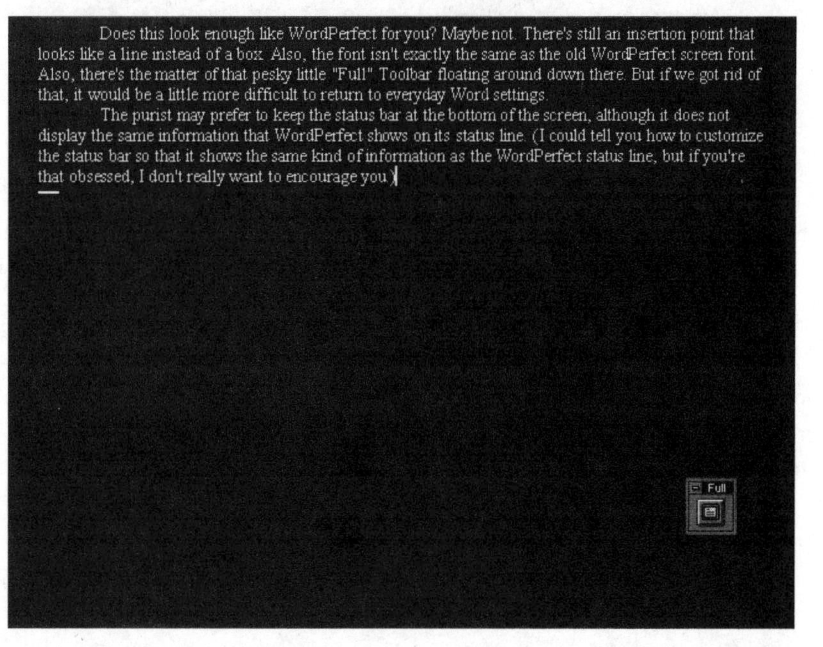

►► **NOTE**

If you don't like the WYSIWYG, check Draft Font in the Show area of the View tab of the Options dialog box (see Figure B.4). You'll still see some basic formatting, but much of it will be represented either by bold or underlining, and size changes will not be reflected in the screen font.

For strange only-the-people-at-Microsoft-understand-them reasons, all of the changes I just had you make persist from one document to another, *except for the horizontal and vertical scroll bars*. They'll reappear in other documents unless you expressly remove them.

You can still get to the hidden menus a couple of ways. You can use the Alt+key shortcuts if you remember them. They're often the first letter of the menu name in question, but not always, of course.

►► **TIP**

Start with any menu, even the Control menu (Alt+hyphen) and then use the arrow keys to slide along to the menu you want.

You can even select the menus with the mouse by clicking in the tiny one-pixel line across the top of the screen. It's a little like playing Pin the Tail on the Donkey.

If you get tired of this arrangement, click your heels together three times and repeat after me.… No, click the Full Screen button on the Full Screen Toolbar (the one floating in the lower-right corner of the screen).

►► Denial Part Two: Using WordPerfect "Navigation" Keys

In word-processing jargon, *navigation* means getting around a document. The basic navigation keys in Word are covered in Chapter 3. If you miss your old WordPerfect cursor-movement key combinations (such as Home Home ↑ to get to the top of a document, instead of Word's Ctrl+Home), there's something you can do about this.

To use WordPerfect navigation keys:

1. Select Tools ➤ Options.
2. Click the General tab (see Figure B.5).
3. Check off Navigation Keys for WordPerfect Users.
4. Click OK.

This purportedly changes the functions of PageUp, PageDown, Home, End, Ctrl+PageUp, Ctrl+PageDown, Ctrl+Home, and Esc to their WordPerfect equivalents. Some of these definitely work properly, but, unfortunately, the implementation is far from perfect. For example, PageUp still doesn't go to the top of a page (as opposed to screen) the way it does in WordPerfect.

If you are dissatisfied with Word's nod toward WordPerfect navigation, then you may be better off trying out the WordPerfect Help feature, which can offer instantaneous Word equivalents when you press a WordPerfect key combination.

►► Word's Help for WordPerfect Users

Word offers extensive WordPerfect Help. This feature can either give you information or actually demonstrate how to get the results you want in Word. WordPerfect Help is there to make your transition smoother. It doesn't make Word work like WordPerfect, but it helps you find equivalent commands for your old favorites.

To check out WordPerfect Help:

1. Select Help ➤ WordPerfect Help. This brings up the Help for WordPerfect Users dialog box (see Figure B.7).

FIGURE B.7

The Help for WordPerfect Users dialog box. Read about the Word equivalents to WordPerfect commands here or have Word demonstrate them for you.

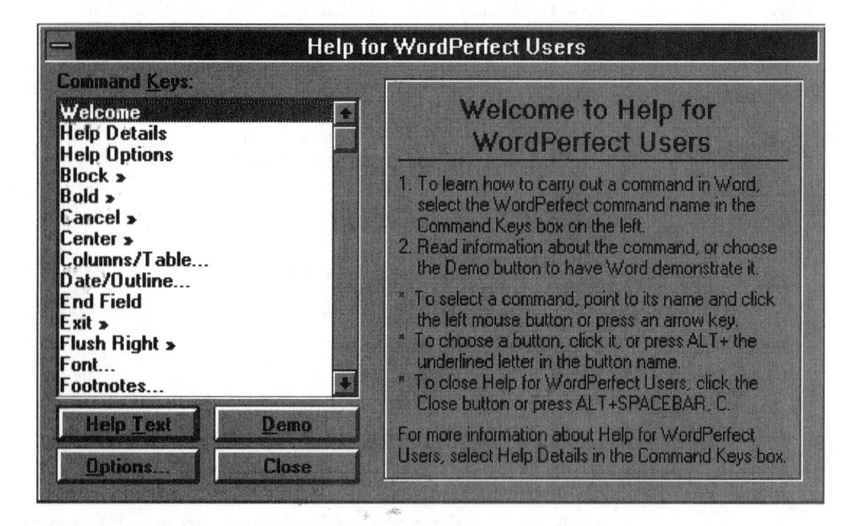

WordPerfect commands are listed in the Command Keys list box. Those with >> after them have demos ready to run. Those with … after them have suboptions.

2. Select a WordPerfect command in the Command Keys list box. The text on the right side of the WordPerfect Help dialog box shows the WordPerfect keyboard shortcut followed by an explanation of the equivalent Word command (see Figure B.8).

► Keep a Coach Handy on the Screen

There are two basic choices at this point: You can click the Help Text button, and a dialog box will appear on the screen, showing the same explanation that was just shown on the right side of the WordPerfect Help dialog box (see Figure B.9).

A dialog box with the explanatory text remains on the screen as long as you want it there as a reminder. Click Demo Now (if it's not grayed

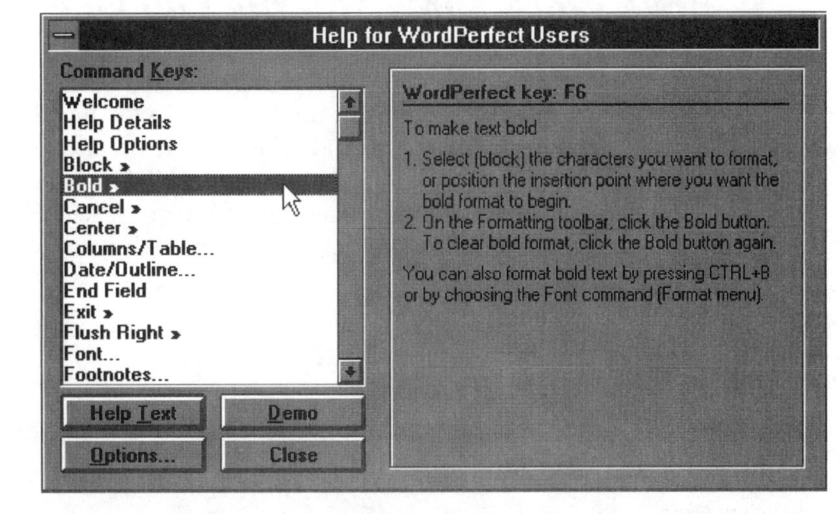

FIGURE B.8

The Help for WordPerfect Users dialog box explains the Word equivalent for the WordPerfect Bold (F6) command.

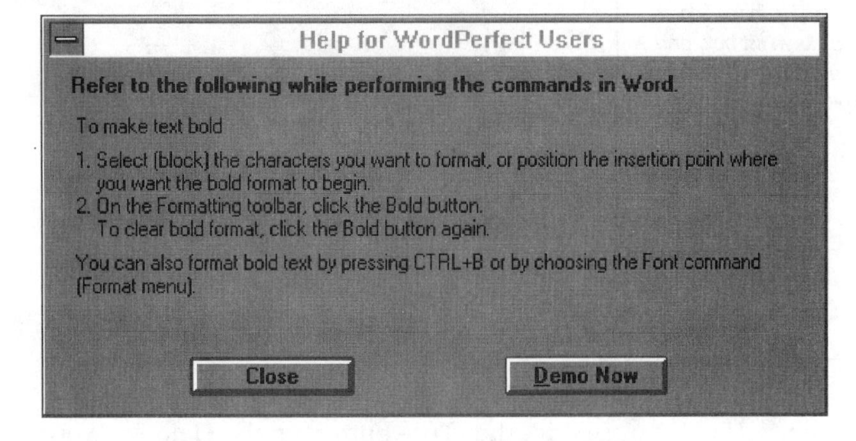

FIGURE B.9

A floating Help Text dialog box. Click Close when you no longer need coaching. Click the Demo Now button to see the demonstration for this command (if there is one).

out) to see the Word procedure demonstrated or click Close when you want to get rid of the dialog box.

▸ Have Word Show You the Equivalent Command

The other choice from the main Help for WordPerfect Users dialog box (Figure B.7) is to click the Demo button and see a Word command demonstrated (this is equivalent to clicking the Demo Now button in the dialog box that remains after you've clicked Help Text). Figure B.10 shows the result of clicking the Demo button with the Search <- command selected.

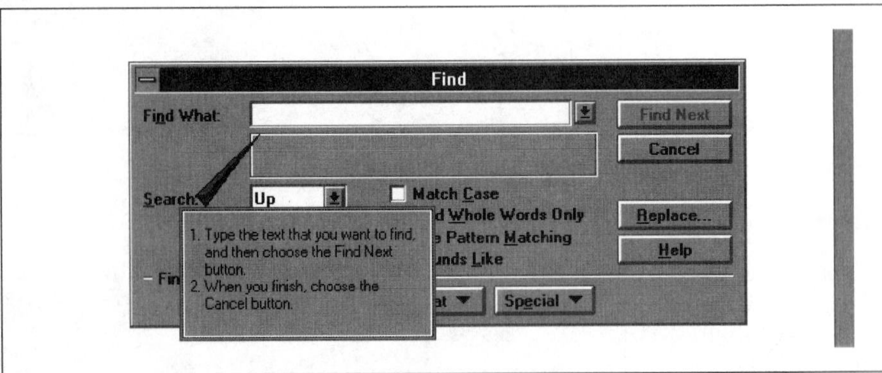

FIGURE B.10 ▸

The end result of the WordPerfect Help demo for the Search <- command. Watch as Word pulls down its own Edit menu, selects Find, chooses Up in the Search drop-down list box, and then attaches a blurb explaining what to do.

The demo really works the Word commands for you, so you can proceed from where the demo leaves you off.

▸ Make Word Respond to WordPerfect Key Combinations

Besides the Close button on the Help for WordPerfect Users dialog box, there is also an Options button. It offers the choice of hooking up the demonstrations so that they play themselves out whenever you press a WordPerfect key combination.

1. From the Help for WordPerfect Users dialog box (Figure B.7), click the Options button. This brings up the Help Options dialog box (see Figure B.11).

FIGURE B.11

The Help Options dialog box. From here you can choose WordPerfect navigation keys, as well as automatic demonstrations (or help text) in response to any WordPerfect key combination.

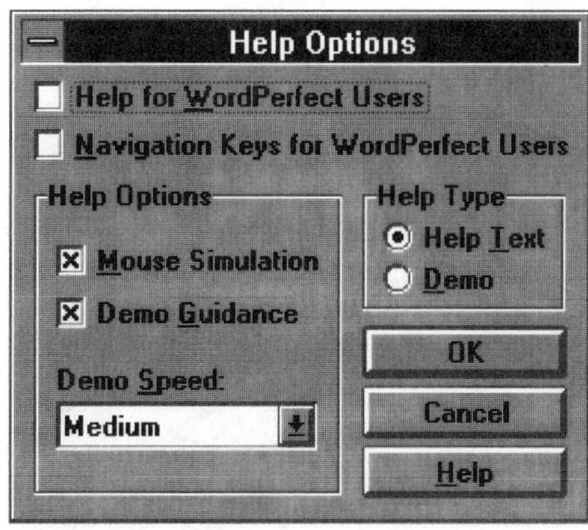

The check box at the top of the dialog box, Help for WordPerfect Users, makes WordPerfect Help context-sensitive. This means that if you press a WordPerfect key combination, WordPerfect Help will automatically come to life, either displaying the appropriate Help Text to help you learn the equivalent Word command, or running its built-in demo (when it has one) to actually show you how to activate the Word command.

The second check box configures the keyboard so that PageUp, PageDown, Home, End, Ctrl+PageUp, Ctrl+PageDown, Ctrl+Home, Ctrl+End, and Esc work the way they do in WordPerfect and not as they do in Word (as explained in the previous section, not all of the keys work the way they really should).

Both of these check-box options are also available on the General tab of the Options dialog box (see Figure B.5).

In the Help Type area to the right, you can select Help Text or Demo. This determines what type of WordPerfect Help will engage when you press a WordPerfect key combination.

The Help Options area on the left controls the details of the demonstrations. If you uncheck Mouse Simulation, then you won't see the pointer floating around and pulling down menus in the demos. If you uncheck Demo Guidance, then you won't get those helpful blurbs and dynamic 3-D–looking pointers explaining the Word dialog boxes. You can choose a slower or faster speed for the demos if they move too fast or slow for your liking. When you've chosen the options you want, click OK.

2. Click Help for WordPerfect Users.
3. Click Demo.
4. Click OK.
5. Click Close.
6. Now to see a live demo, press Ctrl+Home. WordPerfect Help demonstrates the nearest Word equivalent (the Go To command), as shown in Figure B.12.

FIGURE B.12 ▶

WordPerfect Help demonstrates Word's Go To command in response to Ctrl+Home.

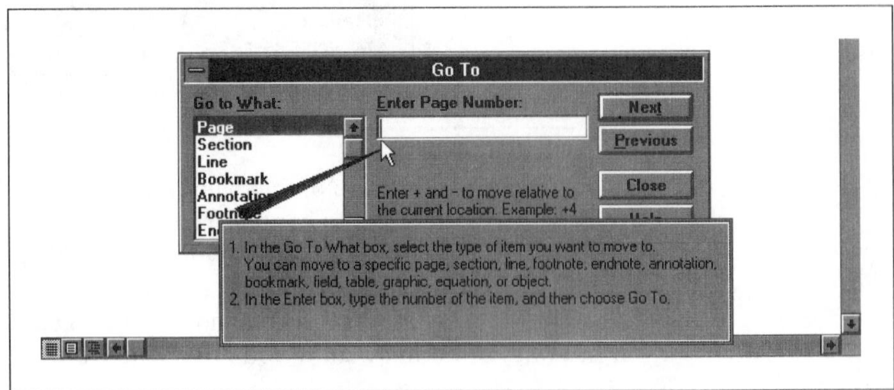

▸▸ **NOTE**

If you have turned on Help for WordPerfect users, you'll see that some Word features work differently. For example, when you select text and then press Delete, Word prompts you with the very WordPerfect-sounding *Delete Block? No (Yes)* in the status bar. If this annoys you, turn it off.

▸▸ Converting WordPerfect Documents

If you're switching over from WordPerfect, then it's likely that you have many WordPerfect documents lying around on your hard disk. Eventually, you'll want to open one up and modify it to create something new.

Fortunately, Word's document-conversion feature has gotten pretty keen and does a pretty spiffy job of converting WordPerfect documents.

It also recognizes WordPerfect documents, no problem, so all you have to do is select File ➤ Open (Ctrl+O) or click the Open button on the Standard Toolbar:

(Yes, this is the normal procedure for opening a document.) Then select the WordPerfect document you want to open and click OK. Word will detect that it is a WordPerfect document and will automatically convert it. The conversion will be pretty good.

►► NOTE

Word can only convert WordPerfect documents through version 5.2. If you have a document that was prepared in WordPerfect 6.0 or later, save it first in an earlier WordPerfect format, and then open it in Word.

Check your page numbers to see if they came through OK (they don't always). And check the Page Setup in general to see if Word did anything weird in response to your document formatting in WordPerfect. Otherwise, there shouldn't be any problems. Save the document under a different name so you can keep the clean source document in WordPerfect.

►► *If You Loved the Advance Feature...*

I was never a very big fan of WordPerfect's Advance feature, which allows you to move text (or anything, really) on the page to a precise location or to a location relative to something else on the page. I guess this feature is useful if you need to fill in a paper form precisely.

Word has added an Advance field code to produce similar results to those of the WordPerfect Advance command. Field codes are explained in Chapter 32, but I'll run through the particulars of the Advance field here.

The syntax for the Advance field is

{ ADVANCE [\ *switches*] }

There are six field-specific switches for the advance command. They are:

SWITCH	WHAT IT DOES
\l *n*	Moves the insertion point *n* points to the left
\r *n*	Moves the insertion point *n* points to the right
\u *n*	Moves the insertion point *n* points up
\d *n*	Moves the insertion point *n* points down
\x *n*	Places the insertion point *n* points to the right of left margin
\y *n*	Places the insertion point *n* points below the top margin

▸▸ **NOTE**

A point is almost exactly equal to 1/72nd of an inch.

The text that follows the Advance field will start from the new location of the insertion point. You can combine switches any way you want, including general switches.

APPENDIX C

Word Commands and Their Shortcuts

▶▶ ***Following*** is a list of Word's most commonly used commands and their shortcuts. The expression Num denotes that you must press the indicated key on the numeric keypad.

COMMAND	SHORTCUT
Align center	Ctrl+E
Align justify	Ctrl+R
Align left	Ctrl+←
All caps	Ctrl+Shift+A
Apply Heading 1	Ctrl+Alt+1
Apply Heading 2	Ctrl+Alt+2
Apply Heading 3	Ctrl+Alt+3
Apply list bullet	Ctrl+Shift+L
AutoFormat	Ctrl+K
AutoText	F3, Ctrl+Alt+V
Bold	Ctrl+B, Ctrl+Shift+B
Bookmark	Ctrl+Shift+F5
Change case	Shift+F3
Citation	Alt+Shift+I
Clear	Delete
Close current pane	Alt+Shift+C
Collapse outline	Alt+_, Alt+Shift+Num (minus)
Copy	Ctrl+C, Ctrl+Ins
Copy format	Ctrl+Shift+C
Copy text	Shift+F2

COMMAND	SHORTCUT
Customize keyboard settings	Ctrl+Alt+Num (plus)
Customize remove menu	Ctrl+Alt+-
Cut	Ctrl+X, Shift+Delete
Delete previous word	Ctrl+Backspace
Delete word	Ctrl+Delete
Demote to body text	Ctrl+Shift+N
Document close	Ctrl+W, Ctrl+F4
Document maximize	Ctrl+F10
Document move	Ctrl+F7
Document restore	Ctrl+F5
Document size	Ctrl+F8
Document split	Ctrl+Alt+S
Edit mail merge data source	Alt+Shift+E
Exit	Alt+F4
Extend down one line	Shift+↓
Extend left	Shift+←
Extend page down	Alt+Page Down
Extend page up	Shift+Page Up
Extend paragraph up	Ctrl+Shift+↑
Extend right	Shift+→
Extend selection	F8
Extend to end of document	Ctrl+Shift+End
Extend to end of line	Shift+End
Extend to end of window	Ctrl+Shift+Page Down
Extend to start of document	Ctrl+Shift+Home
Extend to start of line	Shift+Home
Extend to start of window	Ctrl+Shift+Page Up
Extend up one line	Shift+↑

COMMAND	SHORTCUT
Extend word left	Ctrl+Shift+←
Extend word right	Ctrl+Shift+→
Field click	Alt+Shift+F9
Find	Ctrl+F
Font	Ctrl+D
Font size	Ctrl+Shift+P
Go back	Shift+F5, Ctrl+Alt+Z
Go to annotation	Alt+F11
Go to end of column	Alt+Page Down, Alt+Shift+Page Down
Go to end of document	Ctrl+End
Go to end of line	End
Go to end of row	Alt+End, Alt+Shift+End
Go to end of window	Ctrl+Page Down
Go to next page	Ctrl+Alt+Page Down
Go to previous page	Ctrl+Alt+Page Up
Go to start of line	Home
Go to start of row	Alt+Home, Alt+Shift+Home
Go to start of window	Ctrl+Page Up
Go To	Ctrl+G, F5
Go to start of document	Ctrl+Home
Hanging indent	Ctrl+T
Header/footer	Alt+Shift+R
Help	F1
Help tool	Shift+F1
Hidden	Ctrl+Shift+H
Increase font 1 point	Ctrl+]
Increase font size	Ctrl+>

COMMAND	SHORTCUT
Indent	Ctrl+M
Insert annotation	Ctrl+Alt+A
Insert column break	Ctrl+Shift+↵
Insert date field	Alt+Shift+D
Insert endnote	Ctrl+Alt+E
Insert field	Ctrl+F9
Insert footnote	Ctrl+Alt+F
Insert merge field	Alt+Shift+F
Insert page break	Ctrl+↵
Insert page field	Alt+Shift+P
Insert spike	Ctrl+Shift+F3
Insert time	Alt+Shift+T
Italic	Ctrl+I, Ctrl+Shift+I
Justify	Ctrl+J
Left justify	Ctrl+L
Lock fields	Ctrl+3, Ctrl+F11
Mail merge check	Alt+Shift+K
Mark index entry	Alt+Shift+X
Mark TOC entry	Alt+Shift+O
Menu add	Ctrl+Alt+=
Menu mode	F10
Merge to a document	Alt+Shift+N
Merge to the printer	Alt+Shift+M
Minimize Word	Alt+F10
Move left	←
Move right	→
Move text	F2
New	Ctrl+N

COMMAND	SHORTCUT
Next field	F11, Alt+F1
Next object	Alt+↓
Next window	Ctrl+F6, Alt+F6
Normal style	Ctrl+Shift+N, Alt+Shift+Num 5
Open	Ctrl+O, Ctrl+F12, Ctrl+Alt+F2
Open or close up paragraph	Ctrl+O
Other pane	F6, Shift+F6
Outline demote	Alt+Shift+→
Outline expand	Alt+(plus), Alt+Shift+Num (plus)
Outline move down	Alt+Shift+↓
Outline move up	Alt+Shift+↑
Outline promote	Alt+Shift+←
Outline show first line	Alt+Shift+L
Overtype	Ins
Paste	Ctrl+V, Shift+Ins
Paste format	Ctrl+Shift+V
Previous object	Alt+U
Previous field	Shift+F11, Alt+Shift+F1
Previous window	Ctrl+Shift+F6, Alt+Shift+F6
Print	Ctrl+P, Ctrl+Shift+F12
Print preview	Ctrl+F2, Ctrl+Alt+I
Redo	Alt+Shift+Backspace
Redo or repeat	Ctrl+Y, F4, Alt+↵
Repeat find	Shift+F4, Ctrl+Alt+Y
Replace	Ctrl+H
Reset character formatting	Ctrl+spacebar, Ctrl+Shift+Z

COMMAND	SHORTCUT
Reset paragraph formatting	Ctrl+Q
Restore	Alt+F5
Right justify	Ctrl+→
Save	Shift+F12, Ctrl+S, Alt+Shift+F2
Save as	F12
Select all	Ctrl+A, Ctrl+Num 5
Select column	Ctrl+Shift+F8
Select table	Alt+Num 5
Show all headings	Alt+Shift+A
Show Heading 1	Alt+!
Show Heading 2	Alt+@
Show heading 3	Alt+#
Show Heading 4	Alt+$
Show heading 5	Alt+%
Show Heading 6	Alt+^
Show heading 7	Alt+&
Show Heading 8	Alt+*
Show Heading 9	Alt+(
Shrink font	Ctrl+<
Shrink font 1 point	Ctrl+[
Shrink selection	Shift+F8
Small caps	Ctrl+Shift+K
Space 1 1/2 line	Ctrl+5
Space double space	Ctrl+2
Space single space	Ctrl+1
Spell check	F7
Spike	Ctrl+F3

COMMAND	SHORTCUT
Start of column	Alt+Page Up, Alt+Shift+Page Up
Style	Ctrl+Shift+S
Subscript	Ctrl+=
Superscript	Ctrl+(plus)
Symbol font	Ctrl+Shift+Q
System info	Ctrl+Alt+F1
Thesaurus	Shift+F7
Toggle field display	Shift+F9
Underline	Ctrl+U, Alt+U
Underline double	Ctrl+Shift+D
Undo	Ctrl+Z, Alt+Backspace
Unhang	Ctrl+Shift+T
Unindent	Ctrl+Shift+M
Unlink fields	Ctrl+6, Ctrl+Shift+F9
Unlock fields	Ctrl+4, Ctrl+Shift+F11
Update fields	F9, Alt+Shift+U
Update source	Ctrl+Shift+F7
Update table autoformat	Ctrl+Alt+U
View field codes	Alt+F9
View normal	Ctrl+Alt+N
View outline	Ctrl+Alt+O
View page	Ctrl+Alt+P
Word underline	Ctrl+Shift+W

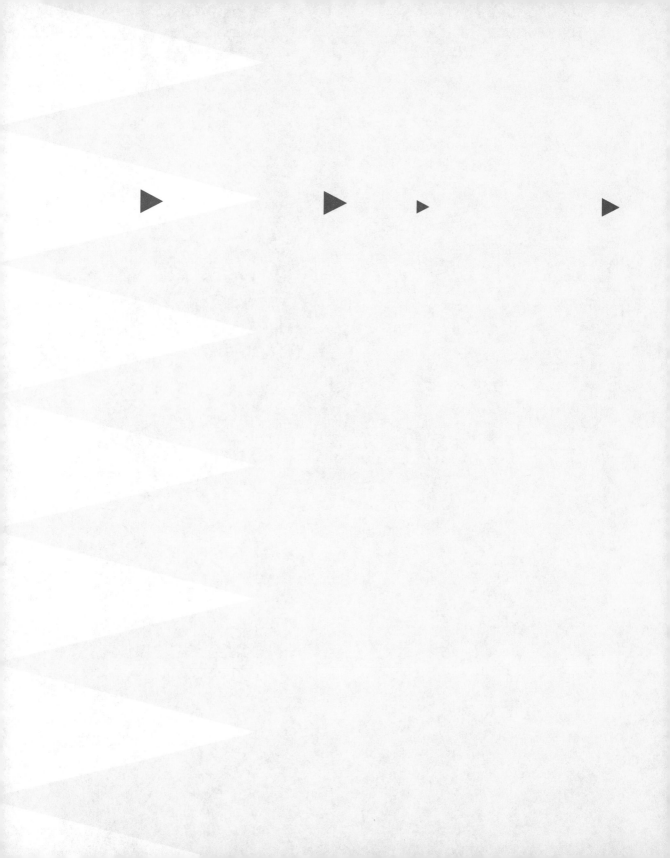

APPENDIX D

Character Sets and Codes

▶▶ **Characters** 0–127 are the standard ASCII characters; these will not change from font to font. Characters 128–255 will change, however.

CHARACTER	ASCII VALUE
NUL	0
SOH	1
STX	2
ETX	3
EOT	4
ENQ	5
ACK	6
BEL	7
BS	8
HT	9
LF	10
VT	11
FF	12
CR	13
SO	14
SI	15
DLE	16
DC1	17
DC2	18

CHARACTER	ASCII VALUE
DC3	19
DC4	20
NAK	21
SYN	22
ETB	23
CAN	24
EM	25
SUB	26
ESC	27
FS	28
GS	29
RS	30
US	31
sp	32
!	33
“	34
#	35
$	36
%	37

CHARACTER	ASCII VALUE
&	38
‘	39
(	40
)	41
*	42
+	43
,	44
-	45
.	46
/	47
0	48
1	49
2	50
3	51
4	52
5	53
6	54
7	55
8	56
9	57
:	58
;	59
<	60
=	61
>	62
?	63
@	64
A	65

CHARACTER	ASCII VALUE
B	66
C	67
D	68
E	69
F	70
G	71
H	72
I	73
J	74
K	75
L	76
M	77
N	78
O	79
P	80
Q	81
R	82
S	83
T	84
U	85
V	86
W	87
X	88
Y	89
Z	90
[	91
\	92
]	93

CHARACTER	ASCII VALUE
^	94
_	95
ù	96
a	97
b	98
c	99
d	100
e	101
f	102
g	103
h	104
i	105
j	106
k	107
l	108
m	109
n	110
o	111

<table>
<tr><th>CHARACTER</th><th>ASCII VALUE</th></tr>
<tr><td>p</td><td>112</td></tr>
<tr><td>q</td><td>113</td></tr>
<tr><td>r</td><td>114</td></tr>
<tr><td>s</td><td>115</td></tr>
<tr><td>t</td><td>116</td></tr>
<tr><td>u</td><td>117</td></tr>
<tr><td>v</td><td>118</td></tr>
<tr><td>w</td><td>119</td></tr>
<tr><td>x</td><td>120</td></tr>
<tr><td>y</td><td>121</td></tr>
<tr><td>z</td><td>122</td></tr>
<tr><td>{</td><td>123</td></tr>
<tr><td>|</td><td>124</td></tr>
<tr><td>}</td><td>125</td></tr>
<tr><td>~</td><td>126</td></tr>
<tr><td>DEL</td><td>127</td></tr>
</table>

APPENDIX E

Field Codes and Their Switches

►► General Switches

All field codes can include general switches, which are mostly used for formatting purposes. The four types of general switches are

Switch Type	Used for
*	Text formatting
\#	Numeric formatting
\@	Date and time formatting
\!	Locking the result

General switches are explained in depth in Chapter 32. The rest of this appendix will explain each individual field code and the *field-specific* switches that pertain to each.

►► Field Codes and Field-Specific Switches

For each field code in Word, I'll give the syntax (that is, the form of the field code), an explanation of the field, and a list of the field-specific switches you can use with the field.

As a matter of convention, the name of the field code will appear in all caps, anything optional will appear between square brackets, and any variable (anything that can be different every time) will be italicized.

►► = (Formula)

The = field is also called the Formula field. It takes this form:

{ =*expression or formula* }

It always consists of the = sign and then either a mathematical expression (using the normal mathematical operators— +, –, /, *, and so on— as well as logical operators) or a formula. Formulas can include bookmarks; references to table cells, rows, or columns; and so on.

▶▶ Advance

Advance fields take this form:

{ ADVANCE [*switches*] }

The Advance field moves the insertion point relative to its current location or to the left or top margin.

The switches control the direction and distance that the insertion point moves. They are as follows:

Switch	Moves the insertion point
\l *n*	Moves the insertion point *n* points to the left
\r *n*	Moves the insertion point *n* points to the right
\u *n*	Moves the insertion point *n* points up
\d *n*	Moves the insertion point *n* points down
\x *n*	Places the insertion point *n* points to the right of the left margin
\y *n*	Places the insertion point *n* points below the top margin

▶▶ **NOTE**

A point is almost exactly equal to 1/72nd of an inch.

▶▶ Ask

Ask fields take this form:

{ ASK *bookmark "prompt text"* [*switches*] }

The field displays a dialog box that includes the prompt text and a text box. Whatever is entered into the text box is assigned to the bookmark.

The field-specific switches for Ask are

\d "*default text*"	Used to supply default text (highlighted) in the text box.
\o	Prompts only once during a mail merge (instead of once for each resulting document).

▸▸ Author

The Author field takes this form:

{ AUTHOR ["*New Name*"] }

By itself, the { AUTHOR } field code displays the name of the author of the document (from the User Info tab of the Options dialog box—Tools ➤ Options). With a new name in quotation marks, as a variable, or input with a prompt, the field stores the new author name.

▸▸ AutoNum

The AutoNum field takes this form:

{ AUTONUM }

This field is used to number paragraphs. Placed at the beginning of a paragraph, it displays a number. It counts all the preceding paragraphs that also start with the AutoNum field and have the same paragraph style (Normal if nothing else), and displays the next number in that sequence. If you rearrange, copy, or insert paragraphs with AutoNum, the numbers will always reflect the current order.

▸▸ AutoNumLgl

The AutoNumLgl field takes this form:

{ AUTONUMLGL }

This field is used to number paragraphs in traditional legal format. Placed at the beginning of a paragraph, it displays a number. It counts all the preceding paragraphs that also start with the AutoNumLgl field and have the same paragraph style (Normal if nothing else) and displays the next number in that sequence. If you rearrange, copy, or insert paragraphs with AutoNumLgl, the numbers will always reflect the current order.

If you use AutoNumLgl field codes with more than one paragraph style, then each style gets its own sequence, starting with 1., 2., 3.; followed by 1.1, 1.2, 1.3; and then 1.1.1, 1.1.2, and so on. The precedence of the styles is determined first of all by their heading levels if they are numbered, and otherwise strictly by the order in which they appear.

AutoNumOut

The AutoNumOut field takes this form:

{ AUTONUMOUT }

This field is used to number paragraphs in traditional outline format. Placed at the beginning of a paragraph, it displays a number. It counts all the preceding paragraphs that also start with the AutoNumOut field and have the same paragraph style (Normal if nothing else) and displays the next number in that sequence. If you rearrange, copy, or insert paragraphs with AutoNumOut, the numbers will always reflect the current order.

If you use AutoNumOut field codes with more than one paragraph style, then each style gets its own sequence, starting with I., II., III.; followed by A., B., C.; and then 1., 2., and so on. The precedence of the styles is determined first of all by their heading levels if they are numbered, and otherwise strictly by the order in which they appear.

AutoText

The AutoText field takes this form:

{ AUTOTEXT *entry* }

This field displays the contents of the AutoText *entry*.

▸▸ BarCode

The BarCode field takes this form:

{ BARCODE "*text*" [*switches*] }

This field inserts a postal bar code based on the literal *text* enclosed in quotation marks.

The field-specific switches for BarCode are

bookmark \b	Creates a postal bar code based on the text contained in *bookmark*.
\f "*letter*"	Inserts a Facing Identification Mark (FIM). If "*letter*" is "A", it inserts a courtesy reply mark. If "*letter*" is "C", it inserts a business reply mark.
\u	Identifies the bar code as a US postal address.

▸▸ Bookmark

The Bookmark field takes this form:

{ *bookmark* [*switches*] }

You don't literally type the word "bookmark." Instead, you type the bookmark name. This field displays the contents of *bookmark*. This is the same as the Ref field.

The field-specific switches for *bookmark* are

\f	Includes and increments footnote, endnote, or annotation numbers.
\n	Inserts paragraph numbering (if any) from the marked paragraph.

►► Comments

The Comments field takes this form:

{ COMMENTS [*"new comments"*] }

By itself, the { COMMENTS } field code displays the comments in the Summary Info dialog box. With new comments in quotation marks, as a variable, or input with a prompt, the field stores the new comments.

►► Compare

The Compare field takes this form:

{ COMPARE *expression1 comparison expression2* }

It compares *firstexpression* with *secondexpression* using the *comparison* operator. If the comparison is true, then it returns a value of 1. If the comparison is false, it returns 0. The expressions can be bookmarks, strings, numbers, other fields that return values or mathematical formulas. For string expressions of more than one word, enclose the string in quotation marks. Valid *comparison* operators are

=	is equal to
<	is less than
<=	is less than or equal to
>	is greater than
>=	is greater than or equal to
<>	is not equal to

For the = and <> operators, the second expression can include the wild-card characters ? and *; ? for any single character to match or * for any number of characters.

▸▸ CreateDate

The CreateDate field takes this form:

{ CREATEDATE }

It displays the creation date of the document it's in.

You can, of course, add the \@ general field switch for date and time "picture" formatting to control the appearance of the date. The \@ options are explained in Chapter 32.

▸▸ Database

The Database field takes this form:

{ DATABASE [*switches*] }

It displays the result of a database query. Usually inserted with the Insert ➤ Database command, this field is a difficult one to construct by hand.

The field-specific switches for Database are

\c *instructions*	The instructions that ODBC uses to make the connection to the database.
\d "*path\ filename*"	The path and file name of the database.
\s *instructions*	The SQL instructions that query the database.
\f *number*	Inserts data into the Word document starting from the data record *number.*
\t *number*	Inserts data into the Word document ending with the data record *number.*
\l "*number*"	Applies a format from the Table AutoFormat dialog box.

\b *number* Specifies which attributes of the format set by the \l switch apply to the table:

0	None
1	Borders
2	Shading
4	Font
8	Color
16	AutoFit
32	Heading rows
64	Last Row
128	First Column
256	Last Column

You can add the numbers together to specify more than one attribute. If you leave out the number, the switch defaults to 16, AutoFit.

►► Date

The Date field takes this form:

{ DATE [\l] }

It displays the current date. The only field-specific switch is \l. It specifies that the date be displayed with the last format chosen for a date (via Insert ➤ Date and Time).

You can, of course, add the \@ general field switch for date and time "picture" formatting to control the appearance of the date. The \@ options are explained in Chapter 32.

►► DDE

The DDE field takes this form:

{ DDE *application document* [*place-reference*] }

It creates a dynamic data exchange (DDE) link with another Windows application. When DDE is updated, it displays current information from the source document.

The *application* instruction is the name of the Windows application. The *document* instruction is the file name of the source document. The optional *place-reference* switch varies in format from application to application. For example, if the source document is a spreadsheet, the *place-reference* would generally be a range named or specified from cell to cell.

►► DDEAuto

The DDEAuto field takes this form:

{ DDEAUTO *application document* [*place-reference*] }

It creates a dynamic data exchange (DDE) link with another Windows application that updates itself automatically whenever you open the document the field is in.

The *application* instruction is the name of the Windows application. The *document* instruction is the file name of the source document. The optional *place-reference* switch varies in format from application to application. For example, if the source document is a spreadsheet, the *place-reference* would generally be a range named or specified from cell to cell.

►► EditTime

The EditTime field takes this form:

{ EDITTIME }

It displays the editing time, in minutes, since the document's creation. Editing time is defined as the time the document is open.

►► Embed

The Embed field takes this form:

{ EMBED *application* [*switches*] }

Inserts an object created in another application, using OLE. You can't insert the Embed field by hand (Insert ➤ Object and Edit ➤ Paste Special can insert the field automatically), but you can edit an existing Embed field code.

You can't change the *application*. The only field-specific switch is \s, which returns the object to its original scale and cropping when it is updated. (The general * mergeformat switch has the opposite effect, keeping the current scale and cropping when the field is updated.)

►► EQ (Equation)

The EQ (Equation) field takes this form:

{ EQ [*switches*] }

EQ produces a mathematical equation assembled from the switches and their contents. Field-specific switches for EQ are

\a(*element1, element2, etc.*) Draws a two-dimensional array using any number of elements. The following options can come between the \a switch and the elements in parentheses:

\al	Align left within columns
\ac	Align center within columns
\ar	Align right within columns
\co*n*	*n* columns (default is 1)
\vs*n*	*n* points of vertical spacing between lines
\hs*n*	*n* points of horizontal spacing between columns

\b(*element*) — Brackets a single element in a size appropriate to the element. The default brackets are parentheses. The following options can come between the \b switch and the element in parentheses:

- \lc*c* — Draws the left-bracket character using the character specified for *c*. If you specify {, [, (, or <, then Word uses the corresponding closing character as the right bracket. If you specify any other character, Word uses that character for both.
- \rc*c* — Draws the right-bracket character using the character specified for *c*.
- \bc*c* — Draws both bracket characters using the character specified for *c*.

\d( ) — Specifies precisely where the next character is drawn. The following options can come between the \d switch and the empty parentheses:

- \fo*n* — Forward *n* points
- \ba*n* — Back *n* points
- \li — Draws a line from the end of the displaced character to the beginning of the next character.

\f(*numerator*, *denominator*) — Creates a fraction with *numerator* and *denominator* centered above and below the division line.

\i(*lower-limit, upper-limit, integrand*) — Creates an integral. The following options can come between the \i switch and the elements in parentheses:

\su	Changes the symbol to a capital sigma (Σ) and creates a summation.
\pr	Changes the symbol to a capital pi (∏) and creates a product.
\in	Creates an in-line format with the limits displayed to the right of the symbol instead of above and below.
\fc*c*	Substitutes a fixed-height character specified by *c* for the symbol.
\vc*c*	Substitutes a variable-height character specified by *c* for the symbol. The symbol matches the height of the third element.

\l(*element1, element2, etc.*) — Creates a list of values separated by commas or semicolons.

\o(*element1, element2, etc.*) — The \o switch overstrikes each successive element on top of the previous ones. Any number of elements is permitted. Each character is printed within an invisible character box. The following options can come between the \o switch and the elements in parentheses:

\al	Aligns the left edges of the characters' boxes.
\ac	Aligns the centers of the characters' boxes. This is the default.
\ar	Aligns the right edges of the characters' boxes.

\r(*element* [, *root*])	Draws a radical (√), using one or two elements. A single element appears as a square root. With two elements, the first element—the exponent—is drawn above the radical, and the second element is drawn inside.
\s(*element1*) [(*element2*) (*etc.*)]	Positions elements as superscripts or subscripts. Each \s code can have one or more elements. If more than one element is specified, the elements are stacked and left-aligned. The following options can come before any parenthetical elements: \ai*n*() — Adds space above a line in a paragraph by the number of points specified by *n*. \up*n*() — Moves a single element up the number of points specified by *n*. The default is 2. \di*n*() — Adds space below a line in a paragraph by the number of points specified by *n*. \do*n*() — Moves a single element down the number of points specified by *n*. The default is 2.
\x(*element*)	Creates a border for an element. When used without options, this code draws a box around the element. The following options can come between the \x switch and the element in parentheses: \to — Top border \bo — Bottom border \le — Left border \ri — Right border

►► FileName

The FileName field takes this form:

{ FILENAME [\p] }

It displays the file name of the document. The option \p switch causes it to display the entire path as well as the file name.

►► FileSize

The FileSize field takes this form:

{ FILESIZE [*switches*] }

It displays the size of the document in bytes. Field-specific switches are

\k	Displays the result in kilobytes, rounded to the nearest whole number.
\m	Display the results in megabytes, rounded to the nearest whole number.

►► Fillin

The Fillin field takes this form:

{ FILLIN ["*prompt*"] [*switches*] }

It displays a dialog box prompting for the text to appear in the place of the field. The field-specific switches for Fillin are

\d "*default*"	Specifies a default result in the dialog box.
\o	Prompts only once during a mail merge.

►► FormCheckbox

The FormCheckbox field takes this form:

{ FORMCHECKBOX }

It inserts a check box in a form. You cannot insert this field manually, nor can you modify it.

►► FormDropdown

The FormDropdown field takes this form:

{ FORMDROPDOWN }

It inserts a drop-down list in a form. You cannot insert this field manually, nor can you modify it.

►► Formula (=)

See the = field entry at the beginning of this appendix.

►► FormText

The FormText field takes this form:

{ FORMTEXT }

It inserts a text box in a form. You cannot insert this field manually, nor can you modify it.

►► GotoButton

The GotoButton field takes this form:

{ GOTOBUTTON *destination display text* }

It shows the display text on the screen as a clickable field result or button (you can also insert a graphic into this field to have the button display as a graphic). Double-clicking the button jumps the reader to the destination, which can be any acceptable Go To destination (Go To is explained in Chapter 3) such as a bookmark, page number, table, and so on.

▸▸ If

The If field takes this form:

{ IF *expression1 comparison expression2 "true text" "false text"* }

It compares *expression1* with *expression2* using the *comparison* operator. If the comparison is true, it displays the true text. If the comparison is false, it displays the false text. The expressions can be bookmarks, strings, numbers, other fields that return values or mathematical formulas. For string expressions of more than one word, enclose the string in quotation marks. Valid *comparison* operators are

=	is equal to
<	is less than
<=	is less than or equal to
>	is greater than
>=	is greater than or equal to
<>	is not equal to

For the = and <> operators, the second expression can include the wild-card characters ? and *; ? for any single character to match or * for any number of characters.

▸▸ IncludePicture

The IncludePicture field takes this form:

{ INCLUDEPICTURE *filename* [*switches*] }

It inserts the named graphic file. If you include the path with the file name, you must type each backslash twice; for example, c:\\art\\picture.bmp. Field-specific switches are

\c *converter*	Specifies the file name of the graphics filter to use.
\d	Specifies that Graphic information not be stored in the document.

►► IncludeText

The IncludeText field takes this form:

{ INCLUDETEXT *filename* [*bookmark*] [*switches*] }

It inserts the named source document or the contents of *bookmark* in the named document. If you include the path with the file name, you must type each backslash twice; for example, c:\\work\\report.doc. The only field-specific switch is

\c *converter*	Specifies the file name of the converter to use.

►► Index

The Index field takes this form:

{ INDEX [*switches*] }

It builds and inserts an index based on entries marked with the XE field. Field-specific switches are

\b *bookmark*	Builds an index for the section of the document marked by *bookmark*.
\c *n*	Creates an index with *n* columns.
\d "*c*"	Defines the separator character (*c*) for sequences defined by the \s switch (default is "-").

\e "*c*"	Defines the separator character between an index entry and its page number (default is ", ").
\f "*entry type*"	Creates an index using only the specified entry type (using only XE fields with the same "*entry type*" text).
\g "*c*"	Defines the separator character (*c*) used in a page range (default is "–").
\h "*heading text*"	Inserts a heading between groups in the index (include A in the heading text string to have the sequential letter of the alphabet in each heading).
\l "*c*"	Defines the separator character (*c*) used between page numbers (default is ", ").
\p *letter1-letter2*	Limits the index to entries beginning with letters between *letter1* and *letter2*, inclusive. Use ! for *letter1* to include all symbols at the beginning.
\r	Runs index subentries on the same line as the main entry.
\s *sequence-name*	When there are Seq fields in the document, includes the sequence number before the page number, joined by whatever character is specified with the \d switch.

►► Info

The Info field takes this form:

{ [INFO] *info-type* ["*new value*"] }

Displays the current value of *info-type* or assigns "*new value*" to it. *info-type* may be any of the following:

AUTHOR

COMMENTS

CREATEDATE

EDITTIME

FILENAME

FILESIZE

KEYWORDS

LASTSAVEDBY

NUMCHARS

NUMPAGES

NUMWORDS

PRINTDATE

REVNUM

SAVEDATE

SUBJECT

TEMPLATE

TITLE

The Info field for any of the above info types is the same as the field by the same name (each of which are listed in this Appendix).

▸▸ Keywords

The Keywords field takes this form:

{ KEYWORDS "*new keywords*" }

By itself, it displays the keywords from the Summary Info dialog box. With new keywords in quotation marks, as a variable, or input with a prompt, the field stores the keywords.

▶▶ LastSavedBy

The LastSavedBy field takes this form:

{ LASTSAVEDBY }

It displays the name, taken from the Summary Info dialog box, of the last person who saved the document.

▶▶ Link

The Link field takes this form:

{ LINK *application filename* [*place-reference*] [*switches*] }

It inserts a link in the document to the named file or to the referenced place in the file. Field-specific switches are

\a	Link updates automatically.
\b	Inserts the linked object as a bitmap.
\d	Does not store graphic data in the document.
\p	Inserts the linked object as a graphic.
\r	Inserts the linked object in RTF (rich text format).
\t	Inserts the linked object in text-only format.

▶▶ MacroButton

The MacroButton field takes this form:

{ MACROBUTTON *macroname display text* }

It shows the display text on the screen as a clickable field result or button (you can also insert a graphic into this field to have the button display as a graphic). Double-clicking the button runs the named macro.

►► MergeField

The MergeField field takes this form:

{ MERGEFIELD *fieldname* }

It merges the data from the data source into the main document during a mail merge.

►► MergeRec

The MergeRec field takes this form:

{ MERGEREC }

It inserts the number of the current data record during a mail merge.

►► MergeSeq

The MergeSeq field takes this form:

{ MERGESEQ }

It inserts the number of the current data record during a mail merge, counting only records included in the merge.

►► Next

The Next field takes this form:

{ NEXT }

It inserts the next record during a mail merge into the current document. Place it before the second set of MergeField fields and thereafter.

▸▸ NextIf

The NextIf field takes this form:

{ NEXTIF *expression1 comparison expression2* }

It compares *firstexpression* with *secondexpression* using the *comparison* operator. If the comparison is true, it merges the next data record into the current document during a mail merge. If false, it merges the next data record into a new document. The expressions can be bookmarks, strings, numbers, other fields that return values, or mathematical formulas. For string expressions of more than one word, enclose the string in quotation marks. Valid *comparison* operators are

=	is equal to
<	is less than
<=	is less than or equal to
>	is greater than
>=	is greater than or equal to
<>	is not equal to

For the = and <> operators, the second expression can include the wild-card characters ? and *; ? for any single character to match or * for any number of characters.

▸▸ NoteRef

The NoteRef field takes this form:

{ NOTEREF *bookmark* [\f] }

It displays the reference mark of the footnote or endnote marked by *bookmark*. Include the \f switch to retain the formatting of the mark.

▸▸ NumChars

The NumChars field takes this form:

{ NUMCHARS }

It displays the number of characters in the document, taken from the Summary Info dialog box.

▸▸ NumPages

The NumPages field takes this form:

{ NUMPAGES }

It displays the number of pages in the document, taken from the Summary Info dialog box.

▸▸ NumWords

The NumWords field takes this form:

{ NUMWORDS }

It displays the number of words in the document, taken from the Summary Info dialog box.

▸▸ Page

The Page field takes this form:

{ PAGE }

It displays the current page.

▶▶ PageRef

The PageRef field takes this form:

{ PAGEREF *bookmark* }

It displays the page number of a bookmark.

▶▶ Print

The Print field takes this form:

{ PRINT "*printer codes*" }

It sends printer codes to the printer.

▶▶ PrintDate

The PrintDate field takes this form:

{ PRINTDATE }

It displays the date the document was last printed. You can, of course, add the \@ general field switch for date and time "picture" formatting to control the appearance of the date. The \@ options are explained in Chapter 32.

▶▶ Private

The Private field takes this form:

{ PRIVATE }

It stores data for a document converted from other file formats in case the document ever needs to be converted back.

▸▸ Quote

The Quote field takes this form:

{ QUOTE "*text*" }

It inserts the specified text into the document.

▸▸ RD (Referenced Document)

The RD (Referenced Document) field takes this form:

{ RD *filename* }

It identifies a file to be included in a table of contents, table of authorities, or index. The field is autmatically formatted as hidden text.

▸▸ Ref

The Ref field takes this form:

{ REF *bookmark* }

It displays the contents of *bookmark*. It's equivalent to the Bookmark field, also listed in this Appendix.

The field-specific switches for Ref are

\f	Includes and increments footnote, endnote, or annotation numbers.
\n	Inserts paragraph numbering (if any) from the marked paragraph.

▸▸ RevNum

The RevNum field takes this form:

{ REVNUM }

It displays the number of document revisions, using statistics from the Summary Info dialog box.

►► SaveDate

The SaveDate field takes this form:

{ SAVEDATE }

It inserts the date and time the document was last saved, using statistics from the Summary Info dialog box. You can, of course, add the \@ general field switch for date and time "picture" formatting to control the appearance of the date. The \@ options are explained in Chapter 32.

►► Section

The Section field takes this form:

{ SECTION }

It displays the number of the current section.

►► SectionPages

The SectionPages field takes this form:

{ SECTIONPAGES }

It displays the total number of pages in the current section.

►► Seq (Sequence)

The Seq (Sequence) field takes this form:

{ SEQ *identifier bookmark* [*switches*] }

It displays a sequential number, counting all the previous Seq fields with the same *identifier*. The identifier word can be anything. Include a bookmark to cross-reference the contents of the bookmark. Field-specific switches are

\c	Inserts the most recent sequence number.
\h	Hides the field result.
\n	Inserts the next sequence number (this is the default).
\r *n*	Resets the sequence number to *n*.

▸▸ Set

The Set field takes this form:

{ SET *bookmark "text"* }

It defines the contents of *bookmark*.

▸▸ SkipIf

The SkipIf field takes this form:

{ SKIPIF *expression1 comparison expression2* }

It compares *firstexpression* with *secondexpression* using the *comparison* operator. If the comparison is true, it skips the next data record into the current document during a mail merge. If false, it does not. The expressions can be bookmarks, strings, numbers, or other fields that return values or mathematical formulas. For string expressions of more than one word, enclose the string in quotation marks. Valid *comparison* operators are

=	is equal to
<	is less than
<=	is less than or equal to
>	is greater than
>=	is greater than or equal to
<>	is not equal to

For the = and <> operators, the second expression can include the wild-card characters ? and *; ? for any single character to match or * for any number of characters.

►► StyleRef

The StyleRef field takes this form:

{ STYLEREF "*style-name*" [*switches*] }

It displays text from the nearest paragraph with the named style. Field-specific switches are

\l	Tells Word to search from the bottom of the page instead of the top.
\n	Inserts any paragraph numbering from the referenced paragraph.

►► Subject

The Subject field takes this form:

{ SUBJECT ["*new subject*"] }

By itself, the { SUBJECT } field code displays the subject of the document (from the User Info tab of the Options dialog box—Tools ➤ Options). With a new subject in quotation marks, as a variable, or input with a prompt, the field stores the new subject.

►► Symbol

The Symbol field takes this form:

{ SYMBOL *character-number* [*switches*] }

Displays the character that corresponds to the specified character-number in the ANSI character set. Field-specific switches are

\f "*font name*"	Specifies the font.
\h	Inserts the symbol without affecting the line spacing.
\s *n*	Specifies the font size as *n* points.

▸▸ TA (Table of Authorities Entry)

The TA (Table of Authorities Entry) field takes this form:

{ TA [*switches*] }

It defines the text and page number for a table of authorities entry. The field is formatted as hidden text. Field-specific switches are

\b	Boldfaces the page number in the entry.
\c *n*	Defines the category number as *n*.
\i	Italicizes the page number in the entry.
\l "*long citation text*"	Defines the long citation for the entry.
\r *bookmark*	Includes the range of pages marked by *bookmark*.
\s "*short citation text*"	Defines the short citation for the entry.

▸▸ TC (Table of Contents Entry)

The TC (Table of Contents Entry) field takes this form:

{ TC "*text*" [*switches*] }

It defines the text and page number for a table of contents entry. The field is formatted as hidden text. The field-specific switches are

\f *entry-identifier*	Identifies the entry as a certain type, using a one-letter *entry-identifier*, for use in tables of just those entry types.
\l *level-identifier*	Identifies the level of the entry using a one-letter *level-identifier.*
\n	Suppresses the page number for the entry.

►► Template

The Template field takes this form:

{ TEMPLATE [\p] }

It displays the file name of the document's template from the Summary Info dialog box. The \p switch adds the path to the file name.

►► Time

The Time field takes this form:

{ TIME }

It displays the current time. You can, of course, add the \@ general field switch for date and time "picture" formatting to control the appearance of the date. The \@ options are explained in Chapter 32.

►► Title

The Title field takes this form:

{ TITLE ["*New Title*"] }

By itself, the { TITLE } field code displays the name of the title of the document (from the Summary Info dialog box). With a new title in quotation marks, as a variable, or input with a prompt, the field stores the new title.

▸▸ TOA (Table of Authorities)

The TOA (Table of Authorities) field takes this form:

{ TOA \c *category* [*other switches*] }

It builds and inserts a table of authorities based on entries marked with the TA field. Field-specific switches are

\b *bookmark*	Builds a table of authorities for the section of the document marked by *bookmark*.
\c *n*	Builds a table of authorities only with entries with category number *n*.
\d "*c*"	Defines the separator character (*c*) between a sequence number and a page number for sequences defined by the \s switch (default is "-").
\e "*c*"	Defines the separator character (*c*) between a table-of-authorities entry and its page number (default is a tab with dot leaders).
\f	Removes the formatting applied to the entries.
\g "*c*"	Defines the separator character (*c*) used in a page range (default is "–").
\h	Includes the category heading for the entries in a table of authorities.
\l "*c*"	Defines the separator character (*c*) used between page numbers (default is ", ").
\p	Replaces five or more page references for the same authority with "passim."

\s *sequence-name*	When there are Seq fields in the document, includes the sequence number before the page number, joined by whatever character is specified with the \d switch.

►► TOC (Table of Contents)

The TOC (Table of Contents) field takes this form:

{ TOC [*switches*] }

It builds and inserts a table of contents based on entries marked with the TC field. Field-specific switches are

\a	Builds a table of figures with neither labels nor numbers.
\b *bookmark*	Builds a table of contents for the section of the document marked by *bookmark*.
\c *n*	Builds a table of authorities only with entries with category number *n*.
\d "*c*"	Defines the separator character (*c*) between a sequence number and a page number for sequences defined by the \s switch (default is "-").
\f *entry-identifier*	Builds a table of contents using only TC fields with the same single-character *entry-identifier*. (The default *entry-identifier* is c. Including no identifier is equivalent to specifying c as the identifier.)
\l *identifier1-identifier2*	Builds a table of contents using only a range of entry levels specified by the \l switch in the TC fields.
\n	Builds a table of contents without page numbers.

\o "*heading No-headingNo*"	Builds a table of contents using paragraphs formatted with built-in heading styles numbered in the specified range.
\p	Specifies the separator character used between a table entry and its page number (default is a tab with dot leaders).
\s *sequence-name*	When there are Seq fields in the document, includes the sequence number before the page number, joined by whatever character is specified with the \d switch.
\t "*style1, style2, etc.*"	Builds a table of contents using paragraphs formatted with the styles listed in quotation marks.

►► UserAddress

The UserAddress field takes this form:

{ USERADDRESS "[*New Address*]" }

By itself, the { USERADDRESS } field code displays the name of the user address (from the User Info tab of the Options dialog box). With a new address in quotation marks, as a variable, or input with a prompt, the field stores the new user address.

►► UserInitials

The UserInitials field takes this form:

{ USERINITIALS ["*New Initials*"] }

By itself, the { USERINITIALS } field code displays the user initials (from the User Info tab of the Options dialog box). With new initials in quotation marks, as a variable, or input with a prompt, the field stores the new user initials.

►► UserName

The UserName field takes this form:

{ USERNAME [*"New UserName"*] }

By itself, the { USERNAME } field code displays the user name (from the User Info tab of the Options dialog box). With a new name in quotation marks, as a variable, or input with a prompt, the field stores the new user name.

►► XE (Index Entry)

The XE (Index Entry) field takes this form:

{ XE *"text"* [*switches*] }

It defines the text and page number for an index entry. The field is formatted as hidden text. To indicate a subentry, include the main entry text, then a semicolon, and then the subentry. The field-specific switches are

\b	Boldfaces the page number for the index entry.
\f *entry-identifier*	Identifies the entry as a certain type, using a one-letter *entry-identifier*, for use in indexes of just those entry types.
\i	Italicizes the page number for the index entry.
\r *bookmark*	Includes the range of pages marked by *bookmark* in the page number for the entry.
\t "*text*"	Inserts the text in quotation marks instead of a page number (such as in "See" entries).

APPENDIX F

WordBasic Commands by Category

Once you start getting further into creating macros, you will realize that there's far more to it than simply recording actions and playing them back. If you plan to edit your macros or even to write them from scratch, then you'll need to know about Word's macro language.

The macro language is called WordBasic, and it's more or less a full-fledged programming language. That means that, in addition to the commands specific to Word, it has all kinds of commands for constructing programs (or in this case, macros) and controlling how they flow.

In this appendix, I'll break the WordBasic commands down into several categories. Each of these categories can be further broken down into subcategories. I'll describe and discuss each type.

NOTE

There is some overlap between the different categories. Some commands fall into more than one category; when that is the case, I've listed them in both (or in each).

WordBasic Command Categories

There are six different general types of WordBasic commands. The categories are as follows:

Editing

Environment

File Operations

Formatting

Programming Commands

Tools

►► Editing

Editing commands generally correspond to commands on the Edit menu, but they also include some commands from the Tools and View menus and some that relate to basic operations such as moving around a document and selecting. The subcategories of the Editing commands are as follows:

AutoCorrect

AutoText

Editing

Finding and Replacing

Moving the Insertion Point and Selecting

Outlining and Master Documents

Proofing

► AutoCorrect

These WordBasic commands all deal with the AutoCorrect command on the tools menu. They include:

GetAutoCorrect$()

ToolsAutoCorrect

ToolsAutoCorrectDays, ToolsAutoCorrectDays()

ToolsAutoCorrectInitialCaps, ToolsAutoCorrectInitialCaps()

ToolsAutoCorrectReplaceText, ToolsAutoCorrectReplaceText()

ToolsAutoCorrectSentenceCaps, ToolsAutoCorrectSentenceCaps()

ToolsAutoCorrectSmartQuotes, ToolsAutoCorrectSmartQuotes()

Commands followed by parentheses return a 0 (zero) if the selection is unchecked and a –1 if the selection is checked. Without the parentheses, they toggle the setting from its previous position, check the corresponding box if they're followed by a 1, or uncheck it if followed by a 0 (zero). The ToolsAutoCorrect command models the AutoCorrect dialog box and can be used to create new entries. The GetAutoCorrect$() replaces the string in parentheses with its AutoCorrect replacement, if there is one.

▸ AutoText

These WordBasic commands all deal with the AutoText command on the tools menu. They include:

AutoText

AutoTextName$()

CountAutoTextEntries()

EditAutoText

GetAutoText$()

InsertAutoText

Organizer

SetAutoText

AutoText displays the AutoText dialog box. EditAutoText is used to add new AutoText entries, based on a selection. SetAutoText is used to create a new entry without requiring a selection. GetAutoText$() converts the string in parentheses to its AutoText equivalent. Organizer models the Organizer dialog box for moving AutoText entries, styles, macros, and so on from one template to another.

▸ Editing

There are many WordBasic commands in this entry. Most correspond to commands on the Edit or Insert menu. They include:

AutoMarkIndexEntries

Cancel

ChangeCase, ChangeCase()

CopyText

DeleteBackWord

DeleteWord

EditClear

EditCopy

EditCut

EditFind

EditGoTo

EditLinks

EditObject

EditPaste

EditPasteSpecial

EditPicture

EditRedo

EditRepeat

EditReplace

EditTOACategory

EditUndo

ExtendMode()

Insert

InsertAddCaption

InsertAutoCaption

InsertBreak

InsertCaption

InsertCaptionNumbering

InsertColumnBreak

InsertCrossReference

InsertIndex

- InsertPageBreak
- InsertPageNumbers
- InsertSpike
- InsertSymbol
- InsertTableOfAuthorities
- InsertTableOfContents
- InsertTableOfFigures
- MarkCitation
- MarkIndexEntry
- MarkTableOfContentsEntry
- MoveText
- OK
- Overtype, Overtype()
- Spike
- ToolsOptionsEdit

Many of their functions are apparent from their names, such as Delete-Word and EditUndo. OK completes a CopyText or MoveText action.

▸ Finding and Replacing

Commands in this category all correspond to options related to Edit ➤ Find and Edit ➤ Replace. They include:

- EditFind
- EditFindClearFormatting
- EditFindFont
- EditFindFound()
- EditFindLang
- EditFindPara
- EditFindStyle
- EditReplace

EditReplaceClearFormatting

EditReplaceFont

EditReplaceLang

EditReplacePara

EditReplaceStyle

RepeatFind

They model the Find and Replace dialog boxes (except RepeatFind, which repeats the last Find action).

▶ Moving the Insertion Point and Selecting

The commands in this category correspond to keyboard shortcuts for insertion-point movement and selection. They include:

AtEndOfDocument()

AtStartOfDocument()

Cancel

CharLeft, CharLeft()

CharRight, CharRight()

ColumnSelect

EditSelectAll

EndOfColumn, EndOfColumn()

EndOfDocument, EndOfDocument()

EndOfLine, EndOfLine()

EndOfRow, EndOfRow()

EndOfWindow, EndOfWindow()

ExtendMode()

ExtendSelection

GetSelEndPos()

GetSelStartPos()

GetText$()

GoBack

GoToAnnotationScope

GoToHeaderFooter

GoToNextItem

GoToPreviousItem

HLine

HPage

HScroll, HScroll()

Insert

LineDown, LineDown()

LineUp, LineUp()

NextCell, NextCell()

NextField, NextField()

NextObject

NextPage, NextPage()

NextWindow

OtherPane

PageDown, PageDown()

PageUp, PageUp()

ParaDown, ParaDown()

ParaUp, ParaUp()

PrevCell, PrevCell()

PrevField, PrevField()

PrevObject

PrevPage, PrevPage()

PrevWindow

SelectCurAlignment

SelectCurColor

SelectCurFont

SelectCurIndent

SelectCurSentence

SelectCurSpacing

SelectCurTabs

SelectCurWord

SelType, SelType()

SentLeft, SentLeft()

SentRight, SentRight()

SetSelRange

ShrinkSelection

StartOfColumn, StartOfColumn()

StartOfDocument, StartOfDocument()

StartOfLine, StartOfLine()

StartOfRow, StartOfRow()

StartOfWindow, StartOfWindow()

TableSelectColumn

TableSelectRow

TableSelectTable

VLine

VPage

VScroll, VScroll()

WordLeft, WordLeft()

WordRight, WordRight()

Options with parentheses can include a number that specifies how many times to repeat the action, so CharLeft(7) moves the insertion point seven places to the left. If you include any other number, besides zero, after the first number, text between the present insertion-point position and the new position is selected. For example, CharLeft(7,1) will move the insertion point seven places to the left and select all the text between the old location and the new location of the insertion point.

► Outlining and Master Documents

Commands in this category correspond to outlining commands (such as the ones on the Outlining Toolbar) and master/subdocument commands. They include:

CreateSubdocument

DemoteToBodyText

InsertSubdocument

MergeSubdocument

OpenSubdocument

OutlineCollapse

OutlineDemote

OutlineExpand

OutlineLevel()

OutlineMoveDown

OutlineMoveUp

OutlinePromote

OutlineShowFirstLine, OutlineShowFirstLine()

OutlineShowFormat

RemoveSubdocument

ShowAllHeadings

ShowHeadingNumber

SplitSubdocument

ViewMasterDocument, ViewMasterDocument()

ViewOutline, ViewOutline()

ViewToggleMasterDocument

CreateSubdocument

DemoteToBodyText

InsertSubdocument

MergeSubdocument

OpenSubdocument

OutlineCollapse

OutlineDemote

OutlineExpand

OutlineLevel()

OutlineMoveDown

OutlineMoveUp

OutlinePromote

OutlineShowFirstLine, OutlineShowFirstLine()

OutlineShowFormat

RemoveSubdocument

ShowAllHeadings

ShowHeadingNumber

SplitSubdocument

ViewMasterDocument, ViewMasterDocument()

ViewOutline, ViewOutline()

ViewToggleMasterDocument

▶ Proofing

Commands in this category correspond to the Spelling, Grammar, Thesaurus, and Hyphenation commands on the Tools menu. They include:

CountToolsGrammarStatistics()

ToolsGetSpelling, ToolsGetSpelling()

ToolsGetSynonyms, ToolsGetSynonyms()

ToolsGrammar

ToolsGrammarStatisticsArray

ToolsHyphenation

ToolsHyphenationManual

ToolsOptionsGrammar

ToolsOptionsSpelling

ToolsSpelling

ToolsSpellSelection

ToolsThesaurus

▸▸ Environment

Environment commands control the setup of Word, its appearance, the commands on the Windows and View menus, and the format of date and time displays. The subcategories of Environment commands are as follows:

Customization

Date and Time

Environment

View

Windows

▸ Customization

Commands in this category control the appearance of Word command shortcuts, such as Toolbars, menus, keyboard shortcuts, and macros. They include:

AddButton

ChooseButtonImage

CopyButtonImage

CountKeys()

CountMenuItems()

CountMenus()

CountToolbarButtons()

CountToolbars()

DeleteButton

EditButtonImage

KeyCode()

KeyMacro$()

MenuItemMacro$()

MenuItemText$()

MenuMode

MenuText$()

MoveButton

MoveToolbar

NewToolbar

PasteButtonImage

RenameMenu

ResetButtonImage

SizeToolbar

ToolbarButtonMacro$()

ToolbarName$()

ToolbarState()

ToolsCustomize

ToolsCustomizeKeyboard

ToolsCustomizeMenuBar

ToolsCustomizeMenus

▶ Date and Time

Commands in this category either display dates and times in various formats or perform calculations and comparisons on dates and times. They include:

Date$()

DateSerial()

DateValue()

Day()

Days360()

Hour()

InsertDateField

InsertDateTime

InsertTimeField

Minute()

Month()

Now()

OnTime

Second()

Time$()

TimeSerial()

TimeValue()

Today()

ToolsRevisionDate()

ToolsRevisionDate$()

Weekday()

Year()

▸ Environment

Commands in this category correspond to options in the Tools ➤ Options dialog box, particularly the Environment tab of that dialog box. They include:

AppInfo$()

Beep

CommandValid()

DOSToWin$()

Environ$()

Err

Error

GetPrivateProfileString$()

GetProfileString$()

GetSystemInfo, GetSystemInfo$()

IsDocumentDirty()

IsExecuteOnly()

IsMacro()

IsTemplateDirty()

LockDocument, LockDocument()

MacroFileName$()

MicrosoftSystemInfo

ScreenRefresh

ScreenUpdating, ScreenUpdating()

SelInfo()

SelType, SelType()

SetDocumentDirty

SetPrivateProfileString, SetPrivateProfileString()

SetProfileString, SetProfileString()

SetTemplateDirty

ViewMenus()

WaitCursor

WinToDOS$()

For commands such as IsDocumentDirty, "dirty" means changes have been made to it since it was last saved.

▶ View

Commands in this category correspond primarily to commands on the View menu, but also to Preview and to the View tab of the Options dialog box. They include:

ClosePreview

CloseViewHeaderFooter

FilePrintPreview, FilePrintPreview()

FilePrintPreviewFullScreen

FilePrintPreviewPages, FilePrintPreviewPages()

Magnifier, Magnifier()

ShowAll, ShowAll()

ShowNextHeaderFooter

ShowPrevHeaderFooter

ToggleFull

TogglePortrait

ToolsOptionsView

ViewAnnotations, ViewAnnotations()

ViewBorderToolbar

ViewDraft, ViewDraft()

ViewDrawingToolbar

ViewEndnoteArea, ViewEndnoteArea()

ViewEndnoteContNotice

ViewEndnoteContSeparator

ViewEndnoteSeparator

ViewFieldCodes, ViewFieldCodes()

ViewFooter, ViewFooter()

ViewFootnoteArea, ViewFootnoteArea()

ViewFootnoteContNotice

ViewFootnoteContSeparator

ViewFootnotes, ViewFootnotes()

ViewFootnoteSeparator

ViewHeader, ViewHeader()

ViewMasterDocument, ViewMasterDocument()

ViewMenus()

ViewNormal, ViewNormal()

ViewOutline, ViewOutline()

ViewPage, ViewPage()

ViewRibbon, ViewRibbon()

ViewRuler, ViewRuler()

ViewStatusBar, ViewStatusBar()

ViewToggleMasterDocument

ViewToolbars

ViewZoom

ViewZoom100

ViewZoom200

ViewZoom75

ViewZoomPageWidth

ViewZoomWholePage

▶ Windows

Commands in this category correspond to options on the Windows menu as well as to general Windows options that control other applications running under Windows, not just Word. They include:

Activate

AppActivate

AppClose

AppCount()

AppGetNames, AppGetNames()

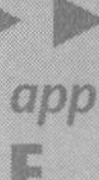

AppHide

AppMaximize, AppMaximize()

AppMinimize, AppMinimize()

AppMove

AppRestore, AppRestore()

AppShow

AppSize

AppWindowHeight, AppWindowHeight()

AppWindowPosLeft, AppWindowPosLeft()

AppWindowPosTop, AppWindowPosTop()

AppWindowWidth, AppWindowWidth()

ClosePane

CountWindows()

DocClose

DocMaximize, DocMaximize()

DocMinimize, DocMinimize()

DocMove

DocRestore

DocSize

DocSplit, DocSplit()

DocWindowHeight, DocWindowHeight()

DocWindowPosLeft, DocWindowPosLeft()

DocWindowPosTop, DocWindowPosTop()

DocWindowWidth, DocWindowWidth()

ExitWindows

FileNameFromWindow$()

HelpActiveWindow

IsMacro()

NextWindow

OtherPane

PrevWindow

Window()

WindowArrangeAll

WindowList

WindowName$()

WindowNewWindow

WindowNumber

WindowPane()

►► File Operations

File Operations commands deal with disk access, documents and templates, and other file-management issues. The subcategories of File Operations commands are as follows:

Application Control

Disk Access and Management

Documents, Templates, and Add-ins

► Application Control

Commands in this category have more to do with Windows in general than with Word in particular, although they can affect Word as they can any running application or any application to be started. They include:

AppActivate

AppClose

AppCount()

AppGetNames, AppGetNames()

AppHide

AppInfo$()

AppIsRunning()

AppMaximize, AppMaximize()

AppMinimize, AppMinimize()

AppMove

AppRestore, AppRestore()

AppSendMessage

AppShow

AppSize

AppWindowHeight, AppWindowHeight()

AppWindowPosLeft, AppWindowPosLeft()

AppWindowPosTop, AppWindowPosTop()

AppWindowWidth, AppWindowWidth()

ControlRun

DDEExecute

DDEInitiate()

DDEPoke

DDERequest$()

DDETerminate

DDETerminateAll

DialogEditor

ExitWindows

FileExit

GetSystemInfo, GetSystemInfo$()

MicrosoftAccess

MicrosoftExcel

MicrosoftFoxPro

MicrosoftMail

MicrosoftPowerPoint

MicrosoftProject

MicrosoftPublisher

MicrosoftSchedule

MicrosoftSystemInfo

RunPrintManager

SendKeys

Shell

They are fairly advanced in general, and you will probably not want to work with them until you are comfortable manipulating the Windows environment.

▶ Disk Access and Management

Commands in this category also deal with issues outside of Word proper. They control the active disk and directory, the creating and deletion of directories, and so on. They include:

ChDefaultDir

ChDir

Connect

CopyFile

CountDirectories()

DefaultDir$()

Files$()

GetAttr()

GetDirectory$()

Kill

MkDir

Name

RmDir

SetAttr

► Documents, Templates, and Add-ins

Commands in this category correspond to commands on the File menu, as well as file-management commands. They include:

AddAddIn, AddAddIn()

AddInState, AddInState()

ClearAddIns

Converter$()

ConverterLookup()

CopyFile

CountAddIns()

CountDocumentVars()

CountFiles()

CountFoundFiles()

DeleteAddIn

DisableInput

DocClose

DocumentStatistics

FileClose

FileCloseAll

FileConfirmConversions, FileConfirmConversions()

FileFind

FileList

FileName$()

FileNameFromWindow$()

FileNameInfo$()

FileNew

FileNewDefault

FileNumber

FileOpen

FilePageSetup

FilePrint

FilePrintDefault

FilePrintPreview, FilePrintPreview()

FilePrintPreviewFullScreen

FilePrintPreviewPages, FilePrintPreviewPages()

FilePrintSetup

FileRoutingSlip

Files$()

FileSave

FileSaveAll

FileSaveAs

FileSendMail

FileSummaryInfo

FileTemplates

FoundFileName$()

GetAddInID()

GetAddInName$()

GetAttr()

GetDocumentVar$()

GetDocumentVarName$()

InsertFile

Kill

LockDocument, LockDocument()

MacroFileName$()

Name

Organizer

PathFromMacPath$()

SaveTemplate

SelectionFileName$()

SetAttr

SetDocumentVar, SetDocumentVar()

ToolsOptionsFileLocations

ToolsOptionsPrint

Many of these are also fairly advanced and should be used with caution (particularly commands such as Kill, which deletes files).

▸▸ Formatting

Formatting commands generally correspond to commands on the Format menu and control the appearance of the document. The subcategories of Formatting commands are as follows:

Borders and Frames

Bullets and Numbering

Character Formatting

Drawing

Footnotes, Endnotes, and Annotations

Paragraph Formatting

Section and Document Formatting

Style Formatting

▸ Borders and Frames

These WordBasic commands correspond to options in the Borders and Shading dialog box. They include the following commands:

BorderBottom, BorderBottom()

BorderInside, BorderInside()

BorderLeft, BorderLeft()

BorderLineStyle, BorderLineStyle()

BorderNone, BorderNone()

BorderOutside, BorderOutside()

BorderRight, BorderRight()

BorderTop, BorderTop()

FormatBordersAndShading

FormatDefineStyleBorders

FormatDefineStyleFrame

FormatFrame

InsertFrame

RemoveFrames

ShadingPattern, ShadingPattern()

ViewBorderToolbar

Commands followed by parentheses can be set to On or Off. Without the parentheses, they toggle the setting from its previous position. The Format… commands correspond to formatting choices on the dialog box.

▶ Bullets and Numbering

These WordBasic commands correspond to options in the Bullets and Numbering dialog box. They include the following commands:

DemoteList

FormatBullet

FormatBulletDefault, FormatBulletDefault()

FormatBulletsAndNumbering

FormatDefineStyleNumbers

FormatMultilevel

FormatNumber

FormatNumberDefault, FormatNumberDefault()

PromoteList

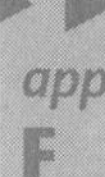

RemoveBulletsNumbers

SkipNumbering, SkipNumbering()

ToolsBulletListDefault

ToolsBulletsNumbers

ToolsNumberListDefault

Commands followed by parentheses can be set to On or Off. Without the parentheses, they toggle the setting from its previous position.

► Character Formatting

Commands in this category correspond mainly to options on the Font dialog box, accessible from the Format menu. They include:

AllCaps, AllCaps()

Bold, Bold()

CharColor, CharColor()

CopyFormat

CountFonts()

CountLanguages()

DottedUnderline, DottedUnderline()

DoubleUnderline, DoubleUnderline()

Font, Font$()

FontSize, FontSize()

FontSizeSelect

FontSubstitution

FormatAddrFonts

FormatChangeCase

FormatDefineStyleFont

FormatDefineStyleLang

FormatFont

FormatRetAddrFonts

GrowFont

GrowFontOnePoint

Hidden, Hidden()

Italic, Italic()

Language, Language$()

NormalFontPosition

NormalFontSpacing

PasteFormat

ResetChar, ResetChar()

ShrinkFont

ShrinkFontOnePoint

SmallCaps, SmallCaps()

Strikethrough, Strikethrough()

Subscript, Subscript()

Superscript, Superscript()

SymbolFont

ToolsLanguage

Underline, Underline()

WordUnderline, WordUnderline()

▶ Drawing

Most of the commands in this category are drawing commands, such as the commands on the Drawing Toolbar. The rest deal with inserting and displaying drawing objects. They include:

DrawAlign

DrawArc

DrawBringForward

DrawBringInFrontOfText

DrawBringToFront

DrawCallout

DrawClearRange

DrawCount()

DrawCountPolyPoints()

DrawDisassemblePicture

DrawEllipse

DrawExtendSelect

DrawFlipHorizontal

DrawFlipVertical

DrawFreeformPolygon

DrawGetCalloutTextbox

DrawGetPolyPoints

DrawGetType()

DrawGroup

DrawInsertWordPicture

DrawLine

DrawNudgeDown

DrawNudgeDownPixel

DrawNudgeLeft

DrawNudgeLeftPixel

DrawNudgeRight

DrawNudgeRightPixel

DrawNudgeUp

DrawNudgeUpPixel

DrawRectangle

DrawResetWordPicture

DrawReshape

DrawRotateLeft

DrawRotateRight

DrawRoundRectangle

DrawSelect, DrawSelect()

DrawSelectNext

DrawSelectPrevious

DrawSendBackward

DrawSendBehindText

DrawSendToBack

DrawSetCalloutTextbox

DrawSetInsertToAnchor

DrawSetInsertToTextbox

DrawSetPolyPoints

DrawSetRange, DrawSetRange()

DrawSnapToGrid

DrawTextBox

DrawUngroup

DrawUnselect

FormatCallout

FormatDrawingObject

FormatPicture

InsertDrawing

SelectDrawingObjects

ToggleScribbleMode

ViewDrawingToolbar

▶ Footnotes, Endnotes, and Annotations

This category is fairly self-explanatory. Commands in it deal with inserting, editing, updating, and displaying notes and annotations. They include:

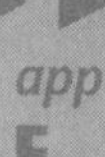

AnnotationRefFromSel$()

EditConvertAllEndnotes

EditConvertAllFootnotes

EditConvertNotes

EditSwapAllNotes

GoToAnnotationScope

InsertAnnotation

InsertFootnote

NoteOptions

ResetNoteSepOrNotice

ShowAnnotationBy

ViewAnnotations, ViewAnnotations()

ViewEndnoteArea, ViewEndnoteArea()

ViewEndnoteContNotice

ViewEndnoteContSeparator

ViewEndnoteSeparator

ViewFootnoteArea, ViewFootnoteArea()

ViewFootnoteContNotice

ViewFootnoteContSeparator

ViewFootnotes, ViewFootnotes()

ViewFootnoteSeparator

▸ Paragraph Formatting

Commands in this category include all formatting commands that take place at the paragraph level, most of which are available on the Paragraph dialog box, accessible from the Format menu. They include:

CenterPara, CenterPara()

CloseUpPara

CopyFormat

FormatDefineStylePara

FormatDefineStyleTabs

FormatDropCap

FormatParagraph

FormatTabs

HangingIndent

Indent

InsertPara

JustifyPara, JustifyPara()

LeftPara, LeftPara()

NextTab()

OpenUpPara

ParaKeepLinesTogether, ParaKeepLinesTogether()

ParaKeepWithNext, ParaKeepWithNext()

ParaPageBreakBefore, ParaPageBreakBefore()

ParaWidowOrphanControl, ParaWidowOrphanControl()

PasteFormat

PrevTab()

ResetPara, ResetPara()

RightPara, RightPara()

SpacePara1, SpacePara1()

SpacePara15, SpacePara15()

SpacePara2, SpacePara2()

TabLeader$()

TabType()

UnHang

UnIndent

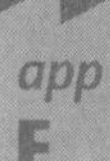

▶ Section and Document Formatting

Commands in this category deal with all the formatting that takes place at the document level or section by section. They include:

CloseViewHeaderFooter

FormatAutoFormat

FormatColumns

FormatHeaderFooterLink

FormatHeadingNumber

FormatHeadingNumbering

FormatPageNumber

FormatSectionLayout

GoToHeaderFooter

InsertSectionBreak

ShowNextHeaderFooter

ShowPrevHeaderFooter

ToggleHeaderFooterLink

ToggleMainTextLayer

TogglePortrait

ToolsOptionsAutoFormat

ViewFooter, ViewFooter()

ViewHeader, ViewHeader()

▶ Style Formatting

Commands in this category govern defining styles, inserting them, changing them, and removing them. They include:

CountStyles()

FormatDefineStyleBorders

FormatDefineStyleFont

FormatDefineStyleFrame

FormatDefineStyleLang

FormatDefineStyleNumbers

FormatDefineStylePara

FormatDefineStyleTabs

FormatStyle

FormatStyleGallery

NormalStyle

Organizer

Style

StyleDesc$()

StyleName$()

▶▶ Programming Commands

The commands in this category all deal with the structure of programs. They're for working with variables, taking input from users, displaying output, creating dialog boxes, and controlling the flow of the programs. If you've never done any programming, you'll find some of these commands difficult to work with. They include:

Basic File Input/Output

Branching and Control

Definitions and Declarations

Dialog Box Definition and Control

Strings and Numbers

▶ Basic File Input/Output

The commands in this category enable programs to take input from users or from source files and to display or print output. They include:

Close

Eof()

Input

Input$()

Line Input

Lof()

Open

Print

Read

Seek, Seek()

Write

Commands such as Open, Close, and Eof handle sequential files (input files). The Input, Input$(), and Print commands are explained in Chapter 34.

► Branching and Control

Most of the commands in this category will look familiar to anyone who's done any programming. They enable programs to loop (repeat a sequence of commands) or make decisions based on different cases. They include:

Call

For...Next

Function...End Function

Goto

If...Then...Else

On Error

OnTime

Select Case

Stop

Sub...End Sub

While...Wend

The commands separated by … work together to create loops.

▶ Definitions and Declarations

The commands in this category are used to declare and define variables and dialog boxes. They include:

Declare

Dim

Let

Redim

Declare and Let are used with variables. Dim and Redim are used with arrays and dialog boxes.

▶ Dialog Box Definition and Control

Commands in this category are used to create and manipulate dialog boxes, which can then draw from existing dialog boxes in Word or take input from users. They include:

Begin Dialog…End Dialog

CancelButton

CheckBox

ComboBox

Dialog, Dialog()

DialogEditor

DlgControlId()

DlgEnable, DlgEnable()

DlgFilePreview, DlgFilePreview$()

DlgFocus, DlgFocus$()

DlgListBoxArray, DlgListBoxArray()

DlgSetPicture

DlgText, DlgText$()

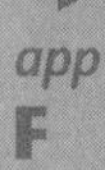

DlgUpdateFilePreview

DlgValue, DlgValue()

DlgVisible, DlgVisible()

DropListBox

FilePreview

GetCurValues

GroupBox

InputBox$()

ListBox

MsgBox, MsgBox()

OKButton

OptionButton

OptionGroup

Picture

PushButton

Text

TextBox

These are advanced commands and they are difficult to work with unless you are comfortable with the workings of dialog boxes.

▶ Strings and Numbers

The commands in this category are used for converting strings to numbers and vice versa, as well as for manipulating strings and numbers (such as extracting portions of strings or performing calculations on numbers). They include:

Abs()

Asc()

Chr$()

CleanString$()

InStr()

Int()

LCase$()

Left$()

Len()

LTrim$()

Mid$()

Right$()

Rnd()

RTrim$()

Selection$()

Sgn()

SortArray

Str$()

String$()

UCase$()

Val()

▶▶ Tools

Tools commands deal with advanced Word features such as fields, forms, bookmarks, OLE, mail merge, and help. The subcategories of commands include:

Bookmarks

Dynamic Data Exchange (DDE)

Fields

Forms

Help

Macros

Mail Merge

Object Linking and Embedding

Tables

Tools

▸ Bookmarks

Commands in this category are used to create, edit, refer to, or work with bookmarks. Remember that bookmarks can be used as variables with other macros. These commands include:

BookmarkName$()

CmpBookmarks()

CopyBookmark

CountBookmarks()

EditBookmark

EmptyBookmark()

ExistingBookmark()

GetBookmark$()

SetEndOfBookmark

SetStartOfBookmark

▸ Dynamic Data Exchange (DDE)

Commands in this category deal with the semi-obsolete DDE Windows feature. (It's mostly been supplanted by OLE, but Word can still work with DDE to retain backward compatability with older Windows applications.) These commands include:

DDEExecute

DDEInitiate()

DDEPoke

DDERequest$()

DDETerminate

DDETerminateAll

SendKeys

▶ Fields

Commands in this category deal with fields. Many Word commands insert fields into documents, and fields can be used to do many of the things that macros do. Chapter 32 explains fields in detail. These commands include:

CheckBoxFormField

CountMergeFields()

DoFieldClick

DropDownFormField

EnableFormField

FormFieldOptions

GetFieldData$()

GetMergeField$()

InsertDateField

InsertDateTime

InsertField

InsertFieldChars

InsertFormField

InsertMergeField

InsertPageField

InsertTimeField

LockFields

MergeFieldName$()

NextField, NextField()

PrevField, PrevField()

PutFieldData

TextFormField

ToggleFieldDisplay

ToolsManageFields

UnlinkFields

UnlockFields

UpdateFields

UpdateSource

ViewFieldCodes, ViewFieldCodes()

Most of these commands either insert fields or update or otherwise control them.

▶ Forms

The commands in this category deal with on-screen forms created with form fields. They're used either to insert form fields, to control the contents of form fields, or to turn on and off the document protection that makes the forms usable. They include:

AddDropDownItem

CheckBoxFormField

ClearFormField

DropDownFormField

EnableFormField

FormFieldOptions

FormShading, FormShading()

GetFormResult(), GetFormResult$()

InsertFormField

RemoveAllDropDownItems

RemoveDropDownItem

SetFormResult

TextFormField

ToolsProtectDocument

ToolsProtectSection

ToolsUnprotectDocument

For more on forms, see Chapter 33.

▶ Help

The commands in this category all correspond to commands on the Help menu. It's that simple. They include:

Help

HelpAbout

HelpActiveWindow

HelpContents

HelpExamplesAndDemos

HelpIndex

HelpKeyboard

HelpPSSHelp

HelpQuickPreview

HelpSearch

HelpTipOfTheDay

HelpTool

HelpUsingHelp

HelpWordPerfectHelp

HelpWordPerfectHelpOptions

▶ Macros

What? Macro commands about macros? That's right. The commands in this category run other macros (even at a predetermined time), keep

track of macros, or even record them. They include:

CommandValid()

CountMacros()

DisableAutoMacros

IsExecuteOnly()

IsMacro()

KeyMacro$()

MacroCopy

MacroDesc$()

MacroFileName$()

MacroName$()

MacroNameFromWindow$()

MenuItemMacro$()

OnTime

Organizer

PauseRecorder

REM

ShowVars

ToolbarButtonMacro$()

ToolsMacro

▸ Mail Merge

The commands in this category all correspond to options of the Merge command on the Tools menu (many of these options appear on the Merge Toolbar). They include:

CountMergeFields()

GetMergeField$()

InsertMergeField

MailMerge

MailMergeAskToConvertChevrons, MailMergeAskToConvertChevrons()

MailMergeCheck

MailMergeConvertChevrons, MailMergeConvertChevrons()

MailMergeCreateDataSource

MailMergeCreateHeaderSource

MailMergeDataForm

MailMergeDataSource$()

MailMergeEditDataSource

MailMergeEditHeaderSource

MailMergeEditMainDocument

MailMergeFindRecord

MailMergeFirstRecord

MailMergeFoundRecord()

MailMergeGotoRecord, MailMergeGotoRecord()

MailMergeHelper

MailMergeInsertAsk

MailMergeInsertFillIn

MailMergeInsertIf

MailMergeInsertMergeRec

MailMergeInsertMergeSeq

MailMergeInsertNext

MailMergeInsertNextIf

MailMergeInsertSet

MailMergeInsertSkipIf

MailMergeLastRecord

MailMergeMainDocumentType, MailMergeMainDocumentType()

MailMergeNextRecord

MailMergeOpenDataSource

MailMergeOpenHeaderSource

MailMergePrevRecord

MailMergeQueryOptions

MailMergeReset

MailMergeState()

MailMergeToDoc

MailMergeToPrinter

MailMergeViewData, MailMergeViewData()

MergeFieldName$()

ToolsAddRecordDefault

ToolsRemoveRecordDefault

Be sure you've mastered mail merge the normal way before you start trying to control mail merges with macros.

▸ Object Linking and Embedding

Commands on this menu relate to the Windows OLE standard that allows Windows applications to open documents created in other applications and to even start those other applications themselves. They include:

ActivateObject

ConvertObject

EditLinks

EditObject

EditPasteSpecial

EditPicture

FileClosePicture

InsertChart

InsertDatabase

InsertEquation

InsertExcelTable

InsertObject

InsertPicture

InsertSound

InsertWordArt

The EditPasteSpecial and Insert… commands create OLE links. The other commands control those links.

Tables

The commands in this category correspond to commands on the Table menu as well as more sophisticated commands for controlling tables. Word tables can be almost as complicated as spreadsheets. These commands include:

FieldSeparator$, FieldSeparator$()

InsertExcelTable

NextCell, NextCell()

PrevCell, PrevCell()

TableAutoFormat

TableAutoSum

TableColumnWidth

TableDeleteCells

TableDeleteColumn

TableDeleteRow

TableFormula

TableGridlines, TableGridlines()

TableHeadings, TableHeadings()

TableInsertCells

TableInsertColumn

TableInsertRow

TableInsertTable

TableMergeCells

TableRowHeight

TableSelectColumn

TableSelectRow

TableSelectTable

TableSort

TableSortAToZ

TableSortZToA

TableSplit

TableSplitCells

TableToText

TableUpdateAutoFormat

TextToTable

▸ Tools

The commands in this category all correspond to commands on the Tools menu, which cover a wide variety of special Word features. They include:

ToolsAdvancedSettings

ToolsCalculate, ToolsCalculate()

ToolsCompareVersions

ToolsCreateEnvelope

ToolsCreateLabels

ToolsCustomize

ToolsHyphenation

ToolsHyphenationManual

ToolsLanguage

ToolsMergeRevisions

ToolsOptions

ToolsOptionsAutoFormat

ToolsOptionsCompatibility

ToolsOptionsEdit

ToolsOptionsFileLocations

ToolsOptionsGeneral

ToolsOptionsPrint

ToolsOptionsRevisions

ToolsOptionsSave

ToolsOptionsUserInfo

ToolsOptionsView

ToolsProtectDocument

ToolsProtectSection

ToolsRepaginate

ToolsReviewRevisions

ToolsRevisionAuthor$()

ToolsRevisionDate()

ToolsRevisionDate$()

ToolsRevisions

ToolsRevisionType()

ToolsShrinkToFit

ToolsUnprotectDocument

ToolsWordCount

The ToolsOptions… commands are used to control Word's environment. The rest deal with the current document directly.

GLOSSARY

Glossary of Word's Menu Commands

▶▶ **W*ord*** for Windows 6 comes with a wealth of new features reached with a variety of new menu commands. Sure, some of your old friends are still there (such as File ➤ New and Tools ➤ Customize...), but many of the shortcuts have changed, as Microsoft has tried to integrate the Windows version of Word with the Macintosh version. Hence this alphabetized list of menu commands, created especially for you by taking the program disks and banging a few nails into them.

For each entry, the command is listed first, followed by the shortcut (if there is one) in parentheses, and then a brief description of what the command does. If a command appears only under particular circumstances, I'll point that out. So read on, MacDuff!

You can change any of Word's predefined shortcuts in the Customize dialog box (reached with Tools ➤ Customize...).

Edit ➤ AutoText... Use to instruct Word to insert text automatically.

Edit ➤ Bookmark... (Ctrl+Shift+F5) Use to mark places in your document that you want to visit frequently.

Edit ➤ Clear (Delete) Removes any text from highlighted cells.

Edit ➤ Copy (Ctrl+C) Places a copy of the highlighted material in the Clipboard, leaving the original alone.

Edit ➤ Cut (Ctrl+X) Removes the highlighted material, placing it in the Clipboard.

Edit ➤ Find... (Ctrl+F) Use to locate specific text strings, formatting, styles, or special characters.

Edit ➤ Go To... (Ctrl+G) Use to go to specific pages, sections, bookmarks, etc.

Edit ➤ Links... Use to make adjustments to the settings that link documents to one another.

Edit ➤ Object Use to make adjustments to objects you have embedded in your Word document.

Edit ➤ Paste (Ctrl+V) Places a copy of whatever material is contained in the Clipboard at the insertion point.

Edit ➤ Paste Special... Works the same as Edit ➤ Paste, but brings up a dialog box with a variety of Paste options (for instance, allows you to paste Excel spreadsheets or to paste the material without any formatting).

Edit ➤ Repeat (Ctrl+Y) Instructs Word to perform the most recent command again. This has various functions, depending upon what you have just done.

Edit ➤ Replace... (Ctrl+H) Use to locate specific text strings, formatting, styles, or special characters and replace them with other text strings, formatting, styles, or special characters (you can even replace material with the Clipboard contents).

Edit ➤ Select All (Ctrl+A) Selects all text in your document.

Edit ➤ Undo (Ctrl+Z) Undoes your most recent action. Like Edit ➤ Repeat, the precise function of this command will vary depending upon what you have just done.

File ➤ Close (Ctrl+W) Closes the active document pane.

File ➤ Exit (Alt+F4) Exits Word for Windows entirely.

File ➤ Find File Use to help you locate files on your or other drives, based upon search criteria that you specify.

File ➤ New... (Ctrl+N) Begins a new, untitled document.

File ➤ Open... (Ctrl+O) Opens a saved document from disk.

File ➤ Page Setup... Use to specify all aspects of your page's appearance, with respect to the printer (that is, margins, page orientation, page size, etc.).

File ➤ Print... (Ctrl+P) Use to print documents.

File ➤ Print Preview (Ctrl+F2) Use to see how your documents will look before you actually print them.

File ➤ Save (Ctrl+S) Saves your document to disk.

File ➤ Save All Saves all open documents to disk.

File ➤ Save As... (F12) Allows you to save your document under a different name, format, etc.

File ➤ Summary Info... Use to fill in or change basic information about the document, such as the author's name. This information can be valuable when used with File ➤ Find File...

File ➤ Templates... Use to choose templates or add-ins.

Format ➤ AutoFormat... (Ctrl+K) Examines your document, looking for ways to improve the appearance of it. Will make certain formatting changes automatically.

Format ➤ Borders and Shading... Use to assign borders and shading to paragraph elements.

Format ➤ Bullets and Numbering... Use to create numbered or bulleted lists.

Format ➤ Change Case... (Shift+F3) Use to change the casing in the selected text (e.g., from ALL CAPS to Sentence casing, and so on).

Format ➤ Columns... Use to specify how many columns you wish and to fine-tune the amount of white space, among other things.

Format ➤ Drawing Object... Use to edit drawn objects you have inserted in your document.

Format ➤ Drop Cap... Use to automatically create drop caps.

Format ➤ Font... (Ctrl+D) Use to change the font, size, or letter style of the selected text.

Format ➤ Frame... Use to edit frames in your document.

Format ➤ Heading Numbering... Automates the number of headings for different parts of a document.

Format ➤ Paragraph... Use to apply formatting to paragraphs, including indents, tabs, space between paragraphs, and more.

Format ➤ Picture... Use to crop, size, and stylize pictures you have imported into your document.

Format ➤ Style... (Ctrl+Shift+S) Use to apply existing styles to text or to create new styles.

Format ➤ Style Gallery... Use to browse through the existing styles in Word's various templates and sample documents.

Format ➤ Tabs... Use to determine where tabs will go and what kind they will be. You can also assign tab leaders from here.

Help ➤ About Microsoft Word... Gives information about the version of Word you are using.

Help ➤ Contents (F1 or Shift+F1) Gives you help on whatever function you happen to be using.

Help ➤ Examples and Demos Brings up examples of Word's features and offers to demonstrate how to use them.

Help ➤ Index Brings up a help index so you can quickly find the topic you are looking for.

Help ➤ Quick Preview Shows how to use Word quickly. You can also get tips if you are a WordPerfect user.

Help ➤ Search for Help on... Allows you to search for help on specific topics. You can type in key words, and this command will help you find them.

Help ➤ Technical Support Brings up information that will explain to you how to get technical support from Microsoft.

Help ➤ Tip of the Day... Shows a tip on how to use Word efficiently. There is a new tip each day!

Help ➤ WordPerfect Help... Tells WordPerfect users how to do something in Word that they were used to doing differently in WordPerfect.

Insert ➤ Annotation (Alt+Ctrl+A) Use to place annotations in your documents.

Insert ➤ Break... Use to insert various kinds of breaks (section, page, column, and so on).

Insert ➤ Caption... Use to place a caption in your document.

Insert ➤ Cross-reference... Use to place a cross-reference mark in your document, linking two or more parts. These are handy because they update automatically when you shift information about.

Insert ➤ Database... Inserts information from a database into your document as a table.

Insert ➤ Date and Time... (Alt+Shift+D, Alt+Shift+T) Use to place preformatted date and time fields in your document. Using fields that update automatically can be a surefire way of keeping track of latest drafts and such.

Insert ➤ Field... Use to place any of Word's hundreds of different types of fields. A field is not text itself, rather it is a code to Word to insert a specific kind of text or specific information.

Insert ➤ File... Use to place an entire file within another file.

Insert ➤ Footnote... (Alt+Ctrl+F: Footnote; Alt+Ctrl+E: Endnote) Use to place a footnote (or endnote) mark in your text. Word will automatically update the number sequence if you add or delete footnotes (or endnotes).

Insert ➤ Form Field... Use to put fields (checkboxes, etc.) in forms that you are creating.

Insert ➤ Frame Use to place a frame in your document, where you can place text, graphics, etc., that you want to move around easily on the page. You also use this command to frame existing material.

Insert ➤ Index and Tables... (Alt+Shift+X: Mark Index Entry; Alt+Shift+O: Mark Table of Contents Entry) Use to mark material so Word knows to include it in the Table of Contents or Index.

Insert ➤ Object... Use to insert one of a large variety of objects (such as drawings, spreadsheets, or text files) in your document.

Insert ➤ Page Numbers... (Alt+Shift+P) Use to specify exactly how your page numbers should look and where they should appear. You can also use this command to start page numbering anew in new sections.

Insert ➤ Picture... Use to place pictures *not* created in Word at the insert point.

Insert ➤ Symbol... Use to insert a variety of special characters (such as ®, •, and so forth).

Last Four Files List (File Menu) If this time-saving option is enabled (in the View tab of the Options dialog box), your last four files will appear at the bottom of the File menu. All you have to do to open one is choose its name.

Open Documents List (Window Menu) This list shows all open documents. To make a different document active, select its name from the list.

Table ➤ Cell Height and Width... Use to adjust the height and width of individual cells in a table.

Table ➤ Convert Text to Table... Use to take regular text in your document and turn it into table form.

Table ➤ Delete Cells... Use to delete cells in a table.

Table ➤ Formula... Use to insert special formulas into tables (for example, formulas that will sum the values of specific cells).

Table ➤ Headings Use to automate the creation of headings for the columns of the table.

Table ➤ Gridlines Turns on and off the nonprinting lines that show on-screen.

Table ➤ Insert Cells... Use to insert rows or columns into a table.

Table ➤ Merge Cells Use to combine several cells into one.

Table ➤ Select Column Use to select entire columns in tables.

Table ➤ Select Row Use to select entire rows in tables.

Table ➤ Select Table (Alt+5 on the keypad) Use to select an entire table.

Table ➤ Sort... Use to sort items in a table (alphanumerically).

Table ➤ Split Cells... Use to separate one cell into two or more cells.

Table ➤ Split Table Breaks a table into more than one table.

Table ➤ Table AutoFormat... Gives a list of predefined formats and lets you preview the appearance of the table.

Tools ➤ AutoCorrect... Use this feature to instruct Word to always correct certain mistakes *as you go*. Use with caution, though, as this can be a double-edged sword!

Tools ➤ Customize... Allows you to personalize dozens of different aspects of Word's functionality. You can enable or disable features, determine what appears on-screen, and specify how or where files are to be saved, among many others. Mostly lets you change the contents of Toolbars and menus (including keyboard shortcuts).

Tools ➤ Envelopes and Labels... Use to help automate the process of addressing envelopes or printing out sheets of labels.

Tools ➤ Grammar... Use to reach the Grammar checker, which can help you correct improper grammar and style in your documents.

Tools ➤ Hyphenation... Use to automate the hyphenation of your documents.

Tools ➤ Language... Use to specify which language defaults Word should use in its various document-polishing tools (the Grammar check, the Spelling checker, and so on).

Tools ➤ Macro... Use to access and create macros. Macros are automated series of commands. This feature is fairly advanced, but it can save you a lot of time.

Tools ➤ Mail Merge... Use to automate the process of creating lists of addresses for mass mailings.

Tools ➤ Options... Similar to Tools ➤ Customize..., allows you to specify dozens of different aspects of Word's functionality. A collection of options for viewing, spelling, editing, printing, etc.

Tools ➤ Protect Document... Use to protect documents from being changed or even viewed. Several levels of protection are offered, including passwords.

Tools ➤ Revisions... Use to indicate where you've made changes on drafts of material.

Tools ➤ Spelling... (F7) Use the Spelling checker to ensure that you are using standard spelling in your documents.

Tools ➤ Thesaurus... (Shift+F7) Use Word's thesaurus to spice up your prose by finding alternative ways of saying the same thing.

Tools ➤ Word Count... Use to get an exact character, word, page, line, or paragraph count for your document.

View ➤ Annotations Shows you all annotations in a document.

View ➤ Footnotes Shows you all footnotes in a document.

View ➤ Full Screen Removes all extraneous Toolbars, rulers, and scroll bars, leaving just your text.

View ➤ Header and Footer Shows you any headers or footers you have created in your document or allows you to create new ones.

View ➤ Master Document Used when creating large documents, consisting of multiple subdocuments. Facilitates cross-referencing and the creation of an index and TOC.

View ➤ Normal (Ctrl+Alt+N) Shows you your document in Normal view. This is the most simple view, showing formatting and special characters but not footers or headers, nor where items will print on the page.

View ➤ Outline (Ctrl+Alt+O) Shows you your document in Outline view. This view is ideal for organizing large documents, as it allows you to quickly move around large blocks of text.

View ➤ Page Layout (Ctrl+Alt+P) Shows you your document in Page Layout view. This is the most robust view, showing items exactly where they will print on the page, including margins and side-by-side columns. It is very slow, however.

View ➤ Ruler Shows the rulers.

View ➤ Toolbars... Allows you to show or remove any of Word's eight Toolbars on-screen.

View ➤ Zoom... Allows you to enlarge or shrink the document on-screen for better viewing. This will not change the actual printed *size* of the document.

Window ➤ Arrange All Shows all open document windows so you can see them simultaneously.

Window ➤ New Window Opens a new pane (windows) for the active document.

Window ➤ Split (Ctrl+Alt+S) Divides the main window of the current document in two so you can scroll in separate parts of the document simultaneously or view different parts in different views.

▸▸ Index

Note to the Reader:
Boldface numbers indicate pages where you will find the principal discussion of a topic or the definition of a term. *Italic* numbers indicate pages where topics are illustrated in figures.

▸ Numbers and Symbols

▸ A

▶ B

C

D

► E

► F

Index

G

▸ H

 **I**

J

K

L

M

► O

P

▶ Q

R

► S

► T

U

V

▶ W

 X

 Z

[1639] *Mastering Word 6 for Windows*

GET A FREE CATALOG JUST FOR EXPRESSING YOUR OPINION.

Help us improve our books and get a ***FREE*** full-color catalog in the bargain. Please complete this form, pull out this page and send it in today. The address is on the reverse side.

Name ______________________ **Company** ______________________

Address ______________________ **City** __________ **State** ____ **Zip** ________

Phone ( ) ______________

1. How would you rate the overall quality of this book?

- ❑ Excellent
- ❑ Very Good
- ❑ Good
- ❑ Fair
- ❑ Below Average
- ❑ Poor

2. What were the things you liked most about the book? (Check all that apply)

- ❑ Pace
- ❑ Format
- ❑ Writing Style
- ❑ Examples
- ❑ Table of Contents
- ❑ Index
- ❑ Price
- ❑ Illustrations
- ❑ Type Style
- ❑ Cover
- ❑ Depth of Coverage
- ❑ Fast Track Notes

3. What were the things you liked *least* about the book? (Check all that apply)

- ❑ Pace
- ❑ Format
- ❑ Writing Style
- ❑ Examples
- ❑ Table of Contents
- ❑ Index
- ❑ Price
- ❑ Illustrations
- ❑ Type Style
- ❑ Cover
- ❑ Depth of Coverage
- ❑ Fast Track Notes

4. Where did you buy this book?

- ❑ Bookstore chain
- ❑ Small independent bookstore
- ❑ Computer store
- ❑ Wholesale club
- ❑ College bookstore
- ❑ Technical bookstore
- ❑ Other ______________

5. How did you decide to buy this particular book?

- ❑ Recommended by friend
- ❑ Recommended by store personnel
- ❑ Author's reputation
- ❑ Sybex's reputation
- ❑ Read book review in __________
- ❑ Other ______________

6. How did you pay for this book?

- ❑ Used own funds
- ❑ Reimbursed by company
- ❑ Received book as a gift

7. What is your level of experience with the subject covered in this book?

- ❑ Beginner
- ❑ Intermediate
- ❑ Advanced

8. How long have you been using a computer?

years ______________

months ______________

9. Where do you most often use your computer?

- ❑ Home
- ❑ Work
- ❑ Both
- ❑ Other ______________

10. What kind of computer equipment do you have? (Check all that apply)

- ❑ PC Compatible Desktop Computer
- ❑ PC Compatible Laptop Computer
- ❑ Apple/Mac Computer
- ❑ Apple/Mac Laptop Computer
- ❑ CD ROM
- ❑ Fax Modem
- ❑ Data Modem
- ❑ Scanner
- ❑ Sound Card
- ❑ Other ______________

11. What other kinds of software packages do you ordinarily use?

- ❑ Accounting
- ❑ Databases
- ❑ Networks
- ❑ Apple/Mac
- ❑ Desktop Publishing
- ❑ Spreadsheets
- ❑ CAD
- ❑ Games
- ❑ Word Processing
- ❑ Communications
- ❑ Money Management
- ❑ Other ______________

12. What operating systems do you ordinarily use?

- ❑ DOS
- ❑ OS/2
- ❑ Windows
- ❑ Apple/Mac
- ❑ Windows NT
- ❑ Other ______________

13. **On what computer-related subject(s) would you like to see more books?**

---

14. **Do you have any other comments about this book? (Please feel free to use a separate piece of paper if you need more room)**

PLEASE FOLD, SEAL, AND MAIL TO SYBEX

SYBEX INC.
Department M
2021 Challenger Drive
Alameda, CA
94501

Double-clicking on Word's hotspots...

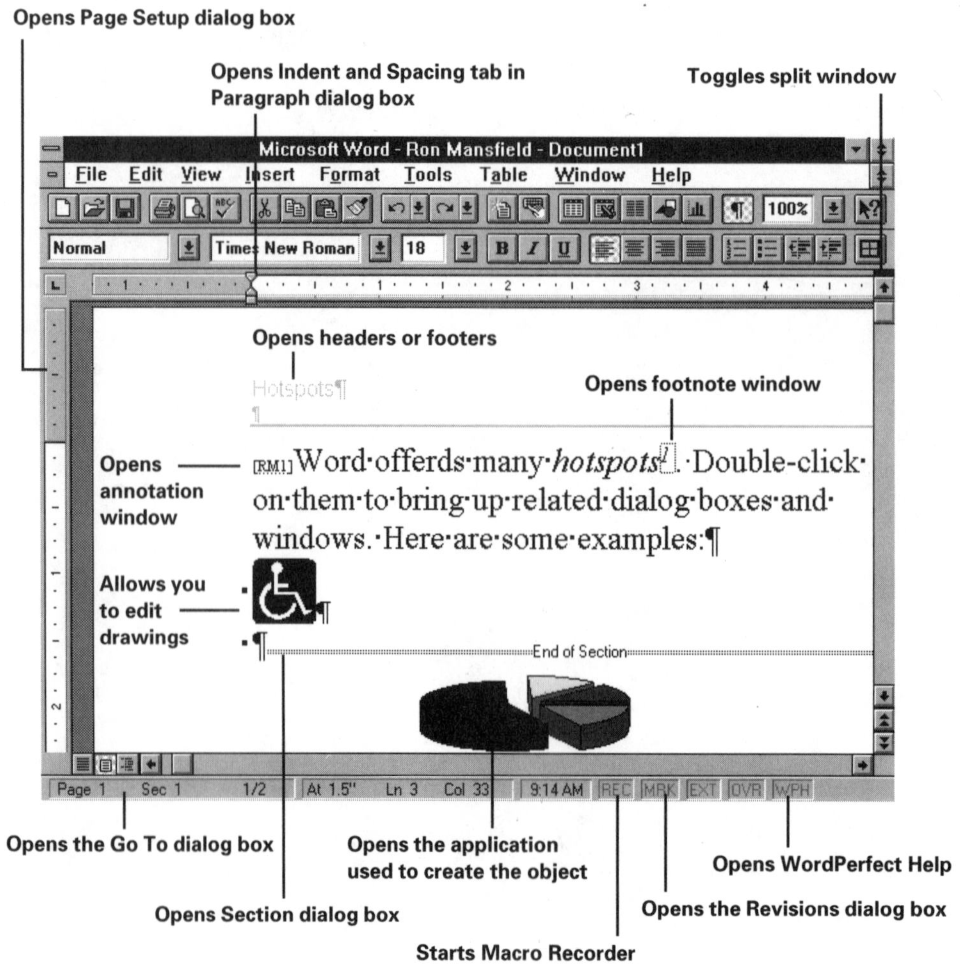